The Corporate Litigator

Committee on Corporate Counsel
Section of Litigation
AMERICAN BAR ASSOCIATION

The Corporate Litigator

Francis J. Burke, Jr., and Michael L. Goldblatt
Co-Editors

A previous version of Chapter 1 appeared in
2 *Preventive Law Reporter* 118 (1984). A previous
version of Chapter 9 appeared in 40 *The Business Lawyer* 631 (1985).
A previous version of Chapter 17 appeared in
10 *Litigation* (1984). Chapter 18 previously appeared in
12 *Litigation* (1986). Chapter 23 previously
appeared in 13 *Litigation* (1986). A previous
version of Chapter 24 appeared in 6 *Litigation* (1980).
Previous versions of Chapter 25 and Chapter 29
appeared in 10 *Litigation* (1984).

Printed in the United States of America.

Library of Congress Catalog Card Number: 89-80487

ISBN: 0-89707-427-0

94 93 92 91 90 5 4 3 2 1

Contents

Section II

Handling Litigation Utilizing the Corporate Law Department / 69
Section Introduction: William R. Hedden

Section III

Establishing the Relationship between Outside Counsel and the Corporate Client / 85
Section Introduction: Stephen M. Kite-Powell

Section VI

The Use of Computers in Litigation / 341
Section Introduction: Dennis A. Estis

Section VIII

Appendix of Forms

Forms for Section II
Handling Litigation Utilizing the Corporate Law Department / 763

Forms for Section III
Establishing the Relationship between Outside Counsel and the Corporate Client / 777

Forms for Section IV
Managing the Cost of Corporate Litigation / 821

Forms for Section V
Alternatives to Litigation / 857

Forms for Section VI
The Use of Computers in Litigation / 891

Preface

Francis J. Burke, Jr., and Michael L. Goldblatt

The publication of this book marks the completion of one of many projects undertaken by the Committee on Corporate Counsel of the Section of Litigation of the American Bar Association. It is a book that will serve the needs of both inside and outside counsel as an authoritative source on corporate litigation.

Most of the articles and forms in this book are derived from materials presented in programs sponsored by the Committee on Corporate Counsel at past American Bar Association meetings. Our subcommittee reviewed the extensive available materials and selected the best articles for inclusion in this book. A few articles from *Litigation* magazine were also selected. All articles were then reviewed to ensure that their content was timely. In many cases extensive revisions were made so that the most current citations would be included in the book.

Production of the book is the work of several individuals, including members of the committee, staff of the American Bar Association, and the lawyers and consultants who prepared the articles and forms included in the book. Paul H. Dawes and James P. Melican, former Co-Chairmen of the Committee on Corporate Counsel, provided significant support and guidance throughout the book project. Several members of *The Corporate Litigator* Subcommittee assisted with editorial responsibilities, including:

- Dennis A. Estis, of Greenbaum, Rowe, Ravin, Davis & Bergstein, Woodbridge, New Jersey
- Shelby R. Grubbs, of Grant, Konvalinka & Grubbs, Chattanooga, Tennessee
- William R. Hedden, of Schering-Plough Corporation, Kenilworth, New Jersey
- John A. Irvine, of Boyar, Norton & Blair, Houston, Texas

Francis J. Burke, Jr., and Michael L. Goldblatt are Co-Chairmen, *The Corporate Litigator* Subcommittee, Committee on Corporate Counsel, Section of Litigation, American Bar Association. Mr. Burke is a member of Streich, Lang, Weeks & Cardon, Phoenix, Arizona, and Mr. Goldblatt is Associate General Counsel of Tidewater, Inc., New Orleans, Louisiana.

- Stephen M. Kite-Powell of International Paper Company, Memphis, Tennessee

Harry J. Haynsworth, Professor of Law at the University of South Carolina, Columbia, reviewed the final manuscript, providing a very comprehensive analysis. We are extremely grateful to him for his tireless efforts in the final editing of the book.

The staff of the Litigation Section and the Publications Department of the American Bar Association in Chicago also made a significant contribution to the compilation of this book through the work of several individuals, including Ron Mochel, Susan Yessne, John Fallahay, David Brent and free-lance copy editor Karen Schenkenfelder.

We thank the authors of the articles and forms for granting permission for their materials to be included in the book and for revising their works to make this book both timely and comprehensive. Thanks also to Cary J. Griffith for preparing a bibliography of references.

We also express our deep appreciation to Jennifer L. Goolsby and Suzanne L. Tredway, Secretaries to Francis J. Burke, Jr., for providing the staff support needed to keep track of the efforts of over sixty editors and authors. We thank the firm of Streich, Lang, Weeks & Cardon in Phoenix, Arizona, for providing the resources and support necessary to copy and circulate articles to authors and editors and for compiling and circulating the final manuscript.

Foreword

Paul H. Dawes and James P. Melican

As corporate litigation becomes even more complex, diverse, and expensive, the corporation's lawyer—whether based in the company's law department or a law firm—has been called upon to fulfill increasingly sophisticated tasks. Several years ago, the Section of Litigation of the American Bar Association recognized the need to provide this special practice area with a forum for education, evaluation, and exchange of views and viewpoints. The Committee on Corporate Counsel—now approximately 1,000 highly qualified and experienced lawyers in membership—serves that role.

The committee's name was chosen carefully. It is not a committee of corporate law department litigators, although approximately half of its membership is so employed. The other half consists of members of outside law firms. It is this divergence of perspective that gives the committee its energy and appeal. Our common theme is developing ways to better manage business litigation, particularly complex litigation.

To that end we have twenty-six subcommittees which handle substantive topics, such as SEC, intellectual property, and employment law matters; procedural topics, such as disclosure privileges and ADR; "dollars and cents" topics, such as budgeting, billing, and marketing of law firm services; and, of enormous interest recently, litigation management, including the use of computers and practical ethical issues.

In addition to publishing a quarterly newsletter, meeting annually, and conducting periodic surveys on trends in practice, the committee has been an active sponsor of continuing legal education programs. Typically this entails the preparation of written program materials for distribution to program audiences. Drawing on the unique experiences of many major corporations and distinguished practitioners who serve them, the focus of

Paul H. Dawes and James P. Melican were Co-Chairmen, Committee on Corporate Counsel during 1985–88. Mr. Dawes is a member of Thelen, Marrin, Johnson & Bridges, San Francisco, California. Mr. Melican is the Senior Vice President and General Counsel of International Paper Company, Purchase, New York.

these written materials has been on the practical ways to accomplish tasks, and commentary and opinion.

Innumerable requests for our papers and articles led us to decide to select and update some that are of particular timeliness to the bar. This is the origin of *The Corporate Litigator.* We look forward to supplementing it and receiving new contributions as the committee grows and the relationship between inside and outside corporate litigation changes, as it inevitably does.

Introduction: Managing Corporate Litigation and the Corporate Litigation Environment

Francis J. Burke, Jr., and Michael L. Goldblatt

During the 1980s, the dramatic growth in volume and complexity of corporate litigation has continued to challenge the ability of counsel to represent their clients effectively and efficiently. Effective representation requires that the corporate litigator keep abreast of current techniques, approaches, and legal developments. Efficient representation has proved to be a more elusive goal. In courtrooms, at seminars, and at bar association meetings, corporate counsel have responded to the challenge by developing methods for containing costs and controlling dockets. Likewise, corporate managers have taken a new interest in litigation because of its increased impact on the bottom line.

The Corporate Litigator is designed to be a comprehensive one-volume manual for in-house and outside counsel who represent corporations in litigated matters. In-house corporate counsel will find this book useful in developing litigation management techniques and in finding new methods for controlling the cost of litigation. Similarly, outside corporate counsel will find that the book helps them to be more responsive to in-house counsel, who increasingly are under strict orders to manage outside counsel and the spiraling costs of litigation.

A major theme of *The Corporate Litigator* is the importance of managing the cost of corporate litigation without sacrificing effective representation. Thus, we have included sections on the use of in-house counsel to directly handle litigation, when and how to retain outside counsel, how to establish an effective working relationship between inside and outside counsel, budgeting, effective litigation management, innovative approaches to controlling costs, reducing costs through settlements and alternative dispute resolution, and how and when to use computers.

Inside and outside corporate counsel will also find this book useful as a

Francis J. Burke, Jr., is a member of Streich, Lang, Weeks and Cardon, Phoenix, Arizona, and Michael L. Goldblatt is Associate General Counsel of Tidewater, Inc., New Orleans, Louisiana.

handbook which contains the most commonly encountered substantive questions in representing corporations in litigation and in preventive law programs. The book includes sections on legal audits, corporate compliance programs, internal corporate investigations, ethical issues, the attorney/corporate client privilege, the fiduciary duties of officers and directors, officer and director liability, indemnification and insurance, derivative suits, litigation involving contests for corporate control, and representing clients in criminal investigations.

In this Introduction, we will provide an overview of the major themes addressed in the eight sections of the book. We have also included an Appendix of Forms on many of the topic areas, and the reader should refer to it for documents that can be adapted to their litigation practice.

Section I: Preventing Litigation through Legal Audits and Internal Corporate Investigations

The frequency of litigation may be reduced by an effective compliance program and the practice of preventive law by corporate counsel. Corporate counsel should learn how to apply preventive law to high-risk areas including antitrust, product liability, employment, environmental, and securities law. This book shows that a good compliance program includes legal audits, compliance reviews, employee certifications, procedures for protecting whistle-blowers, and special litigation committees.

A corporation must maintain the confidentiality of its preventive law work product in order to avoid embarrassment and to minimize adverse impact in litigation. The authors show corporate counsel how to structure preventive law activities to maximize the protection afforded by the attorney-client privilege and work-product doctrine. Examples of forms for an antitrust compliance program, a legal audit, and a contract review procedure are included in the Appendix.

Section II: Handling Litigation Utilizing the Corporate Law Department

Over the past twenty years, corporations have expanded the size of their law departments and the role of their in-house lawyers. However, there are strengths and weaknesses inherent to the use of inside counsel for corporate litigation.

Management philosophy and the centralization or decentralization of the corporation's structure significantly affect decisions regarding the appropriate staffing of litigation. To play an effective role in litigation, the in-house manager of corporate litigation must give significant attention to staff organization, training, and career development, and must insist upon compensation packages that will attract talented litigators. In addition to chapters covering these subjects generally, Chapter Four shows corporate counsel how the Pacific Gas & Electric Company uses in-house corporate litigators to handle virtually all of the company's litigation. The success of its program depends upon competitive salaries, a well-organized department, an effective training program, and careful case management.

Section III: Establishing the Relationship between Outside Counsel and the Corporate Client

Once the corporation has decided to seek outside support, an important ingredient of success is an effective relationship between inside counsel and the outside corporate litigator. This section contains chapters by practitioners with experience as in-house and outside corporate counsel, with many practical tips for forming an effective relationship. The authors show that it is essential to determine the proper timing for retaining outside counsel. The experience and depth of in-house counsel personnel, possibilities for alternative dispute resolution, venue, and jurisdictional aspects of the litigation must all be explored before reaching a decision.

When the company has determined to retain the services of outside counsel, thoughtful consideration should be given to the question of who to retain. It is well worth the effort to check lists of recommended counsel, talk to persons in the community, and conduct in-depth interviews in which there is a full and frank discussion of litigation experience, philosophy, staffing, budgeting, billing, reporting, and controlling costs.

Many corporations have found it useful to send outside counsel a written statement of guidelines concerning how the company expects its litigation matters to be handled, and guidelines concerning reporting, budgeting, and billing. Such statements are often accompanied by retention letters signed by inside and outside counsel. The Appendix includes some excellent examples of such policy statements and retention letters.

A common theme identified by the authors is that once the company has retained outside counsel, it must emphasize allocation of responsibilities and good communications. At the earliest stages, inside and outside counsel must establish the overall goals and objectives to be achieved, then devise the best and most cost-effective strategy for achieving those goals. They must create a teamwork relationship and delineate their respective roles. Increasingly, corporate litigators are concluding that, to be effective, inside counsel must be an active participant in the litigation process.

Finally, the corporate litigator must also be sensitive to ethical considerations. As a result of the national and multinational expansion of corporations and law firms, lawyers must become more alert to the requirements of the ethical rules in their daily practice. The corporate litigator can easily fall into representing the adversary of a former client, simultaneously representing clients with adverse interests, or becoming involved as a witness in litigation. The authors of Chapter Nine show that litigators must approach these situations with sensitivity and care in order to avoid disqualification motions and other sanctions.

Section IV: Managing the Cost of Corporate Litigation

The cost of corporate litigation has mushroomed in recent years as cost pressures on corporate law firms have led to steady increases in legal fees. In addition, the broad scope of discovery and increased complexity of modern corporate transactions have led to protracted litigation and lengthy and expensive pretrial discovery proceedings. At the same time, the modern American corporation, faced with an increasingly competitive global marketplace, must find ways to control costs.

Inside and outside corporate litigators have struggled with this tension between the need to control costs and the need to adequately represent the corporate client in the litigation arena. The solution to this dilemma includes careful planning, focusing on the objectives by evaluating the evidence as it is discovered, making strategic choices, deciding upon an acceptable level of risk in the discovery process, avoiding overdiscovery, exercising vigilance in the desire to control costs at every turn, and finding ways to terminate the litigation with an appropriate result at the earliest possible stage. These are difficult tasks that require teamwork between inside and outside counsel.

Because of the importance of these tasks, the section regarding managing the cost of corporate litigation is particularly relevant. It contains a variety of the most insightful current thinking concerning the best ways to manage costs in today's litigation environment.

One of the increasingly popular techniques for focusing the corporate outside and in-house counsel on the strategic choices that must be made is the preparation of a litigation budget. Budgets can be presented in many forms, ranging from simple to complex, sketchy to detailed, and including only fees or also costs and expenses. Their principal benefit is to force the litigator to focus on objectives and map strategies. Some excellent examples have been included in the Appendix of Forms.

Other various techniques are being employed by corporate litigators as a means of controlling litigation costs. One technique is to share resources with others. For example, some companies involved in the defense of toxic-substance litigation have developed an elaborate system for sharing counsel.

Corporate litigators are increasingly being forced to sharpen their management skills. Successful litigation management involves the same attributes as successful business management: planning, organizing, leading, staffing, and controlling. Corporate litigation costs can also be managed by defining those tasks which can be best performed by inside counsel as opposed to outside counsel, and by placing tight operational controls in place to prevent costs from spiraling out of control.

The chapters in this section of the book suggest several steps to reduce discovery costs:

1. Inside and outside counsel should establish objectives, prepare detailed plans and budgets, and monitor the case to assure the limits on costs are being achieved.
2. Counsel can use pretrial conferences under Rules 26(f) and 16 as mechanisms for narrowing issues and thus controlling costs and fees.
3. Avoid needless duplication of the use of discovery devices or of the efforts of multiple counsel.
4. Focus on the acceptable level of risk in the discovery process, and decide on whether to take discovery at all on particular witnesses or on particular topics. Many witnesses need not be deposed, even if they will be called as witnesses by the opposition at trial. But both inside and outside counsel, and perhaps also key executives of the corporate client, must participate in such decisions.
5. Streamline the litigation by focusing on the objectives that have been established, learning the appropriate facts early, developing a theory of the case, and developing evidentiary outlines and proof narratives to keep the corporate litigator focused on the essential facts.
6. The litigation should be terminated as quickly as possible. There are two usual endings for a legal dispute, judgment or settlement. If settlement is the preferred alternative, there is often no excuse for failure to achieve an appropriate settlement as quickly as possible. Counsel will find in this book suggestions for how to be an effective negotiator.

Today's corporate client challenges litigators to achieve successful results cost effectively. We hope this book will help corporate litigators to rethink approaches to the litigation process and to use the most current techniques to achieve efficiencies.

Section V: Alternatives to Litigation

Given the astronomical cost of protracted litigation, corporate clients increasingly are pressing their lawyers to explore possibilities for early termination of disputes through alternative dispute resolution (ADR) procedures such as mediation, arbitration, minitrials, and summary jury trials. Corporate litigators are developing an increasing awareness that they have a professional obligation to learn about the benefits of ADR techniques, to suggest them when appropriate, and to learn how to invoke them when requested.

Alternative forms of dispute resolution provide the corporate litigator with additional capabilities for dealing with such matters as high costs, long delays, adverse publicity, and the quality of the tribunal.

Each ADR mechanism may or may not be useful to a particular case. Mediation can be effective as a means of bringing a third party's viewpoint to negotiations. Minitrials and summary jury trials are often not binding but can give the parties a sense that they have had their day in court and can give the parties the feedback of a neutral fact-finder who has been given an abbreviated version of a trial. In arbitration, of course, rulings are usually binding on the parties.

However, alternative dispute resolution does not work in all cases. For example, referral to ADR will not work if litigation is being pursued for tactical reasons or there is an imbalance of economic power among the litigants. The authors recommend which cases are suitable for ADR and which are not.

Although the state of the art of ADR mechanisms is relatively primitive, there are significant pressures in the direction of ADR. The American Bar Association Committee on Professionalism has recommended that lawyers learn more about ADR. Many of the Fortune 500 corporations have committed to explore ADR mechanisms through commitments to the Center for Public Resources in New York. And the courts have provided impetus to the use of ADR mechanisms. The U.S. Supreme Court has upheld the enforceability of arbitration clauses in a variety of disparate areas. Many lower courts have imposed mandatory procedures for mediation, arbitration, or summary jury trial.

Today's corporate litigator is well advised to become familiar with current ADR techniques. To help with this, the Appendix contains a number of forms dealing with contract language, ADR model procedures, and other ADR issues.

Section VI: The Use of Computers in Litigation Management

We are experiencing an information revolution in which technological advances are bringing ever-increasing amounts of information to our fingertips at a rapidly decreasing cost. Law firms and corporations are making available to corporate litigators the most advanced computer, copying, telecommunications and other technology. Certainly such technology is in some cases necessary and in many cases important as a cost-saving means of managing the available and relevant information. However, there can be a vast difference between having such technology available and being able to use it effectively and cost-efficiently.

In-house counsel can benefit significantly from the use of computers for tracking outside counsel, current litigation pending against the corporation, and legal research prepared by or on behalf of the corporation.

Computers can also assist in-house and outside corporate counsel in the management of discovery. Not long ago, most experts believed that a case had to involve 5,000 to 10,000 documents before computers could be justified. Now, microcomputers are so inexpensive, and the software is so easy to use, that virtually every deposition should be put onto the computer, it makes sense to make a computer document index with as few as 100 to 500 documents, and computers can be of significant help in formulating evidentiary and proof outlines. As the chapters in this section point out, the corporate litigator should become involved in the selection and design of the system, identification of the key issues, selection of the key discovery materials to be computerized, and identification of the types of information to be used during discovery, motion practice, and at trial. The chapters in this section will help the corporate litigator become conversant with computer terms and provide guidance on many of the key computerization decisions. A number of forms to facilitate the use of computers have been included in the Appendix.

Section VII: Substantive Aspects of Representing Corporate Clients in Litigation

Because they recur in so many types of cases involving corporations, we have chosen to cover the substantive rules governing the communications between attorney and corporate client; establishing the fiduciary responsibilities of corporate officers, directors, and employees; and establishing when it is appropriate for the corporation to idemnify or purchase insurance for its officers, directors, and employees.

Of course, in understanding the attorney/corporate client privilege, it is important not only to understand when the privilege attaches, but also when it is waived. The authors of Chapter Twenty-Nine show how the privilege may be lost in derivative litigation, by raising reliance on advice of counsel, through disclosures to auditors, through waiver by a trustee, and other situations.

The last decade has been marked by ferocious battles for control of many of America's largest corporations. Ingenious maneuvers have been developed by bidders, targets, and their counsel. This has led to significant developments in the responsibilities of corporate officers and directors, such as changes in the business judgment rule, which must be mastered by the corporate litigator. The authors of Chapter Thirty guide the reader through recent developments in the fiduciary responsibilities of officers and directors.

Because of the liability insurance crisis and the increasing frequency of civil and criminal challenges to actions of corporate officers, directors, and employees, another timely topic is indemnification and insurance of corporate officials. Chapters Thirty-One and Thirty-Two discuss the rules regarding permissive and mandatory indemnification, the corporate power to purchase directors and officers insurance, typical policy terms, limits of liability, exclusions, typical defense and claims-handling issues, some of the current alternatives to insurance, and shifts in corporate law allowing corporations to adopt charter provisions restricting director liability.

Section VIII: Representing Corporate Clients in Various Litigation Settings

Corporate litigators must deal with a wide variety of complex and specialized areas of the law in representing their corporate clients. This book focuses on three litigation settings: the shareholder derivative suit, the contest for corporate control, and the criminal investigation.

In shareholder derivative litigation, the demand requirement is perhaps the most important threshold issue. Chapter Thirty-Three shows when the demand may be excused, what factors to use in determining whether the rejection was lawful, and whether the board of directors of a corporation may appoint a special litigation committee to deal with the demand for litigation by the corporation.

Another timely topic is the role of litigation in corporate control contests. Numerous litigation alternatives are available to the corporate bidder as well as the target. The authors of Chapter Thirty-Four show how the litigation meshes with business maneuvers and discuss in detail a considerable number of litigation strategies, including challenges to the opponent's disclosures and challenges to a number of offensive and defensive corporate maneuvers.

Increasingly, corporations are becoming the targets of criminal investigations and must retain corporate litigators to represent them and their officers, directors, and employees. Such criminal investigations often involve complex business transactions with interrelated ramifications involving civil and criminal liability and administrative penalties.

Corporate clients often prefer that their regular outside counsel represent them in such matters. The authors of Chapters Thirty-Five and Thirty-Six discuss the bounds of corporate criminal liability and show the corporate litigator how to deal with documentary subpoenas, how to maintain the attorney-client privilege, how to negotiate immunity and engage in plea bargaining.

Finally, Chapter Thirty-Seven shows that the criminal investigation from the perspective of in-house corporate counsel has unique considerations such as the interrelationship between the corporate compliance program and the criminal investigation, whether to discharge or discipline corporate employees pending a criminal investigation, and the question of joint or separate counsel for the corporation and its employees.

Conclusion

This introduction has provided a sampling of the issues and answers that appear in the following chapters and forms. The corporate litigator will find a wealth of additional tips and techniques in the pages that follow. We hope that this book will be of enduring value to practitioners in law firms as well as corporate law departments.

Section I

Preventing Litigation through Legal Audits and Internal Corporate Investigations

Every corporation's first and best defense against the perils of the litigation process is a meaningful compliance and preventive law program. To be effective, such a program must be carefully considered, well documented, and tailored to the preservation of appropriate privileges. However, despite the best efforts and intentions, events will sometimes raise the specter of litigation. At that point, often the best response is to conduct an internal corporate investigation to learn what happened and why. This phase too must be carefully conducted. Because meaningful compliance programs and well-conducted internal corporate investigations can reduce the risk of litigation and make the corporation's response more effective, *The Corporate Litigator* begins with a section on these subjects.

The section opens with a prize-winning chapter written by David Hardy. The chapter begins with the theoretical underpinnings of preventive law and includes extensive treatment of and checklists on how to establish corporate compliance programs and conduct legal audits. The checklists cover several matters, including trade association activities, antitrust compliance, purchasing matters, and exposure to products liability. Forms 1–6, in the Appendix, have been provided by Combustion Engineering Corporation and demonstrate the types of corporate forms needed for an antitrust compliance program.

This section also includes a chapter by Jerold S. Solovy, Joel J. Africk, and David M. Greenwald. Titled "Preserving the Confidentiality of Legal Audit Findings," this chapter emphasizes the steps needed to maximize the protection afforded by the attorney-client privilege and the work-product doctrine. The article also reviews special problem areas, including shareholder litigation, state court litigation, the Freedom of Information Act, ethical considerations, and attorney subpoenas.

Michael L. Goldblatt
Tidewater, Inc.
New Orleans, Louisiana

One

Establishing Corporate Legal Audits and Drafting Compliance Programs

David Hardy

What Is a Legal Audit?

Historic Overview

Credit for inventing and popularizing the phrase "legal audit" belongs to Louis M. Brown, Professor of Law Emeritus at the University of Southern California School of Law.[1] There do not appear to be any earlier uses of the phrase, although clearly the audit concept was by 1965 already being applied to particular corporate legal problem areas.[2]

Professor Brown stated four assumptions to support the desirability of legal audits:[3]

> 1. Often, legal trouble arises because of failure to recognize legal trouble at an early state. Broadly stated, the assumption is that more legal trouble arises by virtue of failure to recognize the potential presence of problems than because of failure to find acceptable solutions to problems after they are recognized.
> 2. If we assume that a problem exists, the solution of which is not legally adequate, the unknown presence of the problem is more dangerous to the legal health of the business than is its knowledgeable presence even though solution is inadequate. If a problem is known to be present, management can at least endeavor to measure the risks involved, set aside some kind of contingency, and avoid surprise if the risk materializes. Furthermore, on some occasions it may be possible to solve a known problem by extra-legal means and thus reduce or eliminate the risk.

David Hardy is of counsel to Buchman, O'Brien & Williams and was formerly Deputy General Counsel of McKesson Corporation in San Francisco, California.
The author extends his gratitude to Paul L. Larsen, Associate General Counsel of McKesson Corporation, whose understanding of corporate compliance efforts has contributed in the most significant ways to the development of this article.

3. As a practical matter, management would welcome an appropriate procedure whereby it is advised of legal problems at early stages. Management would, of course, seek to measure the value of such information in terms of its costs to the business, including the cost to obtain and act on the information, which cost is to be compared with the cost (often unknown) to the business of the failure to obtain the information.
4. If legal problems can be discovered early, then solution is more available and often less expensive than it would be after the problem is matured.

The Brown legal audit, as originally conceived, drew an analogy from the audit of financial statements in suggesting that minimum professional standards might be established to set the extent and scope of the examination. Professor Brown saw the legal audit as standing on its own footing, but theorized that the legal issues to be examined, or at least some of them, could be obtained by exploring and examining the legal implications underlying the accountants' statements, and by analyzing the transaction flow, i.e., the step-by-step course of legal conduct of the activities of the business in relation to third parties to develop other legal issues.

Professor Brown's concept of the legal audit as a general technique for practicing preventive law does not appear to have significantly varied over the years. He included excerpts from his original article in his jointly authored provocative and stimulating law school casebook.[4] Current views of Professors Brown and Dauer are set forth in the *Preventive Law Reporter,*[5] in Part III of a long-continuing article entitled "A Synopsis of the Theory and Practice of Preventive Law." In summary, Brown and Edward A. Dauer write, "A legal audit is essentially a professional review of the legal affairs of the business, done periodically and culminating in a summary report to management." However, the authors refer to the collateral benefit of affording legal staff the opportunity to assist management in policing transactions.

Other Types of Legal Audits

Having identified the scope and purposes of the "traditional" corporate legal audit, it seems reasonably clear that legal audits, in the context of organized corporate compliance efforts, may involve differing purposes, and do involve a significantly different approach and require significantly different legal techniques.

To the extent that a corporate compliance program is the exercise of preventive law, then the broad purpose is the same. However, the point is that specific purposes must be more narrowly aimed. Increasing legislative and administrative constraints (including the increasing attempts to criminalize unacceptable conduct by corporations and corporate officials) involve a different matrix of factual problems and legal considerations. Among other things, the compliance legal audit may well involve significant potential legal risks, including criminal, and the possibility of imminent litigation.

Any legal audit can be distinguished from other corporate audits. The legal audit emphasizes measuring compliance or noncompliance with a set of legal standards. Other corporate audits may have tangential legal effects, but the primary objective is appraising conduct against a nonlegal set of standards, even though discrepancies revealed by the audit may have legal overtones. Sometimes these standards are set by company policy, which obviously will take legal considerations into account.[6] Lawrence Perlman and Kelley V. Rea—pioneers in this area—have identified over a dozen specific areas that might be covered by legal audits with tangential legal impact:[7]

1. Contract management audits
2. Ethics and securities law compliance audits (directed to top officers, directors, and consultants)
3. Internal audits (with principal focus on financial and operational integrity, protection of proprietary information, and EDP and data center security; secondary audits relate to compensation and expense records, third-party practices, company investments and internal controls)
4. Trade regulation compliance audits
5. Escheat law compliance audits
6. Audit committee reviews
7. Personnel audits (including equal opportunity, affirmative action, age discrimination, equal pay)
8. Litigation audits (cover reviews of existing litigation and reviews of other audit results to detect litigation risk potential or any legal problems, trends, etc.). In another sense, all legal audits have a litigation dimension because sizing the legal risks must take into account potential litigation.
9. Environmental safety and OSHA audits
10. Purchasing audits
11. Audits performed in the course of an acquisition or joint venture
12. Clayton Act Section 8 audits
13. Record retention audits (audits to determine whether records are being retained in accordance with the company's record retention schedule—these audits are also "incorporated" into several of the other audits)

One particular proposal for a legal audit should be noted in passing:

Curzan and Pelesh's article titled "The Changing Role of Outside Counsel: A Proposal for a Legal Audit."[8] The authors suggest the establishment of a legal compliance committee by the board of directors which would engage outside counsel on a periodic basis to review the significant legal affairs of the corporation. The "auditor" counsel would not have a prior client relationship to the corporation and primarily would perform its audit by reviewing the work of the inside general counsel and his or her law department. "Auditor" counsel would report to the special board committee, which would be obligated to report significant legal problems to the board with a recommendation. This proposal not only raises broad issues of corporate governance beyond the scope of this chapter, but the possibility of duplication of effort also seems to raise questions as to the most cost-effective delivery of corporate legal services. It is also predicated upon a generalization that is not supportable. The proposal explicitly assumes that the natural inclination of inside corporate counsel is "to temporize and downplay the significance of legal issues; to find answers at the operational level and not to direct these issues to the board of directors. [In the authors' experience] corporate counsel tends not to seek out problems that may require reference to the board and disclosure to the public."[9]

Another particular type of legal audit is that conducted by an acquiring corporation at the time of a negotiated acquisition. Although compliance issues are important and in certain cases could be critical, such an audit has other primary objectives, akin to those of the "traditional" legal audit.

Still another type of legal audit is the litigation audit, which covers reviews of existing litigation and reviews of other audit results to detect litigation risk and other potential claims. (Broadly, of course, all legal audits have a litigation dimension, because any analysis of legal risks must take into account potential litigation. For a litigation audit checklist, see, in general, Gonser and Wilhelm's article, "A New Direction in Preventive Law: The Litigation Audit."[10]

The remainder of this chapter will focus on corporate compliance programs with particular emphasis on legal audits conducted in that context.

Structuring and Implementing Compliance Programs

Legal audits in the compliance context follow upon the establishment of compliance programs, and compliance programs follow upon corporate policy decisions to establish or to formalize codes of conduct. The first question in implementing a code of conduct is compliance with what?

A major factor in elevating the consciousness of compliance efforts was the SEC questionable-payments program in the mid-1970s, and the consent decrees and voluntary programs that followed thereon. The major scope of interest was in the areas of foreign practices, political payments, and other questionable domestic payments.

Formal antitrust compliance programs have been around for at least a couple of decades. The Electrical Equipment Conspiracy cases in the 1960s are replete with references to antitrust compliance efforts that were customarily circumvented, with disastrous results. The felonization of antitrust violations also occurred in the mid-1970s and undoubtedly gave a large shove to organized antitrust compliance efforts.[11]

The passage of the Foreign Corrupt Practices Act (FCPA) in 1977 responded to the SEC's questionable-payments program with broad provisions prohibiting bribery in foreign operations. In addition, however, the FCPA mandated that public companies maintain accurate records and devise and maintain more stringent internal accounting controls. Still more companies became involved in establishing and communicating formal codes of conduct.

Antiboycott legislation and the explosion of environmental regulation, often with criminal overtones, added new areas of law to the organized compliance effort.

My former company, faced with a consent decree that mandated formal compliance efforts only in one area of its business (the sale of wines and spirits), determined that varying levels of organized compliance efforts did not seem appropriate, particularly in the context of a broad code of conduct. Accordingly, it established a program designed to ensure compliance with all laws throughout the company, although the level of interest and activity varies from area to area.

Elements of a Compliance Program

The basic requirements of any compliance program are the same:

- Participation by the board of directors, usually with supervision expressly delegated to an audit committee. (Although note that a few commentators still doubt that legal compliance is an appropriate subject for audit committee jurisdiction.)
- The adoption and communication of a corporate policy statement that contains a commitment that the business of the company will be conducted in accordance with applicable rules of law. Often such a policy statement will also take the opportunity to encourage lower-level management to directly consult the law department if any problems arise.

- Recognition that the program is a management program, in which primary responsibility for implementation rests with the operating officers of the company. This is the most important single element of any compliance program.

The question arises as to how, if at all, a compliance program can deal with exceptions—endemic but minor violations of law (truck drivers going 60 mph), broadly unenforced laws, overseas problems that take time to cure, meeting unlawful competitive practices in the marketplace, and similar matters. In most cases, it is impractical to provide a formal written exception procedure. Additionally, boards of directors do not like to be forced to deal with exceptions. This problem is one of the reasons to have a senior management compliance committee interface with the audit committee. At the least, certain problems, if not material, can be dealt with over a longer time span—what could be called a "time-controlled solution." Any significant exceptions to the standard of compliance must be brought to the attention of this committee, which decides at what stage to report to the audit committee.

Implementing the Program

Implementing a compliance program is a five-step process:

1. Periodic review by the audit committee assures the board of directors that the program is being continuously implemented credibly and effectively.
2. A top-management compliance committee, by some name, is charged with guiding, staffing, reviewing, and reporting on the program.
3. In appropriate areas, corporate internal audit capabilities are used to ascertain potential or actual problems and to refer such special problems for special handling.
4. Assuming the corporation has its own law department, the law department participates by conducting legal audits, sometimes euphemistically referred to as legal surveys, and by preparing written educational materials, leading compliance reviews, and undertaking other educational efforts.
5. Outside counsel participates in formal investigations, when regulatory or criminal impact develops, and when top management needs special "comfort."

The legal audit, as part of the compliance program, is the subject of much of the remainder of this article, so it will not be dealt with in detail here.

Compliance Reviews

Ultimately, the purpose of a compliance program is to ensure that the corporation's public policy is communicated, understood, and adhered to. Typically, the program will use periodic educational seminars on a continuing basis. For convenience, these seminars are herein referred to as "compliance reviews."

The coverage of the compliance review will vary depending upon the circumstances. Commonly, those personnel who are in a position to get the company in trouble are required to participate at periodic intervals.

Compliance teams are organized to conduct the compliance reviews. A senior operating manager will preside at each review with the responsibility of introducing the program and remaining available during the meeting. The introduction might cover these points:

- A review of corporate public policy with specific reference to compliance with law
- The need to be forthcoming in both questions and responses
- A statement that senior management's and attendees' presence is mandated by the board of directors to emphasize the seriousness of the principles that will be discussed at the meeting
- An explanation that the program is to protect both the individual and the corporation
- If considered necessary, a statement that transgressions will be dealt with from the vantage point of management having clearly enunciated the corporate policy to all those concerned with its implementation and having clearly affirmed the seriousness of its intent

The lawyer then conducts the review, advising and instructing on the laws applicable to the operations of the clients being addressed. Presentation details at the compliance reviews will vary with the particular program.

The program is conducted in seminar form with client participation and lawyer-client interaction. In appropriate circumstances, the compliance review team can include representatives of the accounting and internal audit departments for discussions of internal control and record-keeping issues. The amount of time can vary from a half-day to several days. In my experience, four hours is the longest that a single session should last.

Preferably, the size of the group should not be larger than twenty, with twelve probably being ideal. However, as the program continues, repeat seminars can involve a larger group.

Handouts, visual aids, and other teaching materials should be copiously utilized. Presentations simulating real-life situations have been used effectively. One prominent outside antitrust lawyer is said to use blown-up visuals of indictments, pictures of the chief executive officer behind bars, and similar attention-holding materials. I suspect most of us will be satisfied with a somewhat less dramatic presentation.

Considerations of cost-effectiveness suggest that the reviews be held at the time and place of meetings already scheduled by operating personnel for other purposes. However, at the beginning of a program, separate scheduling will emphasize a corporate commitment in the strongest way.

Internal Audit Legal Referral

It is clearly important to use an internal audit function in the internal controls and record-keeping of a compliance program. Perhaps less obvious is the use of internal auditors as a source of input of legal problems for solution. Thus, the "internal audit legal referral."

Internal auditors can use legal checklists tailored to specific legal problems and covering items that an auditor can reasonably be expected to detect in the course of a regular audit. A typical example is a checklist covering specific state liquor laws. The internal auditors can be educated with printed materials and at their regular departmental meetings to be alert to certain specific matters.

In this context, the internal auditors, although not lawyers, are performing functions akin to those in a legal audit, even though their activities are limited. Protection of confidentiality requires special consideration. Internal written procedures and flow charts can specify that in this area the auditor's client is the corporate law department. Also, "findings" with respect to possible legal problems can be written up separately from the regular audit findings and transmitted to the law department for advice or resolution.

Expectations should be realistic, but with experience in the program, the internal audit department can significantly reduce the expenditure of lawyers' time in the conduct of legal audits.

Procedural Details

The basic underpinnings and procedural details of a compliance program should be set forth in a manual furnished to each lawyer. Depending on the circumstances, the manual can contain copies of policy statements, consent decrees, written program educational matter, and checklists. In general, it can serve as a source of relevant information to facilitate training of individual lawyers and to assist in their conduct of the program. Forms 1 through 6 in the Appendix are examples of a manual and accompanying forms and checklists that can be used in an antitrust compliance program.

Employee Certificates

It seems to be customary practice at the time of instigating formal compliance programs to prepare and distribute a booklet describing the program and containing a suitable certificate whereby each employee confirms understanding of, and compliance with, the corporate policies and programs. New employees should also receive the booklet and execute the certificate. A sample certificate appears as Form 4 in the Appendix.

The use of certificates to periodically reaffirm compliance is also a common practice, particularly if the organization, or some part thereof, instigated a formal program because of the discovery of significant preexisting problems. There is a difference of opinion about the usefulness of obtaining certificates on a regular basis. Some companies use general ones, containing a representation that an individual has complied with the corporate program. Others are more specific, requiring disclosure of knowledge of price fixing, price discrimination, and similar items. Some even require that a manager vouch for the actions of his or her subordinates. The literature is conflicting, and the effectiveness of such certificates debatable.

Whistle-Blower Protection

A controversial technique is to provide some kind of employee "safe harbor" whereby individual employees can get advice or report violations without following the chain of command and without fear of reprisal if they report a violation by their superiors. This practice is probably most used in distribution or consumer businesses, where employees handle cash or valuable merchandise and employee dishonesty is a significant problem. Although the downside is obvious, there are now some laws that provide protection to corporate whistle-blowers, and further developments in this area can be anticipated.

Investigation of Compliance Problems

An important element in any compliance program is the conduct of external and internal investigations occurring upon the discovery of a potentially serious compliance problem. At this point, the legal risks to the corporation are at their highest, since there may be a concurrent external investigation with criminal overtones pending or threatened, or civil litigation may be a strong possibility. When appropriate, investigations should be formally instigated at the audit committee level, with counsel being instructed to investigate and provide legal advice in anticipation of litigation.

Counsel should conduct interviews only after the interviewees have received a written direction to cooperate and have been advised that the attorney-client privilege is that of the corporation and not that of the individual employee and may be waived by the corporation. Consideration must be given to the need for *Miranda* warnings and to the availability of separate outside counsel to individual employees. (The issue of handling fee advances and payments is beyond the scope of this chapter.)

Significant problems arise when individual employees exercise fifth amendment rights or are advised by a separate counsel to consider seeking criminal immunity in exchange for testimony. I have heard of corporate policies or practices that mandate immediate termination of employment when fifth amendment rights are exercised before a grand jury. The potential harm that can be done by disgruntled former employees makes it appropriate to use a case-by-case decision process.

The particular area where most corporations should bring in outside counsel at the beginning is a formal compliance investigation, particularly when a concurrent external investigation with criminal overtones is pending or threatened, or when material civil litigation is a possibility.

Possible Problems with Compliance Programs

In the long run, formal compliance programs and other compliance efforts represent affirmative response to the increasingly recognized need for a "control environment" throughout the public corporation. In many cases, compliance programs were established as a response to a specific crisis. As elsewhere in the corporate world, there is a need for perspective so that compliance efforts do not become bureaucratic exercises with a life of their own. An ongoing program should have room for flexibility, material should be cut to fit operating needs, presentations should be sharpened, premeeting preparation expected, and day-to-day problems concentrated upon. This challenge to the management must be handled by individual corporations in the light of their own culture and environment.

It is fair to ask whether a bona fide compliance program can be a liability. At least two jury instructions have permitted the jury to consider the existence of compliance effects in determining corporate intent in Sherman Act cases.[12] Such efforts have also been considered by the court in granting judgment to a defendant.[13] In my experience, prosecuting and regulatory agencies, upon examination, have considered compliance programs favorably in determining whether or not to recommend prosecution or impose other sanctions. (However, participation in meetings by executives who have been educated by a compliance program may be evidence of a conscious and deliberate intention to join a conspiracy.)

From the standpoint of the law department, there is a real risk of turning the lawyers into police officers, with a resultant breakdown in communications and in the ability to effectively deliver legal services. For this reason alone, management should continually emphasize the educational aspects of the program, possibly even in the context of the legal audit.

Nothing could be more adverse than a compliance program that is not bona fide or that is inherently ineffective. The adoption of a corporate policy statement and implementation of a program requires a continuing corporate commitment. (General Electric's "Directive 20.5" was a resounding order for antitrust compliance. However, to quote Fuller, "[20.5]. . . obviously was regarded merely as a sheet of paper, unheeded by anyone. . . . As a matter of fact, there was later testimony that if an employee. . . failed to *violate* the GE directive, he was summarily shunted off to a less profitable job."[14] To quote an expert: "[A] 'paper' compliance program will probably do more harm than good. After all, a 'red herring' by any other name is still a fish. And, a fish when caught either gets cooked or it begins to smell bad."[15] The trial courts gave no credence to a defense or mitigation based on 20.5.[16]

In 1984 John G. Harkins, Jr., stated his impression that, conversely, the absence of a compliance program would be weighed in determining whether to instigate an enforcement action, as it should in principle, representing a failure to management, and supervision. (Note one purported quirk: The Justice Department will not consider an antitrust compliance program in mitigation or in the exercise of prosecutorial discretion, unless the program has a safe harbor for whistle-blowers.[17]

A number of cases have considered the effect of corporate policies on the question of whether the employee in fact acted to benefit the corporation.[18] The contrary line of authority strictly adheres to the historic rule that corporate criminal liability can be imposed upon *respondeat superior,* based upon the activities of the employee.[19] A few other cases have demonstrated the advantageous uses of Compliance Programs.[20] The cases that exist support the conclusion that the weak, improperly implemented or "paper" compliance program can greatly hurt the corporate defendant.[21] (Sam Miller has done seminal work in sorting out conflicting theories of corporate criminal liability in these situations.[22])

The Compliance Legal Audit— Who, Where, When, What, and Why

Who: Inside versus Outside Counsel

Assuming an ongoing compliance legal audit program and enough law department resources, cost-effectiveness alone suggests the use of inside counsel. Additionally, paralegal personnel can be used effectively, particularly for document review and similar tasks. However, there are exceptions to the rule that inside counsel should be used if possible:

- If significant litigation has commenced, in most cases any legal audit efforts should be solely in conjunction with that litigation and should be conducted by trial counsel in the course of their usual litigation activities.
- If a formal audit committee investigation is being conducted, any peripheral legal auditing should be conducted by the counsel engaged for trial investigation.
- If counsel is engaged because of grand jury activity or because a significant regulatory investigation (such as an IRS tax fraud inquiry) is under way, any peripheral legal auditing should be conducted by counsel engaged for that matter.

The obvious reason for these exceptions is the potential problems resulting from the conduct of routine compliance activities in a high-risk environment.

There is, of course, another view, which holds that the purported objectivity of outside counsel renders it the choice to perform legal audits. I disagree with this view. However, if the law department appears to be cast in the role of police officer, its effectiveness could be compromised. For that reason, the education purposes discussed earlier should be emphasized.

Where

At the commencement of a formal compliance program, the program's planners should consider examining all units and facilities. If overall auditing is impractical or otherwise inappropriate, then concentration should be on high-risk areas, using sampling and written questionnaires to identify particular candidates.

Follow-up can be either periodic or determined by using the techniques that originally identified the high-risk areas.

When

Assuming a positive cost/benefit ratio, timing is pretty much a function of where and why, giving consideration also to the litigation and investigatory consideration discussed under "Who." After an initial compliance legal audit program is completed, experience permits a sharpening of focus and attention to high-risk, high-exposure activities.

What

How a legal audit should be done is discussed in the next section of this chapter.

Why

There are at least three reasons for a compliance legal audit program, any of which could separately justify the program. A compliance legal audit program provides comfort to the board of directors that the corporate code of conduct is not just an empty writing, but rather is in place as a fundamental element of corporate policy.

Obviously, legal audits may identify problem areas. We are back to the basics of preventive law, and Professor Brown's four assumptions (described at the beginning of this chapter) are still valid.

In many cases, however, a compliance legal audit program is justified alone on its potential for lawyer education. It is possible for there to be compliance programs without legal audits; I doubt that there can be effective compliance programs that do not focus on a continuing education of company personnel as to the reasons for compliance and the specifics of how to comply. The lawyers who participate in legal audits of specific units and locations learn directly what the problems are in the real world and are better equipped to provide practical advice. At the same time, lower-level managers have direct access to inside counsel in an institutional context, which encourages them to share their problems.

The Elements of and Procedure for a Compliance Legal Audit

The Checklist

The lawyer performing the audit should use a checklist to ensure that all areas and issues of concern are covered. The development of the checklist also serves to develop the audit program itself in a logical and complete form. In addition, the checklist permits the lawyer performing the audit to benefit from the experience of the senior lawyers in the specialized fields of law involved.

Retention of Checklist

There are differing opinions about the retention of the checklist after the audit has been performed. Any generalization is probably both impractical and dangerous.

One school of thought believes that at the completion of the audit, the lawyer should use the checklist and any interview notes to prepare a carefully drafted file memorandum setting forth the audit findings. Thereupon, the checklist and the lawyer's interview notes should be destroyed. (I once heard a prominent food and drug lawyer argue that internal food company quality control audit reports should have a retention period of not more than ten seconds! Conversely, in such products liability fields as drugs and toxic substances, longer retention periods appear to be more and more justifiable.)

The other view is that the work-product and attorney-client privileges provide adequate protection, and that the single copy of the completed checklist should be preserved with the findings memorandum in law department files, to provide a record of the scope of the audit as long as needed. Obviously, the completed checklist should not be duplicated or distributed in any event.

On balance, I am of the view that, assuming it has not been used as a convenient notepad during survey interviews, a carefully drafted checklist can be preserved, but that it is not necessary if the closing file memorandum makes the scope of the audit clear. Accordingly, the better practice seems to be routine destruction.

Approach to Drafting Checklist

The checklist should be drafted in a way that avoids the possibility that its subsequent production could be embarrassing or worse. As an extreme example, the checklist would not have an item "Sherman Act violated: ___ Yes ___ No." Instead, the checklist would provide, "Determine the applicability of the Sherman Act and compliance therewith— ___ Relevant matters reviewed ___ See comment."

Straightforward factual questions without substantive connotations can provide for yes and no answers: "Does the operation have approved written purchase order terms and conditions? ___ Yes ___ No ___ See comment."

The Overall Checklist

An overall checklist should include a section on general compliance, which should cover the following points:

- Applicability of consent decrees and cease and desist orders and compliance therewith
- Applicability of specific statutes and regulations and compliance therewith
- Determination of any regulatory jurisdiction by other federal, state, and local agencies over products or activities, excluding agencies acting pursuant to enumerated specific laws, and determination of compliance with requirements thereof
- Determination that corporate requirements for mandatory law department approvals are being obtained: printed or standard forms; advertising, packaging, and labeling; political and charitable contributions, including tickets

- Determination whether any litigation or administrative proceedings are pending or threatened and/or whether local counsel is being used without appropriate approvals

Trade Association Activities

In most organizations, trade association memberships and participation in trade association activities are of great enough potential risk that a series of questions should be directed specifically to this area. The following list of obvious potential items was developed by McKesson, but certainly no originality is claimed:

- Possible antitrust violations by, and litigation against, the association over at least the past five years
- Competent legal counsel attending all meetings and writing minutes
- Pricing activities or discussions
- Restrictive membership qualifications
- Use of expulsion
- Availability of services to nonmembers
- Engagement in cost studies, product standardization, certification practices, or industry self-regulation
- Engagement in cooperative buying or selling
- Engagement in lobbying
- Credit report function
- "Rump sessions" before or after meetings
- Social gatherings
- Membership inclusion of different industry levels: suppliers, distributors, customers

Antitrust Compliance

In most organizations, antitrust compliance will be a major area of concern. The development of this portion of the checklist permits a focus on areas of particular concern. One way to structure this portion of the checklist is to break down the items functionally (which may result in an overlap beyond antitrust considerations).

Depending on the circumstances, the pricing section would cover such items as these:

- How pricing authority is defined
- How price-exception authority is defined
- An examination of the differences, or lack thereof, between the company's prices and those of its competitors and the justifications for any price similarity
- The maintenance of written price and discount lists

- Any variance in price lists, geographical or otherwise, for the same product, and the justification therefor
- The existence of sales at other than listed prices and, if such sales exist, the maintenance of written justifications
- The interchange, publication, or other distribution of prices or price lists, in advance or otherwise
- Whether any competitors are customers or suppliers
- The details of any price leadership in the industry and the methods of setting competitive prices
- If meeting competition is a factor, whether prices are met, not beat, the use of written price deviation forms, the substantiation set forth therein, and the retention of the forms
- Whether two- or three-tier pricing is used
- The use of volume discount schedules, and how they are justified
- Minimum order size
- Seasonal price fluctuations
- Promotional price reductions
- The suggestion or endorsement of retailer or distributor prices in print, package, or otherwise

When appropriate, sections of the checklist would cover relations with suppliers. These sections would include such items as the following:

- A determination of whether contracts are used and, if used, the audit procedure would also require an examination of the contracts themselves, at least through the use of a sampling procedure
- Territorial restrictions in contracts
- Price maintenance provisions in contracts
- Output or requirement provisions
- "Evergreen" provisions
- State laws affecting termination of agreements
- "Favored nation" provisions
- Reciprocal purchasing arrangements
- Exposure to charges of inducing discriminatory low prices

Where appropriate, sections of the checklist would deal with sales and distribution activities (not otherwise covered), including advertising, promotions, and merchandising activities:

- Who the operation sells to—distributors, retailers, consumers
- Existence of independent sales agents
- Existence of exclusive sales arrangements

- Refusals to sell to individual customers or classes of customers and circumstances thereof, including unilateral nature of determination and maintenance of adequate written justification
- Existence of written distribution or sales representative agreements; practices regarding termination and maintenance of written justification
- Existence of understandings not to sell in certain markets, domestic and foreign
- Existence of joint selling or marketing arrangements with competitors
- Existence of exclusive agents or distributors and an examination of surrounding circumstances
- Existence of sales below cost
- Existence of advertising programs and provision of advertising or promotional services or allowances and, if these exist, existence of a written program making them available to all direct or indirect customers or competing customers on a proportionately equal basis
- Reliance upon independent distributors to communicate advertising, merchandising, and promotional plans and/or to distribute advertising, merchandising, and promotional payments to indirect customers; if they are relied upon, existence of appropriate supervisory or audit programs to assure proportionately equal treatment
- Customer identification or retail price information in advertisements
- Allocation practices during shortages

The preceding lists of specific suggestions are intended to show how many sections of the checklist can be designed. The basic idea is to review functionally a particular part of the corporate operations in the light of the substantial legal issues and problems that apply to the operation, and then to formulate a series of factual questions, the answers to which will disclose a legal problem. A sample antitrust compliance checklist is included as Form 5 in the Appendix.

Other Operational Areas

There are, of course, many other operational areas that lend themselves to treatment similar to that just discussed. The following items should be included in the checklist to cover purchasing matters:

- The existence of written purchase orders and acknowledgments and other standard forms is verified.

- Standard practices—i.e., rejection of the other party's terms and conditions, inspection on receipt, and the like—are reviewed.
- Inquiry is made into the existence of single-source purchasing of essential materials, and the legal status of any such commitments is reviewed.
- Particular attention is addressed to the issues of warranty, indemnity, and limitation of liability. I recall one case where field officials executed a tank car agreement with liability-shifting provisions that resulted in a $1.4 million personal injury judgment in the trial court because written corporate procedures calling for review of indemnity provisions were not being followed.
- When applicable, the checklist should cover standard practices with respect to obtaining and giving statutory Food, Drug, and Cosmetic Act guarantees and similar guarantees under other federal and state laws.

With regard to product liability exposure, the examination overlaps into purchasing and sales documentation and other practices, particularly in the warranty area. In addition, however, appropriate questions deal with products that require warnings as to hazards, methods of use, storage, or disposal. The entire chain of documentation, as well as the packaging and labeling, is examined to determine the adequacy of such warnings and the extent to which currently accurate data are obtained and passed on.

The checklist inquires into practices in the field such as whether representatives ever recommend substances, practices, and procedures based on customer advice as to end use, and whether the company refuses to furnish products when a disclosed use could be hazardous.[23]

In general, you should consider including a checklist on all those other areas of operations where legal risks are involved. Examples are:

- Trademark and copyright protection and practices
- Patent and trade secret protection and practices (including licensing procedures)
- Equal employment opportunity compliance and employee termination practices
- Franchising practices
- Antiboycott practices
- Real property—fee and leasehold
- Escheat practices
- Risk of disregard of corporate entity of subsidiaries (what is the impact of the corporate cash management system?)

- Local property tax procedures (are local consultants or counsel, used on a contingent fee basis?)
- Advertising and promotional programs
- Insurance and risk management practices
- Consumer credit practices
- Interlocking directorates
- Conflicts of interest

In some areas, the only question for the checklist may be an inquiry as to whether the company is obtaining required legal or other corporate staff reviews. A sample license and joint venture review procedure is shown as Form 6 in the Appendix.

Noncheckhlist Areas

There are still other areas of potential legal exposure where the checklists are either a less important element of the legal audit or where considerations of technical expertise render the lawyer inappropriate to conduct the audit alone. Compliance with environmental laws is a typical example. Various types of audits are inherent in an environmental compliance program.[24]

Compliance with the Foreign Corrupt Practices Act is an important element of many compliance programs. Here, however, the checklist seems a less important tool, and personal interviewing and document examination become even more fundamental. The books, records, and financial controls issues, in the audit context, are primarily for the internal auditors. The key problem in the foreign payments area is to identify exposures. This requires an inquiry into such things as payments to foreign consultants and agents, cash transfers to foreign subsidiaries, payments of salaries or fees outside the country of residence or domicile of the recipient, questionable invoicing procedures, supported payments and "back to back" arrangements. The lawyer's role is essential, but different techniques must be emphasized to produce the raw data for analysis.

The Lawyer's Survey

The primary intent of surveys is to bring the lawyer to the facts, to permit the identification of existing and potential problem areas, and to better equip that lawyer to conduct operations-oriented compliance reviews.

The survey should develop basic information about the competitive environment of the operating unit. The relevant facts include size, product lines, number and relative size of competitors, classes of customers, and supplier relationships.

The process of learning about the unit will inevitably reveal potential legal problems. They should be identified so that they can be evaluated.

It is not the purpose of the survey to educate local management about relevant laws, although the opportunity to do so may often, or even usually, present itself. The lawyer must use judgment about the feasibility and desirability of doing this, within the time available to conduct the survey.

While the checklist is an aid to assure complete coverage of relevant legal areas, it certainly is not a substitute for intelligent inquiries designed to provide complete information. If the checklist is used as a convenient notepad to record information, then it and any other notes should be destroyed immediately after the survey report has been prepared.

Particular circumstances, including time restraints, will dictate whether interviews should be conducted separately or with a group of employees. Initial and follow-up interviews separately with the local manager seem appropriate, with the rest of the information being obtained in sessions with one or more small groups of key employees. Information so gathered will suggest the desirability of further individual interviews.

On-the-spot legal advice given to local management should be confined to very serious matters—those involving high risks, clear violations of important criminal statutes or basic corporate policy, and serious exposure to liability. An example is possible price-fixing activity.

The survey portion of the legal audit program should contemplate that most legal problems identified will be subject to a more thorough factual and legal analysis after the audit has been completed.

Document Review

Practically any legal audit should serve to update and improve record retention practices and to secure compliance with record retention policies. In addition, in many and perhaps most instances, only a review of documents can adequately determine legal exposures.

Perlman and Rea[25] suggest that sampling techniques can be employed for screening fairly uniform documents, such as contracts, nondisclosure agreements, or price exception reports. They state the inspection of 50 percent of the documents in a file of similar documents achieves a high probability of finding sensitive or problem documents.

Like Perlman and Rea, I adhere to the view that key words or subjects facilitate the audit process. Their example, in the antitrust area, is that "market share" and "pricing" and files of that nature are screened fully. My own list in the same area is taken from John T. Loughlin's classic article, "The Naughty Words of Antitrust."[26] Loughlin identifies twelve categories of "naughty" antitrust words:

1. Guilty-complex words: "destroy after reading," "no copies"
2. Power words
3. Planning and intent words

4. Words delineating markets or market shares
5. Bragging words
6. Overselling words: "To you Jim and to you alone, the price is a below-cost two bucks a dozen"
7. Overcompetitive and undercompetitive words: "Let's cut him off at the knees"; "Let's make a diplomatic approach to that unethical competitor"
8. Words disparaging competitors
9. Loose words about competition and prices
10. Conclusionary words on antitrust subjects
11. Helpfully intended words by friends
12. Unnecessary words

With thought, similar key words and subjects can be developed for other areas of legal significance. With a checklist in hand and the key words and subjects in mind, it is possible to screen selected files effectively in a reasonable time. Paralegal personnel can be used very effectively in this area.

The Audit Report

Immediately upon completion of the audit, the lawyer who conducted it should prepare a report. The report should cover the following topics:

- Competitive environment
- Identification of legal problems, with as many facts as possible to facilitate resolution
- Any on-the-spot legal advice given to local management
- An indication that all relevant items on the checklist were covered in the audit
- A statement as to the scope of the document review and its results. If appropriate, copies of specific documents can be appended.

The effective implementation of the legal audit requires that the legal problems identified be written up so that they can be properly analyzed and resolved. The process could generate written materials that contain statements indicating possible law violations of varying degrees of seriousness.

The attorney-client privilege and the attorney work-product rule may insulate audit reports from later discovery, but they may not. These reports probably stretch the traditional ambit of the work-product rule to some extent.[27] In any event, that privilege is only conditional. Despite *Upjohn v. United States,*[28] state courts may limit the attorney-client privilege to a corporate control group. In the event of stockholder litigation, *Garner v. Wolfinbarger*[29] is still with us. For an optimistic update, see Kirby's article titled "New Life for the Corporate Attorney-Client Privilege in Shareholder Litigation."[30]

Risks arising from future discovery should be reduced, to the extent possible. Consider the following:

- Reports should be written with the understanding that what is written may subsequently be discovered. This does not require distortion or incompleteness, but give thought to what is written. Do not state legal conclusions; avoid opinion and speculation. Do not represent something as fact unless you are sure it is. Concede the incomplete nature of the information and the need for additional research and analysis.
- Audit reports probably should not be retained after they have served the purpose of identifying legal problems for solution. An appropriate retention period would be only until the next audit of the same unit, or until all problems identified are resolved, whichever occurs first.
- There should be a standard procedure for retention. Selective destruction of particular sensitive reports appears to be the worst of evils.

Review and Follow-up

Each audit report should be reviewed to determine the significance of the legal problems identified and to determine what appropriate corrective action should be taken. Individual law department structures will determine the responsibility to obtain additional facts, analyze legal issues, and recommend appropriate courses of action. Lawyers not participating in the audit who are assigned particular divisional responsibilities need to be kept informed and perhaps to be used to handle the problems that have been identified with their particular managements.

Conclusion

This chapter has attempted to demonstrate that corporate compliance efforts must be designed and implemented in the light of the specific environment of a given corporation. There is no body of generally accepted corporate compliance practices that provides standards by which to measure compliance efforts. Such guidance as has been furnished by courts or regulatory agencies is spotty and not necessarily consistent.

Notes

1. Brown, *Legal Audit,* 38 S. CAL. L. REV. 431 (1965).
2. *See* Wald, *Anti-Trust Audits,* 1 CORP. PRAC. COMM. 17 (1959).
3. Brown, *supra,* note 1, at 431–32.

4. L. M. BROWN & E. A. DAUER, PLANNING BY LAWYERS: MATERIALS ON A NONADVERSARIAL LEGAL PROCESS (1978).
5. Vol. 1, no. 3 (Jan. 1983), PL Publishers.
6. For this distinction, and for much more, I express my gratitude to Lawrence Perlman and Kelley V. Rea, General Counsel and Assistant General Counsel, respectively, of Control Data Corporation, for their outline entitled "Newer Methods of Introducing and Implementing a Legal Audit and Corporate Compliance Program" presented in San Francisco in October 1982 at the 14th Corporate Section Meeting of the Conference of American Legal Executives. No one covering this ground can avoid treading in the Perlman and Rea footsteps.
7. Perlman & Rea, *supra* note 6.
8. 56 NOTRE DAME LAW. 838 (1981).
9. *Id.* at 848.
10. 68 A.B.A. J. 446 (1982).
11. A significant amount of material is available on antitrust compliance programs and legal audits in connection therewith. Following is a selected bibliography; most of the materials listed cite other valuable material: Anderson, *Antitrust Compliance in Action,* ANTITRUST BULL. 731 (Winter 1975); BRADLEY, ANTITRUST ADVISOR, ch. 8 (2d ed. 1978) (includes detailed suggested questions in substantive antitrust areas for use in audits); GARRETT, ANTITRUST COMPLIANCE (1978); HANCOCK, MATERIALS AND ANTITRUST COMPLIANCE (2 vols. 1983) (contains an FTC Memorandum, "An Outline of an Antitrust Compliance Program" with its own bibliography, appendix to vol. 2 at 1553); McLaury, *Compliance Programs under the Robinson-Patman Act and Other Antitrust Laws,* 37 ANTITRUST L. J. 96 (1968); Shenefield, *Compliance Programs as Viewed from the Antitrust Division,* NATIONAL INSTITUTE ON PREVENTIVE ANTITRUST (1979), *reprinted in* 48 ANTITRUST L.J. 73 (1980). All of volume 73, issue 1 of the *Antitrust Law Journal* is devoted to the proceedings of that institute. Included is a dramatization, "Presentation of an Antitrust Compliance Program to Management," and a panel discussion, "Varied Approaches to Antitrust Compliance." *See also* Forms 1–4 in the Appendix for samples of antitrust legal audit compliance materials.
12. United States v. Koppers Co. (D.C. Conn., Criminal No. 73–85, June 26, 1980); *In re* Corrugated Container Antitrust Litig., M.D.L. No. 301 (S.D. Tex. 1979).
13. Di-Wal, Inc. v. Fibreboard Corp., 1980 Trade Cas. (CCH) ¶ 73,155 (N.D. Cal. 1970).
14. FULLER, THE GENTLEMEN CONSPIRATORS 87 (1962).
15. Cyrus V. Anderson, quoting himself in Anderson, *supra* note 11.
16. *See* BANE, THE ELECTRICAL EQUIPMENT CONSPIRACIES (1973).
17. Speech by Ky P. Ewing, Jr., Apr. 28, 1981, *reported in* LAWYER'S BRIEF, no. 9, May 15, 1981.
18. United States v. Beusch, 596 F.2d 871 (9th Cir. 1979) (Bank Secrecy Act); United States v. Basic Constr. Co., 711 F.2d 570 (4th Cir.), *cert. denied,* 194 S. Ct. 371 (Sherman Act); United States v. Hanger 1, Inc., 406 F. Supp. 60 (N.D. Ala. 1975), *rev'd on other grounds,* 563 F.2d 1155 (5th Cir. 1977) (False Claims Act). *See* United States v. American Radiation & Standard Sanitary Corp., 433 F.2d 174, 204 (3d Cir. 1979), *cert. denied,* 410 U.S. 948 (Sherman Act).

25

19. United States v. Hilton Hotel Corp., 467 F.2d 1000 (9th Cir. 1972), *cert. denied,* 409 U.S. 1125; C.I.T. Corp. v. United States, 150 F.2d 85 (9th Cir. 1945).

20. TRW Inc. v. FTC, 647 F.2d 942 (9th Cir. 1981) (Clayton Act § 8, Issuance of FTC Cease and Desist Order improper); Peter Kiewit Sons' Co. v. United States Army Corps of Engineers, 534 F. Supp. 1139 (D.D.C. 1982), *rev'd,* 714 F.2d 163 (D.C. Cir. 1983) (showing that plaintiff was a "responsible bidder" despite prior bid rigging); United States v. FMC Corp., 306 F. Supp. 1106 (E.D. Pa. 1969) (finding of independent pricing decision because employee resisted price discussion overtures, based on compliance program); Corregated Container Antitrust Litig., 1981–1 Trade Cas. (CCH) ¶ 64, 114 (S.D. Tex.) (in analyzing the fairness of settlements, the court consisdered the existence or absence of antitrust compliance programs in evaluating whether the plaintiffs' case was strong or weak against particular settling defendants); Carroll v. Sears, Roebuck & Co., 514 F. Supp. 788 (W.D. La. 1981), *aff'd in part and rev'd in part,* 708 F.2d 1983 (5th Cir. 1983) (relevance to lack of employment discrimination); EEOC v. IBM Corp., 583 F. Supp. 875 (D. Md. 1984) (akin to *Sears, Roebuck*).

21. United States v. Greyhound Corp., 363 F. Supp. 525 (N.D. Ill. 1973), 370 F. Supp. 881 (1974) (contempt of court); United States v. Phelps Dodge Indus., Inc., 1984–1 Trade Cas. (CCH) ¶ 65, 987 (S.D.N.Y. 1984) (violation of FTC Cease and Desist Order); Montgomery Ward & Co. v. FTC, 691 F.2d 1322 (9th Cir. 1982) (cease and desist order, Magnuson-Moss Warranty Act).

22. Miller & Levine, *Recent Developments in Corporate Criminal Liability,* 24 SANTA CLARA L. REV. 41 (1984).

23. For additional discussion of product liability considerations, see Dauer & Kolmar, *Lawyers' Roles in Products Liability Prevention for the Small Business Client,* 1 PREVENTIVE L. REP. 1 (Apr. 1983); Ross, *The Role of Lawyers in Product Liability Prevention for the Large Corporate Client,* 2 PREVENTIVE L. REP. 104 (Feb. 1984).

24. For a reference to such audit practices, see *Structuring Corporate Compliance Programs for Pollution Control Requirements,* 35 BUS. LAW. 1459, 1476–78, 1487–89 (1980).

25. Perlman & Rea, *supra* note 6.

26. 54 A.B.A. J. 246 (Mar. 1968).

27. *See* Chapter 2 for a more detailed description of the attorney-client privilege and work-product doctrine with regard to legal audit reports.

28. 449 U.S. 383 (1981).

29. 430 F.2d 1093 (5th Cir. 1920).

30. 69 A.B.A. J. 174 (Feb. 1983). See chapters two and thirty for a more detailed discussion of the attorney-client privilege and work-product doctrine.

Two

Preserving the Confidentiality of Legal Audit Findings

Jerold S. Solovy, Joel J. Africk, and David M. Greenwald

A legal audit is an internal corporate investigation of questionable corporate practices, usually conducted under the auspices of a committee of the board of directors and directly supervised by either in-house or outside counsel. A corporation may initiate a legal audit upon learning information that suggests illegal conduct or misuse of funds, in response to an ongoing government investigation or agency subpoena, or pursuant to a consent decree entered into with the SEC or other government agencies.

A corporation should maintain the confidentiality of its legal audits to minimize the corporation's exposure to adverse proceedings by public and private litigants. Maintaining confidentiality also will diminish adverse publicity and embarrassment to the corporation. Corporations, therefore, should structure legal audits to maximize the protections of confidentiality afforded by the attorney-client privilege and the work-product doctrine.

Structuring a Legal Audit to Maximize the Protection of the Attorney-Client Privilege

Although the facts discovered during the course of a legal audit are not themselves privileged, a corporation may be able to shield portions of the audit by preserving the attorney-client privilege.[1] To establish that the privilege applies, a corporation must establish the traditional elements of a privilege claim. The elements of a privilege claim were set forth concisely by Judge Wyzanski in *United States v. United Shoe Machinery Corp.*:[2]

1. the privilege applies only if the person who asserts the privilege is or seeks to become a client;

Jerold S. Solovy is a member and Joel J. Africk and David M. Greenwald are associates of Jenner & Block, Chicago, Illinois.

2. the person to whom the communication was made is an attorney or his subordinate, acting in his capacity as an attorney with respect to the communication;
3. the communication relates to a fact of which the attorney was informed by the client in confidence;
4. the communication relates to the seeking of legal advice or assistance and not for the purpose of committing a crime or tort; and
5. the privilege has been claimed and not waived.[3]

Only Communications with a Client Are Privileged

The attorney-client privilege protects communications between the attorney and his or her client, but not between the attorney and third parties. Although this requirement is easily applied with respect to individuals, the definition of "client" in the corporate setting is considerably less clear.

Defining the "Client"

In *Upjohn Co. v. United States*,[4] the Supreme Court held that communications between legal counsel and lower-echelon managers of a corporation were protected by the attorney-client privilege when the information necessary to supply the basis for legal advice was not available from "control group" management, when the communications concerned matters within the scope of the employees' duties, when the employees were aware that they were being questioned in order for the corporation to secure legal advice, and when the communications were considered confidential when made and kept confidential.[5]

In *Upjohn*, the company discovered that a foreign subsidiary had paid foreign government officials to secure government business. After learning of the payments, Upjohn's general counsel conferred with the chairman of the board and outside counsel.[6] Upjohn then commenced an internal investigation and, as a part of that investigation, sent questionnaires to all of its foreign managers. In a letter accompanying the questionnaire, the chairman emphasized the company's need to know the full extent of such payments and explained that counsel had been directed to conduct an investigation. Recipients of the questionnaire were instructed to send their responses directly to the general counsel and to treat the investigation as highly confidential. General counsel and outside counsel also interviewed the questionnaire recipients and other employees.[7]

At the conclusion of the audit, Upjohn voluntarily submitted to the SEC a preliminary report disclosing certain questionable payments on SEC Form 8-K. Upjohn also submitted a copy of the report to the IRS along with a list of the names of all persons who had been interviewed and who had responded to the questionnaire. The IRS issued a summons demanding production of all files regarding the investigation, including the completed questionnaires and notes or memoranda of oral interviews. When Upjohn refused to comply with the summons, the IRS sought enforcement.[8]

The district court found that Upjohn had waived the attorney-client privilege and ordered enforcement of the IRS summons. On appeal, the Sixth Circuit rejected the waiver argument relied on by the district court, but ruled that the communications in question were not privileged if they were made by employees who were not in Upjohn's "control group"—in other words those persons "not responsible for directing Upjohn's actions in response to legal advice." Because the record was unclear on this issue, the Sixth Circuit remanded to the district court for a determination of who was within Upjohn's "control group."[9]

The Supreme Court reversed and upheld Upjohn's assertion of the privilege. Noting that the purpose of the privilege is "to encourage full and frank communication between attorneys and their clients," the Supreme Court criticized the Sixth Circuit's application of the control group test because it "overlook[ed] the fact that the privilege exists to protect not only the giving of professional advice to those who can act on it but also the giving of information to the lawyer to enable him to give sound and informed advice."[10] The Court recognized that the first step in resolving any legal problem is to ascertain the facts and to focus on those that are legally relevant. In the corporate context, the Court noted, the individuals with legally relevant information may be middle- or lower-level employees.[11]

The Court in *Upjohn* "decline[d] to lay down a broad rule" to govern the extent of the privilege's reach,[12] and therefore left open many questions to be resolved on a case-by-case basis. For example, the Court expressly refused to decide whether the privilege protects communications from former employees during the course of legal audits.[13] However, Chief Justice Burger, in his concurrence, expressed his belief that the privilege should apply to communications from former employees.[14]

Post-*Upjohn* decisions have generally taken an expansive approach to defining the "client." The Ninth Circuit, for example, has extended the protection of the privilege to communications by former employees. In *In re Coordinated Pretrial Proceedings in Petroleum Products Antitrust Litigation*,[15] the plaintiff sought to disqualify the defendant corporation's attorney from representing past and present corporation employees, asserting that such representation prevented plaintiffs from inquiring into predeposition conferences between the employees and the corporation's attorney.[16] The court said that communications between the employees and attorney for the corporation were privileged regardless of whether they were represented by the same attorney. (State courts have not uniformly followed the *Upjohn* decision, as described later in this chapter.) In another case decided after *Upjohn*, one court has upheld the privilege in the absence of one of the *Upjohn* factors.[17]

Employees Generally Not Considered Individual Clients of Corporate Counsel

Although the corporation may enjoy the attorney-client privilege with respect to communications between an employee and its attorney, the employee does not automatically become a client of the attorney. For example, in *United States v. Keplinger*,[18] the court held that employees who had been questioned by their employer's counsel could not assert the attorney-client privilege with respect to those communications because no attorney-client relationship existed between the employees and the corporation's attorneys.

The defendants, employees of Industrial Bio-Test Laboratories, Inc. (IBT), were charged with various counts involving false and fraudulent statements in connection with laboratory safety studies. Before trial, the defendants attempted to suppress certain testimony and materials on the ground of an attorney-client privilege. The trial court determined that no attorney-client relationship existed. The Seventh Circuit affirmed, noting that the trial court had found that the defendants never sought or inquired about individual representation, and IBT's attorneys had neither believed nor represented to the defendants that they were acting as counsel to the employees.

Note that if an attorney fails to make clear to an employee that the attorney is representing the corporation and not the employee, the attorney may be disqualified from representing the corporation in later litigation against the employee. An employee has, however, a heavy burden to establish that corporate counsel was providing dual representation of the corporation and the individual. In *In re Grand Jury Investigation No. 83-30557*,[19] the court held that an employee seeking to prove that he was being represented individually by corporate counsel must show: (1) he approached corporate counsel for the purpose of seeking legal advice; (2) he made it clear that he was seeking advice in his individual capacity; (3) counsel sought to communicate with the employee in an individual capacity mindful of possible conflicts; (4) communications were confidential; and (5) communications did not concern the employee's official duties or general affairs of the company.[20]

Only Communications with an Attorney or Attorney's Agent Are Privileged

The attorney-client privilege protects communications with in-house or outside counsel when counsel is acting in the capacity of an attorney.

In-House Counsel

In-house counsel enjoy the full protection of the privilege for communications in a legal capacity. In *In re Sealed Case*, [21] the D.C. Circuit Court of Appeals held that status as house counsel does not dilute the privilege, but does require a clear showing that communications with house counsel were in a professional legal capacity. The Federal Circuit Court of Appeal concurred in *U.S. Steel Corp. v. United States*, [22] and held that status as in-house counsel alone cannot serve as the sole basis for denying access to confidential information in cases before the Court of International Trade.[23]

Specially Appointed Counsel

Specially appointed counsel also enjoy the protection of the privilege for advice given in the capacity of attorney. Indeed, one court has extended the privilege to an officer serving a hybrid role as privately retained counsel and government investigator. In *In re LTV Securities Litigation*,[24] the court refused to allow discovery of the contents of communications with a "special officer" appointed pursuant to a consent decree with the SEC.[25] The court observed that the functions and obligations of the special officer were a hybrid of those of a government investigator and privately retained counsel. Specifically, the court noted that the corporation did not control the special officer's duties, was obligated to cooperate fully with the special officer, could not assert any corporate privilege against the officer except with respect to matters prepared in the course of the SEC investigation, and was obligated to authorize all employees, officers, and directors to testify under oath.[26] The special officer was obligated to furnish the SEC with all materials or information in his possession before submitting them to the corporation.[27]

Analyzing the case as if the special officer had been either the corporation's privately retained counsel or a government investigator, the court concluded that the bulk of his work would be protected from disclosure under either role.[28] Although recognizing that the material was not privileged under traditional theories, the court emphasized the utility of special officers in SEC investigations and the benefits of having such officers for all concerned, including the shareholders. A finding of no privilege in this context, the court recognized, would have discouraged corporations from self-investigation and would force the SEC to commit significantly greater resources to its investigations.[29]

Only communications to and from specially appointed counsel acting in a legal capacity are entitled to protection.[30] Where an attorney serves solely as an investigator and and not as a legal adviser, the communications are not privileged. For example, in *SEC v. Canadian Javelin Ltd.*,[31] the court held that no attorney-client relationship existed between the corporation and its special counsel, and therefore the privilege did not apply.[32] In *Canadian Javelin*, the SEC moved for an order to compel deposition testimony and production of documents from an attorney who had been named as special independent counsel to the corporation's compliance committee pursuant to an injunction entered against the corporation in an earlier case.[33] The earlier injunction gave the special counsel the obligation to review all information disseminated by the corporation, to take all reasonable steps to ensure compliance with the decree, and to notify the SEC and the corporation's board of directors in the event of noncompliance. The injunction was silent as to the attorney-client privilege.

The court found that no attorney-client relationship existed between the corporation and the special independent counsel. The court noted that he was not appointed to render advice, but to monitor compliance. The court also observed that the corporation did not have any legitimate expectation of confidentiality because counsel was obligated to disclose the corporation's activities to the SEC.[34]

A similar result was reached in a slightly different factual setting in *Osterneck v. E. T. Barwick Industries.*[35] In *Osterneck*, private party plaintiffs subpoenaed attorneys who had acted as special counsel to Barwick pursuant to an SEC consent decree.[36] The decree provided that the disclosure of any information or materials to the special counsel did not constitute a waiver of the attorney-client privilege. It further provided that any privileged material would be released to the SEC only upon a judicial determination that such disclosure would not constitute a waiver.

The attorneys who had acted as special counsel to Barwick refused to comply with the plaintiffs' subpoenas on the ground that the material requested was privileged.[37] Granting plaintiffs' motion to compel the depositions, the court held that special counsel was not retained to render legal advice but to investigate and report the facts.[38] In support of its holding, the court noted that only a minute portion of the final report of special counsel consisted of legal advice.[39]

Agents of Counsel

The attorney-client privilege also applies to communications with an agent of an attorney.[40] The privilege applies to a subordinate or agent of the attorney only when the attorney is using the agent to facilitate the rendering of legal advice, and when the agent is acting under the direct supervision of the attorney.[41]

Only Communications Made for the Purpose of Securing Legal Advice Are Privileged

To be protected by the attorney-client privilege, communications must relate to the seeking of legal advice.[42] The privilege is not lost merely because the communication contains some nonlegal information.[43] However, when an attorney acts as business adviser or scrivener, communications are not privileged.[44]

If a document is prepared for simultaneous review by legal and nonlegal personnel, it is not privileged. Courts have typically held that such documents were not prepared primarily for the purpose of providing legal advice.[45] Also, as noted, communications incident to an attorney-conducted investigation do not constitute *per se* legal advice.[46]

Summary documents that are created based on attorney-client communications, but that do not reveal any individual communications, may be not privileged if they were prepared for purposes other than securing legal advice.[47]

Communications from an Attorney to a Client

Generally, the attorney-client privilege protects communications from an attorney to a client as well as communications from the latter to the former. There is some conflict, however, as to whether a communication from an attorney to a client is itself privileged or is privileged only to the extent that its disclosure would reveal a confidential communication from a client to his attorney.

Some courts have protected virtually all of the attorney's communications to his or her client. For example, in *In re LTV Securities Litigation*,[48] the court recognized that there was a split of authority, and noted that several courts had held that communications from attorney to client were not encompassed within the attorney-client privilege unless they revealed confidential client communications. The court rejected this approach, however, as failing "to deal with the reality that lifting the cover from the advice will seldom leave covered the client's communication to his lawyer."[49] Instead, the court adopted the "broader rule" which protects from disclosure any communication from an attorney to a client when made in the course of giving legal advice.[50]

Other courts have adopted a narrower view and have held that communications from attorney to client are privileged only to the extent that their disclosure would reveal a confidential communication from a client.[51]

Waiver of the Attorney-Client Privilege

Even if all the prerequisites for asserting the attorney-client privilege are met, a corporation can be found to have waived the protection afforded by the privilege. Whenever a corporation discloses confidential communications to third parties, including government agencies, the disclosure may constitute a waiver both as to the communication that has been disclosed and other communications relating to the same subject. In addition, a corporation may be found to have waived the privilege if it has used privileged communications in a manner inconsistent with maintaining confidentiality.

Disclosure to Third Parties

To be privileged, communications must remain confidential; disclosure of privileged communications to someone outside the attorney-client relationship generally waives the privilege.[52]

However, disclosure of a privileged communication to a third party for the purpose of preparing a joint or common defense does not waive the privilege. For example, the court in *In re Bevill, Bresler & Schulman Asset Management Corp.*[53] found that the joint defense privilege protects communications between an individual and an attorney for another when communications are part of an effort to set up a common defense strategy. The party asserting the privilege must show that "(1) the communications were made in the course of a joint defense effort, (2) the statements were designed to further the effort, and (3) the privilege has not been waived." In a non–legal audit context, the court in *Sobol v. E.P. Dutton, Inc.*,[54] held that disclosure of documents to a former employee, for the purpose of preparing a common defense, was not a waiver of the attorney-client privilege. In *Roberts v. Carrier Corp.*,[55] the district court held that disclosure to a sister corporation does not constitute waiver. In *Schachar v. American Academy of Ophthalmology, Inc.*,[56] the court stated, "It is now well established that attorneys facing a common litigation opponent may exchange privileged communications and attorney work-product in order to prepare a common defense without waiving either privilege. . . . [C]ourts have applied the joint defense privilege to cases of 'potential' litigation as well."[57] And in *Levingston v. Allis-Chalmers Corp.,*[58] the court held that disclosure to attorneys of co-parties does not waive the privilege where the communications are designed to further a joint or common interest.

Authority to Waive Privilege

As a general matter, authority to waive the attorney-client privilege rests with the corporation's management and is normally exercised by its officers and directors.[59] The managers must exercise the privilege in a manner consistent with their fiduciary duty to act in the best interests of the corporation and not themselves as individuals.[60] When control of a corporation passes to new management, the authority to assert and waive the corporation's attorney-client privilege passes as well.[61] A manager's power to waive the corporation's attorney-client privilege, therefore, terminates when the manager loses his or her job.[62]

Limited Disclosure to Government Agencies

An important issue in connection with many legal audits is whether disclosure of the results of the audit to the SEC, IRS, or other government agencies constitutes a waiver of the attorney-client privilege. Two separate principles affect the determination of whether the privilege has been waived. The first is the general principle that disclosure of privileged material constitutes a waiver of the privilege with respect to the material disclosed.[63] The second is the principle of involuntary waiver, in which disclosure of a portion of a privileged communication can result in a waiver as to other communications regarding the same subject matter. At a minimum, waiver will be found for so much of the withheld information "as will make the disclosure complete and not misleadingly one-sided."[64]

In applying these principles, the courts consider the extent to which a disclosure to the government has been voluntary, and whether there are policy concerns supporting a finding of privilege notwithstanding the waiver.

Protecting Documents That Have Been Disclosed. When corporations voluntarily disclose documents or communications to federal agencies, the documents and communications may lose the protection of the privilege and be subject to discovery by other parties, including private plaintiffs, in other litigation. Corporations have argued that these voluntary disclosures to government agencies amount to a limited waiver of the privilege solely for the benefit of the public agency's review, and should not be considered as a waiver for purposes of private civil litigation. Faced with these arguments, often grounded on considerations of public policy, the courts have reached conflicting results.

In *Diversified Industries v. Meredith*,[65] the Eighth Circuit held that disclosure to the SEC of a corporate report describing a "slush fund" amounted to only a limited waiver of the attorney-client privilege and refused to order the corporation to produce the report for inspection by private plaintiffs in the pending litigation. The Eighth Circuit explained, "To hold otherwise may have the effect of thwarting the developing procedure of corporations to employ independent outside counsel to investigate and advise them in order to protect stockholders, potential stockholders and customers."[66]

Unlike the Eighth Circuit, the District of Columbia Circuit has rejected the doctrine of limited waiver. In *Permian Corp. v. United States*,[67] the court held that the attorney-client privilege had been waived when the party asserting the privilege permitted the disclosure of the documents to the SEC for the purpose of expediting consideration of its registration statement. In *Permian*, Occidental Petroleum had been sued in connection with a proposed exchange offer for shares of Mead Data. A substantial number of documents were produced by Occidental in that litigation pursuant to a stipulation that inadvertent production of a privileged document would not constitute a waiver of the attorney-client privilege.[68]

At the same time, the SEC was investigating the adequacy of Occidental's registration statement for the proposed offer. In an effort to expedite SEC approval, Occidental agreed to allow the SEC access to the documents produced to Mead, since Mead had organized the documents around certain issues. In connection with this agreement, Occidental and the SEC reached an agreement giving Occidental notice of all documents produced by Mead and providing for a restrictive endorsement preventing certain further disclosure.[69]

The Department of Energy then sought to obtain from the SEC certain of the documents relating to Permian's pricing practices. Occidental brought suit when the SEC indicated that it would produce the documents.[70]

The District of Columbia Circuit held that Occidental had waived the attorney-client privilege by allowing disclosure of the documents to the SEC.[71] First, the court held that no purpose was served by a limited waiver. Second, the court stated that the privilege was not designed to allow a client "to pick and choose among his opponents, waiving the privilege for some and resurrecting the claim of confidentiality to obstruct others." Finally, the court refused to recognize a public policy rationale in favor of cooperation with the SEC that would override the requirements of the privilege.[72] The court concluded that any privilege had been waived, stating, "the attorney-client privilege should be available only at the traditional price: a litigant who wishes to assert confidentiality must maintain genuine confidentiality."[73]

Likewise, although the court in *In re Penn Central Commercial Paper Litigation*,[74] recognized that witness cooperation was less likely if statements were subject to discovery in later civil proceedings, the court found that this public policy reason was inadequate to "break new legal ground" and ordered production of the transcript of an attorney's testimony before the SEC and the documents that were given to the SEC. Further, the court in *In re Subpoenas Duces Tecum (Fulbright & Jaworski)*,[75] relying on *Permian*, held that the privilege was waived by disclosure to the SEC even though the transmittal letter had stated the documents were confidential and the submission of them to the SEC was not a waiver of any privilege. In contrast to *Fulbright & Jaworski*, the court in *Teachers Insurance & Annuity Association of America v. Shamrock Broadcasting Co.*,[76] held that disclosure to the SEC constitutes a complete waiver of the attorney-client privilege unless, at the time of disclosure, the company specifically has reserved the right to assert the privilege in subsequent proceedings.

Protecting Documents That Have Not Been Disclosed. A partial production of privileged documents exposes a corporation not only to the risk that a disclosed document or communication will be subject to discovery by other parties, but also the risk that additional documents and communications relating to the same subject matter will lose the protection of the privilege. The party seeking disclosure typically argues that the corporation cannot select only those portions of a confidential communication that it wants to disclose.

Decisions in this area depend on the particular facts of the cases, including the importance of the documents for a fair determination of the companies' disclosures, the nature of the person or entity requesting the material, and the efforts taken by the company to maintain some limited disclosure of privileged materials. In any event, there is a substantial risk that disclosures to a government agency will result in a waiver both as to disclosed documents and as to nondisclosed documents regarding the same subject matter.

The issue of selective production of privileged documents arose in the Sixth Circuit's decision in *United States v. Upjohn Co.*[77] In *Upjohn*, the company had submitted to the SEC two reports concerning its internal investigation that were subsequently made available to the IRS.[78] The Sixth Circuit addressed the issue of waiver only in a footnote, but stated that the company's voluntary disclosures to the SEC amounted to a waiver only with respect to the facts actually disclosed.[79]

In reversing the Sixth Circuit, the United States Supreme Court did not address the waiver issue even though it was argued strongly by the government.[80] By ultimately upholding Upjohn's privilege claim, however, the Supreme Court implicitly approved the Sixth Circuit's holding that there had been no waiver.

Similarly, in *Byrnes v. IDS Realty Trust*,[81] the court held that the corporation did not waive the privilege by including a memorandum of counsel in a detailed response to an SEC request for information that would explain a disparity between figures on an earnings statement and later audited figures. In *United States v. Lipsky*,[82] disclosures in a report to the IRS and on SEC Form 10-K concerning questionable political contributions did not result in a waiver of the attorney-client privilege with respect to all of the details underlying an investigative report prepared by the corporation. And in *In re Grand Jury Subpoena Dated July 13, 1979,*[83] the court held that disclosure of independent counsel's report to the SEC, grand jury, and IRS did not result in a waiver of the attorney-client privilege with respect to the underlying documentation. This finding was based in part on the policy argument that voluntary cooperation with government agencies and grand juries might be significantly curtailed if cooperation amounted to a waiver of the attorney-client privilege.

Other courts, however, have found a waiver based upon a selective disclosure of otherwise privileged materials. The District of Columbia Circuit, in a case decided after *Upjohn*, found that selective disclosure waived the privilege.[84] In *In re Sealed Case*, outside counsel for the defendant conducted an internal investigation into possible illegal foreign payments and illegal political contributions and submitted a final report to the SEC along with notebooks containing the lawyers' notes of interviews and certain corporate records and documents.[85] The grand jury subpoenaed and received all the documents that had been produced to the SEC. During testimony before the grand jury, the corporation's in-house general counsel revealed that there were thirty-eight additional documents that had not been produced to the SEC or the grand jury.[86] The grand jury subpoenaed these documents, and the corporation moved to quash. The district court granted the motion to quash, except with respect to portions of eight documents that the court held were subject to production because the attorney-client privilege and work-product protection had been waived. The corporation's lawyer refused to produce the documents to the grand jury, and the corporation was held in contempt. The corporation appealed.[87]

The court of appeals held that the privilege had been waived and that the claim of privilege was being used in a manner inconsistent with the purposes of the privilege. First, the court noted that the corporation's final report to the SEC had emphasized that it was based on a review of all relevant files and that those files all had been made available to counsel conducting the investigation. Second, the court observed that the corporation had allowed the SEC access to its files, asserting that all relevant supporting documents were being made available, when in fact two of the documents in question had been removed. Third, the court emphasized that the two documents in question were particularly significant because they impeached the official version of the report and cast doubt on its veracity. Rejecting the corporation's argument that disclosure would prompt corporations to avoid voluntary cooperation with the government, the court stated that the SEC or any other government agency could expressly agree to limitations on further disclosure consistent with their legal responsibilities. Finding that the corporation had "attempted to manipulate its privilege, by withholding vital documents while making a great pretense of full disclosure of their contents," the court held that the privilege had been waived.[88]

The Eighth Circuit, in *United States v. Cote*, a case decided before *Upjohn*, ordered disclosure of all work papers underlying the preparation of an amended tax return that had been filed with the IRS.[89] The facts in *Cote* presented a strong case for disclosure. The accountant had testified that the information contained in the work papers had been transcribed onto the amended returns.[90] Moreover, in a footnote, the court acknowledged that certain of the work papers might remain privileged to the extent that they contained expressions that were not part of the information revealed on the tax returns.[91]

Disclosure of Special Litigation Committee Reports

Special Litigation Committee (SLC) reports are likely to be discoverable upon a motion to terminate a derivative action. In *Joy v. North*,[92] the court held that upon a motion to terminate, an SLC must disclose its report and supporting data. The court determined that the motion to terminate operated as a waiver of the attorney-client privilege.

Similarly, in *In re Continental Illinois Securities Litigation*,[93] the trial court had ordered public disclosure of an SLC report upon the motion of several newspapers for access during a hearing on a motion to terminate. The Seventh Circuit declined to adopt a per se rule of disclosure upon a corporation's motion to terminate. Instead, the court held that the presumption of public access to information before the court outweighed the corporation's need for confidentiality.[94]

Compare this to the court's decision in *In re Dayco Corp. Derivative Securities Litigation*,[95] holding that privilege is not waived when an SLC report is not released to the court or the public but only portions of the SLC's findings are released. Similarly, the court in *Watts v. Des Moines Register & Tribune Co.*,[96] held that shareholders may discover the bases for the SLC's conclusions but not why certain factors were or were not considered. In *Abbey v. Computer & Communications Technology Corp.*,[97] the court stated, "Plaintiff will be limited to taking the deposition of the Special Litigation Committee with a view toward establishing just what was done in the course of its investigation, and why. This will include production of the documentary materials utilized or relied upon by the Committee during its investigation."

Inadvertent Disclosure

Sometimes a corporation inadvertently discloses privileged documents, particularly in cases with large numbers of documents. The courts are split as to whether inadvertent disclosure of privileged documents constitutes a waiver of the privilege.[98]

Advice of Counsel

The attorney-client privilege may be deemed waived when the privileged communication is itself an issue in the litigation, such as when the corporation raises an "advice of counsel" defense. For example, in *Panter v. Marshall Field & Co.*,[99] the court held that where defendants assert advice of counsel as a defense to shareholders' suit alleging violations of securities laws, the defendants have waived the attorney-client privilege with respect to all communications to or from counsel concerning the transaction for which advice was sought. In *Handgards, Inc. v. Johnson & Johnson,*[100] the advice-of-counsel defense to a claim that suits were instituted in bad faith was held to have waived attorney-client privilege as to all documents and communications relating to the advice. And the court in *Garfinkle v. Arcata National Corp.*[101] held that the defendant's pleading of opinion letter as a defense waived the attorney-client privilege as to all relevant documents bearing on the attorney's advice.

However, in *Standard Chartered Bank PLC v. Ayala International Holdings*,[102] the court held that the privilege is waived when communications are themselves an issue in the litigation only where: (1) the very subject of privileged communications is critically relevant to the issue to be litigated, (2) there is a good-faith basis for believing such essential privileged communications exist, and (3) there is no other source of direct proof on the issue. The implied waiver principle will not be expanded, however, to every case in which fraud or reliance is an issue, and the moving party alleges that a legal opinion was the actual impetus for the opponent's actions.

In *Barr Marine Products Co. v. Borg-Warner Corp.*,[103] the court held that an affirmative "meeting competition" defense does not directly raise advice of counsel and therefore does not constitute a waiver.

Refreshing Recollection

The attorney-client privilege also may be waived by using privileged documents for the purpose of refreshing the recollection of a witness.[104]

The Crime-Fraud Exception

The attorney-client privilege will not apply where legal advice has been obtained in furtherance of an illegal or fraudulent act.[105] For example, in *In re Antitrust Grand Jury (Advance Publications)*,[106] the court held that communications made with intent to further violate the Sherman Act would be a sufficient basis for application of the crime-fraud exception. In *In re Grand Jury Subpoena Duces Tecum Dated September 15, 1983 (Marc Rich & Co. A.G.)*,[107] the court held that fraudulent conveyance was a sufficient basis for application of the crime-fraud exception. And in *Irving Trust Co. v. Gomez*,[108] the court held that the intentional or reckless tort of refusing to release funds without a basis for belief that the customer was not entitled to his money was sufficient basis for application of the crime-fraud exception.

To establish the crime-fraud exception, a party seeking discovery need make only a prima facie showing that the advice was obtained in furtherance of an illegal or fraudulent act.[109] One need not show that a crime or fraud has occurred—only that a crime or fraud was the objective of the communication.[110]

The circuits are split over the applicable standard for making a prima facie showing that advice was obtained in furtherance of an illegal or fraudulent act. At least two circuits have held that there must be a showing that there is probable cause to believe that a crime or fraud was committed.[111] The District of Columbia Circuit has required a showing that "offers evidence that if believed by the trier of fact would establish the elements of an ongoing or imminent crime or fraud."[112] In practice, the standards may not be very different.[113]

In addition, a link must be drawn between the privileged communication and the crime or fraud. In *In re Antitrust Grand Jury (Advance Publications),*[114] the court stated, "[M]erely because some communications may be related to a crime is not enough to subject that communication to disclosure; the communication must have been made with an intent to further the crime." The court in *Pritchard-Keang Nam Corp. v. Jaworski*[115] found that a report of the results of a questionable-payments investigation was not itself in furtherance of crime or fraud, and therefore was not subject to disclosure under the crime-fraud exception.

The attorney's ignorance of a client's purpose is irrelevant.[116]

Recommendations for Preserving the Privilege in Legal Audits

When a corporation commences a legal audit, the audit should be structured to maximize the corporation's protection under the privilege. The following recommendations may help the corporation preserve the privilege:

- Consider carefully the timing of a legal audit. If a corporation delays an audit in the face of legitimate questions requiring investigation, the corporation may be forced by a government agency to appoint special counsel, and thereby lessen its entitlement to confidentiality.
- If in-house counsel will conduct the legal audit, counsel should receive a specific directive from the board of directors. If outside counsel will handle the audit, the company should

send a retention letter. The directive or letter should make clear that counsel has been asked to provide legal advice, not just to investigate and report facts.

- Management personnel should not conduct a legal audit. If nonlegal personnel must be used, the attorneys should direct their work.
- If nonlegal experts are necessary, the attorney and not the corporation should hire them. Express authority to hire nonlegal experts should be given in the directive to in-house counsel or in the retention letter to outside counsel. It may be desirable to use experts the corporation does not regularly retain in a business capacity.
- The attorney should send a letter of retention to each nonlegal expert, setting forth the nature of the expert's obligation and the necessity of expert information in rendering legal advice. The letter of retention also should state that all communications and information are confidential.
- Where corporate employees will be interviewed, an appropriate high-ranking corporate executive should send a letter to all employees who will be questioned or interviewed, emphasizing the importance of the investigation, the need for full cooperation from all employees, and the confidential nature of the investigation. The letter also should state that the purpose of the investigation is to provide legal advice to the corporation.
- If an investigation will include questioning middle- or lower-level employees, the attorney should memorialize the fact that the information sought is not available from higher-level employees and the reasons why it is not available.
- The attorney should restrict communications with lower-level employees to matters within the scope of their employment.
- The attorney or corporation should inform employees who are interviewed or questioned that the attorney does not represent them individually.
- All interviews should be conducted by legal personnel, who should take notes of witness interviews. Notes should incorporate impressions, analyses, and opinions of counsel, which would be protected by the work-product privilege. Where a witness to the content of the interview may be required, an investigator working for the attorney should be present. Keep a record of all persons present during oral interviews with employees.

- Do not disclose the contents of privileged communications or documents beyond those who have a need to know.
- Keep all privileged communications and documents segregated from business documents.
- Clearly mark each privileged document as an "attorney-client communication" and instruct all recipients concerning the need for confidentiality.
- Avoid mixing business advice with legal advice in a privileged communication.
- Where disclosure to a government agency is required or advisable, attempt to obtain a commitment from the agency to maintain the confidentiality of all communications.
- Be aware of statutes and regulations regarding agency disclosure. Take advantage of statutory or regulatory schemes that decrease the risk of further disclosure. (See the section on the Freedom of Information Act later in this chapter.)
- If possible, maintain custody and control of any privileged documents disclosed to government agencies by allowing the agencies access to the documents without relinquishing possession.
- Do not use privileged information to refresh the recollection of a witness or to provide an expert with a basis for an expert opinion.
- In deciding whether to have employees sign interview statements or transcripts, consider the requirement under Federal Rule of Civil Procedure 26(b)(3), which stipulates that signed statements and transcripts be produced, upon request, to the person making the statement.

Structuring a Legal Audit to Maximize the Protection of the Work-Product Doctrine

The work-product doctrine, established in *Hickman v. Taylor*,[117] can be a valuable means of preserving the confidentiality of legal audit findings. In *Hickman*, the Supreme Court held that an attempt by a party to obtain written statements, private memoranda, and personal recollections prepared by an adverse party's attorney in the course of his legal duties, without showing necessity or justification, "falls outside the arena of discovery."[118] The Court indicated that this protection was not absolute, at least with respect to written statements and documents containing relevant and nonprivileged facts, and that discovery might be permitted if the party seeking access established adequate reasons.[119] With respect to witnesses' oral statements to the attorney, whether memorialized or not, the

Court held that no showing "under the circumstances of this case" would justify an order for production.[120] The Court did not foreclose the possibility that this type of material may be discoverable in "a rare situation."[121]

Federal Rule of Civil Procedure 26(b)(3) substantially codified the doctrine of *Hickman v. Taylor*. Its application depends on a number of factors, including the nature of the information, the nature of the proceedings, the identity of the parties, and the need for the information by the corporation's adversary. Rule 26(b)(3) provides that:

1. documents or tangible things;
2. prepared in anticipation of litigation or for trial;
3. by or for another party, or by or for that party's representative;
4. are protected against discovery unless the party seeking disclosure can demonstrate:
   a. substantial need; and
   b. that it would experience undue hardship without discovery.

Although Rule 26(b)(3) is limited to the discovery of "documents and tangible things," the Court in *Hickman* clearly was concerned not only with documents and tangible things, but also with mental impressions.[122]

Documents Protected by the Work-Product Privilege

To be protected by the work-product doctrine, Rule 26(b)(3) requires materials to have been prepared in anticipation of litigation. Although there is some contrary authority, most courts have held that documents prepared during internal legal audits satisfy this test. For example, in *Upjohn v. United States*,[123] the government conceded applicability of the work-product doctrine to documents prepared in the course of a legal audit.

Even before *Upjohn*, the Second and Third Circuits had extended work-product protection to legal audits. In *In re Grand Jury Subpoena (John Doe, Inc.)*,[124] the Second Circuit held that interview notes and memoranda, questionnaires, and summaries compiled by outside counsel pursuant to a legal audit of possible illegal foreign payments were prepared in anticipation of litigation.[125]

Two pre-*Upjohn* decisions, however, denied work-product protection to legal audit reports. In *Diversified Industries v. Meredith*,[126] the full court concluded that the report, which detailed the results of an investigation by outside counsel regarding the alleged existence of a "slush fund," was protected by the attorney-client privilege and therefore did not address the panel's treatment of work product. The panel opinion had concluded that the report was not prepared in anticipation of litigation, however. The panel reasoned that because the law firm was employed to inform the corporation's board of directors of what had transpired so that the board could formulate remedial measures, the firm's legal audit was not prepared in anticipation of litigation.[127]

In *Litton Systems, Inc. v. American Telephone & Telegraph Co.*,[128] the court held that interview memoranda compiled under the direction of in-house counsel regarding suspected bribes and unfounded "finder's fees" in the corporation's sales department were not prepared in anticipation of litigation. The court noted that the only anticipated litigation would be criminal prosecutions of the employees involved.[129]

When documents have been prepared in anticipation of litigation, but not in anticipation of the litigation in which the protection of the doctrine is asserted, the weight of modern authority provides that the documents should be treated as work product, at least where the subsequent case is related to the case for which the work product was created.[130]

Documents may be denied work-product protection if they are used for business purposes. In *Simon v. G.D. Searle & Co.*,[131] the plaintiff moved to compel discovery of "risk management" documents prepared by Searle, many of which included products liability aggregate case reserve information based on reserve estimates obtained from Searle's legal department. Searle's individual case reserves embodied the attorney's estimates of anticipated legal expenses, settlement values, length of time to resolve the litigation, geographic considerations, and other factors.[132] However, based on the rationale that the aggregate reserves were used by risk management documents for a variety of business planning purposes, and that the risk management department was not involved in giving legal advice or in "mapping" litigation strategy in any individual case, the court held that the aggregate reserve information contained in the documents was not protected by the work-product doctrine, at least to the extent that individual case reserve figures were not revealed.[133]

Extent of Work-Product Protection

Unlike the absolute protection afforded by the attorney-client privilege, the work-product doctrine affords only a qualified protection. Rule 26(b)(3) provides that the court can order disclosure of work-product if the party requesting it has substantial need of the materials and cannot obtain the substantial equivalent without undue hardship. The rule further provides, however, that the court "shall protect against disclosure" of the mental impressions and opinions of the attorney or other representative.

Hickman, Rule 26(b)(3), and the cases addressing the extent of work-product protection all recognize a distinction between material such as witness statements, which do not reveal any of the attorney's mental processes ("ordinary work product"), and materials such as notes of oral interviews of witnesses, which reveal the opinions, conclusions, and mental impressions of the attorney ("opinion work product").[134] Not surprisingly, ordinary work product typically receives less protection.

Ordinary Work Product

Courts have reached different conclusions when asked to determine what constitutes a showing of substantial need sufficient to justify disclosure of ordinary work product. The cases appear to turn on their facts. For example, the Third Circuit has reached different results in two cases. In *In re Grand Jury Investigation (Sun Co.)*,[135] the court stated that a grand jury might be entitled to employee questionnaires in order to impeach or corroborate the testimony of a witness, but that the desire to impeach never would justify production of the attorney's memoranda of oral interviews. Since no employee had yet been called to testify, the court refused to order disclosure.[136] However, in *United States v. Amerada Hess Corp.*,[137] the court held that avoidance of time and effort was sufficient to justify disclosure of a list of persons interviewed during an internal investigation where the list contained no mental processes, was of very limited substantive content, and disclosure presented none of the dangers of *Hickman*.[138]

Opinion Work Product

Unlike ordinary work product, opinion work product is discoverable, if at all, only upon a showing of extraordinary need. Some courts have held that opinion work product is absolutely privileged, and not discoverable under any circumstances.[139]

Other courts have noted that a showing of extraordinary need or special circumstances might justify disclosure of opinion work product. For example, in *Sporck v. Peil*,[140] the Third Circuit held that opinion work product is accorded "almost absolute protection from discovery because any slight factual content that such items may have is generally outweighed by the adversary system's interest in maintaining the privacy of an attorney's thought processes and in ensuring that each side relies on its own wit in preparing their respective cases."[141] In *Upjohn*, the Supreme Court stopped short of ruling that opinion work product is always protected.[142]

Waiver of Work-Product Protection

The standards of waiver for the attorney-client privilege differ from those for the work-product doctrine, reflecting the differences between their underlying policies. In contrast to the attorney-client privilege, the purpose of which is to protect confidential communications between an attorney and client and thereby the relationship itself, the purpose of the work-product doctrine is to promote the adversary system by protecting the fruits of an attorney's trial preparation from an adversary.[144]

Disclosure to Third Parties

Despite the policy differences between the attorney-client privilege and the work-product doctrine, either privilege may be lost by disclosure to third parties. Courts have held that work-product protection is waived if materials are disclosed to anyone other than one with a common interest.[145]

Disclosure to Government Agencies

When a corporation discloses work product to the government, the court may permit private parties and other government agencies access to the materials.[145]

Refreshing Recollection

The protection of the work-product doctrine may be waived by using protected documents to refresh the recollection of a witness before his or her testimony at deposition or trial. In *James Julian, Inc. v. Raytheon Co.*,[146] the court ordered production of a binder of documents compiled by counsel and used to refresh the recollection of deposition witnesses, even though it recognized the binder as constituting opinion work product. The court held that the binder was opinion work product because it comprised a few documents selected from thousands discovered in the case, and the selection process "could not help but reveal important aspects of [counsel's] understanding of the case."[147]

Also, in dictum in *Sporck v. Peil*,[148] the court interpreted Federal Rule of Evidence 612 to require the disclosure of documents a deponent has used to refresh his or her memory only where opposing counsel lays a proper foundation. Counsel must first elicit specific testimony from the deponent and then ask the deponent which, if any, documents "informed that testimony." The deponent will be compelled to disclose only the documents he actually used to refresh his memory, not all documents counsel showed him in preparation for his testimony, which are protected as opinion work product.

In denying a motion to compel discovery of files reviewed by a deponent before his deposition, the court in *Aguinaga v. John Morrell & Co.*[149] held that the purpose of Federal Rule of Evidence 612 is to allow an adverse party to have access to writings that "have an impact on the testimony of the witness." However, "'proper application of Rule 612 should never implicate an attorney's selection, in preparation for a witness' deposition of a group of documents he believes critical to a case.'"[150]

Testimonial Use

Work-product protection also can be waived through testimonial use of the materials. In *United States v. Nobels*,[151] the Court held that defense counsel's use of testimony of an investigator waived work-product protection with respect to matters covered in his testimony. In *Coleco Industries, Inc. v. Universal City Studios*,[152] the court held that where privileged documents were selectively disclosed for "testimonial use" to support a partial new trial in a separate action, fairness requires an implied waiver of all work-product protection relevant to the same issue in the instant action.

Advice of Counsel

The work-product privilege may be deemed waived when the privileged document is itself an issue in the litigation, for example, when the corporation raises an "advice of counsel" defense. (Compare this to the authority to waive the attorney-client privilege, as described earlier.)

Noting that "a consistent line of cases has developed an exception to the work-product privilege where the party raises an issue which depends upon an evaluation of the legal theories, opinions and conclusions of counsel," the court in *Coleco Industries, Inc. v. Universal City Studios*[153] held that the corporation's reliance on advice of counsel as a defense waived the work-product privilege.

The Crime-Fraud Exception

Like the crime-fraud exception to the attorney-client privilege, crime or fraud has been held to waive the work-product doctrine. According to the court in *In re Antitrust Grand Jury (Advance Publication)*,[154] the standard to be applied with respect to the crime-fraud exception differs between ordinary and opinion work product. "When there has been an ongoing client crime or fraud, any privilege to fact work-product is waived and the 'scale tips in favor of disclosure.'"[155] To discover opinion work product, however, there must be a showing that "otherwise protected communications or materials are made in furtherance of a crime or fraud."[156]

Upon a prima facie showing of fraud, the Seventh Circuit held that a client may not assert work-product protection and an attorney may not assert work-product protection with respect to ordinary work product.[157]

But where there was no allegation of attorney fraud, another court held that no intrusion will be allowed upon opinion work product.[158]

Unlike the attorney-client privilege, an attorney's knowledge of the crime or fraud is relevant in the context of a work-product protection; if the attorney is ignorant of the crime or fraud, work-product protection is waived only as to information furnished to the attorney and not as to the attorney's mental impressions, conclusions, opinions, or legal theories.[159] To determine whether communications were made in furtherance of a crime or fraud, the court should review the documents *in camera*, and at least one court has held that it was plain error for a court to grant disclosure without such a review.[160]

Recommendations for Preserving the Confidentiality of Work Product Pertaining to a Legal Audit

In addition to the steps recommended to maximize the corporation's protection under the attorney-client privilege set forth earlier, further precautions will maximize the protection afforded by the work-product doctrine:

- Stress that the audit is being conducted in anticipation of litigation. If in-house counsel will conduct the legal audit, he or she should receive a specific directive from the board of directors indicating that the audit has been undertaken in anticipation of litigation. Include possible government investigations, private litigations, shareholder class or derivative suits, and litigation that the corporation might bring against directors or employees to recover damages for illegal conduct. If outside counsel will conduct the audit, the company should send a retention letter reciting these matters.
- Counsel should conduct all interviews. Counsel's interview notes or interview memoranda should state that the documents contain counsel's "impressions and conclusions" concerning the interview. Do not include lengthy verbatim entries.
- Segregate work-product materials and maintain their confidentiality. Disclosure of protected documents may result in waiver.
- Do not use work-product materials to refresh the recollection of a witness or to provide an expert with a basis for an opinion.

Special Problem Areas
Shareholder Litigation

In actions brought by shareholders, courts have been less willing to protect confidential materials. Because corporate management owes fiduciary duties to its shareholders, courts have justified disclosure of privileged documents to shareholders by invoking various analogies to the attorney-client privilege exceptions, such as the joint client exception. This is particularly true in shareholder derivative actions, where the shareholders are literally suing on behalf of the corporation.[161] However, courts have been more sympathetic to claims of work product, especially when the confidential material has been created in anticipation of shareholder litigation. Recognizing the realities of the adversarial relationship between the corporation and its shareholders, courts have been reluctant to order disclosure.[162]

The *Garner* Doctrine

The issue of shareholder access to privileged corporate communications is not limited to legal audits. Indeed, most of the significant cases in this area have not concerned audits. In *Garner v. Wolfinbarger*, perhaps the most influential decision in this area, the Fifth Circuit held in a shareholder derivative suit that:

> where the corporation is in suit against its stockholders on charges of acting inimically to stockholder interests, protection of those interests as well as those of the corporation and of the public require that the availability of the privilege be subject to the right of the stockholders to show cause why it should not be involved in the particular instance.[163]

In reaching its decision, the court analogized the exception to the fraud and joint client exceptions to the attorney-client privilege.[164]

The *Garner* court set forth a number of factors that it believed indicated the presence or absence of "good cause": the number of stockholders involved in the corporation; the bona fides of the stockholders; the nature of the claim and whether it is obviously colorable; the necessity of the information to the stockholders; the availability of the information from other sources; whether the acts complained of are criminal or illegal; whether the communication sought involves past or prospective actions; whether the communication involved advice regarding the litigation itself; the extent to which the information sought is identified; and the risk of revealing information for which the corporation has independent reasons for seeking confidentiality, such as trade secrets.[165]

The *Garner* decision has been criticized by some commentators.[166] However, most federal courts have followed *Garner*.[167] But the state courts have not uniformly embraced the *Garner* doctrine. California courts, for example, have squarely rejected the *Garner* rule, and held that there is "no extraordinary avenue . . . available to [shareholders] to pierce the [corporation's] privilege."[168] Other states have upheld the rule.[169] (For a discussion of state privilege issues, see the section titled "State Court Litigation" later in this chapter.)

Extending *Garner* beyond Derivative Actions

In a derivative suit, the derivative shareholder purports to represent the corporation itself. Where the suit is direct, rather than derivative, some courts have been reluctant to extend the *Garner* doctrine. The Ninth Circuit has invoked this distinction in refusing to apply *Garner* in an individual shareholder action, although the court allowed the requested discovery based on a finding of waiver.[170]

In this case, *Weil v. Investment/Indicators, Research & Management, Inc.*, the court distinguished Weil's individual action from the derivative suit in *Garner* and therefore refused to pass on the merits of *Garner*. In addition, the court noted that Weil was a former, not present, shareholder of the corporation.[171]

To the extent that the Ninth Circuit intends to limit the broad application of *Garner*, the limitation represents an important shift from prior cases extending *Garner* beyond shareholder derivative litigation:

- In *Aguinaga v. John Morrell & Co.*,[172] the *Garner* doctrine was applied in a union context, granting former union members access to attorney-client communications and work product.
- In *Helt v. Metropolitan District Commission*,[173] the *Garner* doctrine was applied where the beneficiary of a pension plan sought to discover correspondence between attorneys for the pension plan and the plan's trustee.
- In *Donovan v. Fitzsimmons*,[174] the Secretary of Labor, bringing suit on behalf of beneficiaries of a pension fund, was granted access to privileged materials on the basis of *Garner*.
- In *Cohen v. Uniroyal, Inc.*,[175] the *Garner* rationale was applied in a shareholder class action where the plaintiffs were not shareholders at the time of the allegedly fraudulent conduct.
- In *Broad v. Rockwell International Corp.*,[176] the *Garner* rationale was applied where a corporation was sued by debenture holders.

- In *Bailey v. Meister Brau, Inc.*,[177] although the court recognized that *Garner* was not direct support, it applied the rationale to compel deposition testimony concerning communications between the corporation and its attorneys in a suit by a shareholder of a different corporation where one of the defendants was an officer of both corporations simultaneously and owed fiduciary duties to the plaintiff.

Attorney-Client Privilege

In *In re LTV Securities Litigation*,[178] the court applied *Garner* but found that there was not "good cause" to justify disclosure of an attorney's after-the-fact remedial advice. In *LTV*, the plaintiff class alleged that defendants had violated the federal securities laws by overvaluing inventory through manipulative accounting.[179] The plaintiffs sought disclosure of communications that took place after the allegedly wrongful conduct.[180] The court sustained the corporation's assertion of the attorney-client privilege and explained:

> Once accused of wrongdoing, management's need to consult counsel in confidence is self-evident. Moreover, the interests of the corporation at such time are not necessarily coincidental with shareholder plaintiffs complaining of past misconduct. The Plaintiff class is frozen when corporate wrongdoing ends. From that time on, the class interests are adverse to the corporation which has allegedly defrauded it, and possibly adverse to nonparty shareholders as well.[181]

The *LTV* decision provides support for corporations seeking to preserve the confidentiality of legal audit findings. Like the information requested in *LTV*, the information gathered pursuant to a legal audit almost always will be gathered after the termination of the allegedly wrongful conduct and frequently after accusations of wrong doing. *LTV* is strong support for the proposition that such materials are not discoverable under the "good cause" exception of the *Garner* rationale.

Work Product

In *In re International Systems & Controls Corp. Securities Litigation*,[182] the Fifth Circuit held that the *Garner* principle does not apply to the work-product doctrine and therefore refused to order production of binders containing information accumulated during a special review of illegal foreign payments. In holding that *Garner* does not apply to work-product materials, the court stated that the mutuality of interest rationale of *Garner* does not apply once there is sufficient anticipation of litigation to bring the documents within the work-product doctrine. "To hold otherwise would be to ignore modern corporate realities."[183]

State Court Litigation

Although the question of the confidentiality of legal audits frequently arises in federal court, counsel also should investigate any applicable state law. The Supreme Court's decision in *Upjohn* does not establish state law guidelines, and several states have established different rules governing the application of the attorney-client privilege to corporations:

- In *Alpha Beta Co. v. Superior Court (Sundy)*,[184] the California court held that attorney-client privilege will attach to communications with a corporate employee only where the employee is the natural person to be speaking for the corporation with respect to the subject matter of the communications.
- In *Consolidation Coal Co. v. Bucyrus-Erie Co.*,[185] the Illinois Supreme Court rejected the *Upjohn* approach and adopted the "control group" test, which protects communications between counsel and corporate decision makers or those "who substantially influence corporate decisions."[186] As a practical matter, the only communications that will ordinarily be protected are those made by top management who have the ability to make a final decision.
- In the Minnesota case of *Leer v. Chicago, Milwaukee, St. Paul & Pacific Railway*,[187] the court noted various tests for determining the identity of a corporate client but failed to adopt any of them, holding that the statements of an employee to the corporation's attorney regarding an accident witnessed by the employee are not protected under any of the tests.
- In *Macey v. Rollins Environmental Services (N.J.), Inc.*,[188] the New Jersey Superior Court, citing *Upjohn* favorably, interpreted the state codification of the attorney-client privilege broadly and held that it protects communications between corporate counsel and the corporation's officers and employees.
- In *Marriott Corp. v. American Academy of Psychotherapists, Inc.*,[189] decided less than one month after *Upjohn* and without citing it, the Georgia appeals court applied a modified "subject matter" test, based upon *Diversified Industries v. Meredith*,[190] in defining the corporate client. The *Diversified* court held that the attorney-client privilege protects an em-

> ployee's communication if "(1) the communication was made for the purpose of securing legal advice; (2) the employee making the communication did so at the direction of his corporate superior; (3) the superior made the request so that the corporation could secure legal advice; (4) the subject matter of the communication is within the scope of the employee's corporate duties; and (5) the communication is not disseminated beyond those persons who, because of the corporate structure, need to know its contents."[191]

The work-product rules of *Hickman v. Taylor* and Rule 26(b)(3) also are binding only in federal courts. Individual states may apply different standards to determine the availability of work-product protection. For example, the court in *People v. Boclair*[192] held that the opinion work-product privilege is not absolute. The court held that handwritten notes taken during a witness interview are not work product per se, and that it is within the trial judge's discretion to determine whether documents are privileged. The court upheld the trial court's excising of privileged and irrelevant portions of counsel's notes after an *in camera* review and its order to counsel to produce the remainder of the notes to the state's attorney.

Freedom of Information Act

Counsel who produce documents to a government agency following a legal audit should also be aware that those documents may be disclosed to the public pursuant to the Freedom of Information Act (FOIA).[193] However, the disclosure obligations under FOIA are not absolute. FOIA includes exemptions for confidential commercial information, intra-agency and inter-agency memoranda, and investigative files.[194] FOIA exemptions do not prohibit disclosure—they merely permit nondisclosure.[195]

Several federal statutes also provide exemptions to FOIA disclosure. The Hart-Scott-Rodino Antitrust Improvements Act of 1976 exempts from FOIA disclosure all information and documentary material filed pursuant to the premerger notification requirements.[196] The Federal Trade Commission Improvements Act of 1980 exempts from FOIA disclosure any material received by the FTC in an investigation conducted to determine whether any person has violated any provision of a law administered by the FTC and provided pursuant to compulsory process or provided voluntarily in place of compulsory process.[197] The Antitrust Civil Process Act exempts from FOIA disclosure any documentary material, answers to written interrogatories, or transcripts of oral testimony provided pursuant to 15 U.S.C. § 1314 (regarding civil investigative demands).[198]

In addition, several agencies have adopted regulations governing the confidentiality of information and the duty to disclose pursuant to

FOIA.[199] It also may be possible to protect documents from FOIA disclosure requirements by allowing interested government agencies access to the documents without relinquishing possession.[200]

Attorney Subpoenas

The confidentiality of client communications generated during a legal audit may also be affected by an attorney's legal and ethical obligation to reveal confidential information in certain circumstances.[201] Although an attorney may not be compelled to disclose privileged communications, an attorney may be compelled to testify concerning his or her fees and the sources of those fees,[202] and may be required to testify about matters concerning an ongoing crime or fraud. (See the earlier discussion of the crime-fraud exception.) This problem, which often arises when an attorney is subpoenaed to appear before a grand jury seeking documents or information relating to the attorney's representation of a client, undermines the confidentiality of the attorney-client relationship and in some cases may require the attorney's disqualification from further representation of a client.[203]

A number of courts have held that a prosecutor is required to show the relevance of and need for information before a lawyer must respond to a grand jury subpoena requesting client information.[204] Most courts, however, have held that no such showing is required, and have required attorneys to respond to grand jury subpoenas and assert any claims of privilege on a question-by-question or document-by-document basis.[205]

The ABA has taken the position that an attorney should not be required to testify as to matters he or she has learned of in the course of representing a client. In its Grand Jury Policy and Model Act (1977–82), the ABA adopted the following policy statements:

> 1. *Grand Jury Principle #29.* No attorney, his agent or employee, shall be questioned by the grand jury concerning matters he has learned in the legitimate investigation, preparation or representation of his client's cause or be subpoenaed to produce before the grand jury private notes, memoranda, and the like constituting his professional work-product.
> 2. *Grand Jury Principle #23.* All stages of the grand jury proceedings should be conducted with proper consideration for the preservation of press freedom, attorney-client relationships, and comparable values.

In July 1985, the United States Justice Department established internal guidelines governing the use of attorney subpoenas. The guidelines provide in part that before subpoenas are issued to attorneys, reasonable attempts shall be made to obtain the information voluntarily or from alternative sources. The guidelines further require the express authorization of the Assistant Attorney General of the Criminal Division before such subpoenas may be issued. In approving the issuance of attorney subpoenas in criminal cases, the guidelines direct the Assistant Attorney General to ascertain that: (1) there are reasonable grounds to believe that a crime has been or is being committed; (2) all of the information sought is reasonably needed for the successful completion of the investigation or prosecution; and (3) reasonable attempts to obtain the information from alternative sources have proved to be unsuccessful. In civil cases, there must be reasonable grounds to believe that the information is reasonably necessary to the successful completion of the litigation. In all cases, the Assistant Attorney General is required to ascertain that the government's reasonable need for the information outweighs the potential adverse effects upon the attorney-client relationship; that the subpoenas are narrowly drawn; and that the subpoenas are limited as to subject matter and period of time. Finally, under the guidelines, federal prosecutors may not seek information protected by a valid claim of privilege. It should be noted, however, that the guidelines do not create substantive rights in witnesses. Courts have refused to consider challenges to subpoenas based upon the Justice Department's alleged failure to adhere to these guidelines.[206]

In response to prosecutors' increasing use of attorney subpoenas, the Massachusetts Supreme Judicial Court passed a disciplinary rule requiring judicial approval before the issuance of subpoenas to attorneys "where the prosecutor seeks to compel the attorney/witness to provide evidence concerning a person who is represented by the attorney/witness." The rule, which became effective January 1, 1986, deems it "unprofessional conduct," punishable by the customary array of sanctions, for a prosecutor to issue such a subpoena without prior judicial approval.

Ethical Considerations and Dual Representation

Another problematic issue that arises in the legal audit context is whether a corporation's counsel should represent corporate employees and, if not, the extent to which corporate counsel should inform employees about their individual legal rights. When a corporation believes it is in its best interest to waive the attorney-client privilege regarding employee communications, such communications are subject to discovery, unless the employee may assert an individual attorney-client privilege. An employee may do so only if the communication satisfies the *United Shoe* test discussed in the first part of this chapter. If counsel represents only the corporation and has informed the employee of that fact, no individual privilege arises to protect the employee.

Under certain circumstances, a corporation may choose to have its counsel also represent its employees. Where corporate officers, directors, or employees are the subjects or targets of a grand jury investigation, for example, a corporation may wish to offer joint representation in order to retain control over the case and enable counsel to plot joint strategy. Joint representation may provide counsel with increased information and facilitate interviewing grand jury witnesses.

Multiple representation may, however, lead to disqualification of counsel on motion of the government in a criminal case or an adverse party in a civil case, and may disqualify a lawyer and the lawyer's firm from participating in the litigation.[207] Even if counsel is not disqualified, counsel may have difficulty adequately representing individuals' interests, which may conflict with those of the corporation or those of other individuals represented by corporate counsel. For example, it may be in an individual's best interest to accept an offer of immunity from the government, but such an offer may undermine the corporation's case. In certain circumstances, the Code of Professional Responsibility and the Model Rules of Professional Conduct may prohibit the representation of more than one client in this situation.[208] In criminal cases, moreover, this joint representation by counsel may also increase the possibility that counsel will be subpoenaed by the grand jury, which may lead to disqualification, as described in the preceding section of this chapter.

Even if a corporation decides that its attorneys will not represent its directors, officers, and employees, a number of ethical questions remain unanswered. In conducting a legal audit in which corporate counsel is not counsel for those interviewed, what should an attorney tell the employees or directors about their individual rights? Should an attorney merely inform interviewees that he or she represents the company and does not represent them, or should the attorney explain that the corporation has the right to waive the privilege, and that disclosure may expose the employee to criminal or civil liability? Should an attorney suggest that an interviewee consult separate counsel before speaking to him or her? Corporate counsel's task obviously becomes more difficult in such a case, because such admonitions may chill employees' willingness to provide complete information, and the corporation's best interests may be thwarted.

Notes

1. *E.g.*, Upjohn Co. v. United States, 449 U.S. 383 (1981); Diversified Indus. v. Meredith, 572 F.2d 596 (8th Cir. 1978) (en banc); *In re* Grand Jury Subpoena Dated July 13, 1979, 478 F. Supp. 368 (E.D. Wis. 1979).
2. 89 F. Supp. 357 (D. Mass. 1950).

3. *Id.* at 358–59. *See also* VIII WIGMORE, EVIDENCE § 2292 (McNaughton rev. ed. 1961).
4. 449 U.S. 383 (1981).
5. *Id.* at 394–95.
6. *Id.* at 386.
7. *Id.* at 386–87.
8. *Id.* at 387–88.
9. *Id.* at 388–89.
10. *Id.* at 389–90.
11. *Id.* at 390–91.
12. *Id.* at 386.
13. *Id.* at 394 n.3.
14. *Id.* at 402–03.
15. 658 F.2d 1355 (9th Cir. 1981), *cert. denied*, 455 U.S. 990 (1982).
16. *Id.* at 1356, 1359.
17. Baxter Travenol Laboratories, Inc. v. Lemay, 89 F.R.D. 410, 412–14 (S.D. Ohio 1981) (claim of privilege upheld even though the communications did not concern the matters within the scope of the employee's duties). *See also* Leucadia, Inc. v. Reliance Ins. Co., 101 F.R.D. 674 (S.D.N.Y. 1983).
18. 776 F.2d 678 (7th Cir. 1985), *cert. denied*, 106 S. Ct. 2919 (1986).
19. 575 F. Supp. 777 (N.D. Ga. 1983).
20. *See* Chase Manhattan Bank v. Higgerson, No. 17864/84, slip op. (N.Y. Sup. Ct. Oct. 11, 1984) (employee defendant sought to disqualify investigating counsel from representing company in litigation arising out of investigation on grounds that employee thought counsel was representing him personally—disqualification ordered on other grounds).
21. 737 F.2d 94, 99 (D.C. Cir. 1984).
22. 730 F.2d 1465, 1468–69 (Fed. Cir. 1984).
23. *See also In re* LTV Sec. Litig., 89 F.R.D. 595, 601 (N.D. Tex. 1981) ("*Upjohn* laid to rest suggestions that House Counsel are to be treated differently from outside counsel with respect to activities in which they are engaged as attorneys."); Valente v. PepsiCo., Inc., 68 F.R.D. 361, 367 (D. Del. 1975) (privilege protects communications with in-house counsel); Burlington Indus. v. Exxon Corp., 65 F.R.D. 26, 36 (D. Md. 1974) (privilege protects communications with in-house counsel); Hasso v. Retail Credit Co., 58 F.R.D. 425, 427 (E.D. Pa. 1973) ("[H]ouse counsel does not stand in any different shoes than private counsel."). *But see In re* Grand Jury Investigation (Sun Co.), 599 F.2d 1224, 1233 at n.2 (3d Cir. 1979) (leaving open the question of whether communications to in-house counsel are protected by the attorney-client privilege).
24. 89 F.R.D. 595 (N.D. Tex. 1981).
25. *Id.* at 614–22.
26. *Id.* at 614.
27. *Id.* at 614–15.
28. *Id.* at 615–18.
29. *Id.* at 618–22.

30. *In re* Grand Jury Subpoena Duces Tecum Dated Sept. 15, 1983 (Marc Rich & Co. A.G.), 731 F.2d 1032, 1036–37 (2d Cir. 1984); *In re* Grand Jury Proceedings, 658 F.2d 782, 784 (10th Cir. 1981).
31. 451 F. Supp. 594 (D.D.C.), *vacated and remanded with instructions to transfer*, [1979 Transfer Binder] FED. SEC. L. REP. (CCH) ¶96,742 (D.C. Cir. 1978) (per curiam).
32. *Id.* at 596.
33. *Id.* at 595.
34. *Id.* at 596.
35. 82 F.R.D. 81 (N.D. Ga. 1979).
36. *Id.* at 82–83.
37. *Id.* at 83.
38. *Id.* at 85.
39. *Id.* at 85–86. *See also* Henderson v. National R.R. Passenger Corp., 113 F.R.D. 502 (N.D. I11. 1986) (communications between employees and an attorney acting as EEOC representative, who investigated claims and reported solely to Amtrak legal department, were not privileged because the attorney did not work for Amtrak's benefit and employees "had no expectation of privacy").
40. United States v. United Shoe Mach. Corp., 89 F. Supp. 357, 358 (D. Mass. 1950).
41. *Compare* United States v. McPartlin, 595 F.2d 1321, 1335–37 (7th Cir.), *cert. denied*, 444 U.S. 833 (1979) (statement made to investigator employed by co-defendants' counsel is privileged); United States v. Cote, 456 F.2d 142, 143–44 (8th Cir. 1972) (attorney-client privilege applies to work papers of accountant prepared at direction of attorney for aid in rendering legal advice), *with* Dabney v. Investment Corp. of Am., 82 F.R.D. 464, 465–66 (E.D. Pa. 1979) (privilege not available to a law student who was not acting under the direct supervision of a member of the bar); United States v. Brown, 478 F.2d 1038, 1039–40 (7th Cir. 1973) (privilege does not prevent disclosure of accountant's notes of oral conversation with client and attorney when accountant was retained by the client and instructed by the client to attend the meeting).
42. United States v. United Shoe Mach. Corp., 89 F. Supp. at 358–59 (correspondence between company and counsel was privileged only insofar as it was prepared to solicit or give legal opinion).
43. Chubb Integrated Sys. Ltd. v. National Bank of Wash., 103 F.R.D. 52, 66 (D.D.C. 1984) (attorney-client privilege from discovery not lost in a patent case merely because the communication contains technical data); Crane Co. v. Goodyear Tire & Rubber Co., 27 Fed. R. Serv. 2d (Callaghan) 1058, 1059–60 (N.D. Ohio 1979)(inclusion of technical information in communication to attorney does not foreclose privilege); Burlington Indus. v. Exxon Corp., 65 F.R.D. 26, 39 (D. Md. 1974) (privilege not lost in patent area because technical information included).
44. *In re* Diasonics Sec. Litig., 110 F.R.D. 570, 573 (D. Colo. 1986); *In re* Grand Jury Subpoena Duces Tecum Dated Sept. 15, 1983 (Marc Rich & Co. A.G.), 731 F.2d at 1037; North Carolina Elec. Membership Corp. v. Carolina Power & Light Co., 110 F.R.D. 511, 517 (M.D.N.C. 1986); SEC v. Gulf & W. Indus., 518 F. Supp. 675, 683 (D.D.C. 1981).

45. FTC v. TRW, Inc., 479 F. Supp. 160, 163 (D.D.C. 1979), *aff'd*, 628 F.2d 207 (D.C. Cir. 1980)(document that was prepared for legal and nonlegal review not considered to have been prepared primarily for legal advice); United States v. International Business Mach. Corp., 66 F.R.D. 206, 213 (S.D.N.Y. 1974) (same); United States v. Aluminum Co. of Am., 193 F. Supp. 251, 252–53 (N.D.N.Y. 1960) (copy of document that was originally addressed to attorney sent to corporate president in response to independent request for similar information was not privileged).

46. Osterneck v. E.T. Barwick Indus., Inc., 82 F.R.D. 81, 85 (N.D. Ga. 1979) (attorneys "were employed not for their legal acumen but for their skill as investigators").

47. *See, e.g.,* Simon v. G.D. Searle & Co., 816 F.2d 397 (8th Cir.), *cert. denied,* 108 S. Ct. 268 (1987) ("risk management" documents prepared for general business purposes, but based on privileged case reserve information, held not privileged, at least to the extent that they revealed only aggregate information and not individual privileged communications).

48. 89 F.R.D. 595 (N.D. Tex. 1981).

49. *Id.* at 602.

50. *Id. See generally* 2 J. WEINSTEIN & M. BERGER, WEINSTEIN'S EVIDENCE ¶503(b)[03] (1985 & Supp. Dec. 1985) (suggesting that the *LTV* rule is the proper one); United States v. Amerada Hess Corp., 619 F.2d 980, 986 (3d Cir. 1980) (attorney-client privilege applies to communications of attorney); Burlington Indus. v. Exxon Corp., 65 F.R.D. at 37 (self-initiated attorney communications protected); Jack Winter, Inc. v. Koratron Co., 54 F.R.D. 44, 46 (N.D. Cal. 1971) (self-initiated attorney communications protected).

51. Schlefer v. United States, 702 F.2d 233, 245 (D.C. Cir. 1983) (confidential communication from an attorney to client is protected when it is based on confidential information supplied by client); Mead Data Cent., Inc. v. United States Dep't of the Air Force, 566 F.2d 242, 253–54 (D.C. Cir. 1977) (same in FOIA exemption context); North Carolina Elec. Membership Corp. v. Carolina Power & Light Co., 110 F.R.D. 511, 514 (M.D.N.C. 1986) (communications protected by privilege only if they tend to reveal confidential client communications); Ohio-Sealy Mattress Mfg. Co. v. Kaplan, 90 F.R.D. 21, 28 (N.D. Ill. 1980) (same); *In re* Ampicillin Antitrust Litig., 81 F.R.D. 377, 388 (D.D.C. 1978) (same); United States v. International Business Mach. Corp., 66 F.R.D. at 211, 215 (same); SCM Corp. v. Xerox Corp., 70 F.R.D. 508, 520–23 (D. Conn.), *appeal dismissed*, 534 F.2d 1031 (2d Cir. 1976) (same); Attorney Gen. of the United States v. Covington & Burling, 430 F. Supp. 1117, 1120–21 & n.1 (D.D.C. 1977) (attorney-client privilege protects communications from attorney to client only to the extent that it would reveal confidential communication from client or would reveal, by subsequent communication, an admission by adoption); United States v. United Shoe Mach. Corp., 89 F. Supp. at 359 (attorney communications privileged to the extent that they are based on confidential communications from client).

52. United States v. El Paso Co., 682 F.2d 530, 540 (5th Cir. 1982), *cert. denied*, 466 U.S. 944 (1984) (disclosure of tax pool analysis and underlying documentation to outside accountants for tax audit purposes waives attorney-client privilege); *In re* John Doe Corp., 675 F.2d 482, 488–89 (2d Cir. 1982) (disclosure of a business ethics review to an attorney for an underwriter waives attorney-client privilege for the review; conversation with corporation's

accountant for purposes of financial statement audit waives privilege with respect to contents of conversation); Triax Co. v. United States, 11 Cl. Ct. 130, 134 (1986) (voluntary disclosure of privileged communications to Government Accounting Office by Air Force constituted waiver of all communications on the same subject); Chubb Integrated Sys. Ltd. v. National Bank of Wash., 103 F.R.D. at 67 (disclosure of attorney-client communications to adversary in separate litigation waived privilege with respect to instant lawsuit); Eglin Fed. Credit Union v. Cantor, Fitzgerald Sec. Corp., 91 F.R.D. 414, 418–19 (N.D. Ga. 1981) (attorney-client privilege waived with respect to board minutes that had been made available to accountants for audit purposes); SEC v. Texas Int'l Airlines, Inc., [1979 Transfer Binder] FED. SEC. L. REP. (CCH) ¶ 96,945 (D.D.C. 1979) (summary of decision) (disclosure of documents to corporation's investment banker constitutes waiver of privilege with respect to documents).

53. 805 F.2d 120, 126 (3d Cir. 1986).

54. 112 F.R.D. 99 (S.D.N.Y. 1986).

55. 107 F.R.D. 678 (N.D. Ind. 1985).

56. 106 F.R.D. 187 (N.D. Ill. 1985).

57. *Id.* at 191.

58. 109 F.R.D. 546 (S.D. Miss. 1985).

59. Commodity Futures Trading Comm'n v. Weintraub, 471 U.S. 343, 348 (1985).

60. *Id.* at 348–49.

61. *Id.* at 349.

62. Allen v. Burns, Fry, Ltd., 83 C 2915, slip op. (N.D. Ill. June 4, 1987) (available on LEXIS).

63. *In re* Penn Cent. Commercial Paper Litig., 61 F.R.D. 453, 463–64 (S.D.N.Y. 1973).

64. First Fed. Sav. & Loan v. Oppenheimer, Appel, Dixon & Co., 110 F.R.D. 557, 567–68 (S.D.N.Y. 1986); Teachers Ins. & Annuity Ass'n of Am. v. Shamrock Broadcasting Co., 521 F. Supp. 638, 641 (S.D.N.Y. 1981) (disclosure of part of a document or communication amounts to waiver of privilege with respect to undisclosed portion to the extent necessary to make disclosure complete); Duplan Corp. v. Deering Milliken, Inc., 397 F. Supp. 1146, 1161–62 (D.S.C. 1974) (voluntary waiver as to certain communications waives privilege as to similar communications).

65. 572 F.2d 596 (8th Cir. 1978) (en banc).

66. *Id.* at 611.

67. 665 F.2d 1214, 1219–20 (D.C. Cir. 1981).

68. *Id.* at 1215–16.

69. *Id.* at 1216.

70. *Id.* at 1217.

71. *Id.* at 1222.

72. *Id.* at 1220–22.

73. *Id.* at 1222.

74. 61 F.R.D. at 463–67.

75. *In re* Subpoenas Duces Tecum (Fulbright & Jaworski), 738 F.2d 1367, 1370 (D.C. Cir. 1984).

61

76. 521 F. Supp. at 642–46.
77. 600 F.2d 1223 (6th Cir. 1979), *reversed*, 449 U.S. 383 (1981).
78. 600 F.2d at 1225.
79. 600 F.2d at 1227 n.12.
80. Brief for the United States and the Federal Respondent at 22–26, Upjohn Co. v. United States, 449 U.S. 383 (1981).
81. 85 F.R.D. 679, 682, 688–89 (S.D.N.Y. 1980).
82. 492 F. Supp. 35, 43–44 (N.D. Tex. 1979).
83. 478 F. Supp. 368, 372–73 (E.D. Wis. 1979).
84. *In re* Sealed Case, 676 F.2d 793 (D.C. Cir. 1982).
85. *Id.* at 801–03.
86. *Id.* at 803–04.
87. *Id.* at 804–05.
88. *Id.* at 817–25.
89. United States v. Cote, 456 F.2d 142, 143–45 (8th Cir. 1972).
90. *Id.* at 145.
91. *Id.* at n.4. *See also In re* Weiss, 596 F.2d 1185, 1186 (4th Cir. 1979) (court compelled an attorney to testify before a grand jury because he already had testified and produced documents before the SEC and because the grand jury already possessed the documents and a transcript of his SEC testimony).
92. 692 F.2d 880, 893–94 (2d Cir. 1982), *cert. denied*, 460 U.S. 1051 (1983).
93. 732 F.2d 1302 (7th Cir. 1984).
94. *Id.* at 1314.
95. 99 F.R.D. 616, 619 (S.D. Ohio 1983).
96. 525 F. Supp. 1311, 1329 (S.D. Iowa 1981).
97. Civil Action No. 6941, slip op. at 7 (Del. Ch. Apr. 13, 1983).
98. *Compare* International Business Mach. Corp. v. United States, 471 F.2d 507, 509–11 (2d Cir. 1972), *appeal dismissed*, 480 F.2d 293 (2d Cir. 1973) (en banc), *cert. denied*, 416 U.S. 980 (1974) (no waiver when party asserting privilege was ordered by court to produce extraordinary number of documents on expedited basis and all reasonable precautions had been taken); Transamerica Computer Co. v. International Business Mach. Corp., 573 F.2d 646, 647–51 (9th Cir. 1978) (same); Standard Chartered Bank PLC v. Ayala Int'l Holdings, 111 F.R.D. 76 (S.D.N.Y. 1986) (inadvertent disclosure of one isolated document did not automatically effect a waiver where the isolated document was produced in conjunction with over 1,000 pages of documents and where counsel took care to withhold all other allegedly privileged documents concerning the same subject matter); Kansas-Nebraska Natural Gas v. Marathon Oil Co., 109 F.R.D. 12, 21 (D. Neb. 1985) (inadvertent production of one privileged document among 75,000 pages that were produced does not waive privilege where party attempted to screen such documents from production), *with In re* Grand Jury Investigation of Ocean Transp., 604 F.2d 672, 674–75 (D.C. Cir.), *cert. denied*, 444 U.S. 915 (1979) (complete waiver as to documents produced in response to grand jury subpoena where documents were produced with no indication of privileged status); Hartford Fire Ins. Co. v. Garvey, 109 F.R.D. 323, 331 (N.D.

Cal. 1985) (inadvertent production where there was a "complete failure to take reasonable precautions" waived the privilege); Chubb Integrated Sys. Ltd. v. National Bank of Wash., 103 F.R.D. 52, 67 (D.D.C. 1984) (weight of authority recognizes that waiver can occur through inadvertence); Mendenhall v. Barber-Greene Co., 531 F. Supp. 951 (N.D. Ill. 1982) (inadvertent production attributable to client's carelessness waived privilege).

99. 80 F.R.D. 718, 720–21 (N.D. Ill. 1978).

100. 413 F. Supp. 926, 928–29 (N.D. Cal. 1976).

101. 64 F.R.D. 688, 689–90 (S.D.N.Y. 1974).

102. 111 F.R.D. 76 (S.D.N.Y. 1986).

103. 84 F.R.D. 631, 635 (E.D. Pa. 1979).

104. R.J. Hereley & Son Co. v. Stotler & Co., 87 F.R.D. 358, 359 (N.D. Ill. 1980) (attorney-client privilege waived by deponent's use of a privileged document to refresh his recollection); Julian v. Raytheon Co., 93 F.R.D. 138, 146 (D. Del. 1982) (plaintiff waived attorney-client and work-product privileges to an attorney-assembled binder of nonprivileged documents by using the binder to prepare witnesses for their depositions); Wheeling-Pittsburgh Steel Corp. v. Underwriters Laboratories, Inc., 81 F.R.D. 8, 8–11 (N.D. Ill. 1978) (ordering production of correspondence with attorney when used by witness to refresh recollection before deposition); Bailey v. Meister Brau, Inc., 57 F.R.D. 11, 13 (N.D. Ill. 1972) (plaintiff waived attorney-client privilege with respect to documents used by witness to refresh his recollection at a deposition); Marshall v. United States Postal Service, 88 F.R.D. 348, 350–51 (D.D.C. 1980) (privilege waived only as to documents used to refresh recollection, but not as to all communications on the same subject). *But see* Leucadia, Inc. v. Reliance Ins. Co., 101 F.R.D. 674, 679 (S.D.N.Y. 1983) (finding that the legislative history of the amendments to Federal Rule of Evidence 612 indicates that Congress did not intend to bar the assertion of the attorney-client privilege with respect to writings used by a witness to refresh his memory and, therefore, holding that the mere fact that a deposition witness looked at a document protected by the attorney-client privilege in preparation for a deposition is inadequate to destroy the privilege); Jos. Schlitz Brewing Co. v. Muller & Phipps (Hawaii) Ltd., 85 F.R.D. 118, 119–20 (W.D. Mo. 1980) (correspondence file of attorney-witness not discoverable even though he "looked at" it before his deposition); 3 J. WEINSTEIN & M. BERGER, WEINSTEIN'S EVIDENCE ¶ 612[04] (1982 & Supp. Dec. 1982) (waiver should be found only when witness has consulted a writing embodying his own communication and his testimony discloses a significant part of the communication).

105. *In re* Antitrust Grand Jury (Advance Publications), 805 F.2d 155, 162 (6th Cir. 1986); *In re* Grand Jury Subpoenas Duces Tecum, 773 F.2d 204, 206 (8th Cir. 1985); United States v. Horvath, 731 F.2d 557, 562 (8th Cir. 1984); Clark v. United States, 289 U.S. 1 (1933).

106. 805 F.2d 155 (6th Cir. 1986).

107. 731 F.2d 1032, 1038–39 (2d Cir. 1984).

108. 100 F.R.D. 273 (S.D.N.Y. 1983).

109. Coleman v. American Broadcasting Cos., 106 F.R.D. 201, 207 (D.D.C. 1985); *In re* Sealed Case, 754 F.2d 395, 399 (D.C. Cir. 1985); United States v. Horvath, 731 F.2d at 562; *In re* Grand Jury Subpoena Duces Tecum Dated Sept. 15, 1983 (Marc Rich & Co. A.G.), 731 F.2d at 1038–39; *In re* Grand Jury

Proceedings, 689 F.2d 1351, 1352 (11th Cir. 1982), *cert. denied,* 104 S. Ct. 3524 (1984).

110. *In re* Grand Jury Subpoena Duces Tecum Dated Sept. 15, 1983 (Marc Rich & Co. A.G.), 731 F.2d at 1039.

111. *In re* Antitrust Grand Jury (Advance Publications), 805 F.2d 155, 165–66 (6th Cir. 1986) (adopting standard articulated by Second Circuit).

112. *In re* Sealed Case, 754 F.2d at 399.

113. Coleman v. American Broadcasting Cos., 106 F.R.D. at 207 n.8 (citing probable cause standard with approval).

114. 805 F.2d at 165–66.

115. 751 F.2d 277 (8th Cir. 1984), *cert. dismissed*, 472 U.S. 1022 (1985).

116. *In re* Sealed Case, 754 F.2d at 402; United States v. Horvath, 731 F.2d at 562.

117. 329 U.S. 495 (1947).

118. *Id.* at 510.

119. *Id.* at 511–12.

120. *Id.* at 512.

121. *Id.* at 513.

122. *See In re* D.H. Overmyer Telecasting Co., 470 F. Supp. 1250, 1255 & n.6 (S.D.N.Y. 1979) (content of communications between co-counsel held protected by *Hickman* although Rule 26(b)(3) was inapplicable).

123. 449 U.S. 383, 399 (1981).

124. 599 F.2d 504, 511 & n.5 (2d Cir. 1979).

125. *In re* International Sys. & Controls Corp. Sec. Litig., 91 F.R.D. 552, 557 (S.D. Tex. 1981), *vacated on other grounds*, 693 F.2d 1235 (5th Cir. 1982) (special audit work papers met the anticipation-of-litigation requirement because the corporation knew from the initial SEC inquiry that involvement in SEC proceedings was likely and shareholder suits were quite possible); *In re* LTV Sec. Litig., 89 F.R.D. 595, 612 (N.D. Tex. 1981) (outside counsel's response to an SEC subpoena held to have been prepared in anticipation of litigation); United States v. Lipshy, 492 F. Supp. 35, 44–45 (N.D. Tex. 1979) (internal investigation of political payments by the corporation's general counsel was prepared in anticipation of litigation where the investigation took place at the same time that the IRS was conducting a general investigation of the corporation's tax liability, where there was a possibility of an SEC enforcement action regarding disclosure violations, and where shareholder suits were also possible). *See also In re* Grand Jury Investigation (Sun Co.), 599 F.2d 1224, 1229 (3d Cir. 1979) (interview memoranda and questionnaires compiled as a result of an internal legal audit by outside counsel regarding possible illegal foreign payments were prepared in anticipation of litigation).

126. 572 F.2d 596 (8th Cir. 1978) (en banc).

127. *Id.* at 604.

128. 27 Fed. R. Serv. 2d (Callaghan) 819 (S.D.N.Y. 1979).

129. *Id.* at 821.

130. *Compare* Levingston v. Allis-Chalmers Corp., 109 F.R.D. 546 (S.D. Miss. 1985) (court adopts "intermediate approach," finding no work-product privilege where the cases are not at all related); *In re* International Sys. & Controls Corp. Sec. Litig., 91 F.R.D. 552, 557 (S.D. Tex. 1981), *vacated on other grounds*, 693 F.2d

1235 (5th Cir. 1982) (work-product protection prevents disclosure in shareholder suit of materials prepared for SEC proceedings); *In re* LTV Sec. Litig., 89 F.R.D. at 612 (anticipation of suit by federal agency protects material in late shareholder suit), *with* Panter v. Marshall Field & Co., 80 F.R.D. 718, 724 (N.D. Ill. 1978) (weight of authority extends work-product protection to documents produced in anticipation of prior terminated litigation regardless of interconnectedness of issues); Eagle-Picher Indus., Inc. v. United States, 11 Cl. Ct. 452, 457 (1987) (weight of modern authority is that the work-product immunity applies to documents prepared in anticipation of unrelated terminated litigation).

131. 816 F.2d 397 (8th Cir.), *cert. denied,* 108 S. Ct. 268 (1987).

132. *Id.* at 400–01.

133. *Id.* at 401–02. *But see* Tronitech, Inc. v. NCR Corp., 108 F.R.D. 655 (S.D. Ind. 1985) (audit letter analyzing financial implications of a lawsuit, prepared by corporate counsel at the request of and for use by corporation's accounting firm, held privileged).

134. Hickman v. Taylor, 329 U.S. at 511–13; Upjohn Co. v. United States, 449 U.S. at 399–402; *In re* Grand Jury Subpoena (John Doe, Inc.), 599 F.2d 504, 512–13 (2d Cir. 1979).

135. 599 F.2d 1224 (3rd Cir. 1979).

136. *Id.* at 1232–33; *In re* Grand Jury Subpoena (John Doe, Inc.), 599 F.2d at 512 (government's desire to examine questionnaires and interview memoranda in order to decide whether to offer immunity was not sufficient need even for ordinary work product); Donovan v. Fitzsimmons, 90 F.R.D. 583 (N.D. Ill. 1981) (same).

137. 619 F.2d 980, 988 (3d Cir. 1980).

138. *Id.* at 988. *See also In re* International Sys. & Controls Corp. Sec. Litig. (Koenig), 693 F.2d 1235, 1240 (5th Cir. 1982) (witness's present lack of recollection sufficient to establish substantial need); Panter v. Marshall Field & Co., 80 F.R.D. at 725 (death of witness sufficient to allow production of work product); *In re* Grand Jury Proceedings, 73 F.R.D. 647, 653–54 (M.D. Fla. 1977) (materials subpoenaed by grand jury that were prepared in anticipation of prior completed litigation held not protected by work-product doctrine, with the court relying on the strong policy in favor of grand jury's authority and need to accomplish its investigative duties).

139. *In re* Grand Jury Proceedings (Duffy), 473 F.2d 840, 841–42, 848 (8th Cir. 1973) (attorney notes, memoranda, and recollections of oral conversations held absolutely privileged from disclosure to grand jury); *In re* Grand Jury Investigation (Sturgis), 412 F. Supp. 943, 949 (E.D. Pa. 1976) (file memorandum of attorney's telephone conversation with client absolutely protected).

140. 759 F.2d 312, 316 (3d Cir.), *cert. denied*, 106 S. Ct. 232 (1985).

141. *In re* International Sys. & Controls Corp. Sec. Litig. (Koenig), 693 F.2d 1235, 1240 (5th Cir. 1982) (opinion work product entitled to "almost absolute protection"); *In re* Sealed Case, 676 F.2d 793, 809–10 (D.C. Cir. 1982) (opinion work product can be discovered only upon "extraordinary justification"); *In re* Subpoena (Murphy), 560 F.2d 326, 336 (8th Cir. 1977) (opinion work product enjoys a nearly absolute immunity, discoverable only in "very rare and extraordinary circumstances"); Eagle-Pitcher Indus., Inc. v. United States, 11 Cl. Ct. 452, 457 (1987) (discovery of opinion work product "is allowed sparingly").

65

142. Upjohn Co. v. United States, 449 U.S. at 399–402.

143. *See generally* United States v. American Tel. & Tel. Co., 642 F.2d 1285, 1299 (D.C. Cir. 1980).

144. Schachar v. American Academy of Ophthalmology, Inc., 106 F.R.D. 187, 191 (N.D. Ill. 1985) (attorneys facing a common litigation opponent may exchange privileged communications and attorney work product in order to prepare a common defense without waiving privilege); United States v. American Tel. & Tel. Co., 642 F.2d at 1298–1300 (common interest a relevant factor in determining whether disclosure constitutes a waiver; no waiver where both parties are pursuing similar claims against a common adversary); D'Ippolito v. Cities Serv. Co., 39 F.R.D. 610 (S.D.N.Y. 1965) (disclosure to Department of Justice, admittedly not on same side of litigation, results in waiver of work-product protection). *But see* Triax Co. v. United States, 11 Cl. Ct. 130, 133 (1986) (disclosure of privileged documents to the General Accounting Office by the Air Force did not constitute waiver, because the GAO was not an adversary in litigation and disclosure was not "inconsistent with the adversarial process"); Chubb Integrated Sys. Ltd. v. National Bank of Wash., 103 F.R.D. at 67 (voluntary disclosure of work product to adversary in separate litigation waives the privilege with respect to adversaries in lawsuits concerning the same subject matter).

145. *Compare In re* Sealed Case, 676 F.2d 793, 817–25 (D.C. Cir. 1982) (grand jury granted access to documents that related to documents previously supplied to the SEC), *with* GAF Corp. v. Eastman Kodak Co., 85 F.R.D. 46, 51–52 (S.D.N.Y. 1979) (plaintiff's disclosure to government of written analysis of documents that had been produced by defendant does not constitute waiver of work-product protection).

146. 93 F.R.D. 138, 144–46 (D. Del. 1982).

147. Shelton v. American Motors Corp., 805 F.2d 1323, 1329 (8th Cir. 1986) (in-house attorney not compelled to testify about even the existence of a document where she "engaged in a process of selecting and compiling documents in preparation for litigation [and] the mere acknowledgment of the existence of those documents would reveal counsel's mental impressions, which are protected as work-product"). In Berkey Photo, Inc. v. Eastman Kodak Co., 74 F.R.D. 613 (S.D.N.Y. 1977), the court refused to order disclosure of notebooks that had been prepared by an attorney and reviewed by the party's experts. However, the court was not confident that it had reached the correct result and suggested that similar discovery would be allowed in the future. *Id.* at 614–17. According to the court in *James Julian*, the *Berkey* decision "put the bar on notice that in the future a contrary result would obtain." 93 F.R.D. at 145.

148. 759 F.2d 312, 317–18 (3d Cir.), *cert. denied*, 106 S. Ct. 232 (1985).

149. 112 F.R.D. 671 (D. Kan. 1986).

150. *Id.* at 683. Bloch v. Smithkline Beckman Corp., Civil Action No. 82-510, slip op. (E.D. Pa. Apr. 9, 1987) (use of privileged documents to refresh a witness's recollection does not automatically waive the privilege but will be evaluated on a case-by-case basis to ensure that a party does not make "unfair use" of the work-product privilege); Bogosian v. Gulf Oil Corp., 738 F.2d 587 (3d Cir. 1984) (rules do not require disclosure of opinion work-product documents shown to a party's expert); WEINSTEIN & BERGER, *supra* note 56, at ¶ 612[04] (court should require showing of need before compelling disclosure of protected

documents). *See also* Omaha Public Power Dist. v. Foster Wheeler Corp., 109 F.R.D. 615, 616–17 (D. Neb. 1986) (expressing doubt that Federal Rule of Evidence 612 is applicable to deposition testimony, but applying the *Sporck* standard that a party must first elicit testimony from a deponent and then ask the witness to identify which documents, if any, informed that testimony).

151. 422 U.S. 225, 236–40 (1975).

152. 110 F.R.D. 688 (S.D.N.Y. 1986).

153. *Id.* at 690.

154. 805 F.2d 155, 162–64 (6th Cir. 1986).

155. *Id.* at 163.

156. *Id.* at 164. *See also* Grand Jury Subpoena Duces Tecum Dated Sept. 15, 1983 (Marc Rich & Co. A.G.), 731 F.2d at 1038 (advice sought to further a crime or fraudulent scheme renders any work product unprotected); *In re* Sealed Case, 676 F.2d at 811–13 (crime-fraud exception applied to work-product privilege); *In re* John Doe Corp., 675 F.2d 482, 492 (2d Cir. 1982) (use of work product in aid of criminal scheme may be "rare occasion" on which opinion work product is not immune).

157. *In re* Special Sept. 1978 Grand Jury (II), 640 F.2d 49, 63 (7th Cir. 1980).

158. *In re* International Sys. & Controls Corp. Sec. Litig., 91 F.R.D. at 559–60, *vacated on other grounds*, 693 F.2d at 1242.

159. *In re* Antitrust Grand Jury (Advance Publications), 805 F.2d at 164; *In re* Special Sept. 1978 Grand Jury II, 640 F.2d at 63.

160. *In re* Antitrust Grand Jury (Advance Publications), 805 F.2d at 166.

161. *E.g.*, Garner v. Wolfinbarger, 430 F.2d 1093, 1102–03 (5th Cir. 1970), *cert. denied*, 401 U.S. 974 (1971).

162. *E.g.*, *In re* International Sys. & Controls Corp. Sec. Litig., 693 F.2d at 1239–40.

163. Garner v. Wolfinbarger, 430 F.2d at 1103–04.

164. *Id.* at 1102–03.

165. *Id.* at 1104.

166. *See, e.g.*, Kirby, *New Life for the Corporate Attorney-Client Privilege in Shareholder Litigation*, 69 A.B.A. J. 174 (1983); Block & Prussin, *After* Upjohn, *The* Garner *Rule Still Creates Uncertainty in Area of Corporate Attorney-Client Privilege*, 3 BUS. ADVOC. 5–6 (Spring 1981). *But see* WEINSTEIN & BERGER, *supra* note 56, at ¶ 503(b)[05] (*Garner* approach is sound).

167. *See* Quintel Corp., N.V. v. Citibank, N.A., 567 F. Supp. 1357, 1363 (S.D.N.Y. 1983) (ordering disclosure); *In re* LTV Sec. Litig., 89 F.R.D. 595 (N.D. Tex. 1981); Ohio-Sealy Mattress Mfg. Co. v. Kaplan, 90 F.R.D. 21, 31–32 (N.D. Ill. 1980) (ordering disclosure); Cohen v. Uniroyal, Inc., 80 F.R.D. 480 (N.D. Ill. 1978); Valente v. PepsiCo, Inc., 68 F.R.D. 361 (D. Del. 1975); Bailey v. Meister Brau, Inc., 55 F.R.D. 211 (N.D. Ill. 1972). *But see* Shirvani v. Capital Investing Corp., Inc., 112 F.R.D. 389, 390–91 (D. Conn. 1986) (rejecting *Garner* doctrine).

168. Hoiles v. Superior Court of Orange County, 157 Cal. App. 3d 1192, 1199 (4th Dist. 1984).

169. Neusteter v. District Court, Denver, 675 P.2d 1 (Colo. 1984); Beard v. Ames, 96 A.D.2d 119, 468 N.Y.S.2d 253 (4th Dept. 1983).

67

170. Weil v. Investment/Indicators, Research & Management, Inc., 647 F.2d 18, 23 (9th Cir. 1981).

171. *See also* Shirvani v. Capital Investing Corp., 112 F.R.D. at 390–91 (rejecting *Garner* doctrine in action brought directly against the corporation by shareholders).

172. 112 F.R.D. 671, 676–82 (D. Kan. 1986).

173. 113 F.R.D. 7, 9–10 (D. Conn. 1986).

174. 90 F.R.D. 583, 584–87 (N.D. Ill. 1981).

175. 80 F.R.D. 480, 482–85 (E.D. Pa. 1978).

176. [1976–1977 Transfer Binder] FED. SEC. L. REP. (CCH) ¶ 95,894 at 91,303 (N.D. Tex 1977).

177. 55 F.R. D. 211, 213–14 (N.D. Ill. 1972).

178. 89 F.R.D. 595, 607–08 (N.D. Tex. 1981).

179. *Id.* at 598.

180. *Id.* at 607.

181. *Id.* at 608.

182. 693 F.2d 1235 (5th Cir. 1982).

183. *Id.* at 1239. *But see* Donovan v. Fitzsimmons, 90 F.R.D. 583, 588 (N.D. Ill. 1981) (*Garner* rationale must be addressed in the work-product context "lest the work-product immunity swallow up the *Garner* exception in its entirety").

184. 203 Cal. Rptr. 752, 756 (Ct. App. 5th Dist. 1984).

185. 432 N.E.2d 250, 256–58 (Ill. 1982).

186. *Id.* at 257.

187. 308 N.W.2d 305, 308–09 (Minn. 1981), *cert. denied*, 455 U.S. 939 (1982).

188. 432 A.2d 960, 961–64 (N.J. Super. Ct. App. Div. 1981).

189. 277 S.E. 2d 785, 790–92 (Ga. Ct. App. 1981).

190. 572 F.2d 596 (8th Cir. 1978) (en banc).

191. *Marriott Corp.*, 277 S.E.2d at 791–92.

192. 119 Ill. 2d 368 (1987).

193. 5 U.S.C. § 552.

194. 5 U.S.C. § 552(b).

195. Chrysler Corp. v. Brown, 441 U.S. 281, 293–94 (1979).

196. 15 U.S.C. § 18a(h).

197. 15 U.S.C. § 57b-2(f).

198. 15 U.S.C. § 1314(g).

199. *See, e.g.,* 17 C.F.R. § 240.24b-2 (1984) (exclusive means of objecting to public disclosure by SEC of documents required to be filed by 1934 act); 17 C.F.R. § 240.0-4 (1984) (certain investigative documents considered confidential); 17 C.F.R. § 230.122 (1984) (same); 17 C.F.R. § 200.83 (1984) (procedures for requesting confidential treatment by SEC); 17 C.F.R. § 200.80 (1984) (general SEC rules regarding documents and FOIA requests); 40 C.F.R. § 2.100–2.309 (1984) (EPA regulations regarding FOIA requests and confidentiality determinations).

200. *E.g.*, Forsham v. Harris, 445 U.S. 169, 182–86 (1980) (materials were not agency records subject to FOIA disclosure even though agency had access to them). *See also* 15 U.S.C. § 78x (definition of "records" for FOIA purposes includes documents "filed with or otherwise obtained" by the SEC).

201. *See, e.g.*, SEC v. National Student Marketing Corp., 457 F. Supp. 682, 712–14 (1978). *See generally* Burke, *The Duty of Confidentiality and Disclosing Corporate Misconduct*, 36 BUS. LAW. 239 (1981); Hoffman, *On Learning of a Corporate Client's Crime or Fraud—The Lawyer's Dilemma*, 33 BUS. LAW. 1389 (1978).

202. *In re* Grand Jury Subpoena (Doe), 781 F.2d 238 (2d Cir.) (en banc), *cert. denied*, 106 S. Ct. 1515 (1986); *In re* Grand Jury Subpoena Duces Tecum (Shargel), 742 F.2d 61 (2d Cir. 1984).

203. *See generally* MODEL CODE OF PROFESSIONAL RESPONSIBILITY DR 5-102 (withdrawal as counsel when lawyer becomes witness), DR 4-101(d)(2) (permitting attorney to reveal confidence when required by an order of court); MODEL RULES OF PROFESSIONAL CONDUCT Rules 1.6, 3.3 (1983).

204. *In re* Grand Jury Subpoena (Legal Serv. Center), 615 F. Supp. 958, 963–64 (D.C. Mass. 1985), *citing In re* Special Grand Jury No. 81-1 (Harvey), 676 F.2d 1005, *vacated on other grounds*, 697 F.2d 112 (4th Cir. 1982); United States v. Badalamenti, 614 F. Supp. 194, 198–99 (S.D.N.Y. 1985).

205. *In re* Grand Jury Subpoena (Doe), 781 F.2d at 244–47; *In re* Grand Jury Investigation (Harvey), 769 F.2d 1485, 1487 (11th Cir. 1985); *In re* Klein, 776 F.2d 628, 633 (7th Cir. 1985); *In re* Proceedings (Doe), 754 F.2d 154 (6th Cir. 1985); *In re* Grand Jury Proceedings (Schofield), 721 F.2d 1221, 1222 at n.1 (9th Cir. 1983).

206. *E.g.*, *In re* Klein, 776 F.2d at 634–35.

207. *In re* Gopman, 531 F.2d 262 (5th Cir. 1976); United States v. RMI Co., 467 F. Supp. 915 (W.D. Pa. 1979). *See also* Doe v. A Corp., 709 F.2d 1043 (5th Cir. 1983) (attorney disqualified from representing class in action against former client where he would have had opportunity to use confidential information against former client); *In re* Coordinated Pretrial Proceedings in Petroleum Prods. Antitrust Litig., 658 F.2d 1355, 1361 (9th Cir. 1981), *cert. denied,* 102 S. Ct. 1615 (1982). (Canon 9 is sufficient ground for disqualification in itself, but appellate court will affirm a disqualification order "only where the impropriety is clear and is one that would be recognized as such by all reasonable persons"); Smith v. New York, 611 F. Supp. 1080, 1091 (S.D.N.Y. 1985) (Canon 5 is satisfied by the clients' informed consent); United States v. Occidental Chem. Corp., 606 F. Supp. 1470 (W.D.N.Y. 1985) (corporate counsel may also represent former employees where there is no actual conflict of interest); United States v. Linton, 502 F. Supp. 871, 877 (D. Nev. 1980) (consent to and waiver of objections to conflict of interest not sufficient if confidential information involved: "the ethical requirement to utilize on behalf of one client confidential information obtained from another client could conceivably result in counsel's disqualification to represent both clients"). *But see* Vegetable Kingdom, Inc. v. Katzen, 653 F. Supp. 917 (N.D.N.Y. 1987) (noting that motions for disqualification are increasingly filed merely to harass opposing counsel, the court denied the motion and imposed sanctions on movant).

208. *See* CODE OF PROFESSIONAL RESPONSIBILITY DR 5-105, EC 5-14, 5-15, 9-1, 9-2; MODEL RULES OF PROFESSIONAL CONDUCT ER 1.6, 1.7, 1.8(f), 1.13(e); United States v. Marshall, 488 F.2d 1169 (9th Cir. 1973).

Section II

Handling Litigation Utilizing the Corporate Law Department

Prudent corporate management has always required evaluation of all department functions to ensure the effective and responsive delivery of necessary services. In recent years, due to the loss of affordable product liability coverage and associated insurance company claims-handling service, corporate law departments have come under particular scrutiny. The primary area of concern has been litigation, particularly its frequency, seriousness, and volume; the cost-effectiveness of outside counsel providing services; and the feasibility of bringing more litigation responsibility in-house. These considerations are complex and vary greatly from one corporation to another. The articles collected for this section provide some thoughtful comments and helpful advice for evaluating your corporate needs.

In Chapter 3, Thomas B. Leary raises issues pertaining to the use of inside counsel. He reviews means to determine which cases are appropriate to be handled in-house. He describes factors that affect the litigation decision, including management philosophy and corporate decentralization. Based on the role of in-house counsel in litigation, Mr. Leary discusses the management of in-house staff, including determination of the type and size of staff required, recruitment and training of personnel, and establishment of long-term goals and career development. The company can then develop flexibility to meet changing or unforeseen legal needs by adding outside assistance.

Moving to a specific example of in-house staffing to handle litigation, Robert L. Bordon in Chapter 4 shows you how Pacific Gas & Electric set up its law department to handle all of the company's litigation needs. PG&E's philosophy is that in order to perform litigation in-house, it must maintain a qualified firm that is competitive with private practice. Although most corporations find the diversity of litigation and number of attorneys necessary to maintain a trial litigation department too costly, this article provides an excellent guide for those considering bringing all or a major portion of their litigation in-house. The chapter refers to Forms 7-9 in the Appendix, which provide details of PG&E's training program.

The importance of an effective corporate litigation department is obvious. More than ever before, the result of poor client advice or litigation strategy is likely to be adverse decisions, class actions, criminal liability, and punitive damages. Economic health and public image are closely tied to how well a company handles its litigation. A review of this section will help to assess your law department, your litigation philosophy, and whether your litigation needs are being delivered as required and in a cost-effective manner.

William R. Hedden
Schering-Plough Corporation
Kenilworth, New Jersey

Three

The Size and Organization of Corporate Legal Staffs

Thomas B. Leary

Corporate legal staffs are increasingly visible. They have grown in size and in influence, and people have begun to recognize that corporate staffs are law firms in their own right. The internal organization of these in-house law firms, and the interaction between inside and outside counsel, are subjects of ongoing interest.

Growth of In-House Staffs

There is a tendency to overstate the extent to which legal work is being transferred from the "outside" to the "inside." It is true that corporate staffs grew dramatically from the early 1960s to the early 1980s. But there also was a dramatic increase in the amount of government regulation (which requires lawyering) during the same period. Much of this regulation was either industry-specific or of a kind that requires extensive internal compliance—and inside lawyers may have been best qualified to handle it. The overall growth in demand was probably more significant than the shift from one kind of lawyer to another. The recent leveling in the size of corporate staffs is consistent with this explanation, because government regulation has also leveled off or actually decreased.

In the future, the head count of mature organizations is likely to remain relatively stable or actually decline, unless there is a movement toward re-regulation. There are likely to be increases in the legal head count of smaller and younger companies as they mature. An expanded legal staff is a capital investment, which a company is more apt to make when future needs can be seen more clearly.

Some continued internalization of legal functions also seems likely—particularly in the area of litigation support and even courtroom advocacy itself. However, there probably will not be as dramatic a change as some people hope for or fear, and few corporations should find it feasible to train and retain first-class trial lawyers.

Thomas B. Leary, formerly Assistant General Counsel at General Motors Corporation, is a member of Hogan & Hartson, Washington, D.C.

Areas of Law Appropriate and Inappropriate for In-House Staff

We have moved away from the primitive notion that routine matters should be handled inside and complex ones referred outside. The difficulty of matters is not what is significant, but rather their predictability. If a general counsel can anticipate that certain kinds of legal problems are apt to recur, it is sensible to consider the capital investment required for an internal capability. Otherwise, it will probably still pay to go outside.

An example might be the capability to handle mergers and acquisitions. Some companies are committed to acquisition programs on an ongoing basis; they may even have a department dedicated to the activity. It may be prudent for them to develop an in-house legal capability. A company that acquires (or divests) only occasionally has entirely different needs.

Litigation is another example. A manufacturer may anticipate that it will continually come up against multiple product liability or warranty cases involving claims that a particular product or component is defective. The basic engineering facts are going to be similar. It may be efficient for inside lawyers, assisted by inside engineering experts, to do almost all of the trial preparation and, in some instances, to actually try the cases. If a major jury trial is anticipated, however, or the jurisdiction is relatively unfamiliar, outside lawyers might have an expertise that the inside staff cannot match.

In summary, you cannot say that any area of law is "appropriate" or "inappropriate" for particular kinds of lawyers. It all depends.

Determining the Size of In-House Staff

In addition to the factors outlined so far, the size of the staff may be affected by the company's overall management philosophy. Some chief executives believe in small internal staffs in all areas and prefer to rely heavily on purchased services; others do not. The consequences for legal staff size are obvious.

The extent to which a company is decentralized or engaged in widely diverse enterprises is also significant. For example, my former employer, General Motors, is larger than General Electric, but its legal staff is considerably smaller. This may reflect the fact the GE is more decentralized and in more varied businesses.

There are some overall constraints on the size of a professional organization that may affect decisions about staff expansion. Problems of management efficiency will be discussed later on. For the moment, note simply that a growing staff will eventually require an internal management structure. Increasing numbers of senior lawyers may have to function as administrators, an activity that is unfamiliar and uncongenial to many professionals. This must be taken into consideration in determining the optimal balance between inside and outside activity.

Steps in Creating an Efficient In-House Staff

Like so many other issues, the appropriate solution depends on the needs of a particular company and staff. A staff that is expected to serve as a full-service law firm will be built up differently than a staff whose primary mission is the coordination of outside legal work. A small company has different needs than a large one. Some companies are extensively regulated; others are not. In some cases, it makes sense only to hire experienced lawyers, with specialized knowledge, in the anticipation that they will devote their legal careers to a particular kind of work for the company. In other cases, it may be appropriate to recruit directly from law schools; to hire lawyers on the basis of general aptitude, rather than specific legal expertise; to expect some movement of lawyers from one specialty to another; and to accept a relatively high attrition rate.

The transition from the former to the latter mode has presented a significant challenge for some corporate legal staffs in recent years. An organization structure has to be created for the first time. The company has to learn a new method of recruitment, in direct competition with outside law firms. Training and career development programs have to be developed. It may not be easy to integrate young lawyers, fresh from the campus, with older lawyers who may have different attitudes, aptitudes, and career expectations.

There are no easy or broadbrush solutions to these problems, but the first step is to recognize that they exist. Fortunately, counsel in other companies, who have already faced these problems, are usually willing to share their experiences.

Management of In-House Staff

The demands on an in-house staff may grow to the point where it is simply impossible for one general counsel to oversee all of the organization's legal work personally. Some kind of management structure will have to be devised, with an appropriate delegation of authority. Two contrasting models may be adapted: (1) a staff organized around substantive areas of law and (2) a staff organized around the operating units of the client company. There are advantages and disadvantages of each. The ultimate choice of one model, or something in between the two, will probably be strongly influenced by the overall structure of the corporation.

A centralized staff organized by substantive areas facilitates a high level of internal specialization and legal expertise. It promotes a unified approach to the legal problems of a widespread organization, and the "remoteness" from day-to-day client operations may enhance professional independence. On the other hand, that same remoteness undercuts the intimate familiarity with operations that may be an inside lawyer's great strength. Accordingly, a staff organized on substantive lines will typically have some ad hoc arrangements under which designated lawyers have special responsibility for the legal affairs of particular operations.

A staff organized around operating units maximizes familiarity with the business and fosters close client relationships. Legal services may be provided faster and at less cost. On the other hand, it is difficult for lawyers "in the field" to develop a real substantive expertise in specialized areas, and there is a risk that they may identify too closely with individual units at the expense of overall corporate interests. Accordingly, a decentralized organization will typically have at least a skeleton "headquarters" staff, consisting of experts in particular substantive areas with some corporatewide jurisdiction.

Additional problems arise when legal staffs, however organized, become so large that some senior lawyers have to devote substantial amounts of time to administrative responsibilities. The internal culture that prevails in the corporation may emphasize administrative functions when allocating rewards, and this may blunt the development of individual professional skills. Lawyers must become "managers" whether they have any particular aptitude or not. This emphasis may also lead to a proliferation of titles and layers of legal management, in an effort to provide opportunities for lawyers to be "promoted" like other corporate managers. Lawyers may seek assignments on the basis of perceived opportunities for promotion, rather than individual aptitudes.

A law firm model may be better for a professional group, because senior lawyers are not necessarily required to be administrators. Reporting lines can be informal and project-specific. The concept of a "partner" is alien in the normal structure of a corporation, however, and personnel policies have to be adjusted to reflect the special needs of a professional group.

The point here is that the issue of legal staff management involves much more than just the efficient allocation of particular parcels of legal work. It requires attention to long-term career development, in the context of overall corporate personnel policies. If in-house staffs are going to compete effectively for legal talent, they cannot neglect this issue.

Relationships with Outside Counsel

Tension may be perceived between a corporation's desire to move some work inside and its desire to continue strong relationships with outside counsel. This issue is just part of a larger topic: the decline of "client loyalty." It is simply no longer possible for law firms to assume that an established relationship with a client will continue indefinitely; clients are beginning to shop around with other law firms, as well as bring matters inside. This creates tension because it is now harder for outside law firms to engage in long-term planning; they may be more reluctant to subsidize legal work on small matters with revenues (actual or anticipated) from large matters; and they may be reluctant to turn down new business from a client's competitors if they cannot count on a continuing relationship with the client.

There is nothing unusual about this kind of fluid relationship in the normal business context. Corporations review their make/buy decisions all the time; they consider both long-term and short-term contracts for goods and services; and they buy a "full line" or they buy selectively. The reason it seems particularly difficult in the area of legal services is that inside and outside counsel have not yet become entirely comfortable discussing these things on a businesslike basis. We were bred in a tradition that it was somehow unprofessional to talk about the commercial aspects of legal representation.

We need to talk more candidly, not only about immediate matters, but also about long-range planning. It is not unusual right now for outside lawyers to give their clients a full briefing about the capabilities of their firm and its future directions. It is unusual, however, for them to seek equivalent information about the future directions of the corporate client's staff. Both sides need to be better informed in order to work toward a rational allocation of legal effort. For one thing, information may well lead to efficiencies that can be reflected in billing rates.

Determining Whether and to What Extent to Use Outside Counsel

As indicated, the decision to use inside or outside counsel is strongly influenced by the likelihood that particular legal problems will recur. Recurring problems may justify the investment in an in-house capability. This could apply to litigation, if cases of a particular kind or in a particular jurisdiction can be expected to continue. General Motors, for example, developed the in-house capability to try substantial numbers of workers' compensation cases in the state of Michigan; this was viewed as high-volume work for the foreseeable future in a familiar jurisdiction.

Short-term decisions are more likely to be made on a purely ad hoc basis. A matter that is handled inside this year may be farmed out next year if the staff is swamped. Sometimes outside counsel is brought in purely for internal political considerations—the staff may want reinforcement when rendering an opinion that management may not like. Sometimes outside counsel is employed to enhance the external credibility of an opinion.[1]

Outside counsel can be employed in various ways. Sometimes corporate staffs want to "rent an associate" in order to lend a hand when internal personnel are unavailable; sometimes corporate staffs are only interested in consultation at the partner level and intend to handle all the backup work themselves. Sometimes inside and outside lawyers work literally side by side on projects. There is no limit to the kinds of arrangements that are possible. In all cases, however, it is important that lines of responsibility be clearly understood, and somebody—either inside or outside—has to be clearly in charge of the project.

In making either short- or long-term decisions about outside counsel, it is important to remember that inside counsel are not necessarily "cheaper." Outside counsel's hourly charges appear to be large when compared with the salaries of staff lawyers reduced to an hourly basis. But the gaps may narrow drastically when fringes and corporate overhead are fully allocated, as they should be. Moreover, the differences that may have existed in the overall compensation levels of inside and outside lawyers continue to narrow as corporate staffs increasingly compete for the same talent and offer comparable opportunities. It is a mistake for a corporation to plan on the basis that it can hire "cheaper" lawyers than the lawyers it retains. You tend to get the level of competence you pay for, regardless of whom you pay.

The important consideration is not hourly cost, it is efficiency. Outside lawyers may do some things more efficiently because they have developed a broader expertise in particular areas of practice; inside lawyers may do some things more efficiently because they know the business better and require less startup time. Ideally, however, they should be lawyers of equivalent caliber.

How to Later Expand or Contract as Company's Needs Change

Expansion is easier than contraction. Although times are changing, there are still more apt to be implicit reciprocal expectations of lifetime employment in corporate staffs than in law firms. Moreover, it may be more difficult to measure the productivity of in-house lawyers—for one thing, they typically do not account for their time. If demand for service declines, productivity will probably decline faster than head count.

To the extent that corporate staff size is driven by a one-way ratchet, it may be prudent to let staff growth lag anticipated demand—to defer the investment in human capital until the need is clear and convincing. One corporate general counsel recently expressed the concept as "staffing . . . for the valleys of activity and not the peaks."[2] If this requires the use of outside services that appear to be more expensive, the expense is justified because the company is "laying off" a risk. In fact, the ability to respond with people—either to accommodate an unexpected surge in demand or a deliberate shortfall in supply—is one of the most important services that a private firm can offer. And, like any other kind of insurance coverage, this protection normally involves some premium. The premium should be less to the extent the risk is less, however, and open communication about long-range plans can help to make it so.

Conclusion

The questions posed do not have any broadly applicable answers. Each situation is different. These comments are intended merely as a stimulus to thought, not as a substitute for it.

Notes

1. *See* Aibel, *Successful Teaming of Inside and Outside Corporate Counsel*, 38 Bus. Law. 1587 (1983).
2. *Id.* at 1588.

Four

The Organization and Staffing of an In-House Counsel Office in Order to Handle Litigation Directly

Robert L. Bordon

This chapter discusses handling litigation in-house by a company with a commitment to a first-rate law department that is capable of handling all of its litigation. It begins generally with the economies of an in-house department, which explains why we operate as we do at PG&E and sets the stage for the balance of the chapter.

Commitment to hiring and retaining top law students and lawyers has been and is a primary concern for PG&E. To attract top law students, we must meet the competition. As will be discussed later, we do just that.

You'll be asked, "If we meet the competition, and pay those extraordinarily high (outrageous) salaries, why not just go outside?" Your answer: "Because, even with those high salaries, it is far more economical to do it ourselves." Virtually all of PG&E's legal work is handled by the law department. We have conservatively estimated that the cost to the company of the law department's services is less than $100 per hour. (This assumes a certain number of hours per attorney and includes all overheads plus direct and indirect costs, such as salaries, imputed office rent, library, and support staff. Inasmuch as the major commercial firms in San Francisco bill their first-year associates at $100 per hour and partners up to $250 per hour and more, PG&E could not obtain the same legal services from a law firm at anywhere near the cost at which the law department provides them.

What about efficiency? Would a law firm do the same work in more or less time? Again, our studies show that the major firms staff similar cases with more lawyers than do we. This means that if a major case were sent to an outside firm for handling, not only would the hourly cost per firm attorney be substantially higher ($150–$175 per hour versus $100 per hour), but the firm would also expend more than twice the attorney time

Robert L. Bordon is an attorney with Pacific Gas and Electric Company, San Francisco, California.

on the case. Thus, the cost of sending a case out is more than two times the cost of doing it in-house.

What about quality? This gets back to whom you hire. If you pay the same, you can hire the same quality attorney that the firms do.

Recruitment

We have limited our recruiting for the past several years to Stanford, Boalt, and Harvard. While we have interviewed only at those schools until this past year, we have always sought and attracted some students and lawyers (lateral hires usually up to three years out) from other top schools. Our department primarily comprises attorneys from those three schools and from Hastings. While we seek students who were in the top quarter of their class, many of our members were Law Review and Order of the Coif. Many come with unusual educational backgrounds (four have Ph.D.'s) and work experience, which we find very useful.

A major part of our success in attracting and retaining the top law students from the best law schools is the company's long-standing commitment to meet the salaries for associates paid by the seven to nine major commercial law firms in San Francisco.

When interviewing law students, it has become apparent that any corporation is at a disadvantage compared to its competition. We are unable to offer the lure of partnership and associated financial rewards. Moreover, we must overcome a strong bias against corporate law departments. Most law students of the caliber we seek are conditioned to believe that the best graduates go to major business law firms. We thus must stress that in all respects, other than partnership compensation, we are similar to the competition and offer other compensating rewards. (The other rewards are largely intangibles, such as closer client contact, the ability to shape policy, the opportunity to gain responsibility very early in a career, and a practice involving issues of great public importance.) The bottom line is, though, that if we were unable to meet the competition's starting salary, our ability to hire the best students would be impaired.

How do you market yourself? First, money. You have to pay the same starting salary to compete for the best. Second, money. You have to convince the students that they'll continue to do well if they stay with you for their career. Third, money. Look for ways to make them happy and keep them motivated. We use bonus plans, stock plans, and an array of benefits. Fourth, stress the intangibles just described. Let the law schools and students know what you have to offer. Provide each school with an informational packet containing your "résumé."

Because students want to know the type of attorneys with whom they will be associating, our packet also includes the biography of the department's members. (Since we are not listed as a firm in Martindale-Hubbel, we have to supply our own listing.) We also include our annual report, list of company benefits, and some glossy material from our company's personnel department.

Develop a high profile. We maintain contact with deans, professors, and placement directors at the three law schools. We appear on panels. We have even thrown a cocktail party to meet large numbers of students. When we are seeking laterals, we use the school placement services and, of course, local advertising.

Pattern your interviewing methods after your competition. Do it yourself. Do not use your personnel department. We conduct the normal fly-out and call-back interviews that the firms do. This always includes at least a half-day of interviews at the office and lunch or dinner. Our hiring committee has a member assigned to follow each prospect. We try to match personality and background so that the prospective hire feels comfortable with his or her contact on our committee and with us. We follow up with letters, phone calls, and dinners with spouses.

If you get into this on more than a very modest scale, you may wish to hire a professional consultant to assist. We engaged Management Team Consultants, Inc. for a one-day seminar, which we found very useful. We learned through written material, lecture, video presentation, and a workshop how to conduct effective interviews, follow up, and sell ourselves. We videotaped the presentation so that new members of the committee can learn the methods quickly and inexpensively. (You will be amazed to see how contrary to your hiring goals is the typical trial lawyer's cross-examination style.)

Training

Our training consists of an orientation training program provided to all new hires and further specific training for all attorneys new to litigation.

The general department program is a rather formal and lengthy program. (See Form 7 in the Appendix.) This program was developed with the assistance of a management consultant. It is administered by a committee in our department consisting of a member from each section and headed by a senior attorney. Form 7 explains the program now in effect. The in-house training sessions were very successful and included one specifically directed toward litigation with a sitting judge as a participant.

The formal course ensures that every lawyer is introduced to the department and receives basic information and training. The further training within the litigation section is the most important part of the new trial lawyer's education. In earlier years, we simply threw the new lawyer into the water to see if he would sink or swim. (When I started seventeen years ago, that was all that was done. There was no training whatsoever.) That has given way to a variety of teaching tools. However, a quick introduction to the practice is the best way to learn.

Supervisor

Each new attorney is assigned to a more senior attorney in our section, designated as the supervisor. It is the responsibility of the supervisor to see that the new attorney has a balanced case load. That is, we like to provide each attorney with some small cases of his or her own, some medium-sized cases to work on with a more experienced attorney, and a role in some large cases. If the load gets uneven, the supervisor lets me know, so that I can make adjustments in assignments. The supervisor helps to resolve conflicts when the attorney receives competing demands on his or her time and helps to set priorities. The supervisor ensures that the attorney is getting an appropriate number of research assignments while also making enough deposition and court appearances.

The supervisors meet regularly and are rotated from time to time to assure that each attorney is treated in a like manner. Although each attorney remains in the program five years, he or she should require only minimal supervision after two.

Hands-On Training

New attorneys are encouraged to attend depositions, court appearances, and trials to watch and learn. Most are thrown into court on their own very quickly. Within weeks they may make court appearances and take a deposition. We will have a senior attorney watch the first few. Thereafter we will read the transcripts of selected proceedings and critique their performance. Within six months, each new attorney has probably handled an arbitration and may even have tried a small court or jury case. Each will soon assist on a larger trial. Within one year we expect each attorney to have a sizable case load of small and medium cases and to be assisting on a fair number of large cases.

Meetings

Every Friday morning our entire section meets to discuss new cases, developments in the law, trial tactics, and items of general interest. Attorneys are sometimes assigned to make presentations on specific topics. If someone has attended an educational course, that person is expected to give a report. The meetings are also the forum for resolving upcoming calendar conflicts. We have found that it works best when we spend a few minutes stating conflicts and asking for volunteers. This provides an opportunity to spread the appearances among all the newer attorneys. It also has developed a great esprit among the trial lawyers.

Open-Door Policy

Our best training device is the open-door policy. Every attorney, new and experienced, is encouraged to discuss his or her cases with other attorneys. This goes on all the time, every day. Often the new attorneys will pick out someone with whom they have a good rapport. However, since each is assigned at least one case with five different attorneys, the new attorney will learn many different styles and approaches.

Settlement Committee

Although the settlement committee is part of our case management, it is also a training tool. Every attorney must present his or her case to the settlement committee no later than receipt of notice of trial-setting conference. This provides time for further work in light of the feedback received. Through this meeting, each attorney learns if he or she has been preparing the cases in an acceptable manner.

Advancement

About four years ago, we eliminated titles in our department. We also made all offices the same size. Thus, each attorney primarily looks to his or her annual merit review and bonus review to see how he or she is progressing, and only the law department's management committee knows how each is doing relative to the next. Without titles there seems to be less worry about status and "advancement." Now, advancement means more pay, receiving bigger cases to handle, and, if desired, the opportunity to participate in the management of the office. Moving up the salary ladder also makes the attorney eligible for additional benefits not available to an attorney who is lower paid and rated.

Some attorneys desire to move out of the department and into management. Several managers of departments, vice presidents, and the current chairman of the board, vice chairman, and most members of the company's executive committee are alumni of our law department. The chairman (and the recently retired chairman) were once trial lawyers in the law department.

The flip side of advancement is termination. We have a very careful review process, which is administered by a review committee. The committee recommends to the department's management committee whether an attorney should be retained or not.

Case Management

The most important part of case management is assigning a capable attorney to handle the case in the first place. I don't believe in a lot of management of professionals. Nevertheless, we do a number of things to ensure that cases are receiving appropriate handling.

When a new case comes to the company, my administrative assistant (a senior paralegal) reviews the file and provides me with a preliminary assessment of the case. This includes the reserve to be set, the attorney(s) to be assigned, and the "ranking." The ranking is a numerical value assigned to each case based on its exposure, complexity, and expected time demands. For example, a small case may be given a 2, and a large tort case a 7. (The numbers do not work with the very large commercial and real property disputes. These are generally assigned to a team and are assumed to be very time-consuming and complex.) After some discovery, attorneys are requested to advise whether the reserve and the ranking should be changed.

The ranking helps us determine which cases require more attention and whether we are spending money appropriately. It also provides me with a method (albeit crude) of determining whether case loads are evenly balanced among the attorneys.

Of our 1700 active cases, a majority are tort (large and small), small commercial, and real property disputes. To facilitate the handling of this mass of cases, several years ago we prepared a Litigation Checklist and an Initial Case Analysis. (See Forms 8 and 9.) These forms are placed in every new case file. They are particularly helpful to the new attorney as a guide. The senior attorneys do most of this in their own fashion, but some use these as a reminder.

Settlement Committee

The settlement committee is composed of senior attorneys, only two of whom must be convened to hold a settlement case review. This review is the final check that a case is well prepared. It is also the time for settlement authority to be determined. I have delegated certain authority to the committee so that most cases can be settled without my involvement. The committee makes recommendations to me on larger cases. This provides me with a collective analysis and is far more accurate than trying to do it all alone.

Paralegals and Investigators

We have a lead paralegal who ensures that work loads of the paralegals are evenly balanced and that all attorneys have their projects completed.

Ideally we should not have as much competition for these services as we do. But we operate on a budget.

Budgets

Our department is trying to operate on a budget. It is particularly difficult for litigation. But, being part of a larger entity, we have no choice. A law firm with an increasing load will hire more lawyers and paralegals and smile all the way to the bank. We don't. This is probably the toughest part of an in-house practice. How do you handle growing case loads on a fixed budget? I suppose that seeking budget variances is the only sensible approach. Obviously, if you attempt to operate on too lean a budget, you will reach a point where your efficiencies will disappear, your practice will become mediocre, and your cost savings will change into expensive verdicts.

You can do the work in-house, and save money. But you have to be willing to spend money. This may mean spending more for lawyers than for most other employees of your company. But why not? You are doing this already with your outside firms. And, if you spend it on your lawyers—good lawyers—you'll save in the long run. You must get the necessary commitment right from the start and see that it never wanes. Hire well, pay well, train well, and monitor performance. Then, when the tough case comes in, you'll be ready, willing, and able to handle it yourself and save a substantial sum of money in the process.

Section III

Establishing the Relationship between Outside Counsel and the Corporate Client

Effective litigation management for any corporation, large or small, dictates a systematic approach, regardless of whether the corporation has an in-house legal staff or relies upon outside counsel to provide its legal services. Establishing the relationship between outside counsel and the corporate client (whether the "client" is the corporation or in-house counsel) is a key to successful litigation management. To that end, Section III focuses on the relationship between in-house and outside counsel from its inception through the term of its existence. This section looks at three aspects of that relationship: (1) retaining outside counsel, including the selection process; (2) establishing the roles of inside and outside counsel during the course of handling a particular piece of litigation; and (3) ethical considerations of those relationships, notably potential conflicts of interest.

The first step in creating the relationship between inside and outside counsel is the selection and retention of outside counsel. Thus, the first portion of the section begins with a chapter on that topic. In Chapter 5, Robert E. Bouma discusses the timing of retention of outside counsel. He also examines the selection process, including tips on how to approach the outside litigator and what questions to ask. Mr. Bouma recommends that inside counsel evaluate in writing the performance of the outside attorney and maintain records of evaluations for each lawyer and firm that has represented the company in the past.

The next portion of Section III includes three articles on the subject of establishing the roles of inside and outside counsel in handling litigation. In Chapter 6, M. Elaine Jacoby draws the important distinction between monitoring litigation and managing it by controlling it and directing it. She focuses on ways to effectively manage litigation. Chapter 7, by Michael J. Plishner, focuses on a model in which inside and outside counsel have agreed to jointly manage the litigation. Mr. Plishner emphasizes the importance of carefully selecting the entire team and describes the many ways for dividing case responsibilities and communicating effectively. In Chapter 8, Nancy C. Dreher explores how the law department can control costs through work sharing and tight operational controls.

Forms 10–19 in the Appendix supplement these articles. These forms include counsel retention letters, statements of corporate litigation philosophy, reporting formats, and fee agreements. Four variations of letters to outside counsel are included. Forms 10 and 11, from Aetna Corporation, emphasize joint planning between inside and outside counsel regarding strategy and use of resources. Form 12, from a mythical Cartoonah Corporation, contains strict commandments for outside counsel, emphasizes strong management of the litigation by inside counsel, contemplates shared work, and requires detailed budgets and reports. Forms 13–15, from Security Pacific National Bank, contemplate more delegation to outside counsel, who must develop a strategic plan at the outset and periodically report to inside counsel. Form 16, from Xerox Corporation, requests that outside counsel adhere to litigation principles developed by the American Corporate Counsel Association. Finally, Forms 17–19 are samples of alternative fee agreements: a contingent fee, a modified contingent fee, and a fixed fee plus bonus.

The relationship between outside counsel and the corporation can be dramatically affected by ethical rules concerning conflicts of interest. Therefore, the final portion of Section III is devoted to a chapter on this topic. Chapter 9, by Samuel R. Miller and Irwin H. Warren, discusses applicable case law and rules under the Canons of Ethics, Model Code of Professional Responsibility, and the Model Rules of Professional Conduct. The article covers five key situations: problems of successive representation in representing the adversary of a former client, ethical implications of attorney movement between law firms and corporate legal departments, ethical implications of the movement of attorneys in and out of government, conflicts arising from simultaneous representation of clients with adverse interests, and rules governing the role of lawyer as witness.

Stephen M. Kite-Powell
International Paper Company
Memphis, Tennessee

Five

Selection and Retention of Litigation Counsel

Robert E. Bouma

While this chapter is primarily directed to the issues of choosing and employing outside counsel in litigation matters, it is important to note at the outset that inside counsel should, if feasible, take certain steps *before* the litigation actually begins. The approach varies, of course, depending upon whether the inside lawyer is with the company that has been threatened with the lawsuit or the company that is considering instituting the lawsuit.

If associated with the company threatened with a lawsuit, inside counsel should attempt to ascertain promptly the relevant facts by interviewing appropriate company officials and employees and by reviewing relevant documents. The depth of such an examination depends upon a number of factors, including whether the initiation of the lawsuit is imminent or whether action will not be taken by the other side until a response is received. Once inside counsel has marshaled the facts and formed preliminary conclusions, possibilities for resolving the dispute short of litigation should be explored with management. If resolution of the dispute through alternative dispute techniques does not appear feasible, inside counsel should then consider more closely the company's possible counterclaims as well as defenses. Counsel should also investigate and weigh venue and jurisdictional aspects, including the advisability of taking the initiative and commencing the lawsuit before the other party acts. This latter approach can often offer an advantage with respect to choice of forum.

On the other hand, if a lawyer is with the company that intends to commence the litigation, there is a critical need for advance factual and legal investigation. Special consideration should be given to possible remedies, enforceability and collectibility of any favorable judgment, probable legal and other costs, and the potential disruption of management's normal duties. Again, the possibility of resolving the matter short of litigation through an alternative dispute method should be considered.

In either event, it is critical that key management and inside counsel consult together at an early stage. A strong communications link between

Robert E. Bouma, formerly General Counsel of Household International, Inc., is a member of McDermott, Will & Emery, Chicago, Illinois.

senior management and the in-house legal group is absolutely essential at all stages of the litigation.

Timing—When to Retain Counsel

In many instances prelitigation activities can be carried out solely by inside counsel. In others it may be entirely appropriate to involve outside counsel before litigation begins. The relevant factors to consider include the size of the inside legal staff, the philosophy of the general counsel, the staff's expertise in the area in question, and its past litigation experience.

One point at which outside counsel should become involved is when the company has made a final decision to commence the lawsuit. In such a case, especially where the company may wish to move for injunctive or other extraordinary relief, various tactical issues need to be explored with outside counsel. Another case for involvement of outside counsel is where it appears imminent that the company will be named as a defendant in a lawsuit and it is probable that the plaintiff will be seeking a restraining order or other immediate judicial relief. Also, where it appears that the suit may be brought in a particular location, the outside firm's knowledge and views on local judges, court rules, and practices can be an important asset in a final decision.

In short, each situation is different, and there is no "bright-line" test of when outside counsel should be retained. My own view is that inside counsel should not instinctively move to retain outside counsel whenever litigation appears to be a possibility but, rather, should evaluate carefully the timing issue and act only after making an informed determination that retention of outside counsel is appropriate at a particular time.

Choice of Counsel—Selection Process

Once inside counsel has determined that the services of outside counsel are necessary, there are a number of factors to consider in selecting the most appropriate lawyer to represent the company's interests. Because the partners in the litigation or trial departments of a law firm can vary widely in their experience and ability to handle a particular type of matter, the in-house lawyer's focus must always be on finding the most appropriate *individual* lawyer within a firm to handle the case, and not on which *firm* may have the best overall reputation, be it in the litigation field or more generally. The approach should in short be to retain a specific individual and not a firm, and if a particular lawyer is not available to handle or direct a matter, the inside lawyer should consider retaining another highly recommended lawyer in another firm.

The in-house lawyer's starting point in a search for this individual lawyer should be through personal contacts. The in-house lawyer should consult others in the company's corporate law department and members of other corporate law departments where contacts exist. The inside lawyer should also consider consulting with attorneys in outside firms with whom he or she has worked and in whom he or she has a high level of confidence with respect to their recommendations. If the case is of any meaningful significance, the retaining lawyer should be imaginative and aggressive in seeking out lawyers who can give personal recommendations. Even though certain lawyers contacted may not have retained litigation counsel in the particular locale, they may well be able to suggest someone who has, and the inside lawyer should then pursue this avenue of inquiry.

In seeking recommendations, one should explain briefly the nature of the matter and the type of lawyer desired. The nature of the matter will affect not only the expertise that is required, but also whether the "best," most experienced (and therefore often the most expensive) litigator is actually needed. In many cases there is no such requirement, and inside counsel must focus on and come to grips with that fact early on.

From my perspective, law directories, such as Martindale-Hubbell, may be consulted for backgrounds and clientele of a firm or an individual lawyer, but they should not take the place of an informed decision based upon personal experiences, references, and interviews. Only if all other avenues have failed should the ratings in such directories be the basis for selecting an attorney.

Before the selection process is begun, it is axiomatic that inside counsel must decide whether the local lawyer is to handle the matter entirely or whether that lawyer is to play a liaison, "mail-drop," or other supporting role. In some instances, if a lawyer in another locale has acquired special expertise about the company, its products, and the governing legal principles from handling the same type of matter previously and he or she has performed well in that role, you may well want to assign primary responsibility for the matter to that individual. While this choice may appear to increase your costs because of the involvement of two firms, the determining factor should always be the potential impact of the matter on your company. If the impact may be substantial, then such an approach may well save the company money overall.

Criteria for Choice of Counsel

As we all know, each matter is different, and the selection criteria will vary according to your needs as well as the type of case. However, a number of criteria apply in most, if not all, instances:

- *Size of firm*—The number of lawyers and support staff that can be brought to bear on a matter is a crucial consideration if the case has the potential to develop into a major broad-based lawsuit or series of lawsuits.

- *Reputation*—The standing of the lawyer and the firm with the local bench and bar is very important.
- *Educational and professional background*—This would also include membership in the American College of Trial Lawyers and similar litigation-oriented organizations.
- *Experience*—This covers not only past involvement in similar types of matters, but overall actual trial experience. Inside counsel should not hesitate to ask about the litigation matters the lawyer has handled, including any involving the subject matter of the suit, how many have actually been tried, and the results.
- *Possible conflicts of interest*—Inside counsel should explain fully at the outset the scope of the company's operations and stress the importance of a thorough check by the firm as to conflicts. In my experience, this area is often overlooked or the search undertaken is inadequate. Nothing is more harmful than the firm discovering a conflict after the lawyer has been retained and has been working on the matter.
- *Availability*—This relates to the particular attorney you have selected to handle your matter. Key issues are how fast you expect your matter to move and what preexisting commitments the lawyer has. Avoid being shuffled to another attorney in the firm without your prior knowledge and approval. Your attitude here will be affected by the importance of the case.
- *Billing issues*—The firm's fee structure and sensitivity to staffing and cost considerations and its willingness to comply with your billing and budgeting policies must be discussed at the outset.
- *Responsiveness*—Does the lawyer understand your needs in terms of frequency of reporting, advance review of briefs, approval of research projects, retention of experts, etc.? Does he or she understand who has the final say as between outside and inside counsel? Does outside counsel understand that this is a relationship between equals? If not, then you should go elsewhere despite the presence of other positive factors.

The Retention Process

The key point here is a simple one: Outside counsel should not be retained until the inside lawyer is fully satisfied that this person meets the necessary criteria. In short, a decision should not be made before having a full and frank discussion with the outside lawyer. "Full and frank" means just that. As noted previously, the time to explain fully one's expectations of outside counsel and to learn about outside counsel's attitudes is at the outset.

One of the key subjects to be discussed at the beginning is the law department's policies regarding billing for legal fees. Failure to have a dialogue on this subject at the beginning of a new relationship inevitably results in later misunderstandings and disagreements. Neither party should be embarrassed or hesitant to discuss this subject, and to do so in detail. If the discussion is not specific and frank, it will not be meaningful. More particularly, inside and outside counsel should discuss and reach an understanding on at least the following items:

- *Billing rates*—What are the hourly rates for each lawyer and paralegal who will be assigned to the matter? Can the rates be increased without the inside counsel's prior approval?
- *Frequency of billing*—Will bills be sent monthly, quarterly, on completion, or on some other basis?
- *Format and detail of bills*—How detailed a description of services is needed? Will the bill identify what services each lawyer and paralegal performed during the billing period and how many hours were expended by each?
- *Disbursements*—What are routine disbursements? What types of disbursements must receive advance approval? Are there any special requirements, such as for air travel?

The best approach to this general subject is a written policy on legal fees and disbursements. This focuses attention on this important subject and helps ensure that it is adequately addressed. However, such a policy, sent in the mail after a retention has been made, is not an adequate substitute for an upfront exchange of views.

Another subject that must be discussed early on is staffing, which encompasses the following issues:

- Which, and how many, lawyers and paralegals are to be assigned to the case?
- What are their levels of experience and expertise?
- What will be the duties of each individual assigned to the matter? This item is especially important, because clients differ with respect to the tasks and activities the inside staff plans to become involved in, either by reason of philosophy or staffing restrictions.
- What commitments to other matters, such as cases about to be tried, do the various lawyers assigned to your matter have?

The subject of reporting relationships, as with billing and staffing, should be discussed with your new counsel promptly. Inside counsel should explain in detail his or her requirements, and an understanding should be reached with respect to such items as the following:

- *Frequency of reporting*—Does inside counsel expect to receive status reports regularly, e.g., monthly or quarterly, or is a more informal arrangement desired?
- *Advance review of briefs, motions, etc.*—Is outside counsel to submit drafts of briefs and motions to inside counsel for prior review and approval?
- *Review of projects, legal research, travel, etc.*—In what instances must outside counsel secure approval in advance?
- *Tactics and strategy*—How actively will inside counsel be involved, and under what circumstances must decisions on how to proceed be approved by inside counsel?
- *Contacts with management*—When, how, and by whom are contacts to be made with company representatives? Many inside counsel, for instance, require that all contacts within the company be made only through them or with their prior approval.

One of the most fertile grounds for misunderstanding and frustration in the relationship between in-house and outside counsel arises from the failure to establish the relationship between the two at its inception or at the beginning of a particular litigation. Defining roles is critical to the success of any effective approach to managing litigation. Once those roles have been defined, they should not be changed without good reason, since proper use of corporate resources, both in and outside the corporate legal department, can be used to effectively reduce the cost of litigation.

The inside lawyer must also make an initial evaluation of the outside lawyer's sensitivity to cost considerations. While this may be difficult to gauge, the inside lawyer should be able to get a sense, through discussion and questioning, of the outside lawyer's true as opposed to apparent appreciation of cost-benefit considerations. One approach is to exchange views on the discovery and motion practice that should be pursued in the particular matter. If the outside lawyer urges an overly expansive or "shotgun" discovery program, or an early motion solely to "educate the court," inside counsel should be wary. There are no precise ground rules here, of course, since each case is different, but in any event these warning signals should not be ignored. Indeed, it is only through such discussions that the inside lawyer will be able to form an intelligent conclusion concerning the willingness of the outside lawyer to comply with inside counsel's requirements and expectations. Forms 10–19 in the Appendix show several different styles of counsel retention letters, statements of corporate litigation philosophy, reporting formats, and fee agreements.

The Feedback Process

After the litigation is finally resolved, the corporate law department should evaluate in writing the performance of the outside attorney. All too often this is not done or, if undertaken, is done poorly. One approach is to maintain a book, which can be organized by geographic location, containing evaluations for each lawyer and firm that has represented the company in the past. A book of this type should contain at least the following information:

- The name of the individual lawyers involved, and their firm
- The type of matter involved
- The name of the member of the corporate law department who worked with outside counsel
- The manner in which the matter was resolved
- A detailed evaluation of the firm's performance, and how it measured up to the law department's criteria and expectations
- A recommendation as to whether the firm should be retained on future matters and, if so, which specific types of litigation matters

Some companies include similar information about opposing counsel as well. This serves as a double check against possible conflicts as well as an information source for future cases.

In sum, retention of outside counsel in litigation matters is an important and time-consuming process. It is not to be done lightly or haphazardly. The key is the *individual* lawyer who is going to be responsible for the litigation matter. The time to determine whether that person is the right person, and whether the law department's involvement and policies are truly acceptable to that individual, is at the outset of the relationship. Time spent here pays immeasurable future benefits for the client and the inside lawyer.

Six

Managing the Litigator

M. Elaine Jacoby

Management versus Monitoring

Frequently, one hears lawyers speak of "managing" or "monitoring" litigation as though the terms were synonymous. They are not. Before addressing the subject of managing the litigator, we should be clear on what is meant by litigation management. Management implies a degree of control or direction, a degree of involvement, that monitoring does not. Monitoring suggests checking, keeping tabs. A nurse or paramedic monitors the patient's vital signs; the doctor makes decisions on treatment. The litigation manager is also a decision maker who is deeply involved in every stage of the litigation. This is not to say that monitoring, rather than managing, litigation is never appropriate. Under particular circumstances, it may constitute the best use of in-house counsel's time. For example, a high volume of matters with low potential for damages may not justify the time that would be required for in-house counsel to manage them. But this article focuses on techniques for managing, rather than monitoring, litigation.

In-house litigation managers who have had experience as litigators in private practice undoubtedly have some advantages over their corporate colleagues who have no background in litigation. As in most areas of the law, one of those advantages is simply knowing the language, the special lingo of the litigator. (This may not be a major advantage, however, if one is managing litigation in many different jurisdictions; even the experienced litigator may learn that the lingo of litigation in the New York State courts, for example, is of little use when he or she has to deal with demurrers and MSCs—mandatory settlement conferences—in California.)

Perhaps the most important advantage for in-house counsel who have litigated is their sense that they know what litigation is all about and do not have to accept whatever course of action outside counsel embark on.

M. Elaine Jacoby is a member of Epstein, Becker, Borsody & Green, Princeton, New Jersey, and was formerly Assistant Vice President–Legal at Beneficial Management Corporation, Peapack, New Jersey.

In contrast, in-house counsel who have no litigation experience are commonly perceived as dependent on outside counsel for advice, strategy, and results. This perception may not be completely true, but there is probably some basis for it. Nonlitigators can be effective litigation managers, however, if they refuse to be intimidated by the assignment itself and by outside counsel. In fact, they often have strengths that corporate litigators lack. They may have more in-depth knowledge of the business and its operating management and personnel. If they have been involved in compliance programs, they probably know the applicable laws and regulations, as well as the regulatory agencies' staffs, better than any litigator.

In addition to refusing to be intimidated by litigation and the litigator, if nonlitigators are to be effective, they must be willing to commit the necessary time and energy to litigation management. This is essential; you *cannot* manage litigation if you are not permitted to or do not want to make a major commitment to it. The amount of time and effort you have to put into litigation management depends on a number of factors: Do you have one case to manage or many? Do the matters involve relatively simple legal issues or complex ones? Is the jurisdiction one that you are familiar with? Whatever the answers to these questions, the commitment still has to be major in comparison to your commitment to your other responsibilities. If you are going to do it well, you simply cannot put it at the bottom of your list of priorities.

You should also recognize that managing litigation may produce more pressure and require more of your time than seems warranted at certain times. When a case is first filed against your company, or a decision has been made that you will file suit, you should spend as much time as possible investigating the factual background and developing strategy with outside counsel. Major discovery events, such as key depositions, are likely to require extra time. And, if the matter goes to trial, clearly you will need more time on it in the weeks or months (depending on its complexity and importance) immediately before trial.

Finally, managing litigation *includes* managing the litigator—who is a person, of course. Some lawyers take more kindly to supervision by inside counsel than do others. Your interpersonal skills may be more important to your effectiveness as a litigation manager than will your specific legal experience. You need to develop a relationship with outside counsel that is based on mutual respect. You need not dictate to the litigator in order to manage the lawsuit, but you can make clear that you are, ultimately, the decision maker. Most litigators who regularly represent corporations have no difficulty accepting the role of the in-house litigation manager, but the relationship does require a degree of sensitivity on your part, as well as on the part of outside counsel.

Suggestions for Effective Litigation Management

Personally investigate the factual background of the matter. Review documents and talk to witnesses. Start immediately, before retaining outside counsel, if time permits. It is very important for you to know all of the facts and to communicate to the litigator the additional background that may affect interpretation of the facts—background of your witnesses, particular business practices of your company, the corporate culture. Unless you are fully aware of the facts, you will be unable to make the judgments about the strengths and weaknesses of the case that are necessary for real management. Continue to serve as a resource for factual information throughout the case.

Retain outside counsel. Your law department should have some kind of file listing attorneys who have represented the company in the past. This is often the best place to begin your search, since you know that, at the least, the attorney has some familiarity with the company. To the extent he or she already understands the corporate culture, communication will be much easier.

If your law department file contains no evaluative material on the attorneys listed, try to obtain an oral evaluation from another attorney in the company who previously worked with those you are considering, or review whatever files you can find on the matters they previously handled. If you can find no attorney listed in the department file who seems appropriate, there are a number of avenues to explore to find a litigator. You can request a referral from outside counsel in another location; you can consult Martindale-Hubbell for litigation attorneys in the area where the lawsuit was or will be filed; you can check with trade associations to which your company belongs. Generally, you should be aiming at finding a particular lawyer, rather than retaining a firm. To that end, conduct interviews by telephone or in person before making a decision.

For future reference, consider developing a better file on outside attorneys for your department. If you have access to a computer or even a word processor, you can create a roster, including evaluations, of all outside attorneys retained by your company.

Use a calendar system to control your docket and track important dates. Again, a computer-assisted plan for docket control is invaluable. If you have no access to a computer or word processor, use a manual system. It is essential that you be aware of key dates as much in advance as possible. Do not assume that outside counsel will remind you; in fact, you should be prepared to remind him or her when you have not received papers to review within a reasonable amount of time before a filing deadline.

Communicate your expectations to the litigator, and follow through on what you have said you want. Your retainer letter (or agreement, if you prefer more formality) should spell out the essentials—what copies of documents, correspondence, and so forth should be sent to you; whether you want regular status reports; what you expect in the way of staffing and statements for services; and any particular cost containment requirements (such as no first-class travel). Be prepared to remind outside counsel orally of the contents of the retainer letter.

As early as possible, decide what the guiding principles for the particular matter should be, and communicate them to the litigator. Specific objectives and strategy will vary according to the guiding principles. For several examples of letters that can be sent to counsel, see Forms 10–19 in the Appendix. Additionally, know what your authority is. If you are new to the company or have never managed a lawsuit, find out what your general counsel or management expects of you and the dollar amount of authority you have to approve attorney's fees and to settle the case.

The "guiding principle" in a case is often closely related to your company's corporate culture. Thus, you may have the same guiding principle in most cases, e.g., an economically justifiable result. If this is the overall objective, you will need an estimate from the litigator of potential liability and the cost of defending the matter through trial. It also may mean aiming at a quick settlement (based, perhaps on a percentage of the potential damages that is proportionate to the likelihood of success, plus the estimated cost of defense). More specifically, this principle may mean limiting discovery by the defense. (But do so in a logical way. Interrogatories are much cheaper than depositions, for example, but tend to provide much less useful information. In certain kinds of cases, such as employment cases, quick depositions of the plaintiff tend to be more cost-effective than interrogatories.) In other cases, another or an additional principle may be necessary, e.g., delay until a legislative effort or some other extrajudicial process is completed. In a matter where delay is necessary, you should not rule out settlement; as a matter of fact, settlement negotiations may themselves effectively delay the lawsuit. Extensions of time to answer pleadings, discovery, and motions are also helpful. Extensive discovery of the plaintiff's case will, of course, keep your adversary busy. Alternatively, the guiding principle may be to send a message that your company is not an easy target. This principle suggests an aggressive defense, including early and thorough discovery of the plaintiff's documents and depositions of its witnesses, motions, and so on.

Whatever the guiding principle, make sure that you communicate it to the litigator. Communication is essential to developing a good working relationship. If you are unable to meet with him or her, communicate by telephone as much as possible, and keep notes of your conversations, with dates, in the file.

Require some kind of game plan from the outside counsel, preferably in writing (a letter), and make clear that strategy decisions require consultation. Let the litigator know what your needs are—for example, the lead time you are likely to require to respond to requests for information, or the need for a particular decision.

Review drafts of pleadings, motions, briefs, and interrogatories carefully, and watch particularly for factual inaccuracies. Ask for explanations as to why a particular deposition should be taken, motion should be brought, and so forth. Conduct discussions by telephone (if not face to face) as much as possible; again, *take notes* so you have record of contacts and decisions.

Follow your instinct in challenging an approach, e.g., interrogatories that seem burdensome. Are they likely to provoke a costly battle and possibly a decision against the company? Is delay (if that is the objective) worth it? And do not hesitate to require a redraft of anything you are dissatisfied with.

Participate in legal analysis. Ask for copies of memoranda associates prepare for the partner in charge or, if an associate is handling the matter, the results (even if in letter form) of his or her legal research. Read key cases. Make an independent judgment as to how the law applies to the facts in your case.

Participate in discovery and trial preparation. Be involved directly in collecting documents and information to respond to document demands and interrogatories; you should know far better than outside counsel where to look and whom to ask, and you should be able, in many cases, to predict the kinds of documents, statistical information, and so forth that should be developed or retained for use in the suit. This does not mean that you have to review every document yourself if thousands are involved, but do as much as you can and get assistance from in-house resources (paralegals or, if you have none, other support staff or even managers).

Attend key depositions if possible. Be involved in preparing key defense witnesses for their depositions—in person, if possible, or by telephone or through suggestions to the litigator. Company executives and employees often feel much more comfortable when "their" lawyer is present. Always obtain copies of deposition transcripts and read them. They are especially important if you have not been able to attend the depositions, since transcripts will give you a much better feel for the witness than a summary of the testimony prepared by outside counsel.

Be involved in settlement strategy and negotiations. No matter what the principle involved, never close your mind to settlement, and try to influence your client not to do so. In an article in the *Harvard Business Review* (March/April 1985), Roger Fisher spoke for at least some corporate counsel when he said, "Once we have given a case to outside counsel we are likely to see it as 'their problem,'" and we therefore don't think about settlement. Fisher rightly stresses the importance of developing not only a litigation strategy, but also a settlement strategy. This is an area in which you can and should play a major, if not dominant, role. The litigator can become so involved in depositions, briefing, trial preparation, and so forth that he or she neglects to consider how to settle the case. You should not neglect to do so.

While the traditional approach is that the plaintiff makes the settlement demand, you need not accept that approach, waiting for his or her lawyer to make a demand while your attorney's fees are mounting. Explore other approaches with your outside counsel, including soliciting a settlement demand, requesting a settlement conference, making an offer of judgment, and so on. If you feel that the litigator is, for whatever reason, unable to make a breakthrough in settlement negotiations, consider bringing in separate counsel or taking on the role of negotiator yourself. You may be better at it than the litigator. (He or she would, of course, be present at any meeting you have with the adversary.)

Obtain estimates from outside counsel of costs (including attorney's fees and expert's fees) at various stages of the proceedings, as well as an estimate of the likelihood of success, and use these numbers to formulate a range within which it would make economic sense to settle. Even if other considerations militate against settlement, this is a useful process. The result may lead you or your client to decide on settlement after all. Numbers of this kind generally make a great deal of sense to corporate management, and you will need them for support if you decide to recommend a settlement.

Keep a running tab of what the case has cost. It is a simple matter to set up a computer program to do this for all litigation, and your accounting department may already have a program to which you can obtain access and that you can modify. If you do not have a computer readily available, your secretary or paralegal can set up a manual system. The current cost of the case should, in any event, be at your fingertips, either at the front of your paper file or on your computer. Consult it when discussing or considering settlement.

Evaluate the performance of outside counsel. This should be an ongoing process through the litigation. It is as necessary as evaluation of the people you supervise in your office. If counsel is not performing up to your expectations, as set out in your retainer letter and in periodic discussions, you need to let him or her know.

In evaluating, use outside counsel's statements for services. Know what you are paying for; statements should contain detailed accounts of specific work performed and time spent by individual lawyers and paralegals.

If you think that a particular charge is unreasonable or unjustified, tell the litigator right away.

Make your own judgment of the quality of the work based on your review of counsel's work product. Be aware, however, that the best litigator in the world cannot turn a loser of a case into a winning one. But you can evaluate the advice and efforts he or she makes to contain the damage in such a situation, either through settlement efforts or otherwise.

Enjoy the work! Managing litigation can be very satisfying because of your real involvement in the case and your sense of responsibility for the results.

Seven

In-House and Outside Counsel: Staffing for Joint Management of Litigation

Michael J. Plishner

Once the company has determined that outside counsel should be used in connection with a piece of litigation, many issues must be resolved between in-house corporate counsel and retained outside counsel. Some involve the nitty-gritty: the organization of the particular case and how it will be handled and the work accomplished day to day; joint planning with respect to specific discovery, motions, the use of experts, and other pretrial and trial activities; in some instances, the division of specific tasks and the responsibility for particular discovery, briefing, and so forth between the staffs of inside and outside counsel; methods for instituting appropriate cost control measures such as budgeting, quarterly and annual reviews of litigation expenses, and the like.

But it is perhaps even more important, at the time outside counsel are retained, to establish the basic relationship between in-house and outside counsel in the sense of the big picture. Issues that must be considered here include the structure of case management as between in-house and outside counsel; staffing issues; procedures for decision making; basic orientation for the outside lawyer with respect to the company and its people, and the matters at issue in the case; and mechanisms for coordination and communication. These issues are key to a successful relationship between in-house and outside counsel and will bring about the best possible result for the company in the most efficient manner. See Forms 10–16 in the Appendix, which illustrate four variations on the relationship between inside and outside counsel. Some thoughts on these big-picture issues follow.

Roles of In-House and Outside Counsel in the Management of the Litigation

At the outset of any new relationship with retained counsel (and even perhaps in beginning a major new litigation matter with an outside counsel who has been used regularly before), it is critical that in-house and out-

Michael J. Plishner is a member of McCutchen, Doyle, Brown & Enersen, San Francisco, California.

side counsel work out an arrangement that clearly defines the roles both are expected to play. This determination must be based upon the company's desires and philosophy concerning how deeply it wishes in-house lawyers to be involved in the day-to-day aspects of the litigation. Many of the other matters concerning the relationship between inside and outside counsel in terms of decision making, coordination, reporting, and the like turn upon this initial philosophical decision. There are today, I think, really three possible models of inside/outside participation:

1. In some situations, outside counsel may be expected to "run" the litigation, keeping in-house counsel informed of its status and consulting with in-house counsel before making major decisions (such as whether to conduct certain types of discovery, whether and when to file certain motions). This kind of hands-off approach is becoming less and less common, and these days is generally found only in companies with very small legal staffs that cannot spend time on litigation matters on an ongoing basis.
2. At the other extreme, the company may wish in-house and outside counsel to essentially merge their respective staffs, creating a joint venture in which members from each are used in a largely interchangeable way to do whatever needs to be done in the litigation. This arrangement, of course, implies that the management of the team, day-to-day decision making, and most details (except for the most trivial) will be discussed between inside and outside counsel. It also means that methods will have to be set up to ensure the level of communication and coordination that this kind of joint venture approach requires.
3. Finally, the balance of participation may be something in between—strong and ongoing joint management of the litigation process by both in-house and outside counsel, with many tasks performed solely by the outside lawyer's staff; with some (including those which tend to be very time-consuming and expensive), such as review of the company's documents and preparation of interrogatory responses, to be done by in-house lawyers and/or paralegals; with direct and significant involvement by in-house lawyers in writing all briefs, and with no decision, large or small, that is likely to have more than a nominal impact on the client's bill, to be made by outside counsel without clearance from an authorized in-house lawyer.

The third approach seems by far the most common today in matters in which outside counsel are brought in at all. And, as the description makes obvious, such an arrangement requires that substantial attention be paid to establishing the management structure and the lines of communication to make it work; in short, it requires a real team approach to litigation. Since this is the most common arrangement, I will focus on it in this chapter.

The key to making this kind of arrangement work lies in appropriate staffing (both in-house and outside), an understanding of how decisions are to be made, and a structure and method for proper planning and communication.

Team Structure and Staffing

Team Leaders

In the team approach just described, it is of course important that there be a designated team leader on each side who is to be the prime contact person for coordinating the relationship. In-house, this will be the attorney who is charged with overall responsibility for the case. Most often this will be a senior staff attorney; in some companies, and where the matter is significant enough, it may be the director of litigation (or someone with similar responsibilities) or even the general counsel. The designated person should, ideally, be able to devote enough time to understand the case as well as the outside lawyer in charge. The team leader should also have the authority to independently make most day-to-day decisions as to litigation strategy and to approve most expenditures necessary for the litigation. And this person should have the respect and the ear of the company's general counsel and management so that the decisions he or she makes will not be second-guessed, and management will feel comfortable that he or she will consult within the organization before acting where a *major* company decision is involved.

From the side of outside counsel, the team leader will be the partner in charge—the attorney whom the company has hired and who has been designated to manage the case during its pretrial phase and to try it if that becomes necessary. From the company's standpoint, several things are critical with respect to this individual: He or she must be able to devote the time necessary to "know" the case backward and forward, taking a hands-on approach and not simply turning the matter over to underlings until it is time for trial, or until the chairman of the board's deposition is to be taken. That does not mean that in-house lawyers should refuse to deal with anyone other than the designated lead lawyer. Indeed, it must be recognized that outside lawyers won't (and can't) devote one hundred percent of their time to any one case, and in a major piece of litigation it is not only appropriate, but highly desirable, that there be an extremely able junior partner or senior associate involved, who is capable of coordinating the day-to-day management of the case to the extent and when necessary. Nonetheless, it is critical to ensure that the person the company hires as its lawyer has the reputation of being someone who is clearly *involved* in every step of the litigation and be always available to the client when needed. The lawyer in charge must also, of course, be an able and aggressive litigator, a creative thinker, and probably above all, a good manager, both of cases and of people.

Other Members of the Litigation Team

From the in-house side, the lead staff attorney may well be the only team member. In the model we are looking at here, a single in-house lawyer will most often be designated to work with and oversee all the activities of the outside counsel who has been retained for the case. The lead staff lawyer will generally keep a senior in-house lawyer who is in charge of litigation for the company (or the general counsel) regularly advised of developments, but from the standpoint of day-to-day contact with outside counsel, this one individual will be the "point man."

In the case of a very large piece of litigation, however, one or more other staff attorneys from in-house counsel's staff may be designated to work on the matter, under the direction of the designated in-house lead lawyer. These other attorneys will be assigned responsibility for working with outside counsel on particular areas of the case, and their functions may be divided any number of ways. They may, for example, be divided along functional lines: one in-house lawyer may be in charge of discovery, experts, and fact gathering; another may be in charge of legal analysis and motion practice; and the team leader may be in charge of overall coordination, dealing with the company's management in connection with the case, arranging for and dealing with company witnesses, and the like. Alternatively, if several in-house lawyers are to be involved, they may choose to divide their responsibilities along the lines of particular case issues: one may be in charge of certain claims that are being defended against or certain factual issues that are key to the case; another may deal with other claims or fact areas, or perhaps be in charge of counterclaims or cross-claims that are significant to the matter.

Regardless of how responsibilities are divided among the in-house attorneys, these staff lawyers will have several roles—to oversee portions of the case from the company's standpoint, to work directly with outside counsel in the conduct of the case, and to work with the senior in-house lawyer in a coordinated approach that assures the job is done right by outside counsel and at a reasonable cost, but without simply duplicating the work that is otherwise being done by the outside lawyers.

What of the other members of the team assembled by outside counsel? It is critical that the in-house staff attorney in charge have some say not only in who he or she is hiring as the partner in charge, but also in the composition of the other team members (be it one, two, or many) of outside counsel's staff. In this area, house counsel can probably do more up front to control both the scope and the cost of the litigation effort than in any other.

House counsel and the outside lawyer in charge must reach an understanding as to *what* it is that the case requires in terms of staffing and, to some extent, *whom* it requires.

In deciding on "what," they must jointly determine the significance of the case, the magnitude of the dollar exposure involved, and the risks (monetary and otherwise) of an adverse judgment. In the first instance, it is up to the company to decide what "level" of defense (or prosecution) of the action it is prepared to undertake, and to advise the outside lawyer what it expects. Is this a case in which the partner in charge should, with the assistance of a single junior lawyer, handle the case from beginning to end? Does it require a group of lawyers at various levels of experience, along with a number of paralegals? Aside from the primary area of expertise for which the lead lawyer has been hired (for example, securities litigation), are there other areas of expertise (for example, certain areas of high technology or regulatory expertise) that mandate calling in lawyers from within the firm with that background—often or from time to time—to assist? What really is needed here is a detailed review, analysis, and clear meeting of the minds between in-house and outside counsel, as to just what *this* case requires in terms of staffing—given the risks presented by the case and the company's desires.

Now what about the question of "who"? What involvement, if any, should in-house counsel have in picking the members of the staff to be used by retained outside counsel? Frankly, as more and more companies have taken to "interviewing" a number of firms before deciding on counsel for a new piece of major litigation, they have learned how important it is to have some view not only of who will be the partner in charge, but also of which other lawyers will be assigned to work on the matter. With a sizable piece of litigation that is of significance to the company, that may go on for several years, and that requires—all agree—a number of lawyers provided by outside counsel, knowing just who will be on the outside litigation team being proposed can be almost as important as picking the lead lawyer.

Of course, there are limits to what house counsel can do to ensure who will be on that team a year or two down the road. Junior associates may well change as they come and go from the law firm, or simply because it may turn out that they are not right for the particular job that needs to be done at the time. Neither the firm nor the company's wishes can change that. On the other hand, the number 2 man or woman on the proposed team can usually be counted on as someone who is likely to be there for the duration and should certainly be scrutinized in any hiring interview as closely as the lead lawyer.

There is an important reason for doing this that is often overlooked in the quest for the ultimate trial lawyer for the litigation. Often the in-house staff attorney will end up spending a good part of the next three to four years with the person who is second in command on the day-to-day details of the case. Therefore, these questions ought to be asked:

- Can this person be expected to manage the paralegals and young lawyers who will have to do much of the paperwork and routine discovery in the matter?
- Does this person seem capable of dealing with opposing counsel in all of the nitty-gritty of the case?
- Is he or she a good idea person?
- Will he or she be able to deal effectively with the basic motion and deposition practice, which you will probably all agree it is unnecessary to call on the lead lawyer to do?

The point is simply this: Much as you might wish otherwise, no one lawyer will in fact be able to take full charge of a major piece of litigation, and in-house counsel should make sure he or she knows, before signing up counsel for a case, who *other than* the lead lawyer will be taking a major management role—not every lawyer who may come in contact with the case over the next three years, because that simply cannot be predicted—but *who else* will be the *key person* or the *key people* to the functioning of the case over that period.

Consultation and Decision Making

Perhaps one of the greatest causes of friction between in-house and outside counsel during the course of any piece of litigation comes as a result of miscommunication between the two as to when, how often, and under what circumstances house counsel expect to be consulted and involved in decisions that have to be made in the case. The appropriate level of consultation is not always easy to determine in the abstract. Unfortunately, the appropriate line between "too much" and "too little" often is defined only when it is realized that outside counsel has already made a decision that house counsel would have wanted to be involved in.

The extremes are easy to define: Almost all house counsel who intend that the case be handled cooperatively between inside and outside attorneys will assume that they will be consulted with respect to the preparation of major pleadings, significant motions, substantial discovery, the hiring of outside consultants, and other items that are likely to have an important impact on the cost of the litigation or the overall case strategy. At the other end of the spectrum, it is fair to assume that very few in-house lawyers will want to be bothered for their approval of a routine extension of time or wish to review in advance basic correspondence to opposition lawyers or co-counsel about simple discovery disputes. Keeping house counsel informed after the fact will almost always suffice in such instances.

Beyond those easy extremes, however, we get into the vagaries of personal style. Some in-house lawyers will insist that the ultimate decision-making role is theirs (as indeed it is) and that they should be consulted frequently, even daily, as to case strategy and immediate plans and activities. They will want to review and approve *any* pleading that is to be filed on the company's behalf, and they will want to see in draft form and approve all but the most routine correspondence in which a position of any sort is taken on behalf of the company. These lawyers see themselves as hands-on managers of the litigation, which is certainly a perfectly appropriate role to take. With other in-house attorneys who still consider themselves very much as involved participants in the ongoing activities of the litigation, it may be seen as appropriate for outside counsel to report in, perhaps once a week or so, for a detailed review of both immediately past and future events as well as longer-term plans and strategies. Review of briefs (well enough in advance of filing to permit real and substantial input) may also be requested, but more routine matters may be left for the lawyer on the scene to handle and report on.

To achieve the desired balance of involvement, house counsel and retained outside counsel should sit down together at the outset and specifically define the role the in-house lawyer wishes to have in decision making. Then it is the job of the outside lawyer to try, in all except emergency circumstances beyond his or her control, to maintain the level of consultation that has been agreed upon.

It is a serious mistake for outside lawyers to be *at all* defensive about how much or how often they are willing to consult. This should not be seen as a test of the client's confidence in the lawyer, but rather as a decision the client has every right to make as to just how involved *it* wishes to be in *its* litigation. Where the client insists on intimate involvement in the case, the role of the outside attorney is to counsel and advise, to give his or her best judgment in the decision-making process, and to let the client make those decisions which it wishes to make for itself rather than permit its outside lawyer to make. Short of decisions that create an ethical violation, a risk of misleading the court, or a strategic blunder the outside lawyer believes requires him or her to withdraw from the case, it is, after all, the client's province to decide as it wishes, and to decide just *who* will decide for it.

Orientation of Outside Counsel

Having established some of the ground rules for the relationship between in-house and outside counsel, it is also important to make an early effort to introduce the key outside lawyers to the client, its business, and the matter at issue.

Clearly, one of the major advantages in-house lawyers have over their outside counterparts in dealing with litigation is their intimate knowledge of the company, its people, what it does, its corporate philosophy, and the inner "mystique" that distinguishes it from any other business entity. Having decided to hire outside attorneys, in-house counsel is responsible for trying to pass on to them as much of this special knowledge as possible. A well-planned visit to the company and the facilities most relevant to the lawsuit can certainly help. However, it is important that this go beyond simply an introduction to the particular case and a preview of the relevant files. Counsel should try to arrange formal interviews and some informal social contact with company managers whose areas are involved in the litigation, and who can also give a sense of the company as a whole.

A chance to view the entirety of the processes at issue in the case may also be important. For example, assume the case is a class action attacking the claims-handling procedures of an insurer, alleging that claims are routinely handled to the detriment of the policyholders. In this kind of case, it would help to have the orientation of retained counsel include discussions with the senior officers responsible for claims as to the policies and procedures and how the company operates its claims function; separate discussions with several claims managers and claims handlers as to how they do their job day to day; if appraisals are relevant, similar discussions with people, top to bottom, in that area as well; a walk-through of one of the company's claims-handling facilities, with a step-by-step explanation of how claims are processed and particular problem files dealt with; discussions with marketing and underwriting people about their separate, though related, areas—so that counsel can see how the product is sold to the consumer and thus what the policyholder's expectations may be, and can understand how the policy provisions that may bear on the obligations in issue in fact came about.

In cases in which the industry's manufacturing processes are relevant, counsel should be given a complete tour of the plant and an opportunity to consult with production people and engineers. Not too many years ago, when I took part in a major antitrust case involving the uranium mining industry, an executive of our client suggested that the only way to understand the real economics of mining was to tour an open-pit and an underground mine, and a uranium processing mill. A group of lawyers, representing a number of the defendants, along with several of our economic experts, went to New Mexico and did just that. The company executive was absolutely right. We learned more about many of the real issues in the case in that two-day orientation than we had in the prior year of reading texts on mining economics.

Creativity on the part of those in the know—the in-house lawyers and key managers in the area or areas directly involved in the litigation—is what is critical here in making the orientation a meaningful and useful tool for advancing on the outside lawyer's learning curve and making him or her a more effective advocate for the client's position.

There is one other key part to this orientation process. The flip side of introducing the company to the outside lawyer is, of course, introducing the newly retained lawyer to the company's management personnel. Outside counsel should be given a chance to meet with those who have ultimate responsibility for the case, and who may eventually (or, hopefully, even sooner than that) have to evaluate proposals for settlement. Each should get to know the other so that they begin to build a level of confidence that will enhance the credibility of the outside lawyer when he or she is asked to evaluate the case and offer settlement recommendations. In addition, since the responsible manager may in some cases find outside counsel's bill as a line item on his or her monthly P&L and will certainly have a say in how much the company wishes to spend in defense of the case, it is important that in-house counsel do whatever possible to permit the relevant manager to get to know, and establish a rapport with and trust in, the outside lawyer retained for the case.

Mechanisms for Communication and Coordination

A useful method for focusing many of the issues and decisions that need to be made at the outset of a case is for outside counsel to prepare a litigation strategy and plan. Done within the first month or two after counsel is retained, it will, of course, be based upon incomplete and preliminary information. Yet it is an important start. It should include the outside lawyer's outline of the case issues, both factual and legal; an overall plan for action in the case; a strategy or a series of strategies with alternative levels of involvement and the risks and benefits of each; and a tentative estimate of costs in the form of an early litigation budget. If carefully prepared, this litigation plan can be used as a jumping-off point for the necessary discussions with in-house counsel about case staffing, methods of coordination, decision-making responsibilities, and the like. It also can and should be updated, along with more detailed plans and more sophisticated budgeting efforts, as the case proceeds.

Once the case is under way, it is important to have appropriate reporting mechanisms to keep house counsel informed of the status of the case. Such mechanisms can also be used, of course, as a recognized and routinized method for advising and consulting on long-range activities, as well as for making decisions on strategy.

One such mechanism that can be set up at the outset of the representation is a written status report. The size and scope of the litigation can determine how frequently it is prepared and its format. In large cases, it may well be issued as a weekly report; in smaller cases, or where inside counsel does not wish to be updated this frequently, a monthly or even quarterly report may do.

The level of detail will be tailored to the case and the desires of in-house counsel, but the items covered will generally be the same:

- Projects that have been completed since the prior report
- Projects that are under way and are to be accomplished in the short term, with the status of each such project (in the case of a weekly report, "short-term" means, perhaps, the next two weeks; in the case of a monthly report, say, a month)
- Longer-term projects that are under way, again with the status of each
- Plans, for discussion purposes, for possible additional projects, both immediate and longer-term.

The "projects," of course, will be determined by the case, but will generally fall into such categories as review of company documents, interviewing company personnel and/or other witnesses, conduct of discovery matters (both by and against the company), preparation of and responding to motions, development of factual issues, legal research and analysis, work with outside experts and consultants, and the like. The status report should also have a brief section reporting on significant events that have happened in the case since the last report: the filing of motions by the opposition or co-defendants, new discovery requests, significant results in recent depositions, agreements with co-counsel on sharing of work, etc.

Where house counsel is located in the same city as the retained outside lawyers, a weekly or biweekly status meeting is a useful adjunct to this kind of status report. In essence, the status report can form the agenda for a weekly (or other periodic) oral update on case developments, the status of ongoing work, and plans and strategies for the future. Where the case is sizable enough to involve a team of lawyers and paralegals, this status meeting can take the form of a one-hour working lunch of the team, including, of course, house counsel.

A multitude of functions can be served by this process: Team members (including paralegals) can be kept up-to-date on all aspects of the case status. In this way, even the most junior member of the team feels involved in the overall effort and comes to understand his or her part in it. Team members can individually report on what each is doing. This enables house counsel to get to know each team member personally; he or she gets to see each in action and understand what each is up to. Ultimately, when the monthly bill is received, this whole process gives the in-house lawyer a much clearer picture of what the client is actually paying for. Outside lawyers and in-house counsel both get to participate regularly in planning for the case—and, amazing as it may seem, on occasion they will find that the most useful suggestions on strategy may come from a young lawyer or a paralegal who has been spending all of his or her time in the trenches.

Weekly status meetings like this represent the ideal form of lawyer-to-lawyer communication to keep house counsel informed and directly involved. Of course, where the client is located far from the city in which the action is pending, this will be impossible. An alternative is the use of the weekly or other periodic status report, along with regular telephone reporting by lead outside counsel to the in-house lawyer in charge. Even in this situation, however, it seems useful to try to set up a team meeting—perhaps for a whole day once a quarter—for a full-scale update and review of case status and strategy.

Conclusion

The relationship between inside and outside attorneys in the management of a major piece of litigation will not always be perfect. As in most other relationships, there will be occasions on which there are misunderstandings and a need to redefine the respective roles of the participants. To make the relationship work, it is critical that in-house and outside counsel try to define the company's expectations at the outset of the representation, and that they keep open lines of communication thereafter. When problems arise, they should be dealt with quickly, without defensiveness, and be put behind the participants. With this kind of approach, and with the belief that management of litigation is a team effort between the inside and outside lawyers, they can achieve the overall objective—providing the best possible result for the company in the most efficient and cost-effective way.

Eight

Sharing the Work Load

Nancy C. Dreher

It is becoming increasingly common for pretrial and trial activity to be shared between inside and outside counsel. In some cases, this is happening because able people on in-house staffs want hands-on experience. It is also happening, or should be happening, because there are cost efficiencies to be achieved through the use of a team consisting of inside and outside lawyers. In-house counsel needs to decide very early on how active a role he or she wants, or wants the people on staff, to take in pretrial, settlement, and trial. That role needs to be clearly established from the beginning.

How Inside Counsel Can Help

In my experience, there are some aspects of pretrial and trial where inside counsel can be especially helpful. These are discussed in the following paragraphs.

Providing Background About the Industry and the Client

In-house counsel brings a valuable asset to the litigation process: knowledge about the inner workings of the company and the industry in general. In-house counsel, for example, will often know instinctively where the "bones are buried," how management views the litigation, and the potential for a counterclaim. In-house counsel also knows the personalities involved to a greater extent than outside counsel. It is important for in-house counsel to share this information with outside counsel. Otherwise, the corporation will spend unnecessary sums to educate its outside lawyers the hard way.

Assisting in Planning and Budgeting

The strategic plan, operating plan, and budget will tend to be better management tools if they are the result of a joint effort by inside and outside counsel. The planning process includes much more than outside counsel's

Nancy C. Dreher, formerly a member of Leonard, Street and Deinard, Minneapolis, Minnesota, is a United States Bankruptcy Judge for the District of Minnesota.

putting numbers to paper. In many respects, in-house counsel has substantial insight into the process and what the client really wants.

Discovery Plans and Discovery Papers

At one time or another, all of us have struggled with the inarticulately phrased request for production of documents or interrogatory. This can be avoided if inside counsel helps to phrase discovery requests and interrogatories or reviews them with a keen eye toward careful drafting. For example, in litigation between two competitors, it is a fair bet that the adversaries keep the same types of files, answer to the same regulatory agencies, and in general conduct business in the same way. Inside counsel usually knows or can find out the key words to use in a request or an interrogatory. Inside counsel can probably also look at any request to be sent to the other side and more accurately assess the volume of material that is likely to be produced. Inside counsel also generally has a much better grasp of the industry, or in some cases the corporate transaction involved, and thus can gauge what it is reasonable to expect the other side to have in the way of factual response. Outside counsel does not have these advantages. Inside counsel should thus try to stay close to the offensive discovery process, if possible.

Responding to Interrogatories and Discovery Requests

In-house counsel has far greater insight than outside counsel with respect to documents that may be responsive to discovery requests, the burden of gathering them, their true competitive sensitivity from the corporation's viewpoint, and the logistics of production. It is, therefore, generally appropriate for in-house counsel to play an active role in this aspect of discovery.

For example, corporate managers will almost always view most of their documents as highly sensitive, confidential information. Excessive use of confidential protection procedures, however, inevitably leads to discovery disputes and overly cumbersome proceedings. I have found it much more efficient to have inside counsel interface with corporate personnel when resolving this issue.

The same problem arises with respect to the question of excessive burden. Responding to the other side's discovery requests is always a burden and is never any manager's top priority. In-house counsel can often more effectively persuade, cajole, or bludgeon in-house personnel into assisting in responding to the other side. It is also appropriate for in-house counsel, in many cases, to draft answers to interrogatories as they relate to matters within their special area of knowledge.

Furnishing Technical Support

Increasingly, law firms have been required to use computerized litigation support systems. This can range from simple full-text retrieval of depositions to highly sophisticated programs of document organization, retrieval, and analysis. Working through in-house counsel, the client may bring its own computer capabilities or that of its affiliates into play. In-house counsel can play an especially helpful role, first in recognizing the expertise that is available within the organization and second in providing it to outside counsel.

Location of and Working with Experts

In-house counsel can also play an especially helpful role in finding, selecting, and working with experts, especially technical or industry experts. Rather than having outside counsel search a broad potential pool of available sources, in-house counsel may be able to pinpoint potential experts. In a recent case that I tried as a private practitioner, for example, in-house counsel was able to quickly identify a range of potential experts, make the initial contacts and arrangements, and begin the selection process. Technical experts, moreover, seem to be more comfortable when they are working with someone who is knowledgeable in the business or the technology involved. Often in-house counsel can provide this comfort level to a greater degree than outside counsel.

Sharing or Providing Legal Assistants, Clerks, and Coders

An efficiently managed case uses legal assistants to do meaningful, necessary tasks that cannot be done by secretaries and should not be done by lawyers. Too often, however, legal assistants perform tasks that are not needed or that are far below their abilities. A properly managed law office should be able to provide the client not only with highly trained career legal assistants, but also with a range of staff in the form of clerks, coders, temporaries, and lesser legal assistants to do lesser functions. Too often, however, all work that falls between secretary and lawyer is categorized as legal assistant and billed at one rate. In-house counsel and outside counsel should explore together a full range of options in any case that may involve extensive use of legal assistants. For example, in-house counsel may wish to lend a legal assistant from the corporate office for the purpose of ensuring that a legal assistant who knows the industry, transaction, or parties works on the case. Or in-house counsel may wish to directly subcontract the clerking and coding functions, rather than having a law firm do the job at its overhead rates. By doing so, in-house counsel can keep tighter rein on the work being performed and the costs that are generated.

Trial and Trial Preparation

As in all phases of litigation, the role of inside counsel in trial preparation and trial can be tailored to the case and in-house counsel's view of the role he or she wants to take. In my experience, however, the following activities are especially suited to in-house counsel:

- *Working with and preparing the company's employees to testify*—Especially in cases where outside counsel has represented the company on a limited basis, there is great value in having in-house counsel engaged in the process of preparing witnesses whom he or she knows and may work with regularly. Most witnesses have a much higher comfort level with the process if this occurs.
- *Liaison with experts*—The same reasons that make it helpful to have in-house counsel involved in pretrial selection and preparation of experts suggest that he or she can play a special role in liaison with and preparation of experts at trial.
- *Daily attendance at or contact with the trial process*—In a case of any magnitude, someone needs to be the client on a daily basis. The jury should not see the corporate defendant personified in the form of its lawyers. Even if not present, moreover, someone from the corporation needs to be available on short notice to handle the myriad of issues that come up daily at trial. This role can, and in my experience usually does, fall on in-house counsel.
- *Serving as point person for settlement*—Cases often settle just before or just after a trial has started. In-house counsel's role is to be ready with authority to make decisions when the occasion arises. The in-house counsel who has closely monitored the proceedings day by day does a much better job at settling than one who has not.
- *Providing technical and logistical support*—Even when the case is well prepared for trial, new matters will arise during trial. In my experience in private practice, these included locating a former employee who became important during the plaintiff's case, and the need, as the other side's expert testified, to conduct an experiment in our client's laboratory to test the hypothesis upon which that testimony was based. These tasks logically fell to in-house counsel.
- *Furnishing a different view*—Trial counsel will tend to take a particular view of the case. One of the most effective roles in-house counsel can perform is to test from his or her own vantage point the themes and proposed presentation of trial

counsel. I followed a practice, for example, of suggesting that in-house counsel review tapes of my proposed opening statement and closing arguments. To the extent inside counsel was willing, I reviewed major briefs with him or her for the specific purpose of getting someone else's view.

Tight Operational Controls

While litigation costs cannot be avoided, they can be trimmed if outside and inside counsel work toward that goal. Tight operational controls can dramatically reduce the costs of much litigation without jeopardizing the prosecution or defense of the case. The following paragraphs present a few examples.

Take More Risks

I recently attended a mock trial using Irish lawyers, an Irish judge, and Irish rules. In Ireland, discovery is virtually nonexistent. The lawyers did quite well on their feet examining witnesses they had never seen and never deposed. They made their two or three points and, while the examinations were not flawless, they were good enough. It is riskier to try a case without deposing everyone in sight, but it can be done. The concept of pleading fewer claims and defenses, asking fewer interrogatories, looking at fewer documents, and taking fewer depositions is here to stay. While all of this increases the risk, that increased risk can often be justified on a cost/benefit basis. In any event, inside and outside counsel should do a considerable amount of cost/benefit thinking as the case goes on.

Try to Develop an Amicable Working Relationship with the Other Side

In my experience, the most expensive litigation has been that in which counsel's personality has interjected itself into the case. It is not possible in all cases to maintain a good working relationship with the other side, but that is a goal to seek.

Develop a Settlement Strategy

Settlement strategy should be an upfront and constantly reviewed issue. It is increasingly common to consider settlement options before lawsuits are started or in the very early stages before substantial costs are incurred. Settlement should generally be explored before anyone incurs substantial litigation costs, because those costs themselves sometimes make settlement much more difficult.

Complete Discovery as Quickly as Possible

There are times when it is necessary to take a considerable time to complete discovery. But, in general, the shorter the discovery deadlines, the lower the costs. Perhaps the flip side is even more the rule—the longer counsel has to complete discovery, the more it will cost. Early discovery cutoffs and a fixed trial date will almost always reduce the cost of trial preparation. Inside and outside counsel should carefully do a cost/benefit analysis when anyone suggests a request for a delay in the discovery cutoff or the trial date.

Limit the Number of Lawyers

It is seldom necessary to have more than one lawyer in one place at one time, either at a deposition, a court appearance, or meetings. As one client said, "Lawyers come in pairs," but the cost of doing that has become increasingly prohibitive. In the pretrial stage, in-house counsel should carefully scan the bills to see if double-teaming is occurring. My former firm now has many clients with standard retainer agreements that contain a prohibition against double-lawyering without prior approval.

Use Informal Discovery Procedures Wherever Possible

Lawyers are accustomed to sending interrogatories, issuing requests for production, and taking depositions in order to obtain information. That is the most expensive way to get information. I am always surprised at how much can be learned and developed outside the formal discovery process and at how seldom lawyers use these informal techniques. A most mundane example is the telephone book. It is easier to locate a witness in the phone book than it is to send an interrogatory. Also, while in private practice, I used a private investigator to develop all types of factual evidence. The investigator's rates are lower than those of a lawyer. A wealth of financial information on industries and adversaries is available in state and federal regulatory agencies throughout the country. And, the well-placed interview of a potential witness will often generate as much or more information than a formal and more expensive deposition. Inside and outside counsel should both work creatively to develop facts through these types of informal channels.

Control and Manage Document Inspections and Productions

It is very important that a lawyer be present at most document inspections for the purpose of quickly scoping out the task and managing and directing further conduct of the document inspection. If that does not happen, more often than not, paralegals will spend days looking at materials that may have little or no relevance to the litigation. They will then cleanse, code, and computerize every piece of paper they have seen, no matter what its importance may be to the litigation.

An example from my experience in private practice proves the point. At a document production, we received more than fifty banker's boxes of material. I personally spent three hours scoping out the inspection, identifying what was clearly extraneous, and deciding how much more effort needed to be expended on particular categories of materials. I also found the metaphorical "smoking gun." That three hours of time saved the client considerable sums. Moreover, it is immensely wasteful to have a legal assistant dealing with any document that will never be looked at again. Worthless or unimportant materials should simply be put aside, and no one should spend any time on them.

Avoid Discovery Motions Wherever Possible

I know of no judge or magistrate who wants to hear a discovery motion. Both sides should avoid discovery motions at all costs. Both sides should also agree to stipulate to confidential protective orders without court involvement.

Keep the Team Interested; Hold Disciplined Staff Meetings

In major litigation, it is very important to keep the lines of communication open and to keep members of the team apprised of developments. That does not mean that counsel should encourage any kind of unnecessary chatting over developments in the case. Those types of conversations serve little or no purpose. Rather, to keep people at all levels knowledgeable with respect to what is happening, it is efficient and helpful to memo copies of correspondence and similar documents to persons who are working on the case.

On larger cases, while in private practice, I used a "task list," which is prepared weekly and circulated to everyone involved. These lists allow persons who are on the team to know the assigned tasks, the assignment date, the due date, and any information about how to complete the task. While task lists are cryptic, they are an easy way for everyone to know what other team players are doing.

Also, in cases of great magnitude, it is important that all members of the team feel some sense of direction. A regular staff meeting attended by most of the people involved, with a clear agenda and minutes, helps immensely to keep team members aware of and interested in what is occurring.

Computerize with Care

The computer has its place, to be sure. For example, while in private practice we used extensive litigation support in a case that involved $150 million in potential liability, multiple defendants, and hundreds of thousands of documents. At a second's notice, the support system allowed us to prepare "hit lists" of every document where any witness was mentioned. Use of hit lists was of invaluable assistance in preparing witness kits. The computer could do other amazing and wonderful things. Had the case gone to trial for twelve to fifteen weeks, as originally expected, the fortune we put into developing the program would have been worth its weight in gold.

However, computerization is not necessary and helpful in every case. Inside and outside counsel should jointly discuss the decision to computerize or even consider computerizing any case before taking steps to do so. Even the best computer system has its flaws. Every step should be taken to avoid excessive and unnecessary difficulty with the software.

Conclusion

There are no simple answers to controlling the cost of litigation. One thing is certain, however: It is much more difficult to control litigation costs when inside counsel and outside counsel are working on two different tracks. Application of standard management tools and techniques to the litigation process, coupled with a keen view toward the cost/benefit trade-off of most strategic decisions, can provide some answers to escalating litigation budgets.

Nine

Conflicts of Interest and Ethical Issues for the Inside and Outside Counsel

Samuel R. Miller and Irwin H. Warren

At one time, it was easy to practice law without the canons of ethics that govern conflicts of interest "getting in the way." Most corporations' inside legal staffs, if they existed at all, were minuscule. The law—common, statutory, and especially regulatory—with which corporations were concerned was much simpler and more limited. Corporations tended to use one law firm for the bulk of their work in any one city. The law firms themselves operated in a much simpler environment. Firms were relatively small, they tended to be located in one city, and their attorneys tended to be either general practitioners or specialists in only a few areas. A handful of major corporate clients would dominate most firms' practices.

However, the nature of legal practice has changed dramatically. Corporations have greatly expanded in size; they may have subsidiaries or divisions located all across the United States and in foreign countries. As a result of internal expansion or mergers and acquisitions, corporations may be involved in a whole host of unrelated businesses. A seamless and ever-thickening web of common law, statutes, and regulatory requirements covers their every move. The general counsel of a company now is likely to have a staff ranging from a handful to 100 or more inside counsel. Corporations may retain a number of law firms in different cities or even in the same city.

Law firms have also changed. Many firms have opened branch offices in two, three, or even a half-dozen or more different cities and foreign countries. Thanks to modern travel and telecommunications, firms centered in one city often represent clients located thousands of miles away. Firms now commonly have 100, 200, or even 300 attorneys. Individual attorneys tend more and more to specialize in particular areas of the law; many firms have found success through a "boutique" approach that permits them to offer their clients specialists in a number of areas.

Samuel R. Miller is a member of Morrison & Foerster, San Francisco, California. Irwin H. Warren is a member of Weil, Gotshal & Manges in New York City. The authors gratefully acknowledge the assistance of Deborah E. Townsend, associate attorney with Morrison & Foerster, in updating this article.

Finally, another wrinkle has been added to the fabric by virtue of the increased size of government legal staffs. More and more attorneys spend part of their careers in government. Law firms and corporate legal staffs increasingly look to the government to recruit experienced attorneys with specialties in particular areas of the law.

Given this combination of changed circumstances, the canons of ethics governing conflicts of interest cannot help but get in the way of current legal practice from the perspective of both corporations and law firms. Lawyers in firms spend an increasing amount of time running conflict checks in order to determine whether they can accept a matter even from a client of long standing. Inside counsel spend more and more time contemplating whether or not to consent to one of the company's outside law firms representing an adversary. Law firms and corporations that believe they have scrupulously adhered to the canons of ethics may suddenly find themselves in the midst of conflicts when the law firm discovers that one of its branch offices thousands of miles away represents an adversary of the corporation. And with the ever-increasing turnover of attorneys between private firms, government, and corporation legal staffs, a mounting problem is the identification of a "Typhoid Mary"—the attorney who joins a firm or legal staff and brings with him a "taint" from his prior employer that may result in disqualification.

Consequently, attorneys have had to become ever more alert to the rules of professional conduct governing conflicts of interest.[1] This chapter focuses on the provisions of the ethical rules concerning conflicts of interest that are of particular importance in terms of the regularity with which they are implicated and the drastic consequences that result from a failure to follow them.[2]

This chapter discusses the following topics:

- Problems of successive representation: representing an adversary of a former client
- Ethical implications of attorney movement between law firms or corporate legal departments
- Ethical implications of the movement of attorneys in and out of government
- Conflicts arising from simultaneous representation of clients with adverse interests
- Rules governing the role of lawyer as witness

The article discusses the applicable case law under the canons of ethics and Model Code of Professional Responsibility (Model Code). It also highlights the changes in ethical standards incorporated into the new Model Rules of Professional Conduct (Model Rules). It points out distinctions that have developed among various circuits. As will be clear, disqualification issues are intensely fact-specific and, perhaps more than many other areas of the law, court-specific. In the area of ethics and disqualifications, the circuits split on standards, and individual judges differ on how the same standards should be applied to the same fact situation. Some courts have recognized and taken into account the realities of modern legal practice, while others have adopted a strict approach that ignores these considerations. Hopefully, this article will alert practitioners to many ethical issues and will suggest some practical steps that may be helpful in avoiding conflicts problems.

Problems of Successive Representation: Protecting the Confidences of Former Clients

Problems of successive representation arise when an attorney seeks to represent a new client whose interests are adverse to those of a former client. No provision of the Model Code specifically addresses the problem of successive representation. However, in deciding motions for disqualification in this context, courts have been guided by canon 4 and canon 9 of the Model Code and the applicable ethical considerations and disciplinary rules thereunder. Canon 4 requires that a lawyer "preserve the confidences and secrets of a client." Canon 9 requires that an attorney avoid even the appearance of impropriety.

As a general rule, courts have forbidden counsel from representing a new client in a matter against a former client if the two matters are "substantially related" unless the former client consents.[3]

Obligation to Protect the Confidences of a Former Client

Under Ethical Consideration (EC) 4-6, the obligation of a lawyer to preserve the confidences and secrets of a client continues after the termination of the employment.[4] Thus, the lawyer must refrain not only from divulging the client's secrets or confidences, but also from acting for others in any matters in which knowledge of the client's affairs acquired in the course of the earlier employment can be used to the former client's disadvantage.[5]

The ethical obligation to preserve a client's confidences is not confined to information that is subject to the attorney-client privilege; it extends to all knowledge and information acquired from a former client or from others in the course of the representation of the former client.[6] The confidences protected under canon 4 also include "intangibles" arising from the very nature of the lawyer-client relationship.[7]

Courts, therefore, have been quite sensitive to situations in which the law firm "was privy to [the client's] practices and procedures, and had access to internal papers.[8] Courts will not inquire into whether some or all of the confidences of the client could have been obtained elsewhere or might be known by the new client, but will seek instead to protect against the possibility of confidences passing through the attorney.[9]

The Substantial-Relationship Test

In determining the need for disqualification of a law firm under canon 4 because of a current representation adverse to the interests of a former client, courts have uniformly applied a "substantial-relationship" test.[10]

In the seminal case of *T.C. Theatre Corp. v. Warner Brothers Pictures*,[11] the court enunciated the following test for disqualification:

> [T]he former client need show no more than that the matters embraced within the pending suit wherein his former attorney appears on behalf of his adversary are *substantially related* to the matters or cause of action wherein the attorney previously represented him, the former client. The Court will assume that during the course of the former representation confidences were disclosed to the attorney bearing on the subject matter of the representation. It will not inquire into their nature and extent.[12]

Courts have diverged, however, in determining whether two matters are "substantially related." Most courts have sought to find similarities in the subject matters or factual context of the successive representations.[13] In *Realco Services, Inc. v. Holt*,[14] the court stated:

> If the client in the prior representation might have imparted confidential information to his lawyer to aid the lawyer in dealing with particular issues, and if issues arise in the second suit which would permit the use of such confidences *against* the original client, the substantial relationship test is met, and disqualification is required.[15]

The Second Circuit has approved a narrower standard, requiring that the relationship between the prior and current representation be "patently clear" before counsel may be disqualified.[16] The Second Circuit has also noted that a high standard of proof should be imposed on a party seeking to disqualify his former counsel.[17]

In situations in which an attorney moves from one firm to another, the Seventh Circuit has recently developed a new test for determining whether a substantial relationship exists.[18] This new test is discussed below.[19]

To avoid inquiry into the content of the attorney-client relationship or the substance of the very communications and confidences that canon 4 protects, many courts presume that confidential information passed during the prior representation if a substantial relationship is shown to exist.[20]

Who Is Subject to Disqualification?

In the context of canon 4, even if only one attorney in the firm represented the former client and was privy to the client's confidences, the firm as a whole is disqualified from representing a new client in a substantially related matter adverse to the former client.[21]

At least until recently, attempts to screen attorneys or create a "Chinese wall" to avoid disqualification of an entire firm in successive representation cases have not succeeded.[22] However, as discussed below, an exception to this rule has recently been developed in certain (but not all) courts in the situation in which a lawyer changes jobs and the new law firm is retained by an adversary of a client of the former firm.

Even in the situation in which a law firm switches sides, some judges have criticized the automatic imputation of one attorney's knowledge to the entire firm. In *Analytica, Inc. v. NPD Research, Inc.*,[23] the court disqualified a firm in an action against a former client of one partner, ruling that the presumption of shared confidences among firm members was irrebuttable. However, Judge Coffey, in dissent, argued that the time has come to abandon the irrebuttable presumption that the knowledge of one attorney is the knowledge of the entire firm. As he stated:

> The irrebuttable presumption that all information is shared among every attorney in a firm ignores the practical realities of modern day legal practice. The practice of law has changed dramatically in recent years, with many lawyers working in firms consisting of 20, 30, 60, 100 or even 300 or more attorneys, and with some firms having offices located throughout the country or even throughout the world. Additionally, the trend within law firms has been toward greater specialization and departmentalization. Surely, it defies logic and common sense to establish a presumption, with no opportunity for rebuttal, that every individual lawyer in such a multi-member and multi-specialized firm has *substantial knowledge* of the confidences of each of the firm's clients. Recognizing these realities of the modern practice of law, we must continue to take a more realistic view toward the law of attorney disqualification by allowing the presumption that confidences have been shared throughout a firm to be rebuttable.[24]

Courts have refused to allow disqualified counsel to violate canon 4 indirectly by communicating with other counsel and have disqualified otherwise acceptable lawyers who have been tainted by communications with another attorney or firm disqualified pursuant to canon 4.[25]

In *Trone v. Smith*,[26] the Ninth Circuit rejected efforts by a law firm to remain as plaintiffs' counsel by parsing out the defendants so as to represent plaintiffs against all defendants except the one whom the firm had previously represented. The Ninth Circuit noted, "Fiduciary obligations and professional responsibilities may warrant disqualification of counsel in appropriate cases even in the absence of a strict contractual attorney-client relationship."[27]

In *Kevlik v. Goldstein*,[28] the First Circuit recently ruled that a party to a lawsuit has standing to move to disqualify opposing counsel under the principles of canon 4 and canon 9 even if the moving party was not the aggrieved former client. In this case, a civil rights claim based on police misconduct was brought against a municipality. The incident giving rise to the suit grew out of the arrest of three individuals. One of the individuals consulted an associate of a law firm regarding criminal charges following the arrest. The associate withdrew from representing the individual after a day or two when he learned that his firm represented the municipality's insurance carrier. When the two other individuals involved in the incident brought a civil suit against the municipality, the law firm appeared as the municipality's counsel. Counsel for the plaintiffs thereafter moved to disqualify the firm on the ground that it had previously represented an individual involved in the incident who would be called as a witness for the plaintiffs. The First Circuit affirmed the order disqualifying the municipality's counsel. The court held that the plaintiffs had standing to raise the disqualification issue even though they were not the aggrieved party.[29] The court further held that a conflict of interest existed, since the municipality's lawyers were in a position to possibly use privileged information gained from a former client against that client.[30]

The *Kevlik* case is significant because it raises the prospect that a firm may be disqualified when its former client is merely a witness, not just when the firm is involved in a suit against its former client.

If counsel is disqualified, courts may prohibit the firm from transferring its files or communicating its work product to new counsel.[31]

Successive Representation Problems in the Corporate Context

Several successive representation problems that have arisen in the corporate context deserve mention. One issue addressed by various courts is whether company counsel can be disqualified in a suit by the company against a former employee when the employee has previously consulted with counsel for the company. In *E.F. Hutton & Co. v. Brown*,[32] the outside general counsel and local counsel of E.F. Hutton were disqualified in a suit by the company against a former vice president. Before the institution of the civil suit, Hutton's counsel had represented the vice president in an SEC investigation and bankruptcy hearing relating to the same transactions at issue in the suit. The employee had asserted in these proceedings that he was being represented individually by the counsel for the company, and counsel did not indicate otherwise. The court, therefore, found that there was an attorney-client relationship between company counsel and the former employee. The court ruled that the attorney for two formerly joint clients should be disqualified in litigation between the joint clients in a matter that was the subject of the former representation. The court noted, however, that the result might have been different if company counsel had clearly enunciated to the employee that counsel was representing only the corporation.

In somewhat similar circumstances, the court in *Meehan v. Hopps*[33] reached a contrary result. In *Meehan*, the receiver of a corporation sued an individual who was chairman of the board of the company on a theory of breach of fiduciary duties. The individual moved to disqualify the firm, arguing that he had established a personal attorney-client relationship with the firm. He argued that the company's attorneys had provided services to him in a number of transactions and that he had provided confidential information to the attorneys. The court denied the motion for disqualification, stating:

> The attorney for a corporation represents it, its stockholders and its officers in their representative capacity. He in nowise represents the officers personally. It would be a sorry state of affairs if when a controversy arises between an attorney's corporate client and one of its officers he could not use on behalf of his client information which that officer was required by reason of his position with the corporation to give to the attorney.[34]

Conflicts may also arise when corporate counsel attempts to take sides in an intracorporate dispute. In *Brennan's, Inc. v. Brennan's Restaurants, Inc.*,[35] an attorney who formerly represented all the family members in a closely held business was disqualified from representing one family faction against another. Similarly, in *Goldstein v. Lees*,[36] the court held that it was improper for the former general counsel of a company to represent a director who was a minority shareholder in a proxy fight for control of the corporation.

In *Wilson P. Abraham Construction Corp. v. Armco Steel Corp.*,[37] the court determined that counsel for one co-defendant engaged in a joint defense in a criminal antitrust conspiracy action could not subsequently represent a plaintiff in a civil antitrust action against his former co-defendants. In *Abraham Construction*, it was not a former client of the attorney who sought to disqualify him, but rather co-defendants of a former client. The court held that when information is exchanged between various co-defendants and their attorneys engaged in the joint defense, an attorney who is the recipient of such information breaches his or her fiduciary duty if later, in representing another client, the attorney is able to use this information to the detriment of a co-defendant. As the court stated:

> Just as an attorney would not be allowed to proceed against his former client in a cause of action substantially related to the matters in which he previously represented that client, an attorney should also not be allowed to proceed against a co-defendant of a former client wherein the subject matter of the present controversy is substantially related to the matters in which the attorney was previously involved, and wherein confidential exchanges of information took place between the various co-defendants in preparation of a joint defense.[38]

However, in these circumstances, the court ruled that the co-defendants could not rely on the presumption that confidential information had been exchanged and required the co-defendants to prove that the attorney had actually received confidential information.[39]

In a somewhat related context, counsel for a party in an antitrust suit that started the litigation as a plaintiff but became a defendant was recently disqualified in order to prevent inadvertent disclosures to other defendants of information counsel had acquired in strategy sessions with counsel for other plaintiffs.[40]

Consent or Waiver

The former client can consent to the firm's representing a new client against it.[41] The Eleventh Circuit recently found that, in the context of canon 4, a client may waive even a "serious and pervasive" conflict of interest.[42] However, courts will not accept a claim by a law firm of consent in advance or a blanket consent (for example, a general release to the firm after the prior representation ends). Rather, the consent must be made with full knowledge of all the facts and implications of the particular, now-adverse representation.[43]

The Ninth Circuit found de facto consent to adverse representation in *Trust Corp. v. Piper Aircraft Corp.*[44] In *Piper*, one party delayed bringing the motion for disqualification until shortly before trial, although the potential conflict had been disclosed two and one-half years previously. A number of courts have followed the *Piper* court's lead, voicing a concern that disqualification motions were being abused as tactical weapons.[45] Other courts, however, have granted disqualification motions after a long delay and even at the commencement of trial.[46]

Impact of Canon 9

Canon 9 requires that an attorney avoid even the appearance of impropriety. Some courts have relied on canon 9, as well as on canon 4, in upholding the disqualification of an attorney who has switched sides.[47]

Some circuits have ruled that disqualification may be based upon canon 9 alone.[48] The Second Circuit, on the other hand, has indicated that "appearance of impropriety is simply too slender a reed on which to rest a disqualification order except in the rarest cases."[49]

Impact of the New Model Rules

Rule 1.9 of the Model Rules codifies the substantial-relationship test. Rule 1.9 provides in pertinent part, "A lawyer who has formerly represented a client in a matter shall not thereafter: (a) represent another person in the same or a substantially related matter in which that person's interests are materially adverse to the interests of the former client unless the former client consents after consultation."

Rule 1.9 abandons disqualification in successive representation cases based upon canon 9's appearance-of-impropriety test. The Model Rule does not attempt to define "substantially related matter." The comments to rule 1.9 note that the scope of a matter may depend on the facts of a particular situation or transaction and the degree of the lawyer's prior involvement.[50] The comments state:

> [W]hen a lawyer has been directly involved in a specific transaction, subsequent representation of other clients with materially adverse interests clearly is prohibited. On the other hand, a lawyer who recurrently handled a type of problem for a former client is not precluded from later representing another client in a wholly distinct problem of that type even though the subsequent representation involves a position adverse to the prior client.[51]

According to the comments to rule 1.9, "The underlying question is whether the lawyer was so involved in the matter that the subsequent representation can be justly regarded as a changing of sides in the matter in question."[52]

Pursuant to rule 1.9, disqualification from subsequent representation can be waived by the former client "if there is disclosure of the circumstances, including the lawyer's intended role in behalf of the new client."[53] Rule 1.10 of the Model Rules changes the result in successive-representation cases when a lawyer changes firms. This is discussed in the next section.

Ethical Implications of Attorney Movement Between Law Firms or Corporate Legal Departments

As discussed above, canon 4 mandates protection of the confidences of a client, including former clients. When a law firm sues a former client on behalf of a current client, canon 4 comes into play, with the courts using the substantial relationship test to determine the necessity for disqualification.

Most commonly, this situation arises when the former client no longer uses the law firm. However, the client that has remained loyal to the firm, only to discover that one of the individual lawyers at the firm suddenly has moved to a firm "on the other side," is also entitled to protection under canon 4. The movement of an attorney, no less than the movement of a client, will implicate canon 4. And in the current period of law firms' opening up offices in many cities, merging with other law firms, and developing specialty practices, and with the growth of in-house corporate legal staffs, attorney movement is the rule, not the exception. This has long been the case, of course, with associate-level attorneys; but increasingly, even partners of law firms have become inclined to move. As will be discussed, the implications of the attorney's movement will vary depending on the attorney's work in the former job and in the new one and on the measures taken by the new firm to avoid ethical problems.

The Circumstances and Extent of Disqualification

As a general rule, even if only one attorney was privy to the former client's confidences, "the firm as a whole is disqualified whether or not its other members were actually exposed to the information."[54] The knowledge of each attorney, in effect, is imputed to the entire firm.

Certain courts, however, have interpreted the Model Code, and canon 4 in particular, in a flexible, practical manner when dealing with the movement of attorneys from one law firm or legal staff to another. This practical approach to imputation of knowledge must be considered in two contexts: imputation of knowledge at the old firm and imputation at the new firm. Courts have been inconsistent in their treatment of the issue in both contexts. Some courts reject the notion that presumptions of shared confidences are rebuttable at all;[55] other courts disagree.

The Second Circuit in *Silver Chrysler Plymouth, Inc. v. Chrysler Motors Corp.*[56] dealt with the issue of imputation of knowledge at the old firm. The defendant corporation in *Silver Chrysler* moved to disqualify the plaintiff's attorney and his law firm on the ground that the attorney previously had been associated with the law firm representing the defendant. The court denied the motion. The court took a practical "facts of life of big firm legal practice" approach in denying the disqualification motion:

> Even after an initial association with a firm upon graduation, it is not uncommon for young lawyers to change their affiliation once or even several times. It is equally well known that the larger firms in the metropolitan areas have hundreds (collectively thousands) of clients. . . . [I]t would be absurd to conclude that immediately upon their entry on duty they become the recipients of knowledge as to the names of all the firm's clients, the contents of all files relating to such clients, and all confidential disclosures by client officers or employees to any lawyer in the firm. . . . [A] rational interpretation of the Code of Professional Responsibility does not call for disqualification on the basis of such an unrealistic perception of the practice of law in large firms.[57]

The court's analysis was based on the specific facts concerning the nature of the attorney's role while at his former law firm: "[Although] an inference may arise that an attorney formerly associated with a firm himself received confidential information transmitted by a client to the firm, that inference is a rebuttable one."[58] The court looked to see whether the attorney had worked at all on matters for the corporation and, if so, at the nature and quantity of work that was performed. In *Silver Chrysler*, disqualification was denied even though the attorney had worked on some matters for the corporation, because the total time expended by him was minimal and the matters on which he had worked were not deemed sufficiently related to, or to have involved confidences regarding, the matters being handled by his new firm.[59] Because the inference of knowledge of confidences at the former firm had been rebutted, the court did not have to reach the issue of imputed knowledge at the new firm, and it denied the disqualification motion.

This "rebuttable presumption" approach has recently been adopted by the Seventh Circuit.[60] Current cases in the Seventh Circuit employ three-level inquiry in attorney-movement cases:

> First, the trial judge must make a factual reconstruction of the scope of the prior legal representation. Second it must be determined whether it is reasonable to infer that the confidential information allegedly given would have been given to a lawyer representing a client in those matters. Third, it must be determined whether that information is relevant to the issues raised in the litigation pending against the former client.[61]

If, after evaluating the facts according to this three-part standard, the court finds that a substantial relationship does exist, it should presume that the attorney received confidential information during his or her prior representation and therefore may properly be disqualified. This presumption, however, is a rebuttable one.[62] "[Although a] very strict standard of proof must be applied. . . [i]f the attorney can clearly and persuasively show that he was not privy to the confidences and secrets of the client" while at his old firm, he will be able to rebut the presumption that such information was disclosed to him at his former firm.[63]

It will not always be easy to rebut this presumption, however.[64] If the attorney, while at the former firm, was involved in the matter or otherwise cannot rebut the presumption of knowledge of confidences of the former firm's clients, the attorney's knowledge will then ordinarily be imputed to his or her new firm, and that new firm may be subject to disqualification.[65] Courts may use a more lenient standard of imputing shared confidences when considering the disqualification of co-counsel.[66]

The rebuttable presumption approach of the Second and Seventh Circuits in attorney movement cases has been followed in the Sixth Circuit and other courts.[67] In *Manning v. Waring, Cox, James, Sklar & Allen*, the Sixth Circuit denied a motion to disqualify a law firm with a "tainted" attorney, stating that the firm had effectively rebutted the presumption of shared confidences by the erection of screening devices before the attorney in question joined the firm.[68] Other courts have refused to follow these circuits. The Eighth Circuit declined to follow *Silver Chrysler* and disqualified a lawyer employed by a state government's legal staff because he previously had been associated with the law firm for a corporation that the state was suing.[69] The court held that the inference of shared confidences among partners and associates at a firm is virtually irrebuttable.[70]

The Efficacy of Screening and Chinese Walls

Equally important, the unilateral efforts by the new firm to avoid disqualification by attempting to screen the new tainted attorney from matters relating to his former firm's client, or to establish so-called Chinese walls around him are likely to be accepted by some courts but rejected by others.[71]

The Second Circuit, for example, rejected such unilateral screening in *Cheng v. GAF Corp.*[72] In *Cheng*, disqualification of the new firm was ordered even though the individual attorney and his new firm had both taken substantial steps to insulate the attorney from the matter in question. The Second Circuit specifically rejected the district court's conclusion that the "risk of disclosure of confidential information is negligible," holding instead that "one of the purposes of disqualification is 'to guard against the danger of inadvertent use of confidential information.' "[73]

> Although [the individual attorney now] may not be personally involved in the *Cheng* defense, he is a member of a relatively small firm. . . . [I]t is unclear to us how disclosures, admittedly inadvertent, can be prevented throughout the course of this representation. . . . [T]here exists a continuing danger that [the attorney] may unintentionally transmit information he gained through his prior association with *Cheng* during his day-to-day contact with defense counsel.[74]

This approach has been followed by certain courts outside the Second Circuit as well.[75]

The Seventh Circuit, in contrast, has recently indicated that such unilateral screening may well suffice to prevent disqualification of the new firm in situations where the conflict has arisen because an attorney moved from one firm to another. It further has been indicated that such screening is appropriate and effective regardless of whether the attorney in question was a partner or an associate at either the old firm or the new firm.[76] This approach has recently been followed by the Sixth Circuit in *Manning*.[77]

The Seventh Circuit has rejected "screening defenses," however, when the screening was not put into place until the disqualification motion was made[78] or when the screening was informal rather than a clearly prescribed "institutional mechanism."[79]

In *Nemours Foundation v. Gilbane, Aetna, Federal Insurance Co.*, a district court in Delaware accepted the institutional screening defense in an attorney-movement situation based upon its interpretation of rules 1.10 and 1.11 of the Model Rules.[80] The court's analysis began by noting that there is now an explicit exception to imputed disqualification in the case of former government attorneys, under model rule 1.11. The court then found that model rule 1.10's comment indicated the drafters' intent that a pragmatic approach be used in vicarious disqualification cases and that the analysis under rule 1.10 applies not only to former government attorneys but also to lawyers in law firms generally.[81] The court concludes that there is "no substantial reason against extending the exception to vicarious disqualification from the case of a former government attorney to private attorneys generally."[82] For the reasons discussed in a following section, the authors question the reasoning of the court in *Nemours* in light of rule 1.10's silence with respect to the efficacy of screening where a private attorney switches firms.

In dealing with attorney movement under the Model Code, courts have treated corporate law departments and individual in-house counsel in the same way as law firms and attorneys working at such firms.[83] Similarly, the government agency or legal staff that hires or retains an attorney may be subject to disqualification in the same manner as a private-sector client or law firm.[84]

Consent

As noted above, a former client can consent to its former law firm's representing a new client against it.[85] By the same token, a client can consent to the movement of an attorney from the firm representing it to the firm opposing it. In this context, the screening and Chinese walls, which, if unilaterally imposed, would not be deemed sufficient by certain courts, may be made a condition of the consent. In *Cheng*, for example, the Second Circuit distinguished its prior decision in *Armstrong v. McAlpin*[86] on the ground that, inter alia, "the tainted attorney's former employer in *Armstrong* [the government agency] agreed to the representation as long as proper screening techniques were used; here, Cheng and [the legal aid office, the attorney's] former employer, have objected to the representation since the [defendant's law] firm hired [the attorney]."[87]

The New Model Rules of Professional Conduct

Unlike the Model Code, the newly adopted Model Rules, in rule 1.10, deal directly with the concept of imputed disqualification resulting from the movement of attorneys.[88] As noted in the commentary to rule 1.10:

> [I]t should be recognized that today many lawyers practice in firms, that many to some degree limit their practice to one field or another, and that many move from one association to another several times in their careers. If the concept of imputed disqualification were defined with unqualified rigor, the result would be radical curtailment of the opportunity of lawyers to move from one practice setting to another and of the opportunity of clients to change counsel.[89]

The comments to rule 1.10 stress that the term "firm" includes lawyers "employed in the legal department of a corporation or other organization."[90]

Rule 1.10 takes a middle ground between the positions of the Second and Seventh Circuits in dealing with the issues of attorney movement and imputation of knowledge of confidences at the old and new firms.

As the comments make clear, subparagraph (a) of rule 1.10 adopts the rule of imputed disqualification with respect to lawyers currently associated in a firm in order to ensure that the firm itself meets its obligation of loyalty to its clients; that is, the firm of lawyers "is essentially one lawyer for purposes of the rules governing loyalty to the client," and "each lawyer is vicariously bound by the obligation of loyalty owed by each lawyer with whom the lawyer is associated."[91] With respect to attorney movement, however, and particularly the issue of imputed knowledge at the attorney's former firm, the comments note that the "fiction that the law firm is the same as a single lawyer is no longer wholly realistic."[92] The comments specifically reject the "per se rules of disqualification" such as the conclusive presumption that a partner in a law firm has access to all confidences of all clients in the firm. The comments note that this is factually unrealistic and "exaggerates the difference between a partner and an associate in modern law firms."[93]

The new Model Rules also reject the pure "appearance of impropriety" approach. The commentary concludes that "[a] rule based on a functional analysis is more appropriate for determining the question of vicarious disqualification. Two functions are involved: preserving confidentiality and avoiding positions adverse to a client."[94]

Thus, subparagraphs (b) and (c) of rule 1.10 require an analysis of a situation's particular facts. As noted thereafter in the commentary, these paragraphs "operate to disqualify the [new] firm only when the lawyer involved has actual knowledge of information [of the old firm's client] protected" by the confidentiality rules.[95] Similarly, the commentary notes that as long as the conditions of rule 1.10(b) and (c) concerning confidentiality have been met, the consideration of avoiding positions adverse to a client resulting from attorney movement is not a problem.

In short, the new Model Rules appear to adopt the approach of the Second Circuit in *Silver Chrysler* and of the subsequent Seventh Circuit decisions, which hold that the inference of knowledge obtained by an attorney in his or her former employment is rebuttable. Significantly, however, rule 1.10 does not contain any provision for screening at the new firm of an attorney who fails to rebut the presumption of knowledge acquired in the former employment. The commentary does not discuss the question of screening at all. Nevertheless, the failure to provide for screening in rule 1.10 is highlighted by the fact that rule 1.11 (dealing with movement of attorneys in and out of government) expressly does provide for screening to avoid disqualification of a former government lawyer's new private law firm. The commentary to rule 1.11 notes that "[t]he provisions for screening and waiver are necessary to prevent the disqualification rule from imposing too severe a deterrent against entering public service."[96] No such discussion appears in the commentary to rule 1.10. In this regard, the new Model Rules appear to follow the approach of the Second Circuit in *Cheng* rather than the Seventh Circuit approach in the *LaSalle/Schiessle* line of cases.

Practical Approaches to Dealing with the Problem of Attorney Movement

The key to dealing with the problem of disqualification resulting from attorney movement in private practice is to be aware of the potential pitfalls and to take steps to avoid them in advance. The following are some suggestions:

- Know the law of your jurisdiction: Does it allow screening of a tainted attorney, and, if so, under what circumstances? If you are in a jurisdiction that allows screening, set up the screening in a timely manner (that is, before the attorney arrives); and be sure to set up formal, institutional screening procedures, including memoranda to all firm personnel and rules governing access to files.
- When considering employing an attorney, investigate your own records to determine whether there are any matters as to which the attorney's current employer (be it law firm or corporation) is on the other side of the litigation or other matter in which you are involved.
- Find out whether the individual attorney is involved in any matters against your company or your law firm. The nature and extent of any such involvement should also be examined.
- Particularly in instances in which, under cases such as *Silver Chrysler* or *LaSalle*, you perceive that a question or genuine problem may arise, raise the issue with the attorney in question and, if necessary, with the attorney's current employer. It is often a viable alternative for that current employer to obtain the affected clients' consent to the attorney's new job, particularly if adequate screening is assured. As a practical matter, most firms, corporations, and clients will not want to impede unnecessarily the professional advancement of an attorney when there is no real danger of the disclosure of confidences that canon 4 is designed to protect. In those instances in which consent cannot be obtained, it is just as well to find out in advance, rather than test this issue by a disqualification motion in court.
- If any attorney with your firm or legal staff leaves, be sure that his or her new employer or firm is not on the other side on any matters involving your company or your client.

Employment of Former Government Attorneys

Lawyers increasingly spend all or part of their careers in government. Hoping to obtain a background in a field of specialization, they may begin their careers with an agency, or they may develop a name for themselves in private practice and then spend time in government service. Law firms and, increasingly, private corporations are hiring individuals who have had government experience. Such hiring, however, may prove to be a trap for the unwary: a law firm or corporate legal staff may find itself disqualified from handling particular matters, or even a broad range of matters, involving the agency at which the newly hired attorney once worked.

Alternatively, in order to avoid disqualification, it may find that it must "neutralize" the former government lawyer in question by screening him or her from important cases. The key is to understand, before hiring the lawyer, the limitations and obligations imposed by the ABA Model Code and Model Rules, the ABA Formal Opinion on the subject, and the regulations of the particular government agencies in question.[97]

The Model Code and ABA Formal Opinion 342

DR 9-101(B) mandates refusal of employment on a matter by an individual lawyer who had substantial responsibility with respect to that matter while a public employee.[98] DR 5-105(D) provides that when an individual attorney is disqualified from a matter, the attorney's entire firm is disqualified.[99] The combination of DR 9-101(B) and DR 5-105(D) could lead to draconian results, disqualifying law firms or corporate legal departments in a wide variety of matters. Accordingly, the ABA, in Formal Opinion 342,[100] undertook an extensive analysis of the rationales for the Model Code's disqualification provisions, noted the special considerations that apply when government attorneys are involved, and provided its own interpretation of some of the elements of the canons (for example, what is a "matter" and what constitutes "substantial responsibility"). More important, it established guidelines that would permit screening so as to avoid the imputation of disqualification to an entire firm or legal department. The courts have given great weight to Formal Opinion 342.[101]

When Does DR 9-101(B) Apply?

The applicability of DR 9-101(B) will vary depending on the situation; it turns on the identity of the individual in question, the precise nature of that person's role and responsibility while with the government, and the nature of the matter that his or her law firm or corporate law department wishes to handle.

At the outset, DR 9-101(B) by its terms applies only to a matter as to which the attorney, while with the government, had substantial responsibility. "Substantial responsibility" is defined in Formal Opinion 342 as a responsibility that requires the attorney to become personally involved in the investigation or deliberative process regarding the transaction or facts in question.[102] It means far more than mere presence at an agency at the time in which a matter was before it. For example, an attorney did not have substantial responsibility merely because he was an attorney with the SEC Enforcement Division at the time a matter was being investigated or litigated if he had nothing to do with that matter. Similarly, supervisory personnel with overall responsibility for a department may not be deemed to have had substantial responsibility on a matter even though attorneys in that department were handling the matter. The key is the quality of the involvement by the individual: what did the person know, to what information did he or she have access, and in what way was he or she involved.[103]

The nature of the matter is also significant. Obviously, if an attorney was handling a particular litigation for an agency and then left the agency to work for a law firm that was on the other side, the matter is identical.[104] Under Formal Opinion 342, many subjects of responsibility are not deemed "matters" as to which disqualification or screening procedures or both would apply. For example, work by a former government attorney in drafting, formulating, or participating in hearings concerning the adoption of an agency rule is not considered to be a matter that would prevent the attorney from litigating—even against that agency—about the meaning, interpretation, or application of the rule on behalf of a client of the firm.[105] The improprieties that DR 9-101(B) is intended to forestall are reasonably possible only if specific information (as distinct from general agency expertise or contacts) to which a former government lawyer may have had access in one matter is likely to be useful in a subsequent matter.[106] But even where DR 9-101(B) may not require a former government attorney to withdraw, the attorney's withdrawal may be forced by other ethical considerations, such as DR 4-101(B), which prohibits the use of a client's confidences or secrets to a third person's advantage.[107]

Policy considerations may also play a role. Because DR 9-101(B) appears under the maxim of canon 9, "A Lawyer Should Avoid Even the Appearance of Professional Impropriety," some courts have applied an appearance-of-impropriety standard to former government attorneys in their later representations.[108] However, Formal Opinion 342 clearly states that the "appearance of professional impropriety" language of canon 9 is not a standard or test embodied in DR 9-101(B), but is a policy consideration supporting the existence of the rule.[109] The majority of courts follow the reasoning of Formal Opinion 342 with respect to the appearance-of-impropriety test,[110] particularly in criminal cases.[111]

Avoiding Disqualification of Firms or Legal Staffs

Even in those situations in which the individual former government attorney would be disqualified, the attorney's law firm or corporate legal staff can avoid the imputation of disqualification by following the procedures outlined in Formal Opinion 342. Disqualification can be avoided by a two-part process involving screening of the former government attorney by the attorney's law firm or legal staff and obtaining from the interested government agency a waiver of imputation of disqualification. Allegations of mere appearance of impropriety provide an insufficient basis to disqualify a law firm when there have been screening and a waiver from the government agency. Thus, in *Armstrong v. McAlpin*,[112] disqualification of the law firm was rejected even though the firm had hired the attorney in charge of an SEC investigation and enforcement action regarding the very matters as to which that law firm was subsequently retained to bring suit.

Waiver

Agencies have specific rules of practice concerning the hiring and use of former agency lawyers.[113] The attorney and law firm or law department should examine these before even beginning discussions about possible employment.

Screening

Formal Opinion 342 sets out the requirement of screening. To protect the firm or department from disqualification, all steps should be taken to minimize any possibility or claim of participation, assistance, or involvement in any way at the firm or legal department by the former government lawyer in the matter in question. Screening procedures should be explicit and tailored to the requirements of each individual case.[114] The following procedures are guidelines:

1. The former government lawyer should not participate or share in the fees that are received with respect to the matter as to which he or she is disqualified. For attorneys who are hired as associates or as legal staff counsel and who thus are on salary, this normally presents no problem. When a former government lawyer is brought in as a partner of a law firm or otherwise would ordinarily share in a percentage of the profits, the law firm either should make a flat fee arrangement with the attorney or else have that partner's share calculated after deduction of the fees attributable to the matter(s) as to which he or she has been disqualified.[115]
2. The former government attorney should be instructed not to have anything to do with the matter, either as an active participant or even in informal discussions with other attorneys or employees.
3. All attorneys in the firm or legal departments should be advised of the former government lawyer's disqualification from particular matters. They further should be instructed not to discuss with that attorney any matters as to which he or she had substantial responsibility while with the govern-

ment. The precise matters, if known, should be listed. To be safe, the governmental agency at which the attorney worked also should be clearly identified, and all attorneys should be urged not to speak with the former government lawyer about any matters involving or arising out of that agency. One or more attorneys with the firm or in the legal department should be used as "screening points" (that is, individuals who would like to speak with the former government attorney about a subject falling within the attorney's expertise should clear the question or matter with these screening points before initiating discussion of the matter; if there is some question as to the propriety of the discussion, the screening point attorney may be able to make the inquiry without disclosing the matters involved).

4. All nonlegal personnel (such as paralegals and filing room personnel) should be advised that they are not to speak with the former government lawyer about any specified matter or any matter involving his or her former agency; in addition, they should be instructed not to provide to such attorney access to the files of or documents relating to specified matters, which should be clearly identified.
5. The firm or legal staff should decide on the screening measures it intends to take and should discuss these with the agency personnel responsible for granting waivers before the attorney is hired. Care should be taken to obtain the waiver as to specific matters where possible.

Model Rules of Professional Conduct Concerning Successive Government and Private Employment

The new Model Rules deal with the question of movement of attorneys in and out of government and private employment in far greater detail than does the Model Code. The Model Rules, however, are quite consistent with the approach taken by the ABA in Formal Opinion 342 concerning the movement of attorneys. Rule 1.11 of the Model Rules, entitled "Successive Government and Private Employment," is the governing rule.

Several factors should be stressed. In rule 1.11(a),[116] the new Model Rules follow the approach of decisions such as *Armstrong v. McAlpin* and Formal Opinion 342 in disqualifying the former government lawyer from the private matter while permitting his or her law firm to continue or undertake representation in a private matter so long as the disqualified lawyer is screened from participating in the matter and a consent is obtained from the government agency. In rule 1.11(b),[117] the new Model

Rules adopt the approach of *Handelman v. Weiss*,[118] disqualifying the attorney individually and permitting his new firm to participate only if it follows screening procedures and the subsequent litigation does not involve the government agency that the attorney formerly represented. Although the government must be given notice of the firm's involvement and be allowed to satisfy itself that the firm's screening is adequate, it may not veto the firm's participation by withholding consent.[119]

Rule 1.11(b)[120]—like rule 1.10—"operates only when the lawyer in question has knowledge of the information, which means actual knowledge; it does not operate with respect to information that merely could be imputed to the lawyer."[121] Protection extends only to information that the lawyer has gained "by use of governmental power" (i.e., by subpoena) and that the government generally keeps confidential.[122]

Counsel for law firms and corporate legal staffs—as well as the former government lawyers—should note the proscription in rule 1.11(c) (2)[123] against the government lawyer's "negotiat[ing] for private employment with any person who is involved as a party or as attorney for a party in a matter in which the lawyer is participating personally and substantially."

Relevant Federal Statutory Provisions

Former government lawyers should be aware that the federal government may bring an action under provisions of the Ethics in Government Act that restricts postemployment activity of federal officials and employees. The act at 18 U.S.C. § 207 (1982)[124] prohibits certain post–executive branch representation activities for varying periods of time. Section 207(a) prohibits former government employees from engaging in representation regarding any matter in which the former employee participated "personally and substantially" while employed by the government. Section 207(b) provides for a two-year "cooling-off" period by prohibiting a former employee from entering a personal appearance respecting any matter that was "actually pending" for one year before his or her termination. Sections 207(c)[125] and (d) apply to high-level employees of the executive department such as cabinet officers and agency heads, who are restricted for one year from representing a client before, or communicating so as to influence, the government entity for which they served, in connection with any matter pending before that government entity or in which the entity has a "direct and substantial interest."

Canon 5: Simultaneous Representation of Multiple Clients

Canon 5 provides that "A Lawyer Should Exercise Independent Professional Judgment on Behalf of a Client." This canon and its ethical considerations and disciplinary rules are aimed principally at preventing lawyers from simultaneous representation of conflicting interests.[126] In general, canon 5 forbids, in the absence of consent, the representation of one current client whose interests are adverse to those of another current client, even if the subject matter of the two representations is entirely different.[127] As will be discussed, the substantial relationship test used in the context of canon 4 ordinarily is not applicable in this canon 5 context.

Application of Canon 5

The courts have been zealous in enforcing the principles of canon 5 concerning multiple representation, applying its terms quite literally and without the somewhat more limited approach to disqualification used in the context of canon 4.[128] In the canon 5 context, courts have not been hesitant to rely on the "appearance of impropriety" language of canon 9 in ordering disqualification.[129] Significantly, considerations of canons 5 and 9 have been held to apply with full force to large, multicity, multi-office law firms, even if the simultaneous representation was unknowing and not deliberate.[130]

Canon 5 applies when one client "is likely to be adversely affected" by its law firm's simultaneous representation of another client. Canon 5 governs when the attorney "cannot exercise independent judgment and vigorous advocacy" on behalf of one without injuring the other, or when the lawyer (or firm) has "put himself in a position where, even unconsciously he will be tempted to 'soft pedal' his zeal."[131] The attorney should avoid situations not only in which there is an actual conflict but also in which conflict is likely to develop.[132] As with canon 4, problems arise most frequently in the context of litigation, but canon 5 is not so limited in its application. Any simultaneous representations, both on behalf of and adverse to an existing client, may trigger canon 5's application.

Courts use varying standards to determine when an attorney or firm must withdraw in a canon 5 situation. In considering whether disqualification is appropriate, some courts evaluate whether there is an "actual" conflict or a "potential" conflict[133] and order disqualification only if they find an actual conflict. Other courts reject the word "potential" as overly broad, as the Oregon Supreme Court did in returning to an approach based on actual, likely, and unlikely conflict.[134] Under this standard, an attorney may never represent two clients with actual conflicts of interest, and may represent clients with likely conflict of interests only if the attorney complies with DR 5-105(C)'s disclosure and consent exception.

Several state bar ethics committees have attempted to define the meaning of "adverse" in specific areas. The District of Columbia and Colorado bars, while noting the general inappropriateness of joint representation of both parties in a divorce action, also agreed that such representation is not improper where there is no evidence of coercion and the attorney is confident that the interests of each can be adequately represented.[135] The Colorado opinion further states guidelines for real estate transactions (the purchaser and seller must have substantially agreed on all terms in order to be nonadverse) and sales of a business (representation of buyer and seller not prohibited per se, but a situation justifying dual representation is difficult to conceive of).

Those courts that have considered simultaneity in the canon 5 context have adopted an expansive view. Status as a present or former client is to be determined as of the time of the filing of the complaint;[136] otherwise, a law firm could always convert a present client to a former one by withdrawing from the representation of one client. The Third Circuit, in *IBM v. Levin*, held that IBM was a present client of a law firm even though the firm had no specific IBM project on hand the day the complaint was filed and the law firm worked on a fee-for-services basis and was not on retainer to IBM.[137] The Tenth Circuit likewise held proper the disqualification of an attorney who had represented an employee in an annulment matter while representing defendant employer in a Title VII sex discrimination investigation by the EEOC, in which the employee was an interested party. This holding was in spite of the fact that settlement negotiations on the discrimination charges between the EEOC and defendant employer were terminated before the attorney began to represent the employee; the court held that the charges, and thus the possibility of litigation, still remained alive.[138]

The Second Circuit has expressly rejected the substantial-relationship test in the context of canon 5 (as opposed to canon 4—former client).[139] The Third Circuit likewise has not required any substantial relationship between the matters in which the law firm's client is involved,[140] nor have district courts in Florida and Illinois.[141] As the Second Circuit described the very broad test for canon 5's applicability, "Where the relationship is a continuing one, adverse representation is prima facie improper . . . and the attorney must be prepared to show, at the very least, that there will be no actual or *apparent* conflict in loyalties or diminution in the vigor of his representation."[142]

The court continued:

> Putting it as mildly as we can, we think it would be questionable conduct for an attorney to participate in any lawsuit against his own client without the knowledge and consent of all concerned. . . . '[W]ith rare and conditional exceptions, the lawyer may not place himself in a position where a conflicting interest may, even inadvertently, affect, or give the appearance of affecting, the obligations of the

> professional relationship.' . . . In *Grievance Committee v. Rottner*, Connecticut's highest court held that the maintenance of public confidence in the bar requires an attorney to decline employment adverse to his client, even though the nature of such employment is wholly unrelated to that of his existing representation.[143]

However, the Second Circuit adopted a limited exception using the substantial-relationship test in the canon 5 context when one of the adverse representations involved representation of a broad-based, multiparty organization such as a multiemployer bargaining unit or trade association.[144] In *Glueck*, the court used the substantial-relationship test to determine whether canon 5 "should be applied to suits brought by an [incorporated] association's law firm against an association member"; it refused to adopt a rule that all members of the association are, per se, clients of the law firm for purposes of canon 5.[145]

The court may rely upon the law firm's own reaction to the simultaneous representation to find that there is indeed a violation of the ethical rules; for example, if members of the firm evidence their view that there may be a violation of the canons, such as by seeking consent to dual representation, the court may consider such evidence in determining that there is a violation.[146]

The Role of Consent

Canon 5's proscription is not absolute; simultaneous representation is permitted if the clients grant their consent under the terms of DR 5-105(C). However, courts have carefully examined defenses to disqualification motions based on consent. For consent to be effective, there must be full disclosure of all the facts and implications of the simultaneous representation by the attorney to both clients involved in the conflict situation. Express consent must be given by both clients based upon the full disclosure.[147] Occasionally, the likelihood of an adverse effect may be so powerful as to preclude the possibility of client consent.[148]

Equally important, courts will not imply consent. Courts also will not presume or impute knowledge of either the fact or the implications of simultaneous representation to the client.[149] This is so even if the client is a major corporation that has its own in-house legal staff supervising or even working with the outside law firm.[150] Rather, the courts require clear proof of the disclosure.[151]

The Necessity of Adequate Representation

Consent, by itself, is not enough to avoid canon 5 disqualification in the simultaneous representation context. In *addition* to the consent of both clients, it must be "obvious that [the lawyer] can adequately represent the interest of each."[152] Thus, simultaneous representation will not be deemed proper, even with consent, "where the public interest is impaired or where there is a great likelihood that one party will be prejudiced."[153]

The factors bearing upon the issues of whether it is obvious that the attorney can adequately represent both clients include the nature of the litigation or other matters involved, the type of information to which the lawyer may have access, whether the clients are in a position to protect their interest or to know whether they may be disadvantaged as a result of the multiple representation, the questions in dispute, and whether a government body is involved.[154]

Although, as noted above, the substantial-relationship test applicable in a canon 4 (former client) situation does not generally apply to a canon 5 (current clients) situation, that test has been used by the Ninth Circuit to determine the issue of adequacy of representation. In *Unified Sewerage*, the Ninth Circuit held that, *upon consent of both clients*, a lawyer could "adequately represent" both clients in different litigations where there was no substantial relationship between the two matters.[155]

An Illinois district court used a "reasonable and informed observer" standard, where such an observer would "at once appreciate the importance of a party's right to be represented by counsel of his or her choice and the ability of a lawyer to keep clearly in focus the interests of clients whose circumstances are not identical."[156]

Relief to Be Applied by the Court

Although courts generally disqualify the law firm when a canon 5 violation has been found, arguably, disqualification is not required in all cases.[157] For example, laches has been recognized as a defense to a canon 5 disqualification motion.[158] Disqualification is a matter of discretion and equity. Among the relevant considerations is whether a party waived its right to obtain an attorney's disqualification by delaying and permitting the attorney to represent other clients well into the course of a matter. The *Jackson* court noted that a litigant may not delay filing a motion to disqualify in order to use the motion later as a tool to deprive an opponent of counsel of his or her choice after substantial preparation of the case had been completed.

Assuming the court finds a violation of canon 5 requiring disqualification, the cases vary as to which representation may continue; the attorney does not have the choice of deciding which client to represent.[159] Some cases indicate that the representation should continue as to the first-retained client.[160] Another case suggests that the first-retained client has the choice of either discharging the attorney or discontinuing its action against the second client.[161] The Third Circuit has held that if the second client is dissatisfied with and unwilling to consent to the joint representation, the attorney must cease representing the first client.[162] When a court finds a conflict, it may disqualify the attorney from representing either client,[163] or both clients.[164] The confusion in the circuits should be resolved by a clear, equitable rule. Fairness would seem to dictate that the first client ought to have the option to either retain or terminate employment of the attorney or firm at issue, but that the attorney should not represent the second client. Any rule should allow for some discretion on the part of the court, which might appropriately exercise it when both clients were taken on at about the same time or when circumstances make it impossible to say who was the first client. Courts should consider the impact of disqualification on the client's interests as well as the propriety of the attorney's conduct.

Because the considerations underlying canon 5 (for example, desire that the attorney vigorously represent his or her clients) differ from those underlying canon 4 (protection of confidences of a client), the relief ancillary to a disqualification order differs in the context of canon 5. Thus, in contrast to the situation that often arises under canon 4, if disqualification pursuant to canon 5 is ordered, the court may well permit the attorney both to turn over his or her work product to and consult with new counsel for a reasonable period of time in order to ameliorate the impact on the other client.[165]

Canon 5 and the Simultaneous Representation of a Corporation and Its Officers and Employees

The issue of simultaneous representation frequently arises when in-house counsel or attorneys from one outside law firm are asked to represent one or more of the corporation, its current officers and employees, or former officers, directors, and employees. The approaches of the courts vary, especially when grand jury proceedings are involved, but no hard and fast rule precludes such multiple representation.[166] However, some courts have based disqualification in the context of simultaneous representation upon the interference with the effective functioning of the grand jury.[167]

One court ordered disqualification of counsel in a criminal antitrust action from representing a defendant corporation as well as three company employees who had been granted immunity and could be called as government witnesses against the company.[168] The court rejected the clients' waiver of any conflicts and found that the continued representation of the immunized witnesses by corporate counsel would create an impermissible appearance of impropriety.

The Model Rules of Professional Conduct

The new Model Rules address the issue of simultaneous representation in rule 1.7, which provides as follows:

> (a) A lawyer shall not represent a client if the representation of that client will be directly adverse to another client, unless:
> (1) the lawyer reasonably believes the representation will not adversely affect the relationship with the other client; and
> (2) each client consents after consultation.
> (b) A lawyer shall not represent a client if the representation of that client may be materially limited by the lawyer's responsibilities to another client or to a third person, or by the lawyer's own interests, unless:
> (1) the lawyer reasonably believes the representation will not be adversely affected; and
> (2) the client consents after consultation. When representation of multiple clients in a single matter is undertaken, the consultation shall include explanation of the implications of the common representation and the advantages and risks involved.[169]

The Model Rules represent a substantial clarification of the attorney's obligations, if not a change in the applicable standards. For example, the comments note that "loyalty to a client prohibits undertaking representation *directly adverse* to that client without that client's consent. . . . Thus, a lawyer ordinarily may not act as advocate against a person the lawyer represents in some other matter, even if it is wholly unrelated."[170]

The new Model Rules thus impose a "directly adverse" standard, even while adhering to the case law rejecting the substantial-relationship test. As the commentary states, "[S]imultaneous representation in unrelated matters of clients whose interests are only generally adverse, such as competing economic enterprises, does not require consent of the respective clients. Paragraph (a) applies only when the representation of one client would be directly adverse to the other."[171]

The standard of obviousness of the current Model Code is also replaced. As noted in the comments to rule 1.7, "when a disinterested lawyer would conclude that the client should not agree to the representation under the circumstances, the lawyer involved cannot properly ask for such agreement or provide representation on the basis of the client's consent."[172] Of particular note in this regard is rule 1.7(b), governing simultaneous representation of parties whose interests in litigation only may conflict, such as co-plaintiffs or co-defendants. The commentary suggests looking to such issues as substantial discrepancies in the parties' testimony, incompatibility in positions in relation to an opposing party, or even substantially different possibilities of settlement among such clients.[173]

The commentary also specifically recognizes that given the large size of corporations, litigation by an attorney against a corporate client, based on consent, may be permissible:

> [T]here are circumstances in which a lawyer may act as advocate against a client. For example, a lawyer representing an enterprise with diverse operations may accept employment as an advocate against the enterprise in an unrelated matter if doing so will not adversely affect the lawyer's relationship with the enterprise or conduct of the suit and if both clients consent upon consultation.[174]

The commentary recognizes as well that lawyers may find themselves arguing different positions on the same issues in different cases for different clients. It suggests that this is permissible but perhaps subject to limitations. Specifically, the commentary notes:

> A lawyer may represent parties having antagonistic positions on a legal question that has arisen in different cases, unless representation of either client would be adversely affected. Thus, it is ordinarily not improper to assert such positions in cases pending in different trial courts, but it may be improper to do so in cases pending at the same time in an appellate court.[175]

Finally, the commentary to model rule 1.7 states, "A lawyer for a corporation or other organization who is also a member of its Board of Directors should determine whether the responsibilities of the two roles may conflict. The lawyer may be called on to advise the corporation in matters involving actions of the directors." After listing a variety of factors to be considered in this regard, the commentary concludes, "If there is material risk that the dual role will compromise the lawyer's independence of professional judgment, the lawyer should not serve as a director."[176]

Some Practical Points for Dealing with Simultaneous Representation Issues

The key to dealing with canon 5 problems is the same as in canon 4 situations: identifying the problem or potential problem and taking steps in advance to avoid it. The following are some suggestions:

- Identify potential problems at the earliest possible moment. This requires knowing who you are representing at all times. Before accepting any matter from an existing client or new client, check to be sure you are not representing the party on the other side. For large firms, computerized information retrieval systems are essential. This, in turn, requires detailed information input (as when "new matter" sheets are prepared). It is helpful in this regard if corporate clients provide counsel with a list of all its subsidiaries and affiliates.

- When a potential conflict of interest exists, determine whether you can adequately represent both clients. If you conclude that you can, contact both clients to obtain consent. The request for consent must explain the implications of the simultaneous representation to each client.
- If you are the inside counsel and consent is sought from you, fully analyze the situation to see whether consent should be given. Among the factors you might consider are the nature of the case, whether the parties are subsidiaries in discreet lines of business, the nature of the records and identity of personnel likely to be the subject of discovery, and the nature of the law firm's current representation of your company.
- Wherever possible, *the consent should be in writing*. While the outside firms and inside counsel both may feel somewhat uncomfortable about this, it will help to focus both the company and law firm on the nature of the representation being proposed and the scope of the consent being given. This will protect the client by making clear the risks of and the limitations upon the adverse representation; it will protect the law firm against subsequent complaints about or other challenges to the adverse representation. For an excellent example of the reasons why written consent should be obtained and for a form of consent letter, see *Interstate Properties v. Pyramid Co.*[177] At a minimum, if the circumstances are inappropriate for such a letter, a detailed file memo should be prepared concerning the request and the consent; but the protections and certainty are less, of course.
- The consent letter is equally essential in the context of simultaneous representation of clients whose interests are not adverse at the moment—but may become so in the future. Full disclosure may also avoid subsequent canon 4 (protection of confidences) problems if litigation arises between the two clients. When a company consents to a law firm's representing it, knowing that the firm will continue to represent another primary client on the same or related matters, the court may find that there was no intention of confidences and that information disclosed by the new client was not expected to be confidential and kept from the primary client.[178] Such a written letter may also be useful in the situation in which corpo-

rate counsel is simultaneously representing the entity and company officers or employees.

The Lawyer as Witness: Problems under Canon 5
Model Code Provisions

Under ABA Model Code DR 5-101(B) and DR 5-102(A), a lawyer should not accept employment in contemplated or pending litigation, and the lawyer and his or her firm should withdraw as trial counsel, if the "lawyer learns or it is obvious that he or a lawyer in his firm ought to be called as a witness on behalf of his client." This general rule is subject to the following four exceptions:

1. The testimony will relate solely to an uncontested matter.
2. The testimony will relate solely to a matter of formality, and there is not reason to believe that substantial evidence will be offered in opposition to the testimony.
3. The testimony will relate solely to the nature and value of legal services rendered in the case by the lawyer or lawyer's firm to the client.
4. Withdrawal would work a substantial hardship on the client because of the distinctive value of the lawyer or lawyer's firm as counsel in the particular case.

Pursuant to DR 5-102(B), a lawyer and the lawyer's firm may continue representation if the "lawyer learns or it is obvious that he or a lawyer in his firm may be called as a witness *other than on behalf of his client*. . . until it is apparent that his testimony is or may be *prejudicial* to his client."[179]

ABA Formal Opinion No. 339 identifies three primary reasons for the rule forbidding a lawyer to act both as trial counsel and as a witness on behalf of his client: (1) the client's interest in having testimony from a witness who is "not subject to impeachment for interest in the outcome of the trial"; (2) the client's entitlement to an advocate whose effectiveness cannot be impaired by reason of testifying as to contested issues; and (3) the "handicap [to] opposing counsel in challenging the credibility of the lawyer-witness." The opinion also notes that it is "unseemly" for a lawyer to argue his or her own credibility or that of a lawyer in the firm.[180]

ABA Formal Opinion No. 339 sets forth the reason DR 5-102(B) requires that a lawyer withdraw if that lawyer or another lawyer in the same firm is called to testify other than on behalf of a client and it is apparent that the lawyer's testimony is or may be prejudicial to the client: "the prejudice likely to result from the prospect of unfavorable testimony being elicited from a party's trial advocate."

Testimony on Behalf of a Client

Under DR 5-102(A), if a lawyer or another lawyer in the firm ought to be called as a witness on a contested matter on behalf of a client, both the lawyer and the firm are subject to disqualification.

Determination of When the Lawyer Ought to Be Called as a Witness

Most courts independently assess whether a lawyer ought to be called as a witness and do not rely on assertions from the client or counsel that the lawyer will not be called.[181] The Third Circuit has stated (in dictum) that a lawyer ought to be a witness only when he "has crucial information in his possession which must be divulged" or is an "indispensable witness."[182] The Fifth Circuit rule is that an attorney ought to testify when he has information making it "obligatory to place [himself] on the witness stand in order to advance the [client's] case completely and zealously."[183]

In *J.P. Foley & Co. v. Vanderbilt*,[184] the court found that a lawyer ought to be a witness on behalf of a client when the facts indicated that the lawyer had attended relevant meetings in the absence of the client and therefore was the only person who could testify on behalf of the client on that subject matter, and it appeared that the lawyer's testimony would be "pivotal," even if on rebuttal.

In *MacArthur v. Bank of New York*,[185] the court cited *J.P. Foley* and then announced a much more specific test: "Defendant's argument that [the attorney's] testimony would merely corroborate other testimony, even if accurate, is unavailing. The test is whether the attorney's testimony could be *significantly useful* to his client; if so, he ought to be called."[186]

Also adopting an expansive view is *Supreme Beef Processors v. American Consumer Industries*.[187] In this case, the court ordered disqualification even though counsel's testimony was cumulative because "[t]he client is entitled to every scrap of favorable evidence that is available, not only the favorable evidence that is *essential* to his case."[188]

Other courts, however, have adopted a less expansive view of when a lawyer ought to testify.[189]

Of particular interest to corporate counsel are cases in which courts have disqualified attorneys who participated in negotiations or who drafted agreements that were at issue in a pending case.[190]

In *MacArthur v. Bank of New York*,[191] Judge Sofaer rejected the argument that a strict rule of disqualification would preclude a law firm from serving clients on a continuous basis:

> [D]efendant objects that the effect of the court's ruling [disqualifying counsel *sua sponte*]. . . would be to prevent a law firm from maintaining a continuing relationship with a client. That fear is groundless. A lawyer can choose. . . to participate

> actively in a client's business affairs—not just as an adviser, but also as a negotiator and agent. . . . Such conduct is entirely proper. But if an attorney chooses to become intimately involved in the client's business, then he or she must be prepared to step aside if the matters involved result in litigation. This may be displeasing to firms that wish to have some members act as businessmen and others as litigators. But when these firms place themselves in the position of having an attorney acquire information that makes his testimony necessary, they must accept the consequences.[192]

Some courts have recognized an exception to the general rule of disqualification if the lawyer is a *party* to the litigation as well as a potential witness.[193]

Effect of the Client's Waiver of Any Conflict or Consent to the Lawyer's Testimony

Several courts have ruled that a client may not waive the mandates of DR 5-102(A).[194] As the court in *Supreme Beef Processors* stated:

> The first legal issue concerns whether a client may waive the protection of DR 5-101 and DR 5-102. Although these disciplinary rules are for the protection of clients, they are also for the protection of the bar and the integrity of the court. I therefore hold that these disciplinary rules may not be waived by the client.[195]

In *MacArthur*, the court stated, "[A] second feature of DR 5-102(A) is that the stricture is mandatory: the party cannot choose between the attorney's testimony and his representation.[196] The court went on to say, "[N]or may the client waive the rule's protection by promising not to call the attorney as a witness." In addition, the court held, "[W]here neither party moves for disqualification, the court must intervene to ensure that the mandate of DR 5-102(A) is followed."[197] Thus, in *MacArthur*, the court disqualified counsel *sua sponte during trial.*

In response to criticism that motions to disqualify were being used for tactical advantages in litigation, and especially in light of the California Supreme Court's decision in *Comden v. Superior Court*,[198] the California Rules of Professional Conduct were amended in 1979 to permit a lawyer to continue as trial counsel with the client's informed consent even if the lawyer ought to be a witness in the trial.

As modified, rule 2-111 (A)(4) of the California Rules of Professional Conduct provides:

> If upon or after undertaking employment, a member of the State Bar knows or should know that the member ought to be called as a witness on behalf of the member's client in litigation

> concerning the subject matter of such employment, the member may continue employment only with the written consent of the client given after the client has been fully advised regarding the possible implications of such dual role as to the outcome of the client's cause and has had a reasonable opportunity to seek the advice of independent counsel on the matter.

In addition, the modified California rule does not require disqualification of the firm if one lawyer will testify.

The Substantial Hardship Exception

Most courts have been reluctant to permit trial counsel to testify under the substantial hardship exception. In *Draganescu v. First National Bank*,[199] the attorney representing the heirs of an intestate in a suit against the bank for negligent failure to prepare a will was disqualified despite the clients' claim that they would suffer substantial hardship because they were Romanian. The attorney could speak Romanian and had known the decedent for many years; further, other lawyers were reluctant to take cases involving Romanians on a contingent fee basis.

In *United States ex rel. Sheldon Electric Co. v. Blackhawk Heating & Plumbing Co.,*[200] the court rejected as insufficient a showing that the law firm had represented the client for ten years and that 450 hours had been expended in connection with the case.[201]

In *MacArthur v. Bank of New York*, the court stated that "absent extreme hardship to the client, the mandate of 5-102(A) has been strictly invoked."[202]

In *General Mill Supply Co. v. SCA Services, Inc.*,[203] the court noted that the substantial hardship exception should include a requirement that the client had not knowingly caused or did not reasonably foresee the need for the lawyer's testimony. The court stated that the exception should apply when the lawyer-client team came unexpectedly upon a disqualification situation against which they neither actually did nor could have safeguarded themselves.[204]

Some courts, however, have been more liberal in applying the substantial-hardship exception.[205]

For example, in *Montcalm Publishing Corp. v. Pustorino*, the court considered substantial hardship, as well as the lack of necessity of the lawyer as witness and his lack of active participation in the actual case, to deny a motion to disqualify the attorney's law firm from representing the client.[206]

Testimony Other than on Behalf of a Client

As noted, under DR 5-102(B) a lawyer may be disqualified as trial counsel if his or her testimony is or may be prejudicial to the client. This rule was not designed to permit one side to call opposing counsel as a witness and thereby attempt to disqualify him or her as counsel.[207] Thus, the burden is on the party moving to disqualify to demonstrate what prejudice may occur and that "the likelihood of prejudice occurring is substantial."[208] One formulation of the meaning of "prejudicial" testimony is testimony "sufficiently adverse to the factual assertions or account of events offered on behalf of a client, such that the bar or the client might have an interest in the lawyer's independence in discrediting that testimony."[209]

Impact of the New Model Rules

Rule 3.7 of the ABA Model Rules governs the situation in which a lawyer may be a witness. Under rule 3.7, a lawyer shall not act as an advocate at a trial in which the lawyer is likely to be a necessary witness except when "(1) the testimony relates to an uncontested issue; (2) the testimony relates to the nature and value of legal services rendered in the case; or (3) disqualification of the lawyer would work substantial hardship on the client."

In this respect, rule 3.7 does not differ markedly from practice under the Model Code. The comments to rule 3.7 note that combining the roles of advocate and witness can prejudice the opposing party. The comments do not define "substantial hardship" but note that this determination will require a balancing of the interests of the client and those of the opposing party. In this regard, the comments indicate that it is relevant that one or both of the parties could reasonably foresee that the lawyer would probably be a witness. One change under rule 3.7 is that the showing of substantial hardship does not necessarily require a finding of the "distinctive value" of the lawyer, a requirement under DR 5-101(B)(4).

The most important difference between practice under the Model Code and rule 3.7 of the Model Rules is that there is no rule of imputed disqualification of an entire firm if one of the firm's lawyers will testify on behalf of the client.[210] This is a significant difference which reduces the incentive for making a motion to disqualify for tactical advantage. In this regard, rule 3.7(b) states that a lawyer may act as an advocate in a trial in which another lawyer in the lawyer's firm is likely to be called as a witness, unless there is a conflict of interest between the lawyer's testimony and the position of the client. If, however, the testimony of the lawyer is likely to be prejudicial to the client, disqualification may be appropriate. The comments note in this regard:

> [I]f there is likely to be substantial conflict between the testimony of the client and that of the lawyer or a member of the lawyer's firm, representation is improper. . . . If a lawyer who is a member of a firm may not act as both advocate and

witness by reason of conflict of interest, rule 1.10 disqualifies the firm also.[211]

Notes

1. There is considerable literature on the subject of conflicts of interest. *See generally Corporate Legal Ethics—An Empirical Study: The Model Rules, the Code of Professional Responsibility, and Counsel's Continuing Struggle Between Theory and Practice*, 8 J. CORP. L. 601 (Summer 1983); *Developments in the Law—Conflicts of Interest in the Legal Profession*, 94 HARV. L. REV. 1244 (1981).

2. This article discusses the applicable provisions of the American Bar Association (ABA) Model Rules of Professional Conduct (Model Rules), adopted by the House of Delegates of the ABA in August, 1983, and the ABA Model Code of Professional Responsibility (Model Code), originally adopted in 1969.

   The Model Code consists of three parts: the canons are 9 short, general "statements of axiomatic norms"; the ethical considerations (EC) are 136 aspirational guidelines "toward which every member of the profession should strive," but which are not mandatory; and the 41 disciplinary rules (DR) state "the minimal level of conduct below which no lawyer should fall without being subject to disciplinary action."

   Most state courts have adopted all or at least substantial portions of the Model Code. On July 19, 1984, the New Jersey Supreme Court adopted a new code of ethics for the state's lawyers based on the new ABA Model Rules. Currently over half of the states have adopted the Model Rules in some form. Even in states where the Model Rules have not been adopted, courts have referred to provisions of the new Model Rules in deciding conflicts questions. *See, e.g.*, Alexander v. Superior Court, 141 Ariz. 157, 685 P.2d 1309 (1984).

3. *See generally* Greene, *Everybody's Doing It—But Who Should Be? Standing to Make Disqualification Motions Based on an Attorney's Representation of a Client with Interests Adverse to Those of a Former Client,* 6 U. PUGET SOUND L. REV. 205 (1983); Note, *Attorney's Conflict of Interests: Representation of Interest Adverse to That of Former Client*, 55 B.U.L. REV. 61 (1975).

4. EC 4-6 provides in pertinent part: "The obligation of a lawyer to preserve the confidences and secrets of his client continues after the termination of his employment."

5. *See* MODEL CODE EC 4–5, which provides:

   > A lawyer should not use information acquired in the course of the representation of a client to the disadvantage of the client and a lawyer should not use, except with the consent of his client after full disclosure, such information for his own purposes. Likewise, a lawyer should be diligent in his efforts to prevent the misuse of such information by his employees and associates. Care should be exercised by a lawyer to prevent the disclosure of the confidences and secrets of one client to another, and no employment should be accepted that might require such disclosure.

6. EC 4–4 provides in this regard, "The attorney-client privilege is more limited than the ethical obligation of a lawyer to guard the confidences and secrets of his client. This ethical precept, unlike the evidentiary privilege, exists without

regard to the nature or source of information or the fact that others share the knowledge." *See also* Brennan's, Inc. v. Brennan's Restaurants, Inc., 590 F.2d 168, 172 (5th Cir. 1979).

7. Marco v. Dulles, 169 F. Supp. 622, 629 (S.D.N.Y.), *appeal dismissed*, 268 F.2d 192 (2d Cir. 1959) (decided under analogous provisions of the ABA Canons of Professional Ethics, the predecessor of the Model Code).

8. Fund of Funds, Ltd. v. Arthur Andersen & Co., 567 F.2d 225, 236 (2d Cir. 1977).

9. *See, e.g.*, NCK Org. Ltd. v. Bregman, 542 F.2d 128 (2d Cir. 1976); Cord v. Smith, 338 F.2d 516, 524–25 (9th Cir. 1964). *But see* Allegaert v. Perot, 434 F. Supp. 790 (S.D.N.Y.), *aff'd.*, 565 F.2d 246 (2d Cir. 1977) (plaintiff could not disqualify counsel for defendant even though the firm had access to plaintiff's information during course of prior plaintiff-defendant joint venture, since plaintiff knew that information conveyed to the law firm would not be kept from the defendant, which was the firm's long-standing client); Christensen v. United States Dist. Court for the Cent. Dist. of Cal., 844 F.2d 694 (9th Cir. 1988) (adopting *Allegaert* rule that substantial relationship test is inapplicable where former client had no reason to believe confidential information was not disclosed to current client, a senior partner at the same law firm as former client's counsel).

10. *See* Kevlik v. Goldstein, 724 F.2d 824, 850–51 (1st Cir. 1984); LaSalle Nat'l Bank v. County of Lake, 703 F.2d 252, 255 (7th Cir. 1983); Cheng v. GAF Corp., 631 F.2d 1052, 1056 (2d Cir. 1980), *vacated on other grounds*, 450 U.S. 903 (1981); *In re* Corrugated Container Antitrust Litig., 659 F.2d 1341, 1346 (5th Cir. 1981); Trone v. Smith, 621 F.2d 994, 998 (9th Cir. 1980); Westinghouse Elec. Corp. v. Gulf Oil Corp., 588 F.2d 221, 223 (7th Cir. 1978); T.C. Theatre Corp. v. Warner Bros. Pictures, 113 F. Supp. 265, 268 (S.D.N.Y. 1953).

11. 113 F. Supp. 265 (S.D.N.Y. 1953).

12. *Id.* at 268 (emphasis added).

13. *See, e.g., Trone*, 621 F.2d at 999–1000; General Elec. Co. v. Valeron Corp., 608 F.2d 265, 267 (6th Cir. 1979), *cert. denied*, 445 U.S. 930 (1980).

14. 479 F. Supp. 867 (E.D. Pa. 1979) (emphasis in original).

15. *Id.* at 871.

16. *See* Government of India v. Cook Indus., Inc., 569 F.2d 737, 739–40 (2d Cir. 1978); Silver Chrysler Plymouth, Inc. v. Chrysler Motors Corp., 518 F.2d 751, 754–55 (2d Cir. 1975).

17. *See* Evans v. Artek Sys. Corp., 715 F.2d 788, 791 (2d Cir. 1983).

18. *See LaSalle Natl'l Bank*, 703 F.2d at 255–56; Freeman v. Chicago Musical Instrument Co., 689 F.2d 715, 722 (7th Cir. 1982). *See generally* Peterson, *Rebuttable Presumptions and Intra-Firm Screening: The New Seventh Circuit Approach to Vicarious Disqualification of Litigation Counsel*, 59 NOTRE DAME L. REV. 399 (1984).

19. *See infra* notes 38–63 and accompanying text.

20. *See* Wilson P. Abraham Constr. Corp. v. Armco Steel Corp., 559 F.2d 250, 252 (5th Cir. 1977); Cord v. Smith, 336 F.2d at 524; *T.C. Theatre Corp.*, 113 F. Supp. at 268. *See also* People ex rel., Deukmejian v. Brown, 29 Cal. 3d 150, 156–57, 172 Cal. Rptr. 478, 480–81, 624 P.2d 1206, 1208 (1981) (State

Attorney General disqualified from suing a state agency after he had met with the agency on the issue in question; court applied rule that the attorney-client relationship raises an irrefutable presumption that confidences were disclosed).

21. Trone v. Smith, 621 F.2d 994, 999 (9th Cir. 1980); Cheng v. GAF Corp., 631 F.2d 1052, 1057–58 (2d Cir. 1980), *vacated on other grounds*, 450 U.S. 903 (1981).

22. *See* Analytica, Inc. v. NPD Research, Inc., 708 F.2d 1263, 1266–67 (7th Cir. 1983); *Cheng*, 631 F.2d at 1057–58. *See generally* Comment, *The Chinese Wall Defense to Law-Firm Disqualification*, 128 U. PA. L. REV. 677 (1980).

23. 708 F.2d 1263 (7th Cir. 1983).

24. *Id.* at 1274 (emphasis in original).

25. *See, e.g.*, Fund of Funds, Ltd. v. Arthur Andersen & Co., 567 F.2d 225, 234–36 (2d Cir. 1977).

26. 621 F.2d 994 (9th Cir. 1980).

27. *Id.* at 1002.

28. 724 F.2d 844 (1st Cir. 1984).

29. *Id.* at 847–48.

30. *Id.* at 849–51.

31. *See* First Wis. Mortgage Trust v. First Wis. Corp., 584 F.2d 201 (7th Cir. 1978) (en banc); Valley Title Co. v. Superior Court, 124 Cal. App. 3d 867, 885–87, 177 Cal. Rptr. 643, 653–54 (1981).

32. 305 F. Supp. 371 (S.D. Tex. 1969).

33. 144 Cal. App. 2d 284, 301 P.2d 10 (1956).

34. *Id.* at 290, 301 P.2d at 14.

35. 590 F.2d 168 (5th Cir. 1979).

36. 46 Cal. App. 3d 614, 120 Cal. Rptr. 253 (1975).

37. 559 F.2d 250 (5th Cir. 1977).

38. *Id.* at 253.

39. *Id.*

40. Trinity Ambulance Serv., Inc. v. G & L Ambulance Servs. Inc., 578 F. Supp. 1280 (D. Conn. 1984).

41. *See In re* Yarn Processing Patent Validity Litig., 530 F.2d 83, 89 (5th Cir. 1976).

42. Cox v. American Cast Iron Pipe Co., 847 F.2d 725 (11th Cir. 1988).

43. Westinghouse Elec. Corp. v. Gulf Oil Corp., 588 F.2d 221 (7th Cir. 1978).

44. 701 F.2d 85 (9th Cir. 1983).

45. *See, e.g.,* Hannan v. Watt, 147 Ill. App. 3d 456, 497 N.E.2d 1307, 100 Ill. Dec. 945 (Ill. App. 1 Dist. 1986); Cox v. American Cast Iron Pipe Co., 847 F.2d 725; River West Inc. v. Nickel, 188 Cal. App. 3d 1297, 234 Cal. Rptr. 33 (Cal. Ct. App. 1987).

46. *See* Kevlik v. Goldstein, 724 F.2d 824, 850–51 (1st Cir. 1984); *Valley Title Co.,* 124 Cal. App. 3d at 883–84, 177 Cal. Rptr. at 652–53. *See also* Dewey v. R.J. Reynolds Tobacco Co., 109 N.J. 201, 536 A.2d 243 (1988) (refusing to disqualify law firm at point of trial because of undue hardship to client, but sanctioning firm for failing to deal with conflict by denying compensation for work performed for client from that point on).

47. *See, e.g.*, Cheng v. GAF Corp., 631 F.2d 1052, 1058–59 (2d Cir. 1980), *vacated on other grounds*, 450 U.S. 903 (1981); Trone v. Smith, 621 F.2d 994, 999 (9th Cir. 1980); Arkansas v. Dean Food Prods. Co., 605 F.2d 380 (9th Cir. 1980), *overruled on other grounds, In re* Multi-Piece Rim Prods. Liab. Litig., 612 F.2d 377 (9th Cir. 1980).
48. *In re* Coordinated Pretrial Proceedings in Petroleum Prods. Antitrust Litig., 658 F.2d 1355, 1360–61 (9th Cir. 1981), *cert. denied*, 455 U.S. 990 (1982); *In re* Corrugated Container Antitrust Litig., 659 F.2d 1351, 1349 (5th Cir. 1981).
49. Board of Educ. v. Nyquist, 590 F.2d 1241, 1247 (2d Cir. 1979).
50. The text of the Model Rules and the comments thereto appear in the ABA/BNA LAWYERS' MANUAL ON PROFESSIONAL CONDUCT (LAWYERS' MANUAL) (1984). In this article, citations to the comments to the Model Rules will be to the *Lawyers' Manual. See* LAWYERS' MANUAL ¶ 01:124.
51. *Id.*
52. *Id.*
53. *Id.*
54. *Trone*, 621 F.2d at 999; *see also Cheng*, 631 F.2d at 1055–56, 1057–58. *See generally* DR 5-105(D) (if one attorney at a firm is disqualified, no other attorney at the firm may handle the matter).
55. *See, e.g.*, Price v. Admiral Ins. Co., 481 F. Supp. 374 (E.D. Pa. 1979) (irrebuttable presumption of shared confidences among partners in case involving former government attorney arising under canon 9).
56. 518 F.2d 751 (2d Cir. 1975).
57. *Id.* at 753–54.
58. *Id.* at 754.
59. *Id.* at 756–57.
60. *See generally* Peterson, *supra* note 18.
61. LaSalle Nat'l Bank v. County of Lake, 703 F.2d 252, 255–56 (7th Cir. 1983).
62. *Id.* at 257; Freeman v. Chicago Musical Instrument Co., 689 F.2d 715, 722, 723 (7th Cir. 1982).
63. *LaSalle Nat'l Bank*, 703 F.2d at 257.
64. *See, e.g.*, Schiessle v. Stephens, 717 F.2d 417 (7th Cir. 1983) (presumption not overcome when unrebutted affidavit of attorney from former firm stated that the partner who had switched firms had been the partner in charge of the matter at his former firm and had conducted numerous discussions with the client concerning the litigation).
65. *Id.* (new firm disqualified); *LaSalle Nat'l Bank*, 703 F.2d 252 (disqualification of plaintiff's law firm ordered when one of its new associates failed to overcome presumption of access to confidences of the defendant while in his former employment). *See also* Cheng v. GAF Corp., 631 F.2d 1052 (2d Cir. 1980), *vacated on other grounds*, 450 U.S. 903 (1981) (defendant's law firm disqualified when, in the middle of a case, it hired as an associate an attorney for a legal aid office that had been representing the plaintiff, even though that attorney had not handled the case at the legal aid office and his exposure to the client and his confidences had been relatively limited—and even though the new firm "screened" him from the matter); Motor Mart, Inc. v. Saab Motors, Inc., 359 F. Supp. 156 (S.D.N.Y. 1973) (disqualification ordered because plaintiff's attorney, in the course of former role as counsel for defendant, had represented

defendant in "essentially the same type of suit" and thus had had an opportunity to learn of defendant's policies, practices, and procedures generally).

66. *See, e.g.,* General Elec. Co. v. Industra Prod. Inc., No. F87-50 (DC N. Ind. Apr. 20, 1988) (presumption of shared confidences, which disqualified an entire firm because of one lawyer's conflict of interest, could extend to co-counsel firm but is rebuttable); Smith v. Whatcott, 774 F.2d 1032 (10th Cir. 1985) (co-counsel relationship alone does not warrant disqualification).

67. *See, e.g.*, Manning v. Waring, Cox, James, Sklar & Allen, 849 F.2d 222, 225 (6th Cir. 1988) (allowing the presumption of shared confidences to be rebutted by "specific institutional screening mechanisms"); Cook v. Cook, 559 F. Supp. 213, 215 (E.D. Pa. 1983) ("the inference that a lawyer possesses confidences which might have been given to members of his former firm is rebuttable").

68. *Manning*, 849 F.2d at 224.

69. Arkansas v. Dean Food Prods. Co., 605 F.2d 380, 385–86 (9th Cir. 1980), *overruled on other grounds, In re* Multi-Piece Rim Products Liability Litigation, 612 F.2d 377 (9th Cir. 1980).

70. *Id.* at 386.

71. *See, e.g.*, Atasi Corp. v. Seagate Technology, 847 F.2d 826, 831 (Fed. Cir. 1988) (noting that two district courts, under the relevant Ninth Circuit law, had allowed Chinese wall defenses, but declining to recognize either Chinese wall or "cone of silence" defenses in the instant case, since the Ninth Circuit itself had not yet spoken definitively on these defenses).

72. 631 F.2d 1052 (2d Cir. 1980), *vacated on other grounds*, 450 U.S. 903 (1981). *Accord*, United States v. Uzzi, 549 F. Supp. 979 (S.D.N.Y. 1982). For an example of an early case rejecting a Chinese wall approach (without using the term), *see* W.E. Bassett Co. v. H.C. Cook Co., 201 F. Supp. 821 (D. Conn.), *aff'd*, 302 F.2d 268 (2d Cir. 1962).

73. 631 F.2d at 1057 (quoting *Silver Chrysler*, 518 F.2d at 754).

74. *Id.* at 1058 (footnote omitted).

75. *See, e.g.*, Amoco Chems. Corp. v. D.C. MacArthur, 568 F. Supp. 42, 46–47 (N.D. Ga. 1983) (disqualification of new firm ordered when attorney changed sides; court observed that it would not allow screening when attorney moved from purely private-sector law firm rather than from government legal staff).

76. In Schiessle v. Stephens, 717 F.2d 417 (7th Cir. 1983), the Seventh Circuit stated:

> Factors appropriate for consideration by the trial court [concerning the adequacy of 'institutional mechanisms' for screening] might include, but are not limited to, the size and structural divisions of the law firm involved, the likelihood of contact between the 'infected' attorney and the specific attorneys responsible for the present representation, the existence of rules which prevent the 'infected' attorney from access to relevant files or other information pertaining to the present litigation or which prevent him from sharing in the fees derived from such litigation.

Id. at 421 (citing LaSalle Nat'l Bank v. County of Lake, 703 F.2d 252, 259 (7th Cir. 1983)).

77. Manning v. Waring, Cox, James, Sklar & Allen, 849 F.2d 222, 225 (6th Cir. 1988).

78. *LaSalle Nat'l Bank*, 703 F.2d 252; *see also Atasi*, 847 F.2d at 831.
79. *Schiessle*, 717 F.2d at 421.
80. 632 F. Supp. 418 (D. Del. 1986).
81. *Id.* at 424–25.
82. *Id.* at 427. This rationale was also noted approvingly in dicta in *Manning*, 849 F.2d at 226.
83. *See, e.g.*, Chugach Elec. Ass'n v. United States Dist. Court, 370 F.2d 441 (9th Cir. 1966), *cert. denied*, 389 U.S. 820 (1967) (disqualification ordered because one party's attorney previously had been general counsel for the opposing party); Hull v. Celanese Corp., 513 F.2d 568 (2d Cir. 1975) (disqualification of plaintiff's attorney ordered when, while litigation was pending, defendant's in-house counsel switched sides to become a party plaintiff in a title VII suit).
84. Arkansas v. Dean Food Prods. Co., 605 F.2d at 385–86.
85. *See supra* note 41 and accompanying text. *See also* Interstate Properties v. Pyramid Co., 547 F. Supp. 178 (S.D.N.Y. 1982).
86. 625 F.2d 433 (2d Cir. 1980) (en banc), *vacated on other grounds*, 449 U.S. 1106 (1981) (law firm that hired a former government attorney avoided disqualification by screening the former government lawyer).
87. *See* Cheng v. GAF Corp., 631 F.2d 1052, 1058 n.7 (2d Cir. 1980), *vacated on other grounds*, 450 U.S. 903 (1981).
88. Rule 1.10 of the Model Rules provides as follows:

> (a) While lawyers are associated in a firm, none of them shall knowingly represent a client when any one of them practicing alone would be prohibited from doing so by Rules 1.7, 1.8(c), 1.9 or 2.2.
>
> (b) When a lawyer becomes associated with a firm, the firm may not knowingly represent a person in the same or a substantially related matter in which that lawyer, or a firm with which the lawyer was associated, had previously represented a client whose interests are materially adverse to that person and about whom the lawyer had acquired information protected by Rules 1.6 and 1.9(b) that is material to the matter.
>
> (c) When a lawyer has terminated an association with a firm, the firm is not prohibited from thereafter representing a person with interests materially adverse to those of a client represented by the formerly associated lawyer unless:
>
> (1) the matter is the same or substantially related to that in which the formerly associated lawyer represented the client; and
>
> (2) any lawyer remaining in the firm has information protected by Rules 1.6 and 1.9(b) that is material to the matter.
>
> (d) A disqualification prescribed by this Rule may be waived by the affected client under the condition stated in Rule 1.7.

89. LAWYERS' MANUAL, *supra* note 50, ¶ 01:126–01:127.
90. *Id.* ¶ 01:125.
91. *Id.* ¶ 01:126.
92. *Id.*
93. *Id.* ¶ 01:127.
94. *Id.*
95. *Id.*

96. *Id.* ¶ 01:129.

97. *See generally* Comment, *Toward a New Ethical Standard Regulating the Private Practice of Former Government Lawyers*, 13 GOLDEN GATE L. REV. 433 (1983).

98. DR 9-101(B) states, "A lawyer shall not accept private employment in a matter in which he had substantial responsibility while he was a public employee."

99. DR 5-105(D) provides, "If a lawyer is required to decline employment or to withdraw from employment under a Disciplinary Rule, no partner, or associate, or any other lawyer affiliated with him or his firm, may accept or continue such employment."

100. ABA Comm. on Ethics and Professional Responsibility, Formal Op. 342 (1975).

101. *See, e.g.*, Armstrong v. McAlpin, 625 F.2d 433 (2d Cir. 1980) (en banc), *vacated on other grounds*, 499 U.S. 1106 (1981); Kesselhaut v. United States, 555 F.2d 791 (Ct. Cl. 1977) (en banc) (per curiam). *Cf.* Amoco Chems. Corp. v. D.C. MacArthur, 568 F. Supp. 42, 47 (N.D. Ga. 1983) (noting the policy considerations that allow screening of a former government lawyer, but not a private-sector lawyer, who joins a new firm).

102. Some ethics committees use the language of Model Rule 1.11, which requires the attorney to have "participated personally and substantially," when interpreting DR 9-101(B) under the gloss of Formal Opinion 342. *See* D.C. Bar Legal Ethics Comm., Formal Op. 177 (1986); Ill. State Bar Ass'n Comm. on Professional Ethics, Op. 85–10 (1986).

103. D.C. Bar Legal Ethics Comm., Formal Op. 177 (1986) (where a supervisory attorney's only involvement is to delegate a matter, the task is sufficiently clerical in nature so that it does not constitute substantial participation, but where he or she is consulted in any aspect of a case, the supervisory attorney will be considered to have had substantial responsibility for that case). *See* Securities Investor Protection Corp. v. Vigman, 587 F. Supp. 1358 (C.D. Cal. 1984) (the head of an SEC regional office who signed a civil complaint found to have substantial responsibility); United States v. Uzzi, 549 F. Supp. 979 (S.D.N.Y. 1982). *See also* Cheng v. GAF Corp., 631 F.2d 1052 (2d Cir. 1980), *vacated on other grounds*, 450 U.S. 903 (1981).

104. *See, e.g.*, Armstrong v. McAlpin, 625 F.2d 433 (2d Cir. 1980) (en banc), *vacated on other grounds*, 499 U.S. 1106 (1981). For a broad approach to the definition of a matter requiring disqualification, *see* General Motors Corp. v. City of New York, 501 F.2d 639 (2d Cir. 1974).

105. Formal Op. 342, *supra* note 100, at 6.

106. Brown v. District of Columbia Bd. of Zoning Adjustment, 486 A.2d 37 (D.C. App. 1984).

107. *See, e.g.*, D.C. Bar Legal Ethics Comm., Formal Op. 189 (1987).

108. Wagner v. Lehman Bros. Kuhn Loeb, 646 F. Supp. 643 (N.D. Ill. 1986); Kessenich v. Commodity Futures Trading Comm'n, 684 F.2d 88 (D.C. Cir. 1982); *In re* Opinion No. 569 of Advisory Comm. on Prof. Ethics, 511 A.2d 119 (N.J. 1986); Cleary v. District Court in and for the Eighteenth Judicial Dist., 704 P.2d 866 (Colo. 1985) (in circumstances not involving vertical intra-agency relationships, the presumption that an appearance of impropriety has been created may be rebutted by contrary evidence).

109. Formal Op. 342, *supra* note 100, at 3.

110. *In re* Opinion No. 569 of Advisory Comm. on Prof. Ethics, 511 A.2d 119, at

121, n.4 (N.J. 1986) (New Jersey remains one of the few states to adhere to the appearance-of-impropriety rule).

111. United States v. Washington, 782 F. 2d 807 (9th Cir. 1986) (case remanded for evidentiary hearing to determine whether attorney in fact received confidential information—appearance of impropriety an insufficient threat to override Sixth Amendment rights); United States v. Judge, 625 F. Supp. 901 (D. Hawaii 1986) citing Board of Educ. of New York City v. Nyquist, 590 F.2d 1241, 1247 (2d Cir. 1979); Thompson v. State, 330 S.E.2d 348 (Ga. 1985).

112. 625 F.2d 433, (2d Cir. 1980) (en banc), *vacated on other grounds*, 449 U.S. 1106 (1981).

113. *See, e.g.*, Securities and Exchange Commission's Regulation Concerning Conduct of Members and Employees and Former Members and Employees of the Commission, 17 C.F.R. § 200.735 (1984).

114. Max Jordan Bauunternehmung v. United States, 8 Cl. Ct. 793 (1985).

115. *See* D.C. Bar Comm. on Legal Ethics, Op. 162 (1985).

116. Rule 1.11(a) provides:

> Except as law may otherwise expressly permit, a lawyer shall not represent a private client in connection with a matter in which the lawyer participated personally and substantially as a public officer or employee, unless the appropriate government agency consents after consultation. No lawyer in a firm with which that lawyer is associated may knowingly undertake or continue representation in such a matter unless:
>
> (1) the disqualified lawyer is screened from any participation in the matter and is apportioned no part of the fee therefrom; and
>
> (2) written notice is promptly given to the appropriate government agency to enable it to ascertain compliance with the provisions of this Rule.

117. Rule 1.11(b) provides:

> Except as law may otherwise expressly permit, a lawyer having information that the lawyer knows is confidential government information about a person acquired when the lawyer was a public officer or employee, may not represent a private client whose interests are adverse to that person in a matter in which the information could be used to the material disadvantage of that person. A firm with which that lawyer is associated may undertake or continue representation in the matter only if the disqualified lawyer is screened from any participation in the matter and is apportioned no part of the fee therefrom.

118. 368 F. Supp. 258 (S.D.N.Y. 1973).

119. Kovacevic v. Fair Automotive Repair, Inc., 641 F. Supp. 237 (N.D. Ill. 1986); *see also* Kadish v. Commodity Futures Trading Comm'n, 548 F. Supp. at 1035; *In re* Marriage of Thornton, 486 N.E.2d 1288 (Ill. App. 1985).

120. *See supra* note 117.

121. LAWYERS' MANUAL, *supra* note 50, ¶ 01:130.

122. Rule 1.11(e) provides:

> As used in this rule, the term 'confidential government information' means information which has been obtained under governmental authority and which, at the time this rule is applied, the government is prohibited by law from disclosing to the public or has a legal privilege not to disclose, and which is not otherwise available to the public.

123. Rule 1.11(c) provides:

> Except as law may otherwise expressly permit, a lawyer serving as a public officer or employee shall not:
>
> (1) participate in a manner in which the lawyer participated personally and substantially while in private practice or nongovernmental employment, unless under applicable law no one is, or by lawful delegation may be, authorized to act in the lawyer's stead in the matter; or
>
> (2) negotiate for private employment with any person who is involved as a party or as attorney for a party in a matter in which the lawyer is participating personally and substantially.

124. *See* Regulations Concerning Post Employment Conflict of Interest, 5 C.F.R. § 737 (1987).

125. The suit against former White House Deputy Chief of Staff Michael Deaver for his alleged attempts to later lobby the White House on behalf of the Government of Canada and the Commonwealth of Puerto Rico was brought pursuant to 18 U.S.C. § 207(c). *See* Deaver v. Seymour, 822 F.2d 66 (D.C. Cir. 1987) (denying Deaver's request for declaratory and injunctive relief from independent counsel's exercise of prosecutorial authority).

126. The principal provisions of the Model Code concerning simultaneous representation of multiple clients are EC 5-1, EC 5-14, EC 5-15, EC 5-16, EC 5-19, and DR 5-105.

127. *See generally* Moore, *Conflicts of Interest in the Simultaneous Representation of Multiple Clients: A Proposed Solution to the Current Confusion and Controversy*, 61 TEX. L. REV. 211 (1982).

128. *See, e.g.*, Westinghouse Elec. Corp. v. Kerr-McGee Corp., 580 F.2d 1311 (7th Cir.), *cert. denied*, 439 U.S. 955 (1978); IBM v. Levin, 579 F.2d 271 (3d Cir. 1978); Cinema 5, Ltd. v. Cinerama, Inc., 528 F.2d 1384 (2d Cir. 1976); Estates Theatres, Inc. v. Columbia Pictures Indus., 345 F. Supp. 93 (S.D.N.Y. 1972).

129. *See, e.g.*, IBM v. Levin, 579 F.2d at 283; *Cinema 5*, 528 F.2d at 1387.

130. *Kerr-McGee*, 580 F.2d at 1321; *Cinema 5,* 528 F.2d at 1387.

131. *Estates Theatres*, 345 F. Supp. at 99.

132. *Id.* at 100 n.16.

133. Clay v. Doherty, 608 F. Supp. 295, 302 (N.D. Ill. 1985).

134. *In re* Johnson, 707 P.2d 573 (Or. 1985).

135. D.C. Bar Comm. on Legal Ethics, Opinion 143 (Nov. 13, 1984), 1 LAWYERS' MANUAL 554; Colo. Bar Ass'n Ethics Comm., Opinion 68 (Apr. 20, 1985), 1 LAWYERS' MANUAL 806.

136. *See* Ransburg Corp. v. Champion Spark Plug Co., 648 F. Supp. 1040 (N.D. Ill. 1986); Unified Sewerage Agency, Etc. v. Jelco, Inc., 646 F.2d 1339 (9th Cir. 1981); Fund of Funds v. Arthur Andersen & Co., 435 F. Supp. 84 (S.D.N.Y. 1977), *aff'd in part, rev'd in part on other grounds*, 567 F.2d 225 (2d Cir. 1977).

137. IBM v. Levin, 579 F.2d at 281.

138. Equal Employment Opportunity Comm'n v. Orson H. Gygi Co., Inc., 749 F.2d 620 (10th Cir. 1984).

139. *Cinema 5*, 528 F.2d at 1387.

140. IBM v. Levin, 579 F.2d at 280, 281 (disqualification ordered where law firm

which from time to time represented IBM on labor matters disqualified from representing another client in antitrust suit against IBM).

141. Ransburg Corp. v. Champion Spark Plug Co., 648 F. Supp. at 1043–44 (substantial relationship that does not apply to canon 5 which concerns itself with an attorney's duty of loyalty to present clients); Harte Biltmore Ltd. v. First Pa. Bank, 655 F. Supp. 417, 420–21 (S.D. Fla. 1987) (substantial relationship test not applicable where, as a result of merger, members of the same law firm simultaneously represent and oppose client in two different matters).

142. *Cinema 5*, 528 F.2d at 1387 (emphasis in original).

143. *Id.* at 1386–87 (citation omitted); *accord* IBM v. Levin, 579 F.2d at 280 (citing *Cinema 5*, 528 F.2d at 1386–87, and taking a very broad view of the various subjective intangibles that could constitute the adverse effects that could satisfy canon 5, and allowing simultaneous representation only when clients consent thereto).

144. Glueck v. Jonathan Logan, Inc., 653 F.2d 746, 749–50 (2d Cir. 1981).

145. *Id.* at 749–50. The law firm was disqualified in *Glueck*, with the Second Circuit taking an expansive approach in finding a substantial relationship between the representation entailed through the association (collective bargaining) and the adverse representation involved in the suit (wrongful discharge claim by an executive who was not a member of the collective bargaining unit).

146. IBM v. Levin, 579 F.2d 271, 280–81 (3d Cir. 1978).

147. Model Code DR 5-105(C); Unified Sewerage Agency v. Jelco Inc., 646 F.2d 1339, 1345–46 (9th Cir. 1981); IBM v. Levin, 579 F.2d at 280–81; Estates Theatres, Inc. v. Columbia Pictures Indus., 345 F. Supp. 93, 97 (S.D.N.Y. 1972). For an excellent discussion of the issue of consent, including the steps to be taken to obtain (and later prove) it, see Interstate Properties, Inc. v. Pyramid Co., 547 F. Supp. 178 (S.D.N.Y. 1982).

148. *See* Clay v. Doherty, 608 F. Supp. 295, 302 (N.D. Ill. 1985) (there may be classes of cases where the likelihood of adverse effect under DR 5–105(B) is so powerful as to justify automatic prohibition, nor will client's consent to the representation automatically justify the lawyer's maintenance of employment). *Cf.* Smith v. City of New York, 611 F. Supp. 1080, 1091 (D.C.N.Y. 1985) (canon 5 did not preclude city from tendering, or police officers fully advised of their options from accepting, representation by corporation counsel who were authorized to cast away officers' counterclaim as "bargaining chip" to obtain favorable overall settlement).

149. Westinghouse Elec. Corp. v. Kerr-McGee Corp., 580 F.2d 1311, 1321 (7th Cir.), *cert. denied*, 439 U.S. 955 (1978).

150. IBM v. Levin, 579 F.2d at 281–82.

151. United Sewerage Agency, Etc. v. Jelco, 646 F.2d 1339, 1346 (9th Cir. 1981); IBM v. Levin, 579 F.2d at 282. *See Interstate Properties*, 547 F. Supp. at 182–83.

152. Model Code DR 5-105(C); *Unified Sewerage Agency*, 646 F.2d at 1346–51.

153. *Unified Sewerage Agency*, 646 F.2d at 1350 (footnote omitted).

154. *Id.*

155. *Id.* at 1351; *see also* Pennwalt Corp. v. Plough, Inc., 85 F.R.D. 264, 270–72 (D. Del. 1980) (denying disqualification of plaintiff's counsel in an action being prosecuted by it against a sister corporation of another one of the firm's clients;

the opinion suggests that the absence of a substantial relationship between the two members was one factor in holding that there was no violation of canon 5).

156. Clay v. Doherty, 608 F. Supp. at 302.

157. *Compare* Cinema 5, Ltd. v. Cinerama, Inc., 528 F.2d 1384, 1387 (2d Cir. 1976) ("Whether such adverse representation, without more, requires disqualification in every case, is a matter we need not now decide."), *with* IBM v. Levin, 579 F.2d at 279 (if violation of canon 5 is shown, "it would ordinarily be error for the court to fail to declare the disqualification," and citing cases that doubts should be resolved in favor of disqualification).

158. Jackson v. J.C.Penney Co., 521 F. Supp. 1032, 1034–35 (N.D. Ga. 1981).

159. Estates Theatres, Inc. v. Columbia Pictures Indus., 345 F. Supp. 93, 100 S.D.N.Y 1972); *Pennwalt*, 85 F.R.D. at 272.

160. *Estates Theatres*, 345 F. Supp. at 100; *see Cinema 5*, 528 F.2d at 1386.

161. *Kerr-McGee*, 580 F.2d at 1322.

162. IBM v. Levin, 579 F.2d 271. It should be noted that the language of EC 5-19 seems to imply that the client who is dissatisfied with the simultaneous representation should get new counsel, but the case law is to the contrary.

163. Moore v. Margiotta, 581 F. Supp. 629 (E.D.N.Y. 1984) (plaintiffs' firm disqualified from representing both subclasses in a class action where court determined that there were conflicts between the relief sought by each subclass).

164. Margulies by Margulies v. Upchurch, 696 P.2d 1195 (Utah 1985) (conflict of interest created by law firm's representation of limited partnership of physicians in commercial litigation while at the same time representing medical malpractice plaintiffs in action against those physicians, required that the firm withdraw from both actions, not just one of them at the firm's option); *Harte Biltmore*, 655 F. Supp. at 421 (disqualifying attorney from representing First Pennsylvania Bank after he had withdrawn from representing Harte in an adverse representation to the Bank, and strongly suggesting that withdrawal would have been required from both clients in any case); Picker Int'l Inc. v. Varian Assoc., Inc., 670 F. Supp. 1363 (N.D. Ohio 1987) (after two law firms, one of which represented plaintiff and one of which represented defendant, merged, the resultant law firm was disqualified from representing either party).

165. IBM v. Levin, 579 F.2d 271, 275, 283 (3d Cir. 1978).

166. *See, e.g., In re* Coordinated Pretrial Proceedings in Petroleum Prods. Antitrust Litig., 658 F.2d 1355 (9th Cir. 1981), *cert. denied*, 455 U.S. 990 (1982) (refusing to disqualify company counsel from representing present and former employees in civil antitrust suit); *In re* Special Grand Jury, 480 F. Supp. 174 (E.D. Wis. 1979) (refusing to disqualify law firm that was being paid by the corporation from representing present and former employees who were witnesses before a grand jury). For a discussion of numerous decisions in this area, see generally Miller, *The Problems of Multiple Representation in the Investigation and Prosecution of Corporate Crime*, 29 FED. BAR NEWS & J. 217 (1982).

167. Pirillo v. Takiff, 462 Pa. 511, 341 A.2d 896, *aff'd per curiam*, 466 Pa. 187, 352 A.2d 11 (1975), *appeal dismissed and cert. denied*, 423 U.S. 1083 (1976). *See also In re* Grand Jury Empaneled Jan. 21, 1975, 536 F.2d 1009 (3d Cir. 1976).

168. United States v. RMI Co., 467 F. Supp. 915 (W.D. Pa. 1979), *appeal dismissed*, 661 F.2d 279 (3d Cir. 1981).

169. LAWYERS' MANUAL, *supra* note 50, ¶ 01:117.

170. *Id.* ¶ 01:118 (emphasis added).

171. *Id.* In contrast, when representation of one client may be "materially limited" by the attorney's responsibilities to another client or third person, the consent of the former client only to the representation is required under rule 1.7(b).

172. *Id.*

173. *See, e.g.*, Sellers v. Superior Court, 742 P.2d 292 (Ariz. Ct. App. 1987) (interpreting rule 1.7 as contemplating "an informed risk-benefit balancing approach" to the question of joint representation of co-parties where testimonial discrepancies exist).

174. *Id.* ¶01:119.

175. *Id.*

176. *Id.* ¶ 01:120.

177. 547 F. Supp. 178 (S.D.N.Y. 1982). *Cf.* IBM v. Levin, 579 F.2d 271 (the problems that arise when the consent is not memorialized).

178. *See* Interstate Properties, Inc. v. Pyramid Co., 547 F. Supp. 178 (S.D.N.Y. 1982); *see also* Allegaert v. Perot, 565 F.2d 246 (2d Cir. 1977).

179. MODEL CODE DR 5-102(B) (emphasis added).

180. ABA Comm. on Ethics and Professional Responsibility, Formal Op. 339 (1975). *See also* MODEL CODE EC 5-9, EC 5-10. *See generally* Note, *Disqualification of Counsel under the Advocate-Witness Rule: Fair or Futile?*, 48 U. CIN. L. REV. 794 (1979).

181. *See* J.P. Foley & Co. v. Vanderbilt, 523 F.2d 1357, 1359 (2d Cir. 1975); Brotherhood Ry. Carmen v. Delpro Co., 549 F. Supp. 780, 789 (D. Del. 1982); MacArthur v. Bank of New York, 524 F. Supp. 1205, 1209 (S.D.N.Y. 1981); J.D. Pflaumer, Inc. v. United States Dep't of Justice, 465 F. Supp. 746, 748 (E.D. Pa. 1979).

182. Universal Athletic Sales Co. v. American Gym, Recreational & Athletic Equip. Corp., 546 F.2d 530, 538 n.21 (3d Cir. 1976), *cert. denied*, 430 U.S. 984 (1977).

183. Cossette v. Country Style Donuts, Inc., 647 F.2d 526, 530–31 (5th Cir. 1981).

184. 523 F.2d 1357 (2d Cir. 1975).

185. 524 F. Supp. 1205 (S.D.N.Y. 1981).

186. *Id.* at 1208 (emphasis added).

187. 441 F. Supp. 1064 (N.D. Tex. 1977).

188. *Id.* at 1068 (emphasis in original).

189. *See* Zions First Nat'l Bank v. United Health Clubs, Inc., 505 F. Supp. 138 (E.D. Pa. 1981) (lawyer who prepared and recorded standard leasehold mortgage need not be disqualified where his client stated that he would not be called and the opposing party made no specific showing that lawyer's testimony would be necessary); Norman Norell, Inc. v. Federated Dep't Stores, Inc., 450 F. Supp. 127, 129–30 (S.D.N.Y. 1978) (lawyer-witness whose testimony would be necessary on certain issues because of his "particular knowledge" disqualified); United States *ex rel.* Sheldon Elec. Co. v. Blackhawk Heating & Plumbing Co., 423 F. Supp. 486, 488 (S.D.N.Y. 1976) (lawyer-witness with "knowledge crucial" to his client's case disqualified; court chastised counsel for stating that he would not testify, noting that his failure to do so would "likely result in ineffective assistance of counsel for his client," *id.* at 489 n.5).

190. *See, e.g.*, MacArthur v. Bank of New York, 524 F. Supp. 1205 (S.D.N.Y. 1981); *Supreme Beef Processors*, 441 F. Supp. 1064; *Sheldon Electric*, 423 F. Supp. 486; Greenebaum-Mountain Mortgage Co. v. Pioneer Nat'l Title Ins. Co., 421 F. Supp. 1348 (D. Colo. 1976).

191. 524 F. Supp. 1205 (S.D.N.Y. 1981).

192. *Id*. at 1211.

193. Bottaro v. Hatton Assocs., 680 F.2d 895, 897 (2d Cir. 1982).

194. *See* General Mills Supply Co. v. SCA Servs., Inc., 697 F.2d 704, 715 (6th Cir. 1982) (disqualification affirmed despite clients' waiver); *MacArthur*, 524 F. Supp. at 1209; Supreme Beef Processors v. American Consumer Industries, 441 F. Supp. 1064, 1068 (N.D. Tex. 1977); Draganescu v. First Nat'l Bank, 502 F.2d 550 (5th Cir. 1974), *cert. denied*, 421 U.S. 929 (1975) (applying the rule of disqualification to co-counsel).

195. *Supreme Beef Processors*, 441 F. Supp. at 1068 (footnote omitted).

196. 524 F. Supp. at 1209.

197. *Id*. at 1209–10.

198. 20 Cal. 3d 906, 576 P.2d 971, 145 Cal. Rptr. 9, *cert. denied*, 439 U.S. 981 (1978) (adopting a broad rule disqualifying a lawyer-witness and his firm).

199. 502 F.2d 550 (5th Cir. 1974), *cert. denied*, 421 U.S. 929 (1975).

200. 423 F. Supp. 486 (S.D.N.Y. 1976).

201. *See also* Connell v. Clairol, Inc., 440 F. Supp. 17, 19 (N.D. Ga. 1977) (no substantial hardship even despite a "dearth of competent counsel in the Atlanta area"); *Norman Norrell*, 450 F. Supp. at 130–31 (disqualification ordered because no showing of counsel's "distinctive value" to the client despite recognition of his "unique loyalty and diligence").

202. 524 F. Supp. at 1209.

203. 697 F.2d 704 (6th Cir. 1982).

204. *Id*. at 713.

205. *See* Greenebaum-Mountain Mortgage Co. v. Pioneer Nat'l Title Ins. Co., 421 F. Supp. 1348, 1352 (D. Colo. 1976); *see also* ABA Formal Op. No. 339 (1975) (giving as examples of substantial hardship the existence of a complex action that had been in preparation for a long time coupled with an unanticipated development making the lawyer's testimony necessary, or a "long or extensive professional relationship with a client" resulting in "an extraordinary familiarity with the client's affairs").

206. 3 LAWYERS' MANUAL 368–69 (N.Y. Sup. Ct., N.Y. County, Oct. 27, 1987).

207. Kroungold v. Triester, 521 F.2d 763, 766 (3d Cir. 1975); Zions First Nat'l Bank v. United Health Clubs, Inc., 505 F. Supp. at 140.

208. Rice v. Baron, 456 F. Supp. 1361, 1371 (S.D.N.Y. 1978) (citing Freeman v. Kulicke & Soffa Indus., 449 F. Supp. 974, 978 (E.D. Pa. 1978)).

209. *Id*. at 1371 (citing *Freeman*, 449 F. Supp. at 977).

210. LAWYER'S MANUAL *supra* note 50, ¶ 01:154. *See also Montcalm* (reaching the same result through case law).

211. *Id*.

Section IV

Managing the Cost of Corporate Litigation

As the cost of litigation has grown dramatically in recent years, corporate managers have increasingly turned their attention to efforts to manage their internal legal budgets to obtain the most cost-effective representation possible. It is imperative that corporate litigators who want to be effective and competitive understand and appreciate the techniques that have been used to make their work cost-effective. This section addresses these techniques with chapters discussing four aspects of cost management: (1) litigation budgets, (2) managing the case to improve efficiencies, (3) innovative approaches to controlling litigation costs, and (4) managing litigation costs through effective settlements.

The first portion of this section contains two chapters on the hows and whys of preparing a litigation budget. Chapter 10, by Alfred H. Hoddinott, Jr., and David M. Balabanian, maintains that budgets are now required by many corporations and are viewed not only as a road map for the litigation, but as indicia of counsel's commitment to efficiency and cost-effectiveness. The authors explain how to prepare a budget (including computer techniques) and suggest uses of budgets in the litigation environment. The authors also have provided Forms 20–22 in the Appendix, which demonstrate budget and projection formats. Chapter 11, by R. Doak Bishop, begins with budgeting theory, then focuses in detail on the preparation of various types of budgets. The article concludes with a discussion of the costs of budgeting and the use of budgets to control litigation costs. Form 23 in the Appendix demonstrates a number of budget formats discussed in Mr. Bishop's article.

The second portion of the section contains two chapters that focus on managing the case to improve efficiencies. In Chapter 12, Edward Lowenberg draws on his in-depth experience in defending toxic-substance litigation to present an innovative proposal for the coordinated defense of litigation: sharing counsel, stipulating that contribution and indemnity cross-claims will be deemed filed, and sharing costs and litigation risks. Mr. Lowenberg has also provided Forms 24–29 in the Appendix, which illustrate a number of agreements and motions necessary to effectuate such a coordinated defense. In Chapter 13, Ralph I. Miller focuses on the lawyer who is supervising the litigation team, and provides guidelines for the efficient delegation of tasks to other lawyers and the appropriate supervision of team members.

The third portion of the section contains four chapters offering insightful and imaginative proposals for controlling litigation costs. Chapter 14, by Peter M. Saparoff, includes insightful strategies and helpful citations for using the Rules of Civil Procedure for limiting the scope of the litigation and keeping attorney's fees under control. Mr. Saparoff includes some specific proposals for monitoring and controlling plaintiffs' attorney's fees, especially in class action litigation. In Chapter 15, Steven R. Steinberg provides an alternative to the traditional approach that "more is better." He argues persuasively that while some cases certainly demand that no stone be left unturned, most cases require that critical decisions be made regarding the costs and the anticipated benefits of turning each stone. In Chapter 16, Thomas J. Kavaler shows that the process of cutting costs demands that the client appreciate the risks inherent in a decision not to take certain discovery and suggests ways counsel can help clients make risk management decisions. Chapter 17, by David D. Leitch, focuses on the role of litigator as corporate problem solver and suggests ways the litigator can emphasize the needs of the client and the main issues of the case.

The final portion of the section consists of three chapters that focus on managing litigation costs through effective settlements. In Chapter 18, James C. Freund brings his perspective as a merger negotiator to the process of negotiating disputes. He describes the differences between negotiating and litigating and offers practical suggestions for finding a compromise and deciding when to settle. Chapter 19, by Paul H. Dawes and Richard A. Lapping discusses how counsel can prepare for special issues that can arise in the settlement of complex litigation, notably preventing disclosure of confidential information, the need to obtain bankruptcy court approval of a settlement, and determination of settlement authority in cases involving the federal government. Finally, in Chapter 20, Samuel R. Miller and Leigh Shields explore the risks attendant to a settling defendant in a multidefendant lawsuit.

The articles included in this section contain some of the most current thinking by experienced corporate litigators on the best methods for controlling the spiraling costs of litigation. The articles in this section are not only interesting but extraordinarily useful in day-to-day practice.

John A. Irvine
Boyar, Norton & Blair
Houston, Texas

Ten

Controlling Legal Costs: Budgeting for Litigation

Alfred H. Hoddinott, Jr., and
David M. Balabanian

The Current Status of Litigation Budgeting

Litigation budgeting first became the subject of wide comment at the beginning of the 1980s. Many lawyers regarded this development with considerable skepticism, even cynicism, and predicted that the difficulties inherent in projecting the costs of litigation would cause litigation budgeting to go the way of the Hula Hoop once the economy revived. That has not proved to be the case. On the contrary, despite a long-lasting economic recovery, interest in budgeting for litigation has grown along with the increased emphasis on making litigation a cost-effective means of resolving disputes.

While some corporations have used litigation budgets for years (Xerox Corporation has used them in one form or another since 1975), the use of litigation budgets has only recently become widespread. Their basic forms are rapidly becoming a matter of common knowledge. Lawyers who only two or three years ago had never seen a litigation budget (and doubted that one was possible) now prepare them routinely. More and more clients request them and regard a lawyer's familiarity with and receptivity to budgeting as a measure of the lawyer's commitment to efficiency and cost-effectiveness.

The Need for a Cost-Conscious Approach to Litigation

While the roles of in-house and outside counsel may diverge in many respects, both the litigation attorney and his or her corporate counterpart will do well to recognize and respond to the growing demands of corporate management for heightened cost-consciousness in litigation. In our

Alfred H. Hoddinott, Jr., is Assistant General Counsel, Litigation, at Xerox Corporation, Stamford, Connecticut. David M. Balabanian is a member of McCutchen, Doyle, Brown & Enersen, San Francisco, California.

increasingly litigious society, the costs associated with litigation often represent the major share of a company's total legal budget. Corporate managers, under pressure to estimate, monitor, and, wherever possible, reduce costs, and to evaluate the results of specific resource allocations, may nevertheless find they have little or no influence over litigation expenses once a lawsuit has been passed to outside counsel. This need not and should not be the case. Corporations and business-oriented law firms are developing the tools to help management play a more active role in planning and conducting litigation. Properly used, the litigation budget can be the key to this increased participation.

What Is a Litigation Budget?

A litigation budget consists of a set of assumptions about the tasks to be accomplished during the course of a lawsuit and the costs associated with those tasks. The nature of litigation makes exact predictions impossible, and budgeting is perhaps better viewed as art than science. The process of drafting a budget, however tentative, nonetheless provides corporate and outside counsel with a unique opportunity to tailor legal services to the specific needs and concerns of the client. By voicing its cost control objectives while the litigation is still at the planning stage, the client, through house counsel, can achieve greater economy and predictability in its legal expenses. A litigation budget encourages and facilitates cost control decisions by providing a graphic, concrete means of balancing the cost of a given legal task against its perceived potential benefit.

On a larger scale, budgeting can be helpful in assessing the merits of the lawsuit as a whole. A reasonably accurate budget allows outside and house counsel to examine the alternative courses the litigation might take as a result of potential strategic decisions and, accordingly, to weigh the risks and benefits of continued litigation against those of settlement. To provide the greatest possible savings to the client, this critical overall cost/benefit analysis must be undertaken as early as possible in the life of the lawsuit and reviewed frequently as the litigation progresses. A well-drawn budget, regularly updated by corporate and litigation counsel, is the key to this effort.

For outside counsel, the inspiration to budget is not drawn solely from the prospect of increasing cost-effectiveness. The creation and use of a budget can assist the outside attorney in organizing and carrying out his or her litigation objectives. In the course of drafting a budget, corporate and outside counsel are compelled to anticipate the litigation tasks that lie ahead. This planning process clarifies goals, giving both attorneys a better sense of the best and worst directions the litigation might take.

Finally, budgeting requires an exchange of expertise and information between the outside lawyer and the in-house counterpart. During the course of budgeting discussions, outside counsel may become aware of the client's especially strong desire to protect its public image, or its special concern about the protection of information it considers privileged or proprietary. Perhaps outside counsel will discover that the in-house staff has research or computer capabilities to lend to the litigation effort.

Similarly, house counsel, having acquired a clearer picture of the company's potential exposure and the timetable that will govern the litigation, will also develop a better understanding of the need for prompt, precise responses to litigation counsel's request for information or decisions.

Creating a Budget

The process of budgeting need not be overwhelming in its complexity. Indeed, a budget that attempts to compute in minute detail every expense associated with a lawsuit could hamstring the litigation and be a constant source of controversy between in-house and outside counsel, as well as cost more than it is worth. Rather, a budget should be designed to provide a realistic estimate of legal tasks and their attendant costs while preserving the flexibility necessary to effective litigation. Accordingly, there are no hard and fast rules for the construction of budgets. While some companies now require staff and outside attorneys to use standard budgeting forms and procedures, counsel will generally look to the type and size of case involved in determining when to prepare a budget and how comprehensive it should be.

In a small, relatively simple case, a fairly accurate budget for the entire course of the litigation may be prepared as soon as the suit is filed. Where exposure is limited and facts are few, an early cost projection will give counsel a clear idea of the settlement value of the case.

A different approach may be warranted in more complex cases where potential liability is substantial and extensive facts must be collected and analyzed. If the merits of such a case cannot be realistically appraised at its outset, counsel may decide to delay preparation of a comprehensive budget until initial discovery has been completed. Moreover, where protracted litigation appears likely, an attempt to predict the overall posture and dimensions of the lawsuit many months or even years in advance is, in all probability, pointless.

A more useful strategy under these circumstances is to formulate a rather general forecast of the volume and complexity of the legal services required, and then to compose a series of detailed cost projections, as needed, throughout the course of the litigation. The time span covered by each of these partial budgets may reflect natural divisions in the unfolding sequence of events in the action, or may correspond to fiscal periods defined by the client.

Whatever budgeting approach is ultimately selected, its effectiveness will be greatly enhanced if its execution is a joint effort of in-house and outside counsel. In the context of planning and budgeting a lawsuit, both attorneys develop an understanding of the key issues in the case; each becomes attuned to the needs and expectations of the other. Furthermore, the usefulness of the budget as a tool for predicting and regulating costs is a function of the accuracy of its assumptions about future legal maneuvers as well as the extent to which it reflects the client's specific goals and concerns.

Whenever possible, house counsel should follow through on their involvement in the planning process with direct participation in the litigation itself. The eventual size of a litigation bill reflects numerous day-to-day decisions, e.g., whether the depositions of remote witnesses are really necessary, whether another round of interrogatories is cost-justified. A cautious and competent outside attorney will be justifiably reluctant to forgo any potentially useful source of information. In contrast, an involved, informed in-house attorney can take responsibility for decisions of this nature. Thorough familiarity with the reasoning behind the budget's assumptions also gives house counsel a fair and accurate vantage point from which to evaluate the performance and cost-efficiency of the outside law firm.

The Elements of a Budget

A litigation budget consists of the following basic elements:

- Description of the legal tasks that in-house and outside counsel assume will be necessary, and a realistic estimate of the number of hours required for each. The hours can be either those of outside counsel and their legal assistants or of the in-house legal staff. Indeed, one of the more useful ways to use a budget is as a gauge on the expense and cost-effectiveness of previously uncontrolled inside legal time.
- The number and level (partner or associate) of attorneys, paralegals, or legal assistants needed, together with the hourly rate at which the outside firm bills for services at the necessary staffing levels.
- An estimate of disbursements for travel, copying, deposition costs, etc.

Budget Form

The Appendix contains two sample budgets prepared by the McCutchen, Doyle firm for actual cases. They illustrate possible budgeting techniques for two types of cases. Form 20 demonstrates the feasibility of budgeting discrete phases of a medium-sized contract case, and also addresses the problem of how to budget for alternate contingencies. Form 21, a detailed budget for the final pretrial year of an antitrust case, shows the utility of budgeting and planning for complex litigation. In addition, Form 22 illustrates the Xerox requirements for legal bills, which enables the company to receive detailed billing information so that it can compare actual expenses to budgeted expenses.

These are, of course, not the only alternatives available, and there is much to be said for additions at both ends of the spectrum. For instance, many companies that have much recurring litigation (e.g., product liability cases for a company that manufactures consumer products) budget for an entire case as soon as it is brought, whatever its anticipated duration. Thus, in a single budget they would include pleadings, motions, legal research, factual investigation, discovery, miscellaneous expenses, trial preparation, and trial. Such a system helps focus on the entire case at an early stage, when making the cost/benefit analyses necessary to determine settlement possibilities increases the opportunity for savings.

At the other end of the spectrum is some sort of aggregation of all of the cases a corporation has at any particular time. While the lawyers involved in a particular case will have intimate knowledge of its specific facts and budgetary assumptions, the general counsel of a major corporation will have responsibility for literally hundreds of lawsuits at any given time. The general counsel may wish to have a summary of all the cases reflecting bottom-line numbers for past and current actual expenses and what had been budgeted for those expenses, as well as the forecasts for the coming year.

Such information makes it possible to spot significant trends and also identify for closer scrutiny those cases which show major variations between budgeted and actual costs or a dramatic escalation in costs. Experience has shown that while there may be wide swings in individual cases, expenses generally even out over the total, so that overall expenditures tend to be within an acceptable range of the original plan.

The Impact of Litigation Budgeting on Staffing Decisions

Preparation of a litigation budget requires answering certain questions about staffing, including:

- What level of person is going to perform the task?

- How many people will be required?
- How long will they take?
- Will they be inside or outside personnel?

Many of these variables are interrelated (e.g., can a senior person perform the task in fewer hours than a junior?). The level of the person to be used for each task is determined to a great measure by the nature of the task. Basic legal research is well done by a junior associate. Arguing a motion for summary judgment is more likely reserved for the senior lawyer on the case. A deposition can be taken by a spectrum of legal talent in between, depending on its importance to the case. Also relevant is how expeditiously the task can be performed by any particular level of person, and how economically. A senior partner costs more than other partners, and partners cost more than associates. But an experienced lawyer may require two or three hours to prepare for and argue a motion, while a novice will spend ten to fifteen hours to prepare for what he or she has never done before.

Similar considerations exist with respect to the number of people assigned to any given task. Again, its nature will determine the number of people involved. A large file search cannot realistically be done by a single person. Many tasks may require several people at different levels. A file search might be most expeditiously conducted by a number of legal assistants, with a single lawyer in a supervisory capacity, rather than a number of junior lawyers.

Another factor is the amount of time available for the task. If the task must be completed within a tight time frame because of the exigencies of strategy or, as is more likely, because the court or the rules have set a deadline, then more people are required. The budget reflects these variables.

Another time factor is how long the task takes to complete. Is it a simple one that can be quickly and easily performed by one person? Or is it something requiring supervision, review, and constant change? Basic research on an isolated point of law for an internal memorandum is quickly and easily done by a junior associate. But the brief to accompany a motion for summary judgment may be made up of segments prepared by a number of lower-level lawyers; it is then reviewed and perhaps redrafted by a more senior lawyer.

A further staffing variable, for budgetary purposes, is whether the task can be performed by in-house personnel. Even when that is so, other considerations are still necessary to determine if there is a real saving in taking any particular task in-house. Perhaps a specific example will make the point: Assume a file search is required. Assume further that outside legal assistants are billed at $40 per hour, while in-house legal assistants cost the company about $25 per hour. It would seem a clear choice to use the in-house staff, since they are cheaper and probably know more about the company and its files. But what if the case involves an area of law with which the in-house staff is unfamiliar, so that it might have difficulty spotting the most pertinent documents? And what if the files are located in a city that is distant from the location of the in-house staff, so that hotel and living expenses must be set against the difference in the hourly rates? The advantages of using in-house staff for any given task may disappear when all of the factors are weighed.

The advantages of the budgeting process with respect to staffing do not inure solely to the benefit of the corporation. Budgeting also serves as a useful tool for the law firm in its own internal planning. It provides a means to focus on what mix of partners, associates, and support staff will be required—and over what period of time.

As the various alternative strategies for the litigation are weighed, their impact on the firm and its staff also becomes evident. The budget supplies information, not just as to the staff required for a particular case, but also with respect to income, expenses, the effect of disbursements on cash flow, and the availability of personnel for the staffing of other matters the firm may be handling.

The Role of the Computer in Litigation Budgeting

As with so many other business and legal tasks, computers have invaded the small world of the legal budget. Whether simple or sophisticated, a computer not only makes creating the budget easier, but also increases the data available and facilitates data manipulation.

As an example, the Xerox budgets of the type shown in Forms 20 and 21 are now created on Xerox 8010 computers using Spreadsheet software. Spreadsheet (or any other spreadsheet software) turns a simple computer into an electronic calculator that performs various functions instantaneously and with total accuracy. For instance, with just the number of hours and the hourly rates available, the computer is able to make all of the necessary computations when the hours are allocated to a particular financial quarter and to add in the necessary disbursements. If the final result of a budget suggests that it needs adjustment, small changes can easily be made, and the computer will recalculate the figures and create a new budget. As the budget is updated each quarter in the Xerox system, the computer simplifies those calculations. The existing budget is called up from the computer's memory and is updated by inserting actual expenses for the quarter immediately preceding. The computer then readjusts the assumptions and recalculates the yearly budget.

The computer's ability to store, retrieve, and manipulate data can also be used in other budget-related operations. Several corporations, such as Control Data, use computers to store basic data concerning every dispute involving the company. Examples of the type of data captured in a single place include the case name, date commenced, identification number, jurisdiction, parties, counsel, nature of the claims, status, budgetary information, value assessment (exposure/possibility of recovery), and closing information. Still other companies use computers for docket and schedule control.

The advantage of having all of this information in a single database is obvious. The computer can be used to organize cases by:

- Type of case
- Outside counsel
- Inside counsel
- Opposing counsel
- Court or state
- Size of case
- Amount of exposure

Two or more categories can be sorted in relation to each other, such as exposure on any particular type of case, or the case load of a particular in-house attorney, to see if he or she can handle more work.

The Effective Use of Budgeting

Properly prepared and used, the litigation budget can greatly assist management in its efforts to monitor and control rising legal costs. To be effective, however, a budget should be viewed as a living document, not as a rigid blueprint that counsel must follow slavishly. Once in-house and outside counsel have prepared a budget, they should schedule regular conferences to update and revise it, and should further revise it whenever a change in the complexion of the lawsuit calls for a reconsideration of strategy or a recalculation of costs. Should actual billings differ greatly from budgetary predictions, inside and outside counsel must reexamine their original assumptions and determine whether fresh approaches or personnel are needed.

The budget should not be allowed to obscure issues that transcend cost. For example, a loss in a given case could set a negative precedent, resulting in a proliferation of similar claims. The client may be facing criminal charges or a serious erosion of its public image. In these and similar situations, management must determine whether cost or policy issues are more critical.

Conclusion

Cost control in litigation will not "just go away." Our clients have seen that it works, and they will not let it go away. Therefore, it is up to both inside and outside counsel to see that it becomes a means of ensuring that the client obtains superior legal services in an economic fashion, without causing friction among any of the individuals involved. Conscientiously and wisely used, the budget can facilitate that end.

Eleven

Litigation Planning and Budgeting: Theory and Cost Control

R. Doak Bishop

Litigation Budgeting

A simple budget, which merely estimates the expected fees for certain stated activities, can easily be made for any lawsuit. The attorney begins by preparing a list of tasks that he or she expects will be undertaken and performed in preparing the case for trial.[1] He or she then decides how many people will be assigned to each task, the level of person required for each, and the amount of time each is expected to devote to the tasks.[2] At this point, it should be a simple matter to fill in the billing rate for each level of personnel and multiplying the estimated time for each task by the billing rate on a line-by-line basis. The lines are then summed to arrive at a grand total for the case. An example of a simple budget is found in Schedule A of Form 23, in the Appendix.

This is the way that most litigation budgets are prepared today; the extend of the information they convey is limited. It is very similar to the traditional open-ended budget in which counsel submits a single budget estimate, which can be accepted or rejected by the client. But the client is not informed about possible alternatives or given a real choice to make. As a result, some attorneys have recently begun to give the client two or more alternative budgets for the case as a whole in order to provide the client with some options.[3] But the basic problems remains: The client is not given the detailed information, which is necessary to control the direction of the lawsuit. On the other hand, if the client is faced with a list of alternatives for each potential task (i.e., each individual deposition or set of interrogatories), he or she is likely to be overwhelmed with unnecessary detail and to have inadequate time to analyze each of the alternatives.

Because the case will ultimately be won or lost on the basis of the legal theories and because discovery programs may vary widely for separate issues, the critical level for presenting budget options is not that of the law-

R. Doak Bishop is a member of Hughes & Luce, Dallas, Texas.

suit as a whole or that of the individual tasks, but at the issue level. This will provide management with an opportunity to compare the strengths and weaknesses of the issues (as identified in the planning stages) against the costs of alternative discovery approaches to those issues. The practical budgeting system described below, which combines traditional budgeting techniques with certain features of more sophisticated budgeting theories, will be referred to in this chapter as "issue budgeting," because it focuses upon alternative budgeting for the issues in the case.

Issue budgeting may be done either at the level of the individual issues or at the level of selected issues clustered together. The latter may be used to indicate discrete strategies or scenarios, or it may be used simply to indicate that all of the issues grouped together will require development of the same facts and evidence. In that case, deletion of one, but not all, of the clustered issues will not save the client money, so there is no need to budget those issues separately. The same may be true even when the facts may differ somewhat between two issues if all of the same depositions and other discovery will be required for both. For instance, if the same three depositions are slated for two discrete issues, and are allocated 70 percent to issue A and 30 percent to issue B, the deletion of issue A will not necessarily mean that the depositions will not be taken—this depends on the importance of issue B and the significance of the depositions to that issue. The percentage of time for a given task allocated to a particular issue may be misleading in this regard. These are the types of things that should be identified and analyzed in the "decision packages," which will be discussed below.

Since budgeting is a practical tool and not an academic exercise, it may not be necessary or reasonable (even when preparing separate budgets for each issue) to prepare alternative budgets for every possible issue in the case. There will often be issues of such overwhelming importance (in cases of great significance to the client) that the level of activities and of funding will be obvious. Likewise, there may be issues so marginal that only the barest of discovery programs can be justified. In such cases, it would be a waste of effort to prepare alternative budgets when the choice is clear-cut. But for other issues, the choice will not be so easy, and management will need a set of pretrial alternatives to permit it to combine the planning and budgeting functions and to make rational funding choices. Inside and outside counsel should jointly discuss and decide which issues to budget alternatively.

When preparing such options, counsel should make each alternative budget as realistic as possible within the basic assumptions made for that option, and the assumptions underlying each alternative should be clearly identified. Counsel should avoid falling into a rut of presenting three alternatives for each issue (arbitrarily assuming a comprehensive list of tasks, a minimal list, and an intermediate list), although such a pattern will, at times, be called for. A worst-case analysis (in which the opposing side demands the fullest possible discovery) may be included as a standard alternative, and in any event, counsel must factor into the budget the opposing side's likely discovery plan and both sides' probable response to the other's discovery program. For example, if one side demands maximum discovery, the other will probably do the same. Trial counsel is employed for his or her judgment, and the exercise of that judgment should exclude wasting time in preparing unrealistic, arbitrary alternatives just for the sake of saying that an option has been presented; each option should present a definite scenario and purpose and be based upon clearly identifiable assumptions. An example of alternative budgets for a breach-of-contract issue is set forth in Schedules B and C of Form 23.

The first step in issue budgeting is the preparation of a strategic plan for the prosecution or defense of the lawsuit. The strategic plan should, at a minimum, list the issues and rank them in terms of their importance to the success of the lawsuit. For example, if the plaintiff is asserting six theories for recovery, the litigation plan should include a judgment as to which of the issues are considered strongest, which are considered marginal, and which are considered as having potential, with a list of the problem areas that must be overcome for each. Ideally, the strengths and weaknesses of each issue should be quantified. This type of analysis will be important in determining the extent of activities and expenditures to be authorized for each issue.

The next step is to take the litigation plan and develop a pretrial program to meet the plan's objectives. This program should be categorized into the ultimate legal (and in some cases, the important factual) issues in the case, and a pretrial budget should be made for each such issue or cluster of issues. This will only be necessary for the pretrial aspects of the case, because this is the area in which the greatest expense of the lawsuit will be concentrated.

From a mechanical standpoint, a budget for a pretrial program is developed in much the same way as a traditional budget. A list of attorney tasks or activities must first be made, and then segregated according to the issues. There will undoubtedly be overlaps, because a single set of interrogatories, request for admissions, or request for production of documents may cover several different issues. The same may, of course, be true for a single deposition or motion. Therefore, each separate issue budget should list in its pretrial program each task with which that issue will be concerned (even if that task is also listed in other issue budgets). The overlaps are harmonized by listing beside each task that is designated in more than one budget, a percentage representing the portion of the total time required for the task that will be devoted to that issue. Similarly, the dollar amounts listed beside each task in each budget will be only the amount reflecting the proportion of the task's total time devoted to that issue. For example, if the purpose of a given deposition is to develop evidence for antitrust, breach-of-contract, and fraud issues, the deposition should be listed in the issue budget for each of these causes of action with a parenthetical next to it. Thus 60 percent might be specified in the antitrust budget, indicating that 60 percent of the total cost of the deposition will be allocated to that issue, and varying percentages would appear in the other sections, such as 30 percent under breach of contract and 10 percent under fraud, so that the percentages add up to 100 percent. In this way, the total cost is included but spread among the relevant theories.

The development of the list of tasks is one of the most difficult, yet critical, steps in preparing a budget. It is important that this list be as comprehensive as possible for each issue. In preparing this list, it may be helpful for planning purposes to group the activities into various phases of the case, such as investigative/research, pleadings, discovery, motions, and trial preparation.[4] Examples of lists of tasks classified by phases of the case are shown in Schedules A, B, and C of Form 23, with Schedules B and C addressing a single breach-of-contract issue. These cover the activities to be performed by the attorneys. Examples of lists of tasks for the paralegals working on the case are shown in Schedules A and E of Form 23, with Schedule E representing the paralegal tasks for the same breach-of-contract issue budgeted in Schedules B and C. The final part of the total case budget for fees, which is not segregated into separate issue budgets, will be the trial and post-trial stages of the lawsuit. Schedule D shows this phase of the overall budget. A budget for these phases is also incorporated in the simple budget shown in Schedule A.

Once the activity lists have been prepared, the lawyer tasks are assigned to different levels of attorneys, depending upon the staffing of the case and the difficulty and significance of the task. For example, research may be delegated to young associates, some depositions may be assigned to senior associates or young partners, while other depositions and hearings may be handled by more senior partners.

When the staffing level for each activity has been assigned, then the time for each task must be estimated. Estimating the time for completion of each task may be difficult at first, but as lawyers grow accustomed to budgeting (and perhaps generate and maintain historical records on the time it takes to accomplish various kinds of activities with different staffing levels), the estimation process will become easier and more precise. After the time has been estimated, it will be a simple matter to add in the billing rate for the various staffing levels involved, multiply it by the number of hours estimated for the task, and reach a projected cost for each activity listed. The estimated costs for all tasks are then added together, and a grand total for the issue is determined. This procedure is followed for each controlling legal issue or cluster of issues, and in certain instances, it may be done for selected, highly important and discrete, factual issues.

One of the more important aspects of the issue budgeting system is the preparation of a "decision package" for each issue for which alternative budgets are made. These decision packages will often overlap with the litigation plan, and may be included within it. They should identify the differing assumptions underlying each alternative budget, the significant differences in the list of tasks, the risks run by deletion of these tasks, and (to the extent counsel can do so) a cost/benefit analysis of the various options for each issue. Counsel should rank the decision packages according to the priority he or she gives to each issue and to each alternative approach to each issue. An example of a simple decision package is found in Schedule H of Form 23.

This system of litigation budgeting has major advantages over traditional budgeting techniques. It focuses the attention of inside and outside counsel where it properly belongs: on the controlling legal and factual issues. It permits the general counsel to make decisions on the funding of cases at the issue level, which is the level on which the case will be ultimately decided. General counsel does not have to become bogged down in the decision making on each individual task or activity, nor is he or she limited to choosing from among one or two self-contained, total budgets for the whole case. Moreover, litigation budgeting fits smoothly into the analytical and planning process and provides the manager with the appropriate level of detail and flexibility to make rational decisions and to mold the case budget to the needs and the resources of the company.

Expense Budgeting

Another part of the overall budget that should be developed for each case is the expense budget. Counsel should approach preparation of this budget in very much the same way as the issue budgets. The first step in preparing the expense budget is to identify the separate items of expense. The next step is to estimate the quantities of particular items to be consumed, the number of trips that will be required to a certain locale, the number of days required for each trip, the number of photocopies that must be made, and so on. The cost of each such item can be readily obtained and applied to the quantity estimates so that cost projections can be made for each. (One item that is slightly more difficult to estimate is the cost of expert witnesses, although this can and should be included with the best estimate possible.) The figures for each are then summed to provide a grand total for all expenses.

Certain optional items might be included in the expense budget as well, such as the cost of a computer system for controlling documents or the cost of employing a social science firm to aid in selecting the jury, analyzing the issues and arguments to be presented, or communicating persuasively with the jury. These expenses will not be cost-effective in every case, but they can be very useful in some large cases and should be included on any standard list of expense items. They can easily be crossed off the standard list if they do not apply in a given situation. An example of an expense budget is included in Schedule F of Form 23.

Periodic Budgeting

Since one of the purposes of litigation budgeting is to aid management in anticipating and controlling the company's cash flow, it may be necessary to provide a breakdown of the estimated costs of the lawsuit on a periodic basis, such as monthly or quarterly. An example of a monthly budget is provided in Schedule I of Form 23. This can best be prepared after completion of the issue budgets, the trial and posttrial budget, and the expense budget.

To assist management in controlling its cash flow on a periodic basis, it is not necessary to segregate the estimated time by issues, or to separate either the attorney's time from that of the paralegals or the fees from the expenses. A single periodic estimate is all that is necessary. In preparing such a breakdown, it may be helpful to counsel to do so by phases of the case, since the activities in each phase will occur more or less in the same time frame, and this overall time frame may be estimated (for a case in a given court) with some degree of accuracy. For example, counsel may predict that the investigative/research phase of the case will last 30–60 days, the pleadings phase approximately 30–60 days, the discovery phase 180–270 days, the motion phase 30–60 days, trial preparation 30–60 days, and trial 15–30 days. By reviewing the activities listed within each phase and their estimated costs, and by then allocating them within the predicted time range for that phase of the case, counsel can (with some reasonable degree of accuracy) estimate the monthly or quarterly bill for fees. By then factoring in the expense budget amounts, the overall expected bill can be projected by month or by quarter.

Computers

Although a discussion of the use of computers in litigation is beyond the scope of this article, counsel should recognize their potential value in litigation budgeting, particularly when alternative budgets are contemplated. Personal or microcomputers can easily and quickly recompute whole columns of numbers when one or more numbers are varied due to changing assumptions. Thus, alternative budgets for the same issue can be developed in a fraction of the time that it would take to calculate and draft them by hand. But even for more traditional budgets, collecting, storing, structuring, calculating, restructuring, and recalculating data (which are necessary functions for the preparation of budgets) are what computers do best. In setting out to create a budget, trial counsel would do well to consider using a computer.

The Timing and Precision of Budgeting

Computer programmers have a saying about the output of their machines: "Garbage in, garbage out." The same thing is true of making budgets. If outside counsel is required to render a budget before getting his or her arms around the case, the resulting product may be less than useful. The optimum time for preparing the budget is after counsel has had an opportunity to interview the critical witnesses, review the most important documents, do the initial research, and generally ask about and get an idea of the number of issues, witnesses, and documents involved. If counsel plans for a 5000-document and twenty-witness case, and then learns that it is a 100,000-document and sixty-witness case, the initial budget will be worthless and, perhaps, even misleading.

A different way of dealing with this problem is by providing a range of time and dollar figures in the initial budget spanning a worst- to a best-case analysis. This type of initial budget would ideally set certain specified pretrial stages of the case at which outside counsel would provide increasingly refined and definitive budgets. When insufficient information is available, this should solve the problem of premature budgeting.

The planning function of a budget must also be considered in deciding when to prepare the budget. If the preparation of a thorough and fully considered budget is delayed while the case progresses, so will the planning process. While it may be argued that this prevents counsel from getting too locked in to a set strategy with no freedom to react to changing circumstances, the other side of the argument is that it retards the strategic planning process and encourages counsel to improvise the case development. It is only with such a plan that counsel can control the case, rather than having the case control counsel; besides, there is nothing inherent in the nature of a plan that prohibits counsel from alertly reacting to new or unexpected developments and altering the plan as necessary. Indeed, counsel is more likely to spot and react quickly to exigencies requiring such changes when working from a plan than in the absence of one.

Just as plans can and do change in the light of new developments, so do budgets (as will be discussed more fully). A budget, however well planned and detailed, is not and cannot be static, and neither inside nor outside counsel should expect it to be so. Understanding the imprecise and fluid nature of budgets should prevent outside counsel from harboring any irrational fears of the process. But by the same token, changes in the budget should not always be one-sided; counsel must be alert to delete tasks that become obsolete and should not permit the budget to dictate spending on unnecessary activities. In light of the nature of the process and its importance and relationship to planning, a full budget should be prepared (in the most precise detail possible) as early as counsel can reasonably get his or her arms around the case, and the budget should be refined and altered as necessary thereafter.

Costs of Budgeting

There are, inevitably, certain costs associated with the very process of preparing a budget. These must be taken into account in determining what type of budget to prepare for a given case; the cost of preparing the budget in attorneys' time must be compared to the benefit to be obtained from use of the budget. It obviously makes no sense to require full issue budgets for numerous issues in a case in which only $3000 is at stake. Only the preparation of a simple traditional budget, at most, could be justified for such a small case.

In very large cases, of course, much more extensive budgets should be prepared. Outside counsel may be required to spend considerable time on such a budget. In that situation, outside counsel should discuss with management the billing of the time for the preparation of the budget (whether hourly or by fixed fee), since this in and of itself is a service to the client. With less extensive budgets, counsel may wish to bill the time to firm administration or some other internal account, rather than to the client. But however it is handled, it should be a matter of prior consultation and agreement between the company and its lawyers.

Controlling Litigation Costs with the Budget

The budget itself does not actually control costs, except as it serves as a self-fulfilling prophecy—a target at which counsel should aim. The control is provided by management (or counsel) periodically comparing actual costs against estimated costs and then taking affirmative steps to determine and correct the reasons for any deviation.

Of course, a budget is merely a forecast of future costs based upon estimates.[5] (The estimates, in turn, are based upon a set of stated assumptions, which are necessarily imprecise.[6]) If the estimates are incorrect for any reason, then the budget will not provide an accurate model with which to compare actual costs. Similarly, if changing conditions alter the strategic or tactical plans in the midst of operations, as often happens with litigation, then the budget will also be inaccurate as a model.

In either of these situations, the budget should not be permitted to arbitrarily dictate the maximum level of expenditures in light of the circumstances. But neither should the budget be ignored, for the budget permits management to plan the financial operations of the company by gauging the periodic future inflow and outflow of cash. Without a budget to work from, management will be unable to plan rationally for the cash flow drain resulting from litigation. As soon as budgetary estimates are determined to be erroneous or conditions change sufficiently to require alteration of the budget, the budget should be revised in consultation between inside and outside counsel.

When costs begin to exceed budget estimates, the situation should be analyzed to determine the reason for the discrepancy.[7] This is the initial critical step in using a budget to control costs. Once the analysis is complete, the second critical step in cost control should occur: Either management or counsel should take appropriate action to regulate or limit costs or to revise the budget. If the difference resulted from carelessness, waste, or lack of knowledge of the budgeted figures, then the matter should be discussed with the responsible parties, and cost control procedures (such as advance approval before costs are incurred) should be tightened to ensure that the differential will not recur.

Of course, discovering and correcting budgetary variances in a timely manner requires a review and comparison of actual costs and budgeted costs *at least* periodically, preferably monthly. To provide tighter control over ongoing costs, counsel should consider the use of microcomputers to furnish daily time records, much as accountants do, rather than waiting until the end of the month to learn what costs have been incurred. Without some sort of periodic review and comparison of actual and budgeted costs, a budget will be of no use as a device to control costs. Periodic budget review is the sine qua non of cost control.

Just as important as periodic review is periodic consultation between inside and outside counsel. Such consultation provides outside counsel with an opportunity to discuss upcoming activities and any changes in the litigation plan or program. Such changes are, of course, frequent in litigation because of the necessity of responsiveness to the opposing party's actions. Unfortunately, the issues to be raised and the activities to be undertaken are not solely within the control of one party or the other.[8] Periodic consultations on the budget can often prevent unpleasant surprises and hard feelings—on both sides.

Conclusion

Litigation budgeting is a relatively new idea among practicing trial lawyers. But now that the concept has achieved some level of acceptance, it is time to critically examine the nature of such budgets and their usefulness in controlling the case. The issue budgeting system described and recommended in this chapter, which integrates the planning and budgeting functions and which focuses on the critical level (the issues) for appraising options and controlling costs in litigation, is a practical approach that will aid inside counsel in carrying out the mission of actively overseeing and managing the company's litigation. It should also provide a useful bridge between the well-developed and sophisticated management theories of budgeting for the enterprise and the practical necessities of litigation.

Notes

1. Quinn, *Litigation Budgets Ease Inside Counsel's Concern*, Legal Times, Jan. 17, 1983, at 15, col. 3.
2. *Id.*
3. Lempert, *Litigation Budgeting: Yes After All*, Legal Times, March 22, 1982, at 2, col. 3.
4. *See generally* Quinn, *supra* note 1.
5. W. RAUTENSTRAUCH & R. VILLERS, BUDGETARY CONTROL 247 (New York 1968).
6. Quinn, *supra* note 1, at 15, col. 2–3.
7. RAUTENSTRAUCH & VILLERS, *supra* note 5, at 246.
8. Lempert, *supra* note 3, at 2, col. 4.

Twelve

Shared Use of Counsel in the Defense of Toxic-Substance Litigation—Petrochemicals

Edward Lowenberg

It is significant that in its bankruptcy filing, Manville cited the increasing and oppressively burdensome costs of its asbestos litigation as a cause of that corporation's decision to seek the protection of bankruptcy. The goal of containing the costs of multiparty toxic-substance litigation and, at the same time, enhancing the effectiveness of the defendants' case preparation and trial presentation becomes a higher priority when viewed in the context of the Manville alternative. Having invited a comparison between asbestos litigation and toxic-substance litigation involving petrochemicals, this chapter will attempt to distinguish toxic-petrochemical litigation and suggest a means of attaining the enhanced cost and trial efficiencies that is available to all industries involved in the manufacture, production, and/or distribution of generic or similar substances.

Toxic-substance lawsuits involving petrochemical products or petrochemical-containing products are substantially different from their predecessors, the asbestos and drug exposure lawsuits. Asbestos has, through accepted medical diagnostic practices, been linked at least synergistically to certain human cancers. Certain drug formulations have similarly been linked to human disorders through compelling epidemiological statistical correlations. With a few notable exceptions, however, the majority of the growing number of lawsuits involving petrochemical products, such as mineral spirits, toluene, xylene, kerosene, gasoline, benzene, and other solvents, are notable for the lack of scientific or medical proof of causation. These cases can be effectively defended on the causation issue absent masochistic, albeit traditional, defense practices.

Similarly, the suspected, if not known, linkage between certain chemicals and human ills has been set forth in the sales and product-handling literature of the petrochemical industry for several decades. The issue of adequacy of warnings can be effectively presented to the fact finder at the

Edward Lowenberg is Litigation Counsel for Exxon, its affiliates and subsidiaries, Houston, Texas.

time of trial absent the redundancy and/or inertia of multiple-defense counsel.

There does exist a potential for greater expenses attendant to the trial of a petrochemical lawsuit than an asbestos lawsuit. In the petrochemical lawsuits, the courts and testifying experts have moved to the front, if not out in front, of the generally accepted opinions and literature of the scientific and medical community. The shared use of competent experts provides a defense efficiency second, if not equal, to the efficiencies and effectiveness of the shared use of trial counsel in toxic-substance lawsuits involving mass or multiple corporate defendants.

The Problem of Single-Counsel Representation

In multidefendant litigation involving the same or similar generic products, it may no longer be appropriate, efficient, or effective for each defendant to be represented by a separate law firm. In a Beaumont, Texas, jury trial, over seventy original defendants and third-party defendants showed up at the courthouse with separate counsel, accompanied by assorted associate counsel and over fifty in-house and insurance carrier representatives to offend the jury with their presence, even though only seven attorneys had by agreement of all been assigned "speaking" trial roles. The duplicative pleadings and presence of "spectator" counsel certainly taxed the resources of the court, the clerk, and the client corporations and/or their carriers. What became apparent from that experience was that a different approach to multidefendant litigation was needed that could more efficiently use and fund trial counsel, expert witnesses, and case administration, and at the same time provide for the most cost-effective effort.

The different approach needed may be the concept of the shared use of defense counsel. It has been tried in a growing number of cases and has shown itself to be a "better mousetrap" for litigation efficiencies and a very cost-effective means of containing litigation cost.

Several objections have been raised to sharing a single law firm or, alternatively, to grouping defendants with like products or along producer and distributor tiers with two or more law firms (depending on the number and categories of defendants). These objections are categorized and rebutted in the following paragraphs.

Entitlement to Multiple Counsel

Objection: The insured is entitled to one counsel to represent its interests or uninsured vulnerability and one counsel for the interest covered by its insurance.

This can be resolved by inviting the insured's manager or house counsel to explore the benefits and enhanced likelihood of a defense verdict from the joint use and funding of single or several, as opposed to multiple, counsel. This author is ready and willing to provide your carrier or insured with the names and numbers of satisfied users of the shared counsel approach to multidefendant litigation. The entitlement to multiple counsel for a single-party defendant can be waived, or merely left unexercised, while the sharing approach is attempted.

Possible Inherent Conflicts

Objection: There may be inherent conflicts among the defendants reflecting indemnification demands and/or differences in the supply volume or products of the prospective "sharing" defendants.

In the actual experience of one company that has participated in over sixty informal sharing agreements, no dispute arose between the sharing co-defendants that could not be resolved out of court between the corporate and insurance lawyers and managers. In one instance, a perceived indemnification conflict was resolved by agreement to preserve the prospective dispute until after the defense against the plaintiff's cause had been concluded. That matter was subsequently resolved amicably between the parties.

The differences between the sharing defendants may require a revision of the usual equal-share formula for allocating litigation costs. The flexibility and informality of the agreement allows the parties the ability to negotiate and, if necessary, separate to the use of different trial counsel, if that is what the circumstances mandate.

Uncertainty about Potential Conflicts

Objection: There is no way of knowing at the onset of litigation whether or what prospective or, as yet, unknowable conflicts may arise between the sharing co-defendants.

There is also no way of knowing whether the prospective or unknowable conflicts will ever arise. The benefits of a shared and cost-efficient initial discovery effort more than offset the possibility of a later need for the use of separate counsel. The insured, of course, appreciates the efforts of the insurer to avoid potential conflicts and to subordinate cost efficiencies to the greater duty of the fiduciary insurer to its insured. However, the insured's management, aided by informed house counsel, can waive (and has waived in a growing number of cases) the possible conflicts objection and can authorize the use of shared-counsel agreements.

Ethical Issues Concerning Solicitation

Objection: Retained outside counsel cannot ethically solicit additional clients, nor as a practical matter can one insurer's representative solicit another insurer's insured to participate in a sharing of a single-counsel arrangement.

The effort to organize and invite co-defendants to share the use and costs of a single law firm can be and will be willingly undertaken by one of the growing number of informed in-house company counsel responsible to toxic-substance litigation. Many of these in-house counsel are employed by self-insureds.

Need for Cross-Action and Contribution Claims

Objection: The operation of state statutes for contribution among joint tort-feasors may require the existence of a pleading cross-acting or otherwise seeking contribution from co-defendants.

All defendants, or counsel-sharing co-defendants, can jointly move the entry of an agreed order to have "necessary" contribution or cross-actions deemed extant and answered without the need to file same. This will be appreciated by court, the clerk of the court, and the numerous legal secretaries who would otherwise be required to read, file, or prepare the duplicative, identical, unnecessary separate pleadings of multiple co-defendants. (See Forms 26 and 27 in the Appendix for a sample cover page and motion.) Cross-actions and contribution claims usually provide no benefit to the defense of the original lawsuit, and more often signal the plaintiff that defense counsel are levering each other to produce settlement.

Risks of Sharing Proprietary Information

Objection: The separate corporate defendants will be forced to share proprietary or confidential data, either directly or through their shared counsel, with competitors in the marketplace who happen to be counsel-sharing co-defendants.

The basic formulation of many petrochemical substances and products is, if not generic, so well known to competitors in the marketplace that the "trade secret" objection is of little consequence. Moreover, the allegations, e.g., cancer, neuropathy, levied against petroleum-based products have not as yet claimed that secret additives are the causative factor, but rather, that all of the defendants' basic products are contaminated with some naturally occurring element that may be carcinogenic or toxic.

In any event, any "confidential" data imparted to trial counsel need not be shared with co-defendants unless the cooperating defendants elect to share such information. Otherwise, the confidentiality of communications between individual defendants and their shared counsel would remain privileged and confidential as between the counsel and each client. The author is aware of no instance in a sharing-of-counsel case where there has been a need to disclose proprietary or confidential data to either trial counsel or co-defendants.

One Answer to the Problem: Sharing Trial Counsel

As implemented, the shared use of trial counsel can involve retaining a single law firm to represent a large number of co-defendants. For example, in one such case, thirty-four cross-industry corporate defendants from the petrochemical and steel industries shared the use and costs of one defense firm in defending a leukemia/death lawsuit. Alternatively, depending on the number of defendants and their categories of interest (e.g., manufacturers and distributor tiers of defendants), the defendants may choose to group themselves around two or more law firms. However, single–law firm representation has worked without difficulties for sharing defendants from diverse industries, e.g., petrochemical, steel, pharmaceutical, and rubber manufacturers and distributors.

The Steering Committee

The retained counsel is directed by a *small* steering committee, the members of which are chosen by all of the sharing defendants. Due to the increasing frequency of petrochemical toxic-substance lawsuits, a degree of familiarity and mutual confidence has developed between the usual company contacts and, in some instances, insurance carrier representatives or counsel responsible for administering these lawsuits. The steering committee representative (or, if appropriate, a single in-house or insurer contact) takes the responsibility for handling noncase dispositive minsterial matters with the shared outside law firm, and contacts each defendant's representative only where unanimity is required on major tactical, expense, or case dispositive matters.

The steering committee does not act to prevent all communications between retained counsel and any defendant but does cut down on unnecessary and repetitive contacts. Although the functions of a steering committee may vary, the committee can generally perform the following activities:

- Develop a plan and evaluate defense strategy and needs
- Establish in-house work groups and assign or solicit volunteers for specific projects, e.g., discovery, research, locating in-house experts, to avoid duplication of efforts
- Implement quick feedback to outside counsel where unanimity is required from all sharing defendants

- Distribute the regular written progress reports of retained counsel, although direct mailing from such counsel is preferable
- Review the fairness of the cost allocation formula in use
- Open communications, if needed, with nonsharing co-defendants

Setting Up a Sharing Arrangement

Time is the major factor in whether a sharing of trial counsel can be put together. The method recommended for setting up a sharing of trial counsel and organizing a defense steering committee is as follows.

Upon discovering the existence of a toxic tort lawsuit, preferably before service is made, call and telex all potential like-situated co-defendants and invite them to share, for your joint defense, a single law firm (or as previously mentioned, group yourselves in logical categories or tiers of defendants with two or more law firms). Follow up the call and telex with an overnight letter (enclosing pleadings, if available) identical to the telex. A proposed form for such a letter appears in the Appendix as Form 24. This sets out the terms and conditions of a flexible sharing agreement that can be terminated or revised as circumstances require.

The agreement is not a contractual apportionment of prospective liability, nor does it bind any party to stay the course for trial. A more formal, fixed agreement has been proposed by Peter N. Sheridan, Product Liability Counsel for the Ciba Geigy Corporation,[1] and will not be discussed here.

You may initially share the costs entirely by equal share until there is a reason to use a different formula for allocating costs. Alternatively, you may choose to institute a billing practice where each defendant's customized work is billed 25 percent to the entire group of defendants and 75 percent to the defendant needing the customized work. This enables companies with in-house counsel to further defray litigation costs by doing some of their own customized work. It also recognizes that the numerous products of a major petrochemical defendant may require more trial counsel hours of study than a single product line of a defendant that is a "mom and pop" solvent manufacturer.

The basic counsel-sharing agreement, as set out in Form 24, calls for co-defendant nonaggression, sharing costs, not opposing dismissal of unnecessary party defendants, and the right to withdraw from the agreement. Implicit in the sharing arrangement is the prospect of using some in-house medical staff, company testing laboratories, health professionals, and other in-house experts, as appropriate, for a first-run cost-efficient analysis of the lawsuit. Other cooperation agreements, which contemplate sharing information and agreements not to file contribution claims, agreements to toll the statute of limitations, and similar matters, are set forth as Forms 28 and 29 in the Appendix.

Benefits

Besides cost-effectiveness, other benefits of the sharing arrangement include:

- Discouragement of a divide-and-conquer approach by plaintiff's counsel to the traditional multiple defense counsel.
- Avoidance of adverse jury reaction to legions of three-piece-suited counsel.
- Avoidance of the "cost of litigation" justification for settling a defendable case. The aggregate cost of a three-week trial for thirty law firms is in no way comparable to the cost of funding a defense team from one competent law firm.
- Avoidance of a divide-and-settle approach to litigation by some defense counsel who assume others will settle and don't want to be the last one out of the case. Occasionally, this leads to full lifeboats and a perfectly solid but empty ship.
- Avoidance of counterproductive attacks on co-defendant products.
- Avoidance of defense inertia, which can occur when multiple defense counsel seek to have their clients avoid being perceived as the target and when each counsel, by reason of the innocuous product to which his or her client has been linked, assumes that someone else must be representing the true target. When this occurs, a totally frivolous case can remain undefended.

The drawbacks of a shared use of defense counsel are mostly prospective and either never arise or can be resolved amicably. Sharing trial counsel does not violate antitrust law, criminal or civil conspiracy statutes, or the rules of the courts.[2]

The interests of judicial economy and efficiency are so in tune with this approach to multiple-defendant toxic-substance litigation that pretrial orders can be, and have been, entered to preclude any cooperating co-defendants from being prejudiced at trial by "evidence" of their cooperative litigation defense efforts. For example, see the proposed form of language for inclusion in an appropriate pretrial order provided in the Appendix as Form 25.

The shared use of trial counsel and the organization of this approach to the defense of cases with multiple defendants requires an initial effort on the part of some in-house counsel. The timing of the organizational effort is critical. It is hoped that the insurers' representatives and the in-house counsel located nearest to the courthouse (and the first to be served) will act as an early-warning system alerting other co-defendants of the lawsuit's existence and permitting the implementation of this nontraditional, but more trial-effective and cost-efficient, approach to the defense of toxic-substance litigation.

Notes

1. Sheridan, Sindell *and Its Sequelae—or—from a Defendant's Perspective, How to Manage Multiple-Party Litigation under Nontraditional Theories of Litigation,* 17 FORUM 1116–38 (Spring 1982).
2. *See* Moore, *Conflicts of Interest in the Simultaneous Representation of Multiple Clients: A Proposed Solution to the Current Confusion and Controversy,* 61 TEX. L. REV. 211–88 (Oct. 1982).

Thirteen

Executive Skills for Litigators: Leadership and Management Techniques for Trial Lawyers

Ralph I. Miller

Lawyers who supervise litigation teams are chief executives, constantly exercising leadership, managing subordinates, and delegating tasks. Often these executive efforts are unsophisticated because lawyers have little opportunity for academic or practical exposure to management theories. Fortunately, that is easy to change.

Lawyers have developed the ability to absorb a great mass of facts quickly and to play roles in the courtroom. These talents, which have been honed by law school and law practice, can serve as the foundation for development of management skills by litigators. Certain precepts of good management practice are also available to all lawyers through their training in contract law doctrines.

Executive Skills Can Be Learned

The ability to accomplish an organization's goals through teamwork is a crucial capability for executives, and a substantial body of literature has developed to help corporate employees become better managers. Many executives attest that management skills can be learned,[1] but lawyers tend to be unaware of management principles, just as executives are often ignorant of fundamental rules of courtroom advocacy.

The absence of management training for lawyers is easy to explain. Business executives are usually exposed to management theory in college, at seminars, or from the executives to whom they report.[2] The trek up the organizational ladder places most managers over a series of ever-larger groups of subordinates that the executive must organize, motivate, and control. Lawyers rarely have similar opportunities.

Even though the absence of management training for lawyers is excusable, the effects of mismanagement on litigation are not. Lawyers have not served their clients well by merely preparing a litigation plan in a ma-

Ralph I. Miller is a member of Thompson & Knight, Dallas, Texas.

jor case[3]—they must also implement that plan through effective leadership and delegation. Weak management skills can cause inadequate trial preparation in larger cases, often doing as much damage to a client's interests as can ineffective advocacy.

Fortunately, lawyers are quick learners. The principles of good staff management are not too complex, and some of those precepts are analogous to legal doctrines with which all lawyers are familiar. With a modest amount of effort, any litigator can absorb the basic principles of good personnel management. Through practice, the lawyer can then build a good management style on a solid theoretical foundation.

Delegation Is a Necessary Evil

In traditional management theory, executives should accomplish their work primarily through "delegation" of jobs to subordinates.[4] Effective delegation is a difficult thing for most corporate managers to learn,[5] and lawyers seem to face the same barriers in passing parts of a lawsuit down the chain of seniority.

Delegation entails a necessary element of risk,[6] and lawyers are understandably reluctant to trust others with the welfare of their clients. This risk can be reduced, however, by knowing what can be delegated, by using sound techniques for delegation, and by proper supervision as the job progresses.

Resistance to delegation appears to be a natural human tendency, and it often manifests itself in lawsuits as procrastination in assigning projects that more senior lawyers had hoped to complete themselves. The first step toward becoming a good manager is acceptance of two facts about delegation: (1) delegation is necessary, and (2) delegation is hard work.

Clients sometimes make the task of delegation more difficult, but a rational explanation usually removes any misunderstandings. Frequently a client wants the most senior lawyer to take all the depositions, or argue all the motions, or cross-examine all the witnesses at trial. This flattering request may appeal to the ego of the senior lawyer,[7] and junior lawyers may be reluctant to question the uniqueness of the attorney in charge of the case.

If a case has legitimately grown beyond the ability of one lawyer to handle it efficiently, lawyers do a disservice to their clients by acquiescing to restrictions the client may try to impose on delegation.[8] A litigation plan with objectives and deadlines can also help explain to the client why delegation is necessary. Even if the senior lawyer could theoretically take all the depositions before the trial setting, the schedule may show that the last depositions should be completed early enough to allow adequate summarization and briefing. Most clients will withdraw restrictions on delegation if they hear a well-reasoned justification for the need to delegate.

Effective delegation requires a surprising amount of effort. Managers come to accept the need to devote most of their time to the process of managing, but lawyers often feel they should be "working" instead of supervising. After lawyers accept the need to delegate, they must then give some thought to the right way to accomplish that delegation.

Divide to Conquer

Successful division of responsibility in litigation often depends on creativity in dividing the litigation tasks. Most young trial lawyers have little need to classify the various aspects of a case. Young trial lawyers traditionally prove themselves by trying the smaller cases assigned to them and performing discrete tasks they are given in larger cases. To delegate successfully, however, a lawyer must divide trial preparation into its component parts and match the skills required for each task with the people who have both the ability and the desire to apply those skills.

One author has distilled a four-step test from management literature for portions of a project that can be delegated:

> Although a great many people believe that delegation is a bit like money in that more is always preferable to less, thoughtful writers on the topic have identified four assumptions that must be satisfied before delegation can be successful:
>
> 1. Delegatees having training, ability, and skill in the . . . area.
> 2. Delegatees care about and have a commitment to the organization in general and the delegated area in particular.
> 3. The area of delegation lends itself to measurement.
> 4. The delegator is secure both emotionally and job-wise.[9]

This author concludes that these requirements may "preclude delegating 'hot potato' issues where no one knows what a good decision is and no one wants to get stuck with it" and urges managers to delegate subparts if the whole project fails his four criteria for delegation.[10]

Lawyers tend to feel that cases are difficult to fragment, but in reality pretrial preparation is always a series of distinct activities. Even within a single category of activities, different skill levels may be required. All depositions, for example, are rarely of equal significance in a large case. Motions, discovery requests, and even witness examinations usually cover a spectrum of importance and complexity. Frequently the lawyers or legal assistants are paired with tasks on the basis of scheduling convenience or stereotyped assignments. A better approach would be a rational designation of responsibilities at the beginning of the case that seeks to match tasks with the individuals most appropriate to complete them. After drawing up that plan for delegation, the supervising litigator can then turn to the process of passing the tasks to members of the team.

Use the Independent Contractor Analogy

Classic management theory requires that delegation include the latitude for the delegatee to make decisions on the way to accomplish the task. For lawyers, it is probably helpful to think of the distinction between employees and independent contractors: Unlike an employee, the independent contractor is supposed to retain some discretion concerning the manner of performing the contract. A successful executive strives to create relationships like that with an independent contractor, rather than imposing the role of master and servant. One author explains the importance of including discretion in a true delegation this way:

> Almost any task can be delegated, or it can be assigned. If it is delegated, it is entrusted pretty completely to the employee, and few strings are tied to him as he carries out the responsibility. A brief, and almost accurate, explanation is that we let the worker plan and run a delegated task. We decide with him the goal to reach, and he is given the least possible supervision in reaching it. Otherwise it is a sham delegation.[11]

Just as a "turnkey" construction contract shifts responsibility for completion from the owner to the contractor, a proper delegation moves responsibility to the subordinate. Subordinates sometimes become adept at placing a delegated task back on the manager's desk with a question, excuse, or incomplete effort. Junior lawyers, like all other subordinates, may resist effective delegation by attempting to volley a job back to the delegating lawyer. A classic article has described the mechanism by which the "monkey" may jump from the subordinate's back to the manager's back if the manager is not vigilant.[12]

After illustrating some of the ways in which subordinates may cleverly return a delegated job to the manager, the authors of that article explain:

> What we have been driving at in this monkey-on-the-back analogy is to transfer initiative from manager to subordinate and keep it there. We have tried to highlight a truism as obvious as it is subtle. Namely, before a manager can develop initiative in his subordinates, he must see to it that they *have* the initiative. Once he takes it back, they will no longer have it and he can kiss his discretionary time good-bye. [The manager's time] will all revert to subordinate-imposed time [to complete the tasks that were not fully performed by the subordinates].[13]

In rendering the best professional services for clients, lawyers must seek to satisfy both the professional requirement that experience levels must be adequate and the management rule that junior lawyers should be allowed to exercise some initiative.

In the context of complex litigation, confusion frequently arises over the authority of junior lawyers to make decisions on strategy and approach. Out of an abundance of caution, the junior lawyers frequently feel they have no authority, and they take every decision to the senior attorney for approval. By devoting a little time to designating the tasks over which junior lawyers have decision-making authority, the senior lawyer can avoid unnecessary harassment. The junior lawyers, in turn, can gain new motivation and challenge.

Defining the Task Is a Fine Art

Management theory places great emphasis on the importance of defining tasks carefully.[14] This is a particular problem in complex lawsuits because the tasks often need to evolve as they are accomplished. Until legal research is done, for example, the issues to be researched are usually impossible to define. Giving the best definition possible for a task is still much more effective, however, than leaving the task undefined.

Litigators may find it helpful to ask themselves how comfortable they would feel if they had to sue the person to whom an assignment was given for breach of contract if the work is not done satisfactorily. One recent management book suggests that goals for subordinates may even sound legalistic:

> Don't worry if the goal sounds legalistic. This may be unavoidable; after all, optimal goals and legal language have something in common: they're both designed to tie down loose ends. So if the goal sounds as if it's been drafted by lawyers, that's okay.[15]

In a very real sense, you are making a contract when you delegate work. Review that contract with your legal training to see if the delegation has been properly defined. Consider the following issues:

- Will that contract be easier to enforce if it is in writing? Probably so—write a memo!
- Will there be problems of ambiguity? Define terms.
- Is time clearly of the essence? If so, is the time of completion specified? Set an action date.
- How has force majeure been defined? Is notice required if force majeure will operate? Be sure you are advised if the project stops.

- Are the effects of breach clearly disclosed to the other party, so you can recover for consequential damages? Tell people why an assignment is important.
- Is this merely an agreement to agree? Get a commitment, not a promise to "do it if I get time."

Although they may not be aware of it, most lawyers have already learned the standards by which a good work assignment should be evaluated. Just write your contract carefully.

To follow the contract analogy further, supervising litigators should be sure to obtain acceptance of the terms of a delegation memorandum, even if the result is essentially a contract of adhesion. To assure that target dates are reasonable, the people undertaking the tasks can be asked to estimate the time they will need before the deadlines are set. There should be a clear understanding, however, that the deadlines cannot be extended unilaterally, and a modification of the contract will be necessary.

Individual accountability is also very important in work assignments. One individual should be responsible for accomplishing each task, even if others are specified to assist. Assigning two people to accomplish a task "jointly" may be good office politics, but usually it is bad management practice.

Seek a Balance in Supervision

Even if a task has been properly delegated initially, skill is needed to maintain the right level of supervision. One author notes:

> You've got to trust your subordinates. But at the same time, you've got to watch them. The interplay between trusting and monitoring forms an important part of the art of management.[16]

Within litigation teams, lawyers are probably well advised to err on the side of too much supervision rather than too little. An early status check can do little harm if a project is on track, but it can avoid a disaster if the work has gone awry.

If a legal assistant is assigned to summarize a long deposition, for example, it can be very useful to have the summary checked by the assigning lawyer after the first fifty pages are summarized. If the summary looks good, the assigning lawyer can reinforce the assignment by assuring the legal assistant that the job is going well. If the summary is too general or too detailed, however, the supervising lawyer can easily correct the scope. If any changes are suggested, the summaries on the next fifty pages can quickly be checked to be sure the new approach is right.

After the initial review of the assignment, periodic checks on progress are usually desirable. Trial lawyers always have a reminder system for deadlines, and the supervising lawyer can easily include checkup dates in this system for tasks assigned to other lawyers or legal assistants.[17]

Intermediate deadlines can help to assure that tasks are progressing. Trial lawyers face many competing demands for their time,[18] yet they are usually careful to meet their deadlines and be prepared when they must appear in court. Corporations have long used presentations and quarterly reviews as devices to create artificial deadlines, and lawyers may find that some of these procedures apply in a complex case.

The memorandum for an associate assigned to a long brief may include, for example, dates when an oral report is due on research, when an outline of major headings is to be circulated, and when a "working draft" with blanks is to be ready, as well as the traditional date for a first draft. Entry of these dates on the associate's calendar, combined with a desire to avoid embarrassment, will probably provide ample incentive to keep the brief moving forward. Corporate counsel may wish to take a similar approach to supervision of outside counsel.

Recognize and Reward Success

Management theory requires that success be recognized and rewarded, but the reward need not be economic. One author suggests:

> The reward for success should be greater than any penalty for failure. Upon completion of the task or project, those involved should evaluate the entire process used to improve proper delegation in the future.[19]

Anyone who performs a delegated task well should receive some recognition. For a brief delivered promptly by the mail room runner, a telephone call to express appreciation may be enough. For a word processor who stays late to finish a motion, a memorandum of commendation, with a copy to the office administrator, may be in order. For victory snatched from the jaws of defeat through skillful cross-examination, nothing less than a round of applause at a firm luncheon may suffice.

Managers must make a concerted effort to provide recognition and reward. Even after a favorable verdict has been obtained, the executive litigator should not turn to the next crisis until the good work of the trial team has been properly commemorated. Selecting and providing rewards is difficult and tedious work, but good executives accept the need to devote a significant amount of time to arranging recognition for good work by subordinates.

Sound management practice also prohibits the superior from usurping credit for the ideas and accomplishments of subordinates. If a trial lawyer has progressed from one-person cases to supervision of multilawyer suits, it may seem unnatural to acknowledge that part of the credit for success belongs to the supporting cast. Yet failure to give credit will inevitably undercut the success of delegation in future cases.

Lawyers Must Manage as Well as Lead

Although delegation is done at many levels in an organization, the responsibility to motivate and inspire the whole group rests on the lawyer in charge of the team. Just as each lawyer must develop a personal style for persuasion in the courtroom, so each executive must develop a personal style in motivating subordinates. The courtroom style, however, is not necessarily the right management style.

Management literature draws a distinction between leaders, who derive their authority from the consent of subordinates, and managers, who receive their authority from the organization.[20] If possible, managers should be good leaders,[21] but sometimes effective management requires that popularity as a leader be sacrificed to promote the organization's goals.[22]

Trial lawyers are persuaders by profession, and that background, combined with the structure of most law firms or corporate law departments, may interfere with effective management of subordinates. Lawyers who are accustomed to arguing to dubious judges and juries may tend to approach the members of the litigation team in the same way—as doubters to be convinced by advocacy. There is no reason to stifle this natural tendency,[23] but the lawyer in charge of a litigation team must recognize that some tasks have to be imposed because they are too unattractive to be sold. Further, the process of asking for an expression of interest before assigning a project must not convey the impression that the job can be returned if the recipient finds it less pleasant than expected.

The lack of structure in many law firms may make the role of a litigation manager more difficult. Although senior partners rarely have much difficulty in directing a junior associate to accomplish something, lawyers near the same level of seniority may find it necessary to negotiate assignments with each other. The same lack of delineation of authority may occur among associate general counsel in a corporate law department. The senior lawyer in charge of a team or office should recognize these potential problems and define the lines of authority clearly.

If the supervising lawyer has done a good job of planning and delegation, most tasks should be accomplished smoothly, but occasionally a member of the team will simply fail to perform. When that happens, the lawyer in charge must manage the problem forcefully.

The lawyer in charge of a litigation team must diagnose the cause of performance failures and act decisively to correct each problem. Sometimes the pairing of skills with assignments was imperfect, and the original recipient proves incapable of doing the job. In those instances, the manager should promptly redelegate the project to someone else.

If the delegatee was capable but not conscientious, a courteous but firm request for corrective action is appropriate. Management credibility develops only if subordinates learn that they must do it right or do it over. If suggestions for improvement are friendly and constructive, the junior lawyer will often feel genuine appreciation for the guidance, rather than the resentment that the manager may fear. Regardless of the effect on the manager's popularity, however, the senior litigator must compel specific performance if subordinates breach the "contracts" they have undertaken.

Practice Management as You Practice Law

Although the fundamentals can be learned quickly, management, like law, improves with practice. Once a supervising lawyer becomes aware of some of the issues that are debated by professional managers, self-evaluation of management skills becomes possible. Litigators can begin to build a better understanding of their own leadership style and to note ways their own delegation habits may conflict with the conventional wisdom of management theories.

For those with an academic interest in management, the articles and books cited in the notes to this chapter will provide a good introduction to the theory of delegation. To keep abreast of changing concepts, a supervising litigator might invest in a subscription to one of the publications of the American Management Association, such as *Management Review* or *Supervisory Management*.

For the future, there is hope that trial lawyers are building a body of literature in legal publications (like this anthology) to promote better management skills in corporate legal departments and law firms. Tailoring management approaches to litigation offers great promise for lowering client costs, for improving staff morale, and for simplifying the lives of executive litigators. In our adversary context, the well-managed trial team is more likely to represent the client's interests effectively. Finding the time to develop executive skills is not easy for a busy trial lawyer, but the benefits far outweigh the cost. We can all manage to be better managers.

Notes

1. Lawrence A. Appley, the long-time president and then chairman of the American Management Association, was a principal proponent of the concept that professional management can be taught. S. FEINBERG, MANAGEMENT'S CHALLENGE: THE PEOPLE PROBLEM 57 (1976).
2. One author notes that delegation is frequently best learned by observing effective management skills of an experienced superior. Brill, *Delegation: It's Harder Than It Looks*, J. SYS. MGMT. 36, 37 (Feb. 1979).

3. Chapters 10 and 11 discuss the preparation of a litigation plan, and this chapter assumes that a litigation plan has been developed.

4. "The core concept of management is getting things done through other people—any activity that involves leading any group of people toward the attainment of common objectives in any walk of life. . . . He who does things himself is an individual producer and not a manager." S. FEINBERG, *supra* note 1, at 58. *See* Brill, *supra* note 2, at 36.

5. Brill, *supra* note 2; Krein, *How to Improve Delegation Habits*, MGMT. REV. 58 (May 1982).

6. Ford, *Delegation Without Fear*, SUPERVISORY MGMT. 2 (July 1983); Krein, *supra* note 5, at 60.

7. One author has noted that the "workaholic" with an "inflated self-image" frequently finds it impossible to delegate. Sandage, *The Art of Delegating*, REAL ESTATE TODAY, 18, 19 (Aug. 1980).

8. A client's legitimate concern about "double teaming" should not be confused with a restriction on delegation. Sending a junior lawyer to take a deposition is delegation, but bringing a junior lawyer to watch a deposition may or may not be delegation, depending on the role the observer will play.

9. Ford, *supra* note 6, at 4.

10. *Id.* at 7–8.

11. D. LAIRD & E. LAIRD, THE TECHNIQUES OF DELEGATING 107 (1962).

12. Onken & Wass, *Management Time: Who's Got the Monkey?* 52 HARV. BUS. REV. 75–80 (Nov./Dec. 1974). When the original version of this chapter was discussed at a program of the Litigation Section in Los Angeles, several participants recommended this article.

13. *Id.* at 79 (emphasis in original).

14. Ford, *supra* note 6, at 5; Krein, *supra* note 5, at 59.

15. R. LEFTON, V. BUZZOTTA & M. SHERBERG, IMPROVING PRODUCTIVITY THROUGH PEOPLE SKILLS 240 (1980).

16. Brill, *supra* note 2, at 37.

17. "Delegating requires constant communication, agreeing on the work to be done and the time needed to do it, agreeing on procedures and resources, counseling, and monitoring." M. PARSON, AN EXECUTIVE'S COACHING HANDBOOK 11–12 (1986).

18. Supervising trial lawyers may be reassured to find that their disjointed days are not unlike those of many other executives. One author notes, "Executives have sensed for years that this series of interruptions with the task at hand sandwiched in represents a true picture of the way they do business, but only recently has such a routine been thoroughly documented." Peters, *Leadership: Sad Facts and Silver Linings*, HARV. BUS. REV. 165 (Nov./Dec. 1979).

19. Sandage, *supra* note 7, at 20.

20. "Management is the accountability that we have to formulate and achieve the objectives of the organization of which we and our employees are members. Leadership is the responsibility we have to represent our followers' needs and goals and help them achieve what they want. A leader deals in emotions, excites camaraderie and unity, and guides vague notions into concrete actions. A manager determines, organizes, and directs programs, and compromises among

differing desires." Plachy, *Leading vs. Managing: A Guide to Some Crucial Distinctions*, MGMT. REV. 58, 61 (Sept. 1981).

21. An author who had studied eighty successful chief executive officers concluded, for example, "To use a popular distinction, they viewed themselves as *leaders* not *managers.*" Bennis, *The Five Key Traits of Successful Chief Executives,* INT'L MGMT. 60 (Oct. 1981) (emphasis in original).

22. "The managership-leadership dichotomy is a reciprocal relationship: the more you choose to manage, the less you choose to lead. . . . Managers are not managers unless they are continually creating 'disgruntlements' by choosing between conflicting demands." Plachy, *supra* note 20, at 61.

23. Harry Levinson, a psychologist who has written extensively on motivation theory, contends that the "reward-punishment psychology" should be replaced by practices that include "group appraisal and appraisal by subordinates" and consideration of "the personal goals of the individual first." H. LEVINSON, THE GREAT JACKASS FALLACY 106–07 (1973). Using persuasion rather than coercion is consistent with this approach.

Fourteen

Use of Pretrial Conferences to Control Costs and Fees

Peter M. Saparoff

Much attention has recently been focused on the need for controls on fees and expenses in class action litigation.[1] Although examination of attorney's fees and expenses has traditionally occurred after trial or settlement, courts now recognize that to effectively control attorney's fees, they must turn their attention to the pretrial stage as well:

> The courts. . . have the ultimate power and responsibility to prevent abuse. One important step in this direction is for the court to supervise the conduct of class actions from their inception.[2]

Recent amendments in rule 16 of the Federal Rules of Civil Procedure involving the scope and objectives of pretrial conferences and in rule 26(f) of the Federal Rules regarding the parties' right to a discovery conference have expanded the district courts' authority and the parties' opportunity to prevent excessive pretrial fees and expenses by seeking a simplified organizational structure for plaintiffs' attorneys, restricting the number, duration, form, and manner of discovery; and proposing specific limitations on attorney's hourly charges and expenses. This chapter examines common causes of the fee problem, procedural mechanisms available to parties seeking to control fees and expenses, and the recent pretrial orders of district courts implementing fee guidelines in complex federal class action suits.

Typical Organizational Structure in Complex Class Action Suits

During the last two decades, the predominant organizational model for complex class action suits involving multiple plaintiffs' attorneys has been

Peter M. Saparoff is a member of Gaston & Snow, Boston, Massachusetts. He gratefully acknowledges the assistance of Nancy Ballard in 1984 and of Robert Waddick in 1987, both third-year law students at Northeastern University School of Law at the respective times.

a multilayered committee structure. A typical organizational hierarchy is the one approved by California District Court Judge Lucas in *In Re Equity Funding Corp. of America Securities Litigation:*[3]

1. All plaintiffs' attorneys who filed suit before consolidation of individual cases or certification of the class constituted the "Committee Counsel," the first tier in the hierarchy. The "Committee" was charged with ultimate authority for all plaintiffs' pretrial activities. Each attorney had an equal voice in the decisions or activities of the Committee and in selecting a "Steering" or "Executive" Committee, the second tier.
2. The "Steering Committee" commonly consists of four to eight attorneys elected by the Committee of Counsel. The Steering Committee assumed responsibility for the general supervision of the case, receiving and executing orders of the court, representing issues to the court, organizing subcommittees and distributing work to the subcommittees. Members of the Steering Committee usually elect a Chairperson or Co-Chairpersons to act as lead counsel (tier three).
3. Subcommittees of the Committee of Counsel, organized by the Steering Committee, undertook the research, wrote briefs and memoranda, and dealt with individual plaintiffs and subclasses. Typical subcommittees include the discovery subcommittee, pretrial memorandum committee, briefing committee, class certification committee, etc.
4. A Liaison Counsel or the "Liaison Committee" is usually appointed by the Steering Committee. The Liaison Counsel is responsible for maintaining communication among attorneys and sometimes, individual class members or subclasses. (Some courts have authorized the creation of other subordinate bodies to deal with individual plaintiffs or subclasses.)

In the past several years, all parties have become disenchanted with many aspects of the multilayered committee approach to class action litigation. Probably the most thorough and revealing analysis of the potential problems and abuses of a complex class action case was undertaken by Judge McGlynn in his district court opinion discussing his attorney's fees awards in *In Re Fine Paper Antitrust Litigation*.[4] Judge McGlynn's opinion describes a plaintiffs' attorneys' organization wherein uninvolved lawyers were recruited to provide voting blocs for firms desiring steering committee positions. Other attorneys were apparently encouraged to join as co-counsel to share in assignments that would result in substantial attorney's fees in hopes that similar favors would be returned in the future.[5] The district court explained in great detail the inefficiency, political maneuvering, and duplication of effort that resulted from "an organizational structure consisting of tiers of committees and subcommittees with numerous 'Chairmen' and scores of 'Co-chairmen' for virtually every task in the case."[6]

In awarding attorney's fees, the district court reduced plaintiffs' 161 attorneys' requested charges of $21,000,000 for 70,000 attorney hours and over 16,000 paralegal hours to $5,464,123, disallowing thousands of hours for overattendance by plaintiffs' attorneys at pretrial conferences (counsel billed approximately $500,000 for 1446 hours of preparation, travel, and attendance at pretrial conferences); duplication of effort on the pretrial memorandum (51 plaintiffs' lawyers devoted 4500 hours to the pretrial memorandum at a requested cost to the class of over $1,000,000); unproductive research on the issue of damages (4200 hours); excessive time spent on discovery related to the issue of class certification (1310.7 hours); overattendance at depositions (approximately 1500 hours billed to the class for preparation and taking of one third-party witness); and unnecessary review of documents by attorneys not closely related to or responsible for the subject matter of the documents. The court also recalculated work performed by partners that could have been done by associates and compensated partners for that work at an associate's rate.

In its appellate decision, the Third Circuit stated, "We have found more in the trial court's opinion with which we wholeheartedly approve than we have found necessary to reverse."[7] Among other things, the Third Circuit did not approve the district court's "across the board 50% reduction in pretrial memorandum time" (4500 hours requested).[8] Neither did the Third Circuit approve the district court's reduction in fees for overattendance at depositions (approximately 1500 hours requested).[9] In disapproving cuts made by the district court, the Third Circuit noted that the district court had failed to specifically identify the entries comprising the disallowed hours.[10] In addition, the Third Circuit rejected the district court's application of "hypothetical national rates" to determine attorney's fees.[11]

A recent Second Circuit opinion disagreed with the *Fine Paper* appeals court decision on the last two points. In *In Re Agent Orange Product Liability Litigation*,[12] the Second Circuit held that the district court had the power to make cuts in fee applications without the item-by-item specificity required by *Fine Paper*.[13] The *Agent Orange* decision also held that the use of national hourly rates to determine attorney's fees is proper in multiparty class action suits where there is an adequate evidentiary basis.[14] The court maintained that its opinion was not inconsistent with *Fine Paper* on this point, claiming that *Fine Paper* "may be read to condemn only national hourly rates not based on an adequate evidentiary record."[15]

In response to *Fine Paper* and other less notorious but nonetheless unwieldy and expensive committee structures,[16] courts have begun to require simplified organizational structures (or have simply appointed lead counsel themselves) and have begun to place explicit limitations on attorney's fee charges.

Attorney's Fee Factors Appropriate for Pretrial (Presettlement) Consideration

The amount of attorney's fees that can be recovered from the common fund by plaintiffs' attorneys lies within the broad discretion of the district court.[17] Typically, district courts calculate attorney's fees by multiplying the hours reasonably expended by the attorney(s) for the benefit of the class by a rate commensurate with the rates charged by other attorneys with similar experience doing similar kinds of work in the community. This "lodestar" figure can then be increased or decreased according to other factors such as exceptional quality of representation, risk borne by plaintiffs' attorneys, and the size of the award.[18]

However, the Supreme Court has restricted the instances in which a district court may allow a quality multiplier.[19] In *Blum v. Stenson* the Court determined that the quality of representation is presumed to be reflected in the initial lodestar figure.[20] Therefore, any adjustment to the lodestar would be proper only in "the rare case where the fee applicant offers specific evidence to show that the quality of service rendered was superior to that one reasonably should expect in light of the hourly rates charged and that the success was exceptional."[21] *Pennsylvania v. Delaware Valley Citizens' Council* reaffirmed *Blum*, pointing out that determining fee awards based on the lodestar approach "leaves very little room for enhancing the award based on post-engagement performance."[22]

Pretrial activities that have been disallowed by courts include hours spent locating a named plaintiff or providing essentially personal (as opposed to class) services;[23] time spent attending conferences and representing the interests of governmental entities rather than the class;[24] hours charged for negotiating fee arrangements with individual clients;[25] time spent trying to compete with or oust lead counsel;[26] time consumed in investigation, clerical work, or review and proofreading that could be done by nonlawyers;[27] hours spent working on briefs that are substantially similar to previously submitted briefs;[28] time charges for two or three lawyers when one attorney could have done the job;[29] time spent inefficiently trying to locate experts;[30] charges for intraoffice meetings;[31] and hours billed for unnecessary motions.[32]

The frequency of requests for what many courts believe to be excessive attorney's fees has led to the potential for sanctions being assessed against a plaintiff's attorney who requests compensation for an excessive number of hours. In *Jacquette v. Black Hawk County, Iowa*,[33] a civil rights case in which plaintiff's attorney sought $91,710.98 in fees pursuant to 42 U.S.C. § 1988 after a $1500 settlement had been reached, the Eighth Circuit stated,

> This court cannot understand, in the absence of finding of bad faith, misconduct, or serious neglect by one or more of the parties or its attorney, how this case could remain in district court for almost three years, and generate such an astounding expenditure of legal time. . . . If [plaintiff's attorney's] hours were expended on frivolous claims, unnecessary and extended motion practice or were expended vindictively and in bad faith harassment of defendants then the district court should so state and a finding of bad faith would be warranted.[34]

The court of appeals then remanded the case for an evidentiary hearing, imposed on plaintiff's counsel the burden to explain the reason for expenditure of the excessive number of hours as found by the trial court, and instructed the district court to consider assessing defendant's attorney's fees against the plaintiff's attorney if bad faith were found.[35] Although the disparity between the amount of the settlement and the requested fees was almost guaranteed to arouse suspicion in *Jacquette*, the Eighth Circuit's opinion is indicative of courts' growing impatience with both plaintiffs' attorneys and defense attorneys who initiate pretrial maneuvers for purely tactical or bargaining advantage.

Early discussion of the limits of compensable time works to the advantage of both plaintiffs' attorneys and defendants. The plaintiffs' attorneys learn before they expend time and money what charges the court is likely to reimburse and what charges will not be allowed. As discussed later in this chapter, early attention to fee issues may also encourage a judge to be particularly sensitive to the economic ramifications of his or her pretrial rulings (i.e., whether modification of protective orders is appropriate, whether restriction of one form of discovery rather than another will result in greater expense, and whether document requests responses should be submitted in the form most accessible to plaintiffs' attorneys). Early consideration of attorney's fees and expenses is important to defendants, both because they will be asked directly or indirectly to bear the plaintiffs' attorneys' costs in virtually every settlement arrangement, and because many of the plaintiffs' attorneys' activities directly affect the work and expenses of their own lawyers. *The Report of the Commission on Professionalism to the Board of Governors and the House of Delegates of the American Bar Association*[36] emphasized the importance of pretrial orders vis-à-vis attorney's fees:

> Experience indicates that issuance of pretrial orders by judges can be useful. The orders should outline precisely the procedures to be followed by counsel and could, among other things, limit the number of lawyers participating in depositions and appearing before the Court in oral arguments. Orders such as these will help minimize the size of requested fee awards.

Pretrial Procedures for Seeking Order to Limit Fees and Expenses

To grapple with the incidence of discovery abuse and the high cost of resolving complex cases, the Federal Rules Advisory Committee initiated a number of changes extending the authority of judges over pretrial cases management generally and over discovery in particular.[37]

Rule 26(f)—Discovery Conference

Although in most jurisdictions the authority of the court to exercise considerable control over the discovery process has been settled for some time,[38] Federal Rule of Civil Procedure 26(f), adopted in 1980, confirmed that power by explicitly giving the court discretion to convene a discovery conference on its own motion, and requiring the court to convene a conference upon motion by a party.[39] Of the few courts that have considered discovery conference requests, several have recognized that consideration of plaintiff's attorney's fees is appropriate in formulating a discovery plan.[40] In one case, a district court judge expressed regret that he hadn't early in the proceedings exercised the foresight to cite guidelines for attorney's fees and expenses such as those suggested in *In Re Continental Illinois Securities Litigation*.[41]

A party's motion for discovery conference must include a statement of the issues before the court; a proposed plan and discovery schedule; any limitation proposed to be placed on discovery; any other proposed orders with respect to discovery; and a statement showing that the attorney making the motion has made a reasonable effort to reach agreement with opposing attorneys on the matters set forth in the motion.[42] Following the discovery conference, the court must enter an order tentatively identifying the issues for discovery, establishing a plan or schedule for discovery, describing any limits to be placed on discovery, and determining "such other matters. . . as are necessary for the proper management of discovery in the action."

The power of the court to control attorney expenses by placing restrictions on discovery is broad but not unbounded. Limitations as to amount, kind, geographical location, number of attorneys who will be compensated, and duration of the discovery period are all within the sound discretion of the district court.[43] The Third Circuit in *Fine Paper* rejected plaintiffs' argument that they were afforded too little time for discovery and trial preparation, stating,

> [An appellate court] will not interfere with a trial court's control of its docket except upon the clearest showing that the procedures have resulted in actual and substantial prejudice to the complaining litigant.[44]

The trial court may not, however, restrict the scope of discovery for purposes of economic efficiency. Relevancy to the subject matter is the only permissible boundary on the scope of discovery.[45]

A court may also combine a discovery conference with a rule 16 pretrial conference. Although rule 26(f) contains no explicit provision for continued control or monitoring, such power has been implied from the court's power to establish a schedule and its general authority to determine "matters necessary for the proper management of discovery in the action."[46]

Case Management through Pretrial Conferences—The New Rule 16

In 1983, Federal Rule of Civil Procedure 16 was retitled from "Pretrial Procedure; Formulating Issues" to "Pretrial Conferences; Scheduling; Management" and extensively amended. The purpose of the rule 16 amendments was to shift the emphasis away from a pretrial conference model that focused primarily on trial issues and toward a process of judicial management that embraces the entire pretrial phase, especially motions and discovery.[47] Consequently, the scope of the new rule has been considerably expanded:

> (a) PRETRIAL CONFERENCES; OBJECTIVES. In any action the court may in its discretion direct the attorneys for the parties and any unrepresented parties to appear before it for a conference or conferences before trial for such purposes as
> 1. expediting the disposition of the action;
> 2. establishing early and continuing control so that the case will not be protracted because of lack of management;
> 3. discouraging wasteful pretrial activities;
> 4. improving the quality of the trial through more thorough preparation; and
> 5. facilitating the settlement of the case.[48]

Subsection (b) of rule 16 directs the courts to hold a scheduling conference as soon as practicable but not more than 120 days after the filing of a complaint and to issue a scheduling order limiting the time to join other parties, amend the pleadings, file and hear motions, and complete discovery; announcing the next conference date; and dealing with other appropriate matters. If the scheduling conference cannot be held within 120 days after the complaint is filed, an order may be issued after some communication with the parties (i.e., via the mail or telephone).[49] Although a conference is discretionary unless a party requests it, rule 16(b) mandates that a scheduling order be issued in every case unless there is a local exemption rule. Consequently the court must, unless excused by local rule, set limitations on discovery. Moreover, the court is bound to "secure the just, speedy, and inexpensive determination of every action"[50] and to discourage wasteful pretrial activities.[51] Either party to a class action suit can reasonably claim that not only *may* a judge set out his or her guidelines for reimbursement of plaintiff's attorney fees but that in order to comply with rule 16, he or she *must* do so upon request.[52]

There is no uniform practice in the district courts concerning the responsibility for preparing pretrial orders under rule 16. In some courts the judge dictates the orders in the presence of counsel; in others orders are prepared by party attorney(s) and submitted to the court. In still others the judge may draft a proposal and request oral or written comments from counsel. Finally the minutes of pretrial conference may constitute the discovery order.[53]

A scheduling order pursuant to rule 16 cannot be modified except by leave of the judge or a magistrate upon a showing of good cause. Subsection (f) of rule 16 mandates sanctions if a party or party's attorney fails to obey a scheduling or pretrial order or fails to participate in good faith in pretrial conference.[54] In lieu of or in addition to any other sanctions, the judge must assess against the noncomplying party, or the attorney representing him or her, the reasonable expenses including attorney's fees incurred because of the noncompliance unless the judge finds that the noncompliance was substantially justified or that other circumstances make such an assessment unjust.[55]

Local Rules

Although the Federal Rules impose no limitation on the number of interrogatories, depositions, or document requests a party may make,[56] many if not most federal court districts have limited the number of interrogatories a party can pose through local rule, and individual judges in some districts have done the same through order or practice. Several state courts have also adopted interrogatory limitations.[57] Attorneys seeking scheduling orders that restrict the number and duration of discovery requests should check local court rules to see if a rule has already been promulgated to support the discovery proposal.

Use of Rule 26(e) Protective Orders and Sharing of Information

Plaintiffs' attorneys in securities fraud cases can often save considerable time and expense if they are able to obtain information discovered in previous private litigation or in prior SEC investigations. Discovery such as depositions, documents, responses to requests for admission, and answers to interrogatories are filed with the court and thus become matters of public record unless the discovered party moved in the previous proceeding that they not be filed.[58]

Discovery not filed with the court generally becomes the property of the discovering party and, in the absence of a court limitation on use, can be made available to litigants in other suits. Defendants wishing to limit the future transfer of the fruits of discovery to litigants in other cases can move for a protective order. Federal Rule of Civil Procedure 26(c) allows a court "for good cause shown . . . [to] make any order which justice requires to protect a party or person from annoyance, embarrassment, oppression or undue burden or expense." Many defendants move for protective orders as a matter of course, but by restricting the persons who have access to discovered information or restricting the use of discovery already obtained, defendants effectively increase plaintiffs' cost of litigation by preventing reuse of information and requiring costly and time-consuming duplication of discovery. Plaintiffs' attorneys and other parties (not affected by the fruits of the protected discovery) who are faced with proposals by defendants for severe fee restrictions should oppose such protective orders or seek modification of outstanding orders that prevent them from obtaining useful information inexpensively. A growing number of courts have required the party seeking to establish "good cause" for imposing a protective order to demonstrate that the disclosure "will work a clearly defined and very serious injury."[59]

Orders modifying protective orders should be given if the factors that gave rise to the need for the protective order are no longer present. For instance, in *United States v. American Telephone & Telegraph Co.*,[60] the district court judge granted the government's motion for access to documents previously produced by AT&T in two ongoing suits.[61] The Seventh Circuit upheld the district court's modification of protective order on the grounds that "the relaxation of the protective order in this case has only the effect of permitting MCI counsel to make the depositions and their analyses of data available to government counsel. We are impressed with the wastefulness of requiring government counsel to duplicate the analysis and discovery already made."[62] If the plaintiffs before the court are entitled to the substance of already discovered material by virtue of their undertaking a lawsuit, there does not appear to be a good-faith reason for a defendant's refusal to accept modification of a protective order while contending that plaintiffs' attorney's fees must be limited.

Defendants, on the other hand, can take advantage of the plaintiffs' access to already discovered materials and urge that charges for plaintiffs' attorney's time not reflect work that duplicates material already available to them. Access to government investigative information or material produced in suits involving issues substantially similar to issues before the court have caused judges to reduce attorney hours and/or refuse to offer a bonus multiplier to increase the lodestar amount.[63]

Pretrial Proposals for Limiting Plaintiffs' Attorney's Fees

The following proposals for limitations on attorney's fees have been included in pretrial or discovery conference orders, proposed in rule 26(f) or rule 16 motions by class action defendants, or considered in postsettlement attorney's fee hearings and could be explored in early scheduling or discovery conferences.[64]

Proposals for Simplification of Organization

One approach to limiting potential attorney's fees is to seek a simple plaintiff's attorney committee structure. Courts have recently become less enchanted with the broad-based "democratic" committee model and have begun appointing two or three "lead counsel" and/or a "steering committee" whose responsibility it is to supervise work, present material to the court, and receive and execute court orders.[65] Court appointment of lead counsel obviates the opportunity for much of the political maneuvering that has plagued cases like *Fine Paper*. Lead counsel usually is (are) given the authority to distribute work and appoint subcommittee members. His (her or their) decisions should only be overruled by a majority of the plaintiff's counsel.[66]

In addition, a liaison attorney may be appointed either by the court or lead counsel to receive and distribute pertinent notices, orders, and other communications from the court to counsel and class members. All plaintiff's attorneys should have access through the liaison attorney to documents produced throughout the litigation but should not need to receive each and every discovery document. As Judge Grady stated in his pretrial order in *In Re Continental Illinois Securities Litigation*, "[I]t makes no sense to designate a small number of attorneys to represent a class and then compensate them for time spent communicating with other attorneys for individual class members. If the attorneys for the class are competent, there is no need for a legion of other lawyers to be looking over their shoulders; if they are not competent, the legion will do no good anyway."[67]

Although complicated organizational structures have resulted in some abuse and much unintentional duplication of effort, courts are still reluctant to get too involved in the running of the plaintiff's organization.[68] Also, courts may not be receptive to suggestions from defendants on the plaintiffs' attorneys' organizational structure, as adverse parties are not normally permitted to tell each other how to run their practices. Defendants are likely to achieve greater success in controlling the fees of plaintiffs' attorneys by describing the potential for inefficiency and duplication inherent in a multiple-attorney class action suit (particularly one involving a democratic or consensually operated committee structure) and proposing specific limitations on time and expense charges rather than specifically seeking to influence the structure of plaintiffs' attorneys' litigation organization.

Monitoring of Attorneys' Activities

Although specific pretrial proposals should, of course, be tailored to the individualized needs and potential problems presented in a particular case, proposals to limit attorney time charges and expenses generally fall into the catagories described in the following paragraphs.

Accounting for Time by Activity

Probably the single most effective means of encouraging cost efficiency is for the court to require that plaintiffs' attorneys submit their time records chronologically by activity rather than by attorney.[69] Where multiple firms are involved, the accounting should be presented both generally and by firm so that the judge and the parties both have a clear, concise picture of how much time and money is being spent on each facet of the case. Judges are far more likely to declare that an excessive number of hours were spent on a pretrial memorandum than to state that a particular attorney or firm wasted *x* number of hours.[70] Moreover, accounting by activity should prove valuable to the parties in settlement negotiations because the cost of further proceedings can be translated more readily into a specific amount. Undoubtedly, the plaintiffs' bar will quickly become astute at estimating the cost of pretrial procedures once accounting for attorney's fees by activity becomes standard practice.

Limitations on Discovery

Limitation on the number of interrogatories, depositions, or document requests directly saves money for plaintiffs as well as defendants. Use of a central depository and negotiation by the parties on the form in which document request responses will be given also should bring savings, based on the overall economic impact to the parties as well as traditional tactical considerations.[71]

Attorney Compensation for Participation in Discovery or Court Appearances

Judge Grady, in *In Re Continental Illinois Securities Litigation*,[72] ordered that depositions, pretrial conferences, motions, and settlement negotiations be attended by only one attorney billing time. The Second Circuit has, somewhat reluctantly, affirmed disallowance of charges for multiple plaintiff's attorneys in motions and negotiations even when the defendants had multiple attorneys present.[73] Defendants seeking to limit the number of plaintiff's representatives compensated in court appearance may receive a more sympathetic hearing if they offer to abide by the restrictions they propose.

Limitation of Plaintiffs' Attorney's Expenses

Clear delegation of reimbursable expenses should be part of a proposal for limiting attorney's fees. For instance, reimbursement should be limited to necessary travel, hotel accommodations, and meals when (if) counsel must travel out of state. Conferences between counsel whose offices are at different points should be by telephone.[74]

Explication of Limits of Compensable Attorney Hours

The limits of compensable legal research and billing rates should be clearly stated in an early pretrial order. In *In Re Flight Transportation Securities Litigation*, defendants proposed in their motion for a Rule 26(f) discovery conference that because class representation is not given to attorneys who are not experienced in the field that is the subject of litigation, the court should deny compensation for general research in the areas of law known to plaintiffs' counsel.[75]

Defendants should also propose that the court explicitly state that time will be compensated according to the level of the work, not the level of the person doing it, i.e., senior partner rates should only be paid for work that warrants the attention of a senior partner. If a senior partner spends time reviewing documents or doing research a beginning associate could do, the partner should be paid at the rate of a beginning associate.[76] Although valuations of the level of skill required for various tasks admittedly involve subjective determination, courts regularly make such assessments in reaching a settlement award after the work has been done, so prior negotiations should help rather than inhibit responsible and efficient delegation of tasks.

Limitations on "Document Review"

One of the most chronic problems in multidistrict litigation highlighted by Judge McGlynn in *Fine Paper* involves half a dozen or more attorneys or law firms "document reviewing," or reading all the paperwork generated in the course of the trial and settlement preparation. Noting that one of the principal advantages of a class action is the avoidance of duplicated legal effort, Judge Grady in the *Continental Illinois* pretrial order stated that he would allow no compensation for time spent reading another lawyer's work except when a senior lawyer is required to approve a junior associate's document before filing or a lawyer is required to read something prepared by someone else in order to perform his or her task.[77]

Billing Judgment Should Be Exercised

The court should make clear in its pretrial order that plaintiffs' attorneys should not charge for duplicated hours, pursuits down blind alleys, or otherwise unnecessary hours and leave the court to ferret out the excessive hours. The Supreme Court recently instructed attorneys that hourly charges in the class action suit must meet the normal "billing judgment" standards that are used in the private sector.[78] Defendants should also be prepared to show that they will not and are not overstaffing, pursuing claims based on their delaying or bargaining potential, or billing for unnecessary work, as courts may ask for defendants' attorneys' billed hours to help determine whether plaintiffs' attorneys expended hours unnecessarily.[79]

Periodic Monitoring of Time and Expense Charges

In complex suits or suits that will obviously take some time to resolve, the court should order that time sheets be submitted to the court at frequent intervals. This will enable the court to monitor the reports periodically for insufficient record keeping or for such problems as duplication of effort, excessive hours, or double-billing.[80] The *Manual for Complex Litigation* recommends use of magistrates, where available, or appointment of a master to oversee factual issues relating to the fee determination, but many litigants fear that involvement of more personnel will lead to uneven application of reasonableness-of-expenses judgments. Moreover, litigants are usually required to pay the expenses of a master.[81]

Conclusion

The more information about the work of the attorneys and the economic realities of various organizational structures and pretrial procedures available to the court, the more likely it is that fair, reasonable, and adequate, but not excessive, attorney's fees will be awarded. A pretrial conference pursuant to Federal Rule of Civil Procedure 16 or 26(f), with considerable time devoted to fee issues, should be held early in the proceedings, and the court's expectations and procedures regarding the fee determination should be made clear to all parties.

In complex cases involving a number of different attorneys representing various class members of subclasses, defendants should urge the court to direct that an organizational structure be agreed upon that minimizes duplication of work, review of other attorneys' work, and power struggles within the attorneys' ranks. Attorneys representing individual clients should be advised that only work benefiting the class will be compensated from any settlement fund. Defendants should be prepared to demonstrate that they, too, are pursuing resolution of the suit in good faith and in a cost-efficient manner. Defendants' attorneys' billing charges should not reflect wanderings down blind alleys, superfluous motions, and overstaffing.

Defendants and plaintiffs should seek to adopt a discovery plan designed to limit the expenses of both parties through extrajudicial negotiation or pursuant to rule 26(f).

Finally, defendants should request that plaintiffs' attorney's fees be accounted for by activity rather than by attorney or firm, that explicit limitations be imposed on expenses such as travel, review of documents, interattorney conferences, number of attorneys to be compensated per disposition of pretrial conferences, etc., and that accounting be submitted to the court for review at regular intervals.

Notes

1. *See In re* Agent Orange Prod. Liab. Litig., 611 F. Supp. 1296 (D.C.N.Y. 1985), *aff'd in part, rev'd in part*, 818 F.2d 226 (2d Cir. 1987); *In re* Fine Paper Antitrust Litig., 98 F.R.D. 48, 84–85 (E.D. Pa. 1983), *aff'd in part, rev'd in part and remanded*, 751 F.2d 562 (3d Cir. 1984); *In re* Continental Ill. Sec. Litig., 572 F. Supp. 931 (N.D. Ill. 1983); Liebman v. J.W. Petersen Coal & Oil Co., 63 F.R.D. 684, 701 (N.D. Ill. 1974).
2. Liebman v. J.W. Petersen Coal & Oil Co., 63 F.R.D. at 701.
3. (General Management Order No. 1), M.D.L. Docket No. 142 (D.C. Cal. July 24, 1974).
4. 98 F.R.D. 48, 751 F.2d 562.
5. Several of the attorneys were joined and many of the assignments were made after a partial settlement had been obtained. *Fine Paper*, 98 F.R.D. at 73–76.

6. *Id.* at 70.
7. *Fine Paper*, 751 F.2d at 601.
8. *Id.* at 594.
9. *Id.* at 599–600.
10. *Id.* at 596.
11. *Id.* at 591.
12. 818 F.2d 226 (2d Cir. 1987).
13. *Id.* at 236–37, *citing* Ohio-Sealy Mattress Mfg. Co. v. Sealy Inc., 776 F.2d 646 658 (7th Cir. 1987).
14. *In re* Agent Orange Product Liab. Litig., 818 F.2d 226, 233 (3d Cir. 1984).
15. *Id.* at 233.
16. *See, e.g.*, Liebman v. J.W. Petersen Oil & Coal Co., 63 F.R.D. 684, 695 (N.D. Ill. 1974); *In re* Master Key Antitrust Litig., 1978-1 Trade Cas. (CCH) ¶ 61,887 (D. Conn. 1977). *See also* Miller, *Of Frankenstein Monsters and Shining Knights: Myth, Reality, and the "Class Action Problem,"* 92 HARV. L. REV. 664, 667 (1979).
17. Liebman v. J.W. Petersen Oil & Coal Co., 63 F.R.D. at 670. Although a fair number of settlements provide for a common fund and the defendant agrees to pay plaintiffs' attorneys, the plaintiff's attorneys' fees are considered part of the plaintiffs' fund. *See* Jones v. National Distillers & Chem. Corp., Fed. Sec. Rptr. (CCH) ¶ 97,288 (S.D.N.Y. 1980); Halsbind v. Sanders Technology, Fed. Sec. Rptr. (CCH) ¶ 98,011 (S.D.N.Y. 1981).
18. Lindy Bros. Builders Inc. of Philadelphia v. American Radiator & Standard Sanitary Corp., 487 F.2d 161, 167–68 (3d Cir. 1973), *aff'd in relevant part, vacated on other grounds*, 540 F.2d 102, 116–17 (3d Cir. 1976); City of Detroit v. Grinnell, 495 F.2d 448 (2d Cir. 1974), *aff'd in relevant part, rev'd in part,* 560 F.2d 1093, 1098 (2d Cir. 1977); Viosin v. Bartell Media Corp., Fed. Sec. Rptr. (CCH) ¶ 99,014, at 94,806 (S.D.N.Y. 1982). The United States Supreme Court recently approved the lodestar approach in determining an attorney's fee award under section 1988 but cautioned district courts to be sure to exclude hours not reasonably expended due to overstaffing, the inexperience of counsel, and duplication of work. Hensley v. Eckerhart, 461 U.S. 424, 103 S. Ct. 9133, 76 L. Ed. 2d 40 (1983).
19. Pennsylvania v. Delaware Valley Citizens' Council for Clear Air, 478 U.S. 546, 106 S. Ct. 3088, 92 L. Ed. 2d 439 (1986); Blum v. Stenson, 465 U.S. 886, 104 S. Ct. 1541, 79 L. Ed. 2d 891 (1984).
20. Blum v. Stenson, 465 U.S. at 899, 104 S. Ct. at 1549.
21. *Id.*
22. 478 U.S. at ______ , 106 S. Ct. at 3098. *But see Agent Orange Prod. Liab. Litig.*, 818 F.2d at 235 (inclusion of quality factors within the initial lodestar figure should not apply to instances in which district court uses national hourly rates).
23. Kamens v. Horizon Corp., Fed. Sec. Rptr. (CCH) ¶ 98,007, at 91,217–18 (S.D.N.Y. 1981).
24. *In re* Master Key Antitrust Litig., 1978-1 Trade Cas. (CCH) ¶ 61,887 (D. Conn. 1977).

25. Liebman v. J.W. Petersen Coal & Oil Co., 63 F.R.D. at 690–91.

26. *Id.* at 690; Cole v. Schenley Indus., No. 71-102, 563 F.2d 35 (S.D.N.Y. 1979).

27. Brown v. Gillette, 536 F. Supp. 113, 121 (D. Mass. 1982) (Title VII case); Steinberg v. Carey, 470 F. Supp. 471, 479 (S.D.N.Y. 1979).

28. *In re* Fine Paper Antitrust Litig., 98 F.R.D. 48 (E.D. Pa. 1983), *aff'd in part, rev'd in part and remanded*, 751 F.2d 562 (3d Cir. 1984).

29. Seigal v. Merrick, 619 F.2d 160, 164 (2d Cir. 1980); Steinberg v. Carey, 470 F. Supp. at 479 n.35.

30. Brown v. Gillette, 536 F. Supp. at 122.

31. *Id.*

32. Steinberg v. Carey, 470 F. Supp. at 479.

33. 710 F.2d 455 (8th Cir. 1983).

34. *Id.* at 461.

35. *Id.* at 462.

36. 112 F.R.D. 243, 285 (1986).

37. *See* P. CONNELLY, E. HOLLEMAN & M. KUHLMAN, JUDICIAL CONTROLS AND THE CIVIL LITIGATION PROCESS: DISCOVERY (Fed. Jud. Center 1978); Kirkham, *Problems of Complex Litigation*, 83 F.R.D. 497 (1979); Sherman & O'Kinnard, *Federal Court Discovery in the '80s: Making the Rules Work*, 95 F.R.D. 246, 269 (1983).

38. *See, e.g., In re* Fine Paper Antitrust Litig., 685 F.2d 810, 817 (3d Cir. 1980); Eli Lilly & Co. v. Generix Drug Sales Inc., 460 F.2d 1096, 1105 (5th Cir. 1972).

39. FED. R. CIV. P. 26 (f) provides:

> At any time after commencement of an action the court may direct the attorneys for the parties to appear before it for a conference on the subject of discovery. The court shall do so upon motion by the attorney for any party if the motion includes: (1) A statement of the issues as they then appear; (2) A proposed plan and schedule of discovery; (3) Any limitations proposed to be placed on discovery; (4) Any other proposed orders with respect to discovery; and (5) A statement showing that the attorney making the motion has made a reasonable effort to reach agreement with opposing attorneys on the matters set forth in the motion. Each party and his attorney are under a duty to participate in good faith by the framing of a discovery plan if a plan is proposed by the attorney for any party. Notice of the motion shall be served on all parties. Objections or additions to matters set forth in the motion shall be served not later than ten days after service of the motion.
>
> Following discovery conference the court shall enter an order tentatively identifying the issues for discovery purposes, establishing a plan and schedule for discovery, setting limitations on discovery, if any; and determining such other matters, including the allocation of expenses, as are necessary for the proper management of discovery in the action. An order may be altered or amended whenever justice so requires.
>
> Subject to the right of a party who properly moves for a discovery conference to prompt convening of the conference, the court may combine the discovery conference with a pretrial conference authorized by Rule 16.

40. *See, e.g., In re* Continental Ill. Sec. Litig., 572 F. Supp. 931 (N.D. Ill. 1983).

41. Kansas-Nebraska Natural Gas Co. Inc. v. Marathon Oil Co., 109 F.R.D. 12, 31 (D. Neb. 1985).

223

42. FED. R. CIV. P. 26(f) (1)–(5).

43. Stich v. United States, 730 F.2d 115 (3d Cir. 1984).

44. *In re* Fine Paper Antitrust Litig., 685 F.2d 810, 817–18 (3d Cir. 1980), *cert. denied sub nom.* Alaska v. Boise Cascade Corp., 103 S. Ct. 801 (1983).

45. The Advisory Committee specifically rejected proposals to limit the scope of discovery to claims or defenses rather than to any "subject matter involved in the action," so the discovery conference provisions should not be read as authorizing the court to narrow the general scope of discovery. *See* Sherman & O'Kinnard, *supra* note 37, at 247 n.7.

46. FED. R. CIV. P. 26(f).

47. Sherman & O'Kinnard, *supra* note 37, at 273.

48. A scheduling conference may also be requested by either party or by a magistrate authorized by district court rule. ADVISORY COMMITTEE R. 16, n. 8 to subsection (b).

49. Subsections (b)–(f) provide:

(b) SCHEDULING AND PLANNING. Except in the categories of actions exempted by district court rule as inappropriate, the judge, or a magistrate when authorized by district court rule, shall, after consulting with the attorneys for the parties and any unrepresented parties, by a scheduling conference, telephone, mail, or other suitable means, enter a scheduling order that limits the time

(1) to join other parties and to amend the pleadings;
(2) to file and hear motions; and
(3) to complete discovery.

The scheduling order also may include:

(4) the date or dates for conferences before trial, a final pretrial conference, and trial; and
(5) any other matters appropriate to the circumstances of the case.

The order shall issue as soon as practicable but in no event more than 120 days after filing of the complaint. A schedule shall not be modified except by leave of the judge or a magistrate when authorized by district court rule upon a showing of good cause.

(c) SUBJECTS TO BE DISCUSSED AT PRETRIAL CONFERENCES. The participants in any conference under this rule may consider and take action with respect to

(1) the formulation and simplification of the issues, including the elimination of frivolous claims or defenses;
(2) the necessity or desirability of amendments to the pleadings;
(3) the possibility of obtaining admissions of fact and of documents which will avoid unnecessary proof, stipulations regarding the authenticity of documents, and advance rulings from the court on the admissibility of evidence;
(4) the avoidance of unnecessary proof and of cumulative evidence;
(5) the identification of witnesses and documents, the need and schedule for filing and exchanging pretrial briefs, and the date or dates for further conferences and for trial;
(6) the advisability of referring matters to a magistrate or master;
(7) the possibility of settlement or the use of extrajudicial procedures to resolve the dispute;
(8) the form and substance of the pretrial order;
(9) the disposition of pending motions;

(10) the need for adopting special procedures for managing potentially difficult or protracted actions that may involve complex issues, multiple parties, difficult legal questions, or unusual proof problems; and

(11) such other matters as may aid in the disposition of the action.

At least one of the attorneys for each party participating in any conference before trial shall have authority to enter into stipulations and to make admissions regarding all matters that the participants may reasonably anticipate may be discussed.

(d) FINAL PRETRIAL CONFERENCE. Any final pretrial conference shall be held as close to the time of trial as reasonable under the circumstances. The participants at any such conference shall formulate a plan for trial, including a program for facilitating the admission of evidence. The conference shall be attended by at least one of the attorneys who will conduct the trial for each of the parties and by any unrepresented parties.

(e) PRETRIAL ORDERS. After any conference held pursuant to this rule, an order shall be entered reciting the action taken. This order shall control the subsequent course of the action unless modified by a subsequent order. The order following a final pretrial conference shall be modified only to prevent manifest injustice.

(f) SANCTIONS. If a party or party's attorney fails to obey a scheduling or pretrial order, or if no appearance is made on behalf of a party at a scheduling or pretrial conference, or if a party or party's attorney is substantially unprepared to participate in the conference, or if a party or party's attorney fails to participate in good faith, the judge, upon motion of his own initiative, may make such orders with regard thereto as are just, and among others any of the order provided in Rule 37(b)(2)(B), (C), (D). In lieu of or in addition to any other sanctions, the judge shall require the party or the attorneys representing him or both to pay the reasonable expenses incurred because of any noncompliance with this rule, including attorney's fees, unless the judge finds that the noncompliance was substantially justified or that other circumstances make an award of expenses unjust.

50. FED. R. CIV. P. 1.

51. FED. R. CIV. P. 16(a)(3).

52. *See* Sherman & O'Kinnard, *supra* note 37, at 277–78.

53. Balbanian, *Pretrial Orders in the Complex Case*, in FEDERAL DISCOVERY IN COMPLEX CIVIL CASES 113, 114–15 (1980).

54. *See In re* Sanction of Baker, 744 F.2d 1438, 1440 (10th Cir. 1984), *cert. denied*, 105 S. Ct. 2016, 85 L. Ed. 2d 299 ("[N]either contumacious attitude nor chronic failure is a necessary threshold to the imposition of sanctions . . . intent [of rule 16(f)] is to impose the sanction where the fault lies"); Titus v. Mercedes Benz of N. Am., 695 F.2d 746 (3d Cir. 1982) (sanctions imposed for attorney's lack of preparation for pretrial conferences and failure to prepare pretrial order).

55. FED. R. CIV. P. 16(f).

56. Sherman & O'Kinnard, *supra* note 37, at 263 n.72. In 1979 the Advisory Committee decided against inserting a numerical limit on interrogatories, although it had proposed limiting the number to thirty unless a court ordered otherwise in its 1978 proposed amendments. *See Amendments to the Federal Rules of Civil Procedure*, 85 F.R.D. 521, 539 (1980).

57. *See, e.g.*, TEX. RULES CIV. PROC. R. 168(5) (1981) (no party may require more than thirty answers or serve more than two sets of interrogatories).

58. *See* FED. R. CIV. P. 5(d); Note, *Non-Party Access to Discovery Materials in Federal Courts*, 94 HARV. L. REV. 1085–88 (1981).

59. *In re* Continental Ill. Sec. Litig., Fed. Sec. Rptr. (CCH) ¶ 91,457 (7th Cir. 1984); United States v. International Business Mach. Inc., 67 F.R.D. 40, 46 (S.D.N.Y. 1975); *In re* Hulkins, 598 F.2d 176, 186, 191 (D.C. Cir. 1979).

60. No. 74-1698 (D.D.C. 1974).

61. Litton Sys. Inc. v. American Tel. & Tel. Co., No. 76-2512 (S.D.N.Y. 1976); MCI Communications v. American Tel. & Tel. Co., No. 74-633 (N.D. Ill. 1974).

62. American Tel. & Tel. Co. v. Grady, 594 F.2d 594, 596–97 (7th Cir. 1978). Defendants' arguments that parties will be less likely to make full discovery disclosures if the information is not restricted in use has earned little favor in the courts. Since a defendant's obligation to respond to discovery is not discretionary, judges do not believe defendants should be given an incentive to do what they are obligated to do under the federal rules.

    But see Litton Sys. Inc. v. American Tel. & Tel. Co., No. 76-2512, slip op. at 5 (S.D.N.Y. 1979) (expedited preparation of the government's case against defendant does not by itself constitute "good cause" for modification of the protective order). *See also* Seattle Times v. Rhinehart, No. 82-172, N.Y. Times, May 22, 1984, at A19, col. 1 (S. Ct. May 21, 1984) (defendants not entitled to use discovery for extrajudicial purposes that would subject plaintiff and third parties to public harassment).

63. *See, e.g.*, Meer v. United Brands Inc., Fed. Sec. Rptr. (CCH) ¶ 96,794 (S.D.N.Y. 1979) (requested award reduced because information from U.S. Attorney General, defendant's investigation committee reports, and SEC was available to plaintiffs).

64. Since economy of action and resources are criteria for class certification, exploration of attorney's fee limitations is appropriate even before class certification. *See In re* Continental Ill. Sec. Litig., 572 F. Supp. 931 (N.D. Ill. 1983); *In re* Greeman Sec. Litig., 94 F.R.D. 274, 276 (S.D. Fla. 1982) (court's ability to control attorney's fees considered in whether to certify class under FED. R. CIV. P. 23(a)).

65. *See, e.g.*, *In re* Greeman Sec. Litig., 94 F.R.D. at 282.

66. *Id.* at 283.

67. *In re* Continental Ill. Sec. Litig., 572 F. Supp. at 934.

68. Many judges hesitate to become involved in matters tangential to the subject of the litigation. *See In re* Greeman Sec. Litig., 94 F.R.D. at 283. Increasingly, however, judges feel the need to appoint magistrates or masters or even guardians ad litem to oversee complicated cases involving dozens of plaintiffs' attorneys. *See* MANUAL FOR COMPLEX LITIGATION § 417 (Supp. 1981).

69. *See* Wabasha v. Solem, 580 F. Supp. 488 (D.S.D. 1984).

70. *See, e.g.*, *In re* Fine Paper Antitrust Litig., 98 F.R.D. 48, 81 (E.D. Pa. 1983), *aff'd in part, rev'd in part and remanded*, 751 F.2d 562 (3d Cir. 1984); Liebman v. J.W. Petersen Coal & Oil Co., 63 F.R.D. 684, 699 (N.D. Ill. 1974).

71. Federal Rule of Civil Procedure 34 requires a party to produce documents pursuant to a request either as they are kept in the ordinary course of business or according to the categories in the plaintiff's request. Although the rule appears to give the option as between the choice to the defendant, the advisory comments indicate that a defendant may at times be required to organize or present the information in a manner that is useful to the discovering party.

Courts have, for instance, ordered defendants to translate documents written in Japanese and to program their computer to provide information to plaintiffs in a reasonably useful form. *See* Japanese Elec. Prods. Antitrust Litig., MDL 189 Pretrial Order 154 (E.D. Pa 1979); Kozlowski v. Sears, Roebuck & Co., 73 F.R.D. 73, 76 (D. Mass. 1976).

72. 572 F. Supp. at 933.

73. *See* Seigal v. Merrick, 619 F.2d 160, 164 (2d Cir. 1980).

74. *See In re* Continental Ill. Sec. Litig., 572 F. Supp. at 934.

75. *In re* Flight Transp. Sec. Litig., No. 4-82-874, at 13 (D. Minn. Sept. 1, 1983) (defendants' motion for a pretrial conference). *See also In re* Continental Ill. Sec. Litig., 572 F. Supp. at 933 (pretrial order).

76. *See In re* Fine Paper Antitrust Litig., 98 F.R.D. 48, 85 (E.D. Pa. 1983), *aff'd in part, rev'd in part and remanded*, 751 F.2d 562 (3d Cir. 1984).

77. *In re* Continental Ill. Sec. Litig., 572 F. Supp. 931, 933 (N.D. Ill. 1983).

78. Hensley v. Eckerhart, 461 U.S. 424, 103 S. Ct. 1933, 76 L. Ed. 2d 40 (1983). *See also* Zeffiro v. First Pa. Bank, 574 F. Supp. 443, 446 (E.D. Pa. 1983); State of Arizona v. Maricopa County Medical Soc'y, 578 F. Supp. 1262, 1265 (D. Ariz. 1984) (hours excluded from fee award for plaintiff's attorneys' failure to exercise billing judgement).

79. *See* Jacquette v. Black Hawk County, Iowa, 710 F.2d 455, 461 n.13 (8th Cir. 1983); Stastny v. Southern Bell Tel. & Tel. Co., 77 F.R.D. 662 (W.D.N.C. 1978); Naismith v. Professional Golfer's Ass'n, 85 F.R.D. 552, 562–63 (N.D. Ga. 1979).

80. *See* MANUAL FOR COMPLEX LITIGATION § 1.47 (Supp. 1981).

81. For advantages and disadvantages of using a master in discovery and fee determination, *see* McKinstry, *Use of Master in Major Complex Cases*, in FEDERAL DISCOVERY IN COMPLEX CIVIL CASES 213 (1980).

Fifteen

Fifteen Suggestions for Cutting Discovery Costs

Stephen R. Steinberg

Let's identify one of the sources of our problem—Federal Rule of Civil Procedure 26:

> GENERAL PROVISION GOVERNING DISCOVERY.
>
> (a) Discovery Methods. Parties may obtain discovery by one or more of the following methods:
>
> [(i) oral depositions; and/or (ii) written depositions; and/or (iii) written interrogatories; and/or (iv) production of documents or things; and/or (v) requests for admission.]
>
> (b) Discovery Scope and Limits . . .
>
> (1) *In General*. Parties may obtain discovery regarding any matter, not privileged, which is relevant to the subject matter involved. . . . It is not ground for objection that the information sought will be inadmissible at the trial if the information sought appears reasonably calculated to lead to the discovery of admissible evidence.

Theoretically, we can use five different discovery devices to investigate one fact or line of inquiry, which may or may not result in admissible evidence at trial. We know that the judges do not have the time to decide whether a proposed discovery inquiry falls outside of the rule. We also know that it is improper to instruct a witness not to answer, except on privilege grounds. Discovery can, unless litigators exercise restraint, go on and on while needless costs mount.

Possibly we should consider exerting our varying levels of influence to get the scope of discovery under the rule narrowed. If the rule were limited, so would be discovery and its costs. Do we really need to ask for and discover every paper that has any relationship to the subject matter of the dispute? Do we really need to depose everyone who ever wrote, read, touched, talked about, or saw every piece of paper ever written or produced in discovery under the present rules? Do we really need interrogato-

Stephen R. Steinberg is a member of Fulbright Jaworski & Reavis McGrath, New York City.

ries and depositions on every meeting or conversation held? Do we really need limitless interrogatories; do we really need interrogatories at all? How much of the massive amount of discovery now permitted and taken really winds up helping to resolve the dispute?

But if we do not use the existing rule to its fullest in advocating our clients' causes, are we guilty of poor practice, sloppy practice, or malpractice? Is one solution, given the present rule, that client and lawyer agree at the beginning to limit the scope and extent of the discovery that will be used in the case? Should they? Is the client expert enough in the business of litigation to be able to make such an agreement, or does the client have the legitimate right to rely on the litigator to call these shots? Should the lawyer be asking for a waiver beforehand? In the outcome and during the litigation process, it is the client's money that is at stake, and some clients are astute enough to make the hard choices when it comes to saving or spending their money.

But we do have "the rule," and we do have clients who pay the bill. Here are 15 concrete approaches we should use to try to limit discovery costs:

1. Focus very early on your objectives: What does the law require you and the other side to prove? What are the legal issues? What is your strategy of prosecution or of defense? And what do you think your adversary's strategy will be? Determine who the key witnesses are on both sides, and limit discovery requests to these persons. (Wait until later and only if necessary to depose or seek documents from the lower levels; start with the decision makers or prime actors.) Find out early where the important documents are. Be prepared to produce these documents quickly and offer key depositions early so that you can seek the same from your adversary. And try to get an agreement with the adversary to limit numbers of witnesses, interrogatories, days of deposition, type of documents, subject matter, persons from whom documents should be sought. If you want to accomplish these goals, you must establish a working relationship with your adversary.
2. If you see that your adversary is uncooperative or that you are on a runaway train, try to get the court to intervene early. Try to get the judge to agree to hear discovery disputes orally or on a letter application or short notice. And if the case merits it, try to interest your adversary or the judge in a discovery master, who is a private practitioner who would be paid such a person's regular high hourly

rates, to decide disputes or recommend decisions to the court.

3. Make your venue and dispositive pleading motions quickly, and let the judge know that these may narrow discovery if decided quickly.
4. Do not argue about every discovery matter that you and your adversary disagree on. The "cost" of these disputes usually far outweighs the substantive litigation benefit. Limit making motions to matters you reasonably believe may affect the substantive outcome. In other words, be prepared to make concessions on discovery. And do not use sanctions motions as a weapon; they cost more than they are worth to the ultimate outcome. When things get bad enough, most judges get the picture themselves.
5. Cut down slavish reliance on computerized litigation support and retrieval systems. Depending on volume, review documents early for hot and substantive documents, and read them early on. The layers of cost created by coders, paralegals, etc. before senior litigators see the "evidence" could be reduced by getting our hands dirty early on.
6. Do not double- and triple-team depositions. It may be necessary for more than one lawyer to prepare for taking or defending a deposition, but seldom is more than one lawyer necessary at the deposition. And when you are taking a deposition, if your paralegal has done the proper job in preparing the documents, see whether you really need the paralegal at the deposition. Or else prepare yourself; you need to know the documents anyway!
7. Have your client's depositions taken at your client's place of business, and take your adversary's depositions at your adversary's place of business. The economic loss in dragging clients downtown is clear, and immeasurable time savings arise from access to documents not previously identified or persons to get information from at once.
8. Have younger lawyers argue those few discovery motions you are compelled to make.
9. Avoid cross-claims among defendants; try to get standstill agreements. Concentrate discovery on the adversary; do not create new ones.
10. If your client has the personnel, have them prepare initial drafts of answers to fact interrogatories. And since they may be initially closer to the facts, ask them for suggestions

for areas of document requests and depositions (and, if necessary, interrogatories).

11. Do not prepare deposition summaries for every deposition. Use your PC—disks of depositions are available. It is much less costly to use PCs for full text or searches than to pay for a paralegal's and a typist's time.
12. In dealing with technical matters, use the client's in-house "experts" first, before going to outside experts to help you in discovery.
13. Keep your client advised (either orally or in writing, depending on your relationship) of what is going on in discovery and what you plan. Discovery should not be a big, unknown hole into which the client pours money.
14. Do not recommend discovery on the basis of the burden it will place on other parties or the delay it will cause in the lawsuit. Our clients are too smart for that.
15. Do not forget that it really is not necessary to turn over every stone and dig up every tomb. But we must focus early on the substantive needs of the litigation in order to try to cut down discovery costs. Litigate the case, not your adversary or procedural differences.

Sixteen

Facing Up to the Costs of Cutting Costs

Thomas J. Kavaler

Handling the kind of major litigation that we are concerned with here—drawing on inside and outside lawyers—as in doing the tango, takes both of them, working cooperatively, to control costs. While the prevalent stereotype features the cost-conscious in-house counsel and the spendthrift big-firm litigator, thoughtful observers of the scene have long recognized that costs can truly be contained only when both of these players share a common goal and a common understanding of the ways in which that goal can be achieved.

It is axiomatic that costs must be—and can be—controlled in major litigation and in all other kinds of litigation. But what is often overlooked is that the most effective means of cutting costs can often be by increasing risk. If the increased risk being assumed is justified by the costs being saved, then the process is effective.

In deciding to abandon the "spare no expense" philosophy of litigating major cases, inside and outside counsel must both realize that they are thereby also abandoning the stance that victory is the only acceptable result, which all too often becomes "victory at any cost." Provided you are prepared to risk doing things that may, to some extent, diminish the likelihood of your succeeding at trial, costs can be saved quite simply in many areas. However, a price that inside counsel must be prepared to pay for these savings is the diminution of one of the things typically purchased from outside counsel in major litigation: comfort.

Whereas inside and outside counsel may share a tendency to view inside counsel as "the client" vis-à-vis outside counsel, in reality there is an ultimate client behind inside counsel: the corporate entity, as personified by its business managers, who, after all, are running the very business that inside counsel represents. Although businesspeople are widely reputed to be risk takers, lawyers—both inside and outside—are widely regarded as being highly risk-averse. Thus, it is not at all unusual to find inside and outside counsel striving mightily to cross all the t's and dot all the i's in major litigation for no better reason than to avoid the possibility that, if things do not work out right, there may be recriminations from the busi-

Thomas J. Kavaler is a member of Cahill Gordon & Reindel, New York City.

ness managers predicated upon the assumption that some action left untaken would have altered the outcome had it been undertaken. If this premise is examined at the outset of major litigation, rather than at its conclusion, counsel and the ultimate client can agree upon a level of acceptable risk, which in turn can lead to some truly effective cost-saving measures.

Discovery Costs

For example, perhaps the most widely acknowledged cause of enormous expense in all litigation, and especially in major litigation, is the entire area of discovery. Contemporary litigators tend to regard comprehensive discovery as inevitable in all cases and, similarly, tend to forget that discovery as we know it today is barely fifty years old. Current concepts of discovery have evolved since the adoption of the Federal Rules of Civil Procedure in 1938. Before that, trial lawyers (the prehistoric ancestors of today's litigators) conducted their cross-examinations in court, before the judge and jury, and not in depositions. Granted, they were sometimes surprised—and sometimes unpleasantly so—by the answers elicited by their questions, but they certainly spent substantially less time and money preparing to go to court as distinguished from going to court. If we recognize that only 5 percent of all cases commenced ever reach the courtroom for trial, then it is evident that in 95 percent of all cases, depositions are not really being taken in preparation for trial but, rather, are being taken for purposes of enhancing the taking party's settlement posture or for purposes of grounding what is hoped to be a dispositive motion.

Let's focus on the other 5 percent of the cases, that is, the ones that will actually be tried. Where is it written that it constitutes malpractice to announce that you are ready to try the case without having precluded, to a mathematical certainty, the possibility that the other side might call even a single witness whose (multiday) deposition you have not already taken? Have litigators lost entirely the skills that enabled their predecessors, the trial lawyers, to cross-examine undeposed witnesses at trial? What of the numerous matters that even today are resolved by arbitration, wherein there is generally no prehearing deposition discovery and wherein lawyers necessarily examine adverse witnesses without benefit of prior sworn testimony? Why is it that lawyers are capable of examining witnesses they haven't deposed in an arbitration—and their clients are willing to have them do so—but then the same lawyers and the same clients will not even consider entering a courtroom to try a case without having deposed every conceivable adverse witness to within an inch of his or her life?

In virtually every case, it should be possible to determine early on which witnesses one can, with an acceptable degree of risk, refrain from deposing entirely. These include witnesses whose deposition will not enhance the settlement posture of the case or help to ground a potentially dispositive motion. But they also include those witnesses whose appearance at the trial is unlikely (either for reasons of geography, health, age, or disposition toward the adversary or because a realistic assessment of the adversary's trial strategy suggests that they will not be called even though they are available), and also those witnesses whose testimony is reasonably predictable so that the risk of confronting such a witness at trial without having taken a deposition can be quantified. Another type of witness who need not be deposed is one whose trial testimony cannot possibly be harmful, regardless of what it may be. This is the same witness who, at trial, will escape with no cross-examination because he has scored no points. If you are not planning to cross-examine him at trial, why do you need to take his deposition?

A closely related type of witness whose deposition can safely be omitted is the witness who, because of the substantive law that applies to the case, cannot do you any legal harm. I offer an example from my own practice. Approximately a year ago, I tried a libel case to a federal court jury on behalf of one of the major television networks. Although the plaintiff named in excess of two dozen witnesses on his list of trial witnesses, we deposed only one of them: the plaintiff himself. As to all of the others, we were prepared to accept as a reasonable risk the possibility that they would take the stand and testify to matters that might arguably go to the truth or falsity of the broadcast. However, since I knew that none of these two dozen individuals had spoken to the reporters who prepared the broadcast, I was highly confident that, on cross-examination, each one would have to admit that he or she had never conveyed the substance of his or her trial testimony to the reporters before the broadcast, and thus the plaintiff would be unable to establish the element of actual malice (or knowing falsity) that was an essential part of his prima facie case. Thus, in deciding to forgo some two dozen depositions, we were able to effect substantial cost savings while taking what we viewed as only a minimal risk.

The important point to focus on here is that the risk is—and properly ought to be—the client's. It is not the proper role of either inside or outside counsel to decide to create a totally risk-free environment without regard to cost. However, it is essential that these risks be fully discussed and appreciated by all concerned before being undertaken, lest what was viewed as a prudent cost-saving mechanism at the time it was undertaken comes to be viewed, post hoc, as a sin of omission with tragic consequences.

The decision to adopt this sort of "less is more" strategy necessarily influences the choice of counsel. All other things being equal, it is relatively easy to shine in the cross-examination of a trial witness who testifies for one hour on direct but whose deposition you have previously taken for three days in the comfort and serenity of your own office. Much more difficult is the cross-examination of the undeposed witness. This requires a lawyer whose particular skill and experience lies in this area, backed up by a client who has faith in that skill and experience. While this approach may result in some unpleasant surprises in some cases, they will only rarely affect the outcome, and it will, at the same time, result in significant savings in all cases where it is used.

There is, however, one inevitable downside to this approach, and it is not an insignificant one. Trying a case on this basis deprives inside and outside counsel of the ability to report to the client that they have left no stone unturned and that the adverse result obtained is either the natural consequence of the facts or a result of imperfections in the judicial system. This is why it is so necessary for the ultimate client to understand the risks to be taken and to weigh those risks against the savings to be achieved.

Choosing One Cause of Action

This same "less is more" approach can be adopted in other areas as well. For example, while major corporations are more often defendants than plaintiffs, it is not unheard of for them to initiate litigation. Because corporate counsel are so used to being on the receiving end of prolix complaints that contain innumerable causes of action, when it is their turn to be a plaintiff, there is an understandable tendency to want to assert numerous causes of action. However, since you are only going to get one recovery, all you need is one cause of action, provided it is a good cause of action. Pleading half a dozen alternative causes of action simply gives the defendant the opportunity to engage in motion practice directed at one or two of those causes of action, while simultaneously urging the court that the entire suit should be stayed until the motion that is addressed to those causes of action is resolved. It also needlessly broadens the scope of discovery to which the plaintiff will be exposed and which the plaintiff will feel obligated to take of the defendant. Moreover, it is often the case that if all the causes of action survive until the trial stage, the jury will be confused by instructions on alternate theories of law. Jurors frequently have more difficulty understanding the concept of pleading in the alternative than do lawyers who draft complaints.

However, here, once again, the decision to forgo potentially available theories of relief must be that of the ultimate client. The executive whose responsibility covers the relevant business area must understand that, while he or she is certainly going to minimize costs by a quantifiable factor, there is at least a remote possibility that he or she will not prevail on the selected cause of action, whereas there might exist or might later be determined to have existed some other theory that might have been successful. Once again, the question is one of balancing the risk/reward ratio. And again, the balance should be struck by the real client, or at least with the client's knowledge and acquiescence.

Multidefendant Cases

What of the all too common phenomenon of the multidefendant case, that is, one in which neither inside nor outside counsel for your corporation is in a position to dictate the scope of discovery, even from the defense point of view? This type of litigation is very common where, for example, all members of an industry are being sued for an alleged common failing or where numerous competitors are being sued in an antitrust context or where the plaintiff has alleged any conspiracy that involves a number of large corporate defendants.

If one is willing to assume a certain degree of risk, these kinds of cases present perhaps the best area for potential cost savings. For example, in a case with a dozen defendants, each of whom is a major player in the industry and each of whom has roughly equivalent exposure, why is it necessary for a lawyer (or, God forbid, two lawyers) representing each of those dozen defendants to attend each and every deposition, status conference, examination of documents, physical inspection of the plant, or other proceeding that produces a written record? Assuming a certain commonality of interests, why can't X Corporation and its fancy outside law firm rely upon Y Corporation's fancy outside law firm to attend a pretrial conference and report to the court that the parties require another six months to complete discovery, without fear that something of value will be lost to X Corporation by not getting a chance to second this view in person?

Another example from my own practice comes to mind. I am currently representing a major broker-dealer in a case brought against more than a dozen parties by a plaintiff who was, simultaneously, a customer of my client and several other broker-dealers. In this lawsuit, the former customer makes allegations against both the broker-dealers with whom it dealt and numerous other players in the commodities markets, all of whom are charged with having conspired to violate the antitrust and commodities laws. In this case there are necessarily worldwide depositions of each of the defendants, numerous representatives of the plaintiff, nonparty witnesses, and several far-flung experts. Defense counsel have gotten together and agreed to a division of labor whereby the lawyers for one of the defendants take the lead role in deposing a given witness for the plaintiff or, indeed, several witnesses for the plaintiff. The lawyers for the other defendants do not attend these depositions, although they receive transcripts. Since the deposition usually continues for several days, it is possible for lawyers not attending to contact the lawyer taking the deposition at the end of the first day of the deposition and satisfy themselves that things are proceeding in a manner consistent with their interests and expectations. To the extent they have suggestions for lines of inquiry that should be pursued, these can be conveyed to the lawyer taking the deposition, who can incorporate them in the next day's proceedings.

Similarly, when the deposition of one of the defendants is taken, the other defendants need not all be represented by their dozen-odd counsel, provided that they have in advance worked out some arrangement whereby an objection by any defendant at a deposition inures to the benefit of all defendants and the defendants will not cross-examine one another's witnesses during the plaintiff's discovery, but rather will make one another's witnesses available informally to other defense counsel for trial preparation should the case survive to that stage. Similarly, at routine status conferences, it is not necessary for each of the dozen-plus defendants to send even a young associate for the simple purpose of observing first-hand what the plaintiff or the court has to say. Pretrial conferences in this case are transcribed, and the transcripts are available from the official court reporter within several days after the conference. Even if they were not, a single defense lawyer attending on behalf of a single defendant would be more than capable of circulating a memorandum to absent counsel for all defendants describing what transpired.

Of course, such coordination by agreement among counsel is commonplace in many cases. What I am suggesting goes one step further: Where such an agreement is not readily forthcoming for one reason or another, consider putting the same procedures into effect unilaterally. That is, if ten other lawyers are going to attend the deposition of the plaintiff in Timbuktu, decide that you probably don't have enough to add to that deposition to make it worth your while to attend. If ten other lawyers are going to attend the pretrial conference and you have nothing unique to raise, don't go. Someone will tell you what happened.

In each of these instances, it is possible that something untoward will happen while you are absent. That is the risk. However, the cost savings are obvious and, once again, there is a balance to be struck. But here, too, the ultimate client must be aware of and content with the decision to undertake this risk, or else inside and outside counsel will be confronted with the question "Where were you when the plaintiff testified that. . . ?" The client must know, in advance, that you will not be there.

Document Review

The same philosophy can apply to the phenomenally time-consuming, and therefore expensive, process of reviewing documents produced by other parties in litigation. Why is it necessary that each of a dozen defendants should separately and independently review the two million documents produced by the plaintiff? Why can't that be delegated to one of the defendants, who has as much at stake as anyone, and to that defendant's reputable, experienced, competent outside counsel? Why can't the other defendants rely upon that one defendant and its counsel to do an adequate job? The answer is that of course they can, but here again what is being sacrificed is the comfort factor. Should the case not turn out well, will the ultimate client turn to the inside and outside counsel and say, "How did you guys miss this document?" He won't if he has been briefed in advance that a decision is being made to save X dollars in document review costs by relying on the review being conducted by the outside or inside counsel for a fellow defendant (who, in turn, will presumably be relying on you to perform some other function in the case).

Once again, this is commonly done by agreement in large cases where counsel establish various committees to conduct various aspects of trial preparation. But in a case where such an agreement is not forthcoming, you could consider the risk/reward ratio of simply not doing something that will be done by someone else with a similar exposure and therefore a similar interest in seeing that it is done well.

Repetitive Litigation

Another example is repetitive, patternlike litigation—not necessarily small, but also not novel. For example, your company routinely hires sales representatives from the competition. They have employment contracts. They get sued. You defend them. You usually prevail—or settle cheap—and anyway, it is more cost-effective than training your own. Why not let your outside lawyer delegate some of these cases to a trusted associate? Sure, you increase the risk somewhat (very little, I submit), but you also cut the costs.

Risk versus Expected Return

There is a common theme in each of these examples: Lawyers who by inclination and experience want to leave no stone unturned should be encouraged to leave many stones untouched. This is a difficult enough proposition to sell to lawyers under any circumstances, but it becomes impossible when they do not receive adequate assurances that they will not be criticized after the fact for nonfeasance by a client who is unhappy with—and surprised by—the outcome. Traditionally, one of the benefits outside counsel have "sold" to inside counsel is comfort, or, phrased differently, hiring a prestigious outside firm gives inside counsel the ability, in the event of an unsuccessful outcome, to turn to senior management and say, "But I hired Blank, Blank & Blank—what more could I have done?" backed up by outside counsel, who says, "But I did everything it was possible to do—what more could I have done?" Inside and outside counsel both have to be willing to forgo this security blanket in appropriate circumstances. The calculus is always this: How much money can be saved by eliminating certain pretrial activities that are reasonably expected not to significantly affect the ultimate outcome of the case, balanced against the incremental risk of an adverse outcome (or, sometimes, where liability is inevitable, the risk that damages will be higher than they might otherwise be)?

To be avoided at all costs is the "we had to burn the village down to save it from the enemy" syndrome. Thus, a defendant's verdict in a case where the *ad damnum* is $1 million, achieved after expending legal fees of $1.5 million, will only in the rarest circumstances be regarded as a victory by the business types who are the clients. Assuming that a "victory at any price" defense in such a case would cost $1.5 million and assuming further that there is no way that the damages can exceed the *ad damnum*, it is readily apparent that any cost-saving measures that will bring the legal fees under a million dollars are justified. Let us assume that, at the outset, counsel believes damages can be cut in half with a maximum defense. For an expenditure of $1.5 million in legal fees, you might save $500,000. This is obviously not cost-justified. If you can cut your legal fees down to $500,000, while only increasing the odds of losing the full $1 million from one out of two to three out of four, you will have saved a million dollars while theoretically risking an additional $250,000. If you can scale your legal fees down to $250,000, while at the same time increasing the odds of losing the full million dollars to four out of five, you would still be ahead.

The problem is that, too often, inside counsel demands outside counsel reduce the cost from $1.5 million to $250,000, but is unwilling to see the risk increase above fifty-fifty. The demand to outside counsel is to cut costs without increasing risk. Given that limitation, outside counsel is relegated to the sort of relatively minor cost cutting that results from eliminating first-class air travel, secretarial overtime, courier-delivered drafts, and things of that nature. It takes a lot of forgone secretarial overtime and a lot of coach travel to equal the savings that can be achieved by skipping one five-day deposition in a city 2,000 miles from your lawyer's office. That is where the big savings are.[1]

If outside counsel are willing to forgo the comfort of only examining at trial the previously deposed witness in all cases, if inside counsel are willing to forgo the comfort of being able to tell line managers that they have left no stone unturned, and if business people are willing to engage in the same level of risk taking in litigation that they engage in when conducting their day-to-day business affairs, then the costs of major litigation can indeed be cut substantially.

Note

1. Even many of these comparatively minor "savings" sometimes can turn out to be penny wise but pound foolish. For example, a rule that prohibits first-class air travel per se can often increase disbursements rather than decrease them. Consider the following scenario: You have already insisted that your outside lawyer travel solo and do the work himself and not delegate it to associates. You have hired a busy lawyer, so he has no incentive to expand his billable hours to fill out his day. Now he has to conduct a deposition or a hearing in a remote city. Let us assume that three hours of preparation time is required and that the proceeding is to commence at 11:00 A.M. If the lawyer can fly first-class, it is quite feasible for him to leave his home early that morning and catch an early flight to the distant city. Given the greater space available in a first-class seat, he has both the room to spread out his papers to work on the plane and the privacy to be reasonably sure that his seatmate is not looking over his shoulder to examine what may be confidential materials. These goals are simply impossible to achieve in coach. Assuming the lawyer is never permitted to fly first-class, he will probably elect to fly coach the night before, leaving after the end of his normal working day and arriving in the remote city that evening. I assume he will not charge you for the time he spends in the coach cabin of the airplane watching the movie or reading a novel, but you certainly will be charged for the cost of the hotel room that he stays in for the extra night in the distant city and, most likely, for the dinner he has when he gets there, since eating airplane food is above and beyond the call of duty. Thus, the differential between coach and first-class travel has to exceed the cost of dinner and the hotel room before it makes sense to require the lawyer in this example to fly coach. This is not an argument for first-class travel at all times; rather, it is simply an argument against coach travel at all times.

Seventeen

Streamlined Litigation

David D. Leitch

> "Our life is frittered away by detail. . . simplify, simplify."
> —Henry David Thoreau

Cost-effectiveness has now become a major concern in every case, large or small. Yet, historically, the trial bar has been obsessed with the notion that the hallmark of any good litigator is thorough preparation. One primer on the art of trial advocacy has put it this way: "Pre-trial preparation is the key element in all successful trials; there can be no substitute for being prepared for trial. . . . The most common advice given by the experienced advocate to the fledgling trial lawyer is to be prepared."[1]

Trial lawyers have an ethical obligation to prepare themselves adequately. "Competent handling of a particular matter includes inquiry into and analysis of the factual and legal elements of the problem, and use of methods and procedures meeting the standards of competent practitioners. It also includes adequate preparation."[2]

The admonition to prepare thoroughly, however, does not tell us how we go about the process of becoming thoroughly prepared or how much preparation is enough. In an era less cost-conscious, the trial lawyer's response to such concerns could simply be that "more is better." This became the accepted, traditional approach. Even today, corporate litigation is frequently pursued as though thorough preparation can only be achieved by putting more lawyers on the case, writing more memoranda, putting more counts in the complaint and affirmative defenses in the answer, serving more interrogatories, taking more depositions, and filing more discovery motions designed to pry lose every last document in our opponent's possession. Once the firm assembles this arsenal of information, it is reviewed, analyzed, and reorganized in the last few weeks before trial in an effort to prepare the best case possible. But "more is better" is never cost-effective. It is like swatting flies with a sledgehammer.

Few litigators would question the continuing legitimacy of the trial bar's obsession with thorough preparation. But if the increasing need for

David D. Leitch is an associate with Weil, Gotshal & Manges in New York City.

cost-effectiveness has made "more is better" unacceptable, what is to take its place? How can the corporate litigator simultaneously pursue the dual objectives of cost-effectiveness and thorough preparation?

As a trial lawyer, you must do two things. First, redefine your relationship with the client. Discard the attitude that you are simply a warrior. Instead, embrace the belief that you are in the business of corporate problem solving. Help your client identify and realize both its short- and long-term objectives, rather than simply responding to the exigencies of a single litigation. Second, remain faithful to the goal of thorough preparation, but employ case management techniques that help identify and assemble the necessary proof without overkill. The following guidelines provide a blueprint for a successful approach.

Be a Problem Solver First and Litigator Second

Far too often, the pursuit of litigation as an art form triumphs over the search for commonsense solutions to problems. It may be inspiring to read a deposition transcript and relive how your brilliant use of documents destroyed the credibility of a witness who shaded the truth. And knowing how to destroy a witness's credibility in this manner will be essential to the success of any litigator.

But if your client's case could have been settled on favorable terms ten depositions ago, your preoccupation with the process of litigation has prevented you from finding the most cost-effective solution to your client's problem. The client will prefer the result to the process, the settlement to the slashing examination. You will be serving the client best when you obtain the most result with the least process.

Develop an Overview of the Client's Objectives at the Outset

When a corporation retains you as litigation counsel, your first step should be to ask two questions: (1) What are the client's objectives in this situation? (2) Could other corporate objectives be affected by either suing or failing to sue?

Be prepared to help the client crystallize these objectives, for the client may have only a vague understanding of what they are. In corporate litigation, the client's needs and objectives are often conflicting and unclear. For example, the client may desperately wish to set a precedent or take a hard-nosed position but believe that a lengthy battle will imperil its financial health.

Once objectives have been identified, prioritize them. Then identify the means available to accomplish each objective. Fully advise the client about the costs, advantages, and disadvantages of each approach.

Occasionally, you will find total victory is subordinate to other client needs. Litigation against a competitor may require disclosure through discovery of sensitive confidential information about customers, marketing information, manufacturing processes, or competitive strategies. It may be in the client's best interest to forgo litigation against a competitor in order to preserve the confidentiality of this sensitive information. Or a client may not wish to alienate a good customer by initiating litigation until it has exhausted other means of dispute resolution. Initiate litigation only after you have ascertained the extent of the client's commitment to litigate and after you have determined that litigation appears the best method of attaining your client's objectives.

Do Not Cut Corners

Once the decision to litigate is made, do not attempt to save money by cutting corners or taking a half-hearted approach. Lower costs do not necessarily mean greater cost-effectiveness. There is a world of difference between giving the client more service and simply reducing the volume of legal services provided. Such an approach breeds chronic underpreparation, and the dollars the client saves on its monthly statements will be lost in the courtroom or at the bargaining table. In addition, the lawyer who attempts to reduce expense in this manner increases the risk of failing to satisfy his or her ethical responsibility to prepare. You will only be adequately prepared by devoting thorough attention to the client's problem.

Get to Know Your Case as Well as You Can as Soon as You Can

Use informal interviews of your client's employees and your review of the client's files to obtain as detailed and objective an overview of the facts as is possible before launching a formal discovery program. Do not rely on conversations with corporate counsel or a few key executives. Speak directly with the key actors in the events giving rise to the litigation. Likewise, do not rely on the company's employees to provide you with the relevant documents. Have members of your litigation team review the relevant files. The objectives are to make sure that all potential legal issues are identified at the outset, objectively assess the merits of the case, enable you to forecast the cost and burden of discovery, and formulate short- and long-run strategic objectives.

Nail down the elements of each claim or defense at the outset. Never begin discovery (much less get near the courtroom) without a clear idea of what you and your opponent must prove to the jury to prevail at trial. Even prepare tentative jury instructions. Preparing jury instructions at the beginning of the case forces you to develop an understanding of what you must prove to the jury. This will help give discovery a greater sense of direction, making it leaner, more issue-oriented, and more cost-effective.

Analyze the damages issues as soon as possible. Too often, damage issues are not addressed until the merits of the case are developed. Cost-effectiveness requires that the amount of provable damages be considered both at the outset, when first formulating case strategy, and throughout the pretrial period. Only in this way can you subject projected expenses to meaningful analysis.

The Federal Rules of Civil Procedure now require early inquiry into the merits. As a result of the 1983 amendments to rule 11, counsel must inquire into the merits of a "pleading, motion, or other paper" before signing it. Under the amended rule, the signature of an attorney or a party "constitutes a certificate by him that he has read the pleading, motion or other paper; that to the best of his knowledge, information, and belief formed after reasonable inquiry it is well grounded in fact and is warranted by existing law or a good faith argument for extension, modification, or reversal of existing law." Counsel and parties who sign pleadings in violation of the rule are subject to sanctions, including costs and attorney's fees occasioned by the violation.[3] Rule 26(g), also adopted in 1983, contains similar provisions regarding the signing of discovery requests, responses, and objections.

Develop a Theory of the Case at the Beginning

Perhaps James McElhaney has described it best:

> The theory of the case is the basic, underlying idea that explains not only the legal theory and factual background, but also ties as much of the evidence as possible into a coherent and credible whole. . . . It is the basic concept around which everything else revolves.[4]

Once you develop an overview of your client's objectives and understand the relevant facts and legal principles, select several strong, consistent and understandable case themes. Keep them simple. Write them down, refer to them continuously, and make sure every step develops these case themes. Do not be afraid to abandon weak or inconsistent theories. Develop your strongest themes fully, and discard the rest. Too often litigators succumb to the temptation to raise every possible theory. The jury will reject your weak themes and disbelieve the rest. And the client dollars spent to bolster weak themes are almost always wasted.

The 1983 amendments to Federal Rule of Civil Procedure 16 reduce the temptation to plead every conceivable theory. Rule 16(c)(1) can be used to eliminate frivolous claims and defenses at any time before trial. The rule provides that "formulation and simplification of issues, including elimination of frivolous claims and defenses" are now appropriate subjects for binding pretrial orders and discussion at pretrial conferences. A formal summary judgment motion is no longer required to eliminate meritless claims and defenses, and the rule 16(c)(1) procedure can be initiated by either party or the court on its own motion.

Know the Industry

Learn about the industry involved, not only to facilitate your understanding of the case, but to maximize your ability to effectively communicate with the jury about what happened. At the beginning, learn as much as possible from your client's employees. Use your experts to further develop your knowledge. And, once you have obtained a solid understanding of the industry, translate industry jargon into simple language. As Socrates says in Plato's *Phaedo,* the oldest treatise on rhetoric, one can communicate with people in terms of their experience. To be effective, present your case to the jury in terms a layperson can understand—the terms of his or her own experience. If industry jargon is particularly complex or your case involves difficult concepts, consider hiring a college professor knowledgeable in the industry to help you. Such a person will know how to teach others and how to simplify confusing terms and concepts. Prepare a glossary of translated terms for your litigation team, and ask for leave to distribute copies to the jury at trial.

Communicate with Opposing Counsel

Periodic face-to-face communication with opposing counsel can create an atmosphere that facilitates early identification of issues in dispute and the positions of the parties, resolution of disputes without judicial intervention, and early settlement of cases that should not proceed through discovery or trial. Written communication will often obfuscate issues and positions rather than clarify them. Face-to-face communication enables counsel to raise questions, expose ambiguity and error, and reduce the case to its essentials. This reduces both cost and delay. As soon as possible, create an atmosphere of dialogue and common sense. Follow up informal face-to-face communication with a letter. If you fear that informal meetings may suggest weakness in your position or a lack of resolve, use judicially supervised conferences. The pretrial conference procedures set forth in Federal Rule of Civil Procedure 16 (described in detail below) facilitate obtaining this type of judicial involvement.

Organize and Supervise Effectively

Far too often, litigators fail to appreciate the importance of skillful management. The following guidelines will result in better manpower management and increased efficiency in almost any case.

Place Ultimate Authority in the Hands of One Lawyer with Clear Lines of Authority

> A committee is a group
> That works all day.
> Everybody puts in a color
> And it comes out gray.
> —Anonymous

Do not supervise litigation by committee. Do not vest ultimate authority in two (or more) lawyers at the same level of seniority. Such a management team will spend too much time swapping ideas about what ought to be done rather than effectively implementing management decisions. Management will be far less decisive, and decisive management is essential for cost-effectiveness. Attaining consensus will be tortuous and time-consuming through a committee.

Place supreme authority for managing the case in one lawyer. Valuable worker-hours will be wasted if subordinates do not know who will provide them with essential information. Make sure subordinates know exactly who they must account to, who has authority, and who can give definitive directions, criticism, and answers.

Delegate Authority

In a labor-intensive personal service industry like the practice of law, cost-effectiveness is maximized by delegating authority to the lowest competent level. Partners should not perform tasks that associates can perform. Associates should not perform tasks best suited for paralegals or skilled legal secretaries. Successful delegation does require that the lawyer responsible for assignments understand them clearly. It also requires that the supervising lawyer monitor the tasks delegated and provide constructive feedback to the delegatee.

Manage without Meetings

One of the most common symptoms of disorganization is too many meetings attended by too many people. An excess of meetings indicates only that objectives are too diffuse, or that jobs have not been clearly defined or vested with enough responsibility. If a meeting must be held, have one person supervise it. Meetings are more effective if the participants come prepared, so make sure each person who will be attending becomes aware of the agenda beforehand. Circulate written agendas before the meeting if time permits. Identify in writing the assignments and decisions made at the meeting. Otherwise, meetings will degenerate into bull sessions, or people will leave with different understandings of what has been accomplished or what remains to be done.

Keep People Informed

Timely, effective communication between members of your litigation team about developments in the case is essential. It is inexcusable to have an associate working day and night on a massive rule 37 motion after the supervising partner has tentatively decided not to file it. It is even worse to find out two days after settlement that the firm copy center just finished those 3000 copies you requested two weeks ago. Yet events like this occur in major litigation with alarming frequency. Regularly give everybody information about the progress of the litigation. Tailor the exact procedures used to the needs of the case. One approach is to have a brief team meeting first thing every Monday morning at which you review the previous week's progress and the current week's objectives. Make sure all lawyers and paralegals working on the case attend.

Help the Court Implement Effective Judicial Management Strategies

Judge William W. Schwarzer has said that far too many lawyers fear active judicial management. They fear that judicial limitations will hamper their own trial preparation in unforeseen ways. "As a result, counsel will often comply with burdensome and even abusive discovery which the court on request might have limited."[5] Counsel's fear of judicial management is unfounded if claims and defenses are not frivolous and discovery objectives and requests are legitimate. Counsel will be able to litigate far more cost-effectively with sound judicial management than without it. Empirical studies have demonstrated that increased judicial control during the pretrial process accelerates the processing and termination of cases.[6]

Sound judicial management can help identify issues, set time limits, manage discovery, and resolve discovery disputes. If ground rules for the litigation cannot be agreed upon with opposing counsel, your goal must be to help the court shape judicial control that is well tailored to the case. Small or simple cases may need only a modest amount of judicial control, while large cases may require a great deal. An extremely broad range of judicial management options and procedures is available to litigants and the court under Federal Rules of Civil Procedure 16 and 26(f). Efficient use of these rules to shape realistic ground rules for the litigation can reduce costs and delays.

The 1983 amendments to rule 16 expand the trial court's ability to implement early and ongoing judicial management. The amended rule changes the role of pretrial conferences. The rule shifts the emphasis away from a single conference focused solely on the trial and toward a process of judicial management that embraces the entire pretrial phase, especially motions and discovery. Rule 16(a) sets forth the purposes of the pretrial conference:

- Expediting disposition of the action
- Establishing early and continuing control so that the case will not be protracted because of lack of management
- Discouraging wasteful pretrial activities
- Improving the quality of the trial through more thorough preparation
- Facilitating settlement

Some degree of judicial management is mandatory under rule 16(b). The court must prepare a scheduling order limiting the time to join additional parties, amend pleadings, file and hear motions, and complete discovery. The order must be prepared as soon as practicable, but no later than 120 days after the filing of the complaint. The order is mandatory in all cases except those exempted by local rule.

Rule 16(c) specifies a broad range of topics that are proper subjects for discussion at any pretrial conference. They can be made the subject of a binding pretrial order under rule 16(e). These subjects include formulating and simplifying issues, amending pleadings, resolving discovery and evidentiary disputes, eliminating cumulative proof at trial, identifying witnesses and exhibits for trial, settlement, pending motions, and adoption of special procedures for complex cases. Under rule 16(f), the court may impose sanctions against a party or the party's attorney for failure to obey a pretrial order or attend a pretrial conference.

Rule 26(f) provides an additional means to identify issues, set time limits, and eliminate discovery abuse. Under the rule, the court may hold a discovery conference on a motion of any party or its own motion. The party's motion must state the issues, propose a discovery schedule, propose deadlines and other limitations on discovery, and state that counsel unsuccessfully attempted to stipulate these issues with opposing counsel.

Use the Federal Rules of Civil Procedure Creatively

Before preparing discovery requests, become familiar with the law regarding discovery of the matters at issue. Make sure your requests are narrowly drafted, technically correct, and phrased so that the judge will be able to easily understand and enforce them. This will minimize the risk that your opponent will be able to legitimately object or answer evasively. This, in turn, reduces the need to rely on expensive rule 37 motions to obtain the needed discovery.

Use rule 30(b)(6) to reduce your client's offensive discovery burden. Under this rule, a party may name as the deponent a corporation, partnership, or government agency "and describe with reasonable particularity the matters on which examination is requested." The organization so named must then "designate one or more officers, directors, or managing agents or other persons who consent to testify on its behalf, and may set forth, for each person designated, the matters on which he will testify." An early 30(b)(6) deposition ties your opponent down to a position that will be difficult to alter at trial, because its principal factual witness on a particular issue usually provides the 30(b)(6) testimony on that issue. Upon completion of the 30(b)(6) deposition, you will have a good sense of what must be accomplished through further discovery to prepare your case for trial. This will often enable subsequent discovery to be lean and focused, saving both time and money.

Use requests for admission under rule 36 rather than interrogatories. Use this method to nail down points that are indisputable and to establish the authenticity and foundation of documents. The request to admit has numerous advantages over interrogatories.[7] Interrogatories are all too often simply "a lazy lawyer's way to obtain evasive answers."[8]

Obtain information from government sources. A well-drafted request for information pursuant to the Freedom of Information Act may accomplish your discovery objectives with far less expense and inconvenience than one of the traditional methods. Much of what you obtain from the government will be admissible under an exception to the hearsay rule.[9]

In large cases, consider a statement of contentions and proof rather than interrogatories to clarify issues. The court can require each party to file such statements pursuant to its authority to implement procedures for narrowing and identifying issues under rules 16 and 26(f). These statements should set forth each legal and factual contention of the parties and indicate the witnesses and documents that will be used at trial to support them. These statements should be specific. Do not write them in a conclusory or argumentative style. Revised statements are filed periodically with the court to reflect the additional discovery and to facilitate a narrowing of the issues.[10]

Expert discovery will be more focused and productive if the parties' experts prepare written reports summarizing the subject matters, facts, and opinions (and the basis therefore) to which each expert is expected to testify. Deposition of experts should be delayed until after the submission of such reports. If your opponent will not agree to such a procedure, ask the court to require it pursuant to its inherent power to enter orders establishing a plan for discovery under rules 26(d) and (f).

Use rules 26(b) and (c) to curb discovery abuse. Rule 26(b) limits discovery methods under the following circumstances:

- The discovery sought is unreasonably cumulative or duplicative, or is obtainable from some other source that is more convenient, less burdensome, or less expensive.
- The party seeking discovery has had ample opportunity to obtain through discovery the information sought.
- The discovery is unduly burdensome or expensive, considering the needs of the case, the amount in controversy, limitations on the parties' resources, and the importance of the issues at stake in the litigation.

The court may invoke appropriate discovery limitations on its own initiative or pursuant to a motion under rule 26(c). The advisory committee note makes it clear that the objectives of these provisions are to "guard against redundant or disproportionate discovery" and "encourage judges to be more aggressive in identifying and discouraging discovery overuse."

When defending, consider the offer of judgment procedure provided by rule 68 to encourage settlement on your client's terms. Under rule 68, a party can offer to "allow judgment to be taken against him for the money or property or to the extent specified in his offer, with costs then accrued." If the offer of judgment is not accepted and the final judgment is not more than the amount of the offer, the offeree is liable for the costs incurred by the offeror after the date of the offer.[11]

Maintain Control of the Facts

Control the facts to identify the essential evidence and tailor it to your themes and legal theories. Controlling the facts throughout discovery will enable trial preparation to proceed with discovery rather than await its completion.

Streamline Your Document Control System

As soon as a prospective deposition exhibit is identified, mark it with a permanent exhibit sticker and number. Use the same number to identify the document throughout discovery and at trial. This will eliminate the need to identify the exhibit again with a new number each time it is used. It will also eliminate the need to renumber exhibits before trial according to the order in which they will be introduced. This saves time and expense.[12]

Use a Theme Development System to Organize Your Proof

A theme development system is simply an organizational framework upon which you assemble your proof for trial. The core of such a system is provided by the evidentiary outline and the proof narrative.

The evidentiary outline is an outline of the major factual propositions you will be trying to establish at trial. These propositions should reflect your basic case themes and cover each element of each claim or defense. The outline is easy to prepare. You need to refer only to the factual and legal research you have completed and your list of themes. Prepare the outline at the beginning of the case, before you begin discovery. In larger cases, the evidentiary outline can provide the format for a subject matter index to documents or for any trial briefs or settlement negotiation documents that are prepared.

While the evidentiary outline indicates *what* you must prove at trial, the proof narrative helps you determine *how* to prove it. It does this by segregating the isolated facts developed during discovery in terms of the factual propositions contained in the evidentiary outline.

Each section of the proof narrative relates to one of the factual propositions in the evidentiary outline. Each of these sections contains subsections relating to jury instructions, method of proof, and gaps in proof for the proposition. The method of proof subsection is further subdivided according to the methods of proof used at trial: stipulations of counsel, admissions in pleadings, written discovery responses, witnesses, and documents. The relevant facts are simply coded to the applicable subsection of the method of proof as they are developed. For each witness and document identified in the method of proof subsection, include a brief summary of the evidence and identify any possible evidentiary problems (e.g., availability of a witness or foundational problems for a document). You can also include subsections that summarize your evidence, your opponent's position, the need for further discovery, and the desirability of filing any motions relating to proof of the applicable proposition. These additional subsections enable you to analyze on an ongoing basis the facts developed during discovery. Final determination of the evidence to be used at trial is made at the close of discovery.

Use of the evidentiary outline and proof narrative throughout discovery will provide several benefits:

- It will keep you focused on the issues throughout discovery, which enables discovery to proceed with greater direction and a minimum of overkill.
- It will tailor the evidence to your theories and prevent you from becoming overwhelmed by unessential evidence.
- It will ease preparation for depositions and drafting of written discovery.

- It will allow counsel to more effectively evaluate contemplated discovery in light of how it will help establish necessary elements of proof, whether its objectives have been accomplished by completed discovery, and whether it can correct evidentiary problems and eliminate gaps in proof.
- It will facilitate cost-effective decision making regarding the filing of discovery motions to obtain requested discovery that has been withheld.
- It will foster development of realistic expectations about the likelihood of success on the merits, as counsel must continually consider whether the available evidence supports proffered legal theories.
- It will foster cost-effective and principled decisions regarding the desirability of summary judgment motions, motions in limine, and settlement.
- It will facilitate the preparation of time-saving and case-winning devices such as summary exhibits, composite exhibits, and graphic aids.
- It will organize the proof available for use at trial, making final preparation for trial less costly, time-consuming, and harried.

The evidentiary outline and proof narrative are particularly useful in complex cases—such as antitrust cases—that require proof of a pattern of conduct consisting of numerous seemingly unrelated acts or events. If you use a document-numbering system like the one just described, it is easy to code documents and the key deposition testimony relating to them, especially if depositions are searched by computer. When using these tools, do not lose your flexibility. Remain open through discovery for new claims or theories consistent with your basic themes.

Notes

1. Smithburn & Seckinger, Trial Techniques 13 (1983).
2. Model Rules of Professional Conduct Rule 1.1 comment (1983).
3. *See* Eastway Constr. Corp. v. City of New York, 762 F.2d 243 (2d Cir. 1985).
4. McElhaney, *Trial Notebook: The Theory of the Case* 6 Litigation no. 1, at 51 (Fall 1979).
5. Schwarzer, Managing Antitrust and Other Complex Litigation 57 (1982).
6. *See* Flanders, Case Management and Court Management in United States District Courts (Federal Judicial Center 1977).
7. *See* Epstein, *Rule 36: In Praise of Request to Admit,* 7 Litigation no. 3, at 30 (Spring 1981).
8. Pollack, *Discovery—Its Abuse and Correction,* 80 F.R.D. 219, 224 (1978).
9. Fed. R. Evid. 803(8); *see also* Zenith Radio Corp. v. Matsushita Elec. Indus. Co., 505 F. Supp. 1125, 1143–50 (E.D. Pa. 1980).

10. *See, e.g.,* United States v. American Tel. & Tel. Co., 461 F. Supp. 1314, 1345–46 (D.D.C. 1979).

11. *See* Marek v. Chesny, 473 U.S. 1 (1985).

12. *See* Sullivan & Rez, *Let's Get Rid of Big Cases,* 7 LITIGATION no. 4, at 8 (Summer 1981).

Eighteen

Bridging Troubled Waters: Negotiating Disputes

James C. Freund

I spend most of my professional hours negotiating mergers and other business deals. Lately, though, I have gotten involved in trying to resolve some commercial disputes, both before and after litigation has begun.

Going in, I thought this would not be too difficult. Cutting up a finite pie seemed a lot easier than pulling together all the pieces of a complicated transaction.

I was dead wrong. Resolving disputes is hard work, in some respects even harder than making a deal. But I found that my experience in putting deals together gave me a fresh perspective on settlement. Here, then, are an outsider's thoughts on how to settle a dispute.

The starting point is the group of difficulties that come from the mere fact of litigation. These include the client's ambivalence, the special problems a litigator faces, the tricky matter of getting talks going, the mood of distrust, and the lack of a problem-solving mentality.

We begin with ambivalence. I was really struck by how ambivalent everyone was, right up to the moment of final settlement, about whether the matter should be settled.

In an acquisition, the prevailing mood is, "Let's get it done." All the pressure drives the parties toward an agreement. The businesspeople want the deal done yesterday; the investment bankers sweat over their contingent fees; the lawyers get caught up in the frenzy. The emphasis is on being constructive—finding ways to solve problems and get on with the transaction. A corporate lawyer whose heart is not in it—who tries to delay (or worse, sabotage) an agreement—is anathema. The bogeyman of all concerned is a "busted deal."

But when the parties are at loggerheads in a dispute over a business practice or a broker contract, the mood is entirely different. Often, at least some of the parties or lawyers (invariably those on the other side)

James C. Freund is a member of Skadden, Arps, Slate, Meagher & Flom, New York City.

prefer that the conflict remain unresolved. Even the party with *more* to gain from a negotiated settlement sometimes seems ambivalent about settling. One minute, he tells you to go ahead and see what you can work out; the next, he has second thoughts and is ready to go back to war.

Settling differences is tough enough work if your heart is really in it. When lawyers reflect their clients' hot-and-cold moods, the task becomes monumental.

The real keys for a lawyer settling a dispute are, first, to overcome the client's ambivalence and get him or her committed to a settlement and, second, to persuade the adversary that the proposed resolution is sufficient to give up the fight.

The litigator who is handling the case (assuming it has ripened into a lawsuit) bears a special burden in accomplishing these tasks. Up to now, the litigator has been busy throwing his weight around: alleging total fraud and depredation, seeking trebled recompense, ridiculing the adversary's claims as lacking merit. The litigation papers—with everything larger than life and choking on adverbs (the opponent's argument is characterized as "patently absurd," the simplest contractual phrase is "hopelessly ambiguous")—are enough to send shivers up a corporate lawyer's spine. The litigators tend to be combative types, and their contacts during the lawsuit, sometimes reflecting the emotions of their respective clients, are often of the bristling variety.

Rigidity in Litigation

To shift abruptly to talking about settlement requires a sizable psychological adjustment. What makes it even more difficult is that the lawyers have no way of knowing whether a settlement will ultimately be reached. The left hand is negotiating while the right prepares to resume the conflict. I think this uncertainty deters trial lawyers from taking positions that imply vulnerability, from swapping meaningful compromises, even from making conciliatory noises, for fear that these concessions will somehow make things more difficult if they have to go back to the mat.

In short, there can be a rigidity in shepherding the litigation that is antithetical to the search for compromise, a search that lies at the core of striking a deal.

The litigator may also have trouble, of a more subtle variety, in the home camp. Clients like their gladiators to be tough, to stand up for them forcefully, and successful litigators often cultivate a hawkish image. So it may be hard for a litigator to prod a client in the direction of settlement. Yet many business deals get done only when the lawyers are able to move their clients away from intractable positions toward compromise solutions. For a litigator—poised to defend the client's honor through the last appeal—the conciliatory approach is a hard road to travel without running the risk of being seen as a softy who is reluctant to fight and ready to give away the store.

Assuming that litigation has started, there is often a lot of foot-shuffling before settlement talks begin. The principal fear is that making the first move shows weakness. So each side waits for the other side to blink first, which might happen one day—and, if we wait long enough, pigs will probably fly, too.

In a messy dispute, the distrust each side feels for the other hinders the ability of lawyers to negotiate. The plaintiff feels the defendant has committed a serious tort or breach of contract; the defendant, certain he or she has done nothing wrong, harbors a sense of betrayal at being hauled into court. What basis is there for trust between the parties?

Yet trust is basic to successful negotiating. Has each party received accurate information from the other about the subject of the dispute? Will a party use information learned in the negotiations to the adversary's disadvantage? Will the other side renege tomorrow on what it agreed to today? If the settlement involves future conduct—as it often must to bring the full range of settlement options into play—can the other party be trusted to live up to its end of the bargain? Without trust, striking a deal is more than difficult.

In corporate transactions, lawyers and businesspeople start by assuming that they can trust their opposite numbers. In litigation, trust is hard to win and harder to maintain. But when the opposing lawyers can create an atmosphere of mutual trust, this climate can go a long way (assuming the lawyers have some influence with their clients) toward closing the gap between positions that had been irreconcilable.

In deal making, most good lawyers start with the attitude that everything is ultimately soluble. All you have to do is reduce what sound like sacred principles to mundane dollars, then throw in a face saver, and the parties are shaking hands.

Central to this attitude is the sense that the other side's problems are *your* problems, too. If your adversary cannot solve a particular tax issue, for instance, there may be no deal at all. So you have to help develop a structure that works for the other side.

This attitude of ultimate solubility is conspicuously absent in litigation. The parties' positions always seem irreconcilable—just read the briefs. There is no disposition to solve the other side's problems; everyone is having a hard enough job solving his or her own.

Still, the crux of accommodation is often to figure out what your adversary's *real* problem is (since he or she may have been less than forthcoming on this score) and then to come up with a creative solution. But my sense is that litigators, influenced by their clients' huffing and puffing, often do not bother themselves with their adversaries' problems.

Finding a Compromise

These are some of the problems that are inherent in litigation. The other group of difficulties is related to finding an acceptable compromise. This group includes problems in assessing what will happen if the parties do not settle and the litigation proceeds, the absence of usable settlement models, and the confinement of a negotiation in which the only real question is who will pay how much to whom.

In deal making, if negotiations prove unsuccessful, one party or the other can walk away. This threat keeps a negotiator from taking too unreasonable a position, unless his or her leverage is terrific (as when the other party needs the deal to avoid takeover by a raider).

So, when a corporate lawyer decides whether to stick or yield on certain major points, the key question is whether the issue is a "deal breaker." If it is, then the alternative to compromise is clear: no deal. Someone has to budge if the project is worth doing; otherwise, both sides go home.

But in litigation there is no neutral walkaway. The alternative to settling is to try the case—to let the judge (or jury or arbitrator) decide. The consequences of not settling will be determined by a third party. And, at the moment you attempt to settle, no one knows for certain how the trier of fact would come out. Yet in order to evaluate the proposed settlement, you need to assess how much your client will win or lose if you take the case to judgment.

To estimate a range of potential settlements, you not only have to evaluate how well *you* will do in the case, but also how well your adversary believes *he* will make out (which may be different from what he *says* during the negotiations). Of course, what is in your adversary's mind can be influenced by what you do and say as you go about the process of trying to lower his expectations.

The central problem in valuing the litigation alternative is that a judge cannot just whack up the pile of dollars at issue somewhere in the middle, which is where the parties are heading when they try to settle. If the judge finds for the plaintiff, the plaintiff will probably get much of what he or she reasonably claims; if the judge finds for the defendant, the plaintiff gets nothing. So the negotiated settlement is almost bound to be at odds with the litigation result.

Even if the two sides could agree on the *likely* outcome, it would not be usable as a settlement figure. The potential loser would say, "I'd rather take my chances; I sure can't do worse."

So the parties need to decide two things—the likely outcome, and just how likely it is to occur—in order to discount back to a fair settlement. These are truly tough calls, and if a jury is involved, the prospects are even more inscrutable.

(Well, say some litigators, it is not all that hard: Try the winners, and settle the losers. This reminds me of Will Rogers's advice on the stock market: "Don't gamble; take all your savings and buy some good stock and hold it till it goes up, then sell it. If it don't go up, don't buy it.")

Another problem in settling litigation, as compared with negotiating a deal, is the scarcity of good models on which to rely. In an acquisition, opposing counsel argue over a number of points, but we have a plethora of precedents for how most issues are usually resolved, and these precedents provide sort of a built-in standard of reasonableness. I know what can be yielded—others have done so before me, so my client will not feel too exposed—and, conversely, where I should stand firm.

In contrast, many commercial trials have their own unique facts and dynamics. While analogies may be available and damages measurable within a range, litigators often lack useful benchmarks.

One reason I underestimated the difficulty of dispute resolution is that, in contrast to deal making, where it is necessary to agree on a large number of points, resolving a dispute often requires agreement on only a single dollar figure. Once the bucks are right, everything else falls into place.

I assumed that fighting over one issue would be easier than trying to sort out dozens of equally important issues. I discovered, though, that the very narrowness of the negotiations makes it *harder* to resolve disputes than to arrange a complex transaction.

When the agreement depends on a single number, nothing is settled until everything is settled. In a deal, there may be a hundred issues, but they are sprinkled throughout the process, and you can make progress on them as you go, swapping *A* for *B* (or perhaps conceding *A,* in hopes of getting a reciprocal concession on *B* down the road). No single issue—other than price, which is usually the first big issue resolved—takes on disproportionate importance. In litigation, much more pressure is placed on the final breakthrough.

As a nonlitigator, when I may be called in to help settle a dispute, I do not face certain problems. There is no backlog of hostility to overcome; I am better able to create an atmosphere of mutual trust; and I have no reluctance to initiate settlement talks, since that is why I am on the scene in the first place. I simply call up the other lawyer and say, in effect, let's see if it is possible to work out a negotiated settlement before my partner tears you apart in court.

Dealing with the other side, I am able to come up with suggestions and fresh approaches to overcoming obstacles without carrying any special baggage from the litigation. I am not ambivalent—everyone realizes that my function is to try to negotiate a settlement—and I am inclined to believe that everything is soluble, without worrying too much about what my attitude might convey to the other side. Whenever I find myself too far out on a limb, I can always point to my litigating partner—whom I portray as a large lion just before feeding time—waiting impatiently for the negotiations to break down, so he can get back to his real task of attacking our adversary in court.

As for managing my own client, I am able to say, look, if you want litigation advice, my partner will tell you the risks and rewards. If you want to know what I think it will take to settle this case, I'll tell you that. Then you can make up your mind which way to go.

The Two-Lawyer Team

My experience suggests that, at least in some cases, a two-lawyer team—a litigator and a negotiator—has a flexibility of approach that either lawyer alone lacks.

In suggesting this, I intend no disrespect to my litigating colleagues, for whom I have the utmost admiration. In particular, I find no substance in the charge sometimes leveled that litigators do not want to settle because, with all the bravado of their papers, they have talked themselves into thinking that their side of the case is stronger than it really is. In my experience, good litigators—no matter how much they may want to try the case—provide the client with a fair assessment of risks and rewards and recommend settlement if they think that is the appropriate course. Behind all the noise and posturing, they understand what a crapshoot litigation is.

My point, though, is that it is often hard for one person to play two contrasting roles. Having a litigator and a negotiator team may increase your effectiveness by allowing each person to play a single role to the hilt. This approach may also help to keep the other side off balance, not knowing who will prevail in the councils of your client. The team approach can also help your client to decide whether to fight or settle, since each lawyer advises on only one of the options.

This approach calls for good teamwork. You and your partner need to be on the same wavelength, with neither of you committed to litigating or settling at any cost but realizing that the scales can tilt either way as the negotiations proceed.

It is a mistake to refrain from initiating talks indefinitely out of a fear that the overture will convey weakness. Obviously, timing can be important. The day after your side has been trounced on a motion or has suffered a setback in discovery is not the best time to hoist the white flag.

But, generally speaking, if it is in your client's best interests to settle, and the other side makes no move in that direction, you should try to open a dialogue.

A good litigator knows how to get across a sense of confidence in the case, and so is not unduly concerned that the adversary will perceive him or her as having cold feet. In fact, some litigators go one step further and suggest that they are initiating talks because they know their adversary cannot make the first overture; given his lousy case, it would obviously be a terrible sign of weakness for *him* to do so.

The realistic approach is to look at the cost to both sides if the case continues and say, "Before our clients make us rich, shouldn't we look at the alternatives?" Weakness and strength will be apparent from the course of the settlement discussions, not from who makes the first move.

When to Settle

Is it better to try to settle the dispute before or after the lawsuit has started? There are pros and cons to both.

Settling early makes sense for a number of reasons. Starting the talks is easier before litigation begins simply because no one *wants* to litigate if there's an alternative. Once the lawsuit starts, picking the right time to talk can be a delicate operation. Also, at the early stage, neither party has made a big litigation investment of time, effort, or fees; the momentum and passions of the contest are yet to come, and less animosity stands in the way.

Sometimes, though, only a lawsuit can induce a recalcitrant adversary to come to the table. (But it can also work the other way. Sometimes the threat has force, but once the lawsuit has been filed, the pressure to settle dissipates, and the parties dig in for a pitched battle.)

Discovery may give you a keener sense of the strengths and weaknesses of both cases. This perspective can help you assess the case if it goes to trial. Litigation may also work off some of the parties' venom. As they see their legal bills mounting with no trial in sight, they may be more receptive to working things out.

So there are the pros and cons to settling early or late. But all things being equal, you are better off trying to settle the dispute early, provided you can put yourself in a position to understand the relative merits of each party's case.

It is important to prepare for negotiating a settlement. Many litigators, who spend countless hours preparing for trial, motions, and even depositions, spend very little time getting ready for settlement discussions. Think about it: If you are not prepared, and your adversary is, the adversary has an advantage.

The core of good preparation for settlement is to flush out the strengths and weaknesses of both sides' cases. How do you do this without starting a lawsuit and going through discovery?

In one of the matters I handled, where the dispute was heavily fact-laden, I got each party to spell out its factual case. To be sure, there was a lot of posturing, some real vagueness in crucial spots, and (as might be expected) an absence of common ground on even the most trivial elements. Still, the exercise served an important educational function, not the least of which was to isolate the major issues, leaving us all better off than if we had been flying totally blind. It also showed everyone that the two sides could talk rationally without going to court.

Bargaining Tips

Once you resolve to try to settle the case, make or receive the first overture, and develop a sharp sense of the strengths and weaknesses of both sides of the dispute, it is time to start the long, hard bargaining.

Here are some thoughts on conducting the negotiations.

- First, be persistent. There is no quick fix in settlement discussions. One case I handled involved settlement talks, interspersed with litigation maneuvers, that went on for several years. You simply have to stick with it, no matter what the frustrations. Instant gratification is for bowlers.
- Second, listen. Once you get into the talks, do not do all the talking. Listen to what your adversary has to say. And particularly listen, with an analytical ear, to the unspoken messages, like what has been curiously omitted from your adversary's position. You can learn a lot by creative listening.
- Third, ask questions. Prepare and ask probing questions. You might get some interesting answers. At worst, your adversary's ducking and weaving, or outright refusal to answer, can itself provide useful information.
- Next, equalize the authority. Make sure the other lawyer has as much authority as you do to reach a settlement or at least has as much clout with his or her client as you have with yours. "I'll sell this one to my client if you sell it to yours" is a familiar refrain in negotiations. If your adversary is handicapped in this regard, watch out: The game is being played with a loaded deck.
- Make an effort to persuade the other side that it is in his or her interest to settle. It must be in *your* interest, or you would not be at the table, but your adversary may not yet see any

convincing advantages. Probe to find out the reasons for this reluctance. Then deal directly with the rationale.

- Be creative. Something other than whacking up a pot of cash may bring the parties together. Never underestimate the power of tax advantages. If you are unskilled in that department, bring in an expert.
- Business arrangements may offer a way out. If the parties can have commercial relations, the value to the recipient of goods and services is always substantially higher than the cost to the furnisher, an economic fact of life that can help to bridge large gaps.
- The subject matter of the dispute can itself provide grist for the settlement mill. If, for example, there is a question about the value of disputed property, it may be possible (if the property is divisible, such as a natural resource) to use some of it directly in the settlement, instead of reaching an impasse trying to agree on the equivalent dollar value.
- Time is also significant. Payments spread out over a number of years have both a financial and psychological dimension. The recipient can say, "I settled for $5 million." The payor can say, "It cost me $3.5 million—the net present value of the payments—to get rid of the case."
- If your initial discussions have isolated several difficult issues, try to attack these separately. By chopping the overall settlement into parts, you may achieve a series of small accords, which, taken together, pave the way for the ultimate resolution.
- Start with a reasonable offer. Do not highball (or lowball) it. You can get a reasonable dialogue going only if you show that you mean business.
- On the other hand, it is foolish to start with your best offer, even if you label it as such and ooze sincerity. You adversary will not believe you. Besides, an adversary wants the satisfaction of seeing you move in his or her direction.
- Give a reason for any proposal you make. Show the other side how you arrived at it. Your adversary will have a different number, to be sure, but if you can get your adversary to explain the rationale for his or her number, then there will be some basis for moving the numbers closer together. It is easier to argue about rationales than about numbers.
- To reach a deal, the plaintiff has to come in with a number that he or she has a good chance of topping by taking the case to trial. The defendant's offer, in turn, must force the

plaintiff's counsel to tell his or her client that the court might well grant less or at most not enough more to warrant the expenses of trial and the delays in getting the money.

- Do not bid against yourself. Find out your adversary's number before sweetening your offer.
- If you go into a negotiating session with a number and dress it with appropriate rationale, do not change the number at the same session. Stick for that day, at least.
- Once you get into the bargaining, do not make a myriad of small concessions. A few meaningful concessions encourage the other side to reciprocate. And each number should have its own rationale. Be sure to tell your adversary how you arrived at your new stopping point.
- When the bidding starts to get close, slow down on "splitting the difference"—thereby changing your position without any commitment on the part of the other side to the intermediate figure.
- Finally, keep cool. As settlement nears and the tension builds, minor points often tend to be magnified way out of proportion. Do not get caught up in your client's ego or indignation. As George C. Nathan said, "No one can think clearly when his fists are clenched. In a litigious world, it takes a cool head to resolve hot disputes."

Nineteen

Settlement of Complex Litigation: Preserving Confidentiality, Anticipating Bankruptcy, and Other Problems

Paul H. Dawes and Richard A. Lapping

Privileges

Settlement conferences and discussions about settlement frequently bring together the client and its insurer (who may or may not bear the cost of defense) or the client and its adversary and the adversary's counsel. Taking a hard look at the merits of the case usually requires candor and frank discussion that may lead to a damaging admission by the client. If no settlement is reached, the adversary may offer the client's statement into evidence or may seek to interrogate the insurer about the client's statement to the insurer.

The rules of evidence provide some protection against an adversary's later use of a client's statement made in settlement negotiations, although a number of important exceptions may suspend the protection. To protect communications between clients and insurers in certain litigation-related situations, the majority of jurisdictions uphold application of the attorney-client privilege, although the availability of the privilege is judicially created and requires close observance to see that the underlying policy objectives are met.

Preventing Disclosure of Conduct and Statements Made in Settlement Negotiations

Statements Made in Settlements Generally Not Admissible to Prove Liability or Damages

Federal Rule of Evidence 408 provides:

> Evidence of (1) furnishing or offering or promising to furnish, or (2) accepting or offering or promising to accept, a valuable consideration in compromising or attempting to compromise a

Paul H. Dawes is a member and Richard A Lapping is an associate of Thelen, Marrin, Johnson & Bridges, San Francisco, California.

> claim which was disputed as to either validity or amount, is not admissible to prove liability or invalidity of the claim or its amount. *Evidence of conduct or statements made in compromise negotiations is likewise not admissible.* This rule does not require the exclusion of any evidence otherwise discoverable merely because it is presented in the course of compromise negotiations. This rule also does not require exclusion when the evidence is offered for another purpose, such as proving bias or prejudice of a witness, negativing a contention of undue delay, or proving an effort to obstruct a criminal investigation or prosecution. [Emphasis added.]

Twenty-four states have rules that are based on or similar to Rule 408 of the Federal Rules of Evidence. For example, section 1152(a) of the California Evidence Code provides:

> Evidence that a person has, in compromise or from humanitarian motives, furnished or offered or promised to furnish money or any other thing, act or service to another who has sustained or will sustain or claims that he or she has sustained or will sustain a loss or damage *as well as any conduct or statements made in negotiation thereof,* is inadmissible to prove his or her liability for the loss or damage or any part of it. [Emphasis added.][1]

Formal settlement techniques, such as mediating, may also be protected. In 1985 California enacted a protective statute applicable to any statement or any admission made in the course of a mediation.[2] Although mediation is not defined in the statute, the section applies only if the parties explicitly invoke it in a written agreement executed before the mediation.[3]

The protection afforded by Federal Rule of Evidence 408 is not available unless the point of threatened litigation has been reached. Statements made in the course of business communications between companies before that point have been held admissible.[4]

Two principal exceptions that undermine this protection are the exception for admissions connected to an offer of compromise and the exception that allows admissibility for a purpose other than proving liability or damages.

Admission of Statements Independent of the Offer of Compromise

The second sentence of Rule 408 would appear unequivocal on the point that, once compromise negotiations have begun in a case where litigation has at least been threatened, no contemporaneous conduct or statement by any of the participants is admissible. Nonetheless, courts have stated that "evidence concerning negotiations may be admitted to establish admissions of fact rather than 'hypothetical or provisional concessions conditioned upon the settlement's completion.' "[5] The court in *Hiram Ricker & Sons* admitted this testimony: "[Jarvis] passed me a yellow sheet of paper saying, 'This is what we owe you. If you agree and sign a release absolving us from any and all damage and all future bills we will pay you.' It was $44,000."[6]

Notwithstanding a contrary pronouncement in the legislative history of section 1152 of the California Evidence Code, a forerunner of Federal Rule of Evidence 408, California courts recognize a similar exception. In *Moving Picture Machine Operators Union v. Glasgow Theatres,*[7] a letter was admitted (over objection) that stated, "Mr. Glasgow admits he owes as follows" and that "defendants are prepared to pay this amount in full satisfaction of the matter sued upon in your complaint."[8] The court concluded that the intention of the defendant was "to make no concessions but to exact all that he deemed himself entitled to" and that the statement was not connected to an offer of compromise.[9]

The 1965 enactment of section 1152(a) of the California Evidence Code was intended to overrule a similar decision in *People v. Forster*.[10] According to the contemporaneous comment of the Law Revision Commission:

> The rule excluding offers is based upon the public policy in favor of the settlement of disputes without litigation. The same public policy requires that admissions made during settlement negotiations also be excluded. The rule of the *Forster* case that permits such statements to be admitted places a premium on the form of the statement. The statement "Assuming for the purposes of these negotiations, that I was negligent . . ." is inadmissible; but the statement "All right, I was negligent! Let's talk about damages . . ." may be admissible. . . . The rule of the *Forster* case is changed by § 1152 because that rule prevents the complete candor between the parties that is most conducive to settlement.

The Advisory Committee on the Federal Rules of Evidence has also criticized placing premiums on the formulation of statements:

> The practical value of the common law rule has been greatly diminished by its inapplicability to admissions of fact, even though made in the course of compromise negotiations, unless hypothetical, stated to be "without prejudice," or so connected with the offer to be inseparable from it.[11]

In light of the clear legislative intent to dispense with a party's sentence formulation as a basis for the admissibility of statements made in the course of settlement negotiations, the exception articulated in *Glasgow Theatres* may be limited to its facts or to similar situations, such as the rendering of an account stated—held admissible in *Truestone v. Simi West Industrial Park II,*[12] the only reported case to follow *Glasgow Theatres.* Alternatively, *Glasgow Theatres* and *Truestone* may be characterized as cases where the parties discussed *termination,* not *compromise,* of the litigation, taking the cases outside the general rule.[13]

Admissibility of Settlement Negotiation Statements for Another Purpose

Most formulations of the rule excluding evidence of settlement negotiations limit its applicability to admissibility on disputed issues of liability and damages. But where the conduct or statement is offered for some other purpose, admissibility is upheld.

For example, regarding communication about a different claim, the court in *Fieldson Associates v. Whitecliff Laboratories*[14] upheld admission of correspondence regarding the compromise of a dispute contract claim. The letters had made no mention of lost profits arising from the very transaction discussed in them. The plaintiff claimed lost profits in the litigation. The proponent sought to demonstrate that the plaintiff had failed to mention the lost-profits issue at a time when it would have been natural to do so.[15]

Regarding mitigation of damages, in *Urico v. Parnell Oil Co.,*[16] admission of testimony detailing settlement discussions was upheld. The defendant contended that the plaintiff had failed to mitigate its damages; the plaintiff had adduced statements from settlement discussions to attribute to the defendant blame for the plaintiff's inability to mitigate damages. Specifically, in a clear-cut liability situation, the plaintiff contended that defendants who had damaged his truck were informed that the plaintiff had insufficient cash to pay for truck repairs, but the defendant had refused to advance repair funds unless the plaintiff waived his other claims.[17]

In another case, the plaintiff offered statements from settlement negotiations to rebut the assertion by the defendant in a default hearing that it had not been aware of the issues in the lawsuit until it was filed.[18]

With regard to class actions, the court permitted inquiry into the conduct and negotiations that led to subclass settlement.[19]

In another case, a statement from negotiation of a civil claim was offered to establish that the defendant committed a crime. However, the court held that the Rule 408 policy justification is inapplicable to criminal prosecutions. The public interest in disclosure and prosecution of crime is greater than the public interest in settlement of civil suits.[20]

Evidence of a settlement between the plaintiff and the insurer of a cross-defendant was admitted in a contract action to impeach the testimony of the plaintiff's witness.[21] In *John McShain, Inc. v. Cessna Aircraft*

Co.,[22] a settlement agreement between plaintiff purchaser and a third-party defendant aircraft mechanic was admitted to prove bias or prejudice. However, the trial court must determine that the potential prejudice from such evidence does not outweigh its probative value.[23] The trial court's determination will not be overturned absent an abuse of discretion.[24]

Settlement negotiations, and particularly offers made in the course of negotiations, are admissible in a subsequent action against an insurance company because they are not offered to prove the original loss.[25]

Protecting the Confidentiality of the Client's Communications with the Client's Insurance Carrier

Unlike communications made to the adversary in settlement negotiations, the confidentiality of a client's consultations with its insurer has not been preserved by statute or rule. Available protection for this class of confidential communications depends on the application of the attorney-client privilege by means of an agency theory or the joint-defense doctrine. However, the requisite requirements may not be met where the insurer has no duty to defend (most often the case with directors and officers liability policies) or where the interests of the client and the carrier have or may become divergent.

Use of the Attorney-Client Privilege to Preserve the Confidentiality of Client-Insurer Communications in the Settlement Process

The Insurer's Duty to Defend. The threshold issue in applying the attorney-client privilege to protect communications between the client and its insurer is whether and on what basis the insurer can be placed in the role of attorney. (This assumes that the insurer will always be in the role of client. It is conceivable that an insurance carrier could designate in-house counsel to jointly represent both insured and insurer in defense of a claim.) Those courts that recognize the attorney-client privilege with respect to some communications between a client and its carrier do so on the basis that the insurer acts as an agent for the attorney it designates to defend the action.

The prevailing rule is that a communication made by an insured to its liability carrier pertaining to a covered event is privileged, provided the policy requires the insurer to defend the insured through its attorney, and the communication is intended for the information and assistance of the attorney.[27] Some courts reject this agency theory and protect only communications made directly to the attorney.[28]

Some, but not all, communications may take on the character of attorney work product, and may thereby be protected from disclosure.[29]

Directors and Officers Liability Insurance—No Duty to Defend. Directors and officers liability policies seldom contain an undertaking by the insurer to defend the action.[30] No case has addressed the confidentiality of communications between a covered officer or director and the carrier under one of these policies. Indeed, cases that have embraced the application of the attorney-client privilege to insurer-insured communications have stressed the duty to defend.[31]

A number of courts appear to have embraced a broader insurer-insured privilege that emphasizes the policy objectives similar to those underlying the attorney-client privilege rather than the policy clause creating the insurer's duty to defend.[32] However, the insurance policies in each case did require the insurer to defend.

The fact that, even without the duty to defend, an insurer can exert significant control over the litigation may sway a court to recognize the privilege: "D & O insurance policies indirectly afford insurance companies the right to control litigation without the duty to defend through clauses that forbid the incurring of 'costs, charges, and expenses' without the company's consent."[33] Indeed, in a settlement context, the insurer may exert great leverage without regard to a duty to defend. An insurer's ability to refuse to fund a settlement offer may trigger both a fiduciary duty and a relationship that will support a privilege for confidential communications:[34]

> The fiduciary duty of an insurer for good faith rests on the reservation of exclusive right to contest or negotiate the claim of liability brought against the insured, and so withhold from the insured the right to settle without consent of the insurer. . . . Such terms of agreement repose in the insurer the power to act for the insured, akin to authority a client vests in an attorney, or a principal in an agent—each a relationship of inherent fiduciary obligation.

The foregoing passage was quoted in *J.E. Dunn Construction Co. v. Sprinkle,*[35] in a discussion of Missouri's broad protection for insurer-insured confidential communications.

The Joint-Defense Doctrine

An additional, independent ground for invoking the attorney-client privilege to protect communications between the client and its insured is the joint-defense doctrine, which holds that "waiver [of confidentiality] is not to be inferred from the disclosure in confidence to a co-party's attorney for a common purpose."[36] In *Davis v. Costa-Gavras,*[37] relying on the joint-defense doctrine, the court protected all communications between and among executives of a defendant motion picture studio, the defendant's attorneys, the defendant's defamation insurance carrier's attorneys, and an unrepresented defendant that took place at a "pre-production libel review" for the film *Missing* that later became the subject of a libel action:

> Plaintiffs further contend that Hauser's [the unrepresented defendant's] presence at the meeting belies any assertion that the communications made during the meeting were confidential. Several Universal attorneys and executives as well as counsel for Universal's defamation insurer attended the meeting.[38]

Although not directly at issue, the presence of insurance carrier attorneys clearly did nothing to weaken the joint-defense doctrine.

An unanswered question is whether the sometimes divergent interests of the director or officer on one hand, and the insurance carrier on the other, will defeat the necessary common purpose. The existence of the conflict was recently noted by Bisceglia:

> Although the company has a duty to defend in good faith, a director cannot but notice that his interests and the company's not only do not coincide but directly oppose each other. The director wants to be cleared or, failing that, to be covered. The insurance company wants to pay as little as possible in judgment or settlement. The insurance company's interests would thus be served by a finding of dishonest behavior or other excluded misconduct [rather than mere negligence].[39]

Such a conflict may, in some circumstances, require retention of separate counsel. The court in *San Diego Navy Federal Credit Union v. Cumis Insurance Society, Inc.*[40] held that when an insurance company reserves a right to deny coverage to an insured, the lawyer hired by the insurance company automatically faces a conflict of interest. The insured then has the right to obtain independent counsel at the insurer's expense. However, the right to insist on independent counsel is the right of the insured, and the insured has the power to waive or otherwise forgo the right.[41]

Bankruptcy Ramifications

Approval of Settlement in Bankruptcy Court

The need to obtain bankruptcy court approval of a settlement can arise in a number of situations. The two most common situations are where one of the parties to the litigation is either a bankruptcy trustee or a debtor in possession or where the litigation itself takes place in the bankruptcy court as an adversary proceeding. The governing rule for approval of a bankruptcy court settlement is Bankruptcy Rule 9019, which provides in relevant part:

> (a) *Compromise.* On motion by the trustee and after a hearing on notice to creditors, the debtor and indenture trustees as provided in Rule 2002(a) and to such other entities as the court may designate, the court may approve a compromise or settlement.

The bankruptcy courts have discretion in approving settlements.[42] Indeed, the discretion of the bankruptcy court permits it to approve a settlement just above the lowest level of reasonableness.[43] Approval at that level, however, is not required.[44]

Factors Governing Settlement

In determining whether it is appropriate for a trustee or debtor in possession to settle a particular piece of litigation, the bankruptcy court reviews the following factors:[45]

- The probability of success in the litigation
- The difficulties, if any, to be encountered in the matter of collection
- The complexity of the litigation involved, and the expense, inconvenience, and delay necessarily attending it
- The paramount interest of the creditors and a proper deference to their reasonable views in the premise

The settling parties must make a presentation to the court in sufficient detail that if a disgruntled party appeals, a reviewing court can distinguish the basis for the bankruptcy court's approval from a mere boilerplate approval of the trustee's suggestions.[46] In reviewing the facts and details brought to its attention at the hearing, the bankruptcy court is not finally "to decide the numerous questions of law and facts raised . . . but rather to canvass the issues and see whether the settlement 'fall[s] below the lowest point in the range of reasonableness.'"[47]

The Overly Pervasive Settlement

Of the four factors governing settlement previously listed, the first three are hardly unique to bankruptcy—all litigants, in evaluating whether to settle, should examine the probability of success, the difficulties of collection, and the expense of the litigation. The fourth factor, the paramount interest of creditors, requires consideration of the entire realm of circumstances affecting the bankruptcy. Settlement of a major case can significantly affect the bankruptcy proceedings, for example, whether the debtor can reorganize or must liquidate.

A court-approved settlement must be made on notice to all creditors and interested parties.[48] If the settlement is approved and no appeal is taken, or the appeal is decided adversely, the terms of the compromise are binding on all creditors and parties in interest to the bankruptcy. It is not uncommon that a cause of action is the major asset of a bankruptcy debtor. Where that is the case, the decision to settle can have major implications for the creditors interested in the availability of the proceeds of that asset. Accordingly, "[u]pon timely objection, the court is to consider whether a settlement is a *de facto* plan of reorganization and thus requires procedural protections of Chapter 11 of the Bankruptcy Code."[49]

Tactical Suggestions for Obtaining Settlement Approval

Bankruptcy court approval of settlements and compromise under the current bankruptcy rules is not substantially different than under the former bankruptcy rules promulgated pursuant to the 1898 Bankruptcy Act. For this reason, the following suggestions for advancing settlement in bankruptcy have retained their usefulness:[50]

1. *Apply for Court Approval Promptly.* The settling party, in particular, should provide that the settlement agreement is subject to bankruptcy court approval, and that the trustee must apply for such approval within a definite time period. Trustees often procrastinate.
2. *Monitor the Trustee's Efforts.* The settling party should not only prod the trustee into applying for court approval, but also review the substance of the trustee's application. Very often, the trustee may leave out a material settlement term, or distort others. An objecting party could thus legitimately claim that the trustee was misleading the court and creditors.
3. *Provide for Any Failure to Get Court Approval.* If the bankruptcy court declines to approve the proposed settlement, the trustee and settling party will have to continue litigating. Neither party wants his settlement agreement or evidence submitted in the bankruptcy court to be evidence in the ensuing trial. Although it is questionable whether this could happen, the careful practitioner will expressly provide that neither the parties to the proposed settlement nor any third-party may rely on anything done to effect the proposed settlement.
4. *Consider the Hearing on the Settlement as a Trial.* As we have emphasized, counsel for the trustee, the settling party and the objector, in particular, should be prepared for the introduction of evidence at the hearing on approval of the settlement. The objector's counsel should not be stampeded into trial without having had pretrial discovery, if necessary. At the same time, counsel for the objector should be prepared to offer his own evidence, or at least show the weakness of the trustee's evidence.
5. *Do Not Act Until the Approval Order Is Final.* Neither the trustee nor the settling party should rely on an order approving

a settlement until it has become final and is no longer subject to review. In bankruptcy and most reorganization cases, any such order will become final within ten days of entry. This ten-day appeal period is substantially shorter than the thirty-day appeal period under the Federal Rules of Civil Procedure. Accordingly, we suggest, out of an excess of caution, that the parties not rely on their settlement until the appeal period has expired. In fact, careful drafters will make appropriate provision in the settlement agreement.

Structuring the Settlement Agreement to Survive Bankruptcy

Some litigation is settled on the basis that the defendant promises to pay some specified sum at some future time. Whenever such a settlement is contemplated, the parties should be aware of the impact of a subsequent bankruptcy by the party obligated to make the payment.

One of the first precautions the creditor should consider is obtaining collateral from the debtor at the time of the settlement to support any future payments. However, if the debtor files a petition in bankruptcy within ninety days of granting the security interest in the collateral, the debtor or the bankruptcy trustee may avoid the transfer of the security interest as a preference under section 547 of the Bankruptcy Code.[51]

A creditor may be tempted to argue that its agreement to forgo a larger claim and settle the case arguably constitutes "new value" given to the debtor in exchange for the security interest, thus qualifying the settlement transaction as an exception to the present rule.[52] However, a court will likely consider the creditor's claim in the litigation to be "antecedent debt" for which the creditor received part payment in the form of a security interest. In that case, the transaction could be subject to avoidance as a preference.[53] If the creditor loses its collateral, it will be relegated to the status of an unsecured creditor with only a pro rata share of any proceeds remaining after expenses of administration and other priority claims are paid.

Although the debtor cannot waive before bankruptcy the trustee's right to avoid preferences, the creditor may insist on a provision that revives the original claim amount if the debtor declares bankruptcy within the preference period.[54] Where the settlement includes a substantial compromise in the amount of the plaintiff's claim, revival of the larger claim will increase the pro rata share available to the settling plaintiff. Of course, if the claim was in dispute before the bankruptcy, the trustee or debtor in possession may continue to defend by objecting to the amount of the creditor's claim. Such objections are litigated in bankruptcy court as contested matters.[55]

Dischargeability of Obligations Incurred in a Settlement Agreement

If the plaintiff's complaint includes allegations of fraud, embezzlement, larceny, or willful and malicious injury, it may be nondischargeable under section 523 of the Bankruptcy Code, which precludes discharge of such debts. Often the complaint will also contain one or more causes of action that do not allege a nondischargeable basis of liability. If the settlement agreement does not address whether the basis for liability is predicated on the dischargeable or nondischargeable causes of action, and if the defendant later files for bankruptcy, the creditor's ability to obtain deferred payments under the settlement agreement may depend on having the defendant's liability under the settlement agreement determined to be nondischargeable.

The creditor must act quickly: Bankruptcy Rule 4007(b) is in effect a statute of limitations. It provides a relatively short time in which a creditor may object to the discharge of debts arising under circumstances specified in section 523 (c) of the Bankruptcy Code. The nondischargeability proceeding must be commenced not later than sixty days after the first date set for the meeting of creditors held pursuant to section 341(a). If a complaint to determine the dischargeability of the debt is not timely filed, the debt is discharged.[56]

In determining the dischargeability of the debtor's obligations under the settlement agreement and any judgment thereon, the bankruptcy court makes an independent determination based on all relevant evidence—it is not bound by collateral estoppel or by the record in the state court action.[57] *In re Daley* involved a settlement of a complaint containing twenty-one counts of breach of contract and fraud. The plaintiffs won a partial summary judgment on the breach of contract claims and stipulated to a dismissal with prejudice of the fraud claims. The Ninth Circuit rejected the debtor's argument that the bankruptcy court was precluded by the doctrines of res judicata and collateral estoppel from reconsidering the fraud claims as a basis for nondischargeability. Interpreting the holding in *Brown v. Felsen*[58] that "the bankruptcy court is not confined to a review of the judgment and record in the prior state-court proceeding when considering the dischargeability of [a] debt," the Ninth Circuit held that the bankruptcy court could inquire beyond the dismissal of the fraud claims reflected in the state court's record.

The Ninth Circuit found unpersuasive the debtor's attempt to distinguish *Brown v. Felsen* on the basis that the settlement in *Brown* made no mention of the theory of liability—fraud or contract—on which the liability was premised.[59] Moreover, the agreed-upon dismissal with prejudice in *Daley* did not bind the plaintiffs to the terms of their bargain: "It makes little sense, however, to resolve a federal dischargeability question according to whether or not the parties in state court waived their right to engage in hypothetical litigation in an inappropriate forum."[60]

From plaintiff's standpoint, no planning is required at the settlement stage to take advantage of the bankruptcy court's independent review of the grounds for nondischargeability of the debt arising from the settlement agreement. Indeed, in both *Daley* and *Brown v. Felsen,* an important policy consideration was the desire to avoid "needless litigation by forcing 'an otherwise unwilling party to try [nondischargeability] questions to the hilt in order to protect himself against the mere possibility that a debtor might take bankruptcy in the future.' "[61]

From the defendant's standpoint, recitals and stipulations in the settlement agreement that the obligation would be dischargeable in bankruptcy may bind the plaintiff, but as a practical matter their inclusion in a preliminary draft would only alert the plaintiff to the need for bankruptcy-planning devices such as a security interest and a clause reviving the debt in the event of bankruptcy.

Settlement of Litigation with the Government—Attorney General Settlement Guidelines

The authority to settle litigation on behalf of or against the United States has been delegated to Assistant Attorneys General.[62] Section 0.160 generally grants settlement authority in the amount of $750,000, with settlement authority for any greater amount assigned to the Deputy Attorney General.[63] The regulation states in relevant part:

> (a) Subject to the limitations set forth in paragraph (c) of this section the Assistant Attorneys General of the litigating divisions are authorized, with respect to matters assigned to their divisions, to:
>
> (1) Accept offers in compromise of claims on behalf of the United States in all cases in which the difference between the gross amount of the original claim and the proposed settlement does not exceed $750,000 or 10 percent of the original claim, whichever is greater;
>
> (2) Accept offers in compromise of, or settle administratively, claims against the United States in all cases where the principal amount of the proposed settlement does not exceed $750,000;
>
> (3) Accept offers to compromise all nonmonetary cases.
>
> . . . .
>
> (c) Any settlement, regardless of the amount or circumstances, should be referred to the Deputy Attorney General:
>
> (1) When for any reason, the compromise of a particular claim, as a practical matter, will control or adversely influence

the disposition of other claims totalling more than the $750,000 designated in the preceding part of this section.

(2) When the Assistant Attorney General is of the opinion that because of a question of law or policy presented, or because of opposition to the proposed settlement by the agency or agencies involved, or for any other reason, the offer should receive the personal attention of the Deputy Attorney General.

The authority to settle nonmonetary cases conferred in subsection (a)(3) above, whether settlement agreement or consent decree, has been limited by a recent memorandum from the Office of the Attorney General to all Assistant Attorneys General and all United States Attorneys.[64] The memorandum sets forth policy guidelines on consent decrees and settlement agreements. These new policy guidelines prohibit consent decrees that:

- convert a department or agency's discretionary authority to revise, amend, or promulgate regulations into a mandatory duty;
- commit a department or agency to expend funds not appropriated or not budgeted; or
- divest a department or agency of discretionary power committed to it to respond to changing circumstances, to make policy or managerial choices, or to protect the rights of third parties.

In like fashion, the new guidelines prohibit settlement agreements that interfere with the department or agency's authority to revise, amend, or promulgate regulations, or commit the department or agency to expend funds that have not been appropriated or budgeted.

In addition, in any settlement agreement where a secretary or agency administrator agrees to limit the exercise of his or her discretion in a particular way, the sole remedy for failure to comply with the settlement terms shall be the revival of the suit.

Termination of Derivative Actions against a Corporation

Intertwined with the decision to settle is the decision to simply stop litigating. In the context of shareholder derivative litigation, such a decision can be implemented by a motion to terminate a derivative suit against directors of the corporation. The decision to make such a motion should be made by a "special litigation committee" of the board of directors, comprising only disinterested directors.[65]

Whether the special litigation committee's decision to terminate the litigation will be respected may depend upon which of the two leading lines of cases the jurisdiction embracing the state of incorporation applies to the review of the committee's decision. The New York case of *Auerbach v. Bennett*[66] and cases following it limit judicial review of the decision to terminate the litigation to the issues of good faith and the independence or disinterestedness of the members of the special litigation committee. By contrast, cases following the Delaware case of *Zapata Corp. v. Maldonado*[67] allow judicial inquiry into both of the foregoing issues as well as into the merits of a committee's decision under a de novo application of the business judgment rule by the reviewing court in "demand excused" cases.[68]

Notes

1. Section 1154 of the California Evidence Code provides identical protection to the party who indicates a willingness to accept an offer of settlement.
2. CAL. EVID. CODE § 1152.5.
3. *Id.* § 1152.5(c).
4. Big O Tire Dealers, Inc. v. Goodyear Tire & Rubber Co., 561 F.2d 1365 (10th Cir. 1977), *cert. dismissed,* 434 U.S. 1052 (1977).
5. Urico v. Parnell Oil Co., 708 F.2d 852, 854 (1st Cir. 1983), *quoting from* Hiram Ricker & Sons v. Students Int'l Mediation Soc'y, 501 F.2d 550, 553 (1st Cir. 1974).
6. *See also* NLRB v. Gotham Indus., Inc., 406 F.2d 1306, 1313 n.9 (1st Cir. 1969) ("As a simple example, if a party says the defendant broke his arm and he would settle for so many dollars, the dollar amount would be admissible, but the assertion he broke his arm would be admissible if he later claimed it was his leg."); Vulcan Hart Corp. (St. Louis Div.) v. NLRB, 718 F.2d 269, 277 (8th Cir. 1983) ("[T]o the extent that either party makes an independent admission of fact, the evidence is admissible.").
7. 6 Cal. App. 3d 395, 86 Cal. Rptr. 33 (1970).
8. 6 Cal. App. 3d at 405.
9. *Id.*
10. 58 Cal. 2d 257, 23 Cal. Rptr. 582, 373 P.2d 630 (1962).
11. Notes of Advisory Committee on Proposed Rules (citation omitted).
12. 163 Cal. App. 3d 715, 725, 209 Cal. Rptr. 757 (1984).
13. A collection of various state and federal cases on this topic may be found in Annot., 15 A.L.R.3D 13 (1967).
14. 276 Cal. App. 2d 770, 81 Cal. Rptr. 332 (1969).
15. 276 Cal. App. 2d at 773.
16. 708 F.2d at 854.
17. *Id.*
18. Breuer Elec. Mfg. Co. v. Toronado Sys. of Am., Inc., 687 F.2d 182, 217 U.S.P.Q. 24 (7th Cir. 1982).
19. *In re* General Motors Corp. Engine Interchange Litig., 594 F.2d 1106 (7th Cir. 1979), *cert. denied,* 444 U.S. 870 (1979).
20. United States v. Gonzalez, 748 F.2d 74, 78 (2d Cir. 1984).

21. County of Hennepin v. AFG Indus., Inc., 726 F.2d 149 (8th Cir. 1984).
22. 563 F.2d 632 (3d Cir. 1977).
23. *Id.* at 635; FED. R. EVID. 403.
24. 563 F.2d at 635.
25. White v. Western Title Ins. Co., 40 Cal. 3d 870, 887, 221 Cal. Rptr. 509, 710 P.2d 309 (1985). *See also* CAL. EVID. CODE § 1152(b) (requiring admission of prior and subsequent offers of compromise where evidence of one such offer has been admitted in an action for breach of an insurance contract's implied covenant of good faith and fair dealing).
26. *See* People v. Ryan, 197 N.E.2d 15, 17 (Ill. 1964); Brakhage v. Graff, 206 N.W.2d 45, 47–48 (Neb. 1973).
27. Heffron v. Los Angeles Transit Lines, 170 Cal. App. 2d 709, 718, 339 P.2d 567 (1959). *See also* Hollien v. Kaye, 194 Misc. 821, 87 N.Y.S.2d 782, 785 (1949); People v. Ryan, 197 N.E.2d at 17.
28. *See, e.g.,* Jacobi v. Podevels, 127 N.W.2d 73, 76, 23 Wisc. 2d 152 (1964); Gottlieb v. Bresler, 24 F.R.D. 371, 372 (D.D.C. 1959).
29. *See, e.g.,* Cataldo v. County of Monroe, 238 N.Y.S.2d 855, 858, 38 Misc. 2d 768 (1963), *aff'd,* 243 N.Y.S.2d 986 (1963).
30. *See* Chapter 32. *See also* Johnston, *Corporate Indemnification and Liability Insurance for Directors and Officers,* 33 BUS. LAW. 1993, 2016, 2023 (1978).
31. *See Heffron,* 170 Cal. App. 2d at 718.
32. *See Cataldo,* 238 N.Y.S.2d 855; Cain v. Barker, 540 S.W.2d 50, 53 (Mo. 1976); Puckett v. Broome, 385 S.W.2d 762, 770 (Tenn. App. 1964).
33. Bisceglia, *Practical Aspects of Directors and Officers Liability Insurance—Allocating and Advancing Legal Fees and the Duty to Defend,* 32 U.C.L.A. L. REV. 690, 704 (1985).
34. *See* Craig v. Iowa Kemper Mut. Ins. Co., 565 S.W.2d 716, 723 (Mo. App. 1978).
35. 650 S.W.2d 707, 710 n.1 (Mo. App. 1983).
36. United States v. McPartlin, 595 F.2d 1321, 1336 (7th Cir.), *cert. denied,* 444 U.S. 833 (1979).
37. 580 F. Supp. 1082 (S.D.N.Y. 1984).
38. *Id.* at 1098.
39. Bisceglia, *supra* note 33, at 708.
40. 162 Cal. App. 3d 358, 208 Cal. Rptr. 494 (1984).
41. McGee v. Superior Court, 175 Cal. App. 3d 226, 221 Cal. Rptr. 421, 424 (1985). *See also* Previews, Inc. v. California Union Ins. Co., 640 F.2d 1026 (9th Cir. 1981) (holding that in a conflict of interest situation, the insurer's obligation to defend extends to paying reasonable value of legal services and costs performed by independent counsel selected by the insured).
42. United States v. Aweco, Inc. (*In re* Aweco, Inc.), 725 F.2d 293, 297–98 (5th Cir. 1984), *cert. denied,* 469 U.S. 880, 105 S. Ct. 224, 83 L. Ed. 2d 182 (1984).
43. *In re* Lion Capital Group, 49 B.R. 163 (Bankr. S.D.N.Y. 1985).
44. *Id.* at 176.
45. *In re* Lion Capital Group, 49 B.R. at 175; Drexel v. Loomis, 35 F.2d 800, 806 (8th Cir. 1929).

46. *In re* Lion Capital Group, 49 B.R. at 176; *In re* Boston & Providence R.R. Corp., 673 F.2d 11, 12 (1st Cir. 1982).
47. *In re* Lion Capital Group, 49 B.R. at 175, *quoting from* Anaconda-Ericsson, Inc. v. Hessen (*In re* Teltronics Servs. Inc.), 762 F.2d 185, 187, 189 (2d Cir. 1985).
48. BANKR. R. 9019(a).
49. *In re* Lion Capital Group, 49 B.R. at 175; *accord In re* White Transp. Corp. Sec. Litig., 730 F.2d 1128 (8th Cir. 1984), *cert. denied,* 469 U.S. 1207, 105 S. Ct. 1169, 84 L. Ed. 2d 320 (1985).
50. Cook & Goldstein, *Settling with the Bankruptcy Trustee: More or Less Litigation?* 5 LITIGATION 19, 22 (Fall 1978).
51. 11 U.S.C. § 547(c).
52. *See* Bankruptcy Code § 547(c).
53. *Id.* at § 547(b).
54. If the creditor is also an insider, as defined in section 101(28) of the Bankruptcy Code, than the preference period is one year rather than ninety days. 11 U.S.C. § 547(b)(4)(B). For a survey of decisions applying the Bankruptcy Code's definition of "insider" in the context of corporations and partnerships, see Annotation, *Who Is "Insider" within Meaning of Bankruptcy Code of 1978 (11 U.S.C. §§ 101* et seq.*),* 71 A.L.R. FED. 197 (1985).
55. *See* BANKR. R. 9014.
56. 11 U.S.C. § 523(c); Advisory Committee Note to Rule 4007(c).
57. *In re* Houtman, 568 F.2d 651, 653–54 (9th Cir. 1978); *In re* Daley, 776 F.2d 834, 13 C.B.C.2d 927, Bankr. L. Rep. (CCH) ¶ 70,853 (9th Cir. 1985), *cert. denied,* ____ U.S. ____ , 106 S. Ct. 2279, 90 L. Ed. 2d 721 (1986).
58. 442 U.S. 127, 138–39, 99 S. Ct. 2205, 2213, 60 L. Ed. 2d 767 (1979).
59. *In re* Daley, 776 F.2d at 837.
60. *Id. quoting from* Brown v. Felsen, 442 U.S. at 137. *See also In re* Gross, 654 F.2d 602 (9th Cir. 1981) (contract judgment in state court does not constitute a binding election of remedies precluding consideration of fraud claim in dischargeability proceeding); Williams v. Colonial Discount Co., 207 F. Supp. 362 (N.D. Ga. 1962) (bankruptcy court may make independent determination of unlitigated malicious damage issue); Greenberg v. Schools, 711 F.2d 152, 156, 8 C.B.C.2d 1407 (11th Cir. 1983) (settlement agreement does not extinguish the original fraud claim on which it was based).
61. *In re* Daley, 776 F.2d at 837, *quoting from* Brown v. Felsen, 442 U.S. at 135.
62. 28 C.F.R. § 0.160 (1987).
63. *Id.*
64. *See* Memorandum, Office of the Attorney General, Department Policy Regarding Consent Decrees and Settlement Agreements, at 3 (Mar. 13, 1986), *reprinted in* 34 U.S. ATTORNEYS BULL. no. 7, at 186 (May 16, 1986).
65. *See generally* Block & Prussin, *Termination of Derivative Suits against Directors of Business Judgment Grounds: From* Zapata *to* Aronson, 39 BUS. LAW, 1503 (1984).
66. 47 N.Y.2d 619, 393 N.E.2d 994, 419 N.Y.S.2d 920 (1979).
67. 430 A.2d 779 (Del. 1981).
68. For additional discussion of this issue, see chapters thirty and thirty-three.

Twenty

Contribution, Indemnity, and Settlements in Multidefendant Cases

Samuel R. Miller and Leigh Shields

This chapter will discuss the issues faced by a defendant in a multidefendant case in attempting to reach a settlement with the plaintiff. A chief concern of a defendant faced with claims governed by the principles of joint and several liability is that even a relatively innocent or insignificant defendant may be saddled with the entire judgment if he or she is found liable. Thus, in a variety of multidefendant cases, a defendant will look for various vehicles to ensure an equitable sharing of exposure, including asserting cross-claims for indemnity or contribution. On the other hand, when a defendant in a multidefendant case does settle with the plaintiff, the settling defendant wants to ensure against exposure to further litigation on such cross-claims from the nonsettling defendants. This chapter will discuss the issues faced by a defendant involved in the partial settlement of a multidefendant case. It will examine the law in various fields, including securities and antitrust litigation.

General Principles of Indemnity and Contribution

A defendant in a multidefendant case will immediately seek to determine whether claims for indemnity or contribution may be asserted. Contribution is an equitable doctrine based on the principle that a person who discharges a liability shared with another should not bear the sole burden of payment. It involves the sharing of losses among tortfeasors by requiring each to pay a proportionate share of the loss.[1] Rights of contribution among tortfeasors are governed by statute in many jurisdictions[2] and by judicial decision in others.[3]

Twenty-one states have adopted some version of the Uniform Contribution Among Tortfeasors Act (1955 version),[4] (hereinafter cited as the Uniform Contribution Act). Section 1(b) of the Uniform Contribution Act states that the "right of contribution exists only in favor of a tortfeasor who has paid more than his pro rata share of the common liability, and

Samuel R. Miller is a member and Leigh Shields is an associate of Morrison & Foerster, San Francisco, California.

his total recovery is limited to the amount paid by him in excess of his pro rata share." Section 2 states that the "relative degrees of fault [of the tortfeasors] shall not be considered in determining the pro rata share." Thus, under the Uniform Contribution Act, the judgment is allocated by dividing the judgment by the number of defendants, without regard to the relative fault of each defendant. The rule in the Uniform Contribution Act that contribution is allocated on a pro rata basis has been modified in some states to permit an allocation of liability based on the relative degree of fault of the joint tortfeasors.[5]

Under section 4 of the Uniform Contribution Act, a defendant who settles in "good faith" with the plaintiff is protected from contribution claims brought by nonsettling defendants.[6] This type of provision, generically knows as a "settlement bar statute," is critical as far as ensuring that a defendant who settles is not kept in the litigation by nonsettling codefendants.

While contribution involves a proportionate sharing of the loss, indemnification entails the shifting of the entire loss from one tortfeasor who has been compelled to pay it to another. Rights of indemnity may arise from express contractual language, such as an agreement by a manufacturer to indemnify a wholesaler or retailer for all losses or damages the wholesaler or retailer may incur due to injury to a third party caused by a product failure.

Indemnity rights may also be implied under the doctrine of implied equitable indemnity.[7] Under this doctrine, the entire loss is shifted from one tortfeasor to another, even in the absence of an express agreement, where such loss shifting is equitable. This doctrine has been applied in a variety of contexts, such as where one defendant has been an active wrongdoer and another defendant has only been passive.[8]

Claims for indemnity or contribution do not accrue in most circumstances until judgment has been entered and a defendant has paid more than his or her "fair share" of the judgment.[9] Nevertheless, in many states, a cross-complaint or third-party complaint for indemnity or contribution may be filed at the time that the defendant answers the complaint or during the course of pretrial proceedings.[10]

Thus, an immediate strategic question facing a defendant in a multidefendant case is whether to assert such a cross-complaint in the case in chief or whether to wait until the case against the plaintiff is resolved by settlement or judgment. An obvious advantage of not asserting such a cross-complaint is that the defendants can form a united front against the plaintiff. A disadvantage of waiting to assert such a claim is that the rights of indemnity or contribution of various defendants may not be adjudicated in the main trial on the merits unless such cross-claims are asserted. Thus, the determination of these issues may involve additional litigation.

Moreover, in some cases, there may be tactical advantage to asserting a cross-complaint and thereby unequivocally pointing the finger at another defendant, who may be painted as the real culprit.

If there is any doubt as to whether claims for indemnity or contribution have accrued, a tolling agreement may be negotiated among co-defendants to ensure that no such claim is waived.

Principles of Indemnity and Contribution under the Federal Securities Laws

Federal law, not state law, governs the existence of rights to indemnity or contribution under the federal securities laws.[11]

Indemnification under the Federal Securities Law

The general rule under the federal securities laws is that indemnification will not be allowed at least where the defendant acted with more than ordinary negligence.[12] *Globus I* expressly reserved the question of whether indemnification could be denied where the defendant seeking indemnification was guilty only of negligence, not intentional wrongdoing. However, several subsequent cases have extended the limitation on indemnity to negligent conduct as well.[13]

The rationale for denying indemnification to joint tortfeasors under the federal securities law is to uphold the strong policy of investor protection by insisting upon vigilance and diligence by all persons charged with actively complying with those standards.

Several exceptions to the general rule precluding indemnity may exist. One exception applies where the liability of a joint tortfeasor is imposed only by operation of law.[14] Thus a corporate defendant may be able to obtain indemnity from its agents where it is liable only by reason of the principles of *respondeat superior.*[15] This exception may be important in circumstances where there has been a change in management after the acts that are the subject of the litigation.

Contribution in Securities Litigation

Several sections of the federal securities laws specifically authorize contribution.[16] Virtually all courts that have considered the question have held that a right to contribution exists in actions under section 10(b) of the Securities Exchange Act of 1934.[17]

Although there is a general consensus that a right to contribution exists, courts differ with respect to how liability should be apportioned among the defendants. Several cases have awarded contribution on a pro rata (i.e., per capita) basis. Under this approach the judgment is divided evenly among the various defendants, regardless of their relative fault.[18] As noted, the pro rata approach is the approach of the Uniform Contribution Act.

On the other hand, at least some courts have seriously considered applying concepts of relative culpability.[19] In *McLean v. Alexander,* all the defendants except the corporate issuer's accountant settled during trial, the judgment was rendered against the accountant. Although the finding of liability against the accountant was later reversed, the district court's handling of the contribution claims departed from a pro rata approach. The *McLean* court adopted a relative-fault measure of damages based on considerations of "equity and common sense."[20] Noting the "vast difference between the defendants and the degrees of their wrongdoing," the court held the accountant liable for 10 percent of the plaintiff's damages and the sellers considered together as one entity liable for the other 90 percent.[21]

Procedures to Extinguish Contribution Claims in Securities Cases

Until recently, parties and courts struggled to find a procedural mechanism whereby a settling defendant could be sure that claims for contribution by nonsettling defendants would be cut off as a part of the settlement with the plaintiff. Unlike the procedures under the Uniform Contribution Act or other state law, the federal securities laws contain no provision that a good-faith settlement precludes the right of a nonsettling defendant from obtaining contribution from settling defendants.

In *Altman v. Liberty Equities Corp.,*[22] the court refused to approve a provision of a partial settlement permanently enjoining the nonsettling defendants from prosecuting claims for indemnification or contribution against the settling defendants on the ground that a right to contribution in an action under section 10(b) existed under federal law and that it would be unjust to cut off the remaining defendants' rights to contribution at an early stage of the litigation.[23]

In light of this possibility, efforts have been made to structure settlement to afford the settling defendants some protection against claims for contribution. One method that has been employed is for the plaintiff to agree, as part of the settlement, to indemnify the settling defendant from liability on any contribution claims.[24] Such indemnification agreements have been employed in a variety of settlement contexts.[25] Another method that has been employed to avoid contribution claims is a "judgment reduction" type of settlement in which the plaintiff agrees to release the nonsettling defendants from the settling defendant's share of total damages. This type of approach has met with some approval.[26]

Even when the settlement does not use such a judgment-reduction clause, several courts have refused to require settling defendants to pay contribution. For example, in *Gould v. American-Hawaiian Steamship Co.*,[27] the court denied the contribution claim of the nonsettling defendant on the ground that the nonsettling defendant had not been required to pay more than his equitable share of plaintiff's damages and thus had no right to contribution against the settling defendant. Similarly, in *Herzfeld v. Laventhol, Krekstein, Horwath & Horwath*,[28] the court found that the nonsettling defendant had no right to contribution against the settling defendants on the ground that the settling defendants had already paid more than one-half of plaintiff's damages. However, in these cases, the courts based their determinations not to permit contribution on after-the-fact determinations that the settling defendants paid a "fair share." Thus, these cases cannot assure a settling defendant at the time of settlement that contribution claims will be cut off.

In several recent federal securities cases, courts have protected settling defendants from contribution claims through application of a settlement bar rule.[29] In *Nelson v. Bennett*, the Eastern District of California applied a federal settlement bar rule as a matter of federal common law.[30] The court analyzed the settlement agreement under the rule, concluding that it was fundamentally fair and equitable and then dismissed all cross-claims for contribution or indemnity asserted against the settling defendant. The factors considered by the court in evaluating the equities of the settlement agreement were "the possible uncollectibility of any larger judgment which might be entered against the settling defendants, the adequacy of the settlement amount in light of the comparative culpability of the settling defendants and the uncertainties of establishing such liability, and the participation of a magistrate or judge in the settlement negotiations."[31]

Also relying on federal common law and considering similar factors, the court in *In re NuCorp Energy Securities Litigation* determined that the settlement represented "the settling defendants' 'fair' or 'proper' share of the total damages" and dismissed all federal securities law claims for contribution against the settling defendants.[32]

In *First Federal Savings & Loan Association v. Oppenheim, Appel, Dixon & Co.*,[33] the Southern District of New York dismissed claims for contribution on the pleadings after adopting the state settlement bar statute as the federal rule of decision. The *First Federal Savings* litigation arose out of claims made by various savings and loan institutions against Comark, a dealer in government securities, and Marine Midland Bank. During the course of the trial, Marine Midland reached a sliding-scale settlement with the plaintiffs, under which Marine Midland agreed to pay the plaintiffs a base settlement amount of $3 million with the payment of an additional settlement amount of up to $2 million contingent upon the amount of money subsequently recovered by plaintiffs from other potential defendants. Thereafter, First Federal Savings and other plaintiffs sued Comark's accountants, who in turn sought contribution from Marine Midland. The court adopted the New York release statute as the rule of decision governing contribution claims against the settling tortfeasor as to both state law and federal securities laws claims.[34] Under the New York release statute,[35] the settlement reduced the plaintiff's claim against the nonsettling tortfeasors by the greater of the amount stipulated in the judgment, the amount of consideration, or the amount of the released tortfeasor's equitable share of the damages.

In *Smith v. Mulvaney,*[36] the Ninth Circuit reversed a district court's conclusion that settling defendants had paid their fair share of the judgment and were not liable for contribution on federal securities law claims. There, the nonsettling defendant, Mrs. Smith, sought to bring claims for contribution against the settling defendants after a substantial judgment had been entered against her. The district court granted summary judgment as to the claims for contribution based upon its prior approval of the partial settlement under Federal Rule of Civil Procedure 23(e) and its "judicial notice" of Mrs. Smith's greater culpability.[37] The Ninth Circuit embraced the rule that contribution claims should be determined based on relative culpability. However, the Ninth Circuit found there was inadequate support in the record for the district court's conclusion that defendants had paid their proper share of the judgment and remanded the case to the district court.[38]

Recently, in *Kirkorian v. Bonelli,*[39] Chief Judge Robert Peckham of the Northern District of California interpreted *Smith v. Mulvaney* as approving "in principle the proposition that a proper fairness hearing could protect settling defendants from contribution claims under the federal securities law."[40] Applying the factors enunciated in *Nelson v. Bennett* and *In re Nucorp Energy Securities,* Judge Peckham approved a partial settlement in which certain defendants contributed 25 percent of the total claimed losses and thereby barred any claims against the settling defendants by the nonsettling defendants for indemnity or contribution under state or federal law. The *Kirkorian* decision is significant because it reflects a judicial willingness to apply a settlement bar rule before trial without a full-blown evidentiary hearing on the relative culpability of the various defendants. Thus, *Kirkorian* will encourage partial settlements in federal securities cases.

If the parties to a partial settlement are uncertain as to whether a district court will adopt a federal settlement bar rule, an alternative strategy to achieve "total peace" in a case involving both federal securities claims and state law claims is for the plaintiff to settle the state law claims and dismiss the federal securities claims. This would remove any uncertainty regarding the ability to extinguish claims for contribution if the applicable state law bars contribution claims after a good-faith settlement. Thus, because application of state law may become critical on the issue of whether contribution claims are barred, a defendant involved in multistate litigation should carefully choose a settlement forum to take advantage of favorable state laws.

Partial Settlement on Multidefendant Antitrust Litigation

Defendants in antitrust litigation are jointly and severally liable for the full amount of damages awarded to the plaintiff.[41] This liability results in great exposure for each individual defendant because there is no right to contribution among antitrust co-conspirators.[42] Thus, a settling defendant has no right to contribution, and a claim for contribution cannot lie against a settling defendant.[43]

The Reduction of Judgment by the Amount of the Settlement in Antitrust Cases

An antitrust plaintiff "who has recovered any item of damage from one co-conspirator may not again recover the same item from another conspirator; the law, that is, does not permit a plaintiff to recover double payment."[44] Thus, any judgment against nonsettling defendants in an antitrust lawsuit is offset by the amount collected by plaintiffs in settlements with defendants' co-conspirators. But the amount received from a settling defendant is subtracted from the actual damages fixed by the jury verdict only *after* the award is trebled.[45]

Effect and Legality of Most-Favored Nations Clauses in Settlement Agreements

A settlement agreement may provide that plaintiff reduce the settling defendant's obligation if the plaintiff later settles with another defendant on more favorable terms. Such clauses have been called "most-favored nation" clauses. Some courts have enforced these provisions in the antitrust context.[46] At least one antitrust decision, however, has invalidated a so-called most-favored nation clause, reasoning that these clauses restrict plaintiff's ability to settle.[47]

Section 23.23 of the *Manual for Complex Litigation (Second)* criticizes most-favored nation clauses as undesirable. The manual states that in the unusual circumstances where such a clause is found warranted, its operative effect should terminate after a specified length of time, and the court should be vested with broad discretion to void or limit the clause if its continuation would be unfair or inequitable.

A less strict type of most-favored nation clause allows the plaintiff to enter into subsequent, more favorable settlements without refunding any settlement proceeds to the defendant with whom the plaintiff has already settled if there is a material change in circumstances relevant to the litigation or if there are financial or other differences among the defendants. Thus, in *Fisher Brothers v. Phelps Dodge Industries, Inc.*,[48] the court denied a defendant's motion to require enforcement of a most-favored nation clause because it found that the allegedly more favorable settlement occurred in materially changed circumstances.

Effect and Legality of Sharing Agreements among Antitrust Co-Conspirators

In some antitrust cases (and other types of cases), the defendants may contract privately to share liability proportionately by entering into "sharing agreements."[49] A typical sharing agreement in the antitrust context may provide for the division of liability among defendants on the basis of market share. The sharing agreement could include provisions that (1) a settling defendant must obtain from plaintiff an agreement to reduce the judgment against other defendants by the greater of the sum paid by the settling defendant or the amount of the judgment attributable to the sales of settling defendant; (2) a settlement agreement cannot provide for the settling defendant's voluntary cooperation with plaintiff in the prosecution of the action; and (3) the settling defendant will promptly notify the other defendants of the terms of the settlement.

It has been argued that sharing agreements reduce the likelihood of settlement because plaintiffs are reluctant to agree to claims reduction provisions and will be less likely to agree to discount settlements with defendants in financial difficulty.[50] According to the *Manual for Complex Litigation (Second),* sharing agreements are discoverable and may be admissible at trial to show bias on the part of a witness.[51]

Indemnity and Contribution Rights in Civil RICO Litigation

Unlike the federal securities laws, the Racketeer Influenced and Corrupt Organizations Act (RICO)[52] does not contain a provision authorizing contribution. This statutory silence has resulted in uncertainty with respect to the right to contribution in RICO cases. Several federal district courts, however, have recently ruled that there is no right to contribution in a RICO suit.[53] In *Boone v. Beacon Building Corp.*, a New Jersey district court granted a motion to dismiss the contribution cross-claims of numerous co-defendants against the Township of Gloucester in litigation concerning damages arising from the plaintiffs' purchase of a home near a toxic land fill. The court reasoned that, although silent on the contribution issue, the RICO statute "closely tracks the language of § 4 of the Clayton Act," and that the issue of contribution under the antitrust laws was resolved by the Supreme Court when it held in *Texas Industries v. Radcliff Materials*[54] that there is no such right.[55]

RICO decisions also follow the antitrust rule that amounts received from settling defendants are credited against a subsequent judgment only after the damage award is trebled.[56]

Extinguishment of Claims for Contribution or Indemnity under State Law

As noted, the court in *First Federal Savings*[57] relied on New York's release statute, under which a release given in good faith by an injured party to one tortfeasor relieves the settling party from liability to other parties for contribution.

Other states, including California, have similar statutory provisions. The California Code of Civil Procedure in section 877 provides in pertinent part:

> Where a release, dismissal with or without prejudice, or a covenant not to sue or not to enforce a judgment is given in good faith before verdict or judgment to one or more of a number of tortfeasors claimed to be liable for the same tort . . . it shall discharge the party to whom it is given from all liability for any contribution to any other parties.

Pursuant to section 877.6 of the California Code of Civil Procedure, any party may request a hearing on the issue of the "good faith" of the settlement entered into by the plaintiff and one or more alleged tortfeasors. Pursuant to Section 877.6 of the Code of Civil Procedure, a court determination that the settlement was made in good faith shall bar any other joint tortfeasor from any further claims against the settling tortfeasor for equitable comparative contribution, or partial or comparative indemnity, based on comparative negligence or comparative fault.

In *Tech-Bilt Inc. v. Woodward-Clyde & Associates,*[58] the California Supreme Court set forth the standards to be applied in determining the good faith of a settlement. The court directed trial courts to inquire whether the amount of the settlement is within the "reasonable range of the settling tortfeasor's proportional share of comparative liability for the plaintiff's injuries." In other words, some element of proportionality is required. However, the court in *Tech-Bilt* cautioned that a nonsettling defendant may not overturn a settlement merely by showing that the settlement figure is disproportionately low. Factors such as the financial condition and insurance policy limits of the settling defendant must be taken into consideration. To be subject to challenge, the settlement must be so far "out of the ballpark" in relation to these factors as to be inconsistent with equitable objectives of the statutory scheme.[59]

Chief Justice Rose Bird dissented in *Tech-Bilt,* predicting that the definition of a good-faith settlement provides no certainty as to whether a settlement will be upheld and will clog the trial courts with minitrials on the issue of whether the settlement is within the "reasonable range" of expected liability.

One issue raised by the *Tech-Bilt* standard is whether a nonsettling defendant challenging a settlement may take discovery from the plaintiff's lawyer on the basis of the lawyer's evaluation of the exposure and damages in the case. If the lawyer for the nonsettling defendant tries to inquire into the thought processes of the settling lawyers, questions arise as to whether the work-product or attorney-client privileges may be invaded. This issue remains unresolved.

Conclusion

Mechanisms to achieve partial settlements that will extinguish cross-claims for contribution or indemnity from nonsettling defendants should be given judicial recognition. That recognition will encourage settlement of complex, multiparty litigation. Adoption of the *Tech-Bilt* standards and the development of a federal "settlement bar" rule as in *In re Nucorp* and *Kirkorian* provide means of accomplishing this goal.

Notes

1. *See* Adamski, *Contribution and Settlement in Multiparty Actions under Rule 10b-5,* 66 IOWA L. REV. 533, 534 (1981).
2. *E.g.,* CAL. CIV. PROC. CODE §§ 875–80; N.Y. CIV. PRAC. LAW §§ 1401–04. For a listing of the provision of state law recognizing rights of contribution, see Note, *The Right to Contribution for Response Costs under CERCLA,* 60 NOTRE DAME L. REV. 345, 356 n.92 (1985).
3. *See, e.g.,* George's Radio v. Capital Transit Co., 126 F.2d 219 (D.C. Cir. 1942).
4. 12 U.L.A. 63 (1975).
5. *See* 12 U.L.A. at 75 (1986 Supp.).
6. *See, e.g., In re* MGM Grand Hotel Fire Litig., 570 F. Supp. 913, 927 (D. Nev. 1983).
7. *See generally* PROSSER & KEETON, THE LAW OF TORTS § 51 (1984).
8. *See id.* § 51 at p. 343. *See also* American Motorcycle Ass'n v. Superior Court, 20 Cal. 3d 578, 594, 146 Cal. Rptr. 182 (1978).

9. *See* People *ex rel.* Department of Transportation v. Superior Court, 26 Cal. 3d 744, 751, 163 Cal. Rptr. 585 (1980) (California law of equitable indemnity); Albert v. Dietz, 283 F. Supp. 854 (D. Hawaii 1968) (contribution rights).
10. *See American Motorcycle Ass'n,* 20 Cal. 3d at 604–06.
11. *See* Heizer Corp. v. Ross, 601 F.2d 330, 331 (7th Cir. 1979) (contribution); Professional Beauty Supply, Inc. v. National Beauty Supply Inc., 594 F.2d 1179, 1182 (8th Cir. 1979) (contribution); Globus, Inc. v. Law Research Serv., Inc. [*Globus I*] 418 F.2d 1276 (2d Cir. 1969), *cert. denied,* 397 U.S. 913 (1970) (indemnity).
12. *Globus I,* 418 F.2d at 1288. *See also* Laventhol, Krekstein, Horwath & Horwath v. Horwitch, 637 F.2d 672, 676 (9th Cir. 1980), *cert. denied,* 452 U.S. 963 (1981); Heizer Corp. v. Ross, 601 F.2d 330 (7th Cir. 1979); Premier Corp. v. Economic Research Analysts, 578 F.2d 551, 555 (4th Cir. 1978).
13. *See, e.g.,* Laventhol, Krekstein, Horwath & Horwath v. Horwitch, 637 F.2d at 676; Gould v. American-Hawaiian Steamship Co., 387 F. Supp. 163, 167–68 (D. Del. 1974), *vacated on other grounds,* 535 F.2d 761 (3d Cir. 1976); Kennedy v. Josephthal & Co., [1982–1983 Transfer Binder] FED. SEC. L. REP. (CCH) ¶ 99,204 (D.Mass. 1983).
14. *See* Block & Barton, *Contribution and Indemnification under the Federal Securities Laws,* 11 SEC. REG. L.J. 351, 353–55 (1984).
15. *See, e.g.,* Handel-Maatschappij, etc. v. Farradyne Elec. Corp., 37 F.R.D. 357, 359 (S.D.N.Y. 1964); deHaas v. Empire Petroleum Co., 286 F. Supp. 809, 816 (D. Colo. 1968), *aff'd in part, vacated in part,* 435 F.2d 1223 (10th Cir. 1970); Maryville Academy v. Loeb Rhoades & Co., Inc., 530 F. Supp. 1061, 1071 (N.D. Ill. 1981).
16. *See, e.g.,* Securities Act of 1933 § 11(f), 15 U.S.C. § 77k(f) (civil liability for false registration statements); Securities Exchange Act of 1934 § 9(e), 15 U.S.C. §78i(e) (civil liability for manipulation of security prices); Securities Exchange Act of 1934 § 18(b), 15 U.S.C. § 78r(b) (civil liability for false and misleading statements in documents filed with the SEC).
17. *See generally* Adamski, *supra* note 1, at 539; Sirota v. Solitron Devices, Inc., 673 F.2d 566 (2d Cir.), *cert. denied,* 459 U.S. 838 (1982); Globus Inc. v. Law Research Serv., Inc. [*Globus II*], 318 F. Supp. 955 (S.D.N.Y. 1970), *aff'd,* 442 F.2d 1346 (2d Cir.), *cert. denied,* 404 U.S. 941 (1971); *In re* Olympia Brewing Co. Sec. Litig., 674 F. Supp. 597, 616 (N.D. Ill. 1987).
18. *See, e.g.,* Herzfeld v. Laventhol, Krekstein, Horwath & Horwath, 540 F.2d 27, 38 (2d Cir. 1976). *See generally* Ruder, *Multiple Defendants and Securities Law Fraud Cases: Aiding and Abetting, Conspiracy, In Pari Delicto, Indemnification, and Contribution,* 120 U. PA. L. REV. 597, 650 (1972); Adamski, *supra* note 1, at 556.
19. *See, e,g.,* Smith v. Mulvaney, 827 F.2d 558, 561 (9th Cir. 1987); Gould v. American-Hawaiian Steamship Co., 387 F. Supp. at 171; McLean v. Alexander, 449 F. Supp. 1251, 1274–76 (D. Del.1978), *rev'd on other grounds,* 599 F.2d 1190 (3d Cir. 1979).
20. 449 F. Supp. at 1275–76.
21. 449 F. Supp. at 1272–73.
22. 54 F.R.D. 620 (S.D.N.Y. 1972).
23. *See also* Muth v. Dechert, Price & Rhoads, 391 F. Supp. 935, 939 (E.D. Pa.

1975); *In re* National Student Marketing Litig., 517 F. Supp. 1345 (D. Colo. 1981).

24. *See* Adamski, *supra* note 1, at 546; Seiffer v. Topsy's Int'l, Inc., 80 F.R.D. 272, 278 (D. Kan. 1978); McLean v. Alexander, 449 F. Supp. at 1266.

25. *See In re* MGM Grand Hotel Fire Litig., 570 F. Supp. 913, 928–29 (D. Nev. 1983).

26. *See* Adamski, *supra* note 1, at 546; McLean v. Alexander, 449 F. Supp. at 1266.

27. 387 F. Supp. 163 (D. Del. 1974), *vacated on other grounds,* 535 F.2d 761 (3d Cir. 1976).

28. 540 F.2d 27 (2d Cir. 1976).

29. *See* Kirkorian v. Borelli, FED. SEC. L. REP. (CCH) ¶ 93,782 (N.D. Cal. 1988); Nelson v. Bennett, 662 F. Supp. 1324 (E.D. Cal. 1987); *In re* Nucorp Energy Sec. Litig., 661 F. Supp. 1403 (S.D. Cal. 1987); First Fed. Sav. & Loan Ass'n v. Oppenheim, Appel, Dixon & Co., 631 F. Supp. 1029 (S.D.N.Y. 1986).

30. 662 F. Supp. at 1335–38.

31. *Id.* at 1338.

32. 661 F. Supp. at 1408–09.

33. 631 F. Supp. 1029 (S.D.N.Y. 1986).

34. *Id.* at 1032–37.

35. N.Y. GEN. OBLIG. LAW § 15-108.

36. 827 F.2d 558, 562 (9th Cir. 1987).

37. *See* Smith v. Mulvaney, FED. SEC. L. REP. (CCH) ¶ 92,084 (S.D. Cal. 1985), *rev'd,* 827 F.2d 558 (9th Cir. 1987).

38. 827 F.2d at 562.

39. FED. SEC. L. REP.(CCH) ¶ 93,782 (N.D. Cal. 1988).

40. *Id.* at p. 98,692.

41. Solomon v. Houston Corrugated Box Co., 526 F.2d 389, 392 n.4 (5th Cir. 1976).

42. Texas Indus., Inc. v. Radcliff Materials, Inc., 451 U.S. 630 (1981).

43. *See generally* Note, *Contribution between Joint Tortfeasors Denied under the Federal Antitrust Laws,* 65 MARQ. L. REV. 281 (1982).

44. Zenith Radio Corp. v. Hazeltine Research, 401 U.S. 321, 348 (1971).

45. Hydrolevel Corp. v. American Soc'y of Mechanical Engineers, Inc., 635 F.2d 118, 130 (2d Cir. 1980), *cert. denied,* 456 U.S. 989 (1982); Flintkote Co. v. Lysfjord, 246 F.2d 368, 398 (9th Cir.), *cert. denied,* 355 U.S. 835 (1957).

46. *See, e.g., In re* Ampicillin Antitrust Litig., 82 F.R.D. 652, 655 (D.D.C. 1979); *In re* Corrugated Container Antitrust Litig., 1983-1 Trade Cas. (CCH) ¶ 65,451 (S.D. Tex. 1983), *rev'd,* 752 F.2d 137 (5th Cir.) (remanding for evidentiary hearing), *cert. denied,* 105 S. Ct. 3536 (1985).

47. *See In re* Chicken Antitrust Litig., 560 F. Supp. 943, 948 (N.D. Ga. 1979).

48. 614 F. Supp. 377 (E.D. Pa. 1985).

49. *See generally* Note, *Sharing Agreements among Defendants in Antitrust Cases,* 52 GEO. WASH. L. REV. 289 (1984).

50. *Id.* at 206. *See also* MANUAL FOR COMPLEX LITIGATION (SECOND) § 23.23 (1986).

51. MANUAL FOR COMPLEX LITIGATION (SECOND) § 23.23 (1986).

291

52. 18 U.S.C.A. § 1961 *et seq.*

53. *See* Boone v. Beacon Bldg. Corp., 613 F. Supp. 1151 (D.C.N.J. 1985); *In re* Olympia Brewing Co. Sec. Litig., 674 F. Supp. 597 (N.D. Ill. 1987); Jacobson v. Western Mont. Prod. Credit Ass'n, 643 F. Supp. 391 (D. Mont. 1986); Delta Holdings, Inc. v. National Distillers & Chem. Corp., [1986–1987 Transfer Binder] FED. SEC. L. REP. (CCH) ¶ 92–910 (S.D.N.Y. 1986); Seminole Elec. Coop., Inc. v. Tanner, 635 F. Supp. 582 (M.D. Fla. 1986).

54. 451 U.S. 630 (1981).

55. Boone v. Beacon Bldg. Corp., 613 F. Supp. at 1154.

56. Liquid Air Corp. v. Rogers, 834 F.2d 1297, 1310 (7th Cir. 1987); *In re* National Mortgage Equity Corp. Mortgage Pool Certificates Sec. Litig., 636 F. Supp. 1138, 1152 (C.D. Cal. 1986).

57. 631 F. Supp. 1029 (S.D.N.Y. 1986).

58. 38 Cal. 3d 488, 213 Cal. Rptr. 256 (1985).

59. 38 Cal. 3d at 499–500.

Section V

Alternatives to Litigation

As a matter of unfortunate fact, although litigators live by rules that proclaim they "shall be construed to secure the just, speedy, and inexpensive determination of every action,"[1] they do not always use those rules to avoid expense and delay. Rather, the present Chief Justice of the United States went on record in 1980 for the proposition that "[d]elay and excessive expense now characterize a large percentage of all civil litigation,"[2] and his predecessor, Chief Justice Burger, in his now-famous address to the Pound Conference, noted that to meet the needs of the coming century, "[w]ays must be found to resolve minor disputes more fairly and more swiftly than any present judicial mechanisms make possible."[3] Accordingly, it behooves lawyers competing for corporate clientele to familiarize themselves with current concepts and mechanisms for alternative dispute resolution (ADR).

This section contains five insightful and thought-provoking discussions of alternatives to litigation. Several perspectives are represented: authors include in-house counsel, consultants, a federal judge, and lawyers engaged in private practice. Mechanisms discussed range from the traditional approaches of mediation and arbitration to more recent innovations, i.e., summary jury trials and minitrials. These discussions are supplemented by Forms 30–35 in the Appendix from the Center for Public Resources in New York, including suggested contract provisions and model procedures for alternative dispute resolution.

In Chapter 21, James P. Melican and James W. Quinn use two hypothetical cases to show which kinds of disputes are amenable to alternative dispute resolution. The authors then describe existing ADR mechanisms, including arbitration, court-annexed arbitration, and minitrials, and the kinds of cases in which ADR should at least be considered.

Chapter 22, by Frederic C. Nelson, addresses a specific ADR technique: the minitrial. This chapter focuses on five practical issues: How should the parties evaluate a dispute for minitrial potential? How should one party attempt to convince another that a minitrial makes sense? How should the minitrial proceeding itself be structured? How should the parties choose the third party neutral? And how should the parties structure the settlement discussions that follow the "information exchange"?

Chapter 23 looks at another specific technique: the summary jury trial. The author, Judge Thomas Lambros, developed the summary jury trial in 1980 after seven years as a judge of the Ohio Court of Common Pleas and thirteen years on the federal bench. Judge Lambros has written elsewhere that, while trying cases that should have settled:

> It occurred to me that if only the parties could gaze into a crystal ball and be able to predict with a reasonable amount of certainty what a jury *would* do in their respective cases, parties and counsel would be more willing to reach a settlement.[4]

As arbitration has been used for some years and is subject under most arbitration clauses to relatively standardized rules of procedure, it is perhaps the most "mature" ADR procedure available. In Chapter 24, Geraldine Soat Brown provides excellent advice to litigators considering or engaged in the growing field of arbitration. She speaks from a wealth of experience in and with arbitration, having represented architects, contractors, owners, and the American Arbitration Association itself.

In Chapter 25, Barbara Ashley Phillips and Anthony Piazza address ADR through mediation. They provide a thorough catalog of the benefits of mediation, as well as a checklist for lawyers involved in the mediation of disputes.

Lawyers may be sure that in the future, alternative procedures will be followed in an increasing percentage of cases. Because most lawyers practicing today have had little if any formal instruction in ADR procedures, most readers should find the articles in this section helpful.

Shelby R. Grubbs
Grant, Konvalinka & Grubbs
Chattanooga, Tennessee

Notes

1. Fed. R. Civ. P. 1.
2. Dissenting statement of Justices Powell, Stewart & Rehnquist to Order of Apr. 29, 1980, amending Rules 4, 5, 26, 28, 30, 34, 37, 45.
3. Burger, *Agenda for 2000 A.D.—A Need for Systematic Anticipation,* 70 F.R.D. 83, 93 (1971).
4. Lambros, *The Summary Jury Trial,* 103 F.R.D. 461 (1984).

Twenty-One

Controlling Litigation Costs with Alternative Dispute Resolution

James P. Melican and James W. Quinn

Lawyers, businesspeople, jurists, and the general public have all decried the delays and consequent injustice caused by our present system of litigation. "Justice delayed is justice denied" is no longer dismissable as a cliché, but is in fact a truism, an actuality faced by consumers and businesspeople alike when disputes arise. Delay in resolving a dispute can destroy business relations and customer goodwill that have been established and cultivated at great effort and cost over a number of years.

Reasons for Using Alternative Techniques

The principal reason for pursuing alternative forms of dispute resolution is to control this delay and the legal costs. This concern over costs is not a theoretical one. As corporations, facing difficult times or declining markets, look to find ways to reduce costs by closing plants, laying off workers, and cutting back on executive positions, they cannot be expected to preclude legal expenses from the same scrutiny. An increasing number of clients complain that legal bills have grown too fast, particularly when compared with the progress of the lawsuit. There are, of course, other important reasons for opting for alternative dispute resolution mechanisms:

- Publicity concerning certain large commercial disputes may be adverse to the interests of both parties in that the process of litigation may necessarily involve the disclosure of trade secrets, business practices, financial, and other matters. Moreover, publicity concerning litigation often spawns additional plaintiffs' suits, particularly in the consumer products field. In the instance of disputes that are raised to class status, such litigation and its potential liability create an *in terrorem* effect on a defendant manufacturer separate from the merits of the case.

James P. Melican is Executive Vice President and General Counsel, International Paper Company, New York City. James W. Quinn is a member of Weil, Gotshal & Manges, New York City.

- The parties may not wish to risk an adverse precedent, which may have ramifications in other pending or future litigation.
- In intercorporate disputes, the private atmosphere and informality of alternative proceedings can create and preserve a climate more conducive to the friendly resolution of the dispute (and hence the continuance of business relations) than does the adversarial court procedure.
- Parties who wish to continue commercial relations notwithstanding a dispute may wish to avoid a win-or-lose, all-or-nothing situation, which results from a court decision.
- Further benefits may inure by "elevating" the quality of the resolution process. Parties may choose third-party specialists in the field in question, who are experienced in the trade and knowledgeable as to the trade's customs and practices.
- Alternative means of resolution can also alleviate the stress litigation can impose on the litigants. For example, studies have shown that certain forms of court-annexed compulsory arbitration are efficient in reducing costs and delay, and also highly satisfactory to the attorneys and litigants involved, precisely because the highly charged courtroom atmosphere has been eliminated. Additionally, using such alternative methods can prevent significant interruptions in an individual's life or a company's day-to-day operations.
- In the context of voluntary arbitration, there are inherent and traditional limitations on recovery to be considered, which translate into advantages to the manufacturer in disputes with consumers. For example, punitive damages are not awarded in traditional consensual arbitration because the power to do so is regarded as a judicial prerogative.

Examples

Two cases, showing opposite extremes of complexity and monetary significance, demonstrate some of the problems encountered and the need for alternative forms of dispute resolution:

Case A

XYZ Corporation has a multimillion-dollar contract to supply airplane engines by a fixed date and at a modest profit to an airplane manufacturer. ABC Corporation is a supplier to XYZ of a unique and vital component, and also operates on a low profit margin. XYZ has found that ABC's component does not conform with its recent specifications and has concluded that the part is unsuitable for use in its engine. ABC claims that the component is in compliance with these specifications and fit for its intended purpose. Because of the great expense involved, ABC refuses to rebuild the component. Not only is XYZ unable to perform the contract until ABC redesigns, but it is threatened with the loss of its engine contract and consequential liability if it does not adhere to production and delivery schedules.

A resolution as to which company is correct will require evaluation of thousands of engineering and other documents. Deadlines, costs, and damages are crucial to both parties, and litigation would be slow and costly. Furthermore, the court dockets are currently swollen, with a three-year delay for the trial of civil matters.

Case B

Mr. Smith and Mr. Jones, after carefully shopping for new cars, decide to purchase brand-new Studebreakers for $10,000 each. After Mr. Smith has enjoyed his car for the first 5000 miles, it experiences a series of problems that result in costly and lengthy repairs, during which Mr. Smith is denied the use of his car. The dealer claims that the necessary repairs are not covered under the warranty because the problems did not arise from any defect, but instead from the manner in which Mr. Smith used his car. After incurring a total of $1500 in repairs, losing the use of his car for over twenty days in two months, facing additional repair bills, and getting nowhere with his letters to Studebreaker, Inc., Mr. Smith, upon weighing the time and costs involved in litigating his rights, rationally chooses to sell his car and swears never to buy another Studebreaker again.

Mr. Jones also has been experiencing similar problems and has obtained no satisfaction from his visits, telephone calls, or letters to the dealer and manufacturer. Instead of selling his car, however, Jones sees his brother-in-law the lawyer. His brother-in-law, while knowing that the federal Magnuson-Moss Consumer Warranty Act provides for an award of attorney's fees in such litigation, tells Jones that because they're family, he'll waive his usual hourly fee and take the case on a small retainer. Jones's brother-in-law, who subscribes to the Center for Automotive Safety's newsletter, reads about other owners of Studebreakers who are having problems. Jones's brother-in-law informs Jones that he is going to make him famous by making him a named plaintiff, and they subsequently commence a class action.

The filing of the class action is reported throughout plaintiff's bar, and Jones's brother-in-law receives numerous phone calls from attorneys across the country and their clients. Together they form a group called Consumers Against Studebreaker Hazards ("CASH") and call a press conference during which they announce the institution of a nationwide federal class action. If this were not enough, various state attorneys general, aspiring to their respective states' gubernatorial mansions, hold press conferences at which they announce that in the public interest, they are commencing their own investigations and hearings into what may be the most pervasive instance of consumer fraud in their state's history. The ensuing publicity concerning this class action and the 500,000 putative class members it purports to represent, as well as the investigations of the attorneys general, results in widespread adverse publicity and, in time, sharply decreases sales in showrooms across the country.

Finding a Solution

Clearly, no single panacea is available to instantly solve the problems raised by theses examples. Some years ago, then–Chief Justice Warren E. Burger opined about one alternative:

> Well, there are a great many problems that should not come to judges at all and can be disposed of in other ways—better ways. I can suggest one basic way that must be developed more widely in this country, and that is the use of private arbitration . . . . [M]any lawyers, including the best lawyers in the country, press their clients in a great many large business engagements between corporations to agree that all disputes between them will be resolved by private arbitration without resort to courts and without judicial review. This is one area we've got to enlarge. . . . We must use this highly-acceptable device that in the long run is probably less expensive and at least as efficient and fair as any judicial process. . . . There are many advantages in private arbitration over litigation in the courts. Much, if not most, of the factual material, what we would normally call the evidence in the case, can be reduced to writing by agreement and submitted to the arbitrators. Only the matters on which the parties can't agree as to the facts and the evidence are then presented to the arbitrators in the place of the conventional form of testimony under oath with direct and cross-examination by the lawyers. This is a device widely used in Europe. We need to use it more in this country.[1]

Voluntary arbitration, of course, is but one (although perhaps the most popular) alternative means of dispute resolution. Other forms include conciliation, mediation, court-annexed compulsory arbitration, dispute resolution centers, and minitrials, to name a few.

Several fundamental truths have given rise to the exploding interest in managing civil litigation, big or small, corporate or consumer:

- Existing court procedures for dispute resolution are fostering corporate and consumer ill will and are unnecessarily expensive in terms of attorney time and other costs. It has been estimated that $80 billion is spent annually on intercorporate litigation alone. Tens of billions more are spent on individual civil litigation arising from automobile accidents, family disputes, and other problems of everyday life. Moreover, many disputes like those between manufacturers and their consumers, beyond proving costly and time consuming, have fallen woefully short in achieving redress, even when a resolution to the conflict is obtained.[2]
- On an international basis, there is a continuing and growing reluctance on the part of foreign companies from other cultural traditions to enter into joint ventures with Americans because of the litigiousness they associate with the United States.
- It is time to acknowledge the basic premise that the most effective way to control legal costs is to prevent the continuation of the dispute, i.e., to force settlements at an early stage, before these massive costs are incurred.
- At the heart of achieving an early settlement of a dispute is the necessity to find the means that can reconvert what has become a "lawyer's dispute" back into a "people problem," e.g., that will allow for dialogues between the parties on the merits of the controversy, and thereby narrow the area of the dispute, dispose of collateral issues, and encourage a fair and equitable settlement.
- Most litigants—individual or corporate—desire to have their dispute heard on the merits and resolved "fairly," which is precisely what alternate dispute resolution is best designed to do.
- In sum, the objective is the formation and implementation of "mechanisms that can produce an acceptable result in the shortest possible time, with the least possible expense and with a minimum of stress on the participants."[3]

Summary of Potential Methods of Dispute Resolution

Early Dispute Intervention—Corporate Negotiation

When the parties enter into a contractual relationship, both sides should consider designating those management personnel from each side who will be responsible for resolving conflicts that arise. Their authority and responsibilities are defined bilaterally, with a working relationship and familiarity with the subject contract developed between the sides *before* any conflict. Similar channels of communication should be open with the respective parties' house counsel *before* the stage at which litigation becomes foreseeable. This method has been quite successful in international disputes, particularly in Europe.

Mid-Dispute Intervention and Third-Party Involvement—Mediation and Conciliation

Mediation and conciliation, long present on the labor scene, also represent informal alternative methods of dispute resolution and should be used as a first attempt to resolve the conflict. Both methods are also extensions of the bilateral negotiations between the parties and now include negotiations with a third-party intervenor.

Succinctly, mediation is a process in which the mediator acts as a go-between in an attempt to bring the parties together to arrive at a solution to their problems. The mediator, however, does not decide the dispute. Rather, the final resolution is a decision solely of the parties, and the mediator's only function is to act as an intermediary to bring the parties together to resolve the dispute themselves.

In proceedings involving conciliation, the conciliator takes a more active role in actually resolving the dispute. The dispute is referred to a conciliator, who investigates the subject matters of the dispute and attempts to reconcile opposing contentions. The conciliator then formulates proposals for settlement, which the parties are free to accept or reject. Again, similar to mediation, the conciliator does not finally decide the dispute. The ultimate decision remains that of the parties, although they now have had the advantage of having an independent third party recommend a decision after investigation of the facts.

Mediation and conciliation may both be provided for in the initial contract between the parties, or may be the subject of an agreement after the dispute has arisen. The agreement should provide for how the mediation or the conciliation is to be chosen and how the proceedings are to be conducted. The final resolution to be achieved by these methods (as well as by the "early dispute" negotiations between the parties) is a function of the goodwill and faith of the parties. Forms 30–32 in the Appendix, developed by the Center for Public Resources in New York City, contain a proposed mediation procedure and possible contract language regarding negotiation, mediation, and minitrials.

Quasi-Litigation Alternatives

Arbitration and the minitrial (a hybrid offspring of conciliation and arbitration) are more formalized methods of dispute settlement than mediation or conciliation. In essence, in arbitration both sides have agreed to submit (sometimes without the assistance of lawyers) their dispute to one or more impartial, nonjudicial arbitrators. The parties are, in cases involving binding arbitration, bound to abide by whatever decision is reached. Arbitration differs from conciliation in that the decision given by the arbitration is binding on the parties and may be enforced against a recalcitrant party.

A minitrial has been referred to as a confidential, nonbinding information exchange or formalized structure for settlement negotiations, which consists of limited discovery, summary presentation by lawyers and experts for both parties, who put forth their clients' best case to representatives of top management with settlement authority. Additionally, an independent finder of fact may be retained to render a report on the merits of each side's case and the likely outcome. The minitrial also contemplates good-faith negotiations in light of the minitrial's results, to settle the dispute in order to reduce legal costs. See Forms 33–35 in the Appendix, which show potential minitrial procedures developed by the Center for Public Resources.

Mandatory (Court-Annexed) Arbitration

Unlike traditional arbitration, court-annexed arbitration is compulsory rather than voluntary, and the award is not binding. By definition, court-annexed arbitration is a method of disposing of civil litigation after a lawsuit has already been filed, whereas traditional arbitration occurs before any litigation is commenced. There may be one or several arbitrators, typically assigned by a judge from among a pool of volunteer lawyers rather than chosen by the parties.

Court-annexed arbitration, which began in the Philadelphia Court of Common Pleas more than thirty years ago, is today being used fairly extensively.[4] When Pennsylvania in 1951 enacted the enabling act providing for court-annexed arbitration at the option of the county courts of common pleas, the jurisdictional amount was limited to cases involving $1000 or less. Today, the maximum limit is $20,000 in Pennsylvania and in most of the states ($15,000 in California). In two currently functioning federal court programs, the monetary ceilings are considerably higher ($100,000 in the Northern District of California and $50,000 in the Eastern District of Pennsylvania).

Potential Areas of Application for Alternative Dispute Resolution Mechanisms

The following paragraphs briefly highlight some of the areas of dispute in which alternate forms of resolution are ripe for continued discussion and consideration.

Consumer Warranty Litigation

The Magnuson-Moss Warranty—Federal Trade Commission Act of 1975[5] contains provisions that permit a warrantor to establish an independent informal "dispute settlement mechanism" (i.e., an arbitration procedure) in accordance with rules established by the FTC.[6] The incentive provided by the act is straightforward. If such a resolution mechanism is established in compliance with the FTC rules and is incorporated in the written warranty furnished to the consumer, an individual suit to enforce the warranty cannot be instituted until the consumer has resorted to this dispute resolution procedure. So far, two different types of mechanisms have been established in compliance with the act and FTC regulations (e.g., HOW arbitrations, established by the National Association of Home Builders, and the Chrysler Corporation Automobile Warranty Program). Similar non–FTC-authorized arbitration programs have been established for consumers of appliances (the Major Appliance Consumer Action Panel (MACAP)), consumers of automobiles (AUTOCAP, Consumer Appeals Board, American Automobile Association, Better Business Bureau, and pursuant to recently enacted "lemon laws"), retail buyers of furniture (the Furniture Consumer Advisory Panel (FCAP)), and utility users (under the auspices of the Pennsylvania Public Utility Commission).

Mass Products Injury Cases

The settlement facility created in connection with asbestos litigation is an example of the use of alternative dispute resolution for mass products injury cases.

Environmental Law—Toxic Torts Conflicts

Some of the problems that have been addressed in the area of environmental law and toxic torts include disposal of hazardous wastes, granting of oil and gas leases in wilderness areas, airport development, and open-pit mining. Many of the disputes involve sizable dollar amounts of business investment, actual or potential legal costs, and regulatory requirements.

One especially frustrating example of what can go on is the case of the Hampton-Roads refinery in Portsmouth, Virginia—a proposal at least a decade old and one that may still be five years from its first drop of oil. The president of the Hampton-Roads Energy Company first approached the State of Virginia in 1970 with a proposal for a $100 million refinery. The story reads like something out of Kafka. Apart from the various state and local agencies saying yes and no and maybe over about six years—and the company changing its mind about siting once or twice—one spectacular row started over the environmental impact statement and is still in the courts today. The costs of all this—and they may not be over yet—

have been staggering. The out-of-pocket costs for the company from the permitting process alone were more than $6 million, with maybe half of that just in legal fees. The Army Corps of Engineers has no doubt spent at least as much as the company on legal fees, and who knows how much in time and trouble. Yet a similar dispute involving the Snoqualmie Dam in Washington State was solved through mediation in less than a year.

Regulatory Disputes between the Government and the Private Sector

The Environmental Protection Agency and the Federal Aviation Administration have in recent years experimented with a relatively new technique known as "regulatory negotiation," which brings together representatives from the agency, industry, public interest groups, and other interested parties to design mutually acceptable rules that can form the basis for regulations. Supporters of the "reg neg" process, as the approach is known, believe that rules produced in this manner will be less likely to be challenged—or overturned—in court.

For the past several years, the Department of Health and Human Services' Grant Appeals Board, which hears disputes between HHS and organizations that receive funds from the agency, has offered parties the option of resolving their conflicts with the help of a specially trained mediator. Such an approach, the staff attorneys who mediate these cases say, can improve communication and more easily produce results that satisfy both sides.

The Merit Systems Protection Board, formerly known as the Civil Service Commission, and the Land Sale Fraud Division of the Department of Housing and Urban Development have turned to arbitration to resolve some of their cases. Officials at the two agencies say the procedure can reduce the time spent on litigation, allowing the agencies to use their resources more efficiently.

Transnational Corporate Disputes

Arbitration clauses have long been included in international contracts. But international arbitration has been an area of particularly rapid growth in the legal profession in the last few years, and there are numerous reasons for this growth. Most obvious is the steady increase in U.S. trade activities overseas.

The need for a neutral forum and neutral rules to resolve international disputes becomes particularly acute when one of the parties in a dispute is a foreign government or a government-owned business. Nowhere has the neutrality of arbitration been showcased more dramatically than in the establishment of the Iran–United States Claims Tribunal that was set up in The Hague as a condition of the release of the U.S. hostages in Iran. In numbers alone, the tribunal's contribution to the practice of arbitration has been enormous; it has sifted its way through nearly 800 major cases and several thousand minor ones involving billions of dollars in contested claims between U.S. and Iranian parties, including the governments of both nations.

Also adding to the growth of the international arbitration practice in the last decade or so has been a new set of arbitration rules issued by the United Nations Commission on International Trade Law (UNCITRAL), the ratification by the United States in 1970 of the New York convention of 1958, and a stream of recent U.S. court decisions that have upheld decisions reached by arbitrators in other forums. The UNCITRAL rules have become widely accepted in a relatively short period of time, because the lesser developed countries appear to trust a product of the United Nations more than the rules issued by an organization such as the International Chamber of Commerce, which they suspect of having a pro-Western bias.

Intercorporate Contractual Disputes

Examples of intercorporate contractual disputes handled through alternative resolution include minitrials involving TRW and Telecredit, NASA, and the Space Communications Company.

Compulsory Arbitration of Medium-Sized Civil Disputes

In jurisdictions that have adopted some form of mandatory court-annexed arbitration, the bulk of the claims involve either property damage from automobile cases or disputes between retailers and consumers relating to nonpayment for allegedly defective products or services. These programs appear to have met with at least some success in handling this type of relatively simple matter with reduced cost and time.

An example is the Detroit mandatory diversion program. In Detroit, civil suits under a specified amount must first be heard by a panel of arbitrators-mediators, who confer and reach a conclusion. This proceeds very quickly; the lawyers must state their cases in brief, outline form, and the panels can hear as many as two or three of these cases in an hour. The parties are free to reject the panel's decision, but only if they are willing to risk a substantial penalty if the court decision is not substantially different from the panel's. If a party rejects the mediator's decision and fails to do at least 10 percent better in court, the party pays a hefty portion of his or her opponent's court fees. In almost 70 percent of all civil cases, the matter never goes past the mediation phase. Reportedly, this has reduced court dockets by up to 4000 cases.

There have been a number of other recent studies of mandatory court-annexed arbitration, most of which have focused on three key issues: whether the process accelerates the resolution of disputes, whether it appears to be substantially less expensive to the litigants and to the state, and whether the litigants are generally satisfied that they have had their day in court. Provided the programs are effectively administered (some early failures in this regard are discussed in the studies), the answer to all three questions appears to be yes.

For example, a recent analysis shows that the state and federal arbitration programs in Pennsylvania have resulted in quicker decisions for the litigants. In the federal courts, the median time for disposition of arbitration cases has been six months from the date when the pleadings were complete, whereas the median time for all other civil cases in that court has been thirteen months. In the state courts, the average disposition time for arbitration cases is less than half of the average time for civil cases in the last year for which statistics were available.[7] In the first year of the California program, about 24,000 smaller-value (i.e., under $15,000) cases were diverted to the judicial arbitration program in the superior courts of the thirteen counties that were required to adopt it. A Rand study estimated that, if this same percentage held throughout the five-year life of the California statute, the courts might save from 200 to 400 civil jury trials per year—a savings of about 10 to 20 percent in the thirteen largest counties.[8]

Perhaps the most interesting issue is whether the litigants have been generally satisfied. To obviate constitutional objections,[9] all of the statutes and court rules of which the authors are aware provide that the arbitration is not binding and that either party is entitled to a trial de novo. Most do, however, have some financial disincentives built into the mechanism. In California,[10] if the judgment upon the trial de novo is not more favorable than the arbitration award in either the amount of damages awarded or the type of relief granted, the court is directed to order the party to pay to the county the costs of the arbitration and to pay the other party all court costs, including fees for expert witnesses. Despite this deterrent, in the first year of the California program, the rate of requests for de novo trial averaged about 40 percent. However, there is good reason to believe, based on results in other states, that few such cases will in fact ever go to trial. In Philadelphia, a review of one sample of almost 800 appeals indicated that only 1 1/2 percent of the cases originally referred to court-annexed arbitration required disposition by judge or jury.[11]

If the Philadelphia numbers are even close to accurate, they would suggest that compulsory arbitration is working. But whether the concept spreads still further probably depends on whether the state legislatures become convinced that the public interest in the expeditious and economical resolution of cases is being so well served that they are willing to risk charges that they are tampering with the citizen's right to a jury trial. That is, after all, a subject on which many attorneys, perhaps particularly trial attorneys, have strong philosophical convictions.

Notes

1. *"As I See It—Slow Justice Is Inadequate Justice": An Interview with Chief Justice Warren E. Burger,* 108 FORBES no. 1, at p. 21 (July 1, 1971).
2. *See* N.Y. Times, July 28, 1983, at A19, col. 1 (report of the conclusions of a Rand Corporation study finding that only 37 percent of the $600 million that defendants and insurers have spent on lawsuits in connection with asbestos damage suits has gone to compensate plaintiffs).
3. Former Chief Justice Warren E. Burger, STATE OF THE JUDICIARY ANN. REP. (Jan. 24, 1982).
4. Levin, *Court-Annexed Arbitration,* 16 J.L. REFORM 537, 539 (1983). *See also* CONNELLY & SMITH, DESCRIPTION OF THE MAJOR CHARACTERISTICS OF THE RULES FOR SELECTED COURT-ANNEXED MEDIATION/ARBITRATION PROGRAMS (ABA Comm. to Reduce Court Costs and Delay 1982); *see generally* Hensler, *What We Know and Don't Know about Court Administered Arbitration,* 69 JUDICATURE 270 (1986).
5. 15 U.S.C. §§ 2301 *et seq.* (1976).
6. *Id.* at § 2310.
7. Barbara W. Mather, Court-Annexed Arbitration in Pennsylvania (unpublished speech delivered to the Conference of Chief Justices, Jan. 31, 1983).
8. D. HENSLER, A. LIPSON & E. ROLPH, JUDICIAL ARBITRATION IN CALIFORNIA: THE FIRST YEAR xi (Rand Institute for Civil Justice 1981).
9. *See* Application of Smith, 381 Pa. 233, 112 A.2d 625 (1955), *appeal dismissed sub nom.* Smith v. Wissler, 350 U.S. 858 (1955).
10. CAL. CIV. PROC. CODE § 1141.21.
11. Mather, *supra* note 7.

Twenty-Two

Common Problems on the Road to a Successful Minitrial

Fredric C. Nelson

While the minitrial is a relatively recent development in alternative dispute resolution (ADR), the advantages it offers litigants, particularly in commercial disputes, has attracted a great deal of attention. This chapter offers the reader aware of the general characteristics of a minitrial a brief review of the problems most often encountered in negotiating and conducting a minitrial, and how those problems may be solved. Forms 33–35 in the Appendix, developed by the Center for Public Resources in New York City, demonstrate the basic procedures that are commonly used in a minitrial.

The issues most often confronted in negotiating and conducting a minitrial are the following:

- How should the parties evaluate a dispute for minitrial potential?
- How should one party attempt to convince another that a minitrial makes sense?
- How should the minitrial proceeding itself be structured?
- How should the parties choose the third party neutral?
- How should the parties structure the settlement discussions that follow the information exchange?

Evaluating a Case for Minitrial Potential

On their face, certain factors are good indications that a minitrial makes sense, but many cases that have not conformed to the minitrial "profile" also have been resolved through mini-trials.[1]

One good candidate is a case in which two, or few, parties are involved. While it is certainly possible to conduct a minitrial involving numerous parties, the difficulties encountered in multiparty cases probably will be more substantial than in two-party litigation. Convincing two parties to conduct a minitrial is likely to be easier than convincing multiple parties

Fredric C. Nelson is a member of Thelen, Marrin, Johnson & Bridges, San Francisco, California.

to do so. Also, the likelihood of reaching a settlement probably is inversely proportional to the number of parties involved. The more parties involved, the greater the chances of complications in reaching a compromise.

Another case with minitrial potential is one in which the parties have an ongoing business relationship. Experience has proved that minitrials are most likely to succeed when the parties are highly motivated to reach a settlement. One important motivating force may be the existence of an ongoing business relationship. The minitrial offers a means to resolve a dispute quickly, before animosities get out of control, and to preserve those relationships in the process.

A third viable candidate for a minitrial is a case in which there is a straightforward commercial dispute. Claims of fraud, dishonesty, or bad faith may make a minitrial less likely to succeed. If the case is a straightforward commercial dispute, however, the parties may preserve their dignity and resolve the matter on a sensible, economic basis. Therefore, again, the motivation to settle may be greater if reputation or personal issues are not on the line.

It bears repeating that, although these characteristics may indicate greater minitrial potential, minitrials have been conducted successfully in cases far different from this profile. The most important factor, of course, is a clear motivation to settle at an early date.

Convincing the Other Party that a Minitrial Makes Sense

Because the minitrial is still just emerging as an effective ADR measure, many trial lawyers, who are most comfortable in traditional litigation, are likely to be skeptical about it. This may be true for several reasons. A lack of awareness of the minitrial concept may, quite naturally, breed suspicion. In addition the lawyer, as "gladiator," may be reluctant to recommend that the client try to resolve the matter at an early stage rather than rely upon the lawyer's skills as advocate to achieve an all-out win. Counsel may also feel that adopting the minitrial process would be an indication of weakness.

When dealing with this sort of skepticism, the most effective approach is to emphasize that a minitrial is not really new or revolutionary at all. Rather, it is but one form of a proceeding that most litigators are very familiar with, namely, a settlement conference. True, it is more structured and requires greater preparation than do most settlement conferences. Nevertheless, it should not be viewed as a foreign proceeding. The similarities between a minitrial and traditional litigation should be emphasized, and the differences downplayed.

Most practitioners have concluded that if the party proposing the minitrial does so correctly, it will not be seen as an indication of weakness by the opposition. To the contrary, if approached in the right way, the opposition should conclude that the proponent is confident enough about the case that he or she is not afraid to lay his cards on the table during the minitrial.

Concern is frequently expressed regarding the strategic implications if the minitrial does not result in a settlement. Does revealing what one perceives to be the greatest strengths of one's case place a party at a significant disadvantage later if the matter is not settled? There is, of course, some risk in "previewing" one's case for the opponent, and this risk must be weighed against the potential gain from reaching a settlement. In most cases today, however, the broad scope of discovery means there probably will be few real surprises for the opposition. Also, given the abbreviated nature of the minitrial, frequently only the general contours of the case are explored, not the sort of details that are most likely to reveal those surprises, if they exist in the first place.

In some cases the level of acrimony between the litigants is such that the proposal for a minitrial (or *any* proposal for that matter) is unlikely to receive a warm response, even though it may make great sense. In those cases, the party interested in pursuing a minitrial can take one of two steps.

First, he or she can bring in another person, previously uninvolved in the litigation, to discuss the minitrial with the opposition. This third party can be either another lawyer from the outside counsel's firm or an in-house lawyer. The third party may also be a business person who may productively make the proposal directly to his or her counterpart on the other side.

If this first option is unattractive for any reason, firms such as the Center for Public Resources or EnDispute are available, typically for a fee, to help initiate and facilitate negotiations leading to a minitrial or some other ADR mechanism.[2]

Structuring the Proceeding

To save legal expenses and to avoid the possibility that disagreements over the terms of the minitrial agreement will scuttle the proceeding early on, the parties may decide to use form minitrial agreements that have been prepared for general use.[3] This is a recommended procedure, since it should circumvent at least some threshold arguments and also because it should save substantial time and legal expenses.

However, even these form agreements provide choices with respect to certain fundamental aspects of the minitrial. The following are several of the most important issues the parties will confront.

First, how much discovery should be permitted before the "information exchange"? While each case is unique, generally speaking the bare minimum should be allowed. This is so because the minitrial is usually seen as a means to resolve a dispute quickly and economically. Of course, if the minitrial is begun after discovery has gotten under way, the issue may be somewhat academic. Thus, it is best to explore the possibility of a minitrial early in the proceedings. In any event, discovery should be limited, if possible, to the central issues in the case. By nature, many peripheral issues will not be explored in any minitrial. Time simply will not allow it. These same issues should not be the subject of discovery.

Second, how much time should the parties allow for the minitrial hearing itself? Experience has shown that one day should suffice for practically all minitrials.[4] The proceeding necessarily will be abbreviated. In all but the most complicated cases, the central issues can be covered in a one-day hearing.

Third, the selection of a panelist or panelists to serve along with the "neutral" can be a very important step, since these are the individuals who will actually attempt to settle the matter. While each case may suggest the need for peculiar expertise or qualifications, usually the most important factor is objectivity. This may suggest several things:

- The panelists probably should be businesspeople and not lawyers. Lawyers may act in a less conciliatory role than businesspeople would, and to a degree, this may undermine settlement prospects.
- The businesspeople should not be identified in any way with the dispute in question. If a businessperson has something at stake, that is likely to color his or her judgment on settlement.
- If possible, the businesspeople should come from a division whose bottom line will not be affected by a settlement. Again, objectivity is the key, and a businessperson who is concerned about the bottom line is less likely to be objective.

Choosing the "Third Party Neutral"

Discussions with lawyers who are unfamiliar with minitrials indicate that one of their prime reservations concerns the selection of the individual who will serve as the "third party neutral." While it might be expected that the selection of the neutral would be a significant obstacle to a successful minitrial, in practice this simply has not proved to be the case. In fact, assuming some flexibility and a desire on the part of both parties to select an objective, fair neutral party, this may well be one of the easiest aspects of the minitrial.

In those instances where there may be suspicion, it may be best to select a neutral party who is well known and whose credibility and qualifications are unquestioned. This may diffuse any suspicion. Various panels of well-respected lawyers or retired judges are available from which third party neutrals may be chosen.[5]

If one party is highly suspicious, it may make sense to retain a well-known or well-respected individual at an early stage merely to assist the parties in negotiating and implementing the minitrial. Yet another neutral party may be selected later to hear the controversy. While this would increase the expense, it may be a small price to pay if it means the difference between success or failure in settling the case.

Structuring the Settlement Discussions

At the close of the "information exchange," the parties will engage in discussions designed to lead to settlement. Two important questions must be considered with regard to the structure of the settlement negotiations.

First, should the lawyers for the parties be present? While it is difficult to generalize, it may well be best if only the businesspeople "panelists" participate in the settlement discussions. As an advocate, the lawyer may find it difficult to serve, at least in part, as a conciliator. In addition, the lawyer already may have advised the client regarding the settlement value of the case, and it may be easier for the client to reach a settlement if he or she is doing so "privately," without the presence of counsel. Finally, the settlement negotiations should be informal, while businesslike. The fewer people involved, the better.

The second important question concerns whether the third party neutral should be present during the settlement discussions. This is a more difficult issue to analyze. If the representatives of the parties have gotten to know the third party neutral and have developed rapport with him or her, this persons's presence may be very helpful. If, on the other hand, the parties are not familiar with the third party neutral, his or her presence may inhibit the sort of give and take that can be instrumental to a creative settlement.

At the least, the neutral party must be available to give an opinion concerning legal issues involved in the case or an opinion based upon his or her experience in trying cases, either as a lawyer or judge.

Conclusion

The probability of success in conducting a minitrial relates largely to the parties' flexibility, objectivity, and desire to resolve the matter quickly and privately. The common pitfalls should be anticipated, and the prospects for their avoidance analyzed before starting down the road to a minitrial. Such forethought should enhance the prospects for a successful minitrial, with all the benefits that flow from it.

Notes

1. *See, e.g., Report of Subcommittee on Alternative Means of Dispute Resolution, Committee on Corporate Counsel,* A.B.A. LITIGATION SEC. 37–45.
2. Numerous Fortune 500 companies have become members of the Center for Public Resources, a nonprofit corporation dedicated to, among other things, furthering the cause of alternative dispute resolution. Many of those companies have signed the "ADR Pledge," which obligates them to seriously explore ADR in certain circumstances. In and of itself, the pledge facilitates early exploration of ADR in general and minitrials in particular.
3. See Form 35 in the Appendix, which is a form minitrial agreement prepared under the auspices of the Center for Public Resources.
4. *See* SUBCOMMITTEE REPORT, *supra* note 1, at pp. 27–28.
5. For example, the Center for Public Resources has compiled a judicial panel consisting of well-known lawyers, former judges, and academics.

Twenty-Three

Summary Jury Trials

Thomas D. Lambros

Most cases settle. Although the jury trial continues to be at the core of our system of justice, the expense and burdens of taking a case that far suggests that it should be a method of last resort.

Fair settlements can be reached in even the most complex cases through the thoughtful use of other methods. One that has proved particularly valuable is the summary jury trial.

A summary trial is an abbreviated presentation to an advisory jury to show the parties, the lawyers, and the judge how jurors react to the dispute. The procedure is nonbinding, unless all parties agree otherwise, and so it does not impair the constitutional right to a trial by jury.[1] Summary jury trials foster settlements by immersing the parties in the trial experience and giving them an advisory verdict.

The summary jury trial is my way of linking the great heritage of the jury trial with modern methods of resolving disputes. Before joining the federal bench in 1967, I was a trial judge on the Court of Common Pleas for Ashtabula County, Ohio. On both the state and federal benches, as I watched the growth of court dockets across the country, I saw a need for new, efficient procedures that retain the good aspects of the jury trial while encouraging settlements. So I invented the summary jury trial as a way to reduce the stresses on the judicial system while safeguarding the time-tested process of trial by jury.

The summary jury trial is not intended to replace the traditional jury trial. Instead, judges can use it to settle cases when negotiations fail.

How Summary Jury Trials Help

In the right case, a summary jury trial is effective for a variety of reasons. The parties are generally more receptive to settlement after they see how jurors react to the conflicting evidence, test the strengths and weaknesses of their arguments, and have the satisfaction of speaking their piece in court.

Thomas D. Lambros is a United States District Judge for the Northern District of Ohio.

A summary jury trial often produces the same sorts of psychological strains on the litigants as a full-blown jury trial. The specter of an approaching summary jury trial usually intensifies the parties' efforts to settle.

Because the parties are required to attend the summary jury trial, the procedure is particularly effective when the trip through the legal labyrinth begins to tax their patience. And when the summary jury trial shows them what they have been too blinkered to see on their own when they were sitting across the table glaring at each other, settlement discussions may become more meaningful.

Summary jury trials are also valuable because they conserve resources. Court dockets are more crowded than ever, and the costs of litigation are spiraling upward. Summary jury trials result in substantial savings because they settle cases at an early stage.

The savings are twofold. First, the costs to the parties are reduced because the litigation is abbreviated. The costs they avoid include lawyers' fees for prolonged court appearances, expenses of support staff and paralegals, fees of expert witnesses, and the other costs to the litigants when they have to spend weeks on end in a courtroom. Second, because summary jury trials facilitate settlements, they free up court time for those cases that really require full jury trials.

When to Use a Summary Jury Trial

In every case, the judge should consider whether a summary jury trial will make a settlement more likely. Whether it will be the most effective way to settle a case depends more on the dynamics of the controversy than on the causes of action involved. Summary jury trials have been used in cases ranging from simple negligence and contract actions to complex mass-tort and antitrust cases.

The summary jury trial is intended for hard-core cases that defy settlement and appear destined for trial. A summary jury trial is appropriate if the discussions have reached an impasse, but the judge believes that he or she can break the deadlock by exposing the parties to the objective verdict of an impartial jury.

Federal and state judges have the authority to manage their dockets by using alternative methods to settle cases. Under Federal Rule of Civil Procedure 16(c)(7), a district court may adopt a local rule specifically authorizing summary jury trials. Even without a local rule, Federal Rule 16(c)(7) empowers a district judge to "consider and take action with respect to the possibility of settlement or the use of extrajudicial procedures to resolve the dispute." The judge's broad pretrial management powers under rule 16 plus the mandate of rule 1 that the Federal Rules be applied "to secure the just, speedy and inexpensive determination of every case" give the judge the authority to conduct summary jury trials.

Lawyers should consider requesting summary jury trials. The final pretrial conference is when the judge and counsel most often explore alternatives to the full-scale war of a jury trial. Particularly then, lawyers should ask themselves, Have I done everything I can to resolve this case favorably to my client? Is there an alternative to exposing my client to the stress and expense of trial? Is my client (and am I) too emotionally involved in the case to evaluate it objectively?

The summary jury trial is effective when settlement seems impossible because of a client's unyielding attitude. The procedure is a safe and inexpensive way to show a recalcitrant client that his or her case is weak.

It may also be helpful if a client feels that settlement would be an admission of weakness. The psychological satisfaction of courtroom combat is important to many litigants. A summary jury trial gives them the opportunity to tell their story to an impartial group of their peers. Having had their day in court, they may no longer regard settlement as cowardly.

Navigating the Summary Jury Trial

The summary jury trial has three phases: pretrial conferencing; jury selection and formal presentations; posttrial discussion and conferencing.

Before the Trial

Effective pretrial conferencing is essential. At the beginning of the litigation, the judge should suggest a summary jury trial, so that counsel will be prepared if this alternative is later adopted. In subsequent conferences, the judge should thoroughly explore settlement and again raise the possibility of a summary jury trial. The decision to use a summary jury trial is usually made at the last regularly scheduled pretrial conference.

Once the judge decides to use a summary jury trial, the remainder of the conference is devoted to questions about the procedure. With proper preparation, the proceedings will go smoothly and quickly. To ensure that everyone understands the process, the judge should distribute a written explanation (or a copy of this article) to the lawyers and their clients.

During the conference, the judge should make sure that all necessary discovery has been completed. The judge should also rule on all pending motions on the merits, so that the parties' presentations will closely parallel the actual trial.

Because the summary jury trial is nonbinding, evidentiary and procedural rules should be few and flexible. Nevertheless, at the conference, the lawyers should raise any questions about the materials they want to present, including any opinions, and the judge should rule on anticipated objections and consider motions *in limine.*

No later than three working days before the date of the proceedings, counsel should submit proposed jury instructions and briefs on any novel issues of law. Each party should file a trial memorandum and may submit proposed voir dire questions. If necessary, the court may require the parties to submit exhibit lists and lists of witnesses whose testimony will be summarized.

If the case warrants, the judge should schedule an additional conference right before the summary jury trial. It is a good idea to require the litigants to be there. The final conference is an excellent opportunity for the parties to engage in intensive settlement discussions. At this point in the litigation, the lawyers are practically ready for trial. The strengths and weaknesses of each side's case are coming to light. The parties realize that the verdict of the advisory jury will unalterably affect their bargaining positions and that all further settlement demands will be measured against it.

The Trial Proceedings

If the case does not settle, the proceedings begin. A summary jury trial is like a regular jury trial, only shorter. A venire of a sufficient number is called to provide a jury of six; alternates are unnecessary for this abbreviated proceeding.

To expedite jury selection, the jury commissioner gives the prospective jurors a questionnaire asking for name and occupation; martial status; spouse's name and occupation; names and ages of children; previous knowledge of the parties, counsel, or the case; and any prejudicial attitudes toward the parties or their causes. In certain cases involving complex issues, a more detailed inquiry is appropriate.

While the potential jurors complete their questionnaires, the judge again meets with counsel. Often, the imminence of a summary jury trial produces a settlement.

If not, the judge calls the court to order and makes a few introductory remarks. He briefly explains the nature of the case, as well as the summary jury trial procedure. He says that the lawyers have reviewed the relevant materials, interviewed the witnesses, and condensed the evidence, which they will present to the jury in narrative form. He tells the jurors that they will later be instructed on the applicable law and the use of a verdict form.

The jurors are told that the proceeding will be completed in a single day and that their verdict will help the parties to resolve the dispute. The nonbinding character of the trial is not emphasized. The jurors take an oath to return a true verdict based on all the evidence.

After this introduction, the judge conducts a brief voir dire, generally posing questions to the full panel of jurors. The judge and the lawyers also have the jurors' responses to the profile questionnaire. Counsel may exercise challenges for cause, as well as two peremptory challenges. The first six jurors seated after the challenges constitute the panel.

Before the formal presentations, each side should give a five-minute overview so that the jury can see the entire landscape of the controversy. Normally, the lawyers then have one hour each for their presentations.

Usually, the plaintiff devotes forty-five minutes to its case-in-chief, followed by the defendant's presentation of about the same length. The parties may then use their remaining fifteen-minute periods for rebuttal and surrebuttal. In complex cases, counsel should be given additional time so they have an opportunity to make comprehensive presentations.

Regardless of the time allotted, the lawyers should remember the overall goal of brevity. Just as the summary jury trial is a streamlined version of a formal trial, so should the attorneys' presentations be pared to the bone.

Summary jury trials eliminate the long, drawn-out process of direct and cross-examination. There is no time for pettifoggery or verbal sophistry. The most effective presentations are those that, early on, highlight the unique personality of the case.

The lawyers' presentations are limited to summaries of evidence that would be admissible at trial. Although counsel are permitted to mingle representations of fact with legal arguments, they should be responsible and restrained in their arguments. They may summarize, comment on, and quote from the evidence, depositions, interrogatories, responses to requests for admissions, and sworn statements of potential witnesses.

In the absence of a sworn statement from a witness, the lawyer may summarize the witness's probable testimony on the basis of his or her conversations with that witness. But the lawyer must tell his or her adversary beforehand of this plan, so that the adversary, too, has an opportunity to speak to the witness.

Physical evidence, including documents, may be exhibited during the lawyers' presentations and submitted for the jury's examination during deliberations. One effective way to present documents is to prepare an exhibit notebook for each juror, as well as an enlargement of each exhibit to display during counsel's oral presentation.

Although most objections should be handled before the proceeding, the court may entertain objections at trial if counsel exceeds the limits of propriety. Besides applying the rules of evidence in a practical way, the judge should ensure that the representations made by counsel accurately reflect the nature and the weight of the evidence.

For example, if the plaintiff tries to establish a crucial fact by the rather questionable testimony of one witness, and the defendant can present five independent witnesses to refute that testimony, the plaintiff's lawyer should not be allowed to assert the crucial fact as irrefutable truth. The lawyers should also be reminded of Disciplinary Rule 7-106 of the Code of Professional Responsibility, which forbids them from asserting personal knowledge of the facts in issue, or personal opinions as to the justness of a cause or the credibility of a witness.

Given the general flexibility of a summary jury trial, there are few hard and fast limitations on the lawyers' presentations. A lawyer should not hesitate to ask the judge to adapt the proceeding to the requirements of the particular case. For example, the judge may permit key witnesses to testify in an abbreviated form, especially in a case that turns on the credibility of a particular witness's testimony.

A lawyer may also be allowed to use a videotape to summarize his or her case or to show the jury actual witnesses or physical evidence. This method was used in a personal injury case before Judge Lee R. West, of the United States District Court for the Western District of Oklahoma. The tape gave an overview of the plaintiff's case, and it included an animated reconstruction of the accident scene. It also showed the litigant's injuries and their effect on his everyday life.

At the close of the lawyers' presentations, the judge should give the jurors a practical understanding of the applicable law. The judge should avoid unnecessary detail and should explain to the jurors, in a straightforward manner, the basic principles they need to apply to decide the case fairly.

The jurors are told that they should attempt to return a unanimous verdict. They are given a verdict form containing specific interrogatories, a general liability inquiry, and an inquiry about damages. The judge may tell the jurors that if, after diligent efforts, they are unable to reach a unanimous verdict, they may return separate verdicts. He or she may distribute separate verdict forms initially or wait until after the jury reports a deadlock to mention separate verdicts.

After the Trial

Once the jury has been excused to deliberate, the judge may engage the parties in further settlement negotiations. These negotiations have a special urgency, since they are conducted in the shadow of an impending verdict.

When the jurors complete their deliberations, they return either a consensus verdict or separate verdicts. Then the judge, the attorneys, the parties, and the jurors talk. The judge may ask the jurors to give their perceptions of the attorneys' presentations or to explain the reasoning behind the verdict. The lawyers are encouraged to discuss the case with the jurors.

If the case cannot be settled during or immediately after the summary jury trial, another conference is scheduled for about a month later. The delay gives the parties a chance to digest the results of the advisory procedure.

During the subsequent conference, the discussion focuses on the advisory verdict and the jurors' comments on the case. Everyone must recognize that another jury would probably return a similar verdict if the case goes to trial. Settlement is the next logical step. If the case still cannot be settled, it is set down for a regular jury trial, which is normally held within a month, but which may be postponed if settlement negotiations continue.

Conclusion

Summary jury trials focus the parties on the essential issues. So, if the regular trial does go forward, it takes less time and runs more smoothly than it otherwise might.

The traditional jury trial is still the foundation of our system of justice. But the summary jury trial has proved to be effective in resolving complex disputes because it provides a objective prediction of how a regular jury would decide the case.

Note

1. In addition, the Seventh Circuit Court of Appeals has ruled that a federal judge may not require litigants to participate in a nonbinding summary jury trial. Strandell v. Jackson County, Ill., 838 F.2d 884 (7th Cir. 1987). *But see* McKay v. Williams, 120 F.R.D. 43 (E.D. Ky. 1988) (summary jury trial ordered under local rule notwithstanding *Strandell*).

Twenty-Four

Some Practical Thoughts on Arbitration

Geraldine Soat Brown

You represent the general contractor for a large office building. As in many construction projects, there are a variety of disputes about the work. The owner complains that delays in completing construction are holding up his use of the building. Your client believes that the delays are the owner's fault and that he has a claim against the owner for additional work performed. A subcontractor who has not completed his work is demanding full payment. A lawsuit by someone is in the wind.

Will the action be in state or federal court? Can all the disputes be joined in one action? What discovery will be needed? Will you need expert witnesses? Should you ask for a jury? Are there any standard legal defenses available, like the statute of limitations? How much will the litigation cost the client? How long before a judgment can be expected?

The answers to these key questions are affected by one fact: The construction was governed by the American Institute of Architects (AIA) standard form, "General Conditions for Construction Contracts."[1] Your client's contracts with the owner and the subcontractors incorporated those general conditions by reference, including the provision that:

> Any controversy or claim arising out of or related to the Contract or the breach thereof. . . shall be decided by arbitration in accordance with the Construction Industry Arbitration Rules of the American Arbitration Association then obtaining unless the parties mutually agree otherwise.[2]

This tongue-twisting provision means that your client's disputes with the owner, and even his dispute with the subcontractor, may be subject to arbitration. Your client's situation is not unusual in the construction industry, because the AIA's forms are used widely.

As increasing costs and lengthening delays in courtroom litigation accelerate the search for alternative means to resolve disputes, attorneys who have mastered the rules of procedure and evidence are often finding themselves in arbitration, where those rules may not apply. The spread of

Geraldine Soat Brown is a member of Miller, Shakman, Nathan & Hamilton, Chicago, Illinois.

arbitration clauses is not confined to the construction industry, but extends throughout a variety of commercial activities. For example, the United States Supreme Court has ruled that some antitrust claims and even claims under section 10(b) of the Securities Exchange Act and under RICO may be arbitrated rather than resolved in court.[3] This chapter's observations about practical considerations that will influence your decision to seek or to resist arbitration apply to most disputes in which there is an apparent agreement to arbitrate. Litigators who have a general commercial practice must now be familiar with the special procedures governing arbitration as well as with the traditional rules.

Choice of Forum

As every litigator knows, the choice of the forum and the fact finder can be critical to the outcome of the case. Thus, as you review your client's problem, the most basic question remains: Is it to my client's advantage to have this dispute resolved by arbitration? If it is, you may decide not to resist your opponent's demand for arbitration, or you may need to compel your opponent to arbitrate. If you decide that arbitration is not a favorable forum for your client's position, you may decide to waive arbitration or to explore the possibilities for resisting an opponent's attempt to compel arbitration.

To make this choice, you must know how arbitration differs from courtroom procedures and how those differences affect your client's case. Bearing in mind that specifics will vary according to the wording of the arbitration agreement involved and the applicable arbitration statute, in general, arbitration differs from litigation in the following ways.

The forum, the fact finder, and the procedure are determined not by civil procedure or evidence rules, but by the parties' arbitration agreement and the arbitration statute of the applicable jurisdiction. Arbitration statutes like the Uniform Arbitration Act (the UAA, passed by thirty states) and the Federal Arbitration Act[4] make the parties' choice of arbitration specifically enforceable and enable the prevailing party to convert the arbitrator's award into a judgment that can be enforced by the usual court procedures. Under these statutes, a valid arbitration award must be rendered in accordance with the procedures contained in the arbitration agreement.

The AIA form contracts provide that claims or disputes shall be decided by arbitration in accordance with the Construction Industry Arbitration Rules of the American Arbitration Association (AAA) then in effect, unless the parties mutually agree otherwise. However, an arbitration agreement that does not specify the particular arbitrators or even the method for selecting them may still be enforced. Both section 3 of the UAA and 9 U.S.C. § 5 authorize a court to appoint the arbitrators in these circumstances.

The rules of evidence and civil procedure that usually apply to courtroom litigation are not mandated in arbitration proceedings. An arbitration need only afford the parties a full opportunity to be heard and to present evidence.[5] Although the arbitrator decides the admissibility of evidence, he or she is not required to comply with legal rules of evidence.[6] Instead, hearsay and other usually inadmissible evidence can be accepted by the arbitrator.[7] Under AAA rule 32, evidence can be submitted by affidavit.

The arbitrator, who may decide both fact and law questions,[8] is not a judge and need not even be a lawyer. Arbitrators are selected by the parties in accordance with the procedure established in the arbitration agreement or by the court. The agreement may name a particular arbitrator or allow each party to designate an arbitrator. A designated arbitrator may not be disqualified for interest or bias, for this person is not expected to be neutral.[9] Unless this kind of designation procedure is part of the agreement, an arbitrator normally must be neutral. An award by an arbitrator selected as a neutral arbitrator may be vacated upon a showing of bias or partiality.[10]

The AAA maintains panels of experienced arbitrators from which neutral arbitrators may be selected. The construction industry panel, for example, includes architects, contractors, and attorneys who have handled construction suits. In practice, after a dispute is submitted, the AAA sends to each party a list of names from the National Panel of Construction Arbitrators, with a brief description of the qualifications of each potential arbitrator. Each party is instructed to strike the name of an arbitrator that is not acceptable and to number the remaining names in the order of preference. From the list of acceptable arbitrators, and in the order of mutual preference, the AAA invites an arbitrator to serve. Arbitrators appointed by the AAA are governed by the Code of Ethics for Arbitrators in Commercial Disputes and by the ethical standards for arbitrators applied by the courts of the relevant jurisdiction.[11]

Arbitration procedures are designed to get to the facts of the dispute. The arbitrator, selected for his or her expertise, may bring personal knowledge to bear on the decision.[12] The arbitrator may ask questions and seek out evidence he or she believes is needed to make a fair decision.[13] Conversely, legal defenses may be more difficult to assert. Arbitration has no explicit procedure for pretrial motions to dismiss for failure to state a claim. A suit to stay arbitration can be brought only because there is no agreement to arbitrate, not because the claim lacks legal merit. Nonlawyer arbitrators in particular may be inclined to deal with the facts instead of determining at the threshold defensive issues like the statute of limitations or the statute of frauds.

The broad discovery allowed in civil practice may not be available. There are no express provisions for discovery in either the UAA or the Federal Arbitration Act beyond the arbitrator's ability to compel production of witnesses and documents at the hearing by subpoenas. Most prehearing procedures in arbitration are arranged by agreement. Arbitration agreements can provide for certain types of discovery or pretrial motions. The standard AIA forms do not; however, you may work out an agreement with the opposing party or request that the arbitrator establish a procedure pursuant to his or her powers under AAA rule 29. The AAA Construction Industry Rules allow for a prehearing conference at the request of the parties or at the discretion of the AAA "to arrange for an exchange of information and the stipulation of uncontested facts to expedite the arbitration proceedings."

Finally, and perhaps most significantly, the grounds for vacating an arbitrator's award are narrowly circumscribed by statute. The award may be simple and conclusory and need not make specific findings of fact on each point.[14] Generally, it may not be vacated for error of law or fact. Section 13 of the UAA allows modification of an award for an "evident mistake in description" or "evident miscalculation," but the UAA limits the grounds for vacating an award to five:

1. The award was procured by corruption, fraud, or other undue means.
2. There was evident partiality by an arbitrator appointed as a neutral arbitrator or corruption or misconduct prejudicing the rights of any party.
3. The arbitrator exceeded his or her powers.
4. The arbitrator refused to grant a continuance for good cause, refused to hear evidence material to the controversy, or conducted the hearing so as to prejudice substantially the rights of the party.
5. There was no arbitration agreement.

Courts have necessarily been wary of turning an application to vacate an arbitration award into a trial de novo of the issues heard before the arbitrator. What can be presented to show that the arbitrator exceeded his or her powers varies from state to state, but the Illinois Supreme Court reviewed the case law and concluded that it demonstrates "the clear intent [of the UAA] that judicial review of an arbitrator's award would be more limited than appellate review of a trial court's decision."[15] The court quoted with approval the comment that:

> The question for the court is whether the construction of the

> contract made by the arbitrator is a reasonably possible one that can seriously be made in the context in which the contract was made.[16]

Thus, even gross errors of judgment in law or a gross mistake of fact will not vitiate an award unless these mistakes or errors are apparent on the face of the award.[17] This view is shared by other states.[18] It is also the view of the federal courts.[19]

In light of these distinctions between arbitration and civil litigation, you should discuss with your client some of the following issues.

How well do we know the facts and theories of our own case? Because arbitration is designed to avoid the normal civil suit delay between complaint and trial, you may have to develop files, facts, and law in short order. For example, upon the filing of a party's arbitration demand, the AAA's Chicago office asks the parties to select a date for hearing within the next two months. This is not to say that arbitration will occur in two months; the arbitrator is required by section 12 of the UAA to grant reasonable requests for continuance. However, the policy that arbitration is a speedy resolution of disputes is notice that counsel cannot expect a delay comparable to that for court cases.

How well do we know our opponent's case? Are we in a position to go forward without extensive discovery? Is our case premised on customs and practices in the trade that an experienced layperson might understand better than a judge? Does the force of our case rest on its "jury appeal"? Is our case based on sophisticated legal issues that would be best decided by a judge?

Are we looking for equitable relief? The power of the arbitrator to grant equitable relief is determined by the scope of the agreement unless contrary to the applicable law. AIA contracts incorporate by reference AAA rules that allow the arbitrator to grant any remedy or relief that is just, equitable, and within the terms of the parties' agreement.[20] However, the arbitrator retains no jurisdiction after the award. Enforcement of an equitable order entered in the award is left to the court in a suit to enforce the arbitration award.

Finally, what are the client's financial resources? Initial arbitration filing costs may be higher than court costs. Under the AAA rules there is a filing fee for a claim or counterclaim based on a percentage of the claim. In addition, AAA construction arbitrators donate their time for the first day of hearings but customarily receive compensation for their time during the second and following hearing days. But the legal time involved in discovery and briefing is diminished in arbitration, and a client (particularly a plaintiff) may be able to have a claim adjudicated much faster and at a considerable savings.

A caveat is necessary here. While arbitration is designed to be relatively speedy and inexpensive, arbitrators are not judges and do not devote full time to hearing the dispute. Hearing days are scheduled at the convenience of the arbitrator and usually with the agreement of the parties. As a result, an arbitration can take months to conclude with only a few hearing days each month.

Demand for Arbitration

If you decide to arbitrate, the first step is to prepare a demand for arbitration to serve on the other parties. A demand is not a complaint; it need not follow the formalities of a complaint. The AAA has specific "Demand for Arbitration" forms to initiate proceedings under AAA auspices. Under the AAA rules, the demand must state the nature of the dispute, the amount involved, and the remedy sought. The AAA then notifies the opposing party, who is permitted to file an answering statement within seven days. Failure to file an answer is not deemed an admission; instead, it is a denial of the claim.[21]

You may demand arbitration only with a party who has agreed to arbitrate, but arbitration agreements have a surprisingly long reach. Contractors, architects, subcontractors, and sureties have been held to arbitration agreements because their contracts incorporated by reference the AIA's "General Conditions for Construction Contracts," which in turn provide for arbitration of disputes arising from the agreement.[22] A party claiming third-party beneficiary rights under a contract containing an arbitration clause may be bound to arbitrate that claim.[23] In *P.R. Post Corp v. Maryland Casualty Co.,*[24] an award in an arbitration between an owner and a contractor was treated as prima facie evidence of the liability of the contractor's surety.

Courts have taken opposing views about whether arbitration of disputes covered by separate arbitration agreements can be consolidated in one proceeding without consent of all the parties. In similar fact situations (arbitration between the owner and the contractor and between the owner and the architect), a Minnesota court ordered consolidation,[25] while a Massachusetts court refused to consolidate.[26] Federal courts have likewise taken differing views, with the Second Circuit favoring consolidation[27] and the Ninth Circuit refusing consolidation.[28] The AIA "General Conditions" attempt to restrict consolidation:

> No arbitration arising out of or relating to the Contract Documents shall include, by consolidation, joinder or in any other manner, the Architect, the Architect's employees or consultants, except by written consent containing a specific reference to the Agreement and signed by the Architect, Owner,

> Contractor and any other person or entity sought to be joined. No arbitration shall include, by consolidation or joinder or in any other manner, parties other than the Owner, Contractor, a separate contractor as described in Article 6 and other persons substantially involved in a common question of fact or law whose presence is required if complete relief is to be accorded in arbitration.

The United States Supreme Court has agreed to hear a California case staying an arbitration in which third parties could not be joined.[29]

It is important to remember that arbitration is a contractual right that can be waived by inconsistent actions. Filing a court action inconsistent with an arbitration demand can be deemed a waiver of arbitration. Your client need not, however, abandon its security. The filing of a mechanic's lien is generally not in itself considered a waiver of arbitration.[30] If the arbitration is not concluded before the statutory deadline for filing suit to foreclose the mechanic's lien, or to enforce the bond under the Miller Act in the case of federal contracts, contractors may, without waiving arbitration, file a court action asking to stay court proceedings during the arbitration but to retain jurisdiction to enforce the arbitrator's award.[31]

Compelling Arbitration

Your client may have come to you to enforce the arbitration agreement after your opponent has filed a complaint in federal or state court. Section 2 of the UAA and 9 U.S.C. § 3 specifically set out procedures for this situation. If the action is in state court in a state that has adopted the UAA, the first step is to serve a demand for arbitration and to file with the court an application to compel arbitration under section 2(a) of the UAA. This should be done before any responsive pleading or discovery is filed in the court action. The application to compel should allege the existence of a valid arbitration agreement covering some or all of the issues involved in the court proceeding, allege that the court proceeding indicates your opponent's refusal to proceed to arbitration, and request an order under section 2(a) and section 2(b) compelling your opponent to arbitrate and staying the state court action during the pendency of the arbitration.

Under the UAA, the sole defense to such an application to compel arbitration is the lack of an agreement to arbitrate. If an agreement to arbitrate exists, the court must stay the court proceedings relating to that issue and order both parties to arbitrate. The party opposing arbitration may not raise the merits of any issue in the case in chief.[32] If the opposing party denies there is an agreement to arbitrate, "the court shall proceed summarily to the determination of the issues so raised and shall order arbitration if found for the moving party."[33] In practice, this means that proceedings on the court case are halted until the court determines whether arbitration is the appropriate forum for the case and determines what issues should go to arbitration.

The Federal Arbitration Act sets out a similar procedure. A suit may be filed to compel an opponent to arbitrate,[34] and any pending federal action may be stayed until arbitration is concluded.[35] Use of the Federal arbitration Act to compel arbitration is complicated by the case law interpreting these seemingly straightforward statutes.

At the outset, the Federal Arbitration Act is not an independent basis for federal jurisdiction.[36] A party may initiate a petition to compel arbitration in the federal district court only if the court "save for such agreement, would have jurisdiction under Title 28. . . ." Second, in *Bernhardt v. Polygraphic Co. of America,*[37] the Supreme Court ruled that the limitations of 9 U.S.C. §§ 1 and 2 must be read into the remaining sections of the act. In other words, federal substantive law (which favors the enforceability of arbitration agreements) applies only if the contract is a "maritime transaction" or "a contract evidencing a transaction involving [interstate] commerce." Without a finding of "interstate commerce," a federal court sitting in a diversity case must apply the substantive arbitration policy of the governing state law.

This distinction can determine the outcome, as the *Bernhardt* case shows. The plaintiff there brought suit in a Vermont court, and the defendant removed to the federal court on the basis of diversity jurisdiction. The defendant also moved, under 9 U.S.C. § 3, to stay the federal case pending arbitration. The Supreme Court held that although the arbitration agreement might be valid and enforceable under federal law, because "interstate commerce" was not involved, the forum state's law, which would not enforce arbitration agreements, must be applied. Conversely, state courts may have to apply the Federal Arbitration Act where interstate commerce is present.[38]

Thus, whether the transaction involves interstate commerce can determine whether the claim actually goes to arbitration. As under the UAA, the only issue in a federal court proceeding either to compel arbitration[39] or to stay a federal proceeding pending arbitration[40] is "the making of the arbitration agreement or the failure, neglect or refusal to perform the same."[41] In making this finding, the federal courts have interpreted their role very narrowly.

Much of the case law on efforts to stay or compel arbitration centers on two issues: Is there an agreement to arbitrate between these parties, and if so, is the present dispute covered by that agreement? On the second issue, the federal court "is to determine whether the parties agreed to arbitrate that dispute. The court is to make this determination by applying the 'federal substantive law of arbitrability. . . . The Arbitration Act establishes that, as a matter of federal law, any doubts concerning the scope of arbitrable issues should be resolved in favor of arbitration. . . .' "[42] Issues of "procedural arbitrability," such as laches or termination of the agreement, are for the arbitrator.[43]

In contrast, state courts have differing views on whether the arbitrator or the court determines the scope of the arbitration agreement. In an early and leading case under the UAA, the Minnesota Supreme Court held that where the issue of the scope of the arbitration agreement is questionable, arbitration should be ordered, and the issue should be resolved in the first instance by the arbitrators.[44] Other courts seem to have reserved for themselves a larger role in determining whether the dispute is covered by the arbitration agreement. In *Roosevelt University v. Mayfair Construction Co.*[45] and *J&K Cement Construction, Inc. v. Montalbano Builders, Inc.*,[46] the courts reviewed authorities and concluded that under a broad or "generic" agreement that "all disputes" are to be arbitrated, the court in the first instance should refer "all types of disagreements" to the arbitrators, but that the scope of a "specific" arbitration agreement limiting arbitration to specified disputes is to be determined by the court. This allows the court to determine in each case whether the arbitration agreement covers the dispute.

The federal courts also take a different approach to the initial issue of whether an arbitration agreement exists between the parties. Under the UAA, that issue is to be determined "summarily" by the court. Under the Federal Arbitration Act,[47] a jury trial on issues of fact may be demanded.[48] Further, federal courts have developed a doctrine of "severability": Arbitration clauses as a matter of federal law are separable from the contract in which they are imbedded.[49] Thus, in an action to compel arbitration, the federal court will decide the issue of fraud in the inducement of the contract only if it is alleged that the fraud induced the arbitration clause itself rather than the contract generally. Fraud alleged to have induced the entire contract is an arbitrable issue. In contrast, in state courts arbitration may be stayed while the issue of fraud in the inducement of the contract is decided by the court.[50]

In short, the allegation that "interstate commerce" exists, which determines whether federal or state arbitration law is to apply, may well determine the success of a federal action to compel arbitration. However, construction projects often meet this test. For example, courts have found that interstate commerce was involved in a contract where the general contractor and subcontractor transported materials to the construction site in a different state,[51] or where the contract called for subcontracts and equipment shipped from other states and nonresident employees were involved in the project.[52]

In either state or federal court, a reference of issues to arbitration stays the court action only on those issues.[53] To avoid fighting a war on two fronts, you must appeal to the court's discretion to stay the other proceedings in the court suit until the arbitration is concluded.

Resisting Arbitration

If you and your client decide that arbitration should be avoided, the same principles previously discussed apply, with particular emphasis on the need to object to jurisdiction. Under section 12 of the UAA, participation in arbitration proceedings without objection to the arbitrator's jurisdiction waives that objection.

The simplest way to avoid arbitration is by mutual waiver. Filing an action in court is a waiver of your right to demand arbitration. If your opponent then proceeds to defend the court action without raising a demand for arbitration, he or she has also waived arbitration.[54]

On the other hand, under section 5 of the UAA, refusing to participate in arbitration proceedings does not constitute an effective revocation of the agreement to arbitrate, for the arbitrator may determine the dispute even if a party fails to appear. It is possible to raise the absence of any agreement to arbitrate when your opponent tries to confirm the award,[55] but if that issue is determined in favor of arbitration, all other defenses that could have been brought in the arbitration will have been lost.

The UAA provides three opportunities to object to arbitration. First, when your opponent "commences or threatens" an arbitration proceeding, you may bring an action in court to stay that arbitration by showing that there is no agreement to arbitrate. Section 2(b) of the UAA provides that the absence of an arbitration agreement, "when in substantial and bona fide dispute, shall be forthwith and summarily tried and a stay [of arbitration] ordered if found for the moving party." As previously noted, the court may order the arbitrator to decide the issue of arbitrability as a threshold matter. If so, the issue must be raised to the arbitrator, or it is waived. It may be possible to schedule preliminary hearings before the arbitrator to determine that issue alone.

The second opportunity for objecting to arbitration is in the arbitration proceeding itself. A timely objection to arbitration at the beginning preserves the objection even if the party then participates in the arbitration on the merits.[56] However, a party may not participate until the award is rendered and then object to the arbitrator's jurisdiction.

The final opportunity to object to arbitration may arise under section 12(a)(5) of the UAA, when the lack of arbitrability may be asserted as a defense to confirming the award, if the objection was asserted in the arbitration proceedings, and if the objection was not "adversely decided" in an earlier proceeding to stay arbitration.

Unlike the UAA, the Federal Arbitration Act has no explicit procedure for staying threatened arbitration proceedings. Instead, in a case where federal jurisdiction otherwise exists, an action may be brought in federal court for an injunction against the arbitration proceedings under the court's general equity power.[57]

Section 19 of the UAA expressly provides for appeals from orders denying an application to compel arbitration. Some states also allow interlocutory appeals from orders compelling arbitration.[58] On the other hand, it has not been easy to determine the appealability of a federal court order staying or compelling arbitration. Whether a federal order to arbitrate or to stay arbitration may be appealed has depended upon the exact procedural status of the order, rather than upon the substance of the relief granted or withheld.[59] However, in 1988 Congress amended the Federal Arbitration Act to add a new section, 9 U.S.C. 15, that allows immediate appeal from orders denying arbitration, and providing that appeal may not be taken from interlocutory orders directing arbitration to proceed.

Unique Opportunity

Arbitration agreements—whether in the construction industry or any other commercial activity—allow counsel a unique opportunity to structure the forum and procedure in which future disputes will be resolved. In advising a client who is about to enter into an agreement containing an arbitration clause, you should attempt to anticipate potential disputes and draft the arbitration agreement to preserve the procedures your client will need to present his or her case fully, while retaining the benefits the client hopes to achieve in agreeing to arbitration.

Notes

1. AIA form A201.
2. *Id.*
3. Mitsubishi Motors Corp. v. Soler Chrysler-Plymouth, Inc., 473 U.S. 614, 87 L. Ed. 2d 444 (1985); Shearson/American Express, Inc. v. McMahon, 107 S. Ct. 2332, 96 L. Ed. 2d 185 (1987).
4. 9 U.S.C. § 1 *et seq.*
5. Reisman v. Ranoel Realty Co., 303 A.2d 511 (Pa. Super. Ct. 1973).
6. Gozdor v. Detroit Auto. Inter-Ins. Exch., 216 N.W.2d 436 (Mich. App. 1974).
7. Pierre v. General Accident Ins., 474 N.Y.S.2d 622 (N.Y. App. 1984).
8. Verdex Steel & Constr. Co. v. Board of Supervisors, 509 P.2d 240, 244 (Ariz. App. 1973).
9. *See, e.g.*, Astoria Medical Group v. Health Ins. Plan, 11 N.Y.2d 128 (1962) (party permitted to name as an arbitrator a member of its board of directors).
10. UAA § 12; 9 U.S.C. § 10.
11. Merit Ins. Co. v. Leatherby Ins. Co., 714 F.2d 673, 681 (7th Cir. 1983).

331

12. American Almond Prods. Co. v. Consolidated Pecan Sales Co., 144 F. 2d 448, 450 (2d Cir. 1944).
13. AAA Rule 31.
14. Sperry Int'l Trade, Inc. v. Government of Israel, 602 F. Supp. 1440 (S.D.N.Y. 1985); Del Bianco & Assocs., Inc. v. Adam, 6 Ill. App. 3d 286 (1972).
15. Garver v. Ferguson, 76 Ill. 2d 1, 9 (1979).
16. *Id.*
17. *Id.* at 10.
18. Raisler Corp. v. New York City Housing Auth., 32 N.Y.2d 274, 283 (1973); Ray Wilson Co. v. Anaheim Memorial Hosp. Ass'n, 166 Cal. App. 1081 (1985); Grudem Bros. Co. v. Great W. Piping Corp., 213 N.W.2d 920, 923 (Minn. 1973); Foley Co. v. Grindsted Prods., Inc., 662 P.2d 1254 (Kan. 1981).
19. French v. Merrill Lynch, Pierce, Fenner & Smith, Inc., 784 F.2d 902 (9th Cir. 1986).
20. AAA Rule 43.
21. AAA Rule 7.
22. ADC Constr. Co. v. McDaniel Grading, Inc., 338 S.E.2d 733 (Ga. App. 1985); Bigge Crane & Rigging Co. v. Docutel Corp., 371 F. Supp. 240 (E.D.N.Y. 1973); Exchange Mut. Ins. Co. v. Haskell Co., 742 F.2d 274 (6th Cir. 1984).
23. Jeanes v. Arrow Ins. Co., 494 P.2d 1334, 1337 (Ariz. App. 1972).
24. 68 Mich. App. 182 (1976), *modified,* 403 Mich. 543 (1978).
25. Grover-Dimond Assocs. v. American Arbitration Ass'n, 211 N.W.2d 787 (Minn. 1973).
26. Stop & Shop Cos., Inc. v. Gilbane Bldg. Co., 304 N.E.2d 429 (Mass. 1973).
27. Sociedad Anonima de Navegacion Petrolera v. Cia. de Petroleos de Chile, S.A., 634 F. Supp. 805 (S.D.N.Y. 1986).
28. Weyerhaeuser Co. v. Western Seas Shipping Co., 743 F.2d 635 (9th Cir. 1984).
29. Volt Information Sciences, Inc. v. Stanford University, No. 87-1318, *appeal from* 195 Cal. App. 3d 349 (1987).
30. *See* Annot., 73 A.L.R.3d 1042 (1976); Annot., 73 A.L.R.3d 1066 (1976).
31. United States *ex rel.* Capolino Sons, Inc. v. Electronic & Missile Facilities, Inc., 364 F.2d 705, 708 (2d Cir. 1966); Frederick Contractors, Inc. v. Bel Pre Medical Center, Inc., 334 A.2d 526, 531 (Md. 1975).
32. UAA § 2(e).
33. UAA § 2.
34. 9 U.S.C. § 4.
35. *Id.* § 3.
36. Moses H. Cone Memorial Hosp. v. Mercury Constr. Corp., 460 U.S. 1, 25 n.32 (1983); Commercial Metals Co. v. Balfour, Guthrie & Co., Ltd., 577 F.2d 264, 269 (5th Cir. 1978).
37. 350 U.S. 198 (1956).
38. Southland Corp. v. Keating, 465 U.S. 1 (1984).
39. 9 U.S.C. § 3.
40. *Id.* § 4.
41. Prima Paint Corp. v. Flood & Conklin Mfg. Co., 388 U.S. 395 (1967).

42. Mitsubishi Motors Corp. v. Soler Chrysler-Plymouth, Inc., 473 U.S. 626, 87 L. Ed. 2d 444, 454 (1985).
43. Stroh Container Co. v. Delphi Indus., Inc., 783 F.2d 743 (8th Cir. 1986).
44. Layne-Minnesota Co. v. Regents of Univ. of Minn., 123 N.W. 2d 371 (Minn. 1963); *see also* University of Ala. v. Modern Constr., Inc., 522 P.2d 1132, 1138 (Ala. 1974).
45. 28 Ill. App. 3d 1045 (1975).
46. 119 Ill. App. 3d 663, 670–71 (1983).
47. 9 U.S.C. § 4.
48. *See* Austin v. A.G. Edwards & Sons, Inc., 349 F. Supp. 615 (M.D. Fla. 1972).
49. *Prima Paint,* 388 U.S. at 402.
50. *See* Atcas v. Credit Clearing Corp. of Am., 197 N.W.2d 448, 456 (Minn. 1972) *and cases cited therein*; Annot., 11 A.L.R.4th 774 (1982).
51. Metro Indus. Painting Corp. v. Terminal Constr. Co., 287 F.2d 382 (2d Cir. 1961).
52. American Home Assurance Co. v. Vecco Concrete Constr. Co., 629 F.2d 961 (4th Cir. 1980).
53. UAA § 2; 9 U.S.C. § 4.
54. Hilti, Inc. v. Griffith, 68 Ill. App. 3d 528 (1978).
55. UAA § 12.
56. Board of Educ. v. Champaign Educ. Ass'n, 15 Ill. App. 3d 335, 341–42 (1973).
57. 9 MOORE'S FEDERAL PRACTICE ¶ 110.20[4.-1] at 249 (2d ed. 1987).
58. *See* Annot., 6 A.L.R.4th 652 (1981).
59. 9 MOORE'S FEDERAL PRACTICE, *supra* note 57, at 246. *See* Moses H. Cone Memorial Hosp., 460 U.S. at 8.

Twenty-Five

How to Use Mediation

Barbara Ashley Phillips and Anthony Piazza

Litigation is expensive and consumes a great deal of time. Mediation is a quick and inexpensive way to uncover and assess the options for resolving a dispute. Corporate litigators are turning more frequently to mediation as a tool for gauging the necessity for and managing the course of litigation.

The vast majority of lawsuits settle before trial. Yet until recently, trial lawyers have only infrequently used mediation in preparing and settling cases. Some lawyers may have feared that early settlements are against the economic interests of lawyers, even though most of them agree that resolving disputes is a lawyer's stock in trade; the better a lawyer's record in solving clients' problems, the better and busier the lawyer.

Essentially, mediation is a turbocharged negotiation. Unlike arbitration and other means of adjudication, the parties retain complete control. The parties and their lawyers develop the procedures for the mediation. If they do not like the mediator, they get another one. If they fail to produce results, they may end the mediation at any time.

Mediation proceedings are informal. The parties need not submit evidence or produce witnesses, although they may exchange information and make witnesses available.

The mediator does not make findings of fact or law. He or she meets with the parties in either joint or individual session. Private caucuses allow the parties to test their perceptions and positions in a confidential setting against those of an impartial third party.

When necessary, the mediator can help the parties select experts, stipulate for prompt decisions on controlling questions of law, and select other courses of action, such as fact-finding or a minitrial. Since the stated issues in a complaint often conceal the underlying dispute, the parties may want to redefine the issues. In mediation, unlike adjudication, this can easily be done.

Barbara Ashley Phillips is President and Founder and Anthony Piazza is Director of Professional Services for American Intermediation Service, San Francisco, California.

One important aspect of mediation is that the parties agree in advance that all disclosures to the mediator are confidential and privileged. As a result, the parties can communicate to the mediator facts that may ease a settlement but that they would not want disclosed to the other parties.

The confidentiality and reduced adversarial nature of the process also help to protect business relationships in intercorporate disputes, and to preserve the privacy of corporate affairs. Thus, for example, claims involving termination of upper-level business managers are frequently resolved through mediation, as are disputes that would require extensive discovery of sensitive business documents.

Use of Mediators

Consider some specific applications of the process in the context of litigation. Mediation can be used to accomplish the following objectives:

- Open communications where a high level of hostility or distrust among the parties make direct negotiations impossible or unwise.
- Break an impasse by permitting parties to explore options without taking responsibility for suggesting them, and by allowing them to test the other side's responses without disclosing confidential information or a willingness to compromise a position previously taken.
- Develop choices by exploring the underlying interests of each party. Clients often box themselves in by adopting positions on issues that may bear little relationship to their actual interests. Framing causes of action or defenses often reinforces this tendency by forcing the parties to define issues by external rules—the legislature or the courts. Negotiations may then deteriorate into an exchange of statements of principle with a price attached. In mediation, although legal rights and liabilities are important to bargaining, the mediator can probe statements of principle for the interests they are intended to serve. The issues under discussion can then be reframed to reflect these interests. For example, a community group might file suit to enjoin a proposed expansion of a hospital. The group's underlying interest might be to prevent deterioration of the neighborhood through demolition of homes, increased traffic, parking problems, and noise. To state a cause of action for injunctive relief, however, the community group may be forced to allege due process violation in the procedure for granting government approval for the project. Through

mediation, the parties can develop changes that could not be obtained through litigation alone—such as including moderate-income apartments or a parking garage in the project.
- Take personalities out of the dispute. Mediation focuses on developing and assessing options, rather than on assigning blame.
- Enable the parties to compare their positions to an objective standard. The adversary process distorts perceptions. The mediator provides advocates with an independent view and an opportunity to assess the strength of their positions. The mediator can also improve the exchange of information, which can prevent the facts from being distorted.
- Help construct a durable settlement and reduce later conflict. To avoid recurrence of problems, the parties must achieve procedural, substantive, and psychological satisfaction.

Parties to a mediation can achieve procedural satisfaction when a party trusts the fairness of the process. That parties are willing to resort repeatedly to litigation suggests that it provides procedural satisfaction. The formality and ceremony of courts and the robes of judges seem to assure procedural fairness.

In mediation, the parties satisfy themselves about procedure through procedural agreements. Parties who retain control of whether and how they participate and what kind of result they obtain are usually satisfied with the procedure.

Substantive satisfaction requires that the parties perceive the settlement as fair and reasonable. This means that the parties must satisfy their real underlying interests. Not all interests can (or should) be satisfied. But where one interest cannot be satisfied, the mediator can help the parties find a substitute. Litigation, which so often deals with issues rather than interests, is weak in this regard.

Psychological satisfaction means that the parties feel good about having been through the process. Ventilating feelings, having the opportunity to tell your story and knowing that it has been heard, and being treated as an equal in the bargaining process all help to ensure psychological satisfaction.

Litigants expect these kinds of satisfaction in trial, just as they expect that their lawsuit will, in fact, be tried. Many are deeply disappointed to find that after long involvement with litigation, their best interests are not to go to the mat after all.

Mediation is unique in providing all types of satisfaction, even when settlement is not reached. Because all parties participate in developing procedural agreements and exploring possible results, they have a sense of ownership in the process and a stake in the outcome.

Mediation can lead to early settlement of cases. But even where parties cannot come to a complete agreement, mediation can often do the following:

- Eliminate issues and unnecessary parties
- Clarify issues
- Reduce the emotions in the case
- Simplify the exchange of information that would otherwise proceed though formal discovery
- Produce an agreement on experts to replace a battle of experts
- Change the atmosphere from one of perhaps unbridled hostility to one in which some trust exists

The parties and lawyers who have been educated to the strengths and weaknesses of their case should be more willing to resolve it, and the process of agreeing on procedural matters can often lead the way to broader agreement. The issues are not just when, where, and for how long mediation will be undertaken, but who should be present, whether meetings will be joint sessions or private caucuses with the mediator, what issues will be discussed and in what order, who can speak to the press and what might be contained in any public statement, whether the issues should be reframed, whether nonparties should be included, and so forth.

By contrast, litigation is largely a lawyer's game. Litigation does not provide much opportunity for clients to take part or to examine their assumptions.

The price for mediation is low. Fees for mediators vary, but they are roughly equivalent to the fees of experienced trial lawyers. Mediation may take only a few hours and rarely requires more than a few days of the mediator's time, although the time may be stretched out over a longer period.

The parties may apportion costs equally or in any proportions they agree on. A wealthy party can agree to pay a more substantial percentage of the mediation costs, in order to lower the risk of mediation to a poorer party. Ideally, all parties should share in the cost, since equal apportionment underscores the neutrality of the process and gives all parties an investment in its success.

Settlement rates for mediated cases range around 80 percent, with turnaround time varying from a few days to some months. These figures hold true for all cases, including settlements into eight and nine figures and cases involving hundreds of parties.

When a trial lawyer has a case that is suitable for mediation, the parties have the option of using a mediation firm to invite the other parties to the table. Success rates for obtaining agreements to mediate range as high as 90 percent, and most firms consider such agreements a standard part of their services.

If litigants themselves choose to persuade the other parties to mediate, attorneys should communicate a willingness to reexamine their own positions. Lawyers will not attract many adversaries to mediate by suggesting that through mediation they could learn how foolish and untenable their position is. The message to the opponent's counsel can be something like this:

> I've been thinking over this case. We're both so convinced of our positions, maybe there's something we're both overlooking. It might be worthwhile to get a mediator to help us explore the alternatives, so you and I can learn what's keeping our clients so far apart.

Sometimes an angry client, rather than the lawyer, stands in the way of resolution. In such a case, mediation may appeal to the client as an opportunity to demonstrate before an impartial observer how reasonable his or her position is, and to have someone talk sense to the opponent.

From the perspective of corporate counsel, having clients participate directly in an early and realistic assessment of the options for resolution helps assure that, if litigation through trial is indeed necessary, the client has conducted the risk analysis needed to commit to this route and to accept the necessary costs and risks. Many companies, as part of the war on litigation costs, now make mediation a routine step in handling all their cases. Outside counsel are often directed to offer to mediate early in litigation.

By making mediation a known, routine part of corporate litigation policy, companies avoid any misinterpretation of the offer to mediate. The statement to adversaries is, "We're confident enough to the strength of our position to sit down and discuss it before a neutral third party."

Courts are beginning to explore settlement possibilities in more creative ways than they used to. Some judges refer cases for mediation under the rules providing for special masters. By doing this, the courts relieve the parties from being the first to suggest settlement. The judges can time their suggestions to coincide with the best moment for constructive discussion.

The danger is that the courts will coerce the parties or their counsel into mediation, and so distort the process. Mediation is and must be voluntary. The mediator's power rests on continuing consent, not authority.

The actual participation of the parties whose interests must be satisfied makes the process a powerful way to clear misperceptions, reduce rancor, and provoke a realistic appraisal of the situation.

Checklist for Mediating

Since mediation skills differ considerably from those of other disciplines, particularly trial law, it is important to be able to identify mediators who have been trained specifically for mediation. All parties must remain comfortable with the mediator. A mediator friendly to your side is no advantage, as such a position compromises the mediator's professional impartiality and could destroy the trust of the other side.

You need not choose a mediator expert in the field of the dispute. Such expertise can, in fact, be a handicap, because the parties may look to the mediator as an advice giver or adjudicator.

Mediation services have been developed that offer to put litigants or their representatives in touch with trained mediators, including experienced litigators and former judges. Services like these can also give advice on setting up a mediation and whether it would prove useful.

The following checklist is helpful for lawyers in preparing for mediation:

1. Confirm the agreement of opposing counsel to participate in mediation, the choice of mediator, and the allocation of costs.
2. Make certain that your client understands the purpose and nature of mediation, and that it is voluntary, confidential, and not an adjudication. Your client should also know that he or she waives no other alternatives to litigation.
3. Prepare a summary of the relevant facts and issues. In some cases, the mediator may want a summary before the first meeting. If summaries are required, they should usually be brief—no more than five or six pages.
4. Agree whether the first session is to be a joint meeting or a private caucus. Lawyers may be present or absent as circumstances require.
5. Identify the issues of fact that must be clarified to resolve the dispute. Remember, though, that settlements are most often based not on agreement about what happened in the past, but agreement about what will be done in the future.
6. Consider what information you can share, as well as what information must be kept confidential. The mediator is responsible for obtaining permission to release information to

the other side. It is a good precaution to stress particular matters that should not be disclosed. This should be discussed at the end of each caucus.

7. Summarize the interests in dispute: your client's interest, your own interest, and that of each participant.
8. Summarize the choices you see as possible to resolve the dispute.

Businesses are continually confronted with disputes, many of which cannot be resolved without litigation. Experienced corporate litigators are careful to manage the process of dispute resolution so that litigation is used most appropriately and with greatest effect—as a scalpel, rather than as a truncheon. They are using mediated negotiations as a tool for gaining insight into the points of disagreement and for developing options for resolution.

The small investment required by mediation is paying handsome dividends in efficiency in resolving disputes and in increased client satisfaction.

Section VI

The Use of Computers in Litigation

> [T]he computerized trial support system developed by IBM's counsel. . . was prepared solely for litigation, and it was put in the computerized form so that it could be used in connection with litigation.
>
> . . . .
>
> [T]he trial support system created by IBM's counsel reflects their mental impressions, theories and thought processes, and the Court is not satisfied that information contained in that system can be segregated from such lawyers' mental impressions and theories.[1]

Twenty years ago, the concept of every practicing attorney and every corporate counsel's office being able to assimilate discovery, communicate with each other, provide reasonable methods for efficient litigation management, and be concerned with protecting such a system from divulgence would have been considered near impossible. However, today, with a multitude of different types of computer hardware and software available, solo practitioners, attorneys in medium-sized and large law firms, and attorneys in corporate counsel offices are all able to serve as efficient "information managers" in the complex world of corporate litigation.

The chapters contained in this section emphasize the practical means of using computers in the corporate litigation context, from the standpoint of outside counsel, inside counsel, and corporate counsel. They do not inform attorneys about particular hardware or software systems available in the marketplace. Rather, they seek to enlighten the reader as to the benefits of computerization in the context of corporate litigation and its management. They are also designed to educate the practitioner and corporate counsel as to when such devices should *not* be used. Each chapter clearly cautions that computerized management of litigation is not appropriate for every case, and that each case must be analyzed to determine whether the need for such management outweighs the drawbacks in terms of additional costs. Several of the authors in this section have provided forms (located in the Appendix) that will prove helpful to the practitioner.

In Chapter 26, Michael C. Hallerud demonstrates why the use of computers is particularly beneficial to corporations that have a decentralized structure. The author concentrates on three applications of computer systems in this environment: (1) selection and control of outside counsel; (2) litigation tracking and management; and (3) making a reusable resource system from the company's collection of in-house research. Forms 36–38 in the Appendix are a series of computer forms and reports utilized by Boise Cascade Corporation for such purposes.

Chapter 27 concentrates on the management problems related to discovery and how they can be overcome with the use of computers. The chapter, written by three litigation consultants, James Keane, Alan Silverman, and Sheila Teisher, first concentrates on the kinds of problems that can arise in the discovery context by not using a computer and the advantages that can be realized in using the computer. The authors then explore the various uses of computers in the discovery context, taking particular note of document management. They discuss when the use of computers is appropriate for these activities, the types of systems available, and what is involved in setting up such a system. The authors have also provided Forms 39–47, which consist of computer input forms and computer reports.

In Chapter 28, Kenneth J. Moran and William H. King, Jr., provide an attorney's perspective on when computer support is appropriate. They note that the great volume of documentation handled by trial lawyers today indicates the value of using an automated litigation support system. The authors describe document management systems and why a system, be it computerized or manual, is necessary. Then they provide practical suggestions for deciding whether and how to computerize the document management system. They close the chapter with a discussion of how to protect the information in the system from discovery. Forms 48–50 are examples of document digest, document tracking, and document coding forms suggested by the authors.

The three articles in this section make it clear that today's corporate litigator must recognize the benefits of computer use and be able to fully utilize computer support systems in the litigation context. This not only applies to outside counsel, but also to in-house counsel, who must monitor ongoing litigation and be budget-conscious at the same time. As part of the early planning process in litigation, it will become second nature to the corporate litigator to make decisions regarding whether to use computers, the nature of the systems to be used, and how to realize the most benefit from the systems.

Dennis A. Estis
Greenbaum, Rowe, Ravin, Davis & Bergstein
Woodbridge, New Jersey

Note

1. *In re* IBM Peripheral EDP Devices Antitrust Litig., 5 Computer L. Serv. Rep. 878, 879 (N.D. Cal. 1975).

Twenty-Six

Corporate Litigation Management in a Decentralized Legal Structure

Michael C. Hallerud

Because corporate counsel neither design, manufacture, nor market the products or services of the typical corporation, they are often regarded as merely overhead, and their activities are treated with the same warmth accorded investigative demands from the Internal Revenue Service or the Defense Contract Audit Agency. Nowhere is this more likely to be true than when the corporation is involved in litigation. For many corporate managers, litigation is not only an unwelcome intrusion on their time and a deflection from their principal mission, but it is a confrontation with the unsolicited, negative judgment of an outsider about how the business is managed. Moreover, it is an unpredictable and (from the manager's perspective) uncontrollable expense that disrupts budget discipline and performance.

For these reasons, litigation must be managed by corporate counsel as efficiently and effectively as professional skills and available technology will permit. The efficient and effective management of litigation is difficult enough in any corporation, but is most complex in corporations where the responsibility for the actual administration and delivery of legal services is diffused among legal departments that report directly to semiautonomous operating divisions or groups of the parent corporation.

In such a decentralized legal structure, where the general counsel's office has only a "dotted line" relationship to the division legal departments except for legal matters that are inherently or by decree "corporate" matters, effective comprehensive management of corporate litigation can only be approached through the development and analysis of information and data about the corporation's litigation portfolio. And unless the corporation is very small or so perfect (or perceived as such) that it is never or infrequently sued, the compilation and real-time analysis of litigation

Michael C. Hallerud is a member of Pettit & Martin, San Francisco, California. He was formerly the Assistant General Counsel for The Boeing Company, Seattle, Washington.

information and data can only be accomplished through a computerized system for litigation management.

In the decentralized business and legal structure, most litigation will arise out of and concern most directly the operating divisions or groups. Therefore, it is logical that the direct management of that litigation (whether it is to be tried in-house or by outside counsel) be by the division legal department. After all, that legal staff will know the client better than the corporate legal department and will be better able to tap the division's resources to prosecute or defend the litigation and to get policy guidance on the strategy and tactics to pursue.

However, when litigation is managed in the divisions without a substantial and well-defined role for the general counsel's office, several significant problems will probably develop. First, the division may be primarily populated by business lawyers, not litigation specialists who by experience and training are better equipped to try or to supervise outside counsel in the trial of the matter. Second, some cases have corporatewide significance in their own right, mandating a pivotal role for the general counsel's office. These cases, even though arising out of the division's operations, may involve business or legal principles of corporatewide concern, or the exposure may be so large that the viability of the corporation as a whole, including the uninvolved operating divisions, may be affected. Finally, even where the individual cases may be small in exposure or significance, the collective fiscal impact of all these cases may require their overall management by the general counsel's office.

Thus, with due regard for the primacy of divisional legal departments in any given case, it is a central premise of this chapter that there must be overall corporate supervision of litigation. That supervisory role is an indispensable element of the general counsel's charter to administer and deliver legal services to the corporation as a whole.

Based on these principles, this chapter considers the information development and management techniques that will facilitate management of a company's litigation portfolio. Rather than investigate specific hardware and software recommendations or the design of coding sheets or output reports, this chapter will concentrate on what the hardware, software, and applications ultimately ought to accomplish. This subject is often seriously neglected, perhaps because our fascination with the technology has caused us to overlook *why* we use the technology.

While there are any number of systems that contribute to the management of litigation, this chapter will discuss three systems that have a decidedly positive and immediate impact on outcome and cost containment in a decentralized corporate legal environment: (1) selection and control of outside counsel, (2) interactive litigation tracking and management, and (3) reusable resource systems.

Selection and Control of Outside Counsel

The selection of outside counsel, whether as co-counsel, local counsel, or exclusive trial counsel, is an early milestone in the management of a particular case, and one that will have a material impact on outcome and costs. The selection of outside counsel is based on many factors, including geographical proximity to the action or the underlying events; experience in similar matters; experience with or familiarity to the client, opponent, and court system; the advice or contractual prerogatives of a carrier in insured cases; and the efficiency and effectiveness of the outside counsel in litigation. Because the selection of outside counsel is so significant in any individual case, it follows that the control over the selection process across the entire corporate litigation portfolio will materially affect, for better or worse, the corporation's ability to manage that portfolio.

Corporate lawyers realize that the selection of outside counsel requires both professional and business judgment. They will exercise that judgment more effectively if the influential variables are defined and quantified accurately. For this reason, even a decentralized corporation should maintain a centralized roster of outside counsel who have been approved, disapproved, or nominated for consideration. That roster should track the variables that influence the selection of counsel, such as location, possible conflicts of interest, past involvement and performance on behalf of the corporation, billing history, and so forth. Moreover, the database should be searchable and capable of a sort using any variable. This enables corporate lawyers to consider all available alternatives based on the influence of a given variable on the ultimate selection. Form 36 in the Appendix shows a computerized matter directory used by Boise Cascade Corporation, which can also be used as a roster of outside counsel.

In addition, because the conventional (and correct) wisdom is to hire lawyers, not law firms, any centralized outside counsel roster should identify the specific lawyers within a firm who merit consideration or caution. The roster should also identify the source of information or intelligence about a particular firm or lawyer, so that more detailed questions can be directed when required for making a selection. Identifying the information source also prevents blackballing or canonization without accountability.

The centralized roster of outside counsel, as with any computerized litigation management tool, is a living document. That is, it should be accessible to all corporate litigation managers, and those managers should be regularly solicited for data to update and upgrade the roster.

The centralized outside-counsel roster can also be used, if appropriate, as a control over the selection or use of outside counsel. For instance, the corporation may choose to require higher-level approvals of outside-counsel selection if the proposed selection is not on the roster or contains a disapproval rating. Where the database notes a deficiency associated with a particular lawyer or law firm—for instance, a tendency to overlawyer and overbill or the opposite—the litigation manager who chooses that lawyer or firm will be on notice that special attention may be required to compensate for or avoid that deficiency.

A computerized, current, and searchable outside-counsel roster with realistic variables will advance the process by which outside counsel are selected. Such a roster can also be used to control the selection process appropriately and to improve the use of outside counsel. But what the roster cannot do, fortunately, is to convert the art into a science. The selection of variables, the assignment of values to those variables, and the interpretation of the data all remain, as they should be, professional judgments.

Interactive Litigation Tracking and Management

The effective management of a litigation portfolio in a decentralized corporation with semi-autonomous legal departments requires at least a comprehensive and current list of all pending litigation (including arbitrations and adversary administrative proceedings) and threatened litigation (such as government investigations and presuit demand letters). While such a goal is basic, in the real world it is only attainable with discipline and structure.

An effective litigation tracking system must provide for input into the system of all "new business" in the same way that a private practice firm opens new matters for purposes of accounting, filing, and checking conflicts. Whenever a legal matter, by its size, significance, or character, qualifies as an object to be monitored by the litigation-tracking system, it should be entered in that system by an input document that records the essential objective and subjective data known at that time. The system should also provide prompts requiring the entry of additional data as they become available. Disciplined application of such a system invests each matter with the visibility that makes it manageable by the sectors of the corporation that are accountable for its conduct and disposition.

The design of a litigation-tracking system in a decentralized corporate legal environment depends on how the responsibility for the overall litigation portfolio and individual cases is allocated and how the responsibility is to be discharged. Where the premise is (as it is for this article) that most litigation will be directly managed in the operating divisions, the system must allow and require the recording of information that is essential for the assigned corporate counsel to try or to manage outside counsel in the trial of the litigation. Moreover, the system must track the information that will enable the litigation managers in the general counsel's office to supervise the divisional litigation managers' handling and supervision of litigation, as well as report on the current or historical status of the litigation portfolio for upper management or the board of directors.

An effective litigation-tracking system will of, course, collect and permit retrieval of basic, objective information about any case. These data would include, for instance, case name and number, court, assigned in-house attorneys, outside counsel, opposing counsel, parties (with special attention to those which are or may be adverse), legal costs (often broken down by lawyer, case phase, fees, and disbursements), the allowability of those costs against specific contracts or in specific overhead pools, type of litigation (such as labor, EEO, criminal, personal injury), and formal status. Forms 36 and 37 in the Appendix are computerized case-tracking forms and reports used by Boise Cascade Corporation for these purposes.

Such objective data are useful not only to plot and influence the progress of a given matter, but to analyze or monitor cases that feature a given variable. For instance, the performance of a given division or outside lawyer can be assessed by studying the cases assigned to that lawyer and comparing his or her performance in respect to one or more variables of interest (e.g., discovery costs) against a control measure of performance (such as discovery costs incurred on average by all other lawyers for that type of litigation). This information enables the corporate lawyer to direct scarce management resources to solving problems that involve lawyers or elements of litigation that have an undesirable impact on the company. Moreover, realistic targets will be available through the proper definition and valuation of control measures. The system can also be used to evaluate the causes of litigation (e.g., most EEO cases arise in one factory), the adequacy of insurance coverage for a given category of risk, the proportions of cases resolved by judgment or settlement, the average costs of each category of disposition, and so forth.

In addition to compiling and analyzing objective data, the system might allow for interaction among the corporate attorneys with responsibility for litigation. While that interaction may well occur intermittently by telephone, meetings, or correspondence, more effective management can be achieved if the computerized system allows, within the electronic record of each case, for inquiries, specification of milestones or performance targets, and other narrative entries. These entries would become a permanent part of the electronic record of the case and would afford a more complete picture of the conduct of the litigation than the objective data alone. For instance, the responsible lawyer in the general counsel's office could electronically query the division lawyer assigned to the case about the motion practice proposed in the matter, about specific discovery practices undertaken or considered, or about the wisdom of filing an offer of judgment. Those queries, and the responses to them, would remain in the electronic case file as part of the record of its handling.

Other applications of this interactive concept are intriguing as well. For instance, a corporate lawyer who has had a recent experience with a particular judge or opposing counsel, or who has learned of a new local court rule affecting the attorney-client privilege when a corporate attorney verifies interrogatories (as recently happened in California), or who has noted a new decision affecting a given class of litigation, could globally insert a note in the electronic narrative of each case that, based on its objective characteristics (judge, jurisdiction, type of law, etc.), should be managed to account for that consideration.

The electronic tracking system can be designed, as with electronic messaging, to prompt the assigned corporate lawyer to review any new input in the electronic record of the case. The system can also be used to "tickle" the attorneys for responses, to identify cases for analysis in which no activity has taken place (or for which no entries have been made) for a specified period of time, or to collect all cases in which queries are pending of or by a given lawyer.

In a decentralized legal and business environment, decentralized litigation management generates many practical risks. For instance, the corporation, through its various semi-autonomous divisions or groups, may take conflicting positions, duplicate effort, or work at cross-purposes. A comprehensive, computerized litigation-tracking system can minimize those risks when the corporate or divisional litigation managers use the system to identify cases that present the opportunity for conflict, duplication, or interference. To get these benefits, corporate lawyers should, as appropriate, have access to the system to edit entries or only to read them.

Again, as with the system for selecting outside counsel, the litigation-tracking system does not replace the lawyer, but provides a forum in which to record and measure the lawyer's judgment. The system is a tool by which not only individual cases, but the entire corporate docket, can be better managed.

Reusable Resource Systems

Private practice firms have long maintained collections of in-house research efforts to expedite and economize the disposition of client matters. Many corporate law departments, of course, do the same. However, computer technology has advanced collection and retrieval efforts light years ahead of the card catalog systems that were unavoidably used for so long. Technology can not only be used to collect and retrieve research, but also in conjunction with other litigation management tools to further a corporation's litigation objectives.

A substantial portion of any corporation's legal budget is expended on legal research. That legal research is conducted both in-house and as part of the counseling and litigation services purchased from outside counsel. As with the reinvention of the wheel, it makes no sense in any respect to pay more than once for the same insight. And if your litigation opponent's research and writing are any good, you can avoid paying (at least directly) even once for good work product. Accordingly, one of the first applications for a corporate law department computer system should be a "reusable resource system" or brief bank. Form 38 in the Appendix shows the input form used in the automated brief bank used by Boise Cascade Corporation.

Some inputs into a brief bank can be completely automated with the use of a full-text retrieval system that is integrated with the legal department word-processing system. Integration means that a document created in the word-processing system can be copied directly into and retrieved directly from a compatible parallel data-processing system. Where the corporation's outside counsel uses a compatible word-processing system, legal research done by outside counsel can be telecommunicated directly to the corporation's brief bank.

Where legal research is obtained from sources or in media that do not permit direct electronic entry into the brief bank, deposits can still be made by abstracting the research and listing key words that will enable any user to identify the research document and retrieve a hard copy from a traditional file. Additionally, the incompatible format research could be scanned electronically by means of an optical character reader, which converts the typed page into electronic input reasonably compatible with your computerized brief bank.

Once the hardware and software are specified for the brief bank and it is in operation, all that remains to the collection effort is for the corporate lawyers to specify the documents that should be entered. This effort should take place when the document is created or received. That is, every valuable piece of research should be immediately tagged for entry into the brief bank.

The use of a brief bank in a corporate legal practice is not confined, of course, to litigation. Nor is the utility of a brief bank in litigation confined to saving time and costs of further research. Rather, the brief bank, if its use is enforced for all corporate litigation managers, represents a source of information about pending and past litigation which improves the management of new litigation.

For instance, the use of a brief bank will identify outside counsel (law firms and individual lawyers) who have expertise in a particular area of law or type of litigation, even if those lawyers are not included in the automated outside-counsel roster. The written product of those outside counsel also provides a basis for evaluating their past performance in relation to the consideration of retention in a new matter. A brief bank can also help with the selection of outside counsel in the same way that a library of expert witness testimony assists in the employment of experts. Specifically, it is wise to avoid retaining outside counsel to advance a position incompatible with one that firm or lawyer has previously taken.

A brief bank also records (along with other things) some history of the corporation's litigation experience. Litigation managers who screen that bank may well be apprised, as they might through the use of the litigation-tracking system, of pending matters where the corporation has taken positions or used techniques that are relevant to the matter at hand. Finally, the brief bank has its more traditional use in litigation, namely of eliminating duplication of effort and costs when the same issue is involved in more than one matter.

Conclusion

Computerized techniques for litigation management in corporate practice are indispensable to the effective and efficient advancement of the corporation's objectives in handling litigation: speedy and positive dispositions. Those techniques can also be used to understand the causes of litigation and minimize their recurrence.

However, no system can realize its potential unless its financial and psychic cost for advancing the management of litigation does not exceed its benefits. For that reason, the litigation management tools the corporation uses should reflect the realities of corporate organization and compensate for realities that may make business sense but do not streamline the management of litigation.

Twenty-Seven

Managing Discovery with Computers

James Keane, Alan Silverman, and Sheila Teisher

Thomas J. Watson, Sr., is generally credited with changing IBM from a small company in upstate New York, which manufactured time clocks and bacon slicers, into one of the most powerful and sophisticated multinational corporations in the world. (Incidentally, its success also made it one of the largest users of legal services in the world.) In the early 1950s, when IBM was about to deliver its first electronic computer, Mr. Watson predicted that the total worldwide market for such machines would not exceed 200. Today, there are probably more than 200 computers being used in each of several law firms. You can buy a small computer at your local department store, and your child can operate it.

These facts are presented here to convince litigators that computers are here to stay, that they have found their place in almost every business and profession in the United States, and that they—like those other modern inventions, the telephone and the copying machine—have a legitimate place in the conduct of litigation. The purpose of this chapter, which focuses on the use of computers to manage discovery in complex litigations, is to attempt to remove some of the mystery surrounding computers, so that lawyers will be more receptive to using them in litigation.

Why Use a Computer

Besides the advantages of using a computer, there are problems with *not* using one.

Problems with Not Using a Computer

Manual Filing Systems

As soon as the volume of documents in a case gets too big to keep in a briefcase or to stack conveniently on your desk, you are faced with a systems design decision. Shall you put the documents in a box or a drawer, or punch holes in them and put them in a binder?

James Keane is President of James Keane Company, Gaithersburg, Maryland. Alan Silverman is a partner with Coopers & Lybrand, San Francisco, California. Sheila Teisher was formerly with Coopers & Lybrand, Los Angeles, California.

Suppose you opt for a filing cabinet. You must now decide on a filing sequence. If you are interested in the chronological development of the facts in the case, you might choose to file the documents in chronological sequence. However, when preparing for the deposition of Mr. Brown, it might be nice to collect all documents written by him. For that reason, you might make a second copy of your chronological set and sort these into alphabetical sequence by author. If you wish to prepare a motion for summary judgment on a specific issue, you would like to collect all documents relating to that issue. This could result in yet a third copy filed in issue sequence.

You now have three times the original number of documents. You have created a space problem, copying costs, and a headache in keeping the three sets synchronized as newly discovered documents are added. Such a system becomes unwieldy with only a few hundred documents.

Card Index Systems

Another popular attempt at solving this problem is to leave the original set of documents in one sequence, and to create several card indexes in the various sequences mentioned. The card usually contains key information, such as date, author, recipient, and subject. In addition, each card might contain an abstract or summary of the document written by a paralegal or an associate. The card index system may work quite well with a modest number of documents, but suffers from the same problem of updating as multiple file cabinets.

A premature indication of the advantage of a computer can be seen by an attempt to find a letter written by Mr. Brown to Mr. Green on July 12, 1985, concerning "pricing." This requires searching four separate card indexes: an author index, recipient index, chronological index, and subject index.

Advantages of Using a Computer

You can think of a computer as being merely an electronic set of card index files. In the example, the computer searches each of the four indexes, compares the results for documents satisfying all four conditions, and presents only the relevant documents for consideration by the attorney.

Some of the advantages of using a computer are:

- *Accuracy*—The search would be done with the unfailing accuracy that only an unthinking machine can produce. No mistakes will be made unless introduced by humans.
- *Completeness*—Instructions will be followed faithfully. No index card will be inadvertently overlooked. Every known document will be considered for selection.

- *Speed*—The search will be done many times faster than a battery of humans could do it. Isn't that why people use computers?
- *Feasibility*—In large cases with complex searches, a computer may provide the only feasible way of finding some documents.
- *Cost-effectiveness*—With the hourly rates for paralegals and attorneys rising almost as fast as the cost of computers is declining, a computer is often the least expensive way of managing your documents. Can you justify billing all that paralegal time to your client if a computer does the job at half the price?

When Is Computer Support Appropriate?

Determining when computer support is appropriate is not a simple task. It is generally agreed that you should consider the characteristics of the data, the characteristics of the attorneys and their organization, and the characteristics of the case.

Characteristics of the Data

Number of Documents

The threshold number of documents was once quoted as 5000, but if the law firm has a microcomputer, some kind of computer support might be justified with as few as 100 documents.

Types of Documents

If most of the documents are blueprints or engineering drawings, as in a construction dispute or patent case, there may be little value in using a computer to index them, unless they are first abstracted. Similarly, if the bulk of the documents are complex financial schedules which must each be analyzed by an accountant to calculate damages, then what is the advantage of indexing them? But if a substantial proportion of the documents are from the correspondence files of key executives and might prove liability in a conspiracy case, then a computer index could be invaluable.

Potential Use of Documents

In preparing for depositions or filing pretrial motions, a computer index can be a great help. This help is accentuated in trial, where the preparation time is reduced and the cross-examination takes unexpected turns.

Computer-Originated Evidence

Most companies involved in business litigation have their business records on a computer. A discovery demand for the accounts receivable file may produce a magnetic tape or disk in response. This material is ideal for indexing in a computer; in fact, most of the work has been done for you.

Characteristics of the Attorneys

Willingness to Plan and Manage

Computers are much fonder of systematic planning than most trial attorneys. To make good use of a computer, you must start planning before discovery starts. If the key lawyers are unwilling to plan, don't waste your client's money on using a computer system.

The lawyers must also devote the time and effort to manage the implementation of the system. Vendors, consultants, or clients' staff can help, but the final responsibility must rest with the trial attorney.

Number of Attorneys Involved

The more attorneys there are working on the case, the more essential it is to have a well-organized central file index of documents. A computer system can enforce this discipline and provide a common base of material for all lawyers. If one lawyer takes a key document home, the computer will still allow others to be aware of its existence.

Life Span of the Case

The longer a case lasts, the greater the turnover in legal, paralegal, and clerical staff, and the greater the need for a well-organized document system that is independent of the quirks and whims of individuals. A document index understood only by a former paralegal who is now in the Peace Corps in Namibia will not help at trial. A computer system can provide a consistent and reliable means of passing case knowledge from one generation of attorneys to the next.

Number of Working Locations

By means of computer terminals linked by telephone lines, attorneys in widely separated locations can have access to the same computer index of documents. Without this, indexes would have to be reproduced in each location. Naturally, the documents themselves cannot be available simultaneously in all locations unless they are reproduced on paper or microfilm.

Characteristics of the Case

Complexity of Issues

The more complex the issues, the more potentially relevant facts might appear in any document, and so the more need for indexing. The more people involved, the greater the need to cross-index documents.

Likelihood of Settlement

If a case might settle easily, it might not be worth the significant initial expense to implement the computer system. However, don't wait until the eve of trial to make that decision.

Amount of Money at Risk

The amount of money at risk must justify the initial expense for the system. However, a simple microcomputer system can cost little enough to be used in small to moderate-sized cases solely on the basis of increased productivity and efficiency.

Some Examples

Examples of some types of cases where computers have proved useful include breach of contract, securities litigation, construction disputes, product liability, wrongful termination, patents and trade secrets, and aircraft crashes.

Types of Computer Litigation Systems

Use of Smaller Computers

Litigation can be supported with microcomputers of the type often found even in the smallest law firm. Even word-processing equipment can provide some rudimentary support.

Simple Coding

One of the first myths to be exploded is that computers in some way obviate the necessity for someone to read the documents. The computer only knows as much about the document as it is told by someone who has read it. The advantage is that, with careful control and instructions, the reading can be delegated to nonlawyers, who will capture key information for the computer. The computer can then make available only the selected documents for detailed review by an attorney.

In a simple case, the coders could be given a list of key names and subjects and asked to transcribe information from the document to a simple coding form, such as the one shown in Form 40.

Various Sequence Listings

The coded information can then be fed into a computer and sorted into various sequences. (See Forms 43 and 46.) When sorted, it can be printed in listings or catalogs of the type found in libraries. Possible sequences are:

- Alphabetically by author
- Alphabetically by subject
- Chronologically

These listings typically refer to a "document number." This is merely a sequential number assigned to each document before entry into the computer system, by which the computer can identify unique documents. It is often helpful to keep the physical collection of documents in this numeric sequence in filing cabinets and use the index listings to find them, rather than keep them in chronological sequence.

Minimum Size of Case

With the availability of computer equipment in many law firms, it is possible to justify a simple listing system when you have 500 relevant documents in a single case, and perhaps fewer if you have adopted routine procedures for automated document control.

Limitations of Listings

The listings are merely computer-produced logical equivalents of the card index files discussed earlier. They are more accurate, more complete, more easily reorganized, and more reliable, yet they suffer from the same limitation of becoming unwieldy when you get too many documents. If several lawyers are working in different locations, the problem of updating and distributing several copies of the listings becomes significant.

The listings are also limited in the amount of information they contain. It may not be sufficient for a complex case. Microcomputer programs called filing systems or database management systems (DBMS) are well suited for these types of listings. Most of them even permit some text searching at the computer, though this may become painfully slow as the size of the document collection grows.

Inverted File Retrieval Systems

The next step up in the organization and indexing of documents is the use of an "inverted file" retrieval system. Most of the literature is written about this kind of system, and most of the support vendors offer this kind of support. There are new microcomputer programs especially designed for text management that perform many of the functions that were once available only on larger computers.

What Are They?

In the small computer systems previously discussed, only limited information about a document is captured and sorted in various ways to produce the listings. Access to the documents is by visual inspection of the listings. In a more sophisticated system, more information concerning each document can be captured. This is a function of the larger storage capacity of the computer, the sophistication of the coding operation, and the power of the computer software.

This more detailed information is stored permanently (at least for the life of the case) and is available instantaneously to any qualified person, with appropriate security checks, by means of a computer. The visual inspection of the several lists referred to earlier is done automatically by the computer, and the results of the comparisons of the various listings are presented to the attorney at the computer.

How Do They Work?

Key information from each document is transposed to a coding form and is then transformed into a machine-readable form. The computer then "reads" this information and creates an index, recording the fact that the significant words that have been coded are present in that document.

The computer thus creates two separate files. The first file contains the significant coded information from each document, and this file is in document number sequence. The second file is an alphabetical list of all significant words that appear in any of the documents, together with an indication of the document numbers where the word appears. (See the internal computer indexes in Form 46.) Thus, the second file (or index file) is a cross-reference index to the first file (or document text file).

Consider the search for a letter written by Mr. Brown to Mr. Green on July 12, 1985, concerning pricing. The computer searches the index file and finds that Mr. Brown is mentioned in document numbers:

1257, 1702, 1971, 1694, 1943, 2106

However, the computer could also determine (because this was coded) that Mr. Brown was the author of a more limited list of documents:

1257, 1943, 1971, 2106

A further search of the index file could show that Mr. Green was the addressee of documents numbered:

1157, 1257, 1971, 1943, 1652, 1432, 2354, 2572

The computer then compares these two lists of numbers and determines that the only documents written by Mr. Brown and addressed to Mr. Green are numbered:

1257, 1971, 1943

Adding the additional criteria of date and subject will cause the computer to perform further searches of the index file to find that documents dated July 12, 1985, are numbered:

0936, 1257, 1163, 1943

Also, documents mentioning "pricing" are numbered:

0627, 0794, 1172, 1943

By comparing these lists of document numbers (almost instantaneously), the computer can determine that the only document satisfying all four conditions is document number 1943.

There are many more sophisticated features of most of the software packages used for this application, but this example describes the principle by which the searching is done.

Full Text versus Key Word versus Abstract

One debate that has been raging since the early use of computers in litigation is over merits of putting the full text of a document into the computer, or just some key bibliographic and subject words. In either case, the debate eventually raises the question of including an abstract or summary of the document prepared by a lawyer or paralegal. Full-text systems have the obvious advantage of capturing every word in the document, although to conserve on space, most of these systems exclude "if," "and," "but," and other such common words to keep them from clogging up the electronic indexes.

Another advantage is the virtual elimination of the intellectual part of the coding effort, since no decisions have to be made concerning the important words. You simply feed all words into the computer. Some types of information may be fed directly into the computer without further human intervention, e.g., deposition or trial transcripts.

The elimination of the intellectual decisions from the coding operation is also one of the biggest disadvantages in a full-text system. It is this attorney thought process that makes the strongest argument for work-product protection. In *In Re IBM Peripherals EDP Devices Anti-Trust Litigation,*[1] IBM put forward this argument to protect the privilege of its "key-word" system. The court agreed.

Another former disadvantage of full-text systems is becoming less significant. It basically trades the cost of a more discriminating coding operation at the front end against the cost of storing more information in the computer for the life of the case. As the cost of computer storage comes down and the labor cost of coding goes up, this balance tends to tip in the direction of full-text. The cost of data entry can still make the full-text system expensive, but "smart" optical scanning devices, digital image scanning and laser disk technology, direct data-entry techniques, and computer-assisted transcription may yet make full-text systems cheaper and increasingly attractive.

It is also possible to use a hybrid system. For example, one might use a key-word system and still carry important sections of a document in full text.

Some trial lawyers will demand abstracts or digests with great vehemence. They wish to include their analyses of the key documents in the system. The problem, in a large case, is how to identify key documents until you have them in the system. One can return to these later and enhance the computer record with an abstract as an aide-mémoire as well as a tool to display the distillation of long documents or lengthy excerpts of transcripts. (See sample in Form 46.)

The most effective retrieval strategy, but alas the most expensive, is a combination of indexing, abstracts, and full text.

Steps in the Implementation of a System

Planning Before Discovery Starts

Most cases settle before trial, so why start planning until just before trial and settlement negotiations have broken down? Unfortunately, it takes several months to implement a computer system for litigation support, and the trial attorney and client have to weigh this along with all the other factors when deciding how much money to spend before trial. A well-prepared attorney is usually in a better position to negotiate a favorable settlement, and a well-prepared computer system can enhance that process.

To implement a good computer system, you must capture some information at the discovery site. This is invaluable later when arguing for or against the admission of a document. Such information as production date and location, receptacle number and description, and department and file folder title can be captured by use of a microfilm "target sheet" (Form 39) or a "production source log" (Form 47) or a "file inventory" (Form 42). This information is fed into the computer (see Form 42) and listed in various sequences (Form 43).

Design

The most important phase in the implementation is the design phase. It is at this time that the trial attorney states what the system should do. Although the attorney can get technical help from vendors and consultants, the fundamental decisions cannot be delegated. The value of an expert at this stage is to ask the attorney the kinds of questions that need to be addressed.

Examples of such questions are:

- What types of documents?
- How many of each type?
- Can we cut the volume by gross selection?
- What are the key issues?
- Can we identify key names?
- Do we need special treatment of some documents, e.g., diaries, engineering drawings, invoices?
- How will depositions be handled?
- What about deposition exhibits?

These are just some of a myriad of questions that must be asked and answered before moving on to the detailed design, selection of computer, and development of coding procedures. An attorney with no prior experience in this area might save countless hours and dollars by getting expert help to ensure that all the appropriate questions have been answered.

Training in data processing is not enough. It is also essential to have practical experience in applying data processing to litigation.

Coding

Once all the design questions have been answered, it is possible to choose a computer system and then design a coding form. Coding is the most labor-intensive and, therefore, the most expensive part of the whole operation.

To understand the coding operation, it might be useful to look at a sample coding form such as the one provided as Form 44 in the Appendix. This coding form, or "Document Information Sheet," contains more detail than is required in many systems. It shows the use of a combination of key words, extracts of full text, and summaries or abstracts.

Coding can be divided into a series of steps. Administrative staff can code bibliographic and file description data. They may process ten to fifteen documents per hour. Paralegal or technical staff can read, understand, and code the substance of the documents. Their pace is more likely to be two to five documents per hour.

The coding operation is usually the critical path that controls the flow of documents into the computer. It is here that information from the original document is placed in a form acceptable to the computer. It is here that the quality of the entire system will rise or fall. This coding form must be well designed and implement the attorney's trial objectives.

The coding operation itself must be well managed and staffed with intelligent and well-trained coders. Quality control checks must be placed in the coding pipeline. This work can be boring, and boredom breeds errors. Innovative techniques for managing coders must be devised to maintain interest and quality. The greatest cost in the system is here, and most disappointment in the use of systems can be traced to poor design, poor coding, or poor quality control.

Data Entry

Having coded the information from each document, the next step is to convert this information into a machine-readable form. Unless the coders are keying information directly, this has historically been done by keying the coding sheet information into a computer medium such as a diskette or tape.

Although reasonably mechanical, this step requires tight controls and should be entrusted to experienced professionals.

File Loading, Storage, and Updating

With the information in machine-readable form, it can now be fed into the computer. This process of "file loading" also includes several "editing" steps. The computer is able to check the spelling of names against a previously approved list and ask if the new spelling is correct. It can check for the "reasonableness" of information. For example, are all the dates in numeric form?

The computer then takes the information about the document and stores it in its main file. At the same time, it takes the key words and stores them in the "electronic card index." This information is now available to all approved users of the system.

Information can be added to the file as more documents are discovered, or information can be added to an individual document record. For example, an attorney summary of a key document could be added, or a notation to indicate that this document has been used as a deposition exhibit.

Design Considerations

The design of the system is the most important phase, for it is here that the attorney has the opportunity to tailor the proposed system exactly. This requires some prior knowledge of litigation support systems. Attorneys that have this prior experience, or have access to it with their client's staff, can select a vendor and work with the vendor to design their system. Attorneys without prior experience may need some preliminary help before selecting a vendor.

A solution to this chicken-and-egg dilemma is to work with a consultant familiar with litigation support requirements and familiar with the services available from the vendors. By acting as an "interpreter" between the lawyer and the design process, the consultant can help assure the lawyer that the fundamental design questions have been addressed, and that the proposed system is feasible. They can further assist the lawyer in evaluating the capabilities of qualified vendors, and in estimating the cost of implementing the system.

Types of Documents

One of the first steps in systems design is to attempt to understand the volume and types of documents produced in discovery. Estimates of volume are difficult in the early stages of a case, but attempts should be made to produce estimates that are accurate within an order of magnitude (e.g., will there be 1000, 10,000, 100,000, or 1,000,000 documents?).

For some types of documents, detailed indexing of the contents will mean little. It may be enough for the computer merely to indicate their existence and their title. Examples of such documents might include blueprints, engineering drawings, detailed financial work papers, and instruction manuals. These may be valuable documents, but their value normally cannot be revealed by simple coding; they need to be analyzed by experts. The results of this analysis could be included in the "Abstract" or "Comment" section of the computer record, for example:

> TITLE: Cross-Section of Flange and Hub
>
> COMMENT: The design of the hub shows that this drawing must have been copied from the European implementation, not the American implementation.

See sample records in Form 46.

Correspondence files, minutes of meetings, expense reports, diaries, and other similar documents are usually worthy of coding, in either keyword, full-text, or some combined format. Not every document discovered should be put into the computer system. The trial attorney must define the priorities. These priorities are often dictated by the pending schedule of depositions.

You are usually faced with a trade-off of which documents to put into the computer first—your own documents or those produced by your adversary. If you are a plaintiff, particularly one not facing a counterclaim, you would almost certainly choose to concentrate on documents produced by the defendant. For the same reason, the defendant may choose to concentrate on its own documents. However, if the defendant is aggressively presenting an affirmative defense through depositions, it will be valuable to have the plaintiff's documents in the computer.

Remember, coding is usually the bottleneck in the operation, so you must pay careful attention to the changing priorities of documents in the pipeline as deposition schedules and case strategy change.

Transcripts

Deposition transcripts form an integral part of the evidence to be considered at trial, and also for the preparation of pretrial motions and subsequent depositions. It is helpful to have the deposition transcripts in the computer system in full text. This can be done by rekeying the transcripts, using optical scanning devices, transferring the text from the court reporter's word-processing machines or from their computer-assisted transcription devices.

Computer-Assisted Transcription (CAT)

Court reporting systems now routinely produce a "machine-readable" transcript as a by-product of the normal recording process. A special attachment to the court reporter's machine can produce a magnetic cassette or disk that can be fed directly into a computer. If the deposition site is remote from the computer and time is of the essence, then the "magnetic transcript" can be fed into the computer over telephone lines. Once in the computer, the transcript can be searched for key words just as the collection of documents can.

Enhanced Transcripts

It is also possible to use the computer to "enhance" the transcript and so make it more useful for computer searching. As an example, a line of questioning may concern a meeting between the witness and Mr. Brown, which allegedly occurred on June 23, 1986. After several pages of questioning, the witness may start referring to John Brown as "John" or "Jack" and to the date as "the following Monday" or "three days later." When asking the computer system to find any transcript pages where the witness referred to John Brown or a meeting on June 23, 1986, we humans must give the computer some help by "enhancing" the computer record and supplementing the references to "Jack," "John," and "three days later" by a proper name and actual dates.

Hearing and Trial Transcripts

Deposition transcripts are not the only transcripts that might be indexed in a computer. Trial transcripts and the transcripts of pretrial hearings should also be considered, especially in a case involving many pretrial motions, where the prior positions taken by the court and opposing counsel are key to arguing a later motion.

Exhibits

When putting transcripts into a computer, one is immediately faced with the question of what to do with deposition exhibits. Usually these exhibits will be documents produced in the discovery process and will already be in the document file in the computer. If this is the case, you will need "two-way" indexing. It is necessary to indicate that exhibit number 5 to the Jones deposition is, in fact, document number 1234 in the computer file of produced documents. It is also desirable for the computer record of document number 1234 to show that it was used as Jones deposition exhibit number 5.

A natural outcome of this two-way indexing is the creation of a third file, in addition to the document file and the deposition transcript file. This third file is a file of deposition exhibits. The relationship among the three files is illustrated in the accompanying diagram on page 366, and these files may be linked to the trial exhibit number.

Use at Trial

The most neglected part of the design of computer systems for litigation support is in the support required at trial. Since so many cases never reach trial, this weakness is rarely revealed.

In addition to specific design criteria, there are "environmental" considerations. Among these are:

- The trial site may be remote from the lawyer's and client's hometown.
- The response time required to react to questions is much shorter.
- Most work must be done outside normal working hours.

One major use of a computer system at trial is to argue for or against the admission of documents. If the computer system has been properly designed and implemented, then it should be possible to assemble an "objection book" for each of your opponent's proposed trial exhibits. This objection book might contain the following information about the proposed exhibits:

- When and where produced
- Other versions of the same document
- "Surrounding" documents, e.g., replies or attachments
- Any use of the documents as a deposition exhibit, along with the relevant transcript pages

With this kind of ammunition, a lawyer can be better prepared to argue the admissibility of the proposed exhibits.

Other uses for a computer at trial include the indexing of the trial transcripts and exhibits in a manner similar to that described for deposition exhibits. The computer can also be used to produce listings of exhibits offered and admitted, including rulings on objections.

Relationship among Files Containing Deposition Exhibits

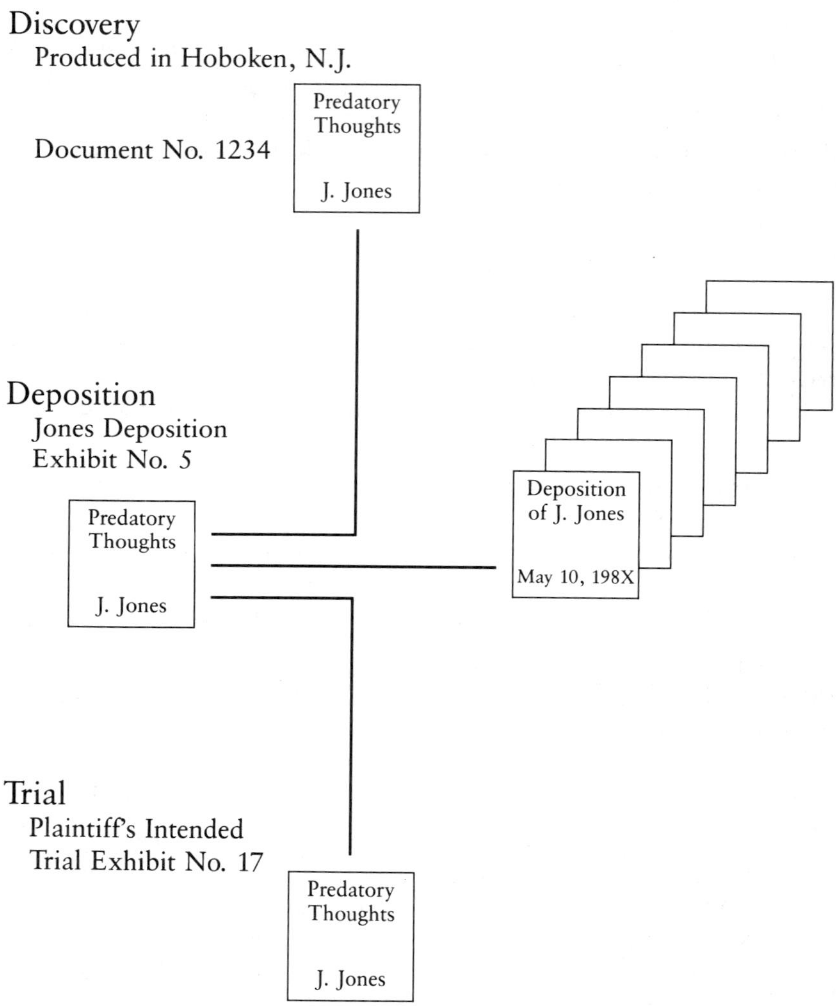

The indexing and analysis of the trial transcript can enable the trial lawyer to collect all testimony relating to a particular subject or issue. In addition to its value as a cross-examination device, it is valuable in preparing motions for summary judgment, for directed verdicts, or for preparing proposed findings of fact in a judge-tried case. Evidence tends to be entered in sequence by witness, but arguments tend to be made in sequence by subject. The computer merely resequences the evidence quickly and accurately.

Cost Considerations

Who Does the Design?

We have already emphasized the absolute necessity for the trial lawyer to be deeply involved in the design process, and the value of a consultant or experienced vendor at this stage. They can minimize the time demands on the lawyer.

This is not the phase of implementation in which to cut corners. False economies here will translate to increased costs later. If done properly, the design will not have to be redone, and will minimize the cost of the other steps. See the data structure sample in Form 45.

Who Does the Coding?

Most litigation support vendors will run the coding operation for you. They are experienced in doing so and have the management structure to ensure adequate supervision and quality control. Of course, they are in business to make a profit on the time of their people, and so this can be an expensive way to go.

A more expensive, and probably less efficient, alternative is to use lawyers or paralegals to do the coding. One of the benefits of the litigation system is removing the burden of reading every single document from the lawyers and then using the computer to retrieve only relevant documents when the lawyer need them. If lawyers do the coding, this advantage is lost. We have heard lawyers argue that the quality of the coding would be higher. That claim is open to question, particularly since few busy trial lawyers will spend eight hours a day filling out document-coding forms.

A trained and seasoned paralegal can compose excellent document summaries and deposition digests, but paralegals usually have much higher billing rates than document analysts used by vendors. Unless the paralegals are extremely skilled and experienced in document coding, the extra expense is hard to justify for a large and diffuse document collection. However, using them to code key documents and important depositions can enhance their knowledge of the case, as well as the lawyer's confidence that the most essential coding was done by a trusted aide.

A third alternative, which combines some of the benefits of each approach is to set up the coding operation under the management of the law firm, with the day-to-day operations managed by a paralegal with appropriate experience or by a qualified consultant. The law firm recruits, trains, and manages the coders in the same way as a vendor manages their operations, but there is no vendor's overhead and profit added to the hourly rate. The closer supervision by the law firm can be valuable.

There is no single best solution. The choice among the alternatives will be strongly influenced by the philosophy of the trial lawyer, the firm's experience, and the budget and time available.

Whose Computer to Use?

The Client's?

In deciding whose computer to use, the least expensive alternative may be the client's computer. If there is spare capacity, then the computer time is "free." There may be an internal transfer of charges, but the net outflow of cash for computer time will only be increased if there are overtime charges for the machine and staff.

One immediate consideration is the question of whether a litigation support software package (i.e., a computer program) is available for the make of machine used by your client. There is also the question of size. A sophisticated on-line litigation support system, doing all the things described in this chapter, uses a lot of computer capacity. The computer software vendors can tell you whether their software will fit the client's machine. If it "almost" fits, it may be worth having your client enlarge its installation.

Even if the software and size of the computer are right and the client has the staff competent enough to implement the software, there is the question of availability and priority. If your client uses its computer for an on-line order-processing application, and the spare capacity offered is from 2:00 A.M. to 4:00 A.M. every other Friday, it may be difficult for you to use this help. If the time available is more ample and convenient, still beware of priorities. Suppose the union payroll has to be run just when you are preparing to cross-examine a key witness?

Some very large corporations are providing litigation support services for inside and outside counsel, and have developed considerable expertise in doing so. If your client is not one of these, you may find it difficult to communicate your requirements to the client's data-processing personnel, and inside counsel may not be able to help much. This is another place where an experienced consultant can be of value.

Another major consideration in the use of the client's system is the preservation of work-product privilege. Many companies have solved this problem to the satisfaction of their lawyers, but it does require special consideration. For a more detailed discussion of this issue, see Chapter 29.

The Law Firm's?

Many law firms have computers large enough for large and sophisticated litigation support systems. With the advent of microcomputers, it is possible for a firm of any size to handle small and moderate-sized cases ranging from 500 to 5000 documents. This can still require a significant investment in hardware and training, and should not be undertaken casually or by assigning it, without controls or supervision, to an inexperienced paralegal.

An Outside Vendor's?

Litigation support vendors are in the business of providing computer support for litigators. They have the machines, the people, and the organization to do so. Although they are in business to make a profit by selling their facilities and skill, the individual trial lawyer is sharing the cost of the system with other lawyers on other cases. (Vendors will check for potential conflicts of interest so that they don't work on both sides of the same case.)

Because of their expertise and tested facilities, it is usually faster to implement a system using a vendor. Their computer is dedicated to litigation support, so there is no question of competing for priority. The selection of a particular vendor involves consideration of the design objectives along with the technical capabilities, experience, and cost of the vendor. This is an important decision.

Dollars and Sense

No matter what system you use, automated or manual, the base cost is the time to read a document at some hourly rate. The computer may add some incremental cost to this process, but will probably save costs by making the lawyers more efficient.

We know of one case where the lawyers were proud of having tried a large document case without a computer. A post mortem revealed that they had spent $12,000 of paralegal time just sorting documents. For that price they could have bought a microcomputer and had $7,000 left over. Law firms can spread costs across many cases and recoup the investment by direct charges to clients for coding and computer usage.

Note

1. MDL 163-RM (N.D. Cal. 1975), 5 COMPUTER L. SERV. 878.

Twenty-Eight

When Computer Support Is Appropriate: An Attorney's Perspective

Kenneth J. Moran and William H. King, Jr.

The past two decades have witnessed dramatic changes in the litigation "environment." New theories of recovery, consumer awareness, ever-increasing jury verdicts, and other trends have made us into the most litigious society in the world. At the same time, changes in the rules governing discovery and evidence have multiplied the volume of information to be assimilated for trial and have increased the time and expense of litigation. As a result, today's attorney must not only possess the traditional legal acumen, but must be an efficient information manager.

Today's trial lawyer is faced with the problem of effectively managing and assimilating a large volume of complex information in a high-stakes environment. As legal costs spiral, the problem is compounded by tighter corporate litigation budgets and the need to exercise cost control. Modern corporate litigation requires a systematic approach in which automation may play a pivotal role through the use of automated litigation support systems.

The American Bar Association has defined an automated litigation support system (ALSS) as "any operation combining men, machines, and methods for processing information for use by attorneys or expert consultants in preparation for and trial of a lawsuit."[1] Stated otherwise, an ALSS involves the use of computers in a team environment to store, analyze, sort, and retrieve selected information for use in discovery or trial or in managing multicase litigation. The "team" may merely consist of the lawyer and his or her secretary creating a small database on a personal computer. In larger or more sophisticated applications, it may involve attorneys, paralegals, in-house data-processing personnel or outside consultants, document coders, and data-entry clerks.

The most familiar ALSS is the document management system. This system uses a computer and database management software to store and retrieve document-based information. While the same principles can be

Kenneth J. Moran and William H. King, Jr., are members of the firm of McGuire, Woods, Battle & Boothe, Richmond, Virginia.

used for docket or case control, complex damage analyses, and budget projections, the focus here will be on document management.

Document Management

Whether a manual or automated system is involved, document management requires a *system.* Nothing is more embarrassing than trying to find a particular exhibit for cross-examination in a pile of papers in a courtroom or at a deposition. Nothing is more frustrating in pretrial preparation than wasting hours finding a particular document or series of related documents. Prevention of these problems begins with a carefully designed approach to document management that can be used with *either* a manual or an automated system.

Design Considerations

The first step in the design of any document system is analyzing the case and understanding the issues and problems it presents:

- What are the prima facie elements necessary to recovery?
- What defenses are available or likely to be used?
- What is the potential exposure and the likelihood of success?
- What is the anticipated cost of the litigation, and what type of budget is involved?
- How many documents will be involved, and what is their importance to the overall case?
- Who are likely to be the key witnesses?
- What staff and equipment are available?
- How much time is available to prepare the case for trial?

The answer to these and other questions often will dictate the type of system to be used.

Document Control

One of the most important but difficult tasks is collecting potentially relevant documents from within the corporation. The task is compounded if many far-flung offices or divisions are involved. This aspect of document management is worth a tome in itself. Suffice it to say, counsel must document the collection activity from initial site interviews to receipt of the documents at a central collection point. The initial "general counsel's letter," search requests, inventory logs, shipping documents, and collection procedures should be retained to verify the scope and responsiveness of the effort. As discussed later in this chapter, computerization, either as part of an overall document system or as a stand-alone system, can assist in these tasks.

The next step is to keep track of the documents obtained so that they can be used and produced in discovery in an orderly manner. Each page of a document should be numbered using a Bates stamp, computer-generated label, or other method. The numbering system may be a simple sequence or a complex "code" indicating producing party, original source, etc. Numbering each page identifies the document in terms of its content and length, thereby precluding future arguments regarding "missing" pages.

If the producing party has numbered its documents, that number may be sufficient for control purposes. The parties may even agree to a common numbering scheme in advance. They can refer to a given document by its number throughout depositions and trial, and even on appeal. This prevents confusion and simplifies exhibit identification during depositions.

Since documents get misplaced or worn with use, the original documents should be numbered and copied. The copies form a "master" set. The originals are then stored as the ultimate archive or fail-safe. Work copies of documents are made from the master set. Frequent use of documents may make microfilm or microfiche desirable. Recent advances in digitalized copying may make this a cost-effective alternative for long-term storage of large document collections.

Document Coding

The next step is to extract relevant information from the individual documents. It would be needlessly time-consuming to have to read and reread each one to determine its relevance or potential use at various points in the trial. Therefore, documents are analyzed and coded using a digest sheet adapted to the issues in the particular case. This form, which may be as simple or detailed as necessary, is used to select documents for potential deposition or trial exhibits.

Form 48 in the Appendix shows a simple digest form. It captures or codes control information (document number, source, type, etc.), bibliographic information (subject, date, author, etc.), key issues or subjects, and a "free text" summary of the contents. The form is designed so that a paralegal or secretary can use it, freeing the attorney from the time-consuming task of document review.

This single form is copied as necessary and filed in lieu of the original document, which may contain many pages and attachments. Separate files can be maintained on potential witnesses, issues, subject matters, etc. These files can be reviewed when necessary, and the required documents selected from the coding forms.

The Decision to Computerize

The preceding discussion suggests a simple approach to document management, whether the system is manual or automated. *Not every case warrants a computerized document system with its associated costs and time requirements!* Rather, the decision to computerize requires a careful cost/benefit analysis.

Advantages

Properly designed and used, an ALSS offers the advantages generally associated with automated data processing: speed, reliability, flexibility, and long-term cost savings.

Speed and Reliability

The creation of a database and some method of digesting are essential elements of any document management system. Once these have been accomplished, it is easy to see how automation can minimize document searches and retrieval time. Where the document base is large and complex, where multiple issues are involved, or where document patterns are important, processing speed may be critical. In the same vein, a computer does *not* think and cannot make subjective errors. If the documents have been coded or indexed accurately, the retrieval will be accurate and complete the first time.

Flexibility

Once computerized, the database becomes "portable." Machine-stored information can be accessed from remote locations using modems, and the microfilm document file can be used to generate hard copy. Therefore, the entire system becomes accessible to the attorney in the office, at depositions, and at trial.

The types of document retrieval are virtually limitless. Documents can be sorted and resorted by a variety of fields such as date, subject, author, and key phrases. Supplementary reports on how the documents are used in litigation also can be generated, and document usage can be tracked from case to case.

Long-Term Cost

While a manual system may be cheaper to design and implement initially, its use is labor-intensive. Conversely, an automated system reduces the cost of maintenance and use. It has been estimated, for example, that once an ALSS has been installed, operation and maintenance amount to only 10–15 percent of the expense of the system over its life.[2] In addition, an automated system reduces the size of the staff and the time required to handle documents. This can affect the personnel problem of dealing with a large litigation team when a case has been concluded.

The Decision-Making Process

The question of when to computerize does not lend itself to a simple answer. While cost is an important consideration, a number of factors need to be addressed. Many of the factors suggested with regard to a manual system are equally relevant to this cost/benefit analysis. Futhermore, the decision is not just the trial counsel's, but should involve the client, in-house counsel, outside consultants, etc.

Cost

An ALSS can be an expensive undertaking. At one time, for example, it was estimated that the minimum cost of an automated document management system was $75,000, and that the cost per document would range between $3 and $13.[3] Recent advances in available software and other technologies may reduce these costs. Naturally, the cost of an ALSS grows proportionately to the size and sophistication of the application. Much of the cost is related to personnel for document coding and data entry. These costs remain relatively fixed even as the cost of hardware and software decreases.

An ALSS characteristically has higher start-up costs than a manual system. Document analysis and coding may amount to 44 percent of the total price of the system, with data entry constituting an additional 20 percent.[4] A given system may have its own special costs, such as the need for remote terminals, trial support (portable terminals, microfilm reader, etc.), ongoing programming for expanded or unanticipated uses, and periodic training and retraining.

At the same time, however, the cost of computer technology (hardware and software) has tended to decrease. Thus, automated document management systems are no longer the domain of large firms or clients with a mainframe computer or cases with 10,000 documents or more. Small document bases can be effectively handled through the use of personal computers and off-the-shelf software. Readily available database management software often can be tailored for specific document applications. Some vendors advertise prepackaged document system software for smaller databases for less than $2000.

In addition, costs may be reduced in a number of ways:

- Through the use of in-house legal and corporate data-processing resources, including hardware, systems managers, programmers, data-entry personnel, and in-house paralegals
- Through the use of prepackaged software

- Through the use of service bureaus and time-sharing for data processing

The cost/benefit analysis should consider the entire life of the system, as well as its application in future litigation. If access to documents will be required over a five- or ten-year period, the initial costs may be amortized through reduced personnel and/or facility costs.

Exposure

The cost of the system should be weighed against the potential exposure involved in the litigation, including the exposure to punitive damages. This requires a careful analysis of the litigation: Are multiple suits involved? Are multidistrict procedures imposed? What is the potential for class actions, shareholder suits, or concurrent government actions? Will "special" legal factors such as collateral estoppel and indemnity increase the ultimate exposure? Finally, is the client self-insured?

Time

An ALSS requires *adequate* time for document collection, system design ("taxonomy"), hiring, training, and installation. One observer has noted:

> An ALS system has unique characteristics: little time for planning, design and start-up; rapid hiring and training of project staff; exceptionally high requirements for learning among all participants, combined with very little time for learning; the necessity for integrating disparate functions on the run; oppressive deadlines; and a heterogeneous collection of documents to be classified and indexed.[5]

Like any data-processing application, a document system requires time for proper design and the creation of an accurate database. Otherwise, it is "garbage in, garbage out." If adequate time is not available, the system may be expensively useless.

While requirements vary from system to system, document coding and data entry typically consume the greatest amount of time. In a recent national product liability case, for example, three million pages of documents were processed by 150 coders in a six-month period working six days per week. While that may not be typical, the complexity of the documents can add to the requisite coding time as well as the skill required by the document coder.

In analyzing the time component, the following questions should be addressed:

- How much lead time is available, and when are the likely discovery cutoff and trial dates?
- If there is little lead time, can the document tasks be separated using computerization for part of the requirements?

- If in-house (client) resources are used, what is the competition for those resources, and will the law department be given priority?
- What are the prospects for a quick settlement?
- How much travel time will be required?

The Database

Does the size and/or complexity of the database warrant the expense of automation? Historically 5000 to 10,000 documents have been used as a rule of thumb as the cost-effective threshold for an ALSS.[6] However, the advent of personal computers and more sophisticated word-processing systems has greatly reduced that number. Computers can now be used to effectively handle as few as 500 documents.

The types of documents involved and their potential use frequently is more important than numbers. If the document base consists of blueprints, engineering drawings, or complex financial or testing records, there may be little advantage to attempting to index and abstract them. Conversely, internal memoranda, reports, and correspondence may make an automated system invaluable. Again, this analysis should be forward-looking, since the database will grow over time as new types of documents become relevant or assume greater importance.

Additional considerations include the following questions:

- Are document "patterns," such as by author or chronology, important?
- Is there a need to access, identify, and produce documents periodically?
- Will the same set or subsets of documents be produced in multiple discovery responses?
- Is the database fairly complete initially, or must additional documents be located and added over time?
- What is the availability of personnel and time for manual searches and retrievals?

Summary

The foregoing considerations are not all-inclusive, and each lawsuit or application undoubtedly will produce its own unique considerations. The cost/benefit analysis is not static and should be based over the entire life of the litigation in terms of start-up expenses, projected uses, changing personnel, and exposure. Therefore, the client and corporate counsel ultimately may be in the best position to decide whether to automate.

System Design and Installation

Preliminary Review

Once a tentative decision has been made to computerize a document management system, detailed analysis and review are required to define the potential database, the uses of the system, and the personnel requirements. This preliminary review should be conducted by attorneys familiar with the litigation and the client. The assistance of a data-processing consultant may be necessary. Proper initial design will avoid the expense and inconvenience of later changes. As described later, attorney input at this stage may protect the system from future discovery.

Sources of Documents

For the corporate defendant, the major source of documents will be intracompany files. These may include inter- and intracompany correspondence and memoranda, board of directors' minutes, development and testing records, production records, quality assurance files, financial records, and perhaps claims and lawsuits. However, documents from outside the company may also prove relevant, and portions of treatises, industry standards, and government reports may be added to the database. As the litigation proceeds, documents produced by other parties, deposition exhibits and/or testimony, and trial exhibits may be incorporated as well.

Document collection logs and "selected" office files should be reviewed to determine the type of documents involved, their potential relevance to the litigation, and the magnitude of the task. This review should include an estimate of the ultimate number of documents to be coded and their location, the identification of key witnesses and employees, and the type and form of the documents' contents. Consideration should be given to a method of handling documents that are currently being used in company operations.

As suggested previously, document collection frequently becomes difficult in a corporate setting. A simple database can be created to help keep track of documents as they are received, numbered, copied, and reviewed. A computer record such as the one in Form 49 is created for each file or box of documents. The database can be used to project personnel and time requirements, and it preserves an audit trail for the collection process if there are future discovery disputes.

Full Text versus Abstracting

Full Text

The increased processing speed of the latest computers and the large amounts of memory available have resurrected the debate over full text versus document abstracting (coding). Each has its own advantages and costs.

In a full-text system, the entire contents of a document are placed into the database in machine-readable form. Some records such as claim summaries, testing data, project reports, and budget information may already be in this format stored on disk or magnetic tape. However, most company records, particularly correspondence and memoranda, are not, and will have to be "formatted" and retyped by data-entry personnel.

Full text offers the advantage of content accuracy, eliminating judgmental errors by the document coder. However, data-entry, computer storage, and retrieval time are increased, thereby increasing the overall cost of the system. Furthermore, the full-text approach relies less on attorney input and may subject the system to discovery.

Document Coding

To counter these problems, most document systems use the "abstract" or "indexing" method, in which information from the document is coded and entered in summary form. Abstracting introduces a subjective element into the system, and increases the margin of error. It also accentuates the need for properly trained individuals performing document review and data entry.

There are two basic approaches to coding: a bibliographic review designed to identify documents by author, date, or type, and a subjective review for issues and key words. For large or complex document collections, the two may be combined to eliminate duplicate documents and identify a smaller subset for subjective coding.

Initially, documents are reviewed for:

- Document identification number
- Document date
- Number of pages
- Source of the document
- Addresses
- Presence of marginal notations

Once duplicates have been eliminated from the database, the coders make the second review. At this time, they extract and code the following information:

- The subject or subjects of the document
- Subject codes related to factual or legal issues
- Potential claim of privilege
- Key word, names, or places
- A free-text summary of contents

As the system is used, additional coding to track document usage may be required.

The first page of a sample coding is shown as Form 50 in the Appendix. This form is quite similar to the manual digest sheet discussed previously.

Hybrid Systems

On occasion, a hybrid system using coding for some documents and full text for others may be the most advantageous. Many court reporters, for instance, use computer-aided transcription (CAT) for depositions. They are able to provide the transcript on a computer disk in machine-readable form. Available software packages allow the computer to search the transcript for names, key words, etc. This system may be used to augment the document database.

The same type of software can also be used to search pleadings and correspondence in machine-readable form. Legal memoranda, discovery responses, and letters prepared by a word-processing system can be transferred to the database on disk. Other documents may be typed using an optical character recognition (OCR) typewriter font to facilitate rapid data entry by optical scanning.

Personnel Requirements

As a general rule, experience suggests that document coders can process approximately 80–120 documents per day extracting bibliographic information. More subjective or issue-type coding will reduce the rate to 45–70 documents. Similarly, data entry will vary based on individual skills; however, documents normally can be entered at a rate of 150–200 per day.

Given the personnel requirements and hardware costs, the use of outside resources bears consideration. A number of vendors market off-the-shelf software for document management and offer a wide range of support, ranging from consultants to turnkey systems.

The extent to which outside support will be employed involves a number of trade-offs. Turnkey systems, service bureaus, and time-sharing can reduce the hardware costs and perhaps programming costs. However, while outside vendors may have elaborate quality control procedures, their knowledge of the issues involved in the litigation is at best secondhand. Moreover, the knowledge gained by a law firm or in-house counsel in developing a document management system enhances the overall knowledge of the case, and may provide expertise that can be used in other matters. One possible compromise is the use of attorneys and paralegals in systems design and to supervise document coding. Once the coding forms have been completed, the outside vendor can provide data entry and storage.

An effective document management system requires accurate coding of the source documents. It is tempting to reduce costs in this area by hiring unskilled personnel to perform essentially repetitious and "routine" tasks. This may create a frequent turnover of people and result in an unusable database. To avoid these problems, consider the following approaches to staffing, motivation, and supervision:

- Proper and detailed training to include the use of written coding manuals
- Proper supervision and the use of verification steps for coding and data entry
- Employment of educated individuals seeking part-time work (e.g., college students, potential paralegals)
- A comfortable work environment with good lighting, pleasant furnishings, break areas, etc.
- Bonuses or merit pay
- Stressing the need for information security

The Output

The system should be designed to facilitate retrieval on any of the fields of coded data. It should also be able to search for key words in the text fields (e.g., title, abstract). Planning for the output during the initial design stages helps ensure that all the needed information is abstracted; otherwise the documents may have to be reviewed and coded a number of times.

The uses of a document system are limited only by the imagination. The system can be used to find documents by a particular author or dealing with particular subjects. It can generate "privilege" lists in discovery and can compare deposition exhibits. Through the use of modems and communication software, the data become rapidly available regardless of the location.

Protection from Discovery

The Discovery Standard

The creation and installation of a computerized document management system involves considerable time and expense. If the system were discoverable and could be used by the opposing party to gain access to the database, the expense and effort would be largely wasted.

The scope of civil discovery is quite broad, and the federal rules expressly recognize the discoverability of "data compilations."[7] Therefore, machine-readable business records are routinely subject to discovery to the same extent as manual records.[8] A court may even require the producing party to assist in interpreting its computer records[9] and to bear the costs of producing those business records.[10]

There are, however, two recognized exceptions to the discovery rules—materials prepared in anticipation of litigation ("ordinary work product") and the mental impressions, conclusions, or opinions of attorneys or their representatives regarding the litigation ("opinion work product"). Ordinary work product is afforded limited immunity and may be discovered upon a showing of "substantial need" and "undue hardship" in obtaining the "substantial equivalent of the materials by other means."[11] Opinion work product is afforded absolute immunity from discovery.[12] These two exceptions generally form the argument against the discovery of an ALSS.

Application to Litigation Support Systems

A number of articles have been written concerning the discoverability of a litigation support system.[13] However, there appears to be little case law in this area. The leading decision is *In re IBM Peripheral EDP Devices Antitrust Litigation,*[14] in which plaintiffs sought discovery of IBM's document management system. In its answers to interrogatories, IBM indicated that its attorneys had developed a computerized trial support system containing "summaries and analyses" of documents produced to the plaintiffs. Additional discovery was sought in an effort to use that system to "identify documents pursuant to search criteria designated by plaintiffs." The court held that the document management system had been prepared solely for the litigation, and that the documents contained in the database were otherwise available through normal discovery procedures. Plaintiffs failed to show undue need or hardship or the unavailability of alternative means to obtain equivalent information. Finally, the court noted, "The trial support system created by IBM's attorneys reflects their mental impressions, theories and thought processes." The information in the system could not be segregated from those impressions and theories.

The IBM decision suggests that courts will address the question of discoverability on a case-by-case basis, and will use a balancing process in applying the ordinary work-product and opinion work-product exceptions. In determining whether substantial need or undue hardship exists under the *ordinary work-product* doctrine, the court may consider the following criteria:

- The importance and relevancy of the requested materials
- The requesting party's ability to specify or identify the materials requested (avoidance of a fishing expedition)
- The cost incurred in developing and implementing the document management system
- The requestor's financial ability to duplicate the system
- The time constraints involved

- The nature of the documents and the expertise of the producing party in identifying relevant materials[15]

Under the *opinion work-product* exception, the court generally will consider the ability to segregate the mental impressions and opinions of attorneys from the remainder of the system.[16]

Effect on System Design

The few reported decisions suggest that maximum protection will be afforded to opinion work product. Therefore, attorney involvement at *all* stages in the design, installation, and use of a computerized document management system is crucial. Furthermore, the system should be created solely for use by attorneys and their representatives, and should not be employed for general corporate applications. The following specific suggestions should help protect against discovery:

- Use of attorneys or paralegals to supervise the coding of information or actually to do the coding
- The use of abstract coding with free-text summaries rather than the full text
- Locating the system in-house or with an attorney rather than using a service bureau
- Attorney input into the design and the use of the system's output.
- Formulation of the input and output to prevent segregation of data
- Limiting access to the system and its output

Conclusion

While most large document productions require some type of well-conceived document management system, not every case warrants computerization. The decision to computerize should be based on a thorough cost/benefit analysis over the entire life of the system. This decision ultimately rests with the client and in-house counsel with the advice of the trial attorney and perhaps outside consultants.

Once these parties have decided to use a computerized document management system, the maximum amount of time and energy should be spent on understanding the litigation and designing the system. Attorney involvement at all stages of the system will help ensure proper design and protect the system from discovery.

Notes

1. Model Definition § 1 (American Bar Association, Section on Science and Technology 1978).
2. Emerson, *Support Systems for Litigation Management,* Legal Automation News, Oct. 15, 1981, at 1.

383

3. *Id.;* AMERICAN LEGAL SYSTEMS, CAPABILITY STATEMENT (1981).
4. Emerson, *supra* note 2.
5. ALEXANDER GRANT & CO., AUTOMATED LITIGATION SUPPORT—A LITIGATOR'S PRIMER 13 (1981).
6. *Id.*, Sherman and Kinnard, *The Development, Discovery and Use of Computer Support Systems in Achieving Efficiency in Litigation,* 79 COLUM. L. REV. 267 (1979).
7. *See* FED. R. CIV. P. 26(b), 34(a).
8. *See, e.g.,* Adams v. Dan River Mills, Inc., 54 F.R.D. 220 (W.D. Va. 1972); *see also* MANUAL FOR COMPLEX LITIGATION, ¶ 2.715 at 75 (Federal Judicial Center 1977).
9. Lodge 743, Int'l Ass'n of Machinists, AFL-CIO v. United Aircraft Corp., 220 F. Supp. 19 (D. Conn. 1963), *aff'd,* 337 F.2d 5 (2d Cir. 1964), *cert. denied,* 380 U.S. 908 (1965).
10. *See, e.g.,* Bills v. Kennecott Corp., 108 F.R.D. 459 (C.D. Utah 1985).
11. FED. R CIV. P. 26 (b)(3).
12. *E.g.,* Duplan Corp. v. Moulinage et Retorderie de Chavanoz, 509 F.2d 730 (4th Cir. 1974), *cert. dismissed as improv. granted*, 420 U.S. 997 (1975).
13. *See, e.g.,* Fromholz, *Discovery, Evidence, Confidentiality and Security Problems Associated with the Use of Computer Based Litigation Support Systems,* 1977 WASH. U. L. Q. 445; Sherman & Kinnard, *supra* note 6, at n. 15.
14. 5 COMPUTER L. SERV. REP. 878 (N.D. Cal. 1975).
15. *See* A.H. Robins Co., Inc. v. Aetna Casualty & Sur. Co., Chancery No. G 3321-2, Cir. Ct. of City of Richmond, Va., 6 VADA NEWSLETTER 1 (1981).
16. *See* Natural Union Elec. Corp. v. Matsushita Elec. Indus. Co. Ltd., 494 F. Supp. 1257 (E. Pa. 1980) (discovery of production and sales data permitted, since it was not the product of any attorney input, distinguishing *IBM Peripherals,* 5 COMPUTER L. SERV. REP. 878).

Section VII

Substantive Aspects of Representing Corporate Clients in Litigation

The corporate litigator must deal with each client through its officers, directors, and employees. This may involve interviews of officers, directors, or employees to determine the relevant facts involved in the litigation; conferring with corporate officials to decide upon an appropriate strategy in litigation; defending the actions of corporate officials when they are charged with having contravened their corporate responsibilities; or conferring concerning business alternatives that may affect the litigation. In fulfilling these roles as interviewer, advocate, defender, and counselor, the corporate litigator must be cognizant of the substantive rules that govern the attorney-client relationship, establish the boundaries of proper officer or director actions, and protect officers and directors against unwarranted liability. This section therefore includes chapters concerning three aspects of representing corporate clients: the attorney-corporate client privilege, the fiduciary responsibilities of officers and directors, and the indemnification and insurance of corporate officials.

The section begins with a chapter on the attorney-corporate client privilege. Chapter 29, by Samuel R. Miller and Breck C. Tostevin, looks at some specific applications of the attorney-corporate client privilege in a number of special situations: internal corporate investigations, the attorney who is also an officer or director, the shareholder derivative action, and the special litigation committee in the shareholder derivative action. The authors also discuss waiver situations where the board of directors invokes a defense of reliance on counsel, where management of the corporation passes to a new entity or management, where privileged material has been inadvertently produced, and where privileged material has been disclosed to underwriters, auditors, or potential purchasers. Finally, the article discusses the impact of the work-product doctrine on these situations.

Chapter 30, by William L. Stern and Michelle L. Kerr, contains an extensive and excellent discussion of the fiduciary duties of directors under state law and also under federal securities and other statutes. Starting with a discussion of state common law and statutory law, the article discusses the duty of loyalty, the duty of care, and the business judgment rule. The chapter also describes fiduciary standards under federal securities law and under statutory extensions of fiduciary responsibility.

The final two chapters in the section address the related topics of officers and directors liability, indemnification, and insurance. In Chapter 31, Dennis J. Block, Nancy E. Barton, and Stephen A. Radin discuss indemnification and insurance of corporate officials. The chapter is particularly timely in light of the increase in contests for corporate control, the increased number of challenges to actions by boards of directors, and increased civil and criminal enforcement activity by government agencies, which frequently name individual officers and directors as defendants. The chapter focuses on corporate laws of California, Delaware, and New York and the Model Business Corporation Act in discussing circumstances in which indemnification is mandatory, in which it is permissible, and where a court may order indemnification. The authors consider whether it is appropriate to advance costs of litigation by paying counsel fees and whether a corporation is permitted to indemnify its officers and directors beyond the boundaries explicitly authorized by statute. The authors then provide an introduction to directors and officers insurance, including the corporate power to purchase it and typical policy coverage. In light of the insurance coverage crisis, the article concludes with a discussion of alternatives to insurance.

Chapter 32 provides a different perspective on the topic of D & O insurance; author James B. Wallace is vice president of an insurance brokerage. The chapter describes the general nature of directors and officers insurance and the indemnification of directors and officers by corporations, explaining typical policy language and how various choices of wording can affect the corporate insured. The article concludes with a discussion of typical defense and claims-handling issues in a directors and officers insurance policy.

These four articles provide an in-depth analysis of the critical and sensitive issues that arise when the corporate litigator must work with officers, directors, and employees of the corporate client in the litigation setting. A reading of these articles should show the corporate litigator the key traps for the unwary.

Francis J. Burke, Jr.
Streich, Lang, Weeks & Cardon
Phoenix, Arizona

Twenty-Nine

Attorney-Client Privilege and Work-Product Protection in the Corporate Context

Samuel R. Miller and Breck C. Tostevin

A leading definition of the attorney-client privilege is found in Wigmore's *Evidence in Trials at Common Law:*

> (1) Where legal advice of any kind is sought (2) from a professional legal advisor in his capacity as such, (3) the communications relating to that purpose, (4) made in confidence (5) by the client, (6) are at his instance permanently protected (7) from disclosure by himself or the legal advisor, (8) except the protection be waived.[1]

When the client is a corporation, courts have adopted various approaches in defining the scope of the attorney-client privilege.[2]

The Control Group Test

Until the United States Supreme Court's decision in *Upjohn v. United States,*[3] the most widely accepted test in the federal courts for the attorney-client privilege in the corporate context was the "control group" test first used in *Philadelphia v. Westinghouse Electric Corp.*[4] Under this test, an employee's statement to corporate counsel is not privileged unless the employee "is in a position to control or even to take a substantial part in a decision about any action which the corporation may take upon the advice of an attorney, or (unless) he is an authorized member of a body or group that has the authority."[5] The control group test had been widely accepted by the federal courts.[6]

Application of the control group test, which focuses on the authority of the communicating employees to take discretionary action on the attorney's advice, generally limits the protection of the privilege to communications between upper-echelon corporate employees and counsel. Proponents of this test assert that limiting the scope of the attorney-client privilege in a corporate context prevents the corporation from creating a

Samuel R. Miller is a member of Morrison & Foerster, San Francisco, California. Breck C. Tostevin was, at the time of this writing, a summer associate at Morrison & Foerster.

"zone of silence" around corporate affairs. However, the control group test has also been criticized as being too artificial and too narrow. Critics point out that this application excludes middle-management personnel, who often are the real decision makers in the corporate structure. It has also been noted that the control group test ignores the fact that corporate counsel must obtain information from corporate personnel at various levels before rendering informed legal advice.

The Subject Matter Test

A more expansive formulation of the attorney-client privilege in the corporate context was established in *Harper & Row Publishers, Inc. v. Decker.*[7] The court held that communications by a company employee outside the control group to a corporation's attorney are privileged:

> [W]here the employee makes the communication at the direction of his superior in the corporation and where the subject matter upon which the attorney's advice is sought by the corporation and dealt with in the communication is the performance by the employee of the duties of his employment.

A modified *Harper & Row* subject matter approach was endorsed by the Eighth Circuit in *Diversified Industries, Inc. v. Meredith.*[8] At issue in *Diversified Industries* was the discoverability of a report prepared by a corporation's outside counsel after the law firm's investigation of an alleged corporate slush fund. The Eighth Circuit ruled that the employee interviews conducted by the corporation's law firm, as well as the law firm's report, were protected by the attorney-client privilege. In so holding, the court stated its test for the privilege as follows:

> The attorney-client privilege is applicable to an employee's communication if (1) a communication was made for the purpose of securing legal advice; (2) the employee making the communication did so at the direction of his corporate superior; (3) the superior made the request so that the corporation could secure legal advice; (4) the subject matter of the communication is within the scope of the employee's corporate duties; (5) the communication is not disseminated beyond those persons who, because of the corporate structure, need to know its contents.[9]

The Supreme Court Decision in *Upjohn Co. v. United States*

In *Upjohn Co. v. United States,*[10] the United States Supreme Court was asked to resolve the conflict among the federal courts between those adopting the control group test and those embracing a more expansive subject matter approach. In *Upjohn,* the IRS summoned the product of a corporation's internal investigation of questionable payments by employees of the corporation or its subsidiaries. The company resisted the summons on the grounds of attorney-client privilege and the work-product doctrine. The Sixth Circuit Court of Appeals[11] rejected the company's claim of privilege, holding that the control group test was the proper approach in determining the scope of the attorney-client privilege.

The Supreme Court reversed, ruling that the questionnaires, memoranda, and notes at issue in *Upjohn* were privileged. Although the Court declined to specifically embrace the subject-matter test or "lay down a broad rule," it did hold on the facts before it that the control group test was too narrow. The Court noted that the control group test frustrates the very purpose of the attorney-client privilege by discouraging the communication of relevant information from middle-level and lower-level corporate employees to attorneys seeking to render legal advice to the corporation. The Court also dismissed the "zone of silence" argument, stating that the privilege does not prevent an opposing party from seeking information directly from company employees; it merely bars the more convenient route through a lawyer's files.

Further, the Court in *Upjohn* reversed the lower court's ruling that there was no work-product protection for summoned materials. The Court left unresolved the question of whether the attorney-client privilege also protected counsel's notes and memoranda of interviews with former employees. However, it ruled that such materials were covered by the work-product doctrine.

Although the Court in *Upjohn* declined to enunciate a general rule on the scope of the attorney-client privilege, it emphasized the following factors that should give guidance in defining the privilege:

- The communications were made by corporate employees to corporate counsel upon orders of superiors to enable the corporation to secure legal advice.
- The information sought concerned matter within the scope of the employees' corporate duties.
- The employees were aware that the reason for the communications with counsel was so that the corporation could obtain legal advice.
- The communications were ordered to be confidential, and they remained confidential.

The Corporate Privilege after *Upjohn*

Even after *Upjohn*, the Illinois Supreme Court adhered to the control group test rejected by the U.S. Supreme Court.[12] Some federal courts have also read the *Upjohn* decision narrowly.[13]

On the other hand, a number of courts have taken a broader view of the corporate attorney-client privilege after *Upjohn*. For example, in *In re International Systems and Controls Corp. Securities Litigation,*[14] the attorney-client privilege was found to extend to communications between an attorney and *any* employee as long as the communication dealt with matters within the scope of the employee's corporate duties, the employee was informed he or she was being questioned so that the corporation could obtain legal advice, and the communication was considered and maintained as confidential by the company.

The Ninth Circuit extended the corporate privilege to communications with *former* employees in *In re Coordinated Proceedings in Petroleum Products Antitrust Litigation.*[15] The court ruled that corporate counsel may need the knowledge of former employees to advise the company regarding legal problems. The district court in *United States v. King*[16] followed *Coordinated Proceedings.* In *King,* a corporate attorney interviewed a former employee (after termination) with respect to a federal criminal investigation of the corporation's banking transactions. The court held that the attorney-client privilege attaches to such conversations under *Coordinated Proceedings* and *Upjohn,* because the conversation related to a criminal investigation of the corporate client.[17]

In *Baxter Travenol Laboratories, Inc. v. Le May,*[18] the court reaffirmed its earlier holding that, in light of the *Upjohn* decision, the attorney-client privilege attaches to "communications between corporate counsel and an employee of the client corporation, which concerns matters that occurred prior to the employee's employment with the corporation (i.e., matters not within the scope of the employee's corporate duties) but which, in all other aspects, fall within the analysis of [*Upjohn*]."[19]

Attorney Acting as Special Investigator of Potentially Wrongful Activities

When an attorney supervises or conducts a factual investigation in order to render legal advice to a corporate client, the communications requested or received from employees or former employees of the client during the investigation should be protected by the attorney-client privilege.[20] Similarly, a report that incorporates counsel's impressions of the interviews and contained legal conclusions and communications by counsel with the board of directors should fall within the privilege.[21]

However, when the attorney has been retained for some purpose other than the rendering of legal advice, such as the monitoring of a consent decree, communications with the attorney may not be protected by the privilege. In *SEC v. Canadian Javelin, Ltd.,*[22] lawyers were appointed as special counsel to monitor the company's compliance with an earlier consent judgment involving securities violations. The court rejected the attorney's claim of privilege and permitted the SEC to depose special counsel. The court held that the counsel's limited engagement was not for the purpose of rendering legal advice and did not constitute an attorney-client relationship in the traditional sense.[23]

With in-house counsel, special care must be taken to establish that a communication claimed to be privileged is made to or by the attorney acting as legal counsel and not as a business adviser or policymaker.[24] For example, in *In re Sealed Case,*[25] the court ruled that the former general counsel of a company could testify before a grand jury investigating bid rigging that he observed the president of the company making hurried telephone calls from an airport on the morning certain bids were due. The court further allowed testimony that the former general counsel saw the president of one of his client's competitors walking in an airport concourse behind the president of his client. The court concluded that these observations were not within the scope of the counsel's legal role and therefore not privileged.

Attorney-Client Privilege when Attorney Is Also an Officer or Director

Similarly, when a director or officer is also an attorney and gives advice to the board during deliberations, difficult questions may arise as to what capacity the attorney is serving. The client faces greater difficulty in preserving the attorney-client privilege when a corporate attorney provides advice in more than one capacity.[26] In *SEC v. Gulf & Western Industries, Inc.*, communications made between corporate officials and the company's outside general counsel/director were deemed not privileged because the general counsel "arguably received information in his role as director of Gulf & Western or in his various other [non-general counsel] roles."[27]

Attorney-Client Privilege in Shareholder Suits

Federal courts have recognized a limitation on the corporation's ability to assert the attorney-client privilege in shareholder derivative suits against the management of the company. In such cases, federal courts have held that the corporation's attorney-client privilege is a qualified privilege that may be overcome by a showing of "good cause." The leading case establishing this principle is *Garner v. Wolfinbarger.*[28] In *Garner,* the court rejected the view that a corporation's right to assert the attorney-client privilege is absolute as against its shareholders. The court identified the following factors that should be considered in determining whether good cause has been shown:

- The number of shareholders bringing the suit and the percentage of stock they represent
- The nature of their claims
- The necessity of obtaining the information and its availability from other sources
- Whether the alleged misconduct of the corporation was criminal, illegal but not criminal, or of doubtful legality
- Whether the communication concerned past or prospective actions
- Whether the communication was of advice concerning the litigation itself
- Whether the shareholders were "blindly fishing"
- The risk of revealing trade secrets or other confidential information

A number of cases have found "good cause" to overcome the attorney-client privilege.[29] Some courts have extended *Garner* in several respects.[30] Other courts have restricted the application of the *Garner* exception. In *In re International Systems and Controls Corp. Securities Litigation,*[31] the Fifth Circuit applied the *Garner* rule in the context of a class action. However, the court also ruled that the *Garner* principles governing discoverability of communications protected by the attorney-client privilege were not applicable to efforts to obtain attorney work product. In the Ninth Circuit, the *Garner* rules do not apply to class actions under the holding of *Weil v. Investment Indicators, Research and Management, Inc.*[32] In *Weil,* the Ninth Circuit ruled that the *Garner* exception was inapplicable where the action was not a derivative suit and the plaintiff was not currently a shareholder.[33]

Moreover, a number of courts applying *Garner* have refused to apply the exception to communications after the events giving rise to the litigation.[34] In addition, state courts may not extend the *Garner* principle to decisions based upon the state evidence rules. The California courts have rejected the *Garner* exception, ruling that, unlike the federal privilege rules, privilege in California is governed by statute and the courts are not free to create exceptions.[35]

Special Litigation Committees: Reliance on a Report Prepared by Counsel to Dismiss a Shareholder Derivative Suit

When faced with a derivative suit, corporations commonly establish a special litigation committee (SLC) composed of independent directors, who determine whether continuation of the action is in the best interests of the corporation. The investigation into the merits of the claims is generally conducted by special counsel under direction of the SLC. Where a corporation has moved to terminate the derivative action based upon the SLC's determination that the action is not in the corporation's best interests, courts consider the methodology and thoroughness of the SLC's investigation.[36]

Several courts have considered whether the submission of the SLC's report to the court, even under seal, constitutes a waiver of the attorney-client privilege or work-product doctrine with respect to some or all of the committee's investigative files and activities:

- In *Joy v. North,*[37] the court held that by making its motion for summary judgment based upon the SLC's determination to terminate the litigation, the corporation waived the attorney-client privilege with respect to the committee's report. The *Joy* court also held that the work-product doctrine did not apply to the extent that the special counsel's work was communicated to the SLC.
- In *In re Continental Illinois Securities Litigation,*[38] the court reached a similar result based upon different reasoning. The court held that where the defendant corporation had introduced the SLC's report into evidence in support of its motion to terminate a derivative suit, the presumption of public access to court records overrode the corporation's interest in preservation of the attorney-client privilege or work-product doctrine.
- On the other hand, in *In re Dayco Derivative Securities Litigation,*[39] the court held that there was no waiver of the attorney-client privilege where special counsel's report to the SLC was not released to the court or the public, but only portions of the "findings" of the committee were publicized in a two-page press release.[40]

Reliance-on-Counsel Defense and Waiver of the Attorney-Client Privilege

Recent cases such as *Smith v. Van Gorkom*[41] have stressed that the business judgment rule protects informed decisions of a board of directors. In establishing that a decision was made after adequate deliberation, a board of directors may argue that it consulted with counsel and that counsel recommended a particular course of action. However, some courts have ruled that invocation of the defense of reliance on counsel "waives the attorney-client privilege with respect to all communications, whether written or oral, to and from counsel concerning the transactions for which counsel's advice was sought."[42]

A commonly cited case on this issue is *Handguards Inc. v. Johnson & Johnson.*[43] In this private antitrust action, plaintiff claimed that defendant had attempted to restrain trade by bringing patent infringement actions in bad faith. The court held that since the defendant intended to call the attorneys who had litigated the prior suits as witnesses to testify that the prior actions were brought in good faith and on the basis of competent legal advice, defendants waived the attorney-client privilege as to communications and documents relating to the good-faith prosecution of the prior actions. The court further held that by raising the "good faith" defense and by calling its lawyers as witnesses, the defendant waived the attorney's work-product protection.

Who Holds the Corporate Attorney-Client Privilege, and Who Can Waive It?

When the client is a corporation, the entity itself through its current management holds the attorney-client privilege. The U.S. Supreme Court in *Commodity Futures Trading Commission v. Weintraub* explained:

> [F]or solvent corporations, the power to waive the corporate attorney-client privilege rests with the corporation's management and is normally exercised by its officers and directors. The managers, of course, must exercise the privilege in a manner consistent with their fiduciary duty to act in the best interests of the corporation and not of themselves as individuals.[44]

Moreover, when managerial authority passes to new people or a new entity, so too passes the authority to claim the privilege:

> [W]hen control of a corporation passes to new management, the authority to assert and waive the corporation's attorney-client privilege passes as well. New managers installed as a result of a takeover, merger, loss of confidence by shareholders, or simply normal succession, may waive the attorney-client privilege with respect to communications of former officers and directors. Displaced managers may not assert the privilege over the wishes of current managers, even as to statements that the former might have made to counsel concerning matters within the scope of their corporate duties.[45]

In *Weintraub,* the Court held that the trustee of a corporation in bankruptcy can waive the attorney-client privilege of the corporate debtor over the objections of the corporation's former officers.[46]

Similarly, at least one court has held that senior in-house counsel may waive the corporation's privilege, presumptively because he or she is the agent of the corporation with authority to waive the privilege in testimony before the grand jury.[47] The *Weintraub* decision underscores the necessity of distinguishing between representation of the corporation as opposed to directors and officers in their individual capacities.[48]

In *In re Bevill, Bresler & Schulman Asset Management Corp.*,[49] the Third Circuit held that a corporate officer cannot prevent the corporation from waiving the company's attorney-client privilege. To assert a personal claim of privilege, a corporate officer must show (1) the officer approached counsel to seek legal advice, (2) the officer made it clear he or she was seeking legal advice in an individual capacity, (3) the counsel communicated with the officer in the officer's individual capacity, and (4) the conversation did not concern matters within the general affairs of the company.[50] Where there is joint representation of both a corporation and its principal shareholders and/or officers, the privilege may remain as to the individual even after the corporation waives, and vice versa.[51]

Waiver by Disclosure to Underwriters, Auditors, or Potential Purchasers

Numerous courts have held that the disclosure of privileged materials to unnecessary third persons defeats a claim of privilege.[52] Lack of meticulous care to preserve the privilege has been held to negate the privilege even where the opposing party recovered the documents in question out of the garbage.[53] Other courts have mitigated this strict rule concerning inadvertent disclosure.[54]

Work-Product Doctrine

The work-product doctrine enunciated by the Supreme Court in *Hickman v. Taylor*[55] provides a qualified privilege for the work papers, notes, memoranda, and reports gathered or prepared by counsel and their agents in anticipation of litigation. The *Hickman* Court held:

> [T]he general policy against invading the privacy of an attorney's course of preparation is so well recognized and so essential to an orderly working of our system. . . that a burden rests on the one who would invade that privacy to establish adequate reasons to justify production.[56]

The work-product doctrine was later codified and now appears as Federal Rule of Civil Procedure 26(b)(3), which provides:

> [A] party may obtain discovery of documents and tangible things. . . prepared in anticipation of litigation or for trial by and for another party or by and for that other party's representative (including his attorney, consultant, surety, indemnitor, insurer, or agent) only upon a showing that the

> party seeking discovery has *substantial need* of the materials in the preparation of his case and that he is *unable without undue hardship* to obtain the substantial equivalent of the materials by other means. In ordering discovery of such materials when the required showing has been made, the court *shall* protect against disclosure of the mental impressions, conclusions, opinions, or legal theories of an attorney or other representative of a party concerning litigation. [Emphasis added.]

While the rule expressly provides that the work-product doctrine only protects materials "prepared in anticipation of litigation," determining "whether a document has [been so prepared] is a slippery task."[57] However, the Supreme Court in *Upjohn v. United States*[58] clearly suggests that, if the collection or preparation of documents is prompted by a concern about the potential for litigation, the documents will enjoy work-product protection even if they were prepared before litigation was first threatened. Work product extends, at a minimum, to discovery in related subsequent litigation, and the weight of authority holds that work-product protection is available in subsequent litigation regardless of relatedness.[59]

Applicability of Work-Product Doctrine to Internal Corporate Investigations

The work-product doctrine can be a particularly effective tool in maintaining the confidentiality of internal corporate investigative reports. Work-product protection is potentially broader than attorney-client privilege because it is not limited to attorney-client communications. Courts have consistently held that investigative reports prepared in anticipation of or in response to litigation are entitled to work-product protection.[60]

Under federal law, materials prepared by nonlawyers will nonetheless be protected work product if they were prepared by the party's representative in anticipation of litigation.[61] The Supreme Court recently rejected, however, work-product protection for accountants as not analogous to attorney work product; an attorney works as a "confidential advisor and advocate," while an accountant is "a disinterested analyst charged with public obligations."[62]

Waiver of the Work-Product Protection

Like the attorney-client privilege previously discussed, the protection of the work-product doctrine can be lost through disclosure. It is important to note, however, that the *Garner* exception to the attorney-client privilege in the context of shareholder derivative suits has been ruled inapplicable to work-product protection.[63]

Since the primary purpose of the work-product rule is to protect the adversary process, not the client's confidence, disclosure to a third party does not automatically waive the privilege.[64] Disclosure does not waive federal work-product protection "unless it substantially increased the opportunities for potential adversaries to obtain the information."[65] If the transferor and transferee have a common interest in a particular issue against a common adversary, disclosure is consistent with the nature of the work-product privilege.[66] Similarly, disclosure of some documents will not destroy work-product protection for other documents of the same character.[67]

Notes

1. 8 WIGMORE, EVIDENCE IN TRIALS AT COMMON LAW § 2990 (1961).
2. *See generally* Miller, *Corporate Attorney Client Privilege and the Work Product Doctrine Protection from Compelled Disclosure in Criminal Investigation of a Corporation,* 12 U.S.F. L. REV. 569 (1978); Marcus, *The Perils of Privilege: Waiver and the Litigation,* 84 MICH. L. REV. 1605 (1986).
3. 449 U.S. 383 (1981).
4. 210 F. Supp. 483 (E.D. Pa. 1962).
5. 210 F. Supp. at 485.
6. *See, e.g.,* United States v. Upjohn, 600 F.2d 1223 (6th Cir. 1979), *rev'd,* 449 U.S. 383 (1981); *In re* Grand Jury Investigation, 599 F.2d 1224 (3d Cir. 1979); Virginia Elec. Power Co. v. Sun Shipbuilding & Dry Dock Co., 68 F.R.D. 397 (E.D. Va. 1975); United States v. IBM Corp., 66 F.R.D. 206 (S.D.N.Y. 1974).
7. 423 F.2d 487 (7th Cir. 1970).
8. 572 F.2d 596 (8th Cir. 1978).
9. *Diversified Indus.,* 572 F.2d at 609.
10. 449 U.S. 383 (1981).
11. United States v. Upjohn, 600 F.2d 1223 (6th Cir. 1979), *rev'd,* 449 U.S. 383 (1981).
12. Consolidated Coal Co., 432 N.E.2d 250 (Ill. 1982).
13. Permian Corp. v. United States, 665 F.2d 1214, 1221 (D.C. Cir. 1981) (holding that privilege must be "narrowly construed" because it "inhibits the truth-finding process").
14. 693 F.2d 1235 (5th Cir. 1982).
15. 658 F.2d 1355, 1361 n.7 (9th Cir. 1981), *cert. denied,* 445 U.S. 990 (1982).
16. 536 F. Supp. 253 (C.D. Cal. 1982).
17. *Id.* at 239. *See also In re* Fortune Sys. Sec. Litig., No. C-83-3348A WHO (N.D. Cal. Nov. 6, 1986) (attorney-client privilege extends to protect predeposition discussions between former employees of corporation and corporate counsel, but only for information the employees acquired during their employment with the corporation; matters after they left employment not privileged); *In re* Data Gen. Corp. Antitrust Litig., MDL No. 369 MHP (N.D. Cal. Aug. 1, 1986) (privilege extends to prevent one party from retaining as a consultant a former employee of the other party who possesses knowledge of privileged information regarding the litigation); Porter v. Arco Metals, Div. of Atlantic Richfield, 642 F. Supp.

1116, 1118 (D. Mont. 1986) ("It is apparent from the *Upjohn* decision that while the attorney-client privilege may extend to Arco's former employees, it applies only to communications between those employees and company's counsel.").

18. 514 F. Supp. 1156 (S.D. Ohio 1981), *appeal dismissed without opinion,* 708 F.2d 721 (6th Cir. 1982).

19. *Id.* at 1157. *But see* Leer v. Chicago, Milwaukee, St. Paul & Pac. Ry. Co., 308 N.W.2d 305 (Minn. 1981), *cert. denied,* 455 U.S. 939 (1982) (communications relating to employer, but not matters within the employee's duties, are not privileged).

20. *See* Upjohn Co. v. United States, 449 U.S. 383 (1981) (communications from Upjohn employees to counsel, at direction of corporate supervisors and in order to secure legal advice from counsel, protected from compelled disclosure); Diversified Indus., Inc. v. Meredith, 572 F.2d 596 (8th Cir. 1978) (en banc) (when outside counsel was retained to conduct a special investigation into corporate bribes and to advise company on legal consequences, communications held privileged); *In re* LTV Sec. Litig., 89 F.R.D. 595 (N.D. Tex. 1981) (privilege applies to factual data gathered by special counsel hired during an SEC investigation); *In re* Dayco Corp. Derivative Sec. Litig., 99 F.R.D. 616 (W.D. Ohio 1983) (interviews and materials prepared by special review committee of board of directors in cooperation with law firm investigating potentially improper payments abroad were privileged and work product).

21. Joy v. North, 692 F.2d 880, 893–94 (2d Cir. 1982), *cert. denied,* 460 U.S. 1051.

22. 451 F. Supp. 594 (D.D.C. 1978).

23. *See also* Osterneck v. E.T. Barwick Indus., Inc., 82 F.R.D. 81 (N.D. Ga. 1979) (claim of privilege rejected where the attorney was employed as special counsel to a special review committee set up under an SEC consent decree).

24. *See In re* Sealed Case, 737 F.2d 94, 99 (D.C. Cir. 1984) (company must make a "clear showing" that in-house counsel was acting in a professional legal capacity); Coastal Corp. v. Duncan, 86 F.R.D. 514, 521 (D. Del. 1980); North Am. Mortgage Investors v. First Wis. Nat'l Bank of Milwaukee, 69 F.R.D. 9, 11 (E.D. Wis. 1975).

25. 737 F.2d 94 (D.C. Cir. 1984).

26. SEC v. Gulf & W. Indus., Inc., 518 F. Supp. 675 (D.D.C. 1981).

27. *Id.* at 683. *See also* Elgin Fed. Credit Union v. Cantor, Fitzgerald Sec. Corp., 91 F.R.D. 414, 418–19 (N.D. Ga. 1981) (privilege for company board minutes lost when minutes were made available to accounting firm for audit purposes).

28. 430 F.2d 1093 (5th Cir. 1971).

29. *See* Broad v. Rockwell Int'l Corp., [1976–1977 Transfer Binder] FED. SEC. L. REP. (CCH) ¶ 95,894 (N.D. Tex. Feb. 18, 1977); *In re* Transocean Tender Offer Sec. Litig., 78 F.R.D. 692, 696–97 (N.D. Ill. 1978); Cohen V. Uniroyal, Inc., 80 F.R.D. 480, 484–85 (E.D. Pa. 1978); Panter v. Marshall Field & Co., 80 F.R.D. 718, 723 (N.D. Ill. 1978); Valente v. PepsiCo, 68 F.R.D. 361, 367–70 (N.D. Ill. 1978).

30. Broad v. Rockwell Int'l Corp., [1976–1977 Transfer Binder] FED. SEC. L. REP. (CCH) ¶ 95,894 (N.D. Tex. Feb. 18, 1977) (exception applies to bondholders as well as shareholders); Cohen v. Uniroyal, Inc., 80 F.R.D. 480 (E.D. Pa. 1978) (exception applies to communications occurring before the shareholders are

shareholders); Bailey v. Meister Brau, Inc., 55 F.R.D. 211 (N.D. Ill. 1972) (exception applies to communications between parent corporation and subsidiary); Valente v. PepsiCo, 68 F.R.D. at 369 (same).

31. 693 F.2d 1235, 1239 n.3 (5th Cir. 1982).

32. 647 F.2d 18 (9th Cir. 1981).

33. *See also* Shirvani v. Capital Investing Corp., Inc., 112 F.R.D. 389, 391 (D. Conn. 1986) (court questioned justification for the *Garner* exception and concluded that good-cause exception to privilege was not necessary to protect interests of shareholders in suit against company).

34. *See* Garner v. Ohio Seely Mattress Mfg. Co., 90 F.R.D. 21, 31 (N.D. Ill. 1980); *In re* LTV Sec. Litig., 89 F.R.D. 595, 607–08 (N.D. Tex. 1981); PRINCIPLES OF CORPORATE GOVERNANCE § 7.11(d) (Discussion Draft). *See also In re* International Sys. & Controls Corp. Sec. Ltd., 693 F.2d 1235, 1239 (5th Cir. 1982) ("once there is sufficient anticipation of litigation to trigger the work product immunity, we think this mutuality [between shareholders and management] is destroyed").

35. Hoiles v. Superior Court, 157 Cal. App. 3d 1192, 1198–99 (1984); Dickerson v. Superior Court, 135 Cal. App. 3d 93, 99–100 (1982).

36. *See generally* Block & Prussin, *Termination of Derivative Suits against Directors on Business Judgment Grounds: From* Zapata *to* Aronson, 39 BUS. LAW. 1503 (1984).

37. 692 F.2d 800 (2d Cir. 1982), *cert. denied,* 460 U.S. 1051.

38. 732 F.2d 1302 (7th Cir. 1984).

39. 99 F.R.D. 616 (S.D. Ohio 1983).

40. *See also* Kubushiki Kaisha Hattori Seiko v. Gruen Indus., Inc., No. 84 Civ. 22267 slip op. (S.D.N.Y. Apr. 24, 1986) (attorney-client privilege waived as to contents of documents summarized in a conclusory manner in a declaration by client's counsel).

41. 488 A.2d 858, 872–73 (Del. Super. 1985).

42. Donovan v. Fitzsimmons, 90 F.R.D. 583, 588 (D.D.C. 1981) ("advice of counsel" defense amounts to substantial need required to overcome work-product doctrine). *See also* Coleco Indus., Inc. v. Universal City Studios, 110 F.R.D. 688 (S.D.N.Y. 1986) (reliance on advice-of-counsel defense against claim that corporation misrepresented its ownership rights waives attorney-client privilege with respect to that advice); Panter v. Marshall Field & Co., 80 F.R.D. 718, 721 (N.D. Ill. 1978) (waiver found in securities action where defendant relied on advice of counsel regarding legality of merger); Garfinkle v. Arcata Nat'l Corp., 64 F.R.D. 688 (S.D.N.Y. 1974) (waiver found where defendant relied on advice of counsel concerning the exemption of stocks from registration requirements); Broad v. Rockwell Int'l Corp., [1976–1977 Transfer Binder] FED. SEC. L. REP. (CCH) ¶ 95,894 (N.D. Tex. 1977) (assertion of reliance on advice of counsel as an affirmative defense in an action brought by debenture holders waived attorney-client privilege in entirety from outside counsel about any aspect of the merger). *But see* Standard Chartered Bank v. Ayala Int'l Holdings, 111 F.R.D. 76 (S.D.N.Y. 1986) (bank's counterclaims, including justifiable reliance on lender's oral representations, did not impliedly waive attorney-client privilege as to communications in which attorneys advised that guarantees be in writing); Chase Manhattan Bank v. Drysdale Sec. Corp., 587 F.Supp. 57 (S.D.N.Y. 1984) (same).

43. 413 F.Supp. 926 (N.D. Cal. 1976).

44. 105 S. Ct. 1986, 1991 (1985).

45. *Id.*

46. *See also* Odmark v. Westside Bancorporation, Inc., 636 F. Supp. 552 (W.D. Wash. 1986) (former officers and directors did not have individual attorney-client relationship with savings and loan association's former counsel that would permit them to assert the privilege as against the FSLIC, which "stepped into the shoes" of the S&L when declared receiver for it); Baer v. Abel, 637 F. Supp. 343 (W.D. Wash. 1986) (FSLIC exclusive holder of attorney-client privilege between savings and loan association and law firm, and individual officers and directors of S&L did not have separate attorney-client privilege with law firm); *In re* Diasonics Sec. Litig., 110 F.R.D. 570 (D. Colo. 1986) (privilege remains with the parent corporation after separation of former subsidiary).

47. Velsicol Chem. Corp. v. Parsons, 561 F.2d 671 (7th Cir. 1977), *cert. denied,* 435 U.S. 942 (1978). *But See* Leucadia, Inc. v. Reliance Ins. Co., 101 F.R.D. 674 (S.D.N.Y. 1983) (former director giving attorney work product to opposing party did not waive work-product protection).

48. *See, e.g., In re* Grand Jury Proceedings, 570 F.2d 562 (2d Cir. 1978) (an individual officer or director may not avail himself of the corporate attorney-client privilege); United States v. Delillo, 448 F. Supp. 840 (E.D.N.Y. 1978) (same); *In re* Diasonics Sec. Litig., 110 F.R.D. 570 (counsel's advice to directors seeking to rescind previous merger was obtained in their personal capacity, and attorney-client privilege could not be asserted by the corporation itself).

49. 805 F.2d 120 (3d Cir. 1986).

50. *See also In re* Grand Jury Investigation, 575 F. Supp. 777 (N.D. Ga. 1983) (same test applied to former employees seeking to invoke an independent attorney-client privilege).

51. *In re* Grand Jury Subpoena Duces Tecum (Vesco), 391 F.2d 1029 (S.D.N.Y. 1975).

52. *See* United States v. El Paso Co., 682 F.2d 530 (5th Cir. 1982) (disclosure of tax pool analysis to auditors waived attorney-client privilege); *In re* John Doe Corp., 675 F.2d 482 (2d Cir. 1982) (a company's disclosure of a special investigation report to its underwriters and its outside auditors in connection with public securities offering waived the attorney-client privilege as to the final report and prior drafts); SEC v. Gulf & W. Indus., Inc. 518 F. Supp. 675, 683 (D.D.C. 1981) (no privilege where communications made in presence of third parties or widely disseminated); Elgin Fed. Credit Union v. Cantor, Fitzgerald Sec. Corp., 91 F.R.D. 414, 418–19 (N.D. Ga. 1981) (privilege for company board minutes lost when minutes were made available to accounting firm for audit purposes); SEC v. Texas Int'l Airlines, Inc., [1979 Transfer Binder] FED. SEC. L. REP. (CCH) ¶ 96,945 (D.D.C. 1979) (summary of decision) (disclosure of documents to corporation's investment bankers waives privilege as to documents). *See also* United States v. American Tel. & Tel. Co., 642 F.2d 1285, 1299 (D.C. Cir. 1980) (voluntary disclosure to a third person generally waives attorney-client privilege, although disclosure to party with common interests does not constitute waiver of work product); *In re* Diasonics Sec. Litig., 110 F.R.D. 570 (D. Colo. 1986)(disclosure of corporate counsel's advice by joint director to his personal attorney waived corporate privilege). *But see* United States v. Gulf Oil

Corp., 760 F.2d 292 (1985) (Department of Energy attempted to subpoena documents Gulf Oil received from another oil corporation pursuant to a merger agreement, and the court held that the disclosure to Gulf as potential purchaser did not waive work-product privilege for documents prepared for litigation).

53. *See* Suburban Sew 'n Sweep, Inc. v. Swiss-Bernina, Inc., 91 F.R.D. 254 (N.D. Ill.1981). *See also* O'Leary v. Purcell Co., 108 F.R.D. 641 (D.N.C. 1986) (attorney-client privilege waived as to documents in the possession of defendant's former employee, where defendant made no attempt to retrieve the documents and did not have policies to protect confidentiality of documents).

54. *See* Mendenhall v. Barber-Green Co., 531 F. Supp. 951 (N.D. Ill. 1982) (evidentiary privileges cannot be waived by neglect); Connecticut Mut. Life Ins. Co. v. Shields, 18 F.R.D. 448 (S.D.N.Y. 1955) (requiring indication that client intended to waive privilege); Transamerica Computer Co. v. IBM, 573 F.2d 646 (9th Cir. 1978) (rush of extremely rigorous discovery schedule excuses inadvertent disclosure); Standard Chartered Bank v. Ayala Int'l Holdings, 111 F.R.D. 76 (disclosure of single sentence relating to attorney's advice as part of large document production did not waive attorney-client privilege). *But see* Weil v. Investment Indicators, Research & Management, Inc., 647 F.2d 18 (9th Cir. 1981) (holding bare assertion of no subjective intent to disclose is not enough to preserve privilege).

55. 329 U.S. 495 (1947).

56. *Id.* at 512.

57. United States v. El Paso Co., 682 F.2d 530 (5th Cir. 1982); LARKIN, FEDERAL TESTIMONIAL PRIVILEGES § 11.02 at 11–17 (1985) (applying requirement in practice has proved to be "troublesome").

58. 449 U.S. 383 (1981).

59. *In re* LTV Sec. Litig., 89 F.R.D. 595, 612 (N.D. Tex. 1981); Panter v. Marshall Field Co., 80 F.R.D. 718, 724 (N.D. Ill. 1978). *See also* FTC v. Grolier, Inc., 462 U.S. 19, 25 (1983); *In re* Murphy, 560 F.2d 326, 334–35; United States v. Leggett & Platt, Inc., 542 F.2d 655, 659 (6th Cir. 1976), *cert. denied,* 403 U.S. 945 (1977).

60. *See In re* International Sys. & Controls Corp. Sec. Ltd., 693 F.2d 1235, 1240–41 (5th Cir. 1982) ("modern corporate reality" dictates that litigation is anticipated whenever there is even a hint of scandal); *In re* Dayco Corp. Derivative Sec. Litig., 99 F.R.D. 616 (S.D. Ohio 1983) (interviews and materials prepared by special review committee of board of directors in cooperation with law firm investigating company's involvement with Foreign Transactions Co. were protected work product); *In re* LTV Sec. Litig., 89 F.R.D. at 611–13 (applying work-product doctrine to factual data gathered by special counsel hired during an SEC investigation); Massachusetts v. First Nat'l Supermarkets, Inc., 112 F.R.D. 149 (D. Mass. 1986) (work-product doctrine protects from discovery the identities of persons interviewed by client's attorney, and the dates and places of those interviews, as distinguished from asking the identity of persons with knowledge of the case). *But cf.* United States v. El Paso Co., 682 F.2d 530, 542 (5th Cir. 1982) ("in-house tax counsel's internal audit and analysis of potential tax liability not prepared in anticipation of litigation and therefore not protected work product"); *In re* Grand Jury Subpoena Dated Dec. 19, 1978, 599 F.2d 504, 510 (2d Cir. 1979) ("To the extent that an internal corporate investigation is made by management by itself, there is. . . no work

product protection," and "participation of general counsel does not automatically cloak the investigation with legal garb.").

61. *See, e.g.,* United States v. Nobles, 422 U.S. 225, 239–40 (1975) (agent for attorney); Duplan Corp. v. Deering Milliken Inc., 397 F. Supp. 1146, 1171 (D.S.C. 1974) (domestic and foreign patent agents).

62. United States v. Arthur Young & Co., 104 S. Ct. 1495, 1503 (1984).

63. *See in re* International Systems & Controls Corp. Sec. Ltd., 693 F.2d 1235, 1239 (5th Cir. 1982).

64. *See* United States v. American Tel. & Tel. Co., 642 F.2d 1285, 1299–1300 (D.C. Cir. 1980); WRIGHT & MILLER, FEDERAL PRACTICE AND PROCEDURE § 2024 at 210 (1970).

65. American Standard, Inc. v. Bendix Corp., 71 F.R.D. 443, 446 (S.D. Mo. 1976). *See also* United States v. American Tel. & Tel. Co., 642 F.2d at 1299 ("mere showing of a voluntary disclosure to a third person . . . should not suffice in itself for waiver of work product privilege"); GAF Corp. v. Eastman Kodak Corp., 85 F.R.D. 46 (S.D.N.Y. 1969) (disclosure of documents as part of voluntary cooperation with the government would not waive work-product protection); Stix Prods., Inc. v. United Merchants & Mfrs., Inc., 47 F.R.D. 334, 338 (C.D.N.Y. 1969).

66. United States v. American Tel.& Tel. Co., 642 F.2d 1285, 1299 (D.C. Cir. 1980).

67. Duplon Corp. v. Deering Milliken, Inc., 540 F.2d 730 (4th Cir. 1976) (concept of subject matter waiver not applicable to Rule 26 (b) (3)).

Thirty

General Legal Principles Respecting Fiduciary Responsibilities for Corporate Officers and Directors

William L. Stern and Michelle L. Kerr

Corporate officers and directors are fiduciaries for the corporation and stockholders. Their fiduciary responsibility is expanding. Today's corporate fiduciary can no longer hope to get by acting merely as a prudent person acting in good faith, but must also possess certain threshold skills and technical knowledge. The pressures for more stringent fiduciary standards encroach from all sides: from the courts, through their expansion of legal doctrines affecting the duties of corporate officers and directors; from the legislatures, through statutes aimed at curing perceived abuses; and from regulatory bodies, who have taken on an increasingly more activist role.

The costs and risks of litigating fiduciary issues are also changing. The considerations in litigating with the government, particularly an agency with which the corporate client has continuing dealings, are different from private litigation. In a derivative action brought by a shareholder on behalf of the corporation, the plaintiff is entitled to a jury trial if the corporate claim presents a legal issue.[1] Hence, the ultimate evaluation of the reasonableness of conduct may well be made by a jury of lay persons rather than a court. By whomever judged, however, fiduciary conduct will be determined by hindsight.

Common Law Standards and Their Statutory Supplements

Common law duties that directors and officers owe the corporation are the duties of loyalty and care. The duty of loyalty prohibits any personal gain by a director or officer at the expense of the corporation and its shareholders. The duty of care requires that an officer or director conduct the affairs of a corporation with such care as a reasonably prudent person would use under similar circumstances.

William L. Stern is a member and Michelle L. Kerr was formerly an associate of Severson, Werson, Berke & Melchior, San Francisco, California.

Duty of Loyalty

The duty of loyalty concerns the actions of a director or officer in his or her official capacity which conflict in any way with his or her personal interest. By assuming office, an individual commits allegiance to the corporate enterprise and acknowledges that the corporation's best interest must prevail over his or her individual interest. Accordingly, directors and officers must promote the shareholders' common interest and must not use their position to obtain any personal advantage beyond that enjoyed by fellow shareholders.[2] The scope of this duty is understandably broad. The recurring situations fall into four categories: conflicting and competing interests, usurpation of corporate opportunity, the purchase and sale by corporations of their own shares, and the sale of corporate control.

The Duty to Avoid Conflicting and Competing Interests

Problems concerning a director's or officer's duty of loyalty most commonly arise when an officer or director enters into a transaction with the corporation. Similarly, a conflict may be presented by a contract between the corporation and another corporation in which the director or officer also holds a position or interest.

Historically, contracts between a director or officer and the corporation were voidable at the request of the corporation or its stockholders without regard to the contract's fairness.[3] Today, the courts give these contracts strict scrutiny. When self-dealing is present, courts apply a test of "inherent fairness": The burden is on the interested director or officer to demonstrate good faith and the transaction's fairness to the corporation.[4] This test is generally applied in state courts as well.[5] "The essence of the test is whether or not under all the circumstances the transaction carries the earmarks of an arm's length bargain."[6]

The Delaware Supreme Court has provided a more specific definition of the "fairness" doctrine:

> The concept of fairness has two basic aspects: fair dealing and fair price. The former embraces questions of when the transaction was timed, how it was initiated, structured, negotiated, disclosed to the directors, and how the approvals of the directors and the stockholders were obtained. The latter aspect of fairness relates to the economic and financial considerations of the proposed [transaction], including all relevant factors. . . . However, the test of fairness is not a bifurcated one as between fair dealing and price. All aspects of the issue must be examined as a whole since the question is one of entire fairness.[7]

Clauses in some corporate charters and bylaws sanction contracts between management and the corporation and absolve a director or officer from consequent liability. Such clauses have been generally upheld.[8] However, they function only to shift the burden of demonstrating the fairness of the contract to the challenger; they will not prevent a transaction being voided if unfairness is shown.[9]

Many states have enacted statutes that control dealings between a corporation and its officers or directors. Section 144(a) of the Delaware General Corporation Law is illustrative:

> No contract or transaction between a corporation and 1 or more of its directors or officers, or between a corporation and any other corporation, partnership, association or other organization in which 1 or more of its directors or officers are directors or officers, or have a financial interest, shall be void or voidable solely for this reason, or solely because the director or officer is present at or participates in the meeting of the board or committee which authorizes the contract or transaction, or solely because his or their votes are counted for such purposes, if:
>
> (1) The material facts as to his relationship or interest and as to the transaction are disclosed or are known to the board of directors or the committee, and the board or committee in good faith authorizes the contract or transaction by the affirmative votes of a majority of the disinterested directors, even though the disinterested directors be less than a quorum; or
>
> (2) The material facts as to his relationship or interest and as to the contract or transaction are disclosed or are known to the shareholders entitled to vote thereon, and the contract or transaction is specifically approved in good faith by vote of the shareholders; or
>
> (3) The contract or transaction is fair as to the corporation as of the time it is authorized, approved or ratified by the board of directors, a committee or the shareholders.[10]

In seeking approval for an interested transaction, the officer and director must fully disclose the extent of his or her interest and the terms of the deal. Any material omission or inaccuracy will render the transaction voidable or, if the contract has been consummated, the interested party may be forced to turn over any profit to the corporation.[11]

In some states, an interested director's presence may count toward a quorum.[12] When the board acts to approve a suspect contract, an interested director should, after disclosure, abstain from voting. The fact that an interested director votes will not void the contract, however, if the interested director's vote was unnecessary to approve the transaction.[13] But if the director's vote was necessary, the resolution will be deemed not to have passed.[14]

If the transaction has not satisfied the requirements of the applicable statute, the "inherent fairness" test is applied.[15] On the other hand, satisfying the statutory provisions is no guaranty that the transaction is valid. It may still be attacked if it violates other statutory provisions or common law principles.[16]

The most frequent application of the requirement of fairness in self-dealing involves cases of sales to or purchases from the company by its directors and officers.[17] Financial transactions are also scrutinized. A director may be a creditor of the corporation[18] or may also enforce a loan by foreclosing on corporate property. Loans given by officers or directors to the corporation may be voidable if they are unfair, but they are not void per se.[19] An officer or director cannot, however, use his or her position to obtain an advantage over another creditor.[20]

Conflicting interests and the application of the inherent fairness test have also arisen in a claim by directors to profits in the form of bonuses,[21] to a lease of corporate assets to the directors as individuals,[22] to mortgage transactions between a corporation and its directors or officers,[23] and to agreements between the president of a parent corporation and the manager of its wholly owned subsidiary.[24]

Interests in Competing Enterprises

A director's or officer's fiduciary relationship to the corporation is not an absolute bar against holding an interest in a competing enterprise,[25] but if a director or officer holds such an interest, he or she must act in good faith and not violate any fiduciary duty to the corporation.[26] Thus, an officer or director with an interest in a competing venture must not actively use his or her position to prevent the corporation from competing with the personal venture.[27] Nor may an officer or director use information in a personal competing venture that the officer or director has learned in his or her official corporate capacity.[28]

Even if a corporation is profitable, an officer or director cannot plan for the creation of a competing business and commit acts of disloyalty, such as purchasing equipment for the corporation at a price in excess of its fair market value, soliciting the corporation's customers for the competing business, using the names of the corporation's customers on the competing business's customer list, using the corporation's money for trips to benefit the competing business, planning the competing business during the corporation's business hours, permitting a kickback to be paid to one employee, and recommending salary increases for disloyal employees.[29] If a director or officer resigns from the corporation to form a competing business, he or she will be liable for breaching his or her duty of loyalty for the conduct that began before the resignation was effective, even though most of the improper conduct occurred after the resignation was effective.[30]

When a director or officer has breached this duty to the corporation, the courts may impose a constructive trust for the benefit of the corporation upon the profits from the competing business.[31] Or the courts may award the corporation the amounts it would have earned from the diverted business.[32] Courts may even impose a constructive trust on the competing business itself, allowing the corporation to use the business's property as it sees fit.[33] Unless the officer or director proves the value of his or her services to the corporation, the court may require him or her to forfeit the entire compensation received or accrued while engaging in disloyal conduct in addition to paying the corporation for damages resulting from disloyal activities. That is what the court did in *Chelsea Industries, Inc. v. Gaffney.*[34]

Usurpation of Corporate Opportunity

Closely related to the prohibition against improper competition is the bar on usurpation of corporate opportunities. When a director or an officer encounters a business opportunity that the corporation might be interested in, he or she must first make the venture available to the corporation before taking advantage of it personally. The leading case of *Guth v. Loft, Inc.*[35] holds that a corporate officer or director is presented with a business opportunity that the corporation is financially able to undertake may not undertake it personally if the opportunity is, from its nature, in the line of the corporation's business and of practical advantage to it, and is one in which the corporation has an interest or a reasonable expectancy, and if by embracing the opportunity the self-interest of the officer or director will be brought into conflict with the corporation.

The difficulty in this otherwise straightforward area lies in determining what a corporate opportunity is.[36] In determining this, courts generally consider the totality of circumstances.[37] Courts direct their attention to the following considerations:[38]

- Whether the opportunity was one in which the corporation had an interest or expectancy
- Whether the opportunity was essential, necessary, or merely desirable to the corporation's reasonable needs and aspirations
- Whether the opportunity embraced areas adaptable to its business and in which it might easily or logically expand
- Whether the opportunity was prospectively harmful or unfair

- Whether the corporation had the financial ability to acquire the opportunity
- Whether the opportunity included activities that the corporation had fundamental knowledge of; practical experience in; facilities, equipment, or personnel for; or the ability to pursue

Opportunities for which the corporation has an interest must be made available to it. But if, after full disclosure, the board in good faith rejects the venture, a director or officer is free to pursue the opportunity.[39] An officer will not be relieved of liability for usurping a corporate opportunity even if a corporation is financially unable to pursue the opportunity unless the corporation is insolvent.[40] Otherwise, directors would refrain from exerting their strongest efforts on behalf of the corporation and be tempted to make an inaccurate assessment of the corporation's financial ability.[41] In some jurisdictions, an officer will be absolved from usurping a corporate opportunity only if the corporation is financially unable to undertake it, the opportunity is disclosed to the shareholders and they reject the opportunity, and such action is not detrimental to corporate creditors.[42]

In *International Bankers Life Insurance Co. v. Holloway,*[43] the court held that directors and officers were personally liable for any profits they made at the expense of the corporation. In addition, where the officers or directors acted with malice toward the corporation, punitive damages could be awarded.[44] The court said, "We should not say to defaulting fiduciaries, that the most for which they can be held accountable in equity are the profits which would have remained theirs had they not been called to account." The court went on to say:

> It is consistent with equitable principles for equity to exact of a defaulting corporate fiduciary not only the profits rightfully belonging to the corporation, but an additional exaction for the unconscionable conduct. There should be a deterrent to conduct which equity condemns and for which it will grant relief. The limits beyond which equity should not go in its exactions are discoverable in the facts of each case which gives rise to equitable relief.[45]

Even a corporate officer who is not unjustly enriched as a result of usurping a corporate opportunity may be found liable to the corporation for damages equal to the profit the corporation would have received on the opportunity.[46]

Purchase and Sale by Corporations of Their Own Shares

The key issue in evaluating fiduciary conduct in connection with the purchase or sale of corporate shares is whether the transaction was designed to further bona fide business objectives or to perpetuate existing management. Generally, directors and officers breach their duty of loyalty if they use assets of the corporation, or corporate mechanisms, to protect their own position in the corporation.[47] Often this occurs when corporate fiduciaries make use of the issuance, sale, or purchase of stock by their corporation to maintain or to obtain voting control and thus perpetuate their position.[48] If, however, the action taken to maintain or obtain control is motivated by a valid corporate purpose, courts will uphold the transaction even though incident to the action is the protection of the directors' positions.[49]

Jurisdictions differ as to the test to be applied to determine the legality of a defensive mechanism to protect their control of the corporation. The differing views and some of the cases applying these views are discussed in detail in the section of this paper on the business judgment rule. The business judgment rule will therefore only be summarized in this section of the paper.

Under the business judgment rule, directors are presumed to have acted properly and in good faith and are called to account for their actions only when they are shown to have engaged in self-dealing or fraud, or to have acted in bad faith.[50] The plaintiff has the initial burden of proving the director's interest or bad faith, then the burden shifts to the director to prove that the transaction was fair and reasonable to the corporation.[51] (As discussed in more detail later in this chapter, Delaware places the initial burden on the director in evaluating defensive tactics for corporate control.) "[T]he business judgment rule's presumption is rebutted only where retention of control is the 'primary,' 'sole' or 'predominant' motive underlying the disputed decision."[52]

Until recently, this standard was hard for plaintiffs to overcome and allowed considerable leeway for corporate stock purchases. For example, courts allowed a corporation to enter into a merger agreement involving the exchange of shares, even though the exchange was for the express purpose of increasing the likelihood of consummation of the merger and discouraging a hostile tender offer;[53] to issue stock to a "white knight";[54] to bring a lawsuit to enjoin a proposed merger on antitrust grounds and to acquire other companies to make the merger less attractive and to exacerbate the antitrust problems;[55] and to acquire dissidents' shares, provided it is done to eliminate a threat to the business and is not accomplished for the sole or primary purpose of perpetuating the control of management.[56]

Recently, however, courts have found breaches of fiduciary duty where there is no significant justification for a transaction and there is evidence that management's decision was based on self-interest. In *Norlin Corp. v. Rooney, Pace Inc.*,[57] the court ruled that a target company's directors breached fiduciary duty by issuing new voting stock to a wholly owned subsidiary and a newly created employee stock option plan (ESOP) to concentrate voting control in their hands. The court noted that the stock transferred was to be voted by the directors and members, who also served as directors of the ESOP; the ESOP was created the same day the stock was issued to it; and no rationale was offered for the transfer except to oppose the acquisition. The directors failed to satisfy their burden that the transfer was fair and reasonable.[58] That the takeover in itself might not have been in the best interests of the corporation did not justify the use of defensive tactics that were not fair and reasonable.[59]

Transfer of shares to an ESOP has been held invalid where the transfer was made after an acquirer took control of the target corporation;[60] and where the ESOP was approved only after a tender offer was announced, the shares were purchased from shareholders at prices below the tender offer, and there was no evidence showing what threat was posed to employees or how the ESOP would benefit the shareholders.[61]

Courts have also struck down corporate stock purchases outside the ESOP context. In *Condec v. Lunkenheimer Co.,*[62] the directors issued 75,000 shares of authorized but unissued stock in their corporation in exchange for stock in another publicly held corporation after an outside corporation acquired slightly over 50 percent of the previously outstanding shares. The directors claimed that they opposed the attempted takeover due to the tenderor corporation's excessive debts and low profits, yet the court held otherwise. The court found they were motivated by self-interest because the stock issuance was done in haste without any factual investigation by the target company to justify its conclusion that the offeror's proposed acquisition would be detrimental to the target company's shareholders.

The courts have also found breaches of fiduciary duty where management, in anticipation of a proxy contest, acquired outstanding purchase warrants for no business purpose, created an employee stock purchase plan to move shares into friendly hands, and testified falsely as to the timing and motivation of the various transactions;[63] where there was a sham sale of shares with a secret repurchase and hold harmless from the corporate insider to the purchaser to strengthen management's position in a contest for corporate control;[64] and where a target company acquired another company for the sole purpose of creating an antitrust problem for the tendering company.[65]

Sale of Corporate Control at a Premium

If the directors and officers are also major shareholders, they owe a duty of loyalty to the minority shareholders. This duty arises in connection with a sale of corporate control when the officers or directors are selling shareholders. If the sale will cause corporate harm, the seller's profit will be scrutinized by the court.[66] The courts determine whether the sale is entirely fair to minority shareholders.[67]

In *Perlman v. Feldmann,*[68] the chairman of the board marshaled a group of shareholders which together sold a controlling interest in the corporation at twice the market price of the stock. Although there was no demonstrable harm to the corporation, the court held that there was a reasonable expectancy of corporate harm in the future which justified return of the premium to the corporation. The holding was buttressed by the particular facts underlying the sale. Feldmann had sold control of a steel-making company to a syndicate of end users in the face of a steel shortage during the Korean War. The court felt that Feldmann and his cohorts "in selling control to a potential customer had appropriated to their personal benefit a corporate asset: the premium which the company's product could command in a time of market shortage."[69]

Jones v. H.F. Ahmanson & Co.[70] is a classic example of breach of the majority shareholders' duty to the minority. In that case, the majority shareholders of a closely held savings and loan association transferred their shares to a holding company in exchange for holding company shares. The holding company went public, leaving the minority with unmarketable shares in a nonpublic subsidiary. The holding company then offered to exchange its shares with the minority shareholders at a much less favorable exchange rate than that afforded the majority shareholders.

A similar breach was found in *Brown v. Halbert.*[71] Halbert was chairman of the board, president, and majority shareholder of a savings and loan association. He secretly negotiated with another savings and loan association for the sale of his controlling shares at two and a half times book value, though he knew the outsider's plans to change management would likely devalue the minority's shares. After his sale, he encouraged minority stockholders to sell their stock at less than book value, forecasting doom for their investment if they did not. The court held that as a majority shareholder-director, Halbert owed the other shareholders the duty to act with full disclosure when contemplating a sale of control, so that every opportunity to obtain the same advantage was afforded the minority shareholders. The court found Halbert had breached his duty and ordered that his premium be divided evenly among all those who sold their stock. When a sale of corporate control is made, director-shareholders have a fiduciary obligation to make reasonable inquiry into the acquirer's motives.[72]

On the other hand, in *Wellman v. Dickinson,*[73] the court held that there was no breach of fiduciary duty by a dissident director who sought to promote a tender offer for his company and in fact received a premium for his stock.

This duty to minority shareholders also arises in the context of short-form mergers. A majority of states have statutes permitting a substantial majority of the shareholders to eliminate the minority by merging without requiring any shareholder vote.[74] A valid corporate purpose is required in some states[75] but not in others.[76] In the context of a cash-out merger, a director of the acquiring corporation that is a majority shareholder of the target corporation has the burden of establishing the fairness of a merger to the minority shareholders of the target corporation,[77] as do directors of the target corporation who are also employees of the acquiring-majority-shareholder-corporation.[78]

Courts have also considered whether "greenmail" payments by a corporation are a breach of directors' fiduciary duties to shareholders. For example, in *Heckmann v. Ahmanson*,[79] a California appellate court affirmed the imposition of a constructive trust on a majority shareholder's "greenmail" profits. In *Heckman,* Disney Corporation acquired another corporation having sizable debt three days after a "raider" informed Disney that it would make a tender offer for 49 percent of Disney's outstanding shares. Disney bought back all the raider's stock, borrowing the entire sum. The plaintiffs, Disney shareholders, moved to preliminarily enjoin the "greenmail" payment, and the trial court granted the motion. The Court of Appeal affirmed, noting the short time between the tender offer and the repurchase, and shifting to the directors the burden of demonstrating that the transaction was entered in good faith and that it was inherently fair to the corporation.[80]

In contrast to *Heckman,* in *Polk v. Good,*[81] the Delaware Supreme Court upheld Texaco's repurchase of 9.9 percent of its stock from the Bass Group at a premium of 3 percent over market where Texaco was concerned that Bass would make a hostile move while Texaco was acquiring Getty Oil Company. The court held that the decision of the Texaco board of directors was protected by Delaware's business judgment rule because after a reasonable investigation, the board had a justifiable belief that there was a threat to Texaco. The court noted that the transaction was approved by ten outside directors and that it was supported by advice rendered by an investment banker and legal counsel.[82]

The duty of loyalty, both at common law and under statute, imposes high standards on officers and directors. In any transaction that pits their own interest against that of the corporation or its shareholders, officers and directors must scrupulously maintain the appearance and the fact of full disclosure and unquestioned fairness.

The Duty of Care

Corporate officers and directors have a duty to exercise due care in the management of corporate affairs and assets. Officers are generally held to a higher standard of care than directors because of their greater familiarity with the affairs of the corporation.[83] As to directors, the law historically tied their standard of care to the care of an individual managing his or her own affairs.[84] This standard was relaxed, however, and in 1891 the Supreme Court defined the care expected of corporate directors as "that which ordinarily prudent and diligent men would exercise under similar circumstances. . . . What may be negligent in one case may not be want of ordinary care in another, and the question of negligence is therefore ultimately a question of fact, to be determined under all circumstances."[85]

Today the common law standard of care is supplemented in most states by statute. The law of the state in which the corporation is incorporated governs.[86] Most of these statutes are similar to section 8.30(a) of the Model Business Corporation Act:

> (a) A director shall discharge his duties as a director including his duties as a member of a committee:
> (1) in good faith;
> (2) with the care an ordinary prudent person in a like position would exercise under similar circumstances; and
> (3) in a manner he reasonably believes to be in the best interest of the corporation.

The Official Comments to this section provide some elucidation of the wording:

> (1) The reference to "ordinarily prudent person" embodies long traditions of the common law, in contrast to suggested standards that might call for some undefined degree of expertise, like "ordinarily prudent businessmen." The phrase recognizes the need for innovation, essential to profit orientation, and focuses on the basic director attributes of common sense, practical wisdom and informed judgment.
>
> (2) The phrase "in a like position" recognizes that the "care" under consideration is that which would be used by the "ordinarily prudent person" if he were a director of the particular corporation.
>
> (3) The combined phrase "in a like position . . . under similar circumstances" is intended to recognize that (a) the nature and extent of responsibilities will vary, depending upon such factors as the size, complexity, urgency, and location of activities carried on by the particular corporation, (b) decisions must be made on the basis of the information known to the directors without the benefit of hindsight, and (c) the special background, qualifications, and management responsibilities of a particular director may be relevant in evaluating his compliance with the standard of care. Even though the quoted

> phrase takes into account the special ground, qualifications, and management responsibilities of a particular director, it does not excuse a director lacking business experience or particular expertise from exercising the common sense, practical wisdom, and informed judgment of an "ordinarily prudent person."[87]

Most states lack statutes governing the standard of care for officers. Under the Model Business Corporation Act, an officer with discretionary authority must meet the same standard of conduct required of directors, but his or her ability to rely on information provided by others may be more limited given the officer's obligation to be familiar with corporate affairs.[88]

The Business Judgment Rule

In evaluating a manager's compliance with the duty of care in the decision-making process, courts follow the "business judgment" rule.[89] Courts define the rule differently. Some courts use language similar to the standards set forth in section 8.30(a) of the Model Business Corporation Act. [90] Under Delaware law and that of most states:

> [The business judgment rule] is a presumption that in making a business decision the directors of a corporation acted on an informed basis, in good faith and in the honest belief that the action taken was in the best interests of the company. . . . Absent an abuse of discretion, that judgment will be respected by the courts. The burden is on the party challenging the decision to establish facts rebutting the presumption.[91]

Under the business judgment rule, courts will not second-guess the director's decision in the absence of fraud, bad faith, gross overreaching, or abuse of discretion.[92] The presumption of good faith is heightened when the majority of the board consists of independent outside directors.[93]

The requisites for the application of the business judgment rule are that: (1) the directors must be disinterested; (2) the directors must inform themselves, before making a business decision, of all material information reasonably available to them; and (3) having become so informed, they must act with the requisite care in the discharge of their duties.[94]

Where the business judgment rule applies, the standard of care is gross negligence in Delaware and probably in other jurisdictions as well.[95] Although there is language in some cases suggesting that it is possible to collect damages from directors for negligence even where the business judgment rule applies, as a practical matter only gross negligence will render a director liable for a mistake in judgment. As the court stated in *Joy v. North*:

> While it is often stated that corporate directors and officers will be liable for negligence in carrying out their corporate duties,

> all seem agreed that such statement is misleading. . . . Whereas an automobile driver who makes a mistake in judgment as to speed or distance injuring a pedestrian will likely be called upon to respond in damages, a corporate officer who makes a mistake in judgment as to economic conditions, consumer tastes or production line efficiency will rarely, if ever, be found liable for damages suffered by the corporation.[96]

The business judgment rule does not apply outside a decision-making context,[97] such as where directors abdicate their functions or fail to act.[98] Presumably, if a director is being charged with a breach of a duty for inattention to his or her duties, the general standard of care previously articulated should apply.

The business judgment rule governs only where the directors are shown not to have a self-interest in the transaction at issue.[99] Once self-dealing or bad faith is demonstrated, the duty of loyalty supersedes the duty of care, and the burden shifts to the director to "prove that the transaction was fair and reasonable to the corporation."[100]

Applications of the Business Judgment Rule

Despite the strong language that a director will virtually never be liable for a mistake in judgment, the courts have recently, in an increasing number of cases, held a director liable, most often for decisions made to protect the director's control over the corporation.

Routine Management Decisions. The business judgment rule precludes liability for everyday business matters unless there is self-dealing or bad faith. This includes such decisions as the sale of corporate property,[101] voluntary tax payments to local authorities,[102] or choosing lawyers.[103]

Derivative Suits. Several recent cases have applied the business judgment rule to evaluate whether the requirements of derivative suits have been satisfied.[104] The business judgment rule comes into play in several ways: in reviewing the board's refusal to act pursuant to the shareholder's demand; in determining whether demand would be futile; in efforts by independent disinterested directors to dismiss the action as inimical to the corporation's best interests; and as a defense to the merits of the suit.[105]

In *Aronson,* the court applied the business judgment rule to determine whether, in a derivative action, the demand required of shareholders on the board would have been futile. The court held that demand would have been futile if a reasonable doubt is created that: (1) the directors are disinterested and independent and (2) the challenged transaction was otherwise the product of a valid exercise of business judgment.[106] The plaintiff must allege facts that support a reasonable doubt that the challenged transaction was the product of a valid exercise of business judgment.[107]

There is a split in authority as to whether the wide discretion afforded directors under the business judgment rule applies when a special litigation committee (a disinterested committee selected by interested directors) recommends dismissal of a suit.[108] In New York, the business judgment rule limits judicial scrutiny of the recommendations of a special litigation committee to the committee's disinterested independence and the sufficiency of the investigation.[109] The Delaware and Connecticut courts recognize that there may be a conflict of interest and have adopted a stricter standard of review: If a derivative action is properly brought, an independent committee of directors may obtain a dismissal only if the trial court finds (1) that the committee was independent, acted in good faith, and made a reasonable investigation; and (2) that in the court's independent business judgment as to the corporation's best interest, the action should be dismissed.[110]

Corporate Control. Historically, even when reviewing the defensive tactics voted on by directors to maintain control of a corporation, courts took a hands-off approach. In the absence of self-dealing, fraud, overreaching, or lack of good faith, the courts refused to second-guess an informed decision to reject a takeover proposal.[111] Courts have recently taken a less deferential and closer look at director's decisions pertaining to control of the corporation.[112] Courts now focus on two issues: (1) whether the motive of the director was self-perpetuation, and (2) whether the decision was an informed one.

Smith v. Von Gorkom[113] began the trend in Delaware away from judicial deference and toward scrutiny. In *Smith,* the issue was whether the board had made an informed business judgment in submitting to the shareholders a proposal to purchase a corporation for $55 per share, $17 per share above market price, based on a two-hour board meeting. The court reversed summary judgment in favor of the directors, despite a number of mitigating circumstances: a substantial per-share premium; the board members' excellent qualifications and up-to-date familiarity with the corporation's affairs; a subsequent three-month search for better offers; and the shareholders' approval. The *Smith* decision thus portends a rule of judicial scrutiny that precludes a merger or sale of corporate control, absent an emergency, without a significant formal study of the company's market value or solicitation of bids or both.[114]

Since *Smith,* the Delaware Supreme Court has articulated an even stricter standard for reviewing a decision to adopt a defensive mechanism to maintain corporate control:

> [W]hen the business judgment rule applies to adoption of a defensive mechanism, the initial burden will lie with the directors. The "directors must show that they had reasonable

> grounds for believing that a danger to corporate policy and effectiveness existed. . . . [T]hey satisfy that burden 'by showing good faith and reasonable investigation. . . .'", *Unocal,* 493 A.2d at 955 (citing *Cheff v. Mathes,* 199 A.2d at 554–55). In addition, the directors must show that the defensive mechanism was "reasonable in relation to the threat posed." *Unocal,* 493 A.2d at 955. Moreover, that proof is materially enhanced, as we noted in *Unocal,* where, as here, a majority of the board favoring the proposal consisted of outside independent directors who have acted in accordance with the foregoing standards. *Unocal,* 493 A.2d at 955; *Aronson,* 473 A.2d at 815. Then, the burden shifts back to the plaintiffs who have the ultimate burden of persuasion to show a breach of the directors' fiduciary duties. *Unocal,* 493 A.2d at 958.[115]

To satisfy the directors' burden, they must have analyzed the nature of the takeover bid and its effect on the corporate enterprise.[116] The board under appropriate circumstances may consider:

> the inadequacy of the bid, the nature and timing of the offer, questions of illegality, the impact on constituencies other than shareholders, the risk of nonconsummation, and the basic stockholder interests at stake, including the past actions of the bidder and its affiliates in other takeover contests.[117]

The reason for the stricter business judgment rule is the "omnipresent specter that a board may be acting primarily in its own interests, rather than those of the corporation and its shareholders."[118] This higher standard of scrutiny has been followed in some jurisdictions,[119] but not in others.[120]

The higher standard of scrutiny has been applied to evaluate various defensive tactics used during a takeover contest. For example, the court struck down a sell tender and transfer to an ESOP as a defensive tactic where the only threat to the corporation was that the shareholders might prefer an option to the tender offer and the self tender actually precluded any other options.[121] By contrast, in *Unocal Corp. v. Mesa Petroleum Co.,*[122] the court upheld a self-tender that excluded from participation a shareholder making a hostile tender offer where the board satisfied its burden of showing that it acted in good faith, that it made a reasonable investigation in determining that the tender offer was inadequate and coercive, and that the exchange offer was reasonably related to the threat that minority shareholders would be forced to accept highly subordinated "junk bonds."

The court reached a similar result in *Ivanhoe Partners v. Newmont Min. Corp.,*[123] in which it approved a corporation's decision to avoid a hostile tender offer by declaring a substantial dividend to make the corporation a less attractive target and to help its largest shareholder to engage in a street sweep of the corporation's stock, increasing its ownership of the corporation to 49.7 percent, and by entering into a standstill agreement with the shareholder that allowed the corporation to maintain control of the board of directors.[124]

In both *Unocal* and *Ivanhoe,* the threat to the shareholders was not only that the hostile tender offer was inadequate and coercive, but also that the offeror, T. Boone Pickens, had been involved in several attempts to acquire and break up other corporations, resulting in the payment of "greenmail" or severe restructuring of the target companies.[125]

The courts have evaluated the use of poison pills implemented during a takeover contest[126] as well as a poison pill implemented to ward off future takeover attempts. The court in *Moran v. Household International, Inc.*[127] upheld a plan adopted to ward off future hostile bids because it permitted certain types of hostile tender offers, the directors had satisfied their burden of showing a reasonable investigation and a good-faith belief that there was a danger to corporate effectiveness, and the board's response to any actual takeover bid would be subject to further review.

The court struck down a poison pill plan adopted to oppose a hostile tender offer where management opposed the plan without considering its value to the shareholders, the board adopted the poison pill based only on a conclusory and biased opinion of an investment adviser that did not even mention whether the tender offer price was fair, the hostile bidder would incur a huge capital loss, the corporation would be saddled with a heavy long-term debt, and the shareholders would not necessarily be better off.[128]

Even if the board of directors' investigation shows that a tender offer is inadequate, a poison pill will not be upheld if the triggering prices are unreasonably high, thereby preventing tender offers, of if the price is unsupported by the board's investigation.[129] On the other hand, directors may adopt poison pills that encourage bidding and may even selectively enforce or waive rights under a previously adopted poison pill to promote additional bidding.[130]

In *Revlon, Inc. v. MacAndrews & Forbes Holdings, Inc.,*[131] the Delaware Supreme Court held that a lockup option and a no-shop provision were breaches of fiduciary duty to shareholders. After several earlier bids and defensive moves by Revlon, Pantry Pride bid $56.25 cash per share. In response, Revlon entered into a leveraged buyout agreement with Forstmann Little, whereby Forstmann agreed to pay $57.25 per share, in cash and debt securities, and agreed to protect noteholders who had threatened litigation against Revlon's directors; Forstmann received a lockup option on two Revlon divisions, at a price far below their actual value, if anyone were to acquire more than 40 percent of Revlon's shares and a no-shop provision. The court stated that although lockups are not per se illegal where they encourage bidders to enter the bidding, in this case the lockup destroyed the bidding, the bid was not substantially higher than the previous bid, and "a significant by-product of that action [was] to protect the directors against a perceived threat of personal liability."[132] The court also held that the no-shop provision was impermissible at the stage of the negotiations when a takeover was inevitable, since at that point, "a board's primary duty becomes that of an auctioneer responsible for selling the company to the highest bidder.[133]

Revlon has not foreclosed the use of lockup options and no-shop provisions where they encourage bidding rather than foreclose it.[134] In *Samjeus Partners I v. Burlington Industries, Inc.*,[135] the court approved a merger agreement where the no-shop clause was actually a "window-shop" clause—i.e., it allowed the board to consider other bids, but not solicit them; there was no auction-ending lockup agreement, and, in fact, bids were increased after the merger; and the board reached all of its decisions after thorough consultation with its financial and legal advisers.

Revlon's requirement that directors act as auctioneers responsible for selling the company to the highest bidder, rather than defenders of the corporate structure, applies only when the sale of the company is inevitable.[136] The transfer of 49.7 percent of a corporation's shares by a street sweep is not a sale where the corporation retains its independence and control of the corporation.[137] However, in *Black & Decker Corp. v. American Standard, Inc.*,[138] the court held that a recapitalization plan, approved as an alternative to a hostile tender offer, that effectively transferred control of the corporation to management would be a sale of the corporation, and the directors therefore had a duty to sell to the highest bidder, which they breached by adopting retirement and severance plans that provided for substantial payments of company funds if the hostile tender offer succeeded.

Even in jurisdictions that do not apply Delaware's stricter standard for evaluating directors' duties in adopting defensive tactics during a hostile takeover, courts have taken a less deferential approach to these types of decisions. For example, like *Revlon*, *Hanson Trust PLC v. ML SCM Acquisition, Inc.*[139] also struck down the use of lockup options in a "fast-moving bidding contest." Applying New York's business judgment rule, the court concluded that "where directors make decisions likely to affect shareholder welfare, the duty of due care requires that a director's decision be made on the basis of 'reasonable diligence' in gathering and considering material information."[140] Although the directors' deliberations were not as grossly negligent as those in *Smith*, the directors breached their duty of care in that the board relied on their financial adviser's conclusory oral opinion that the option prices were "within the range of fairness" without inquiring into the basis of their opinion or the range of fair value; the board never sought any documents to support the adviser's opinion; the board never inquired into the effect on the company if the options were exercised or how the opinion would be exercised; and the board failed to use available time to obtain the critical information. That the transaction had been proposed by management directors having an interest in the arrangement should have prompted the independent directors to more closely scrutinize the transaction to protect the shareholders.[141]

Cases Not within Business Judgment Rule

A handful of cases find a breach of fiduciary duty as a result of a director's inattention to his or her responsibilities, rather than a conscious decision to act. In those cases, the business judgment rule does not apply. A director's inaction is measured by the common law duty of care as supplemented by statutory duties. It is unclear whether the standard of care is negligence or gross negligence. Some cases suggest that negligence may be sufficient to find liability, although the conduct of the directors in these cases appears to exceed mere negligence.[142]

For example, in *Francis v. United Jersey Bank,*[143] the New Jersey Supreme Court held that a director was personally liable in negligence for failing to prevent the misappropriation of trust funds by other directors who were also officers and shareholders of the corporation where the director had made only one visit to the corporate offices, made no effort to assure that the policies and practices of the corporation complied with industry custom or law, and generally "never made any effort to discharge any of her responsibilities as a director."[144] According to the *Francis* court, directors must keep informed about the activities of the corporation; maintain familiarity with the financial status of the corporation by reviewing financial statements and, in some circumstances, assuring that bookkeeping methods conform to industry custom and usage; and, if the director discovers an illegality, object, resign, or consult counsel.[145]

In addition, in *Selheimer v. Manganese Corp.,*[146] the corporation owned a small New Jersey plant that, for lack of a nearby railroad, could not economically produce the company's product in any substantial quantity. The corporation offered its stock to the public, representing that the proceeds would be used to purchase another plant that could produce in quantity. The directors failed to make more than token efforts to put the new plant in operation, and instead the corporation squandered the proceeds on unprofitable operations at the old plant. The court felt that the directors' conduct could be portrayed "if not as fraudulent, then assuredly as imprudent beyond explanation," and that the "actions of the managing defendants were palpably careless, reckless and wanting in that diligence and skill of reasonably prudent men and not the result of judgment or acts of ineptitude."[147] This negligence holding appears to stand on its own; it should be noted, however, that *Selheimer* also involved self-dealing by the same directors. Some of the squandered funds went to buy equipment from intermediaries which apparently kicked back some of the purchase price to defendants, who also granted themselves unauthorized salaries.

Although the Pennsylvania Supreme Court affirmed the trial court's finding of liability for negligence, it reversed the lower court's measurement of damages. The trial court had awarded the plaintiff corporation the difference between the amount realized by the public offering and the amount realized upon the sale of the corporation's assets at the time of its demise—that is, all of the losses the corporation incurred during its existence as a public corporation. The high court reversed, holding that the defendant directors were liable only for whatever damage their negligent actions had proximately caused:

> In adopting this measure of damages—tantamount to attributing all Manganese's losses to defendants' conduct—we believe the chancellor erred. The duty of reimbursement should be limited to those losses which were proximately caused by the negligent and wasteful conduct of defendants. As this Court said in *Hunt v. Aufderheide et al.*, 330 Pa. at page 368, 199 A. at page 348: "* * * the value of its [the corporation's] diverted assets marks the maximum of its recovery." The record does not substantiate a finding that all Manganese losses were attributable to the defendants' misconduct. The nexus between Manganese's losses and defendants' negligent and wasteful actions must act as the basis for reimbursement. To establish such relationship the matter must be remanded to the court below.[148]

The case of *DePinto v. Provident Security Life Insurance Co.*,[149] began in 1958, came before the federal district court on five separate occasions, was appealed to the court of appeal four times, and was decided in 1969—eleven years after the suit was instituted. DePinto was an obstetrician who held a directorship in United, an insurance company. The charge against him was that he had not faithfully discharged his duties. There were no allegations of self-dealing, fraud, or bad faith. He knew nothing of the company's financial condition, and he paid little attention to its affairs. When a takeover was attempted, DePinto resigned at the request of the controlling shareholder, leaving no one to effectively oppose it.

In the first trial, the trial court empaneled an advisory jury, which exonerated DePinto. The district judge disregarded the jury's verdict and entered a judgment against all defendants, including DePinto. The court of appeal ruled that the defendants were entitled to a jury trial and that the judge could not award damages in excess of a jury verdict.[150] In the next trial, DePinto's case was severed from the other defendants', and the jury returned a verdict of $314,794 against him alone. The damages were measured according to the amount United lost in the transfer of assets to the raiding party—the loss proximately caused by DePinto's negligence in failing to oppose the transaction. The court of appeal affirmed:

> The jury could have found that DePinto's failure to make a reasonable investigation as to whether the ultimate plan would adversely affect United, his resignation from the board of directors in compliance with Kelly's request and without having made such an investigation, and his failure, as a member of the board of United, to fight for the best interests of United, considered together, constituted negligence and a breach of fiduciary duty and was a proximate cause of the loss sustained by United as a result of the October 18, 1957 transaction.[151]

The lesson of *DePinto* is that even outside directors may be held liable for negligence by inaction, and resignation from the board may not save an individual from liability for negligence after having assumed a directorship. Furthermore, defending a lawsuit can take years and cost enormous amounts in defense, even if the defendant is ultimately exonerated.

Cases similar to *DePinto,* based upon allegations of negligent mismanagement and nonmanagement, provide some further guidance on corporate fiduciaries' liability. In *Stern v. Lucy Webb Hayes National Training School,*[152] the defendant fiduciaries had failed to supervise the management of the charitable organization's investments or even to attend the board and committee meetings. The court held defendants had breached their duty of care, yet it awarded plaintiff no relief except to order procedures to prevent a recurrence of the breach. And in *Harman v. Willbern,*[153] the court exonerated a director who was not involved in the day-to-day operation of the corporation from liability for failing to prevent the majority shareholder from looting the corporation. The court noted there was no evidence that the director would, "in the ordinary course of events, have seen any reports or statements which would have made the transactions suspect"; the director had a "substantial financial stake" in the corporation; and he checked in "periodically" with the officers in charge of day-to-day operations.[154]

Liability to Third Persons

A corporate officer or director has a fiduciary responsibility toward the corporation, but usually not toward third persons.[155] A director or officer may still be held liable to a third person for his or her torts, even though committed in his or her official capacity.[156] However, "[d]irectors or officers of a corporation do not incur personal liability for torts of the corporation merely by reason of their official position unless they participate in the wrong or authorize or direct that it be done. . . . They are not responsible to third persons for negligence amounting merely to nonfeasance, to a breach of duty owing to the corporation alone; the act must also constitute a breach of duty owed to the third person."[157]

In a recent California case, the court held that the business judgment rule does not define the standard of care that directors or officers owe to third parties who might be injured by their personal conduct.[158] Such a rule seems to hold directors to a higher standard of care to third-party strangers than to their own beneficiaries, i.e., the corporation or shareholders. Whether other courts will follow this rule is unclear.

In several recent cases, courts have held directors or officers liable for negligence to third persons. An example is *National Iranian Gas Co. v. Basco Industries, Inc.*,[159] in which the court found the president of a corporation liable to a purchaser of equipment for negligence in directing employees to destroy the equipment while it was still in the corporation's possession. And in *Frances T. v. Village Green Owners Association*, the California Supreme Court held that a condominium owner who was raped in her dwelling sufficiently pled a cause of action for negligence against members of the board of directors of the condominium association—in their personal capacities—based on their having ordered her to remove lighting she had installed to protect herself after a previous break-in and by failing to take action to repair the hazardous lighting condition within a reasonable period of time.[160]

Common Law Defense of Reliance upon Others

Directors often rely in good faith upon others in situations when they are later alleged to have breached their fiduciary duties. Reliance on advice of counsel is a defense.[161] State statutes commonly specify the sort of reliance that will excuse a director from any personal liability. Most of these statutes are similar to section 8.30(b) and (c) of the Model Business Corporation Act.

Section 8.30(b) states:

> (b) In discharging his duties a director is entitled to rely on information, opinions, reports, or statements, including financial statements and other financial data, if the prepared or presented by:
>
> (1) one or more officers or employees of the corporation whom the director reasonably believes to be reliable and competent in the matters presented;
>
> (2) legal counsel, public accountants, or other persons as to matters the director reasonably believes are within the person's professional or expert competence; or
>
> (3) a committee of the board of directors of which he is not a member if the director reasonably believes the committee merits confidence.

This defense is limited, however, by section 8.30(e), which provides:

> (c) A director is not acting in good faith if he has knowledge concerning the matter in question that makes reliance otherwise permitted by subsection (b) unwarranted.

No states have statutes governing an officer's entitlement to rely on others. However, section 8.42 was recently added to the Model Business Corporation Act, and it permits officers to rely on information to the same extent as directors under section 8.30(b)(1) and (2), but does not permit them to rely on "a committee of the board of directors," as directors are allowed to do by section 8.30(b)(3).

In addition, general statutory provisions in the statutes of some states allow directors to rely in good faith without any consequent liability upon any records of their corporation. Section 141(e) of the Delaware Corporations Code is illustrative:

> A member of the board of directors, or a member of any committee designated by the board of directors, shall, in the performance of his duties, be fully protected in relying in good faith upon the records of the corporation and upon such information, opinions, reports or statements presented to the corporation by any of the corporation's officers or employees, or committees of the board of directors, or by any other person as to matters the member reasonably believes are within such other person's professional or expert competence and who has been selected with reasonable care by or on behalf of the corporation.

All these provisions should afford directors some comfort. As discussed above in the context of the business judgment rule, however, this "safe harbor" is unavailable to the extent that they rely on information not worthy of reliance.[162]

Reliance upon Others According to the Securities and Exchange Commission

The Securities and Exchange Commission (SEC) has aggressively expressed its views on the standards of fiduciary conduct by directors. Its concepts of directors' duty are generally more stringent than the case law and may be a preview of future trends. Illustrative of the SEC's position on reliance by directors on management is the *Stirling Homex* matter.[163]

In its release, the SEC sharply criticized the reliance of two outside directors on information supplied by management and the company's independent accountants. Stirling Homex built and sold large developments of modular homes. The company went public in early 1970. To show increased sales, it improperly recorded or fabricated nearly all its reported sales. There was a constant drain on the company's cash and, to continue operations, Stirling Homex had a second offering in July 1971. Sales previously booked did not materialize, and a year later the company filed for bankruptcy.

Management deliberately misled the outside directors about the financial condition and operations of the company. The outside directors protested their lack of information, and one even tendered his resignation in protest but was persuaded to stay on the board. Both outside directors relied on the information given them by the independent accountants (one of the so-called "Big Eight") and by management portraying the company's financial condition as relatively healthy, yet the SEC concluded:

> While this reliance was understandable, it resulted in their making no significant effort to analyze or familiarize themselves generally with these accounting practices, and in the opinion of the Commission, it resulted in their failure to understand the implications of these accounting practices and their susceptibility to abuse. While they periodically asked general and conclusory questions, they frequently obtained only superficial answers which they accepted without further inquiry.
>
> While the Commission recognizes the difficulties which may confront outside directors, particularly in a situation such as this, where management as part of a fraudulent course of conduct to deceive the public was not willing either to take the outside directors into their confidence or to keep them even reasonably well informed, this case illustrates a situation where *these directors, in the opinion of the Commission, did not provide the shareholders with any significant protection in fact, nor did their presence on the board have the impact upon the company's operations which shareholders and others might reasonably have expected.*[164]

The SEC position was expanded in 1978 in its report in *In re National Telephone Co., Inc.* relating to the activities of the outside directors of National Telephone Co.[165] In that case, the outside directors knew of, and failed to correct, misleading financial information that the company was disseminating to the public. The SEC went beyond the criticisms of *Stirling Homex* to set forth affirmative obligations of the board of directors:

> When important events central to the survival of the company are involved, directors have *a responsibility affirmatively to keep themselves informed of developments within the company* and to seek out the nature of corporate disclosures to determine if adequate disclosures are being made. [Emphasis added.]

In addition to an affirmative duty of directors to keep themselves informed, the SEC found:

> [a] need for *adequate, regularized procedures* under the overall supervision of the Board to ensure that proper disclosures are being made. Such procedures could include, among other things, a functioning *Audit Committee* with authority over disclosure matters, or *any other procedure which involves the Board of Directors in a meaningful way in the disclosure process.* [Emphasis added.]

Statutory Indemnity for Corporate Officers and Directors

Indemnification of corporate agents and employees is frequently governed by express statutes, which typically distinguish between actions by shareholders and actions by nonshareholder litigants. The recent crisis in director liability has triggered a wave of reform legislation. Since 1986, thirty states have enacted or proposed legislation designed to reduce directors' personal liability to money damages. These legislative initiatives generally follow one or more of seven different approaches:

1. Authorize a charter provision eliminating or limiting personal liability of directors, with some exceptions
2. Require proof of more than simple negligence
3. Expand the corporation's right to indemnify its directors
4. Authorize the corporation to provide reimbursement other than through conventional insurance
5. Expand the criteria directors may consider in reaching decisions
6. Allow corporations to provide rights aside from indemnification
7. Place a cap on monetary awards

Delaware's law[166] is illustrative of the first approach to reform. Under the new law, a corporation can adopt a provision eliminating or limiting the personal liability of a director to the corporation or its stockholders, with some exceptions. Those exceptions include breach of the director's duty of loyalty, bad-faith acts or omissions, intentional misconduct, knowing violations of law, and any improper personal benefit. Several other states have adopted similar laws or have similar bills pending.

Fiduciary Standards under the Federal Securities Law

The morass of federal rules and regulations spawned by the Securities Act of 1933 and the Securities Exchange Act of 1934, together with related provisions, are viewed as a federal law of corporations supplementing the laws of the several states.[167] Federal securities laws rely primarily on a system of disclosure in connection with the issuance and subsequent trading of securities. These laws impose upon directors and officers fiduciary responsibilities that, although analogous to common law and state statutory traditions, expose directors and officers to a stricter standard of care.

The scope of this paper allows only for a cursory review of six significant portions of the federal securities law:

1. Section 11 of the Securities Act of 1933
2. Section 12 of the 1933 Act
3. Section 14(a) of the Securities Exchange Act of 1934
4. Section 16(b) of the 1934 Act
5. Section 10(b) of the 1934 Act and rule 10b-5 thereunder, promulgated by the SEC
6. The "control person" provisions of sections 15 and 20 of the 1933 and 1934 acts

Provisions of the Securities Act of 1933

The Securities Act of 1933,[168] enacted in the wake of the stock market crash of 1929, was designed to provide investors with full disclosure of material information concerning public offerings of securities, to protect investors from fraud, and to promote ethical standards of honesty and fair dealing through the imposition of specific civil liability. The 1933 Act provides for compulsory registration (with certain exceptions) as a prerequisite to the issuance or sale of any "security."

The term "security" is defined in section 2(1) of the 1933 Act, and it is interpreted broadly to include any investment in a common enterprise in which the investor is led to expect profits "solely from the efforts of a promoter or a third party."[169] Some state courts, in construing their own securities laws, have followed California's lead to find a "security" even where the investor takes an active role in the enterprise, so long as the funds advanced are part of the "risk capital" for the initial development of the business.[170] The United States Supreme Court has declined to decide whether the "risk capital" test should apply to the federal securities laws.[171]

False or misleading statements are prohibited under the 1933 Act and are punished both criminally and through private actions for damages under sections 11 and 12. Although the 1933 Act (and the 1934 Act) preempt inconsistent state law, both are incident to Congress's power to regulate interstate commerce; thus, purely intrastate transactions are still governed by the various states' blue-sky laws.

Section 11 of the 1933 Act

The main provision of the 1933 Act as it relates to corporate officers and directors is section 11.[172] Section 11 imposes civil liability upon issuers of securities and other specified individuals who file securities registration statements that contain any untrue statement of a "material" fact or any omission of a "material" fact. Among those persons who may be potentially liable under section 11 are all those who sign the registration statement, all directors of the issuer at the time of the filing, and all prospective or incoming directors. Thus, a nonsigning officer cannot be held liable under section 11.

Rule 405 of the Securities and Exchange Commission Rules defines "materiality," as it relates to section 11 liability, as all matters "as to which an average prudent investor ought reasonably to be informed before purchasing the security registered." The Supreme Court's view is similar: "A fact is material if there is substantial likelihood that a reasonable shareholder would consider it important in deciding how to vote."[173] Yet a plaintiff does not have to prove that he or she actually relied on the untrue statement or omission, unless the plaintiff bought after the issuer had made its financial statement generally available for at least a twelve-month period after the effective date of the registration statement.[174]

A director or signing officer may escape section 11 liability in several ways. The principal defenses are that the purchaser knew of the untruth or omission when acquiring the security, or that the director exercised due diligence under the statute. The "due diligence" defense applies differently to the two portions of the registration statement, commonly called the "expertised" and "nonexpertised" portions. The "expertised" part is that portion of the registration statement which purports "to be a copy of. . . a report or valuation of an expert."[175] To avoid liability for defects in the expertised portion, the nonexpert director or signing officer need only prove that "he had no reasonable ground to believe and did not believe. . . that the statements therein were untrue or that there was an omission to state a material fact."[176] The director or officer does not have to prove that he or she believed the statements to be true or personally made a reasonable investigation.[177]

The nonexpertised part of the registration statement is that portion which does not derive from an expert's report or valuation. As to those portions, the director must prove "he had made a 'reasonable investigation,' and that he therefore had reasonable ground to believe and did believe. . . that the statements therein were true and that there was no omission to state a material fact."[178] To determine what constitutes a "reasonable investigation" and "reasonable ground for belief," the statute applies the standard of a prudent man in the management of his own property.[179] Thus, liability for negligence under section 11 of the federal securities law differs significantly from common law theories of liability: The director or signing officer has an *affirmative* duty to conduct a reasonable investigation, even in the absence of self-dealing. In short, this person bears the burden of proving his or her compliance with the exculpatory portions of the statute.

In *Feit v. Leasco Data Processing Equipment Corp.*,[180] inside and outside directors were both sued under section 11 for alleged material misrepresentations in a prospectus issued in connection with a tender offer for the stock of another company. The court noted that the extent of a director's duty to investigate depends on several factors:

> What constitutes "reasonable investigation" and a "reasonable ground to believe" will vary with the degree of involvement of the individual, his expertise, and his access to the pertinent information and data. What is reasonable for one director may not be reasonable for another by virtue of their differing positions.[181]

An inside director has an affirmative duty to investigate the company's activities:

> Inside directors with intimate knowledge of the corporate affairs and of the particular transactions will be expected to make a more complete investigation and have more extensive knowledge of facts supporting contradictory conclusions in the registration statements than outside directors.[182]

The inside director in *Feit* was held liable, whereas the outside director was exonerated. Indeed, Judge Weinstein noted that though the inside director's honesty may be unquestioned, his burden is nearly impossible to meet:

> [The decision in *Escott v. BarChris Construction Corp.*, 283 F. Supp. 643 (S.D.N.Y. 1968),] imposes such stringent requirements of knowledge of corporate affairs on inside

> directors that one is led to the conclusion that liability will lie in practically all cases of misrepresentation. Their liability approaches that of the issuer as guarantor of the accuracy of the prospectus.[183]

Section 12 of the 1933 Act

Section 12(1) of the 1933 Act prohibits the offer or sale of a security in violation of the act's registration provision, section 5.[184] This section applies only to "sellers," however.

The mere title of "officer" or "director" should not, of itself, suffice for section 12(1) liability. This has been an unsettled area of law, with some courts taking the narrow view that the term "seller" encompasses only the actual parties to the sale,[185] while others took a more liberal view and include in the term "seller" all "substantial participants" in the sale.[186] However, in *Pinter v. Dahl*,[187] the Supreme Court held that only those who pass title to securities or solicit the plaintiff's purchase are liable under section 12.

Whereas section 12(1) prohibits registration violations, section 12(2) prohibits "sellers" from making any material misstatement or omission in connection with the offer or sale of a security.[188] The same uncertainty over who is a "seller" applies under section 12(2). In any event, the "seller" is exculpated if able to prove that he or she did not know, or in the exercise of reasonable care could not have known, of the untruth or omission.[189]

Sections 12(1) and 12(2) are a specie of strict liability; no proof of fraud, intent to deceive, knowing misrepresentation, or recklessness is required. A purchaser need only prove that a statement in a registration statement or prospectus (or, indeed, even an oral representation) was untrue or misleading. Neither reliance nor causation is required. The civil remedy under section 12 is rescission or damages.[190]

Liability under the Securities and Exchange Act of 1934

The 1934 Act was intended principally to protect investors involved in secondary trading. It was designed to control manipulation of stock prices through regulation of securities transactions occurring over anonymous exchanges, to impose regular reporting requirements on companies whose stock is listed on national exchanges, and to provide for full disclosure of material information to investors.[191] The 1934 Act also established the Securities and Exchange Commission and empowered it with "an arsenal of flexible enforcement powers."[192]

Section 14(a)

With the recent advent of corporate takeovers, increasingly more companies have found themselves locked in proxy solicitation battles involving a bewildering array of scenarios. A major objective of the 1934 Act's disclosure provisions was the regulation of proxy solicitations. Corporate management and its directors are being exposed to ever-increasing liability for strategic decisions made during hostile tender offers, for paying "greenmail," and for pursuing certain defensive tactics. Many of these issues involve section 14(a) of the 1934 Act.

Section 14(a) makes it unlawful for an individual to solicit or to permit the use of his or her name to solicit any proxy in contravention of the SEC's rules and regulations. This provision "was intended to promote the free exercise of the voting right of stockholders by insuring that proxies voted be solicited with explanation to the stockholder of the real nature of the questions for which authority to cast his vote is sought."[193]

The SEC promulgated rule 14a-9[194] to flesh out the antifraud character of section 14. It prohibits the use of any proxy or related communication that is false or misleading with respect to any material fact, or that omits any material fact necessary to prevent the statement from being misleading. The rule applies to corporate officers and directors.

In *J.I. Case Co. v. Borak,*[195] the Supreme Court declared that these provisions allow for direct private rights of action as well as derivative suits. The elements of either action include (1) the solicitation of proxies by the defendants, (2) a false or misleading statement or omission in the solicitation, which is (3) material, (4) a causal connection between the violation and the plaintiff's injury, and (5) damages.

In *Mills v. Electric Auto-Lite Co.,*[196] the Supreme Court declared that a proxy defect need only have "a significant propensity to affect the voting process" in order to be a violation of section 14a-9, but that "a cause of action cannot be established by proof of a defect so trivial, or so unrelated to the transaction for which approval is sought, that correction of the defect or imposition of liability would not further the interest protected by Section 14(a)."

The courts have wrestled with section 14(a)'s elements of causation and materiality. In suits seeking to recover illegal corporate payments that the proxy failed to reveal, courts tend to require "transactional causation"; in short, the authorization of the payments must have been the primary purpose of the proxies and not merely incidental to the directors' reelection. On the other hand, if the section 14(a) suit attacks only the election itself and seeks no money damages, the courts will presume causation if the nondisclosure was material.[197]

Courts have been particularly aggressive in interpreting section 14(a) and rule 14a-9 so as to root out self-dealing. Indeed, the Second Circuit's expansive holding in *Maldonado v. Flynn*[198] suggests that management may have an *affirmative* duty to disclose matters impugning its directors' objectivity:

> Since self-dealing presents opportunities for abuse of a

> corporate position of trust, the circumstances surrounding corporate transactions in which directors have a personal interest are directly relevant to a determination of whether they are qualified to exercise stewardship of the company. . . . For this reason, Rule 14a-9 specifically sets out minimum standards and, *going beyond the Rule, it has been recognized that shareholders are entitled to truthful presentation of factual information "impugning the honesty, loyalty or competency of directors" in their dealings with the corporation to which they owe a fiduciary duty.*[199]

Directors are liable even for negligent misstatements in proxy solicitations. Claims of good faith and lack of scienter will fall on deaf ears. This is true even for outside directors.[200] Directors who breach their duty to fully and fairly disclose material facts in proxy materials they issue to shareholders are jointly and severally liable to plaintiffs for the entire harm resulting from the breach.[201] The measure of such damages is not confined to out-of-pocket loss, but embraces loss of possible profits unless they are wholly speculative.[202]

Section 16

Section 16 imposes strict liability on corporate "insiders" for short swing trading profits.[203] Section 16(a) requires every officer, director of a registered company, and beneficial owner of more than 10 percent of any class of equity security registered under section 12 to file with the Securities and Exchange Commission both a statement of the number of shares owned and any changes in share ownership. Section 16(b) provides that should any such individual make any purchase or sale of securities within six months of an earlier sale or purchase, that person must surrender to the corporation the profit realized.

Where there are multiple sales, damages are not based on a "first-in, first-out" measure, but by matching the highest sale with the lowest purchase, matching the next highest sale with the next lowest purchase, and so on. Thus, an errant director or officer could conceivably purchase and sell the company's stock several times within six months, incur a net loss on the trades, yet still be liable to the company for significant damages.

The following have been held to be sales within section 16(b): chairman of the board's sale of stock held by his mother,[204] exercise of option,[205] election to convert debenture to stock ,[206] and a pledge to a bank to secure a loan which was then sold by the bank with the pledgor's knowledge.[207] But in *Merrill, Lynch, Pierce, Fenner & Smith v. Livingston,*[208] the Ninth Circuit held that a securities salesman who was given the honorary title "vice president" was not within section 16(b), since he received no additional responsibilities nor did that title give him any greater access to inside information.

Although it is not necessary to show that the defendant actually took advantage of or even had access to inside information, most courts follow a "pragmatic" approach and find liability only if the particular transaction presented the possibility for the type of abuse with which Congress was concerned. In *Kern County Land Co. v. Occidental Petroleum Corp.,*[209] the Supreme Court held that, at least in the takeover/merger area, section 16(b) liability should not follow automatically whenever a transaction falls within the section; rather, the courts should examine each transaction to determine whether it presents an opportunity for the insider to capitalize on undisclosed information. Thus, corporate officers and directors who sold transferable warrants to underwriters have been held not to be within the section even though the underwriters later exercised the warrants and sold the stock; the court felt that once the warrants were sold, the insiders could not benefit from any price fluctuations.[210] Under the pragmatic approach of *Kern County,* the courts ask:

- Is the transaction in question of a type that may be characterized as unorthodox?
- Did the insider have control over the timing of the decision involved in the transaction?
- Did the insider have access to inside information, irrespective of whether that information was in fact used?[211]

Rule 10b-5

Rule 10b-5[212] was promulgated by the SEC pursuant to the general antifraud provision of the 1934 Act, section 10(b).[213] To date, it has spawned over 70,000 actions. The rule applies to *all* purchases and sales of securities, whether or not registered, yet its definition is still somewhat uncertain. Rule 10b-5 creates substantial concern even for directors and officers who have no personal interest in the securities transaction. The rule affects corporate directors and officers in two respects: its regulation of insider trading, and corporate mismanagement.

Misuse of Inside Information. A director or officer may not trade for his or her own account in the stock of the company when he or she knows material inside information undisclosed to the public. This principle was established in *SEC v. Texas Gulf Sulphur Co.*[214] The "disclose or abstain" rule so commonly cited in insider trading cases finds its source in *Texas Gulf Sulphur*: "Either disclose [the information] to the investing public, or . . . abstain from trading in or recommending the securities concerned while such inside information remains undisclosed."[215] As a practical matter, because inside directors are usually unable to disclose the information on their own, and because they fear liability for improper or incomplete disclosure should they attempt it, insiders often follow the creed, Don't trade at all. The New York Stock Exchange has formulated considerations that guide insiders in purchasing their own securities on a pattern basis to prevent 10b-5 suits against them.[216]

"Inside information" includes all "material" information about the company's past, present, or projected operations that originates from an internal corporate source and that is not generally available in the marketplace.[217] As for what information is "material," the director or officer must assume that the courts will adopt a broad view. Judge Waterman proffered this definition in *Texas Gulf*:

> The basic test of materiality is whether a *reasonable* man would attach importance in determining his choice of action in the transaction in question. . . . This, of course, encompasses any fact which in reasonable and objective contemplation *might* affect the value of the corporation's stock or securities.[218]

The SEC takes a somewhat "bootstrapping" position: The very fact that a director or officer purchased shares may be evidence that he or she considered the undisclosed information to be material.[219]

As a result of two Supreme Court rulings, insider trading cases must be divided into two classes: true insider trading and outsider trading occasioned by an insider's "tip." Although no formal or statutory classification exists to define "insiders," a prudent officer and director should assume that, given his or her unique access to inside information, he or she will be deemed an insider.[220] The rule in *Chiarella v. United States* is simple: "Insiders must disclose material facts which are unknown to the . . . persons with whom they deal and which, if known, would affect their investment judgment."[221]

As for outsider cases, an officer or director who "tips" outsiders to inside information can be liable for misusing that information. To be liable as a "tipper," however, the insider must personally benefit, either directly or indirectly, from the disclosure.[222]

In addition to the case law under rule 10b-5 that has evolved to regulate insider trading, the SEC has promulgated rule 10b-6. That rule, subject to certain exceptions, prohibits issuers and "affiliated purchasers" from buying up securities that are being offered as the subject of a public offering.[223] Rule 10b-6(c)(2) defines "affiliated purchasers" to include persons who act in concert with the issuer in making the offering and affiliates who directly or indirectly control the issuer. The Ninth Circuit held recently that rule 10b-6 applies to a CEO of a company who served as board chairman and was the company's largest shareholder.[224]

So far, most insider trading cases under rule 10b-5 have been brought by governmental agencies. Although a private action or derivative action is available, private plaintiffs have experienced difficulty surmounting the elements of standing, causation, and damages. The recent insider trading scandals involving Ivan Boesky are illustrative. At least two class actions have been brought by former shareholders who sold their stock in various target corporations at the time Boesky was buying stock in those companies on the basis of material nonpublic information about impending takeovers.[225] The biggest hurdle for these plaintiffs is causation: Unless they can show the stock price increases were caused by insider trading and not other market factors, they will lose. Standing is also a problem because, as *Dirks* makes clear, rule 10b-5 does not proscribe trading on inside information per se, it does so only where the person trading owes a fiduciary duty to the plaintiff.

To provide greater monetary disincentive to insider trading, Congress passed the Insider Trading Sanctions Act of 1984,[226] which authorizes the SEC to recover civil penalties "up to" three times the profit gained or loss avoided from a person who violates, or aids and abets another's violation of, the securities laws by trading on material nonpublic information. (H.R. 5133, just discussed, would amend the act to make treble damages automatic.) For purposes of the act, "profit gained" or "loss avoided" is measured by the difference between the purchase or sale price of the security and the value of that security as measured by the trading price of the security a reasonable period after public dissemination of the nonpublic information. Moreover, the act makes clear that tipping or trading in regard to derivative securities is unlawful to the same degree as tipping or trading with respect to the underlying security. The act provides for a five-year statute of limitations.

In November 1988, the President signed into law new provisions increasing penalties for insider trading.[227] The bill imposes civil penalties on inside traders and their supervisors, including broker-dealers and investment advisers. The law expressly makes tipping a primary violation of the 1984 Insider Trading Sanctions Act and thus subject to the act's civil penalty provisions. The maximum penalty is three times the profit gained or loss avoided. Contemporaneous traders enjoy a private right of action, but damages will not be trebled in private suits.

For the first time, brokerage firms will have to set up detection programs to ferret out and prevent insider trading. And a supervisory system will have to be established to oversee trading of securities in a firm's account and employee accounts. Formerly, there was no affirmative duty of securities firms to prevent insider trading.

Criminal penalties increase from $100,000 to $1 million for violations of the 1934 Act, and from $500,000 to $2.5 million for corporations and partnerships. Jail terms increased from five to ten years. Finally, the law empowers the SEC to award bounty payments to persons who report violations of insider trading rules of up to 10 percent of the penalty imposed or settlement retained.

Corporate Mismanagement. Rule 10b-5 also provides a cause of action against directors and officers who breach their fiduciary duties to the corporation in connection with a purchase or sale of corporate securities.

A recurrent type of claim under rule 10b-5 is a derivative suit by a minority shareholder alleging that the corporation was caused to issue its own securities for inadequate consideration, often in the context of a battle for control, and usually in such a way as to benefit the majority or controlling shareholder. In *Santa Fe Industries v. Green,*[228] the Supreme Court seemed to abolish such actions: "[O]nce full and fair disclosure has occurred, the fairness of the terms of the transaction is at most a tangential concern of [section 10(b)]."[229]

It was once widely believed that *Santa Fe* abolished further inroads by rule 10b-5 in the regulation of corporate management. Not so. The lower courts have significantly eroded the *Santa Fe* holding and have found the following facts to constitute violations of rule 10b-5: failure to disclose facts that could be used by minority shareholders to enjoin a transaction under state law[230] and failure by directors to disclose the inflationary effect of stock repurchase plan on the company's stock price.[231]

Although *Santa Fe Industries* has been largely ignored, the mere breach by director or officer under state law will not necessarily constitute a violation of rule 10b-5. To establish materiality, most courts require that plaintiff prove that he or she had a reasonable probability of winning a state court injunction had the undisclosed information about mismanagement been disclosed.[232]

Although the law is in great flux, some conclusions can be drawn. If the directors labor under some kind of conflict of interest or are in some fashion not fully independent of management, the safest course is for them to make full disclosure of a transaction relating to corporate management even as to matters not requiring shareholder approval. In cases where the board is truly disinterested, however, management's full disclosure to the board may be tantamount to full disclosure to shareholders, thus negating any corporate deception.[233]

In sum, *Santa Fe* and its progeny suggest that rule 10b-5 is alive and well, but that more than mere unfairness is required. Only if corporate action requires shareholder approval or if the directors are interested will nondisclosure, coupled with unfairness, provide the basis for a claim of deception of a corporation in a derivative action under rule 10b-5. Even then, nondisclosure alone may not suffice without a showing that had the corporate malfeasance been disclosed, state court remedies would have been available.

"Control Person" Liability

Section 15 of the 1933 Act imposes joint and several liability on any person who controls a person liable under section 11 or 12 "unless the controlling person had no knowledge of or reasonable grounds to believe in the existence of the facts by reason of which the liability of the controlled person is alleged to exist." Section 20(a) of the 1934 Act provides that "every person who. . . controls any person liable under any provision of this title. . . shall also be liable jointly and severally with and to the same extent as such controlled person to any person to whom such controlled person is liable, unless the controlling person acted in good faith and did not directly or indirectly induce the act or acts constituting the violation or cause of action.

The term "control" is not defined in either act, but the SEC defines the term to encompass "the possession, directly or indirectly, of the power to cause the direction of the management and policies of a person."[234] Thus, mere inaction can give rise to "control person" liability, but courts are split on whether more than mere negligence must be shown. In the case of broker-dealers, who have a statutory duty to supervise their agents, "indirect participation" alone may suffice.[235] But for other defendants, most courts require "culpable participation."[236]

Statutory Extensions of Fiduciary Responsibility

In recent years, several statutes and court rulings have expanded the scope of fiduciary responsibilities of corporate officers and directors into detailed and technical areas of business activity, and have created specific liabilities for breach of those newly imposed responsibilities. The effect of the statutes is to impose, in addition to existing statutory responsibilities, requirements of certain minimum skills upon officers and directors. These statutory duties are not likely to be satisfied by the defense of the prudent person acting in good faith.

ERISA

The Employment Retirement Security Act of 1974 (ERISA)[237] was designed to provide uniform standards for the operation of pension plans by establishing detailed criteria under which employees become entitled to pensions and by regulating the administration of pension plan assets. This complex statutory scheme defines "fiduciary" as any person who exercises discretionary authority or control with respect to the management of a plan, any person who exercises any authority or control respecting disposition of assets of a pension plan, and any person who has any discretionary authority or responsibility concerning the administration of a plan.[238]

Officers of a corporation whose employees are covered by a plan are frequently involved with the pension plan and may be making decisions with respect to payment of benefits or eligibility for benefits or other matters of administration of the plan. The board of directors can be fiduciaries under the plan if, for example, the plan reserves the right to the board of directors to make amendments. ERISA expressly establishes a fiduciary standard of its own to the effect that:

> a fiduciary shall discharge his duties with respect to a plan . . . with the care, skill, prudence, and diligence under the circumstances then prevailing that a *prudent man acting in a like capacity and familiar with such matters* would use in the conduct of an enterprise of a like character and with like aims.[239]

Where the trustees of the benefit plan are also corporate officers and directors, a conflict of interest often arises. This conflict becomes acute in the case of hostile takeovers where the plan trustees have it within their power to commit a large block of stock to one side or the other. Despite the dual role, pension plan fiduciaries must act *solely* for the benefit of the plan's beneficiaries.[240] In such cases, the "business judgment" rule is discarded, and the courts subject the directors' decision making to an "intensive and scrupulous" investigation. It is no defense that the plan in fact benefited from the transaction.[241]

The liabilities for breach of fiduciary duty include the restoration of any losses to the plan and any profits realized by the fiduciary as a result of the breach, and attorney's fees to a party prevailing in an action against the fiduciary.[242]

A pension plan will often involve more than a single fiduciary under the broad definitions of fiduciary. In *United States v. S. & Vee Cartage Co.,*[243] the court rejected the officers' defense that ERISA liability is limited to plan administrators. While the act permits co-fiduciaries specifically to allocate responsibilities among themselves and provides that a fiduciary is not liable for the breach of another fiduciary to whom specific duties were assigned, the act also requires each fiduciary to use reasonable care to prevent another fiduciary from committing a breach and further provides that one fiduciary is liable for the breach of duty by another if the latter party's failure to comply with his or her duties enables the former to commit some breach of duty.

The Foreign Corrupt Practices Act

The Foreign Corrupt Practices Act of 1977 (FCPA)[244] made various kinds of payments to foreign officials unlawful. The act describes the prohibited conduct in detail. FCPA also established detailed record-keeping and internal accounting control requirements, which generally apply to public companies and are not specifically directed to foreign transactions or corrupt practices. FCPA added section 13(b)(2) to the 1934 Act. This section requires the maintenance of accounts "which, in reasonable detail, accurately and fairly reflect the transactions and dispositions of the assets of" the corporation.[245] It also requires corporations to "devise and maintain a system of internal accounting controls sufficient to provide reasonable assurance" that the corporation's transactions are carried out with the authority of management, and recorded in a manner that permits preparation of financial statements in accordance with generally accepted accounting principles, that "access to assets" is permitted only where authorized, and that the assets of record are compared with existing assets at reasonable intervals and "appropriate action is taken with respect to any differences."[246] Directors will be responsible for seeing that these procedures are implemented and properly maintained. This may best be accomplished by the board's auditing committee.

The Heightened Duties Owed by Financial Institutions' Directors and Officers

The Financial Institutions Regulatory and Interest Rate Control Act of 1978 establishes a broad and complex scheme of restrictions on management practices of banks and financial institutions, including loans to insiders and interlocking directorships. Not only the corporation, but "any officer, director, employee, agent or other person participating in the conduct of the affairs" of the institutions is subject to monetary penalties and removal from office for violations of the various statutes and regulations, including portions of the Federal Reserve Act relating to insider transactions, bank reserves, and interest deposits; the Bank Holding Company Act; and the Federal Deposit Insurance Corporation Act.[247] Violation of FIRA encompasses "any action (along or with another or others) for or toward causing, bringing about, participating in, counseling or aiding or abetting" a violator.[248] The broad definitions of "violation" and "participation in a violation" and the complexity of the business activities that are regulated by FIRA impose new duties of inquiry upon officers and directors and, as a practical matter, probably new standards of minimum skill and judgment beyond the traditional prudent person acting in good faith.

A substantial amount of case authority suggests that officers and directors of financial institutions must exercise a greater degree of care than must ordinary directors and officers. The notion of a higher duty is supported by cases suggesting that a financial institution director or officer is like a trustee for depositors' assets,[249] by cases specifically stating that directors and officers of financial institutions have duties that are greater[250] or at least as great[251] as those owed by ordinary directors and officers, and by recent cases implying that special consequences flow from the extensive regulation of federally insured institutions.[252]

Furthermore, federal courts have recognized a private right of action against directors of national banks for knowing violations of the National Bank Act, 12 U.S.C. §§ 21–216.[253] These rights preempt any state law rights of action based on acts in violation of the National Bank Act, but do not preempt federal securities law actions.[254] In addition, 12 U.S.C. § 503 creates a private right of action against directors or officers of member banks of the Federal Reserve System for knowing violations of statutes governing interaffiliate transactions and loans and other transactions between the bank and its directors or officers—specifically 12 U.S.C. §§ 375, 375a, 375b, and 376—or for knowing violations of certain criminal statutes—18 U.S.C. §§ 217–20, 655, 1005, 1014, 1906, or 1909.[255]

Liability for Payment of Taxes

Corporate officers can be held personally liable for the company's failure to pay FICA and withholding taxes.[256] The liability is separate from that of the corporation and may be enforced against all officers whose duties relate to tax withholding.[257] This liability has been expanded so that the officer's personal bankruptcy will not even discharge it,[258] and it exists even though the officer acted on the orders of a superior.[259]

Liability under the Antitrust Laws

A corporate officer who causes the company to violate the antitrust laws may be civilly liable both to the person injured "in his business or property"[260] and to the corporation for negligence in causing it to violate the laws.[261] But the law does not impose any duty upon directors or officers to detect price fixing by their company, other than through the traditional duty of supervising one's employees.[262]

The case of *American Society of Mechanical Engineers, Inc. v. Hydrolevel Corp.*[263] holds that a nonprofit association could be civilly liable for antitrust violations committed by its agents with authority to act on the association's behalf. *Hydrolevel* suggests that a corporation is strictly liable for preventing antitrust violations committed by persons having apparent authority to act on its behalf.[264] It is unclear, however, to what extent an officer or director who did not directly participate in or knowingly approve of the antitrust violation can be held vicariously liable.

Notes

1. Ross v. Bernhard, 396 U.S. 531, 532–33 (1970).
2. W. KNEPPER, LIABILITY OF CORPORATE OFFICERS AND DIRECTORS, § 202.50 (1978).
3. Wardell v. Union Pac. Ry. Co., 103 U.S. 651 (1880).
4. Pepper v. Litton, 308 U.S. 295, 306 (1939).
5. *E.g.,* Tenison v. Patton, 95 Tex. 284, 67 S.W. 92, 95–96 (1902); Kennerson v. Burbank Amusement Co., Inc., 120 Cal.App.2d 157, 171–72, 260 P.2d 823, 831–32 (1953).
6. Pepper v. Litton, 308 U.S. 295, 306 (1939).
7. Weinberger v. UOP, Inc., 457 A.2d 701, 711 (Del. 1983), *quoted in* Drobbin v. Nicolet Instrument Corp., 631 F. Supp. 860, 880 (S.D.N.Y. 1986) (applying Nevada law).
8. Piccard v. Sperry Corp., 48 F. Supp. 465 (S.D.N.Y. 1943), *aff'd per curiam,* 152 F.2d 462 (2d Cir.), *cert. denied,* 328 U.S. 845 (1946).
9. Abeles v. Adams Eng'g Co., 35 N.J. 411, 428–30, 173 A.2d 246, 255–56 (1961); La Vin v. La Vin, 283 App. Div. 809, 128 N.Y.S.2d 518, 519, *aff'd*, 307 N.Y. 790, 121 N.E.2d 20 (1954).
10. DEL. CODE ANN., tit. 8, § 144(a) (1986).
11. Teren v. Howard, 322 F.2d 949, 953 (9th Cir. 1963); Heit v. Bixby, 276 F. Supp. 217, 232 (E.D. Mo. 1967); Guth v. Loft, Inc., 23 Del. Ch. 255, 5 A.2d 503, 511 (1939).
12. CAL. CORP. CODE § 310 (c) (West 1987); DEL. CODE ANN., tit. 8, § 144 (b) (1986); N.Y. BUS. CORP. LAW § 713(c) (McKinney 1987).
13. Rinn v. Asbestos Mfg. Co., 101 F.2d 344, 346–47 (7th Cir.), *cert. denied*, 309 U.S. 555 (1939).
14. Goldie v. Cox, 130 F.2d 695, 717 (8th Cir. 1942).
15. *See, e.g.,* Drobbin v. Nicolet Instrument Corp., 631 F. Supp. 860, 882–83 (S.D.N.Y. 1986).
16. *See* Fliegler v. Lawrence, 361 A.2d 218, 222 (Del. 1976); Edelman v. Fruehauf Corp., 798 F.2d 882, 886 (6th Cir. 1986).
17. *See, e.g.,* South Georgia Holding Co. v. Hiatt, 2 F. Supp. 91, 93 (M.D. Ga. 1933).
18. R.J. Engstrom Corp. v. Interceptor Corp., 555 F.2d 277, 283 (10th Cir. 1977).
19. *Id.;* Western Inn Corp. v. Heyl, 452 S.W.2d 752, 760–61 (Tex. App. 1970).
20. Belcher v. Welb, 176 Wash. 446, 452, 29 P.2d 702, 704 (1934).
21. Jordan v. Jordan Co., 94 Conn. 384, 389, 109 A. 181, 184 (1920).
22. Commercial Banking & Trust Co. v. Tenant's Realty Co., 37 Ohio App. 566, 175 N.E. 36, 37 (1931).
23. Stack v. Welder, 137 Cal. App. 647, 653, 31 P.2d 426, 428–29 (1934).
24. *In re* Westec Corp., 434 F.2d 195, 202 (5th Cir. 1970).
25. Guth v. Loft, Inc., 23 Del. Ch. 255, 5 A.2d 503, 514–15 (1939).
26. Hopper v. Western Tablet & Stationery Corp., 66 F.2d 172, 173 (6th Cir. 1933); Detroit Fidelity & Sur. Co. v. First Nat'l Bank of Wichita Falls, 66 S.W.2d 406, 407 (Tex. App. 1933).

27. Singer v. Carlisle, 26 N.Y.S.2d 172, 181 (1940), *aff'd*, 261 App. Div. 897, 26 N.Y.S.2d 320, *app. denied,* 261 App. Div. 956, 27 N.Y.S.2d 190 (1941); Hall v. Dekker, 45 Cal. App.2d 783, 787–88, 115 P.2d 15, 17–18 (1941).
28. Burg v. Horn, 380 F.2d 897, 899–900 (2d Cir. 1967); Bancroft-Whitney Co. v. Glen, 64 Cal. 2d 327, 346, 49 Cal. Rptr. 825 (1966).
29. Chelsea Industries, Inc. v. Gaffney, 389 Mass. 1, 10–19, 449 N.E.2d 320, 325–29 (1983).
30. *E.g.,* McRoberts Protective Agency, Inc. v. Landsell Protective Agency, Inc., 61 App. Div. 2d 652, 403 N.Y.S.2d 511, 513 (1978).
31. Red Top Cab Co. v. Hanchett, 48 F.2d 236, 238 (N.D. Cal. 1931).
32. McRoberts Protective Agency, Inc. v. Landsell Protective Agency, Inc., 403 N.Y.S.2d at 514.
33. Des Moines Terminal Co. v. Des Moines Union Ry. Co., 52 F.2d 616, 627–28 (8th Cir. 1931).
34. 389 Mass. 1, 449 N.E.2d 320, 326–30 (1983).
35. 23 Del. Ch. 255, 5 A.2d 503, 511 (1939).
36. W. KNEPPER, *supra* note 2, at § 3.01.
37. Paulman v. Kritzer, 74 Ill. App. 2d 284, 219 N.E.2d 541, 546 (1966).
38. Miller v. Miller, 301 Minn. 207, 222 N.W.2d 71, 81 (1974).
39. Thilco Timber Co. v. Sawyer, 236 Mich. 401, 210 N.W. 204, 205 (1926).
40. Klinicki v. Lundgren, 67 Ore. App. 160, 678 P.2d 1250, 1253 (1984); Nicholson v. Evans, 642 P.2d 727, 731 (Utah 1982); Irving Trust Co. v. Deutsch, 73 F.2d 121, 124 (2d Cir. 1934) (applying New York Law), *cert. denied*, 294 U.S. 708, *rearg. denied,* 294 U.S. 733 (1935); Electronic Dev. Co. v. Robson, 148 Neb. 526, 28 N.W.2d 130, 139–40 (1947).
41. All of the above-cited authorities.
42. Lussier v. Mau-Van Dev., Inc., 4 Hawaii App. 359, 667 P.2d 804, 813 (1983).
43. 368 S.W.2d 567, 576–77 (Tex. 1963).
44. *Id.* at 583.
45. *Id.* at 584.
46. CST, Inc. v. Mark, 360 Pa. Super. 303, 520 A.2d 469 (Pa. 1987).
47. *See, e.g.,* Norlin Corp. v. Rooney, Pace Inc., 744 F.2d 255, 265 (2d Cir. 1984).
48. *E.g., id.;* Yasik v. Wachtel, 25 Del. Ch. 247, 17 A.2d 309, 313 (1941).
49. First Mortgage Bond Homestead Ass'n v. Baker, 157 Md. 309, 145 A.876, 879–81 (1929).
50. *E.g.,* Crouse-Hinds Co. v. Internorth, Inc., 634 F.2d 690, 702 (2d Cir. 1980).
51. *Id.; see also* Norlin Corp. v. Rooney, Pace Inc., 744 F.2d 255, 265 (2d Cir. 1984).
52. D BLOCK, N. BARTON & S. RADIN, THE BUSINESS JUDGMENT RULE 81 (1987).
53. Crouse-Hinds Co. v. Internorth, Inc., 634 F.2d 690 (2d Cir. 1980).
54. Treadway Cos., Inc. v. Care Corp., 638 F.2d 357 (2d Cir. 1980).
55. Panter v. Marshall Field & Co., 646 F.2d 271 (7th Cir.), *cert. denied,* 454 U.S. 1092 (1981).
56. Kaplan v. Goldsamt, 380 A.2d 556, 559 (Del. Ch. 1977). *See also* Rosenfeld v.

Fairchild Engine & Airplane Corp., 309 N.Y. 168, 128 N.E.2d 291, *reh'g denied,* 309 N.Y. 807, 130 N.E.2d 610 (1955).

57. 744 F.2d at 266.
58. *Id.* at 267.
59. *Id.*
60. Frantz Mfg. Co. v. EAC Indus., 501 A.2d 401 (Del. Super. 1985).
61. Buckhorn, Inc. v. Ropak Corp., 656 F.Supp. 209, 231–32 (S.D. Ohio 1987) (applying Delaware law).
62. 43 Del Ch. 353, 230 A.2d 769, 772 (1967).
63. Podesta v. Calumet Indus., Inc., [1978 Transfer Binder] FED. SEC. L. REP. (CCH) ¶ 96,433 (N.D. Ill. 1978).
64. Consolidated Amusement Corp. v. Rugoff, [1978 Transfer Binder] FED. SEC. L. REP. (CCH) ¶ 96,584 (S.D.N.Y. 1978).
65. Royal Indus., Inc. v. Monogram Indus., Inc., [1976–1977 Transfer Binder] FED. SEC. L. REP. (CCH) ¶ 95,863 at 91, 136 (C.D. Cal. 1976).
66. Gerdes v. Reynolds, 28 N.Y.S.2d 622 (1941); W. KNEPPER, *supra* note 2, at § 6.03, p. 138.
67. Weinberger v. UOP, Inc., 457 A.2d 701 (Del. Sup. 1983).
68. 219 F.2d 173 (2d Cir.), *cert. denied,* 349 U.S. 952 (1955).
69. Essex Universal Corp. v. Yates, 305 F.2d 572, 576 (2d Cir. 1962) (Judge Lumbard's remarks explaining the court's theory in the *Perlman* decision).
70. 1 Cal. 3d 93, 81 Cal. Rptr. 592 (1969).
71. 271 Cal. App. 2d 252, 76 Cal. Rptr. 781 (1969).
72. DeBaun v. First W. Bank & Trust Co., 46 Cal. App. 3d 686, 120 Cal. Rptr. 354 (1975).
73. 682 F.2d 355, 367–68 (2d Cir. 1982), *cert. denied,* 460 U.S. 1069.
74. *See, e.g.,* MODEL BUSINESS CORP. ACT § 11.04 (1984).
75. *See, e.g.,* Cross v. Communications Channels, Inc., 116 Misc. 2d 1019, 456 N.Y.S.2d 971 (Sup. Ct. 1982).
76. *See* Weinberger v. UOP, Inc., 457 A.2d 701.
77. *Id.; see also* Singer v. Magnavox Co., 380 A.2d 969, 976 (1977).
78. Sealy Mattress Co. of N.J. v. Sealy, Inc., 532 A.2d 1324, 1333–35 (Del. Ch. 1987) (majority shareholder breached duty of loyalty by paying minority shareholder unfair price, by manipulating corporation's values, and by failing to disclose material facts).
79. 168 Cal. App. 3d 119, 214 Cal. Rptr. 177 (1985).
80. *Id.* at 128.
81. 507 A.2d 531 (Del. Super. 1986).
82. *Id.* at 537.
83. Bates v. Dresser, 251 U.S. 524, 530 (1920); MODEL BUSINESS CORP. ACT § 8.42 comment (1984).
84. Hun v. Cary, 82 N.Y. 65 (1880).
85. Briggs v. Spaulding, 141 U.S. 132, 144 (1891).
86. Galef v. Alexander, 726 F.2d 51, 58 (2d Cir. 1980).
87. MODEL BUSINESS CORP. ACT § 8.30 comment (1984).

88. *Id.* § 8.42(a) and comment thereto.

89. *E.g.,* Norlin Corp. v. Rooney, Pace Inc., 744 F.2d 255, 264 (2d Cir. 1984). Some courts and commentators distinguish between the "business judgment rule" and the "business judgment doctrine." The distinction is that the business judgment rule has traditionally operated as a shield to protect directors from liability for decisions made by them, while the business judgment doctrine provides for judicial deference to directors' good-faith actions where the actions themselves are challenged, such as in an action seeking injunctive relief. *See, e.g.,* Revlon, Inc. v. MacAndrews & Forbes Holdings, 506 A.2d 173, 180 n.10 (Del. 1986); Auerbach v. Bennett, 47 N.Y.2d 619, 629–31, 419 N.Y.S.2d 920, 926–27, 393 N.E.2d 994 (1979); D. Block, N. Barton & S. Radin, *supra* note 48, at 3.

90. Model Business Corp. Act § 8.30 comment (1984).

91. Aronson v. Lewis, 473 A.2d 805, 812 (Del. 1984) (citations omitted); *see also generally* Norlin Corp. v. Rooney, Pace, Inc., 744 F.2d 255, 264 (2d Cir. 1984).

92. Panter v. Marshall Field & Co., 646 F.2d 271, 293 (7th Cir.), *cert. denied*, 454 U.S. 1092 (1981).

93. *Id.* at 294; *but see* Norlin Corp. v. Rooney, Pace Inc., 744 F.2d 255, 266 n.12 (2d Cir. 1984).

94. Aronson v. Lewis, 473 A.2d at 812.

95. *Id.;* Smith v. Von Gorkom, 488 A.2d 858, 874–78 (Del. 1985). *See also* Hanson Trust PLC v. ML SCM Acquisition, Inc., 781 F.2d 264, 275 (2d Cir. 1986).

96. Joy v. North, 692 F.2d 880, 885 (2d Cir. 1982) (citations omitted), *cert. denied,* 460 U.S. 1051 (1983).

97. Kaplan v. Centex Corp., 284 A.2d 119 (Del. Ch. 1971).

98. Aronson v. Lewis, 473 A.2d 805, 812 (Del. 1984).

99. Treadway Cos., Inc. v. Care Corp., 638 F.2d 357, 382 (2d Cir. 1980); Aronson v. Lewis, 473 A.2d 805, 812 (Del. 1984).

100. *Id.;* Panter v. Marshall Field & Co., 646 F.2d 271, 293 (7th Cir.), *cert. denied*, 454 U.S. 1092 (1981). *Cf.* Bennett v. Propp, 41 Del. Ch. 14, 187 A.2d 405, 409 (Del. 1962).

101. Fornaseri v. Cosmomart Realty & Bldg. Corp., 96 Cal. App. 549, 557, 274 P. 597 (1929).

102. Kelly & Wyndham, Inc. v. Bell, 266 A.2d 878 (Del. 1970).

103. Fairchild v. Bank of Am., 192 Cal. App. 2d 252, 13 Cal. Rptr. 491 (1961).

104. *E.g.,* Aronson v. Lewis, 473 A.2d 805, 1812 (Del. 1984); Joy v. North, 692 F.2d 880 (2d Cir. 1982), *cert. denied*, 460 U.S. 1051 (1983). *See also* Burks v. Lasker, 441 U.S. 471 (1979).

105. Aronson v. Lewis, 473 A.2d 805, 812 (Del. 1984).

106. *Id.* at 814.

107. *Id.* at 815.

108. D. Block, N. Barton & S. Radin, The Business Judgment Rule, 265 (1987).

109. Auerbach v. Bennett, 47 N.Y.2d 619, 419 N.Y.S.2d 920, 393 N.E.2d 994 (1979).

110. Joy v. North, 692 F.2d 880, 891 (2d Cir. 1982), *cert. denied*, 460 U.S. 1051

(1983) (applying Connecticut law and citing Zapata Corp. v. Maldanado, 430 A.2d 779 (Del. 1979)).

111. Pogostin v. Rice, 480 A.2d 619, 627 (Del. 1984). *See also* Panter v. Marshall Field & Co., 646 F.2d 271 (7th Cir.), *cert. denied,* 454 U.S. 1092 (1981).

112. Greene & Palmiter, *Business Judgment Rule Tightened for Takeovers,* Legal Times, Jan. 20, 1986, at S3.

113. 488 A.2d 858 (Del. 1985).

114. *Id. See, e.g.,* Sealy Mattress Co. of N.J. v. Sealy, Inc., 532 A.2d 1324, 1337 (Del. Ch. 1987) (directors breached duty of care by approving merger without determining whether price was fair, without considering facts that bear on that issue, and without independent financial or legal advice).

115. Moran v. Household Int'l Inc., 500 A.2d 1346, 1356 (Del. 1985).

116. Ivanhoe Partners v. Newmont Min. Corp., 535 A.2d 1334, 1341 (Del. Super. 1987).

117. *Id.* at 1341-42.

118. Unocal Corp. v. Mesa Petroleum Co., 493 A.2d 946, 954 (Del. 1985).

119. *E.g.,* Dynamics Corp. of Am. v. CTS Corp., 794 F.2d 250 (7th Cir. 1986), *rev'd on other grounds,* 107 S. Ct. 1637 (1987); Gelco Corp. v. Coniston Partners, 652 F. Supp. 829, 845 (D. Minn. 1986).

120. *Cf.* Norlin Corp. v. Rooney, Pace Inc., 744 F.2d 255 (2d Cir. 1984).

121. AC Acquisitions v. Anderson, Clayton & Co., 519 A.2d 103 (Del. Ch. 1986); *see also* Frantz Mfg. Co. v. EAC Indus., 501 A.2d 401 (1985) (invalidated transfer to ESOP made after acquiror took control); Buckhorn, Inc. v. Ropak Corp., 656 F. Supp. 209, 231–32 (S.D. Ohio 1987) (striking down transfer to ESOP where no threat to employees and no benefit to shareholders).

122. 493 A.2d 946 (Del. 1985).

123. 535 A.2d 1334 (Del. 1987).

124. *See also* Polk v Good, 507 A.2d 531 (Del. 1986) (upholding greenmail payment in circumstances described earlier in chapter).

125. *Unocal,* 493 A.2d at 952, 956–57; *Ivanhoe,* 535 A.2d at 1342.

126. *E.g.,* Dynamics Corp. of Am. v. CTS Corp., 794 F.2d 250 (7th Cir. 1986), *reversed on other grounds,* 107 S. Ct. 1637 (1987) ["CTS I"]; Dynamics Corp of Am. v. CTS, 805 F.2d 705 (7th Cir. 1986) ["CTS II"].

127. Moran v. Household Int'l Inc., 500 A.2d 1346 (Del. 1985); CRTF Corp. v. Federated Dept. Stores, Inc., 683 F. Supp. 438 (S.D.N.Y. 1988) (applying New York law). *See also* Gelco Corp. v. Coniston Partners, 652 F. Supp. 829, 849 (D. Minn. 1986).

128. *CTS I,* 794 F.2d at 257–59 (following Delaware law).

129. Buckhorn, Inc. v. Ropak Corp., 656 F. Supp. at 229–30; *CTS II,* 805 F.2d at 714.

130. CRTF Corp. v. Federated Dept. Stores, Inc., 683 F. Supp. at 439–42.

131. 506 A.2d 173 (Del. 1986).

132. *Id.* at 184.

133. *Id.*

134. CRTF Corp. v. Federated Dept. Stores, Inc., 683 F. Supp. at 440; *e.g.,* Hastings-Murtagh v. Texas Air Corp., 649 F. Supp. 479, 484–85 (S.D. Fla.

1986) (applying Delaware law, upholding no-shop and lockup provisions where merger was to avoid bankruptcy rather than hostile tender offer).

135. Samjeus Partners I v. Burlington Indus. Inc., 663 F. Supp. 614, 624–25 (S.D.N.Y. 1987).

136. Ivanhoe Partners v. Newmont Mining Corp., 535 A.2d 1334, 1344–45 (Del. 1987).

137. *Id.; see also* Buckhorn, Inc. v. Ropak Corp., 656 F. Supp. at 228.

138. 682 F. Supp. 772 (D. Del. 1988).

139. 781 F. 2d 264 (2d Cir. 1986).

140. *Id.* at 275.

141. 781 F.2d at 277. *See also* Edelman v. Fruehauf Corp., 798 F.2d 882 (6th Cir. 1986). *See also* Mills Acquisition Co. v. Macmillan, Inc. (Del. Ch.) (New Castle Cty.) Oct 18, 1988, No. 10168, *rev'd*, (Del. Sup. Ct.) Nov. 2, 1988, Nos. 415, 416; City Capitol Associates v. Interco, Inc. (Del. Ch.) (New Castle Cty.) No. 1, 1988, No. 10105.

142. *E.g.*, Francis v. United Jersey Bank, 87 N.J. 15, 432 A.2d 814 (1981); Selheimer v. Manganese Corp., 423 Pa. 563, 224 A.2d 634 (1966); DePinto v. Provident Sec. Life Ins. Co., 323 F.2d 826 (9th Cir. 1963), *reh'g denied,* 383 U.S. 973 (1966); 374 F.2d 37 (9th Cir.), *cert. denied,* 389 U.S. 822 (1967).

143. 87 N.J. 15, 432 A.2d 814 (1981).

144. 87 N.J. at 26–27.

145. *Id.* at 31–33.

146. 423 Pa. 563, 224 A.2d 634 (1966).

147. 423 Pa. at 572, 224 A.2d at 640.

148. 423 Pa. at 586, 224 A.2d at 646–47.

149. 323 F.2d 826 (9th Cir. 1963), *reh'g denied,* 383 U.S. 973 (1966), 374 F.2d 37 (9th Cir.), *cert. denied,* 389 U.S. 822 (1967).

150. 323 F.2d 826 (1963).

151. 374 F. 2d 37, 44 (9th Cir.), *cert. denied*, 389 U.S. 822 (1967).

152. 381 F. Supp. 1003 (D.C. 1974).

153. 374 F. Supp. 1149 (D. Kan), *aff'd*, 520 F. 2d 1333 (10th Cir. 1974).

154. *Id.* at 1335.

155. W. KNEPPER, *supra* note 38, at § 7.07.

156. *Id.* § 7.07 (1978).

157. United States Liab. Ins. Co. v. Haidinger-Hayes, Inc., 1 Cal. 3d 586, 595, 83 Cal. Rptr. 418 (1970).

158. Frances T. v. Village Green Owners Ass'n, 42 Cal. 3d 490, 507–08 n.14, 229 Cal. Rptr. 456 (1986).

159. 507 F. Supp. 563 (E.D. La. 1981).

160. Frances T. v. Village Green Owners Ass'n, 42 Cal. 3d at 510–11, 229 Cal. Rptr. at 468–69.

161. *See e.g.*, Panter v. Marshall Field & Co., 646 F.2d 271, 293 (7th Cir.), *cert. denied*, 454 U.S. 1092 (1981); Linden v. United States, 254 F.2d 560, 568 (4th Cir. 1958); Spirt v. Bechtel, 232 F.2d 241, 247 (2d Cir. 1956).

162. *E.g.*, Smith v. Van Gorkom, 488 A.2d 858 (Del. 1985); Hanson Trust PLC v. ML SCM Acquisition, Inc., 781 F.2d 264 (2d Cir. 1986).

447

163. SEC Litigation Release No. 6960 (July 2, 1975).
164. Securities Exchange Act of 1934, Release No. 11516 (July 2, 1975) (emphasis added).
165. SEC Release No. 14380.
166. DEL. CODE ANN. tit. 8, § 102(b)(7) (Supp. 1986).
167. *See* Friendly, *In Praise of Erie—and of the New Federal Common Law,* 39 N.Y.U. L. REV. 385 (1964).
168. 15 U.S.C. § 77a *et seq.*
169. SEC v. W. J. Howey Co., 328 U.S. 293 (1946).
170. Silver Hills Country Cub v. Sobieski, 55 Cal. 2d 811, 815, 13 Cal. Rptr. 186 (1961).
171. United Housing Found. v. Forman, 421 U.S. 837, 857 n.24 (1975).
172. 15 U.S.C. § 77.
173. TSC Indus., Inc. v. Northway, Inc., 426 U.S. 438, 449 (1976).
174. 15 U.S.C. § 77k(a).
175. 15 U.S.C. § 77k.
176. *Id.* § 77k(b)(3)(C), (D).
177. *Id.*
178. *Id.* § 77k(b)(3)(A).
179. *Id.* § 77k(c).
180. 332 F. Supp. 544 (E.D.N.Y. 1971).
181. *Id.* at 577.
182. *Id.* at 578.
183. *Id.*
184. 15 U.S.C. § 771(1).
185. *See, e.g.,* Collins v. Signetics Corp., 605 F.2d 110, 112 (3d Cir. 1979).
186. *See, e.g.,* SEC v. Holschuh, 694 F.2d 130, 139 (7th Cir. 1982) (company president liable despite having had no contact with offerees).
187. Pinter v. Dahl, ____ U.S. ____, 108 S. Ct. 2063 (1988).
188. 15 U.S.C. § 771(2).
189. Ernst & Ernst v. Hochfelder, 425 U.S. 185, 209 N.27 (1976).
190. 15 U.S.C. §771(1).
191. Ernst & Ernst v. Hochfelder, 425 U.S. at 194–95.
192. *Id.*
193. Mills v. Electric Auto-Lite Co., 396 U.S. 375, 381 (1970) (quoting H.R. REP. NO. 1383, 73d Cong., 2d Sess., 14 (1934); S. REP. NO. 792, 73d Cong., 2d Sess., 12 (1934).
194. 17 C.F.R. § 240.14a-9.
195. 377 U.S. 426, 431 (1964).
196. 396 U.S. at 381.
197. *See* Gaines v. Haughton, 645 F.2d 761, 775 (9th Cir. 1981), *cert. denied,* 454 U.S. 1140 (1982).
198. 597 F.2d 789 (2d Cir. 1979).
199. *Id.* at 796 (emphasis added).
200. Gould v. American-Hawaiian Steamship Co., 535 F.2d 761, 777 (3d Cir. 1976).

201. *Id.* at 778.

202. *Id.* at 781; *see also* Gerstle v. Gamble-Skogmo, Inc., 478 F.2d 1281, 1304 (2d Cir. 1973).

203. 15 U.S.C. § 78p.

204. Whittaker v. Whittaker Corp., 639 F.2d 516, 523 (9th Cir.), *cert. denied,* 454 U.S. 1031 (1981).

205. Booth v. Varian Assocs., 334 F.2d 1, 4 (1st Cir. 1964), *cert. denied,* 379 U.S. 961 (1965).

206. Park & Tilford, Inc. v. Schulte, 160 F.2d 984, 987 (2d Cer.), *cert. denied*, 332 U.S. 761 (1947).

207. Alloys Unlimited, Inc. v. Gilbert, 319 F. Supp. 617 (S.D.N.Y. 1972).

208. 566 F.2d 1119, 1122 (9th CIr. 1978).

209. 411 U.S. 582, 594–96 (1973).

210. Portnoy v. Texas Int'l Airlines, Inc., 678 F.2d 695, 698 (7th Cir. 1982).

211. *See* Tomlinson, *Section 16(b): A Single Analysis of Purchases and Sales—Merging the Objective and Pragmatic Analyses,* 1981 DUKE L.J. 941, 949.

212. 17 C.F.R. § 240.10b-5.

213. 15 U.S.C. § 78j(b).

214. 401 F.2d 833 (2d Cir. 1968), *cert. denied,* 394 U.S. 976 (1969), *reh'g denied,* 404 U.S. 1064 (1972).

215. 401 F.2d at 848.

216. *See* NEW YORK STOCK EXCHANGE, COMPANY MANUAL, part III (1978).

217. *Texas Gulf,* 401 F.2d at 849.

218. *Id.* (citations omitted, original emphasis).

219. Securities Exchange Act, Release No. 10174 (May 25, 1973); *In re* Cady, Roberts & Co., 40 S.E.C. 907 (1961).

220. *See* Chiarella v. United States, 445 U.S. 222 (1980).

221. *Id.* at 227.

222. Dirks v. Securities & Exch. Comm'n, 463 U.S. 646, 662 (1983).

223. 17 C.F.R. § 240.10b-6 (1980).

224. SEC v. Burns, [Current Binder] FED. SEC. L. REP. (CCH) ¶ 93,235 (9th Cir. May 1, 1987).

225. French v. Boesky, No. 86-9102 (S.D.N.Y. Nov. 25, 1986); Orido v. Boesky, No. 86-8937 (S.D.N.Y. Nov. 20, 1986).

226. 15 U.S.C. §§ 78t(d), 78u(d)(1)(2).

227. Pub. L. 100–704, 100th Cong., 2d Sess. (Nov. 19, 1988).

228. 430 U.S. 462 (1977).

229. *Id.* at 478.

230. Goldberg v. Meridor, 567 F.2d 209, 220–21 (2d Cir. 1977), *cert. denied,* 434 U.S. 1069 (1978).

231. Alabama Farm Bureau Mut. Casualty Co. v. American Fidelity Life Ins. Co., 606 F.2d 602, 613 (5th Cir. 1979), *cert. denied,* 449 U.S. 820 (1980). *See also* Pappas v. Moss, 393 F. 2d 865, 868 (3d Cir. 1968) (issuance of shares to insiders at too low a price); Vine v. Beneficial Fin. Co., 374 F.2d 627 (2d Cir.

1967), *cert. denied,* 389 U.S. 970 (1967) (cash-out price paid for shareholders' stock following short-form merger too low).

232. *See, e.g.,* Mayer v. Oil Field Sys. Corp., 721 F.2d 59, 67 (2d Cir. 1983).

233. Maldonado v. Flynn, 597 F.2d 789, 793 (2d Cir. 1979).

234. 17 C.F.R. § 230.405.

235. *See* Buhler v. Audio Leasing Corp., 807 F.2d 833, 836 (9th Cir. 1987); Marbury Management, Inc. v. Kohn, 629 F.2d 705, 716 (2d Cir. 1979).

236. *See, e.g.,* Kersh v. General Council of the Assemblies of God, 804 F.2d 546, 550–51 (9th Cir. 1986). *But see*, Wool v. Tandem Computers, Inc., 818 F.2d 1433 (9th Cir. 1987) where the court found that for standard corporate disclosure documents, it was reasonable to presume collective action by corporate officers.

237. 29 U.S.C. § 1001.

238. *Id.* § 1002(21)(A).

239. *Id.* § 1104(a)(1)(B) (emphasis added).

240. *Id.* § 1104 (a)(1); Donovan v. Bierwirth, 538 F. Supp. 463, 468 (E.D.N.Y. 1981), *aff'd,* 680 F.2d 263 (2d Cir. 1982) (breach of fiduciary duty where corporate directors, serving also as plan trustees, used plan assets to purchase stock so as to foil takeover).

241. *See* Leigh v. Engle, 727 F.2d 113, 122 (7th Cir. 1984).

242. 29 U.S.C. §§1109, 1132(g).

243. 704 F.2d 914, 917 (6th Cir. 1983).

244. 15 U.S.C. §§ 78a, 78m, 78dd-1, 78dd-2, 78ff.

245. *Id.* § 78m(b)(2)(A).

246. *Id.* § 78m(b)(2)(B).

247. 12 U.S.C. §1818(b).

248. *Id.* § 1818(k)

249. *E.g.,* Atherton v. Anderson, 99 F.2d 883, 888 (6th Cir. 1938); Harman v. Willbern, 374 F. Supp. 1149, 1161 (D.Kan. 1974), *aff'd,* 520 F.2d 1333 (10th Cir. 1975).

250. Gadd v. Pearson, 351 F. Supp. 895, 903 (N.D. Fla. 1972).

251. Beverly Hills Fed. Sav. & Loan Ass'n v. FHLBB, 371 F. Supp. 306, 314 (C.D. Cal. 1973).

252. *E.g.,* First Hawaiian Bank v. Alexander, 558 F. Supp. 1128, 1132 (D. Hawaii 1983) (federal common law cause of action for breach of fiduciary duty recognized; similar action for negligence rejected); 12 U.S.C. § 1464(d)(4)(A) (grounds for removal of savings institution director by FHLBB).

253. Marx v. Centron Corp., 747 F.2d 1536, 1540–43 (6th Cir. 1984); Harmsen v. Smith, 542 F.2d 496, 499–502 (9th Cir. 1976) [*Harmsen I*].

254. *Harmsen I,* 542 F.2d at 500–02; Harmsen v. Smith, 693 F.2d 932, 940 (9th Cir. 1982) [*Harmsen II*] (10(b) action not preempted).

255. Marx v. Centron Corp., 747 F.2d at 1547–48.

256. 26 U.S.C. §§ 3403, 6672.

257. White v. United States, 372 F.2d 513, 516 (Ct. Cl. 1967).

258. United States v. Soleto, 436 U.S. 268 (1978).

259. Howard v. United States, 711 F.2d 729 (5th Cir. 1983).

260. Northwestern Oil Co. v. Socony-Vacuum Oil Co., 138 F.2d 967 (7th Cir. 1943).

261. Knopfler v. Bohlen, 15 App. Div. 2d 922, 225 N.Y.S.2d 609 (1962); Borden v. Cohen, 231 N.Y.S.2d 902 (Sup. Ct. 1962). *See* Forte, *Liabilities of Corporate Officers for Violations of Fiduciary Duties Concerning the Antitrust Laws,* 40 IND. L.J. 313 (1965).

262. Graham v. Allis-Chalmers Mfg. Co., 40 Del. Ch. 335, 182 A.2d 328 (1962), *aff'd,* 41 Del. Ch. 78, 188 A.2d 125 (1963).

263. 456 U.S. 556 (1982).

264. *Id.* at 570–72.

Thirty-One

Indemnification and Insurance of Corporate Officials

Dennis J. Block, Nancy E. Barton, and Stephen A. Radin

"Indemnification" refers to reimbursement by the corporation to directors and officers of liabilities, including judgments, amounts paid in settlement, expenses, and attorneys' fees, arising out of their service to the corporation. "Insurance," commonly called directors' and officers' liability insurance (D&O insurance), is carried both to reimburse the corporation for indemnification payments made to its directors and officers and to cover the directors and officers in circumstances where corporate indemnification is unavailable.

The law surrounding indemnification and insurance is evolving quickly, as corporations and state legislators struggle to cope with the D&O insurance crisis of the mid-1980s. Premiums skyrocketed, deductibles increased at an extraordinary rate, and coverage shrank. At the same time, policy durations became shorter and shorter, and the policies themselves included an increasing number of exclusions.

The fear of liability without insurance has led many directors and potential directors either to resign their positions or to decline to accept the opportunity to serve in the first instance. As *Business Week* observed in a 1986 cover story:

> Concerned about increasing legal hassles and time demands, scores of directors are quietly stepping down. Some prominent executives confide that when their current terms expire, they will not stand for reelection to outside boards. Many more are turning away all invitations to serve. A number of troubled companies, which need strong directors, are facing mass defections. . . . [All this] comes just as many boards face a rash of proposals for takeovers, divestitures, stock repurchases, and

Dennis J. Block and Nancy E. Barton are members, and Stephen A. Radin is an associate, at Weil, Gotshal & Manges in New York City. The authors gratefully acknowledge the assistance of Richard W. Slack and James G. Flynn.

management buyouts that cry out for scrutiny by strong outside directors.[1]

D&O insurance is somewhat more available today than was the case one or two years ago, but high costs and shortages still pose substantial difficulties for many corporations.[2]

This chapter focuses upon representative approaches to indemnification and insurance adopted by statutes enacted in the California, Delaware, and New York legislatures and by the Model Business Corporation Act.[3] The California, Delaware, and New York statutes have each recently been amended in ways intended to alleviate the D&O crisis. Other statutes are cited to illustrate particular points.

Indemnification

Mandatory Indemnification

Under the Delaware norm, indemnification is mandatory where the person to be indemnified has been "successful on the merits or otherwise."[4] The Model Act provides that the corporate official must have been "wholly successful on the merits or otherwise."[5] California requires that the director be "successful on the merits."[6]

"Successful" or "Wholly Successful"

The Delaware statute mandates partial indemnification in cases of partial success.[7]

In *Merritt-Chapman & Scott Corp. v. Wolfson* (*Wolfson II*),[8] the court awarded partial indemnification to two defendants who, pursuant to a plea bargain, were successful on one count of a criminal indictment (conspiracy to violate federal securities laws) but unsuccessful on a related count (in one case, perjury; in the other, filing false annual reports with the Securities and Exchange Commission and the New York Stock Exchange). By contrast, in an earlier proceeding, *Merritt-Chapman & Scott Corp. v. Wolfson* (*Wolfson I*),[9] the court held that the prosecution's agreement to drop the 10b-5 element of a conspiracy count alleging "perjury, filing false statements with the SEC, obstruction of justice, and fraud upon the corporate shareholders in violation of SEC Rule 10b-5" did not constitute partial success. *Wolfson II* arose after the convictions in *Wolfson I* had been reversed on appeal, thus necessitating a new trial.[10]

Similarly, in *Green v. Westcap Corp.*, [11] the court ordered a corporation to indemnify a former corporate officer for legal expenses incurred in successfully defending a criminal action in which he was alleged to have defrauded and embezzled funds from the corporation.[12] The corporation had argued that any decision regarding indemnification should await the conclusion of related civil litigation, particularly since the judge who directed the judgment of acquittal had stated explicitly that "not guilty" did not imply innocence, and that he believed the officer seeking indemnification would be punished in a civil court.[13] Rejecting this argument, the court emphasized that indemnification was sought only for the successful defense of the criminal charge, and that a grant of such indemnification would not establish any right to indemnification for expenses incurred in any other litigation.[14]

The Model Act rejects Delaware's partial-success rule by requiring that the person to be indemnified must be "wholly successful."[15] According to the drafters of the Model Act, "a defendant is 'wholly successful' only if the entire proceeding is disposed of on a basis which involves a finding of nonliability."[16] Before its recent amendment, the New York statute also employed "wholly successful" language.[17]

Two courts have held that settlements—at least where there is no payment or assumption of liability by the person to be indemnified—"surely" constitute "success on the merits or otherwise."[18] No court has addressed a case in which a corporate agent, as an individual, agrees to make a payment or assume liability as part of a settlement.

In *Lussier v. Mau-Van Development, Inc.*,[19] and *Haenel v. Epstein*,[20] the courts construed "successful" and "wholly successful," respectively, to include finality. Thus, where a favorable trial verdict has been appealed, the corporate agent is not successful until the entry of a favorable and final appellate ruling.

"On the Merits or Otherwise" or "On the Merits"

The "on the merits *or otherwise*" formulation recognizes that while an "occasional defendant" who has in fact done something wrong may be "entitled to indemnification because of procedural defenses not related to the merits of the litigation (for example, the statute of limitations or disqualification of the plaintiff), it is unreasonable to require a defendant with a valid procedural defense to undergo a possibly prolonged and expensive trial on the merits in order to establish eligibility for mandatory indemnification."[21]

California, unlike Delaware, New York, and the Model Act, requires that the director be successful "on the merits."[22]

Permissive Indemnification

Where indemnification is not mandatory, state corporation laws provide for permissive indemnification where the requisite standards of conduct are satisfied. Most statutes provide separate but similarly worded standards for indemnification in third-party actions and actions brought by or in the right of the corporation. Exceptions—most important in the context of derivative actions—are then added.[23]

These standards define the outer limits for which voluntary indemnification is permitted. Directors whose conduct falls within these bounds are not necessarily entitled to indemnification.[24] A substantial number of corporations, it should be noted, have adopted bylaws obligating the corporation to indemnify directors to the maximum extent permitted by the applicable statute.

Third-Party Actions

Most statutes (including Delaware's) provide that indemnification may be granted if the person involved acted:

- in "good faith";
- "in a manner he reasonably believed to be in *or not opposed to* the best interests of the corporation"; and
- with respect to a criminal proceeding, with "no reasonable cause to believe his conduct was unlawful."[25]

California permits indemnification where the person involved acted:

- "in good faith";
- "in a manner such person believed to be in the best interests of the corporation"; and
- "in the case of a criminal proceeding, [with] no reasonable cause to believe the conduct . . . was unlawful."[26]

New York permits indemnification where the person involved acted:

- in "good faith";
- "for a purpose which he reasonably believed to be in . . . the best interests of the corporation"; and
- in criminal proceedings, with "no reasonable cause to believe that his conduct was unlawful."[27]

New York's statute adds that conduct undertaken in service for any entity other than the corporation (for example, another corporation, partnership, joint venture, trust, or employee benefit plan) need only be "not opposed to . . . the best interests of the corporation."[28]

The Model Act authorizes indemnification where the person involved

- acted "in good faith"; and
- "reasonably believed":
  - "in the case of conduct in his official capacity with the corporation, that his conduct was in its best interests"; and

- "in all other cases, that his conduct was *at least not opposed to* its best interests"; and
- in the case of any criminal proceeding,... [that he] had no reasonable cause to believe his conduct was unlawful."[29]

In third-party actions, unlike the case in derivative actions, most statutes authorize indemnification both of reasonable expenses, including attorneys' fees, and of judgments, fines, penalties, and amounts paid in settlement.[30] The termination of an action by judgment, order, settlement, conviction, or plea of nolo contendere or its equivalent does *not* by itself create a presumption that the standard of conduct required for indemnification has not been satisfied.[31]

Derivative Actions

As previously noted, most statutes use similarly worded standards to judge indemnification in third-party and derivative actions. Thus, the California, Delaware, New York, and Model Act standards set forth for third-party actions are followed in the derivative action context, with exceptions tailored to the specialized nature of derivative actions.[32]

One exception found in most statutes precludes indemnification of directors adjudged liable to the corporation. Significantly, a judicial determination that a duty has been breached is not enough to preclude indemnification[33] (although, until the recent amendment of the New York statute, that state had required only a judicial determination that a duty had been breached—not an adjudication of liability[34]). Moreover, many jurisdictions explicitly provide that the court in which the action is pending may, in view of all the circumstances of the case, determine that a director "adjudged to be liable to the corporation" is nevertheless entitled to indemnification.[35] A consent decree does not result in an adjudication against the party consenting to it, and therefore has been held not to preclude indemnification.[36]

Other exceptions include judgments and amounts paid in settling or otherwise disposing of derivative actions. The logic underlying this rule is the avoidance of the circularity that many believe would result if funds received by the corporation (the ultimate plaintiff on whose behalf the suit is brought) were simply returned to the defendant director who paid them.[37] The prohibition is still the law in Delaware (and in most jurisdictions that follow the Delaware model), with section 145(a) of the Delaware statute authorizing indemnification in third-party actions for "expenses (including attorneys' fees), judgments, fines and amounts paid in settlement," and section 145(b) authorizing indemnification in derivative actions merely for "expenses (including attorneys' fees)."[38] New York amended its indemnification statute in 1986 to permit indemnification of amounts paid to settle derivative actions where court approval is obtained.[39] California amended its statute in 1987 to bar indemnification of "amounts paid in settling or otherwise disposing of a pending [derivative] action without court approval," thus implying that indemnification is available after obtaining court approval (arguably of either the settlement or the indemnification, depending upon how one reads the statute).[40] These New York and California statutes reflect a trend in legislative enactments during the mid-to-late 1980s permitting indemnification of judgments and/or settlements in derivative actions, in some jurisdictions with court approval but in a substantial number of jurisdictions without court approval.[41]

Finally, state indemnification statutes that are not exclusive permit indemnification beyond that otherwise authorized by the statute.[42] While no court has yet decided whether indemnification barred by one provision of an indemnification statute—such as indemnification of judgments or amounts paid to settle derivative actions—is permissible pursuant to an exclusivity provision, four statutes have addressed the issue. Virginia's recently amended nonexclusivity statute specifically permits indemnification granted pursuant to that provision to include indemnification of liability arising out of a derivative action.[43] Pennsylvania's statute goes one step further, and declares that indemnification of liability arising out of a derivative action is "consistent with the public policy" of Pennsylvania.[44] Iowa's nonexclusivity provision, however, expressly prohibits indemnification with respect to derivative actions greater than that already provided by statute.[45] California's statue similarly bars indemnification pursuant to that state's nonexclusivity provision in "circumstances in which indemnity is expressly prohibited" by specific provisions in the statute.[46]

Authorization

Permissive indemnification generally must be authorized on a case-by-case basis. Specifically, the corporation must determine that indemnification is proper in the circumstances because the person to be indemnified has met the applicable standard of conduct.[47]

The determination may typically be made by the board of directors, special counsel, or shareholders. A board decision must be by a majority vote of a quorum consisting of directors who are not parties to the proceeding.[48] Where a quorum cannot be obtained, the Model Act permits the decision to be delegated to a committee consisting of two or more directors who are not at the time parties to the proceeding. Directors who are parties to the proceeding may participate in the delegation process.[49]

Most states, including Delaware, New York, and California, permit authorization by "independent" or "special legal counsel" chosen by a majority vote of nonparty directors if the board does not have the requisite number of nondefendant directors or if a quorum of nonparty or disinterested directors so directs.[50] Most statutes do not define what constitutes "independent" or "special legal counsel." As the drafters of the Model Act have noted:

> "Special legal counsel" should normally be counsel having no prior professional relationship with those seeking indemnification, should be retained for the specific occasion, and should not be either inside counsel or regular outside counsel. It is important that the selection process be sufficiently flexible to permit selection of counsel in light of the particular circumstances and so that unnecessary expense may be avoided. Hence the phrase "special legal counsel" is not defined in the statute.[51]

Statutes enacted in Minnesota, North Dakota, Ohio, and Washington do define the term. The Minnesota and North Dakota statutes provide that " '[s]pecial legal counsel' means counsel who has not represented the corporation or a related corporation, or a director, officer, employee, or agent whose indemnification is in issue."[52] Ohio and Washington require the passage of five years and three years, respectively, from counsel's previous association with the corporation and the person to be indemnified.[53]

A shareholder decision, under most statutes—including those of Delaware and New York—is based upon the votes of all shareholders.[54] California does not allow voting of shares owned by the person seeking indemnification.[55] The Model Act precludes voting of shares controlled by shareholders who are parties to the proceeding.[56]

Court-Ordered Indemnification

The judiciary's power to order indemnification may arise in two contexts. First, a director entitled to mandatory indemnification may enforce that entitlement.[57] Second, the court may, in its discretion, and within certain limitations set forth in particular statutes, order indemnification notwithstanding the director's ineligibility for permissive indemnification under the applicable standard.[58]

The Model Act, for example, authorizes court-ordered indemnification in the mandatory indemnification context and in any other case where the corporate official is determined "fairly and reasonably entitled to indemnification in view of all the relevant circumstances"—even if the standard the corporation is required to apply prohibits indemnification. The only limitation upon the court's power is that where the director has been "adjudged liable to the corporation," indemnification is limited to reasonable expenses.[59]

Advancing Costs of Litigation

The Official Comment to the Model Act states:

> It is often critically important to a director who is made a party to a complex proceeding that the corporation he served have power to make advances for expenses at the beginning of and during the proceeding. Adequate legal representation and adequate preparation of a defense may require substantial payments of expenses before a final determination, and unless the corporation may make advances for expenses, a defendant may be unable to finance his own defense. . . . [But] during the early stages of a proceeding (when advances are often needed) the facts underlying the claim cannot be fully evaluated and the board of directors therefore cannot accurately ascertain the ultimate propriety of indemnification.[60]

Statutes authorizing advances of costs must reconcile these opposing considerations.

Until July 1, 1986, Delaware, like most states, permitted advances "as authorized by the board of directors in the specific case upon receipt of an undertaking to repay" the advance unless there ultimately was an affirmative determination that the person was entitled to indemnification.[61] Delaware's legislature has now changed the law by deleting the words "as authorized by the board of directors in the specific case," and by providing that the advanced expenses need not be repaid unless and until an affirmative determination is made that the person to whom expenses were advanced is *not* entitled to indemnification.[62] Similar standards are now the law in California and New York as well.[63]

Under the law of most states, there is no requirement conditioning advancement upon a finding that the applicable standard of conduct has been met,[64] and no requirement that the decision to advance expenses be made by disinterested directors, independent counsel, or stockholders, as is the case with permissive indemnification.[65] This is because advances:

> only become permanent obligations of the company if indemnification is later determined to be proper. Rather than director self-dealing, the primary risk posed to the company by such advances is that the officials to whom the advances are paid will be unable to repay the company if they are not

ultimately indemnified. The requirement that company officials undertake to repay the advances of litigation expenses is an attempt to minimize this risk.[66]

The term "undertaking" is generally not defined in the statutes, but according to one of the Delaware draftsmen means nothing more than a promise to repay.[67] The Model Act's "undertaking" requirement specifies that the undertaking is an "unlimited general obligation" which "need not be secured and may be accepted without reference to financial ability to make repayment."[68]

Types of Litigation Covered

Assuming the applicable statutory requirements are satisfied, corporations may award permissive indemnification to directors for expenses incurred in any "threatened, pending, or completed action, suit, or proceeding, whether civil, criminal, administrative, or investigative and whether formal or informal."[69]

Most statutes refer to directors who are or may become "parties" to an action or proceeding, and thus fail to differentiate between a director's status as a plaintiff or defendant. In *Hibbert v. Hollywood Park, Inc.*,[70] plaintiff directors sought and were awarded indemnification for litigation expenses incurred during a proxy contest. The court noted that the litigation sought, *inter alia*, to compel the defendant-directors to attend board meetings—i.e., the litigation was not "entirely initiated without regard to any duty the plaintiffs might have had as directors." In this context, the court awarded indemnification on the ground that sections 145(a) and (b) of the Delaware statute failed to limit indemnification to defendants.[71] Moreover, the court noted that the corporation's bylaw authorization of indemnification regardless of the director's role in the litigation was "broad enough to include an individual who acts as an intervenor or *amicus curiae* in any particular case."[72]

In *Parker, Chapin, Flattau & Klimpl v. Blackman*,[73] two directors filed suit against two other directors in a dispute involving control of the corporation. Before an adjudication on the merits, the defendant directors sold their stock, and the action was terminated. The attorneys representing the plaintiff directors sued the corporation for payment of their legal fees. The court held that the action had been brought by the directors in their capacity as shareholders, and the directors' attorneys therefore had no claim against the corporation for attorneys' fees.[74]

Statutes enacted in Massachusetts and Texas limit indemnification to actions taken to defend an action or proceeding.[75]

Mandatory indemnification is limited in all jurisdictions to conduct "in defense of any action, suit, or proceeding."[76]

Exclusivity

Most statutory indemnification provisions are not exclusive—i.e., they do not prohibit indemnification in situations beyond the boundaries explicitly authorized by the statute. Thus, for example, section 145(f) of the Delaware statute states:

> The indemnification and advancement of expenses provided by, or granted pursuant to, the other subsections of this section shall not be deemed exclusive of any other rights to which those seeking indemnification or advancement of expenses may be entitled under by-law, agreement, vote of stockholders or disinterested directors or otherwise, both as to action in his official capacity and as to action in another capacity while holding such office.

Section 721 of New York's statute, as amended in 1986, is even more explicit:

> The indemnification and advancement of expenses granted pursuant to, or provided by, this article shall not be deemed exclusive of any other rights to which a director or officer seeking indemnification or advancement of expenses may be entitled, whether contained in the certificate of incorporation or the by-laws or, when authorized by such certificate of incorporation or by-laws, (i) a resolution of shareholders, (ii) a resolution of directors, or (iii) an agreement providing such indemnification, provided that no indemnification may be made to or on behalf of any director or officer if a judgment or other final adjudication adverse to the director or officer establishes that his acts were committed in bad faith or were the result of active and deliberate dishonesty and were material to the cause of action so adjudicated, or that he personally gained in fact a financial profit or other advantage to which he was not legally entitled.

California allows broader indemnification than that otherwise permitted in its statute by "bylaw, agreement, vote of shareholders or disinterested directors or otherwise," but only "to the extent such additional rights to indemnification are authorized in the articles of the corporation."[77] The California statute specifies, however, that no charter provision may provide for indemnification for conduct "from which a director may not be relieved of liability" or "as to circumstances in which indemnity is expressly prohibited" by specific provisions in California's indemnification statute.[78]

The courts have not yet resolved the issue whether nonexclusivity clauses permit indemnification otherwise prohibited by the applicable indemnification statute. One court—*PepsiCo, Inc. v. Continental Casualty Co.*[79]—has rejected the argument that public policy bars indemnification pursuant to a nonexclusivity clause of a settlement of claims alleging violations of § 10(b) of the Securities Exchange Act of 1934,[80] but commentators seem to agree that nonexclusivity clauses are subject to public policy constraints.[81]

The *PepsiCo* court also held that Delaware's nonexclusivity clause permits the corporation to indemnify without following the procedural requirements of section 145(d) otherwise governing permissive indemnification.[82] Two Delaware observers, however, have concluded that while section 145(f) "does provide support for wide-ranging agreements or by-laws which broaden or enlarge upon indemnification rights granted in various other subsections" of that state's indemnification statute, "[i]t is doubtful that a Delaware court would be quite this sweeping in its language in a case . . . involving the outer limits" of section 145(f)'s nonexclusivity provision.[83]

Pennsylvania's nonexclusivity statute eliminates the issue of public policy constraints by expressly providing that indemnification authorized by a corporation pursuant to a nonexclusivity provision is permitted "whether or not the corporation would have the power to indemnify the person under any other provision of law." The Pennsylvania provision expressly declares such indemnification to be "consistent with the public policy" of Pennsylvania.[84]

The Model Act allows indemnification of directors where "consistent" with the statute.[85] The drafters of the Model Act note that their formulation is *not* synonymous with exclusivity: "Situations may well develop from time to time in which indemnification is permissible under [this section] but would be precluded if all portions of [the statute] were viewed as exclusive."[86]

Insurance

The Need for Insurance

The need for D&O insurance coverage arises from gaps in state indemnification statutes, including expenses for directors adjudged liable to the corporation and judgments or amounts paid in settlement of derivative actions, and from the possibility that the corporation may refuse or be unable to pay. Refusal to indemnify, for example, may occur in the aftermath of a hostile takeover. Inability to pay may stem from bankruptcy or other causes. Another need for insurance arises from public policy considerations imposed by federal securities laws. Public policy prohibits indemnification for securities law violations predicated upon intentional or reckless conduct.[87] In addition, the SEC's long-standing view is that an issuer's indemnification of directors or officers against liability under the Securities Act of 1933[88] is against public policy.[89] The SEC enforces this policy by threatening to deny acceleration to registrants who fail to disclose the policy and undertake that if a claim for indemnification against such liability is made, "the registrant will, unless in the opinion of its counsel the matter has been settled by controlling precedent, submit to a court of appropriate jurisdiction the question whether such indemnification by it is against public policy as expressed in the Act and will be governed by the final adjudication of such issue."[90]

One commentator has explained the practical effect of the SEC's policy as follows:

> [M]ost public offerings would be impossible if the registrant, after filing its "price amendment" (*i.e.*, setting the price at which the issue will be sold), had to wait while the statutory twenty-day period, which starts afresh after every amendment, ran again. The market will not hold still that long. The Commission has, however, discretion to accelerate the effective date of a registration statement, permitting it to become effective on the same day that the price amendment is filed, and will normally do so for a cooperative registrant. The power to grant or deny acceleration has thus been an effective club to insure respect for a number of the SEC's policies, including that with respect to indemnification.[91]

The SEC does not regard the maintenance of D&O insurance to be contrary to public policy, even if the corporation pays the cost of the insurance.[92] Public policy limitations against insurance for one's own fraud, however, may still be applicable. In this connection, Wisconsin has recently adopted a statute permitting "indemnification, allowance of expenses and insurance for any liability incurred in connection with . . . any proceeding involving a federal or state statute, rule or regulation regulating the offer, sale or purchase of securities, securities brokers or dealers, or investment companies or investment advisors."[93]

Statutory Provisions Authorizing Insurance

Virtually every indemnification statute empowers corporations to purchase and maintain liability insurance for directors and officers both for indemnifiable and nonindemnifiable liabilities. Delaware's statute is typical:

> A corporation shall have power to purchase and maintain insurance on behalf of any person who is or was a director,

> officer, employee or agent of the corporation . . . against any liability asserted against him and incurred by him in any such capacity, or arising out of his status as such, whether or not the corporation would have the power to indemnify him against such liability under the provisions of this section.[94]

Limitations on the extent of insurance coverage are supplied by the applicable insurance law or by public policy considerations.[95]

New York's statute is more specific, authorizing corporations to provide insurance for corporate officials in "instances in which they may not otherwise be indemnified," so long as the policy contains retention and coinsurance provisions "acceptable to the superintendent of insurance."[96] The statute bars insurance against liability for payments other than defense costs whenever "a judgment or other final adjudication" establishes that the insured committed "acts of active and deliberative dishonesty" or "personally gained . . . a financial profit or other advantage to which he was not legally entitled," or when the insurance relates "to any risk the insurance of which is prohibited under the insurance law of this state."[97]

Underlying these limitations, however, is the statute's declaration that it is "the public policy of this state to spread the risk of corporate management, notwithstanding any other general or special law of this state or of any other jurisdiction including the federal government."[98] New York's only reported decision on the subject placed considerable emphasis on this expression of public policy.[99]

Notice to Shareholders

New York mandates that a corporation notify shareholders of the purchase or maintenance of insurance payments.[100] The Delaware, California, and Model Act provisions do not require shareholder notification.

Policy Coverage

Most currently available policies follow a traditional two-part structure. First, the company reimbursement part insures the corporation for indemnification payments, whether mandatory or permissive. Second, the directors' and officers' reimbursement part insures directors and officers in situations where the corporation cannot or does not indemnify them.[101]

Ambiguities in D&O policies, as in other kinds of insurance policies, are generally resolved against the insurer, which drafted the policy, and in favor of the insured.[102]

Losses Covered

The typical D&O policy insures for any losses—including damages, judgments, settlements, costs, and expenses—incurred in the defense of actions, suits, or proceedings arising out of claims made for "wrongful acts." Generally, "wrongful acts" include "any breach of duty, neglect, error, misstatement, misleading statement, omissions or other act done or wrongfully attempted by the insureds."[103] The inclusion of settlements is significant because state indemnification statutes generally preclude indemnification for amounts paid in settlement of derivative actions.

Among the losses generally *not* covered are fines, penalties, and other matters that are uninsurable under the applicable law.[104]

D&O policies often exclude certain conduct from coverage, most commonly the receipt of a personal profit or advantage to which the insured was not legally entitled, unauthorized remuneration, dishonesty, short-swing profit liability under section 16(b) of the Securities Exchange Act, libel and slander, pollution, ERISA violations, bodily injury or property damage, and nuclear accidents.[105]

Recently, insurers have added exclusions for claims arising out of contests for corporate control.[106] The court in *KDT Industries, Inc. v. Home Insurance Co.*[107] construed an exclusion denying coverage for losses "arising from any attempt to gain control or from any gaining of control of the Company or any claim made by any minority stockholder of the Company"[108] narrowly to allow coverage of two derivative actions in which the "primary allegation"[109] was that the corporation paid too high a price for assets purchased from a shareholder who had recently taken control of the corporation.[110] The court emphasized that "[a]lthough control was an issue, it was only incidental," since liability "hinged on the fairness of the challenged transaction."[111] The court noted its view that the shareholder plaintiffs in these cases "would have been upset about this particular sale of assets even if there had been no preceding takeover."[112]

Exclusions for claims brought by corporations against their own directors and officers have also been added to some policies.[113] This type of exclusion was prompted by actions brought by Chase Manhattan Bank and Bank of America against their insured officers.[114]

Misrepresentation

D&O insurers, like other insurers, may deny liability on the ground of misrepresentation or omission of material facts in the insured's application. Whether particular alleged misrepresentations and/or omissions provide grounds for a denial of liability, of course, depends upon the specific question asked by the insurer and the specific response provided by the insured.[115] The insurer may waive its right to rescind a policy either by failing to make inquiries concerning information "distinctly implied" in facts that are disclosed,[116] or by failing to seek rescission in a timely manner after learning of misstatements and/or omissions.[117]

Two cases—*Bird v. Penn Central Co.*[118] and *Shapiro v. American Home Assurance Co.*[119]—have focused attention upon the way a material misrepresentation by one director or officer affects the insurance coverage of "innocent" directors. In *Bird*, Lloyd's challenged a $10 million policy obtained by Penn Central two years before the corporation's collapse. Lloyd's contended that the chairman of the corporation's finance committee had falsely represented in the company's application that none of the directors and officers seeking coverage knew of any acts or omissions that "might afford valid grounds for any future claim."[120] The court, denying a motion for summary judgment made by outside directors who had no knowledge of any probable claims, held that Lloyd's would be entitled to rescind if materiality and reliance were adequately established at trial.[121]

In *Shapiro*, the court held that material misrepresentations by the former president of an insured corporation defeated coverage under the policy as to all insureds, including those officers and directors who had no knowledge of the misrepresentations.[122] The president had grossly overstated the corporation's earnings, and had falsely stated that he knew of no acts or omissions by the company's officers and directors that might give rise to a claim under the policy.[123]

Significantly, the *Shapiro* court suggested that there was no legal reason why policies could not be negotiated that would adequately protect innocent directors whose corporations were willing to pay higher premiums in return for such coverage.[124] In a subsequent decision in the same case (involving a Securities Act liability policy rather than a D&O policy), the court held that two innocent directors and officers were covered by policies that included severability provisions stating the policies were to be construed as "separate contract[s] with each Insured," and that references "to the Insured shall be construed as referring only to that particular Insured, and the liability of the Insurer to such Insured shall be independent of its liability to any other Insured."[125]

Advancement

From a practical perspective, the advancement of litigation costs may be as important to directors and officers as insurance for ultimate judgments or settlements. Until recently, most D&O policies either did not specifically address this issue or provided that the insurer could at its option advance expenses, so long as if it were ultimately established that the insurer had no liability under the policy all monies advanced would be repaid.[126] A substantial body of case law is now developing interpreting such provisions.

Most prominently, the Third and Ninth Circuits in *Little v. MGIC Indemnity Corp.*[127] and *Okada v. MGIC Indemnity Corp.*[128] have held that a specific provision—stating that "[t]he Insurer may at its option . . . advance on behalf of the Directors or Officers . . . *expenses* which they have incurred in connection with claims made against them"[129]—mandates advancement of litigation costs upon request by the directors and officers.

The *Little* and *Okada* courts each cited the general rule that ambiguous provisions in insurance contracts are strictly construed against insurers, and concluded that the applicable policy language was ambiguous because the "loss" provision included defense costs within the insurer's duty of contemporaneous payment (the policies' definitions of loss were held to impose such a duty) but the "advancement option" provision did not clearly exclude defense costs from the scope of this duty.[130] The *Little* and *Okada* courts noted that separate provisions in each of the policies required the insured to obtain the insurer's consent before incurring any "costs, charges, and expenses," but granted the insurer (in the provision quoted above) the option whether to advance "expenses."[131] In the *Little* court's words, "[o]ne could reasonably understand the option clause . . . to apply only to one type of expenditure within the broader category of 'costs, charges, and expenses,' and because 'expenses' is not defined, one could then conclude that defense costs do not fall within its meaning."[132]

At least two district courts have reached a similar conclusion in other cases involving similar policy language,[133] but several other district courts have reached the opposite conclusion, holding that insurers are not obligated to advance defense costs under policy language virtually identical to that construed in *Little* and *Okada*.[134] Two district courts—*PepsiCo, Inc. v. Continental Casualty Co.*[135] and *Mt. Hawley Insurance Co. v. Federal Savings & Loan Insurance Corp.*[136]—have construed policies that did not include the "insurer may at its option . . . advance . . . expenses" provision found in *Little* and *Okada* to impose a duty to advance defense costs.[137] One court has labeled the issue moot until after resolution of other factual questions (for example, whether the insured's alleged actions fall within the policy's coverage).[138]

Some insurance carriers have now revised their policies in light of decisions such as *Little* and *Okada* to provide specifically that the insurer is not required to advance defense expenses.[139] The district court in *Little* concluded that a policy which clearly excludes advancement of defense costs would be unconscionable under Pennsylvania law.[140] The Third Circuit expressly declined to address this issue.[141]

Allocation

A practical problem arising in any litigation involving multiple defendants, not all of whom are insured by the same carrier, is the allocation of costs and expenses, including attorneys' fees. Since the D&O policy covers only directors and officers, the insurance company in such a case would be required to pay only that portion of the losses and expenses attributable to the directors and officers. The insurance carrier is not obligated to pay the portion of the losses and expenses attributable to the corporation (which is an insured, but only with respect to its obligation to indemnify its directors and officers) or any third party.[142]

Failure to resolve the allocation issue before litigation expenses begin mounting may have serious consequences. For example, the insured directors may wish to settle a case that the insurance company has determined is directed primarily at the corporation or some third party, thus forcing litigation over who should bear the larger part of the settlement and legal expenses—the corporation or the insurer.[143]

Responses to the Current D&O Crisis

Corporations, state legislatures, and commentators have developed four general approaches to the problems caused by the D&O crisis of the mid-1980s.

Negotiation and Unconventional Arrangements

Several commentators have suggested that insurance carriers may be willing to act more flexibly than corporate managers expect. Corporations may, according to this view, obtain coverage by identifying areas of concern to potential carriers and tailoring exclusions to respond specifically to these problem areas. Corporations may also be able to negotiate unconventional arrangements, including differing premiums with different insurers for separate layers of coverage, or the purchase of insurance only for liabilities exceeding a specified level of coverage.[144]

Maximizing Indemnification Rights

As previously discussed, state indemnification statutes typically provide that permissive indemnification must be authorized on a case-by-case basis by the board of directors, special counsel, or shareholders. Corporations may, at least according to numerous commentators, maximize their directors' indemnification rights[145] by enacting charter or bylaw provisions stating that permissive indemnification "shall"—as opposed to "may"—be authorized to the full extent permitted by law.[146]

Commentators have similarly recommended the adoption of charter or bylaw provisions mandating the advancement of expenses, subject only to an undertaking to repay if the board (or, to provide protection in the event of a change in control, a court) later determines that indemnification is not permitted by law.[147]

Commentators have also recommended the adoption of charter or bylaw provisions that place the burden of proving that the applicable standards have *not* been met upon the corporation. Such a provision, for instance, could mandate "that the corporation *must* make indemnification on demand unless, within a specified time, the board of directors affirmatively determines that the agent has *not* met the required standard."[148]

Commentators have also suggested that charter and bylaw indemnification provisions should include a statement that the specified indemnification rights are a "contract" between the director or officer and the corporation, thus adding the element of a direct bargained-for agreement, and at least arguably complicating unilateral modification or repeal by the corporation (following, for example, the official's termination, a change in control, or an adverse change in a state law). Commentators have also suggested that this same end can be achieved, perhaps more successfully, by executing separate indemnification contracts for each director and officer.[149]

A final suggestion has been to establish outside funding mechanisms that would segregate funds and automatically permit their release whenever certain procedures are followed. Such devices include letters of credit that require a bank or other third party to take the risk that the corporation will not pay the indemnification (for example, because of bankruptcy or a new board's refusal to pay after a change in control), and trust funds set up to release assets upon an independent trustee's determination that the claimant is entitled to indemnification.[150] Care should be taken to ensure that such trusts are structured in a way that will prevent creditors (and/or a receiver) from reaching the trust assets in the event of insolvency.[151]

To a large degree, the legality of these various proposals for maximizing indemnification will hinge on how courts construe the nonexclusivity provisions found in statutes similar to those enacted in California, Delaware, and New York. For example, to the extent these provisions attempt to make authorization for permissive indemnification or advancement automatic or mandatory in every instance, they may be viewed as conflicting with the express language of state indemnification statutes (including those in California, Delaware, and New York) requiring authorization on a case-by-case basis.[152] Legislation enacted in 1986 in Delaware deleted the "specific case" requirement for the advancement of expenses, although not for the ultimate authorization of indemnification at the conclusion of the litigation.[153] One court applying Delaware law—*Security America Corp. v. Walsh, Case, Coale, Brown & Burke*[154]—has upheld irrevocable and unamendable trusts established in the face of an imminent change of control to provide for the continued advancement of expenses to the outgoing directors.

469

Legislative Solutions: Limitations on Directors' Liabilities and Expansion of Indemnification Rights

As of mid-1988, 39 states have adopted director-protection statutes as at least a partial solution to the D&O crisis. Most prominent among the statutes enacted to date is section 102(b)(7) of the Delaware General Corporation Law, which authorizes the adoption by shareholders of charter provisions eliminating or limiting a director's liability to the corporation or its stockholders for monetary damages for breach of fiduciary duty, so long as such provisions do not apply to (1) breaches of the director's duty of loyalty, (2) "acts or omissions not in good faith or which involve intentional misconduct or a knowing violation of law," (3) unlawful payments of dividends or unlawful stock purchases or redemptions, and (4) "transaction[s] from which the director derived an improper personal benefit."[155]

As of mid-1988, legislation modeled to one extent or another upon the Delaware statute's authorization of liability limiting or eliminating charter provisions has been enacted in Alaska, Arizona, Arkansas, California, Colorado, Georgia, Idaho, Iowa, Kansas, Kentucky, Louisiana, Maryland, Massachusetts, Michigan, Minnesota, Montana, Nebraska, Nevada, New Jersey, New Mexico, New York, North Carolina, Oklahoma, Oregon, Pennsylvania, Rhode Island, South Carolina, South Dakota, Texas, Utah, Virginia, Washington, and Wyoming.[156] The Louisiana, Mayland, Nevada, New Jersey, and Virginia statutes differ from the Delaware model by providing protection for corporate officers as well as directors.[157]

Five additional states—Florida, Indiana, Maine, Ohio, and Wisconsin—plus Kentucky and Virginia (which, as noted above, also have adopted Delaware section 102(b)(7)-type provisions) have responded to the D&O crisis by enacting statutes that tighten the standard of directorial culpability for directors of all corporations chartered in those jurisdictions. There is no requirement that the corporation adopt a charter provision and/or seek shareholder approval in order to benefit from these statutes.

Florida's statute provides that a director is not liable for monetary damages for any breach of his duties as a director unless the breach constitutes (i) a violation of criminal law, except where the director "had reasonable cause to believe his conduct was lawful or had no reasonable cause to believe his conduct was unlawful," (ii) a "transaction from which the director derived an improper personal benefit, either directly or indirectly," (iii) unlawful payments of dividends or unlawful stock purchases or unlawful sales of assets, (iv) in a derivative action, "conscious disregard for the best interest of the corporation, or willful misconduct," or (v) in a nonderivative action, "recklessness or an act or omission which was committed in bad faith or with malicious purpose or in a manner exhibiting wanton and willful disregard of human rights, safety, or property."[158]

Indiana's statute provides that a director is not liable for failure to act in compliance with his duties as a director unless the conduct constitutes "willful misconduct or recklessness."[159] Kentucky's statute bars monetary relief unless the director's breach of duty constitutes "willful misconduct or wanton or reckless disregard for the best interests of the corporation and its shareholders."[160]

Maine's statute provides that a "director shall not be held personally liable for monetary damages for failure to discharge any duty as a director unless the director is found not to have acted honestly or in the reasonable belief that the action was in or not opposed to the best interests of the corporation or its shareholders."[161]

Virginia's statute precludes directorial liability for conduct "in accordance with [the director's] good faith business judgment of the best interests of the corporation."[162]

The Ohio and Wisconsin statutes similarly tighten the standard of directorial culpability, but authorize the corporation to "opt out" of this standard (as opposed to Delaware's statute, which allows corporations to "opt in") by charter provision. Ohio's statute limits a director's liability for monetary damages unless it is proved, "by clear and convincing evidence," that the act or omission was "undertaken with deliberate intent to cause injury to the corporation or undertaken with reckless disregard for the best interests of the corporation," unless the corporation "opts out."[163] Wisconsin's statute provides directors with immunity from personal liability unless the person asserting such liability proves (i) "a wilful failure to deal fairly with the corporation or its shareholders in connection with a matter in which the director has a material conflict of interest," (ii) a violation of criminal law, except where the director had no reasonable cause to believe his or her conduct was unlawful, (iii) "a transaction from which the director derived an improper personal profit," or (iv) "[w]ilful misconduct," except if the corporation "opts out."[164]

Another legislative measure adopted by a substantial number of states, including New York, specifically authorizes in the statute's nonexclusivity provision the adoption in a corporation's certificate (or, if authorized by the certificate or bylaws, in a board or shareholder resolution or an indemnification agreement) of indemnification rights not otherwise authorized by the statute, provided that no indemnification may be made to a director or officer "if a judgment or other final adjudication adverse to the director or officer establishes that his acts were committed in bad faith or were the result of active and deliberate dishonesty and were material to the cause of action so adjudicated, or that he personally gained in fact a financial profit or other advantage to which he was not legally entitled."[165] Additional variations of this approach have been adopted in California, Florida, Georgia, Iowa, Louisiana, Massachusetts, Mississippi, Missouri, Nevada, New Jersey, North Carolina, Oregon, Pennsylvania, Tennessee, Virginia, Washington, and Wisconsin.[166]

Delaware's statute, it should be noted, has for years provided that statutory indemnification "shall not be deemed exclusive of any other rights to which those seeking indemnification or advancement of expenses may be entitled under any bylaw, agreement, vote of stockholders or disinterested directors or otherwise" without setting forth any limitations such as deliberate dishonesty or willful misconduct.[167]

A second way state legislatures have expanded indemnification rights has been to permit indemnification of judgments and/or amounts paid to settle derivative claims. In Delaware, as in many states, such indemnification is not allowed, the theory being that otherwise funds received by the corporation (the ultimate plaintiff on whose behalf the suit is brought) pursuant to a monetary judgment or settlement would simply be returned to the defendant director who had paid them.[168] As discussed earlier in the chapter, a trend in legislative enactments of the mid-to-late 1980s has been to permit such indemnification, in some jurisdictions with court approval but in a substantial number of jurisdictions without court approval.[169]

The Pennsylvania and Virginia statutes combine both the nonexclusivity and the indemnification in derivative action approaches. The Pennsylvania statute permits indemnification or advancement of expenses under any "bylaw, agreement, vote of shareholders, vote of directors or otherwise," except where a court determines that the act or omission giving rise to the indemnification constituted "willful misconduct or recklessness."[170] The statute also expressly authorizes indemnification in situations not otherwise provided for by statute including liability from any "threatened, pending or completed" derivative action, and declares such indemnification to be consistent with the public policy of Pennsylvania.[171] The Virginia statute similarly specifically authorizes "any further indemnity, including indemnity with respect to a proceeding by or in the right of the corporation" except indemnity against "willful misconduct or a knowing violation of the criminal law."[172]

Alternatives to D&O Insurance

Captive Insurance

One alternative to D&O insurance is the creation of a wholly owned offshore insurance subsidiary. Until recently, captive insurance subsidiaries were almost without exception domiciled in offshore places such as Bermuda or the Cayman Islands, which are free from U.S. insurance regulations.[173] The Tax Reform Act of 1986, however, eliminated the most important tax advantages for U.S. owners of offshore captives, and as a result captive subsidiaries are increasingly being set up in U.S. states.[174]

The use of such a "captive" insurer raises at least two important questions. First, a court may view any "insurance" by a subsidiary not as insurance but rather a "cover" for indemnifying the parent's directors and officers, particularly if the insurer-subsidiary reimburses its parent's directors on a dollar for dollar basis.[175]

California permits corporations chartered in that jurisdiction to own "all or a portion" of a company issuing insurance policies so long as (1) such insurance is authorized by the corporation's charter, or (2) the insurance company is organized and regulated by the insurance laws of the jurisdiction of its organization, procedures for processing claims are in place which do not permit the insurance company "to be subject to the direct control of the corporation that purchased the policy," and the policy provides for "some manner of risk sharing."[176] Arizona, Colorado, Hawaii, Louisiana, Maryland, Nevada, New Jersey, New Mexico, Ohio, Pennsylvania, and Texas have also enacted statutes that in one form or another authorize alternatives to D&O insurance such as self-insurance.[177] The General Corporation Law Section of the Delaware Bar Association rejected such a change in its statute in 1986 on the ground that " 'insurance' without any genuine risk sharing" was "fundamentally circular."[178]

Second, the creation of a captive insurer may also have significant tax consequences. As emphasized most recently by the Ninth Circuit in *Clougherty Packing Co. v. Commissioner*,[179] the "premiums" paid are typically not deductible for federal income tax purposes, since such arrangements may not involve a distribution of risk.[180] The court in *Crawford Fitting Co. v. United States*,[181] however, allowed a taxpayer to deduct premium payments to a captive insurer owned by the same stockholders as several affiliated manufacturing companies (the stockholders' respective interests in the captive were *not* in proportion to their interests in the affiliated manufacturing companies), and which offered insurance coverage to both affiliated and unaffiliated companies.[182] The court concluded that rather than "a parent company . . . trying to deduct nondeductible costs of self-insurance by paying 'insurance premiums' for risks that were being retained," the captive arrangement "was legitimately organized to enable [the corporation] to secure insurance at a reasonable price, without substantial limitations on the types and amounts of risk, . . . in return for the payment of legitimate premiums."[183] In addition, the court emphasized that the captive's ownership placed the risks outside the "economic family," since the "economic risk of loss" was "shifted and distributed among the shareholders of the captive insurance company and its insureds."[184]

To minimize these problems, commentators have recommended that corporations choosing to insure through a captive company take measures to delineate clearly the captive company's separate corporate status and to spread risk. Most notably, a captive company might achieve this with the following characteristics and practices:

- Sufficient capitalization to ensure that it can operate without routinely turning to its parent for funding over and above reasonable premiums
- Independent managers with control over the determination of claims
- Business conducted in accordance with standard trade practices, including standard premium charges and limitations upon liability
- Equity shares issued to third parties
- Reinsurance contracts obtained from established reinsurers
- Insurance of corporations other than just its parent[185]

Insurance Pooling Arrangements

A second alternative to D&O insurance solves many of the problems raised by captive insurance companies by spreading risk through an insurance pooling arrangement in which a group of companies form an insurance company insuring all members of the group. A number of industries have formed such offshore captive pooling arrangements, the most prominent of which is A.C.E. Insurance Co., which was organized in late 1985 by thirty-three major U.S. corporations, including Chase Manhattan, Dow Chemical, Ford, General Electric, IBM, Shell Oil, U.S. Steel, and Upjohn.[186]

Notes

1. *The Job Nobody Wants: Outside Directors Find that the Risks and Hassles Just Aren't Worth It*, Bus. Wk. 56 (Sept. 8, 1986). *See also* Korn/Ferry International Fourteenth Annual Board of Directors Study (Feb. 25, 1987) at 23 (among individuals who declined an invitation to serve on a board of directors, the "predominate reason" in 1986 for 14.2 percent was "increasing legal liability," while in 1985 only 2.5 percent declined for that reason).
2. *See Long-Term Changes, Softening Seen in D&O Liability Markets*, 2 Liability & Ins. Bull. (BNA), No. 38, at 6 (Apr. 11, 1988); Goldwasser, *An Assessment of Directors' and Officers' Liability Insurance in 1988*, in Directors' and Officers' Liability Insurance 1988, 9, 11 (Practising Law Institute 1988).
3. *See* Cal. Gen. Corp. Code § 317 (hereinafter cited as Cal. § ____); Del. Gen. Corp. Law § 145 (hereinafter cited as Del. § ____); N.Y. Bus. Corp. Law §§ 721–26 (hereinafter cited as N.Y. § ____); Model Business Corp. Act §§ 8.50–8.58 (hereinafter cited as Model Act § ____).

4. DEL. § 145(c). *See also* N.Y. § 723(a).
5. MODEL ACT § 8.52.
6. CAL. § 317(d).
7. *See* DEL. § 145(c) ("To the extent that [the person to be indemnified] has been successful. . . he shall be indemnified."). *See also* CAL. § 317(d); N.Y. § 723(a).
8. 321 A.2d 138, 141 (Del. Super. 1974).
9. 264 A.2d 358, 359–60 (Del. Super. 1970).
10. *See* United States v. Wolfson, 437 F.2d 862 (2d Cir. 1970).
11. 492 A.2d 260 (Del. Super. 1985).
12. *Id.* at 262.
13. *Id.* at 265.
14. *Id.* at 265–66. *Cf.* Galdi v. Berg, 359 F. Supp. 698, 700–02 (D. Del. 1973) ("dismissal without prejudice solely because the same charge is being litigated in other presently pending actions" held not to constitute partial success).
15. MODEL ACT § 8.52.
16. *Id.* at § 8.52 Official Comment at 250.
17. *See* former N.Y. BUS. CORP. LAW § 724(a).
18. *See* Wisener v. Air Express Int'l Corp., 583 F.2d 579, 583 (2d Cir. 1978) (applying Illinois law); B & B Inv. Club v. Kleinert's Inc., 472 F. Supp. 787, 789–91 (E.D. Pa. 1979) (applying Pennsylvania law).
19. 667 P.2d 830, 833–34 (Hawaii Ct. App. 1983).
20. 88 A.D.2d 652, 653, 450 N.Y.S.2d 536, 537 (N.Y. App. Div. 1982).
21. MODEL ACT § 8.52 Official Comment at 250.
22. *See* CAL. § 317(d); DEL. § 145(c); N.Y. § 723(a).
23. *See, e.g.*, CAL. § 317(b), (c); DEL. § 145(a), (b); N.Y. § 722(a), (c). *But see* MODEL ACT § 8.51 (§ 8.51(a) includes standards for permissive indemnification in third-party and derivative actions without differentiation, then §§ 8.51(d) (1) and 8.51(e) state two situations in which permissive indemnification will not be permitted in derivative actions).
24. *But see* MINN. BUS. CORP. ACT § 302A.521 (all indemnification mandatory).
25. DEL. § 145(a) (emphasis added).
26. CAL. § 317(b).
27. N.Y. § 722(a).
28. *Id.*
29. MODEL ACT § 8.51(a) (emphasis added).
30. *See* CAL. § 317(b); DEL. § 145(a); N.Y. § 722(a); MODEL ACT §§ 8.50(4), 8.51(a).
31. *See* CAL. § 317(b); DEL. § 145(a); N.Y. § 722(b); MODEL ACT § 8.51(c).
32. *See* CAL. § 317(b); DEL. § 145(b); N.Y. § 722(a), (c); MODEL ACT § 8.51(a).
33. *See, e.g.*, CAL. § 317(c)(1) ("adjudged to be liable to the corporation in the performance of [a] duty to the corporation and its shareholders"); DEL. § 145(b) ("adjudged to be liable to the corporation"); N.Y. § 722(c) ("adjudged to be liable to the corporation"); MODEL ACT § 8.51(d) ("adjudged liable to the corporation").
34. *See* former N.Y. § 722(a).

35. *See* CAL. § 317(c)(1); DEL. § 145(b); N.Y. § 722(c).

36. Cambridge Fund, Inc. v. Abella, 501 F. Supp. 598, 617 (S.D.N.Y. 1980).

37. *See* D. DEMOTT, SHAREHOLDER DERIVATIVE ACTIONS: LAW AND PRACTICE § 6:08, at 6–54 (1987); 1 E. FOLK, R. WARD & E. WELCH, FOLK ON THE DELAWARE GENERAL CORPORATION LAW § 145.5 (1988). This policy rationale is not universally accepted. *See* Herzel, *Law Should Allow Indemnity for Derivative Suits*, Legal Times, Mar. 31, 1986, at 11:

> An example will make it easier to understand the other side of the story.
> Suppose a very wealthy individual would like to set up a trust and appoint as trustees several individuals in whom he has confidence. These individuals would like to serve, but they are afraid because they know that some of the wealthy person's relatives are very disputatious and litigation would be likely and very expensive and risky. To solve this problem, the wealthy individual says: 'I have talked with my lawyers and I am willing to exculpate you in my trust instrument against liability for anything except actions taken in bad faith. That should solve your problem. My lawyers tell me that it would be illegal for me to attempt to protect you against actions taken in bad faith, and I know that you don't expect or need that protection.' The individuals agree.
> Is there anything wrong with a legal rule that permits this? In fact, trust law permits exactly that and has for a long time. If there isn't anything wrong with trust law on this point, why should the rule be different for corporate directors? Usually, legal rules covering trustees are far more stringent than for directors.

"[C]orporation statutes could," according to this view, "require stockholder approval of any bylaw or charter provision allowing exculpation for directors and officers." *Id.*

38. The omission in section 145(b) of "judgments, fines and amounts paid in settlement" was intentional. *See* Arsht & Stapleton, *Delaware's New General Corporation Law: Substantive Changes*, 23 BUS. LAW. 75, 79–80 (1967); Sebring, *Recent Legislative Changes in the Law of Indemnification of Directors, Officers and Others*, 23 BUS. LAW. 95, 103 (1967).

39. N.Y. § 722(c).

40. CAL. § 317(c)(2). California's pre-1987 statute barred indemnification of "amounts paid in settling or otherwise disposing of a threatened or pending [derivative] action, *with or without court approval*." Former CAL. § 317(c)(2) (emphasis added).

41. As of mid-1988, the states other than New York and California that permit indemnification of judgments and/or settlements in derivative actions to one extent or another include Arizona, Florida, Indiana, Louisiana, Maine, Maryland, Massachusetts, Michigan, Minnesota, Missouri, Nevada, North Dakota, Oregon, Tennessee, Texas, Vermont, Wisconsin, and Wyoming. *See* ARIZ. GEN. CORP. LAW § 10-005(B); FLA. GEN. CORP. ACT § 607.014(2); IND. BUS. CORP. LAW § 23-1-37(8); LA. BUS. CORP. LAW § 12:83(A); ME. BUS. CORP. ACT § 719(1); MD. GEN. CORP. LAW § 2-418(b)(2)(i) & (ii); MASS. BUS. CORP. LAW § 67; MICH. BUS. CORP. ACT § 21.200(562); MINN. BUS. CORP. ACT § 302A.521(2); MO. GEN. & BUS. CORP. LAW § 351.355(2); NEV. GEN. CORP. LAW § 78.751(2); N.D. BUS. CORP. ACT § 10-19.1-91(2); OR. BUS. CORP. ACT § 98(2); TENN. BUS. CORP. ACT § 48-18-502; TEX. BUS. CORP. ACT § 2.02-1(E); VT. BUS. CORP. ACT § 1852(15); WIS. BUS. CORP. LAW § 180.049; WYO. BUS. CORP. ACT § 17-1-105.1(a).

A proposal to amend section 145(b) to allow indemnification of judgments and amounts paid in settlement of derivative actions was rejected by the General Corporation Law Section of the Delaware Bar Association in 1986. *See* Veasey & Finkelstein, *New Delaware Statute: Allows Limits on Director Liability and Modernizes Indemnification Protection*, 6 BUS. LAW. UPDATE 1, 2 (July/Aug. 1986).

42. Nonexclusivity provisions are discussed elsewhere in this chapter.

43. VA. STOCK CORP. ACT § 13.1-704B.

44. 42 PA. STAT. § 8365(c).

45. IOWA BUS. CORP. ACT § 496A.4A(7).

46. CAL. § 204(a)(11).

47. *See* CAL. § 317(e); DEL. § 145(d); N.Y. § 723(b); MODEL ACT § 8.55(a).

48. *See* CAL. § 317(e)(1); DEL. § 145(d); N.Y. § 723(b)(1); MODEL ACT § 8.55(b)(1).

49. MODEL ACT § 8.55(b)(2).

50. *See, e.g.*, CAL. § 317(e)(2); DEL. § 145(d); N.Y. § 723(b)(2)(A).

51. MODEL ACT § 8.55 Official Comment at 256.

52. MINN. BUS. CORP. ACT § 302A.521(1)(e); N.D. BUS. CORP. ACT § 10-19.1-91(1)(d).

53. OHIO GEN. CORP. LAW § 1701.13(E)(4); WASH. BUS. CORP. ACT § 23A.08.025(6)(c). *See also* Schmidt v. Magnetic Head Corp., 97 A.D.2d 151, 161–62, 468 N.Y.S.2d 649, 656–57 (N.Y. App. Div. 1983) (an "independent legal counsel" is "an attorney who is free from past connections with the corporation or the person to be indemnified").

54. DEL. § 145(d)(3); N.Y. § 723(b)(2)(B).

55. CAL. § 317(e)(2).

56. MODEL ACT § 8.55(b)(4).

57. *See, e.g.*, Green v. Westcap Corp., 492 A.2d 260 (Del. Super. 1985); Merritt-Chapman & Scott Corp. v. Wolfson, 321 A.2d 138 (Del. Super. 1974).

58. *See* CAL. § 317(c), (e)(4); DEL. § 145(b); N.Y. §§ 722(c), 724(a); MODEL ACT § 8.54.

59. MODEL ACT § 8.54.

60. MODEL ACT § 8.53 Official Comment at 251–52.

61. Former DEL. § 145(e). *See also* CAL. § 317(f).

62. DEL. § 145(e).

63. *See* CAL. § 317(f); N.Y. §§ 723(c), 725(a). *See also* MODEL ACT § 8.53(a)(2).

64. *See* Johnson v. Gene's Supermarket, Inc., 453 N.E.2d 83, 87–89 (Ill. Ct. App. 1983).

65. *See* Security Am. Corp. v. Walsh, Case, Coale, Brown & Burke, No. 82 C 2953 (N.D. Ill. Jan. 11, 1985) (available on LEXIS and WESTLAW).

66. *Id.*, slip op. at 9.

67. Comment, *Law for Sale: A Study of the Delaware Corporation Law of 1967*, 117 U. PA. L. REV. 861, 883 (1969) (citing interview with Ernest L. Folk). *See also* CONN. STOCK CORP. ACT § 33-320a(f) (explicitly requiring nothing more than an "agreement. . . to repay").

68. MODEL ACT § 8.53(b). *See also* ME. BUS. CORP. ACT § 719(4) (defining "understanding" in terms similar to Model Act.

477

69. Model Act § 8.50(7). *See also* Cal. § 317(a), (b), (c); Del. § 145(a), (b). *Cf.* N.Y. § 722(a) (referring to "an action or proceeding,. . . whether civil or criminal").

70. 457 A.2d 339 (Del. 1983).

71. *Id.* at 344.

72. *Id.* at 343.

73. 566 F. Supp. 1112 (S.D.N.Y. 1983).

74. *Id.* at 1115–16.

75. *See* Mass. Bus. Corp. Law § 67; Tex. Bus. Corp. Act § 2.02-1(B).

76. *See* Cal. § 317(d); Del. § 145(c); N.Y. § 723(a); Model Act § 8.52.

77. Cal. § 317(g).

78. Cal. § 204(a)(11) (citing Cal. § 204(a)(10)).

79. 640 F. Supp. 656, 660 (S.D.N.Y. 1986).

80. 15 U.S.C. § 78a *et seq.*

81. *See generally* 1 R. Balotti & J. Finkelstein, The Delaware Law of Corporations and Business Organizations § 4.16, at 197–98 (1988); J. Bishop, The Law of Officers and Directors: Indemnification and Insurance, ¶ 6.03[1][a], at 14–15 (1981 & Supp. 1987); Herzel & Harris, *Uninsured Boards Mount Weak Defense*, Nat'l L.J., Apr. 21, 1986, at 19; Arsht & Stapleton, *supra* note 38, at 80 (nonexclusivity provision included "so that other rights to indemnification may still exist by contract, by-law or charter within such limits of public policy as the court may establish"); Sebring, *supra* note 38, at 105 ("no doubt a court would be guided by public policy considerations").

82. 640 F. Supp. at 660–61.

83. R. Balotti & J. Finkelstein, *supra* note 81, at § 4.16, at 198.

84. 42 Pa. Stat. § 8365(c).

85. Model Act § 8.58(a).

86. Model Act § 8.58 Official Comment at 261.

87. *See, e.g.*, Globus v. Law Research Serv. Inc., 418 F.2d 1276, 1288 (2d Cir. 1969), *cert. denied*, 397 U.S. 913 (1970) (stating that "one cannot insure himself against his own reckless, wilful, or criminal misconduct," and emphasizing that its holding barring indemnification was premised upon the defendant's "actual knowledge" of misstatements in an offering circular; in the court's words, "a sin graver than ordinary negligence" had been committed). *See also* Johnston, *Directors' and Officers' and Related Forms of Liability Insurance*, in Securities Law Techniques § 122.03[3] (A. Sommer ed. 1987).

88. 15 U.S.C. § 77a *et seq.*

89. *See* 17 C.F.R. §§ 229.510, 229.512(i).

90. *Id.* § 229.512(i).

91. J. Bishop, *supra* note 81, ¶ 9.04[1][b] at 11–12.

92. *See* 17 C.F.R. § 230.461(c).

93. Wis. Bus. Corp. Law § 180.059.

94. Del. § 145(g). *See also* Cal. § 317(i); Model Act § 8.57.

95. *See* Arsht, *Indemnification under Section 145 of the Delaware General Corporation Law*, 3 Del. J. Corp. L. 176, 179–80 (1980); Klink, Chalif, Bishop & Arsht, *Liabilities Which Can Be Covered under State Statutes and Corporate*

By-Laws, 27 BUS. LAW. 109, 127 (1972) (Del. § 145(g) "is a corporation law, not an insurance law. . . . If a risk were not insurable before Subsection (g), the subsection's enactment did not make it so."). *But see* National Union Fire Ins. v. Seafirst Corp., 662 F. Supp. 36, 39 (W.D. Wash. 1986) (public policy considerations do not bar insurance of bank personnel against liability for deliberate wrongdoing or dishonesty).

96. N.Y. § 726(a)(3).

97. *Id.* § 726(b).

98. *Id.* § 726(e).

99. *See* Flintkote Co. v. Lloyd's Underwriters, N.Y.L.J. 6 (July 27, 1976) (N.Y. Sup. Ct. 1976), *aff'd*, 56 A.D.2d 743, 391 N.Y.S.2d 1005 (N.Y. App. Div. 1977) (upholding insurance for legal fees and expenses—not fines or penalties—incurred by two officer-directors who pleaded nolo contendere after having been indicted for criminal violations of the Sherman Act).

100. N.Y. §§ 725(c), 726(d).

101. *See generally* Johnston, *Directors' and Officers' and Related Terms of Liability Insurance*, in SECURITIES LAW TECHNIQUES § 122.03[2][a] (A. Sommer ed. 1987); Comment, *Practical Aspects of Directors' and Officers' Liability Insurance—Allocating and Advancing Legal Fees and the Duty to Defend*, 32 U.C.L.A. L. REV. 690, 699–700 (1985).

102. *See, e.g.*, Little v. MGIC Indem. Corp., 836 F.2d 789, 793 (3d Cir. 1987); Okada v. MGIC Indem. Corp., 823 F.2d 276, 281 (9th Cir. 1986); KDT Indus., Inc. v. Home Ins. Co., 603 F. Supp. 861, 866–69 (D. Mass. 1985).

103. *See* Johnston, *supra* note 101, at § 122.03[2][f].

104. *See id.* § 122.03[2][f]. *See also* MGIC Indem. Corp. v. Home State Sav. Ass'n, 797 F.2d 285, 287–88 (6th Cir. 1986) (corporation's settlement of a criminal charge by making full restitution for allegedly illusory loan commitments held not to be a claim for payment on account of a wrongful act within the meaning of an insurance policy: "Home State suggests that there was a *potential* for demands against the officials for the payment of money, but a mere potential for such claims is not enough to meet the condition imposed by the policy. The agreement was that MGIC would pay if, during the policy period, 'claims *are* made against the Directors and Officers.' (Emphasis supplied.) That condition is not satisfied, in our view, where claims might have been made during the policy period, but were not.").

105. *See* Johnston, *supra* note 101, at § 122.03[2][g]; Mallen & Evans, *Surviving the Directors' and Officers' Liability Crisis: Insurance and the Alternatives*, 12 DEL. J. CORP. L. 439, 454–57 (1987); Olson, *The D&O Insurance Gap: Strategies for Coping*, Legal Times, Mar. 3, 1986, at 25; Ichel & Thompson, *Directors' and Officers' Insurance Coverage: An Overview and Current Problems*, in DIRECTORS' AND OFFICERS' LIABILITY INSURANCE 1988, 157, 186–90 (Practising Law Institute 1987).

106. *See* Johnston, *supra* note 101, at § 122.03(2)(g)(v); Mallen & Evans, *supra* note 105, at 456; Olson & Morgan, *D&O Exclusions Extend to Takeover Context*, Legal Times, Mar. 10, 1986, at 23; Hertzberg, *Insurers Beginning to Refuse Coverage on Directors, Officers in Takeover Cases*, Wall St. J., Jan. 20, 1986, at 3.

107. 603 F. Supp. 861 (D. Mass. 1985).

108. *Id.* at 862.

109. *Id.* at 868.

110. *Id.* at 863–65, 868–69.

111. *Id.* at 869.

112. *Id.*

113. *See* Johnston, *supra* note 101, at § 122.03[2][g][ix]; Olson & Morgan, *supra* note 105, at 25; Sloane, *Insurer-Management Liability Rift Seen Growing*, N.Y. Times, Dec. 19, 1985, at D8.

114. *See* Fox v. Chase Manhattan Corp., No. 8192 (Del. Ch. Dec. 6, 1985) (available on LEXIS and WESTLAW) (approving $32.5 million settlement); Bank of Am. v. Powers (Cal. Super. Ct. filed Mar. 1, 1985). *See also* Sloane, *supra* note 113 at D8; National Union Fire Ins. Co. v. Seafirst Corp., No. C85-396R, slip op. (W.D. Wash. Mar. 19, 1986) (available on LEXIS and WESTLAW) (holding that a particular insurance policy covered actions by the corporation against its directors and officers), *aff'd mem.*, 804 F.2d 146 (9th Cir. 1986); Federal Deposit Ins. Corp. v. National Union Fire Ins. Co., 630 F. Supp. 1149, 1157 (W.D. La. 1986) (such an exclusion held inapplicable to FDIC as successor following bank failure).

115. *Compare, e.g.*, Jaunich v. National Union Fire Ins. Co., 647 F. Supp. 209, 210–11 (N.D. Cal. 1986) (granting summary judgment in favor of insurer's rescission of policy because corporation neglected to communicate material information known to it and it had a duty to disclose), *and* F/H Indus., Inc. v. National Union Fire Ins. Co., 635 F. Supp. 60, 61–63 (N.D. Ill. 1986), *vacated in part on other grounds*, 116 F.R.D. 224 (N.D. Ill. 1987) (granting motion to dismiss by insurer against claim that it had improperly refused coverage because the insurance application was "unequivocal in its exclusion of coverage for any claim about which the officers or directors of [the corporation] might have knowledge"), *with* National Union Fire Ins. Co. v. Continental Ill. Corp., 643 F. Supp. 1434, 1438–41 (N.D. Ill. 1986) (insurers' effort to avoid liability on the ground that financial statements attached to policy renewal applications contained materially false information rejected by court because "[b]y the terms of their own forms, neither [insurer] asked [the insured corporation] to represent or warrant the truth of the financial statements. They merely asked [that] the statement be 'attached' ") (footnote omitted); Federal Ins. Co. v. Oak Indus., Inc. [1985–1986 Transfer Binder] FED. SEC. L. REP. (CCH) ¶ 92,519, at 93,120 (S.D. Cal. Feb. 3, 1986) (concluding that the insurer "did not inquire into" and that the insured "was under no duty to disclose its knowledge of any facts or circumstances which would give rise to a claim"); *and* National Union Fire Ins. Co. v. Seafirst Corp., No. C85-396R, slip op. at 5–8 (W.D. Wash. Mar. 19, 1986) (available on LEXIS and WESTLAW) (finding no misrepresentation), *aff'd mem.*, 804 F.2d 146 (9th Cir. 1986). *See generally* Goldwasser & Harley, *Directors' and Officers' Liability Insurance: Difficult Application Questions*, in DIRECTORS' AND OFFICERS' LIABILITY INSURANCE 1988, 553 (Practising Law Institute 1988).

116. *See, e.g.*, *Jaunich*, 647 F. Supp. at 211–15.

117. *See, e.g.*, *Oak Indus.*, [1985–1986 Transfer Binder] FED. SEC. L. REP. (CCH) ¶ 92,519 at 93,120.

118. 334 F. Supp. 255 (E.D. Pa. 1971), *subsequent proceedings*, 341 F. Supp. 291 (E.D. Pa. 1972).

119. 584 F. Supp. 1245 (D. Mass. 1984).
120. 334 F. Supp. at 257, 341 F. Supp. at 292.
121. 334 F. Supp. at 262, 341 F. Supp. at 295–96.
122. 584 F. Supp. at 1252.
123. *Id.* at 1249.
124. *Id.* at 1252.
125. Shapiro v. American Home Assurance Co., 616 F. Supp. 900, 902, 903–05 (D. Mass. 1984), *subsequent proceedings*, 616 F. Supp. 906 (D. Mass. 1985).
126. *See* Johnston, *supra* note 101, at § 122.03[2][j].
127. 836 F.2d 789 (3d Cir. 1987).
128. 823 F.2d 276 (9th Cir. 1987).
129. 836 F.2d at 793–94, 823 F.2d at 279–82 (emphasis added).
130. 836 F.2d at 793–95, 823 F.2d at 280–81.
131. *Id.*
132. 836 F.2d at 795. *See also Okada*, 823 F.2d at 281 ("Nowhere does the policy define expenses, or explain how those expenses differ from the broader language . . . which covers 'costs, charges and expenses.' "). *But see Little*, 836 F.2d at 797 (Stapleton, J. dissenting) ("Because I can think of no 'expense incurred in connection with a claim' that would not also be a 'cost or charge incurred in connection with a claim,' [the] suggested distinction, for me, 'tortures the language of the policy' and reads [the] option . . . out of the agreement of the parties.").
133. *See* American Casualty Co. v. Bank of Montana System, 675 F. Supp. 538, 540–44 (D. Minn. 1987); National Union Fire Ins. Co. v. Federal Deposit Ins. Corp., No. CV 85-6860 RG, slip op. at 9–11 (C.D. Cal. Jan. 12, 1987).
134. *See* Zaborac v. American Casualty Co., 663 F. Supp. 330, 334 (C.D. Ill. 1987); America Casualty Co. v. Federal Deposit Ins. Corp., 677 F. Supp. 600, 605–06 (N.D. Iowa 1987); Luther v. Fidelity & Deposit Co., 679 F. Supp. 1092, 1093 (S.D. Fla. 1986); Enzweiler v. Fidelity & Deposit Co., No. 85-99, slip op. at 2 (E.D. Ky. May 13, 1986) (availiable on LEXIS); Clandening v. MGIC Indem. Corp., No. CV 83-2432-LTL, Tr. op. at 8 (C.D. Cal. May 23, 1983).
135. 640 F. Supp. 656 (S.D.N.Y. 1986).
136. 695 F. Supp. 469 (C.D. Cal. 1987).
137. *See* 640 F. Supp. at 659–60; 695 F. Supp. at 473–76. A subsequent opinion by the same judge who decided *PepsiCo* distinguished that case on the ground that the policy (which was not a D&O policy) at issue in the later case did include the above quoted proviso. *See* Board of Educ. v. CNA Ins. Co., 647 F. Supp. 1495, 1507 (S.D.N.Y. 1986), *aff'd on other grounds*, 839 F.2d 14 (2d Cir. 1988).

    Okada was originally decided by the Ninth Circuit in favor of the insured on the ground that the policy imposed a duty to defend upon the insurer under Hawaii law, and consequently mandated immediate reimbursement of litigation costs. *See* Okada v. MGIC Indem. Corp., 795 F.2d 1450, 1453–55 (9th Cir. 1986), *amended*, 823 F.2d 276 (9th Cir. 1987). The court subsequently retreated from its position that the policy created a duty to defend, and issued an amended opinion finding that the language of the policy was ambiguous. *See* 823 F.2d at 278–82.

138. *See* Bank of Commerce & Trust Co. v. National Union Fire Ins. Co., 651 F. Supp. 474, 476–77 (N.D. Okla. 1986).

139. *See* Johnston, *supra* note 101, at § 122.03[2][j]. *See also* American Casualty Co. v. Bank of Mont. Sys., 675 F. Supp. 538, 544 (D. Minn. 1987) ("It is apparent that insurance companies have no trouble making the policy language clear if they wish to do so.").

140. *See* Little v. MGIC Indem. Corp., 649 F. Supp. 1460, 1478–69 (W.D. Pa. 1986), *aff'd on other grounds*, 836 F.2d 789 (3d Cir. 1987). *See also* Okada v. MGIC Indem. Corp., 608 F. Supp. 383, 387 (D. Hawaii 1985), *aff'd on other grounds*, 823 F.2d 276 (9th Cir. 1987):

> A directors' and officers' policy which did not provide, in the event of suit, for payment of the insureds' attorneys' fees until final judgment—when such suits can last for years and cost astronomical sums to defend—would be virtually impossible to sell to reasonable officers and directors, for it would not truly protect the insureds from financial harm caused by suits against them. An insurance policy should be construed according to the reasonable expectations of the insured.

For discussions of the reasonable expectations doctrine in the context of business insurance policies, see Ostrager & Ichel, *The Role of Bargaining Power Evidence in the Construction of the Business Insurance Policy: An Update*, 18 FORUM 577 (1983); Ostrager & Ichel, *Should the Business Insurance Policy Be Construed against the Insurer? Another Look at the Reasonable Expectations Doctrine*, 33 FED. INS. COUNS. Q. 273 (1983).

141. *See* 836 F.2d at 792 n.1.

142. *See* Okada v. MGIC Indem. Corp., 823 F.2d 276, 282 (9th Cir. 1987); PepsiCo., Inc. v. Continental Casualty Co., 640 F. Supp. 656, 661–62 (S.D.N.Y. 1986).

143. *See* Johnston, *supra* note 101, at §§ 122.03[2][k], 122.04[2].

144. *See From Simple to Bizarre: Ten Ways to Cope with D&O Insurance Crisis*, Corporate Control Alert, May 1986, at 1, 5.

145. *See* Note, *Statutory Responses to Boardroom Fears*, 1987 COLUM. BUS. L. REV. 749, 772 (1987) (observing that since "D&O liability insurance has historically been used to fill in the gaps of available indemnification," a "logical reaction" to the D&O crisis "is an expansion of corporations' ability to indemnify their directors and officers").

146. *See, e.g., From Simple to Bizarre, supra* note 144, at 5–6; Sparks, Johnston & Conan, *Indemnification and Directors and Officers Liability Insurance: The Legal Framework under Delaware Law*, in THE CRISIS IN DIRECTORS' AND OFFICERS' LIABILITY INSURANCE 3, 10–11 (Law & Business, Inc. 1986). *See generally* B&B Inv. Club v. Kleinert's Inc., 472 F. Supp. 787, 793 (E.D. Pa. 1979) (construing such language to provide indemnification "to the greatest extent possible").

147. *See, e.g.*, Olson, *The D&O Insurance Gap: Strategies for Coping*, Legal Times, Mar. 3, 1986, at 25.

148. *Id. See also* PepsiCo, Inc. v. Continental Casualty Co., 640 F. Supp. at 661.

149. *See, e.g., From Simple to Bizarre, supra* note 144, at 6; Johnston, *D&O Insurance Crises: How to Fund Indemnification Arrangements*, INSIGHTS, Aug.

1987, at 3; Olson, *supra* note 147, at 25; Sparks, Johnston & Conan, *supra* note 146, at 11; Rovner, *D&O Indemnity: Discrete Contract Seen as an Option*, Legal Times, Nov. 25, 1985, at 1.

150. *From Simple to Bizarre, supra* note 144, at 7; Johnston, *supra* note 149, at 4–7; Olson, *supra* note 147, at 25.

151. *See* Johnston, *supra* note 149, at 6. *See also* Polance and Graul, *Indemnification Trusts: Tax and Accounting Implications*, INSIGHTS, July 1988, at 19.

152. *See* CAL. § 317(e); DEL. § 145(d); N.Y. § 723(b).

153. DEL. § 145(e). *See also* CAL. § 317(f).

154. No. 82-C-2953 (N.D. Ill. Jan. 11, 1985) (available on LEXIS and WESTLAW).

155. Much has already been written about this statute. *See, e.g.*, Balotti & Gentile, *Elimination or Limitation of Director Liability for Delaware Corporations*, 12 DEL. J. CORP. L. 5 (1987); Richards, *Delaware Shareholders May Limit Directors Liability under New Law,* N.Y.L.J., Aug. 11, 1986, at 35; Veasey, Finkelstein & Bigler, *Delaware Supports Directors with a Three-Legged Stool of Limited Liability, Indemnification and Insurance*, 42 BUS. LAW. 399 (1987); Sparks, *Delaware's D&O Liability Law: Other States Should Follow Suit*, Legal Times, Aug. 18, 1986, at 10; Comment, *Limiting Corporate Director's Liability: Delaware's Section 102(b)(7) and the Erosion of the Duty of Care*, 136 U. PA. L. REV. 239 (1987).

156. *See* ALASKA BUS. CORP. ACT § 10.05.255(c); ARIZ. GEN. CORP. LAW § 10-054(A)(9); ARK. BUS. CORP. ACT § 4-27-202(B)(3); CAL. § 204(a)(10); COLO. CORP. CODE 7-3-101(1)(u); GA. BUS. CORP. CODE § 14-2-171(b)(3); (effective until June 30, 1989); GA. BUS. CORP. CODE § 14-2-202(b)(4) (effective beginning July 1, 1989); IDAHO BUS. CORP. ACT § 30-1-54(2); IOWA BUS. CORP. ACT § 496A.49(13); IOWA GEN. CORP. LAW § 491.5(8); KAN. GEN. CORP. CODE § 17-6002(b)(8); KY. BUS. CORP. ACT § 271.271A(2)(d); LA. BUS. CORP. LAW § 12:24(C)(4); MD. GEN. CORP. LAW §§ 2-104(b)(8), 2-405.2(A); MASS. BUS. CORP. LAW § 13(b)(1-1/2); MICH. BUS. CORP. ACT § 21-200(209)(c); MINN. BUS. CORP. ACT § 302A.251(4); MONT. BUS. CORP. ACT § 35-1-202(2)(e); NEB. BUS. CORP. ACT § 21-2035(2); NEV. GEN. CORP. LAW § 78-036(1); N.J. BUS. CORP. ACT § 14A:2-7(3), 14A:6-14(4), 14A:6–[uncodified section]; N.M. BUS. CORP. ACT § 53-12-1(E); N.Y. § 402(b); N.C. BUS. CORP. ACT § 55-7(11); OKLA. BUS. CORP. ACT § 1006(B)(7); OR. BUS. CORP. ACT § 16(2)(c); 42 PA. STAT. § 8364; R.I. BUS. CORP. ACT § 7-1.1-48(a)(6); S.C. BUS. CORP. ACT § 33-2-102(e); S.D. BUS. CORP. ACT 47-2-58.8; TEX. MISC. CORP. LAWS art. 7.06(B); UTAH BUS. CORP. ACT § 16-10-49.1; VA. STOCK CORP. ACT § 13.1-692.1; WASH. BUS. CORP. ACT § 23A.12.020(d); WYO. BUS. CORP. ACT § 17-1-202(c).

157. *See* LA. BUS. CORP. LAW § 12.24(C)(4); MD. GEN. CORP. LAW § 2-405.a(a); NEV. GEN. CORP. LAW § 78-036(1); N.J. BUS. CORP. ACT § 14A:2-7(3), 14A:6–14(4); VA. STOCK CORP. ACT § 13.1-692.1.

158. FLA. GEN. CORP. ACT § 607.1645(1).

159. IND. BUS. CORP. ACT § 23-1-35-1(e)(2).

160. KY. BUS. CORP. ACT § 271A.202(5).

161. ME. BUS. CORP. ACT § 716.

162. VA. STOCK CORP. ACT § 13.1-690A, C.

163. OHIO GEN. CORP. LAW § 1701.59(D).

164. WIS. BUS. CORP. LAW § 180.307.

165. N.Y. § 721.

166. *See* CAL. § 317(g); FLA. GEN. CORP. ACT § 607.014(7); GA. BUS. CORP. CODE § 14-2-156(f) (effective until June 30, 1989); GA. BUS. CORP. CODE §14.a.856 (effective beginning July 1, 1989); IOWA BUS. CORP. ACT § 496A.4A(7); LA. BUS. CORP. LAW § 12:83E; MASS. BUS. CORP. LAW § 67; MISS. BUS. CORP. ACT § 79-4-8.85(b); MO. GEN. & BUS. CORP. LAW § 351.355(7); NEV. GEN. CORP. LAW § 78.751(6)(a); N.J. BUS. CORP. ACT § 14A:3-5(8); N.C. BUS. CORP. ACT § 55-19(a); OR. BUS. CORP. ACT § 1029(1); 42 PA. STAT. § 8365(a), (b); TENN. BUS. CORP. ACT § 48-18-509(a); VA. STOCK CORP. ACT § 13.1-704B; WASH. BUS. CORP. ACT § 23A.08.025(8); WIS. BUS. CORP. LAW § 180.049.

167. *See* DEL. § 145(f).

168. *See* note 37 and accompanying text *supra*.

169. *See* notes 39–41 and accompanying text *supra*.

170. 42 PA. STAT. §§ 8365(a) & (b).

171. *Id.*

172. VA. STOCK CORP. ACT § 13.1-704B.

173. *See* Johnston, *D&O Insurance Crisis: How to Fund Indemnification Arrangements*, INSIGHTS, Aug. 1987, at 31.

174. *Id. See also* Mallen & Evans, *supra* note 105, at 467 (citing 26 U.S.C. § 832).

175. *See* R. BALOTTI & J. FINKELSTEIN, *supra* note 81, § 4.19, at 200.4–200.6.

176. CAL. § 317(i).

177. *See* ARIZ. GEN. CORP. LAW § 10-005(G) & (H); COLO. CORP. CODE § 7-3-101.5(9); HAWAII BUS. CORP. ACT § 415-5(h); LA. BUS. CORP. LAW § 12:83(F); MD. GEN. CORP. LAW § 2-418(k) (2) & (3); NEV. GEN. CORP. LAW § 78.752; N.J. BUS. CORP. ACT § 14A:3-5(9); N.M. BUS. CORP. ACT § 53-11-4.1(J); OHIO GEN. CORP. LAW § 1701.13(E) (7); 42 PA. STAT. § 8365(a); TEX. BUS. CORP. ACT § 2.02-1(R).

178. Veasey & Finkelstein, *New Delaware Statute: Allows Limits on Directors Liability and Modernizes Indemnification Protection*, 6 BUS. LAW. UPDATE 1, 2 (July/Aug. 1986).

179. 811 F.2d 1297 (9th Cir. 1987).

180. *Id.* at 1298–1307. *See generally* Rev. Rul. 77-316, 1977-2 C.B. 53; Carnation Co. v. Commissioner, 71 T.C. 400 (1978), *aff'd*, 640 F.2d 1010 (9th Cir.), *cert. denied*, 454 U.S. 965 (1981); Mobil Oil Corp. v. United States, 8 Cl. Ct. 555 (1985); Stearns-Rogers Corp., Inc. v. United States, 577 F. Supp. 833, 838 (D. Colo. 1984), *aff'd*, 774 F.2d 414 (10th Cir. 1985).

181. 606 F. Supp. 136 (N.D. Ohio 1985).

182. *Id.* at 137–39, 145–46.

183. *Id.*

184. *Id.* at 145.

185. *See generally* R. BALOTTI & J. FINKELSTEIN, *supra* note 81, § 4.17 at 200.6; Sparks, Johnston & Conan, *supra* note 146, at 18–19; Mallen & Evans, *supra* note 105, at 466–67. *See also* Note, *Protecting Corporate Directors and Officers: Insurance and Other Alternatives*, 40 VAND L. REV. 775, 797–803 (1987).

186. *See* Schauer, *Ailing D&O Insurance Market Looks for Cure,* 6 BUS. LAW. UPDATE 1, 3 (Mar./Apr. 1986); Olson, *supra* note 105, at 25; Hilder, *Big U.S. Firms*

Form Liability Insurer, Wall St. J., Dec. 23, 1985, at 6; Olson, Bogen, Magill & Hatch, *Responding to the D&O Insurance Crisis: Negotiated Indemnification Contracts and Other Alternatives for Director and Officer Protection*, in THE BUSINESS JUDGMENT CONFERENCE: PROTECTING OFFICERS AND DIRECTORS FROM LIABILITY 428, 448–50 (Prentice-Hall Law & Business 1987); Rovner, *Banks Win Approval to Form Captives for Insurance*, Legal Times, Mar. 3, 1986, at 1; Taravella, *Alternative Facilities Easing D&O Market*, Bus. Ins., Oct. 20, 1986, at 26.

Thirty-Two

Directors and Officers Liability and Corporate Reimbursement Insurance: Understanding the Coverage

James B. Wallace

Introduction

Directors and officers liability insurance is not written on a standard form used by all, or even most, insurers. While historically policies did resemble each other structurally and certain common terms were used, substantial substantive differences existed. To further complicate the picture, a number of insurers have redrafted their forms within the past few years. Their expressed purpose was either to clarify the restrictive nature of certain terms or to introduce new provisions restricting coverage. While a common thread of sorts ran through this trend, each insurer also invariably identified and addressed matters of peculiar concern to it. This has resulted in a wider disparity of terms offered under different forms than was historically the case. In addition, when an offer of insurance is made, it invariably includes terms that necessitate amendment of the form by endorsement. Not all insurers have the same concerns, and even when they do, no uniform language has been adopted to address them.

These developments have made it difficult to analyze the quality of insurance being offered. Comparing competing quotes is obviously far more arduous. Nevertheless, it is essential for an insured to understand the differences between various offers of insurance and the extent to which the policy it places will provide protection.

Separate Insuring Agreements

Policies usually contain two separate insuring agreements as follows:

1. *Directors and officers liability insurance agreement*—This provides coverage to the past, present, and future directors

James B. Wallace is Vice President of Johnson & Higgins in New York City.

and officers of the corporation and, most frequently, its subsidiaries, for loss for which they have not been indemnified by the corporation they are serving (parent or subsidiary).

2. *Corporate reimbursement*—This provides coverage to the parent corporation and an insured subsidiary for amounts paid by it to indemnify a director or officers for loss. The coverage for claims against directors and officers of any given subsidiary may not be as broad as that provided to the parent corporation. Sometimes insurers add restrictive terms that apply to a subsidiary acquired during the period of the policy.

While the corporation is an insured, corporate reimbursement does not include coverage for a claim made directly against it. The insurance it enjoys applies to amounts it pays as indemnity to a director or officer in connection with a claim made against him or her.

Identity of Individual Insureds

Not only current directors and officers are insureds, but also past and future holders of such positions. While some policies provide coverage for all directors and officers, others contain restrictive language when identifying the individual insureds. For example, the coverage may only apply to "elected" directors and officers. At times there is an erroneous assumption that the coverage applies to individuals who appear to hold officer titles but who are not, in fact, officers of the corporation. For example, some corporations are structured so that officers of divisions are not corporate officers. It may be possible to gain coverage for claims against these people.

Some individuals who are not officers may hold managerial positions that impose substantial responsibilities upon them. It may be possible to amend the definition of director or officer to include them.

Claims Made Policy

The policy applies to a claim first made during the policy period against a director or officer. This is to be distinguished from an "occurrence" type of policy, which generally applies to injury, damage, or loss that occurs during the period of the policy.

The term "claim" was not defined in earlier policies. Some insurers have now introduced a definition, and this frequently restricts coverage. For example, the term may be defined as a "civil" matter or a "claim seeking monetary damages." This would negate coverage for the defense of a criminal proceeding. Another definition restricts the coverage to an actual suit or legal proceeding of some type. Coverage would not be triggered before the claimant took such a step.

Another important point is that many insurers have added a requirement that the claim be reported to it during the policy period. At times it may prove difficult, if not impossible, to comply with such a requirement, such as with a claim made on the last day of the policy.

Nature and Scope of the Activity to Which the Insurance Applies

Policies historically used the term "wrongful act" to describe the type of conduct that must form the basis of a claim in order to trigger policy coverage. Typically this term was rather broadly defined as:

> any breach of duty, neglect, error, misstatement, misleading statement, omission or other act done or wrongfully attempted by the directors and officers or any of the foregoing so alleged by any claimant or any matter claimed against them solely by reason of their being such directors or officers.

Some insurers have now modified this definition. Invariably these changes give rise to a question of whether this signifies an intent to restrict the coverage. For example, consider a definition stating that wrongful act "shall mean any actual or alleged *negligent* act, error, misstatement, misleading statement, omission or breach of duty. . . ." Does introduction of the word "negligent" affect the coverage substantively?

While historically an issue seldom arose as to whether the conduct of an individual constituted a wrongful act, depending upon the facts involved, a question might arise regarding whether the individual had committed the wrongful act "in his capacity" as a director or officer of the corporation. The situation that typically has given rise to this issue is so-called "outside board activity" at the request or direction of the corporation.

Historically insurers took the position that in acting as a director or officer of another corporation, even at the request or direction of the corporate employer, an individual was not acting in his or her "capacity" as a director or officer of the corporate employer."

Throughout the history of this insurance, attitudes of insurers have fluctuated on whether the coverage should be extended to encompass this exposure. At times they would agree to do so on a rather liberal basis. However, over the last several years they have developed an extremely conservative approach. Today typically either the policy form itself contains an exclusion with respect to claims arising out of service to another organization, or this exclusion is endorsed to the policy. One basic reason for this posture is an insurer's perception that it might inadvertently pyramid one policy limit on another. In addition, insurers note that experience has taught them that service to another organization can broaden the scope of the hazard substantially.

Loss for Which the Policy Responds

The policy limits of liability are available to respond for the costs and expenses of investigation and defense of a claim and amounts paid to respond for liability (damages, judgments, and settlements). Historically policies did not contain a specific agreement that the insurer would defend claims. The manner in which the subject was handled led to the conclusion that the insureds had the right to designate counsel of their own choice. While policies generally did not contain specific language usurping this prerogative, they did contain a requirement that no costs, charges, or expenses be incurred without the insurer's consent. Insurers viewed this language as conferring a right upon them to make certain determinations regarding the reasonableness of defense efforts.

Several insurers have now amended their policies to specifically state that they have no obligation to defend. They have also introduced language designed to give them more control over the appointment of counsel and incurring of defense costs.

Defense fees and expenses are payable within (not in addition to) the limits of liability. The policy will respond for them in the same manner as liability payments, i.e., subject to application of a retention (deductible) and any vertical participation (coinsurance) feature of the policy.

Loss was historically defined in a manner that specifically excluded "fines or penalties." Most insurers have now expanded this exclusionary language to specifically state that loss does not include "punitive or exemplary damages." Other definitions go beyond this. For example, some policies specifically exclude the multiplied portion of any multiplied damage award. Still anther definition also excludes taxes.

Limits of Liability, Retention, and Participation

Limits of liability are provided on an annual aggregate basis for all claims against all directors and officers.

Almost invariably the insurer's obligation to pay is subject to the insured's obligation to first bear a retention (deductible). The amount of the retention applying to the directors and officers liability insuring agreement is relatively low. For example, it might be \$5,000 or \$10,000 per director or officer, with an aggregate (which caps the retention) of \$25,000 (or more) for a "single loss," i.e., claims against several directors or officers arising out of the same circumstances. The retention applicable to the corporate reimbursement insuring agreement is higher. Furthermore, today it may be ten or twenty times more than it was several years ago. A corporate reimbursement retention of $50,000 in 1984 could today be $300,000, $500,000, $750,000, or higher.

Historically policies contained a vertical participation (coinsurance) feature that required the insured to continue to bear a certain percentage of loss above the retention. This was actually 5 percent of the first $1 million of loss. The participation feature for the corporate reimbursement section of the policy has increased in some cases. At other times insurers have eliminated this requirement altogether. Today there is no uniform attitude among insurers regarding the importance of this feature.

In at least one state (New York), a statute mandates that if certain corporations pay the entire premium, policies issued to them must contain a coinsurance feature acceptable to the superintendent of insurance.

Exclusions

Historically policies contained relatively few exclusions. Briefly, these are the part of loss constituting a fine or penalty plus the following claims:

- For libel or slander
- Based upon the gaining of illegal personal profit or gain
- For the return of remuneration improperly received
- For an accounting of SEC 1934 Act section 16(b) profits
- Based upon the failure to maintain insurance
- For (or based upon, or attributable to) bodily injury or property damage
- Resulting in an adjudication of active and deliberate dishonesty
- For which insurance is provided under other policies except with respect to loss in excess thereof
- Insured under a policy previously in force

Other exclusions became fairly common over the course of time. By 1984 one could anticipate underwriters requiring additional exclusions for the following claims:

- Arising from pending and/or prior litigation (as of the date of the first policy)
- Arising from pollution or contamination
- Based upon or for violation of the Employee Retirement Income Security Act of 1974

- Based upon illegal or improper payments to government officials

Of course these were not the only exclusions imposed by underwriters. For example, in connection with any given submission, the insurer might require an exclusion for claims based on antitrust activity.

Within the last several years, insurers began to routinely impose certain newly developed exclusions and also give serious consideration to others. The most common among these are loss that constitutes punitive or exemplary damages or the multiplied portion of any multiplied damage award, as well as the following claims:

- Brought by one insured (including the corporation) against another except for stockholder derivative actions instituted by a person who is not an insured
- Based on resistance to the purchase of the corporation's securities *or* paying a premium for the corporation's securities
- Based upon wrongful acts occurring before either the inception date of the policy or another specified date
- Arising out of directors or officers acting as directors or officers of another organization
- Arising from merger or acquisition activity
- Based upon violation of the securities laws
- Arising from the offering or sale, private or public, of the company's stock or debentures
- Arising out of the performance of professional services for others
- Arising out of the establishment or operation of a captive insurance company
- Arising out of joint venture activity or the corporation acting as a general partner
- Brought by a regulator
- Arising from converting from a mutual to a stock form
- Arising from foreign assets or loans
- Arising from classified loans
- Arising from certain specific activity, e.g., real estate development, mortgage banking, or entering into repurchase agreements
- Arising out of the wrongful acts of a director or officer of a subsidiary committed before the subsidiary was acquired or after it was sold
- Arising out of circumstances that were either reported under a previous policy as having the potential for claim *or* that

formed the basis of an actual claim reported under a previous policy
- Arising out of circumstances that at the inception date of the policy any director or officer should have recognized as having the potential for claim

This list is not exhaustive, but does refer to most of the exclusions relied upon by insurers to circumscribe coverage.

When referring to exclusions, it is appropriate to also refer to "exclusionary language." The reason is that exclusionary language may appear in parts of the policy other than the section (or an endorsement) entitled "Exclusion(s)." For example, "original" applications or proposals contain questions with respect to the knowledge of directors and officers of matters that should be recognized as having the potential for claim. Generally that question is followed by an exclusion for claims arising out of such matters, whether or not they were disclosed in answer to the question. Frequently the exclusion applies to all the directors and officers if one of them should have recognized that given circumstances had the potential for claim. It is obviously easier to determine this with the benefit of hindsight. An insurer viewing the matter after a claim has been made might conclude that the circumstances giving rise to it should have been reported in the application. This exclusion can be extremely onerous. Its presence in an "original" application should be duly noted when considering the replacement of one insurer with another.

Exclusionary language was historically placed in the definition of loss, and those familiar with the insurance understood that this term did not include fines or penalties. Most insurers have expanded that exclusionary language to specifically refer to punitive and exemplary damages. Others have gone beyond this to specifically exclude such things as taxes or the multiplied portion of an award.

Some insurers have introduced exclusionary language into various terms of the policy where one would not generally anticipate encountering such language. For example, the definition of "wrongful act" might use exclusionary language with respect to certain conduct, e.g., efforts to resist purchase of the company's securities. Another example is language inserted into a clause concerned with the acquisition of a corporation, which could be interpreted to negate coverage for claims arising out of the acquisition. These major restrictions on coverage indicate dramatically the need to scrutinize all policy terms for "exclusions." When doing so, note that the term "policy" usually includes the declarations page as well as the application.

Historically not all the exclusions applied to both insuring agreements of the policy. Dishonesty, personal profit and gain, and similar exclusions did not apply to the corporate reimbursement insuring agreement. This meant that when the corporation indemnified a director or officer, the insurer could not deny coverage based upon these exclusions. Today many policies are structured so that all exclusions apply both to the directors and officers liability and to the corporate reimbursement insuring agreements. The fact that a corporation indemnifies a director or officer based upon the conclusion that he or she was not guilty of certain conduct such as dishonesty will not necessarily preclude the insurer from raising an objection to coverage based on its own view of that conduct.

When attempting to analyze the quality of the coverage, it is insufficient to simply note the existence of a certain type of exclusion. The manner in which the exclusion is worded is all-important. A simple example is the so-called bodily injury/property damage exclusion. Some exclusions state that the policy does not apply to a claim for bodily injury/property damage, libel, slander. . . , etc. The word "for" tends to limit the exclusion to a claim made by the party sustaining injury or loss because of bodily injury, property damage, libel, etc. Frequently such claims are the subject of other insurance.

Other bodily injury/property damage exclusions are worded differently and begin with phrases such as "based upon," "attributable to," "arising out of," or "directly or indirectly relating to." Insurers generally interpret this introductory language to negate coverage for claims even remotely related to the specified injury, damage, or offense. Consider, for example, a stockholder derivative suit seeking recovery because the corporation was caused to pay large verdicts as the result of bodily injury or property damage claims. While a corporation normally maintains insurance against such exposures, there are times when the coverage may be inadequate or inapplicable.

A similar observation can be made about any number of exclusions. The specific language used to express the insurer's exclusionary intent is important. For example, merely observing that the policy contains an ERISA exclusion does not come to grips with the issue of the extent to which that exclusion may apply. Does it negate coverage "for breach of fiduciary duty under ERISA" or go beyond this to exclude coverage for any claim "based on, arising out of, directly or indirectly resulting from, in consequence of, or in any way involving" any employee benefit plan?

Other Important Policy Features

Application

Most policies contain a statement that they are issued on the basis of the statements, representations, warranties, and information contained in the application and that the application is considered part of the policy.

Historically applications contained a signature block stating that information was being furnished to the best of the knowledge and information of the individual (president or chairman of the board) signing the application. Most insurers have revised at least this part of the application, and the signature block now usually states that the applicant warrants or represents that the information provided is correct.

As previously noted, original applications for insurance normally contain a question and an exclusion with respect to claims arising out of matters that should be recognized as having the potential for claim. At times this exclusion will apply to any claim made against any director or officer if only one of these individuals should have recognized that certain circumstances had the potential for a future claim. At other times the application will contain a severability clause stating that the exclusion applies only to a claim against the individual having knowledge of the circumstances.

When the coverage is renewed with the same insurer, information is usually provided pursuant to a "short form" or renewal application that does not contain a question or exclusion with respect to circumstances that have the potential for a claim. This renewal application usually incorporates all previous applications. The result is that, with the passage of time, there is less likelihood that the exclusion contained in the original application could form the basis for declining a claim.

Notice of a Potential Claim

Policies normally contain a clause permitting the insured to place the insurer on notice concerning circumstances it has reason to believe could give rise to a claim. Typically clauses conferring such rights also provide that should a claim be made at a future date, it will be treated as made as of the date notice of the circumstances was given to the insurer.

Historically policies were worded in a manner that appeared to permit the insured to report potential claims on a rather liberal basis. For example, a clause might simply state that the insured had a right to report "any circumstances that may subsequently give rise to a claim" against directors and officers. Today such a clause is usually worded in a way the insurer believes tends to restrict its application. For example, the right to report might only be with respect to "a specific wrongful act."

Discovery Clause

Policies normally contain a clause that permits the insured to extend the policy (with one added restriction) for a period of time, if the insurer cancels or refuses to renew. The restriction is that while the coverage continues to apply to claims made during the discovery period, this is only with respect to wrongful acts committed before the effective date of cancellation or nonrenewal.

Historically policies did not specifically address the issue of what might constitute a failure to renew. Today most of them contain a clause stating that the offer of terms that differ in certain respects from those of the expiring policy shall not constitute a refusal to renew. At times this clause is worded in a manner that does not attempt to limit the differences that may be involved and appears to say that the offer of any terms constitutes an offer to renew.

Cancellation

Policies generally contain a clause stating that the corporation will act on behalf of itself and the individual insureds with respect to the giving and receiving of notice of cancellation. Cancellation clauses typically state that the corporation has the right to cancel the policy at any time by following a certain procedure, e.g., providing the insurer with written notice.

Historically policies permitted the insurer to cancel by providing the corporation with written notice to that effect not less than thirty days before the effective date of cancellation. In times when market conditions were favorable to the insured, it might have been possible to negotiate a period of time longer than thirty days.

Today state regulations frequently govern the right of an insurer to cancel or nonrenew a policy. They may specify that such an intent must be expressed in writing no later than a stated number of days before the expiration date of the policy. They may also state that the insurer cannot cancel or nonrenew except for certain specified reasons.

Some policies now contain clauses that purport to cancel or terminate a policy automatically if certain events occur. Acquisition of more than 50 percent of the corporation's voting securities is normally one of the events that triggers such a clause.

Presumptive Indemnity

Today many policies contain a clause stating that the corporation agrees to indemnify directors and officers whenever it is permissible to do so. Generally insurers are thereby seeking to treat claims, whenever possible, under the corporate reimbursement insuring agreement, with its higher (usually substantially higher) retention. The way these clauses are worded is important.

Subsidiaries

Historically policies stated that coverage was automatically provided for subsidiaries created or acquired after the inception date of the policy subject to giving notice within a specified period of time and paying any additional premium required. Insurers frequently took the position that although the policy did not specifically state so, this coverage did not apply to claims arising out of wrongful acts committed before the date the corporation became a subsidiary. Today many policies specifically state that they do not apply to wrongful acts of the directors and officers of the subsidiary committed before the date of acquisition. Some do not provide automatic coverage of any type and require the insurer's consent before the policy will apply.

Defense and Claims Handling

All policies require the insured to report a claim promptly. The term "as soon as practicable" is often used to describe how quickly such action must be taken. At times the word "immediately" is used.

Historically policies were interpreted to permit insureds to choose counsel and defend themselves subject to the insurer's right to be kept advised and possibly refuse to consent to incurring certain costs. Loss included defense costs, but the insurer did not agree to defend.

Today many policies confirm this intent by specifically stating that the insurer has no obligation to defend claims. The extent to which it may have the right to a voice in the selection of defense counsel and incurring of other costs and expenses depends upon the specific language chosen by the insurer to confer such rights upon itself. At the very least, a policy would contain a clause stating that no costs, charges, or expenses will be incurred without the insurer's consent. This would necessarily mean that there must be some communication and cooperation between insurer and insured.

When a claim is reported to an insurer, the insurer generally attempts to initially evaluate whether the matter is likely to result in payment under its policy. At times the insurance company will decide to monitor a claim, at least initially, through its internal facilities. Most frequently, however, insurers refer what appear to be serious claims to outside counsel.

Most claims, and more particularly those that have reached a suit stage, involve allegations that give rise to coverage issues. Therefore, the attorneys acting on behalf of the insurer typically issue a letter reserving the rights of the insurer based on the coverage issues readily identifiable. If they believe that all or a certain aspect of the matter should be the subject of an outright declination, as in the case of a claim for punitive damages, the letter will state this position.

Obviously it is disquieting to receive a communication from the insurer indicating that in its view, the coverage may not apply. However, the fact is that in most instances it is the nature of the allegations that have precipitated the negative comment. In the final analysis, it is frequently the tone of the communication rather than its substantive content that may be the object of legitimate concern. In any event, it is important to avoid the development of an adversarial atmosphere, which may well impede cooperation between insured and insurer. Efforts must be made to develop a working relationship that includes meeting the insurer's legitimate information needs. This is important even from the perspective of the insured. Many cases reach a point where settlement becomes a real prospect. Policies typically state that claims will not be settled without the consent of the insurer, and it is best that at such a stage, the insurer have a complete standing of the matter and be in a position to react promptly.

An issue that frequently arises in connection with the defense of a suit is whether the insurer is obligated to pay defense expenses as they are incurred. Policies historically were written on a "pay on behalf" basis, which led insureds to conclude that, at least in excess of a retention, defense expenses would be paid by the insurer as they were billed. However, insurers seldom interpreted their coverage in this fashion. Moreover, generally (exceptions do exist) they took the position that until coverage issues they had raised were resolved, they were under no obligation to pay defense costs. This issue has been litigated several times, and while courts have not taken a uniform position, decisions more frequently favor the position proposed by the insured.

Today several policies attempt to address the subject by specifying that the insurer has no obligation to make payment under the policy until final disposition of a claim. In keeping with this approach, some insurers have also revised their insuring agreements to state that they will "indemnify" the insured rather than "pay on (its) behalf."

Conclusion

Over the past few years, the quality of the coverage offered by the traditional or conventional market for directors and officers liability and corporate reimbursement insurance has seriously eroded. This and other factors have caused this insurance to become the object of intense criticism and skepticism concerning its value. At the same time, various state laws have been changed to provide directors and officers with further substantial protection. These developments have subjected the insurance to even greater scrutiny.

While much of this is understandable, it is important to remember that historically the coverage has been a valuable tool in the effort to protect directors and officers. Conceptually it can still play the same if not a more valuable role. Changes in the law, while providing further safeguards for directors and officers, do not insulate them to the fullest extent desirable. Insurance can provide meaningful additional protection. The question is whether it will in fact play this role.

Insureds themselves have already cooperated in establishing pooling arrangements to provide quality insurance. Market conditions have been changing in a direction generally favorable to insureds. These beneficial trends will not affect all to the same degree or at the same time, but forces are at work that have resulted in the offer of coverage on improved terms in what is becoming a highly competitive market.

Section VIII

Representing Corporate Clients in Various Litigation Settings

Given the ever-expanding scope of liability for the modern corporation, the corporate litigator must handle a wide variety of litigation settings and a number of substantive areas of the law. This section of the book focuses on three corporate litigation settings: the shareholder derivative suit, the contest for corporate control, and an increasingly common litigation setting that is unfamiliar to most corporate litigators: the criminal investigation. The emphasis is upon general litigation settings and principles affecting the liability of corporations and their directors, officers, and employees, rather than specific substantive topics such as antitrust, product liability, labor relations, or environmental compliance. Based upon the frequency of presentations and the level of attendance at programs sponsored by the Committee on Corporate Counsel and other American Bar Association Committees, these three litigation settings appear to significantly interest a wide variety of corporate litigators.

Chapter 33 addresses the first litigation setting: derivative suits. In this chapter, R. Franklin Balotti and Anne C. Foster commence with an explanation of the rationale and purposes for the demand requirement expressed in Federal Rule of Civil Procedure 23.1 and comparable state rules. The chapter then addresses whether demand on the board of directors may be excused because of futility, and if such demand is made and refused, the applicable standards to determine whether such rejection was wrongful. The chapter discusses whether the board of directors may appoint a special litigation committee, and the standards to be applied by the courts in reviewing the decision by the special litigation committee. Finally, the chapter examines the burden of proof and permissible discovery on motions to dismiss in demand excused cases.

Chapter 34 turns to the next litigation setting: contests for corporate control. In this chapter, Jerold S. Solovy, Arthur M. Martin, Ronald L. Marmer, and David C. Bohan describe the role of litigation for the bidder and the target corporation and discuss offensive and defensive strategies. The chapter also contains a look at the role of civil RICO in takeover battles, and an excellent discussion of rule 11 standards, which can become very important in these hard-fought battles. Given the frequency of contests for corporate control during this decade, this excellent and comprehensive chapter is timely and should prove useful to all corporate litigators.

The final three chapters provide complementary perspectives on the role of the corporate litigator in criminal investigations involving the corporation, its officers, directors, and employees. Chapter 35, by Robert J. Perry, provides an overview of the basic principles of corporate criminal liability. The chapter discusses the range of corporate criminal liability; the liability of officers and agents; frequently used criminal statutes, including conspiracy, RICO, bribery, false statements, mail fraud, and currency reporting; government investigative techniques; and some practical considerations for the corporate litigator.

In Chapter 36, Michael C. Hallerud examines several specific criminal law issues that frequently arise in representing corporations. These issues include employee relations, costs, and risks, including a discussion of whether and how the corporation should discipline employees for violations of the law. It concludes by analyzing the use of outside counsel in criminal cases, including the use of separate counsel for individuals. Form 51 in the Appendix is a sample letter to be sent to employees notifying them of a pending criminal investigation.

In Chapter 37, Jamie S. Gorelick provides an excellent overview of most of the key issues that arise during criminal investigations, including the considerations and potential objections when the corporate client receives an inspector general or grand jury subpoena, relevant issues during the factual investigation, and problems inherent in parallel agency and grand jury investigations. The chapter also discusses the initial contact with the prosecutor; negotiating for nonprosecution of the corporation; immunity for officers, directors, and employees; and plea bargaining and plea agreements.

The excellent chapters in this section should better equip the corporate litigator to apply the most current approaches and techniques in handling shareholder derivative suits, contests for corporate control, and criminal investigations of the corporation and its officers, directors, and employees.

Francis J. Burke, Jr.
Streich, Lang, Weeks & Cardon
Phoenix, Arizona

Thirty-Three

Derivative Litigation: The Demand Requirement

R. Franklin Balotti and Anne C. Foster

The derivative action is a means by which stockholders of a corporation may bring suit on behalf of the corporation, asserting a claim belonging to it. In such a suit, the stockholders are effectively moving to compel the corporation to sue, and the corporation is bringing suit, through the stockholders, against those potentially liable to it.[1] As a result, the corporation is an indispensable party to any derivative suit.[2] To give the corporation the opportunity to bring or maintain the action on its own, the rules of the federal courts and the courts of most states impose the demand requirement, by which the corporation is given such an opportunity unless a plaintiff can show the futility of demand.

Basic Principles Underlying the Demand Requirement

Before instituting a derivative suit, a shareholder is required to make a demand on the board of directors that the board bring suit on behalf of the corporation unless the making of such a demand would be futile. If a demand is not made before bringing suit, the shareholder must state the reasons for not making a demand with particularity in his or her complaint. This requirement is set forth in rule 23.1 of the Federal Rules of Civil Procedure and in comparable state rules. Rule 23.1 provides, in pertinent part, as follows:

> In a derivative action brought by one or more shareholders or members to enforce a right of a corporation . . . [t]he complaint shall . . . allege with particularity the efforts, if any, made by the plaintiff to obtain the action he desires from the directors or comparable authority . . . and the reasons for his failure to obtain the action or for not making the effort.

This requirement of particularity represents a departure from the philosophy of notice pleading embodied elsewhere in the rules of procedure.[3]

R. Franklin Balotti is a member and Anne C. Foster is an associate with Richards, Layton & Finger, Wilmington, Delaware.

Shareholder derivative suits filed in federal court might pose thorny choice-of-law questions. As noted by the court in *Allison v. General Motors Corp.*:

> [B]ecause the demand requirement has both procedural and substantive aspects, questions arising under Rule 23.1 could be governed by both state and federal law. In a diversity case, for example, federal procedural law requires that the reasons for not making a demand be pleaded with particularity, but the source of the demand requirement itself may be state law. Moreover, one could argue that state law should be used to evaluate the adequacy of the reasons given to excuse demand. For example, a state's law might hold that if one-third of the Board of Directors had a financial interest in a transaction, the business judgment rule is inapplicable and a court should not defer to the Board's judgment. In that situation, an allegation that less than a majority of the Board was financially interested should satisfy Rule 23.1, despite contrary federal case law.[4]

Thus, federal courts might follow federal law to determine whether the requirements of rule 23.1 are satisfied, that is, that the complaint states with enough particularity the reasons why demand is excused.[5] However, in *Burks v. Lasker*,[6] the Supreme Court held that state corporate law should be applied as long as it is consistent with federal policy in determining whether disinterested directors may terminate derivative suits. As noted by the court in *Allison*, some federal courts have followed this principle in applying state substantive law to the question of whether the allegations of the complaint state with particularity the reasons for excusing demand.[7]

The purpose of the demand requirement is "to give a corporation the opportunity to rectify an alleged wrong without litigation, and to control any litigation which does arise."[8] Demand is required because "[a] shareholder derivative action is an exception to the normal rule that the proper party to bring a suit on behalf of a corporation is the corporation itself, acting through its directors or a majority of its shareholders."[9] Thus, it is well settled that a stockholder does not have the right to bring a derivative action until the stockholder either has made a demand on the corporation to institute such an action and has been refused, or has demonstrated that the making of such a demand would have been a futile gesture.[10]

The demand requirement of rule 23.1 is "not a mere procedural nicety,"[11] but a substantive rule of "critical importance," which is "fundamental to Delaware corporate jurisprudence."[12] If no demand is made before suit is filed, the plaintiff bears the burden of alleging with particularity in the complaint the reasons why demand would have been futile.[13] In determining the adequacy of a derivative plaintiff's compliance with rule 23.1, courts look only to the matters alleged in the complaint.[14] Although "[a]ll well-plead facts will be assumed to be true and all inferences will be viewed in a light most favorable to the plaintiff, [c]onclusions of law or fact . . . will not be assumed to be true without specific allegations of fact which support the conclusions."[15]

The demand requirement may not be avoided by styling an action as an individual or class action rather than as a derivative action. It is "the nature of the wrong alleged [which] controls, not the pleader's assertion of an intention to sue as a representative of the stockholders rather than in the right of the corporation."[16]

The defense that an action should be dismissed for failure to make a demand can be raised by parties other than the corporation upon whose board such a demand should have been made. In *Kaplan v. Peat, Marwick, Mitchell & Co.*,[17] an accounting firm was sued by stockholders of Chase Manhattan in connection with transactions for which the firm had acted as the company's auditor. The firm moved to dismiss for failure to make a demand upon the Chase Manhattan board. The court of chancery concluded that "the decision as to whether and in what manner a corporation should pursue a corporate claim, is ordinarily for the board of directors to make [and departure from that policy] would prevent particular classes of defendants from raising a Rule 23.1 defense that, if meritorious, would place that litigation-related decision in the directors' hands."[18] As a result, the court held that third parties do have standing to raise such a defense.[19] On appeal, the Delaware Supreme Court affirmed, finding that giving standing to third parties further helps to assure "that the decision as to whether to proceed with the litigation is made by the appropriate party . . . the directors."[20]

In determining the adequacy of a stockholder demand, courts have identified the factors to be considered as follows:

> At a minimum, a demand must identify the alleged wrongdoers, describe the factual basis of the wrongful acts and the harm caused to the corporation, and request remedial relief. In most instances, the shareholder need not specify his legal theory, every fact in support of that theory, or the precise quantum of damages. Decisions as to how and on what theory the corporation will pursue wrongdoers are the proper province of the Board of Directors.[21]

Thus, for example, a letter from a plaintiff's attorney merely stating a "belief" that certain actions taken by the board of directors "are not in the best interests of the shareholders or employees" of the company, without more, does not constitute a demand.[22] Similarly, a broker's meeting with company representatives to discuss alleged mismanagement does not constitute a demand.[23] If these requirements are not met, the communication is not a demand contemplated by rule 23.1, and no response is required by the corporation.

Where an adequate demand is made, however, the board of directors must be allowed a sufficient period of time in which to investigate and respond.[24] An "adequate time" will "vary depending upon the complexity of the issues raised."[25]

Standards for Determining Whether Demand Is Required or Excused

The Aronson *Test: Demand Futility*

In *Aronson v. Lewis*, the Delaware Supreme Court set forth the following test for determining whether demand would be futile and therefore excused:

> [I]n determining demand futility the Court of Chancery in the proper exercise of its discretion must decide whether, under the particularized facts alleged, a reasonable doubt is created that: (1) the directors are disinterested and independent and (2) the challenged transaction was otherwise the product of a valid exercise of business judgment.[26]

Accordingly, the court held that only where "a plaintiff has alleged facts with particularity which, taken as true, support a reasonable doubt that the challenged transaction was the product of a valid exercise of business judgment . . . is demand excused."[27] In *Aronson*, the court held that demand was not excused as futile despite the stockholder's claim that one director's ownership of 47 percent of the corporate stock and personal selection of each of the other directors indicated that the director dominated and controlled the board.

Under *Aronson*, a court is apparently required to look to two separate boards to determine demand futility: (1) the board that acted upon the challenged transaction (to determine if it was the product of a valid exercise of business judgment), and (2) the current board (that is, the board at the time the complaint was filed) to determine if it is disinterested and independent, i.e., that it could impartially consider the demand. As a theoretical matter, there is little justification in requiring the court to examine the prior board or its action, because even if the action challenged was not the product of a valid exercise of business judgment, the current board might well determine that the corporation's interests would be best served by not pursuing the cause of action.

The mere naming of directors as defendants is insufficient to demonstrate futility. As the court stated with respect to this argument urged in support of demand futility in *Aronson v. Lewis*:

> Plaintiff's final argument is the incantation that demand is excused because the directors otherwise would have to sue themselves, thereby placing the conduct of the litigation in hostile hands and preventing its effective prosecution. This bootstrap argument has been made to and dismissed by other courts. *See, e.g., Lewis v. Graves,* 701 F.2d 245, 248–49 (2d Cir. 1983); *Heit v. Baird*, 567 F.2d 1157, 1162 (1st Cir. 1977); *Lewis v. Anselmi*, 564 F. Supp., 768, 772 (S.D.N.Y. 1983). Its acceptance would effectively abrogate Rule 23.1 and weaken the managerial power of directors. Unless facts are alleged with particularity to overcome the presumptions of independence and a proper exercise of business judgment, in which case the directors could not be expected to sue themselves, a bare claim of this sort raises no legally cognizable issue under Delaware corporate law.[28]

Moreover, the mere failure of directors to take action before suit is filed is insufficient to demonstrate futility.[29] The Delaware Supreme Court has held that "mere directorial approval of a transaction, absent particularized facts supporting a breach of fiduciary duty claim, or otherwise establishing the lack of independence or disinterestedness of a majority of the directors, is insufficient to excuse demand."[30] This holding is consistent with the holdings of other Delaware courts in cases preceding[31] and following *Aronson v. Lewis,*[32] as well as with federal precedent.[33] Similarly, the mere allegation that a board has rejected a prior demand is insufficient to excuse demand,[34] nor will the refusal to rescind a transaction demonstrate futility.[35]

Before examining the traditional standards to see if demand is excused, a court must determine what position has been taken by the corporation on whose behalf the derivative action was brought. The Delaware Supreme Court has determined that a corporation "cannot effectively stand neutral [and the] failure to object to a suit brought on its behalf must be viewed as an approval for the shareholders' capacity to sue derivatively."[36] Thus, taking a position of neutrality will lead to excusal of a plaintiff's requirement to make a demand.[37]

For a court to conclude that a director lacks disinterestedness and independence, the director must be a direct and substantial beneficiary of the challenged transaction. Such a benefit exists when an action is brought to challenge a corporate transaction which results in the acquisition by the board of directors of the right to vote a significant amount of stock.[38] In

Pogostin v. Rice, the Delaware Supreme Court described the type of self-interest in a transaction that would taint a director's independence:

> Directorial interest exists whenever divided loyalties are present, or a director either has received, or is entitled to receive, a personal financial benefit from the challenged transaction which is not equally shared by the stockholders. . . . The question of independence flows from an analysis of the factual allegations pertaining to the influences upon the directors' performance of their duties generally, and more specifically in respect to the challenged transaction.[39]

Absent such director interest, courts will not excuse demand under the first prong of the *Aronson* test.[40] However, demand will be excused where a majority of the directors have a direct and substantial interest in the transaction.[41]

The mere threat of personal liability for approving a questioned transaction, standing alone, is insufficient to challenge either the independence or the disinterestedness of directors.[42] A bare allegation of domination and control of directors by one interested in the transaction is insufficient to demonstrate demand futility.[43] The federal cases are to the same effect.[44] Rather, "[t]he question whether a director is controlled by a third party . . . is 'an intensely factual one,' and Rule 23.1 requires that a plaintiff 'assert the facts from which it is believed an inference of control could be drawn.' "[45] Mere financial ties by a majority of directors to the corporation will not necessarily excuse demand,[46] but a direct financial interest in the challenged transaction normally renders a director interested.[47]

In *Grobow v. Perot*,[48] a General Motors stockholder brought suit against the board of directors in connection with the company's payment of over $700 million to a former director in exchange for his General Motors stock. Part of that sum, it was alleged, was given in exchange for the director's promise that he would not publicly criticize the company. In claiming that demand should be excused because of director interest, the plaintiff alleged that the directors of General Motors stood on both sides of the transaction because they had an interest in silencing the former director's public criticisms, which could eventually result in their being forced by public opinion out of office. This argument was rejected by the Court of Chancery and the Delaware Supreme Court, which found that plaintiff had not sufficiently alleged any facts to give rise to the suggestion that the directors of General Motors approved the transaction in response to fears of public criticism.[49]

A plaintiff can establish demand futility by sufficiently pleading facts showing that the transaction complained of was entered into by the board for purposes of entrenchment, thereby demonstrating lack of independence on the part of the board. For example, where the plaintiff's complaint sets forth particularized facts alleging that a defensive tactic adopted by the directors deters all hostile takeover attempts through its limitation on alienability of shares and the exercise of proxy rights, that complaint sufficiently pleads a primary purpose to retain control and casts a reasonable doubt as to the disinterestedness and independence of the board of directors.[50] However, "[s]peculation on motives for undertaking corporate action are wholly insufficient to establish a case of demand excusal."[51]

Absent a showing that the directors are interested, the courts look to see if a plaintiff has established a reasonable doubt that "the challenged transaction was otherwise the product of a valid exercise of business judgment."[52] It must be shown that "the directors were not *capable* of exercising their business judgment with respect to any of the transactions."[53] In *Scopas*, the Delaware Court of Chancery rejected an argument that demand was futile where the plaintiff merely alleged that the transactions were consummated without the authorization of the full board. The court held:

> Demand futility cannot be based on inaction if there is no opportunity to act. Where a challenged transaction was not authorized by the board but was capable of being authorized, the policy behind Chancery Rule 23.1 dictates that the shareholder make demand.[54]

Similarly, the mere fact that proposed charter and bylaw amendments were later withdrawn does not necessarily lead to the conclusion that they were not a product of the board's business judgment.[55]

Courts have found that a reasonable doubt exists as to whether an action was the product of the exercise of business judgment when a complaint sets forth allegations sufficient to support a claim of waste. In *Lewis v. Hett*,[56] the court excused demand where the complaint set forth allegations of a waste of corporate assets. As the court noted, the complaint alleged "that there was no consideration for the substantial payments to be made under the severance agreement . . . that Hett resigned, had no employment contract, and served at the will of the board."[57] Accordingly, the court declined to grant a motion to dismiss holding, "These allegations do create a reasonable doubt that the severance payments constitute a gift or waste of corporate assets and, therefore, that 'the challenged transaction was . . . the product of a valid exercise of business judgment.' "[58]

In *Lewis v. Aronson*, the court stated, "Allegations which raise a reasonable doubt as to whether a transaction constitutes a waste of corporate assets in turn create a reasonable doubt that the transaction was the product of a valid exercise of business judgment."[59] An employment contract that agrees to pay a defendant-director a full salary regardless of services performed and is terminable at will by the defendant-director, while the employer-corporation must give six months' notice before termination, at which time a consulting contract is created that continues through the lifetime of the defendant-director, "suggest[s] that the services [the defendant-director] might render to [the corporation], pursuant to the challenged contract, are so grossly inadequate that no ordinary person of sound business judgment would deem it worth that which the corporation paid."[60]

In *Stein v. Orloff*, the court granted defendants' motion to dismiss for failure to make a presuit demand as to all allegations except one of corporate waste involving a reduction by the board of a stock option price without consideration therefor. At that time, options for three-quarters of the shares were held by one-half of the board members. The court found that because "[t]he Complaint alleges pre-existing options on which the option price was reduced without any consideration being received for the reduction[,]" there exists "a sufficient allegation of facts to state a claim for waste and therefore to create a reasonable doubt that the transaction was the result of a valid exercise of business judgment."[61]

The Test if Demand Is Made and Refused: "Wrongfulness" of the Rejection

If demand is made and refused, the board's decision will be protected unless it was "wrongful," i.e., unless it was not the product of a valid exercise of business judgment.[62] In a demand-rejected case, it is not enough to state that the rejection was "wrongful." Rather, the plaintiff must allege facts with enough particularity to rebut the presumption that the board's rejection is protected by the business judgment rule.[63] Thus, the Third Circuit in affirming dismissal of a demand-rejected derivative suit for lack of standing, held:

> The Supreme Court and, following it, the Court of Appeals have repeatedly stated and applied the doctrine that a stockholder's derivative action, whether involving corporate refusal to bring antitrust suits or some other controversial decision concerning the conduct of corporate affairs, can be maintained only if the stockholder shall allege and prove that the directors of the corporation are personally involved or interested in the alleged wrongdoing in a way calculated to impair their exercise of business judgment on behalf of the corporation, or that their refusal to sue reflects bad faith or breach of trust in some other way.[64]

The *Ash* court further noted that the "[p]revailing doctrine in the state courts is to the same effect."[65]

Where the business judgment rule protects a board's refusal to sue, the shareholder "lacks the legal managerial power to continue the derivative action, since that power is terminated by the refusal."[66]

Special Litigation Committee if Demand Is Excused

If demand is deemed excused, the board may nonetheless appoint a committee of independent directors to determine whether the litigation is in the corporation's best interests, and, if appropriate, to seek a dismissal.[67] A number of states have determined that a special litigation committee of disinterested directors has the ability, in its business judgment, to determine whether the action should be continued. Such ability derives from the duty of the board of directors to govern the affairs and manage the assets of the corporation. Among the states that have considered the question (by state or federal decision) are Alabama, California, Connecticut, Delaware, Massachusetts, Michigan, New York, North Carolina, Ohio and Virginia.[68]

The courts have taken at least two different approaches in reviewing the determination of a special litigation committee that a derivative action should not continue when demand is initially excused.

In *Auerbach v. Bennett*,[69] the New York Court of Appeals determined that the board of directors has the power to seek a dismissal of a derivative action, subject only to judicial review on the sole question of whether an appropriate and sufficient investigation has been made by disinterested members of the board of directors making the decision.[70]

In *Zapata Corp. v. Maldonado*, the Delaware Supreme Court held that the board has the power to appoint a special litigation committee and that the committee has the power to request a dismissal.[71] The court adopted a two-step judicial approach: (1) judicial determination of whether the committee acted independently and in good faith and demonstrated a reasonable basis for its determination that the action should be dismissed; and (2) an application by the court of its "own independent business judgment" (similar to the test used in approving the settlement of a derivative action) to determine whether the action should be dismissed. In applying the second test, the court should consider matters of law and public policy in addition to determining whether the dismissal is in the best interests of the corporation.[72] However, "the second step of the *Zapata* analysis is wholly within the discretion of the court," and the court may therefore decline to express its own independent business judgment.[73]

The Burden of Proof and Permissible Discovery on Motions to Dismiss in Demand-Excused Cases

In *Zapata Corp. v. Maldonado*, the court held, "The corporation should have the burden of proving independence, good faith and a reasonable investigation, rather than presuming independence, good faith and reasonableness."[74] There is some authority that the burden is particularly great where a one-person committee is used. "If a single member committee is to be used, the member should, like Caesar's wife, be above reproach."[75]

To develop a record to assist the court's inquiry into the committee's good faith and independence and the bases supporting the committee's conclusion, the court may order limited discovery.[76] However, the scope of discovery would appear to be limited to "what the Committee did or did not do, and the actual existence of the documents and persons purportedly examined by it."[77] Thus, a plaintiff is "not entitled to discover all the information relating to the Committee's report," but only "sufficient means to discover and examine the independence and good faith of the Committee's investigation."[78]

Discovery in Demand-Refused Cases

Although the question of whether discovery should be allowed in demand-excused cases was decided in *Zapata*, the same issue with respect to demand-refused cases was not decided in Delaware until recently. A derivative suit was commenced after the General Motors board of directors rejected a demand that General Motors rescind its repurchase of shares from former director H. Ross Perot.[79] Plaintiff sought to take discovery in connection with the defendant directors' motion to dismiss for failure to plead wrongful refusal of demand with enough particularity. Defendants moved for a protective order staying discovery pending the outcome of the dismissal motion. Plaintiff argued that in a demand-refused situation, discovery should be allowed to the same extent as in a demand-excused situation.

In distinguishing the demand-excused situation from the demand-refused situation, the court noted that in a demand-refused situation, the board's decision to refuse a demand is presumed to be protected under the business judgment rule, and a plaintiff bears the burden of showing that the refusal was wrongful. Because the function of a motion to dismiss under rule 23.1 is to resolve this very issue, the court held that discovery should not be allowed.[80]

Conclusion

The use of the demand requirement gives a corporation the opportunity to assert (or not assert) claims on its own behalf. Absent a showing of demand futility or wrongfulness of rejection of demand, the decision whether to bring suit will be made either by the board of directors or, if a majority of the board lacks independence, by a special litigation committee. To bring a derivative suit on his or her own, therefore, a stockholder must be certain to comply with the particular requirements of the specific jurisdiction.

Notes

1. Aronson v. Lewis, 473 A.2d 805 (Del. 1984).
2. Maldonado v. Flynn, 413 A.2d 1251 (Del. Ch. 1980), *rev'd on other grounds*, 430 A.2d 779 (1981); Levine v. Milton, 219 A.2d 145 (Del. Ch. 1966).
3. Allison v. General Motors Corp., 604 F. Supp. 1106, 1112 (D. Del.), *aff'd mem.*, 782 F.2d 1026 (3d Cir. 1985).
4. 604 F. Supp. at 1116 n.9 (citations omitted).
5. *See, e.g., Allison,* 604 F. Supp. at 1115 (and cases cited therein).
6. 441 U.S. 471, 486 (1979).
7. *See, e.g.*, Tabas v. Mullane, 608 F. Supp. 759, 764 (D.N.J. 1985) (applying Delaware law); *Allison*, 604 F. Supp. at 1115–16 (and cases cited therein).
8. Aronson v. Lewis, 473 A.2d 805, 809 (Del. 1984). *See* Stroud v. Milliken Enters., Inc., C.A. No. 8969, slip op. at 15 (Del. Ch. Mar. 18, 1988) ("the wisdom of requiring the notification of a board of claims before the filing of a suit [gives] the board a proper opportunity to address the deficiencies by withdrawing the offensive proposals"). *Accord* Cramer v. General Tel. & Elec. Corp., 582 F.2d 259 (3d Cir. 1978), *cert. denied*, 439 U.S. 1129 (1979); Scopas Technology Co. v. Lord, C.A. No. 7559, slip op. at 10 (Del. Ch. Nov. 20, 1984); Stotland v. GAF Corp., C.A. No. 6876, slip op. at 11 (Del. Ch. Sept. 1, 1983), *appeal dismissed as moot*, 469 A.2d 421 (Del. 1983).
9. Daily Income Fund, Inc. v. Fox, 464 U.S. 523, 542 (1984). *See also* D. Block, N. Barton & S. Radin, The Business Judgment Rule: Fiduciary Duties of Corporate Directors and Officers 219–22 (1987).
10. Kaplan v. Peat, Marwick, Mitchell & Co., 540 A.2d 726 (Del. 1988). *See also* Stepak v. Dean, 434 A.2d 388, 390 (Del. Ch. 1981).
11. Richardson v. Graves, C.A. No. 6617, slip op. at 5 (Del. Ch. June 17, 1983).
12. Kaplan v. Peat, Marwick, Mitchell & Co., 529 A.2d 254, 259 (Del. Ch. 1987), *aff'd in part and rev'd in part*, 540 A.2d 726 (Del. 1988). The same principles would seem to apply equally in other jurisdictions.
13. *See, e.g.*, Cramer v. General Tel. & Elec. Corp., 582 F.2d 259, 275 (3d Cir. 1978), *cert. denied*, 439 U.S. 1129 (1979); Aronson v. Lewis, 473 A.2d 805, 815 (Del. 1984); Haber v. Bell, 465 A.2d 353, 357 (Del. Ch. 1983); Bergstein v. Texas Int'l Co., 453 A.2d 467, 469 (Del. Ch. 1982), *appeal denied*, 461 A.2d 695 (Del. 1983); Stotland v. GAF Corp., C.A. No. 7559, slip op. at 10, 11–12 (Del. Ch. Nov. 20, 1984); Lewis v. Aronson, C.A. No. 6919, slip op. at 3 (Del. Ch. May 1, 1985) (opinion of Vice Chancellor Hartnett upholding sufficiency of amended complaint alleging demand futility on remand); Kaufman v. Beal, C.A. No. 6485, slip op. at 6 (Del. Ch. Feb. 25, 1983); In re Kaufman Mut. Fund Actions, 479 F.2d 257, 263 (1st Cir.), *cert. denied*, 414 U.S. 857 (1973).
14. Haber v. Bell, 465 A.2d at 357; Bergstein v. Texas Int'l Co., 453 A.2d at 469; Kaufman v. Belmont, 479 A.2d 282 (Del. Ch. 1984); Stotland v. GAF Corp.,

slip op. at 11; Stein v. Orloff, C.A. No. 7276, slip op. at 3 (Del. Ch. May 30, 1985), *appeal denied*, No. 352, 1986 (Del. Jan. 28, 1986) (ORDER); Lewis v. Aronson, slip op. at 3; Good v. Texaco, Inc., C.A. No. 7501 (Del. Ch. May 14, 1984); Pogostin v. Rice, 480 A.2d 619, 624 (Del. 1984); Kaufman v. Beal, slip op. at 5.

15. Pogostin v. Rice, C.A. No. 6235, slip op. at 6 (Del. Ch. Aug. 12, 1983). *See also* Grobow v. Perot, 539 A.2d 180, 187 (Del. 1988); Lewis v. Honeywell, Inc., C.A. No. 8651 (Del. Ch. July 28, 1987); Haber v. Bell, 465 A.2d 353, 357 (Del. Ch. 1983); Bergstein v. Texas Int'l Co., 453 A.2d 467, 469 (Del. Ch. 1982) *appeal denied*, 461 A.2d. 695 (Del. 1983); Stotland v. GAF Corp., C.A. No. 7559, slip op. at 10, 11–12 (Del. Ch. Nov. 20, 1984); Sundin v. Fisher, C.A. No. 6918, slip op. at 5 (Del. Ch. Feb. 15, 1985), *aff'd sub nom.*, Blosvern v. Fisher, No. 235, 1985 (Del. Jan. 30, 1986) (ORDER); Lewis v. Aronson, C.A. No. 6919, slip op. at 3 (Del. Ch. May 1, 1985); Richardson v. Graves, C.A. No. 6617, slip op. at 5 (Del. Ch. June 17, 1983); Kaufman v. Beal, C.A. No. 6485, slip op. at 5–6 (Del. Ch. Feb. 25, 1983).

16. Elster v. American Airlines, Inc., 100 A.2d 219, 223 (Del. Ch. 1953). *Accord In re* General Motors Class E Stock Buyout Sec. Litig., 694 F. Supp. 1119, 1131 (D. Del. 1988); Lipton v. News Int'l Plc., 514 A.2d 1075 (Del. 1986); MacAndrews & Forbes Holdings, Inc. v. Revlon, Inc., C.A. No. 8126, slip op. at 8 (Del. Ch. Oct. 9, 1985). *See also* Sumers v. Beneficial Corp., C.A. No. 8788, slip op. at 4–5 (Del. Ch. Mar. 9, 1988) (claim that board arbitrarily rejected offer to acquire company's stock at substantial premium constitutes same injury to all stockholders and must be pursued as derivative claim); Colonial Sec. Corp. v. Allen, C.A. No. 6778 (Del. Ch. Apr. 18, 1983) (Plaintiff commenced a purported class action alleging that management's actions constituted impermissible vote buying by management because economic sanctions would be imposed indirectly on the shareholders by the payment of severance benefits if the incumbent slate of directors were defeated. Despite plaintiff's contention that it was adjudicating the individual right of any stockholder to vote his or her shares—and that it was not raising any derivative claims—the court dismissed the suit, holding that plaintiff's complaint must be seen as a derivative claim for waste brought on behalf of the corporation.); Shapiro v. Pabst Brewing Co., C.A. No. 7339 (Del. Ch. July 30, 1985) (claims of entrenchment and waste are derivative claims which may not be pursued individually or as a class action).

17. 529 A.2d 254 (Del. Ch. 1987), *aff'd in part and rev'd in part*, 540 A.2d 726 (Del. 1988).

18. Kaplan v. Peat, Marwick, Mitchell & Co., 529 A.2d at 259.

19. Kaplan v. Peat, Marwick, Mitchell & Co., 529 A.2d at 261–62. *See also* Shlensky v. Dorsey, 574 F.2d 131, 142 (3d Cir. 1978).

20. Kaplan v. Peat, Marwick, Mitchell & Co., 540 A.2d at 730.

21. Allison v. General Motors Corp., 604 F. Supp. 1106, 1117 (D. Del.), *aff'd mem.*, 702 F.2d 1026 (3d Cir. 1985).

22. Seibert v. Harper & Row Publishers, Inc., C.A. No. 6639, slip op. at 6–8 (Del. Ch. Dec. 5, 1984).

23. Blosvern v. Fisher, No. 235, 1985, slip op. at 3 (Del. Jan. 30, 1986) (ORDER).

24. Allison v. General Motors Corp., 604 F. Supp. at 1117; Recchion, Westinghouse Elec. Corp. v. Kirby, 637 F. Supp. 1309, 1319 (W.D. Pa. 1986).

513

25. Recchion, Westinghouse Elec. Corp. v. Kirby, 637 F. Supp. at 1319.

26. 473 A.2d 805, 814 (Del. 1984). *See also* Grobow v. Perot, 526 A.2d 914, 920 (Del. Ch. 1987), *aff'd*, 539 A.2d. 180 (Del. 1988).

27. Aronson v. Lewis, 473 A.2d at 815. Moreover, as one court has noted, "The shareholder derivative suit is designed to permit attacks on improperly motivated business judgments, not poor ones." Lewis v. Hilton, 648 F. Supp. 725, 728 (N.D. Ill. 1986).

The Delaware Supreme Court recently reaffirmed the *Aronson* test, finding that the Court of Chancery had erred in requiring the pleading of particularized facts sufficient to support a "judicial finding" of director interest or lack of independence. Grobow v. Perot, 539 A.2d 180, 186–87 (Del. 1988). In rejecting a more stringent standard than that set forth in *Aronson*, the court noted that the inquiry to be made in such matters is too fact-specific to be governed by a general rule for determining reasonable doubt; moreover, because rule 23.1 motions are generally heard before discovery is taken, some plaintiffs might not be able to meet a more stringent pleading test without the assistance of discovery. *Id.*

28. Aronson v. Lewis, 473 A.2d 805, 818 (Del. 1984). *Accord* Pogostin v. Rice, 480 A.2d 619, 625 (Del. 1984); Phillips v. Bradford, 62 F.R.D. 681 (S.D.N.Y. 1974); Markowitz v. Brody, 90 F.R.D. 542 (S.D.N.Y. 1981); Blosvern v. Fisher, No. 235, 1985, slip op. at 2 (Del. Jan. 30, 1986); Grobow v. Perot, 526 A.2d at 924–25 (Del. Ch. 1987); Sundin v. Fisher, C.A. No. 6918, slip op. at 3–4 (Del. Ch. Feb. 15, 1985); Lewis v. Aronson, C.A. No. 6919, slip op. at 9 (Del. Ch. May 1, 1985); Richardson v. Graves, C.A. No. 6617 (Del. Ch. June 17, 1983); Stotland v. GAF Corp., C.A. No. 7559, slip op. at 15 (Del. Ch. Nov. 20, 1984).

29. Richardson v. Graves, slip op. at 8; Stotland v. GAF Corp., slip op. at 16; Cramer v. General Tel. & Elec. Corp., 582 F.2d 259, 276–77 (3d Cir. 1978), *cert. denied*, 439 U.S. 1129 (1979); Allison v. General Motors Corp., 604 F. Supp. 1106, 1113 (D. Del.), *aff'd mem.*, 702 F.2d 1026 (3d Cir. 1985).

30. Aronson v. Lewis, 473 A.2d 805, 817 (Del. 1984).

31. *See, e.g.*, Haber v. Bell, 465 A.2d 353, 359 (Del. Ch. 1983) ("Allegations that the members of a Board of Directors 'approved or acquiesced in' the action which plaintiffs attack are. . . not sufficient to excuse a demand for redress before suit."); Kaufman v. Beal, C.A. No. 6485, slip op. at 9 (Del. Ch. Feb. 25, 1983) ("mere allegations of approval of a challenged transaction or participation by directors in alleged wrongful conduct, absent a showing of self interest or bias by a majority of the Board, have been held to be insufficient to excuse a demand").

32. *See, e.g.*, Grobow v. Perot, 526 A.2d at 914, 920–21 (Del. Ch. 1987), *aff'd mem.*, 539 A.2d 180 (Del. 1988); Pogostin v. Rice, C.A. No. 6235, slip op. at 9 (Del. Ch. Aug. 12, 1983); Kaufman v. Belmont, 479 A.2d 282, 288 (Del. Ch. 1984); Stein v. Orloff, C.A. No. 7276, slip op. at 10 (Del. Ch. May 30, 1985), *appeal denied*, No. 352, 1986 (Del. Jan. 28, 1986); Sundin v. Fisher, C.A. No. 6918, slip op. at 3–4 (Del. Ch. Feb. 15, 1985); Lewis v. Aronson, C.A. No. 6919, slip op. at 9 (Del. Ch. May 1, 1985); Lewis v. Daum, C.A. No. 6733 (Del. Ch. May 24, 1984).

33. *See, e.g.*, Lewis v. Graves, 701 F.2d 245, 248 (2d Cir. 1983) ("The fact that a corporation's directors have previously approved transactions subsequently challenged in a derivative suit does not inevitably lead to the conclusion that

those directors, bound by their fiduciary obligations to the corporation, will refuse to take up the suit. . . . By virtue of their offices, directors ordinarily participate in the decision making involved in such transactions. . . . Excusing demand on the mere basis of prior board acquiescence, therefore, would obviate the need for demand in practically every case."); Grossman v. Johnson, 674 F.2d 115, 124 (1st Cir.), *cert. denied*, 459 U.S. 838 (1982) ("As for mere 'participation' or 'acquiescence' by the directors. . ., that generality, too, is an insufficient excuse. . . . Bare allegations of 'wrongful participation' or 'acquiescence' are not enough."); Lewis v. Curtis, 671 F.2d 779, 785 (3d Cir.), *cert. denied*, 459 U.S. 880 (1982) ("The majority view is that the mere approval of an allegedly injurious corporate transaction, absent self-interest or bias by a majority of the board, is insufficient to excuse demand."); In re Kauffman Mutual Fund Actions, 479 F.2d 257, 265 (1st Cir.), *cert. denied*, 414 U.S. 857 (1973) ("Where mere approval of the corporate action, absent self-interest or other indication of bias, is the sole basis for establishing the directors' 'wrongdoing' and hence for excusing demand on them, plaintiff's suit should ordinarily be dismissed. . . . If by plaintiff's merely alleging error, the directors are to be presumed incapable of exercising sound business judgment, Rule 23.1 would become virtually meaningless."); Weiss v. Temporary Inv. Fund, Inc., 692 F.2d 928, 943 (3d Cir. 1982), *vacated and remanded on other grounds*, 464 U.S. 1001 (1984) ("The. . .complaint failed to allege that the directors stood to gain any personal advantage from approval of the advisory contracts; rather, it challenged the directors' action only as a breach of their statutory and common law fiduciary duties. . . . We agree with the analysis of the district court that these allegations are insufficient to excuse demand and affirm on that basis."); Allison v. General Motors Corp., 604 F. Supp. 1106, 1114 (D. Del.), *aff'd mem.*, 702 F.2d 1026 (3d Cir. 1985) ("The mere fact that plaintiff names members of the Board of Directors as defendants or even makes conclusory allegations of director wrongdoing does not suffice to excuse demand."); Tabas v. Mullane, 608 F. Supp. 759, 766 (D.N.J. 1985) (quoting Aronson v. Lewis, 473 A.2d at 818).

34. Kaufman v. Safeguard Scientifics, Inc., 587 F. Supp. 486 (E.D. Pa. 1984); Kaplan v. Peat, Marwick, Mitchell & Co., 529 A.2d 254 (Del. Ch. 1987), *aff'd in part and rev'd in part*, 540 A.2d 726 (Del. 1988). *See generally* D. BLOCK, N. BARTON & S. RADIN, *supra* note 9, at 233–34.

35. Grobow v. Perot, 526 A.2d 914, 926 (Del. Ch. 1987), *aff'd*, 539 A.2d 180 (Del. 1988).

36. Kaplan v. Peat, Marwick, Mitchell & Co., 540 A.2d at 731.

37. *Id.*

38. *See, e.g.*, Good v. Texaco, Inc., C.A. No. 7501 (Del. Ch. May 14, 1984) (directors "interested" in derivative action challenging the purchase of stock by the corporation under the terms giving the board voting and control over 5 percent of the corporation's outstanding shares). *See also* Norlin Corp. v. Rooney, Pace, Inc., 744 F.2d 255 (2d Cir. 1984).

39. 480 A.2d 619, 624 (Del. 1984) (citations omitted).

40. *See, e.g.*, Pogostin v. Rice, 480 A.2d at 626 (ten of the fourteen directors deemed to be independent because they were not beneficiaries of the allegedly excessive executive compensation plan); Kaufman v. Belmont, 479 A.2d 282, 288 (Del. Ch. 1984) (only two of the nine board members were "interested"

since they would receive $123,017 in connection with the action challenged in a derivative suit); Lewis v. Daum, C.A. No. 6733 (Del. Ch. May 24, 1984) (only one director of a six-member board was "interested" because the challenged repurchase of that director's stock by the corporation conferred a benefit).

41. *See, e.g.*, Lewis v. Aronson, C.A. No. 6919, slip op. at 11 (Del. Ch. May 1, 1985) (amended complaint pleaded sufficient facts regarding the negotiation of a contract for the purchase of stock from and the employment of one director, raising a reasonable doubt as to the disinterestedness of seven out of ten board members serving on the interlocking boards and thereby excusing demand as to the entire board); Good v. Texaco, Inc., C.A. No. 7501 (Del. Ch. May 14, 1984) (directors "interested" in derivative action challenging the purchase of stock by the corporation under the terms giving the board voting control over 5 percent of the corporation's outstanding shares); Seibert v. Harper & Row, Publishers, Inc., C.A. No. 6639 (Del. Ch. Dec. 5, 1984) (directors "interested" in corporate repurchase of outstanding stock that would give board voting control over approximately 30 percent of corporate stock, even though the repurchased stock was transferred to an employee stock plan and the directors' voting rights might be limited by their fiduciary duties to vote the stock for the corporate employees). *See also* Edelman v. Phillips Petroleum Co., C.A. No. 7899, slip op. at 10–11 (Del. Ch. Feb. 12, 1985), *interlocutory appeal denied*, No. 55, 1985 (Feb. 16, 1985) (denying plaintiff's application for a preliminary injunction, court noted, "The particularized allegations of the complaint . . . directed to the establishment of the EISOP as a means of ensuring control raise a reasonable doubt concerning the interestedness of the Phillips Board. . . . The claim of waste may satisfy the second prong or business judgment exception in *Aronson*. . . . Moreover, given the commitment of Phillips management to use its best efforts to secure approval of the recapitalization plan and the time constraints involved, requiring demand as a preamble to enjoining a shareholder's meeting at which ratification is sought would be a meaningless deferral to the demand rule.") (citations omitted).

42. Aronson v. Lewis, 473 A.2d 805, 815 (Del. 1984).

43. *See, e.g.*, Stroud v. Milliken Enters., Inc., C.A. No. 8969, slip op. at 12 (Del. Ch. Mar. 18, 1988) ("Mere allegations that a director was nominated or elected by a majority shareholder or that the directors would automatically decline to bring suit because they proposed the [subject transaction] are not sufficient, however, to raise a reasonable doubt that the directors are disinterested or independent."); Grobow v. Perot, 526 A.2d 914, 924 (Del. Ch. 1987), *aff'd*, 539 A.2d 180 (Del. 1988) (no doubt raised as to independence when "allegation . . . is conclusory and without particularized factual basis"); Aronson v. Lewis, 473 A.2d at 816 ("The shorthand shibboleth of 'dominated and controlled directors' is insufficient."); Bergstein v. Texas Int'l Co., 453 A.2d 467, 473 (Del. Ch. 1982), *appeal denied*, 461 A.2d 695 (Del. 1983) ("a charge [of domination and control], without some amount of factual foundation, is insufficient"); Stepak v. Dean, 434 A.2d 388, 390 (Del. Ch. 1981) (demand cannot be excused where "the complaint contains only a conclusory allegation as to control by the defendant"); Stein v. Orloff, C.A. No. 7276 slip op. at 10 (Del. Ch. May 30, 1985), *appeal denied*, No. 352 (1986) (Del. Jan. 28, 1986). ("In order to excuse demand there must be allegations of fact which raise a reasonable doubt as to the actual independence of the directors and these facts must demonstrate that the directors are beholden to the controlling person through personal and other relationships."); Sundin v. Fisher, C.A. No. 6918, slip op. at 4 (Del. Ch. Feb. 15,

1985) ("A conclusory allegation of domination and control, without factual support is insufficient to excuse demand."); Lewis v. Aronson, C.A. No. 6919 slip op. at 8 (Del. Ch. May 1, 1985) ("Plaintiff's allegations as to [defendant-director's] stock ownership [more than 50 percent] and designation of the directors are. . . still insufficient to create a reasonable doubt as to the directors' disinterestedness."); Stotland v. GAF Corp., C.A. No. 7559, slip op. at 14 ("there is no presumption that a director is controlled"); Kaufman v. Beal, slip op. at 16–17 (Del. Ch. Nov. 20, 1984) (claims that majority of board was dominated and controlled dismissed "because there is no allegation of facts showing with particularity that there was any such domination and control").

However, when all of the members of the board are appointed by and are employees of the company with whom a particular transaction is undertaken, a reasonable doubt as to the independence of those directors will be raised, and demand will be excused as futile. Sealy Mattress Co. v. Sealy, Inc., C.A. No. 8853 (Del. Ch. July 20, 1987).

44. *See, e.g.*, Grossman v. Johnson, 674 F.2d 115, 124 (1st Cir.), *cert. denied*, 459 U.S. 838 (1982) ("A proper excuse of control or domination calls for particularized allegations and specific facts."); Kaster v. Modification Sys., Inc., 731 F.2d 1014 (2d Cir. 1984); *In re* Kauffman Mut. Fund Actions, 479 F.2d at 257, 264 (1st Cir.) *cert. denied*, 414 U.S. 857 (1973); Cramer v. General Tel. & Elec. Corp., 582 F.2d 259, 276–77 (3d Cir. 1978), *cert. denied*, 439 U.S. 1129 (1979); Allison v. General Motors Corp., 604 F. Supp. at 1115; Tabas v. Mullane, 608 F. Supp. 759, 766–67 (D.N.J. 1985).

45. Weiss v. Temporary Inv. Fund, Inc., 516 F. Supp. 665, 671 (D. Del.), *reargument denied*, 520 F. Supp. 1098 (D. Del. 1981), *aff'd*, 692 F.2d 928 (3d Cir. 1982), *vacated and remanded on other grounds*, 465 U.S. 1001 (1984) (quoting Vernars v. Young, 539 F.2d 966, 968 (3d Cir. 1976)).

46. Haber v. Bell, 465 A.2d 353 (Del. Ch. 1983). For example, the mere receipt by directors of fees for their services as directors is insufficient to render them interested. *See, e.g.*, Grobow v. Perot, 539 A.2d 180, 188 (Del. 1988); *In re* E.F. Hutton Banking Practices Litig., 634 F. Supp. 265, 271 (S.D.N.Y. 1986). Otherwise, "every director who receives a director's fee would be biased." 634 F. Supp. at 271.

47. Bergstein v. Texas Int'l Co., 453 A.2d 467 (Del. Ch. 1982), *appeal denied*, 461 A.2d 695 (Del. 1983); Dann v. Chrysler Corp., 174 A.2d 696 (Del. Ch. 1961); Lewis v. Aronson, C.A. No. 6919, slip op. at 11 (Del. Ch. May 1, 1985).

48. 526 A.2d 914 (Del. Ch. 1987), *aff'd*, 539 A.2d 180 (Del. 1988).

49. *Id.* at 923; 539 A.2d at 188–89.

50. *See* L A Partners, L.P. v. Allegis Corp., C.A. No. 9033, slip op. at 15 (Del. Ch. Oct. 22, 1987) ("[T]he particularized factual allegations sufficiently state a primary purpose to retain control and, therefore, create a reasonable doubt that [the directors] are disinterested. . . [when] circumstances surrounding the execution of the [antitakeover device] and the alleged absence of any business purpose provide independent support for plaintiffs' conclusory allegations as to motive."); Moran v. Household Int'l, Inc., 490 A.2d 1059, 1071 (Del. Ch.), *aff'd*, 500 A.2d 1346 (Del. 1985) ("[T]he plaintiffs' complaints, which set forth particularized facts alleging that the Rights Plan deters all hostile takeover attempts through its limitation on alienability of shares and the exercise of proxy rights, sufficiently pleads a primary purpose to retain control, and thus

casts a reasonable doubt as to the disinterestedness and independence of the board at this stage of the proceedings. . . . Therefore, the plaintiffs' complaints, while setting out derivative causes of action, adequately complied with Chancery Rule 23.1 by demonstrating futility of demand."); Seibert v. Harper & Row Publishers, Inc., C.A. No. 6639, slip op. at 9–12 (Del. Ch. Dec. 5, 1984) (where plaintiff had alleged that board's motive was entrenchment in its repurchase of 30 percent of company's stock for placement in an employee stock plan and a management profit-sharing plan, demand was found to be futile); Good v. Texaco, Inc., C.A. No. 7501, slip op. at 9–11 (Del. Ch. May 14, 1984) (demand found to be futile due to board's obtaining of voting control of 5 percent of company's stock in light of a charter provision requiring 80 percent shareholder approval for director removal).

51. Grobow v. Perot, 539 A.2d 180, 186 (Del. 1988). Thus, an allegation that H. Ross Perot's criticism of the General Motors board could possibly cause sufficient embarrassment to force the other directors from office was insufficient to show a real threat to the directors' positions, particularly when considered in light of the fact that Perot owned only 0.8 percent of the company's voting stock. *Id.*

52. Aronson v. Lewis, 473 A.2d 805, 814 (Del. 1984).

53. Scopas Technology Co. v. Lord, C.A. No. 7559, slip op. at 9 (Del. Ch. Nov. 20, 1984).

54. *Id.* at 9–10.

55. Stroud v. Milliken Enters., Inc., C.A. No. 8969, slip op. at 15 (Del. Ch. Mar. 18, 1988). *See also* Grobow v. Perot, 539 A.2d at 189–90 (second prong of *Aronson* not satisfied when plaintiffs fail to plead facts showing that large premium paid was to buy dissident's silence, and complaint itself set forth two legitimate business purposes).

56. C.A. No. 6752 (Del. Ch. Sept. 4, 1984).

57. Lewis v. Hett, *supra* note 56, slip op. at 10.

58. *Id.*

59. Lewis v. Aronson, C.A. No. 6919, slip op. at 14–15 (Del. Ch. May 1, 1985).

60. Lewis v. Aronson, slip op. at 15.

61. Lewis v. Aronson, slip op. at 14. *See also* Grobow v. Perot, 539 A.2d 180, 191 (Del. 1988) (allegations insufficient to support a claim of waste).

62. Aronson v. Lewis, 473 A.2d 805, 813 (Del. 1984); Zapata Corp. v. Maldonado, 430 A.2d 779, 784–85 n.10 (Del. 1981) ("[W]hen stockholders, after making demand and having their suit rejected, attack the board's decision as improper, the board's decision falls under the 'business judgment' rule and will be respected if the requirements of the rule are met."); Abramowitz v. Posner, 672 F.2d 1025, 1030 (2d Cir. 1982) ("Thus, where a demand is made and refused, absent a showing of wrongful conduct by the voting directors, the stockholder is simply without the legal ability to initiate a derivative action."); Stein v. Bailey, 531 F. Supp. 684, 690–93 (S.D.N.Y. 1982). *But see In Re* Continental Ill. Sec. Litig., 572 F. Supp. 928 (N.D. Ill. 1983), *aff'd*, 732 F.2d 1302 (7th Cir. 1984).

63. *See In re* General Motors Class E Stock Buyout Sec. Litig., 694 F. Supp. 1131, 1132 (D. Del. 1988). However, in determining wrongfulness of demand, a plaintiff is not entitled to discovery. Levine v. Smith, C.A. No. 8833 (Del. Ch.

Dec. 22, 1987); Allison v. General Motors Corp., 604 F. Supp. 1106, 1117 (D. Del.), *aff'd mem.*, 702 F.2d 1026 (3d Cir. 1985); Lewis v. Hilton, 648 F. Supp. 725, 727 n.1 (W.D. Ill. 1986).

64. Ash v. International Business Mach., Inc., 353 F.2d 491, 493 (3d Cir. 1965), *cert. denied*, 384 U.S. 927 (1966); Allison v. General Motors Corp., 604 F. Supp. at 1122. *Accord* Klotz v. Consolidated Edison Co., 386 F. Supp. 577, 582 (S.D.N.Y. 1974); Issner v. Aldrich, 254 F. Supp. 696 (D. Del. 1966); Royston v. Eastern Empire Corp., 393 F. Supp. 1010 (E.D. Pa. 1975).

65. Ash v. International Business Mach., Inc., 353 F.2d at 493. An allegation that directors neglected to fulfill their duty to inform themselves of all material information reasonably available to them in responding to a demand letter has been found sufficient to withstand a motion to dismiss in this context. *See In re* General Motors Class E Stock Buyout Sec. Litig., 694 F. Supp. 1131, 1134 (D. Del. 1988).

66. Aronson v. Lewis, 473 A.2d 805, 813 (Del. 1984); Zapata Corp. v. Maldonado, 430 A.2d 779, 784 (Del. 1981). *See also In re* General Motors Class E Stock Buyout Sec. Litig., 694 F. Supp. 1131, 1133 (D. Del. 1988).

67. Zapata Corp. v. Maldonado, 430 A.2d at 785–89.

68. *See generally* D. Block, N. Barton & S. Radin, *supra* note 9, at 253–62.

69. 47 N.Y.2d 619, 393 N.E.2d 994, 419 N.Y.S.2d 920 (1979).

70. *Accord* Roberts v. Alabama Power Co., 404 So. 2d 629 (Ala. 1981); Genzer v. Cunningham, 498 F. Supp. 682 (E.D. Mich. 1980) (construing Michigan law); Gaines v. Haughton, 645 F.2d 761 (9th Cir. 1981), *cert. denied*, 454 U.S. 1145 (1982); Lewis v. Anderson, 615 F.2d 778 (9th Cir. 1979), *cert. denied*, 449 U.S. 869 (1980) (construing California law).

Although the Supreme Court of North Carolina originally adopted the *Auerbach* approach, *see* Alford v. Shaw, 349 S.E.2d 41 (N.C. 1986), the court recently withdrew that decision and issued a new opinion in which the *Zapata* test was adopted. *See* Alford v. Shaw, No. 132PA85 (N.C. July 28, 1987). The court's rationale was that because a North Carolina statute required that every dismissal of a derivative action be approved by the court with a determination of whether the interests of any stockholder would be substantially affected, then the court must itself "[look] at the proposed action substantively," slip op. at 8, rather than relying "blindly on the report of a corporation-appointed committee which assembled such materials." *Id.*

The Iowa Supreme Court has addressed the issue of special litigation committees by holding that the directors whose conduct is in question are prohibited from being involved in choosing the members of the committee. Miller v. Register & Tribune Syndicate, Inc., 336 N.W.2d 709 (Iowa 1983).

71. *See also* Aronson v. Lewis, 473 A.2d 805 (Del. 1984).

72. *Accord* Joy v. North, 692 F.2d 880 (2d Cir. 1982), *cert. denied*, 460 U.S. 1051 (1983) (interpreting Connecticut law); Abella v. Universal Leaf Tobacco Co., 546 F. Supp. 795 (E.D. Va. 1982) (construing Virginia law); Mills v. Esmark, Inc., 573 F. Supp. 169 (N.D. Ill. 1983) (construing Delaware law). *See also* Hasan v. CleveTrust Realty Investors, 729 F.2d 372 (6th Cir. 1984); *In re* General Tire & Rubber Co. Sec. Litig., 726 F.2d 1075, 1083 (6th Cir.), *modified and reh'g denied*, [1984 Transfer Binder] Fed. Sec. L. Rep. (CCH) ¶ 91,468 (6th Cir. Mar. 8, 1984), *cert. denied*, 469 U.S. 858 (1984) (construing Ohio law).

73. Kaplan v. Wyatt, 484 A.2d 501 (Del. Ch. 1984), *aff'd*, 499 A.2d 1184 (Del. 1985).

74. 430 A.2d 779, 788 (Del. 1981). *Accord* Kaplan v. Wyatt, 499 A.2d at 1188; Lewis v. Fuqua, 502 A.2d 962, 967 (Del. Ch. 1985).

75. Lewis v. Fuqua, 502 A.2d at 967.

76. Zapata v. Maldonado, 430 A.2d at 788. *Accord* Kaplan v. Wyatt, 484 A.2d at 507 ("[T]he type and extent of any discovery in a particular case is a matter left to the discretion of the Court and may be undertaken only if first authorized by the Court."); Lewis v. Fuqua, 502 A.2d at 971 ("Even if the conclusions and recommendations of the Special Litigation Committee had a reasonable basis, this suit should still not be dismissed at this preliminary stage of the proceedings before the plaintiffs have had an opportunity to conduct discovery.").

77. Kaplan v. Wyatt, 484 A.2d at 519.

78. Kaplan v. Wyatt, 499 A.2d 1184, 1192 (Del. 1985).

79. Levine v. Smith, C.A. 8833 (Del. Ch. Dec. 22, 1987).

80. *See also* Allison v. General Motors Corp., 604 F. Supp. 1106, 1117 (D. Del.), *aff'd mem.*, 702 F.2d 1026 (3d Cir. 1985); Lewis v. Hilton, 648 F. Supp. 725, 727 n.1 (N.D. Ill. 1986).

Thirty-Four

The Role of Litigation in Control Contests

Jerold S. Solovy, Arthur M. Martin, Ronald L. Marmer, and David C. Bohan

Takeover contests have become increasingly complex battles for control of corporations, as hostile tender offers are met with competing offers, counteroffers, self-tender offers, and other defensive measures such as "lockup" options and "poison pills." Bidders and targets frequently have been forced to pursue simultaneous strategies of hindering one tender offer while encouraging another, blurring the defensive-offensive labels traditionally applied to the participants and their tactics. For purposes of this chapter, "strategies for defense" are techniques designed to inhibit a corporate acquisition by another corporation, and "strategies for offense" are techniques designed to facilitate an acquisition. With the growing complexity of takeover contests, litigation has emerged as a preeminent defensive and offensive tactic.

The principal federal restrictions on takeover contests are section 14(a) of the Securities Exchange Act of 1934 (the "Exchange Act"),[1] which governs proxy solicitations, and the Williams Act, which is the primary statute governing tender offers. Section 14(a) authorizes the Securities and Exchange Commission (SEC) to prescribe rules governing the solicitation of proxies. The purpose of section 14(a) and the rules promulgated thereunder is to prevent management or individuals opposing management from obtaining authorization for corporate action by means of deceptive or inadequate disclosures in proxy solicitations.[2] The enactment of section 14(a) stemmed from Congress's belief that "[fair] corporate suffrage is an important right that should attach to every equity security bought on a public exchange."[3]

The Williams Act, the principal federal legislation governing tender offers, was enacted in 1968 in response to a wave of cash tender offers exempt from then-existing disclosure requirements. The Williams Act added sections 13(d), 14(d), and 14(e) to the Exchange Act.[4] The purpose of the Williams Act and the rules promulgated thereunder is to protect in-

Jerold S. Solovy, Arthur M. Martin, Ronald L. Marmer, and David C. Bohan are members of Jenner & Block, Chicago, Illinois.

dividual investors by requiring the disclosure of material information relevant to the impact of a possible acquisition of shares or a tender offer and to allow investors enough time within which to make an informed investment decision. In enacting the Williams Act, Congress sought to protect investors not only by furnishing them with necessary information, but also by preventing either target management or the bidder from obtaining any undue advantage that could frustrate the exercise of informed choice.[5]

The SEC has attempted to bolster the regulatory scheme governing tender offers by amending several rules promulgated under the Williams Act. Amendments to rule 13e-4[6] increase the time periods during which self-tender offers must remain open and securities may be withdrawn to coincide with the requirements for third-party tender offers. The amended rule also requires that securities be accepted on a pro rata basis throughout the offer.[7] The SEC also amended rule 14e-1[8] to provide that a tender offer must remain open for ten business days after the announcement of an increase in the amount of securities being sought by the bidder.[9] In addition, the SEC adopted a new rule, rule 14d-10, to make explicit that in third-party tender offers, the bidder's offer must be open to all holders of the class of securities subject to the tender offer and provide that all security holders be offered the highest consideration offered to any security holder. Rule 13e-4, governing issuer tender offers, was similarly amended.[10]

In 1986, the SEC issued a Concept Release seeking public comment on the following issues:[11]

- Whether the Williams Act should apply when a person acquires a "substantial" percentage of a target company's stock during or just after a tender offer
- Whether poison pills should be restricted
- Whether there should be a "self-governance" exception to the new "all holders" rule

The first of these issues were addressed by rules proposed on October 1, 1987.[12] The SEC proposal would require, with some exceptions, that all purchases of securities between the commencement of a tender offer and ten business days of the tender offer's expiration date that would increase the purchaser's ownership of the class of securities subject to the tender offer by 10 percent or more must be made in compliance with the statutes and rules governing tender offers. The same requirements would also apply to a bidder that commences a tender offer by public announcement, until it formally commences a tender offer by some other means or until thirty business days after it subsequently announces that it will not continue the offer. The SEC has also proposed rules that would establish a "cooling off" period after termination of a tender offer, limiting purchases of a target's shares in the absence of a tender offer.[13]

The recent wave of takeover activity, well-publicized insider trading scandals, and the Supreme Court's decision in *CTS Corp. v. Dynamics Corp. of America*[14] have also generated concern on Capitol Hill. Several bills were introduced in the 100th Congress that are intended to curb hostile takeovers as well as limit certain takeover defenses. These bills contained provisions that would, among other things, lower section 13(d)'s 5 percent reporting threshold, require a bidder to make a formal tender offer after purchasing 15 percent of the target's stock, give individuals the right to seek injunctive relief and monetary damages for violations of section 13(d), prohibit bidders from making large purchases of the target's stock after withdrawing a tender offer, prohibit greenmail, and limit adoption of certain takeover defenses during a tender offer.[15]

Most of these bills did not progress. However, S. 1323, the Tender Offer Disclosure and Fairness Act of 1987, was approved by the Senate Committee on Banking on September 30, 1987.[16] The bill stalled when it reached the full Senate because of concerns about potential amendments to allow the SEC to preempt state antitakeover laws.[17] This bill would require more extensive disclosures under section 13(d) and require these disclosures to be filed within five days of acquisition of 5 percent of the target's stock rather than ten days. The bill would also provide that a bidder that obtains 25 percent of a target's stock must make any additional purchases through a formal tender offer, and it would extend the minimum tender offer period from twenty business days to thirty-five business days. It would grant shareholders a cause of action to force the disgorgement of profits obtained in a successful takeover, and it would require an SEC study of abuses in "going private" actions and leveraged buyouts. The committee rejected amendments that would restrict state takeover statutes, and it deleted limitations on poison pills and golden parachutes.[18] The Reagan Administration opposed S. 1323 and similar bills because of their interference with "the market for corporate control" and intrusion into matters that should be left to shareholders.[19] At the time of this writing, it seems likely that legislation similar to S. 1323 will be reintroduced in Congress.

The Role of Litigation in Control Contests

Litigation under the proxy rules, the Williams Act, and state corporation law has become increasingly important in determining the outcome of control contests. Targets use litigation to ward off a takeover attempt or to gain a reprieve during which to consider and implement alternative strategies. Bidders frequently resort to litigation to preempt target actions and to ensure a more favorable forum. Although takeover litigation frequently involves challenges to another party's disclosures, a number of other tactics may also be tested in court.

The Role of Litigation for the Bidder

The bidder generally would prefer not to be involved in any litigation with the target, but should recognize that litigation is almost inevitable. The bidder should therefore develop strategies designed to preempt or limit the target's defensive alternatives.

Challenging Unconstitutional Statutes and Unlawful Acts by the Target

By suing first, the bidder often can choose the most favorable forum for important aspects of the litigation. In particular, a bidder should consider filing a preemptive suit immediately upon commencing its offer. If the bidder has not sued first, and thereby established the forum, the target frequently will bring an action in a state court or state administrative agency. In these state proceedings, typically brought in a forum hospitable to the target, the target seeks to enforce some state regulatory statute that could delay or prevent the offer. Moreover, once these state proceedings are initiated, federal courts may abstain from hearing the bidder's claims under the Williams Act or the United States Constitution until the state proceedings have concluded.

To avoid becoming embroiled in state proceedings in the target's most sympathetic forum, bidders commonly bring preemptive suits in federal courts. These preemptive suits generally seek to enjoin the enforcement of unconstitutional state statutes.

However, even if the bidder's federal lawsuit successfully blocks the target from proceeding in state court, the target may be free to pursue its substantive Williams Act or antitrust claims in a different federal forum. Unless the target's substantive litigation constitutes a compulsory counterclaim to the bidder's pending federal action, the target can sue in virtually any federal district court.[20] In other words, the bidder may not be able to choose the federal forum for the tender offer's main litigation unless the bidder can file a substantive suit against the target (as opposed to a suit to enjoin a state takeover act) in the desired federal court. For example, the bidder may want to commence litigation to invalidate a defensive charter provision of the target.

Obtaining Discovery

In connection with its substantive litigation, the bidder often seeks discovery regarding the background and effect of specific defensive tactics of the target, such as the sale of assets or the issuance of new shares, as well as justifications for statements by the target that the bidder's offer is "inadequate." If the bidder has reason to believe that the target or its allies have engaged in RICO violations, the bidder can probe the background of those suspected offenses. The bidder should prepare discovery requests before making the offer so that they can be served as quickly as possible.

In addition, the bidder should assemble in advance the documents that the target is likely to request and should prepare the witnesses the target is likely to depose.

Working with the Market

As noted, because litigation provides the only substantial public access to the contest for control, the bidder can influence the financial community's perceptions of the contest by pressing a strong litigation posture. Besides generating publicity, litigation challenging the propriety of the target's response also may neutralize the tendency of unsophisticated shareholders to rely solely upon the target's advice concerning the merits of the offer. The bidder often can portray the target's management as placing personal interests above those of target shareholders. For example, a bidder may challenge golden parachutes provided to target management. The bidder also may force the target's management to make embarrassing disclosures.[21]

Switching to Defense

Faced with a competing offer, a counteroffer, or a self-tender offer, the bidder must be prepared to employ defensive strategies similar to those of a target. Such strategies are described later in this chapter.

The Role of Litigation for the Target

Numerous laws, both state and federal, have been enacted to protect target shareholders during tender offers. The target's management is frequently in the best position to see that those statutes are enforced.

Preventing Illegal Acts by the Bidder

The bidder may attempt to obtain a large block of shares at bargain prices without complying with the Williams Act's requirements for prebid disclosure. If a target suspects that someone is engaging in an open-market accumulation scheme, litigation may succeed in flushing out the purchaser. Once the identity of a major open-market purchaser is revealed, the price of the target's stock often will rise, thereby depriving the bidder of bargain prices and ultimately necessitating that the tender offer be made at a higher price.

The bidder also may be in violation of other provisions of the Williams Act. For example, the bidder's Schedule 14D-1 may fail to disclose the bidder's plans for the target or fail to include adequate financial information about the bidder. Targets frequently can use litigation to remedy these violations. In addition, the offer may violate the antitrust laws and force the target to become an unwilling participant in that violation. (Although courts repeatedly have allowed target corporations to enjoin potential Clayton Act violations, the Supreme Court's decision in *Cargill, Inc. v. Montfort of Colorado, Inc.*[22] may reopen the question.) Finally, the offer may violate margin rules, common law principles, or state statutes or regulations (such as state takeover acts or state rules governing regulated industries).

For obvious reasons, a target would prefer to litigate before courts sympathetic to its position, usually in the state or district where the target's headquarters are located or where the target has substantial operations. But the decision on where to litigate should also be influenced by other factors. For example, a target should avoid districts that have denied private rights of action for targets under the Williams Act.

Obtaining Discovery

Depending upon the matters at issue, the target often can depose the bidder's directors, top management, financial officers, outside accountants, and investment and commercial bankers. The target also can obtain documents dealing with the background of the offer. Discovery generally focuses on the financing of the offer, the bidder's "plans or proposals" for an ultimate merger, the bidder's intentions concerning the target's operations, and the integrity of the bidder's management. If the offer raises antitrust issues, the target can seek information concerning the bidder's operations and markets. Moreover, if the target files suit under RICO, discovery can be even more expensive.

Working with the Market

Although most aspects of a takeover proceed in private, litigation is public and may attract substantial attention. In major contests for control, financial reporters frequently attend court hearings and publish accounts of the proceedings, and persons holding large positions in the target's stock may retain counsel to monitor the litigation. Consequently, the financial community forms impressions about the likelihood that the offer will proceed based upon perceptions of who is winning the litigation. The target frequently benefits from publicity concerning the litigation. Indeed, the prospect of public disclosure of some items may be enough to defeat an offer.[23] Particularly where the target has alleged violations under RICO, the bidder may be vulnerable to public disclosure of its links with "racketeers" and "organized crime."

Even where litigation is unlikely to determine the outcome of a control contest, it may benefit a target by creating an environment in which other defensive strategies may be pursued and consummated, although instigating litigation may also subject these strategies to closer scrutiny by a court.

Obtaining Special Remedies

Absent a serious hindrance to the offer such as an antitrust violation, the most common remedy is corrective disclosure. However, some courts have ordered more drastic remedies, such as rescission or sterilization of shares. One court even enjoined a prospective bidder from making a formal offer because the offer would require disclosure of sensitive business information about the target in breach of a confidentiality agreement between the target and the prospective bidder. Thus, in egregious cases, targets should view litigation as a legitimate means for halting an offer.

Switching to Offense

Just as bidders sometimes must shift to defensive strategies, targets pursuing self-tender offers or counteroffers or promoting friendly competing offers must switch to offense. Strategies for offense are discussed in the next part of this chapter.

Representing the Bidder: Strategies for Offense

Challenging the Target's Disclosures

The three primary bases for challenging a target's disclosures are sections 14(a), 13(d), and 14(e) of the Exchange Act. Although none of these sections provides an express private right of action, courts generally have implied rights of action for bidders under each of them.

Section 14(a)—Proxy Regulations

The Supreme Court has held that a private right of action exists under section 14(a).[24] Bidders frequently invoke section 14(a) to challenge disclosures relating to defensive measures enacted or proposed by targets.

Elements. Under *Mills v. Electric Autolite Co.*,[25] in order to establish a section 14(a) violation, a plaintiff must prove that the defendant's proxy materials contain a material misleading statement or omission and that the "proxy solicitation itself, rather than the particular defect in the solicitation materials [is] an essential link in the accomplishment of the transaction."[26] Authorities are split as to whether a plaintiff also must establish that the defendant acted with scienter.

The definition of "materiality" is well settled: "An omitted fact is material if there is a substantial likelihood that a reasonable shareholder would consider it important in deciding how to vote."[27] In applying the standard, the appropriate point of view is that of the reasonable investor, not the sophisticated analyst.[28]

In *Gerstle v. Gamble-Skogmo, Inc.*, the Second Circuit imposed a test of materiality that stresses probability rather than mere possibility.[29] Thus, financial projections and other necessarily speculative information need not be disclosed, unless the predictions regarding future economic and corporate events are substantially certain to hold true.[30] The Third Circuit and the Delaware Court of Chancery have rejected this test, however, in favor of a case-by-case approach.[31]

The trend appears to favor disclosure of soft information such as projections of future performance, although the various courts of appeals have yet to settle on a single approach.[32] The Supreme Court has reserved comment on the issue.[33] Similarly, the disclosure of motives for actions taken or to be taken is unnecessary so long as the underlying facts are disclosed.[34] In addition, nondisclosure of a breach of fiduciary duty or waste of corporate assets has not been considered material for purposes of section 14(a).[35]

The *Mills* requirement that a section 14(a) plaintiff must demonstrate a causal relationship between the violation and the injury for which relief is sought has been termed the "transaction causation" requirement.[36] In challenging a target's disclosures, a bidder must show that the misleading proxy materials directly caused the transaction complained of.[37]

The leading case on the *mens rea* requirement in a rule 14a-9 action brought against a corporate defendant is *Gerstle v. Gamble-Skogmo, Inc.*,[38] in which the Second Circuit relied on differences between the statutory authorization for rules 10b-5[39] and 14a-9[40] to conclude that the rule 10b-5 scienter requirement should not be extended to rule 14a-9.[41] Instead, liability is imposed on those who "merely negligently drafted" the proxy statement.[42]

The Sixth Circuit, however, has extended the scienter requirement under section 14(e) to actions brought under rule 14a-9.[43] A district court has attempted to reconcile the two positions by adopting a negligence standard where the transaction redounded directly to the benefit of the defendant, while reserving the right to apply a scienter requirement where a defendant, such as the outside accountant charged in *Adams*, does not directly benefit from the proxy solicitation.[44]

Standing. In *Mills v. Electric Auto-Lite Co.*,[45] the Supreme Court reaffirmed the existence of a private right of action under section 14(a).

Courts consistently have held that bidders, usually as shareholders but sometimes in their own right, have standing under section 14(a).[46] Courts generally do not award damages to bidders challenging target solicitations as misleading.[47]

Challenging Target's Disclosures under Section 14(a). Bidders generally allege that targets either obtained or are in the process of obtaining shareholder approval of objectionable defensive measures through misleading proxy materials.[48] A bidder may also be able to challenge proxies seeking reelection of directors. In *Goldman v. Lexington Avenue & 42d Street Corp.*,[49] the court found that a director seeking reelection by proxy may be required to disclose firm offers that have been made for the corporation or its assets. The court dismissed the bidder's claim, however, for failure to plead fraud with particularity.

Section 13(d)—Reporting Requirement

Elements. Section 13(d) of the Exchange Act requires a person or group acquiring more than 5 percent of a company's stock to file a Schedule 13D disclosure statement with the SEC within ten days.[50] S. 1323, as approved by the Senate Committee on Banking in 1987, would have required that more detailed disclosures be made within five days of acquiring 5 percent of a company's stock.[51] Other bills introduced in the 100th Congress would have lowered the 5 percent threshold and restricted postdisclosure open-market purchases.

Although section 13(d) traditionally has been used by targets challenging bidders' disclosures, bidders on occasion invoke section 13(d) to claim that the target management, with or without outside allies, has formed a group subject to the requirements of section 13(d).[52] The plaintiff is not required to prove scienter or reliance, because the purpose of these suits is merely to compel the defendants "to file a Schedule 13D, which is complete, accurate, truthful, and not misleading."[53]

Standing. Section 13(d) does not expressly indicate whether private rights of action are intended, although recent proposals have sought to create an express private right of action for injunctive relief and monetary damages. Courts consistently have refused to imply a private right of action for damages in favor of any party under section 13(d).[54] These cases commonly hold that the only legal remedy for misstatements in a Schedule 13D is that provided in section 18(a) of the Exchange Act, which concerns false filings made with the SEC.[55]

Courts are split over whether a private right of action for injunctive relief can be implied under section 13(d). The clear majority of courts have held that both issuers and bidders (as shareholders) can seek injunctive relief under section 13(d), notwithstanding the availability of injunctive relief under section 18(a).[56]

The Eleventh Circuit and several district courts, however, have held that neither issuers nor bidders (even as shareholders) can seek injunctive relief under section 13(d), although this rule has since been softened to permit actions for corrective disclosure. In *Liberty National Insurance Holding Co. v. Charter Co.*,[57] the court of appeals concluded that an issuer may not maintain an action seeking divestiture of the issuer's stock. The court reasoned that implying such a right of action would "tip the balance [of the Williams Act] towards management."[58] However, the Eleventh Circuit has held that issuers may sue to compel corrective disclosures under the Williams Act, and this holding may apply to bidders as well.[59]

Two Supreme Court cases have indicated a possible trend toward implying private causes of action. In *Merrill Lynch, Pierce, Fenner & Smith, Inc. v. Curran*,[60] the Court held that when courts consistently have implied a private right of action under a statute, and Congress then amends that statute without negating the implied private remedy, Congress may have implicitly sanctioned the private right of action. In *Herman & MacLean v. Huddleston*,[61] the Court held that a private right of action for damages exists under section 10(b) of the Exchange Act despite the existence of express remedies under section 11 of the Securities Act of 1933; the Court rejected the notion that the availability of an express remedy in a statute precludes the implication of a private right of action.[62] After *Curran* and *Huddleston*, however, courts continued to split over the question whether a private right of action is available under section 13(d).[63]

Challenging Target's Disclosures under Section 13(d). Most litigation against targets under section 13(d) has focused on the failure of the target's management or its allies, or both, to file a Schedule 13D. In *Jacobs v. Pabst Brewing Co.*,[64] for example, the court refused to dismiss the bidder's claim that an investment adviser allied with the target should have filed a Schedule 13D.[65]

If the target has filed a Schedule 13D, it may be challenged for containing misleading statements or omissions.[66] Increasingly, though, remedies under this section are being limited to corrective disclosure, with an injunction against additional stock accumulation until the disclosure is accomplished.

Section 14(e)—Tender Offer Fraud

Elements. Section 14(e) of the Exchange Act prohibits fraudulent and deceptive practices in connection with tender offers. Because the language of section 14(e) tracks that of section 10(b) and rule 10b-5, the elements of section 14(e) and section 10(b) violations have been deemed identical, except for the 10(b) requirement of a purchase or sale of stock.[68] To establish a violation of section 14(e), therefore, the plaintiff must prove that the defendant made a misleading statement or omission in connection with a tender offer, that the misstatement or omission was material, that the defendant acted with scienter, and that the misstatement or omission caused the plaintiff's injury.[69]

In actions seeking injunctive relief, courts typically assume that the scienter and causation elements are met if the plaintiff demonstrates that the misstatements or omissions are material. The standard for materiality under section 14(e) is the same as that applied in proxy contests: whether "'there is a substantial likelihood that a reasonable shareholder would consider it important in deciding' whether to accept the tender offer."[70] As with other sections of the Williams Act, however, section 14(e) claims are increasingly seen as mooted by curative disclosures.[71]

The Seventh and Second Circuits have held that there can be no violation of section 14(e) unless the prospective bidder actually makes a tender offer.[72] Several courts, however, have indicated that section 14(e) applies to preoffer statements where the offeror "has made public a clear intent to make the offer."[73]

Standing. Although a defeated tender offeror has no private right of action for damages under section 14(e),[74] courts have consistently implied a private remedy for bidders seeking corrective action alone.[75] In addition, one case has held that tendering shareholders may have a private right of action under section 14(e) and rule 14e-1(c), which requires tender offerors to pay the consideration for the tendered shares promptly.[76]

Challenging Target's Disclosures under Section 14(e). If a target disseminates misleading material information or omits to disclose material information during a tender offer, it violates section 14(e). Under rule 14d-9,[77] which has been in effect since 1980, the target must file a Schedule 14D-9 before the target makes any "solicitation or recommendation" to its shareholders. The schedule must describe "the nature of the solicitation or the recommendation" and state "the reason(s) for the [target's] position (including the inability to take a position)." The instructions for completing the schedule add, "Conclusory statements such as 'The tender offer is in the best interest of shareholders,' will not be considered sufficient disclosure."[78] Actionable misstatements or omissions may exist in the target's press releases, shareholder communications, or Schedule 14D-9.[79]

One area that section 14(e) has not been construed to cover is actions for failure to disclose a breach of fiduciary duty. Such a claim is a common law claim for breach of duty and cannot be "bootstrapped" into a federal securities law claim by casting it as a failure to disclose under section 14(e).[80]

Courts are split as to whether and when targets must disclose "soft" financial projections and asset appraisals. The Third and Fourth Circuits have held that whether such information must be released should be decided on a case-by-case basis.[81] The Sixth Circuit, however, has concluded that since such projections are inherently unreliable, they need not be released unless the data they are based on are substantially certain to prove correct.[82] The Delaware Court of Chancery recently adopted the Flynn case-by-case approach.[83]

In *Basic, Inc. v. Levinson*,[84] the Supreme Court resolved a split in the Circuits as to when a corporation must disclose merger discussions. The Third Circuit had held that a potential merger need not be disclosed until the two sides have reached an "agreement in principle," defined as agreement on the fundamental—price and structure—terms of a merger.[85] The Seventh Circuit had also adopted this approach,[86] although it acknowledged an exception for closely held corporations.[87] In contrast, the Sixth Circuit had rejected the agreement-in-principle approach, concluding that a corporation could remain silent about merger negotiations as long as it did not deny that negotiations were taking place or trade in its own stock.[88] A unanimous Supreme Court rejected both the agreement-in-principle approach and that of the Sixth Circuit, adopting instead a fact-dependent assessment of the probability that the merger negotiations would be fruitful and of the magnitude of the transaction to the issuer.[89] If the result of this assessment indicates "a substantial likelihood that the disclosure of the [negotiations] would have significantly altered the 'total mix' of the information made available" to stockholders, the negotiations are material.[90]

Aside from any information that must be disclosed under regulation 14D, rule 14e-2 requires the target to disseminate a statement of its position regarding a tender offer within ten days after the offer is made.[91] The target must recommend acceptance or rejection of the offer, express its intent to remain neutral, or state that it is unable to take a position. When a target's management recommends that shareholders accept or reject an offer, management must disclose any personal advantages or conflicts of interest that might have influenced its decision.[92]

Bidders generally bring actions challenging targets' disclosures as counterclaims to suits brought by the targets themselves. Because the target usually is seeking equitable relief, material misconduct by the target permits the bidder to argue that the target has "unclean hands." However, the bidder risks being too successful, prompting the court to order corrective disclosures that may delay the offer. Bidders, therefore, must carefully consider their approach to the target's disclosures and the relief they intend to seek.

Challenging State Takeover Statutes

Many states have enacted takeover statutes that impose reporting and other regulatory burdens upon bidders beyond those created by the Williams Act. An action to enforce a state takeover law, initiated either by the target or by a state official, can seriously impede the bidder's takeover attempt.

When targets sue to enforce a state statute, they frequently do so in state court and join subsidiaries or other parties whose presence in the litigation will defeat diversity jurisdiction. This prevents the bidder from removing the case to federal court. However, in *Gunter v. AGO International B.V.*,[93] the court recognized an exception to the general rule that for removal based upon federal question jurisdiction, the federal question must be presented by the complaint, not by a defense thereto, and denied a motion to remand a suit to enforce the Florida Insurance Holding Company Act. The court stated that "if the state law upon which the plaintiff relies is entirely preempted by federal law, the case is removable."[94] The bidder may bring an independent action in federal court to challenge the state law's constitutionality, but the abstention doctrine could preclude a speedy resolution of the issue.[95]

To avoid this result, bidders commonly institute preemptive federal court lawsuits challenging each potentially applicable state statute immediately upon commencing their offers. By filing first, and by alleging that the target is acting under color of state law in violation of 42 U.S.C. § 1983, the bidder also should escape the Anti-Injunction Act.[96] Bidders typically allege that the challenged statutes violate both the commerce and supremacy clauses of the U.S. Constitution. The leading authorities for constitutional challenges to state takeover statutes are *Edgar v. MITE Corp.*,[97] and *CTS Corp. v. Dynamics Corp. of America*.[98]

Edgar v. MITE Corp.

In *MITE*, MITE Corporation sought to restrain the Illinois Secretary of State from enforcing the Illinois Business Take-Over Act with respect to MITE's attempted acquisition of Chicago Rivet & Machine. The Illinois Act required a tender offeror to notify the target corporation and the Illinois Secretary of State of the offeror's intention to make a tender offer twenty days before the offer became effective. The act authorized the Secretary to conduct a hearing to determine the offer's substantive fairness and to deny registration if it was deemed unfair. The act required the Secretary to call a fairness hearing if requested to do so by the holders of 10 percent of the shares subject to the offer. The act applied whenever Illinois residents collectively owned 10 percent of the class of shares subject to the offer or the target satisfied two of three tests:

1. It had its principal executive office in Illinois.
2. It was organized under Illinois law.
3. It had 10 percent or more of its stated capital and paid-in surplus represented within Illinois.

The district court granted MITE's request for an injunction, finding that the Illinois Act violated both the supremacy and commerce clauses, and the Seventh Circuit affirmed.[99]

In a sharply divided decision, the Supreme Court held that the act violated the commerce clause because it imposed indirect burdens upon interstate commerce that were excessive in relation to the local interests it served.[100] The majority noted that the act empowered the Secretary of State to adjudicate the fairness of tender offers and thereby to deprive shareholders of the opportunity to sell their shares at a premium, and it provided a disincentive to management to perform efficiently. Because the act could be applied to regulate tender offers involving exclusively nonresident shareholders, as well as foreign corporations with their principal offices in other states, the Court discounted the "local benefits" the act supposedly conferred on Illinois. It concluded that those benefits were outweighed by the act's interference with interstate commerce and that the act was therefore unconstitutional.[101] A three-Justice plurality of the Court also determined that the act impermissibly imposed direct and substantial burdens on commerce, regardless of any counterbalancing "local benefits." Three Justices of the Court would have struck down the act on preemption grounds as well, because the act interfered with the "careful balance struck by Congress" when it passed the Williams Act.[102]

Post-MITE Challenges to State Takeover Statutes

After *MITE*, federal courts preliminarily or permanently enjoined enforcement of a number of comparable "first-generation" takeover statutes.[103] Two state supreme courts also invalidated state takeover laws.[104]

A few courts, however, upheld the constitutionality of state takeover laws. For example, in *Cardiff Acquisitions, Inc. v. Hatch*,[105] the Eighth Circuit substantially upheld the constitutionality of the Minnesota Corporate Takeovers Act. That act empowers the Minnesota Commissioner of Commerce to suspend a tender offer and schedule a hearing within ten days if he determines that the offeror's Minnesota registration statement does not contain all the disclosures required under the act.

The Eighth Circuit distinguished the Illinois Act at issue in *MITE*, noting that the Minnesota statute applies only when at least 20 percent of the target's shareholders are state residents and the target company has "substantial assets" in the state. Moreover, any suspension of a tender offer extends only to Minnesota residents. Thus, the court held that the Minnesota Act burdens interstate commerce only incidentally and that this burden is outweighed by the benefits to Minnesota residents, namely: disclosures akin to those required under the Williams Act, which the Commissioner, unlike the SEC, realistically can scrutinize; and additional disclosures concerning "the impact of the proposed takeover on Minnesota residents."[106] With respect to the challenge to the supremacy clause, the court held that the Williams Act did not preempt the disclosure requirements regarding the tender offer's effect on state residents because they "serve to protect unique and legitimate interests of Minnesota shareholders."[107]

The Eighth Circuit declared unconstitutional on grounds of vagueness provisions of the Minnesota statute requiring "such additional disclosures as the Commissioner by rule prescribed."[108] Significantly, the court declined, on ripeness grounds, to address the constitutionality of the Minnesota act's fair-price provision, which prohibits an offeror from acquiring an equity security from a class of shareholders within two years following a tender offer with respect to that class of shareholders, unless the shareholders are given an opportunity to dispose of their shares on terms "substantially equivalent" to those of the earlier tender offer.

In *Agency Rent-A-Car, Inc. v. Connolly*,[109] the First Circuit vacated a district court order preliminarily enjoining enforcement of the sanctions provisions of the Massachusetts antitakeover statute on preemption grounds, but remanded for a determination of the bidder's commerce clause claim.[110] The plaintiff abandoned its attempted takeover, mooting the case, but in *Newell Co. v. Connolly*,[111] the same statute was found to violate the commerce clause.

Second-Generation Statutes

After *MITE*, several states enacted new takeover statutes or amended existing ones in an attempt to bring their laws into compliance with the supremacy and commerce clauses. One popular approach has been the so-called fair-price provision, variations of which are now in force in Connecticut, Georgia, Illinois, Kentucky, Louisiana, Maryland, Michigan, Mississippi, Pennsylvania, Virginia, Washington, and Wisconsin.[112] These statutes regulate the second step of two-step takeovers, that is, the process by which minority shareholders are bought out after a successful tender offer. Fair-price provisions generally require that under certain circumstances the nontendering minority shareholders receive an amount equal to the highest price paid by the bidder for shares of the target within a specified period of time before the freeze-out.[113]

Variations on the "fair-price" theme abound. In Hawaii, Minnesota, and Missouri if a successful bidder wants to acquire additional shares of the target from a state resident for a period of two years following the bidder's tender offer, the bidder must offer the resident the opportunity to sell his or her shares on the same terms as those offered in the tender offer.[114] In Maine and Pennsylvania, shareholders of the target may force bidders to redeem their shares at fair market value after certain delineated control transactions.[115]

Other forms of regulation of two-step acquisitions also have been enacted. For example, the laws of Indiana, New York, and New Jersey provide that a bidder who accumulates a specified percentage of the target's shares must wait five years before merging with the target or disposing of its assets.[116] A Wisconsin statute dilutes the voting power of shares held by a bidder who accumulates 20 percent of a target's stock.[117] Washington recently passed a statute, designed to prevent a hostile takeover of the Boeing Company and applicable only to that company, which prohibits a target corporation from engaging in a "significant business transaction," such as a merger with an acquiring company, within five years of the acquiring company's acquisition of 10 percent or more of the target's stock.[118]

Another popular approach to state regulation of takeovers has been the "control share" statute, which requires shareholder approval of any tender offer by which a bidder seeks to acquire control of specified percentages of a target's stock. Control share statutes also require a bidder to disclose its plans for the target, and they impose a waiting period between the time the information is disclosed and the time the position may be acquired. During the period immediately following *MITE*, a number of control share statutes were struck down.[119]

CTS Corp. v. Dynamics Corp. of America

In 1987, the Supreme Court surprised most observers when it upheld the constitutionality of the Indiana Control Share Acquisitions Act.[120] The Indiana Act applies only to businesses incorporated in Indiana that meet all of the following requirements:

- The corporation has at least 100 shareholders.
- The principal place of business, the principal offices, or substantial assets are in Indiana.
- Either more than 10 percent of shareholders reside in Indiana, more than 10 percent of shares are owned by Indiana residents, or 10,000 shareholders reside in Indiana.

A bidder that gains a "control share," i.e., acquires shares that would bring its voting power to any of three thresholds (20 percent, $33\frac{1}{3}$ percent, or 50 percent), acquires voting rights only if the bidder is granted those rights by a majority vote of disinterested shareholders.

Both the district court and the court of appeals held the act unconstitutional under *MITE*.[121] The Supreme Court reversed, rejecting claims that the act violated the supremacy and commerce clauses. Without adopting the *MITE* plurality's "broad interpretation of the Williams Act," under which the Illinois statute was preempted because it upset the Williams Act's "careful balance between the interests of offerors and target companies,"[122] the Court found that the statute would not be preempted even under such a broad approach. It emphasized that the Indiana Act protects shareholders against both management and offerors, while the Illinois statute favored management to the detriment of both offerors and shareholders. The Court similarly rejected the commerce clause challenge, stating that the act does not treat out-of-state offerors differently from Indiana offerors and that the act does not subject activities to inconsistent regulations.[123] The Court noted that the act undoubtedly has some effect on interstate commerce, but it emphasized the central role of the states in creating and regulating corporations—a role that inevitably affects some aspects of interstate commerce.[124] The Court's commerce clause analysis stressed Indiana's interest in protecting Indiana shareholders and the fact that the act applies only to businesses incorporated in Indiana.[125]

Current Developments

In addition to reviving existing control share statutes, the *CTS* decision has spawned a flurry of new state legislative action. A number of states have passed or considered statutes based on the Indiana Act, often in response to a takeover bid or a feared takeover bid for a major corporation located in the state. States that have already enacted such legislation include Arizona, Florida, Massachusetts, Minnesota, and North Carolina.[126] Some of the new statutes, such as those of Arizona, Massachusetts, and North Carolina, differ from the Indiana Act in that they apply to businesses incorporated in another state that maintain a substantial presence in the state that passed the legislation.[127] One such statute, passed in Oklahoma, has already been invalidated on its face and as applied to a target corporation that was incorporated in Delaware and of which less than 20 percent of the shares were owned by Oklahoma residents.[128] Applying *CTS* and *MITE*, the court held that the Oklahoma statute violated the commerce clause because it created an "impermissible risk of inconsistent regulation" and because "it imposes an indirect burden on interstate commerce that is excessive in relation to Oklahoma's interest in protection of resident shareholders and businesses."[129]

Delaware has enacted a third-generation statute[130] that prohibits any business combination between a 15 percent stockholder and a corporation for three years after the stockholder obtained the 15 percent holding unless:

- the board approved the business combination or stock acquisition before the stockholder acquired its stake;
- the stockholder had acquired an 85 percent stake at the same time it passed the 15 percent threshold; or
- the combination is approved by the board and by at least two-thirds of the voting stock owned by the other stockholders at an annual or special meeting.

The statute allows corporations to opt out of these provisions in the original articles of incorporation, by board action within ninety days of the effective date of the act, or by affirmative vote of a majority of stockholders.[131]

The Delaware act has twice survived supremacy and commerce clause challenges, with the District Court for Delaware concluding that statutes designed to protect shareholders may have the incidental effect of substantially deterring tender offers so long as a hostile offer that is beneficial to shareholders has a meaningful opportunity to succeed.[132]

Wisconsin's third-generation statute bars business combinations with covered corporations for three years unless the bidder obtains board approval before obtaining a 10 percent position.[133] A federal court enjoined operation of the statute on supremacy clause grounds without reaching the commerce clause.[134] The court reasoned that the Wisconsin statute was at odds with the Williams Act because it vested in directors the ability to prevent a takeover beneficial to stockholders. While the court did not mention the Delaware statute or the cases upholding it, one should note that, unlike the Delaware law, the Wisconsin statute provided no opportunity for shareholders to approve a merger despite opposition from directors.

Massachusetts has taken a slightly different approach, barring takeover attempts for one year unless the bidder disclosed its intent before acquiring a 5 percent position.[135] The First Circuit upheld a preliminary injunction barring enforcement of the act.[136] The court opined that the preacquisition disclosure requirement was likely preempted by the Williams Act requirement that acquisition of a 5 percent position need only be made within ten days after the acquisition.[137] Nevertheless, it limited its holding to striking down the one-year waiting period on dormant commerce clause grounds, concluding that even if the disclosure requirement were valid, the prohibition on a tender offer directly and substantially interfered with interstate commerce.[138]

Some states have placed maximum or minimum limits on the time for which a tender offer must be held open. These limits can interfere with the bidder's plans. Ohio's requirement that a tender offer must be held open for fifty days withstood a motion for a preliminary injunction on supremacy clause grounds, the court reasoning that the longer period did not conflict with Williams Act goals of investor protection.[139] On supremacy clause grounds, Nevada prohibits shareholders from tendering more than sixty days after an offer has been enjoined, at least when delays in state regulatory approvals would combine with the limit to make acquisition impossible.[140]

CTS has also increased interest in federal legislative proposals, with many experts advocating passage of a federal law to preempt states from adopting numerous inconsistent takeover statutes.[141] A potential amendment to S. 1323 that would have preempted state takeover laws caused that bill's sponsor to postpone consideration during the 100th Congress.[142]

Challenging the Target's Defensive Measures: Bounds of the Business Judgment Rule

The business judgment rule rests upon the principle that the management of a corporation is entrusted to its board of directors, which owes the corporation and its shareholders duties of care and loyalty.[143] The rule is designed "to protect and promote the full and free exercise of the managerial power granted . . . directors."[144] It creates a presumption that "in making a business decision, the directors acted on an informed basis, in good faith and in the honest belief that the action taken was in the best interests of the company."[145]

To overcome the business judgment rule, a party challenging board action must show either that the board's decision was uninformed[146] or that the board acted in its own self-interest or in bad faith.[147] The burden then shifts to the board to prove the substantial fairness and reasonableness of the transaction.[148]

In the context of contested takeovers, the business judgment rule historically granted directors wide latitude in devising and implementing defensive strategies.[149] The plaintiff bore the burden of showing bad faith, overreaching, self-dealing or fraud.[150] That the directors would retain control if the takeover defense were successful was not, in and of itself, enough to shift to them the burden of justifying their conduct.[151] Nor was it sufficient to show that "a" motive of the board was to stay in power.[152] Rather, the plaintiff had to demonstrate that the board's "sole or primary motive" was to retain control.[153] This was a burden few plaintiffs could meet.

However, in *Unocal Corp. v. Mesa Petroleum Co.*,[154] the Delaware Supreme Court modified the traditional analysis as applied to takeover defenses. Upholding a Unocal self-tender from which Mesa was excluded, the court declared, "Because of the omnipresent specter that a board may be acting primarily in its own interests, rather than those of the corporation and its shareholders, there is an enhanced duty which calls for judicial examination at the threshold before the protections of the business judgment rule may be conferred."[155] Due to the "inherent conflict" the board confronts in fending off unwanted bidders, the initial burden rests with the directors to show "that they had reasonable grounds for believing that a danger to corporate policy and effectiveness existed because of another person's stock ownership."[156] This burden is satisfied by proof that the board acted in good faith and upon reasonable investigation. Where, however, a complaint makes no factual allegations tending to show that the board's decision was made on an uninformed basis, the complaint may not withstand a motion to dismiss.[157] Additionally, the board must demonstrate that the defensive measure adopted is "reasonably related to the threats posed."[158] Significantly, the board need not rely exclusively upon proof of the likely impact the bidder's conduct would have on the corporation and its shareholders; the board may also demonstrate the likely impact on other constituencies, such as customers, employees, and creditors.

Delaware courts have invoked *Unocal* in scrutinizing poison pills[159] and lockup options and exchange offers.[160] Courts in other jurisdictions also appear to be moving toward stricter scrutiny of defensive measures.[161] In one interesting case, a court found that directors had breached their fiduciary duties during a tender offer by engaging in various defensive maneuvers designed not to obtain the best deal for shareholders but to "save and protect the company for management, at the best possible price for management."[162] The court enjoined the directors "from any further breaches of their fiduciary duties to [the company's] shareholders whatsoever, whether described herein or not."[163]

Recent case law suggests that the degree of protection accorded by the business judgment rule depends in part on the stage at which the board takes the challenged action. Defensive measures are more likely to be upheld when they are implemented before a specific takeover threat emerges.[164] Moreover, once a board of directors decides to sell the company, "[t]he whole question of defensive measures [becomes] moot. The directors' role change[s] from defenders of the corporate bastion to auctioneers charged with getting the best price for the stockholders."[165]

A particular defensive measure is also more likely to be deemed reasonable when it is approved by a board consisting of a majority of outside directors.[166]

In contrast to the increasing scrutiny with which courts are treating defensive measures, some state legislatures are expanding the protection afforded by the business judgment rule. Delaware, for instance, passed a statute allowing a corporation, by shareholder vote, to eliminate or limit director liability for monetary damages for breaches of fiduciary duties except in certain circumstances.[167]

The application of the business judgment rule to particular takeover defenses is examined in the following paragraphs.

Challenging the Target's Charter and Bylaw Amendments

Targets and prospective targets attempting to hamper hostile tender offers have increasingly resorted to special charter and bylaw amendments.[168] Some of the most popular of these "shark repellants" are staggered terms for board members, supermajority voting requirements for mergers and other business combinations, cumulative voting, and fair-price amendments.[169] Bidders often challenge the validity of these shark repellants, either by moving directly to invalidate them or by seeking to enjoin shareholder meetings at which they will be put to a vote.

Shark repellant clauses duly approved by shareholders are generally upheld.[170] Courts have been less inclined to uphold shark repellant clauses adopted by a target's board without shareholder approval.[171] Several courts have refused to enjoin shareholder meetings at which proposed shark repellants were to be voted upon.[172] However, courts have enjoined shark repellants adopted at shareholder meetings that were tainted by inadequate or deceptive proxy materials.[173]

In 1985, the SEC released a study by its Office of the Chief Economist of 649 antitakeover charter amendments adopted between 1979 and May 1985.[174] The study concluded that while antitakeover amendments such as supermajority vote provisions, "blank check" preferred stock, and classified boards generally depress the price of a company's securities, fair-price amendments appear to have very little effect on stock value.

The Investor Responsibility Research Center (IRRC) has concluded that antitakeover amendments are contrary to the best interests of shareholders.[175] Assessing the outcome of takeover battles conducted between 1974 and 1984, the IRRC found that shark repellants discourage takeover attempts and that shareholders in companies with antitakeover charter amendments receive premiums during takeovers that are no higher, and possibly are lower, than shareholders in companies without such provisions. The IRRC released a directory, entitled *Antitakeover Charter Amendments: A Directory of Major American Corporations*, which surveys the charters of 485 of Standard & Poor's 500 companies and reveals that 195 of these companies have antitakeover charter provisions. The vast majority of these measures were adopted for the first time or amended in 1983 or 1984. Eighty-five of the companies surveyed had adopted fair-price provisions, and 154 had classified boards of directors. In addition, 180 of the surveyed companies also had golden parachute arrangements.[176]

Heeding this advice, the Council of Institutional Investors was formed on January 24, 1985. Organized by the late California Treasurer Jessie Unruh, the council was established to enable institutional investors to take a more active role in corporate mergers and takeover battles.[177] The council has expressed its disapproval of greenmail[178] and unequal voting rights.[179]

Challenging the Target's Poison Pill

The "poison pill" has become one of the most popular and controversial defensive weapons in the target's arsenal. A 1987 study by the IRRC found that about 30 percent of the Fortune 500 companies have adopted this weapon.[180] The term "poison pill" has been used to describe a wide variety of antitakeover measures. Initially, the defense involved a dividend distribution to holders of a target's common stock of a new class of preferred stock with special redemption and conversion privileges or special voting rights. If a bidder acquired a specified percentage of the target's shares, holders of the preferred stock could redeem their shares for a specified amount of cash, often equal to the highest price per share paid by the bidder for its shares. In the event of a merger or other business combination, the preferred stockholder could convert his or her shares into common stock of the target or bidder.[181] Poison pills discourage nonnegotiated takeovers by creating large and unattractive corporate liabilities that would pass to the bidder along with control of the target. Where a corporation's charter has vested in the board discretion to fix the terms of new classes of preferred stock and the corporation has sufficient authorized and unissued shares available for the purpose, such poison pills are generally adopted by the corporation's board without shareholder approval.

In November 1985, when the Delaware Supreme Court upheld the legality of a poison pill in *Moran v. Household International, Inc.*,[182] approximately thirty-seven corporations had adopted variants of this defense. Approximately eight months later, in part due to *Moran*, the number had grown to at least 190.[183]

Poison pills are potent antitakeover devices, and some studies indicate that they tend to depress the price of a company's stock.[184] Shareholder lawsuits challenging poison pills have become common, and some institutional investors are demanding that pills already in place be redeemed or be put to shareholder vote.[185] To date, however, none of the shareholder votes that have occurred has resulted in the rejection of a poison pill. The SEC has called for public comment on the question of "whether there should be a governmental response to the proliferation of 'poison pill' plans."[186] Legal challenges to poison pills are likely to gain momentum as a result of the report released in late 1986 by the SEC's Office of the Chief Economist, which concludes that poison pills deter takeovers but decrease shareholder wealth.[187] Although the legality of poison pills is far from a settled issue, an increasing number of courts have demonstrated hostility to them.[188]

In *National Education Corp. v. Bell & Howell Co.*,[189] the court declined to enjoin a potential takeover target from issuing a dividend of "piggyback" preferred stock. The preferred stock had redemption and conversion privileges in the event a bidder acquired 40 percent or more of the target's shares, and an 80 percent approval vote of the preferred was necessary for a merger or other business combination. The court found that because the preferred stock would have independent trading value, it served a purpose other than entrenchment, "even though [entrenchment] may constitute an inevitable by-product to a degree."[190]

Evolution

Poison pill defenses continue to evolve and grow more complex. Currently in vogue is the shareholder rights plan, by which a target's shareholders receive a dividend distribution of long-term contingent rights to acquire additional securities upon the occurrence of certain "triggering events." When issued, the rights attach to and trade with the target's common stock, and may be redeemed by the target for minimal consideration. The rights often are triggered when an "acquiring person" either commences a tender offer for 30 percent of the target's stock or announces that it has already acquired 20 percent. Once triggered, the rights detach from the common stock and become freely transferable; rights certificates are issued, and the rights are redeemable, if at all, only under certain narrowly defined circumstances. The rights of the acquiring person, however, are not triggered; instead, they become null and void. The triggered rights may then be exercised to purchase additional securities of the target, usually shares of a new class of preferred stock. The exercise price, however, is an amount that purports to represent the long-term value of the company, rather than its current market price. Thus the rights ordinarily will be out of the money, that is, exercisable only at a price well in excess of the current market price, when initially issued.

What makes the rights valuable after a triggering event, and what makes them toxic to would-be bidders, are their "flip-in" and "flip-over" features. A flip-in rights plan entitles the rights holder to purchase, for the exercise price, shares of the target with a market value of twice that price. The flip-in provision is triggered if the target and the acquiring person merge or otherwise combine and the target is the surviving entity. A flip-over rights plan allows the rights holder to purchase shares of the acquiring company, again at a 50 percent discount, if the target either does not survive the merger or other business combination or sells most of its assets to the acquiror. Most poison pills have both flip-in and flip-over features.

Another type of poison pill is the "back-end" plan, under which a rights holder, after a triggering event, may exchange his or her stock and rights for a package of securities on favorable terms established in advance by the target's management.[191]

In response to increasing legal attacks and opposition to poison pills by institutional investors, a new version of the poison pill has recently been advocated that allows a bidder to propose a takeover directly to a shareholders' meeting. Such a proposal could only be made by a bidder who owns 1 percent or less of the target's stock and who provides an opinion of an investment banker that the bid is fair.[192] This new version of the pill has already been adopted by a number of corporations.[193]

Future decisions regarding adoption of, or challenges to, poison pill defenses may have to take into account a new statutory context. In addition to federal proposals discussed earlier in this chapter, several state statutes may affect poison pills. Ohio, for example, has enacted a statute allowing corporations to adopt shareholders' rights plans.[194]

Delaware Law

In *Moran v. Household International, Inc.*,[195] the Delaware Supreme Court invited the proliferation of poison pills by upholding the legality of a shareholder rights plan similar in many respects to the generic poison pill. The Household board did not adopt the rights plan "during a battle with a corporate raider, but as a preventive mechanism to ward off future advances."[196] One of two Household directors who voted against the rights plan was also the chairman of Household's largest stockholder. He sued Household and his fellow board members in the Delaware Court of Chancery, alleging that the plan was a sham security and ultra vires under Delaware law, deprived shareholders of their right to entertain tender offers, and was not a proper exercise of the board's business judgment. The court of chancery upheld the plan,[197] and the Delaware Supreme Court affirmed.[198]

The Delaware Supreme Court held that, in adopting the poison pill, the Household board acted within the scope of its authority under Delaware law.[199] The court rejected the plaintiff's argument that the board was powerless to enact the flip-over provision, agreeing with the defendants that the flip-over was akin to antidilution provisions, "which are customary features of a wide variety of corporate securities."[200]

After determining that Household's board had the legal authority to adopt the pill, the court upheld the directors' conduct under the business judgment rule, using the two-pronged inquiry outlined in *Unocal Corp. v. Mesa Petroleum Co.*[201] Regarding the first prong, a reasonable basis for perceiving danger to corporate policy and effectiveness, the court noted that a majority of the Household board consisted of outside, independent directors, and "there was no allegation that the Directors' action was taken for entrenchment purposes." The court found no evidence of gross negligence, noting that the board had been adequately advised by both its investment banker and outside legal counsel.[202] With respect to the second prong, reasonableness of the pill as a defensive measure, the court noted that the pill would not deter all takeovers, because offerors could still commence a tender offer conditioned upon redemption of the rights, acquire slightly less than the triggering percentage of Household's stock (20 percent), and then launch a proxy contest to remove the board and redeem the rights, or pursue other strategies to circumvent the poison pill.

Significantly, notwithstanding the state law focus of the case, the SEC filed an amicus curiae brief urging the Delaware Supreme Court to invalidate the rights plan.[203] The SEC argued that because the rights plan was an "unusually potent" defensive measure that effectively precluded all hostile bids for the company, it contravened federal policy favoring shareholder participation in the consideration of tender offers. The SEC also contended that because the plan was adopted without shareholder approval and forced bidders to deal exclusively with management, it usurped the rights of shareholders to control and manage the corporation. Neither of these arguments succeeded.

In *Revlon, Inc. v. MacAndrews & Forbes Holdings, Inc.*,[204] the Delaware Supreme Court approved a back-end rights plan adopted during a hostile takeover attempt. Under the plan, each Revlon shareholder received a contingent right to exchange one share of Revlon common stock for a one-year 12 percent note in the principal amount of $65. The rights would be triggered whenever an entity acquired 20 percent or more of Revlon's shares, unless the acquiror promptly purchased the remaining shares for at least $65 per share cash. The rights were redeemable at any time before a triggering event for $.10 each. Revlon's plan was adopted in response to a tender offer by Pantry Pride for any and all shares at $45 per share. Revlon's investment adviser had determined that the breakup value of the company was between $60 and $70 per share, and that the company could be sold intact for $50 per share.

The Delaware Supreme Court opined that the Revlon poison pill was a reasonable response to a threatened "bust-up" takeover and that the board had acted in good faith and upon reasonable investigation.[205] During the pendency of the case, however, Revlon announced that it would redeem the rights in connection with any proposal to purchase Revlon's shares for at least $57.25 cash per share. Because all the relevant bids exceeded that amount, the poison pill was no longer an impediment in the contest for Revlon, and the issue of the pill's legality was mooted.[206]

The Delaware Chancery Court has also upheld a corporation's use of a poison pill, coupled with the board's ability to redeem the rights under the pill, as a method to auction the company for the highest price.[207] This approval depended on the court's conclusion that the board was indeed using the poison pill in good faith and not merely to thwart a hostile takeover that would have been beneficial to shareholders.

Post-*Moran* Developments

Moran has been followed in several jurisdictions outside of Delaware.[208] Its rationale, however, tends to yield fact-specific results. The outcome in any individual case depends upon the quality of the board's investigation, the thoroughness of its deliberations, its apparent motivation, the seriousness of the perceived threat, and the reasonableness of its response.[209] In *Gelco Corp. v. Coniston Partners*,[210] the Eighth Circuit affirmed the denial of a preliminary injunction against a poison pill without discussing the substantive issues of the poison pill's legality. The court held that there was no showing of irreparable harm, because if the pill were later held unlawful, the bidder could recover the "difference between the cost of its purchase and the lost liquidation value."[211]

Holstein v. UAL Corp.[212] addressed some other issues raised by the use of poison pills as a defense mechanism. Holstein, a shareholder of UAL, sued UAL and its directors after UAL adopted a poison pill, alleging that the pill was a tender offer and that the corporation's failure to file disclosures violated section 13(e) and rule 13e-4. The court granted a motion to dismiss, holding that adoption of the poison pill did not constitute a tender offer. The court noted that the SEC has indicated that a "back-end" poison pill is a tender offer, but the court stated that even if this view is correct, the plan will not become a tender offer until the shareholder rights become exercisable. The court similarly held that there was no actionable "case or controversy" because a triggering event had not yet become imminent or occurred.

The Seventh Circuit has been openly hostile to the poison pill defense. In *Dynamics Corp. of America v. CTS Corp.*,[213] Judge Posner noted that "we are rather skeptical about the arguments for defensive measures . . . [and] are especially skeptical about the arguments used to defend poison pills." CTS had adopted a poison pill in response to an announcement by Dynamics that Dynamics intended to increase its holdings in CTS from 9.7 percent to 27.7 percent of CTS's outstanding shares by means of a tender offer, and then wage a proxy contest to oust the CTS board. The flip-in provision of CTS's rights plan granted CTS shareholders a nonredeemable right to acquire a package of CTS debt and equity securities at a fraction of its fair market value if a person or group acquired 15 percent or more of CTS's common stock. The flip-over feature of the pill provided that if CTS was acquired through a merger, business combination, or asset sale, CTS's shareholders would have the right to purchase, for $75, stock of the acquiring company with a market value of $150.

The district court granted a preliminary injunction, holding that while the pill was not per se illegal under Indiana law, Dynamics had a "better than negligible" chance of prevailing on its claim that CTS's directors acted with an improper purpose, namely, entrenchment.[214] The district court further found that Dynamics probably would succeed in proving that CTS's poison pill did not bear a reasonable relationship to the perceived threat of a coercive takeover.[215] The court observed that the CTS pill, unlike the one in *Household*, would deter all nonnegotiated takeovers, not merely coercive two-step acquisitions, the threat at which the pill supposedly was aimed. The court also noted that, unlike the Revlon pill, the CTS plan "did not set a price above which offers could be deemed fair."

On appeal, the Seventh Circuit, like the district court, focused on the failure of the CTS board and its investment adviser to determine whether Dynamics' tender offer price was fair.[216] Furthermore, the court rejected CTS's argument that its poison pill was reasonably designed to prevent a "squeeze-out" of minority shareholders, stating that such a pill would be triggered by a majority shareholder rather than CTS's 15 percent threshold, and that it would give minority shareholders the same price received by the majority rather than a higher price. The CTS plan was designed, in contrast, to kill off any tender and allow "management to take the shareholders hostage."[217]

With CTS's poison pill temporarily enjoined, Dynamics proceeded with its tender offer, increasing its ownership of CTS stock to 27.7 percent of the total. In the meantime, on the same day that the Seventh Circuit announced its decision, the CTS board adopted a "back-end" pill, recommended by a committee of outside directors, to limit Dynamics' holdings to under 28 percent. Under this second CTS poison pill, each shareholder would receive a contingent right to exchange his or her common stock for one-year 10 percent notes in the principal amount of $50. The rights would become exercisable if a person or group acquired 28 percent or more of CTS's common stock, and would be distributed five days after the triggering event. (The 28 percent shareholder, of course, would not receive any rights.) Distribution of the rights would be postponed if the bidder purchased its 28 percent ownership interest pursuant to an announced plan to acquire all outstanding shares for at least $50 cash. If the bidder completed its purchase of all CTS's common stock in the time allotted, 120 days, the rights would expire before being noncontingent. Before distribution or a negotiated sale of the company, the rights could be redeemed for $.05 per share.

After the second rights plan was adopted, Dynamics once again moved for a preliminary injunction. The district court denied the motion, holding that "while [Dynamics] has shown fair ground for litigation, its probability of success. . . is decidedly lower than was true in connection with the earlier rights plan, and. . . the balance of hardships does not weigh sufficiently in [its] favor to justify injunctive relief."[218] The court found that the decision to sell was made in good faith and upon reasonable investigation following Dynamics' acquisition of just short of 28 percent of CTS's stock.[219]

On appeal, the Seventh Circuit again questioned the need for a poison pill that would be activated by any acquisition of less than 50 percent of the target's shares, noting that the owner of any fractional interest less than 50 percent could not use this interest to block majority decisions.[220] The court also expressed skepticism regarding the $50 trigger price and the method by which it was determined:

> The trigger price, however, is highly relevant to the issues of reasonableness and good faith, since if set too high it will prevent all tender offers, not just those that are below the corporation's sale value. Since the entire premise of the second poison pill was that it was designed to facilitate the sale of the company, the pill cannot be upheld if the trigger price is an unreasonably high sale price.[221]

Rather than reverse the lower court's decision, however, the Seventh Circuit remanded the case for further fact-finding.[222]

The Seventh Circuit's decisions in the *CTS* litigation contain the most sweeping judicial criticism yet of the poison pill defense, and it should be carefully studied by any bidder intent on challenging a target's pill.[223]

Unlawful Discrimination

In addition to attacking the target's rights plan as a breach of fiduciary duty by the target's directors, bidders should consider whether the plan's disparate treatment of the acquiring person vis-à-vis other shareholders renders the plan ultra vires under applicable state corporation law. In *Amalgamated Sugar Co. v. NL Industries, Inc.*,[224] the district court preliminarily enjoined enforcement of NL Industries' (NLI's) poison pill on this basis. Under NLI's rights plan, the rights belonging to any entity that acquired 20 percent or more of NLI's common stock would be voided if NLI survived a subsequent merger or other business combination with the 20 percent shareholder. However, all other rights holders could avail themselves of the flip-in features of the plan and, for each right owned, pay $50 for $100 worth of NLI common. The district court held that the NLI rights plan subjected the acquiring person's equity and voting rights to "discriminatory dilution," which is forbidden under New Jersey law.[225]

Citing *Amalgamated Sugar* as "helpful authority," a federal district court in Wisconsin concluded that a rights plan similar to NLI's is very likely invalid under Wisconsin law.[226] However, the court declined to issue an injunction against implementation of the plan because the plaintiff had not demonstrated a danger of irreparable harm.

A New York court has enjoined operation of a target's poison flip-in provision that allowed all shareholders other than the bidder to purchase new shares of the target at half price if a bidder acquired more than 20 percent of the target.[227] The court concluded the flip-in provision was an impermissible discrimination between shareholders.

In the second Seventh Circuit opinion of *Dynamics Corp. of America v. CTS Corp.*, however, the Seventh Circuit rejected Dynamics' argument that CTS's second rights plan was ultra vires under Indiana law because the back-end benefits of the plan were unavailable to the 28 percent shareholder whose acquisitions would trigger the rights in the first place. Using Delaware precedent as a guide, the court distinguished discrimination between shares, which is prohibited, from discrimination between shareholders, which is not.[228] The Seventh Circuit noted:

> The case would be different if the poison pill singled out Dynamics, and stripped its shares of rights pertaining to other shareholders' shares. But the poison pill will strip rights from any shareholder who acquires 28 percent of the shares, and Dynamics is not the only shareholder who could do so.[229]

In a later case, the poison pill of a Minnesota corporation survived a challenge based, in part, on a provision of Minnesota corporate law that precludes discrimination within a particular class of stock. In *Gelco Corp. v. Coniston Partners*,[230] the court reasoned that because the Minnesota statute was based upon the Delaware General Corporation Law, Delaware precedents should control. Citing *Providence & Worcester Co. v. Baker*,[231] the same decision relied upon in the second opinion by the Seventh Circuit in the CTS case, the court observed that Delaware courts have permitted discriminatory voting rights within a single class of stock, and, on that basis, upheld the rights plan as a lawful exercise of the board's authority under Minnesota law.

Federal Constitutional Issues

Bidders also have attempted to mount federal constitutional challenges to poison pills, but these efforts appear doomed for lack of any "state action." In *Moran*, for example, the plaintiff argued that if the Delaware General Corporation Law were interpreted to allow a company to adopt a poison pill, the statute would violate the commerce clause and the supremacy clause. The Delaware Supreme Court rejected this argument, holding, "The fact that directors of a corporation act pursuant to a state statute provides an insufficient nexus to the state for there to be state action which may violate the Commerce Clause or the Supremacy Clause."[232] The same result was reached in the second Seventh Circuit opinion in the *CTS* case, where the Seventh Circuit characterized the constitutional argument as "frivolous" because "[t]he commerce clause does not require states to outlaw private contracts that may impede interstate commerce."[233]

Challenging the Target's Lockup Agreements: Sale of Key Assets

An asset lockup is an arrangement by which a target grants a friendly third party the option to acquire significant assets of the target, sometimes referred to as the target's "crown jewels," if a hostile bidder succeeds in obtaining control of the target or accumulates a specified percentage of the target's shares. (Another form of lockup is the stock lockup, by which a friendly suitor acquires an option to purchase newly issued shares of the target. Sales of stock and/or stock options to friendly third parties are discussed in the next part of this chapter.)

Analyzing sales of key assets under the business judgment rule, several courts have upheld the sales.[234] Two 1986 decisions, however, cast serious doubt upon the legality of using asset lockups to deter unwanted suitors.[235] In *Revlon, Inc. v. MacAndrews & Forbes Holdings, Inc.*, the Delaware Supreme Court upheld an injunction preventing Forstmann Little & Co. from exercising a lockup option to purchase certain assets of Revlon. Pantry Pride commenced the bidding for Revlon by announcing a hostile tender offer for any and all shares at $47.50 per share of common stock and $26.67 per share of preferred. The offer was conditioned upon Pantry Pride's obtaining financing and Revlon's redemption of a "back-end" poison pill. In response to Pantry Pride's tender offer, Revlon commenced an exchange offer for up to 10 million shares of common stock, each share to receive a senior subordinated note and a fractional share of a new class of preferred stock. The notes contained covenants restricting Revlon's assumption of new debt, disposition of assets and declaration of dividends. Revlon's exchange offer was oversubscribed, and the company accepted the full 10 million shares on a pro rata basis.

Pantry Pride responded with a new offer of $42 per share, conditioned upon the tender of at least 90 percent of the outstanding stock. This offer was considered equivalent to the prior offer. When Revlon rejected the offer, Pantry Pride increased its bid, first to $50 a share, then to $53. In the meantime, Revlon began negotiations for a leveraged buyout by Forstmann. Revlon and Forstmann reached an agreement whereby each shareholder would receive $56 per share cash, Revlon's management would have an ownership interest in the new company, Forstmann would assume the debt Revlon incurred in issuing senior notes as part of its exchange offer, and Revlon would redeem its poison pill and waive the note covenants.

Pantry Pride increased its offer to $56.25 per share cash, conditioned upon redemption of the pill, waiver of the note covenants, and election of three Pantry Pride directors to Revlon's board. Thereafter, Forstmann met privately with Revlon's investment banker and special counsel to work out a new proposal. Forstmann offered $57.25 per share cash, conditioned upon a lockup option to acquire two Revlon divisions, a "no-shop" provision prohibiting Revlon from negotiating with another potential bidder, redemption of the poison pill and waiver of the note covenants. The lockup option would be triggered if any other bidder acquired 40 percent of Revlon's common stock. The exercise price, $525 million, was approximately $100–$175 million below the market value of the two divisions as determined by Revlon's financial adviser. Finally, Revlon would have to escrow a $25 million "cancellation fee" to be paid to Forstmann if the agreement terminated or if another bidder acquired more than 19.9 percent of Revlon's stock. In return, Forstmann agreed to exchange new debt securities for the newly issued notes, which had suffered in the market.

Revlon's board unanimously approved the transaction with Forstmann. Pantry Pride, which had sued to enjoin enforcement of the poison pill, amended its complaint to include challenges to the lockup option, the cancellation fee, the no-shop provision, and the note covenants. The court of chancery enjoined the lockup, the no-shop and escrow provisions of Revlon's agreement with Forstmann.[236] The court held that Revlon's board had violated its duty to shareholders to seek the highest possible sale price for the company.[237] The directors were motivated, the court found, by concern for their own potential liability to the noteholders, who had threatened to sue if the company waived the restrictive covenants.

On appeal, the Delaware Supreme Court applied *Unocal* in examining each of the defensive measures adopted by Revlon's board. The court upheld the poison pill and the exchange offer, finding that they were reasonably designed to meet the perceived threat of a "bust-up" takeover by a "small, highly leveraged company" financed with "junk bonds."[238] The court then discussed the lockup option granted to Forstmann and the context in which it was approved. It noted that when Pantry Pride increased its offer to $53 per share, the inevitable breakup of the company was apparent. At that point, it became the directors' duty to obtain the best possible deal for the stockholders.[239]

Relying upon *Unocal*, the directors argued that they could properly consider constituencies other than shareholders in deciding the future of the company. Their focus on protecting the noteholders, they contended, demonstrated their good faith. The Delaware Supreme Court disagreed, holding that "such concern for nonstockholder interests is inappropriate when an auction among active bidders is in progress, and the object no longer is to protect or maintain that corporate enterprise but to sell it to the highest bidder."[240]

Significantly, however, the *Revlon* court explicitly rejected the suggestion that lockups are per se illegal under Delaware law. In doing so, the court reaffirmed the holding of *Thompson v. Enstar Corp.*[241] In *Enstar*, the court of chancery declined to enjoin a lockup option that Enstar had granted to Unimar, a friendly bidder, by which Unimar obtained voting control over Enstar Indonesia, a partnership in which Enstar was a partner and that was Enstar's most valuable asset. Enstar remained free to receive and accept tender offers other than Unimar's, but Unimar would retain control of Enstar Indonesia even if Unimar failed in its bid for Enstar. Acknowledging that lockups chill other potential bidders and therefore "must be given careful scrutiny," the court of chancery nevertheless found that the plaintiffs had failed to show a reasonable probability that the lockup was unfair to shareholders or that the directors acted unreasonably in adopting it.[242] The court noted that because the board had been unable to attract other offers, it was not unreasonable to accede to the demands and conditions of Unimar, the one bidder who did surface. Moreover, Unimar's offering price represented a substantial premium over Enstar's historical market value, and was within the range suggested by Enstar's investment adviser.

Although the court in *Enstar* refused to issue an injunction, it cautioned that "if the subsequent offers had been made sooner, a different result might be reached."[243] This was the basis upon which *Enstar* was distinguished from *Revlon:* Whereas the *Enstar* lockup drew a bidder into the contest for corporate control, Revlon's foreclosed further bidding and thereby disadvantaged shareholders.[244]

The *Revlon* court cited and discussed approvingly another case that is likely to inhibit the use of lockup options, *Hanson Trust PLC v. ML SCM Acquisition, Inc.*[245] In *Hanson*, a divided panel of the Second Circuit enjoined Merrill Lynch and related entities from exercising an asset purchase option obtained from SCM Corporation as part of a merger agreement between the parties. Hanson, the hostile bidder, announced a tender offer for any and all shares of SCM at $60 a share. Two weeks later, SCM and its white knight, Merrill Lynch, entered into an agreement by which Merrill Lynch would acquire SCM through a leveraged buyout. Under the terms of the agreement, Merrill Lynch would offer $70 a share for approximately 85 percent of SCM's outstanding common stock and, upon successful completion of the tender offer, purchase the remaining shares for junk bonds in a second-step merger. Some members of SCM's management were to participate in the buyout; they would ultimately own up to 15 percent of the new company. The agreement between Merrill and SCM was conditioned upon the tender of at least two-thirds of SCM's stock in response to Merrill's offer.

Hanson responded by increasing its all-cash bid to $72 a share, subject only to SCM's refraining from granting Merrill any lockups. Merrill then revised its leveraged buyout proposal. Under the revised deal, Merrill would offer $74 a share cash for up to 80 percent of SCM's shares, to be followed by a merger in which the remaining shareholders would receive junk bonds of supposedly equal value. Once again, SCM's management would have an equity interest in the new company. The proposal was conditioned upon the tender of at least two-thirds of SCM's outstanding shares and lockup options to purchase SCM's pigments and consumer foods businesses for a total of $430 million. The purchase option would be triggered if anyone other than Merrill acquired one-third or more of SCM's stock. When SCM's board approved the agreement, Hanson increased its bid to $75 a share, all cash, for any and all shares. This offer was conditioned only upon termination of the lockup.

After Hanson purchased enough shares to trigger the lockup, it brought suit, both as an SCM shareholder and as a competing offeror, to enjoin Merrill from exercising the option. Although the district court did not approve of the board's conduct, it denied Hanson's motion for a preliminary injunction, finding that Hanson had failed to show a breach of fiduciary duty.[246] The court noted that the lockup had been unanimously approved by SCM's independent directors, who acted in good faith in trying to secure for SCM stockholders the benefits of Merrill's offer of $74 per share. The court also noted that the directors justifiably relied on the advice of their investment advisers and legal counsel. The court rejected Hanson's argument that the exercise price of the lockup option was too low, noting the reluctance of courts to get involved in questions of valuation.[247]

On appeal, the Second Circuit reversed.[248] The court of appeals did not dispute the district court's finding that the independent directors acted without self-interest and in good faith, but determined nevertheless that they violated their duty of due care. The court noted that the directors failed to determine the range of fair value for the company or the two divisions that were subject to the lockup.[249] The court rejected the notion that the directors could satisfy their fiduciary obligations merely by relying on the opinions of their advisers, holding that such reliance is warranted only when the directors have become "reasonably familiar" with the opinion. The court also suggested that in approving an asset lockup, directors may have a "heightened duty of care."

Finding that Hanson had met its burden of showing a prima facie breach of the duty of care, the court then examined the evidence to determine whether Merrill and SCM had established the fairness of the transaction. The "critical issue," of course, was the value of the optioned assets, an issue the district court deliberately avoided. Without making a specific determination of value, the court of appeals concluded that the defendants had not offered "legally sufficient" evidence of fair value to overcome Hanson's showing.[250] The court dismissed the defendants' position that the lockup facilitated competitive bidding for SCM, finding instead that it operated to foreclose superior offers, just as it inhibited shareholder resistance to the SCM-Merrill merger. This the directors either knew or should have known.[251]

The *Hanson* and *Revlon* decisions are potentially far-reaching. At a minimum, they call into question the legality of any lockup that has the effect of foreclosing competitive bidding, and make clear that when a company is on the auction block, the board's obligation is to maximize shareholder wealth.[252] *Hanson*, moreover, demonstrates that courts will not permit directors to hide behind the advice of experts in justifying their own conduct.[253]

Under *Hanson* and *Revlon*, "no-shop" agreements, whereby a target agrees not to seek other bids, are also assailable. In *Revlon*, for example, the Delaware court stated that the no-shop provision of the Forstmann-Revlon lockup was "impermissible under the *Unocal* standards when a board's primary duty becomes that of an auctioneer responsible for selling the company to the highest bidder."[254] Similarly, the legality of "best-efforts" clauses (where the target's board agrees to use its best efforts to obtain shareholder approval of a merger agreement) may also be in doubt.[255] Earlier cases had upheld such clauses.[256] In short, any device that frustrates continued free bidding for a corporation's assets is suspect under *Revlon* and *Hanson*.

Challenging the Target's Lockup Agreements: Sale of Stock

The rationale of *Hanson* and *Revlon*, along with that of *Unocal*, suggests that large sales of stock by targets engaged in control contests will receive closer judicial scrutiny than they have in the recent past.[257] For a period, courts seemed more willing to generally permit management to sell newly issued stock to friendly parties in order to maintain control.[258] Those decisions stood in contrast to numerous earlier cases striking down stock sales in control contests.[259]

In *DMG, Inc. v. Aegis Corp.*,[260] the court denied a preliminary injunction in an action by an unsuccessful white knight seeking to enforce an option to buy a majority of the stock of one of the target's subsidiaries. Minstar, Inc. had commenced a tender offer for any and all shares of Aegis. As part of its defensive strategy, Aegis entered into an agreement and plan of merger with DMG at a higher price per share. Aegis also granted DMG an option for a period of one year to acquire 51 percent of the stock of Wellcraft Marine Corp., a wholly owned subsidiary of Aegis, if a third party acquired 40 percent or more of Aegis's stock before the merger. Minstar increased its tender offer price and acquired 77 percent of Aegis's stock. Minstar then installed its own nominees as directors of Aegis. The new board amended Wellcraft's certificate of incorporation to require a two-thirds vote of all outstanding shares for any action by Wellcraft that required shareholder approval. As one factor in support of its conclusion that DMG had failed to demonstrate a likelihood of success on the merits, the court noted that DMG paid nothing for the Wellcraft option. The court expressed "some doubt as to whether or not a valid consideration for the Wellcraft option actually exists."[261]

In contrast, where a lockup option and no-shop agreement are reached in the absence of a competing tender offer, they are likely to be upheld. In *Hastings-Murtagh v. Texas Air Corp.*,[262] the court refused to enjoin a special stockholders meeting at which a merger between Eastern Air Lines and Texas Air Corporation would be approved. The plaintiffs, who were shareholders, employees, and union leaders, contended that lockup and no-shop provisions of the merger agreement were invalid under Delaware law. The court noted that *Revlon* and *Enstar* did not make such provisions void per se; if used to encourage an offer rather than to preclude bidders in an active auction, they will be upheld. The plaintiffs argued that the board acted illegally in precluding a bid from the employees. The court rejected this position, noting a lack of "any legal authority that obligates a board of directors to jeopardize one bid in order to give a group of employees or anyone else an indefinite amount of time in which to develop and finance an acquisition proposal."[263]

Challenging Defensive Self-Tenders and Stock Repurchases

Self-tender offers are governed by rule 13e-4,[264] which requires the filing of a Schedule 13E-4 disclosure statement[265] with the SEC and the dissemination of certain information to shareholders at the time the offer is commenced. The information required to be disclosed is similar to the information required in Schedule 14D-1.[266] The language of rule

13e-4(b)(1)[267] mirrors the language of section 14(e), and bidders can invoke the rule to challenge the target's disclosures.

If the self-tender offer could result in the deregistration or delisting of the target's stock, the transaction also is subject to rule 13e-3,[268] which requires the filing of a Schedule 13E-3 disclosure statement[269] with the SEC and the dissemination to shareholders of certain information, including information regarding the fairness of the transaction. The language of rule 13e-3(b)[270] tracks the language of section 14(e). Section 13(e) creates an implied private cause of action for shareholders challenging improper disclosures under rule 13e-3.[271] Rule 13e-3 also regulates tender offers by affiliates of issuers.

Stock repurchases by a target that do not qualify as tender offers are nevertheless governed by rule 13e-1, which requires the disclosure of information concerning the number of shares to be acquired, the purpose of the repurchases, and the source and amount of funds used.[272]

Target companies may avoid the strictures of rule 13e-4 by repurchasing their stock other than through a tender offer. (However, the target must still make the necessary disclosures under rule 13e-1.) For example, in *SEC v. Carter Hawley Hale Stores, Inc.*,[273] the Ninth Circuit affirmed the district court's denial of the SEC's motion to preliminarily enjoin Carter Hawley Hale from purchasing additional shares pursuant to a stock repurchase program by which it had already accumulated 51 percent of its stock in seven days. Carter Hawley Hale embarked on the repurchase program to prevent a hostile takeover by The Limited. The court of appeals held that the district court did not abuse its discretion in concluding that under the eight-factor *Wellman* test described later in this chapter, Carter Hawley Hale's repurchase program did not constitute a tender offer subject to regulation under the federal securities laws.[274] The district court had reasoned that Carter Hawley Hale's repurchases satisfied only two prongs of the SEC's eight-factor test for identifying a tender offer—i.e., the repurchase program did pressure shareholders to sell and had been publicly announced. The SEC had urged the Ninth Circuit to forsake the *Wellman* test in favor of the more flexible two-factor test set forth in *S-G Securities, Inc. v. Fuqua Investment Co.*,[275] which stated that the tender offer requirement is satisfied by (1) a publicly announced intention by the purchaser to acquire a block of the target company for purposes of acquiring control thereof, and (2) a subsequent rapid acquisition by the purchaser of large blocks of stock through open-market and privately negotiated purchases. The Ninth Circuit declined the SEC's invitation, finding the standard enunciated in *S-G Securities* "vague."[276]

Similarly, in *Maynard Oil Co. v. Deltec Panamerica S.A.*,[277] the district court held that Maynard's well-publicized repurchase of 1.3 million shares in open-market and privately negotiated transactions in order to defeat a hostile tender offer did not constitute a self-tender. Applying the test set forth in *Kennecott Copper Corp. v. Curtiss-Wright Corp.*,[278] and reaffirmed in *Hanson Trust PLC v. SCM Corp.*,[279] the court noted that in its press release Maynard did not establish a particular price at which it would repurchase the stock and did not obligate itself to go forward with the repurchase program.[280] Accordingly, there was no tender offer.

Shareholders may be able to challenge self-tenders on several grounds. A self-tender may be enjoined where its terms or the surrounding circumstances make it coercive.[281] A corporation may also be liable where it makes false or misleading disclosures to shareholders in connection with a self-tender, thus depriving the offer of its voluntary character.[282]

Shareholders may also challenge self-tenders that are discriminatory. As a result of SEC rule making in 1986, self-tender offers are now subject to "all holders/best price" restrictions.[283] The new rules supersede two 1985 decisions that upheld discriminatory self-tenders. In *Unocal Corp. v. Mesa Petroleum Co.*,[284] Mesa commenced a tender offer for 64 million shares or 51 percent of Unocal's common stock at $54 a share, and announced its intention to consummate the acquisition through a back-end merger in which the remaining publicly held shares would be acquired for a package of securities also having an aggregate market value of $54 a share. Determined to oppose what it perceived to be an inadequate price for the company, the Unocal board decided to fight the Mesa plan by instituting a self-tender offer for 87.2 million shares of Unocal common stock not owned by Mesa in exchange for senior debt securities worth $72 per common share. Mesa first sought a preliminary injunction against the discriminatory offer in federal court.[285] The district court declined to issue an injunction, holding that the Williams Act is a disclosure statute and is not designed to regulate the substantive terms of tender offers.[286]

Mesa then turned for relief to the Delaware state courts. Mesa argued that the discriminatory offer violated the fiduciary duties Unocal owed Mesa as a stockholder because it enabled Unocal directors who were stockholders to derive a financial benefit not available to all other shareholders. The Delaware Supreme Court rejected this argument and reversed the lower court's issuance of an injunction. The court noted that Delaware law permits selective dealing with shareholders provided that the directors have not acted out of a sole or primary purpose of entrenchment.[287] The court found that the discriminatory exchange offer was a proper response to what the board believed was a grossly inadequate offer coupled with the threat of greenmail:

> The only difference is that heretofore the approved transaction was the payment of "greenmail" to a raider or dissident posing

> a threat to the corporate enterprise. All other stockholders were denied such favored treatment, and given Mesa's past history of greenmail, its claims here are rather ironic. . . . Thus, while the exchange offer is a form of selective treatment, given the nature of the threat posed here the response is neither unlawful nor unreasonable. If the board of directors is disinterested, has acted in good faith and with due care, its decision in the absence of an abuse of discretion will be upheld as a proper exercise of business judgment.[288]

In response to *Unocal*, which it interpreted as a violation of the fundamental tenet that all shareholders be treated equally in a tender offer, the SEC adopted an "all holders/best price" rule on July 8, 1986.[289] Under amendments to SEC Rule 13e-4, issuer tender offers must be open to all security holders of the class of securities subject to the tender offer, and the consideration paid to any security holder pursuant to the tender offer must be the highest consideration paid to any other security holder.[290] (The same restrictions apply to third-party tender offers under rule 14d-10.[291]) Thus, the Delaware Supreme Court's decision in *Unocal* has effectively been overturned by rule, at least in the case of offers for shares registered under the Securities Exchange Act of 1934.

In recent years, recapitalizations and restructurings have become increasingly popular as a way to deter hostile takeovers and simultaneously provide immediate value to shareholders.[292] Like other defensive measures, a target's decision either to make a self-tender or to repurchase its securities in the open market or in negotiated transactions has generally been protected by the business judgment rule.[293]

However, with the evolution of a more exacting standard of review of measures designed to forestall changes of control, signaled chiefly by *Unocal*, *Hanson* and *Revlon*, courts are likely to be more willing to interfere with a target's defensive acquisition of its own shares. In 1986, the Delaware Court of Chancery enjoined a proposed recapitalization by which Anderson, Clayton would self-tender for 65 percent of its outstanding stock and sell 25 percent of its remaining outstanding shares to a newly formed ESOP.[294] The court found that the recapitalization was intended to provide shareholders with an alternative to a tender offer by a group led by Bear, Stearns for any and all shares for $56 per share. Because the transaction was not "reasonable in relation to the threat posed," however, it failed the second prong of the *Unocal* test. The court noted that stockholders tendering into the Bear, Stearns offer had no assurance that their shares would be accepted for payment, because that offer was conditioned upon the tender of a specified minimum number of shares and the abandonment of the recapitalization plan. Those shareholders would thereby preclude themselves from participating in the cash-heavy front end of the recapitalization and risk a substantial decline in the market price of their shares. Under these circumstances, the Anderson, Clayton offer was coercive:

> [A]n Anderson, Clayton stockholder, acting with economic rationality, has no effective choice as between the contending offers as presently constituted. Even if a shareholder would prefer to sell all of his or her holdings at $56 per share in the [Bear, Stearns] offer, he or she may not risk tendering into that proposal and thereby risk being frozen out of the front end of the [Anderson, Clayton offer], should the [Bear, Stearns offer] not close.[295]

The court noted that although Bear, Stearns could cure the coercive aspect of the Anderson, Clayton offer simply by lifting the conditions on its own proposal, Bear, Stearns "has no legal duty to extend an unconditional offer whereas the [Anderson, Clayton] Board does have a legal duty to its shareholders to exercise its judgment to promote the stockholders' interests."[296] The court concluded that the Anderson, Clayton proposal failed to create a viable alternative for shareholders, was unreasonable in relation to the threat posed, and therefore did not qualify for protection under the business judgment rule. The burden therefore shifted to the target's board to prove the intrinsic fairness of "all aspects of the transaction."[297] Because the board failed to meet this burden, the bidder succeeded in proving a likelihood of success on the merits. Accordingly, the court enjoined Anderson, Clayton from proceeding with its recapitalization until the Bear, Stearns offer had closed.[298]

In *Gelco Corp. v. Coniston Partners*,[299] the court distinguished *Anderson, Clayton* and denied the bidder's request to enjoin the target's exchange offer. The court noted that unlike the situation in *Anderson, Clayton*, Gelco's investment adviser and board had found the offer by Coniston Partners inadequate. (Significantly, the competing offer by Coniston Partners was several dollars per share higher than the "blended value" of the exchange offer.[300]) Moreover, the Gelco exchange offer was part of a restructuring plan adopted nearly one month before the initial offer by Coniston Partners, whereas Anderson, Clayton's offer "had no underlying business purpose other than to react to the hostile offer."[301]

Recapitalization plans do not always succeed in fending off takeover bids. On May 26, 1987, LA Partners, which had proposed that Allegis Corp. sell its recently purchased subsidiaries, Westin Hotel Co., The Hertz Corp., and Hilton International Co., announced its intention to seek shareholder consents to replace a majority of the directors of Allegis. Allegis responded two days later by announcing a recapitalization pursuant to which shareholders would receive a one-time cash dividend of $60 per share while retaining their Allegis shares. Under this plan, the company would add approximately $3 billion of debt. LA Partners unexpectedly announced that it would continue with its planned consent solicitation despite the recapitalization plan. The airline pilots union also proposed its own restructuring plan, and it became apparent to Allegis's directors that its announced recapitalization was not sufficient to prevent a change in control of the board. On June 9, 1987, Allegis announced that it would abandon its "total travel" strategy and sell Westin, Hertz, and Hilton.

Challenging Other Defensive Moves

Use of Employee Benefit Plans

Targets frequently attempt to use employee stock ownership plans (ESOPs) as defensive weapons in takeover battles. Issuing large blocks of stock to an ESOP complicates the bidder's task, since a substantial percentage of the target's stock can be made inaccessible to the bidder. In one case, a federal district court held that the management of a target corporation was justified in establishing an ESOP just before the announcement of a hostile tender offer.[302] The court found that while the burden of proof was on management to justify the fairness of its decision, CPT's management had met that burden.[303]

Two important decisions by the Second Circuit restrict a target company's ability to create and manipulate an employee benefit plan to thwart a hostile takeover. In *Norlin Corp. v. Rooney, Pace, Inc.*,[304] the court prohibited target directors from voting target stock that it had transferred to a newly created ESOP. In so holding, the court reasoned, "When an ESOP is set up in the context of a contest for control,. . . it devolves upon the board [of directors] to show that the plan was in fact entered into to benefit the employees, and not simply to further the aim of managerial entrenchment."[305]

In *Donovan v. Bierwirth*,[306] the Second Circuit condemned the decision by the trustees of a target's pension plan, who were also directors of the target, to use pension plan assets to purchase target stock at a premium in order to defeat a hostile tender offer. Judge Friendly indicated that the only correct course for the trustees would have been to resign their positions as trustees and turn over control of the pension plan to independent trustees for the duration of the offer.[307] In a subsequent opinion, *Donovan v. Bierwirth*,[308] the Second Circuit held that the loss sustained by the beneficiaries by virtue of the trustee's breach of fiduciary duty was to be measured as the difference, if any, between what the ESOP actually earned through the impermissible purchase of target stock and what the plan would have earned had the funds been available for other plan purposes.[309] This difference was to be measured at a reasonable date between the date the suit was filed and the date judgment was entered.[310]

In several tender offer cases, however, targets have employed a technique that may permit target management to exploit the voting power of target stock held by employee benefit plans. The targets simply amended the benefit plans to require that all decisions to tender be made by the employee beneficiaries themselves. In the Bendix–Martin Marietta tender offer, 23 percent of Bendix's stock was held by Bendix's employee benefit plan. The independent trustee of that plan tendered the shares to Martin Marietta. Bendix then amended the plan to permit the employees themselves to decide whether to tender their shares held by the plan. The district court entered a temporary restraining order preventing the trustee from withdrawing any of the tendered shares unless the trustee was specifically ordered to do so by the employee beneficiaries.[311] By the time of the withdrawal deadline, however, employees owning over 4 million of the approximately 4.6 million shares held by the plan ordered the trustee to withdraw their shares.[312]

In the Burlington Northern–El Paso Company tender offer, 8 percent of El Paso's stock was held by two employee benefit plans. Two days after Burlington commenced its tender offer, El Paso amended the plans to provide that the employee beneficiaries were to decide whether to tender shares owned by them. The district court, in an oral opinion, refused to restrain El Paso from implementing the amendments. Within one week, over 90 percent of all plan members had signed forms indicating their desire to tender or not to tender.[313]

Similarly, in *Moran v. Household International, Inc.*,[314] the court upheld the adoption of amendments to Household's ESOP which provided that in the event of a tender or exchange offer the right to tender or exchange would pass through from the ESOP trustee to the individual beneficiaries, and no ESOP shares could be tendered or exchanged without specific instructions from the ESOP beneficiaries. Finding that the board of directors' principal purpose in adopting these amendments was not to retain control, the court held that the board's decision was protected by the business judgment rule.[315]

The United States Department of Labor has taken an active role in some tender offers to ensure that violations of ERISA have not taken place.[316]

Golden Parachutes

Golden parachutes have not been a central weapon in takeover battles, because the fates of tender offers seldom turn on their existence or terms. Thus, few courts have definitively ruled on the validity of golden-parachute agreements for target management. Two decisions, however, have created a procedural paradox for the shareholder who wishes to challenge the agreements. In the first of these cases, *Mills v. Esmark, Inc.*,[317] the court declined to rule on the validity of contracts granted by Esmark guaranteeing the compensation of key officers for up to three years if those officers lost their positions as a result of a hostile takeover of Esmark. The court dismissed the shareholder's complaint because the contract rights were not yet exercisable: "Whether any future merger or acquisition would result in a waste or gift of corporate assets because of these purported agreements is not a matter ripe for consideration here."[318]

In the second case, two months after the *Mills* decision, the Delaware Supreme Court affirmed a court of chancery decision declining to address the merits of a dissident Conoco shareholder's challenge to the validity of nine golden parachutes amounting to $10 million granted before the takeover of Conoco by duPont.[319] The court held that once the merger had taken place, the plaintiff lost his status as a Conoco shareholder and hence his standing to sue.[320]

These cases illustrate the reluctance of courts to become involved with disputes involving compensation to corporate managers.[321] Even where a court does reach the merits, the decision to adopt golden parachutes may be protected by the business judgment rule.[322] Restrictions on the use of golden parachutes are, therefore, more likely to arise through legislation or rule rather than by judicial decree. At least two states—Minnesota and Arizona—have enacted legislation prohibiting adoption of golden parachutes during tender offers.[323] Some of the bills introduced during the 100th Congress have had similar provisions.

Nonetheless, a California court granted an order temporarily blocking initial payments to twenty-five executives of the Signal Cos., Inc. following a friendly merger with Allied Corp.[324] This decision came on the heels of another recent decision which rejected a golden parachute plan as an unlawful entrenchment of management not protected by the business judgment rule.[325]

Restrictions on the use of golden parachutes by corporations were imposed by the Tax Reform Act of 1984.[326] Section 67 of the act provides that a corporation cannot deduct any payment to an officer, shareholder, or highly compensated individual where such payment is contingent on a change in the ownership or effective control of the corporation and the aggregate present value of such payment is more than three times the average annual compensation of the employee for the most recent five years or portion thereof that he or she was an employee of the corporation. Any payment pursuant to an agreement entered into or amended within one year of a change in control is presumed to be contingent on such change in control, unless the contrary is established by clear and convincing evidence. Section 67 of the act further provides that any person who receives an excess parachute payment must pay a nondeductible excise tax equal to 20 percent of such payment. These provisions apply to payments under agreements entered into or renewed after June 14, 1984, and any amendment to a contract entered into before June 15, 1984, is treated as a new contract if it is made after June 14, 1984, and if it amends that contract in any significant relevant aspect.[327] In spite of these restrictions, however, nearly 40 percent of the Fortune 500 companies have awarded golden parachutes to top executives.[328]

Greenmail

Greenmail is the premium that a corporation pays to purchase its own stock held by an individual or group that threatens to launch a tender offer or interfere with the operations of the corporation unless its stock is purchased. Shareholder challenges to greenmail payments have become common but courts have upheld the ability of a corporation to repurchase its own shares at a premium from a hostile or dissident shareholder.[329] For example, in *Pin v. Texaco, Inc.*,[330] the court found that a shareholder failed to state a claim under sections 10(b) and 13(e) in alleging "manipulation" through a greenmail scheme. The court held that the federal securities laws were not implicated because no misrepresentation or nondisclosure had been alleged. In *Polk v. Good*,[331] the Delaware Court of Chancery found that a corporation's greenmail payments were protected by the business judgment rule, "provided the transaction is free from fraud or unfairness."[332] So long as the purpose of the repurchase is not to perpetuate the directors' control of the firm and there is a legitimate threat to the corporate enterprise, the board's decision will be sustained.[333] Of course, when misrepresentations are alleged and the objecting stockholders claim fraud or unfairness or that the directors' goal was to maintain control, stockholder will be able to state a claim for damages or rescission of the greenmail payments.[334]

However, in *Heckmann v. Ahmanson*,[335] the California Court of Appeals upheld a lower court's issuance of a preliminary injunction enjoining a greenmailer from disposing of the profit from the sale of the target's stock. In upholding the injunction, the court found that the plaintiffs had demonstrated a reasonable probability of success on the merits of their claim that company directors and the offeror had breached their fiduciary duties in connection with the greenmail transaction. Noting that the target's directors failed to show that the transaction was entered into in good faith, the court found that such an injunction was proper because if the directors had in fact breached their fiduciary duties, the offeror could be held liable as an aider and abettor.[336]

Heckmann was cited with approval in another recent greenmail case, *Samuel M. Feinberg Testamentary Trust v. Carter*.[337] In *Carter*, a shareholder filed a derivative suit challenging the repurchase by Goodrich of 1 million shares of Goodrich stock from Carl Icahn for $41 million. On the defendants' motions to dismiss, the court held that the plaintiff stated a claim against the Goodrich directors for breach of fiduciary duty and against Icahn for aiding and abetting the directors' breach of fiduciary duty. The court emphasized that the only justification for the payment was prevention of a takeover and that the only beneficiaries were the Goodrich directors and Icahn, not the shareholders.[338]

In 1984, the SEC released a study by its Office of the Chief Economist of eighty-nine instances in which targets repurchased stock. The study concluded that targets that submit to greenmail harm their shareholders because the stock repurchases cause sharp drops in the value of the target's stock.[339]

At least two states have adopted statutes that prohibit greenmail payments unless the payments are approved by shareholders or are offered to all shareholders.[340] Some of the bills introduced in the 100th Congress include similar provisions.

Standstill Agreements

A standstill agreement is an agreement between a target and a substantial shareholder that the target views as a potential tender offeror. In such an arrangement, the shareholder agrees to acquire no more than a fixed percentage of shares in the target in exchange for the target's promise not to oppose the shareholder's stock acquisitions up to that fixed percentage. Such agreements have received mixed reviews from commentators.[341]

In *Enterra Corp. v. SGS Associates*,[342] the court rejected an argument that target management breached its fiduciary duty to the corporation and its shareholders by entering into a standstill agreement because the agreement conflicted with the board's duty to convey to the shareholders all offers to purchase stock in the corporation. Labeling a standstill agreement as essentially a "corporate peace treaty," the court held that target management's decision to enter into such an agreement was protected by the business judgment rule.[343] While retention of control was arguably a motive for entering into the agreement, the court found that the agreement was entered into primarily for a valid business purpose—"to 'create a stable, certain, and cooperative relationship between management and a substantial shareholder.' "[344] In upholding the standstill agreement, the court also noted that target management had promptly informed its shareholders of the existence and substance of the agreement.[345]

In *Ivanhoe Partners v. Newmont Mining Corp.*,[346] the Delaware Supreme Court affirmed the denial of a preliminary injunction sought by a bidder against a target that entered into a standstill agreement with its largest shareholder. To block Ivanhoe's takeover attempt, Newmont had entered into a standstill agreement with its shareholder, Gold Fields, under which Gold Fields agreed to own no more than 49.9 percent of Newmont's stock and to limit its representation on the board of directors to 40 percent of the directors. Along with the declaration of a large cash dividend and a "street sweep" by Gold Fields, in which it increased its share ownership from 26 percent to 49.7 percent, the agreement defeated Ivanhoe's takeover attempt. The court rejected Ivanhoe's request for a preliminary injunction, holding that Newmont's defensive measures were reasonable in relation to the threat posed by Ivanhoe and that they were protected by the business judgment rule.

Use of Special Voting Rights

A target's ability to manipulate voting rights through the issuance of "vote dividends" depends in part upon the law of the target's state of incorporation as well as the target's corporate charter. Two significant decisions, interpreting New Jersey and Delaware law, respectively, illustrate the bases upon which a bidder may attack the target's dilution of the bidder's voting rights.

In *Asarco, Inc. v. MRH Holmes à Court*,[347] Asarco attempted to foil an unfriendly takeover by declaring a stock dividend pursuant to which all common shareholders would receive a distribution of a new series of so-called "blank check" preferred stock. Initially, the preferred had no voting rights. However, if a person or group acquired more than 20 percent of either Asarco's common stock or its new preferred stock, each $\frac{1}{10}$ of a preferred share owned by everyone other than the 20 percent shareholder would have five votes in all matters submitted to the vote of the common shareholders. The preferred owned by the 20 percent shareholder would continue to have no voting rights. The district court found that the plaintiff had failed to demonstrate a likelihood of being able to overcome the protections afforded the target's directors under the business judgment rule,[348] but nevertheless enjoined the dividend on the ground it was ultra vires under New Jersey law.[349] The dividend was unlawful, the court held, because it altered voting rights discriminatorily within a class of stock. The court noted that "equality of voting power among shareholders of the same class, or at least among the same series of a class that has more than one series, is a basic concept in corporate law."[350]

Similarly, in *Unilever Acquisition Corp. v. Richardson-Vicks, Inc.*,[351] the district court enjoined a dividend of preferred stock which, if transferred, would have diminished voting rights for a period of three years. The preferred was to be distributed at the rate of one preferred share for each five common shares. Each share of preferred entitled the holder to cast twenty-five votes on all issues on which the common could vote. In the hands of a transferee, however, the preferred shares had only five votes during the first thirty-six months after transfer. The district court held that the proposed dividend distribution was illegal under Delaware law because it discriminated among shares within a series and because it constituted a restriction on the alienability of voting rights. The target argued that under Delaware law and its own certificate of incorporation, its board was empowered to issue new shares not specifically provided for in the certificate of incorporation merely by filing the necessary certificate with the Delaware Secretary of State.[352]

The district court rejected the target's argument, finding that another provision of the target's certificate of incorporation specifically disallowed discrimination among shares within a single series. The court added, "Under Delaware law, a change in corporate structure of this magnitude, reducing the transferability of a shareholder's ability to vote and the value of his or her asset to this degree, requires stockholder approval which has not been obtained."[353]

Another example of such an action creating special classes of stock is Rockwell International's February 1987 declaration of a stock dividend of one share of Class A common stock for each share of Rockwell common stock. Each Class A share entitles its holder to ten votes, but it may only be transferred to a limited group of purchasers. The Class A shares are convertible to common stock, however, which is then freely transferable. The ultimate effect of this arrangement is gradually to increase the relative voting power of long-term shareholders. A shareholder's challenge to this type of stock reclassification plan was rejected in *Hahn v. Carter-Wallace, Inc.*[354] The court refused to enjoin a plan in which a new class of common stock was to be issued on a share-for-share basis to current holders of common stock. The new shares would have ten votes per share, but most transfers of these shares other than to members of the family that controlled the corporation would convert the new shares into shares of the original class. Applying the business judgment rule, the court found that the plaintiff demonstrated neither a reasonable probability of success on the merits nor the existence of irreparable harm.

Both the *Asarco* and the *Unilever* courts distinguished *Providence & Worcester Co. v. Baker*,[355] in which the Delaware Supreme Court held that a corporation could restrict large shareholders to fewer votes per share than small stockholders, where the corporation's original charter specifically permitted the disparate treatment. In *Asarco*, the district court was unpersuaded by the rationale of *Baker*, but noted that in any event, the Asarco board amended its certificate of incorporation long after the common stock had issued. The *Unilever* court also noted that the board's conduct "strip[ped] the shareholder of the ability to transfer voting rights without prior warning."[356] Thus, although *Baker* remains good law,[357] it does not necessarily foreclose challenges to blank check preferred stock.[358]

In 1984, the New York Stock Exchange (NYSE) suspended its listing standard embodying the "one share, one vote" policy, which prohibits NYSE-listed companies from creating a class of stock with unusual voting provisions that would nullify or restrict voting or voting power disproportionate to the equity interest of the class.[359] In 1986, the NYSE filed a proposed rule change that would allow listed companies to offer equity securities with unequal voting rights.[360] In June 1987, after giving the exchange more than a year to agree on a uniform standard for voting rights, the SEC proposed rule 19c-4, which would require listed domestic corporations to adhere to certain minimum requirements for voting rights.[361]

On July 7, 1988, the SEC issued rule 19c-4[362] prohibiting the listing of securities of an issuer where the issuer has created a class of security or taken any other action with the effect of restricting the voting rights of holders of outstanding shares. Preexisting plans are grandfathered. Some members of Congress challenge the SEC's authority to issue the rule and promise legislation to override it.[363]

Counteroffers for the Bidder

Traditionally, the business judgment rule insulated decisions involving defensive moves, including launching a counteroffer for the bidder. However, some courts have suggested that targets can go too far. Indeed, in the Bendix–Martin Marietta struggle, two courts reached different conclusions on this issue. In *Martin Marietta Corp. v. Bendix Corp.*,[364] the court refused to enjoin Martin Marietta's counteroffer for Bendix, even though financing the counteroffer would harm Martin Marietta's financial condition severely. The court held that Martin Marietta's "board reasonably believes that its offer is in the best interest of. . . Marietta's remaining shareholders."[365] The court also was not persuaded by the fact that at the time the transaction was to occur, Bendix would be Martin Marietta's majority shareholder. The court refused to find that Martin Marietta would owe a fiduciary duty to Bendix. However, in *Martin Marietta Corp. v. Bendix Corp.*,[366] the Delaware Supreme Court denied Martin Marietta's motion to enjoin Bendix's special shareholder meeting, observing that Martin Marietta would breach a fiduciary duty to Bendix as a shareholder.

RICO

The applicability of the Racketeer Influenced and Corrupt Organizations Act (RICO)[367] to control contests is discussed later in this chapter.

Remedies for Violations by the Target

As the cases discussed so far indicate, a bidder's most promising claim against a target is for misleading statements by the management. Remedies for target misstatements range from corrective disclosure to injunctions against future violations.[368] In addition, some bidders have obtained injunctions against shark repellant bylaws and against certain other defensive maneuvers, such as the issuance and sale of new stock.

Representing the Target: Strategies for Defense

Increasingly, courts are deciding challenges to specific actions and practices in takeover battles by looking to the purpose of the Williams Act—to guarantee that shareholders receive full information about tender offers.[369] Since the act was not intended either to promote or to inhibit tender offers, courts are loath to allow its requirements to be shaped into tools favoring either side in a takeover contest. Nonetheless, the Williams Act has been used to challenge nondisclosures by the bidder before, during, and after a tender offer.

Challenging the Bidder's Open-Market and Privately Negotiated Stock Purchases

Two parts of the Williams Act may apply to a bidder's conduct outside a formal tender offer. If the bidder owns more than 5 percent of the target's stock, it must obey the disclosure requirements of section 13(d), and its disclosures may be challenged. The bidder's disclosures may also be challenged under section 14(d) if its stock purchases constitute a de facto tender offer.

Before a tender offer is announced, a prospective bidder may accumulate up to 5 percent of a target's stock through open-market or privately arranged purchases before subjecting itself to section 13(d). Once the bidder or a group of which it is a member acquires more than 5 percent of an issuer's stock, however, the bidder or the group must file a Schedule 13D disclosure statement with the SEC within ten days. (This ten-day period would have been reduced to five days under S. 1323.) Thereafter, the Schedule 13D must be amended when any change occurs that makes the previous disclosure inaccurate or inadequate.[370] A target can sue a person or group that has acquired 5 percent of its shares for failure to properly file or amend a Schedule 13D.[371] Targets also can claim that two or more people accumulating target shares are a "group" for purposes of section 13(d) and therefore must file a disclosure statement.[372] More typically, targets allege that the Schedules 13D filed by potential bidders are false and misleading, particularly concerning the potential bidders' intent to seek control.[373]

In addition to challenges brought under section 13(d), targets have alleged that prebid purchases of its stock are actually tender offers conducted in violation of section 14(d). The term "tender offer" is not defined in the federal securities laws. Absent egregious facts (usually showing the exertion of direct pressure on shareholders), courts generally have refused to deem these prebid purchases tender offers and have refused to integrate these purchases with subsequent formal tender offers.[374]

Some courts have defined "tender offer" according to an eight-factor test proposed by the SEC.[375] Under this test, the court looks for the following characteristics:

1. Active and widespread solicitation of public shareholders for the shares of an issuer
2. Solicitation made for a substantial percentage of the issuer's stock
3. Offer to purchase made at a premium over the prevailing market price
4. Terms of the offer firm rather than negotiable
5. Offer contingent on the tender of a fixed number of shares, often subject to a fixed maximum number to be purchased
6. Offer open only for a limited period of time
7. Offerees subjected to pressure to sell their stock
8. Public announcements of a purchasing program concerning the target company precede or accompany rapid accumulation of a large amount of the target company's securities.[376]

Others have chosen a more flexible approach, focusing on Congress's intent to guarantee that shareholders be fully informed of all information pertinent to their decision whether to tender their shares or not.

Judicial reluctance to label prebid purchases "tender offers" also extends to postbid purchases,[377] although adoption of new legislation or rules could limit purchases made after termination of a tender offer. In *Hanson Trust PLC v. SCM Corp.*,[378] the Second Circuit rejected a target's claim that stock purchases by a bidder after the termination of the bidder's tender offer were a de facto tender offer and violated section 14(d). In that case, Hanson and two affiliated companies made a cash tender offer of $60 per share for all of SCM's outstanding shares. In response to this tender offer, a group consisting of certain SCM managers and Merrill Lynch Capital Markets proposed a leveraged buyout of SCM at $70 per share. Hanson countered this proposal by increasing its cash offer to $72 per share. The SCM–Merrill Lynch group then raised its leveraged buyout proposal to $74 per share and was granted a "crown jewel" lockup option giving Merrill Lynch the right to purchase SCM's two most profitable businesses if any other party acquired more than 66⅔ percent of SCM's outstanding shares. Hanson responded by terminating its cash tender offer and then purchasing 3.1 million, or 25 percent, of SCM's shares on a single day through one open-market and five private purchases. SCM argued that Hanson's purchases immediately following the termination of its tender offer amounted to a de facto continuation of the tender offer and violated section 14(d). The district court issued a preliminary injunction barring Hanson from acquiring any additional SCM shares and from exercising any voting rights with respect to the SCM shares it had purchased.

On appeal, the Second Circuit reversed. The court rejected the application of the *Wellman* eight-factor test, preferring to look at the purpose of section 14(d): "[S]ince the purpose of § 14(d) is to protect the ill-informed solicitee, the question of whether a solicitation constitutes a 'tender offer' within the meaning of § 14(d) turns on whether, viewing the transaction in the light of the totality of the circumstances, there appears to be a likelihood that unless the preacquisition filing strictures of the statute are followed there will be a substantial risk that solicitees will lack information needed to make a carefully considered appraisal of the proposal put before them."[379] In evaluating the totality of the circumstances, the court considered a number of the *Wellman* factors and found them lacking. The court also emphasized, "At least five of the sellers were highly sophisticated professionals, knowledgeable in the market place and well aware of the essential facts needed to exercise their professional skills and to appraise Hanson's offer."[380] The court found no added significance in the fact that Hanson's purchases followed almost immediately the termination of its tender offer and noted that Hanson had already filed with the SEC and made public substantially the same information that SCM contended should have been filed before Hanson made the postbid purchases.

A bidder's liability for pre–tender offer actions may encompass its sales as well as its purchases of the target's stock. In *SEC v. ZICO Investment Holdings, Inc.*,[381] the SEC has charged a bidder, its principal shareholder and his associates, and another company with attempting to drive down the target's price in anticipation of launching a tender offer. The defendants allegedly sold large quantities of the target's stock on the open market before the commencement of the tender offer, creating the impression that the target's market price was weakening.

Challenging the Bidder's Disclosures

The three primary bases for challenging the bidder's disclosures are sections 14(a), 13(d), and 14(e) of the Exchange Act.

Section 14(a)—Proxy Regulations

Section 14(a) of the Exchange Act authorizes the SEC to prescribe rules governing the solicitation of proxies. One such regulation, Rule 14a9,[382] prohibits false and misleading statements in proxy materials.

Elements. The elements of a private right of action under section 14(a) were discussed earlier in this chapter.

Standing. Applying the Supreme Court's broad holding in *J.I. Case Co. v. Borak*[383] that a private right of action exists under section 14(a), courts consistently have granted standing under section 14(a) to target corporations. A nonselling shareholder, in contrast, may be unable to challenge a bidder's disclosure because it cannot prove reliance.[384]

Challenging Bidder's Disclosures under Section 14(a). Targets or their shareholders sometimes allege that bidders obtained or sought to obtain shareholder support through misleading proxy materials.[385]

Section 13(d)—Reporting Requirement

Standing. As previously discussed, courts have split over the question of whether target corporations have a private right of action for injunctive relief under section 13(d). The majority of courts permit such suits. A minority of district courts, purporting to follow the spirit of recent Supreme Court cases, have held that neither issuers nor shareholders can seek injunctive relief under section 13(d).

Challenging Bidder's Disclosures under Section 13(d). Section 13(d) and the rules promulgated thereunder require the filing of a Schedule 13D disclosure statement with the SEC containing, among other information, the identity and background of the person or group making the filing, the source and amount of funds used in making the purchases of securities, the purpose of the purchases, and the purchaser's plans or proposals for future dealings with the issuer or the issuer's securities.

The most common challenge under section 13(d) concerns the 5 percent shareholder's plans.[386] However, targets sometimes challenge the disclosures regarding the source of the 5 percent shareholder's funding,[387] or the identity and background of the person or group making the purchases.[388]

One reaction to the requirement that plans and intentions be disclosed in detail is the so-called "waffling" disclosure, in which the bidder simply enumerates a list of nearly every conceivable thing an owner of a large block of stock might propose to do. In *Dan River, Inc. v. Icahn*,[389] for example, the bidder, Icahn, filed a Schedule 13D containing a long list of actions that Icahn and his associates might consider in deciding whether to seek control of the issuer.[390] The Fourth Circuit approved Icahn's disclosures:

> Icahn's filings appear exceptionally thorough. Icahn clearly and forthrightly set forth its intent to consider extraordinary corporate transactions such as a merger or a sale of substantially all of the corporate assets. . . . The disclosures here give full warning that sweeping changes might take place if Icahn should obtain control.[391]

Section 13(d) disclosure requirements also have been used to obtain an injunction against an impending tender offer where the mandatory disclosure would result in the violation of a preexisting confidentiality agreement. In *General Portland, Inc. v. LaFarge Coppee S.A.*,[392] the potential bidder received confidential information during the course of friendly negotiations with respect to which it signed a confidentiality agreement. When these negotiations failed to result in an agreement and the target realized that a hostile tender offer was impending, it sought and obtained an injunction to prevent the offer on the basis that section 13(d) would require the disclosure of the confidential information in violation of the agreement.[393]

Section 13(d) claims can be important even after the bidder begins a formal tender offer. Two district courts have enjoined tender offers and ordered rescission or divestiture because the bidders had accumulated large blocks of shares on the basis of misleading Schedules 13D.[394] In those cases, the courts reasoned that the section 13(d) violations allowed the bidders to obtain "blocking positions" that inhibited competing offers and made it difficult for the targets to arrange other business combinations.[395] However, the First Circuit recently rejected a target's contention that a bidder who already had obtained 17 percent of the target's shares held an unfair "blocking position": "[W]e think it unlikely that [the bidder's] tactics have given it any 'unfair advantage' that complete disclosure could not cure, or that it has acquired a 'blocking interest' that will ultimately frustrate higher bids by rival offerors and harm [the target's] shareholders."[396]

Section 14(e)—Tender Offer Fraud

Standing. The courts consistently have implied a private right of action on behalf of target corporations seeking injunctive relief under section 14(e).[397] The Eleventh Circuit has implied a private right of action to compel corrective disclosures,[398] but has denied a private right of action seeking divestiture.[399] Whether a target has a private right of action for damages is unclear.[400] As in other areas, a nonselling shareholder may be unable to bring a private action after a successful tender offer.[401]

Challenging Bidder's Disclosures under Section 14(e). Section 14(e) is the enforcement provision for section 14(d). Section 14(d) and the rules promulgated thereunder require the filing of a Schedule 14D-1 disclosure statement with the SEC and the dissemination of certain information to the target's shareholders, including the identity and background of the bidder, the source and amount of the bidder's funds, financial information about the bidder, the purpose of the offer and the plans or proposals of the bidder, and any "additional material information."

Targets have successfully alleged a long list of defects in bidders' section 14(d) filings, but courts are increasingly likely to reject the target's claim unless the bidder's failure to disclose is clearly material. Thus, in *Diamond v. Arend*,[402] the court rejected a series of challenges to a bidder's disclosures as involving immaterial or nondeceptive issues. "The Court is 'not inclined to subject every tender offer to a nit-picking judicial scrutiny.' "[403]

Failure to Disclose Control Purpose. Although nondisclosure of an intent to achieve control is more commonly a prebid section 13(d) violation, the claim also can arise as a section 14(d) violation in tender offers for less than 50 percent of the target's stock.[404] The failure to adequately disclose that the bidder currently has control over the target also can serve as a basis for relief.[405]

Failure to Disclose Postoffer Plans. Targets often allege that bidders have failed to describe adequately their plans to make material changes in the target's management or operations.[406] However, in gauging the accuracy of bidders' disclosures about their future plans for target, courts often recall Judge Ainsworth's statement in one of the first cases interpreting the Williams Act, *Susquehanna Corp. v. Pan American Sulphur Co.*:[407] "Though the offeror has an obligation fairly to disclose its plans in the event of a takeover, it is not required to make predictions of future behavior, however tentatively phrased, which may cause the offeree or the public investor to rely on them unjustifiably."[408]

Failure to Disclose Financial Information about the Bidder. Even in an "any and all" offer, courts have required that bidders reveal substantial financial information about themselves. In *Prudent Real Estate Trust v. Johncamp Realty, Inc.*,[409] the Second Circuit enjoined a tender offer pending the filing of additional disclosures. Judge Friendly explained:

> If the bidder is in a flourishing financial condition, the stockholder might decide to hold his shares in the hope that, if the offer was only partially successful, the bidder might raise its bid after termination of the offer or infuse new capital into the enterprise. *Per contra*, a poor financial condition of the bidder might cause the shareholder to accept for fear that control of the company would pass into irresponsible hands.[410]

The Third Circuit's decision in *Flynn v. Bass Brothers Enterprises, Inc.*,[411] may signal a move toward requiring bidders to disclose asset valuation appraisals, and other "soft information." Traditionally, courts have not imposed a duty on bidders to disclose such appraisals, reasoning that they could mislead shareholders.[412] Noting a trend within the SEC favoring disclosure of "soft information," however, the court in *Flynn* held that in an appropriate case a bidder's asset appraisals must be disclosed. The determination whether such information must be disclosed in a particular case requires balancing the potential aid such information will give a shareholder against the potential harm.[413] Among the factors to be considered are the facts upon which the information is based, the qualifications of those performing the appraisal, and the purpose for which the information was initially intended. The Delaware Court of Chancery has followed the *Flynn* approach.[414]

Despite this move toward greater disclosure, a potential bidder need not reveal which firms it is considering bidding on when it raises funds for acquisitions. Thus, in *Revlon, Inc. v. Pantry Pride, Inc.*,[415] a target was unsuccessful in challenging the bidder's prospectus, where the bidder had revealed its intent to use the capital raised to finance acquisitions.[416]

Failure to Disclose Inside Information about Target Obtained by Bidder. In *Crane Co. v. Westinghouse Air Brake Co.*,[417] the Second Circuit held that a friendly bidder "was an 'insider' with respect to the trading of [the target's] stock" and should have disclosed that it was engaging in "extraordinary buying" of target shares "coupled with . . . large secret sales off the market."[418]

Failure to Disclose Offer's Potential Adverse Impact on Target. In *Sonesta International Hotels Corp. v. Wellington Associates*,[419] the Second Circuit ruled that a bidder violated the Williams Act by failing to disclose details of a substantial debt owed to the target that might have been compromised if the offer were successful. The court also held that the bidder should have disclosed that the target's stock might be delisted from the New York Stock Exchange if the offer were successful.[420]

Other Failures to Disclose. In *Alaska Interstate Co. v. McMillian*,[421] the court enjoined a tender offer because the bidder failed to disclose substantial impediments to achieving control. In *Valente v. Pepsico, Inc.*,[422] the court held that when the bidder had specific plans to merge with the target in the future, the bidder should have described the existence of appraisal rights. However, in *Revlon, Inc. v. Pantry Pride, Inc.*,[423] the court ruled that a bidder need not disclose the identity of a potential target "until the offeror has definitely determined to acquire the target corporation and finally decided on the terms of the offer." Finally, as described later in the chapter, some courts have found violations of the Williams Act where bidders have failed to disclose substantive violations of other statutes, such as the antitrust laws.

Challenging the Substance of a Tender Offer

Courts have thus far refused to sanction the use of the federal securities laws to examine the substance of tender offers. This refusal is rooted in the purpose of the Williams Act, which is to guarantee the availability of all necessary information on tender offers while maintaining strict federal neutrality between the bidder and incumbent management.[424]

In *Santa Fe Industries, Inc. v. Green*,[425] the Supreme Court held that conduct which does not involve either misrepresentation or nondisclosure is not "manipulative" within the meaning of section 10(b) of the Exchange Act[426] and rule 10b-5 thereunder,[427] which prohibit the use of "manipulative or deceptive devices" in connection with the purchase or sale of securities. Under the similar language of section 14(e), a plaintiff may not escape the requirement of alleging and proving misrepresentation or nondisclosure merely by characterizing the defendant's conduct as "manipulative."[428]

For example, courts have held that in the absence of fraud or deception, section 14(e) is not violated by a front-end-loaded, two-tier tender offer (a tender offer for less than all of a target's outstanding stock at one price followed by a second-step merger at a lower price.)[429] In *Radol v. Thomas*,[430] the Court of Appeals accepted the lower court's finding that the two-tier offer was not manipulative. The court also found that acquiescence in the two-step transaction by the target's directors was not a breach of their fiduciary duty and was protected by the business judgment rule.[431] The Fifth Circuit has ruled that, without misrepresentation or nondisclosure, the payment of greenmail does not violate either section 10(b) or section 14(e).[432] Similarly, the Ninth Circuit has rejected a request for injunctive relief based on a bidder's failure to establish firm financing before commencing a tender offer.[433] The court rejected the target's argument that the failure to line up firm financing violated the Williams Act, emphasizing that the act concerns disclosures and does not impose substantive restrictions on the terms of tender offers.[434]

Challenging the Bidder's Compliance with Other Federal Laws

Antitrust Laws

If the bidder's control over the target may substantially lessen competition in a line of commerce, the target may be able to challenge the bidder's efforts under section 7 of the Clayton Act.[435] Through 1986, the cases were split concerning whether a target corporation has standing to bring such an action.[436] In *Cargill, Inc. v. Monfort of Colorado, Inc.*,[437] the Supreme Court emphasized that a competitor must allege an "antitrust injury" to have standing under the Clayton Act. Whether and how *Cargill* will affect lawsuits brought by targets against hostile bidders is unclear, although it is likely that courts will now be more reluctant to afford standing to target corporations.[438] When applicable, section 7 provides one of the best defenses against a hostile tender offer because antitrust violations spawned by the takeover may be incurable.

Takeovers typically are described as horizontal, vertical, or conglomerate. In a horizontal takeover, the combining firms produce or sell the same product in the same geographic area. In a vertical takeover, the combining firms do not produce the same product but possess (or could possess) a customer-supplier or supplier-customer relationship. In a conglomerate takeover, the combining firms do not produce the same product and do not share any special relationship.

Targets successfully have challenged tender offers on the ground that the horizontal effects would substantially lessen competition.[439] In a few instances, targets have successfully alleged anticompetitive vertical effects.[440] Targets have rarely been successful in challenging conglomerate takeovers.[441]

Even in horizontal takeovers, courts tend to view targets' antitrust claims skeptically, recognizing that "target companies are quick to seek refuge in Section 7 against an unfriendly takeover."[442] Courts realize that "[t]he grant of a temporary injunction on antitrust grounds at the behest of a target company spells almost certain doom of a tender offer."[443] As a result, courts often have looked to the Justice Department's Merger Guidelines as a means for gauging the target's likelihood of success. New guidelines, issued in 1982 and revised in 1984, reflect a continued reliance on economic analysis.[444] The revisions address five important areas: (1) market definition and measurement; (2) factors that may affect the significance of concentration and market share data in evaluating horizontal mergers; (3) the treatment of foreign competition; (4) the treatment of efficiencies; and (5) the treatment of failing divisions of healthy firms.[445] The Justice Department statement accompanying release of the 1984 Guidelines indicated, "[T]he revisions are intended to correct any misperception that the Guidelines are a set of rigid mathematical formulas that ignore market realities and rely solely on a static view of the marketplace."[446]

Impact of Other Defenses. In formulating other defenses, targets must consider whether they will compromise viable antitrust claims. Naturally, a counter–tender offer for the shares of the bidder forecloses an antitrust challenge. Contacts with potential white knights also may hinder the target's antitrust defense if acquisition by one of them would create antitrust problems comparable to those created by an acquisition by the bidder.

Attorney's Fees. Several targets that have obtained preliminary injunctions against bidders have been awarded attorney's fees under section 16 of the Clayton Act.[447]

Hart-Scott-Rodino Act. Courts have refused to grant targets a private right of action under the Hart-Scott-Rodino Antitrust Improvements Act of 1976.[448] That act amended the Clayton Act to provide for notification to the Federal Trade Commission and the Antitrust Division of the Justice Department and a review period before the consummation of certain tender offers.[449]

Margin Regulations

Courts generally have refused to permit borrowers or investors to seek private remedies under the margin provisions of section 7 of the Exchange Act.[450] Some courts, however, have held that targets do have standing to challenge bidders' margin violations.[451]

Two courts, while refusing to permit a target to sue directly under section 7, have nevertheless suggested that a target might have standing under section 14(e) to allege that the bidder failed to disclose its section 7 violations.[452] Neither court, however, found a violation of section 14(e). The court in *Revlon v. Pantry Pride* found that there was no section 14(e) violation because the debt in question was exempt from margin requirements. The court in *Nachman Corp. v. Halfred, Inc.* held that section 14(e) was inapplicable because no tender offer had occurred yet.

Margin regulations require more attention in battles for corporate control than they did before the Federal Reserve Board's extension of these regulations to cover junk bonds used to finance a takeover. Under Regulation G, debt securities issued by a shell corporation to finance stock purchases are presumed "indirectly secured" for margin purposes.[453] The SEC reported in June 1986 that although junk bond financing has increased substantially in the last few years, junk bonds are not now, and are not likely to become, the dominant method of financing tender offers.[454] On the other hand, the SEC also found that junk bond financing is used primarily in the largest takeover battles, and suggested that the use of such bonds has leveled off or even declined since the Federal Reserve's action.[455]

Investment Company Act

Section 12(d)(1)(A) of the Investment Company Act of 1940[456] makes it unlawful for an investment company (a company in the business of investing, reinvesting, or trading in investment securities) to acquire more than 3 percent of the outstanding voting stock of another investment company. A target investment company faced with a tender offer from another investment company may be able to use this statute in a manner similar to the antitrust laws.

In *Bancroft Convertible Fund, Inc. v. Zico Investment Holdings, Inc.*,[457] the court affirmed a preliminary injunction against a tender offer it found likely to result in a violation of section 12(d)(1)(A). The court first found an implied private cause of action under section 12(d)(1)(A) and held that a target company has standing to maintain an action.[458] Next, the court rejected the bidder's objection that it fell within the statute's exclusion of privately held companies whose outstanding securities are beneficially owned by not more than 100 persons.[459] Finally, the court rejected the bidder's position that no irreparable harm would result to the target if the tender offer were allowed to proceed. The evidence had shown that the bidder intended to pursue different investment and distribution policies than those of the target, and the court affirmed the district court's conclusion that implementation of these policies would irreparably injure the target.[460]

RICO

The applicability of the Racketeer Influenced and Corrupt Organizations Act (RICO)[461] to control contests is discussed later in this chapter.

Potential Legislation

Although no federal anti-takeover legislation emerged from the 100th Congress,[462] the Supreme Court's decision in *CTS* created renewed Congressional interest in takeover regulation, and it is likely that some of the proposals mentioned elsewhere in this chapter will resurface in future Congresses.

Challenging the Bidder's Compliance with State Takeover and Regulatory Statutes

State Takeover Statutes

State takeover statutes often impose burdensome requirements on bidders. The Supreme Court's decision in *CTS* has given new vigor to state legislative programs, which may provide potent weapons for target corporations. These were described in the section on representing the bidder.

State Regulatory Statutes

Many states have enacted statutes affecting acquisitions in certain regulated industries. Most litigation to date has involved the insurance industry. Although courts have divided on the constitutionality of these statutes, at least two district courts have held that state statutes regulating acquisitions of insurance companies enjoy blanket protection under the McCarran-Ferguson Act and thus are not preempted by the Williams Act.[463]

Many states also have "baby FTC Acts" modeled on the Federal Trade Commission Act.[464] While the literal scope of many of these statutes would permit an interpretation that they apply to securities transactions, most courts have concluded the statutes were not meant to apply.[465]

Challenging the Bidder under State Common Law

Targets often bring common law claims against bidders or their allies, typically alleging that the bidders or those associated with them are breaching their fiduciary duties. In *Martin Marietta Corp. v. Bendix Corp.*,[466] the Delaware Supreme Court, affirming the Delaware Chancery Court, relied upon principles of fiduciary duty to deny Martin Marietta's motion to enjoin a Bendix shareholder meeting that had been called to adopt certain antitakeover amendments. Bendix had made a tender offer for Martin Marietta. Martin Marietta responded by making a counteroffer for Bendix and sought the injunction to prevent Bendix from erecting new obstacles to Martin Marietta's offer. Because Bendix would obtain a majority of Martin Marietta's shares first, the Delaware Supreme Court reasoned that Martin Marietta would owe a duty to Bendix: "In seeking preliminary relief below, Martin [Marietta] is in effect asking the Court of Chancery to assist it in a violation of a duty to its own majority shareholder, Bendix."[467]

Targets, however, should be wary of relying solely upon common law claims of breach of fiduciary duty. As a practical matter, these suits rarely succeed. In *Treadway Companies v. Care Corp.*,[468] the target, Treadway, alleged that one of its directors was affiliated with the bidder, Care Corporation. Treadway claimed that this director breached his fiduciary duty to Treadway because he knew of Care's tender offer in advance and, without disclosing that information to Treadway, sold his 14 percent interest in Treadway to Care. The court rejected Treadway's claim:

> Management—as distinct from the corporation—had no legitimate claim to Cowin's allegiance. Rather, Cowin owed his fiduciary duties to the corporation, and through the corporation to the shareholders. Treadway has not shown that those duties were not fulfilled. Specifically, Treadway has offered no support for the proposition that the duty of good faith that Cowin owed to Treadway carried with it a duty to disclose any information about Care.
>
> . . . .
>
> [W]e decline to impose on Cowin a duty to disclose his negotiations with Care.[469]

Another impediment to fiduciary duty claims in tender offer litigation is standing: The duty allegedly violated must extend to the plaintiff rather than some third party. Thus, in *Jacobs v. Pabst Brewing Co.*,[470] the bidder alleged that an investment adviser allied with the target breached its fiduciary duty to its clients by failing to vote proxies received from those clients in favor of the bidder's slate of directors. The court dismissed the claim, stating that if the investment adviser "has violated a duty, the cause of action must be brought by one of its clients."[471]

In the well-publicized Pennzoil litigation, a Texas state court jury awarded Pennzoil Co. $10.53 billion in damages after finding that Texaco Inc. had improperly seized ownership of Getty Oil Co. from Pennzoil.[472] In December 1983, Pennzoil launched a $100 per share tender offer for 20 percent of Getty's stock. In January 1984, the Getty board voted to accept the offer. Although Pennzoil acknowledged that no formal documents were ever executed, it argued that this favorable vote, a jointly prepared news release, some handshakes and even a champagne toast represented a binding contract. Getty apparently felt differently, and several days later accepted a higher bid from Texaco. After a failed attempt to block the resulting merger,[473] Pennzoil filed suit against Texaco for inducing Getty to breach its "contract" with Pennzoil. The Texas jury awarded Pennzoil the full $7.53 billion in actual damages it sought, along with $3 billion in punitive damages and $470 million in interest.[474] On December 10, 1985, the court affirmed the verdict.[475]

Texaco then applied in federal court for an injunction to preclude a $12 billion appeal bond and to prevent Pennzoil from enforcing the judgment while Texaco appealed. This application was initially granted,[476] but the Supreme Court ruled that the district court should have abstained.[477] On February 12, 1987, a Texas appellate court affirmed the judgment with the exception that it suggested a remittitur of $2 billion of punitive damages.[478] On November 2, 1987, in spite of an amicus curiae brief filed by the SEC stating that Pennzoil's contract with Getty violated rule 106-13, the Texas Supreme Court announced that it would not hear the case. On December 19, 1987, the parties reached a settlement under which Texaco paid Pennzoil about $3 billion.[479]

Remedies for Violations by the Bidder

The primary remedy available to targets is injunctive relief. However, absent incurable hindrances, such as antitrust violations, courts generally will enjoin an offer only temporarily, pending cure of all Williams Act violations. In *Rondeau v. Mosinee Paper Corp.*,[480] for example, the Supreme Court held that the court of appeals erred in enjoining a prospective bidder from voting shares purchased during the period that the bidder had failed to file a Schedule 13D. The Court concluded that, because the prospective bidder eventually filed a proper Schedule 13D, no basis for injunctive relief existed.[481]

Despite *Rondeau*'s holding that shareholders who sell "at an unfairly depressed price have an adequate remedy by way of an action for damages,"[482] several district courts subsequently imposed severe equitable sanctions on bidders who obtained shares in violation of the Williams Act. In *Hanna Mining Co. v. Norcen Energy Resources Ltd.*,[483] the court held that an order requiring the bidder to divest all shares purchased under a false Schedule 13D was warranted:

> Any different result would mean that an acquiring corporation could engage in the most deliberate form of misrepresentation in its statutory filings and when its fraud is discovered merely file corrective amendments and keep the benefits of its wrongful conduct regardless of how that conduct may continue to injure shareholders of the corporation whose stock it has acquired.[484]

Likewise, in *General Steel Industries, Inc. v. Walco National Corp.*,[485] the court ordered that the bidder "offer rescission to all [target] shareholders that sold in the open market during the period of its noncompliance [with section 13(d)] and that the Offer be enjoined pending the completion of that process."[486]

More recently, however, courts have shied away from drastic remedies. In *MacFadden Holdings, Inc. v. JB Acquisition Corp.*,[487] for example, the Second Circuit reversed a district court's injunction ordering a bidder to return shares tendered to it. The district court had found that the tender offeror misrepresented its intention to accept shares before obtaining FCC approval. The Second Circuit concluded that there had been no misrepresentation.

The Fifth Circuit, in *Gearhart Industries, Inc. v. Smith International, Inc.*,[488] reversed the district court's preliminary injunction against a tender offer. The lower court had enjoined the tender offer to prevent the bidder from reaping the benefits of the illegal "blocking position" it had obtained by virtue of its failure to disclose its control purpose in its original Schedule 13D. The Fifth Circuit rejected the lower court's reasoning and held that the injunction was "not justified."[489] Noting that "[t]he *sole* purpose of the Williams Act is full and fair disclosure," the court held that this purpose was satisfied when the bidder amended its Schedule 13D to indicate its control purpose.[490] The court concluded that this amendment "cured any previous violation of section 13(d), at least so far as to preclude injunctive relief."[491]

In *Dan River, Inc. v. Icahn*,[492] the district court permitted a tender offer to proceed once the bidder's disclosure statements were corrected, but ordered that the bidder's stock be "sterilized"—that is, prohibited from voting. The court sterilized the shares that the bidder already owned as well as the shares that the bidder was to purchase pursuant to the offer. The Fourth Circuit reversed, holding that "the order 'sterilizing' [the bidder's] stock cannot be justified on the basis of the insufficient disclosure alleged."[493] The court emphasized that corrective disclosure is the normal remedy for inadequate disclosure. Noting that "the thrust of the disclosure laws is to protect shareholders, not management," the court concluded: "Manifestly, the 'sterilization' order affords shareholders no more 'truthful and complete' information than that already provided by [the bidder] in its filings."[494]

Likewise, in *San Francisco Real Estate Investors v. Real Estate Investment Trust of America*,[495] the First Circuit held that the district court should lift its preliminary injunction against a tender offer once the bidder makes "sufficient disclosure . . . to equip [the target's] shareholders to make a decision."[496] The First Circuit stated:

> [A]n injunction forbidding an acquisition is not, except in the most egregious case, the preferred or even proper remedy. In many situations failure to disclose can be cured by an order requiring appropriate disclosure. And, when that order is insufficient, injunctive relief should be designed to help the victims of the inadequate disclosure, not to hurt them.[497]

Nonetheless, the First Circuit did not preclude remedies beyond corrective disclosures. Indeed, the court endorsed as "sensible" the SEC's threefold test for determining whether additional relief is appropriate. The SEC's test asks the district court to consider "(1) whether a substantial number of shares were purchased after the misleading disclosures and before corrective disclosure, (2) whether the curative disclosure occurred simultaneously with or on the eve of a tender offer, and (3) whether the violation was egregious."[498] Moreover, the First Circuit specifically recalled Judge Friendly's comment in *Electronic Specialty Co. v. International Controls Corp.*: "If the court believes the offeror has improperly depressed the price of the stock before making the offer, it can require rescission and enjoin further solicitation for a period."[499]

Civil RICO Actions

Targets seeking to block tender offers and bidders seeking to block defensive measures should consider using the broad provisions of the Racketeer Influenced and Corrupt Organizations Act (RICO).[500] RICO provides that the following actions are unlawful:[501]

- For any person receiving income from "a pattern of racketeering activity" to use or invest that money in the "acquisition of any interest" in an enterprise affecting interstate commerce
- For any person "through a pattern of racketeering activity" to "acquire or maintain . . . any interest in" an enterprise affecting interstate commerce
- For any person employed by or associated with an enterprise affecting interstate commerce to "participate . . . in the conduct of such enterprise's affairs through a pattern of racketeering activity"

"Racketeering activity" is defined to include a long list of felonies, most prominently mail fraud, wire fraud, and "fraud in the sale of securities."[502] A "pattern of racketeering activity" requires "at least two acts of racketeering activity" within a ten-year period.[503] RICO grants an express civil remedy for treble damages and attorney's fees to "[a]ny person injured in his business or property by reason of" violations of the act's provisions.[504]

The act gives federal district courts jurisdiction over RICO suits but is silent on whether this jurisdiction is exclusive or concurrent with that of the state courts. The issue is hotly debated. The courts of several states disclaim jurisdiction over RICO claims,[505] while other states' courts have acknowledged their concurrent jurisdiction.[506] The Ninth Circuit is the only court of appeals to directly face the issue, concluding state court jurisdiction is concurrent.[507] The Seventh and Fifth Circuits have hinted they agree.[508] Federal district courts have come down on both sides of the question.[509] Unless there is a controlling *state* court decision acknowledging jurisdiction, a RICO plaintiff should sue in federal court, where jurisdiction is assured.[510]

The statute is similarly silent on the question of the applicable statute of limitations. Courts struggling with this question attempted to look to state statutes of limitations, resulting in a "confused, inconsistent, and unpredictable" state of law.[511] In *Agency Holding Corp. v. Malley-Duff & Associates*, the Supreme Court resolved this issue by holding that a uniform four-year limitations period should apply to civil RICO actions.[512]

Applicability of RICO in Tender Offer Litigation

The Supreme Court interpreted civil RICO for the first time in *Sedima, S.P.R.L. v. Imrex Co.*[513] and *American National Bank & Trust Co. v. Haroco, Inc.*[514] The Court's broad interpretation of civil RICO in those decisions may make it easier for plaintiffs to establish RICO violations in takeover litigation.

In *Sedima* and *Haroco*, the Court rejected two judicially created limitations on the use of civil RICO. First, the Court held that a private RICO plaintiff need not prove that the defendant has been convicted of predicate acts of racketeering. Second, the Court held that such plaintiffs are not required to establish a "racketeering injury" that is separate and distinct from the injury caused by the predicate acts themselves.[515] More importantly, the Court made clear its belief that Congress had intentionally drafted RICO with broad language and that limitations on the use of civil RICO must therefore come from Congress, and not from the courts. Although *Sedima* and *Haroco* did not directly address the question of whether civil RICO is applicable in tender offer litigation, these cases have cast doubt on the continuing vitality of pre-*Sedima* decisions in which courts criticized the use of civil RICO in tender offer litigation on the grounds that Congress intended RICO to apply to the infiltration of legitimate businesses by organized crime, and not to "garden-variety frauds."[516] In *Barkman v. Wabash, Inc.*,[517] the court held that a RICO action brought by a former shareholder of the target corporation against the target and the bidder stated a claim. The shareholder alleged, among other things, that the tender offer and a number of related documents were fraudulent, that required disclosures were not made, and that the bidder made payoffs to the deal manager for the tender offer and to the firm retained by the target to render a fairness opinion in order to ensure their silence and cooperation.

Even before *Sedima*, several courts had approved of the use of civil RICO in tender offer litigation. In *Swanson v. Wabash, Inc.*,[518] the court refused to dismiss a class action by shareholders of a target who alleged that the defendants had failed to disclose and misstated certain material facts in connection with a tender offer. In *Hanna Mining Co. v. Norcen Energy Resources, Ltd.*,[519] the court refused to dismiss a target's suit under RICO to enjoin a proposed tender offer. The target alleged that in acquiring its stock, the defendants committed violations of sections 10(b),

13(d), 14(e), and 20(a) of the Securities Exchange Act of 1934. Similarly, in *Spencer Cos. v. Agency Rent-A-Car, Inc.*,[520] the court refused to dismiss a target's complaint that the defendants had violated RICO by filing false Schedules 13D in connection with the purchase of a third company's stock. Spencer, the target company, alleged that Agency financed its purchases of Spencer stock with proceeds of the sale of stock of a third company it had obtained through fraud.

Availability of Injunctive Relief

Section 1964(c) of RICO provides that a private person may sue for violations of section 1962 of the act and "shall recover" treble damages.[521] Section 1964(a) of RICO provides that federal district courts may issue orders to "prevent and restrain" violations of section 1962 of RICO.[522] There is no question that injunctive relief is available in civil RICO suits brought by the United States.[523] It is not clear, however, whether injunctive relief under section 1964(a) is available in private lawsuits, or whether the treble-damages remedy of section 1964(c) is the exclusive remedy for private plaintiffs.

The two courts of appeals to decide the issue have held that injunctive relief is not available to private plaintiffs. In *Religious Technology Center v. Wollersheim*,[524] the Ninth Circuit acknowledged that the statute could plausibly be read either to permit or deny private injunctive relief, but held that Congress did not intend to make such relief available to private plaintiffs.[525] The Fifth Circuit agreed with *Religious Technology Center* in *In re Fredeman Litigation*,[526] also noting a dictum in *Agency Holding Corp.*[527] suggesting Congress intended to preclude injunctive relief. The Second Circuit has twice indicated that it would endorse this view.[528]

Two district courts have expressly held that injunctive relief is available to private plaintiffs.[529] Another court assumed, without discussion, that such relief is available.[530] That position has been endorsed by many commentators.[531]

Although the Supreme Court did not address the availability of private injunctive relief in *Sedima*, it discussed relevant background information in the context of reviewing the legislative history of RICO's provision for private treble damages. The Court noted that Senate Bill 30 limited civil remedies to injunctive action by the United States. During hearings on S. 30 before the House Judiciary Committee, Representative Steiger proposed the addition of private actions for treble damages, which the committee approved. While the bill was being considered by the full House, Representative Steiger offered an amendment to allow private injunctive actions, fix a statute of limitations, and clarify venue and process requirements. The amendment met with some hostility because it had not been presented first to the committee. Representative Steiger withdrew his amendment without a vote being taken by the House. Arguably, the failure to pass the amendment indicates that Congress considered but did not adopt a provision for private injunctive relief.

In some situations this issue can be avoided because the court will have general equitable powers that can be exercised with pendent common law claims. For example, in *USACO Coal Co. v. Carbomin Energy, Inc.*,[532] the district court entered a preliminary injunction freezing the assets of a corporation in an action brought, in part, under RICO. The district court did not address whether RICO authorizes such relief. The Sixth Circuit sustained issuance of the injunction under the lower court's general equitable powers, based on its pendent jurisdiction over common law claims, without reaching the issue of whether section 1964(a) of RICO permits such relief to private plaintiffs.

The "Pattern" Requirement as an Obstacle to Use of RICO

Section 1961(5) of RICO states that a pattern of racketeering "requires at least two acts of racketeering activity . . . the last of which occurred within ten years after the commission of a prior act of racketeering activity."[533] Before *Sedima*, the lower courts gave scant attention to the "pattern" requirement and assumed that the commission of any two predicate acts satisfied the requirements of Section 1961(5).

In *Sedima*, however, the Supreme Court cast considerable doubt on the validity of this interpretation and blamed the proliferation of RICO claims upon "the failure of Congress and the courts to develop a meaningful concept of 'pattern.' "[534] In a lengthy and now famous footnote, the Supreme Court cautioned that while two isolated acts of racketeering are necessary, they "may not be sufficient" to provide the "continuity plus relationship" needed to fulfill the statutory requirement of a pattern.[535] The Court strongly implied that, were it to address this issue, it would require some connection between the predicate acts. The Court granted certiorari in an Eighth Circuit RICO pattern case.[536]

The lower courts have responded with alacrity to the Supreme Court's invitation in *Sedima*, producing a bewildering variety of results. By May 1988, more than forty published decisions of the courts of appeals discussed the pattern requirement,[537] and the numbers have mushroomed since then. All decisions have required that a RICO plaintiff allege more than the irreducible minimum of two predicate acts. The differences have been over just what more is needed.

The Eighth Circuit has taken the most restrictive approach, requiring that there be at least two schemes or episodes of criminal activity.[538] No other circuit has adopted such a strict approach. The Second Circuit has adopted a position seemingly at the opposite extreme, requiring only two "related" predicate acts.[539] Yet the Second Circuit has also required that the plaintiff show that the enterprise represents a continuing threat of criminal activity, rather than that it simply engaged in a short-lived criminal episode. That requirement substantially undercuts the ease with which a plaintiff can meet the Second Circuit's pattern requirement.[540]

The Seventh Circuit has developed a middle road in a long line of cases.[541] The Seventh Circuit's approach has been adopted by most circuits, including the First,[542] Third,[543] Fourth,[544] Ninth,[545] and Tenth.[546] As articulated in *Morgan v. Bank of Waukegan*,[547] this approach looks to several factors including:

> the number and variety of predicate acts and the length of time over which they were committed, the number of victims, the presence of separate schemes and the occurrence of distinct injuries.[548]

In addition, the predicate acts must be ongoing over a period of time and "fairly viewed as separate transactions."[549]

This fact-specific approach makes it almost impossible to say with certainty whether a given set of facts constitutes a "pattern." Indeed, much may depend on the way in which the pleadings are framed. In *Liquid Air Corp. v. Rogers*,[550] the defendant had allegedly converted thousands of plaintiff's gas cylinders by preparing false invoices. The court found a pattern because each false invoice caused a separate injury.[551] In *Brandt v. Schal Associates*,[552] the same court concluded there was no pattern where a contractor allegedly submitted dozens of false invoices to a subcontractor. The court concluded each invoice was geared toward an overall fraud on the contract price, rather than toward causing a distinct injury, so *Liquid Air* did not control.[553]

Two things seem clear. A complaint alleging a single injury upon a single victim will probably not survive the pattern requirement.[554] Similarly, allegations of multiple predicate acts culminating in a single transaction will probably fail.[555]

In the face of the general confusion as to the RICO pattern requirement, a plaintiff should attempt to allege as many predicate acts, victims, injuries, and particularly separate transactions as it responsibly can.

Most takeover attempts involve multiple use of the mails for dissemination of information to stockholders. Yet these multiple acts usually are geared toward a single goal, either effecting or defeating the takeover. Most courts now agree that without more, these multiple acts do not constitute a pattern, even though the purchase from each stockholder might be characterized as a separate "transaction" with a separate victim. For example, in *Walk v. Baltimore & Ohio Railroad*,[556] the plaintiffs were minority shareholders challenging a ten-year series of actions they claimed were designed to freeze them out fraudulently. The court found no pattern:

> This *particular* scheme, limited in scope to the accomplishment of a single discrete objective—forcing out the minority in a single corporate structure—does not pose a sufficient threat of continuing criminal activity.[557]

Nevertheless, some courts might find a pattern on similar or even less expansive allegations. In *Barticheck v. Fidelity Union Bank*,[558] the court found a pattern in the repetition of similar misrepresentations to about twenty investors as part of a scheme to sell worthless limited partnership interests.

Rule 11

Federal Rule of Civil Procedure 11 has radically changed the practice of law. Rule 11 provides that an attorney's or a party's signature on a pleading, motion, or other paper constitutes a certificate that (1) a "reasonable inquiry" of the relevant facts and law was conducted, (2) the pleading, motion, or paper is "well grounded in fact," (3) it is "warranted by existing law or a good faith argument for the extension, modification, or reversal of existing law," and (4) it is "not interposed for any improper purpose," such as harassment, delay, or an unnecessary increase in cost.

Although it appears that no court has yet considered rule 11 sanctions in the context of contests for corporate control, several courts have imposed sanctions for filing frivolous securities or antitrust claims. In *Unioil, Inc. v. E.F. Hutton & Co.*,[559] a noted plaintiffs' securities counsel brought a class action under the federal securities law on behalf of Unioil against certain individuals and brokerage houses. The district court found, and the Ninth Circuit agreed, that counsel had failed to conduct a reasonable investigation before filing suit. The Ninth Circuit upheld a sanction of nearly $300,000 and justified the magnitude of the sanction on the grounds that counsel practiced in securities law and should be held to a higher standard and that counsel's class action imposed substantial costs on the opposing parties.[560] Similarly, in *Frantz v. United States Powerlifting Federation*,[561] the Seventh Circuit directed the award of sanctions for filing frivolous antitrust claims. The court observed that "[a]ntitrust suits are easy to file and notoriously costly to defend" because "[a] single claim in an antitrust case may occasion the expenditure of hundreds or thousands of hours, as opposing counsel try to verify or refute the allegations and theories."[562]

As these decisions indicate, rule 11 raises questions central to litigating takeover contests: In the fast-paced arena of control contests, what factual investigation does rule 11 require before counsel may file suit? Should rule 11 dampen enthusiasm for pursuing innovative legal theories under antitrust, securities, RICO, or state law? Does rule 11's prohibition on filing suit for improper purposes bar litigation brought for the purpose of affecting the adversary's business decisions?

Objective and Subjective Standards

Objective Standards

Rule 11 provides that an attorney certify that he or she has read the "pleading, motion, or other paper; that to the best of the signer's knowledge, information, and belief formed after reasonable inquiry it is well-grounded in fact and is warranted by existing law or a good faith argument for the extension, modification, or reversal of existing law." According to the Advisory Committee Notes, the requirement of a reasonable inquiry "is more stringent than the original good-faith formula and thus it is expected that a greater range of circumstances will trigger its violation." As a result, every court of appeals that has considered the question has held that the new rule 11 incorporates an objective standard of reasonableness.[563] Lawyers "can no longer avoid the sting of rule 11 sanctions by operating under the guise of a pure heart and empty head."[564]

Although rule 11 does not use the word "frivolous," courts consistently have employed a "frivolousness" standard in determining whether sanctions are appropriate.[565] Hence, a pleading, motion, or paper violates rule 11 if it is frivolous, unreasonable, or without foundation, even though not signed in subjective bad faith.[566]

Subjective Standard

Rule 11 also requires that the pleading or motion "is not interposed for any improper purpose, such as to harass or to cause unnecessary delay or needless increase in the cost of litigation." Courts are divided over whether the improper purpose of the signer should be subjectively or objectively tested. Courts that employ a subjective standard hold that a pleading or other paper that is well grounded in fact and law might be the subject of sanction if filed for an improper purpose, while courts that use an objective standard hold that the improper-purpose clause cannot be violated if the complaint is well grounded in fact and in law. The Ninth Circuit has held that the improper purpose of the signer is to be objectively tested, saying that "the subjective intent of the pleader or movant to file a meritorious document is of no moment. The standard is reasonableness."[567]

Other courts have held that rule 11 stipulates that counsel must possess a subjective good-faith belief that a filing is brought for a proper purpose.[568] It is therefore unclear whether an objectively meritorious pleading or other paper may be the subject of sanctions if signed and filed for an improper purpose.

Reasonable Inquiry

Affirmative Duty of Inquiry

Rule 11 expressly imposes an affirmative duty to investigate the facts and law that support a pleading, motion, or other paper.[569] As one court has stated, "The day is past when our notice pleading practice . . . [and] liberal discovery rules invited the federal practitioner to file suit first and find out later whether he had a case or not."[570]

Although related, the prerequisite of a reasonable inquiry differs from the requirement that a pleading or motion be well grounded in fact and warranted by law. A failure to conduct a reasonable investigation may violate rule 11, regardless of the merit of the pleading or motion or the attorney's belief in the merits of the client's case.[571]

Reasonableness of Inquiry

An investigation's reasonableness must be assessed in light of the circumstances of each case.[572] The reasonable-inquiry standard requires at the very least some affirmative investigation on the part of the attorney.[573] It is clear that an investigation need not be to the point of certainty to be reasonable.[574] Rule 11 does not require steps that are not cost-justified or that are unlikely to produce results.[575] Thus, if the lawyer conducted a reasonable inquiry and his or her pleading contained factual errors, courts will be reluctant to impose sanctions on the lawyer.[576] However, short of certainty, the degree of inquiry required by rule 11 is less clear. Courts rely on various factors, such as those set forth in the following paragraphs, to determine whether an investigation is reasonable.[577]

Time Available for Investigation. The thoroughness of the inquiry required by rule 11 depends upon the time available for investigation. A routine pleading or motion demands more extensive investigation than does a motion for a preliminary injunction or a complaint filed shortly before the limitations period expires.[578] For the same reasons, courts hold attorneys to a higher standard of "reasonable inquiry" in signing amended complaints.[579]

Availability of Evidence. Absent time pressures, a reasonable inquiry requires that counsel interview the available witnesses.[580] Counsel should review the relevant documents that are in the client's possession[581] or are otherwise accessible,[582] and explore readily available avenues of inquiry.[583]

Without investigation, counsel cannot represent inferences as facts, whether careless or deliberate.[584]

If the evidence necessary to prove or disprove a claim is in an opposing party's exclusive possession, counsel should request the opposing party to voluntarily disclose the relevant evidence. If this effort is unavailing, rule 11 permits counsel to file a complaint based upon reasonable inferences from whatever evidence is available.[585]

Reliance upon Client's Statements. Rule 11 allows counsel to rely upon a client's statements, but only when it is reasonable to do so. Whether such reliance is reasonable depends upon several factors. First, can the client's statements be corroborated and, if so, at what cost? It generally is unreasonable to rely, to the exclusion of an independent investigation, upon unverified statements that could be readily corroborated.[586] Second, are the statements based upon the client's personal knowledge? It is unreasonable to file a pleading or a motion founded upon unreliable secondhand assertions.[587] Third, are the statements plausible? It is unreasonable to rely upon representations that are implausible on their face.[588] Fourth, how well does counsel know the client? It may be more reasonable to depend upon the statements of a long-standing client that has demonstrated reliability than upon a client unknown to the attorney.[589]

Consultation with the Client. The attorney should confer directly with the client to verify the accuracy of the claims and the client's ability to continue the suit.[590]

Experience of Counsel. The degree of research required by rule 11 depends upon the experience of the attorney or the party signing the pleading or motion.[591] Lawyers with expertise in a particular field are held to a higher standard than that expected of general practitioners.[592]

Costs Imposed on Opposing Party. The requirement of a reasonable inquiry is intended to prevent litigants from imposing the costs due to frivolous filings on their opposing parties.[593] Thus, courts have reasoned, "Just as the gravity of foreseeable injury is relevant to determining a party's standard of care in a negligence case, so should the cost of a foreseeable response by opposing parties be relevant to determining an attorney's standard of reasonable inquiry."[594] Therefore, claims brought on behalf of a large class, which are likely to arouse a vigorous and expensive defense, may require greater investigation than identical claims brought on behalf of a few individuals.

Continuing Duty

Rule 11 does not expressly declare that an attorney bears a continuing duty to amend or to withdraw a paper if, after signing, the attorney learns that it is unfounded or is motivated by an improper purpose. The absence of an explicit statement of such a duty may imply that an attorney does not bear a continuing duty under rule 11. Moreover, the Advisory Committee Notes accompanying the rule state, "The court is expected to avoid using the wisdom of hindsight and should test the signer's conduct by inquiring what was reasonable to believe at the time the pleading, motion, or other paper was submitted."

Nevertheless, the lack of a specific statement on the point in the rule has led to a split of authority. Some courts have stated that there is no continuing duty.[596] Other courts have concluded that rule 11 imposes a continuing duty to withdraw a filing discovered to be unfounded.[597]

A line of cases in the Second Circuit illustrates this split of authority. The circuit originally stated that rule 11 imposes a continuing duty on counsel.[598] It later distinguished *United States v. Carley* and held that there is no continuing duty under rule 11.[599]

Well Grounded in Fact

Rule 11 requires that a document filed with a court be "well grounded in fact." This language articulates a reasonableness standard: A filing is well grounded in fact if it has a reasonable basis in fact.[600] A document violates rule 11 if it is not well grounded in fact, even if it was not brought for an improper purpose.[601] Courts have found filings to be unreasonable on the facts in two types of cases:

1. *No evidence to support filing*—A pleading, motion, or other paper is not well grounded in fact to the extent that there is no evidence to support an essential element of an argument.[602]
2. *Uncontested evidence to the contrary*—A pleading, motion or paper also is not well grounded in fact if it is contradicted by uncontroverted evidence that was or should have been known to the attorney or the party signing the filing.[603]

Warranted by Law

Rule 11 makes clear that a pleading, motion, or paper must be "warranted by existing law or a good faith argument for the extension, modification, or reversal of existing law."[604]

Warranted by Existing Law

A pleading or motion is warranted by existing law if it addresses a question of first impression.[605] A filing also is warranted by existing law if it concerns an issue on which the law is unsettled.[606] However, an attorney is likely to be sanctioned if he or she proceeds in the face of the court's warning that a motion is likely to be denied.[607]

The position taken in a filing need not ultimately prevail to be warranted by existing law.[608] Conversely, that a suit has survived a motion for summary judgment does not mean that it is immune from sanctions.[609]

However, a pleading or motion is unwarranted by existing law if it is contrary to settled precedent.[610] It is no defense to sanctions that counsel was unaware of authority that should have been known to a competent attorney.[611]

Warranted by a Change of Law

As is true of rule 11's other requirements, courts employ an objective standard to determine whether a filing is warranted by a good-faith argument for a change in the law.[612] Thus, a pleading or motion is unwarranted by a good-faith argument for the extension, modification, or reversal of existing law when no reasonable argument can be advanced for a change in the law.[613] Those who make claims that are not clearly warranted by existing law should inform the court that a change in existing law is being sought.[614]

However, rule 11 "is not intended to chill an attorney's enthusiasm or creativity in pursuing legal or factual theories."[615] Further, the rule does not try to "stifle the exuberant spirit of skilled advocacy" or demand that a claim be proven before a complaint can be filed.[616] "Nor is it meant to make lawyers strictly liable if a court rules against them on the merits."[617] Therefore, that an argument has been rejected does not necessarily mean that it is unreasonable.[618] Similarly, an argument for the reversal of existing law that is made to preserve the issue for higher review is not subject to sanctions merely because a lower court is bound by existing law to reject the argument.[619] To ascertain whether a complaint is an effort to change the law, a court should examine with care the arguments counsel adduces.[620]

Duty of Candor

A number of courts have held that rule 11 imposes a duty of candor on an attorney or party to disclose to the court all controlling authority, whether favorable or adverse.[621] These courts reason that a legal theory defeated by an undisclosed adverse decision is not warranted by existing law because it is unsuccessful under prevailing precedent and cannot constitute a good-faith argument for the modification or reversal of existing law because it does not argue that the law should be changed.[622]

Nonetheless, the Ninth Circuit rejected this interpretation of rule 11 when it reversed what formerly was a leading authority for the proposition that rule 11 imposes a duty of candor.[623] The Ninth Circuit reasoned that such a construction would require courts to make fine distinctions as to whether or not an adverse decision should have been called to its attention and would discourage attorneys from zealously representing their clients. Accordingly, it concluded that rule 11 does not require courts to enforce ethical standards that go beyond the language of the rule itself.[624]

However, the Ninth Circuit has taken a different position on the duty to disclose certain "critical facts."[625] The appellate court affirmed the lower court's imposition of sanctions on a labor union that filed a duplicative motion to compel arbitration after the union had appealed the denial of a prior motion and failed to inform the district court of the prior motion. The Ninth Circuit noted that to rely on the court's memory of a motion it heard a few months earlier "is to shift the burden of bringing forth critical facts regarding subsequent motions from counsel to the court."[626]

Improper Purpose

Rule 11 expressly bars any pleading, motion, or paper that is brought for any improper purpose, such as harassment, delay, or an unnecessary increase in costs. The issue of whether a filing is interposed for an improper purpose is subject to a two-part test of objective reasonableness,[627] and subjective good faith.

Under the objective standard, courts infer the purpose of a filing from the consequences of the pleading or motion. Thus, an improper purpose may be inferred when the effect of a pleading or motion is to delay the proceedings.[628] In addition to inferring an improper purpose from the effects of a filing, courts often find an improper purpose on the basis of direct evidence of an attorney's or a party's subjective bad faith.[629] When there is direct evidence of subjective bad faith, some courts have found that a motion was motivated by an improper purpose, even when it was well grounded in fact and warranted by existing law.[630]

Harassment

Absent direct evidence of harassment,[631] courts have found that a pleading or motion is interposed to harass the opposing party when it merely repeats previously unsuccessful claims against the same defendant.[632] A court has also found that a prayer for a damage award could be sanctioned for harassment under rule 11. In *Hudson v. Moore Business Forms, Inc.*,[633] the court upheld the trial judge's decision to impose rule 11 sanctions on attorneys who sued an unemployed woman over fifty years of age for $4.2 million in damages. The trial court noted that the motive and lack of justification for the defendant's unconscionable damage claim raised a strong inference that the defendant's motive in bringing the counterclaim was to harass the woman and deter similar actions from being brought.

Delay

Courts have found that a pleading or motion was prompted by an improper purpose in cases in which the movant stood to benefit financially from delay.[634] On occasion, sanctions have been predicated on direct evidence of subjective bad faith.[635]

Cost

It appears that courts have not yet had occasion to sanction litigants under rule 11 on the sole ground of unnecessarily increasing the cost of litigation. However, one court has warned counsel that the filing of a lawsuit without regard to the merits solely to affect the business decisions of the opposing party may violate rule 11.[636]

Other Improper Purposes

On its face, rule 11 reaches pleadings, motions, and papers prompted by any improper purpose, which includes but is not limited to harassment, delay, and unnecessary increases in cost.[637] For example, the initiation of a lawsuit against a judge for the purpose of compelling the judge to recuse him- or herself from presiding over another case is subject to sanctions.[638] A motion that is filed merely to determine whether it would be resisted by the opposing party is interposed for an improper purpose in contravention of rule 11.[639] The use of unfounded litigation to pursue purely economic or political objectives may violate rule 11.[640]

Available Sanctions

Rule 11 authorizes any appropriate sanction, expressly including reasonable expenses and attorney's fees. The trial court has broad discretion in awarding rule 11 sanctions.[641]

Fees

To be assessed as a sanction, an attorney's fee must be actually incurred and reasonable.[642] Many factors enter into the calculation of a fee's reasonableness:

- *Hours and rate*—The determination of a reasonable fee starts with ascertaining the number of hours worked and the market rate for such services. " 'Reasonable' does not necessarily mean actual expenses."[643] District courts have discretion in awarding attorney's fees and may reduce the number of hours and the rate as is reasonable. However, the district court's discretion in determining the amount of reasonable attorney's fees must be exercised within a reasonable limit.[644] Unless a court states its reasons for reducing the fee requested, a court generally should adopt the hours and rate set forth in an attorney's uncontested affidavit.[645] Even if a party seeking sanctions incurred large legal fees to defend against a pleading or motion, the pleading or motion still might be found to be frivolous.[646]

- *Obligation to mitigate*—Rule 11's purpose is to reduce the costs due to frivolous filings. Courts have reasoned from this premise that the party opposing a pleading or a motion that violates rule 11 bears an obligation to mitigate its attorney's fees.[647] Rule 11 does not intend that the sanctioned party automatically be responsible for the full amount of the prevailing party's attorney's fees.[648] A court, therefore, will not award fees for proceedings that could have been avoided by the party seeking sanctions.[649]
- *Objective reasonableness*—A party that opposes a pleading or motion that violates rule 11 can obtain fees only for work required to respond to the portion of the filing that violates rule 11. Thus, if a filing contains reasonable as well as unreasonable claims, then a court will reduce the award of fees for defending against the filing to the extent that the fees were incurred in response to objectively reasonable arguments.[650]
- *Subjective bad faith*—Although bad faith is not necessary for an award of fees under rule 11, that a party acted in subjective bad faith increases the amount of fees that may be reasonably awarded.[651] Courts sometimes have been lenient with attorneys who have clumsily or nonmaliciously violated rule 11 and who have not exhibited subjective bad faith.[652]
- *Ability to pay*—The reasonableness of the fee depends in part upon the sanctioned party's ability to pay the fee.[653] Absent financial inability to satisfy a sanctions order, failure to pay a fee award may constitute contempt of court.[654]

Expenses

In addition to attorney's fees, rule 11 authorizes the award of all expenses that are actually incurred and reasonable. An "expense" may consist of a loss of funds that otherwise could have been recovered.[655] The reasonableness of an expense is judged by the same factors that determine the reasonableness of a fee award.

Fines

Even though rule 11 does not provide for fines, it has been held that this sanction may be imposed for a violation of the rule.[656] The amount of the fine generally is set without discernible reason.[657] Nonetheless, some courts have suggested that fines should be calculated in the same manner as attorney's fees. According to this proposal, the fine should equal the product of the number of hours of the court's time incurred as a result of the violation multiplied by a reasonable hourly rate for the court's time, viz., $600 per hour.[658]

A fine for a violation of rule 11 may amount to a sanction for criminal contempt.[659] This would be true when the fine bears no relationship to the expenses and fees incurred as a result of the violation of rule 11.[660] In such a case, the imposition of a fine may require compliance with the procedure for criminal contempt set forth by Federal Rule of Criminal Procedure 42.[661]

Other Sanctions

In addition to monetary sanctions, a court may enter any appropriate sanction, which may include dismissal of a pleading or motion,[662] reprimanding counsel,[663] or referring the attorney's conduct for disciplinary proceedings.[664] Courts also have enjoined parties from bringing new suits until outstanding awards have been paid or from refiling similar allegations.[665]

Notes

1. 15 U.S.C. § 78n(a).
2. J.I. Case v. Borak, 377 U.S. 426 (1964).
3. *Id.* at 431, *citing* H.R. REP. NO. 1383, 73d Cong., 2d Sess. 13 (1934).
4. 15 U.S.C. §§ 78m(d), 78n(d), 78n(e).
5. MacFadden Holdings, Inc. v. JB Acquisition Corp. 802 F.2d 62, 66–67 (2d Cir. 1986); SEC v. World-Wide Coin Invs., Ltd., 567 F. Supp. 724, 754 (N.D. Ga. 1983), *citing* Edgar v. MITE Corp., 457 U.S. 624 (1982).
6. 17 C.F.R. § 240.13e-4.
7. *See* Exchange Act Release No. 22,788, [1985–1986 Transfer Binder] FED. SEC. L. REP. (CCH) ¶ 83,954 (Jan. 14, 1986).
8. 17 C.F.R. § 240.14e-1.
9. *See* Exchange Act Release No. 22,791, [1985–1986 Transfer Binder] FED. SEC. L. REP. (CCH) ¶ 83,955 (Jan. 14, 1986).
10. Exchange Act Release No. 23,421B, [1986–1987 Transfer Binder] FED. SEC. L. REP. ¶ 84,016 (Sept. 4, 1986).
11. Exchange Act Release No. 23,486, [1986–1987 Transfer Binder] FED. SEC. L. REP. (CCH) ¶ 84,018 (July 31, 1986).
12. Exchange Act Release No. 24,976 [1987 Transfer Binder] FED. SEC. L. REP. (CCH) ¶ 84,160.
13. *SEC to Propose Rules Aimed at Curbing Market Sweeps That Skirt Williams*

Act, 19 SEC. REG. & L. REP. (BNA) 1384 (Sept. 18, 1987). The rules are not yet in effect.

14. 481 U.S. 69 (1987).

15. *See generally* Langley, *Stricter Rule Urged on Informing SEC of Stock Holdings*, Wall St. J., Mar. 20, 1987, at 15, col. 4; *SEC One Share/One Vote Decision May Spark Takeover Reform, Rinaldo Says*, 20 SEC. REG. & L. REP. (BNA) 251 (Feb. 19, 1988); *Specter Proposes Takeover Reform Bill Covering § 13(d), Greenmail, Poison Pills*, 19 SEC. REG. & L. REP. (BNA) 371 (Mar. 13, 1987); *Simon Proposes Bill to Limit § 13(d) Window, Prohibit Greenmail*, 19 SEC. REG. & L. REP. (BNA) 219 (Feb. 13, 1987); *D'Amato Introduces Comprehensive Proposal for Tender Offer Reform*, 19 SEC. REG. & L. REP. (BNA) 84 (Jan. 16, 1987).

16. *See* S. REP. NO. 265, 100th Cong., 1st Sess. (1987).

17. *See Senate Briefly Considers Tender Offer Reform Proposal*, 20 SEC. REG. & L. REP. (BNA) 917 (June 17, 1988).

18. *See Senate Panel Approves Takeover Bill, Is Neutral on State Antitakeover Laws*, 19 SEC. REG. & L. REP. (BNA) 1479 (Oct. 2, 1987).

19. *See Sprinkel Says Administration Opposes Tender Offer Bill*, FED. SEC. L. REP. (CCH) No. 1240 at 6 (July 15, 1987).

20. *Cf.* Cities Serv. Co. v. Mesa Petroleum Co., 541 F. Supp. 1220 (D. Del. 1982) (bidder's substantive suit against target was compulsory counterclaim to target's substantive suit against bidder and must be brought in district court chosen by target).

21. *See, e.g.*, Plaza Sec. Co. v. Fruehauf Corp., 643 F. Supp. 1535 (E.D. Mich. 1986) (court orders management to make several curative disclosures, including that its tender offer is lower than the value of the company as suggested by management's adviser); Edelman v. Saloman, 559 F. Supp. 1178, 1186–87 (D. Del. 1983) (court orders management to issue curative proxy materials regarding cumulative voting charter amendment; "[S]urely shareholders making a decision on the cumulative voting issue should know that current management misled them in 1981 in an effort to achieve that result."); Telvest, Inc. v. Wisconsin Real Estate Inv. Trust, 489 F. Supp. 250, 255 (E.D. Wis. 1980) (finding that management committed proxy violations and ordering management to send copy of court's decision to shareholders).

22. 479 U.S. 104 (1986).

23. *See, e.g.*, Gerber Prods. Co. v. Anderson, Clayton & Co., 1977-2 Trade Cas. (CCH) ¶ 61,637 at 72,622 (W.D. Mich. Sept. 13, 1977) (offer abandoned after hearing into bidder's questionable payments ordered; target's allegations described in Gerber Prods. Co. v. Anderson, Clayton & Co., 76 Mich. App. 410, 256 N.W.2d 754, 759 (1977)).

24. J.I. Case Co. v. Borak, 377 U.S. at 430–31.

25. 396 U.S. 375 (1970).

26. *Id.* at 383–85.

27. TSC Indus., Inc. v. Northway, Inc., 426 U.S. 438, 449 (1976).

28. *See* Berg v. First Am. Bankshares, Inc., 796 F.2d 489, 495 (D.C. Cir. 1986); Fradkin v. Ernst, 571 F. Supp. 829, 844 (N.D. Ohio 1983); *see also* Kademian v. Ladish Co., 792 F.2d 614 (7th Cir. 1986) (materiality requires an examination of the "total mix" of information available to shareholders at the time of the

proxy); Gerstle v. Gamble-Skogmo, Inc., 478 F.2d 1281, 1297 (2d Cir. 1973) (it is "not sufficient that overtones might have been picked up by the sensitive antennae of investment analysts").

29. Gerstle v. Gamble-Skogmo, Inc., 478 F.2d at 1302.

30. Caspary v. Louisiana Land & Exploration Co., 579 F. Supp. 1105 (S.D.N.Y. 1983), *aff'd per curiam*, 725 F.2d 189 (2d Cir. 1984); Flum Partners v. Child World, Inc., 557 F. Supp. 492, 498–99 (S.D.N.Y. 1983). *Cf.* Keyser v. Commonwealth Nat'l Fin. Corp., 644 F. Supp. 1130, 1143 (M.D. Pa. 1986) (withdrawn tender offer need not be disclosed). *Accord* Walker v. Action Indus., Inc., 802 F.2d 703, 709 (4th Cir. 1986) (no duty to disclose financial projections under section 10(b); contains a review of the state of the law on disclosure of "soft" information), *cert. denied*, 479 U.S. 1065 (1987); Kademian v. Ladish Co., 792 F.2d 614 (no duty to disclose internal valuations); GAF Corp. v. Heyman, 724 F.2d 727, 743 (2d Cir. 1983) (validity of unadjudicated allegations are too speculative to constitute material omissions).

31. *See* Flynn v. Bass Bros. Enters., Inc., 744 F.2d 978, 988 (3d Cir. 1984); Weinberger v. Rio Grande Indus., Inc., 519 A.2d 116 (Del. Ch. 1986).

32. *See* Isquith v. Middle S. Utils., Inc., 847 F.2d 186, 205–06 (5th Cir. 1988) (noting variety of approaches to soft information and declining to establish standard for Fifth Circuit), *cert. denied*, 109 S. Ct. 310 (1988); *see also* Kerr, *A Walk through the Circuits: The Duty to Disclose Soft Information*, 46 MD. L. REV. 1071, 1076–1109 (1987); Hiler, *The SEC and the Courts' Approach to Disclosure of Earnings Projections, Asset Appraisals, and Other Soft Information: Old Problems, Changing Views*, 46 MD. L. REV. 1114, 1157–66 (1987).

33. Basic Inc. v. Levinsen, 108 S. Ct. 978, 984 n.9 (1988).

34. Morrissey v. County Tower Corp., 717 F.2d 1227, 1228–29 (8th Cir. 1983) (charge that company failed to disclose desire to entrench management as motive behind bylaw amendment not actionable).

35. Gaines v. Haughton, 645 F.2d 761, 766–67 (9th Cir. 1981), *cert. denied*, 454 U.S. 1145 (1982); *see also* Kademian v. Ladish Co., 792 F.2d 614. *But see* Bank & Trust Co. v. Hankin, 552 F. Supp. 1330 (E.D. Pa. 1982) (failure to disclose director self-dealing is material and actionable); *cf.* Pavlidis v. New England Patriots Football Club, Inc., 737 F.2d 1227, 1231 (1st Cir. 1984) ("[A]lthough § 14(a) requires any party soliciting proxies, regardless of his status or interest in the transaction, to disclose all material information, a self-dealing insider may have a 'heavier burden of disclosure' in the sense that he will find it more difficult to convince the court that he has met the requirements of § 14(a).").

36. *See* Schlick v. Penn-Dixie Cement Corp., 507 F.2d 374, 382 (2d Cir. 1974), *cert. denied*, 421 U.S. 976 (1975).

37. *See* Mosher v. Kane, 784 F.2d 1385, 1390 (9th Cir.) (a board's failure to act, preventing corporate transactions involving securities, is sufficiently causally connected to state a claim); Sanders v. Thrall Car Mfg. Co., 582 F. Supp. 945, 956–57 (S.D.N.Y. 1983) (fact that directors who engineered "freeze out" merger gained their offices through use of misleading proxy was too attenuated to support private cause of action under section 14(a)), *aff'd per curiam*, 730 F.2d 910 (2d Cir. 1984).

38. 478 F.2d 1281 (2d Cir. 1973).

39. 17 C.F.R. § 240.10b-5.

40. *Id.* § 240.14a-9.
41. *See also* Fradkin v. Ernst, 571 F. Supp. at 842.
42. Gerstle v. Gamble-Skogmo, Inc., 478 F.2d at 1301 n.20; *see also* Gould v. American Hawaiian Steamship Co., 351 F. Supp. 853, 860 (D. Del. 1972), *vacated and remanded on other grounds*, 535 F.2d 761 (3d Cir. 1976); *cf.* Shidler v. All Am. Life & Fin. Corp., 775 F.2d 917 (8th Cir. 1985) (rejecting strict liability as "too blunt a tool to ferret out" section 14(a) violations but not deciding whether negligence is enough).
43. *See* Adams v. Standard Knitting Mills, Inc., 623 F.2d 422, 430 (6th Cir.) (accounting firm not liable for negligent error in proxy financial statements), *cert. denied sub nom.* Adams v. Peat Marwick, Mitchell & Co., 449 U.S. 1067 (1980); *accord* Resource Exploration v. Yankee Oil & Gas, Inc., 566 F. Supp. 54 (N.D. Ohio 1983).
44. *See* Fradkin v. Ernst, 571 F. Supp. at 843.
45. 396 U.S. 375, 391 (1970).
46. *See, e.g.*, Texas Partners v. Conrock Co., 685 F.2d 1116, 1119 (9th Cir. 1982) (4 percent shareholder challenged issuer's proxy statement proposing antitakeover amendment; court holds that proxy statement may have been misleading), *cert. dismissed*, 460 U.S. 1029 (1983); FMC Corp. v. R.P. Scherer Corp., 545 F. Supp. 318, 320 (D. Del. 1982) (bidder, "in its capacity as a tender offeror" and "proxy contestant," sought preliminary injunction against shareholder meeting called to enact antitakeover amendments; injunction denied because bidder failed to show irreparable harm); Unicorp Fin. Corp. v. First Union Real Estate Equity & Mortgage Invs., 515 F. Supp. 249, 262 (S.D. Ohio 1981) (although "injunctive relief is certainly appropriate in these cases," preliminary injunction denied because bidder did not make sufficient showing of likelihood of success on the merits and irreparable injury).
47. *See, e.g.*, Bolton v. Gramlich, 540 F. Supp. 822, 834 (S.D.N.Y. 1982) (bidder claiming damages for funds spent opposing target's "misleading" proxy solicitation was not among those for whose special benefit the statute was enacted).
48. *See, e.g.*, Texas Partners v. Conrock Co., 685 F.2d at 1119 (antitakeover amendment may be invalid because issuer failed to make full disclosure in its proxy materials); Samuel M. Feinberg Testamentary Trust v. Carter, 652 F. Supp. 1066 (S.D.N.Y. 1987) (cause of action stated by shareholders alleging that target failed to disclose payment of greenmail in proxy solicitation relating to antigreenmail amendment); Edelman v. Saloman, 559 F. Supp. at 1187 (charter amendment that eliminated cumulative voting invalidated because issuer failed to make full disclosure in its proxy materials); Telvest, Inc. v. Wisconsin Real Estate Inv. Trust, 489 F. Supp. at 254 (court holds that target's failure to disclose that stock given to REIT manager was being funneled to target's president violated section 14(a)); *cf. In re* Anderson, Clayton Shareholders' Litig., 519 A.2d 669, 678 (Del. Ch. 1986) (under Delaware law, board's misstatements of its attitudes regarding a tender offer are reasonably probable to be found materially misleading).
49. [1987 Transfer Binder] FED. SEC. L. REP. (CCH) ¶ 93,189 (S.D.N.Y. Mar. 18, 1987).
50. *See* 17 C.F.R. § 240.13d-101.
51. *See* S. REP. NO. 265, *supra* note 16, at 18–26.

52. *See, e.g.*, Warner Communications, Inc. v. Murdoch, 581 F. Supp. 1482, 1499–1500 (D. Del. 1984) (while expressing "serious doubt" whether section 13(d)'s disclosure obligations should apply to management groups per se, court holds that management group that entered into a voting or pooling arrangement with third parties is subject to section 13(d)); Jacobs v. Pabst Brewing Co., 549 F. Supp. 1050, 1063–64 (D. Del. 1982) (bidder alleges that management's ally failed to file Schedule 13D).

53. Dan River, Inc. v. Unitex, Ltd., 624 F.2d 1216, 1225 (4th Cir. 1980), *cert. denied*, 449 U.S. 1101 (1981).

54. *See, e.g.*, Kalmanovitz v. G. Heileman Brewing Co., Inc., 595 F. Supp. 1385, 1392–93 (D. Del. 1984), *aff'd*, 796 F.2d 152 (3d Cir. 1985); Sanders v. Thrall Car Mfg. Co., 582 F. Supp. at 961; Schnell v. Schnall, [1981 Transfer Binder] FED. SEC. L. REP. (CCH) ¶ 97,927 at 90,714 (S.D.N.Y. Mar. 30, 1981); Berman v. Metzger, [1981 Transfer Binder] FED. SEC. L. REP. (CCH) ¶ 97,857 at 90,292 (D.D.C. Feb. 9, 1981); Myers v. American Leisure Time Enters., 402 F. Supp. 213, 214–15 (S.D.N.Y. 1975), *aff'd without opinion*, 538 F.2d 312 (2d Cir. 1976).

55. 15 U.S.C. § 78r(a). *See, e.g.,* Sanders v. Thrall Car Mfg. Co., 582 F. Supp. 945.

56. *See, e.g.*, Portsmouth Square v. Shareholders Protective Comm., 770 F.2d 866 (9th Cir. 1985); Gearhart Indus., Inc. v. Smith Int'l, Inc., 741 F.2d 707, 714 (5th Cir. 1984); Indiana Nat'l Corp. v. Rich, 712 F.2d 1180, 1185–86 (7th Cir. 1983); Dan River, Inc. v. Unitex, Ltd, 624 F.2d at 1224; GAF Corp. v. Milstein, 453 F.2d 709, 719–20 (2d Cir. 1971), *cert. denied*, 406 U.S. 910 (1972); Champion Parts Rebuilders, Inc. v. Cormier Corp., 661 F. Supp. 825 (N.D. Ill. 1987); HUBCO, Inc. v. Rappaport, 628 F. Supp. 345 (D.N.J. 1985).

57. 734 F.2d 545, 564–67 (11th Cir. 1984).

58. *See also* Atlantic Fed. Sav. & Loan Ass'n v. Dade Sav. & Loan Ass'n, 592 F. Supp. 1089 (S.D. Fla. 1984) (issuer has no implied right of action for injunctive relief); Equity Oil Co. v. Consolidated Oil & Gas, Inc., 596 F. Supp. 507 (D. Utah 1983) (issuers have no implied right of action for injunctive relief on their own behalf or for the benefit of shareholders); Leff v. CIP Corp., 540 F. Supp. 857, 863 (S.D. Ohio 1982) (shareholders have no implied right of action for injunctive relief against incumbent directors).

59. *See* Florida Commercial Banks v. Culverhouse, 772 F.2d 1513 (11th Cir. 1985).

60. 456 U.S. 353, 378–82 (1982).

61. 459 U.S. 375 (1983).

62. *Id.* at 387.

63. *Compare* Liberty Nat'l Ins. Holding Co. v. Charter Co., 734 F.2d 545, 562–65 (11th Cir. 1984) (despite *Curran*, issuer has no private right of action under section 13(d) for divestiture order) *and* Equity Oil Co. v. Consolidated Oil & Gas, Inc., 596 F. Supp. 507 (D. Utah 1983) (despite *Curran* and *Huddleston*, issuer has no private right of action under section 13(d) on either its own behalf or on its shareholders' behalf) *with* Indiana Nat'l Corp. v. Rich, 712 F.2d 1180, 1182–86 (7th Cir. 1983) (in light of *Curran* and *Huddleston*, issuer has private right of action under section 13(d)) *and* Jacobs v. Pabst Brewing Co., 549 F. Supp. 1050, 1061–62 (D. Del. 1982) (under *Curran*, bidder, as shareholder, has private right of action under section 13(d)).

64. 549 F. Supp. at 1066.

65. *See also* Podesta v. Calumet Indus., [1978 Transfer Binder] FED. SEC. L. REP.

(CCH) ¶ 96,433 at 93,560 (N.D. Ill. May 9, 1978) (management group avoids preliminary injunction against further purchases of shares by voluntarily filing Schedule 13D); Jewelcor Inc. v. Pearlman, 397 F. Supp. 221, 235 (S.D.N.Y. 1975) (management group ordered to file Schedule 13D).

66. *See, e.g.*, Warner Communications, Inc. v. Murdoch, 581 F. Supp. at 1500–01 (management group's amendment to challenged Schedule 13D, to include bidder's allegations that the original Schedule 13D failed to disclose the existence of a section 13(d)(3) group that acquired stock to deter a hostile takeover, did not necessarily cure the omission in the original Schedule 13D).

67. *See* HUBCO v. Rappaport, 628 F. Supp. 345, 354 (D.N.J. 1985).

68. *See, e.g.*, Schreiber v. Burlington N., Inc., 472 U.S. 1, 10 (1985); Smallwood v. Pearl Brewing Co., 489 F.2d 579, 605 (5th Cir.), *cert. denied*, 419 U.S. 873 (1974).

69. *See* Berman v. Gerber Prods. Co., 454 F. Supp. 1310, 1323 (W.D. Mich. 1978); Applied Digital Data Sys., Inc. v. Milgo Elec. Corp., 425 F. Supp. 1145, 1157 (S.D.N.Y. 1977). *But see* Caleb & Co. v. E.I. duPont de Nemours & Co., 615 F. Supp. 96 (S.D.N.Y.) (scienter not required for actions brought under Rule 14e-1(c) regarding prompt payment for tendered shares), *reargument granted,* 624 F. Supp. 747 (S.D.N.Y. 1985). *See generally* Schreiber v. Burlington N., Inc., 472 U.S. 1 (1985) (under either provision, a plaintiff must prove that the defendant's misrepresentation or nondisclosure caused its injury); Connecticut Nat'l Bank v. Fluor Corp., 808 F.2d 957 (2d Cir. 1987) (scienter must be pleaded with particularity).

70. MacFadden Holdings, Inc. v. JB Acquisition Corp., 802 F.2d 62, 69 n.3 (2d Cir. 1986) quoting Prudent Real Estate Trust v. Johncamp Realty, Inc., 599 F.2d 1140, 1146 (2d Cir. 1979)).

71. *See* Danaher Corp. v. Chicago Pneumatic Tool Co., 633 F. Supp. 1066 (S.D.N.Y. 1986).

72. Panter v. Marshall Field & Co., 646 F.2d 271 (7th Cir.), *cert. denied*, 454 U.S. 1092 (1981); Lewis v. McGraw, 619 F.2d 192 (2d Cir.), *cert. denied*, 449 U.S. 951 (1980); Sanders v. Thrall Car Mfg. Co., 582 F. Supp. at 968 (section 14(e) does not reach conduct occurring well in advance of tender offer).

73. Pullman-Peabody Co. v. Joy Mfg. Co., 662 F. Supp. 32, 34 (D.N.J. 1986); *see also* Moravek v. FNB Bancorp, No. 86 C 4571 (N.D. Ill. July 9, 1986) (WESTLAW, 1986 WL 7958).

74. Piper v. Chris-Craft Indus., 430 U.S. 1, 47 (1977).

75. *See, e.g.*, Starkman v. Marathon Oil Co., 772 F.2d 231 (6th Cir. 1985), *cert. denied*, 475 U.S. 1015 (1986); Mobil Corp. v. Marathon Oil Co., 669 F.2d 366, 370 (6th Cir. 1981); Whittaker Corp. v. Edgar, 535 F. Supp. 933, 949 (N.D. Ill. 1982); Bolton v. Gramlich, 540 F. Supp. at 835 (tender offerors, as shareholders, could bring derivative suit against target's board under section 14(e) for damages and injunctive relief); *cf.* Pryor v. United States Steel Corp., 794 F.2d 52, 58 (2d Cir.) (shareholder has standing to sue bidder under section 14(e)), *cert. denied*, 479 U.S. 954 (1986); Plaine v. McCabe, 797 F.2d 713 (9th Cir. 1986) (shareholder has standing to sue target and acquiror even though she did not tender her shares). *But cf.* Kalmanovitz v. G. Heileman Brewing Co., 769 F.2d 152 (bidder who also was shareholder in target had no standing to sue for money damages because his real interest in pursuing claim was as defeated tender offeror, not as shareholder).

76. *See* Caleb & Co. v. E.I. duPont de Nemours & Co., 615 F. Supp. 96.

77. 17 C.F.R. § 240.14d-9.

78. Rule 14d-101, 17 C.F.R. § 240.14d-101. *See also* Rule 14e-2, discussed below.

79. *See, e.g.*, Missouri Portland Cement Co. v. Cargill, Inc., 498 F.2d 851, 874–75 (2d Cir.) (target's statement in advertisement and letter to shareholders implying that increase in price during term of offer would not benefit those shareholders who had already tendered held to violate section 14(e)), *cert. denied*, 419 U.S. 883 (1974); Horowitz v. Pownall, 582 F. Supp. 665, 669 (D. Md. 1984) (summary judgment denied where Martin-Marietta's failure to disclose in its Schedule 14D-9 that its competing tender offer for Bendix would require it to obtain a loan of $900 million may constitute a material omission); Weeks Dredging & Contracting, Inc. v. American Dredging Co., 451 F. Supp. 468, 478 (E.D. Pa. 1978) (target's statement in news report that shares were worth far more than tender offer price and that target's financial picture was "shaping up all right" held to violate section 14(e)); Humana, Inc. v. American Medicorp, Inc., 445 F. Supp. 613 (S.D.N.Y. 1977) (target's statement in press release and letter to shareholders that offer was "inadequate" and "not in the best interests of" the shareholders violated section 14(e) because target failed to include information it had about the offer); Royal Indus., Inc. v. Monogram Indus., Inc., [1976–1977 Transfer Binder] FED. SEC. L. REP. (CCH) ¶ 95,863 at 91,138–43 (C.D. Cal. Nov. 29, 1976) (target's statements in press release and letter to shareholders that exaggerated target's financial condition and wrongly disparaged bidder's financial condition held to violate section 14(e)); *cf.* Plaza Sec. Co. v. Fruehauf Corp., 643 F. Supp. 1535 (E.D. Mich. 1986) (tender offer materials violated Rule 13e-3 (see below) where they falsely described role and independence of committee that investigated proposals, failed to disclose that the purchase price being offered by management was lower than the value of the company as estimated by management's own adviser, failed to disclose relevant financial data, failed to disclose self-serving purpose and effect on shareholders of defensive measures, and failed to adequately describe evaluation of hostile offer and its alternatives). *But cf.* Schreiber v. Burlington N., Inc., 472 U.S. 1 (1985) (failure to disclose golden parachute agreements not actionable under section 14(e) because no causal nexus shown between failure to disclose and damage due to inability to participate fully in prorated tender offer); Feldbaum v. Avon Prods., Inc., 741 F.2d 234, 236–37 (8th Cir. 1984) (target's failure to disclose that market price of its stock probably would decrease if tender offer succeeded not misleading because "[i]t requires no great amount of sophistication to infer from [the facts disclosed] that a decline in . . . price . . . was probable"); Data Probe Acquisition Corp. v. Datatab, Inc., 722 F.2d 1, 5–6 (2d Cir. 1983) (target's statement that it preferred offer with continued employment contracts was unnecessary since contracts had been disclosed), *cert. denied*, 465 U.S. 1052 (1984); Bolton v. Gramlich, 540 F. Supp. at 843 (defeated bidder alleged that target's Schedule 14D-9 failed to disclose conflict of interest of certain trustees; claim dismissed because bidder demonstrated no causal connection to bidder's injury).

80. *See* Field v. Trump, 661 F. Supp. 529, 534 (S.D.N.Y. 1987), *aff'd in part, rev'd in part,* 850 F.2d 938 (2d Cir. 1988); Pullman-Peabody Co. v. Joy Mfg. Co., 662 F. Supp. at 34; Coronet Ins. Co. v. Seyfarth, 665 F. Supp. 661 (N.D. Ill. 1987).

81. *See* Walker v. Action Indus., Inc., 802 F.2d 703, 707–10 & n.11 (4th Cir. 1986) (discussing split in authority and declining to adopt standard), *cert. denied*, 479

U.S. 1065 (1987); Flynn v. Bass Bros. Enters., Inc., 744 F.2d 978 (3d Cir. 1984).

82. *See* Radol v. Thomas, 772 F.2d 244, 253 (6th Cir. 1985) (rule 10b-5 claim), *cert. denied*, 477 U.S. 903 (1986); Starkman v. Marathon Oil Co., 772 F.2d at 238 (rule 10b-5 claim); *see also* Vaughn v. Teledyne, Inc., 628 F.2d 1214, 1221 (9th Cir. 1980) (estimates must be made with "reasonable certainty" before disclosure required in rule 10b-5 and section 14(e) case).

83. *See* Weinberger v. Rio Grande Indus., Inc., 519 A.2d 116 (Del. Ch. 1986).

84. 108 S. Ct. 978 (1988).

85. Greenfield v. Hueblein, Inc., 742 F.2d 751, 756–57 (3d Cir. 1984), *cert. denied*, 469 U.S. 1215 (1985); Staffin v. Greenberg, 672 F.2d 1196, 1206 (3d Cir. 1982).

86. Flamm v. Eberstadt, 814 F.2d 1169. (7th Cir.), *cert. denied*, 108 S. Ct. 157 (1987).

87. Jordan v. Duff & Phelps, Inc., 815 F.2d 429, 434 (7th Cir. 1987), *cert. dismissed*, 108 S. Ct. 1067 (1988); Michaels v. Michaels, 767 F.2d 1185 (7th Cir. 1985), *cert. denied*, 474 U.S. 1057 (1986).

88. Levinson v. Basic Inc., 786 F.2d 741, 744–47 (6th Cir. 1986), *vacated*, 108 S. Ct. 978 (1988).

89. *Basic*, 108 S. Ct. at 987.

90. *Id.* at 983, *quoting* TSC Indus., Inc. v. Northway, Inc., 426 U.S. 438, 449 (1976).

91. 17 C.F.R. § 240.14e-2.

92. *See, e.g.*, Bell v. Cameron Meadows Land Co., 669 F.2d 1278, 1282 (9th Cir. 1982) (target failed to adequately disclose that target's president was compensated for his support of offer); A&K R.R. Materials v. Green Bay & W. R.R., 437 F. Supp. 636, 644 (E.D. Wis. 1977) ("Management must be careful to disclose all possible conflicts of interest in connection with a tender offer."); *cf.* SEC v. Royal Indus., Inc., [1976–1977 Transfer Binder] FED. SEC. L. REP. (CCH) ¶ 95,773 at 90,794 (D.D.C. Nov. 16, 1976) (summary of consent decree; target agrees to disclose that management benefit plan accelerates in event of takeover).

93. 533 F. Supp. 86 (N.D. Fla. 1981).

94. *Id.* at 88.

95. *See, e.g.*, City Investing Co. v. Simcox, 633 F.2d 56, 64 (7th Cir. 1980) (upholding district court's decision to abstain from considering bidder's claim that state takeover statute is unconstitutional). *But see* Martin-Marietta Corp. v. Bendix Corp., 690 F.2d 558, 562–64 (6th Cir. 1982) (overturning district court's decision that action for injunctive relief from Michigan Take-Over Offers Act was barred by doctrine of abstention); National City Lines v. LLC Corp., 687 F.2d 1122, 1126–27 (8th Cir. 1982) (neither *Pullman* nor *Younger* abstention appropriate in case challenging Missouri Takeover Bid Disclosure Act).

96. 28 U.S.C. § 2283. *See* Martin-Marietta Corp., 690 F.2d at 562 (action under 42 U.S.C. § 1983 is an "expressly authorized" exception to Anti-Injunction Act); National City Lines v. LLC Corp., 687 F.2d at 1127 (Anti-Injunction Act inapplicable where federal court lawsuit is filed before state suit).

97. 457 U.S. 624 (1982) (finding Illinois statute unconstitutional).

98. 481 U.S. 69 (1987) (upholding Indiana statute).

99. MITE Corp. v. Dixon, 633 F.2d 486 (7th Cir. 1980), *aff'd sub nom.* Edgar v. MITE Corp., 457 U.S. 624 (1982).

100. 457 U.S. at 643.

101. *Id.* at 646.

102. *Id.* at 634.

103. *See, e.g.*, L.P. Acquisition Co. v. Tyson, 772 F.2d 201, 207–09 (6th Cir. 1985) (Michigan Take-Over Offers Act, even as applied to tender offers for unregistered securities, violates supremacy clause); Mesa Petroleum Co. v. Cities Serv. Co., 715 F.2d 1425, 1428–31 (10th Cir. 1983) (Oklahoma Take-Over Bid Act violates commerce clause); Telvest, Inc. v. Bradshaw, 697 F.2d 576, 579–82 (4th Cir. 1983) (Virginia Take-Over Bid Disclosure Act violates commerce clause); Martin-Marietta Corp. v. Bendix Corp., 690 F.2d at 565–68 (Michigan Take-Over Offers Act violates commerce clause); National City Lines v. LLC Corp., 687 F.2d 1122 (Missouri Takeover Bid Disclosure Act violates commerce clause and supremacy clause); Newell Co. v. Connolly, 624 F. Supp. 126, 127–28 (D. Mass. 1985) (Massachusetts antitakeover statute violates supremacy clause); Bendix Corp. v. Martin-Marietta Corp., 547 F. Supp. 522, 532 (D. Md. 1982) (Maryland Corporate Take-Over Law violates commerce clause and supremacy clause); *see also* Loral Corp. v. Sanders Assocs., Inc., 639 F. Supp. 639 (D. Del. 1986) (court refuses to enter agreed restraining order on the grounds that plaintiff had failed to demonstrate likelihood that Delaware Tender Offer Act, which was "regularly and routinely" enjoined on both commerce clause and supremacy clause grounds, would be enforced against plaintiff).

104. Sharon Steel Corp. v. Whaland, 124 N.H. 1, 466 A.2d 919, 922 (1983) (New Hampshire Security Takeover Disclosure Act violates commerce clause); Esmark, Inc. v. Strode, 639 S.W.2d 768, 733 (Ky. 1982) (Kentucky Take-Over Act violates commerce clause); *see also Colorado Commissioner Cites MITE, Won't Apply State Law to Tender Offers*, 15 SEC. REG. & L. REP. (BNA) 2047 (Nov. 14, 1983). *See generally* Block, Barton & Roth, *State Takeover Statutes: The "Second Generation,"* 13 SEC. REG. L.J. 332 (1986).

105. 751 F.2d 906 (8th Cir. 1984).

106. *Id.* at 912.

107. *Id.* at 914.

108. *Id.*

109. 686 F.2d 1029 (1st Cir. 1982).

110. *Cf.* Baron v. Strawbridge & Clothier, No. 86-2474 (E.D. Pa. May 1, 1986) (WESTLAW, 1986 WL 5163) (section 308 of the Pennsylvania Business Corporation Law, which requires the production of a shareholder list upon a demand by a shareholder for a "proper shareholder purpose," not preempted by rule 14d-5 under the Williams Act, which allows a target's management the option of either mailing a bidder's tender offer materials to shareholders or providing the bidder with a list of shareholders).

111. 624 F. Supp. 126 (D. Mass. 1985).

112. CONN. GEN. STAT. ANN. §§ 33-374a–374c (West 1987); GA. CODE ANN. § 14-2-232(6) (1985); ILL. REV. STAT., ch. 32, § 7.85 (1985); KY. REV. STAT. § 271A.396–400, 405 (1984); LA. REV. STAT. ANN. § 12:132–12:134 (West 1984); MD. CORPS. & ASS'NS CODE ANN. § 3-601 *et. seq.* (1984); MICH. COMP. LAWS §§ 451.901–451.917 (West Supp. 1987); Miss. Shareholder Protection Act; PA. CONS. STAT. § 409.1C (1983); VA. CODE ANN. §§ 13.1-725–728 (1985); WASH.

REV. CODE § 23A.08 425 (1985); WIS. STAT. § 180.725 (1984). *See generally* Romano, *The Political Economy of Takeover Statutes*, 73 VA. L. REV. 111 (1987).

113. *See generally* McKenna & Bittner, *The "Fair Price" Amendment to the Illinois Business Corporation Act*, 67 CHI. B. REC. 64 (1986).

114. HAWAII REV. STAT. § 416 (1985); MINN. STAT. § 302A, 671 (1985); MO. REV. STAT. § 351.407 (1984).

115. ME. REV. STAT. ANN. tit. 13-A, § 910 (1985); PA. CONS. STAT. § 910 (1983).

116. IND. CODE § 23-1-43-1 *et seq.* (1986); N.Y. BUS. CORP. LAW § 912(c) (1986); N.J. Shareholders Protection Act, ch. 74, § 4 (1986).

117. WIS. STAT. § 180.25(9)(a) (1986). *See generally* McKenna & Bittner, *supra* note 113, at 64.

118. 1987 Wash. Legis. Serv. No. 10 at 10 (West). *See New Washington Takeover Law Aimed at Protecting Boeing from Pickens Raid*, 19 SEC. REG. & L. REP. 1266 (Aug. 14, 1987).

119. *See, e.g.*, Gelco Corp. v. Coniston Partners, 652 F. Supp. 829 (D. Minn. 1986) (Minnesota Control Share Acquisition Act violates both commerce clause and supremacy clause), *vacated in part as moot*, 811 F.2d 414 (8th Cir. 1987); Terry v. Yamashita, 643 F. Supp. 161 (D. Haw. 1986) (Hawaii Control Share Statute violates commerce clause); APL Ltd. Partnership v. Van Dusen Air, Inc., 622 F. Supp. 1216 (D. Minn. 1985) (earlier version of Minnesota Control Share Acquisition Act violates commerce clause), *vacated as moot*, No. 85-5346 (8th Cir. Nov. 25, 1985); Icahn v. Blunt, 612 F. Supp. 1400 (W.D. Mo. 1985) (Missouri Control Share Acquisition Act violates both supremacy clause and commerce clause). *See generally* Block, Barton & Roth, *supra* note 104, at 344–52.

120. CTS Corp. v. Dynamics Corp. of Am., 481 U.S. 69 (1987); *see also* Fleet Aerospace Corp. v. Holderman, 796 F.2d 135 (6th Cir. 1986) (striking down Ohio Control Share Acquisition Act), *vacated and remanded in light of CTS*, 107 S. Ct. 1949 (1987).

121. Dynamics Corp. of Am. v. CTS Corp., 637 F. Supp. 406 (N.D. Ill.), *aff'd*, 794 F.2d 250 (7th Cir. 1986).

122. CTS Corp. v. Dynamics Corp. of Am., 107 S. Ct. at 1645.

123. *Id.* at 1649.

124. *Id.* at 1649–50.

125. *Id.* at 1651.

126. *See* 1987 Ariz. Legis. Serv. 32 (West); 1987 Fla. Sess. Law Serv. 517 (West); 1987 Mass. Legis. Serv. 45 (West); 1987 Minn. Sess. Law. Serv. 911 (West); 1987 N.C. Adv. Legis. Serv., no. 2, at 49.

127. *See generally* Danilow & Bentley, *Developments in State Takeover Statutes*, 20 REV. SEC. & COMM. REG. 99 (June 10, 1987).

128. TLX Acquisition Corp. v. Telex Corp., 679 F. Supp. 1022 (W.D. Okla. 1987).

129. *Id.* at 1029.

130. DEL. CODE ANN. tit. 8, § 203.

131. *Id.* at § 203(b).

132. RP Acquisition Corp. v. Staley Continental, Inc., 686 F. Supp. 476, 482 (D. Del. 1988) (denying preliminary injunction because evidence act made favorable

tender offers impossible not persuasive); BNS Inc. v. Koppers Co., 683 F. Supp. 458 (D. Del. 1988) (denying preliminary injunction in absence of evidentiary record as to opportunities for successful offer).

133. 1987 Wis. Act 45, § 2, to be codified at WIS. STAT. § 180.726.

134. RTE Corp. v. Mark IV Indus., Inc., [1987 Transfer Binder] FED. SEC. L. REP. (CCH) ¶ 93,789 (E.D. Wis. May 6, 1988).

135. Massachusetts Take-Over Bid Regulation Act, MASS. GEN. L. ch. 110C, § 3 (1986).

136. Hyde Park Partners, L.P. v. Connolly, 839 F.2d 837 (1st Cir. 1988).

137. *Id.* at 850–53.

138. *Id.* at 847.

139. Veere Inc. v. Firestone Tire & Rubber Co., 685 F. Supp. 1027 (N.D. Ohio 1988).

140. Batus Inc. v. McKay, 684 F. Supp. 637 (D. Nev. 1988).

141. *See, e.g.*, Ingersoll, *Securities Industry Association Urges Congress to Tighten Takeover Regulation*, Wall St. J., Mar. 26, 1987, at 62, col. 1; *Supreme Court Decision Upholding Indiana Takeover Law Remains Key Topic at Hearing*, Daily Report for Executives (BNA), July 13, 1987, at A-16.

142. *See Senate Briefly Considers Tender Offer Reform Proposal*, 20 SEC. REG. & L. REP. (BNA) 917 (June 17, 1988).

143. *See, e.g.*, Norlin Corp. v. Rooney, Pace Inc., 744 F.2d 255, 264 (2d Cir. 1984) (New York law); Minstar Acquiring Corp. v. AMF Inc., 621 F. Supp. 1252, 1260 n.6 (S.D.N.Y. 1985) (New Jersey law); Smith v. Van Gorkom, 488 A.2d 858, 872 (Del. 1985) (Delaware law).

144. *Van Gorkom*, 488 A.2d at 872.

145. *Id. Accord* Treadway Cos., Inc. v. Care Corp., 638 F.2d 357, 381 (2d Cir. 1980) (New Jersey law).

146. *See, e.g.*, *Van Gorkom*, 488 A.2d at 873 (burden satisfied by showing that Trans Union's board was grossly negligent in approving cash-out merger); Hanson Trust PLC v. ML SCM Acquisition, Inc., 781 F.2d 264, 275 (2d Cir. 1986) (although directors' approval of lockup option was not grossly negligent, the "paucity of information and their swiftness of decision-making strongly suggest a breach of the duty of due care," necessitating preliminary injunction).

147. *See, e.g.*, *Norlin*, 744 F.2d at 265 (business judgment rule inapplicable where target's board issued voting stock to a newly created ESOP and a wholly owned subsidiary "to solidify management's control" in face of attempted hostile takeover).

148. *See, e.g.*, *Hanson Trust*, 781 F.2d at 277; *Treadway*, 638 F.2d at 382.

149. *See, e.g.*, *Norlin*, 744 F.2d at 264–65 (citing *Treadway*).

150. Panter v. Marshall Field & Co., 646 F.2d at 293–95.

151. Crouse-Hinds Co. v. Internorth, Inc., 634 F.2d 690, 702–04 (2d Cir. 1980).

152. *Panter*, 646 F.2d at 293–94; Johnson v. Trueblood, 629 F.2d 287, 292–93 (3d Cir. 1980), *cert. denied*, 450 U.S. 999 (1981).

153. *Johnson*, 629 F.2d at 293 (quoting Cheff v. Mathes, 199 A.2d 548, 554 (Del. Ch. 1964)).

154. 493 A.2d 946 (Del. 1985).

155. *Id.* at 954.

156. *Id.*

157. *See* Lewis v. Honeywell, Inc., Civ. A. No. 8651 (Del. Ch. July 28, 1987) (WESTLAW, 1987 WL 14747) (dismissing "conclusory" complaint alleging breach of fiduciary duty in summary rejection of acquisition offer).

158. Unocal Corp. v. Mesa Petroleum Co., 493 A.2d at 955–56.

159. Moran v. Household Int'l, Inc., 500 A.2d 1346 (Del. 1985).

160. Revlon, Inc. v. MacAndrews & Forbes Holdings, Inc., 506 A.2d 173 (Del. 1986); *see also* AC Acquisitions Corp. v. Anderson, Clayton & Co., 519 A.2d 103 (Del. Ch. 1986) (applying *Unocal*, court preliminarily enjoins defensive recapitalization by target). *See generally* Wander & Le Coque, *Boardroom Jitters: Corporation Control Transactions and Today's Business Judgment Rule*, 42 BUS. LAW. 29 (Nov. 1986).

161. *See* Dynamics Corp. of Am. v. CTS Corp., 794 F.2d 250 (7th Cir. 1986) [*CTS I*] (applying Indiana law, but citing *Unocal*, court upholds preliminary injunction against enforcement of target's poison pill), *rev'd on other grounds*, 481 U.S. 69 (1987); Gelco Corp. v. Coniston Partners, 652 F. Supp. 829, 845 (D. Minn. 1986) (applying Minnesota law, court gives "heightened judicial scrutiny" to target's defensive exchange offer, poison pill, and sale of preferred stock to friendly third party, but denies preliminary injunction), *aff'd in part*, 811 F.2d 414 (8th Cir. 1987); Jewel Cos. v. Pay Less Drug Stores Northwest, Inc., 741 F.2d 1555, 1560 (9th Cir. 1984) (applying California law, court recognizes that "the actions of a board of directors in a corporate control transaction may be subject to special scrutiny under both the business judgment rule and the fairness test"); GAF Corp. v. Union Carbide Corp., 624 F. Supp. 1016, 1022 (S.D.N.Y. 1985) (target board has burden of going forward with proof of reasonableness and fairness). *But see* Hanson Trust PLC v. ML SCM Acquisition, Inc., 781 F.2d at 273 (distinguishing *Unocal*, court observes that "under New York law, the initial burden of proving directors' breach of fiduciary duty rests with the plaintiffs"; court nevertheless enjoins target's lockup).

162. Plaza Sec. Co. v. Fruehauf Corp., 643 F. Supp. 1535 (E.D. Mich. 1986).

163. *Id.* at 1546.

164. *Compare* Moran v. Household Int'l, Inc., 500 A.2d at 1350 ("in reviewing a pre-planned defensive mechanism it seems even more appropriate to apply the business judgment rule"), *with CTS I*, 637 F. Supp. at 418 (enjoining enforcement of poison pill adopted "in the heat of a proxy contest"), *aff'd*, 794 F.2d 250 (7th Cir. 1986).

165. Revlon, Inc. v. MacAndrews & Forbes Holdings, Inc., 506 A.2d at 182; *see also* Edelman v. Fruehauf Corp., 798 F.2d 882, 886–87 (6th Cir. 1986) (Michigan law); Hanson Trust PLC v. ML SCM Acquisition Inc., 781 F.2d 264 (2d Cir. 1986) (New York law); Samjens Partners I v. Burlington Indus., Inc., 663 F. Supp. 614 (S.D.N.Y. 1987) (applying Delaware law). *But see* Dynamics Corp. of Am. v. CTS Corp., 805 F.2d 705, 717 (7th Cir. 1986) (suggesting there may be circumstances when defensive measures such as poison pills can raise auction price shareholders receive); Keyser v. Commonwealth Nat'l Fin. Corp., 675 F. Supp. 238 (M.D. Pa. 1987) (Pennsylvania law may allow directors to consider factors other than price to shareholders).

166. Moran v. Household Int'l, Inc., 500 A.2d at 1356. *But see CTS I*, 794 F.2d at 256 ("When managers are busy erecting obstacles to the taking over of the

corporation by an investor who is likely to fire them if the takeover attempt succeeds, they have a clear conflict of interest, and it is not cured by vesting the power of decision in a board of directors in which insiders are a minority. . . . No one likes to be fired, whether he is just a director or also an officer."); Edelman v. Fruehauf, 798 F.2d at 887 (court finds that outside directors "rubber stamped" management's LBO proposal).

167. *See Responses to the D&O Insurance Crisis*, 19 REV. SEC. & COMM. REG. 263, 267 (Dec. 24, 1986). *See also* OHIO REV. CODE ANN., 1987 Legis. Bull. 1 (Anderson); *Ohio Legislature Broadens Scope of Business Judgment Rule*, 18 SEC. REG. & L. REP. (BNA) 1719 (Nov. 28, 1986).

168. *See More Companies than Ever Seeking Antitakeover Amendments, Study Says*, 17 SEC. REG. & L. REP. (BNA) 1960 (Nov. 11, 1985).

169. *See generally* Wander & Le Coque, *supra* note 160.

170. *See, e.g.*, *Lucky Stores' Holders Approve Measure That Clears Way for Restructuring Plan*, Wall St. J., Dec. 23, 1986, at 12 (discussing a San Francisco federal court's refusal to enjoin Lucky Stores' restructuring plan); Seibert v. Gulton Indus., Civ. A. No. 5631 (Del. Ch. June 21, 1979) (WESTLAW, 1979 WL 2710), *aff'd without opinion*, 414 A.2d 822 (Del. 1980) (upholding shareholder-approved charter amendment requiring 5 percent owner to obtain either board approval or 80 percent vote of shareholders before merging with issuer); *see also* Young v. Valhi, 382 A.2d 1372, 1378 (Del. Ch. 1978) (enjoining attempt to circumvent charter provision requiring 80 percent vote to approve mergers; corporation sought to merge into wholly owned subsidiary by means of simple majority vote).

171. *See, e.g.*, Financial Fed'n, Inc. v. Ashkenazy, [1984 Transfer Binder] FED. SEC. L. REP. (CCH) ¶ 91,489 at 98,440 (C.D. Cal. May 9, 1983) (court invalidates board-adopted bylaw amendment disqualifying from board membership any 10 percent owner who had been notified that his actions were illegal, finding that the amendment "was adopted for the sole purpose of excluding Ashkenazy . . . from serving on FFI's board of directors"); Joseph E. Seagram & Sons v. Conoco, Inc., 519 F. Supp. 506, 514 (D. Del. 1981) (board-adopted bylaw restricting the number of shares that could be held by "alien" corporations or individuals violated Delaware statute requiring shareholder approval of any restrictions on stock transfer); Holly Sugar Corp. v. Buchsbaum, [1981–1982 Transfer Binder] FED. SEC. L. REP. (CCH) ¶ 98,366 at 92,240 (D. Colo. Oct. 28, 1981) (court preliminarily enjoins issuer from enforcing board-adopted bylaw amendment limiting right of shareholders to call special meetings); San Francisco Real Estate Investors v. Real Estate Inv. Trust of Am., 701 F.2d 1000, 1006–07 (1st Cir. 1983) (board-adopted bylaw that effectively prohibited anyone from owning more than 9.8 percent of the REIT's shares violated REIT's Declaration of Trust); Telvest, Inc. v. Olson, Civ. A. No. 5798 (Del. Ch. Mar. 8, 1979) (WESTLAW, 1979 WL 1759) (court enjoins board from issuing, without shareholder approval, a new class of preferred stock, a supermajority vote of which was required to approve business combination with a 20 percent shareholder). *But see* Treco, Inc. v. Land of Lincoln Sav. & Loan, 572 F. Supp. 1455, 1460–61 (N.D. Ill. 1983), *aff'd*, 749 F.2d 374 (7th Cir. 1984) (business judgment rule protected board's decision to amend corporate bylaws to increase percentage of shareholder approval necessary for bylaw amendments).

172. *See, e.g.*, Martin-Marietta Corp. v. Bendix Corp., Civ. A. No. 6942 (Del. Ch. Sept. 19, 1982) (available on LEXIS) (court refuses to enjoin shareholder

meeting called to approve two charter amendments), *aff'd on other grounds*, No. 298 (Del. Sept. 21, 1982); FMC Corp. v. R.P. Scherer Corp., 545 F. Supp. 318, 322 (D. Del. 1982) (finding no irreparable harm, court refuses to enjoin vote on charter amendments); FMC Corp. v. R.P. Scherer Corp., Civ. A. No. 6889 (Del. Ch. Aug. 6, 1982) (LEXIS, states library) (same).

173. *See* Texas Partners v. Conrock Co., 685 F.2d 1116, 1120–21 (9th Cir. 1982) (antitakeover amendment may be invalid because issuer failed to make full disclosure in its proxy materials), *cert. dismissed*, 460 U.S. 1029 (1983); Edelman v. Saloman, 559 F. Supp. at 1187 (invalidating charter amendment that eliminated cumulative voting because issuer failed to make full disclosure in its proxy materials); *cf. In re* Anderson, Clayton Shareholders' Litig., 519 A.2d 669 (Del. Ch. 1986) (court enjoins corporate recapitalization approved at shareholder meeting; shareholder vote was flawed because target's representations to shareholders that target was "continuing to discuss" proposed tender offer with hostile bidder, when no substantive negotiations were taking place, were "at least misleading"). *But cf.* Warner Communications, Inc. v. Murdoch, 581 F. Supp. at 1490–91 (target with charter requirement of 80 percent shareholder approval of any tender offer held not obligated to disclose strategy to issue 20 percent of stock to friendly party in event of a hostile tender offer at the mere planning stage "regardless of the strength of management's commitment to ultimately follow through with the defensive tactic").

174. *See Study Shows Fair Price Amendments Have Little Effect on Stock Value*, 17 SEC. REG. & L. REP. (BNA) 1829 (Oct. 18, 1985), *discussing* SECURITIES & EXCHANGE COMMISSION, OFFICE OF CHIEF ECONOMIST, SHARK REPELLANTS AND STOCK PRICES: THE EFFECTS OF ANTITAKEOVER AMENDMENTS SINCE 1980 (1985).

175. *See Shark Repellants Discourage Takeovers, Reduce Shareholders' Returns*, IRRC, 17 SEC. REG. & L. REP. (BNA) 195 (Feb. 1, 1985).

176. *See Institutional Investor Group Issues Directory of Firm Shark Repellants*, 17 SEC. REG. & L. REP. (BNA) at 335 (Feb. 22, 1985).

177. *See Institutional Investors Form Council to Address Corporate Takeover Issues*, 17 SEC. REG. & L. REP. (BNA) 159 (Jan. 25, 1985).

178. *See Institutional Investors Set to Play Larger Role in Takeover, Panel Told*, 17 SEC. REG. & L. REP. (BNA) 362 (Mar. 1, 1985).

179. *See Bill of Rights Seeks to Boost Power of Shareholders*, Wash. Post, Apr. 13, 1986.

180. *See Almost 30 Percent of Fortune 500 Firms Have Adopted Poison Pills, Study Finds*, 19 SEC. REG. & L. REP. (BNA) 223 (Feb. 13, 1987).

181. *See* Note, *Protecting Shareholders against Partial and Two-Tiered Takeovers: The "Poison Pill" Preferred*, 97 HARV. L. REV. 1964 (1984).

182. 500 A.2d 1346 (Del. 1985).

183. Exchange Act Rel. No. 23,486, *supra* note 11.

184. *See Poison Pills Reduce Shareholder Wealth but Stop Raiders, SEC Staff Study Says*, 18 SEC. REG. & L. REP. (BNA) 1577 (Oct. 31, 1986). *But see generally* Lipton, *SEC Wrong on Poison Pills*, Legal Times, Nov. 17, 1986, at 15 (arguing that while prices of target shares do fall immediately after poison pill plans are adopted, shareholders benefit in the long run from such plans).

185. *See* Miller, *Common Defense against Takeovers Faces New Hurdle*, Wall St. J., Nov. 4, 1986, at 24.

186. Exchange Act Rel. No. 23,486, *supra* note 11.

187. *See Poison Pills Reduce Shareholder Wealth but Stop Raiders*, *supra* note 167.

188. *See* Dynamics Corp. of Am. v. CTS Corp., 805 F.2d 705 (7th Cir. 1986) (vacating denial of injunction against second CTS poison pill for further factual determinations); Dynamics Corp. of Am. v. CTS Corp., 794 F.2d 250 (7th Cir. 1986) (affirming injunction against enforcement of first CTS poison pill), *rev'd on other grounds*, 481 U.S. 69 (1987); Buckhorn, Inc. v. Ropak Corp., 656 F. Supp. 209 (S.D. Ohio 1987) (enjoining poison pill; although it was a reasonable response to threat, directors failed to make informed business judgment in setting trigger prices), *aff'd*, 815 F.2d 76 (6th Cir. 1987); Amalgamated Sugar Co. v. NL Indus., 644 F. Supp. 1229 (S.D.N.Y. 1986) (enjoining NL's poison pill). *But see* Tate & Lyle PLC v. Staley Cont'l Inc., FED. SEC. L. REP. (CCH) ¶ 93,764 (Del. Ch. May 9, 1988) (denying preliminary injunction to invalidate poison pill); Harvard Indus., Inc. v. Tyson, [1986–1987 Transfer Binder] FED. SEC. L. REP. (CCH) ¶ 93,064 (E.D. Mich. Nov. 25, 1986) (poison pill was a reasonable response to the threat posed; preliminary injunction denied).

Even the Delaware courts have recently struck down poison pills. *See, e.g.*, City Capital Associates Limited Partnership v. Interco Inc., [Current Binder] Fed. Sec. L. Rep. § 94,084 at 91,064 (Del. Ch. Nov. 1, 1988) (appeal pending, but possibly mooted) (enjoining Rights Plan so that shareholders could vote on roughly equivalent offers); Mills Acquisition Co. v. MacMillan, Inc., [Current Binder] Fed. Sec. L. Rep. § 94,071 (Del. Ch. Oct. 17, 1988) (implying that court would enjoin Rights Plan to allow shareholders to vote for higher offer if bidder removed conditions on offer), *rev'd on other grounds,* [Current Binder] Fed. Sec. L. Rep. § 94,072 (Del. Nov. 2, 1988); *see also* Gibson & Smith, *Pillsbury Agrees to $5.75 Billion Offer by Grand Met After Poison Pill Is Struck Down in Delaware Court,* Wall St. J., Dec. 19, 1988, at A3, col. 1 (quoting Judge Duffy's opinion) ("I conclude that the board's decision to keep the pill in place was not reasonable in relation to any threat posed and, therefore, the board's decision is not protected by the business judgment rule.").

189. Civ. A. No. 7278 (Del. Ch. Aug. 25, 1983) (available on LEXIS).

190. Slip op. at 6. *But see* Asarco, Inc. v. Court, 611 F. Supp. 468 (D.N.J. 1985) (issuance of preferred stock with special voting rights invalid under New Jersey law); Minstar Acquiring Corp. v. AMF Inc., 621 F. Supp. 1252 (S.D.N.Y. 1985) (target's adoption of poison pill debentures and preferred stock improper under New Jersey law).

191. *See generally* Bloomenthal, *Tender Offer Defenses—Poison Pill or Placebo?* 8 SEC. & FED. CORP. L. REP. 145 (Sept. 1, 1986).

192. Burrough & Cohen, *Poison Pill Inventor, Conceding Snags in Defense Plan, Prescribes New Remedy*, Wall St. J., July 20, 1987, at 2.

193. *See* Labaton, *Business and the Law: More Potency for Poison Pills*, N.Y. Times, July 20, 1987, at D2, col. 1.

194. OHIO REV. CODE ANN., 1987 Legis. Bull. 1 (Anderson). *See New Ohio Law to Assist Firms in Rejecting Hostile Takeover Attempts*, 19 SEC. REG. & L. REP. (BNA) 345 (Mar. 6, 1987).

195. 500 A.2d 1346 (1985).

196. *Id.* at 1349.

197. 490 A.2d 1059.

198. 500 A.2d 1346.

611

199. *Id.* at 1353.

200. *Id.* at 1352.

201. 493 A.2d 946 (Del. 1985).

202. 500 A.2d at 1356–57.

203. *See SEC Urges Delaware Court to Void Poison-Pill Preferred Takeover Defense*, 17 SEC. REG. & L. REP. (BNA) 481 (Mar. 22, 1985).

204. 506 A.2d 173, 180 (Del. 1986).

205. *Id.* at 180–81.

206. *Id.* at 181.

207. Facet Enters., Inc. v. Prospect Group, Inc., Civ. A. No. 9746 (Del. Ch. Apr. 15, 1988) (WESTLAW, 1988 WL 36140); *accord* CRTF Corp. v. Federated Dep't Stores, Inc., 683 F. Supp. 422, 439 (S.D.N.Y. 1988) (approving use of poison pill as "shield to fend off coercive offers" and "gavel to run an auction"); *see also* Desert Partners, L.P. v. USG Corp., 686 F. Supp. 1289 (N.D. Ill. 1988) (refusing to enjoin poison pill) (Delaware law).

208. *See, e.g.*, Gelco Corp. v. Coniston Partners, 652 F. Supp. 829 (D. Minn. 1986) (applying Minnesota law but relying in part on *Moran* and *Revlon*, court denies preliminary injunction against target's enforcement of and refusal to redeem poison pill), *aff'd in part*, 811 F.2d 414 (8th Cir. 1987); Horwitz v. Southwest Forest Indus., Inc., 604 F. Supp. 1130, 1136 (D. Nev. 1985) (citing lower court's decision in *Moran*, court denies preliminary injunction against enforcement of Nevada target's poison pill).

209. *Compare* R.D. Smith & Co., Inc. v. Preway, Inc., 644 F. Supp. 868 (W.D. Wis. 1986) (court not persuaded that Preway's board acted in good faith and upon reasonable investigation, but declines to enjoin enforcement of Preway's poison pill due to lack of irreparable harm), *with* Gelco Corp. v. Coniston Partners, 652 F. Supp. 829 (board acted reasonably both in adopting and in refusing to redeem poison pill; motion for preliminary injunction denied), *aff'd in part*, 811 F.2d 414 (8th Cir. 1987).

210. 811 F.2d at 414.

211. *Id.* at 420.

212. 662 F. Supp. 153 (N.D. Ill. 1987).

213. 794 F.2d 250, 255 (7th Cir. 1986) [*CTS I*], *rev'd on other grounds*, 481 U.S. 69 (1987).

214. 637 F. Supp. 406, 417 (N.D. Ill.), *aff'd*, 794 F.2d 250 (7th Cir. 1986).

215. *Id.* at 418.

216. *CTS I*, 794 F.2d at 257.

217. *Id.* at 259.

218. Dynamics Corp. of Am. v. CTS Corp., 635 F. Supp. 1174, *aff'd on rehearing*, 638 F. Supp. 802 (N.D. Ill. 1986).

219. *Id.* at 1178–80.

220. Dynamics Corp. of Am. v. CTS Corp., 805 F.2d 705, 712 (7th Cir. 1986) [*CTS II*].

221. *Id.* at 714.

222. *Id.* at 718.

223. *See also* R.D. Smith & Co., Inc. v. Preway, Inc., 644 F. Supp. 868 (following rationale of *CTS I*).

224. 644 F. Supp. 1229 (S.D.N.Y. 1980).

225. *See* Asarco, Inc. v. M.R.H. Holmes à Court, 611 F. Supp. 468 (D.N.J. 1985) (New Jersey Business Corporations Act prohibits target from issuing as a dividend to all common stockholders preferred stock that, in the event of a 20 percent acquisition, would convert into stock with enhanced voting power for all shareholders other than the 20 percent shareholder).

226. R.D. Smith & Co., Inc. v. Preway, Inc., 644 F. Supp. at 875.

227. *See New York Court Enjoins Enforcement of Discriminatory Flip-In Provision*, 20 SEC. REG. & L. REP. (BNA) 1275 (Aug. 12, 1988), *discussing* Bank of N.Y. Co. v. Irving Bank Corp. (N.Y. Sup. Ct. July 6, 1988). The same court had earlier enjoined the target's bylaw amendments intended to prevent a future board named by the bidder from redeeming the poison pill. Bank of N.Y. Co. v. Irving Bank Corp., 528 N.Y.S.2d 482 (Sup. 1988).

228. *See* Providence & Worcester Co. v. Baker, 378 A.2d 121, 123 (Del. 1977) (upholding charter provision setting varying voting rights depending on the size of a shareholder's holding); *see also* Harvard Indus., Inc. v. Tyson, [1986–1987 Transfer Binder] FED. SEC. L. REP. (CCH) ¶ 93,064 (E.D. Mich. Nov. 25, 1986) (preliminary injunction denied; poison pill discriminates among shareholders, not shares).

229. *CTS II*, 805 F.2d at 718.

230. 652 F. Supp. 829 (D. Minn. 1986), *aff'd in part*, 811 F.2d 414 (8th Cir. 1987).

231. 378 A.2d 121 (Del. 1977).

232. 500 A.2d at 1353.

233. *CTS II*, 805 F.2d at 718.

234. *See, e.g.*, Keyser v. Commonwealth Nat'l Fin. Corp., 644 F. Supp. 1130, 1147 (N.D. Pa. 1986) (upholding lockup plan as "a necessary and integral part of a merger agreement"); *In re* Castle & Cooke Derivative Shareholder Litig., No. C-85-0663 (N.D. Cal. 1985) (upholding board's decision to grant crown jewel asset option exercisable upon shareholder disapproval of proposed merger); Marshall Field & Co. v. Icahn, 537 F. Supp. 413, 422 (S.D.N.Y. 1982) (court refuses to enjoin target's grant to white knight of right of first refusal to buy certain assets); Whittaker Corp. v. Edgar, 535 F. Supp. 933, 950–51 (N.D. Ill. 1982) (court refuses to enjoin target's sale of prized asset); Mobil Corp. v. Marathon Oil Co., [1981–1982 Transfer Binder] FED. SEC. L. REP. (CCH) ¶ 98,375 at 92,285 (N.D. Ohio Dec. 23, 1981) (court refuses to enjoin target's sale of prized asset); *see also* Thompson v. Enstar Corp., 509 A.2d 578 (Del. Ch. 1984) (preliminary injunction denied; plaintiffs failed to meet the burden of proving there was "a reasonable probability that the approval of the lock-up agreements is not fair to the shareholders or that the directors acted unreasonably in adopting them"); GM Sub Corp. v. Liggett Group, Inc., Civ. A. No. 6155 (Del. Ch. Apr. 25, 1980) (available on LEXIS) (sale of asset upheld; "[T]here is nothing offered by GM Sub to show that the price [to be paid for the asset] is in any way inadequate or that the sale is on such unfavorable terms as to constitute a waste of corporate assets."). *But see* Seagram & Sons, Inc. v. Abrams, 510 F. Supp. 860, 861 (S.D.N.Y. 1981) (court issues temporary restraining order preventing target's sale of all its assets); Gimbel v. Signal Cos., Inc., 316 A.2d 599, 617 (Del. Ch.) ("the discrepancy between the values is so

great that an immediate fuller investigation into this matter of fair value should be had"), *aff'd*, 316 A.2d 619 (Del. 1974).

235. *See* Revlon, Inc. v. MacAndrews & Forbes Holdings, Inc., 506 A.2d 173 (Del. 1986); Hanson Trust PLC v. ML SCM Acquisition, Inc., 781 F.2d 264 (2d Cir. 1986).

236. MacAndrews & Forbes Holdings, Inc. v. Revlon, Inc., 501 A.2d 1239 (Del. Ch. 1985), *aff'd*, 505 A.2d 454 (Del. Supr. 1985).

237. *Id.* at 1250.

238. Revlon, Inc. v. MacAndrews & Forbes Holdings, Inc., 506 A.2d at 180–81.

239. *Id.* at 182.

240. *Id.*

241. 509 A.2d 578 (Del. Ch. 1984).

242. *Id.* at 583.

243. *Id.* at 584.

244. Revlon, Inc. v. MacAndrews & Forbes Holdings, Inc., 506 A.2d at 183. *See generally* Note, *Lock-Up Options: Toward a State Law Standard*, 96 HARV. L. REV. 1068, 1081 (1983).

245. 781 F.2d 264 (2d Cir. 1986).

246. 623 F. Supp. 848 (S.D.N.Y. 1985).

247. *Id.* at 857.

248. Hanson Trust PLC v. ML SCM Acquisition, Inc., 781 F.2d 264.

249. *Id.* at 275.

250. *Id.* at 281.

251. *Id.* at 282.

252. *See generally* Finkelstein & Abrams, *Lock-Ups in Contested Takeovers*, 19 REV. SEC. & COMM. REG. 117 (1986).

253. *See generally* Wander & LeCoque, *supra* note 160, at 51–56.

254. Revlon, Inc. v. MacAndrews & Forbes Holdings, Inc., 506 F.2d at 184.

255. *See* ConAgra, Inc. v. Cargill, Inc., 382 N.W.2d 576, 588 (Neb. 1986) (best-efforts clause does not relieve directors of duty to investigate competing offers and recommend them to the shareholders if better than the original offer).

256. *See, e.g.*, Jewel Cos. v. PayLess Drug Stores Northwest, Inc., 741 F.2d 1555 (9th Cir. 1984).

257. *But cf.* Gelco Corp. v. Coniston Partners, 652 F. Supp. 829 (D. Minn. 1986) (upholding sale of preferred stock to friendly third party as a means of "bridge financing" for target's recapitalization), *aff'd in part*, 811 F.2d 414 (8th Cir. 1987).

258. *See, e.g.*, Buffalo Forge Co. v. Ogden Corp., 717 F.2d 757 (2d Cir.) (upholding sale of treasury stock and grant of stock options to one of two competing bidders), *cert. denied*, 464 U.S. 1018 (1983); Treadway Cos. v. Care Corp., 638 F.2d 357, 383 (2d Cir. 1980) (vacating preliminary injunction restraining sale of newly issued stock to white knight); Crouse-Hinds Co. v. Internorth, Inc., 634 F.2d 690, 702 (2d Cir. 1980) (same); Johnson v. Trueblood, 629 F.2d 287, 293 (3d Cir. 1980) (upholding sale of stock to an incumbent director at a price lower than minority shareholders' offer; plaintiffs failed to show that "the sole or primary motive of the defendant was to retain control"), *cert. denied*, 450

U.S. 999 (1981); Marshall Field & Co. v. Icahn, 537 F. Supp. at 422 (upholding white knight's agreement to purchase large block of target's treasury shares provided no other bidder obtained 51 percent of target's stock); Mobil Corp. v. Marathon Oil Co., [1981–1982 Transfer Binder] FED. SEC. L. REP. (CCH) ¶ 98,375 at 92,285 (N.D. Ohio Dec. 23, 1981) (granting white knight option to purchase large block of target's stock and target's principal asset held not to violate target board's fiduciary duties); *see also* Kademian v. Ladish Co., 792 F.2d 614, 627 (7th Cir. 1986) (stock lockup was fully explained in proxy statement and therefore was not "manipulative" under the Williams Act); Data Probe Acquisition Corp. v. Datatab, Inc., 722 F.2d 1, 5 (2d Cir.), *cert. denied*, 465 U.S. 1052 (1984) (vacating preliminary injunction restraining grant of stock option; provided there is full disclosure, imposition of substantive obligations on target's management is an unwarranted extension of the Williams Act); Swanson v. Wabash, Inc., 577 F. Supp. 1308, 1313–16 (N.D. Ill. 1983) (purpose of stock lockup need not be disclosed in tender offer documents, and, without misstatements or omissions, stock lockup is not a manipulative practice). *But see* Gearhart Indus., Inc. v. Smith Int'l Inc., 741 F.2d 707 (5th Cir. 1984) (remanded to district court to determine whether target's transfer of large block of newly issued shares to third party in exchange for third party's subsidiary and third party's agreement to vote with target's directors in next election constituted an interested-director transaction; court labels agreement "particularly suspicious").

259. *See, e.g.*, Chicago Stadium Corp. v. Scallen, 530 F.2d 204, 207 (8th Cir. 1976) ("[D]irectors or officers who cause unissued or treasury shares to be issued to themselves or others solely for the purpose of obtaining or maintaining control of the corporation breach their fiduciary duty to the shareholders."); Klaus v. Hi-Shear Corp., 528 F.2d 225, 233 (9th Cir. 1975) (affirming district court's finding "that the principal purpose of the issuance of stock to ESOP was to dilute Klaus' voting strength"); Consolidated Amusement Co., Ltd. v. Rugoff, [1978 Transfer Binder] FED. SEC. L. REP. (CCH) ¶ 96,584 at 94,485 (S.D.N.Y. Oct. 6, 1978) ("Sale of stock at an inadequate price to specially chosen purchasers. . . violates the fiduciary duty owed by Rugoff to the corporation itself. . . ."); Podesta v. Calumet Indus., [1978 Transfer Binder] FED. SEC. L. REP. (CCH) ¶ 96,433 at 93,557 (N.D. Ill. May 9, 1978) ("[T]he evidence strongly supports the conclusion that Fair and his colleagues adopted the [Employee Stock Ownership Plan], and sold the warrants for the primary, if not the sole, purpose of retaining control of Calumet."); Applied Digital Data Sys., Inc. v. Milgo Elec. Corp., 425 F. Supp. 1145, 1160 (S.D.N.Y. 1977) ("ADDS has produced evidence to support its claim that the sole purpose of this stock sale was to defeat the ADDS exchange offer"); Tully v. Mott Supermarkets, Inc., 337 F. Supp. 834, 848 (D.N.J. 1972) ("[T]his Court finds an incongruity between the purportedly corporate justification for the [sale] of the Treasury stock [to the defendant directors] and the actual corporate situation."); Condec Corp. v. Lunkenheimer Co., 230 A.2d 769, 775 (Del. Ch. 1967) ("I have reached the conclusion that the primary purpose of the issuance of such shares was to prevent control of Lunkenheimer from passing to Condec and to cause such control to pass into the hands of U.S. Industries.").

260. Civ. A. No. 7619 (Del. Ch. June 29, 1984).

261. Slip op. at 7.

262. 649 F. Supp. 479 (S.D. Fla. 1986).

615

263. *Id.* at 484.
264. 17 C.F.R. § 240.13e-4.
265. *Id.* § 240.13e-101.
266. *See id.* § 240.14d-100.
267. *Id.* § 240.13e-4(b)(1).
268. *Id.* § 240.13e-3.
269. *Id.* § 240.13e-100.
270. *Id.* § 13e-3(b).
271. *See* Howing Co. v. Nationwide Corp., 826 F.2d 1470, 1474 (6th Cir. 1987), *cert. denied*, 108 S. Ct. 2830 (1988). Fisher v. Plessey Co., [1982–1983 Transfer Binder] FED. SEC. L. REP. (CCH) ¶ 99,246 (S.D.N.Y. June 22, 1983). *But see* Kalmanovitz v. G. Heileman Brewing Co., 595 F. Supp. 1385 (D. Del. 1984), *aff'd*, 769 F.2d 152 (3d Cir. 1985).
272. 17 C.F.R. § 240.13(e)-1.
273. 760 F.2d 945 (9th Cir. 1985).
274. *Id.* at 952.
275. 466 F. Supp. 1114, 1126–27 (D. Mass. 1978).
276. SEC v. Carter Hawley Hale Stores, Inc., 760 F.2d at 953.
277. 630 F. Supp. 502 (S.D.N.Y. 1986).
278. 584 F.2d 1195 (2d Cir. 1978).
279. 774 F.2d 47 (2d Cir. 1985).
280. Maynard Oil Co. v. Deltec Panamerica S.A., 630 F. Supp. at 506–07.
281. *See, e.g.*, AC Acquisitions Corp. v. Anderson, Clayton & Co., 519 A.2d 103 (Del. Ch. 1986).
282. *See* Lynch v. Vickers Energy Corp., 383 A.2d 278 (Del. 1978) (corporation failed to disclose that a management officer calculated a higher net asset value than that disclosed in the offer and failed to disclose that management had authorized open-market purchases of the corporation's stock for $15 per share before commencing the $12 per share offer); Eisenberg v. Chicago Milwaukee Corp., 537 A.2d 1051 (Del. Ch. 1987) (self-tender enjoined where disclosures implied that offer had a business-oriented, cost-saving rationale unrelated to the actual purpose of acquiring stock at an attractive price after "Black Monday"; where disclosures stated that current market price was only one of several factors, rather than the predominant factor, in determining price; and where corporation failed to disclose potential conflict of interest by directors).
283. SEC Exchange Act Release No. 34-23421, July 8, 1986.
284. 493 A.2d 946 (Del. 1985).
285. *See* Unocal Corp. v. Pickens, 608 F. Supp. 1081 (C.D. Cal. 1985).
286. *Id.* at 1082.
287. Unocal Corp. v. Mesa Petroleum Co., 493 A.2d at 953–54.
288. *Id.* at 957.
289. SEC Exchange Act Release No. 34-23421.
290. 17 C.F.R. § 240.13e-4(f)(8)(i), (ii).
291. *Id.* § 240.14d-10.

292. *See* Block & Hoff, *Recapitalizations and Restructurings*, N.Y.L.J. May 14, 1987, at 5; Lederman & Goroff, *Recapitalization Transactions*, 19 Rev. Sec. & Comm. Reg. 241 (Nov. 19, 1986).

293. *See, e.g.*, British Printing & Communication Corp. v. Harcourt Brace Jovanovich, Inc., 664 F. Supp. 1519 (S.D.N.Y. 1987) (refusing to enjoin defensive recapitalization involving special dividend of cash and additional securities along with increased stock ownership by employee stock ownership plan); Turner Broadcasting Sys., Inc. v. CBS, Inc., 627 F. Supp. 901, 910 (N.D. Ga. 1985) (upholding stock repurchase plan as fair and reasonable); GAF Corp. v. Union Carbide Corp., 624 F. Supp. 1016, 1022 (S.D.N.Y. 1985) (refusing to enjoin an exchange offer under the business judgment rule); Martin-Marietta Corp. v. Bendix Corp., 549 F. Supp. 623 (D. Md. 1982) (refusing to enjoin counter–tender offer for bidder's shares by target); MITE Corp. v. Dixon, 79 C 200, Order at 4–5 (N.D. Ill.Feb. 9, 1979) (refusing to enjoin target's self-tender at higher price than MITE's hostile tender offer), *aff'd on other grounds*, 633 F.2d 486 (1980), *aff'd sub nom.* Edgar v. MITE Corp., 457 U.S. 624 (1982). *But see* Crane Co. v. Harsco Corp., 511 F. Supp. 294, 305 (D. Del. 1981) (refusing to enjoin target from purchasing a large block of its shares at a price higher than tender offer price notwithstanding court's finding of likelihood of success on the merits of bidder's claim that target's directors breached their fiduciary duty; no showing of irreparable harm).

294. AC Acquisitions Corp. v. Anderson, Clayton & Co., 519 A.2d 103.

295. *Id.* at 114. *See also* Eisenberg v. Chicago Milwaukee Corp., 537 A.2d 1051 (enjoining offer that was coercive because of its threat that the stock would be delisted from the New York Stock Exchange). *Cf.* Lieb v. Clark, Civ. A. No. 9012 (Del. Ch. June 1, 1987) (WESTLAW, 1987 WL 11903) (that a self-tender is financially attractive does not make it actionably coercive).

296. AC Acquisitions Corp. v. Anderson, Clayton & Co., 519 A.2d at 114 n.12.

297. *Id.* at 115.

298. *See also* UIS, Inc. v. Walbro Corp., Civ. A. No. 9323 (Del. Ch. Oct. 6, 1987) (WESTLAW, 1987 WL 18108) (target temporarily restrained from purchasing its own stock where it was accused of issuing stock to friendly third party as entrenchment device).

299. 652 F. Supp. 829 (D. Minn. 1986), *aff'd in part*, 811 F.2d 414 (8th Cir. 1987).

300. 652 F. Supp. at 846.

301. *Id.*

302. Danaher v. Chicago Pneumatic Tool Co., 633 F. Supp. 1066 (S.D.N.Y. 1986).

303. *Id.* at 1070–71. *See also* Lieb v. Clark, Civ. A. No. 9012 (Del. Ch. June 1, 1987) (WESTLAW, 1987 WL 11903) (refusing to enjoin tender offer by ESOP that did not have motive or effect of entrenching management and that was not coercive); Edelman v. Phillips Petroleum Co., Civ. A. No. 7899 (Del. Ch. Feb. 12, 1985) (WESTLAW, 1986 WL 6265) (refusing to enjoin recapitalization including a large sale of stock to an ESOP).

304. 744 F.2d 255 (2d Cir. 1984).

305. *Id.* at 266; *see also* Buckhorn, Inc. v. Ropak Corp., 656 F. Supp. 209 (S.D. Ohio 1987), *aff'd*, 815 F.2d 76 (6th Cir. 1987) (enjoining ESOP that was adopted to thwart tender offer and entrench management); Frantz Mfg. Co. v. EAC Industries, Inc., 501 A.2d 401, 407–08 (Del. 1985) (issuing preliminary injunction to halt transfer of shares to ESOP in hasty effort to dilute control

held by bidder based on desire to entrench management); AC Acquisitions Corp. v. Anderson, Clayton & Co., 519 A.2d 103 (enjoining as coercive a recapitalization scheme including a stock sale to an ESOP).

306. 680 F.2d 263 (2d Cir.), *cert. denied*, 459 U.S. 1069 (1982).

307. 680 F.2d at 271–72.

308. 754 F.2d 1049 (2d Cir. 1985).

309. *Id.* at 1056.

310. *Id. See Also* Leigh v. Engle, 727 F.2d 113, 125 (7th Cir. 1984) (administrators of corporation's employee profit-sharing trust violated their fiduciary duties under the Employee Retirement Income Security Act (ERISA) by investing trust assets in other corporations involved in control contests where the administrators were actively involved in the control contests and had substantial interests in them); Sandoval v. Simmons, 622 F. Supp. 1174 (C.D. Ill. 1985). *But cf.* Condec Corp. v. Farley, 573 F. Supp. 1382, 1386–87 (S.D.N.Y. 1983) (refusing to enjoin offensive use of bidder's pension plan funds because Schedule 13D mentioned their use).

311. Martin-Marietta Corp. v. Bendix Corp., 547 F. Supp. 533 (S.D.N.Y 1982).

312. *See* Martin-Marietta Corp. v. Bendix Corp., [1982–1983 Transfer Binder] FED. SEC. L. REP. (CCH) ¶ 99,068 at 95,056 (S.D.N.Y. Sept. 22, 1982).

313. *See* M. Cherno, *Tender Offer Defensive Tactics: Are There Any Limits?* in NEW DIMENSIONS IN SECURITIES LITIGATION 573, 583 (ALIABA Seminar, Boston, Mass. June 2–3, 1983).

314. 490 A.2d 1059 (Del. Ch. 1985), *aff'd*, 500 A.2d 1346 (Del. 1985).

315. *Id.* at 1082.

316. *See, e.g.*, *SEC Loses Bid to Block Carter Hawley; Limited, Inc. Extends Tender to May 14*, 16 SEC. REG. & L. REP. (BNA) 794 (May 11, 1984) (Carter Hawley's lender and trustee for its profit-sharing plan notified that the U.S. Department of Labor is reviewing the bank's actions to determine whether it has violated ERISA). *See also Research Firm Named to Study Effects of Corporate Actions on Pension Funds*, 16 SEC. REG. & L. REP. (BNA) 1758 (Nov. 9, 1984) (Investor Responsibility Research Center, Inc., awarded contract by Department of Labor to study the impact of corporate actions in the face of takeovers on the interest of private pension plans as shareholders).

317. 544 F. Supp. 1275 (N.D. Ill. 1982).

318. *Id.* at 1290–91; *see also* Brown v. Ferro Corp., 763 F.2d 798 (6th Cir.), *cert. denied*, 474 U.S. 947 (1985) (dismissal of challenge to unexercised golden parachutes as premature). *Cf.* Zimmerman v. Bell, 585 F. Supp. 512 (D. Md. 1984) (shareholders' claims justifiable because one of the beneficiaries of the golden parachutes was receiving benefits).

319. Lewis v. Anderson, 477 A.2d 1040 (Del. 1984).

320. *Id.* at 1049. *See also* Kramer v. Western Pac. Indus., Inc., Civ. A. No. 8675 (Del. Ch. Sept. 11, 1987) (WESTLAW, 1987 WL 17043) (shareholder who was cashed out in merger and failed to challenge fairness of merger lacked standing to challenge golden parachutes); Penn Mart Realty Co. v. Perelman, Civ. A. No. 8349 (Del. Ch. Apr. 15, 1987) (WESTLAW, 1987 WL 10018) (shareholder who was cashed out in merger lacked standing to challenge golden parachutes), *appeal dismissed*, 529 A.2d 772 (Del. 1987).

321. *See also* Schreiber v. Burlington N., Inc., 472 U.S. 1 (1985) (withdrawal of

hostile tender offer by bidder and substitution of friendly offer for fewer shares after recognition of golden parachutes for officers of target was not manipulation under section 14(e) because there was full disclosure); Brill v. Burlington N., Inc., 590 F. Supp. 893, 900 (D. Del. 1984) (golden parachutes "are collateral agreements to the tender offer and as such, the provisions of the Williams Act do not apply"); *cf.* Wolgin v. Simon, 722 F.2d 389 (8th Cir. 1983) (because golden parachutes can be ratified by the shareholders of a Missouri corporation, shareholder must make a demand for suit upon all the shareholders before bringing a derivative suit). *But cf.* Zimmerman v. Bell, 585 F. Supp. 512 (D. Md. 1984) (demand on shareholders would have been futile because "the stockholders could only bring a suit against the defendants by demanding that the directors bring an action against themselves").

322. *See* Buckhorn, Inc. v. Ropak Corp., 656 F. Supp. 209, 232–33 (S.D. Ohio 1987), *aff'd,* 815 F.2d 76 (6th Cir. 1987) (upholding golden parachutes under *Unocal* test); *cf.* Orin v. Huntington Bancshares, Inc., 18 SEC. REG. & L. REP. 1719 (BNA) (Ohio Ct. Com. Pleas Sept. 30, 1986) (enforcing golden parachute contracts in suit by recipients); *see also* Koenings v. Joseph Schlitz Brewing Co., 377 N.W.2d 593 (Wis. 1985) (without deciding whether contract was "golden parachute" or applying business judgment rule, court upholds stipulated damages clause).

323. 1987 Ariz. Legis. Serv. no. 7, at 32 (West); 1987 Minn. Sess. Law Serv. 911 (West). *See Arizona Anti-Takeover Bill Signed during Special Session*, 19 SEC. REG. & L. REP. (BNA) 987 (July 3, 1987).

324. Weinberger v. Shumway, No. 547,586 (Super. Ct. San Diego Co., Cal. 1985).

325. *See* Minstar Acquiring Corp. v. AMF, Inc., 621 F. Supp. 1252 (S.D.N.Y. 1985). *Cf.* Kramer v. Western Pac. Indus., Inc. (Del. Ch. Nov. 7, 1986) (WESTLAW, 1986 WL 12787) (challenge to golden parachutes likely to succeed on merits where they were not necessary to induce officers to consider offers and where officers had no intention to continue in office after any acquisition; preliminary injunction denied due to lack of irreparable harm).

326. *See* STAND. FED. TAX. REP. (CCH) extra ed. no. 31 (July 18, 1984).

327. *See also IRS Issues Guidance on Reporting Golden Parachute Payments*, 17 SEC. REG. & L. REP. (BNA) 9 (Jan. 1, 1985).

328. *See Almost 30 Percent of Fortune 500 Firms Have Adopted Poison Pills*, *supra* note 163.

329. *See* Sandler, *Greenmail Is Infuriating Many Stockholders, but Fighting It Still Offers Little Satisfaction*, Wall St. J., Dec. 11, 1986, at 63.

330. 793 F.2d 1448, 1451–52 (5th Cir. 1986).

331. 507 A.2d 531 (Del. Ch. 1986).

332. *Id.* at 536.

333. *Id.* at 536–37.

334. *See* Fry v. Trump, 681 F. Supp. 252 (D.N.J. 1988) (shareholders state derivative claim against directors under §§ 10(b) and 14(a) and Delaware law for breach of fiduciary duty; claim stated against greenmailer for aiding and abetting breach).

335. 168 Cal. App. 3d 119, 214 Cal. Rptr. 177 (1985).

336. 214 Cal. Rptr. at 190.

337. 652 F. Supp. 1066 (S.D.N.Y. 1987).

338. *Id.* at 1081. *But cf. In re* Sea-Land Corp. Shareholders Litig., Civ. A. No. 8453 (Del. Ch. May 22, 1987) (WESTLAW, 1987 WL 11283) (claim against bidder for aiding and abetting successful purchaser's payment, with agreement of board, of premium to bidder in exchange for agreement by bidder not to pursue offer dismissed for failure to allege knowing participation in breach of fiduciary duty).

339. *See SEC Staff Says Greenmail Payments Depress Price of Target's Stock*, 16 SEC. REG. & L. REP. (BNA) 1585 (Oct. 5, 1984).

340. *See* 1987 Ariz. Legis. Serv. no. 7, at 32 (West); 1987 Minn. Sess. Law Serv. 911 (West); *Arizona Anti-Takeover Bill Signed during Special Session*, 19 SEC. REG. & L. REP. (BNA) 1138 (July 31, 1987); *Minnesota Adopts Anti-Takeover Law after Special Legislative Session*, 19 SEC. REG. & L. REP. (BNA) 987 (July 3, 1987).

341. *See, e.g.*, Note, *The Standstill Agreement: A Case of Illegal Vote Selling and Breach of Fiduciary Duty*, 93 YALE L.J. 1093 (1984); Bartlett & Andrews, *The Standstill Agreement: Legal and Business Considerations Underlying a Corporate Peace Treaty*, 62 B.U.L. REV. 143 (1982).

342. 600 F. Supp. 678 (E.D. Pa. 1985).

343. *Id.* at 688.

344. *Id.* (quoting *The Standstill Agreement*, *supra* note 341, at 1096–97).

345. *See also* Mesa Partners v. Phillips Petroleum Co., 488 A.2d 107 (Del. Ch. 1984) (assuming enforceability, court interprets standstill agreement as ordinary contract).

346. 535 A.2d 1334 (Del. 1987).

347. 611 F. Supp. 468 (D.N.J. 1985).

348. *Id.* at 474.

349. *Id.* at 480.

350. *Id.* at 477; *see also* Amalgamated Sugar Co. v. NL Indus., Inc., 644 F. Supp. 1229 (S.D.N.Y. 1986) (relying on *Asarco*, court enjoins poison pill that, when triggered, would dilute the equity and voting rights of 20 percent shareholder).

351. 618 F. Supp. 407 (S.D.N.Y. 1985).

352. *See* DEL. GEN. CORP. LAW § 151(g).

353. Unilever Acquisition Corp. v. Richardson-Vicks, Inc., 618 F. Supp. at 410. *See also* Minstar Acquiring Corp. v. AMF, Inc., 621 F. Supp. 1252 (enjoining poison pill because it unreasonably restrained the alienability of common stock).

354. Civ. A. No. 9097 (Del. Ch. Oct. 9, 1987) (WESTLAW, 1987 WL 18429).

355. 378 A.2d 121 (Del. 1977).

356. 618 F. Supp. at 410.

357. *See CTS II*, 805 F.2d at 718 (citing *Baker*, court refuses to find that poison pill that discriminates against 20 percent shareholder is illegal under Indiana statute patterned after Delaware law).

358. *See also* Telvest, Inc. v. Olson, Civ. A. No. 5798 (Del. Ch. Mar. 8, 1979) (WESTLAW, 1983 WL 8946) (issuance of piggyback preferred stock without shareholder authorization unlawful because it would alter the relative voting rights of common shareholders). *But see* National Educ. Corp. v. Bell & Howell Co., Civ. A. No. 7278 (Del. Ch. 1983) (available on LEXIS) (court refuses to enjoin issuance, without shareholder authorization, of "piggyback preferred

stock" that would increase from 75 to 80 percent the majority necessary to approve a merger; defendant argued that 1983 amendment to Delaware General Corporation Law implicitly overruled *Telvest*, by permitting the board to amend by resolution the target's certificate of incorporation).

359. *See* NEW YORK STOCK EXCHANGE LISTED COMPANY MANUAL ¶ 313.00; *Issuers Urge SEC Not to Adopt Voting Rights Standard for Exchanges*, 19 SEC. REG. & L. REP. (BNA) 1076 (July 24, 1987).

360. *See NYSE Formally Submits Proposal to Allow Unequal Voting Rights*, 18 SEC. REG. & L. REP. (BNA) 1137 (Sept. 19, 1986).

361. SEC Release No. 3,424,623 (June 22, 1987). *See SEC Proposal Would Bar Companies from Disenfranchising Shareholders*, 19 SEC. REG. & L. REP. (BNA) 848 (June 12, 1987).

362. 17 C.F.R. § 240.19c-4.

363. *See* Securities Exchange Act Rel. No. 25,891, 53 FED. REG. 26,376, 26,379 (July 12, 1988); *SEC One Share/One Vote Decision May Spark Takeover Reform, Rinaldo Says*, 20 SEC. REG. & L. REP. 251 (Feb. 19, 1988).

364. 549 F. Supp. 623 (D. Md. 1982).

365. *Id.* at 634.

366. No. 298, 1982 (Del. Sept. 21, 1982).

367. 18 U.S.C. §§ 1961–68.

368. *See, e.g.*, Missouri Portland Cement Co. v. Cargill, Inc., 498 F.2d 851, 875 (2d Cir.) (deeming district court's order that target submit all future defensive material in advance to the district court for approval to be "too severe" and ruling that target merely should be enjoined from making further misleading statements of the type target already had made), *cert. denied*, 419 U.S. 883 (1974); Weeks Dredging & Contracting, Inc. v. American Dredging Co., 451 F. Supp. 468, 479 (E.D. Pa. 1978) (ordering that target send a letter to shareholders correcting past misstatements); Humana, Inc. v. American Medicorp, Inc., 445 F. Supp. 613 (S.D.N.Y. 1977) (enjoining target from disseminating materially false and misleading statements); Royal Indus., Inc. v. Monogram Indus., Inc., [1976–1977 Transfer Binder] FED. SEC. L. REP. (CCH) ¶ 95,863 at 91,145 (C.D. Cal. Nov. 29, 1976) (enjoining target from disseminating materially false and misleading statements).

369. *See, e.g.*, MacFadden Holdings, Inc. v. JB Acquisition Corp., 802 F.2d 62 (2d Cir. 1986).

370. 15 U.S.C. § 78m(d)(2) (1982) (section 13(d)(2)).

371. *See, e.g.*, Dan River, Inc. v. Unitex Ltd., 624 F.2d 1216, 1225 (4th Cir. 1980), *cert. denied*, 449 U.S. 1101 (1981); W.A. Krueger Co. v. Kirkpatrick, Pettis, Smith, Polian, Inc., 466 F. Supp. 800, 802 (D. Neb. 1979); Financial Gen. Bankshares, Inc. v. Lance, [1978 Transfer Binder] FED. SEC. L. REP. (CCH) ¶ 96,403 at 93,425 (D.D.C. Apr. 27, 1978).

372. *See, e.g.*, Wellman v. Dickinson, 682 F.2d 355, 366 (2d Cir. 1982), *cert. denied*, 460 U.S. 1069 (1983); Spinner Corp. v. Princeville Dev. Corp., [1987 Transfer Binder] FED. SEC. L. REP. (CCH) ¶ 93,058 (D. Hawaii 1986) (granting injunction against tender offer by group that failed to disclose its existence as a group), *vacated*, [1987 Transfer Binder] FED. SEC. L. REP. ¶ 93,157 (D. Haw. Jan. 30, 1987); Seilon, Inc. v. Lamb, [1983–1984 Transfer Binder] FED. SEC. L. REP. (CCH) ¶ 99,448 at 96,551 (N.D. Ohio July 27, 1983); Mid-Continent

Bancshares, Inc. v. O'Brien, [1982 Transfer Binder] FED. SEC. L. REP. (CCH) ¶ 98,734 at 93,708 (E.D. Mo. Dec. 11, 1981). *But see* Financial Fed'n, Inc. v. Ashkenazy, [1984 Transfer Binder] FED. SEC. L. REP. (CCH) ¶ 91,489 at 98,437 (C.D. Cal. May 9, 1983) (facts fail to show that any purchasers entered into express or implied agreement to act as a group).

373. *See, e.g.*, Chromalloy Am. Corp. v. Sun Chem. Corp., 611 F.2d 240, 246 (8th Cir. 1979); Kirsch Co. v. Bliss & Laughlin Indus., Inc., 495 F. Supp. 488, 499 (W.D. Mich. 1980).

374. *See, e.g.*, Polinsky v. MCA, Inc., 680 F.2d 1286, 1291 (9th Cir. 1982) ("Appellants' pre–tender offer purchase of Appellee's stock was not a part of the tender offer and, thus, the purchase was not violative of. . . the Williams Act."); Energy Ventures, Inc. v. Appalachian Co., 587 F. Supp. 734 (D. Del. 1984); University Bank & Trust Co. v. Gladstone, 574 F. Supp. 1006, 1011 (D. Mass. 1983); Crane Co. v. Harsco Corp., 511 F. Supp. 294, 302–03 (D. Del. 1981); Kaufman & Broad, Inc. v. Belzberg, 522 F. Supp. 35, 48–49 (S.D.N.Y. 1981). *But see In re* Paine Webber Jackson & Curtis, Inc., [1982–1983 Transfer Binder] FED. SEC. L. REP. (CCH) ¶ 83,310 at 85,695 (SEC Dec. 30, 1982) (holding by SEC administrative law judge that by assembling and acquiring a large block of stock from a number of other brokers, a major brokerage firm commenced a tender offer, even though the transaction ultimately was executed on the Pacific Stock Exchange). *Cf.* Rand v. Anaconda-Ericsson, Inc., 794 F.2d 843, 848 (2d Cir. 1986), *cert. denied*, 479 U.S. 987 (1986) (letter from a creditor to chairman of the board not a tender offer); Pin v. Texaco, Inc., 793 F.2d 1448 (5th Cir. 1986) (private greenmail purchases not a tender offer); SEC v. Carter Hawley Hale, 760 F.2d 945 (9th Cir. 1985) (large open-market purchases not a tender offer); Plessey Co. PLC v. General Elec. Co. PLC, 628 F. Supp. 477, 491 (D. Del. 1986) (American press reports of a British tender offer do not bring the offer within the scope of the Williams Act).

375. *See* Wellman v. Dickinson, 475 F. Supp. 783, 823–24 (S.D.N.Y. 1979), *aff'd on other grounds*, 682 F.2d 355 (2d Cir. 1982), *cert. denied*, 460 U.S. 1069 (1983).

376. *Cf.* Maynard Oil Co. v. Deltec Panamerica S.A., 630 F. Supp. 502 (S.D.N.Y. 1985) (target's announcement of its intention to purchase its own stock privately or in the market, to defeat a tender offer, not itself a tender offer). *But see* Zuckerman v. Franz, 573 F. Supp. 351, 358 (S.D. Fla. 1983) (cash merger proposal satisfied SEC's eight-factor tender offer test and therefore was subject to section 14(e)).

377. *See Allied Stores to Be Bought by Campeau*, Wall St. J., Nov. 3, 1986, at 3, col. 1 (target and hostile bidder reach agreement on acquisition after a federal court allows a large postbid open-market purchase to proceed).

378. 774 F.2d 47 (2d Cir. 1985).

379. *Id.* at 57.

380. *Id.*

381. *See SEC Claims Investors Schemed to Depress Stock Price Prior to Tendering for Fund*, 19 SEC. REG. & L. REP. 1840 (BNA) (Dec. 4, 1987).

382. 17 C.F.R. § 240.14a9.

383. 377 U.S. 426, 430–31 (1964).

384. *See* Bruno v. Cook, 660 F. Supp. 306 (S.D.N.Y. 1987) (granting, in part, motion to dismiss securities fraud claim brought after merger of bidder and target;

plaintiff could not show that the alleged misstatement affected the shareholder vote on the merger, caused plaintiff to enter into or forgo a transaction, or resulted in compensable injury).

385. *See, e.g.*, Berg v. First Am. Bancshares, Inc., 796 F.2d 489 (D.C. Cir. 1986) (finding several omissions or mischaracterizations but dismissing them as immaterial); Keyser v. Commonwealth Nat'l Fin. Corp., 644 F. Supp. 1130 (M.D. Pa. 1986) (rejecting a shareholder effort to enjoin a merger allegedly resulting from solicitation of proxies by means of false information); Pabst Brewing Co. v. Jacobs, 549 F. Supp. 1068, 1073 (D. Del. 1982) (prospective bidder's proxy materials misstated Delaware consent procedure); Camelot Indus. v. Vista Resources, Inc., 535 F. Supp. 1174, 1183 (S.D.N.Y. 1982) (ordering both target and bidder to resolicit proxies with corrected disclosures).

386. *See, e.g.*, Florida Commercial Banks v. Culverhouse, 772 F.2d 1513, 1520 (11th Cir. 1985) (reversing dismissal of claim that Schedule 13D failed to disclose control purpose); Chromalloy Am. Corp. v. Sun Chem. Corp., 611 F.2d at 246 (ordering bidder to disclose its control purpose); General Aircraft Corp. v. Lampert, 556 F.2d 90, 96 (1st Cir. 1977) (affirming finding that bidder failed to disclose its control purpose); Gulf & W. Indus. v. Great Atl. & Pac. Tea Co., 476 F.2d 687, 697 (2d Cir. 1973) (affirming finding that bidder failed to disclose its control purpose); Champion Parts Rebuilders, Inc. v. Cormier Corp., 661 F. Supp. 825 (N.D. Ill. 1987) (preliminary injunction granted against tender offeror group that failed to disclose plans to institute major changes and then resell the target); Homac, Inc. v. DSA Fin. Corp., 661 F. Supp. 776 (E.D. Mich. 1987) (bidder enjoined from further purchases until it amended Schedule 13D to disclose control purpose); K-N Energy, Inc. v. Gulf Interstate Co., 607 F. Supp. 756 (D. Colo. 1983) (bidder's statement that the purpose of its acquisition was "investment only" was false and misleading; bidder ordered to disclose its control purpose); Kaufman & Broad, Inc. v. Belzberg, 522 F. Supp. 35, 44–45 (S.D.N.Y. 1981) (issuer that alleged purchaser failed to disclose central purpose stated claim under section 13(d)); Kirsch Co. v. Bliss & Laughlin Indus., 495 F. Supp. 488, 500 (W.D. Mich. 1980) (injunctive relief granted against purchaser that failed to disclose central purpose).

387. *See, e.g.*, Condec Corp. v. Farley, 573 F. Supp. 1382, 1385 (S.D.N.Y. 1983); Jewelcor Inc. v. Pearlman, 397 F. Supp. 221, 236 (S.D.N.Y. 1975).

388. *See, e.g.*, K-N Energy, Inc. v. Gulf Interstate Co., 607 F. Supp. 756 (D. Colo. 1983); Citizens First Bancorp, Inc. v. Harreld, 559 F. Supp. 867, 872–73 (W.D. Ky. 1982) (bank holding company's dissident management and shareholders formed group to remove current directors).

389. 701 F.2d 278 (4th Cir. 1983).

390. *Id.* at 280 n.2.

391. *Id.* at 285–86.

392. [1982–1983 Transfer Binder] FED. SEC. L. REP. (CCH) ¶ 99,148 (N.D. Tex. Aug. 28, 1981).

393. *Id.* at 95,545.

394. Hanna Mining Co. v. Norcen Energy Resources, Ltd., 574 F. Supp. 1172, 1200 (N.D. Ohio 1982); General Steel Indus., Inc. v. Walco Nat'l Corp., 527 F. Supp. 305 (E.D. Mo. 1981); *see also* Spinner Corp. v. Princeville Dev. Corp., [1987 Transfer Binder] FED. SEC. L. REP. (CCH) ¶ 93,058 (D. Hawaii Nov. 21, 1986) (granting preliminary injunction against tender offer where offerors failed to

disclose existence of bidder group, number of shares owned by group, prior securities law violations by member of group, and financing problems), *vacated*, [1987 Transfer Binder] FED. SEC. L. REP. (CCH) ¶ 93,157 at 95,710 (D. Haw. Jan. 30, 1987); Drobbin v. Nicolet Instrument Corp., 631 F. Supp. 860 (S.D.N.Y. 1986) (enjoining bidder from voting any of its shares until ten days after corrective disclosures are made). *But see* Gearhart Indus., Inc. v. Smith Int'l, Inc., 741 F.2d 707, 717 (5th Cir. 1984) (reversing district court's preliminary injunction against tender offer because bidder obtained "blocking position"; goal of Williams Act is full and fair disclosure, not to tip scales in favor of incumbent management or bidder); Plessey Co. PLC v. General Elec. Co. PLC, 628 F. Supp. 477 (refusing injunction because money damages are available for 13(d) violation); HUBCO, Inc. v. Rappaport, 628 F. Supp. 345 (D.N.J. 1985) (right of action limited to scope necessary to protect shareholders which does not include such "drastic" relief as rescission or sterilization of shares); Scientific Computers, Inc. v. Edudata Corp., 599 F. Supp. 1092, at 1102 (D. Minn. 1984) ("even assuming SCI can prove its creeping acquisition charge, a continuing injunction is not the proper way to deal with misleading 13(d) filings"), *aff'd*, 746 F.2d 429 (8th Cir. 1984).

395. *See also* Spencer Cos. v. Agency Rent-A-Car, Inc., 542 F. Supp. 237 (D. Mass. 1982) (bidder enjoined from voting or exercising any rights with respect to shares of target stock purchased without proper disclosures); SEC Litigation Release No. 9533, *reprinted in* [1981–1982 Transfer Binder] FED. SEC. L. REP. (CCH) ¶ 98,387 at 92,343 (Dec. 21, 1981) (endorsing view that drastic remedies should be imposed when bidder illegally obtains "blocking position").

396. San Francisco Real Estate Investors v. Real Estate Inv. Trust of Am., 701 F.2d 1000, 1010–11 (1st Cir. 1983).

397. *See, e.g.*, Gearhart Indus., Inc. v. Smith Int'l, Inc., 741 F.2d at 714; Scientific Computers, Inc. v. Edudata Corp. (D. Minn. 1984), *aff'd*, 746 F.2d 429; Camelot Indus. v. Vista Resources, Inc., 535 F. Supp. 1174, 1181 (S.D.N.Y. 1982); Wellman v. Dickinson, 475 F. Supp. 783, 817 (S.D.N.Y. 1979), *aff'd*, 682 F.2d 355 (2d Cir. 1982), *cert. denied*, 460 U.S. 1069 (1983).

398. *See* Florida Commercial Banks v. Culverhouse, 772 F.2d 1513, 1519 (11th Cir. 1985).

399. Liberty Nat'l Ins. Holding Co. v. Charter Co., 734 F.2d 545 (11th Cir. 1984).

400. *Cf.* Piper v. ChrisCraft Indus., 430 U.S. 1, 42 n.28 (1977) (defeated tender offeror had no implied cause of action for damages under section 14(e); "the target corporation's standing to sue [is not] in issue in this case").

401. *See* Markel v. Scovill Mfg. Co., 657 F. Supp. 1102 (W.D.N.Y. 1987) (nonselling shareholder unable to show reliance on alleged misstatements), *vacated*, 859 F.2d 148 (2d Cir. 1988).

402. 649 F. Supp. 408 (S.D.N.Y. 1986).

403. *Id.* at 415, *quoting* MacFadden Holdings Inc. v. JB Acquisition Corp., 802 F.2d 62, 71 (2d Cir. 1986).

404. *See, e.g.*, Gulf & W. Indus. v. Great Atl. & Pac. Tea Co., 476 F.2d at 696 (affirming injunction against tender offer; bidder seeking 15 percent of target's shares failed to disclose its intention to seek control).

405. *See* Valente v. PepsiCo, Inc., 454 F. Supp. 1228, 1241–42 (D. Del. 1978).

406. *See, e.g.*, Weeks Dredging & Contracting, Inc. v. American Dredging Co., 451 F. Supp. at 480 (bidder violated section 14(e) by failing to disclose its intent to

change the duties of management upon gaining control of the target); Otis Elevator Co. v. United Technologies Corp., 405 F. Supp. 960, 969 (S.D.N.Y. 1975) (bidder violated section 14(e) by failing to disclose its intent to merge with target); General Host Corp. v. Triumph Am., Inc., 359 F. Supp. 749, 755 (S.D.N.Y. 1973) (bidder violated section 14(e) by failing to disclose its intent to convert certain of target's assets into cash).

407. 423 F.2d 1075, 1085–86 (5th Cir. 1970).

408. *See* Todd Shipyards Corp. v. Madison Fund, Inc., 547 F. Supp. 1383, 1387 S.D.N.Y. 1982); Purolator, Inc. v. Tiger Int'l, Inc., 510 F. Supp. 554, 556 (D.D.C. 1981).

409. 599 F.2d 1140, 1149 (2d Cir. 1979).

410. *Id.* at 1147. *See also* Pabst Brewing Co. v. Kalmanovitz, 551 F. Supp. 882, 889–94 (D. Del. 1982) (tender offer enjoined because bidder failed to disclose financial information concerning two individuals behind tender offer); Riggs Nat'l Bank v. Allbritton, 516 F. Supp. 164, 174 (D.D.C. 1981) (tender offer enjoined because bidder failed to disclose personal financial information); Corenco Corp. v. Schiavone & Sons, Inc., 362 F. Supp. 939, 948–49 (S.D.N.Y.) (tender offer enjoined because bidder failed to disclose any financial information about itself), *aff'd in relevant part*, 488 F.2d 207 (2d Cir. 1973). *But cf.* Plaza Sec. Co. v. Fruehauf Corp., 643 F. Supp. 1535, 1542–43 (E.D. Mich. 1986) (bidder need not disclose financial information regarding chairman of entity that controls bidder); Beebe v. Pacific Realty Trust, 578 F. Supp. 1128, 1147–48 (D. Ore. 1984) (target and acquiror's failure to disclose in proxy solicitation for exchange plan that acquiring company had engaged in a number of leveraged buyouts in the past held not material); Resource Exploration v. Yankee Gas & Oil, Inc., 566 F. Supp. 54, 63–64 (N.D. Ohio 1983) (disclosure of future earnings and other speculative data discouraged).

411. 744 F.2d 978 (3d Cir. 1984).

412. *See, e.g.*, Biechele v. Cedar Point, Inc., 747 F.2d 209 (6th Cir. 1984).

413. Flynn v. Bass Bros. Enters., Inc., 744 F.2d at 988.

414. *See* Weinberger v. Rio Grande Indus., Inc., 519 A.2d 116 (Del. Ch. 1986). *See also* Walker v. Action Indus., Inc., 802 F.2d 703 (4th Cir. 1986) (holding that financial projections need not be disclosed, but declining to adopt the *Flynn* or *Starkman* approach), *cert. denied*, 107 S. Ct. 952 (1987).

415. 621 F. Supp. 804 (D.C. Del. 1985).

416. *Id.* at 808.

417. 419 F.2d 787, 796 (2d Cir. 1969), *cert. denied*, 400 U.S. 822 (1970).

418. *See also* Burlington Indus., Inc. v. Edelman, 666 F. Supp. 799 (M.D.N.C. 1987) (enjoining tender offer where alleged bidder failed to disclose that it had received inside information from target's vice president), *aff'd without opinion*, [1987 Transfer Binder] FED. SEC. L. REP. (CCH) ¶ 93,339 (4th Cir. June 22, 1987); General Portland, Inc. v. LaFarge Coppee S.A., [1982–1983 Transfer Binder] FED. SEC. L. REP. (CCH) ¶ 99,148 at 95,543 (N.D. Tex. 1981) (court enjoins tender offer; prospective bidder received sensitive business information about target and, pursuant to confidentiality agreement, could not purchase target shares without target's consent).

419. 483 F.2d 247, 251 (2d Cir. 1973).

420. *See also* Davis v. Emerson Ins. Agency, 423 F. Supp. 561, 563 (D. Neb. 1976)

(bidder failed to disclose possible deregistration of target's stock); Commonwealth Oil Refining Co. v. Tesoro Petroleum Corp., 394 F. Supp. 267, 277 (S.D.N.Y. 1975) (bidder failed to disclose dollar amounts of possible tax exemption losses).

421. 402 F. Supp. 532, 552–53 (D. Del. 1975).

422. 454 F. Supp. 1228, 1240 (D. Del. 1978).

423. 621 F. Supp. 804, 809 (D. Del. 1985).

424. *See* Pin v. Texaco, 793 F.2d at 1453; *cf.* Hanson Trust PLC v. SCM Corp., 774 F.2d 47, 55 (2d Cir. 1985) (discussion of purpose and adoption of the Williams Act).

425. 430 U.S. 462 (1977).

426. 15 U.S.C. § 78j(b).

427. 17 C.F.R. § 240.10b-5.

428. *See* Schreiber v. Burlington N., Inc., 472 U.S. 1 (1985) (rejection of tendered shares and institution of second tender offer are not manipulative where done openly); Feldbaum v. Avon Prods., Inc., 741 F.2d 234 (8th Cir. 1984); Buffalo Forge Co. v. Ogden Corp., 717 F.2d 757 (2d Cir.), *cert. denied*, 464 U.S. 1018 (1983).

429. *See* Lederman, *Tender Offer Bidding Strategy*, 17 REV. SEC. REG. 917 (Apr. 18, 1984).

430. 772 F.2d 244 (6th Cir. 1985), *cert. denied*, 477 U.S. 903 (1986).

431. *Id.* at 257–58. *See also* Martin-Marietta Corp. v. Bendix Corp., 549 F. Supp. 623, 630 (D. Md. 1982) (court finds two-tier structure not violative of section 14(e), since no deception was involved).

432. Pin v. Texaco, 793 F.2d at 1453.

433. Newmont Mining Corp. v. Pickens, 831 F.2d 1448 (9th Cir. 1987).

434. *Id.* at 1450–53.

435. 15 U.S.C. § 18.

436. *Compare* Central Nat'l Bank v. Rainbolt, 720 F.2d 1183, 1187 (10th Cir. 1983) (target lacked standing because it did not allege antitrust injury), *and* Carter Hawley Hale Stores Inc. v. Limited, Inc., 587 F. Supp. 246, 248–50 (C.D. Cal. 1984) (same), *with* Marathon Oil Co. v. Mobil Corp., 669 F.2d 378 (6th Cir. 1981) (affirming preliminary injunction blocking acquisition of plaintiff by defendant); Grumman Corp. v. LTV Corp, 665 F.2d 10 (2d Cir. 1981) (same), *and* Laidlaw Acquisition Corp. v. Mayflower Group, Inc., 636 F. Supp. 1513, 1516–17 (S.D. Ind. 1986) (target entitled to preliminary injunction against acquisition; court specifically rejects argument that target lacks standing). *See generally* Easterbrook & Fischel, *Antitrust Suits by Targets of Tender Offers*, 80 MICH. L. REV. 1155 (1982) (arguing that targets should not be permitted to block tender offers on antitrust grounds).

437. 479 U.S. 104 (1986).

438. *See, e.g.*, Burlington Indus., Inc. v. Edelman, 666 F. Supp. 799 (M.D.N.C. 1987), *aff'd without opinion*, [1987 Transfer Binder] FED. SEC. L. REP. (CCH) ¶ 93,339 (4th Cir. June 22, 1987); *see also* United States v. BNS Inc., 848 F.2d 945, 954 (9th Cir. 1988) (Beezer, J., dissenting) arguing district court cannot enjoin merger under 15 U.S.C. § 16(b)–(h) at behest of target company).

439. *See, e.g.*, Marathon Oil Co. v. Mobil Corp., 669 F.2d at 383 (6th Cir. Ohio

1981) (enjoining acquisition of oil company by another oil company); Grumman Corp. v. LTV Corp., 665 F.2d at 11 (enjoining acquisition of aircraft manufacturer by company manufacturing aircraft and aircraft components); F&M Schaefer Corp. v. C. Schmidt & Sons, Inc., 597 F.2d 814, 817–19 (2d Cir. 1979) (per curiam) (enjoining acquisition of brewing company by another brewing company); Laidlaw Acquisition Corp. v. Mayflower Group, Inc., 636 F. Supp. 1513 (enjoining acquisition of second largest private school bus firm by the first).

440. *See, e.g.*, Harnischfeger Corp. v. Paccar, Inc., 474 F. Supp. 1151, 1159 (E.D. Wis. 1979) (enjoining acquisition of hydraulic winch purchaser by company manufacturing winches), *aff'd without opinion*, 624 F.2d 1103 (7th Cir. 1979); Filtrol Corp. v. Slick Corp., 1970 Trade Cas. (CCH) ¶ 73,035 at 88,055 (C.D. Cal. Dec. 29, 1969) (enjoining acquisition of supplier of clay adsorbents by clay adsorbent purchaser), *aff'd per curiam*, 428 F.2d 826 (9th Cir. 1970).

441. *See, e.g.*, Missouri Portland Cement Co. v. Cargill, Inc., 498 F.2d at 854 ("Where, as here, the acquisition would be neither horizontal nor vertical, there are 'strong reasons for not making the prohibitions of section 7 so . . . broad as to interfere materially with mergers that are procompetitive in their facilitation of entry and expansion."), *cert. denied*, 419 U.S. 883 (1974). *But see* Allis Chalmers Mfg. Co. v. White Consol. Indus., 414 F.2d 506, 525–26 (3d Cir. 1969) (reversing district court, court grants target's request for preliminary injunction against conglomerate acquisition), *cert. denied*, 396 U.S. 1009 (1970).

442. Grumman Corp. v. LTV Corp., 665 F.2d at 11.

443. Missouri Portland Cement Co. v. Cargill, Inc., 498 F.2d at 870, *cert. denied*, 419 U.S. 883 (1974).

444. *See Merger Guidelines—1984*, TRADE REG. REP. (CCH) No. 655 (Part II) (June 18, 1984).

445. *Id.* at 9.

446. *Id. See generally* P. Tone, *Mergers and Acquisitions: The Antitrust Perspective*, 21ST ANNUAL CORPORATE COUNSEL INITIATIVE (Northwestern University School of Law, Oct. 20–21, 1982).

447. *See* Grumman Corp. v. LTV Corp., 533 F. Supp. 1385, 1391 (E.D.N.Y. 1982) (target that successfully challenged hostile acquisition awarded reasonable attorney's fees in connection with preliminary injunction proceeding); Harnischfeger Corp. v. Paccar, Inc., 503 F. Supp. 102, 106 (E.D. Wis. 1980) (fees awarded both for proceeding in which preliminary injunction was granted and proceeding in which it was affirmed); F&M Schaefer Corp. v. C. Schmidt & Sons, Inc., 476 F. Supp. 203, 207 (S.D.N.Y. 1979) (fees awarded for proceeding in which injunction was granted).

448. 15 U.S.C. § 18(a).

449. *See* Hanna Mining Co. v. Norcen Energy Resources Ltd., [1982 Transfer Binder] FED. SEC. L. REP. (CCH) ¶ 98,742 at 93,740 (N.D. Ohio June 11, 1982) (rejecting target's claim under Hart-Scott-Rodino Act, holding that neither legislative history nor purpose of act indicated any congressional intent to create private right of action); Hammermill Paper Co. v. Icahn, No. 80-47-B (W.D. Pa. Apr. 24, 1980) (available on LEXIS) (issuer has no private right of action under Hart-Scott-Rodino Act).

450. 15 U.S.C. § 78g; *see, e.g.*, First Ala. Bancshares, Inc. v. Lowder, [1981 Transfer

Binder] FED. SEC. L. REP. (CCH) ¶ 98,015 at 91,250–52 (N.D. Ala. May 1, 1981); D-Z Inv. Co. v. Holloway, [1974–1975 Transfer Binder] FED. SEC. L. REP. (CCH) ¶ 94,771 at 96,562 (S.D.N.Y. Aug. 23, 1974); *cf.* Bassler v. Central Nat'l Bank, 715 F.2d 308, 313 (7th Cir. 1983) (bidder has no private cause of action against lender for violation of margin requirements).

451. *See* Pabst Brewing Co. v. Jacobs, [1982–1983 Transfer Binder] FED. SEC. L. REP. (CCH) ¶ 99,042 at 94,952–53 (D. Minn. Mar. 8, 1982); Pargas, Inc. v. Empire Gas Corp., 423 F. Supp. 199, 241–42 (D. Md.) (preliminarily enjoining tender offer on account of, among other things, section 7 violations by bidder), *aff'd per curiam*, 546 F.2d 25 (4th Cir. 1976); Metro-Goldwyn-Mayer, Inc. v. Transamerica Corp., 303 F. Supp. 1354, 1357 (S.D.N.Y. 1969); *see also* Pabst Brewing Co. v. Kalmanovitz, 551 F. Supp. at 885–89 (allowing target to bring action under section 7, court holds that tender offer price, rather than market value of target's shares immediately before tender offer, determines value of shares as collateral for margin purposes).

452. *See* Revlon v. Pantry Pride, Inc., 621 F. Supp. 804, 814 (D. Del. 1985); Nachman Corp. v. Halfred, Inc., [1973–1974 Transfer Binder] FED. SEC. L. REP. (CCH) ¶ 94,455 at 95,594 (N.D. Ill. July 13, 1973).

453. Fed. Res. Bd. No. R-0562 (Jan. 8, 1986).

454. *Noninvestment Grade Debt as a Source of Tender Offer Financing*, [1986–1987 Transfer Binder] FED. SEC. L. REP. ¶ 84,011 (June 20, 1986).

455. *Id.* at 88,170.

456. 15 U.S.C. § 80a12(d)(1)(A).

457. 825 F.2d 731 (3d Cir. 1987).

458. *Id.* at 733–36.

459. *Id.* at 736–38.

460. *Id.* at 738–39.

461. 18 U.S.C. §§ 1961–68.

462. *See Legislators React Cautiously to Wall Street Scandal*, 1986 CONG. Q. WEEKLY REP. 2932 (Nov. 22, 1986).

463. John Alden Life Ins. Co. v. Woods, [1982 Transfer Binder] FED. SEC. L. REP. (CCH) ¶ 98,617 at 93,065 (D. Idaho Dec. 19, 1981); Professional Investors Life Ins. Co. v. Roussel, 528 F. Supp. 391, 402 (D. Kan. 1981). *But see* National City Lines, Inc. v. LLC Corp., 524 F. Supp. 906, 910–11 (W.D. Mo. 1981) (Missouri statute regulating acquisitions of insurance companies preempted by Williams Act), *aff'd on other grounds*, 687 F.2d 1122 (8th Cir. 1982); Gunter v. Ago Int'l B.V., 533 F. Supp. 86, 90 (N.D. Fla. 1981) (Florida statute regulating acquisitions of insurance companies preempted by Williams Act). *Cf.* Mesa Partners II v. Unocal Corp., 607 F. Supp. 624 (W.D. Okla. 1985) (Oklahoma statute regulating purchase of natural resource assets chilled takeovers to point of impinging on Congress's power under commerce clause).

464. 15 U.S.C. § 45(a)(1).

465. *See* Spinner Corp. v. Princeville Dev. Corp., 849 F.2d 388 (9th Cir. 1988) (Hawaii statute); Russell v. Dean Witter Reynolds, Inc., 510 A.2d 972 (Conn. 1986); Cabot Corp. v. Baddour, 477 N.E.2d 399 (Mass. 1985); Lindner v. Durham Hosiery Mills, Inc., 761 F.2d 162 (4th Cir. 1985) (North Carolina statute). *But see* State *ex rel.* Corbin v. Pickrell, 667 P.2d 1304 (Ariz. 1983) (en

banc). The Texas statute may also apply. *See Spinner Corp.*, 849 F.2d at 393, n.6, and cases cited there.

466. No. 298, slip op. at 3 (Del. Sept. 21, 1982), *reprinted in* I 14TH ANNUAL INSTITUTE ON SECURITIES REGULATION 905 (PLI Corporate Law and Practice Series No. 401 1982).

467. *But see* Martin-Marietta Corp. v. Bendix Corp., 549 F. Supp. 623, 634 (D. Md. 1982) (reaching opposite conclusion, stating that Martin-Marietta would not owe a fiduciary duty to Bendix).

468. 638 F.2d 357 (2d Cir. 1980).

469. *Id.* at 377; *see also* Wellman v. Dickinson, 682 F.2d 355, 367 (2d Cir. 1982) (defendant's position as director of target "placed him under no fiduciary duty to reveal to the company's management his intention to use his [company] holdings to effectuate a third-party takeover of the company. . . or to refrain from promoting a takeover by a third-party"), *cert. denied*, 460 U.S. 1069 (1983); Humana, Inc. v. American Medicorp, Inc., [1977–1978 Transfer Binder] FED. SEC. L. REP. (CCH) ¶ 96,286 at 92,826–28 (S.D.N.Y. Jan. 4, 1978) (target alleged that bidder's dealer-manager was breaching its fiduciary duty to target because it had received confidential financial information from target in an unrelated matter; target's motion for preliminary injunction denied); American Medicorp, Inc. v. Continental Ill. Nat'l Bank, 475 F. Supp. 5, 10 (N.D. Ill. 1977) (target, a customer of Continental, sought to enjoin Continental from financing bidder's tender offer because of Continental's actual or potential breach of fiduciary duty; target's motion for preliminary injunction denied); *cf. In re* Sea-Land Corp. Shareholders Litig., Civ. A. No. 8453 (Del. Ch. May 22, 1987) (available on LEXIS) (former shareholders' suit against bidder dismissed because bidder owed no fiduciary duty to corporation or its shareholders); *accord* Fry v. Trump, 681 F. Supp. at 256–57. *See generally* Comment, *Tender Offers and "Chinese Walls": A Bank's Duty of Confidentiality When Financing Acquisition of a Customer*, 1980 WIS. L. REV. 206. *But see* Burlington Indus., Inc. v. Edelman, 666 F. Supp. 799 (granting preliminary injunction barring hostile tender offer where target likely to show that bidder received inside information), *aff'd without opinion*, [1987 Transfer Binder] FED. SEC. L. REP. (CCH) ¶ 93,339 (4th Cir. June 22, 1987); Joseph v. Shell Oil Co., 482 A.2d 335 (Del. Ch. 1984) (granting preliminary injunction against a tender offer by Royal Dutch Petroleum Co., which controlled a majority of the shares of Shell, for the remaining shares; "there is a reasonable probability that the defendants have not offered a fair price for the shares of Shell held by the minority stockholders and that defendants have not made a full and complete disclosure of all pertinent facts with complete candor"); General Portland, Inc. v. LaFarge Coppee S.A. [1982–1983 Transfer Binder] FED. SEC. L. REP. (CCH) ¶ 99,148 at 95,543 (N.D. Tex. Aug. 28, 1981) (court enjoins tender offer; prospective bidder received sensitive business information about target and, pursuant to confidentiality agreement, could not purchase target shares without target's consent). *Cf.* Gilbert v. El Paso Co., 490 A.2d 1050, 1055 (Del. Ch. 1984) (denying target's motion for summary judgment, court holds that shareholders' allegation that target management breached fiduciary duty when it entered into deal with tender offeror that substantially compromised shareholders' right to participate in offer stated a claim of civil conspiracy).

470. 549 F. Supp. 1050 (D. Del. 1982).

471. *Id.* at 1067.

472. *See Pennzoil Wins $10.53 Billion in Suit against Texaco; Verdict Is Called Highest Civil Judgment in History*, Wall St. J., Nov. 20, 1985, at 3.
473. *See* Pennzoil Inc. v. Getty Oil Co., C.A. 7425, slip op. (Del. Ch. 1984).
474. *See How Texaco Turned Big Takeover Victory into Bigger Legal Loss*, Wall St. J., Dec. 20, 1985, at 8.
475. *See Judgment of $11.1 Billion for Pennzoil Co. Is Upheld but Texaco Gets Concession after Hasty Discussion*, Wall St. J., Dec. 11, 1985, at 3.
476. *See* Texaco, Inc. v. Pennzoil Co., 626 F. Supp. 250 (S.D.N.Y.), *aff'd*, 784 F.2d 1133 (2d Cir. 1986).
477. Pennzoil Co. v. Texaco, Inc., 107 S. Ct. 1519 (1987).
478. Texaco, Inc. v. Pennzoil Co., 729 S.W.2d 768 (Tex. Ct. App. 1987).
479. Sullivan & Petzinger, *Settlement Achieved, Texaco and Pennzoil Face New Challenges*, Wall St. J., Dec. 21, 1987, at 1, col. 6.
480. 422 U.S. 49 (1975).
481. *Id.* at 59. *See also* Gearhart Indus., Inc. v. Smith Int'l Inc., 741 F.2d at 715 (reversing district court's preliminary injunction against tender offer because of bidder's failure to disclose its control purpose in original Schedule 13D; bidder's subsequent amendment to Schedule 13D to disclose this purpose "cured" violation); Treadway Cos. v. Care Corp., 638 F.2d 357, 380 (2d Cir. 1980) (injunction denied after curative disclosure: "Since the informative purpose of § 13(d) had thereby been fulfilled, there was no risk of irreparable injury and no basis for injunctive relief."); Chromalloy Am. Corp. v. Sun Chem. Corp., 611 F.2d at 249 (refusing to order additional injunctive relief beyond corrective disclosure). *See also* Hanson Trust PLC v. SCM Corp., 774 F.2d at 60 ("In this context the preliminary injunction, which is one of the most drastic tools in the arsenal of judicial remedies, [citation omitted], must be used with great care, lest the forces of the free market place, which in the end should determine takeover disputes, are nullified."); HUBCO, Inc. v. Rappaport, 628 F. Supp. 345 (D. N.J. 1985) (relief limited to corrective disclosure and injunction until disclosure is made).
482. Rondeau v. Mosinee Paper Co., 422 U.S. at 60.
483. 574 F. Supp. 1172 (N.D. Ohio 1982).
484. *Id.* at 1203.
485. [1981–1982 Transfer Binder] FED. SEC. L. REP. (CCH) ¶ 98,402 at 92,418 (E.D. Mo. 1981).
486. *See also* Spencer Cos. v. Agency Rent-A-Car, Inc., 542 F. Supp. 237, 238 (D. Mass. 1982) (bidder enjoined from "voting or otherwise exercising any rights with respect to shares" of target stock purchased during period misleading Schedule 13D was filed); SEC Litigation Release No. 9533 (Dec. 21, 1981), *reprinted in* [1981–1982 Transfer Binder] FED. SEC. L. REP. (CCH) ¶ 98,387 at 92,343 (endorsing view that district courts have power to order divestiture or rescission).
487. 802 F.2d 62 (2d Cir. 1986).
488. 741 F.2d 707 (5th Cir. 1984).
489. *Id.* at 715.
490. *Id.*
491. *Id. See also* Drobbin v. Nicolet Instrument Corp., 631 F. Supp. 860, 914

(S.D.N.Y. 1986) (refusing to sterilize shares for 14(f) violation, but enjoining voting of shares until ten days after corrective disclosure is made in response to a 13(d) violation); HUBCO, Inc. v. Rappaport, 628 F. Supp. 345, 354 (D.N.J. 1985) (limiting 13(d) right of action to seeking corrective disclosures).

492. 701 F.2d 278 (4th Cir. 1983).

493. *Id.* at 286.

494. *Id.* at 287.

495. 701 F.2d 1000 (1st Cir. 1983).

496. *Id.* at 1010.

497. *Id.*

498. *Id.* at 1009.

499. 409 F.2d 937, 947 (2d Cir. 1969).

500. 18 U.S.C. §§ 1961–68. *See generally* J. Solovy et al., *RICO Update*, 21 REV. SEC. & COM. REG. 81 (May 25, 1988); J. Solovy et al., *Civil RICO in Securities Litigation*, 18 REV. SEC. & COM. REG. 185 (Oct. 9, 1985).

501. 18 U.S.C. § 1962.

502. *Id.* § 1961(1).

503. *Id.* § 1961(5).

504. *Id.* § 1964(c).

505. These include New York, Texas, Ohio, New Jersey, Delaware, and Illinois. Simpson Elec. Corp. v. Leucadia, Inc., 128 A.D.2d 339, 515 N.Y.S.2d 794 (N.Y. App. Div., 2d Dept. 1987); Belfont Sales Corp. v. Gruen Indus., Inc., 112 A.D.2d 96, 491 N.Y.S.2d 652 (N.Y. App. Div., 1st Dept. 1985); Main Rusk Assoc. v. Interior Space Constructors, Inc., 699 S.W.2d 305, 307 (Tex. App. 1985); First Nat'l Bank v. Gonmas, No. 854 1275, slip op. (Ohio Ct. C. Pl. Aug. 20, 1985); Maplewood Bank & Trust Co. v. Acorn, Inc., 504 A.2d 819, 820–21 (N.J. Law Div. 1985); Levinson v. American Accident Reinsurance Group, 503 A.2d 632, 635 (Del. Ch. 1985); Thrall Car Mfg. Co. v. Lindquist, 495 N.E.2d 1132, 1136 (Ill. App. 1st Dist. 1986).

506. These states include California, Pennsylvania, and Washington. Cianci v. Superior Ct., 710 P.2d 375 (Cal. 1985); Village at Camelback Property Owners Ass'n v. Carr, 538 A.2d 528, 537–41 (Pa. Super. 1988); Rice v. Janovich, 742 P.2d 1230 (1987).

507. Lou v. Belzberg, 834 F.2d 730 (9th Cir. 1987), *cert. denied,* 108 S. Ct. 1302 (1988); *see also* Emrich v. Touche Ross & Co., 846 F.2d 1190, 1197 (9th Cir. 1988). In deciding whether a RICO claim was barred by res judicata because it was not raised in a New York state court action, the Second Circuit treated the New York cases cited in note 505 as controlling on the issue of whether these courts would have heard the claim. Cullen v. Margiotta, 811 F.2d 698, 732 (2d Cir.), *cert. denied*, 107 S. Ct. 3266 (1987). While some courts have treated *Cullen* as holding federal jurisdiction was exclusive, it did not do so. *See also* Hampton v. Long, 686 F. Supp. 1202, 1206 (E.D. Tex. 1988) (acknowledging Texas court's denial of jurisdiction for res judicata purposes without holding federal jurisdiction is conclusive).

508. *See* Dubroff v. Dubroff, 833 F.2d 557, 562 (5th Cir. 1987); County of Cook v. Midcon Corp., 773 F.2d 892, 905 n.4 (7th Cir. 1985).

509. *See* Hampton v. Long, 686 F. Supp. at 1205–06 (collecting cases on both sides).

510. Whether a state court has jurisdiction is properly a matter of federal rather than state law, so even a state supreme court decision disclaiming jurisdiction is not final. Yet the only means of facing the state court to hear the claim is through appeal to the United States Supreme Court.

511. Agency Holding Corp. v. Malley-Duff & Assocs., 107 S. Ct. 2759, 2763 (1987) (citation omitted).

512. *Id.* at 2767. *See also* Barkman v. Wabash, Inc., 674 F. Supp. 623 (N.D. Ill. 1987) (four-year limitations period will be applied retroactively).

513. 473 U.S. 479 (1985).

514. 473 U.S. 606 (1985).

515. *See also* Kearny v. Hudson Meadows Urban Renewal Corp., 829 F.2d 1263, 1268 (3d Cir. 1987); Marshall & Ilsley Trust Co. v. Pate, 819 F.2d 806, 809–10 (7th Cir. 1987).

516. *See, e.g.*, Dan River, Inc. v. Icahn, 701 F.2d 278, 290–91 (4th Cir. 1983); *In re* Action Indus. Tender Offer, 572 F. Supp. 846, 850 (E.D. Va. 1983); Bayly Corp. v. Marantette [1982 Transfer Binder] FED. SEC. L. REP. (CCH) ¶ 98,834 at 94,281 (D.D.C. Oct. 19, 1982).

517. No. 85 C 611.

518. 577 F. Supp. 1308, 1318–20 (N.D. Ill. 1983).

519. 574 F. Supp. 1172 (N.D. Ohio 1982).

520. [1981–1982 Transfer Binder] FED. SEC. L. REP. (CCH) ¶ 98,361 at 92,214 (D. Mass. Nov. 17, 1981).

521. 18 U.S.C. § 1964(c) (1970).

522. *Id.* § 1964(a).

523. *Id.* § 1964(b).

524. 796 F.2d 1076 (9th Cir. 1986), *cert. denied*, 107 S. Ct. 1336 (1987).

525. *Accord* Vietnam Veterans of Am., Inc. v. Guerdon Indus., Inc., 644 F. Supp. 951 (D. Del. 1986); DeMent v. Abbott Capital Corp., 589 F. Supp. 1378, 1383 (N.D. Ill. 1984); Kaushal v. State Bank of India, 556 F. Supp. 576, 584 (N.D. Ill. 1983).

526. 843 F.2d 821, 828–30 (5th Cir. 1988).

527. 107 S. Ct. at 2766.

528. *See* Trane Co. v. O'Connor Sec., 718 F.2d 26, 28–29 (2d Cir. 1983); Sedima, S.P.R.L. v. Imrex Co., 741 F.2d 482, 490 n.20 (2d Cir. 1984), *rev'd,* 473 U.S. 479 (1985). *But see* Aetna Casualty & Sur. Co. v. Liebowitz, 730 F.2d 905, 909 (2d Cir. 1984) (indicating that injunctive relief may be available).

529. Chambers Dev. Co. v. Browning-Ferris Indus., 590 F. Supp. 1528, 1541 (W.D. Pa. 1984); Aetna Casualty & Sur. Co. v. Liebowitz, 570 F. Supp. 908, 910–11 (E.D.N.Y. 1983), *aff'd on other grounds*, 730 F.2d 905 (2d Cir. 1984).

530. Vietnamese Fishermen's Ass'n v. Knights of the Ku Klux Klan, 518 F. Supp. 993, 1014 (S.D. Tex. 1981).

531. *See* Belgarde, *Private Civil RICO Plaintiffs Are Entitled to Equitable Relief under § 1964(a)*, 2 RICO LAW REP. 537, 537–38 (1985); Blakey, *The RICO Civil Fraud Action in Context: Reflections on* Bennett v. Berg, 58 NOTRE DAME L. REV. 237, 332 (1982); Fricano, *Civil RICO: An Antitrust Plaintiff's Considerations*, 52 ANTITRUST L.J. 361 (1983); Nachwalter & Blechman, *Is There a Prayer for Private Injunctive Relief after* Religious Technology Center v.

Wollersheim? 2 CIVIL RICO REP. no. 16, part 2 (1986); Strafer, Massumi & Skolnick, *Civil RICO in the Public Interest: "Everybody's Darling,"* 19 AM. CRIM. L. REV. 615, 712 (1982); Wexler, *Civil RICO Comes of Age: Some Maturational Problems and Proposals for Reform*, 35 RUTGERS L. REV. 285, 311–27 (1983).

532. 539 F. Supp. 807, 814–16 (W.D. Ky.), *aff'd*, 689 F.2d 94 (6th Cir. 1982).

533. 18 U.S.C. § 1961(5).

534. Sedima, S.P.R.L. v. Imrex Co., 473 U.S. at 500.

535. *Id.* at 496 n.14.

536. H.J. Inc. v. Northwestern Bell Tel. Co., 829 F.2d 648 (8th Cir. 1987), *cert. granted*, 108 S. Ct. 1219 (1988).

537. J. Solovy et al., *RICO Update*, *supra* note 500.

538. *E.g.*, Terre Du Lac Assoc. v. Terre Du Lac, Inc., 834 F.2d 148, 149–50 (8th Cir. 1987); H.J. Inc. v. Northwestern Bell Tel. Co., 829 F.2d 648 (8th Cir. 1987), *cert. granted*, 108 S. Ct. 1219 (1988); Deviries v. Prudential-Bache Sec., Inc., 805 F.2d 326, 329 (8th Cir. 1986); Superior Oil Co. v. Fulmer, 785 F.2d 252 (8th Cir. 1986).

539. United States v. Ianniello, 808 F.2d 184 (2d Cir. 1986), *cert. denied*, 107 S. Ct. 3229 (1987).

540. *See generally* Beauford v. Helmsley, 843 F.2d 103, 107–10 (2d Cir. 1988) (analyzing "confusing" path of case law and suggesting en banc consideration), *rehearing en banc granted*.

541. *See, e.g.*, Brandt v. Schal Assoc., Nos. 87-2691 & 88-1061 (7th Cir. Aug. 5, 1988) (available on LEXIS); Jones v. Lampe, 845 F.2d 755, 756 (7th Cir. 1988); Medical Emergency Serv. Assocs. v. Foulke, 844 F.2d 391 (7th Cir. 1988); Liquid Air Corp. v. Rogers, 834 F.2d 1297, 1303–05 (7th Cir. 1987); Appley v. West, 832 F.2d 1021, 1027–29 (7th Cir. 1987); Tellis v. United States Fidelity & Guar. Co., 826 F.2d 477, 478–80 (7th Cir.), *cert. granted*, 107 S. Ct. 3255 (1987), *vacated in light of* Agency Holding Corp. v. Malley-Duff & Assocs., Inc.

542. Roeder v. Alpha Indus., Inc., 814 F.2d 22, 30–31 (1st Cir. 1987).

543. Environmental Tectonics v. W.S. Kirkpatrick, Inc., 847 F.2d 1052, 1063–64 (3d Cir. 1988); Saporito v. Combustion Engineering, Inc., 843 F.2d 666, 676 (3d Cir. 1988).

544. Walk v. Baltimore & Oh. R.R., 847 F.2d 1100, 1103–05 (4th Cir. 1988); Eastern Publishing & Advertising, Inc. v. Chesapeake Publishing & Advertising, Inc., 831 F.2d 488, 491–92 (4th Cir. 1987).

545. United Energy Owners Committee, Inc. v. United States Energy Management Sys., Inc., 837 F.2d 356, 360–61 (9th Cir. 1988).

546. Garbade v. Great Divide Mining & Milling Corp., 831 F.2d 212, 214 (10th Cir. 1987).

547. 804 F.2d 970 (7th Cir. 1986).

548. *Id.* at 975.

549. *Id.*

550. 834 F.2d 1297 (7th Cir. 1987).

551. *Id.* at 1304–05.

552. Nos. 87-2691 & 88-1061 (7th Cir. Aug. 5, 1988) (available on LEXIS).

553. *Id.*

554. *See, e.g.*, Medallion Television Enters., Inc. v. SelecTV of Cal., Inc., 833 F.2d 1360, 1364 (9th Cir. 1987); Marks v. Pannell Kerr Forster, 811 F.2d 1108, 1111 (7th Cir. 1987); Lipin Enters., Inc. v. Lee, 803 F.2d 322, 324 (7th Cir. 1986).

555. *See, e.g.*, Medical Emergency Serv. Assocs. v. Foulke, 844 F.2d at 396–97; Eastern Publishing & Advertising, Inc. v. Chesapeake Publishing & Advertising, Inc., 831 F.2d at 492–93; Skycom Corp. v. Telstar Corp., 813 F.2d 810, 818 (7th Cir. 1987); Elliott v. Chicago Motor Club Ins., 809 F.2d 347, 350 (7th Cir. 1986).

556. 847 F.2d 1100 (4th Cir. 1988).

557. *Id.* at 1105. *See also* Roeder v. Alpha Indus., Inc., 814 F.2d at 29–31; International Data Bank v. Zepkin, 812 F.2d 149 (4th Cir. 1987).

558. 832 F.2d 36, 39–40 (3d Cir. 1987).

559. 809 F.2d 548 (9th Cir. 1986), *cert. denied*, 108 S. Ct. 83 (1987).

560. *Id.* at 557–59. *See also* Rice v. Hamilton Oil Corp., 658 F. Supp. 446 (D. Colo. 1987) (awarding sanctions for frivolous securities claim).

561. Slip op., Nos. 87-1149 & 87-1223 (7th Cir. Dec. 31, 1987).

562. *Id.* at 4, 8.

563. *See* Eastway Constr. Corp. v. City of N.Y., 762 F.2d 243, 253–54 (2d Cir. 1985), *cert. denied*, 108 S. Ct. 269 (1987) ("Simply put, subjective good faith no longer provides the safe harbor it once did."); Eavenson, Auchmuty & Greenwald v. Holtzman, 775 F.2d 535, 540 (3d Cir. 1985); Stevens v. Lawyers Mut. Liab. Ins. Co. of N.C., 789 F.2d 1056, 1060 (4th Cir. 1986); Davis v. Veslan Enters., 765 F.2d 494, 497 n.4 (5th Cir. 1985); Albright v. Upjohn Co., 788 F.2d 1217, 1221–22 (6th Cir. 1986); Rodgers v. Lincoln Towing Serv., Inc., 771 F.2d 194, 205 (7th Cir. 1985); O'Connell v. Champion Int'l Corp., 812 F.2d 393, 395 (8th Cir. 1987); Zaldivar v. City of Los Angeles, 780 F.2d 823, 829 (9th Cir. 1986); Burkhart *ex rel.* Meeks v. Kinsley Bank, 804 F.2d 588, 589 (10th Cir. 1986); Donaldson v. Clark, 819 F.2d 1551, 1557 (11th Cir. 1987); Westmoreland v. CBS, Inc., 770 F.2d 1168, 1177 (D.C. Cir. 1985).

564. Zuniga v. United Can Co., 812 F.2d 443, 452 (9th Cir. 1987). *See also* Schwarzer, *Sanctions under the New Federal Rule 11—A Closer Look*, 104 F.R.D. 181, 187 (1985).

565. *See* Hudson v. Moore Business Forms, Inc., 827 F.2d 450, 453 (9th Cir. 1987) ("An objective standard of reasonableness is applied to determinations of frivolousness as well as improper purpose."); Szabo Food Serv., Inc. v. Canteen Corp., 823 F.2d 1073, 1086 (7th Cir. 1987); Insurance Benefit Adm'rs v. Jan Martin, No. 84 C 10355 (N.D. Ill. Sept. 16, 1987) (imposing sanctions for frivolous denial of allegations in the complaint); Kramer, Levin, Nessen, Kamin & Frankel v. Aronoff, 638 F. Supp. 714 (S.D.N.Y. 1986) (sanctioning defendants for filing frivolous affirmative defenses and counterclaims).

566. *See* Zaldivar v. City of Los Angeles, 780 F.2d at 831 (adopting standard set forth in Christiansburg Garment Co. v. EEOC, 434 U.S. 412, 421–22 (1978)); Burkhardt v. Kinsley Bank, 804 F.2d 588; *see also* Lieb v. Topstone Indus., Inc., 788 F.2d 151, 157 (3d Cir. 1986). *But cf.* Hoover Universal, Inc. v. Brockway Imco, Inc., 809 F.2d 1039, 1044 (4th Cir. 1987) (affirming denial of sanction when plaintiff has "a glimmer of a chance of prevailing"); Crosby v. Holsinger, 816 F.2d 162, 164 (4th Cir. 1987) (reversing district court's dismissal and grant of rule 11 sanction for frivolousness) ("A dismissal by a district court *sua sponte*

for frivolousness. . . must be buttressed by much stronger authority than is present here; the action must be clearly foreclosed by authoritative precedent or must have such a tenuous connection with a federal question that no possible facts would entitle the plaintiff to relief.").

567. Zaldivar v. City of Los Angeles, 780 F.2d at 830; *see also* Hudson v. Moore Business Forms, Inc., 827 F.2d at 453 ("[B]ecause of the objective standard applicable to Rule 11 analyses, a complaint that is found to be well-grounded in fact and law cannot be sanctioned as harassing regardless of the attorney's subjective intent."); Oliveri v. Thompson, 803 F.2d 1265, 1275 (2d Cir. 1986), *cert. denied*, 408 U.S. 918 (1987) ("[T]here is no necessary subjective component to a proper Rule 11 analysis."); Brown v. Federation of State Medical Bds. of the United States, 830 F.2d 1429, 1436 (7th Cir. 1987) ("Subjective bad faith is relevant in situations involving malicious prosecution of claims, although not in situations where a party has repeatedly pursued implausible claims."); City of Yonkers v. Otis Elevator Co., 649 F. Supp. 716, 736 (S.D.N.Y. 1986), *aff'd*, 844 F.2d 42 (1988) (bad-faith motive did not justify rule 11 sanctions where signer's argument possessed colorable legal support).

568. *See* Stites v. IRS, 793 F.2d 618, 620 (5th Cir. 1986); Szabo Food Serv., Inc. v. Canteen Corp., 823 F.2d at 1083 (rule 11 has a subjective as well as objective component); *In re* Yagman, 796 F.2d 1165, 1186 (9th Cir. 1986), *cert. denied*, 108 S. Ct. 450 (1987) (subjective "bad faith will. . . support sanctions under either version of Rule 11"); Whittington v. Ohio River Co., 115 F.R.D. 201, 208 (E.D. Ky. 1987) (improper-purpose provision is a subjective requirement; meritorious litigation positions, if taken for purposes of harassment or other improper reason, can violate rule 11).

569. Cleveland Demolition Co. v. Azcon Scrap Corp., 827 F.2d 984, 987 (4th Cir. 1987); McCabe v. General Foods Corp., 811 F.2d 1336, 1340–41 (9th Cir. 1987) (attorney sanctioned for failing to investigate facts before pleading).

570. Hale v. Harney, 786 F.2d 688, 692 (5th Cir. 1986); *see also* Stewart v. RCA Corp., 790 F.2d 624, 633 (7th Cir. 1986) ("Rule 11 *requires* lawyers to think first and file later, on pain of personal liability."); Lieb v. Topstone Indus., Inc., 788 F.2d at 157 (rule 11 "imposes on counsel a duty to look before leaping and may be seen as a litigation version of the familiar railroad crossing admonition to 'stop, look, and listen' ").

571. *See* Brown v. National Bd. of Medical Examiners, 800 F.2d 168, 172 (7th Cir. 1986) (despite sincere belief in the merits of his client's position, attorney had a duty to ascertain the facts and review the law to discover if the facts fit within a recognized entitlement to relief); *see also* Blanchette v. Cataldo, 734 F.2d 869, 871, 879 (1st Cir. 1984) (attorney violated rule 11 by allowing freight claims agent to sign attorney's name to 1900 claims, even though many of the claims possessed merit). *But cf.* FDIC v. Elefant, 790 F.2d 661, 667 (7th Cir. 1986) ("Fees are awarded. . . only when the failure to investigate leads to the taking of an objectively unreasonable position.").

572. *See In re* Yagman, 796 F.2d at 1182.

573. Mohammed v. Union Carbide Corp., 606 F. Supp. 252, 261 (E.D. Mich. 1985).

574. *See* Nemmers v. United States, 795 F.2d 628, 632 (7th Cir. 1986).

575. Szabo Food Serv., Inc. v. Canteen Corp., 823 F.2d at 1083.

576. Greenberg v. Sala, 822 F.2d 882, 887–89 (9th Cir. 1987) (holding that "a complaint based upon a reasonable inquiry should not be found to be factually

frivolous unless some clear authority or a litigant's own clear admission erases the factual underpinning from some essential element of the litigant's pleading").

577. *See* Thomas v. Capital Sec. Serv., Inc., 812 F.2d 984, 988 (5th Cir. 1987); Brown v. Federation of State Medical Bds., 830 F.2d at 1435.

578. *See In re* TCI Ltd., 769 F.2d 441, 446 (7th Cir. 1985); Filippini v. Austin, 106 F.R.D. 425, 432 (N.D. Cal. 1985); Van Berkel v. Fox Farm & Rd. Mach., 581 F. Supp. 1248, 1250 (D. Minn. 1984). *But see* Southern Leasing Partners, Ltd. v. McMullan, 801 F.2d 783, 788 (5th Cir. 1986) (per curiam) ("Failure to do the work of a lawyer cannot be explained away by the approaching limitations bar, as counsel's delay of almost three months in investigating the merits of the case created the problem."); Cabell v. Petty, 810 F.2d 463, 466 (4th Cir. 1987) (complaint violated rule 11 despite impending statutory bar).

579. *See* Fuji Photo Film U.S.A., Inc. v. Aero Mayflower Transit Co., 112 F.R.D. 664 (S.D.N.Y. 1986); Martin v. Supreme Court of N.Y., 644 F. Supp. 1537 (N.D.N.Y. 1986).

580. *See In re* Ginther, 791 F.2d 1151, 1155 (5th Cir. 1986); O'Rourke v. City of Norman, 640 F. Supp. 1451, 1469 (W.D. Okla. 1986); Colorado *ex rel.* Woodard v. Western Paving Constr. Co., 630 F. Supp. 206, 211 (D. Colo. 1986), *aff'd*, 841 F.2d 1025 (10th Cir.), *cert. denied*, 109 S. Ct. 179 (1988); Wold v. Minerals Eng'g Co., 575 F. Supp. 166, 167 (D. Colo. 1983) (cursory telephone conversation insufficient). *But cf.* Foster v. Michelin Tire Corp., 108 F.R.D. 412, 414 n.1 (C.D. Ill. 1985) (reasonable inquiry does not necessarily require interview of key witnesses).

581. *See In re* Ginther, 791 F.2d at 1155; Van Berkel v. Fox Farm & Rd. Mach., 581 F. Supp. at 1249–51.

582. *See* Albright v. Upjohn Co., 788 F. 2d 1217, 1221 (6th Cir. 1986); Fuji Photo Film U.S.A., Inc. v. Aero Mayflower Transit Co., 112 F.R.D. at 666; Florida Monument Builders v. All Faiths Memorial Gardens, 605 F. Supp. 1324, 1325 (S.D. Fla. 1984).

583. Calloway v. Marvel Entertainment Group, 111 F.R.D. 637, 645–47 (S.D.N.Y. 1986).

584. Skycom Corp. v. Telstar Corp., 813 F.2d 810, 819 (7th Cir. 1987) ("Either the lawyers did no investigation or they decided to mistake facts readily knowable.").

585. *See* Oliveri v. Thompson, 803 F.2d at 1279; *In re* Yagman, 796 F.2d at 1186; Jackson Marine Corp. v. Harvey Barge Repair, Inc., 794 F.2d 989, 992 (5th Cir. 1986); Kamen v. American Tel. & Tel. Co., 791 F.2d 1006, 1010–14 (2d Cir. 1986). *But cf.* Lynch v. Cannatella, 810 F.2d 1363, 1377 (5th Cir. 1987) (claims may be dismissed against individual defendants even though defendants "have not cooperated fully with discovery efforts to ascertain the identities of officers actually involved in the incidents alleged").

586. *See* Southern Leasing Partners, Ltd. v. McMullan, 801 F.2d at 788 ("Blind reliance on the client is seldom a sufficient inquiry" under rule 11.); *see also* Nassau-Suffolk Ice Cream, Inc. v. Integrated Resources, Inc., 114 F.R.D. 684, 689 (S.D.N.Y. 1987) (when a lawyer can obtain the information necessary to certify the validity of the claim in a public fashion and need not rely on the client, the lawyer must do so); O'Rourke v. City of Norman, 640 F. Supp. at 1469; Coburn Optical Indus., Inc. v. Cilco, Inc., 610 F. Supp. 656, 659 (M.D.N.C. 1985); Van Berkel v. Fox Farm & Rd. Mach., 581 F. Supp. at 1249–51.

587. *See* Bockman v. Lucky Stores, Inc., 108 F.R.D. 296, 298 (E.D. Cal. 1985); *cf. In re* Curl, 803 F.2d 1004, 1006 (9th Cir. 1986) (attorney has no reason to rely on client on a matter of law).

588. *See In re* Curl, 803 F.2d at 1007; *cf.* Williams v. Whitmill, No. 84 C 4910, slip op. at 4–8 (N.D. Ill. Aug. 8, 1986) (reasonable for counsel to rely upon client's representation that apparently authentic document was genuine).

589. *See generally* Rothschild, Fenton & Swanson, *Rule 11: Stop, Think, and Investigate*, 11 LITIGATION 13, 14–15 (1985).

590. Unioil, Inc. v. E.F. Hutton & Co., Inc., 809 F.2d 548, 557–58 (9th Cir. 1986), *cert. denied,* 108 S. Ct. 83 (1987) (attorney must at least speak to the plaintiff instead of relying solely upon forwarding counsel); Kramer, Levin, Nessen, Kamin & Frankel v. Aronoff, 638 F. Supp. 714, 726 (S.D.N.Y. 1986) (attorney sanctioned for filing answer on behalf of a party who had not hired the lawyer).

591. *Cf.* Oliveri v. Thompson, 803 F.2d at 1278 (counsel may rely on personal experience with similar cases in assessing adequacy of investigation).

592. *See* Unioil, Inc. v. E.F. Hutton & Co., Inc., 809 F.2d at 558–59; Quiros v. Colon, 800 F.2d 1, 2 (1st Cir. 1986); Huettig & Schromm, Inc. v. Landscape Contractors Council of N. Cal., 790 F.2d 1421, 1426–27 (9th Cir. 1986); FDIC v. Elefant, 790 F.2d at 667.

593. *See In re* TCI Ltd., 769 F.2d at 445–50 (7th Cir. 1985).

594. Unioil, Inc. v. E.F. Hutton & Co., Inc., 809 F.2d at 557.

595. *Id.*

596. *See* Pantry Queen Foods, Inc. v. Lifschultz Fast Freight, Inc., 809 F.2d 451, 454 (7th Cir. 1987); Williams v. Whitmill, No. 84 C 4910, slip op. at 9 (N.D. Ill. Aug. 8, 1986) (noting that the disclosure required by a continuing duty might conflict with attorney-client confidentiality).

597. *See, e.g.,* Robinson v. National Cash Register Co., 808 F.2d 1119, 1127 (5th Cir. 1987), *overruled*, 836 F.2d 866 (5th Cir. 1988); Southern Leasing Partners, Ltd. v. McMullan, 801 F.2d at 788; Lee v. Criterion Ins. Co., 659 F. Supp. 813, 821 (S.D. Ga. 1987); Coburn Optical Indus., Inc. v. Cilco, Inc., 610 F. Supp. at 660 ("To persist in claims or defenses beyond a point where they can no longer be considered well grounded violates Rule 11."); Woodfork v. Gavin, 105 F.R.D. 100, 104 (N.D. Miss. 1985) (rule 11 "obligates an attorney . . . to continually review, examine, and re-evaluate his position as the facts of the case come to light.").

598. *See* United States v. Carley, 783 F.2d 341, 345 (2d Cir.), *cert. denied*, 476 U.S. 1142 (1986). *Cf.* Kamen v. American Tel. & Tel. Co., 791 F.2d at 1010 (leaving open issue whether rule 11 imposes a continuing duty to correct a filing); Lane v. Sotherby Parke Bernet, Inc., 758 F.2d 71, 73 (2d Cir. 1985) (per curiam).

599. *See* Oliveri v. Thompson, 803 F.2d at 1274–77 ("Failure to withdraw a paper . . . that later proved to be frivolous . . . does not violate rule 11").

600. *See* Tarkowski v. County of Lake, 775 F.2d 173, 176 (7th Cir. 1985). *Cf.* California Architectural Bldg. Prods., Inc., v. Franciscan Ceramics, Inc., 818 F.2d 1466, 1472 (9th Cir. 1987), *cert. denied*, 108 S. Ct. 698 (1988).

601. *See, e.g.,* Robinson v. National Cash Register Co., 808 F.2d at 1130.

602. *See* MGIC Indem. Corp. v. Weisman, 803 F.2d 500, 505 (9th Cir. 1986) (amended complaint violates rule 11 when no evidence supports element of claim); Mossman v. Roadway Express, Inc., 789 F.2d 804, 806 (9th Cir. 1986)

(summary judgment motion made without supporting affidavits is not well grounded in fact); Albright v. Upjohn Co., 788 F.2d at 1221 (complaint naming pharmaceutical company as one of several defendants despite absence of evidence against particular company is not well grounded in fact); Fontenot v. Upjohn Co., 780 F.2d 1190, 1196 (5th Cir. 1986) (same); National Union Fire Ins. Co. v. Continental Ill. Corp., 116 F.R.D. 252, 254 (N.D. Ill. 1987); Nassau-Suffolk Ice Cream, Inc. v. Integrated Resources Inc., 114 F.R.D. at 691; Wagner v. Allied Chem. Corp., 623 F. Supp. 1407, 1411–12 (D. Md. 1985) (suggesting that a plaintiff may avoid sanctions by consulting an expert before filing suit).

603. *See* Frazier v. Cast, 771 F.2d 259, 263–65 (7th Cir. 1985); O'Rourke v. City of Norman, 640 F. Supp. at 1469–70; Coburn Optical Indus., Inc. v. Cilco, Inc., 610 F. Supp. at 659; Van Berkel v. Fox Farm & Rd. Mach., 581 F. Supp. at 1249–50 (claim concerning accident's date contradicted by uncontested medical records).

604. *See* Cleveland Demolition Co. v. Azcon Scrap Corp., 827 F.2d at 988.

605. *See* Nelson v. Piedmont Aviation, Inc., 750 F.2d 1234, 1238 (4th Cir. 1984), *cert. denied*, 471 U.S. 1116 (1985); John S. Griffith Constr. Co. v. Southern Cal. Cement Masons Negotiating Comm., 607 F. Supp. 809 (C.D. Cal. 1984).

606. *See* Vatican Shrimp Co., v. Solis, 820 F.2d 674 (5th Cir.), *cert. denied*, 108 S. Ct. 345 (1987); Davis v. A.G. Edwards & Sons, Inc., 823 F.2d 105 (5th Cir. 1987); Laborers Local 938 v. B.R. Starnes Co., 827 F.2d 1454, 1458 (11th Cir. 1987); Kamen v. American Tel. & Tel. Co., 791 F.2d at 1013–14; FDIC v. Elefant, 790 F.2d at 667; Eavenson, Auchmuty & Greenwald v. Holtzman, 775 F.2d 535, 544 (3d Cir. 1985). *Cf.* Indianapolis Colts v. Mayor of Baltimore, 775 F.2d 177, 182 (7th Cir. 1985) ("[T]he fact that judges who have ruled on the merits of the pleading disagree provides significant evidence that the pleading was not frivolous or unreasonable.").

607. Fried v. Fried, 113 F.R.D. 103, 106–07 (S.D.N.Y. 1986) (counsel brought meritless action and repeatedly filed unwarranted motions despite the court's warning that sanctions would be imposed).

608. *See* California Architectural Bldg. Prods., Inc. v. Franciscan Ceramics, Inc., 818 F.2d at 1472; Zaldivar v. City of Los Angeles, 780 F.2d at 830–31; Reinhardt v. International Union, United Auto., Aerospace & Agricultural Implement Workers, 636 F. Supp. 864, 868 (E.D. Mich. 1986); Ohio Casualty Ins. Co. v. Prudential Ins. Co., 638 F. Supp. 380, 382–83 (M.D. Pa. 1985).

609. *See* Barrios v. Pelham Marine, Inc., 796 F.2d 128, 132–33 (5th Cir. 1986).

610. *See, e.g.*, Norris v. Grosvenor Mktg. Ltd., 803 F.2d 1281, 1288 (2d Cir. 1986); Stites v. IRS, 793 F.2d at 621; Hale v. Harney, 786 F.2d at 692; Chu v. Griffith, 771 F.2d 79, 81 (4th Cir. 1985); Westmoreland v. CBS, 770 F.2d at 1175; Eastway Constr. Co. v. City of N.Y., 762 F.2d at 254 (rule 11 is violated when "it is patently clear that a claim has absolutely no chance of success under the existing precedents."); Thornton v. Wahl, 787 F.2d 1151, 1154 (7th Cir.), *cert. denied*, 107 S. Ct. 181 (1986) (sanctions imposed on attorney for serious misrepresentation of law and for making preposterous arguments); Szabo Food Serv., Inc. v. Canteen Corp., 823 F.2d at 1080 (the legal basis of complaint was "wacky" and therefore sanctionable). *But cf.* Zaldivar v. City of Los Angeles, 780 F.2d at 834 ("[E]ven if it were squarely on point, a single district court opinion from another circuit cannot alone be sufficient to justify sanctions for failure to adhere to its holding").

611. *See* Hewitt v. Stanton, 798 F.2d 1230, 1233 (9th Cir. 1986); National Survival Game, Inc. v. Skirmish, U.S.A., Inc., 603 F. Supp. 339, 342 (S.D.N.Y. 1985) (defendants sanctioned because they "completely ignored the firmly established precedent directly contradictory to their position"). *But cf.* FDIC v. Elefant, 790 F.2d at 667 (denying sanctions given complexity of the law); Wasyl, Inc. v. First Boston Corp., 813 F.2d 1579, 1583 (9th Cir. 1987) (a pleader need not be correct in her view of the law but must have a "good faith" argument for her view of what the law is or should be); Hoover Universal, Inc. v. Brockway IMCO, Inc., 809 F.2d 1039, 1044 (4th Cir. 1987) (upholding denial of sanctions on the grounds that plaintiff had "a glimmer of a chance of prevailing"); Local 106, Serv. Employees Int'l Union v. Homewood Memorial Gardens, No. 87 C 0403 (N.D. Ill. May 12, 1987) (a reasonable misconstruction of case law on a contract does not entail rule 11 sanctions).

612. *See* Zaldivar v. City of Los Angeles, 780 F.2d at 831; *see also* Burkhart v. Kinsley Bank, 804 F.2d at 590 n.3.

613. *See* Vatican Shrimp Co. v. Solis, 820 F.2d 674; Cabell v. Petty, 810 F.2d at 466; Eastway Constr. Corp. v. City of N.Y., 762 F.2d at 254.

614. Hurd v. Ralphs Grocery Co., 824 F.2d 806 (9th Cir. 1987).

615. Zaldivar v. City of Los Angeles, 780 F.2d at 834 (quoting FED. R. CIV. P. 11 Advisory Committee Notes).

616. Cleveland Demolition Co. v. Azcon Scrap Corp., 827 F.2d at 988.

617. Robinson v. National Cash Register Co., 808 F.2d at 1131.

618. *E.g.*, Hamer v. Lake County, 819 F.2d 1362, 1367 (7th Cir. 1987) ("It is often through vigorous advocacy that changes and developments in the law occur and new precedent is created. Innovative, even persistent advocacy in the face of great adversity must not be unreasonably penalized with hindsight. Subsequent failure is not the test."); Aetna Casualty and Sur. Co. v. Fernandez, 830 F.2d 952, 956 (8th Cir. 1987) ("We are also mindful that excessive 'sanctionitis' under Rule 11 . . . might discourage and 'chill' vigorous and ingenious advocacy, especially in matters of controversial character where there is a reasonable likelihood of achieving potential change in the law."); Eastway Constr. Corp., 762 F.2d at 254 ("Vital changes have been wrought by those members of the bar who have dared to challenge the received wisdom, and a rule that penalized such innovation and industry would run counter to our notions of the common law itself."); Estate of Blas *ex rel.* Chargualaf v. Winkler, 792 F.2d 858, 861 n.4 (9th Cir. 1986) (merely rearguing previously rejected arguments is not sufficient evidence of bad faith or an intent to harass).

619. *See* Gilmore v. Shearson/Am. Express Inc., 811 F.2d 108 (2d Cir. 1987).

620. Szabo Food Serv., Inc. v. Canteen Corp., 823 F.2d at 1082.

621. *See* Filippini v. Austin, 106 F.R.D. 425, 427 (C.D. Cal. 1985); *In re* Ronco, Inc., 105 F.R.D. 493, 498 (N.D. Ill. 1985); WSB Elec. Co. v. Rank & File Comm. to Stop 2-Gate Sys., 103 F.R.D. 417, 420 (N.D. Cal. 1984); Brownlow v. General Serv. Employees Union, 35 Empl. Prac. Dec. (CCH) ¶ 34,886 (N.D. Ill. July 9, 1984).

622. *See* Thornton v. Wahl, 787 F.2d at 1154 (plaintiff's "brief misrepresents existing law; she does not accurately describe the law and then call for change"); O'Rourke v. City of Norman, 640 F. Supp. at 1469. *See generally* Schwarzer, *supra* note 527, at 193–95. *See also* Blackwell v. Department of Offender Rehabilitation, 807 F.2d 914, 915 (11th Cir. 1987) (upholding district court's

imposition of rule 11 sanctions on attorney for his lack of factual candor in his original brief and motion).

623. *See* Golden Eagle Distrib. Corp. v. Burroughs Corp., 801 F.2d 1531 (9th Cir. 1986); *reh'g*, 103 F.R.D. 124 (N.D. Cal. 1984).

624. *See id.* at 801 F.2d 1539–42. *But see* Golden Eagle Distrib. Corp. v. Burroughs Corp., 809 F.2d 584 (9th Cir. 1987) (Noonan, J., dissenting from denial of rehearing en banc). *See generally* Continental Air Lines, Inc. v. Group Sys. Int'l Far East Ltd., 109 F.R.D. 594,, 598 (C.D. Cal. 1986) (no duty of candor under rule 11); Western Co. of N. Am. v. Oil & Gas Comm'n of India, No. 85 Civ. 9858, slip op. (S.D.N.Y. July 2, 1986); Taitt v. Chemical Bank, No. 84 Civ. 8126, slip op. (S.D.N.Y. May 20, 1986), *rev'd*, 810 F.2d 29 (2d Cir. 1987) (failure to note that cited case had been reversed did not violate rule 11).

625. Pipe Trades Council v. Underground Contractors Ass'n, 828 F.2d 609, 615–16 (9th Cir. 1987).

626. *Id.* at 615–16.

627. *See* Lieb v. Topstone Indus., Inc., 788 F.2d at 157; Zaldivar v. City of Los Angeles, 780 F.2d at 831 n.9.

628. *See* Davis v. Veslan Enters., 765 F.2d at 500.

629. *See* Fox v. Boucher, 794 F.2d 34, 36–38 (2d Cir. 1986) (plaintiff brought meritless suit after threatening, "I'm going to get you in court"); Chevron, U.S.A., Inc. v. Hand, 763 F.2d 1184, 1187 (10th Cir. 1985) (plaintiff filed frivolous rule 60(b) motion after stating that she would attempt to delay stipulated dismissal of suit).

630. *See* Cohen v. Virginia Elec. & Power Co., 788 F.2d 247, 249 (4th Cir. 1986).

631. *See* Fox v. Boucher, 794 F.2d at 36–38.

632. *See* McLaughlin v. Bradlee, 803 F.2d 1197, 1205 (D.C. Cir. 1986); Cannon v. Loyola Univ. of Chicago, 784 F.2d 777, 782 (7th Cir. 1986), *cert. denied*, 479 U.S. 1033 (1987) (plaintiff's thirteenth suit in ten years against universities that denied her admission to medical school); Zaldivar v. City of Los Angeles, 780 F.2d at 832 (finding of harassment based on successive filings requires identity of parties and of issues); Cook v. Peter Kiewit Sons Co., 775 F.2d 1030, 1036–37 (9th Cir. 1985), *cert. denied*, 476 U.S. 1183 (1986) (suit that is "carbon copy" of earlier suits was filed to harass defendants); Tarkowski v. County of Lake, 775 F.2d at 176 (history of unfounded litigation establishes prima facie entitlement to attorney's fees); *see also* Greenberg v. Sala, 822 F.2d at 885; Crooker v. United States Marshals Service, 641 F. Supp. 1141, 1143 (D.D.C. 1986); Raffe v. Doe, No. 84 Civ. 6272, slip op. (S.D.N.Y. Oct. 11, 1985).

633. 827 F.2d 450, 456 (9th Cir. 1987).

634. *See* INVST Fin. Group, Inc. v. Chem-Nuclear Sys., Inc., 815 F.2d 391, 402 (6th Cir. 1987), *cert. denied*, 108 S. Ct. 291 (1987); Davis v. Veslan Eters., 765 F.2d at 500; *In re* Oximetrix, Inc., 748 F.2d 637, 644 (Fed. Cir. 1984); Ricci v. Key Bancshares of Maine, Inc., 111 F.R.D. 369, 376–78 (D. Me. 1986) (sanctions imposed against an attorney who filed a motion that was completely specious and intended to obtain delay); Marine Midland Bank v. Goyak, No. 84 Civ. 1204, slip op. at 9–10 (S.D.N.Y. July 12, 1984) ("[T]he defenses alleged . . . are, bluntly stated, stalling operations to delay the plaintiff in obtaining its judgment."). *See also* Cinema Serv. Corp. v. Edbee Corp., 774 F.2d 584, 586 (3d Cir. 1985) (sanctions assessed under Bankruptcy Rule 9011).

635. *See* Chevron, U.S.A., Inc. v. Hand, 763 F.2d at 1187.

636. *See* Burlington Coat Factory Warehouse Corp. v. Esprit de Corp., 769 F.2d 919, 927 n.2 (2d Cir. 1985).

637. *See* Wold v. Minerals Eng'g Co., 575 F. Supp. 166 (plaintiff's motion found to have violated the improper-purpose clause because it was based upon a completely inaccurate factual investigation).

638. *See* Chu v. Griffith, 771 F.2d at 81; Steinle v. Warren, 765 F.2d 95, 101–02 (7th Cir. 1985); *see also* Maier v. Orr, 758 F.2d 1578, 1583–84 (Fed. Cir. 1985) (unfounded recusal motion).

639. *See* Cohen v. Virginia Elec. & Power Co., 788 F.2d at 249.

640. *See* WSB Elec. Co. v. Rank & File Comm. to Stop the 2-Gate Sys., 103 F.R.D. at 421. *But cf.* Zaldivar v. City of Los Angeles, 780 F.2d at 834 (that a suit is inspired by politics does not necessarily mean that it violates rule 11).

641. *See also* Donaldson v. Clark, 819 F.2d at 1557; Anschutz Petroleum Mktg. Corp. v. E.W. Saybolt & Co., 112 F.R.D. 355, 359 (S.D.N.Y. 1986).

642. Anschutz Petroleum Mktg. Corp. v. E.W. Saybolt & Co., 112 F.R.D. at 359 ("The standard to be applied in making an award of attorney's fees is one of reasonableness.").

643. INVST Fin. Group, Inc. v. Chem-Nuclear Sys., Inc., 815 F.2d at 404.

644. Eastway Constr. Corp. v. City of N.Y., 821 F.2d 121, 123–24 (2d Cir.), *cert. denied*, 108 S. Ct. 269 (1987) (allowing award of a fee substantially less than the lodestar amount, but holding that the district judge's award was outside the lower range of permissible discretion and revising the fee upward to the lowest point of permissible discretion); *see also* Cheek v. Doe, 828 F.2d 395 (7th Cir. 1987), *cert. denied*, 108 S. Ct. 349 (1987) (reducing amount of sanctions because litigant appeared pro se and district court failed to provide sufficient statement of reasons for the severity of the sanctions); *In re* Yagman, 796 F.2d at 1185; Marine Midland Bank v. Goyak, No. 84 Civ. 120, slip op.

645. *See* Brown v. Nationwide Mut. Ins. Co., 634 F. Supp. 72, 73 (S.D. Miss.), *modified in part and aff'd in part*, 805 F.2d 1242 (5th Cir. 1986).

646. *See* Unioil, Inc. v. E.F. Hutton & Co., 809 F.2d at 559 ($300,000 sanction substantial but reasonable); *In re* TCI Ltd., 769 F.2d at 448 ("Some frivolous cases impose large costs on defendants when they require counsel to wade through voluminous records or review many cases."); Schwarz v. Folloder, 767 F.2d 125, 134 (5th Cir. 1985).

647. *See* INVST Fin. Group, Inc. v. Chem-Nuclear Sys., Inc., 815 F.2d at 404; Oliveri v. Thompson, 803 F.2d at 1280; *In re* Yagman, 796 F.2d at 1185; United Food & Commercial Workers Union Local No. 115 v. Armour & Co., 106 F.R.D. 345, 349–50 (N.D. Cal. 1985) (reducing fee request because counsel overlitigated the case); Filippini v. Austin, 106 F.R.D. at 433–34; Johnson v. Kut Kwick Corp., 620 F. Supp. 748 (S.D. Ga. 1984).

648. Anschutz Petroleum Mktg. Corp. v. E.W. Saybolt & Co., 112 F.R.D. at 357.

649. *See* Brown v. Capitol Air, Inc., 797 F.2d 106, 108 (2d Cir. 1986); Mossman v. Roadway Express, Inc., 789 F.2d at 806 (fees incurred because of misconduct of party seeking sanctions should not be awarded as sanction); Woodcrest Nursing Home v. Local 144, Hotel, Hosp., Nursing Home & Allied Servs. Union, 788 F.2d 894, 899 (2d Cir. 1986) (affirming denial of sanctions when litigation tactics of party seeking sanctions "hardly represented a model of propriety");

641

Calloway v. Marvel Entertainment Group, 111 F.R.D. at 650–51 (S.D.N.Y. 1986); Michigan Nat'l Bank v. Kroger Co., 619 F. Supp. 1149, 1159 (E.D. Mich. 1985) (parties have duty to mitigate by attempting to resolve legal claims by using the least expensive alternative); Marine Midland Bank v. Goyak, No. 84-1204, slip op.

650. *See In re* Yagman, 796 F.2d at 1184–85; Rodgers v. Lincoln Towing Serv., Inc., 771 F.2d at 205; Medical Emergency Serv. Assocs. v. Foulke, 633 F. Supp. 156, 158 (N.D. Ill. 1986), *aff'd*, 844 F.2d 391 (7th Cir. 1988). *Cf.* FDIC v. Elefant, 790 F.2d at 667 ("Fees are awarded. . . only when the failure to investigate leads to the taking of an objectively unreasonable position.").

651. *See* Lieb v. Topstone Indus., Inc., 788 F.2d at 157–58; Bastien v. R. Rowland & Co., 116 F.R.D. 619 (E.D. Mo. 1987), *aff'd*, 857 F.2d 482 (8th Cir. 1988) ($100,000 sanction imposed upon plaintiffs and their counsel for bad-faith conduct).

652. *See In re* Kelly, 808 F.2d 549 (7th Cir. 1986) (no formal sanctions imposed because the attorney clumsily rather than dishonestly drafted a motion and attorney admitted deficiency of affidavit and assured court that he would not make inadequately substantiated statements in court filings again). *See also In re* Itel Sec. Litig., 596 F. Supp. 226, 235 (N.D. Cal. 1984), *aff'd without opinion*, 791 F.2d 672 (9th Cir. 1986), *cert. denied*, 479 U.S. 1033 (1987).

653. *See* Oliveri v. Thompson, 803 F.2d at 1281; *In re* Yagman, 796 F.2d at 1185 (9th Cir. 1986); Cotner v. Hopkins, 795 F.2d 900, 903 (10th Cir. 1986); O'Rourke v. City of Norman, 640 F. Supp. at 1471; Calloway v. Marvel Entertainment Group, 111 F.R.D. at 651 (although defendant requested $900,000 in attorney's fees, court awarded $200,000, noting that plaintiff's and plaintiff's counsel's ability to pay, defendant's need, and the reasonableness of the fee request must be taken into account).

654. *Cf.* Tinsley v. Mitchell, 804 F.2d 1254 (D.C. Cir. 1986).

655. *See* Davis v. Veslan Enters., 765 F.2d at 500–01 (assessing sanction for interest on judgment lost due to frivolous filing that delayed entry of judgment).

656. *See* Donaldson v. Clark, 819 F.2d at 1557; Glick v. Gutbrod, 782 F.2d 754, 757 n.3 (7th Cir. 1986) (per curiam); Hilgeford v. Peoples Bank, 776 F.2d 176, 178–79 (7th Cir. 1985), *cert. denied*, 475 U.S. 1123 (1986).

657. *See* Nixon v. Rose, 631 F. Supp. 794, 797 (N.D. Ind. 1985), *aff'd without opinion*, 789 F.2d 919 (1986) ($2000 fine); Kearns v. Ford Motor Co., 114 F.R.D. 57 (E.D. Mich. 1987) (court-imposed $10,000 sanction payable to clerk of court imposed under rule 37); Itel Containers Int'l Corp. v. Puerto Rico Marine Management, Inc., 108 F.R.D. 96, 106–07 (D.N.J. 1985) ($5000 fine).

658. *See* Dyson v. Sposeep, 637 F. Supp. 616, 624 (N.D. Ind. 1986); Dominguez v. Figel, 626 F. Supp. 368, 374 (N.D. Ind. 1986); Robinson v. Moses, 644 F. Supp. 975, 982–83 (N.D. Ind. 1986) (court fined plaintiff $3600 for filing a baseless civil rights suit—fine represented amount of judicial resources expended on the case).

659. *Cf.* Eavenson, Auchmuty & Greenwald v. Holtzman, 775 F.2d at 544 (fee award analogous to contempt).

660. *See In re* Yagman, 796 F.2d at 1180–81.

661. *See* Cotner v. Hopkins, 795 F.2d at 903. *But see* Donaldson v. Clark, 819 F.2d at 1558 ("Nothing in the text of Rule 11 or in the Advisory Committee Note

indicates that due process requires a court to follow the procedures called for by Fed. R. Crim. P. 42(b) for criminal contempt proceedings before it can impose a monetary sanction pursuant to Rule 11. Both the note and policy consideration tend to the opposite conclusion.").

662. *E.g.*, Touchstone v. G.B.Q. Corp., 596 F. Supp. 805, 810 (E.D. La. 1984).

663. *E.g.*, *In re* Curl, 803 F.2d at 1007; Larkin v. Heckler, 584 F. Supp. 512, 514 (N.D. Cal. 1984); Huettig & Schromm, Inc. v. Landscape Contractors Council, 582 F. Supp. 1519, 1522–23 (N.D. Cal. 1984), *aff'd*, 790 F.2d 1421 (9th Cir. 1986).

664. *E.g.*, Steinle v. Warren, 765 F.2d at 102; Lepucki v. Van Wormer, 765 F.2d 86, 89 (7th Cir.) (per curiam), *cert. denied*, 474 U.S. 827 (1985).

665. *See* Stelly v. Commissioner, 808 F.2d 442, 443 (5th Cir. 1987); Farguson v. MBank Houston, N.A., 808 F.2d 358, 360 (5th Cir. 1986); Hilgeford v. Peoples Bank, 110 F.R.D. 700, 702 (N.D. Ind. 1986); Van Sickle v. Holloway, 791 F.2d 1431, 1437 (10th Cir. 1986); Cotner v. Hopkins, 795 F.2d at 901 (before filing any future actions, plaintiff was required to demonstrate that action was in good faith and to provide a certification of all pleadings and a list of all previously filed actions); Raffe v. Doe et al., 619 F. Supp. 891, 897–93 (S.D.N.Y. 1985). *See also, e.g.*, Blanchette v. Cataldo, 734 F.2d at 871, 874 (ordering attorney to review up to 1900 claims that he had permitted to be filed without reasonable inquiry); Johnson v. Secretary, Dep't of Health & Human Servs., 587 F. Supp. 1117, 1121 (D.D.C. 1984) (deeming admitted facts alleged by opposing party).

Thirty-Five

Corporate Criminal Liability: An Overview

Robert J. Perry

Scope of Liability

A corporation is criminally liable for criminal acts committed by its agents within the scope of employment and for the benefit of the corporation. The knowledge and criminal purposes of the agents are imputed to the corporation.

Exposure to Criminal Liability

A corporation may be liable for the acts of its agents without regard to their status in the corporate hierarchy. "The corporation may be criminally bound by the acts of subordinate, even menial, employees."[1] The Ninth Circuit has held, "It is the *function* delegated to the corporate officer or agent which determines his power to engage the corporation in a criminal transaction."[2]

Corporations have been convicted for acts by salesmen,[3] clerical workers,[4] truck drivers,[5] and manual laborers.[6]

"Scope of Employment"

An agent's "scope of employment" has been broadly defined and means merely that the criminal act occurred while the employee was carrying out a job-related activity:

> A corporation is held responsible for acts not within the agent's corporate powers strictly construed, but which the agent has assumed to perform for the corporation when employing the corporate powers actually authorized, and in such cases there need be no written authority under seal or vote of the corporation in order to constitute the agency or to authorize the act.[7]

Robert J. Perry is a member of Dalton & Godfrey in Los Angeles, and is of counsel to Epstein Becker Borsody & Green. Formerly, he served as an Assistant United States Attorney in Los Angeles, where he was chief of Financial Investigations.

Employees have been found to have been acting within the scope of their employment while engaging in acts that were specifically forbidden by their corporate employer[8] or that the employer had made good-faith efforts to prevent.[9]

A corporation is liable for crimes committed by its subsidiaries or divisions.[10]

Acting "for the Benefit of the Corporation"

Acting "for the benefit of the corporation" is also broadly defined. A corporation may be criminally liable even though it did not receive any benefit from the employee's criminal acts.[11] The Fourth Circuit has stated:

> We do not accept benefit as a touchstone of corporate criminal liability; benefit, at best, is an evidential, not an operative, fact.[12]

Likewise, the Fifth Circuit has held:

> If it is done with a view of furthering the master's business, then the *expectation or hope of a benefit*, whether direct or indirect makes the act that of the principal. The act is no less the principal's if from such intended conduct either no benefit accrues, a benefit is undiscernable, or, for that matter, the result turns out to be adverse.[13]

Collective Knowledge of Agents

The collective knowledge of its agents may be imputed to a corporation for crimes involving general intent.[14]

Good Faith Efforts to Prevent Criminal Acts

A corporation's good-faith efforts to prevent criminal acts by its employees may not absolve it of criminal liability. Thus, the "due-diligence" defense has been rejected.[15]

Liability of Officers and Agents

Individual Responsibility for Acts

Individuals are responsible for their own acts. Therefore, an agent who commits a criminal act is personally liable even though the agent may have been acting for the corporation in an official or representative capacity.[16]

Responsibility of Officers

Officers may be responsible for the acts of others. More specifically, officers and agents may be personally guilty for aiding and abetting the commission of crimes by lower-ranking employees.[17]

To be liable as an aider and abettor, the officer must associate him- or herself with the venture, participate in it as something the officer wishes to bring about, and through his or her action seek to make it succeed.[18] While the aider and abettor must share the principal's criminal purpose, that person need not know every detail of the illegal conduct or all the persons who were perpetrating the crime.[19] The Ninth Circuit spelled out this responsibility as follows:

> An aider and abettor "is liable for any criminal act which in the ordinary course of things was the natural or probable consequence of the crime that he advised or commanded, although such consequence may not have been intended by him."[20]

An officer's tacit acquiescence to a subordinate's unlawful conduct could result in criminal liability because the officer was aware of the conduct and did not attempt to stop it.[21]

Examples of conduct constituting aiding and abetting have included a corporation president who instructed a bookkeeper to remove invoices of a foreign subsidiary to enable the corporation to evade income taxes,[22] a bank employee who instructed subordinates to make false entries in bank records,[23] and an owner who authorized employees to sign false Medicaid and Medicare claims.[24]

Failure to Control Criminal Acts by Others

An individual may be liable for failing to control the criminal acts of others. In *United States v. Dotterweich*[25] and *United States v. Park*,[26] the Supreme Court upheld convictions of high corporate officials for violations of the Federal Food, Drug, and Cosmetic Act,[27] in which they played no direct role. In these decisions the Supreme Court recognized two duties imposed by the statute due to the public interest in preventing contamination of food and drugs: (1) a duty to implement measures to ensure that violations will not occur, and (2) an affirmative duty to seek out and remedy violations that do occur.

The Supreme Court's analysis in *Park* and *Dotterweich* has been cited with approval in cases involving violations of the Federal Hazardous Substances Act,[28] the Filled Milk Act,[29] and the Migratory Bird Treaty Act.[30]

Congressional Intent to Criminally Punish Corporations

The legislative evidence suggests that Congress intends to punish corporations that perform criminal acts. Several federal statutes specifically mention corporations.[31] In addition, title 1 of U.S.C. § 1, in defining words for acts of Congress, defines "person" to include corporations "unless the context [of the act] indicates otherwise."

Frequently Used Federal Criminal Statutes

Conspiracy

The so-called "darling of prosecutors," the conspiracy statute[32] is frequently used in cases involving more than one defendant. A conspiracy is an agreement between two or more persons to commit an illegal act. The agreement need not be express or formal, and it may be inferred from facts indicating the parties acted in concert with a common design or purpose to achieve a single object:

> To be convicted as a member of a conspiracy, a defendant need not know every objective of the conspiracy, . . . every detail of its operation or means employed to achieve the agreed-upon criminal objective, . . . or even the identity of every co-conspirator, . . . There must, however, be agreement on the "essential nature of the plan," . . . and on the "kind of criminal conduct . . . in fact contemplated."[33]

An earlier court described these characteristics of conspiracy:

> Secrecy and concealment are essential features of successful conspiracy. The more completely they are achieved, the more successful the crime. Hence the law rightly gives room for allowing the conviction of those discovered upon showing sufficiently the essential nature of the plan and their connections with it, without requiring evidence of knowledge of all its details or of the participation of others.[34]

According to the Ninth Circuit, the conspiracy need not be a formal arrangement:

> The government need not show direct contact or specific agreement between the defendants. For the convictions to stand, the government must produce enough evidence to show that each defendant knew or had a reason to know of the scope of the [conspiracy] . . . and had reason to believe that their [*sic*] own benefits derived from the operation were dependent upon the success of the entire venture.[35]

At least one member of the conspiracy must commit an overt act in furtherance of the conspiracy, but that act may be nothing more than making a telephone call[36] or having a conversation.[37]

Each member of the conspiracy is liable for crimes committed by co-conspirators in furtherance of the conspiracy.[38]

Section 371's prohibition of conspiracy "to defraud the United States, or any agency thereof in any manner or for any purpose" has been interpreted to apply to "any conspiracy for the purpose of impairing, obstructing or defeating the lawful function of any department of Government."[39]

A corporation may be convicted for conspiracy with its employees.[40]

The Racketeer Influenced and Corrupt Organizations Act (RICO)

The Racketeer Influenced and Corrupt Organizations Act (RICO)[41] prohibits investing income from a pattern of racketeering activity to acquire an enterprise,[42] using a pattern of racketeering to acquire an enterprise,[43] using an enterprise to conduct a pattern of racketeering,[44] and conspiracy to do any of these.[45]

The definition of "racketeering activity" includes violent state felonies and specific federal crimes including bribery,[46] theft from interstate shipment,[47] mail fraud,[48] wire fraud,[49] and several others. A "pattern of racketeering" requires two acts within ten years.

Under RICO, certain state criminal violations are "predicate offenses" which can form the basis for federal prosecution. RICO has severe criminal penalties, including incarceration for up to twenty years, a fine of $25,000, and forfeiture of the enterprise or the racketeering proceeds to the government.[50]

Bribery of Public Officials

The federal bribery statute[51] has broad scope. It applies to anyone who "directly or indirectly, corruptly gives, offers or promises anything of value" to a "public official" to influence an official act; to influence the public official to commit, collude in, or allow any fraud or "make opportunity for the commission of any fraud" on the United States; or to induce a public official "to do or omit to do any act in violation of his lawful duty."[52] The act covers gratuities and prohibits giving, offering, or promising anything of value to a public official.[53] The act also prohibits public officials from soliciting or receiving bribes and gratuities.[54]

The term "public official" has been broadly defined. In *Dixon v. United States*, [55] the Supreme Court held that an employee of a private firm hired by the City of Peoria, Illinois, to administer Peoria's federal block grant funds was a public official covered by the federal bribery statute even though the private firm had no agreement of any kind with the federal government. The employee was a "public official" because he occupied "a position of public trust with official federal responsibilities."[56]

Bribery of Bank Officials

In October 1984, Congress passed a new bank bribery statute.[57] The statute prohibits the giving, offering, or promising "directory or indirectly" of anything of value to "any officer, director, employee, agent, or attorney of any financial institution, bank holding company, or savings and loan holding company . . . for or in connection with any transaction or business of such financial institution."[58] The statute similarly restricts bank employees from soliciting or receiving things of value.[59]

Violation of the statute involving a thing of value greater than $100 is a felony punishable by up to five years' imprisonment and a $5000 fine or three times the value of anything offered (whichever is greater). If the violation involves a thing of value of less than $100, it is a misdemeanor punishable by imprisonment for up to one year and a fine of up to $1000.

False Statements to the Government

It is a felony to knowingly falsify, conceal, or cover up a material fact, or to make any false, fictitious, or fraudulent statement or representation, or to use any document known to contain false statements "in any matter within the jurisdiction of any department or agency of the United States."[60]

The false-statements statute has broad reach. It has been applied to making false reports regarding oil produced or received from other producers,[61] making false statements in corporate tax returns,[62] making false reports to the Environmental Protection Agency,[63] keeping false business records that are subject to inspection by a governmental agency,[64] and making unsworn, oral false statements to the Federal Bureau of Investigation.[65]

To obtain a conviction under the false-statements statute, the government need not prove the defendant has actual knowledge that the false statements were made in a matter within the jurisdiction of the government.[66]

Mail Fraud

The mail fraud statute[67] prohibits use of the mails to execute "any scheme or artifice to defraud."[68] The statute applies to a scheme that otherwise would not be subject to federal jurisdiction.[69] The statute does not require actual falsity for prosecution. Reckless disregard for truth or falsity is enough to sustain a conviction.[70] The use of the mails need not be central to the scheme to defraud.[71]

Currency Reporting

The Currency and Foreign Transactions Reporting Act of 1970[72] (commonly called the Bank Secrecy Act) obligates financial institutions to file reports with the Treasury Department of currency transactions exceeding $10,000. The term "financial institution" is broadly defined and includes brokers or dealers in securities, a person (including a corporation) who engages as a business in dealing in or exchanging currency, a person who cashes checks or similar instruments, and a person engaged in the business of transmitting funds abroad for others. A single violation of the reporting statute is punishable by imprisonment for up to five years and a maximum fine of $250,000.

Government Investigative Techniques

The Grand Jury

The grand jury is a valuable investigative tool used to investigate corporations. Grand jury subpoenas may be issued on mere suspicion, and corporations may not invoke the privilege against self-incrimination. Attorneys may accompany witnesses to the grand jury, but must remain outside while the witness testifies.

From a prosecutor's perspective, the major drawback to using the grand jury is that it provides notice of the investigation to the suspect. The Department of Justice discourages "forthwith" grand jury subpoenas, and persons or entities who receive subpoenas have time to prepare for their testimony or production of documents.

Search Warrants

Search warrants are issued on sworn affidavits establishing probable cause to search for evidence of specific criminal activity. Search warrants can be executed without notice, and premises may be secured before and during the execution of a warrant. The principal advantage to the government of using search warrants is that evidence is obtained immediately, and suspects have no opportunity to conceal or destroy evidence. The principal disadvantage to using search warrants in investigations of corporations is determining where to search.

Surveillance

The government employs several means of surveillance to investigate criminal offenses. Many of the means discussed here are not frequently employed in investigations of corporations but are available for use in specific cases.

Visual Surveillance

Government agents can conduct visual surveillance of suspects based on mere suspicion. Agents frequently take photographs and occasionally use hidden video cameras to record observations.

Consensual Audio Surveillance

The government frequently records conversations where one of the participants is cooperating with the government. Consensual recording of telephone or face-to-face conversations may be based on mere suspicion.

Wiretaps

In certain investigations, the government may use wiretaps to intercept telephone conversations or may use a covert entry to place a hidden microphone to intercept face-to-face conversations. Such activities are strictly governed by the wiretap statute.[73] Wiretapping must be based on probable cause, which includes a showing that normal investigative techniques have not or will not be successful. Wiretaps are authorized for limited periods not to exceed thirty days and must be approved by the Attorney General or an assistant attorney general authorized to act in the Attorney General's behalf.

The government may use wiretaps only to investigate certain crimes, including bribery, obstruction of criminal investigation, theft from interstate shipment, embezzlement of pension and welfare funds, interstate transportation of stolen property, RICO violations, currency reporting, and drug trafficking.

Mail Covers

The government may request a mail cover be conducted by authorities of the U.S. Postal Service. The mail cover supplies the return addresses of all mail received by the suspect.

Transponders

A transponder is a device that, when installed on a car or plane, will give a signal to indicate its presence. Government agents use transponders to aid surveillance of moving suspects.

Pen Registers

A pen register is a device that displays the numbers called by a telephone. Pen registers may be used on the basis of mere suspicion and are not covered by the restrictions of the federal wiretap statute.

Other Searches

Government agents often search suspects' trash. Such searches can be conducted based on mere suspicion.

Practical Considerations

Corporate officers and their counsel can take a number of steps to prevent and respond to possible criminal violations. Some practical measures are listed here as a starting point:

- Show concern for the need to comply with the law. Provide regular reminders of your company's deep concern that your employees comply with all laws. Make certain that your employees understand that any situation involving even the appearance of impropriety is forbidden.
- Hire a specialist. At the first sign of trouble, bring in an expert to advise you and supervise any investigation done by the corporation.
- Bring corruption to the attention of the government. If you discover an illegal situation involving public officials, bring it to the attention of the proper authorities. Do not wait for the government to come to you. Remember, the government usually has a greater interest in prosecuting its own employees.
- Consider spreading authority among employees. Final authority concentrated in one person can invite corruption. Giving several persons responsibility for final approval of a matter reduces the potential for corruption.
- Institute careful review procedures. Careful review can minimize the potential for corruption.
- Be alert to employee spending habits. An employee's unexplained sudden wealth may indicate involvement in illegal activities.
- Be alert to possible employee drug usage. Consumption of illegal drugs is prevalent in our society. Dependence on drugs can cause an employee to commit illegal acts that could bind the company. Signs of employee drug use include absenteeism, tardiness, lack of concentration, steadily deteriorating or in-

adequate work, unfinished assignments, erratic work, temporary absences during the day, increases in minor illnesses, disinterest in work, sudden moodiness, hand tremors, flushed face, dilated eyes, nodding, poor motor control, and excessive use of health benefits.

Notes

1. Standard Oil Co. v. United States, 307 F.2d 120, 127 (5th Cir. 1962).
2. C.I.T. Corp. v. United States, 150 F.2d 85, 89 (9th Cir. 1945) (emphasis added).
3. United States v. George F. Fish, Inc., 154 F.2d 798 (2d Cir. 1946); Zito v. United States, 64 F.2d 772 (7th Cir. 1933); United States v. Uniroyal, Inc., 300 F. Supp. 84 (S.D.N.Y. 1969).
4. Riss & Co. v. United States, 262 F.2d 245 (8th Cir. 1958) (terminal log clerk); St. Johnsbury Trucking Co. v. United States, 220 F.2d 393 (1st Cir. 1955) (rating clerk).
5. United States v. Harry L. Young & Sons, 464 F.2d 1295 (10th Cir. 1970); Texas-Oklahoma Express, Inc. v. United States, 429 F.2d 100 (10th Cir. 1970).
6. United States v. Illinois Cent. R.R., 303 U.S. 239 (1938) (employee who unloaded cattle from carrier); Dollar S.S. Co. v. United States, 101 F.2d 638 (9th Cir. 1939) (crew member emptying garbage).
7. New York Cent. & H.R.R.R. v. United States, 212 U.S. 481, 493–94 (1909).
8. United States v. Hilton Hotels Corp., 467 F.2d 1000, 1006 (9th Cir. 1972); United States v. American Radiator, 433 F.2d 174, 204 (3d Cir. 1970).
9. Dollar S.S. Co. v. United States, 101 F.2d 638 (9th Cir. 1939).
10. United States v. Wilshire Oil Co., 427 F.2d 969 (10th Cir. 1970); United States v. Johns-Manville Corp., 231 F. Supp. 690 (E.D. Pa. 1963).
11. United States v. Carter, 311 F.2d 934 (6th Cir. 1949); United States v. Empire Packing, 174 F.2d 16 (7th Cir. 1949).
12. Old Monastery Co. v. United States, 147 F.2d 905, 908 (4th Cir. 1945).
13. Standard Oil Co. v. United States, 307 F.2d 120, 128 (5th Cir. 1962) (emphasis added) (holding that corporation was not criminally liable where criminal acts were for the benefit of third persons and resulted in theft of corporate property).
14. Inland Freight Lines v. United States, 191 F.2d 313 (10th Cir. 1951) (reversed on other grounds).
15. United States v. Cadillac Overall Supply Co., 568 F.2d 1078, 1090 (5th Cir. 1978); United States v. Hilton Hotels Corp., 467 F.2d at 1000, 1007 (9th Cir. 1972); United States v. Harry L. Young & Sons, 464 F.2d 1295 (10th Cir. 1970).
16. Kopald-Quinn & Co. v. United States, 101 F.2d 628, 632 (5th Cir. 1939) (affirming conviction of corporation and certain agents of fraudulent sale of worthless stock).
17. 18 U.S.C. § 2 states:

    (a) Whoever commits an offense against the United States or aids, abets, counsels, commands, induces or procures its commission, is punishable as a principal.

> (b) Whoever wilfully causes an act to be done which if directly performed by him or another would be an offense against the United States, is punishable as a principal.

18. Nye & Nissen v. United States, 336 U.S. 613, 619 (1949).
19. United States v. Lane, 514 F.2d 22, 27 (9th Cir. 1975).
20. United States v. Barnett, 667 F.2d 835, 841 (9th Cir. 1982) (citation omitted).
21. Morgan v. United States, 149 F.2d 185 (5th Cir. 1945) (officer permitted sale of ice in violation of price controls).
22. United States v. Berger, 456 F.2d 1349 (2d Cir. 1972).
23. Meredith v. United States, 238 F.2d 535 (4th Cir. 1956).
24. United States v. Precision Medical Laboratories, Inc., 593 F.2d 434 (2d Cir. 1978).
25 320 U.S. 277 (1943).
26. 421 U.S. 658, 673 (1975).
27. 21 U.S.C. § 331(k).
28. United States v. Klehman, 397 F.2d 406 (7th Cir. 1968).
29. Carolene Prods. Co. v. United States, 140 F.2d 61 (4th Cir. 1944).
30. United States v. Frezzo Bros. Inc., 602 F.2d 1123 (3d Cir. 1979).
31. *See* Sherman Act, 15 U.S.C. § 7; Securities Act of 1933, 15 U.S.C. § 77b(2); Securities Exchange Act of 1934, 15 U.S.C. § 78c(a)(1), (9); Food, Drug, and Cosmetic Act, 21 U.S.C. § 321(e); Anti-Kickback Act, 41 U.S.C. § 52; National Housing Act of 1933, 12 U.S.C. § 378; Federal Trade Commission Act, 15 U.S.C. § 714m(f); Wholesome Meat Act, 21 U.S.C. §§ 602, 610, 611; Meat Inspection Act, 21 U.S.C. §§ 88, 90; Navigable Waterways Act, 33 U.S.C. §§ 1, 3, 406, 411, 419, 449, 502; Oil Pollution Act, 33 U.S.C. § 1001(f); Tobacco Statistics Act, 7 U.S.C. §§ 503–04; Export Standards Acts, 7 U.S.C. §§ 586, 589, 596, 599; Interstate Commerce Act, 49 U.S.C. §§ 1(3)(a), 10(3); Commodity Exchange Act, 7 U.S.C. § 473c-3; Communications Act, 47 U.S.C. § 217; Elkins Act, 7 U.S.C. § 41(1).
32. 18 U.S.C. § 371, which provides:

> If two or more persons conspire either to commit any offense against the United States, or to defraud the United States, or agency thereof in any manner or for any purpose, and one or more of such persons do any act to effect the object of the conspiracy, each shall be fined not more than $10,000 or imprisoned not more than five years, or both.
>
> If, however, the offense, the commission of which is the object of the conspiracy, is a misdemeanor only, the punishment for such conspiracy shall not exceed the maximum punishment provided for such misdemeanor.

33. United States v. Gleason, 616 F.2d 2, 16 (2d Cir. 1979) (citations omitted).
34. Blumenthal v. United States, 332 U.S. 535, 557 (1947).
35. United States v. Perry, 550 F.2d 524, 528 (9th Cir. 1977).
36. United States v. McCarty, 611 F.2d 220 (8th Cir. 1979).
37. United States v. Civella, 648 F.2d 1167 (8th Cir. 1981).
38. Pinkerton v. United States, 328 U.S. 640 (1946).
39. Haas v. Henkel, 216 U.S. 462, 479 (1910); Dennis v. United States, 384 U.S. 855, 861 (1965). *See also* United States v. Klein, 247 F.2d 908 (2d Cir. 1957)

(conviction for impeding and obstructing Treasury Department in collection of income taxes).

40. Nye & Nissen v. United States, 336 U.S. 613 (1949); United States v. Hartley, 678 F.2d 961 (11th Cir. 1982).

41. 18 U.S.C. §§ 1961–1968.

42. 18 U.S.C. § 1962(a). The enterprise must be "engaged in, or the activities of which affect, interstate or foreign commerce." 18 U.S.C. § 1962. Purchases of securities that total less than 1 percent of the outstanding securities of an enterprise and that do not confer the power to elect directors are exempted from RICO. *Id.*

43. 18 U.S.C. § 1962(b).

44. 18 U.S.C. § 1962(c).

45. 18 U.S.C. § 1962(d).

46. 18 U.S.C. § 201.

47. 18 U.S.C. § 659.

48. 18 U.S.C. § 1341.

49. 18 U.S.C. § 1343.

50. Russello v. United States, 104 U.S. 196 (1983).

51. 18 U.S.C. § 201.

52. 18 U.S.C. § 201(b).

53. 18 U.S.C. § 201(f).

54. 18 U.S.C. § 201(c), (g).

55. 104 S. Ct. 1172 (1984).

56. 104 S. Ct. at 1180.

57. 18 U.S.C. § 215.

58. 18 U.S.C. § 215(b).

59. 18 U.S.C. § 215(a).

60. 18 U.S.C. § 1001.

61. United States v. Gilliland, 312 U.S. 86 (1941).

62. United States v. Beacon Brass Co., 344 U.S. 43 (1952).

63. United States v. Mahler, 363 F.2d 673 (2d Cir. 1966).

64. United States v. Diaz, 690 F.2d 1352 (11th Cir. 1982).

65. United States v. Rodgers, 104 S. Ct. 1942 (1984).

66. United States v. Yermian, 104 S. Ct. 2936 (1984).

67. 18 U.S.C. § 1341.

68. *Id.*

69. Badders v. United States, 240 U.S. 391 (1916).

70. United States v. Schaflander, 719 F.2d 1024 (9th Cir. 1983).

71. Perreira v. United States, 347 U.S. 1 (1954).

72. 31 U.S.C. § 5322.

73. 18 U.S.C. §§ 2510 *et seq.*

Thirty-Six

Responding to a Criminal Investigation: Some Considerations for Corporate Counsel

Michael C. Hallerud

Corporations are fictional persons that act exclusively through employees or agents who are natural persons. The modern theory of corporate criminal liability avoids any anomalies presented by this incorporeal status by imputing an individual employee's or agent's criminal liability to the corporation itself. In certain circumstances, the vicarious liability of the corporation or the direct liability of its employees or agents may in turn be imputed to still other employees and agents of the corporation. Although in theory, corporate criminal liability derives routinely from the established exposure of corporate employees or agents, only recently have corporations been prosecuted in significant volume.

In response, in-house counsel with a corporate criminal practice must focus on preventing criminal activity by developing and administering a rigorous corporate compliance effort. Where compliance efforts are unsuccessful and the alleged criminal activity becomes the focus of a law enforcement investigation, corporate counsel must strive to avoid indictment or, if necessary, circumscribe the indictment and maximize the likelihood of a favorable disposition (either by plea or at trial).

To succeed in compliance efforts and, if compliance has not been attained, to respond effectively to investigations and indictments, the corporation's policy makers, managers, employees, and agents must cooperate. At the same time, however, those preventive and/or defense mechanisms may split corporate and individual interests.

The Prosecution Decision

Even where a corporate prosecution can be justified as a technical legal proposition, it is still within the prosecutor's discretion whether to pro-

Michael C. Hallerud is a member of Pettit & Martin, San Francisco, California. He was formerly Assistant General Counsel for The Boeing Company, Seattle, Washington.

ceed. The *Principles of Federal Prosecution*[1] and the comments thereto provide a comprehensive glossary of the factors that may be explicitly or implicitly considered in the decision to prosecute.

The principal (formal and informal) consideration in all prosecution decisions is the likelihood of success. Other formal considerations include the strength of the federal interests involved, noncriminal alternatives, and the existence or likelihood of effective criminal prosecution in another federal or state jurisdiction.

Factors that are often, and often futilely, advanced for declining prosecution are claims that only low-level employees were involved; that innocent employees, shareholders, and communities will be hurt (for instance, through a probable bankruptcy triggered by prosecution); that the corporation is critical to some national priority (like national defense); and that prosecution will disrupt settlement prospects with victims or regulators.

Because prosecutors now popularly view the use of criminal laws against corporations as a means of social control and economic regulation, prosecutorial discretion is often heavily influenced by perceptions of the salutary impact of indictment and conviction. In other words, where the corporate culture or climate breeds and either rewards or acquiesces in criminal activity, prosecutors are more motivated to use the criminal justice system to enforce conformity with prescribed norms.

Corporate compliance efforts are thus significant in preventing crimes and avoiding indictment. Among the possible influences on a prosecution decision are the following:

- The level of the officers, employees, and agents whose misconduct has exposed the corporation to liability, and whether that misconduct was geographically and organizationally isolated or widespread
- Whether the company had in place or has since implemented effective systems for preventing, detecting, and correcting criminal activity
- Whether the corporation made a timely disclosure of the criminal activity to the proper authorities and cooperated in the investigation and in the design of remedial measures to compensate victims and prevent repetition
- Whether the corporation took or will take meaningful disciplinary measures against the officers, employees, and agents who are responsible for the misconduct

The U.S. Department of Justice formalized these principles in the "Department of Justice Guidelines Regarding Department of Defense Voluntary Disclosure Program," issued to all U.S. Attorneys by the Criminal Division of the Justice Department on July 17, 1987.

Also, in July 1986, the Department of Defense initiated its Volunteer Disclosure Program to encourage self-policing among defense contractors. That program, in summary, promised that, in any suspension or debarment review, an evaluation of the contractor's present responsibility would be influenced by an effective policy which disclosed wrongdoing by the corporation or its employees, initiated prompt corrective action (including appropriate employee discipline), and was followed by full cooperation with investigating and auditing authorities.

The Justice Department guidelines complement the Department of Defense's consideration of voluntary disclosure for suspension/debarment purposes by similar consideration in the prosecution evaluation. Among the factors to be evaluated by the Justice Department are the following:

- The timelines and quality of the voluntary disclosure
- The corporation's existing prevention/compliance programs
- The loss/benefit from the wrongdoing
- The geographic, organizational, and transactional extent of the wrongdoing
- The level of the employees involved
- The corporation's cooperation with authorities
- The corrective action taken

Where the corporation can marshal these ameliorating facts, it can sometimes avoid indictment. And even where the prosecutor adheres to a decision to press charges, other benefits can nevertheless flow. For instance, the prosecution may agree to reduce the number of counts (and therefore the fines), charge a misdemeanor instead of a felony, indict no individuals (or limit the individuals charged), charge a business entity other than the parent (which may shift some collateral consequences), limit the factual proffer at the time of plea, intercede with administrative agencies that may have been victimized or that have regulatory cognizance over the defendant corporation or individuals, or provide a press statement that may reduce the impact of the indictment or plea on stock prices.

The factors and consequences just described present corporations with substantial incentives to institute compliance programs and take ameliorative measures even after a criminal exposure has become visible. But those factors and consequences also present substantial opportunities for conflict with employees and employee representatives. While it may be salutary to the corporation to institute measures such as internal investigations, discipline, and cooperation with authorities in fixing criminal responsibility of individuals, employees and unions often view these tactics as the ruthless identification of scapegoats whose sacrifice may reduce the risks to the corporation.

Employee Relations, Costs and Risks

Prevention of corporate crime and minimization of its impact neither begin nor end with major employee disciplinary measures. Ideally, a corporation should have already erected effective preventive structures, such as compliance policies and procedures, employee awareness and training programs, and institutionalized detection devices like audits and hot lines. However, this is not an ideal world, and many criminal activities may result from the unauthorized acts of "rogue" employees, agents, or business units, or be vestiges of a corporate environment no longer approved but not yet effectively dismantled.

Employee Discipline

Employee discipline therefore will and must be a permanent feature of any corporate criminal compliance program, and for the same reasons that the criminal justice system itself serves as a corporate and personal control mechanism: correction, deterrence, and punishment. Where compliance has unhappily been unsuccessful, the corporation may have to use employee discipline to protect the broader interests of the corporation, innocent employees, stockholders, and the other communities and constituencies to which a corporation must be responsive. For instance, it may be necessary to discipline employees to preserve any due diligence defenses or equitable appeals the corporation may arguably have against the imputation of individual liability to the corporation or to higher levels of management. Employee discipline is certainly a factor in demonstrating to the Defense and Justice Departments that an effective compliance program is in operation.

Discipline may take many forms. For instance, short of discharge, the company may penalize employees by suspending them, reducing compensation (including bonuses), demoting them, delaying or denying promotions, reassigning them to less desirable positions or locations, and by censuring them orally or in writing. The discipline appropriate to a given situation is totally driven by the circumstances, and no general formulas or rules can be articulated.

The imposition of employee discipline, however appropriate to the corporation's goals, may still violate public policies or private rights. The most common employment causes of action that may be triggered by (or invoked in) employee disciplinary action in the contexts of corporate criminal compliance programs or corrective action are defamation, breach of contract, and actions in derogation of the employment-at-will doctrine.

Defamation

Claims for libel or slander frequently arise out of disciplinary action. The fact of the discipline itself is frequently cited in litigation as the defamatory act. The discipline is "published" in the sense that it is entered in the records of the corporation and known at least to the individual managers who imposed or must effect or consider the discipline. Where the discipline is justified, truth will be a complete defense in most states. In addition, the "publication" in corporate records and to those who have a need to know (which could include prosecutors and debarring officials) may be conditionally privileged by legitimate business requirements.

Of course, even if the discipline is later held to be unwarranted and therefore defamatory, it may arguably not have been published if its dissemination is confined to corporate records and those within the corporation with a need to know. However, there may also be a "compelled publication" of the discipline by the employee himself as he seeks other employment or unemployment compensation. That compelled publication may make the defamation actionable.[2]

Where the fact of discipline or the allegations under investigation are disseminated unnecessarily, such as in the loose comments of auditors or investigators or in a corporate newspaper, liability may still result (even if the actionable comments are true) if there was malice or no justification for the publication.

Breach of Contract

Breach of an employment contract is frequently charged in employment litigation prompted by employee discipline. While the damages may be limited to "make-whole" remedies under this cause of action, it typically has a generous statute of limitations that excuses tardiness in filing.

Many employees are employed under express (usually written) contracts. Typically those contracts are collective bargaining agreements between the corporation and the employee's labor organization. Less common, but by no means rare, especially for senior managers, are individual employment contracts. Express employment contracts usually have actual or implied provisions limiting the employer's procedural and/or substantive disciplinary prerogatives to instances meeting three criteria:

1. The employer has conducted a responsible investigation;
2. The employer has given the employee notice of the charges against him or her and an opportunity to respond;
3. "Cause" for discipline exists.

Enforcement of these contracts depends on their terms and the laws that authorize them. For instance, collective bargaining agreements are typically enforced through grievance arbitration provisions. Where a union, which has some discretion in pursuing a grievance, fails to do so or is unsuccessful, an employee may sue the union for breach of its duty of fair representation and the employer for breach of contract. However, the Supreme Court has recently restricted compulsory resort by unionized employees to contractual arbitration.[3]

Actions in Derogation of the "Employment-at-Will" Doctrine

It is axiomatic that all employees have employment contracts, although not all employment contracts are express or negotiated in the traditional sense. Typically, employees without express (written or oral) employment contracts are employed under terms that are specific only as to compensation and benefits. All other terms of these contracts exist and may be changed at the discretion of the employer. Where there is no express agreement on the duration of the employment or the circumstances (procedural and susbstantive) under which it may be terminated, the employment is considered to be at the will of the employer and the employee. In recent years, "at-will" employees have in many states acquired judicial protection against the employer's traditional and unilateral right to discharge them (and, presumably, to impose lesser discipline) without notice or penalty.

Implied-in-Fact Contracts. In recent years many states have implied procedural and substantive protections against discipline from the facts and circumstances of at-will employment. For instance, offer letters, employee handbooks, personnel policies, and other company practices regulating the relationship or inducing loyalty have been found to create an implied contract or equitable estoppel which forbids the discipline of employees in violation of the representations made by the employer. Where implied-in-fact contracts or equitable estoppels have been found, employees may have a cause of action in contract or in the nature of contract.

Covenant of Good Faith and Fair Dealing. With the erosion of the employment-at-will doctrine in some states has come a cause of action, not for breach of an express or implied contract, but for the *tort* of breach of an implied-in-law covenant of good faith and fair dealing. Because this is not a contract action, it does not depend upon any representations made by the employer or any bargains for which consideration was exchanged. Rather, the employer has been charged with a duty in law, usually owed to longer service employees, to provide the type of procedural and substantive protections against arbitrary discipline commonly associated with traditional just cause provisions in union contracts. Moreover, the damages available include not only traditional contractual "make whole" relief such as backpay, but also damages for pain and suffering, humiliation, and emotional distress, plus punitive damages.

Violations of Public Policy. Employment causes of action for violations of public policy may be at common law (tort or contract) or pursuant to statute. Where an employee has a contract (express or implied) limiting the corporation's right to discipline only where good cause is shown, an employee may have a contract cause of action if the corporation disciplines him or her disproportionately or otherwise unfairly to avoid or minimize its own civil or criminal exposure. Even at-will employees may have a tort cause of action if the discipline is to shift the corporation's exposure or to punish the employees (and intimidate others) for cooperating with the authorities investigating the criminal allegations.

There are also many nonretaliation provisions associated with federal and state statutory systems. Those nonretaliation provisions, like general whistle blower statutes, provide the employee or the government (on behalf of the employee or itself) with a cause of action for discrimination or retaliation for reporting corporate violations or cooperating with the enforcement authorities. For instance, under the False Claims Amendments Act of 1986,[4] individuals are encouraged by the Act's expanded civil remedies to institute private (*qui tam*) actions to recover the government's losses from false claims. Any retaliation by an employer against his *qui tam* plaintiff-employee is actionable and entitles the prevailing employee to reinstatement with full seniority, double back pay *and* interest, and any other special damages, including costs and counsel fees.[5]

Also, The Victim and Witness Protection Act of 1982[6] provides criminal sanctions and actions for injunctions in aid of persons who are harassed or intimidated for reporting crimes or assisting authorities in an investigation or prosecution.[7]

Protective Measures

Where administering a corporate compliance program or instituting corrective action requires employee discipline, the corporation cannot avoid exposure to employment litigation, but it can minimize the exposure somewhat by the following measures:

- The investigation should be thorough, professional, and fully documented. The investigators, whether attorneys, auditors or security personnel, should avoid unnecessary statements to witnesses or other third parties during the investigation. All persons contacted during the investigation should be cautioned not to discuss the investigation except with authorized persons. Such circumstances will minimize the exposure to defamation claims.

- Unless compelling circumstances exist, the individuals subject to discipline should be advised before the final disciplinary decision of the charges against them and given an opportunity to respond in defense or mitigation. This procedure enhances the regularity of the investigation and the discipline process generally and may adduce admissions supporting discipline.
- Discipline should be tied to violations of company policies and procedures, not stated in terms of statutes (especially criminal statutes) or regulations. This practice will minimize the exposure to defamation claims and preserve some flexibility in dealing with prosecutors over whether a crime has been committed.
- In assessing discipline, the corporation should consider its own culpability as a mitigating circumstance. For instance, ineffective policies, training, or supervision may excuse or explain some portion of the employee misconduct triggering the discipline.
- Where the disciplined employee's management shares responsibility, perhaps because of poor training or supervision, the managers should also be disciplined.
- The discipline should be consistent with discipline for similar violations of company policies and proportional to the seriousness of the violations. Consistency and proportionality will diminish the effectiveness of claims that individuals were scapegoats for the corporation's own misdeeds.

Any employment litigation represents a serious exposure in its own right because of the damages that may follow directly, but in the context of a corporate criminal compliance program or corrective action, these actions are potentially more serious. They disrupt compliance and corrective actions and may compromise the defense of the criminal case.

The claims or defenses in employment litigation may bring alleged criminal conduct to the attention of investigators or prosecutors. Where criminal investigations are stalled or accorded low priority, employment litigation may surface witnesses and documentary evidence the authorities have overlooked or undervalued.

Because employment litigation may proceed in parallel with a criminal investigation or prosecution, it may require a corporation, in defending the employment litigation, to assert or forgo factual or legal positions in defense of its discipline that are inconsistent with the arguments to the prosecutor that no crime was committed or that any violations of the law were technical or *de minimis*.

Defense of employment litigation often polarizes employees and creates adversarial relationships that inhibit or may preclude altogether the cooperation between corporations and individuals that can be crucial to a successful defense of the criminal matter. For that reason, a "standstill" agreement that tolls any employment action statute of limitations and defers those disputes is often desirable. Also, a settlement of bona fide employment claim should be explored as soon as the employment dispute arises. However, settlements may appear to be attempts to obstruct justice by influencing testimony of the employee.[8] For that reason, such settlement should be clearly defensible on their own merits.

Settlement of employment claims may also appear to be inconsistent with the corporation's posture of having taken meaningful disciplinary action, which in turn may convince prosecutors and other authorities (such as debarring officials) that appeals to their discretion are insincere. Where employment claims are settled during an investigation, the corporation should consider advising the prosecutor (and the "victim," such as a debarring official or the SEC, in appropriate cases) of the legal, factual, and tactical reasons for the action in order to avoid unfavorable inferences.

Discipline and employment litigation often cause employee morale to decline because they suggest that the corporation is separating itself from the employees, who may feel that they were only following orders or procedures or advancing the corporation's business interests. Settlement of employment litigation or corporate support for a disciplined employee during the pendency of a criminal matter also affects employee (especially managerial) morale because it suggests a lack of corporate resolve or commitment to corporate compliance programs or criminal defense efforts.

Use of Outside Counsel in Criminal Cases

Outside Counsel for the Corporation

In most cases where a matter has been identified as presenting realistic criminal exposure for the corporation, it is important immediately to involve experienced *criminal* counsel for the corporation. A civil lawyer, even an experienced civil litigator, is inadequate in any serious matter. Usually the attorneys selected should be outside counsel, except for matters that are factually and legally simple and involve little actual risk of criminal exposure.

Most corporations lack inside counsel who are fully capable and experienced criminal trial lawyers. But even if such lawyers were in-house, outside counsel provides a valuable appearance of independence. That appearance is significant to prosecutors, who may feel that the factual representations of outside counsel are less subject to corporate "command influence." The appearance may also be significant to separate counsel for individuals, who may have more confidence that the corporation's outside counsel will not cavalierly or secretly sacrifice the individual client's interests.

Outside counsel selected for the corporation must have credibility with prosecutors for the quality of his or her investigation, preparation, and representations. Moreover, he or she must have credibility as a trial adversary, since the corporation's willingness to go to trial and its capability to win—which are significant deterrents to marginal cases—will be evaluated in part based on the conduct and reputation of that outside counsel.

Use of Separate Counsel for Individuals

As with outside counsel for the corporation, the need for separate counsel for individuals should be identified as early as possible. Experienced criminal trial lawyers should be retained to represent the individual witnesses, subjects, and targets whose interests currently or potentially are not wholly congruent with the corporation or whose appearance of independence from the corporation's influence is critical to the corporation's defense.

Outside counsel for the corporation should play a significant role in identifying which employees should be represented separately from the corporation and recruiting the outside counsel to be retained by the corporation on behalf of and recommended to the individuals. It is critical that separate counsel be chosen with due regard for their willingness to work in a joint defense environment with counsel for the corporation and other individuals.

While a corporation will want to minimize the expense and complexity associated with multiple separate counsel, it is important to evaluate the tactical impact of establishing logical groupings of individuals (based on witness, subject, or target status and/or on similarities, dissimilarities, or conflicts in evidentiary contributions, etc.). Each logical grouping of individuals should be assigned separate counsel. Logical groupings with separate counsel improve the efficiency and effectiveness of representation and defuse prosecution concerns over conflicts of interest, which could disqualify lawyers and further disrupt the defense effort.

It is of course the prerogative of each employee and agent to decline any representation or to select individual counsel. It is imperative, however, that the corporation influence that decision constructively by pointing out the advantages of representation generally and of representation by counsel recommended by the corporation in particular. The corporation's willingness to advance the costs of that representation is usually dispositive as a practical matter.

Retaining separate counsel for appropriate individuals is important both to the corporation and to the individuals. For the corporation, the benefits usually include the following:

- Satisfaction of felt moral obligations to employees to protect them from the personal risks of a criminal investigation (which improves employee morale generally and promotes cooperation with the corporation in the defense effort)
- A buffer between the corporation and the employees that diminishes inferences of corporate noncooperation with an investigation (and, therefore, inferences of guilt) when employees are not readily produced with instructions to tell all
- Additional sources of input to the prosecutor and intelligence about the course and direction of the investigation
- Independent representation for individuals who might otherwise be suborned by offers of immunity or plea bargains or intimidated by the prosecutor's power to seek (and almost always deliver) an indictment
- Advance notice of an individual's decision to turn state's evidence and the content of the evidence that will be adduced against the corporation

Individuals usually benefit in the following ways:

- Independent professional representation to assess the natural leverage that prosecutors have from the threat of indictment of individuals or the corporation
- Protection from the real risks of indictment for perjury, obstruction of justice, and false statements when prosecutors, in frustration over the difficulty of making the main case, decide to prosecute individuals for collateral crimes

Despite the importance of the advantages of arranging for separate counsel when appropriate and organizing joint defense efforts, the corporation must continuously recognize that the separate counsel for individuals owe their professional duty to their clients, not to the corporation. This is true even if the corporation is advancing the defense costs.

The benefits to be obtained from providing separate counsel to employees will be forfeited or diminished unless counsel is available or employed before meaningful encounters with the criminal justice machinery. For instance, if employees are interrogated by government investigators or prosecutors before or without assistance of counsel, the corporation may not learn (seasonably or at all) of a significant witness or testimony. The corporation may also have lost an opportunity to dissuade the authorities from all or part of the investigation or prosecution. The unrepresented employee may have lost an opportunity for immunity, become an attractive target of the investigation, or, through poor preparation, exposed him- or herself innocently to liability for false statement or perjury.

Accordingly, as soon as a criminal matter of realistic concern is identified, the corporation should, in addition to securing counsel for the corporation and individuals, take the following steps:

1. "Secure the crime scene" by identifying potential witnesses, subjects, and targets and identifying and preserving physical evidence (e.g., time cards, correspondence).
2. Advise corporate employees and agents who may be witnesses, subjects, or targets of the pendency of the investigation, of their rights to counsel or to deal directly with authorities, and how to contact counsel. This advice should ideally be in writing so that individuals don't misunderstand it and authorities don't suspect obstruction of justice. An example of such an advice memorandum is shown as Form 51 in the Appendix.
3. Immediately begin a comprehensive internal investigation. Counsel should carefully plan the mechanics of this investigation and special problems that may arise, such as coordination of corporate and outside counsel, privileges, and joint defense agreements.

Indemnification of Costs and Judgments

The expense of a criminal defense effort, as well as the financial exposure from possible fines or imprisonment, may constitute a significant practical limitation on an individual's exercise of his or her rights. For this reason, most state corporation laws generally empower corporations to support officers, directors, employees, and agents financially in legal proceedings. This allows individuals and corporations to resist unwarranted claims and encourages capable persons to serve in positions of visibility and responsibility. While each state's law varies somewhat, most are similar to section 145 of the Delaware Corporation Law, which is the basis for the following discussion.

Indemnification

A corporation has the power, but generally not the obligation, to indemnify any current or former director, officer, employee, or agent who, by reason of that status, is or was a party (or is threatened to be made a party) to any civil, criminal, administrative, or investigative proceeding.[9]

The indemnification may be for expenses (including attorney's fees), judgments, fines, and amounts paid in settlement.

The conditions that must be satisfied before this statutory indemnification can be extended are that the indemnitee have acted:

- in good faith; and
- in a manner reasonably believed to be in, or at least not opposed to, the corporation's best interests; and
- in a criminal matter, without reasonable cause to believe the conduct in question was unlawful.

It should be noted that an adverse judgment, settlement, conviction, or nolo contendere plea is not conclusive of ineligibility for indemnification.

Indemnification decisions under the statute are made in each specific instance, not under a blanket or prospective policy. Indemnification is either mandatory or discretionary. Mandatory indemnification, that is, a legally enforceable claim against the corporation for indemnification of expenses, including attorney's fees, arises where a prospective indemnitee is successful on the merits *or otherwise* in an action or any distinct claim therein.[10] Because the prospective indemnitee has prevailed in court, the standards of good faith, etc. found in section 145(a) are inapplicable, and any subjective inquiry behind the objective outcome is irrelevant and not permitted.

A question of discretionary indemnification[11] arises where the prospective indemnitee experiences an adverse outcome or one that is inconclusive. The substantive indemnification standard found in section 145(a) is applied procedurally as follows:

- By the board of directors, assuming a quorum of disinterested directors can be assembled; or
- If no quorum is possible, or if the board otherwise elects, by independent legal counsel; or
- By the stockholders.

Advancement of Defense Costs

While indemnification is a significant benefit for the individual, and therefore a benefit to the corporation, its value is severely limited because, by its nature, indemnification must await the outcome of a proceeding. Except in those limited instances where the potential indemnitee is sufficiently liquid to front what often may well be tens of thousands of dollars in defense costs, or where defense counsel will advance the costs of the representation, indemnification generally comes too late to be of material assistance as a practical matter. Thus, Delaware law provides two alternatives.

The first alternative, in section 145(e), allows (but does not require) corporations to advance the expenses of representation. For officers and directors, the advancement of expenses must be subject to an undertaking to repay the amounts advanced if it should ultimately be determined that indemnification is not required or warranted. For other employees or agents, expenses may be advanced upon such terms and conditions, if any, that the board deems appropriate, including an undertaking.

Unlike indemnification, the advancement of expenses is not subject to any statutory eligibility criteria. But there are practical considerations that a corporation will want to consider. For instance, does the corporation want to distance itself from a target or defendant, as might be the situation in a treason or espionage matter? Or does the corporation want to demonstrate solidarity either to the prosecutor or the advancee? While equity, morality, loyalty, and similar considerations should not be disregarded, the bottom line for the corporation must almost always be its own strategic and tactical self-interest.

In addition to the advancement of expenses under section 145(e), a corporation may under section 145(f), in its bylaws, by employment contracts, or by a vote of disinterested stockholders or directors, provide an enforceable right to advancement of expenses or full indemnification.[12] Section 145(f) does not appear to require any conditions or establish any eligibility standards for such a benefit. Moreover, a corporation may purchase insurance to advance or fund expenses or liabilities, again without regard to whether there would otherwise be corporate power to indemnify.

Because questions of advancements and indemnification must often be confronted at the front end of a proceeding before all facts are known, while emotions may be running high, and while other defensive measures must be simultaneously deployed, it is wise to have mechanisms in place well in advance.

Notes

1. Department of Justice, 1980.
2. Lewis v. Equitable Life Assurance Society, 389 N.W.2d 876 (Minn. 1986).
3. In *Lingle v. Norge Div., Magic Chef, Inc.*, 108 S. Ct. 1877, 100 L. Ed 2d 410 (1988), the Court held that state law claims congruent with union contract claims may be pursued independently if the state law claim does not require interpretation of the collective bargaining agreement.
4. Pub L. No. 99-562, 100 Stat. 3153 (codified at 31 U.S.C. §§ 3729 *et seq.*).
5. 31 U.S.C. § 3730(h).

669

6. 18 U.S.C. §§ 1512 *et seq.*
7. 18 U.S.C. §§ 1512(c), 1513–14.
8. *See* 18 U.S.C. § 1510.
9. DEL. CORP. LAW § 145(a).
10. *Id.* § 145(c).
11. *Id.* § 145(d).
12. *Id.* § 145(f).

Thirty-Seven

Effective Representation of the Corporation, Its Directors, Officers, and Employees in Grand Jury and Agency Investigations

Jamie S. Gorelick

Whether a government inquiry begins with an informal request for information from an inspector general, an agency subpoena, or a grand jury subpoena, corporate counsel must be aware of the dangers and opportunities presented during government investigations. Representing corporations and corporate employees under investigation requires familiarity with largely unwritten rules. The goals of a grand jury or agency representation are threefold: (1) to protect the client's fundamental constitutional and statutory rights; (2) to influence the exercise of prosecutorial discretion by effectively marshaling factual and legal arguments; and (3) ultimately, to seek the least punitive consequence.

A Subpoena: The Process Begins

In many instances, the first indication of government interest in a corporation's activities is a subpoena on the corporation or on an entity or person with whom it does business. In some instances, such as those involving government contracts, the client will have been notified that a referral to the inspector general or a United States attorney has been made. Like many administrative agencies, an inspector general and a United States attorney—through a grand jury—both possess the power to issue a subpoena, and a corporate client must be aware of the particular problems posed by these two situations.

Inspector General Subpoenas

Documents, Not Testimony

The subpoena power of inspectors general appears to be more limited than the comparable grand jury power. Inspectors general have the power

Jamie S. Gorelick is a member of Miller, Cassidy, Larroca & Lewin, Washington, D.C.

to subpoena documents,[1] but appear to be without authority to compel testimony. The court in *United States v. Iannone*[2] so held, but some have argued that the *Iannone* decision is limited to the Department of Energy Inspector General. *Iannone* did involve only the powers of the Department of Energy's Inspector General, but the language of the Department of Energy Organization Act[3] is identical to that of the Inspectors General Act of 1978, which governs most of the inspectors general.[4] Moreover, the Department of Justice itself advocated limiting the subpoena power of inspectors general to the power to obtain documents.[5]

In responding to a document subpoena, the corporation must provide documents through a custodian who can identify the records as authentic and as those called for. This obligation does not, however, extend to providing explanations of the records, descriptions of record-keeping or accounting systems, or any other ancillary information. If an inspector general wants such information, the first opportunity for negotiation is presented.

Third-Party and Financial Records

In general, an inspector general may seek the documents of a third party, even one not otherwise subject to its jurisdiction, "so long as the information sought is relevant and necessary to the effective conduct of the inquiry."[6] But the authority of an inspector general to obtain third-party financial records may be limited. Under the Financial Privacy Act,[7] an individual's financial records can be sought only for a "legitimate law enforcement inquiry," which is defined as "a lawful investigation or official proceeding inquiring into a violation of, or failure to comply with, any criminal or civil statute or any regulation, rule or order issued pursuant thereto."[8] While most investigations will fall within this ambit, audits done by inspectors general arguably do not.

The Financial Privacy Act also provides certain procedural guarantees to individuals whose financial records are sought, including notification to the customer, informing the customer of the nature of the proceeding, and the right to challenge the subpoena in court. The procedures the government is to follow are set forth in the *United States Attorneys' Manual*, section 9-4.800 *et seq*. If there is a prima facie case that the records are irrelevant to a legitimate law enforcement inquiry,[9] the burden shifts to the government to show "a demonstrable reason to believe that the records sought are relevant to [the] inquiry."[10]

Discovery

If an inspector general subpoena is subject to challenge, as overbroad or otherwise improper, some discovery will often be granted. Federal Rule of Civil Procedure 81(a)(3) permits discovery in subpoena enforcement proceedings, although the Advisory Committee Notes indicate that discovery may be limited in order to preserve the summary nature of the proceedings.[11]

Other Agency Subpoenas

Administrative subpoenas may be issued even when there is an ongoing investigation by the Department of Justice, as long as the agency has not itself determined that the matter is a criminal one.[12] Under the Tax Equity and Fiscal Responsibility Act of 1982, an administrative summons may be issued by the IRS while investigating an individual's tax liability unless "a Justice Department referral is in effect with respect to such person."[13] The Internal Revenue Manual requires the suspension of an audit—and referral to the Criminal Investigative Division—when the agent discovers a "firm indication of fraud," but the courts will not second-guess an agent's determination of when a "firm indication of fraud" exists absent a showing of bad faith.[14]

Grand Jury Subpoenas

The Grand Jury

The grand jury has broad powers not limited by most procedural and evidentiary rules. The exclusionary rule is inapplicable to evidence presented to a grand jury,[15] and, except in extraordinary circumstances, the grand jury may rely upon hearsay.[16] Even perjury will not undermine an indictment as long as other competent evidence supports it.[17]

While the grand jury may not be used to prepare for the trial of one already indicted, the careful prosecutor will not indict until after having secured the evidence needed for trial via the grand jury.[18] To prevail on a claim of abuse of grand jury process, a defendant must show that the "sole or dominant purpose" of the grand jury's efforts was trial preparation.[19]

The viability of challenges to grand jury process has diminished considerably since the Supreme Court's decisions in *United States v. Mechanik*[20] and *Bank of Nova Scotia v. Kilpatrick*.[21] *In Mechanik*, the Supreme Court ruled that a petit jury's guilty verdict covers any defect in an indictment related to the grand jury's decision to charge. *Bank of Nova Scotia* extended this holding to constrict the court's supervisory powers over the grand jury. While a district court retains its supervisory authority over the grand jury, it may dismiss an indictment procured improperly only if the error prejudiced the defendants. Thus, in cases of "nonconstitutional error," the standard of prejudice is that articulated in *Mechanik*,[22] whereby dismissal—even under the court's supervisory power—is appropriate only if "the violations substantially influenced the grand jury's decision to indict" or if there is "grave doubt" that the decision was free from substantial influence. The only exception to this rule is if the structural process of the grand jury is so flawed that the proceedings are fundamentally unfair, as where there has been racial or sexual discrimination in the selection of the grand jury.

In light of *Mechanik*, some Circuits have permitted interlocutory review of a broad range of prosecutorial misconduct before the grand jury, including calling witnesses for the purpose of forcing them to assert their fifth amendment rights, harassing witnesses associated with the defendants, failing to present exculpatory evidence, abusing the grand jury's subpoena authority, etc.[23] The Supreme Court has recently granted certiorari to review a decision of the Second Circuit holding that Federal Rule of Criminal Procedure 6(e)'s prohibition of improper disclosure of grand jury matters protects societal interests that do not disappear with a jury verdict, and thus postconviction rather than interlocutory review is required.[24]

Documents and Testimony

Grand juries can subpoena documents and testimony. A grand jury witness has the right to consult with counsel.[25] On rare occasions, subpoenas will call for an appearance "forthwith," but reputable prosecutors do not hold such subpoenas in high regard. They are generally considered appropriate only under exigent circumstances.[26] Ordinarily, a subpoena will call for the appearance of the witness and/or the production of documents in a period of weeks.

Act of Production

Document subpoenas are also subject to the act-of-production protections of *United States v. Doe*,[27] which recognized the testimonial aspects of producing even corporate documents: the existence, authenticity, possession, and control of the documents. Thus, the potential individual liability of the document custodian must be assessed before deciding which individual corporate officer will comply with the corporate document subpoena and authenticate the documents.[28]

A corporation must, however, respond through some custodian. In *Braswell v. United States*,[29] the Supreme Court rejected the argument that the president of a closely held corporation—and the only individual who could produce and authenticate the corporation's records—should be permitted to avoid production by assisting his fifth amendment rights. The Court held that a representative of a "collective entity" acts as agent for the entity and thus cannot assert the privilege as to documents held in a representative capacity. This is true regardless of the corporation's size and whether the subpoena is addressed to the corporation or to the individual as corporate custodian. The Court did acknowledge that, under *Doe*, a sole proprietor—in contrast to the officer of a closely held corporation—still has the opportunity to show that his or her act of production would require testimonial self-incrimination. Upon such a showing, a claim of privilege can still be made.[30]

Also, in a strange twist—labeled by the minority the "judicial creation of a new zone of immunity" and "a peculiar attempt to mitigate the force of its own holding"[31]—the Court held that the act of production is "deemed" one of the corporation, not the individual. Thus, the government "may make no evidentiary use of the 'individual act' against the individual." For example, in a criminal prosecution against the custodian, the government may not introduce into evidence before the jury the fact that the subpoena was served upon and the corporation's documents were delivered by one particular individual, the custodian. The government has the right, however, to use the corporation's act of production against the custodian in that the government may offer testimony—for example, from the process server who delivered the subpoena and from the individual who received the records—establishing that the corporation produced the records subpoenaed. The jury may draw from the corporation's act of production the conclusion that the records in question were authentic corporate records that the corporation possessed and that it produced in response to the subpoena. And if the defendant held a position in the corporation that produced the records, the jury may infer that he or she had possession of the documents or knowledge of their contents. Because the jury would not be told that the defendant produced the records, the Court reasoned that any connection between the defendant and the documents would result solely from the corporation's act of production and other evidence in the case.

The Court left open the question whether "the agency rationale supports compelling a custodian to produce corporate records when the custodian is able to establish, by showing for example that he is the sole employee and officer of the corporation, that the jury would inevitably conclude that he produced the records."[32] One would have thought that *Braswell* presented just such a case, but surely an even closer corporation will have to present that issue.

Objections to Compliance

The majority of the federal circuit courts agree that the government need not make a preliminary showing of relevance in order to enforce a document subpoena.[33]

There are numerous other grounds for objecting to or narrowing document subpoenas. In general, subpoenas may not be "unreasonable" in their scope.[34] The time period covered by the subpoena must be reasonable,[35] and a subpoena must be reasonably particular.[36] Grand jury subpoenas may not be used after an indictment to prepare for trial.[37] And, of course, privileged documents remain protected.[38] In extraordinary cases, a grand jury subpoena will be quashed as a remedy for prosecutorial misconduct.[39]

Target Warnings

The *United States Attorneys' Manual*, in section 9-11.250, requires federal prosecutors to inform individuals who are "targets" of a grand jury investigation of their status at the time they are subpoenaed, although there is no due-process right to be so informed.[40] The *United States Attorneys' Manual* defines a "target" as

> a person as to whom the prosecutor or the grand jury has substantial evidence linking him to the commission of a crime and who, in the judgment of the prosecutor, is a putative defendant.[41]

If an individual is not a target, that person is either a "subject" or a "witness." A "subject" is defined as "a person whose conduct is within the scope of the grand jury's investigation." Often a subject is someone whose level of involvement and culpability the prosecutor has not yet ascertained. A "witness" is defined simply as neither a subject nor a target.

Investigations by Counsel

Effective grand jury representation requires counsel to obtain as much information as possible from actual and potential grand jury witnesses as the investigation progresses. However, counsel must be careful that the information gathered remains privileged or will not be damaging to the client if disclosed.

Joint Defense

Corporate counsel and counsel for individual corporate officers and employees frequently execute joint defense agreements to protect communications among themselves and, thereby, to facilitate communication.[42] The subsequent waiver by one party to the agreement will not waive the privilege of another party.[43] A predicate of the joint defense privilege is that the communication is for the purpose of a joint defense.[44] If clients have adverse interests or communicate other than for the purpose of a joint defense, the communications may not be privileged.[45]

Maintaining the Privilege

The attorney-client privilege does not always protect a lawyer from divulging information about a client. First, the attorney-client privilege does not protect against subpoenas or searches for unprivileged documents given to the attorney by the client.[46] Second, the government is not required to make a showing of need to obtain a grand jury subpoena of a criminal defense attorney representing a client in an ongoing criminal proceeding.[47] In Massachusetts, the Code of Professional Responsibility requires a prosecutor to seek court approval before subpoenaing an attorney, a rule that has been proposed in other jurisdictions.[48] In all jurisdictions, the attorney has the duty to assert the attorney-client privilege, where appropriate, and to afford the client the opportunity to intervene. One court has held that an attorney may not appeal a district court's denial of a motion to quash a subpoena on the attorney because the documents, which had been submitted for *in camera* inspection, had been turned over to the grand jury by the court upon denial of the motion. The lawyer should have refused to comply and litigated any resulting contempt citation.[49] The attorney-client privilege does not protect an attorney from a grand jury subpoena regarding information the attorney received from an attorney representing another target and then conveyed to a client.[50]

The "reverse *Jencks*" rule, whereby the government is entitled to discovery from a defendant of any "statement of a witness" relating to the subject matter of that witness's testimony at trial,[51] requires caution on the part of counsel.[52] If the defense calls a witness other than the defendant, all prior statements—including a statement "adopted" by the witness or a "substantially verbatim recital" contemporaneously transcribed—must be made available to the government. The obligation arguably extends to counsel's notes of witness interviews. As a precaution, counsel should not have potential witnesses adopt written statements or answer questionnaires, should not take "substantially verbatim" statements, and should infuse into his or her notes counsel's impressions, analysis, and reflections, which would be protected work product.[53]

Special Problems Posed by the Need for an Internal Corporate Investigation

Frequently, a corporation will decide to conduct its own internal investigation of an allegation or problem while a criminal or agency investigation is ongoing or about to begin. Pressures for such investigations emanate from the securities laws, the contractual and regulatory obligations of government contractors, directors' concerns, management's desire to evaluate potential corporate exposure or possible remedial measures, etc. Such investigations are often undertaken to blunt agency action.[54]

The submission of a report by counsel to a government agency or to someone outside the corporation carries grave risks of waiver of the privileged nature of the report—as well as underlying documents—as to any other agency or private party.[55] Information shared by a corporate employee with counsel for the corporation is protected only by the corporation's privilege, not the employee's.[56]

Fee Arrangements

Recently, the government has begun more frequently seeking information from attorneys and clients concerning fee arrangements with counsel, sometimes for the purpose of exploring potential conflicts of interest, sometimes for other tactical reasons.[57] In general, the identity of the client and the nature of the fee arrangement are sometimes not considered confidential communications, but where such information might implicate the client in the very matter for which legal advice is sought, the privilege has been held to apply.[58] In light of such efforts, however, and given the potentially wide dissemination of corporate documents, it is wise for corporate fee statements not to particularize counsel's actions on the client's behalf.

Witness Interviews and Obstruction of Justice

The new federal witness tampering statute[59] presents special problems for attorneys monitoring grand jury investigations.[60] Before 1982, federal law prohibited corrupt or coercive efforts to influence witnesses. Under the new law, it is a crime to seek to "influence" a witness's testimony through "misleading conduct." "Misleading conduct" is broadly defined to include concealing a material fact or making a false statement. No intent is required other than "knowing" conduct. A lawyer who interviews a witness before that person's grand jury appearance is likely to seek to "influence" that testimony by testing the witness's memory, refreshing his or her recollection with documents, etc. Thus, if a lawyer suggests to a witness an alternative, nonincriminating interpretation of a transaction or if a defendant tells a potential witness a view of the facts, these actions could give rise to liability. The burden would then be on the defendant to establish the affirmative defense of lack of corrupt intent. The new statute has yet to be used in such a fashion, but on its face it reaches conduct currently common in grand jury practice.

Parallel Proceedings

Parallel criminal and civil and/or administrative proceedings are increasingly common, as criminal investigations emerge from regulatory oversight. They create special problems for potential defendants, as they allow prosecutors to force individuals to choose between protecting their fifth amendment rights and avoiding the negative inference that may be drawn from an assertion of rights in a civil proceeding. The government can take advantage of the overlap between parallel criminal and civil proceedings. Government attorneys involved in a grand jury proceeding may use grand jury materials in a later civil investigation, because such continued use is not "disclosure" within the meaning of rule 6(e), and therefore no prior court authorization is required.[61] Moreover, the grand jury secrecy rule[62] has been held not to bar disclosure of information that, while dealing in a parallel fashion with subjects before the grand jury, does not reveal what actually transpired before the grand jury.[63]

Generally speaking, criminal defendants have been unsuccessful in obtaining stays of civil proceedings pending resolution of a criminal matter, even when the government is able to use the civil proceeding to obtain discovery that would otherwise be unavailable.[64] But courts do have the discretion to issue such stays.[65]

Parallel proceedings can sometimes be used to provide a potential defendant with discovery of the government's case, but the government has had some success in staying civil discovery during the pendency of a criminal matter.[66] While civil discovery may be subject to a protective order to protect a potential defendant during the pendency of a related criminal investigation or trial, at least one court has held that a grand jury may subpoena depositions and discovery material sealed by such a protective order.[67]

Contacting the Prosecutor or Inspector

Questions as to the scope of a document subpoena, the potential liability of a document custodian, and the prosecutorial status of a potential grand jury witness provide the first opportunities for discussions with a prosecutor or investigator. In initial discussions, counsel should seek to determine the thrust and scope of the investigation and the government's assessment of the client's culpability and vulnerability.

If an individual corporate officer or employee is a subject or a target of a grand jury investigation or if there is reason to believe that such a person has legal vulnerability, counsel will ordinarily advise the client not to testify without immunity except in extraordinary circumstances. Even if the individual is merely a witness, there may be grounds for invoking the fifth amendment. Individuals who have been informed that they are merely witnesses are rarely prosecuted, but counsel must assess the individual's status and, if necessary, seek further protection for him or her, as set forth later in this chapter. The status of a witness may change in the course of an investigation.[68]

Representing the Corporation or Individual

After reviewing available documents, interviewing relevant witnesses, sharing information with other counsel pursuant to joint defense agreements, etc., counsel should confer with the prosecutor or the investigator. Depending on the prosecutor's own goals, he may disclose, at least in part, his theory of the case or his assessment of the client's relative culpability and liability. If prosecutorial interest in the client is very low, the government may be agreeable to a formal or informal agreement not to prosecute in exchange for cooperation. If prosecutorial interest is very high and counsel's assessment of liability is very negative, it is sometimes in the client's interest to try to pretermit the investigation with an early disposition. Most frequently, however, the level of prosecutorial interest will lie somewhere in between, and the only course of action is to have a series of meetings and conferences with the prosecutor as the investigation moves forward to try to dissuade the prosecutor from moving against the company.

Negotiating for Immunity

One of the principal opportunities presented by these conferences and, often, one of the goals of a successful representation is obtaining immunity for the corporate officer or employee. An inspector general cannot grant immunity from prosecution, and a demand for immunity—for example, for a document custodian—may trigger referral to or coordination with a grand jury.

Whether to Seek Immunity

In determining whether to seek immunity from a prosecutor, counsel should consider three factors: (1) whether the client needs immunity as a shield from legal liability, (2) whether the client understands and will be able to undertake the obligations of a "cooperating witness," and (3) whether the client can bear the costs and other burdens of the defense.

A prosecutor, in turn, considers the following factors in deciding whether to grant immunity: (1) the culpability of the client relative to the others in the case and, particularly, relative to those against whom the client would testify; (2) the value of the information the client would provide; (3) the client's value as a witness; (4) the ability of the government to obtain elsewhere information the client would provide; and (5) the relative difficulty of obtaining information leading to the client's conviction and of overcoming legal obstacles to such a conviction.

Counsel must convince the government that there are factual and legal obstacles to the successful prosecution of the client. This requires thorough knowledge of the factual and legal basis for the case. Counsel must also convince the prosecutor that the client is a minor actor compared to others under investigation and that the client has information relevant to the prosecution of someone with greater culpability. Finally, the prosecutor must be persuaded that the client would be a credible witness who will provide information difficult to obtain elsewhere.

The Negotiation Process

In negotiating for immunity, a particularly difficult decision is how much to disclose to the prosecutor. If negotiations fail, counsel will have educated the prosecutor. The prosecutor is likely to want a proffer. From a defense standpoint, the best proffer is an oral one on a hypothetical basis. It should describe the subject matter of the testimony but should avoid specifics about what the client will actually say. If a prosecutor insists on a written proffer, it, too, should be as general as possible. In either case, a necessary protection is a letter preventing the direct or indirect use of any information disclosed in the course of discussions with the prosecutor. At a minimum, there should be an agreement that nothing in the proffer will constitute an admission of the witness. Note, however, that in such circumstances, the information may be used to advance the investigation.[69]

Sometimes prosecutors demand to know that a witness will testify to a certain fact. Such a "contingent agreement" is potentially vulnerable to a due-process challenge by a defendant at trial, which provides a basis for dissuading the prosecution from insisting on such a proffer.[70]

Types of Immunity

There are two basic types of immunity: transactional immunity and use immunity. Transactional immunity is an agreement not to prosecute an individual for a particular transaction. Federal prosecutors will grant transactional immunity only in the most extraordinary circumstances. The federal immunity statute[71] provides for use immunity only. Several states, however, provide transactional immunity.

Under use immunity, none of the information a witness provides and no information derived therefrom may be used directly or indirectly against the witness. If the government indicts a defendant whose immunized testimony was presented to the grand jury, it must demonstrate a wholly independent source of evidence.[72] Immunized testimony may influence a prosecution's decision whether to seek indictment.[73] But, where testimony of an immunized witness enables the government to build a case against a co-conspirator who then agrees to testify against the immunized witness, that testimony is not "independent" of the original immunized testimony and cannot be the basis of an indictment.[74]

If the defendant accepts an offer of immunity, the government is bound by the offer and cannot rescind it even if the government never calls the immunized witness to testify.[75] Federal use immunity will extend to state prosecutions.[76] State use immunity extends to federal proceedings, but state transactional immunity cannot confer federal transactional immunity.[77] In a subsequent civil suit, the witness retains the fifth amendment right to refuse to answer.[78]

Immunity Procedures

Immunity can be obtained through several procedures. Formal statutory use immunity, under 18 U.S.C. § 6002, is obtained by the prosecutor petitioning the court.[79] Because they are ancillary to a grand jury proceeding, these proceedings should be held in chambers, and the papers submitted in connection with the proceedings should be under seal.[80]

Informal or letter immunity is secured by a letter from the prosecutor to defense counsel or the witness stating that the prosecutor will not use against the witness any information the witness provides. Letter immunity is often preferable to statutory immunity, because understandings with the prosecutor can be set forth. For example, the letter can describe the scope of the investigation and hence the scope of the immunity. Recent appellate court decisions have upheld the propriety of using informal immunity.[81] In light of these and other developments, prosecutors will probably continue to use letter immunity in the future.

A third, rarely invoked type of immunity is "equitable immunity." This type of immunity arises out of a defendant's reasonable reliance on the prosecutor's oral promise of immunity.[82]

Testimony by the Immunized Witness

Testifying under immunity is not without risk. Witnesses with immunity may have less access to counsel during their appearances than other witnesses. For example, one district court has held that an immunized witness had less need for access to counsel and thus could be questioned by the grand jury for an extensive period without the opportunity to consult with counsel whenever he wished.[83]

Immunized witnesses are not immunized from perjury.[84] After immunity is secured, the client must be prepared to testify truthfully. If the client is called to appear several times before the same grand jury, his or her new testimony must be consistent with earlier testimony. While the government may not bring a witness before a grand jury for the sole purpose of making a perjury prosecution,[85] if a prosecutor feels that an immunized witness is lying, the prosecutor may try to pressure the witness by attempting to elicit contradictory testimony. If it appears that a new appearance by the client might result in a perjury prosecution, counsel should seek a new immunity order or letter.[86] And before the client returns to testify, counsel should request a transcript and a copy of his or her prior testimony.[87]

Appearing without Immunity and Refusing to Appear

If it appears that the prosecutor has no real interest in the client and that the client has no real liability, it may be in the client's interest to testify without immunity. Some clients will refuse immunity even if it is offered, because they object to the notion that they are testifying in exchange for consideration.

By the same token, it will not be in some witnesses' best interest to testify even under immunity. Although the testimony itself is immunized, as already noted, the fifth amendment privilege against self-incrimination does not protect against a prosecutor being influenced by immunized testimony to seek an indictment based upon other evidence.[88] Moreover, a witness may be subjected to civil liability, licensing problems, tax liability, etc.

Sometimes a prosecutor will seek to have a witness immunized against his or her will. Witnesses may be forced to testify under a grant of immunity or be held in contempt unless they can show that the immunity provided does not adequately replace their fifth amendment rights. The circuits are divided on whether immunity from federal prosecution, combined with the requirement of grand jury secrecy, suffices to protect against foreign prosecution and thus permits the compulsion of testimony.[89]

Whether and When to Negotiate

Deciding whether and when to open negotiations on immunity or on a disposition depends on several factors, many of which are out of counsel's control. If the client has received a grand jury subpoena and is either a subject or a target, counsel will generally advise the client not to testify without immunity. The question then becomes whether the client should rest on fifth amendment rights or seek immunity. If counsel is convinced that the client has potential liability and the testimony he or she could provide is already available to the government, negotiations may be indicated. Negotiations can also educate counsel about the prosecutor's case and provide an opportunity to alter the government's view of the client.

On the other hand, if the client is a minor figure in the investigation or has not received a subpoena, initiating negotiation can focus the prosecutor's attention on the client. It is also important to realize that negotiations will educate the prosecutor about the facts of the case, defense strategy, and the existence of exculpatory evidence. If the client is ultimately indicted, this will assist the prosecution.

Often the most favorable immunity decisions and substantive dispositions are arrived at early in the investigation before the prosecutor has reached agreements with others and committed significant resources to the case. If, however, the prosecutor views the client as a central figure in the investigation, the prosecutor is unlikely to pretermit the investigation with an early disposition unless the client provides most of what the prosecutor wants in the way of a plea and testimony.

For many clients, however, the mere fact of an investigation, with attendant publicity, can be as damaging as a trial. An investigation can ruin businesses, reputations, and even mental health. Even subsequent vindication may not outweigh these losses.

Determining whether to negotiate a disposition rests in large part on whether an indictment is likely. An offer to negotiate a disposition may breathe life into a dying case. If an indictment is inevitable, defenses should be saved for trial. Counsel should not educate the prosecutor before indictment, allowing the prosecution to use the grand jury to fill the holes in the case.

Plea Bargaining

There are pros and cons to a negotiated plea. It can limit risks and avoid the embarrassment and expense of a trial. Entry of a plea is generally viewed as a positive factor at the time of sentencing.[90] Under the Federal Sentencing Guidelines, applicable to offenses committed after November 1, 1987, "acceptance of responsibility" by the defendant results in reduction of the "base offense level" that determines sentence length.[91] Mere entry of a plea does not, however, entitle the defendant to this reduction.

Plea negotiations, like immunity discussions, are risky. Factual statements made by counsel should be subject to the negotiated protection of a proffer. At least one court has held that the rule barring the introduction at trial of statements made in plea bargaining negotiations that produce no plea—Federal Rule of Criminal Procedure 11(e)(6)(D)—does not cover derivative evidence.[92]

Frequently, the client is better off proceeding to trial. The government is often far from the promised land at the time it indicts. Particularly in the corporate arena, there are frequently serious questions whether the conduct under investigation—even if fully proved—is criminal. Counsel must realistically look at the government's chances of prevailing and should know the facts and the law of the case as completely as if the case were proceeding to trial. This will also enable counsel to make the prosecutor fully aware of the vulnerabilities of his or her case. Moreover, to make an informed decision on whether to accept a disposition, the client needs sound advice about the government's chances of prevailing at trial. The client must also consider the collateral consequences of a plea, such as losing the right to vote if convicted of a felony, being debarred from government contracts, jeopardizing professional licenses, paying restitution, risking forfeiture, etc.

For the prosecutor, a preindictment disposition provides a certain and "successful" result, eliminating any risk of going to trial. It may also provide information and assistance that would otherwise be unavailable. These factors will affect the prosecutor's willingness to offer an acceptable disposition.

Negotiating Nonprosecution or a Plea

Before seeking to persuade a prosecutor not to prosecute, counsel should determine the internal review procedures for indictment decisions in the prosecutor's particular office. There may be an indictment review committee or other procedure for review of adverse prosecutional determinations or recommendations. The *United States Attorney's Manual* requires that certain types of prosecutions—e.g., for violations of the federal election laws, the Regulation of Lobbying Act, for false statements to federal investigators—have the approval of the Criminal Division of the Department of Justice.

Negotiations with an inspector general or an agency are somewhat more complex in that they cannot guarantee that there will be no criminal prosecution if matters are resolved civilly. There can be an agreement not to make a criminal referral. Note, however, that it has been common practice in recent years for inspectors general to notify the Department of Justice or a United States attorneys' office at the outset of an inquiry. In these circumstances, negotiations with both may be required. Like United States attorneys' offices and the Department of Justice, many inspector general offices have internal review procedures through which counsel should seek appeal of a determination to seek sanctions, civil or criminal.

Presentation of the Facts and the Law

The facts can be presented most effectively to the line prosecutor or investigator. Superiors will be reluctant to overrule a line attorney's evaluation of the facts. Written presentations are effective for focusing arguments and for forcing the government to consider carefully its chances of prevailing at trial. Analysis of the case under the Department of Justice's Principles of Federal Prosecution[93] is also appropriately presented in a written submission. The *United States Attorneys' Manual* commits to specified Department of Justice officials the approval of prosecutions under particular statutes such as the Racketeering Act.[94] Legal and policy arguments are most effectively made to supervisory prosecutors but can also be helpful in addressing particular nonremediable deficiencies in the government's cases with the line prosecutor. It is important, however, not to reveal remediable legal problems, e.g., technical deficiencies in the proposed indictment or statute-of-limitation problems inherent in the government's theory of the case. Every avenue of review should be explored, but counsel should not seek a consultation with a supervisor without, at the very least, informing the line prosecutor of the intention to do so.

Exculpatory Evidence

In some instances, specific affirmative evidence may dissuade a prosecutor from proceeding against a client. There is a line of cases recognizing a prosecutor's duty to present to the grand jury exculpatory evidence of which he or she is aware.[95] Since *Mechanik,* these precedents may no longer be enforceable.

Types of Agreements

There are several types of pleas and several types of plea agreements, depending in part on whether the offense postdated November 1, 1987, the effective date of the Federal Sentencing Guidelines. A conditional guilty plea—under which a defendant preserves the right to appeal certain legal issues—is permitted but uncommon; the procedures outlined in Federal Rule of Criminal Procedure 11(a)(2) must be followed.[96] A nolo contendere plea or an *Alford* plea[97] is often the best result in business or economic crime cases if the client has or may have civil liability in addition to criminal liability. In such a plea, the client does not contest the charges, but the plea cannot be used against the client as an admission in subsequent civil or criminal cases.[98] Federal prosecutors will generally oppose nolo pleas.[99] A nolo plea should not afford the government a basis to debar a government contractor client, but in a recent unreported case, the government has attempted to use such a plea to do so.

An agreement under Federal Rule of Criminal Procedure 11(e)(1)(C) stating that a specific sentence is an appropriate disposition is usually preferable to one leaving the sentence to the court. Under such an agreement, the disposition is submitted to the court in advance, and the plea is entered only if the court agrees to its terms. Courts in some jurisdictions will not accept plea agreements under this provision.

The most common plea is under rule 11(e)(1)(B), in which the government either recommends or does not oppose the defendant's request for a particular sentence. If a sentence of confinement is possible, counsel should understand and fully explain to the client and the court the effect that the parole guidelines will have on the actual time served.[100]

If the offense was committed after November 1, 1987, the entire process of plea bargaining is different. First, parole is eliminated. Second, the Guidelines, as amended in January 1988, suggest that the court may accept a plea agreement that includes dismissal of some of the charges only if "the remaining charges adequately reflect the seriousness of the actual offense behavior."[101] The Guideline sentence will be based upon the entire course of conduct without regard to the actual charges to which the plea is entered. Third, the plea agreement may contain a "non-binding recommendation" on sentence or an agreed upon sentence pursuant to Federal Rules of Criminal Procedure 11(e)(1)(B) and (C), but the court may accept the agreement only if satisfied that the recommended or agreed upon sentence is within the applicable Guideline range or departs from that range for "justifiable reasons."[102] However, the *Prosecutors Handbook on Sentencing Guidelines* promulgated by the Department of Justice urges federal prosecutors not to enter into such agreements.

The key to future plea bargains, therefore, will be agreements on "stipulations of fact relevant to sentencing,"[103] upon which sentences will be calculated. There, prosecutor and defense counsel can agree upon a description of the offense, relevant mitigating and aggravating factors, and even whether a reduction for cooperation is appropriate—as long as the descriptions are truthful and not misleading. An amendment to sections 3B1.1(a)(1) and (2) of the Sentencing Guidelines—defining the "relevant conduct" on which a sentence is based—may require the court to consider all acts committed in preparation for and in the course of the offense, not only those acts constituting the offense itself.[104] Thus, uncharged conduct can significantly affect the sentence. This provision has yet to receive judicial interpretation but could render nonbinding stipulations as to relevant facts underlying a plea.[105]

Fines

Under the Criminal Fine Enforcement Act of 1984,[106] applicable to offenses committed before November 1, 1987, the maximum fine for a single felony has been increased to the largest of one of four possibilities: the statutory maximum; the catchall statutory maximum of $500,000 for a corporation and $250,000 for an individual; twice the defendant's gain; or twice the victim's loss. For related offenses, the maximum is twice the largest amount that could be assessed for any one of them. The Sentencing Guidelines' fine provisions dictate fines based upon, among other criteria, the amount of the loss, and they frequently give rise to more substantial fines than did prior law.

Elements of an Agreement

A plea agreement can be a simple one-line statement or a complex document. It can include the agreed-upon sentence or the agreed-upon sentencing recommendation. Plea agreements under the Federal Sentencing Guidelines will likely not include an agreed-upon sentence. In the absence of a sentencing agreement, a plea agreement can provide for various undertakings by the government, e.g., (1) not to oppose the defendant's sentencing proposal (unless, for post–November 1, 1987, conduct, the recommendation is inconsistent with the federal Sentencing Guidelines); (2) not to allocute; (3) to make the defendant's cooperation or other mitigating factors known to the court (under the Sentencing Guidelines, this must be done by motion of the prosecutor); or (4) to describe the offense in the presentencing report in an agreed-upon manner. The plea agreement can also describe the scope and nature of the cooperation to be rendered, if any. In addition, it can provide ways in which to resolve concerns the prosecutor may have about the defendant's veracity.

If a pretrial disposition is contemplated, it is always best to reach agreement before indictment so that the indictment itself can be negotiated. If this is done, the scope of the government's promise not to prosecute other offenses should be delineated in the plea agreement. If an indictment has already been returned, the agreement should state which charges will be dismissed.[107] Plea agreements often provide that others—family members, employees—will not be prosecuted. Some also provide specifically for restitution under 18 U.S.C. § 3663, and they often state what will happen if either party defaults or if one or more provisions are found to be unenforceable.

Plea Review

The court can reject a guilty plea if it finds that a plea bargain is not in the public interest.[108] But there are limits to this discretion. Such discretion must be exercised on a case-by-case basis. A trial judge may not adopt a blanket policy against accepting certain kinds of plea agreements such as those with single-count pleas to multiple-count indictments.[109]

Scope of Immunity from Subsequent Prosecution

Under the dual-sovereignty doctrine, successive prosecutions by two states or by state and federal governments for the same conduct are not barred by the double-jeopardy clause. As the Supreme Court explained in *Heath v. Alabama:*

> [T]he crucial determination is whether the two entities that seek successively to prosecute a defendant for the same course of conduct can be termed separate sovereigns. This determination turns on whether the entities draw their authority to punish the offender from distinct sources of power.[110]

If two governments seek to enforce two different statutes protecting different interests, the double-jeopardy clause will not bar multiple prosecutions for what otherwise would be viewed as "the same offense."

Successive federal prosecutions will be permitted only if there is no identity in the conduct and elements of the offenses prosecuted.[111] Thus, for example, a multistate bid-rigging conspiracy may be prosecuted in more than one federal jurisdiction if the conduct underlying the initial prosecution involved conduct in only one jurisdiction.[112] For this reason, in negotiating a federal plea in a multijurisdictional case, the agreement should encompass conduct in all possible jurisdictions.

The federal government's "dual-prosecution policy" precludes federal prosecution following state prosecution based upon "substantially the same act" unless there is a compelling federal interest in prosecution.[113] Thus, it is often preferable to conclude any state proceeding first.

Enforcement of Plea Agreements

The Prosecutor's Obligation

Although a prosecutor need not "enthusiastically" support a plea agreement,[114] the prosecutor may not undermine the agreement by his or her conduct.[115] A government promise to "take no position" on sentencing has been subject to interpretation. In some cases the government has maintained that this merely precludes it from recommending a specific sentence rather than allocuting at all.[116]

Rescission

Once the court has accepted a plea agreement, it may not rescind that agreement in the absence of "manifest necessity" even if the court later concludes the plea was unduly unfavorable to the government.[117]

Specific Enforcement

Courts are split on the enforceability of plea agreements that are not in writing.[118] They are similarly split on whether the government can breach an executed plea agreement if the defendant has not yet entered a plea or has otherwise acted to his or her detriment.[119] Courts denying enforcement of plea agreements have reasoned that the defendant has an adequate remedy available in proceeding to trial.[120]

It is clear, however, that if a plea agreement is still in the proposal stage, the putative defendant has no right to its specific enforcement.[121] But if a plea agreement has been entered in reliance upon undertakings by the government, it will likely be enforced.[122]

Conclusion

Preindictment and agency representation is litigation like any other, except that the procedures are undefined and variable. As in the successful trial of a criminal case, however, the client's outcome depends on counsel's knowledge of the facts and the law and his or her ability to marshal the factual and legal arguments.

Notes

1. 5 U.S.C.A. app. I § 69(a)(4) (Supp. 1983).
2. 610 F.2d 943 (D.C. Cir. 1979).
3. 42 U.S.C. § 7138(g)(2).
4. *See* United States v. Exxon Corp., 628 F.2d 70, 76 n.6 (D.C. Cir. 1980), *cert. denied,* 446 U.S. 964 (1980).
5. *See Hearings on H.R. 8588 Before the Senate Subcomm. on Governmental Efficiency and the District of Columbia,* 95th Cong., 2d Sess. 279 (1978) (testimony of John C. Keeney, Acting Assistant Attorney General).
6. United States v. Art Metal–U.S.A., Inc., 484 F. Supp. 884, 887 (D.N.J. 1980).
7. 12 U.S.C. § 3402.
8. 12 U.S.C. § 3401(7).
9. Hancock v. Marshall, 86 F.R.D. 209 (D.D.C. 1980).
10. McGloshen v. United States Dep't of Agriculture, 480 F. Supp. 247, 248 (W.D. Ky. 1979). *See also* Grafstrom v. Securities & Exch. Comm'n, 532 F. Supp. 1023 (S.D.N.Y. 1982); Ling v. United States Dep't of Justice, 507 F. Supp. 1, 2 (S.D. Fla. 1979).
11. *See generally* United States v. Powell, 379 U.S. 48 (1964); Securities & Exch. Comm'n v. Dresser Indus., 628 F.2d 1368 (D.C. Cir. 1980), *cert. denied,* 449 U.S. 993 (1980).
12. *See* United States v. LaSalle Nat'l Bank, 437 U.S. 298 (1978).
13. 26 U.S.C. § 7602(c)(1).
14. Groder v. United States, 816 F.2d 139 (4th Cir. 1987).
15. United States v. Calandra, 414 U.S. 338, 349 (1974).
16. Costello v. United States, 350 U.S. 359, 363 (1956).
17. *Compare* United States v. Udziela, 671 F.2d 995 (7th Cir. 1982), *cert. denied,* 457 U.S. 1135 (1982), *with* United States v. Basurto, 497 F.2d 781 (9th Cir. 1974).

18. *See* Beverly v. United States, 468 F.2d 732 (5th Cir. 1972).
19. United States v. Woods, 544 F.2d 242, 250 (1976), *cert. denied,* 430 U.S. 969 (1977).
20. 475 U.S. 66 (1986).
21. 108 S. Ct. 2369, 101 L.Ed. 2d 228 (1988).
22. 475 U.S. 66, 78 (1986).
23. *See, e.g.,* United States v. Dederich, 825 F.2d 1317 (9th Cir. 1987).
24. United States v. Midland Asphalt Corp., 840 F.2d 1040 (2d Cir. 1988), *cert. granted,* 101 L. Ed. 2d 905 (1988).
25. *In re* Taylor, 567 F.2d 1183 (2d Cir. 1977).
26. *See* Consumer Credit Ins. Agency, Inc. v. United States, 599 F.2d 770 (6th Cir. 1979), *cert. denied,* 445 U.S. 903 (1980).
27. 465 U.S. 605 (1984).
28. *See, e.g., In re* Grand Jury Subpoenas Duces Tecum Dated June 13, 1983, and June 22, 1983, 722 F.2d 981 (2d Cir. 1983); *In re* Schuffman, 386 F. Supp. 177 (S.D.N.Y. 1974).
29. 108 S. Ct. 2284, 101 L. Ed. 2d 98 (1988).
30. *See, e.g.,* United States v. Cates, 43 CRIM. L. REP. (BNA) 2223 (D.C. Md. May 23, 1988).
31. *Braswell,* 101 L. Ed. 2d at 115, 121.
32. 101 L. Ed. 2d at 115, n.11.
33. *In re* Grand Jury Subpoena (Battle), 748 F.2d 327 (6th Cir. 1984), 36 CRIM. L. REP. 2180. *But see In re* Grand Jury Subpoena (Dorokee), 697 F.2d 277 (10th Cir. 1983); *In re* Grand Jury Proceedings (Schofield), 486 F.2d 85 (3d Cir. 1973).
34. FED. R. CRIM. P. 17(d); Hale v. Henkel, 201 U.S. 43 (1906); United States v. United States District Court, 238 F.2d 713 (4th Cir. 1956), *cert. denied sub nom.* Valley Bell Dairy Co., Inc. v. United States, 352 U.S. 981 (1957).
35. *In re* Horowitz, 482 F.2d 72 (2d Cir.), *cert. denied,* 414 U.S. 867 (1973).
36. Roberts v. United States, Misc. No. M 9-150 (RWS) (S.D.N.Y. Mar. 13, 1987); United States v. Reno, 522 F.2d 572 (10th Cir. 1975).
37. United States v. Gibbons, 607 F.2d 1320 (10th Cir. 1979).
38. *E.g.,* Upjohn Co. v. United States, 449 U.S. 383 (1981) (attorney-client privilege and work-product protection); United States v. Helstoski, 442 U.S. 477 (1979) (Speech and Debate Clause privilege).
39. *In re* Grand Jury Subpoenas (Kiefaber), 774 F.2d 969 (9th Cir. 1985).
40. United States v. Washington, 431 U.S. 181 (1977).
41. UNITED STATES ATTORNEYS' MANUAL § 9-11.250.
42. *See In re* Grand Jury Subpoena Duces Tecum Dated Nov. 16, 1974, 406 F. Supp. 381 (S.D.N.Y. 1975).
43. United States v. McPartlin, 595 F.2d 1321 (7th Cir. 1979), *cert. denied,* 444 U.S. 833 (1979); Western Fuels Ass'n v. Burlington N. R.R. Co., 102 F.R.D. 201 (D. Wyo. 1984).
44. *See In re* Bevill, Bresler & Schulman Asset Management Co., 805 F.2d 120, 126 (3d Cir. 1986); Eisenberg v. Gagnon, 776 F.2d 770, 787 (3d Cir. 1985), *cert. denied,* 106 S. Ct. 342 (1985).

45. United States v. Lopez, 777 F.2d 543 (10th Cir. 1985); United States v. Simpson, 475 F.2d 934 (D.C. Cir. 1973), *cert. denied,* 414 U.S. 873 (1973).

46. *See, e.g., In re* Search Warrant B-21778 (Gartley), 513 Pa. 429, 521 A.2d 422 (1987).

47. *In re* Doe, 781 F.2d 238 (2d Cir. 1986).

48. United States v. Klubock, 832 F.2d 664 (1st Cir. 1987) (en banc).

49. *In re* Grand Jury Subpoena Dated June 5, 1985 (Doe), 825 F.2d 231 (9th Cir. 1987).

50. *In re* Grand Jury Testimony of Attorney *X,* 621 F. Supp. 592 (E.D.N.Y. 1985). *See also* Commonwealth v. Maguigan, 511 Pa. 112, 511 A.2d 1327 (1986); Bishop v. Superior Court, 150 Ariz. 404, 724 P.2d 23 (1986).

51. FED. R. CRIM. P. 26.2.

52. *See* United States v. Nobles, 422 U.S. 225 (1975).

53. Upjohn Co. v. United States, 459 U.S. 383, 399 (1981); Hickman v. Taylor, 329 U.S. 495, 513 (1947).

54. *See* Department of Justice Guidelines Regarding Voluntary Disclosure; Department of Defense Federal Acquisition Regulation Supplement, 48 C.F.R. §§ 323, 383 (1987); *The Defense Industry's Initiatives on Business Ethics and Conduct,* 48 FED. CONTRACTS REP. (BNA) 597 (1987); Securities Act Release No. 5466, 3 SEC Docket 647 (Mar. 8, 1974); SECURITIES & EXCHANGE COMM'N, REPORT ON QUESTIONABLE AND ILLEGAL CORPORATE PAYMENTS AND PRACTICES, SENATE COMM. ON BANKING, HOUSING & URBAN AFFAIRS, 94th Cong., 2d Sess. (1976); N.A. KAPLAN ET AL., PARALLEL GRAND JURY AND ADMINISTRATIVE AGENCY INVESTIGATIONS (ABA 1981).

55. *See In re* John Doe Corp., 675 F.2d 482 (2d Cir. 1982); Permian Corp. v. United States, 665 F.2d 1214 (D.C. Cir. 1981); Diversified Indus. v. Meredith, 572 F.2d 596 (8th Cir. 1977) (en banc); Securities & Exch. Comm'n v. Dresser Indus., Inc., 453 F. Supp. 573 (D.D.C. 1978).

56. *See In re* Grand Jury Proceedings, Detroit, Mich., Aug. 1977, 570 F.2d 562, 563 (6th Cir. 1978).

57. *See, e.g.,* United States v. Hirsch, 803 F.2d 443 (9th Cir. 1986); United States v. (Under Seal) (Garber), 774 F.2d 624 (4th Cir. 1985), *cert. denied,* 106 S. Ct. 1514 (1986).

58. *In re* Grand Jury Proceedings (Lawson), 600 F.2d 215 (9th Cir. 1979). *But see* United States v. Hirsch, 803 F.2d 443 (9th Cir. 1986).

59. 19 U.S.C. § 1512.

60. *See generally* Jeffress, *The New Federal Witness Tampering Statute,* 22 AM. CRIM. L. REV. 1 (1984).

61. United States v. John Doe, Inc., 107 S. Ct. 1656 (1987).

62. FED. R. CRIM. P. 6(e).

63. Anaya v. United States, 815 F.2d 1373 (10th Cir. 1987), 41 CRIM. L. REP. 2077. *See also* Standley v. Department of Justice, 835 F.2d 216 (9th Cir. 1987) (list of persons furnished grand jury material by U.S. Attorney not "grand jury material" protected by Privacy Act).

64. *See, e.g.,* Securities & Exch. Comm'n v. Dresser Indus., Inc., 628 F.2d 1368 (D.C. Cir. 1980) (en banc), *cert. denied,* 449 U.S. 993 (1980).

65. *See, e.g.*, Campbell v. Eastland, 307 F.2d 478 (5th Cir. 1962), *cert. denied*, 371 U.S. 955 (1963).

66. *See, e.g.*, *In re* Eisenberg, 654 F.2d 1107 (5th Cir. 1981).

67. United States v. (Under Seal) (*In re* Grand Jury Subpoena), 836 F.2d 1468 (4th Cir. 1988).

68. *See* United States v. Whitaker, 619 F.2d 1142 (5th Cir. 1980); United States v. Jacobs, 547 F.2d 772 (2d Cir. 1976), *cert. granted*, 431 U.S. 937 (1977), *cert. dismissed*, 436 U.S. 31 (1978).

69. United States v. Romaro, 583 F.2d 1, 6 (1st Cir. 1978).

70. *Cf.* United States v. Dailey, 759 F.2d 192 (1st Cir. 1985); United States v. Waterman, 732 F.2d 1527 (8th Cir. 1984), *cert. denied*, 471 U.S. 1065 (1985). *But see* United States v. Cervantes & Pacheco, 826 F.2d 310 (5th Cir. 1987) (informer who received contingent fee may testify).

71. 18 U.S.C. § 6002.

72. Kastigar v. United States, 406 U.S. 441 (1972). *See* United States v. Byrd, 765 F.2d 1524 (11th Cir. 1985); United States v. Hampton, 775 F.2d 1479 (11th Cir. 1985); United States v. Garrett, 797 F.2d 656 (8th Cir. 1986), 39 CRIM. L. REP. 2346.

73. United States v. Byrd, 765 F.2d 1524 (11th Cir. 1985).

74. United States v. Kurzer, 422 F. Supp. 487 (S.D.N.Y. 1976).

75. Plaster v. United States, 789 F.2d 289 (4th Cir. 1986).

76. Murphy v. Waterfront Comm'n, 378 U.S. 52 (1964).

77. United States v. First W. State Bank of Minot, N.D., 491 F.2d 780 (8th Cir.), *cert. denied sub nom.* Thompson v. United States, 419 U.S. 825 (1974).

78. Pillsbury v. Conboy, 459 U.S. 248 (1983).

79. *See* Kastigar v. United States, 406 U.S. 441 (1972).

80. *See* FED. R. CRIM. P. 6(e).

81. *See* United States v. Anderson, 778 F.2d 602, 606 (10th Cir. 1985); United States v. Kilpatrick, 821 F.2d 1456 (10th Cir. 1987).

82. *See* United States v. Society of Indep. Gasoline Marketers of Am., 624 F.2d 461, 473–74 (4th Cir. 1979), *cert. denied*, 449 U.S. 1078 (1981).

83. United States v. Soto, 574 F. Supp. 986 (D. Conn. 1983). *Compare In re* Lowry, 713 F.2d 616 (11th Cir. 1983), *and In re* Earnet, 90 F.R.D. 698 (M.D. Ga. 1981), *with In re* Tierne, 465 F.2d 806 (5th Cir. 1972), *cert. denied*, 410 U.S. 914 (1973).

84. United States v. Apfelbaum, 445 U.S. 115, 121–23 (1980).

85. *See generally* NATIONAL LAWYERS GUILD, REPRESENTATION OF WITNESSES BEFORE FEDERAL GRAND JURIES § 17.3 (2d ed. 1980).

86. *See* United States v. Housand, 550 F.2d 818, 823 (2d Cir. 1977), *cert. denied*, 431 U.S. 970 (1977); People v. Bagby, 65 N.Y.2d 410, 482 N.E.2d 41, 492 N.Y.S.2d 562 (1985). *See also* United States v. Partin, 552 F.2d 621 (5th Cir. 1977), *cert. denied*, 434 U.S. 903 (1977).

87. *See* Bursey v. United States, 466 F.2d 1059, 1080 (9th Cir. 1972), *quoting* United States v. Projansky, 44 F.R.D. 550, 556 (S.D.N.Y. 1968).

88. United States v. Byrd, 765 F.2d 1524 (11th Cir. 1985).

89. *Compare In re* Grand Jury Witnesses, 597 F.2d 1166, 1167 (9th Cir. 1979) (district court's power to prevent disclosure of grand jury testimony obviated any need for further immunity), *and* United States v. (Under Seal) (Araneta), 794 F.2d 920 (4th Cir. 1986). ("The Fifth Amendment Privilege applies only where the sovereign compelling the testimony and the sovereign using the testimony are both restrained by the Fifth Amendment from compelling self-incrimination."), with *In re* Grand Jury Subpoena of Flanagan, 691 F.2d 116, 124 (2d Cir. 1982) ("[W]e prefer not to follow the view of some other circuits that Rule 6(e), F. R.Cr. P., eliminates any real or substantial risk that a witness' immunized grand jury testimony will be used . . . to prosecute him.").
90. FED. R. CRIM. P. 11, and Advisory Committee Note to 1974 Amendment.
91. GUIDELINE § 3E1.1.
92. United States v. Rutkowski, 814 F.2d 594 (11th Cir. 1987), 41 CRIM. L. REP. 2095.
93. UNITED STATES ATTORNEYS' MANUAL § 9-27.00.
94. *Id.* § 9-110.
95. *See, e.g.,* United States v. Litman, 547 F. Supp. 645 (W.D. Pa. 1982). *But see* United States v. Y. Hata Co., 535 F.2d 508, 512 (9th Cir.), *cert. denied,* 429 U.S. 828 (1976). *See* UNITED STATES ATTORNEYS' MANUAL §§ 9-11.252, 9-11.334.
96. United States v. Carrasco, 786 F.2d 1452 (9th Cir. 1986).
97. North Carolina v. Alford, 400 U.S. 25 (1970).
98. *See* FED. R. CRIM. P. 11, Advisory Committee Notes; FED. R. EVID. 803(22).
99. UNITED STATES ATTORNEYS' MANUAL § 9-27.500.
100. *See generally* Miller & Gorelick, *Parole Guidelines Confuse Sentencing Process,* Legal TImes, Aug. 28, 1978, at 9.
101. GUIDELINE § 6B1.2(a).
102. *Id.* § 6B1.2(b).
103. 53 Fed. Reg. 5104 (Feb. 19, 1988).
104. GUIDELINE § 6B1.4.
105. *See Sentencing Commission Holds Hearing on Amendments to Sentencing Guidelines,* 42 CRIM. L. REP. (BNA) 2494 (Mar. 30, 1988).
106. 18 U.S.C. § 3623.
107. FED. R. CRIM. P. 11(e)(1)(A).
108. FED. R. CRIM. P. 11(b), 11(e)(2).
109. United States v. Miller, 722 F.2d 562 (9th Cir. 1983).
110. 106 S. Ct. 433, 437 (1985).
111. United States v. Friedman, 506 F.2d 511 (8th Cir. 1974), *cert. denied,* 421 U.S. 1004 (1975).
112. United States v. Ashland Oil, Inc., 537 F. Supp. 427 (M.D. Tenn. 1982).
113. UNITED STATES ATTORNEYS' MANUAL § 9-2.142.
114. United States v. Benchimol, 471 U.S. 453, 456 (1985).
115. *See, e.g., In re* Palodichuk, 589 P.2d 269, 271 (Wash. Ct. App. 1978); Kluttz v. Warden, 99 Nev. 681, 669 P.2d 244 (1983); *In re* Meunier, 145 Vt. 414, 491 A.2d 1019 (1985).
116. United States v. Corsentino, 685 F.2d 48 (2d Cir. 1982).

117. United States v. Cruz, 709 F.2d 111, 114–15 (1st Cir. 1983); United States v. Blackwell, 694 F.2d 1325, 1338 (D.C. Cir. 1982).

118. *Compare* Siegel v. New York, 691 F.2d 620, 624 (2d Cir. 1982), *cert. denied,* 459 U.S. 1209 (1983) (applying New York law to nullify unwritten promise), *with* United States v. Winter, 663 F.2d 1120, 1133 (1st Cir. 1981), *cert. denied,* 460 U.S. 1011 (1983) (unwritten agreement between informer and federal prosecutor upheld against attack by defendants).

119. *Compare* United States v. Aguilera, 654 F.2d 352 (5th Cir. 1981) (trial judge properly refused to order performance of plea offered by government, since defendant neither accepted nor raised on it), with Cooper v. United States, 594 F.2d 12 (4th Cir. 1979) (constitutional right to fairness in plea bargaining required enforcement of plea-bargaining promises made by government, even though plea offer was withdrawn before defendant's acceptance).

120. Virgin Islands v. Scotland, 614 F.2d 360, 365 (3d Cir. 1980).

121. Mabry v. Johnson, 467 U.S. 504 (1984).

122. United States v. Abbomonte, 759 F.2d 1065 (2d Cir. 1985). *But See* Mabry v. Johnson, 467 U.S. 504, 510, n.11, 104 S. Ct. at 2548 n.11, *discussing* Santobello v. New York, 404 U.S. 257 (1971).

Bibliography

Cary C. Griffith

This bibliography lists selected books and articles on corporate legal departments and outside counsel.

Books

ALLEN, PAUL B., ED. HOW TO KEEP YOUR COMPANY OUT OF COURT. Englewood Cliffs, N.J.: Prentice-Hall, Inc., 1984.

AYRE, J.R. CORPORATE LEGAL DEPARTMENTS: STRATEGIES FOR THE 1980S. New York: Practising Law Institute, 1984.

BALOTTI, R. FRANKLIN, AND FINKELSTEIN, JESSE A. THE DELAWARE LAW OF CORPORATIONS AND BUSINESS ORGANIZATIONS. New Jersey: Prentice-Hall Law & Business, 1988.

BARNETTE, CURTIS H. CORPORATE LAW DEPARTMENTS AND OUTSIDE COUNSEL II. New York: Law and Business.

BASTEDO, WAYNE W. OUTSIDE COUNSEL, INSIDE DIRECTOR: THE DIRECTORY OF LAWYERS ON THE BOARDS OF AMERICAN INDUSTRY. New York: Law Journal Seminars Press, 1981.

BLOCK, DENNIS. THE CORPORATE COUNSELOR'S DESK BOOK. New York: Law and Business, Inc., 1985.

BLOCK, DENNIS J., BARTON, NANCY E., AND RADIN, STEPHEN A. THE BUSINESS JUDGMENT RULE: FIDUCIARY DUTIES OF CORPORATE DIRECTORS AND OFFICERS, 2ND ED. New Jersey: Prentice-Hall Law & Business, 1988.

BURGESS, HAROLD D. SIXTY YEARS AT THE BAR: ANECDOTES OF A CORPORATION LAWYER. Florida: Exposition Press, 1981.

Cary C. Griffith is the Law Librarian for Control Data Corporation, Minneapolis, Minnesota.

CALIFORNIA CONTINUING EDUCATION OF THE BAR. ALTERNATIVE DISPUTE RESOLUTION IN CIVIL CASES. California CEB, July/August 1985.

CARNEY, WILLIAM J. THE CHANGING ROLE OF THE CORPORATE ATTORNEY. Lexington, Mass.: Lexington Books, 1982.

CENTER FOR PUBLIC RESOURCES. CORPORATE DISPUTE MANAGEMENT. New York: Center for Public Resources, 1982.

CHAYES, A. MANAGING THE CORPORATE LEGAL FUNCTION. New York: Mathew Bender, 1985.

CONRAD, ROBIN, AND KRASNOW, ERWIN G. 100 WAYS TO CUT LEGAL FEES & MANAGE YOUR LAWYER. Washington, D.C.: U.S. Chamber of Commerce, 1988.

CORPORATE COUNSEL INSTITUTE—CORPORATE COMPLIANCE PROGRAMS (SIXTH ANNUAL): A COURSE HANDBOOK. New York: Practising Law Institute, 1983.

DEER, RICHARD E. THE LAWYER'S BASIC CORPORATE PRACTICE MANUAL. Philadelphia, Pa.: American Law Institute, 1978.

FROMHOLZ, HALEY J. THE COORDINATION AND MANAGEMENT OF MAJOR LITIGATION. New York: Practising Law Institute, 1982.

GREEN, ERIC. THE CPR LEGAL PROGRAM MINI-TRIAL HANDBOOK. New York: Center for Public Resources, 1982.

HANCOCK, WILLIAM A. LEGAL COMPLIANCE AND EDUCATION PROGRAMS. Chesterland, Ohio: Business Laws, Inc., 1985.

______. MATERIALS ON MINIMIZING MANAGEMENT LIABILITY. Chesterland, Ohio: Business Laws, Inc., 1985.

HAYNSWORTH, HARRY J. THE PROFESSIONAL SKILLS OF THE SMALL BUSINESS LAWYER. Philadelphia, Pa.: American Law Institute, 1984.

HENNING, JOEL. CORPORATE CLIENTS AND THEIR LAWYERS: A COLLOQUY. Chicago: Law Letters, 1982.

HUGHES, ROBERT B. LEGAL COMPLIANCE CHECKUPS: BUSINESS CLIENTS. Glenview, Ill.: Callaghan and Co., 1985.

JONES, RONALD L. PRACTICE PREVENTIVE CORPORATE LAW. Philadelphia, Pa.: American Law Institute, 1985.

MANAGEMENT FOR IN-HOUSE COUNSEL: TECHNIQUES, TOOLS, APPROACHES. Chicago: ABA, 1985.

TRAGER, LESLIE. INSIDER AND EMPLOYEE THEFTS: CORPORATE COUNSEL'S ROLE—TRAPS AND PITFALLS. New York: Practising Law Institute, 1981.

WEISS, STEPHEN J. REPRESENTING DIRECTORS, OFFICERS, AND HOUSE COUNSEL OF PUBLICLY HELD CORPORATIONS. New York: Practising Law Institute, 1981.

YEAGER, DENNIS R. THE ROLE OF OUTSIDE COUNSEL IN THE BUSINESS INVESTIGATION. New York: Practising Law Institute, 1985.

ARTHUR YOUNG AND COMPANY. REPORT OF SURVEY OF CORPORATE LAW DEPARTMENTS COMPENSATION AND ORGANIZATION PRACTICES. New York: Arthur Young and Company, 1982.

Articles

Asbel, Howard J. *Successful Teaming of Inside and Outside Counsel to Serve the Corporate Client.* 38 BUS. LAW. 1587–1603 (Aug. 1983).

Baird, Peter D. *How Lawyers Lose Their Way,* 9 LITIGATION 8 (Fall 1982).

Bennett, Guy. *The Role of the Computer in the Law Firm and Corporate Legal Department.* 10 LEGAL ECON. 53 (Mar.–Apr. 1984).

Bergeisen, Michael D. *How to Manage Litigation and Evaluate Outside Counsel.* 31 PRAC. LAW. 37–44 (Apr. 15, 1985).

Blodgett, Nancy. *Lawyer Shopping: Clients Look for Low Bidders.* 72 A.B.A. J. 17 (July 1, 1986).

Bridges, Terry. *Advice from Outside: A Business Litigator Tells In-House Counsel How to Get More for Their Money from Outside Attorneys.* 5 CAL. LAW. 29 (Oct. 1985).

Brill, Steven. *Jealous Co-Counsel: Inside v. Outside.* 6 AM. LAW. 1 (June 1984).

Brown, Louis M. *Legal Audit.* 38 S. CAL. L. REV. 431 (1965).

______. *Memorandum on Non-Adversarial Law Practice and Preventive Law.* 6 J. LEGAL PROF. 3 (1981).

______. *Update of Legal Audit—A Personal Account.* N.Y. ST. B.J. 282 (Aug. 1982).

Bush. *Dispute Resolution Alternatives and the Goals of Civil Justice: Jurisdictional Principles for Process Choice.* 1984 WIS. L. REV. 893 (1984).

Chayes, Abram. *Corporate Counsel and the Elite Law Firm.* 37 STAN. L. REV. 277–312 (Jan. 1985).

Cohen, Avery. *Outside Lawyer vs. Board of Directors: A Relationship Suffering Rapid Change.* 188 N.Y.L.J. 31 (Dec. 13, 1982).

A Corporate Campaign to Slash Legal Costs. BUS. WK. 90 (May 25, 1981).

Corporate v. Private: Changes in Lawyer Pay. 27 LAW OFF. ECON. & MGMT. 381–82 (Fall 1986).

Coulson, Robert. *Management Control of Corporate Litigation.* 190 N.Y.L.J. 1 (Oct. 13, 1983).

Davis, F.T. *The Corporate Investigation and the Role of the Corporate Lawyer.* 20 GA. ST. B.J. 74 (Nov. 1983).

Desperate Court Treatment of Retained and In-House Corporate Counsel: United States Steel Corporation v. United States. 20 NEW ENG. L.J. 87–122 (1985).

Dillinger, Gary R. *Corporate Practice, Your Outside Counsel Needs a Corporate Handbook.* 71 A.B.A. J. 66 (Nov. 1985).

Doss, M. Kenneth. *Working with Outside Counsel on the Products Case: A Practical Approach.* 28 FOR DEF. 12–18 (July 1986).

Eisler, Kim Isaac. *Getting the Specifics for Outside Counsel.* 98 L.A. Daily J. 5 (Mar. 27, 1985).

Evaluating Cases for ADR Potential. CENTER FOR PUBLIC RESOURCES LEGAL PROGRAM PROCEEDINGS (June 1984).

Fisher, R. *The Changing Role of Corporate Counsel.* 4 J.L. & COM. 45–64 (1984).

Franklin. *The "Mini-Trial": What It Is and What It Isn't: What It Can Do and What It Can't Do.* 4 CONSTRUCTION LAW. (ABA Forum Committee on the Construction Industry 1983).

Friedman, Frank B. *Corporate Environmental Programs and Litigation: The Role of Lawyer-Managers in Environmental Management,* 45 PUB. AD. REV. 766–70 (Nov. 1985).

Frierson, James G., and Michael J. Brown. *Build Your Practice with Legal Audits.* 71 A.B.A. J. (June 1985).

Fuhrman, J. *Cost-Benefit Study Utilized to Plan Bank's Legal Budget.* Legal Times, Nov. 1, 1983, at 2.

Galen, Michele. *More Can Be Less (Major Corporations Spending More Money on Outside Counsel Fees).* 9 Nat'l L.J. 2 (May 11, 1987).

Glasser, Stephen A. *Aetna Pens Guide for Outside Counsel.* Legal Times, Dec. 12, 1983, at 8.

______. *Corporate Lawyers Advise Getting Tough.* Legal Times, July 12, 1982, at 12.

Goldblatt, Michael L. *Corporate Practice: Inside and Outside Counsel Team Up to Serve Corporate Clients.* 21 TENN. B.J. 29 (Nov.–Dec. 1985).

Goldenkranz, Michael B. *The Legal Affairs Log and Litigation Status Report: Two Useful Tools for the General Counsel.* 12 LEGAL ECON. 27 (Feb. 1986).

Goldstein. *Alternatives for Resolving Business Transactions Disputes.* 58 ST. JOHN'S L. REV. 69 (Fall 1983).

Green. *A Comprehensive Approach to the Theory and Practice of Alternative Dispute Resolution.* 34 J. LEGAL EDUC. 245 (1984).

______. *Growth of the Mini-Trial.* 9 LITIGATION 12 (Fall 1982).

Grimes, Larry B. *What to Do 'til the Doctor Comes: Handling Corporate Litigation before Retaining Outside Counsel.* 7 LITIGATION 28 (Summer 1981).

The Growing Field of Alternative Dispute Resolution. 7 AAA LAW. ARB. LETTER (Dec. 1983).

Harnig, E. *Perspectives on Litigation Cost Control.* N.Y. ST. B.J. 6 (May 1983).

Haserot, P. *Can Small Firms Attract Big Business?* Nat'l L.J. 14 (May 5, 1986).

Haynes. *Private Means to Public Ends: Implications of the Private Judging Phenomenon in California.* 17 U.C.D. L. REV. 611 (1984).

Hershman, M. *What Inside Counsel Look for in a Private Firm; Often It's a Second Opinion.* Nat'l L.J. 32 (Feb. 3, 1986).

Holub, Hugh A. *Outside Corporate Counsel.* 99 L.A. Daily J., Feb. 21, 1986, at B3.

Is There a Lawyer in the House? 9 BARRISTER 25 (Summer 1982).

Jealous Co-Counsel. AM. LAW. 1 (June 1983).

Keefe, Arthur John. *How Corporations Can Control Legal Costs.* 69 A.B.A. J. 538 (Apr. 1983).

Killian and Mancini. *Mini Trials: Basic Principles and Guidelines.* CONSTRUCTION BRIEFINGS, No. 85-3 (Mar. 1985).

Kirk, Susan L. *The Importance of the Legal Survey to Inside and Outside Counsel.* INT'L LEGAL PRAC. 132 (Dec. 1984).

Klein, Michael R. *The End Is Not Near: Outside Counsel Will Survive, the Role of In-House Lawyers Will Surely Expand—But They'll Still Need Help.* 96 L.A. Daily J. 4 (June 2, 1983).

______. *Outside Counsel's Sun Hasn't Yet Sunk into the West.* 5 Legal Times, May 23, 1983, at 14.

Landes, Robert N. *Advice on Hiring Outside Lawyers.* 197 N.Y.L.J. 5 (Jan. 29, 1987).

Lempert, Larry. *Companies Take Litigation In-House.* 4 Legal Times, Mar. 1, 1982, at 1.

______. *New Realism Suffuses Inside-Outside Dialogue (Relationship between Corporate Legal Departments and Private Firms).* 6 Legal Times, Feb. 27, 1984, at 36.

______. *Outside's Look In Differs from Inside's Look Out.* 7 Legal Times, Jan. 28, 1985, at 10.

Lorne, Simon M. *Why Outside Counsel Should Stay Outside: One Corporate Lawyer Makes the Case for Keeping General Counsel Off the Board.* 6 DIRECTORS & BOARDS 26–28 (Fall 1981).

Marks. *Cost-Effective Litigation Management: The Role of Alternate Dispute Resolution.* ABA NATIONAL INSTITUTE ON ALTERNATIVE METHODS OF DISPUTE RESOLUTION (Feb. 1983).

Marquis, Joshua. *In-House Counsel Seek Ways to Cut Litigation Expense: Case Management Restrictions Annoy Outside Attorneys: Billings Questioned: Corporate Costs.* 95 L.A. Daily Times 1 (Aug. 20, 1982).

Mathews, Arthur F. *The Role of Outside Counsel.* 61 N.C.L. REV. 483–504 (Mar. 1983).

McBaine, John N. *The Attorney-Client Privilege for Corporations: What Comes Next?* 7 LITIGATION 18 (Summer 1981).

Middleton, M., and Vicki Quade. *Corporations Hunt Ways to Cut Legal Costs.* 68 A.B.A. J. 523 (May 1982).

Mode, Paul J., and Deanne C. Siemer. *The Litigation Partner and the Settlement Partner.* 12 LITIGATION 33 (Summer 1986).

Moore. *Emerging ADR Prospects for Large Construction Disputes.* 2 ALTERNATIVES 11 (Nov. 1984).

Morgan, G. *How Small Firms Can Attract Corporate Litigation.* 70 A.B.A. J. 59 (Oct. 1984).

The New Balance of Power: The Changing Relationship between Inside and Outside Counsel. 8 AM. LAW. 5 (Nov. 1986).

Oster and Wheatley. *"Rent-a-Judge—Private Judging": What It Is and How It Works.* 4 CEB CIV. LITIGATION REP. 65 (1982).

An Ounce of Prevention Is Worth a Pound of Lawsuits. BUS. WK. (Mar. 22, 1982).

Outside Legal Costs for Major Corporations Remain Steady: In-House Attorney Staffs Shrink, Paralegals Grow. 60 OHIO ST. B.A. REP. 22 (Jan. 12, 1987).

Outside-Counsel Honeymoon Lasts Five Years, Study Hints. 8 PA. L.J. REP. 1 (Apr. 15, 1985).

Parker and Radoff. *The Mini-Hearing: An Alternative to Protracted Litigation of Factually Complex Disputes.* 38 BUS. LAW. 35 (1983).

Pollack, E. *Time for In-House Counsel?* AM. LAW. 7 (June 1983).

Propper, Eugene M. *How to Analyze a Target's Litigation Risks.* Nat'l L.J. 30 (Nov. 3, 1986).

Quinn, James W. *Litigation Budgets Ease Inside Counsel's Concern.* 5 Legal Times, Jan. 17 1983, at 15.

Ranii, David. *In-House, Outside Counsel: Can They Bridge the Gap?* Nat'l L.J. 1 (Sept. 10, 1984).

Raylesberg, Alan I. *New Post Can Aid and Control Outside Counsel; Legal Affairs Manager Cuts Costs.* Nat'l L.J. 20 (May 27, 1985).

Reynolds. *Is In-House In?* 6 DISTRICT LAW. 31 (1982).

Rosenthal, Mark M., and Robert A. Miller. *When Your Client's Business Deal Goes Sour.* 71 A.B.A. J. 58 (June 1985).

Ross, Kenneth. *Managing Litigation for the Corporation: The Role of Corporate Counsel.* 6 Nat'l L.J. 20 (Dec. 19, 1983).

______. *Some Rules for a Happy Marriage: Living with Outside Counsel in Litigation.* Nat'l L.J. 10 (Jan. 2, 1984).

Sciamanda, John. *Preventive Law.* 4 ALTERNATIVES TO HIGH COST LITIGATION 9 (Sept. 1986).

Slind-flor, Victoria. *Law Firm Salaries Cast Shadow on In-House Counsels: Corporate Recruiters Tell Young Attorneys Pay Isn't Everything; Stress "Lifestyle Issues."* 99 L.A. Daily J. 1 (Aug. 18, 1986).

Smith, Robert M. *Not-Quite-50 Ways to Limit Expenses for Top Clients: Your Big Accounts Need Not Be Gold Mines for Outside Counsel.* 97 L.A. Daily J. 4 (June 14, 1984).

Survey Probes Relations between Corporate Lawyers, Outside Firms, 8 LITIGATION NEWS 3 (Summer 1983).

Tanenhares, Edward D. *Occupational Disease Litigation Management: The Case for an In-House Director.* 5 Nat'l L.J. 20 (Jan. 17, 1983).

Turk, Harry N. *The Rise of Corporate Law Departments: Pressure on Both In-House and Outside Counsel.* 10 EMPLOYEE REL. L.J. 551–56 (Winter 1984).

Whitefield, Robert. *How to Manage Outside Counsel Efficiently.* 132 Chicago Daily L. Bull. 2 (Dec. 31, 1986).

Whitehead, G. Marc. *In-House, Outside Counsel.* 4 Nat'l L.J. 16 (June 7, 1982).

Appendix of Forms

This appendix contains a wealth of forms developed to support the topics discussed in each section except Section VII. These forms include sample contracts, company policies and procedures, reports, form letters, and other documents that corporations have used in handling litigation.

We suggest that, after you have read a topic of interest in this book, you then page through the relevant section of the appendix for aids to implementing the ideas presented. In addition, the forms are numbered sequentially, and some chapters refer to specific forms by number. For further help in identifying the forms of interest to you, you may want to refer to the list of form titles in the table of contents or to the relevant subjects in the index.

Francis J. Burke, Jr.
Streich, Lang, Weeks & Cardon
Phoenix, Arizona

Forms for Section I:

Preventing Litigation through Legal Audits and Internal Corporate Investigations

FORM 1

Sample Corporate Letter of Instruction on Antitrust Compliance

[Date]

Corporate Letter of Instruction No. 1

Subject: Antitrust Compliance

Effective Date: This corporate letter of instruction (CLI) is effective upon receipt, and supersedes all previous statements on this subject.

Statement of Policy

It is the policy of the corporation to comply with the antitrust laws of the United States, the several states, foreign countries, and various multinational groups such as the European Economic Community. The corporation fully supports the purpose of these laws, which is to assure the effective operation of the private marketplace for goods and services. These laws are intended to prevent and eliminate any agreements and individual conduct that would interfere unreasonably with the operation of the marketplace.

In addition to compliance with the various antitrust laws, it is the further objective of the corporation to assure awareness of the business and personal risks associated with antitrust violations, and to specify programs to assure compliance with these laws. It is intended that through attainment of these objectives, the corporation will achieve the goals of good corporate citizenship through such compliance; avoid criminal prosecution of the corporation and its directors, officers, and employees; and avoid the substantial financial risks associated with noncompliance.

Risks of Noncompliance

The risks of noncompliance with the antitrust laws are extremely severe on both the individuals involved in the violations and on the corporation. For example, certain violations of the federal antitrust laws, described below, constitute a felony and upon conviction, the corporation may be fined up to $1 million and individual employees may be fined up to $100,000. The individuals involved also can be imprisoned up to three years and may be required to pay any resulting fine and the substantial legal costs for their defense out of their own funds. Convicted individuals also would lose their rights under various laws to engage in certain occupations and would risk the discharge of their employment by the corporation.

Equally important, any violation of the federal antitrust laws could result in the payment of treble damages to persons injured in their business or property by such violations. Such damages could amount to millions of dollars, particularly with respect to violations for price fixing and monopolization. A conviction or plea of guilty by the corporation or an officer or employee constitutes a prima facie case of liability in a private treble-damage action against the corporation or such person. In addition, the corporation could be required to divest itself of certain assets, and other assets, such as patents and other proprietary information, might become unenforceable.

Elements of Compliance Program

The antitrust compliance program of the corporation shall consist of the following elements:

- The issuance, dissemination, and administration of this Letter of Instruction
- The Statement of Policy and Antitrust Guidelines for employees, promulgated by the Chairman of the Board
- Special procedures relating to review and approval of acquisitions
- Legal guidelines applicable to the planning and marketing functions of the corporation to be issued separately
- Periodic presentations by the Legal Department to the Operations Committee and various groups of employees of the corporation relating to compliance with the antitrust laws
- Periodic legal reviews of individual operating groups and units in order to assure that local compliance programs are effective

Compliance Guidelines

The antitrust laws affect virtually every area of business activity of the corporation. This section focuses on those activities relevant to the business of the corporation for which it is important to establish clear antitrust guidelines.

Conduct Subject to Criminal Prosecution

The antitrust laws apply to a wide range of business practices, many of which may or may not be lawful depending upon the circumstances of a specific situation. In most situations, a balance must be reached as to what is fair and reasonable competitive conduct. However, a few practices are considered to be so anticompetitive that they are always deemed to be unlawful. The government has confined criminal prosecution to these clear and indefensible antitrust violations. These consist of agreements with competitors relating to prices and other terms and conditions of sale or to costs, dividing up customers or sales areas among competitors, agreements among competitors to curtail or allocate production, agreements among competitors to boycott suppliers or customers, and agreements with suppliers or customers to fix resale prices (as distinguished from the use of bona fide sales agents or sales representatives).

Due to the seriousness of these specific practices, employees are prohibited from engaging in any such activity and must avoid any actions from which any inference could be drawn that they had entered into any such unlawful contract, combination, or conspiracy to restrain trade. For example, no employee may engage in any written or oral communication with a representative of any competitor, supplier, or customer relating to any of the above-described subject areas. If any such subjects are raised at any gathering at which a representative of any such other outside party is present, the employee involved must insist that the discussion terminate immediately, and if this request is not honored, the employee must promptly leave. Employees must be extremely careful that the abovementioned subject areas do not creep into conversations at otherwise legitimate gatherings, such as meetings of trade associations and professional societies, trade shows, local civic activities and business and social clubs, supplier product demonstrations and technical presentations, and even neighborhood conversations. Industry associations and less formal groups at the customer level may try to impose uniform conduct on suppliers to the industry. Employees of the corporation may not engage in discussions regarding, or agree to, any such uniform conduct.

No employee may exchange a price list with a competitor, and any price list of a competitor obtained from a customer or other indirect source must be labeled as to its source. Information relating to bids may not be discussed with a competitor. The corporation may not engage in any continuing joint marketing or selling arrangements with a competitor. (Individual project joint selling arrangements must be approved by the Legal Department.) These prohibitions are only illustrative, and each employee is responsible for using sound judgment in avoiding all conduct that could lead to criminal prosecution of the individual and, as a result, of the corporation.

The above-described practices need not take place within the United States to result in a criminal prosecution. Similar practices carried out in foreign countries that harm interstate commerce or imports into, or exports from, the United States are just as risky. All license agreements and joint venture agreements must be reviewed with the Legal Department. Occasionally, particularly with respect to foreign projects, it may be necessary to team up with a competitor in preparing and presenting a consolidated bid to the foreign client. All such situations must be reviewed in advance with the Legal Department.

Evidence of unlawful conduct of the type described above need not be in writing. Casual conversations may be clearly recalled years later in a grand jury hearing, particularly by another person seeking to gain immunity from criminal prosecution. Where there is a common course of conduct among competitors relating to any of the above-mentioned practices, the government and treble-damage plaintiffs will thoroughly explore any meetings, correspondence, and conversations with competitors to determine whether such parallel conduct was, in fact, agreed upon. It would be criminal obstruction of justice to knowingly destroy written evidence of such an agreement once a government investigation has begun. Even statements to persons outside the corporation, such as the news media or individual customers, relating to price moves still under internal consideration, or public announcements of price moves far in advance of any customer need, could raise questions. Frequently, competitors also are either suppliers or customers of the corporation. It is entirely lawful to carry on bona fide supplier and customer relationships with such other companies, provided that there is no discussion about unrelated situations where the two companies compete.

The above-specified restrictions on employee conduct apply regardless of the business reasons that may be involved. It is no defense that some competition remains in nonprice areas, that discussions among competitors were not the sole cause of a price rise, that ruinous price competition forces out marginal competitors, that the competitors involved do not control the market, that prices are not fixed but only affected in their movement, that prices are simply exchanged and not agreed upon, that a government official is aware of the pricing scheme, or that such discussions are required to verify a competitor's price quoted by a customer, or any other reason.

Trade and Professional Associations and Other Groups

Trade, professional, industry, and similar associations perform many legitimate and useful functions, such as providing members with general business information; informing the government of industry problems and needs; developing voluntary test, performance, and product standards that improve safety and efficiency; and solving environmental, safety, and similar industrywide problems. On the other hand, these associations could be the occasion for discussion of the unlawful subject areas previously mentioned. In addition, codes of conduct issued by some associations dealing with such subjects as minimum fees, joint price advertising, and prohibitions against such competitive activities as bidding and advertising, can inhibit competition. Other questionable association activities include compulsory performance or product standards, unreasonably restrictive membership requirements, exchange of individual company financial data, development of product standards intended to affect pricing, joint engineering of products, agreements not to produce nonconforming products, and certification programs that exclude the products of some competitors.

Accordingly, the Vice President and General Counsel must be notified in advance before the corporation applies for membership in any trade, professional, industry, or similar association. The charter and bylaws and existing programs of such associations must be reviewed, and it must be determined that there is an important and legitimate business need for such membership and that the association has an adequate antitrust compliance program. Associations in which employees with marketing or selling responsibilities, as opposed to engineering or other nonselling duties, attend meetings are especially sensitive. The Vice President and General Counsel shall undertake a review of existing association memberships to assure compliance with this policy. The Legal Department shall maintain appropriate records relating to these associations.

Occasionally, competitors deem it important to make joint presentations to the legislative, executive, and judicial branches of federal and state governments. Companies have a constitutional right to make such presentations. However, since corporate participation in such joint industry activities could have unlawful spillover effects, any participation in such group efforts must be reviewed in advance with the Vice President and General Counsel.

Monopolizing Conduct

Any business unit that is the largest factor in its product or service field should exercise special caution to avoid claims that it is attempting to monopolize such business by forcing out smaller competitors through unfair market strategies and, as a result, gaining unlawful control over the pricing and production of such products or services. Good judgment must be used in determining what market strategies are fair and reasonable.

Competitors who are injured by such unfair market strategies could press claims for treble damages under the antitrust laws for millions of dollars, and the costs of defense could amount to additional millions of dollars. Activities that could raise questions in this area include systematic undercutting of the prices bid by smaller competitors, sales below cost, regional price discrimination aimed at smaller regional sellers, addition of production capacity far beyond current industry needs, new market strategies specifically intended to eliminate or limit a new entrant, extending a commanding market position in one product to another product through coercive tie-in requirements, making new-product announcements unreasonably in advance of ability to supply, or the filing of a fraudulent patent application. These examples are only illustrative.

This is not to suggest that managers may not aspire to become or remain the largest factor in a particular line of business. However, the management of any such business should review carefully with the Legal Department any new market strategy before it is implemented. The antitrust laws do not permit willful maintenance of a monopoly position, or willful attempts to achieve such a position, by taking unfair advantage of a commanding market position, however lawfully attained, but do permit continued growth and development as a result of bona fide new technology, lower manufacturing costs, or the adoption of sales programs already employed by other competitors. The rules of conduct in this area are very imprecise, justifying considerable caution by management.

Acquisition and Disposition of Voting Stock or Assets

The antitrust laws contain limitations on the rights of the corporation to acquire a competitor, supplier, or customer, or a company in a highly concentrated business into which the corporation is an actual or perceived potential entrant, and where the effect of such an acquisition of voting stock or assets would be to substantially lessen competition. The same laws apply to the sale of a business by the corporation.

Accordingly, the acquisition of any of the voting stock or assets of another company, or the sale of any business of the corporation, must be reviewed in advance with the Vice President and General Counsel or his designee to determine that such purchase or sale is lawful under the antitrust laws. In addition, the sponsor of any such acquisition or sale must comply with the review provisions of CLI 2.

Pursuant to the Hart-Scott-Rodino Antitrust Improvements Act of 1976, the corporation must give advance notice to the United States Department of Justice and Federal Trade Commission of any acquisition or disposition of a business meeting the minimum requirements established by the government, and submit a written report. While the rules for determining which transactions are reportable are extremely complex, they generally provide that the acquisition of the voting stock or assets of any company by the corporation is subject to advance notice and reporting, and a waiting period, if such company has total assets or annual net sales amounting to $10 million or more and, as a result of the acquisition, the corporation would hold either $15 million worth or 15 percent or more of the acquired person's assets or voting securities as a result of the transaction. If the corporation already holds a minority ownership interest in another company, the purchase of any additional voting stock in such a company could trigger the reporting requirements and waiting period.

The Vice President and Controller is responsible for preparing such reports, which are to be filed by the Vice President and General Counsel. Following such advance notice, the corporation must observe a waiting period of up to thirty days and possibly longer, if the government requests additional information. Accordingly, the sponsor of any such acquisition or sale should consult with the Vice President and General Counsel to ensure compliance with this advance reporting requirement.

Relationships with Suppliers and Customers

The corporation's business relationships with its suppliers and its customers also could raise antitrust questions, although normal purchasing and selling activities should not raise any concern.

Obviously, any requirement that a supplier of critical raw materials deal exclusively with the corporation could raise an antitrust question if adequate alternative sources were unavailable to competitors. Also, in dealing with suppliers, employees are prohibited from engaging in any type of reciprocity dealing (see Corporate Purchasing Policy).

Business units should avoid any contracts with, or requirements upon, customers that unreasonably restrain trade. As previously noted under the guidelines relating to criminal conduct, the corporation may not attempt to control in any way the resale prices, of its customers, although suggested resale prices, clearly labeled, may be published. It should be noted that the federal law permitting state fair-trading statutes has been repealed. As also previously noted, the corporation may not engage in a boycott of any supplier or customer.

Restriction limiting the type or location of the persons to whom customers sell and exclusive dealing arrangements may not be used without the prior approval of the Legal Department. One product or service may not be tied to the sale of another product or service unless this is essential for technical reasons. Uniform distribution practices among competitors could create a suspicion of industrywide collusion, and as previously noted, employees are prohibited from agreeing with a competitor, directly or indirectly, with respect to any terms and conditions of sale or other disposition of the corporation's products or services.

Restrictions such as those described above may be unlawful whether imposed by a contract, a refusal to deal, or the promise of a benefit.

Finally, except for bona fide bid situations, the antitrust laws make it unlawful to sell the same product at different prices to two competing customers, or in two different regions where the effect may be to substantially lessen competition at the seller or customer level, unless the lower price is granted in good faith to meet the lower price of a competitor, or there has been an advance determination that the lower price is cost-justified. Functional allowances may be granted to wholesalers and similar customers only for bona fide services performed by such customers at the intended distribution level. The law also provides that any promotional allowances or services must be made available to competing customers on proportionally equal terms. The Legal Department should be consulted in making these determinations and for establishing appropriate procedures within business units confronted by such situations.

Training of Personnel

The Vice President and General Counsel shall be responsible for providing appropriate training for employees of the corporation in order to better assure compliance with the antitrust laws. This training should include an annual update of antitrust laws presented to the Operations Committee, and periodic presentations to operating unit management, management trainees, planning and marketing personnel, domestic and foreign sales personnel, purchasing personnel, and personnel who regularly attend trade and professional association meetings. Such presentations may be made through videotape or other means. Officers of the corporation responsible for compliance with the CLI shall be responsible for scheduling and arranging these presentations upon consultation with the Vice President and General Counsel, except as otherwise specifically directed in this CLI or any other corporate directive.

Referral of Matters to Legal Department

As noted above, the antitrust laws regarding many business activities are unclear. The illustrations contained in this CLI should be useful in evaluating analogous situations. The use of these illustrations is not intended to suggest that these practices are invariably unlawful. Indeed, the discussion of these illustrations in many instances may impose standards higher than the law compels. Nevertheless employees are asked to follow these standards to the letter in order to eliminate *any* question of unlawful conduct under the antitrust laws. If an employee has any doubt regarding the legality of a specific situation, the Legal Department should be contacted to review the situation.

All outside inquiries regarding the corporation's practices under the antitrust laws should be promptly and firmly referred to the Vice President and General Counsel without reply, including oral or written requests for information from the United States Department of Justice, the Federal Trade Commission, and the attorneys general of the various states. The Vice President and General Counsel is responsible for responding to all such inquiries.

Responsibility for Compliance

The Statement of Policy and Antitrust Guidelines for employees promulgated by the Chairman of the Board has been delivered to each salaried employee of the corporation and its subsidiaries. A copy thereof shall be incorporated in personnel or other appropriate policy or procedure manuals maintained at the corporate, group, subsidiary, and operating unit levels.

It is the responsibility of the Group Vice Presidents, and the Chief Executive Officers of independent operating units, to assure strict and continuing compliance with this CLI by employees under their supervision. Corporate staff officers are responsible for such compliance within their areas of supervision. In addition, these officers are directed within their respective groups, divisions, subsidiaries, and areas to establish procedures that will assure that every newly hired salaried employee receives a copy of the Statement of Policy and Antitrust Guidelines for Employees and that such newly hired employee's personnel file will include a form signed by such individual acknowledging receipt of this policy.

For the purposes of this CLI, salaried employees of newly acquired companies and businesses shall be deemed new employees. It will be the Legal Department's responsibility to send copies of the Statement of Policy and Antitrust Guidelines for Employees to each such employee.

Other corporate policies and procedures referred to in this CLI contain special compliance responsibilities, which are incorporated herein by this reference.

Maintenance and Revision: Responsibility for maintenance and revision of this CLI rests with the Vice President and General Counsel.

____

Chairman of the Board

FORM 2

Sample Policy Statement and Guidelines on Antitrust Compliance

[Letterhead of Chairman of the Board]

[Date]

TO: ALL SALARIED EMPLOYEES

The attached Statement of Policy and Antitrust Guidelines is herewith distributed to all salaried employees.

The attached statement reaffirms the position of the Company on the important matter of antitrust compliance and provides all salaried employees with specific guidelines to follow. You are expected to read and strictly adhere to these guidelines.

These guidelines also will assist new employees, and personnel who have joined the Company through acquisition, to understand the Company's position on antitrust compliance. You are required to conform to the Company position on this subject.

If you have any questions concerning the attached, please consult with the attorneys assigned to your Group or the Corporate Legal Department.

____

Chairman of the Board

[Company Letterhead]

Statement of Policy and Antitrust Guidelines for Employees

The antitrust laws are a bulwark of our competitive free enterprise system. The Company reaffirms its dedication to the principles of the antitrust laws, and its long-standing policy that requires full compliance with the antitrust laws as an absolute necessity.

You must understand clearly that you personally can be fined as much as $100,000 and can be imprisoned for as long as three years for any antitrust violation you commit. In addition to this fine, you also may be required to pay substantial legal costs for your defense from your own funds. The Company can be fined up to $1 million for each violation of the antitrust laws you commit as an employee of the Company. The Company also can be liable to anyone injured in his or her trade or business because of such a violation for three times the amount of the actual damages, plus the injured person's attorney's fees, which could amount to millions of dollars in expenses to the Company. It should be obvious that neither you nor the Company can afford any antitrust violation.

The antitrust laws forbid agreements or understandings, and concerted action, between personnel of the Company and personnel of any of our competitors for the purpose, and with the effect, of fixing or affecting prices and other terms and conditions of sale, dividing up customers or sales territories, and boycotting suppliers or customers. Agreements with customers to fix resale prices (as distinguished from the use of bona fide sales agents or representatives) also are forbidden by the antitrust laws.

Such understandings and concerted action can be illegal whether formal or informal, express or implied, oral or written. Casual conversations may be recalled years later by personnel of a competitor called to testify before a grand jury looking into practices in your industry. The government and private treble-damage plaintiffs will thoroughly explore any meetings, conversations, and correspondence with competitors to determine if parallel conduct among competitors was, in fact, agreed upon.

The purposes of the Company's antitrust compliance policy are to assure full compliance with these laws and to have our personnel conduct themselves in such a way as to avoid antitrust litigation. Accordingly, you must carefully avoid any conduct that would suggest that you are involved in unlawful concerted action with some competitor. Employees may find themselves in meetings with competitors where the discussion turns naturally to general conditions in the industry. Such conversations, even if purely social in origin, must be avoided, for the government may interpret your conduct as being a subtle form of concerted action. As an employee of the Company, you must avoid *even the appearance* of having engaged in concerted action condemned by the antitrust laws. Here are some specific pointers for your guidance.

Rule One: Don't Talk Prices

In part, this means don't talk about prices, or other terms and conditions of sale, with anyone outside of the Company except your customers. But this isn't all it means. It also means don't even talk about general business conditions with competitors. Don't discuss costs, even in general, with a competitor. This may give the appearance that you're talking prices. And you must avoid the appearance of wrongdoing.

There may be times when you're unavoidably with a group of competitor engineers or salespeople, such as at a trade association or professional society meeting, or a seminar conducted by a supplier. Stay away from "shop talk" in these circumstances. If you can't, then get away from the group. What you're talking about may sound harmless, but salespeople and engineers know the competitive value of even small shop talk. When everyone in an industry knows what everybody else is doing, all may wind up doing the same thing. And where you've talked about it in advance, the antitrust enforcement authorities may suspect that you have agreed to do it. Price fixing is a felony.

Rule Two: Don't Give Our Price Lists to a Competitor: Never Accept a Price List from a Competitor

Where a price list from a competitor is in our files, or where our price lists are in a competitor's files, it looks as if we have talked about prices with a competitor. If you get a price list from a customer (or from some other source other than the competitor itself), make a record of how and from whom the price list was obtained. Never exchange prices orally with a competitor, regardless of the reason. There is simply no justification for talking prices.

Rule Three: Don't Talk about Customers to Competitors

If you violate this rule, you may lose a customer. If you keep the customer, it may look as if you're agreeing with a competitor to stay away from its accounts if it will stay away from yours. Such an agreement is a felony. Your accounts are your own business. Similarly, do not discuss sales territories.

Rule Four: Don't Talk about Bids

If you tell someone what you're going to bid, or have bid, they may make the same bid. When bids are the same, the antitrust enforcement authorities may suspect that you've agreed to submit the same bid. Such an agreement would be a felony. On the other hand, if they make a lower bid, you lose the business. And if they make a higher bid, the antitrust enforcement authorities may suspect that you have an agreement to rotate the business. This too would be a felony.

Rule Five: Don't Make Telephone Calls to Competitors

Telephone lists are kept by the telephone company, and by our own operators. And, by being able to prove the fact of a telephone call through such lists, the antitrust enforcement authorities may infer that you have talked about something that violates the antitrust laws. Don't make calls to competitors on any subject dealing in any way with the marketing or sale of products or services.

Occasionally, you may need to make or receive telephone calls to or from a competitor in connection with safety matters, bona fide trade association activities, technical problems, professional societies, purchases or sales in the ordinary course of business, emergency situations, etc. Exercise great caution to limit the conversation to these lawful matters.

Rule Six: Don't Refuse Anyone's Business without Clearance

If for some reason other than Financial Department objections to a potential customer's credit standing, terms of payment, and the like, or Legal Department or executive objections to proposed contract terms and the like, let the head office know if you plan to turn down business. It can clear the problem with the Legal Department. If you refuse potential business, antitrust enforcement authorities may think you're part of a conspiracy to boycott someone, or are dividing customers with competitors or are trying to monopolize a market. Don't refuse anyone's business or offer any benefit, as a means to fix or affect the resale prices or other terms of sale of any customer. (It is lawful to suggest resale prices clearly labeled as such.)

Rule Seven: Don't Discriminate among Customers

When selling standardized products, do not discriminate in price or promotional allowances between competing customers except to meet competition, or where the Company will realize bona fide cost savings. And in these latter situations, you must check with the Legal Department, or follow procedures developed in cooperation with the Legal Department, to assure that such concessions are lawful.

Rule Eight: Don't Refuse to Buy Because the Supplier Won't Reciprocate

It is the firm policy of the Company to base all purchase decisions solely on quality, price, delivery terms, and other legitimate factors. Company salespeople may not discuss with the Purchasing Department the purchases the Company makes from individual customers or prospective customers. Salespeople may not discuss with customers the purchases the Company makes or could make from such customers.

Rule Nine: Don't Join Trade Associations or Professional Societies without Clearance

Trade associations and professional societies can serve many important functions. However, some information exchanges and standardization programs may diminish competition or foreclose competitors from the marketplace. Do not participate in association programs without discussing them with your Group Counsel. All new Company memberships in trade associations and professional societies must be reviewed in advance with the Vice President and General Counsel.

Conclusion

If you stay away from competitors, you and the Company will avoid the most serious antitrust violations. Remember that many innocent contacts may look like concerted action. Once the Government begins a criminal investigation, it would be a felony to destroy relevant evidence to impede the investigation.

All outside inquiries regarding the Company's practices under the antitrust laws should be promptly and firmly referred to the Vice President and General Counsel without reply, including oral or written requests for information from the United States Department of Justice, the Federal Trade Commission, and the attorneys general of the various states. The Vice President and General Counsel is responsible for responding to all such requests.

FORM 3

Sample Antitrust Compliance Manual

Foreword

(Letterhead of Chairman of the Board)

TO: ALL SALARIED EMPLOYEES

I welcome the opportunity to restate to all salaried employees, worldwide, the Company's policy to comply with the letter and the spirit of the antitrust laws. The antitrust guidelines contained in this booklet are intended to assist each of you in meeting your individual compliance responsibilities. Unlike most laws, antitrust affects virtually every activity of the Company from general management to engineering, sales, marketing, international, licensing, pricing, purchasing, and other functions. All employees, therefore, should pay heed to these guidelines.

Compliance with law in general is an important aspect of doing business. The laws that govern our domestic and foreign business are many and complex. Further, as the Company grows in size and diversity, the interpretation of laws and their effect on the Company's operations, and our business decisions—your decisions and my decisions—can change.

Over the years, the Company has grown significantly. We have succeeded because of newer and better products and services and the conscientious efforts of our employees. This is entirely consistent with the antitrust laws. Our success and growth, however, make it even more important for each of us to understand, and comply with, the antitrust laws.

It is the policy of the Company to comply with the antitrust laws of the United States, the several states, foreign countries, and various multinational groups such as the European Economic Community. These laws are intended to prevent and eliminate any agreements and individual conduct that would interfere unreasonably with the operation of the marketplace. They protect the workability of the markets the Company serves, and accordingly constitute a positive, business-oriented force.

The Company through its compliance is contributing to the overall economic health of the markets in which it participates. Moreover, through its compliance, the Company avoids the substantial financial and other business risks associated with noncompliance, as well as the criminal prosecution of the Company, its officers, and employees.

Company counsel prepared this booklet to assist you in understanding basic antitrust principles and to highlight some of the more frequently encountered applications. The purpose is not to train you to decide antitrust questions, but to help you recognize when they are present so that you can obtain advice from Company counsel, preferably at an early date rather than at the last moment. Due to the nature of these laws, which involve a mixture of law, economics, and government policy, their interpretation and application change over time. Whenever questions arise, it is mandatory that we consult with Company counsel who have expertise in this important area of the law. The Vice President and General Counsel and his staff are anxious to help you achieve your business objectives in ways that do not create legal problems for you or the Company.

I ask each of you, including in particular both new employees and personnel who have joined the Company through acquisition, to read these guidelines carefully and to keep this booklet within reach for easy reference.

____

Chairman of the Board

Introduction

I would like to take this opportunity to mention briefly a few general points about the antitrust laws, which I believe each employee should keep in mind in reviewing these guidelines. These laws apply to a wide range of business practices, the legality of which depend on the circumstances of each situation.

However, a few practices are considered to be so anticompetitive that they always are deemed to be unlawful. These are described in more detail in the guidelines that follow. The most prominent of these is any scheme to fix or affect prices among competitors. Practices such as price fixing constitute a felony crime under the federal antitrust laws, and the individuals who participate in such practices could be imprisoned (and frequently are) under the antitrust laws for up to three years and fined in an amount up to $100,000. In such instances, the Company can be fined as much as $1 million. In addition, the individuals involved might be charged with other federal crimes such as mail or wire fraud and the organized-crime control laws. The number of federal criminal grand juries investigating possible antitrust violations has increased steadily over the last few years. In 1982 alone, the government collected $36 million in antitrust fines, and businesspeople were sentenced to 7000 jail days of incarceration.

Conviction for a felony could involve the individual in substantial personal expenses for legal defense costs, which might not be reimbursed by the Company, and could result in discharge of employment. Also, one's right to vote and to participate in various professions could be terminated. That would be a terrible price to pay for a temporary business advantage. I can think of no greater humiliation than a criminal indictment and conviction. The last section of these guidelines sets forth simple rules of conduct for avoiding these most serious problems.

Such violations also can draw the Company into extremely costly treble-damages litigation brought by private individuals. The cost of defending such claims, including lawyers fees and expenses, easily could amount to millions of dollars. If the Company were to lose or settle such a case, it also could be liable for tens and even hundreds of millions of dollars in damages and the plaintiff's own legal fees. Moreover, as to some violations, the Company's business future could be seriously jeopardized through court orders imposing rigid business restrictions on the Company's future activities.

The enclosed guidelines are intended to acquaint employees with legitimate antitrust concerns so that they can spot potential problems and refer such situations to the Company counsel at an early stage for proper advice. Throughout these guidelines, there are references to various required legal review situations, and these are listed at the end of these guidelines for your convenience. Each operating unit has an assigned Company counsel, who should be contacted in these situations. They are anxious to provide you with practical advice. Any employee should feel free to contact me directly with respect to any ongoing practice within the Company that the employee feels might involve a serious antitrust violation, and I will endeavor where requested to preserve the confidential nature of such communications to the greatest possible extent.

Before closing, I would like to remind you of one important practice. It is important that all employees refer to the Legal Department any requests for information, whether by telephone, in person, or in writing, received from any government representative, or from an outside private party, that relates to the Company's competitive practices. The Legal Department will supervise the preparation of an appropriate response and submit the proper information to the requesting party.

____

Vice President and
General Counsel

The Antitrust Laws

The federal antitrust laws are for the most part very general. They do not identify all of the types of conduct that are or may be unlawful. The four basic federal laws governing the antitrust area are known as the *Sherman Act*, the *Clayton Act*, the *Robinson-Patman Act* and the *Federal Trade Commission Act*.

- *The Sherman Act* contains the broad general rules and policies governing the antitrust field. In general, it prohibits "every contract, combination or conspiracy" that unreasonably restrains trade, and it also prohibits monopolizing (or attempting or conspiring to monopolize) any part of trade or commerce.
- *The Clayton Act* contains three basic prohibitions on conduct that may be anticompetitive and unreasonably restrain trade under certain circumstances. These prohibitions on conduct include: (1) exclusive-dealing agreements, "requirements" contracts, and "tying" arrangements with distributors, retailers, or customers; (2) corporate mergers; and (3) individuals serving at the same time as directors of two or more competing corporations. These guidelines will not deal with the third prohibition, since it is not of direct concern to most employees of the Corporation in their daily activities.
- *The Robinson-Patman Act* (technically section 2 of the Clayton Act) generally prohibits discrimination in prices or services between purchasers, the effect of which is to injure competition. Purchasers who induce discrimination in favor of themselves can also be held liable.
- *The Federal Trade Commission Act* supplements the Sherman and Clayton Acts and prohibits "unfair methods of competition in or affecting interstate commerce and unfair or deceptive acts or practices in or affecting interstate commerce." This act also give the Federal Trade Commission the power to promulgate rules of competitive conduct, violations of which are punishable by substantial fines, and therefore may be more restrictive in some respects than either the Sherman or Clayton Acts.

During recent years, federal authorities have given increasing attention to enforcement of the federal antitrust laws. Congress has recently amended these laws to provide increased penalties for violations and to enlarge the enforcement powers of such authorities.

In addition to the federal laws, many states have their own antitrust laws, frequently patterned after the federal statutes, which reach local activity not involving or affecting interstate commerce.

Activities Subject to Criminal Prosecution

The government has been severe in applying criminal penalties to agreements among competitors intended to limit competition. Agreements such as price fixing or price tampering cause monopoly-like conditions to prevail in markets without any compensating benefit to the public.

The penalties for such unlawful agreements, both under and outside the antitrust laws, are described in the Introduction to these guidelines, and they are severe. All Company employees are expected to take the precautions set forth at the end of these guidelines. Following these simple rules can avoid the most serious situations.

The following are the more common practices among competitors likely to precipitate a criminal action:

- Price fixing/tampering
- Bid rigging
- Customer allocation
- Market allocation
- Production allocation
- Boycotts (joint refusals to deal)
- Joint selling (with exceptions)
- Patent pooling (with exceptions)
- Price exchanges
- Actual or attempted monopolizing

This list is not all-inclusive, and other like agreements among competitors could evolve into a criminal case. Even legitimate transactions with competitors, such as export trade associations, patent infringement settlements, joint research and development, standardization and certification programs, joint appeals for government action, and information exchange programs could result in criminal prosecution and costly treble-damage actions unless carefully monitored and controlled. Please refer in this regard to the following discussion of trade associations in these guidelines.

There literally are no excuses to justify such practices. A violator could not use as a defense the fact that some competition continues (either among other competitors or on other bases such as service or technology), that there is substantial plant overcapacity or rampant discounting, that prices are merely exchanged and not agreed upon, that competing offers need to be verified, that prices were fixed at reasonable levels, or even that the government was aware of the activity.

While the antitrust laws require an *agreement* among competitors to create criminal liability, this term does not mean the same thing as the typical business contract. Such an agreement need not be in writing. A court or jury might infer it from a course of dealing and series of actions among members of an industry. Such conduct might include a pattern of price announcements within the industry or prices that rise or remain constant when demand falls. Pricing actions and announcements intended primarily as a signal to competitors could be construed as a device to facilitate agreement on industry prices. Company employees involved in industries that have been deregulated (e.g., transportation) and no longer are protected from antitrust attack by government immunity must learn through consultation with Company counsel how the antitrust laws now affect their activities. Membership in an export trade association must be approved by Company counsel.

No employee may exchange a price list with a competitor, and any price list of a competitor obtained from a customer or other indirect source must be labeled as to its source. No Company employee may discuss with a competitor anything that relates to pricing or bidding, any aspect of the marketing of products or services, or any other sensitive competitive information. If any representative of a competitor raises such a subject with a Company employee, the employee should request that the discussion stop. If the request is not promptly honored, the Company employee should terminate the discussion. Employees must be extremely careful that prohibited subjects do not creep into conversations with competitors at otherwise legitimate gatherings, such as meetings of trade associations and professional societies, trade shows, local civic activities and business and social clubs, supplier demonstrations and technical presentations, and even neighborhood conversations. Questions regarding communications with competitors should be referred to Company counsel for guidance.

Trade and Professional Associations and Other Groups

Trade, professional, industry, and similar associations perform many legitimate and useful functions, such as providing members with general business information; informing the government of industry problems and needs; developing voluntary test, performance, and product standards that improve safety and efficiency; and solving environmental, safety, and similar industrywide problems.

On the other hand, these associations frequently are the occasion when competitors meet one another, and this fact alone calls for considerable caution. In addition, unless properly monitored by competent antitrust counsel, associations may adopt or undertake restrictive codes of conduct, compulsory performance or product standards, restrictive membership requirements, exchanges of confidential financial data, joint engineering of products, and restrictive certification programs, each of which may involve antitrust problems.

Accordingly, the Company's Corporate Letters of Instruction provide that the Vice President and General Counsel or his delegate will be notified before the Company applies for membership in any trade, professional, industry, or similar association. The purpose of this procedure is to give Company counsel the opportunity to review the charter and bylaws, existing programs, and antitrust safeguards of such associations before a final decision is made to join. Following the decision to join an association, it is the responsibility of each Group Vice President and appropriate Corporate Vice President to assure that an antitrust monitoring program has been set up with Company counsel for that association. Employees who hold individual memberships in such associations, such as ASME and ASTM, will be individually responsible for obtaining guidance from Company counsel with respect to their own activities in order to assure that their conduct will not harm the interests of the Company. The Legal Department maintains appropriate records relating to the associations reviewed by it. Any questions that develop concerning the lawfulness of the conduct of any outside group to which the Company or a Company employee belongs should be referred immediately to Company counsel.

Company employees who attend meetings of an association, whether in this country or a foreign country, should avoid all discussions with representatives of competing firms on subjects not on the agenda for such meetings. Standardization, certification and price, output, credit, or other information exchange programs in which such employees participate should be brought to the attention of Company counsel for their review.

Occasionally, associations and informal coalitions of competitors deem it important to make joint presentations to the legislative, executive, and judicial branches of federal and state, and foreign governments on matters affecting their industry, including questions dealing with exports and imports of goods and services. Companies have a constitutional right to make such presentations. However, since participation in such joint industry activities could have unlawful spillover effects, any participation must be reviewed in advance with the Vice President and General Counsel or his delegate.

Monopolizing Conduct

Any business unit that is the largest factor in its product or service market should exercise special caution to avoid claims that it is attempting to monopolize or is monopolizing such business by forcing out, or precluding, smaller competitors through business practices considered predatory and, as a result, gaining or maintaining unlawful control over the pricing and production of such products or services.

An important point to remember is that the law does not prohibit a company from having a monopoly market share. It only prohibits the company from taking predatory or unreasonably exclusionary actions ("monopolizing conduct") in obtaining or maintaining its monopoly share. Consequently, for a violation to exist, a company must: (1) have a monopoly market share or monopoly power; and (2) use predatory or unreasonable exclusionary conduct to acquire or maintain that monopoly share.

How can a manager determine if the business unit holds a monopoly position? The law defines a monopoly as the *power* of a company, whether or not exercised, to control its prices or limit its production without losing its market share, and to exclude new competition within its market. While there are other facts that might prove the existence of such power, the law presumes (rebuttable) that a firm has a monopoly (but not necessarily unlawful) position if its market share is in the vicinity of 60 percent or more. Where other evidence of monopoly power is present, market shares of 50 percent or somewhat lower may be held sufficient to support such a legal presumption.

The "market" for making this legal presumption frequently is not the market as defined in strategic plans and market reports prepared by Company employees. The "market" for determining whether a company holds a monopoly must include all other available products or services, whether or not identical, that the company's customers could consider as reasonable substitutes for the company's products or services, since such substitutes could influence the company's pricing and levels of production. Under such circumstances, it could not be presumed that the company holds a monopoly. The term "market," therefore, should not be used in preparing strategic plans, market reports, and other written material without due regard for the legal implications involved. The Company's strategic plan and market analysis guidelines require that the term "market," as used in the Company's marketing documents, be defined and that an appropriate disclaimer be used. All strategic plans and significant market reports prepared by the Company must be reviewed with Company counsel.

How can a manager decide if the business unit is engaging in predatory or unreasonable exclusionary conduct? The most frequent antitrust question is whether a monopolist may defend or enhance its market share through competitive pricing by lowering its prices or meeting the prices of a smaller competitor, or whether such a strategy constitutes unlawful "monopolizing conduct." Under recent court decisions, a firm with monopoly power may compete on the basis of price as long as it is not pricing below cost. The courts are not clear on what measure of costs must be met, except that pricing at or above one's own anticipated average total costs does not constitute predatory pricing.

Thus, except as mentioned above, a firm with monopoly power is not legally prevented from offering lower prices or required to maintain uniform prices in order to protect smaller or less efficient competitors. No protective price umbrella is required. Nevertheless, no business unit with a monopoly or near-monopoly share in its market should offer prices below its anticipated average total costs. Business units with high market shares should review all pricing strategies and price changes in advance with Company counsel.

Besides pricing, what other competitive strategies that might exclude competitors are considered unlawful? Is there a double standard—one for the smaller competitor and a higher one for the firms holding a monopoly position? There are no clear answers to these questions, and therefore any major market strategy of such a business unit should be gone over with Company counsel before it is used in order to determine whether the strategy is reasonable under all of the relevant circumstances involved.

Certain strategies have been held lawful in a monopoly situation in addition to competitive pricing. While these strategies may tend to exclude smaller competitors, they also serve overriding business purposes that benefit the public. These strategies include a refusal to license newly developed technologies and more efficient processes, product differentiation through advertising, product changes that improve the product, failure to disclose in advance the introduction of new products, and construction of additional manufacturing capacity in anticipation of increased demand.

Conversely, the courts have been much less receptive to tie-in or exclusive-dealing arrangements and refusals to sell or deal. Under certain circumstances, these strategies could constitute unlawful practices for a firm with a monopoly market share. Disparagement of competitors, dissemination of false or misleading information, sham litigation, and other garden-variety unfair methods of competition obviously should be avoided because of their exclusionary potential and absence of legitimate business purpose. In general, any actions that lack a clear benefit to the public and have a strong potential for excluding competitors should be avoided. Any questions regarding such strategies, and other strategies not mentioned here, should be discussed with Company counsel.

Two further points on monopolization need to be mentioned. First, an attempt to monopolize is as unlawful as actual monopolizing. In this context, market shares in the range of 40 to 50 percent may trigger application of the law, particularly when there are few competitors and substantial barriers to the entry of additional competitors. The purpose or intent of the manager involved also is a critical factor here, as reflected in correspondence, strategic plans, and market reports.

Second, unlawful monopolizing or attempted monopolizing need not involve but a single firm. It is unlawful to conspire with competitors or others to commit either of these offenses. For example, joint attempts to fix or otherwise tamper with prices, and joint action with respect to exclusionary marketing strategies, could trigger the application of this law as well as criminal prosecution described elsewhere in these guidelines.

Mergers and Acquisitions

The antitrust laws apply to acquisitions by the Company of all or a part of the stock or assets of another company, as well as the sale of part of the Company's assets, wherever located. The law also applies to the creation of joint venture companies.

Legal Review Procedures.

Whether or not the law permits the proposed acquisition, sale, or joint venture depends upon the anticipated effect of the transaction on competition. This is an extremely complex area of the law, and Company counsel should be brought into each such situation as soon as serious interest develops. In this regard, the antitrust review procedures provided for in the Corporate Letters of Instruction should be followed. Company counsel must be given enough facts about the companies involved to develop a successful antitrust strategy.

Premerger Notification Requirements

Federal law requires that notice of proposed acquisitions of a specified minimum size must be given to both the Federal Trade Commission and the U.S. State Department of Justice, and that the parties wait for a period of thirty days, or more (if additional information is requested), before closing the transaction while the government studies the antitrust implications. The act covers asset acquisitions, stock acquisitions, joint ventures in company form, and mergers. (Various foreign countries have notification requirements that may apply if foreign assets are included.) The reporting regulations are complex, and questions regarding their potential application to a given situation should be directed to Company counsel.

If reporting requirements apply, both the acquiring and acquired persons must file detailed notification and report forms. In addition, each party must supply copies of certain studies and reports prepared by or for any officers or directors of each company for the purpose of evaluating the acquisition.

Importance of Market Definition

The determination of whether an acquisition, sale, or joint venture creates antitrust problems depends primarily on the determination of the "relevant" product or service market. This subject was discussed previously in connection with monopolizing market strategies. The government has published numerical guidelines that, when applied to the production or sales of competitors within a designated product or service market, provide an indication of whether the proposed transaction would be challenged. The Company's previous written reports defining the market, such as in strategic plans and market reports, would constitute relevant information. Accordingly, for much the same reasons as discussed with respect to monopolizing activities, strategic plans and significant market reports and studies must be reviewed by Company counsel before they are distributed.

In this connection, the federal premerger notification rules require submission to the government of "all studies, surveys, analyses and reports which were prepared by or for any officers or directors . . . for the purpose of evaluating or analyzing the acquisition with respect to market shares, competition, competitors, markets (and) potential for sales growth or expansion into product or geographic markets." The Company's Corporate Letters of Instruction provide that all such acquisition-specific reports and memoranda must be reviewed by Company counsel during their preparation.

International Operations

A substantial and growing part of the Company's business involves international operations. The need to serve foreign markets through exports of goods, services, and technology and foreign joint ventures has increased due to shifts in the Company's mix of products and services and the growth of foreign markets. In addition, as foreign industrial capabilities have increased, competition in various domestic markets has intensified through entry of foreign suppliers into these markets. How do the antitrust laws of this country and foreign countries affect these operations?

Activities Affecting Domestic Markets

The United States antitrust laws apply to the extent international transactions have a direct and substantial effect on competition within this country. Business strategies that would create antitrust concerns when used solely within this country and with respect to domestic competitors, customers, and suppliers, as discussed throughout these guidelines, would cause similar concerns where imports, exports, and foreign firms are involved, and occasionally even where the conduct is foreign-based. If, for example, the Company entered into a foreign-based cartel that fixed the prices or limited the supply of products or services coming into the United States, the antitrust dangers described in the discussion of Activities Subject to Criminal Prosecution would exist.

The size of markets within the country has attracted much foreign competition. Domestic companies are justifiably concerned when foreign competitors enjoy special financing privileges available from their governments and where foreign competitors are government owned or controlled. Lower-cost foreign labor may give foreign competitors a further advantage. The urge to adopt private remedies against such foreign competitors through the use of restrictive business strategies described elsewhere in these guidelines could be intense. In addition, domestic competitors may seek to bring U.S. government pressure to bear against such foreign competition through use of the courts, the Congress, and executive departments. All such activities involving the Company must be reviewed by Company counsel to assure that the Company and its employees are not exposed to significant risks under U.S. antitrust laws.

Joint Ventures and Licensing Arrangements

Joint ventures and technology licensing arrangements with foreign companies, if properly structured, should not present any antitrust difficulty. Consortium arrangements on large-scale projects, long-term research and development and manufacturing joint ventures, and long-term technology-licensing arrangements have important procompetitive aspects such as risk sharing, pooling limited resources and skills, and making technology available to more consumers. Such agreements, however, frequently have come under antitrust scrutiny due to the government's concern with respect to international price-fixing or market allocation cartels, among other potentially restrictive practices. Foreign government participation in these arrangements would not exempt the private firms involved from antitrust scrutiny. Consequently, all joint venture and licensing agreements (both foreign and domestic) must be reviewed in advance with Company counsel to ensure that they do not pose significant antitrust risks and, in the case of investment-type joint ventures, to determine whether the Company must file a preclosing notice under the federal premerger notification law. Additional information on the subject of licensing agreements appears under the discussion of Patents and Trademarks later in these guidelines.

Export Trade Associations and Other Activities Affecting Foreign Markets

To promote export trade, Congress passed the Webb-Pomerene Act and, more recently, the Export Trading Act, which provide certain exemptions from U.S. antitrust laws for joint export activities by competing U.S. companies. Both acts require formal application to and certification by the government. These laws, however, do not provide any immunity with respect to ancillary activities that unreasonably restrain domestic commerce or the export trade of domestic competitors that are not members of the joint export association. Similarly, these laws do not afford their members any protection under the antitrust laws of foreign countries that might be affected by such joint export arrangements. Accordingly, as in the case of trade associations, any participation by the Company in joint export associations must be approved in advance by Company counsel.

Other business activities also may subject the Company to the antitrust or competition laws of foreign countries and international organizations. While it can be assumed for the most part that these foreign laws reach the same types of practices and arrangements as do the U.S. antitrust laws, there are some differences. Indeed, in some cases, practices considered lawful under U.S. law may be considered unlawful in a foreign country, particularly countries that do not have the same type of market economy as the United States.

Perhaps the most prominent foreign antitrust laws are articles 85 and 86 of the Treaty of Rome, which established the European Economic Community (or Common Market) in 1962. The ten member states of the Common Market in which articles 85 and 86 apply are Belgium, Denmark, West Germany, Greece, France, Ireland, Italy, the Netherlands, the United Kingdom, and Luxembourg. Spain and Portugal are negotiating to become members. The general approach of articles 85 and 86 is comparable to the basic U.S. antitrust laws. One important difference, however, is that the Common Market has a preclearance procedure under which all business transactions or agreements that may fall under the broadly defined coverage of articles 85 and 86 must be reported to the Competition Office of the Common Market, which subsequently may clear, exempt, modify, or prohibit the arrangement.

Most of the Common Market countries also have their own antitrust laws, which apply to the extent they are not in conflict with articles 85 and 86. Of these countries, West Germany and the United Kingdom probably have the most well-developed and energetically enforced competition laws. Other countries, such as Canada, Japan, and Australia, also have been active in recent years in promulgating and enforcing antitrust and other trade regulation laws.

Dealings with Suppliers and Customers

There are several areas in which our relationships with our suppliers and customers should be closely scrutinized to avoid antitrust problems. Company employees need to be aware of the antitrust problems associated with these practices, whether they are acting in the role of a supplier (e.g., manufacturer, franchisor, or other selling activity) or as a customer (e.g., purchaser of raw materials or functioning as a distributor or retailer).

Resale Price Fixing

The term "resale price fixing" means any agreement between a seller and its customers to limit their freedom to set their own prices. Any such agreement or understanding with dealers or distributors, whether written or oral, is unlawful. It makes no difference whether the prices are set high, low, or in the middle or whether the majority of the customers are pleased with the arrangement.

A seller is permitted to publish and supply its customers with lists of "suggested resale prices." However, all such lists must be conspicuously marked as suggested prices. Preticketing packaged products without more also is acceptable. But the seller may not exert pressure on nonconforming customers to follow the suggested or preticketed prices. As previously discussed, an unlawful agreement under the antitrust laws may be inferred from a course of conduct of the parties. For example, a pattern of criticism and threats of termination or other coercive actions directed against nonconforming customers may be enough evidence from which to infer an unlawful agreement with conforming customers to punish nonconforming customers, particularly where such actions are followed up by termination of, or refusals to deal with, the offending customers. Ambiguous writings and statements by the seller's employees may increase the antitrust risk. Similarly, offers of benefits, such as promotional allowances, should not be conditioned upon compliance with published resale prices.

Oral or written complaints from conforming customers concerning the pricing practices of other customers in competition with them are particularly troublesome. The Company, when acting as a dealer or distributor, should not join in such complaints. When acting as the seller, Company employees should refer to Company counsel any complaint regarding resale pricing. It is the Company's policy not to engage in resale price fixing, and responses to questions regarding the Company's policy should so state. If a written response is necessary, it should be prepared by Company counsel.

Every termination must be based on good and sufficient business reasons and be communicated in writing. A nonperforming distributor or dealer should be given reasonable advance warnings of possible termination. All termination notices must be reviewed by Company counsel before their transmittal. The groundwork for a proper termination should be laid well in advance in consultation with Company counsel, and files should be reviewed to ensure that the case for legitimate termination is strong.

Refusals to Deal

Any agreement between the Company and a customer or supplier under which the Company or such other party agrees not to sell to, or buy from, another person (or class of persons) may raise antitrust concerns, particularly where the agreement results in the termination of other existing suppliers or customers.

An agreement with distributors or dealers that compels them to purchase all their requirements of a product from the Company or not to deal with the Company's competitors (or an agreement with suppliers compelling them to supply the Company with all of their output) could raise antitrust concerns. Such concern would arise where competitors are foreclosed from essential sources of supply or outlets for their products so as to significantly limit or destroy their ability to enter or remain in the market.

Whether an exclusive dealing agreement or requirements contract is lawful would depend upon a detailed inquiry into such matters as whether the restrictions are industrywide, the number of competitors in the relevant market and their market share, the degree of foreclosure of competitors due to the arrangement, the market share of the participants, and the duration of the arrangement. Such agreements should not be entered into without prior review by Company counsel.

Geographic Restrictions and Dual Distribution

It is lawful for a seller to appoint a sole distributor or dealer in a particular territory, assign a geographic area of responsibility, and require the dealer or distributor to achieve reasonable sales goals set by the seller in the assigned territory. When a customer fails to perform these requirements, a seller may lawfully terminate the customer after proper documentation of the legitimate business reasons for termination.

However, restrictions on sales or advertising outside an assigned territory would raise antitrust concerns if they restrain trade unreasonably. Whether such restrictions are reasonable would depend upon the same factors as discussed with respect to customer restrictions and refusals to deal. Consequently, territorial and other customer restraints should not be imposed or agreed upon without careful consideration and approval by Company counsel.

It is lawful for a seller to compete with its dealers or distributors or other customers. For example, a seller may become a "dual distributor" by selling direct to dealers and also establishing its own dealer or retail network. In such circumstances, however, greater caution is necessary in assigning areas of sales responsibility. Prices and other terms and conditions of sale should not be discussed with such competing dealers. Since the seller has entered into competition with its customers, they might be viewed by some courts as direct competitors. Consequently, any dual-distribution situation should be carefully reviewed and approved in advance and closely monitored by Company counsel.

Tying Agreements

A tie-in occurs when a seller offers a product (the tying product) on condition that the customer also purchases another product (the tied product). Services as well as products may be the subject of a questionable tie-in. Full-line forcing is a form of tie-in that occurs when a seller requires the customer to purchase all or most of an entire line of products in order to obtain any particular part of the line. The legality of such arrangements would depend upon several factors: Are the tying and tied products actually two separate products? Does the seller possess substantial economic power in the market for the tying product? Is there a substantial effect on competition in the tied product? The determination of whether a tie-in exists and whether it is legal is complex, so that any proposal to employ such an arrangement should be discussed in advance with Company counsel.

Reciprocity

Any practice of linking the Company's purchases from a supplier to its sales to that supplier is against Company policy and may violate the antitrust laws. Company employees should not refer to past or contemplated purchases during sales negotiations. Any suggestion or request for reciprocal dealing by persons outside the Company should be brought to the attention of Company counsel.

Price and Service Discrimination

The antitrust laws provide that a seller may not discriminate in price between buyers of the same product where the effect may be to lessen or injure competition among (1) the seller and its competitors, (2) the favored purchaser and its competitors, or (3) the customers of the favored purchaser and their competitors.

The purpose of this area of the law is to protect small competitors, particularly at the purchaser level. The application of this law, which is invoked primarily by private parties, is not always consistent with the aims of the other antitrust laws; nevertheless, injured firms frequently bring potentially costly treble-damage actions in this area, making familiarity with this subject essential. Each Company manager responsible for pricing shall arrange for Company counsel to review any nonuniform pricing in order to control the risk of damages from price discrimination.

Discrimination in price refers to the net price after deducting all discounts, rebates, and allowances. Thus, the granting of free goods, special credit terms, special freight allowances, or the like to a favored buyer may constitute a violation. For the law to apply, there must be at least two completed sales. The law does not apply to discrimination in lease rates, consignment or license fees, or royalties. Further, the disfavored purchaser must have purchased the product within the United States; export sales are not covered by this law. The sale must involve goods, and the products must be of "like grade and quality" and sold within a reasonably contemporaneous time period. Finally, for recovery of damages, there must be proof of actual injury (i.e., lost sales) to the disfavored purchaser, which damages are causally related to the price difference.

The law has several exemptions. One involves charging a lower price due to changed market conditions. Sales to nonprofit institutions and the government are exempt, unless the buying entity involved is engaged in commercial activity in competition with private firms. The law permits the granting of allowances for bona fide services performed at the intended distribution level. Where lower prices are offered in only one area of the country for competitive reasons, it is unlikely that the law will apply unless the lower prices are below the seller's average total costs. Finally, the law does not apply to bona fide bid situations where a good-faith effort is made to become the winning bidder absent a predatory purpose.

In addition, the law does not apply where a lower price reflects lower costs or is granted to meet competition. A seller may discriminate in price if the lower price reflects savings in the cost of manufacture, sale, or delivery resulting from differing methods or quantities in which goods are sold or delivered. This is a complex and difficult defense, usually requiring detailed cost studies prepared before a price concession, such as a quantity discount, is allowed. Any such study must be reviewed by Company counsel.

As to meeting a competitor's price, a seller is protected even if it undercuts a competitor if acting under a reasonable, good-faith belief that it is only meeting an equally low price actually offered by a competitor. Further, a seller may avail itself of the meeting-competition defense in adopting a good-faith local or regional pricing system in response to a competitor's pricing system in the same area. Meeting competition should be used only pursuant to special procedures approved by Company counsel, which include systematic and reasonable methods for obtaining the best information available as to a competitor's lower price. Under no circumstances may a Company employee contact a competitor to verify the competitor's lower price, since such action may appear to be unlawful price fixing.

The most sensitive and risky area of the law relates to the granting of promotional or advertising allowances or promotional services or materials to customers in connection with the resale of a product. Any such allowances, services, or materials should be extended to all competing customers on a proportionately equal basis. Where such benefits are provided to wholesale customers, commitments must be obtained from such wholesalers to redistribute such benefits on a proportionately equal basis. In each instance, there must be a written plan for such benefits that has been approved by Company counsel.

Two other activities should be mentioned here. Before brokers are used, the brokerage program, including broker's fees, should be reviewed by Company counsel. Finally, Company employees engaged in purchasing raw materials, components, and other products for internal consumption or resale must avoid agreements with suppliers intended to injure smaller competitors. However, it is entirely lawful for Company employees to negotiate the best prices, terms, and conditions available to the Company for the purpose of meeting the Company's needs.

Unfair Methods of Competition and Unfair or Deceptive Trade Practices

Federal law prohibits unfair methods of competition and unfair or deceptive acts or practices in interstate commerce. Most states have similar laws, and state courts have allowed plaintiffs to recover damages for competitive harm caused by such practices. While not all such practices amount to antitrust violations, some actions of a predatory nature, as explained below, also may violate the antitrust laws. It is contrary to Company policy to engage in any of the practices described below.

What constitutes an unfair method of competition? There is no precise definition, but the concept is broad enough to cover any unethical or unfair practice directed against a competitor. The following practices have been held illegal: bribing a competitor's or customer's employee; industrial espionage; stealing or otherwise wrongfully obtaining a competitor's trade secrets, designs, technical data, or other proprietary or confidential information; sales promotion lottery schemes; disparaging a competitor or its products or communicating false or unfair statements or rumors about a competitor; or inducing the breach of a contract between a competitor and one of its customers, suppliers, or employees.

What constitutes an unfair or deceptive act or practice? Again, there is no precise definition, but the concept covers any unethical or unfair practice directed against *consumers*. The following types of business activities are illustrative: false or misleading advertising, testimonials and salespeople's representations; misleading packaging and labeling, including failure to disclose the foreign origin of a product; and "bait and switch" tactics, e.g., advertising low-priced products not generally available or usable. Whether an advertisement or product claim is false or misleading depends on the content of the material and the overall impression it creates. All advertising claims should be substantiated before publication. This means that the necessary documentation to prove a claim must be assembled and maintained. All advertisements must be reviewed by Company counsel before publication.

Exemptions from the Antitrust Laws

Congress and the courts have created a number of exemptions to the antitrust laws. Special exemptions exist for many regulated industries. In addition, there are exemptions for organized labor, export trade, lobbying, state or local government action, and certain defense contracts. Only the exemptions most relevant to the Company are discussed in these guidelines.

Transportation Exemption

Commercial motor, rail, and air transportation industries have been regulated by the Interstate Commerce Commission and the Civil Aeronautics Board. Due to this regulation, carriers and shippers have enjoyed a broad statutory immunity from the antitrust laws. New legislation, however, provides for the phased deregulation of the air and surface (motor carrier and railroad) transportation industries and the substitution of competition to determine the price and availability of transportation services. The Civil Aeronautics Board was abolished in 1985, and the regulatory functions of the Interstate Commerce Commission have been sharply curtailed in many areas.

The specific changes brought about by the new legislation are many and complex, and beyond the scope of these guidelines. However, these changes have removed or will shortly remove antitrust immunity from a number of formerly exempt joint activities by shippers and carriers. For example, the standards and basis for challenging carrier certificates of operation have been narrowed. Joint discussion or voting on single-line rates by rate bureaus has been eliminated, and such discussions now will constitute unlawful price fixing.

The important point for Company employees who work in transportation or deal with the transportation industry is that transportation services now are subject to antitrust standards. Accordingly, these guidelines are intended to apply equally to all such activities. Particularly to avoid inadvertent antitrust violations, Company counsel should be consulted regarding the lawfulness of particular activities when any question about them arises.

Government Procurement

The antitrust laws apply generally to federal, state, and local government procurement and projects. In certain circumstances, however, courts have allowed a limited exemption from the antitrust laws for certain commercial activities where the state legislature has provided for the state or local authorities to regulate such activities. No antitrust exemption should be assumed or relied upon unless the subject activity has been reviewed in advance and approved by Company counsel.

Lobbying and Joint Efforts to Influence Government Action

The U.S. Constitution protects business entities when they petition any branch of the government, using joint efforts to obtain legislative, executive, or judicial action, even if the requested action would eliminate competition.

The courts, however, have construed this exemption narrowly to include only bona fide efforts to influence government action. They have held, for example, that the exemption does not apply where the lobbying campaign or joint action is a mere sham, the real purpose being to harass a competitor; where there is an attempt to influence government officials engaged in purely commercial, rather than policymaking or regulatory activities; where concerted efforts to influence government action are accompanied by illegal predatory or fraudulent practices; and where the public official becomes a co-conspirator in a conscious effort to restrain trade.

The greatest antitrust concern in this area is that competitors may exchange information as part of an exempt joint presentation to the government and, in the process, use such information to restrain competition among themselves. Joint efforts by competitors to lobby or influence government action frequently take place through trade or business associations and ad hoc political coalitions. All such joint efforts with competitors must be reviewed in advance with Company counsel to assure that reasonable precautions are taken to avoid any serious antitrust risks.

Protection from Unfair Foreign Competition

The United States has enacted laws under which domestic companies can respond to unfair methods of competition and other predatory practices of foreign firms, such as predatory pricing, within the United States. These laws are directed at such practices as dumping, patent infringement, and foreign government subsidies. They give U.S. companies and trade associations the right to petition the Office of the United States Trade Representative, the Commerce Department, and the International Trade Commission to investigate and take action against violations. Since the harm contemplated by these laws usually affects entire industries, the action to evoke these laws often involves trade associations or other group of competitors. Any participation by the Company in such joint efforts to enforce our rights under these laws should be cleared in advance with Company counsel.

Document Production and Review

The records of a company often become the controlling factor in antitrust cases, particularly as to issues involving the proper market definition, as in monopoly and merger cases, and where the intent of the company is important, as in attempted monopoly and distribution restraint cases. What Company employees write has considerable evidentiary value in court, because writings constitute a contemporaneous and candid statement prepared in the performance of the individual's work on behalf of the Company.

For this reason, these guidelines provide in several areas for the review of certain documents before their dissemination. These antitrust review requirements are listed at the end of these guidelines. The courts have recognized that managers on the front line of the competitive struggle understandably tend to exaggerate, and that they may not always describe a competitive situation objectively. Use of such words as "dominant" to describe one's market position, and defining the market in a manner to give one's operation a dominant market share illustrate the point. Nevertheless, adversaries are certain to use such written statements as evidence against the Company in antitrust cases, many of which are before juries. It often is difficult to explain away such statements.

Review by Company counsel of important documents will help to reduce these risks, but the primary responsibility remains with each employee. One important purpose of these guidelines and related antitrust training within the Company is to make each employee sensitive to statements that could create unnecessary and unjustified antitrust concern. Embarrassing documents cannot be disposed of once an antitrust case begins. Indeed, it would be a serious crime to knowingly destroy written evidence once a government investigation has begun or during the course of a trial.

Company employees should assume that everything they write, in connection with their work, whether in the Company's files, at home, or elsewhere, eventually will become a public record. This should not surprise a sophisticated business person. The Company may have to volunteer documents in order to comply with various laws, such as giving the government notice of an acquisition. Courts have power to order the disclosure of the Company's records whether or not it is a party to the case. Government agencies have almost unlimited rights to obtain the Company's records in the course of carrying out investigations. While company counsel can take certain actions to limit discovery to documents relevant to an investigation or action, they cannot withhold relevant documents because they contain exaggerated or erroneous statements. The only way to prevent this is for each employee to write accurately in the first place. Certain documents prepared by, or under the supervision of, Company counsel are subject to the attorney-client privilege and are immune from disclosure.

Patents, Technology, Copyrights, and Trademarks

The owner of a patent, copyright, or trademark is the recipient of a government-granted monopoly in the United States and many foreign countries with the right to exclude others from the use of an invention, literary or artistic work, or mark. For example, the owner of a product or process patent can prevent the importation (but not exportation) of foreign products that incorporate the patented invention. The owner of a product or process patent also is free to fully exploit such patent rights by licensing others in return for a fee and royalties. The rights to exclude and to license are incentives created by law to foster inventions and in consideration of publicizing such inventions.

Unpatented technology (know-how), which is included in a patent license but which often is licensed separately, does not enjoy statutory protection, unlike patents. Owners of such information must retain such information in secret in order to protect it, and require licensees to maintain the confidentiality of such information. The law protects such proprietary information only in the event of theft and to the extent it has not become public. The owner of an invention has the option of patenting the invention, if patentable, or retaining it in secret. Some inventions are not novel enough to qualify for a patent, but may be retained in secret and perhaps exploited as such.

The courts have permitted certain restraints upon competition in agreements licensing valuable patent rights and know-how in recognition of policy considerations favoring inventions, but the only restraints that will be upheld are those which are reasonably ancillary to the transfer of such rights and reasonable in duration and scope. The following are examples of conduct that could raise antitrust concerns:

- Obtaining a patent by use of fraud or misrepresentation, e.g., intentional failure to disclose "prior art" (always unlawful)
- Enforcing or licensing a fraudulently procured patent (always unlawful)
- Acquiring title to patents and know-how from the original owner
- Requiring a licensee of a patent or know-how to purchase materials or services from the owner of the patent or know-how
- Requiring a licensee to assign to the patent owner title to any future patent that may be issued to the licensee
- Restricting a purchaser of a patented product (or one that incorporates secret know-how) in the resale of that product
- Restricting a licensee's freedom to deal in products or services not within the scope of a licensed patent or know-how
- Agreeing with one licensee not to license others without the original licensee's consent
- Requiring the licensee to take, and pay for, unwanted patents or know-how as a condition to licensing a wanted patent or know-how
- Insisting that a licensee pay royalties in an amount not reasonably related to the licensee's sales of products covered by a patent or know-how
- Requiring a licensee to adhere to a specified or minimum price with respect to the licensee's sale of products incorporating a licensed patent or know-how
- Charging discriminatory royalty rates to different licensees
- Requiring that royalties be paid after the patent or know-how license has expired

Note that these provisions and arrangements for patent and technology licensing may be perfectly lawful under certain circumstances. The legality of arrangements for patent and technology licensing must be determined on a case-by-case basis. The Company could be exposed to disastrous consequences, such as being compelled to license anyone, should its licensing arrangements be found to violate the antitrust laws. It is Company policy that all license agreements must be reviewed by Company counsel, as well as the Patent Department.

Antitrust Rules of Conduct

Rule One: Don't Talk Prices with Competitors

In part, this means don't talk about prices, or other terms and conditions of sale, with a competitor except in bona fide supplier-customer situations. But this isn't all it means. Don't discuss actual costs with a competitor. Stay away from "shop talk" with competitors at trade shows, professional meetings, and the like.

Rule Two: Don't Give Our Price Lists to a Competitor: Never Accept a Price List from a Competitor

Where a price list from a competitor is in your files, or where our price lists are in a competitor's files, it looks as if you have talked about prices with a competitor. Return all price lists received directly from competitors. If you get a price list from a customer (or from some other source other than the competitor itself), make a record of how and from whom the price list was obtained.

Rule Three: Don't Talk to Competitors about Customers

If you violate this rule, you may lose a customer. If you keep the customer, it may look as if you're agreeing with a competitor to stay away from its accounts and that it will stay away from yours. Your accounts are your own business. Similarly, do not discuss sales territories or any subject dealing in any way with the marketing or sale of products or services.

Rule Four: Don't Talk to Competitors about Bids

If you tell someone what you're going to bid, the competitor may make the same bid. When bids are the same or close, the antitrust enforcement authorities may suspect that you've agreed to submit the same bid. On the other hand, if the competitor makes a lower bid, you lose the business. And if either one makes a higher bid, the antitrust enforcement authorities may suspect that you have an agreement to rotate the business.

Rule Five: Don't Make Telephone Calls to Competitors

Telephone lists are kept by the telephone company and by our own operators. By being able to prove the fact of a telephone call, antitrust enforcement authorities and treble-damage plaintiffs may infer that you have talked about something that violates the antitrust laws. Also, competitors may take notes or record your discussion, which could be subpoenaed. Occasionally, you may need to make or receive telephone calls to or from a competitor in connection with safety matters, bona fide trade association activities, technical problems, professional societies, purchase or sales in the ordinary course of business, emergency situations, etc. Exercise great caution to limit the conversation to these lawful matters.

Rule Six: Don't Refuse Anyone's Business Without Clearance

Let the head office know if you plan to turn down business for some reason other than Financial Department objections to a potential customer's credit standing or terms of payment or Legal Department or executive objections to proposed contract terms. The head office can clear the problem with Company counsel. If you refuse potential business, antitrust enforcement authorities and the rejected customer may think you're part of a conspiracy to boycott the customer, or are dividing customers with competitors, or are trying to monopolize a market.

Rule Seven: Don't Impose Resale Restrictions Without Clearance

Don't refuse, or threaten to refuse, anyone's business or offer any benefit as a means to fix or affect resale prices. (It is lawful to suggest resale prices clearly labeled as such.)

Rule Eight: Don't Discriminate among Customers

When selling standardized products, do not discriminate in price or promotional allowances between competing customers except to meet competition, unless you check with Company counsel to assure that such concessions are lawful.

Rule Nine: Don't Refuse to Buy Because the Supplier Won't Reciprocate

It is the firm policy of the Company to base all purchase decisions solely on quality, price, delivery terms, and other legitimate factors. Company salespeople may not discuss with the Purchasing Department the purchases the Company makes from individual customers or prospective customers. Salespeople may not discuss with customers the purchases the Company makes or could make from such customers.

Rule Ten: Don't Join Trade Associations or Professional Societies Without Clearance

The government may suspect that information exchange and standardization programs are part of a price-fixing scheme or a boycott of nonmembers. Do not participate in association programs without discussing them with Company counsel. All new Company memberships in trade associations and professional societies must be reviewed in advance with the Vice President and General Counsel.

Antitrust Review Procedures

The following agreements, reports, and memberships must be reviewed with and cleared by Company counsel for antitrust purposes before their execution, dissemination, or acceptance:

- All joint selling agreements with competitors, including export trade association memberships
- All patent and technology license agreements and joint venture agreements for research and development
- All joint venture agreements establishing a continuing business relationship between the partners, whether for a single project or an indefinite manufacturing or service business.
- All original applications for membership by the Company in trade, professional, industry, or similar associations
- All joint presentations with competitors to the legislative, executive, or judicial branches of federal, state, or foreign governments
- All new market strategies of any operating unit that is the largest factor in its market
- All strategic plans prepared by the Company
- All significant market studies and reports prepared internally or by consultants
- All acquisitions and dispositions of assets or securities
- All reports submitted to any government antitrust agency, including reports under the Hart-Scott-Rodino Pre-Merger Notification Act
- All distribution agreements containing resale restrictions
- All price concessions to less than all competing customers, and all customer-level promotional programs
- All outside inquiries regarding the Company's practices under the antitrust laws and responses thereto

FORM 4

Sample Employee Certificate

[Company Letterhead]

This will acknowledge that I have received and read the STATEMENT OF POLICY AND ANTITRUST GUIDELINES FOR COMPANY EMPLOYEES.

Signature ____

Date ____

FORM 5

Sample Audit Questions

General—Company and Industry Overview

1. List the products manufactured or sold by the company.
2. Describe the end uses/characteristics; prices; industry recognition; special vendors/buyers; special production facilities related to each product.
3. List your competitors by product in the United States and their estimated market share.
4. When did each competitor enter the market? Have any firms exited the market? Are there any potential entrants? Identify and describe each such firm.
5. What are the barriers to entry in each market identified? What do you need to enter and compete effectively?
   - Capital cost (plant, land, and equipment)
   - Raw material (absolute cost)
   - Patents, economies of scale, product differentiation, other
6. Who are the major consumers/customers for the company's products? How strong are they economically? Do they exercise any power over price? Give examples. Would a 5 percent price increase provoke new entry or product substitution?
7. What is the company and industry profitability? How is it measured? How does it compare with other similar businesses?
8. Is there any known or suspected anticompetitive conduct in the subject industry in the United States or abroad? Is there any company or industry history of antitrust or competition litigation or investigation or complaints by government or private parties (any judgments, orders, or consent decrees, etc.)?
9. What is the pricing trend with respect to each product over the past five to ten years? What is the capacity trend? What is the demand trend? What is the profitability trend?

10. Has there been any innovation or new technology over the past five to ten years? Describe and assess any such developments.

Competitor Contacts

1. Have you had contacts with competitors? Explain details and frequency of any contacts with competitors.
2. Do any records reflect competitor contacts (expense accounts, calendars, trip reports, etc.)?
3. Are you aware of any contacts by other company personnel with competitors?
4. Does the company make contact with competitors in any indirect ways (e.g., through consultants, agents, former employees, customers, purchasers)?
5. Does the company have any of the following arrangements with competitors?

    a. Product or information swapping
    b. Customer/supplier relationship
    c. Joint venture
    d. Lease or other business arrangement (e.g., toll milling)
    e. Patent or "know-how" license
    f. Litigation or claims (actual or potential)
    g. Officer or director interlocks or key employee swapping (any with major suppliers or customers?)

    If so, explain nature, purpose, and composition. Where are files located?
6. Do any company employees have social contacts with competitors? Describe.

Price Fixing

1. Have you had any contacts with competitors in the last year about prices (not just "fixing" or "stabilizing" higher or lower prices, but *any* contacts), whether in person, by phone, in writing, or oral and regardless of the place (for example, trade shows, trade associations, bars, customers' premises, company premises, or a hotel room) and whether or not anything came of that contact.
2. Have you had any contacts with competitors about anything that may indirectly affect prices, e.g., limiting production?
3. Do you have or have you had copies of your competitors' prices or price lists (dealers, wholesale or retail)? If yes, how did you get them? Are they publicly available?

Pricing

1. How does the company set prices for its products?
2. Who is responsible for pricing? (Who recommends and approves pricing?)
3. What documents are used or developed in setting prices, and where are they located?
4. How does the company make its pricing decisions known? (Does it use price lists or books, standardized discounts, etc.?)
5. How does the company obtain information about competitor prices?
6. Does the company receive price information from or exchange price information with any competitor (e.g., price lists, invoices)?
7. Does the company or any competitor make advance announcements of price changes under circumstances where "followship" might be inferred?
8. Does the company or its competitors engage in two or more tiered price systems (with lower prices in areas where independent rather than major competitors are present)?
9. Does the company or competitors engage in volume discounts, freight allowances, credit terms, or any other price-related policy that is standard in the industry or followed by others? If so, how did it come about? Any joint meetings, arrangements, or understandings?
10. Does the company or any competitor sell at, near, or below cost? How is cost determined?
11. Has the company or any competitor ever directed its pricing at a particular or potential competitor (to hinder, restrain, or eliminate it)?
12. Is there any pricing flexibility? How is it administered? How is a "special" or "different" price obtained? Who has authority and under what conditions? How is it documented?
13. Have you ever received a complaint from one customer about another customer cutting prices?
14. Do you solicit or receive complaints on prices from anyone?
15. Do you ever act or attempt to act on a complaint (even to the extent of "passing it on to the right person or anyone")?
16. How do your prices compare with competitors and other channels of distribution (yours or a competitor's)?
17. How do your price changes compare to those of your competitors with respect to timing and amount?

18. Have there been any recent changes in pricing practices or policies or business practices?
19. Do you have any customers who are also competitors? If yes, how are the two relations distinguished and controlled (dual distribution relationship)?

Trade Associations

1. To what trade associations or other industry groups does the company or its employees belong? Who is involved? Are there any files?
2. Provide full details as to the name, address, purpose, benefit of membership, type of activity, nature and conduct of meetings (agenda, minutes, presence of antitrust counsel, frequency, who attends), antitrust litigation or investigations, antitrust counsel, and compliance programs and standards.
3. Provide the charter, bylaws, minutes, agenda, and other descriptive documents as to each association.
4. Review each association and its committees as to:
   a. Importance of membership (i.e., competitive advantage)
   b. Membership or access problems (expulsion)
   c. Codes or standards of conduct
   d. Product standardization programs
   e. Standard setting, certification, seal of approval programs
   f. Programs for sharing customer credit or other information (e.g., wages, costs)
   g. Exchange of price, statistical, or other information
   h. Joint lobbying or government representation
   i. Bid depositories
   j. Trade shows
   k. Joint labor negotiations
   l. Joint research and development
5. What contacts or conversations with competitors occur at or outside association meetings? Do they involve sensitive matters?

Customer and Territory Allocation

1. Does the company have any contacts, discussions, or understandings with competitors (including customers) about allocating, reserving, or staying away from customers by any of the following criteria?
   - Name
   - Product lines

- Classifications such as application areas, types of businesses, government sales, accounts
- Territories or geographic areas

2. Do any company dealers allocate or attempt to allocate customers or markets?
3. Has the company ever received a complaint from one customer about another customer selling either outside their territory or into the complainor's territory? What did the company do about it? How did it respond? What records exist regarding such a complaint?

Boycotts

Are you aware of any contacts by company employees with competitors, customers, suppliers, or others concerning agreement or understanding to refuse to do business with any third party?

Refusal to Deal

1. Are there any situations where the company has refused to sell or do business with a customer, or class of customers, or supplier?
   a. Were these customers or suppliers the company has previously done business with, or were they new customers?
   b. What documents exist or existed that record the facts and circumstances?
2. Has the company refused to deal with and/or terminated any dealer, agent, customer, or supplier in the past year?
   a. If yes, what was the basis for the refusal and/or termination?
   b. If yes, has a new distributor been appointed?
   c. What documents exist or existed that record the facts and circumstances?
3. Have there been any complaints from or about any dealer, agent, customer, or supplier the company refused to deal with?
4. Has the company been asked to take, taken, and/or hinted at taking any action toward a dealer, distributor, customer, or supplier in response to or as a result of the request or urging of others?
5. Is there any restriction on providing service, or a particular type of service, to a dealer, supplier, customer, or class of customers?

Resale Price Maintenance

1. Has the company ever told or attempted to persuade (either directly or indirectly) any purchasers as to the price at which they are to resell the company's product?
2. Has the company ever suggested a resale price to dealers or any customer? If so, how is it transmitted to the customer? What is the caption on the price list? Is there any type of follow-up to see if the suggested prices are being used? If yes, describe it. What is done if suggested prices are not followed?
3. Does the company consider resale use in setting price?
4. Does the company consider resale price in setting price?
5. Does the company ever refuse to deal or try to avoid doing business with, criticize, or threaten price cutters?
6. Does the company know at what price its dealers resell its product? If yes, what is the source of this information?
7. Has the company ever received a complaint from one customer about another customer cutting prices? Describe the situation. How did the company respond? What records exist regarding such a complaint?
8. Are there any internal memoranda, letters, notes, or conversations that refer to "price cutters" or words of similar meaning?
9. Are there any restrictions on pricing or resale related to pricing to any customer?

Customer, Territorial, and Other Vertical Restrictions

1. Describe the company's distribution system. Does it use independent dealers or distributors, agents, or other representatives?
2. Provide a copy of each standard type of dealer or distribution agreement. What are the relevant provisions?
3. What oral agreements or understandings does the company have with dealers, distributors, or agents?
4. Are there any territorial, customer, or other restrictions on dealers, distributors, or customers (such as location restrictions, exclusive territories, customer classifications, exclusive customer accounts, areas of primary responsibility, profit passover, exclusive distributorships, limitations on product shipment, service reimbursement allowances, designation of warehouse locations, limitation on customer product use, geographic limitations, resolution of interterritorial disputes,

pricing based on customer classification, pricing based on customer name, limitations on how the product can be promoted for sale)?

5. What is the purpose of each restriction?
6. Is each restriction enforced? How? Is there documentation?
7. Is each restriction reasonable under all the circumstances in the market? (Review the competitive impact of each restriction under rule-of-reason test set forth in *GTE Sylvania*).

Price Discrimination

1. Has the company ever charged a customer or class of customers a lower price than other customers on products of like grade and quality?
2. Have there been secret rebates or other unpublicized price reductions available only to selected customers, such as special services, allowances, or supplies?
3. Were the prices lower to meet equally low prices of competitors on specific sales?
4. If quantity discounts are given, can they be cost-justified?
5. If functional discounts are given, are they valid?
6. Are prices geographically uniform?
7. How does the company price and merchandise a new product in order to gain market entry?
8. Are merchandising and promotional allowances and services given fairly?
9. Does the company sell its products under a delivered-pricing system?
10. Does the company ever meet competitive prices or promotions by making a price change or issuing a special price?
    a. How is the price obtained?
    b. Who has authority, and under what conditions?
    c. How is it documented?
11. Has the company ever obtained a price concession from suppliers not available to its competitors?
12. Has the company ever priced at or below cost?

Promotional Service and Allowance Discrimination

Has the company ever granted rebates, promotional or other allowances, advertising services or payments, advertising or promotional facilities, materials, or other assistance, or other things of value to some customers or type of customers and not others or at different rates to different customers?

Exclusive-Dealing Contracts

1. Has the company ever required or attempted to require any purchaser to deal with, buy, or handle only its product, to the exclusion of a competitor's product? (What is the market? Are competitive products available? What is the effect on competition?)
2. Has the company sold or attempted to sell products or services to anyone only or primarily on the condition that the customer does not handle a competitor's products or services? (What is the policy? What is the market? Are there other outlets for the competitive product?)
3. Is the company the exclusive seller of any product?
4. Has the company ever agreed to purchase all or a significant portion of its requirements for any item from a single supplier or agreed to supply all or a significant portion of the requirements of any single customer for a company product? (What is the product? What is the market? Were any suppliers, competitors, or customers foreclosed from substantial market access?)
5. Has the company ever entered into an "exclusive" contract with anyone?

Tie-In Sales

1. Does the company sell two or more distinguishable products or services together?
2. If it does, are customers permitted to buy each separately?
3. If customers are permitted to buy them separately, are the separate products priced in a way that makes separate purchasing more expensive or more difficult or inconvenient?
4. Do any customers in fact purchase less than the total package of products?
5. Are any unusual credit arrangements offered that inhibit separate purchasing?
6. Does the company require customers to carry a full or substantially complete line of products?
7. As to any potential tie-in, what are the purposes and business justifications? Are the products separate and distinct? Does the company have economic power in the market for the tying product? Is a not insubstantial amount of commerce effected in the tied product? What is the market structure? Is there significant foreclosure of market access to customers or competitors?

Reciprocity

1. Has the company ever agreed by buy any supplier's product only on the condition that the supplier buy a product of the company?
2. Has the company ever agreed or attempted to agree to sell any product to another party on the condition that the party sell its products to the company?
3. Does the company maintain any records by which purchases from or sales to any firm are compared or matched?
4. Does the company distribute purchasing figures to sales personnel or sales figures to purchasing officials?
5. Do purchasing officials accompany sales personnel when calling on customers?
6. Is there any practice or procedure by which buying is concentrated as to customers or potential customers?

Acquisitions, Mergers, and Joint Ventures

1. Is the company considering the purchase or sale of any assets or stock of, or merger with, any corporation? Describe any in detail.
2. Is the company considering any joint ventures, partnerships, or capital, or other contributions to a business or third party, or does it have plans for such contributions to the company by a third party?
3. Is the company considering obtaining financial, contractual, or other control over the business of a third party, or does the company have plans for a third party exercising such control over company business?
4. Review each acquisition or joint venture for compliance with Hart-Scott-Rodino premerger notification requirements; for compliance with the merger standards of section 7 of the Clayton Act and the Justice Department 1982 Merger Guides (and Sherman Act joint venture standards in the case of joint venture) and for potential or existing antitrust problems of the company to be acquired or the joint venture partner.

Monopolization

1. Does the company have a leading or dominant position in any line of commerce? How did it obtain this position?
2. Does the company have a competitive advantage over manufacturers or sellers of similar products? If so, what is it?
3. Has the company by pricing, product availability, new-product strategies, or any other means been able to gain

market share, retain market advantage, discourage or eliminate competitors, or forestall new companies from entering the market? Discuss the reasonableness of and business justification for the practices.

4. Does the company ever target specific competitors' products or geographic markets in business strategies?
5. Have company officials ever expressed in a meeting or document a business strategy to gain a protected position or a predominant position, or to capture a specific market or exploit a specific market?
6. Is the company aware of any threat or potential for monopolization charges against it by the government or a private party?

Patents, Licenses, and Trademarks

1. Describe all company patents, licenses, trademarks, know-how, or other proprietary information.
2. Where are the files?
3. Are there any claims or litigation relating to patents, licenses, or trademarks?
4. Are there any exclusionary, restrictive, or tying terms in the licenses or related agreements?
5. Has the company entered into cross-licensing agreements with competitors or otherwise pooled its patent holdings or know-how with a competitor?
6. Are any of the company's patents known to be invalid? If so, has the company made any efforts to enforce them?
7. Are patent or know-how licenses restricted concerning competing products, resale prices, or customers?
8. Do patent or know-how licenses provide for quotas, patent grant-backs, purchases of unpatented supplies, or royalties payable after some or all patents have expired?
9. Are royalty rates uniform, or do they discriminate in favor of one or more licensees?
10. Does the company insist on package licensing of patents or know-how, whether or not the licensee wants the full package?

Miscellaneous

1. Does the company operate in industries that are wholly or partially exempt from the antitrust laws by statute? If so, is the company operating lawfully within the exemption?

2. Does the company have foreign operations through export sales, foreign subsidiaries, affiliates, licensees, or joint ventures? Are these operations in compliance with U.S. and applicable foreign competition laws?

Unfair Competition or Unfair Deceptive Trade Practices

1. Are you aware of the existence of any unfair or unethical competitive practices by company personnel (such as bribery of competitors or customers; industrial espionage; theft of property or trade secrets, designs, or other proprietary information; sales promotion lottery schemes; disparagement of competitors or their products or communication of false or unfair statements about competitors; or inducement of breach of contract between a competitor and its customers, suppliers, or employees)? Are you aware of any such practices in the industry?
2. Are you aware of the existence of any unfair, deceptive, or unethical practices directed against customers by company personnel (such as false or misleading advertising, testimonials, or sales representations; misleading packaging or labeling; failure to disclose product origin; or "bait and switch" tactics)?
3. Does the company have an advertising substantiation program? Explain it. Where are the files located?

FORM 6

Sample License and Joint Venture Review Procedure

[Date]

To: All Attorneys
From: General Counsel
Re: Legal Review of License Agreements and Joint Venture Agreements

Policy

All domestic and foreign license agreements and joint venture agreements and any amendment or extension of such an agreement are to be reviewed with corporate antitrust counsel for antitrust purposes. Any distribution, marketing, or representation agreement, subcontracting agreement, or other agreement to be executed in conjunction with a license or joint venture agreement and essential to a full understanding of such agreement, must be included in the material submitted for review. This review procedure becomes effective upon receipt of this memorandum.

Definitions

For purposes of this review procedure, a "license agreement" is any agreement under which rights in property owned by the Company, or a subsidiary thereof, in the form of a patent, trademark, or know-how, are granted to a person other than the Company or a subsidiary thereof, or where similar rights are granted to the Company, or a subsidiary thereof, by another person.

A "joint venture agreement" for purposes of this procedure is any agreement with another person under which the Company, or a subsidiary thereof, is to undertake jointly with such other person a commercial activity, such as research and development work, manufacturing, construction or erection work, or the marketing and distribution of goods or services, whether such activity is to be undertaken through establishment of a new corporate entity or a partnership, or simply through a contract.

A joint venture in corporate form may have to be reported as an acquisition to the Federal Trade Commission and the U.S. Department of Justice under the Hart-Scott-Rodino Antitrust Improvements Act of 1976 and a thirty-day waiting period observed before consummating the joint venture.

Exceptions

A standard form of license agreement should be reviewed under this procedure only once. Therefore, if a previously reviewed and approved form is used without substantive change in a subsequent transaction, such license agreement should not be submitted for antitrust review. However, if a subcontracting, distribution, or other agreement or a joint venture agreement is to be executed in conjunction with such a license agreement, this exception does not apply.

These review procedures do not apply to intangible property rights granted by the Company or a subsidiary thereof under a contract for and in connection with the sale in the ordinary course of business of materials, services, or equipment.

Review Procedures

When an attorney becomes aware of a situation involving or a provision in a proposed license agreement or joint venture agreement that raises an antitrust question, the attorney should notify corporate antitrust counsel by telephone at the earliest opportunity. It is expected that most questions will be resolved by telephone at this early stage, causing the least inconvenience to the management and providing the greatest opportunity to make effective legal recommendations that may require consultation among the parties.

Each license agreement and joint venture agreement and related agreements prepared by the Legal Department, other than agreements excepted from these review procedures, should be sent to corporate antitrust counsel for antitrust review at the time it is circulated among management for review and before submission to an outside person. Each license agreement and joint venture agreement prepared by another person should be sent to corporate antitrust counsel for antitrust review as soon as it is received by a Company attorney, unless you intend to change such agreement. In that event, your revised draft should be sent to corporate antitrust counsel for review.

Each agreement submitted for antitrust review should include a review form similar to the form attached to these procedures as Attachment 1. The form should be completed by the submitting attorney. Corporate antitrust counsel will sign and date it upon completion of the antitrust review and then will return it to the sender.

In the unlikely event that a license agreement or joint venture agreement is changed following the antitrust review in a manner that, in the judgment of the responsible attorney, calls for a further antitrust review, the attorney should notify Corporate antitrust counsel promptly by telephone. Corporate counsel will then determine what additional antitrust review, if any, is required.

Other Reviews

This antitrust review does not supersede, or take the place of, the drafting and review of license agreements and joint venture agreements now being done by other attorneys within the Legal Department.

____

General Counsel

Attachment 1

____

(Date)

To: Corporate Antitrust Counsel

Attached for your antitrust review is a

_______ License Agreement

_______ Joint Venture Agreement

between ________________________ and ________________________

(Company) (Name of other party)

Also attached are the following related agreements:

____

____

____

____

(Signature of attorney)

____

(Telephone number and ext.)

Reviewed by:

____

(Signature)

____

(Date)

Forms for Section II:

Handling Litigation Utilizing the Corporate Law Department

FORM 7

In-House Training Procedures

Orientation Training Program

Each newly employed attorney is introduced to the Law Department through the Orientation Training Program. Every reasonable effort is made to assure that she or he is made to feel welcome, is promptly introduced to everyone in his or her section, and is provided answers to any questions.

The section's Professional Training Manager—who is a member of the Department's Professional Training and Development Committee—assures that the new attorney receives orientation training.

The Orientation Training Program includes:

- Signing personnel documents
- Distributing an announcement of the new attorney's arrival
- Viewing the Department's orientation film
- Discussing the film with two senior attorneys
- Introductions within the section
- Assignment to a mentor
- Lunching with the General Counsel, section head, and/or the mentor
- Being furnished a procedures manual and related materials
- Meeting with the Chairman of the Standards Review Committee
- Meeting with the Chairman of the Pro Bono Committee
- Receiving an orientation briefing by the head of the Support Staff
- Receiving an orientation briefing by a senior paralegal
- Receiving an orientation briefing by the Librarian
- Meeting informally with a young attorney
- Meeting with the mentor
- Meeting with the section's Professional Training Manager

- Lunching with a senior representative from each section and being introduced to the section members

Basic Lawyering Skills Program

Each newly employed attorney who has less than two years of lawyering work experience is provided formal training in basic lawyering skills. The purpose is to contribute to his or her expeditious development as a practicing attorney.

The section's Professional Training Manager—who is a member of the Department's Professional Training and Development Committee—assures that the new attorney receives the basic skills training and that all of her or his related questions are answered. Scheduling the training sessions is a responsibility of the Department's Professional Training and Development Coordinator.

The Basic Lawyering Skills Program includes such subjects as:

- Organizing Your Work and Your Office
- Working with Your Secretary
- Information Sources
- The Company's Support Services
- The Practice of Administrative Law
- The Utility Industry
- What the Company Is and What It Does
- Dealing with Personnel in the General Office, the Regions, and Subsidiary Companies
- Legal Writing
- Correspondence Rules and Guidelines
- Legal Opinions
- Oral Reports
- Oral Advocacy
- The Assignment Process
- Practice Tips

Guidelines For Mentor System

A mentor is a wise and trusted counselor. Each new attorney shall be assigned to a mentor. The objectives of the Mentor System are twofold. First, it is intended to expedite assimilation of new attorneys (including lateral hires) into the Law Department by giving them a source of practical information and constructive guidance about the personal and organizational dynamics of the Law Department, the Company, and the bar. Second, it is intended to enhance the professional and personal development of new attorneys.

Characteristics of a Good Mentor

A good mentor:

- is a people-oriented person who has good chemistry with his or her new attorney(s);
- has about ten years' seniority over his or her new attorney(s) in:

  a. years of practice; and
  b. years with the Company;
- has time available for mentoring;
- strives to keep the relationship with his or her new attorney(s) informal;
- is sensitive to the relationship between the Law Department and all other departments and to the relationships between the Company and its various societal constituencies.

Assignment of Mentors

Mentors are assigned as follows:

- Each new attorney *must* be assigned a mentor.
- A mentor should normally be a member of the new attorney's section, but should not be one of his or her supervisors.
- Each mentor should have no more than two new attorneys.
- Selection and pairing of mentors and new attorneys should be made by the Professional Training and Development Committee in consultation with the Section Head and should occur promptly after new attorneys arrive; compatibility should be the key criterion.
- The Professional Training and Development Committee should periodically evaluate the relationship between each mentor and his or her new attorney(s); if any incompatibilities have developed, assignments should be changed.
- Assignments should last as long as the new attorney is subject to the review committee; relationships should be encouraged to continue informally thereafter.

Operation of the Mentor Relationship

Contacts between a mentor and his or her new attorney should relate to matters that directly or indirectly involve the new attorney's career at the Company. Each new attorney should contact the mentor any time he or she desires information or guidance. Each mentor should contact his or her new attorney(s) at least once a month.

As circumstances warrant, and normally with the concurrence of the new attorney, the mentor shall consult with the Section Head and/or the new attorney's supervisor(s) about his or her professional development.

Guidelines for One-On-One Training

The objective of one-on-one training is to improve the substantive skills of junior attorneys who are new to the Law Department (including lateral hires) and are new to a particular section. Improved skills should not only enhance the quality of Department's work product, but also should increase the Department's productivity.

How One-On-One Training Works

The role of one-on-one training is twofold:

1. Comprehensive supervision by the assigning attorney
2. Availability of a senior attorney in each section to act as a trainer (or to be responsible for delegating the training) when the assigning attorney is not available or when the junior attorney needs training that does not relate to an assigned project

The responsibility of the assigning attorneys working with the new attorneys is comprehensive supervision:

- One-on-one training is an explicit responsibility of each assigning attorney re each assigned matter.
- Each assignment should be specific, and the assigning attorney should explain its context.
- The assigning attorney should verify, soon after work has begun, that the junior attorney is on the right track.
- The assigning attorney should help the junior attorney learn time-saving shortcuts in completing assignments.
- The assigning attorney *must* give feedback to the junior attorney following completion of each assignment.

The Professional Training and Development (PT&D) Committee Member has a dual responsibility in one-on-one training:

1. The PT&D Committee Member is responsible for ensuring that new attorneys receive one-on-one training.
2. The PT&D Committee Member will be available to all junior attorneys in his or her section for this purpose.

The trainer should have the following general characteristics:

- Is a senior attorney (so as to be knowledgeable about the substantive areas of law assigned to the junior attorneys)
- Is a good teacher

- Has time available for training

The training operates as follows:

- The trainer should be available to all junior attorneys in the section.
- Each trainer (or delegate) *must* give feedback to each junior attorney whom he or she trains.

The Departmental Program

The Department recognizes the importance of providing a regular forum for the presentation and discussion of important issues facing the Company, the Department, and the legal profession. The issues addressed will respond to concerns Department members have raised as being of particular interest and will be flexible in its format, thereby ensuring that current issues can be presented in a timely manner.

Based upon the recent survey soliciting ideas for the first series of the departmental programs, the first forum has been scheduled to take place on April 24 and will address current issues surrounding the Diablo Canyon facility. The first program will consist of a panel discussion, with Peter Hanschen, head of the Diablo Canyon Rate Case team, as moderator. The panel members will consist of the following individuals:

Kermit Kubitz	Alternative Rate Design
Ward Wogsland	Current Operating Issues
Ivor Samson	The Rate Case
Richard Locke	NRC Licensing and the Seismic Plan

The second departmental forum will take place in early June. The topic will be analyzing financial statements. It will be given by the Company's independent auditors, Arthur Andersen & Co.

The third departmental forum is tentatively planned as a program on stress reduction and management. Proposed future topics include the future of the Company, negotiation and/or conflict resolution, and possibly an outside speaker from the state legislature.

Attending Courses Offered by Organizations Outside the Company

The Law Department supports and encourages each attorney in the Department to attend courses offered by outside organizations that are reasonably relevant to his or her work. Generally, it will be considered normal for each attorney to attend in a year one course offered locally and a second course that may involve travel away from the area, if necessary. If good reason is established, an attorney may be permitted to attend a greater number of courses within a year.

Of course, attendance at courses should be arranged in a manner consistent with the attorney's duty to fulfill his or her responsibilities to the Company.

Requests to attend outside courses should be given to your section training committee member, who will work with the Section Head in processing the request.

This policy has been developed under the current Law Department budget and may change as budgetary constraints or opportunities arise.

Training Within the Sections

Ongoing training of all lawyers within their sections is essential if we are to keep abreast of current developments in our areas of practice and effectively represent our client. Therefore, each member of the Professional Training and Development Committee has been given responsibility for organizing the ongoing lawyer-training activities for his or her section. In that role, the committee member will be working very closely with the Section Head to identify areas and issues where additional emphasis would be beneficial for section members.

Since the sections are so diverse in nature, no specific set of guidelines has been developed for section training. Instead, the training committee members will build on the section activities that currently exist, including strengthening procedures for keeping lawyers informed of recent developments affecting their practice and arranging special presentations and discussions when warranted. When issues would be of interest to members of another section, the section with the greater involvement in the issue will arrange a joint presentation for members of both sections. Similarly, special meetings of small groups of lawyers within a section can also be arranged to address issues of special interest to them but not to the section as a whole.

The Client Employees' Environment

All attorneys are encouraged to take advantage of practical opportunities to spend time in their client employees' working environments. The benefits of such action include the subsequent ability to formulate conclusions and undertake actions based on firsthand knowledge; and the improvement in future communications resulting from enhanced personal relationships.

The extra time required to visit client employees' locations and to inspect related facilities is considered to be an investment in personal training and development.

For each new attorney in a section, the Professional Training Manager shall arrange at least one and, if appropriate, more than one on-site visit to a Company facility that is likely to play a significant role in the work that attorney will do. The visit should take place within the first eight weeks of the new attorney's arrival.

Pro Bono Legal Services Project

Each lawyer is encouraged to volunteer for the Bar Association's Legal Service Corporate Pro Bono Project. The purpose of this project is to involve corporate lawyers in the delivery of legal services to the poor.

The Law Department has participated in this project since 1985. Almost one-third of our attorneys participate. Pro bono work is an important part of your professional development and responsibility. Moreover, it not only enhances the Company's image but is an important consideration in the competitive environment in which we now operate. The guidelines for participating are available. To obtain them or further information or to volunteer, please contact the Professional Training and Development Manager for your section.

The Pro Bono Legal Service Project includes the following:

- Family Law and Landlord Tenant Legal Clinic Training through the Bar Association of San Francisco
- $1 million legal malpractice insurance through the bar association
- Established guidelines for participating

FORM 8

Litigation Checklist

On Receipt of Complaint or Cross-Complaint

1. Proper Service?
   a. On company?
   b. On individual company employee?
2. Consult/write employee who may have individual lawsuit. (See form file.)
3. Statute of Limitations? (CCP §§ 312, 335 *et seq.*)
4. Service within three years? (CCP § 581)
5. Proper venue?
6. Tender our defense to another?
7. Answer or demurrer?
8. Affirmative defenses?
9. Cross-complaints? (File only, or file and serve)
   Permission obtained: Division Manager ________________
   Government Affairs ________________
   (if against government entity)
   a. Express indemnity?
   b. Implied indemnity?
   c. Partial indemnity?
10. Request statement of damages.
11. Notify excess insurer?
12. Write opening letter.
13. Send first set of interrogatories. (Secretary to calendar.)
14. Notice depositions if priority and speed required.
15. Determine earliest possible date case might be sent to trial.
16. Calendar case—mark file and calendar: 30/60/90 days.
17. Consider use of investigators and paralegals.

Thirty-to Sixty-Day Follow-Up

1. Review interrogatory answers.
2. Subpoena records (medical, business, etc.).
3. Notice depositions.

4. Further investigation (meet with investigator, interview witness, visit scene, obtain documents, discuss exhibits, more photographs, etc.).
5. Consider hiring of experts.
6. Calendar case.

On Receipt of At-Issue Memorandum

1. Is counter at-issue needed?
   a. Is estimated time of trial accurate?
   b. Should we demand jury?
2. Determine time between filing at-issue memo and trial setting conference in the county where the action is pending.
3. Is certificate of readiness required?
4. Should a motion for summary judgment or motion for judgment on the pleadings be made?
5. Review discovery:
   a. Witness/party depositions remaining?
   b. Subpoena/request medical or employment records?
   c. Interrogatories?
   d. Requests for admission?
   e. View scene?
   f. Arrange for nonpercipient/expert witnesses?
   g. Requests for documents/things?
   h. Subpoena third-party records?
6. Arrange for I.M.E.

On Receipt of TSC Notice or Pretrial Conference Notice

1. *Case Review: Meet with two members of settlement committee to review case. This is mandatory!* (Obtain additional authority and adjust reserve where necessary.)
2. Send CCP § 998, if appropriate.

After TSC or Pretrial Conference

1. Inform investigator and independent witnesses/experts of trial date. (Each company witness should have a copy of his or her deposition.)
2. Obtain updated medical reports.

3. Notice depositions of experts (CCP § 2037 disclosure).
4. Send final interrogatories/requests for admission.
5. Have exhibits prepared.
6. Break down file for trial. (Consider paralegals for preparation of trial book, deposition summaries, etc.)

Thirty Days before Trial

1. Send notice to produce at trial to parties (CCP § 1987).
    a. Include production of all necessary documents and things.
    b. Ask for investigation file? (Ten days for witnesses, twenty days for documents.)
2. Subpoena third-party witnesses and records.
3. Ensure copying service has *original affidavits* from custodians of records for all records previously subpoenaed. Instruct copying service to deliver records and affidavits to court.
4. Make sure depositions will be filed by court reporters.
5. Make sure proper foundation is laid for introduction of documentary/demonstrative evidence.
6. Prepare trial brief where necessary.
7. Prepare motions in limine.
8. Prepare jury instructions.
9. Prepare notes for voir dire, opening statement, direct examination, and cross-examination.

FORM 9

Initial Case Analysis

Attorney:

Date:

1. *Case Name:*
2. *Court and County:*
   Telephone:
3. *Case No.*
4. *Accounts Receivable No.* — *Investigator:* *Telephone:*
5. *Date of Incident:*
6. *Plaintiff Attorney:*
7. *Other Attorneys:*
8. *Key Witnesses:*

9. *Fact Summary and Legal Analysis* (A brief description of the incident, the Company's involvement, potential problems, Company wit-

nesses, other witnesses, and anticipated legal issues. Where appropriate, you may attach other summaries here in lieu of a new fact summary.):

10. *Liability and Exposure* (opinion as to liability, percentages, and exposure):

11. *Settlement Discussions* (date and amount of each demand and offer and any relevant comments):

12. *Further Preparation* (investigation and discovery plans that are apparent from file review, with *updates* as case proceeds):

13. *Trial-Setting Conference Memo*
Date: ______________________
Appearances: Plaintiffs: ______________________
____
Defendants: ______________________
____

a. Trial Date: ______________________

b. Settlement Conference
Date: ______________________
Time: ______________________
Department: ______________________

c. Discovery End: ______________________

d. Estimated Trial Length: ______________________

e. Notice Is/Is Not Waived: ______________________

f. Jury/Nonjury Case: Number of Jurors: ______________________

g. Jury Demand: ______________________

h. Jury Fees Deposited by: ______________________

i. Peremptory Challenges:
Sides: ______________________
Number: ______________________

j. Reveal Experts: ______________________

k. Fictitious Defendants: ______________________
Dismissed by Stipulation: ______________________

l. Further Orders: ______________________
____
____

14. *Depositions:* Two things *MUST* be done:
    1. List deposition taken on the form below.
    2. Prepare deposition summary immediately after each deposition and insert chronologically, below.
       (The deposition summary can be typed or handwritten. You may wish to use a separate page for each witness. The summary need be no more than a half a page but should include the witness's relationship to the case, his or her demeanor and appearance, what the witness says about the Company, and other key facts.)

	Witness Name	Affiliated with	Date of Deposition
a.			
b.			
c.			
d.			
e.			
f.			
g.			
h.			
i.			
j.			

Forms for Section III:

Establishing the Relationship between Outside Counsel and the Corporate Client

FORM 10

Outside Counsel Relations and Billing Review: Policy, Engagement Memo, and Format for Interim Statement

Policy

Careful review of outside counsel billings is clearly a major responsibility of the Department. Prior reviews have shown a lack of mutual understanding with outside counsel as to *the precise nature of* the engagement and the *controls* we have on that engagement. To make our expectations of outside counsel uniform, we have prepared guidelines for our principal retentions. A copy is attached.

Certain terms in our relationships with outside counsel are so fundamental to the Company that they will apply to all engagements. Others may be added where appropriate. Fundamental engagement concerns include: level of communications and Company controls, use of Company resources, productivity, cost forecasting, and billing procedures.

After a mutual understanding has been reached through the engagement process, billing review becomes a question of whether outside counsel has fulfilled its engagement commitments. The review process is intended to determine that legal work was actually done as efficiently as possible consistent with the terms of the engagement. If problems do emerge in review of the bill, a follow-up by the responsible lawyer is essential, after consultation with the appropriate section head or with the General Counsel. *A lawyer should not approve a bill for processing unless the bill has been substantiated and all open questions resolved.* The Company lawyer must be fully prepared to answer any question concerning the bill.

The attached engagement memo is designed as a model. Variations may be appropriate. Government Relations will obviously vary the model for its retained counsel program. In cases where small legal fees are involved, the letter may be dispensed with. In addition, if you have had a lengthy and satisfactory relationship with outside counsel, you need not send this letter each time. However, you should send it to counsel at least once, even if you already deal with the firm.

The key to successful engagement and billing review is the manner in which the attached is presented to outside counsel from prior practices with the client. Gentle but firm diplomacy will be necessary in those instances. In any event, it will be necessary to discuss the letter with all recipients to make sure that the letter does not result in new communication problems.

Engagement Memo

Date

Re:

Dear _____________ :

In connection with our conversation on your representation of us in the above-captioned matter, this letter sets forth our understanding of the engagement. If you have any questions about it, please get in touch with me as soon as possible.

No Conflict

Before you spend any time on this matter, you will review the project and your records and determine that no conflict exists that would prevent you from fully representing our Company.

Communications

Full and regular communications are essential to our relationship. It almost goes without saying that all developments that could affect this project shall be actively addressed and managed between us, and no significant decision as to the direction or mechanics of the project shall be made without input from us.

Costs

Generally, we expect that there will be no surprise in the project's costs. When decisions could significantly affect our reasonable expectations as to the costs we will incur for this assignment, please discuss them with us before undertaking the work.

Engagement Plan

As soon as possible, we will together determine a plan for all future activity in this project. The plan is a general statement of the strategy to be used to achieve our Company's objectives. Of necessity, it will be highly flexible and frequently reviewed and revised to reflect subsequent developments related to the project.

The plan need not be in writing, but if not, it must be discussed in detail. It shall include the following:

- *Objectives*—We must have an identical, clear understanding, from the beginning, of our Company's overall objectives as they relate to this matter.
- *Strategy*—We will have a common understanding, up front, as to the specific resources and procedures to be used to meet our Company's objectives.
  [For use in litigation letters]
  You will also provide a breakdown of the strategy into stages. At each of these points, we should be able to step back and consider the efficacy of prior stages and the advisability of planned future stages.
- *Staffing*—You will identify the lawyer who is primarily responsible for implementation of the plan and all other lawyers who will do significant work on the project and the expected division of labor.
- *Company resources*—The Company has developed substantial inside support resources (paralegal support, computerized document control and retrieval, computer-aided research, legal research, etc.). It is the Company's policy to use those resources whenever possible. We will reach and implement an understanding of which resources will be provided by us.
- *Cost estimate*—At the outset, we will ask you for your best estimate of the total cost involved in the engagement, and for a breakdown of the work load (partners, associates, and paralegals). If the plan is to be implemented in stages, cost estimates should be discussed by stage. If the cost exceeds $5000, we will ask for periodic updating, more often than quarterly, if appropriate (see the section on billing, which follows). We are particularly concerned about incurring fees for training associates and for duplicating presence at meetings, hearings, and the like. Although we recognize that some of such costs may be appropriate, we should be fully advised in advance of the extent to which such costs will be incurred.

Productivity

It is always a Company objective to handle cases as efficiently as possible consistent with other expressed objectives. Decisions as to the amount of effort or the amount or level of staffing to be applied to meetings (and their frequency), interviews, travel [for litigation, add "court arguments, depositions, procedural objections, number of drafts, negotiation"] should be based on their necessity to successful implementation of the plan.

In preparing memoranda for either internal or external use, we may ask that you provide us with drafts so that our input may be included before the memoranda are distributed. Also, the level to which such memoranda are researched or finally polished should reflect the magnitude of the issue involved and be agreed upon between us before the fact.

Travel and Other Expenses

All decisions relating to the extent and mode of travel and other reimbursable expenses should be made with concern for efficiency and expense.

Billing

All bills should be forwarded for payment to the undersigned. Bills should be rendered monthly if they exceed $2500 but, in any event, no less frequently than quarterly. They should contain the information set forth in the attached sample interim statement.

The undersigned cannot approve a bill for processing unless the bill has been substantiated and all open questions resolved. As primary liaison with our Company client, we must be fully prepared to answer any client question concerning the bill.

Very truly yours,

Interim Statement

Name of Firm

Company Client Name Name of Matter

Monthly Period Covered

1. General Description of Services Rendered:

Total Fee

2. Breakdown by Attorney Time:

	Hours	*Rate*	*Total*
Attorneys			
Paralegals			

Total Fee

3. Breakdown of Time Spent in Listed Categories:
   For example:

	Percent	*Hours*
Drafting and revision	%	hrs.
Research	%	hrs.
Conferences with clients	%	hrs.
Conferences within firm and with nonclients	%	hrs.
Negotiation	%	hrs.
	% 100.0	hrs.

4. For Costs Advanced:

Date	*Item*	*Cost*
		Total costs advanced ______
		Total amount due ________

FORM 11

Roles and Relationship of Inside and Outside Counsel: Initial and Follow-up Letters and Evaluation Checklist

Initial Letter

Dear _____________ :

I'd like to pull together, in writing, some of the points and concerns we've discussed regarding our respective roles and relationship.

As you know, [Company] is very much committed to quality legal service—a commitment that has led us to [outside counsel]. By now you have also become aware that we are equally concerned about efficiency and the cost of those services. We recognize that we cannot "wish" our legal fees lower. We, therefore, have created an approach to our litigation that has proved effective in linking our simultaneous goals of quality service and efficiency.

Our approach is primarily based upon [Company's] ability to perform a number of support functions itself, to evaluate and knowingly elect to accept certain risks by eliminating or curtailing some legal services and some experience and expertise in alternative dispute resolution and negotiations.

Clearly, we are unable to apply our approach without *advance* knowledge of each separate project within a specific retention that our outside firms feel is necessary to undertake. With that advance knowledge, we can help tailor the project in the most cost-effective way possible without giving up quality. Consider, for example, a document review. Unless we know precisely what you and your associates are reviewing for or the methods or purpose of any further organization you may undertake through your paralegals, we are unable to suggest alternative ways (using our people or equipment) or to discuss refraining, delaying, or curtailing portions of your work because we're willing to live with the consequences of the downside risk we're trying to avoid.

We recognize that retentions such as the present matter are fluid, and our assumptions and expectations are constantly changing. To us, this requires that our communications constantly adjust our assumptions and expectations.

As we go forward, I ask that you keep very much in mind the responsibility we place on you to discuss each project in detail before you undertake it. The risk in not doing so is that we rely on unspoken assumptions which explode in the face of "surprise" bills. We then begin scrambling for negotiating positions and harping over bills we perhaps could be thankfully paying.

Our engagement letter with you states this concept as follows:

> Generally, we expect that there will be no surprise in the project's cost. All decisions that could significantly affect our reasonable expectations as to costs we incur for this assignment should be discussed with us before the work is undertaken.

Obviously, as you see potential costs exceeding your initial [amount] estimate, it is essential for you and we to discuss and document these revised estimates so that we can avoid unproductive finger pointing after the fact. My objective at all times is to have an up-to-date plan of attack and current estimate of costs *in writing,* which serves as our current understanding and agreement. I think this makes sense for [outside counsel] and [Company], but it does require good communication and effective documentation of understanding.

If you have any questions or comments about this approach, please call.

Very truly yours,

Follow-Up Letter

Dear ______________ :

We thought our January 17th meeting was excellent. It was certainly the most intense, thought-provoking, and candid we've had with outside counsel—and enjoyable. We each had an agenda, and we covered them exhaustively.

At that meeting we discussed chronicling our mutual expectations for our relationship in the form of a "charter" or "covenant" of our ideal litigation relationship. We hesitate to glorify what follows with such a title, but we think we've fairly set forth what we'd like to see happen over the next year:

Quality Service

You will continue to provide planned and authorized services at the highest professional level. It is understood, however, that we will, together, define guidelines for certain legal services (i.e., appropriate staffing levels and discovery, investigative, or research limitations), and you will not provide services beyond those defined without additional authorization.

Two points here: (1) We are extremely impressed with your legal service, but we, jointly, must decide what level of effort a given matter requires. (2) By going the "authorization" route, we should produce full communication *before* the fact and avoid second-guessing and erroneous perceptions regarding the efficiency with which a matter was handled.

Team Approach

As the bottom line on cost of litigation is a composite of inside and outside expenses, we are both responsible for the implementation of [Company's] litigation objectives—though we will divide certain tasks and services between us. Given that shared overall responsibility for cost-effective and successful litigation services, [outside counsel] and [Company] are committed to a team approach to our objectives rather than "we-they." This means we will openly and candidly communicate about our mutual goals and promptly evaluate (including constructive criticism) our individual and combined progress on assigned tasks.

Support Services

As you know, [Company] has developed paralegal and other support services for litigation matters which we believe can be used at significant cost savings. We seek to provide those services as well as any others we may undertake at the *same level of quality* you expect from your own people. We recognize that initially we may need additional training or direction to reach that level, and we therefore have asked you to commit to helping us do so. We agreed that inside support services are appropriate on litigation matters when they meet the quality, quantity, and deadline standards that would normally apply and when there is a short- or long-term efficiency in this use. You will evaluate our efforts honestly and openly and provide appropriate guidance to help make our efforts succeed.

Communications

We agreed that, as befits a team approach to litigation, communications will be open and candid. You will talk with us, and we will talk with you, initially at least monthly in connection with specific case plans, and we will mutually discuss performances against this letter and our case plans and steps we can take to improve results. With an active level of communications and installation of our planning and evaluation process, we should learn of dissatisfactions in their incipient and correctable stages. It should go without saying that you have access to any level at [Company] that is appropriate for any problem you perceive, including, if applicable, concerns relating to the balance between quality and efficiency. In addition, we will have extensive discussions of our relationship and performances annually.

Objectives and Cost Planning

[Outside counsel] and [Company] have committed to the discipline of a planning process yielding a written "plan" for each pending case. This process will ensure that all [Company] litigation objectives are identified and discussed before either of us undertakes work and that a case plan is established reflecting quality *and* cost-effectiveness by identifying, staffing and assigning (among ourselves) specific case tasks. In addition, the estimated cost for each task, along with any underlying assumptions, will be set forth so that we mutually understand the scope of work and level of staffing. Cost or services in excess of the forecast shall be specifically authorized before undertaken.

In connection with developing the plan for each new case, we will use the objectives outline included in our January 10 letter (attached) as a checklist to guide conversations on each case. Following that discussion, one of us will follow up with a written description and confirmation of the conversation. These case plans should be completed as soon as possible for each pending case, and we should establish deadlines therefor. Case plans will be updated, in writing, at least quarterly.

Innovation in Cost Control

[Outside counsel] and [Company] recognize that the provision of legal services in the most cost-effective manner possible is essential to [Company]. You have agreed to assume an active planning role in this regard by approaching issues of cost-effectiveness in the same manner as you would any substantive legal issue; applying the same level of innovation, good judgment, and dogged determination as we have come to rely upon in substantive areas. Some possible cost control approaches we have discussed are the use of alternative dispute resolution mechanisms; intelligent review and selection of acceptable risks in case planning; use of [Company] support resources; aggressive application of management techniques for staffing to the leanest appropriate levels. [Outside counsel] and [Company] will continue to discuss these approaches and others as part of our long-term objectives as well as in connection with specific cost planning on cases.

[Name], let's continually view our relationship through these principles and discuss any questions or uncertainties as they arise. As a result, we think our excellent relationship can only improve.

Very truly yours,

Evaluation Checklist
Initial Joint Evaluation

1. How important is the matter?
   (a) Financial exposure
   (b) Principle
   (c) Precedent
2. What is the ultimate goal?
   (a) Settle (what range?)
   (b) Litigate
   (c) Possible alternative means of resolution
3. Who should have the responsibility for the matter?
   (a) Company lawyers
   (b) Outside counsel
   (c) Other counsel
   (d) Combination of above
4. What legal work do we anticipate doing?
   (a) Immediate (within the first quarter)
   (b) Long term
5. How should the matter be staffed?
   (a) Levels at outside counsel
   (b) In-house work at the Company
   (c) Potential training
6. Budget
   (a) Immediate estimate (for the first quarter)
   (b) Total estimate
   (c) Actual + ETC = EAC

Update System

1. Normal reporting (as events occur and with quarterly billings)
2. Yearly review (all of the initial evaluation items should again be covered on a formulized basis with a time for the year-end evaluation set when the representation is accepted)

FORM 12

Corporate Statement of Litigation Principles* with Litigation Plan and Budget

This brochure sets forth the basis for your retention by Catoonah Manufacturing Company and for our relationship with you.

Catoonah began to be self-insured for most cases in 1965. We did so to ensure a high-quality, effective defense of our assets and our products and to obtain the opportunity to exercise direct control over cases pending against the Company. Our first concern is to achieve a strong, effective defense. We retain only law firms that have the resources and willingness to provide an excellent defense.

Over the years, Catoonah has been quite successful, but we have found our defense to be quite expensive—a good deal more expensive than was anticipated when the self-insured program was undertaken. Accordingly, we ask our outside counsel to do everything necessary, in cooperation with us, to provide an excellent defense, but at the same time, to use good judgment to avoid duplicative or unnecessary expense. In achieving this balance, we subscribe to the following principles:

- The Company exercises direct control over the cases against it. Accordingly, we have an understanding with outside counsel that retention of a firm is subject to our direct supervision and control.
- Both the in-house staff and outside counsel must do what is necessary to provide an excellent defense. We want the best thinking, strongest advocacy, greatest initiative, perseverance and steadfastness from our outside counsel. While we have primary responsibility for developing a defense strategy for each case, we expect your support and input in preparing a strategy that, barring settlement, will see us successfully through trial and appeal.
- We have an experienced in-house litigation staff which will work closely with you. They have extensive experience and hence are in a position to supply you with substantive information about the Company and to work with you while jointly developing our strategy. All important decisions with

*This statement is modeled after that of a major corporation. It has been altered somewhat, at its request, to ensure anonymity.

respect to the litigation are under our control. However, we look forward to hearing all of your suggestions and criticisms and to working with you in a constructive partnership.

- Catoonah has highly competent in-house experts in various areas, including expertise in technical and financial subjects. We will try to use these experts first before hiring outside consultants. In addition, our in-house experts can be invaluable in assisting in the selection of outside consultants. Retention of outside consultants will in any event be subject to our prior approval.
- We expect you to use good judgement in staffing our cases so as to provide an excellent defense without incurring unnecessary expense. Obviously, this is a matter of judgment. We assume that basic research, collating of documents, summarizing of testimony, and the like will be done by junior lawyers or, when appropriate, paralegals. We expect that only one attorney from your office will attend meetings, arguments, and depositions, although we recognize you may need a "second chair" for trials and major hearings.
- To aid us in developing a common understanding in this area, we have developed a set of guidelines for outside counsel, which is attached to this brochure. Additionally, we expect you to make a plan of anticipated developments in each lawsuit you handle for us and assess what activities, staffing and costs are likely to be involved. A sample litigation plan and budget follows the litigation guidelines. *We expect to receive this plan and budget within ninety days after you are retained.*

We trust that you will adhere to a proposed plan and budget for your defense of each litigated matter in accordance with the guidelines. Please talk openly and often to the Catoonah lawyer who has retained you about any questions or reservations you have about either the guidelines or the planning and budgeting procedure.

We have retained you because we value your expertise and abilities, and we want to get the full benefit of them. If for one reason or another you wish to follow a different procedure, let us know, and we will try to work out an arrangement that is satisfactory and consistent with the principles described above.

Harris C. Houston
Senior Vice President and General Counsel
Catoonah Manufacturing Corporation

Litigation Guidelines
In-House Attorney

Each case will be the responsibility of the Catoonah in-house attorney who has retained your firm. Your firm should deal with this attorney on all matters relating to the lawsuit. However, if you have to discuss a matter with us promptly and the designated attorney is not available, you should contact Newton L. Jacobson, our Product Liability Counsel, and he or someone on his staff will obtain a prompt answer to your questions.

Outside counsel will not deal directly with the business of technical people within Catoonah. The in-house legal staff will serve as a liaison between outside counsel and other Catoonah employees. In exceptional circumstances (for example, when a discovery deadline requires close continuous contact between outside counsel and Catoonah, or when the in-house counsel is out of town for an extended period of time), this rule may be suspended, but only after discussion with the in-house attorney on the case.

Assignment of Firm Personnel

The in-house attorney responsible for the case will be personally in charge of the matter, including billings. Shortly after a case is referred to your firm, you should discuss with the in-house attorney who retained you the names of the people from your firm who will be assigned to the case. If it becomes necessary to substitute an attorney or add additional attorneys, please consult with us before doing so. While you will perform those tasks that require your skill and ability, we expect that you will attempt to minimize legal expenses by relying on a junior attorney or legal assistant for less-demanding tasks. We also know that duplication of efforts and the resultant inefficiencies can sometimes be avoided by a few hours of your direct effort.

Litigation Plan and Handling the Case

During the first three months (ninety days) following the assignment of a new case, your firm should prepare, in consultation with us, an overall plan and budget for this litigation. We recognize that it is difficult at an early stage in a litigation to project accurately what will be required for discovery, motion practice, trial preparation, and trial, but we ask that you take some time to organize your thoughts and reflect them in a litigation plan and budget. The plan can be modified as the case progresses, but should reflect your best judgment as of the time it is prepared.

The plan and budget should be in the format that follows these guidelines. As you can see, these project the activities that would be necessary to proceed through trial with this matter—pleadings, motion practice, discovery, legal and fact research, trial preparation, and trial—and the likely cost of these activities. If you already prepare litigation budgets in a different format, we would be happy to discuss whether your present procedures would adequately meet our needs.

The plan and budget should be submitted to us within three months (ninety days) after your retention on this matter. Thereafter, *the plan and budget should be updated quarterly.* If you find there is no substantial change in the litigation posture of a particular case, you can simply state this in a two-line letter to us, and submit that letter in lieu of a revised plan or budget.

If more than one attorney in the firm is handling cases for Catoonah, we suggest that each attorney in charge of a file put together a litigation plan and budget in accordance with the requested format, and discuss the plan and budget with the partner in the firm who is responsible for the overall management of Catoonah's cases. The partner managing our cases should then send to us the litigation plans and budgets for all of the cases handled by the firm.

Multiparty Cases

Occasionally, Catoonah is only one of numerous defendants in a particular lawsuit. As a result of our experience in many similar cases, we have decided we will explore joining in group defense efforts. The extent of our liability exposure in a multiparty case is sometimes not known until after commencement of discovery, but an effort is made initially to share our proportionate part of the work load with other defendants in the group.

There are some multiparty cases in which we will seek to share counsel with other defendants. In those situations we will seek to cooperate with the other defendants to retain one firm that is acceptable to the group, or to ask our respective law firms to divide the work so as to avoid duplication of effort. We will seek to have your law firm appointed group defense counsel where appropriate, but if the group should choose other counsel, that act should not be interpreted by your firm as a loss of our faith in your firm's abilities. We would no doubt continue to look to your law firm to protect Catoonah's interests in any subsequent proceeding in the multiparty case, as well as in other traditional lawsuits.

Motion Practice and Discovery

All pleadings, motions, and other papers prepared by your firm will be submitted to us in draft for review and comment before service upon other parties and filing with the court, *without exception.*

In general, answers to interrogatories will be prepared by our staff. In addition, unless there are good strategic reasons to the contrary, document productions will be conducted by our staff at our various corporate sites.

We need the maximum possible lead time for functioning on all papers, particularly answers to interrogatories. *We require complete copies of all final documents, including informal correspondence, for our files.* Summarized accounts of these materials, in lieu of the actual documents, will not suffice. These papers should be sent to us promptly.

Emphasis should be given to formulating dispositive motions (dismissal, summary judgment, etc.), as well as necessary investigations, discovery, and legal research. You will not engage in any motion practice without first obtaining the approval of the supervising in-house lawyer.

We take an aggressive posture toward most discovery requests. Please review discovery requests before sending them to the supervising in-house lawyer, and identify those items to which you recommend we object and those which you recommend we answer. The supervising in-house lawyer will supervise the discovery search.

We expect you to discuss a strategy for taking depositions and other discovery of our opponent's case. Your oral or written evaluation of any depositions needed should include a brief explanation of the proposed deponent's location, his or her involvement in the matter, and the purpose for the deposition.

Please do not prepare deposition summaries as a matter of routine without first discussing the matter with the supervising in-house lawyer. Please advise us of your impressions of each witness deposed, and how the deposition of that witness affects our posture in the case.

Legal Research

We have retained your firm in part because of your expertise. Therefore, we do not expect to be billed for any basic legal research to educate your lawyers in the basic field of the lawsuit. Consequently, all legal research you intend to bill to the Company shall be specifically requested or authorized in advance by the supervising in-house lawyer. When you do legal research, please be sure we receive a copy of the results of that research, regardless of whether it is in the form of handwritten notes or a formalized memorandum of law or whatever. You are encouraged to use computer searching of case law. When you do legal research of any type that is applicable to this case as well as other cases your firm is handling, we expect to pay only our proportionate share of costs.

Status Report

In addition to sending to the supervising in-house lawyer copies of all significant correspondence, internal memoranda of fact or law, and court filings, a status report should be sent routinely to the supervising in-house lawyer as significant events may warrant. Such reports should be no longer than one page, and should report only significant events or the absence of significant events. Do not recite the pleadings or the case history. If a case is inactive, the quarterly report will suffice.

Settlement

We may discuss with you the advisability of settlement at very early stages of the litigation. Our experience has led us to conclude that exploration of settlement at early stages in litigation is often beneficial. All settlement discussions will be conducted by house counsel unless you are advised to the contrary. You should not undertake any discussions in this regard (or indirectly imply any interest in settlement) without our prior approval.

Media Coverage

All inquiries from the news media should be forwarded to Newton Jacobson for handling.

Expense Account Practices

While traveling, we expect you to stay at quality hotels and eat enjoyable meals. However, first-class air transportation, luxury hotel accommodations, and lavish meals are not appropriate.

Disbursements for computerized research, research services, extensive copying, computerization of documents, and the like will not be reimbursed unless approved by us *in advance.* Disbursements should not include charges for routine secretarial work, word processing, or office supplies.

Disbursements for overtime and the like should be charged only if required for client effort and not because of other firm or personal priorities or interests. (E.g., charges for an attorney working nights or weekends necessitated by other client or bar activities during the business day should not be chargeable to us.) We will reimburse you for necessary photocopying and other expenses *at your cost.* If research materials are photocopied because of their absence from your own library and you anticipate using such materials for future matters, we expect that cost to be absorbed by the firm.

Billing

Unless we have made other arrangements, separate bills should be presented monthly on a case-by-case basis within thirty days after the end of the month. For expeditious handling, bills should be sent to the in-house attorney assigned to the case.

Invoices should show the name of the attorney who did the work, the date the work was done, the hours that were involved, a description of the services performed, and the amount charged per hour. A sample invoice format is attached following the form for the litigation plan and budget. If time has been written off because of inefficiency or other reasons, please indicate this. Also, in reviewing a statement before it is sent, ensure that a copy of all internal memoranda of fact or law, correspondence, and court filings that the statement covers have been sent to us. If obvious questions are raised by an invoice, such as legal research on a basic point or involvement of attorneys in addition to those on which we have agreed, it would be helpful if the explanations were included along with the billing.

The Company will pay for time spent in transit if travel outside your locale is necessary. If work is done for another client in transit, we will not reimburse transit time. If travel time is devoted to working for one or more clients in addition to the Company, we should be billed only for the proportionate time. Unless agreed to in advance, time away from home or the office that is not in transit or spent performing legal services will not be compensated.

Invoices should be addressed and submitted to the in-house attorney as follows:

Catoonah Manufacturing Company
Legal Department
85 Wilson Lane
Ridgefield, CT

795

Litigation Plan and Budget

Case Name

Privileged and Confidential

	Description of Activity	Responsible Attorney/ Paralegal	Time	Estimated Expenses
Pleadings				
Dispositive and forum motions				
Legal research				
Investigations				
Discovery (including related motions)[a]				
Miscellaneous[b]				
Trial preparation				
Trial				
Total				

[a]Please itemize including, for depositions, the witness name and locale.
[b]Please itemize.

Invoice

Attorney	Date	Hours	Description of Services Rendered
QRS	10/02/83	0.4	Review Judge's Order; conference with XYZ re Order.
WXY	10/02/83	0.2	Conference with QRS re Judge Smith's Order and suing the corporate maker of the note to avoid the possible release of the guarantors.
QRS	10/03/83	0.3	Draft amended complaint.
WXY	10/09/83	0.3	Discussion with QRS re status and strategy, adding parties.
WXY	10/10/83	0.2	Reviewing complaint prepared by QRS.
QRS	10/16/83	2.7	Prepare for pretrial conference.
QRS	10/17/83	4.1	Prepare for hearing; research re release of guarantors; court appearance; conference with WXY; prepare order.
MNS	10/17/83	2.0	Preparation of documents at QRS's instruction.
WXY	10/18/83	1.7	Meeting with Judge Smith; memorandum to client re status.
QRS	10/22/83	0.2	Review and revise memorandum.
WXY	10/30/83	0.1	Conference with client re settlement.
Total Hours		12.2	Total Fees $00.00

Date	Disbursement	Description
10/19/83	$1.20	Copying expenses at . . . cents/ page

Summary by Attorney	Classification	Hours	Rate/Hour	Totals
William X. Yancy	Partner	2.5	00.00	$00.00
Quincy R. Sturgess	Associate	7.7	00.00	00.00
Marcia N. Sotherly	Paralegal	2.0	00.00	00.00

Total Fees	$00.00
Total Disbursement Charges	1.20
Total This Statement	$00.00

FORM 13

Guidelines for Outside Counsel: Statement of Litigation Principles

These guidelines are intended to serve as a framework for outside counsel in providing legal representation to the Company. In those instances where the guidelines do not fit a particular situation, exceptions will be made in order to accommodate the best interests of the Company. However, significant deviations from the guidelines for special situations should be discussed with an appropriate officer in the Office of the General Counsel (OGC).

Retention of Counsel

It is the responsibility of the OGC to retain outside counsel to ensure that the Company is provided with competent legal services on a cost-effective basis. All engagements of counsel are arranged through or approved by the OGC. Matters are referred to counsel on the basis of expertise in a particular area of the law, geographic location, and whenever possible by proven performance in past representation of the Company.

The establishment and maintenance of a good working relationship between counsel and the OGC assigned attorneys is an achievable goal, which should enhance the Company's legal representation and at the same time reduce fees and costs. Accordingly, counsel are encouraged to discuss the issues, tactics, and strategy of litigation and nonlitigation matters with the assigned attorneys. Although frequently personnel in other corporate departments are involved in the business and credit aspects of a particular matter, and of necessity must communicate directly with counsel, the assigned attorney should be kept current on developments and should participate in all decisions concerning legal tactics and strategy. Counsel should provide the assigned attorney with copies of all correspondence and pleadings in litigation matters.

Litigation Evaluation Form

Counsel handling Company liability litigation are to complete and submit a Litigation Evaluation Form (Form 14) on all litigation matters. The form, to accompany the referral letter, should be completed and returned within sixty days from the date of referral. The Litigation Evaluation Form is intended as an aid in the management of Company litigation.

There is particular interest in the Projected Fees and Costs Section of the Form, which requires short-, mid-, and long-term fee and cost projections on each case.

The assigned attorney is to be informed of any significant deviations, so that operating department budgets can be adjusted. The Litigation Evaluation Form may not fit every situation, but so long as the essential elements are covered, the analysis and projections may be submitted in a different format. Counsel are encouraged to provide as much detail as appropriate on each case and should not be confined to short answers.

Billing Practices

Unless other arrangements are agreed upon, the following procedures are to be used in the submission of billing for legal services and costs incurred:

Submit to the assigned attorney monthly billings for services rendered and costs incurred. Include the name of the attorney, paralegal/legal assistant, the date, the time expended, and a brief description of the service rendered. Costs should be identified and itemized. The respective hourly billing rates of the attorneys and paralegals/legal assistants working on a particular matter should be included on the billing statement or provided by separate letter.

Except in unusual circumstances, the Company does not expect to pay for secretarial time, word processing, or extra staffing. Similarly, time expended in review of files upon reassignment of a case within the outside firm and for its convenience should not be charged to the Company. On those rare occasions when the nature of the task or time constraints require extraordinary efforts, billing for extra staffing should be preauthorized by the OGC. Copying and its attendant costs should be limited wherever possible. When the need of extensive copying arises, consideration should be given to the use of the Company's copying facilities.

The use of standard pleadings and cover letters when appropriate is encouraged.

Research

While not every issue researched must be reduced to a writing, whenever outside counsel prepares a formal research memorandum, a copy is to be provided to the assigned attorney. Before outside counsel undertakes research projects requiring more than ten hours of lawyer time, the matter should be discussed with and authorized by the assigned attorney.

Staffing

Counsel retained by the Company in a particular matter bear the responsibility of providing appropriate staffing. Except in extraordinary circumstances, one attorney should conduct depositions and attend motion hearings, settlement conferences, and strategy meetings. The need for more than one trial counsel is to be discussed with the assigned attorney on a case-by-case basis. Clearly the supervising partner need not conduct every deposition, attend every hearing, and be present for every meeting, since many of such functions usually can be performed by an associate. On the other hand, certain matters do require the presence and active participation of the "heavyweight" partner. The decision as to who should do what during the course of a particular matter must be made with the objective of providing the Company with the best legal representation *on a cost-effective basis.*

The assigned attorney should assist in gathering files, contacting witnesses (particularly Company employees and officers), collating information, and providing overall support to outside counsel. The active use of the assigned attorney in this support role can substantially reduce the cost of litigation for the Company.

In cases in which Company personnel are potential witnesses, early interviews of those persons are recommended, since memories fade and personnel resign, retire, or are terminated, and sometimes become hostile. Likewise, if appropriate, securing possession of pertinent Company files is important and should be completed early in the case.

Discovery

The discovery phase of litigation is time-consuming and therefore extremely expensive. The planning and implementation of a reasonable discovery program is an important part of any litigation matter. The Litigation Evaluation Form should assist in this process. Some cases require numerous depositions, extensive written interrogatories, and careful examination of voluminous files. Counsel must judge the necessity of pursuing every avenue of discovery before trial. Some "big" cases, due to the potential exposure, require a maximum effort in the discovery phase. Other cases, potentially less harmful, may not need such full coverage.

Motions

All motions should first be discussed with the assigned attorney. Discretionary motions should be limited to situations where there is a better than even chance of a successful final disposition of the case, or where such a motion provides some worthwhile strategic advantage. Of course, motions that are dilatory in nature or intended to merely educate or harass the opposition are to be avoided.

801

Settlement

It is a fact that over 90 percent of the cases filed against the Company are settled before the trial of the action. Counsel representing the Company must be sensitive to settlement opportunities, particularly in the early stages of litigation. Whenever possible, without impairing the Company's position, discovery programs should be structured so that settlement discussions can commence as soon as possible. Personality conflicts between opposing counsel that inhibit settlement should be avoided. The use of a risk analysis procedure, if appropriate, is encouraged. All settlement overtures by opposing counsel should be passed on to the assigned attorney. The use of the Litigation Evaluation and Settlement Discussion Checklist (Form 15) is helpful in focusing on the aspects of a particular case and assists in explaining the important aspects of a case to senior management as part of the settlement procedure.

FORM 14

Litigation Evaluation Form

Date: ______________________

Case Name: ______________________

Court: ______________________

OGC Contact: ______________________

Gravamen of the Action: ______________________

____

____

Relief Sought: ______________________

____

____

Counsel Assigned to the Case

Law Firm: ______________________

Partner: ______________________

Associate(s): ______________________

Paralegal(s): ______________________

Possible Depositions

Company Officers and Employees: ______________________

Adverse Parties: ______________________

Nonparty Witnesses: ______________________

Possible Document Production

Company Files: ______________________

Company Manuals: ______________________

Adverse Party Books and Records: ______________________________

____

Nonparty Books and Records: __________________________________

____

Projected Legal Fees and Costs

Next Six Months: ____

Next Twelve Months: ____

Up to Trial: ____

Recommended Strategy

Settlement Possibilities

Current: ____

Future: ____

Tactical Pleading

Demurrer: ____

Summary Judgment: _____________________________________

Other: ____

Discovery Tactics

Intensive: ____

Minimal: ____

Remarks:

____

____

____

____

____

____

____

____

____

FORM 15

Litigation Evaluation and Settlement Discussion Checklist

I. Statement of facts
II. Gravamen of the action
III. Damages
   A. General
   B. Special
   C. Punitive
IV. Legal authority
   A. Supporting Company's position
   B. Supporting plaintiff's position
V. Plaintiff's case
   A. Character of plaintiff and evaluation as witness
   B. Sympathy factor
   C. Type of injury claimed
      1. Emotional
      2. Physical
      3. Special damages
   D. Evaluation of opposing witnesses
   E. Evaluation of opposing counsel, including experience, competence, and character
   F. Strongest point of plaintiff's case
   G. Weakest point of plaintiff's case
VI. Company's case
   A. Evaluation of Company's witnesses
   B. Effectiveness as witnesses before a jury
   C. Availability—depositions—statements
   D. Sufficiency of documentary evidence
   E. Experience of Company's trial counsel
   F. Strongest point of Company's case
   G. Weakest point of Company's case
VII. Present status of case
   A. Additional discovery
   B. Time to trial
   C. Prior settlement discussions

1. Offer
2. Demand

D. Fees and costs to date
E. Fees and costs trial preparation and trial
F. Length of trial

VIII. Alternative dispute resolution procedures

A. Arbitration
B. Minitrial
C. Rent-a-judge
D. Other

IX. Trial counsel's evaluation

X. Risk analysis

XI. Settlement proposals

A. By Company
B. By plaintiff

Remarks:

FORM 16

Litigation Principles as Stated in Letters from President and Vice President–General Counsel and in Guidelines for Practice Under the Federal Rules

Letter from Company President
To All Lawyers Representing [Company]

Former Chief Justice Warren E. Burger remarked that "a more productive judicial system is essential for justice," and during his tenure he dedicated himself to the improvement of our system of justice. Yet, despite his efforts and the demonstrable improvement in the efficiency of the federal courts, dissatisfaction still exists in the public and in the business community in particular with the burdens and costs of litigation in this country.

The notorious burden of litigation for American business has grown to the point that it can and does have a significantly negative impact upon the financial results of many of our corporations. Whatever the reason, it cannot continue in an economic world where success demands productivity and cost-effectiveness from business entities. We cannot lose sight of our system of justice as the pillar supporting our individual rights, but neither can we ignore the threat to that system if our companies do not maintain a competitive position in world markets. Unnecessary cost burdens must be addressed and eliminated.

At his confirmation hearings in 1969, the former Chief Justice noted that he could not improve the efficiency of the judicial system by himself. Many in the judiciary, government and the organized Bar followed his leadership and joined in the effort, and yet spiraling legal costs continue as a fact of life. One party to the problem who has not been involved in the solution is the litigant. Of course, no one litigant or class of litigants can provide solutions. Yet, corporations find themselves in court more often than the individual citizen and thus are in a position to provide direct support to efforts at court reform. It is time for the business community to cease complaining about runaway costs and to lend its support to the efforts of the former Chief Justice.

[Company] intends to demonstrate its support through the conduct of its lawyers in the courtroom. We will insist that when you appear on our behalf that you have as one of your primary objectives the support and maintenance of an efficient court system as required by the letter and spirit of the recently amended Federal Rules. Since this is consistent with your professional obligations, I do not see it as a direction that you can find objectionable.

However, I am advised that many misuses and abuses of our judicial system are justified by practitioners on the basis of an obligation to the client. The exhaustion of adversarial opportunities is characterized as the epitome of professional dedication to the client. Our system demands dedication to the client but there must always be trade-offs. The policy question of whether zealous adversary positions should be pursued despite their negative impact on the system is not often brought to the attention of the client and generally are made by the lawyer. Absent client direction, the professional most often will—and perhaps should—follow the advocate track and rationalize his or her conduct on the basis of the client's wishes.

Of course, lawyers have a professional obligation to the courts as well, but the client, too, has an interest in the efficient administration of justice above and beyond the particular issues in a given lawsuit. The professional principles that underlie the lawyer's obligation to the courts have relevance to all our citizenry. It is not a conflicting obligation but rather a limitation on their obligation to the client. I suspect many of you will accept this in principle, but considerable disagreement will exist among you as to its practical application. This is to be expected, especially where the client has given no direction as to its position on specific matters.

To the end that we may both better address the need for supporting the drive to make litigation a more efficient process, I have directed our General Counsel to establish ground rules and principles of behavior for all lawyers representing [Company] to guide their conduct in litigated matters, particularly in the context of the Federal Rules. They will apply to attorneys employed by the Company as well as to those whom we may retain. These rules must, of course, be consistent with the codes of ethics of the profession but are to specifically address those areas where it is the recognized prerogative of the client to decide upon courses of action bearing upon the conduct of litigation. The Corporation expects its interests to be protected as appropriate but not with a disregard for the need for an efficient system of justice. I believe there is ample room for improvement without any impact on the interest of the Corporation.

I trust I can count on your full cooperation with and endorsement of this effort.

[Name]
President
[Company]

Letter from Vice President–General Counsel
To [Company] Attorneys

Our profession is laboring under a perception by businessmen that we are inefficient and unconcerned by costs. Our clients are particularly critical of the economics of the litigation process. I personally believe that, insofar as the Bar as a whole is concerned, much of the criticism is warranted. Whether or not we agree as to the degree of unwarranted cost in the process, we must all agree that the perception exists and that alone is cause for concern.

I hardly need say that I applaud the views espoused by our Chief Executive Officer, [Name], in his letter on litigation practices. An efficient judicial system is key to the climate in which our businesses operate and it is shortsighted to pursue every perceived advantage in a particular lawsuit without giving a thought to the importance of protecting that system. His position of leadership on this issue, however, throws the challenge back where it belongs: on us, as practicing lawyers. [Company] attorneys cannot justify extreme advocacy positions on the ground that the client expects it of us. We are expected to exercise judgment, avoiding futile searches for perfection and battles which are not likely to have a substantive impact on our litigation, but we, nonetheless, are expected to protect our client. The challenge we face is not to unduly impose on the courts while protecting the interest of the Company. I am confident we can improve our practice substantially without foregoing any of the substantive rights of [Company]. I say that even though I am equally convinced that the attorneys representing this Company are already effective litigation managers.

The attached Guidelines were prepared by a committee of the American Corporate Counsel Association. Their focus is the Federal Rules, and upon three of them in particular; but it is expected that the same principles will be applied in all courts. We intend to expand them and amend them as we gain experience with them and as the Rules themselves are expanded and amended. You should accept them as an instruction from the client with all of the professional obligations that that implies. You will not find much foreign to the practices we have followed in the past, and I hope you will use the Guidelines as a means for expanded professional leadership of the Trial Bar.

[Name]
Vice President and General Counsel
[Company]

Attachment

Guidelines for Practice under the Federal Rules
Rule 11

Guideline #1

No cause of action should be pleaded unless that cause of action would be the basis for a lawsuit standing by itself.

Comment: Causes of action are often asserted in litigation which are beyond the one that motivated the lawsuit. The inclusion of these additional causes of actions is generally justified on the ground that: (a) something might occur or be discovered during the course of the lawsuit that would give vitality to these ancillary causes of actions; and (b) there is little additional cost in including these claims.

In practice an ancillary cause of action that standing alone would not have prompted litigation rarely results in significant recovery. On the other hand, these claims often result in a great deal of unnecessary costs and expenses, including additional discovery or motions to dismiss. Moreover, spurious claims constitute unprofessional conduct. The application of an economic test for the inclusion of a cause of action can eliminate overbearing complaints without prejudicing the Company and can eliminate an unjustifiable burden on the courts.

Guideline #2

Whenever litigation is being filed in order to preserve rights due to the running of a statute of limitations, the attorney responsible should, before filing the lawsuit, seek an agreement to toll the statute of limitations for a period sufficient to make a reasonable investigation as to whether or not a lawsuit is warranted.

Comment: One obvious conflict between the requirements of rule 11 and the obligations of an attorney to protect his or her client arises when the attorney's ability to protect a client, for reasons beyond the attorney's control, conflicts with his or her ability to make as thorough an investigation as required by rule 11. In situations where an attorney is unable to make such an investigation before filing the complaint due to pending expiration of a statute of limitations, he or she should file the lawsuit only if, after diligent effort, an agreement cannot be reached with the adversary to toll the statute of limitations of enough duration to make a reasonable inquiry.

Guideline #3

Upon receipt of a complaint, and if possible before an answer is due, the attorney having primary responsibility for defending the Company shall

initiate discussions with opposing counsel in order to determine the following:

- **The precise nature of the claim**
- **The propriety of the lawyer's client as defendant**
- **The prospect of using alternative dispute resolution in resolving the claim**

Such discussions shall not be necessary where communications between the Company's counsel and opposing counsel were had before the filing of the complaint.

Comment: The Company's interests are not advanced by the premature preparation of papers, and the resulting filing of pleadings and motions places a burden on the courts that may not be warranted. This guideline ensures that a dialogue between opposing counsel is initiated and that the essential nature of the dispute is determined before work commences on the case.

The lawyers are asked to candidly discuss the precise nature of the claim, e.g., not simply that the defendant was negligent, but the precise manner in which the Company is alleged to be negligent and how the harm occurred.

Finally, it is also useful at this stage to see if alternative dispute resolution (ADR) is practical before work commences on the assumption of a court or jury trial.

Guideline #4

Plaintiffs and defendants should draft pleadings in a manner that facilitates resolution of disputed issues by rule 12(c). Rule 12(c) motions are to be made as soon as possible after the pleadings are closed.

Comment: It is the obligation of attorneys to define the issues in dispute with enough particularity to resolve matters that can be resolved as issues of law on the pleadings. Combining or obfuscating issues in order to avoid rule 12(c) motions is improper.

Parties who are able to make rule 12(c) motions should make such motions as soon as possible in order to eliminate the lawsuit or refine it to the essential issues of the dispute.

Guideline #5

In initially evaluating a pleading from the perspective of plaintiff or defendant, primary focus shall be given to resolving all or as many of the issues in dispute as possible by means of a rule 56 motion for summary judgment.

Comment: In the past, courts have been reluctant to grant motions for summary judgment, and consequently these motions have not been used as often as they might. The fact remains that the use of rule 56 motions can greatly reduce litigation costs and speed up the trial. While it is our practice to file motions on the basis of cost/benefit trade-offs, attorneys representing the Company shall not decide against filing a rule 56 motion merely on the basis of perceived judicial reluctance to grant such motions. When a complaint is drafted or received, the application of a rule 56 motion shall be considered at the outset. Similarly, rule 56 motions shall be given priority consideration throughout the proceedings as papers are filed or produced by the adversary. The attorney certification requirements of rule 11 should be emphasized in such motions where appropriate.

Guideline #6

It shall be the obligation of attorneys representing the Company to bring to the attention of the court any conduct by other attorneys of record that may merit the imposition of sanctions pursuant to rule 11.

Comment: Unprofessional conduct or actions in violation of the rules often will not come to the attention of the court without a specific motion. As officers of the court, attorneys have a professional obligation to assure that the rules of court are recognized and applied. It is not for the Company's lawyers to decide whether sanctions should indeed be imposed, but without their activist support, the intent of the rules may be frustrated. This obligation requires the application of objective judgment without concern for the possibility of cross-motions for sanctions.

The purpose of the guideline is not to cause secondary litigation over such issues. It is expected that the mere existence of the guideline will induce attorneys to comply with the rules and thus avoid unwanted dispute over conformity therewith. Nonetheless, without occasional motions for sanctions, the spirit of rule 11 will not be universally achieved.

This guideline is identical to guidelines 3 of rule 16 and 4 of rule 26.

Rule 16

Guideline #1

Whether or not local rules may exempt the application of Federal Rule 16, lawyers representing the Company shall, within thirty days of the commencement of court litigation, prepare a strategy for addressing the case. Such strategy shall include an assessment of settlement possibilities and an identification of the key factual and/or legal issues in the case as they then appear to them. Unless early settlement seems likely, the attor-

neys shall also set forth the particular discovery they propose to take with respect to the issues identified. Counsel will identify motions they feel will expedite the litigation or assist in focusing on the issues in the case, and they will allocate the work load under the proposed plan.

The proposed strategy will be reviewed and agreed to by the General Counsel or his or her designee before submission of papers for the first pretrial conference.

Comment: The failure of attorneys to meet early to assess a lawsuit and to agree upon a plan for meeting the issues not only generates costly inefficiencies but also imposes upon the court's time. Planning is the key to all effective enterprises, and while plans for a lawsuit may change as new material comes to light, litigation cannot be permitted to drift without purpose or direction. From the first day of filing, some things are known about the lawsuit that permit intelligent planning of a course of action. Even if nothing were known, the attorneys can plan a strategy to develop the relevant factual and legal issues based on the allegations in the pleadings and the known facts of the Company's business.

Guideline #2

Scheduling orders are consistent with the objective of expediting litigation. Unless excused by local rule, the attorneys representing the Company shall seek the entry by the court of an order consistent with the plan agreed upon pursuant to guideline #1 of rule 16. In no event shall an attorney seek a provision in any order for the purpose of delaying the litigation unless he or she shall advise the court of that purpose and the reasons why delay is necessary or desirable.

Comment: The direction of rule 16 is to provide for judicial management of litigation. This purpose is supported by the Company, and therefore the attorneys representing the Company are expected to support the endeavors of trial judges to manage the court's case load. The requirements of rule 16 are consistent with the professional obligations of attorneys to the Company and with the Company's Guidelines under this rule and rules 11 and 26.

While submissions under this guideline must be in accord with the plan developed under guideline #1, the plan itself should be treated as attorney work product and privileged. This guideline is not intended to waive the Company's rights in that regard.

Guideline #3

It shall be the obligation of attorneys representing the Company to bring to the attention of the court any conduct by other attorneys of record that may merit the imposition of sanctions pursuant to rule 16(f).

Comment: This guideline is identical to guidelines 6 of rule 11 and 4 of rule 26. Although the sanctions applied by the court may differ under the individual rules, the basis for seeking their application is the same.

Rule 26

Guideline #1

Before pursuing any discovery, litigation counsel shall submit to the General Counsel or his or her designee a written statement of the following:

- **The particular discovery method to be used and why it is the most desirable**
- **The lawyer responsible for it and the persons assisting, if any**
- **The issue on which the discovery bears**
- **The fact issues expected to be developed**

No discovery shall be instituted without approval of the General Counsel or his or her designee of the discovery proposed.

Comment: Discovery reputedly is the most abused process in litigation. A requirement that the purpose be justified along with the means proposed will curtail fishing expeditions and avoid use of procedural tools for purposes other than resolution of the substantive disputes.

The desirability of a particular discovery method shall be determined in light of its expense relative to the issues in controversy and the alternative means for discovering the facts. In no case shall discovery be recommended on the basis of the burden it will place upon other parties or the delay it will cause in the proceedings.

This guideline is consistent with guideline #1 of rule 16, requiring the submission and approval of a discovery plan and may be encompassed in the compliance with that guideline.

Guideline #2

The lawyer responsible for the discovery proposed and approved by the Office of General Counsel shall sign the discovery request pursuant to rule 26(g).

Comment: Inasmuch as sanctions may be imposed upon attorneys engaged in improper discovery practice, it is incumbent upon the lawyer responsible for each item of discovery to accept professional responsibility for his or her actions. No attorney will be expected to sign a discovery request that has been modified from his or her proposal unless the attorney shall agree with the modification.

Guideline #3

No lawyer shall sign a response or objection to discovery unless he or she has made a personal professional judgment consistent with rule 26(g) that the correct information has been provided or that the objection is ap-

propriate and not for the purpose of delay or harassment of other parties. Objections to discovery shall not be made without prior notification to opposing counsel and an effort to dispose of the issue without court intervention.

Comment: This guideline is consistent with the professional responsibility of lawyers and their exposure to sanctions for improper use of discovery. No attorney can guarantee that the client has provided all relevant and correct information, but he or she must be reasonable in concluding that the professional obligation has been met.

Guideline #4

It shall be the obligation of attorneys representing the Company to bring to the attention of the court any conduct by other attorneys of record that may merit the imposition of sanctions pursuant to rule 26(g).

Comment: This guideline is identical to guidelines 6 of rule 11 and 3 of rule 16. Although the sanctions applied by the court may differ under the individual rules, the basis for seeking their application is the same.

FORM 17

Fee Agreement on Contingent Fee

[Name and address of Corporate counsel]

Re: [name of case]

Dear ______________ :

This letter will set forth our fee agreement concerning the above-entitled matter:

1. We will be paid at our customary hourly rates for the initial investigation of the case, which we anticipate shall be concluded within the next couple of weeks. Our fees for this stage of the case will not exceed $ ______________ .
2. We will also receive one-third of any recovery, whether by judgment, settlement or other compromise, in this matter, less any fees paid pursuant to paragraph 1 of this agreement. Any court-awarded fees will be considered as part of the recovery and will be added to damages, lost profits, and anything else of value recovered before application of the determination of the firm's fees. If a judgement or settlement is uncollectible, [the Company] will pay us at our customary hourly rates for work performed on this matter.
3. In addition to the fees described in paragraphs 1 and 2 of this letter, [the Company] will reimburse us for any out-of-pocket costs or expenses incurred in connection with this matter, including travel expenses, expert witness fees, process fees, transcript costs, and the like. Costs and expenses will be billed to you monthly.

If this agreement is acceptable to you, please sign the copy of the letter enclosed herewith and return it to me.

Very truly yours,

The above terms are acceptable.

____

FORM 18

Fee Agreement on Modified Contingent Fee

[Name and address of Corporate counsel]

Re: [name of case]

Dear ______________:

Our firm is willing to represent [the Company] in connection with the above-entitled matter on the following basis:

1. Our fee will be the greater of (a) one-third of any recovery, by judgment, settlement, or other compromise, or (b) one-half of our normal hourly rates for time spent on the case. Our present hourly rates are $ ______________ per hour for partners, $ ______________ per hour for associates, and $ ______________ per hour for paralegals and law clerks. You will also be responsible for the full amount of any costs incurred in connection with the case.
2. The fee arrangement set forth in paragraph 1 will be applicable to both any proceedings in the Circuit Court and to any appeal taken by [the defendant] from a Circuit Court judgment in your favor.
3. We will bill you on a monthly basis for time spent on the case at one-half of our normal hourly rates, plus costs. If we succeed in obtaining a recovery and one-third of the recovery exceeds the amount of our monthly billings, you will be required to pay us the difference between one-third of the recovery and our monthly billings, but such payment need not be made until you have received the funds representing the recovery.

If these terms are acceptable to you, please sign the enclosed copy of this letter and return it to me in the self-addressed, stamped envelope that I have included herewith.

Very truly yours,

The above terms are acceptable.

____

FORM 19

Fee Agreement on a Fixed Fee Plus Bonus

[Name and address of Corporate counsel]

Dear ______________ :

Our firm will be pleased to represent [name of company] in connection with [description of matter]. Our representation will be on the following terms:

1. *Preliminary analysis of case.* We will conduct a preliminary analysis of the case, which shall include review of any relevant documents and/or pleadings, discussion of factual background with selected company personnel, and initial examination of applicable legal authorities. This preliminary analysis will be completed by [date]. Our fee for this preliminary analysis will be calculated at our customary hourly rates, but shall not exceed [agreed amount]. Any costs incurred shall be in addition to this amount.
2. *Optional fixed-fee agreement.* Following our preliminary analysis of the case, we will either continue to represent [name of company] on an hourly basis or, at the option of the company, we will enter into a fixed-fee agreement for handling the remainder of the case. A fixed-fee agreement will include separate fee amounts for each of the following:

   - Initial pleadings stage—drafting complaint, answering complaint, drafting or answering counterclaim, preparing or responding to motion to dismiss.
   - Discovery—depending on the case, the fee for discovery may be divided into three parts—minimum discovery, medium discovery, and maximum discovery. Criteria defining each of these categories shall be set forth in the fixed-fee schedule.
   - Motion for summary judgment—this amount is optional, and preparation of a motion for summary judgment will

only be undertaken at the appropriate time in the case after consultation with the client.

- Trial preparation—includes all work done after discovery cutoff date, including interviewing witnesses, assembling exhibits, and preparing the final pretrial order.
- Trial.
- Posttrial motions.

The fees for the above items do not include costs, which shall be billed separately. The consent of the company shall be obtained before incurring any major expenses, including travel expenses, experts' fees, and major copying projects. Moreover, the fees for the above items do not include any interlocutory appeals. Our fee for an interlocutory appeal shall be the subject of a separate fixed-fee agreement or shall be billed on an hourly basis, at the option of the company. Naturally, as indicated by the above categories, the fixed-fee agreement does not include any postjudgment appeals.

3. *Timing of fee payments.* Hourly billing shall be on a monthly basis. Fixed-fee payments shall be determined on a monthly basis by dividing the fee for a particular stage of the proceeding by the number of months that stage is anticipated to last. However, in all cases, the fixed fee for a particular stage of the proceeding shall be due when that stage is concluded. Under both hourly and fixed-fee billings, expenses will be billed monthly.
4. *Bonus for successful completion.* The fixed-fee schedule shall set forth guidelines for payment of an agreed bonus for successful conclusion of the case. The size of the bonus will vary depending on the stage at which the litigation is concluded, with a higher bonus provided for earlier resolution. This system reflects the savings to the company in both administrative time and fee payments that would accompany a quick disposition of the case.
5. *Staffing.* Through discussions with you, we will come to a mutual agreement as to how the case will be staffed. No change in staffing will be made without your prior consent.

The foregoing principles are incorporated into a sample fixed-fee schedule attached hereto. We shall forward a completed schedule to you at the conclusion of our preliminary analysis.

Very truly yours,

Fixed-Fee Schedule for Representation of [Name of Company] in Connection with [Description of Matter]

Description	*Total Fee*	*Monthly Fee*
1. Initial pleading stage	—	—
2. Discovery		
Option 1: Total cost	—	—
Option 2:		
a. Minimum [description of minimum discovery]	—	—
b. Medium [description of medium discovery]	—	—
c. Maximum [description of maximum discovery]	—	—
3. Motion for summary judgment on behalf of company	—	—
4. Response to motion for summary judgment on behalf of another party	—	—
5. Trial preparation	—	—
6. Trial	—	—
7. Posttrial motions	—	—
8. Bonus—Settlement or judgment at or below [above] [amount] ("the bonus amount")	—	—
a. 25 percent of difference between settlement or judgment amount and the bonus amount if case is concluded before the end of initial pleading stage		
b. 15 percent of difference between settlement or judgment amount and the bonus amount if case is concluded before the end of minimum discovery stage		
c. 10 percent of difference between settlement or judgment amount and the bonus amount if case is concluded before the end of entire discovery stage		
d. 5 percent of difference between settlement or judgment amount and the bonus amount if case is concluded at any other time		

Forms for Section IV:

Managing the Cost of Corporate Litigation

FORM 20

Budget Format (Preliminary Injunction, Summary Judgment, Evidentiary Showing)

Work to Be Done through Hearing on Motion for Preliminary Injunction

Complete preparation of complaint, including collection of market and other data still needed; effect service	25 hrs.
[Optional, though recommended: Additional time required to interview & secure assent from employee if one is to serve as joint plaintiff, and to incorporate employee data into complaint]	10 hrs.
Preparation of motion for preliminary injunction and supporting documents:	
• Complete collection and review of authorities, including local court files in recent case involving similar issue	20 hrs.
• Prepare brief in support of motion for preliminary injunction, assuming argument of both illegality of contract termination under California law and ineffectiveness of termination notice, but not potential antitrust issues	25 hrs.
• Prepare affidavits in support of motion, including interviews or other communications with affiants and collection of supporting exhibits from client files (assume two affiants from client and one from consulting firm)	30 hrs.
Review brief in opposition to motion for preliminary injunction; examine authorities not previously cited or identified; check facts asserted in brief and supporting affidavits	10 hrs.

Prepare reply brief in support of motion, including preparation of affidavits refuting statements in defendant's affidavits (assume three additional or supplemental affidavits)	20 hrs.
Prepare for and present oral argument on motion	5 hrs.
Preliminary Injunction Total	145 hrs.
145 hours at assumed composite rate (lawyer and paralegal) of ________________	______
Expenses (principally copying and air courier)	______

Work Required in Resisting Anticipated Defendant's Motion for Summary Judgment

Review defendant's motion for summary judgment and supporting affidavits; review authorities cited and factual assertions made that were not addressed in connection with motion for preliminary injunction	15 hrs.
Preparation of brief and supporting documents in opposition to summary judgment motion:	
• Drafting legal arguments, including necessary additional research	15 hrs.
• Preparation of affidavits refuting representations contained in defendant's affidavits, including interviews with affiants (assume two from client and one from consulting firm)	30 hrs.
• Search of client files for documents needed to meet and refute defendant's showing (assume search by client personnel with assistance from one paralegal)	20 hrs.
Review of defendant's reply brief; consideration of responses to be made at oral argument to new points made	10 hrs.
Preparation for and presentation of oral argument	5 hrs.
Summary Judgment Motion Total	95 hrs.
95 hours at assumed composite rate of ________________	______
Expenses (copying and air courier)	______

Additional Expenses if Discovery Necessary—Either Because Initiated by Us or Because It Becomes Essential to Refutation of Defendant's Evidentiary Showing

Depositions

Prepare deposition notices, including requests for documents to be produced at deposition	5 hrs.

Prepare and take depositions of defendant's president and one other representative of defendant, including review of documents produced; assume two-day depositions and one lawyer taking deposition (with assistance from paralegal for notetaking and document control)	50 hrs.
Prepare three client witnesses for deposition by defendant (assume two from client and one from consulting firm)	20 hrs.
Defend our witnesses at their depositions (assume two days each and one lawyer without assistance)	
	35 hrs.

Documentary Discovery

Collect and produce documents demanded by defendant in connection with depositions of our witnesses (assume use of subpoenas duces tecum only, no discovery motions at this point; assume search of client files to be done by client personnel with some assistance by one paralegal)	20 hrs.
Incorporate documents produced and testimony taken into briefs filed in connection with application for preliminary injunction and/or motion for summary judgment	30 hrs.
Discovery Total	160 hrs.
160 hours at assumed composite rate of __________ (reflecting lower ratio of lawyer to paralegal time than on briefing and arguing motions)	______
Court Reporter charges in connection with depositions	$8000
[Optional: additional cost of videotaping deposition of defendant's president; assume use of law firm equipment and personnel]	$ 500
Discovery Total	______

FORM 21

Litigation Projection

Sour-Grapes Buyer v. International Multinational Corp. et al.

Projection for Remainder of Time until Trial
January 1, 198x–December 31, 198x

Description	*Days Allotted*	*Estimated Fees*
1. *Preparation for IMC's defensive case*—Organize fruits of discovery from IMC, SGB, other defendants, and third-party witnesses as they bear on IMC's defenses. Prepare for trial testimony, prepare trial exhibits and deposition excerpts, prepare charts and other demonstrative aids.	Attorney time: _____ Paralegal time: _____	$ ______________ $ ______________
2. *Motions and briefs relating directly to IMC's case*—Prepare motion for summary judgment pertaining to IMC's conduct; prepare trial brief pertaining to IMC's conduct; prepare necessary evidentiary briefs re matters affecting IMC's case.	Attorney time: _____ Paralegal time: _____	$ ______________ $ ______________
3. *Preparation of IMC's counterclaim case*—Organize fruits of discovery from IMC, SGB, and third-party witnesses as they bear on IMC's counterclaim. Conduct necessary third-party discovery that supports counterclaim damages (e.g., re loss of opportunity claims). Work with IMC personnel to define IMC damages and SGB effects on IMC more clearly. Do necessary legal research to support IMC's counterclaim theories. Work with experts (group or IMC alone) to define and prove IMC's damages. Prepare for trial testimony, prepare trial exhibits and deposition excerpts, prepare charts and other demonstrative aids.	Attorney time: _____ Paralegal time: _____	$ ______________ $ ______________

Task	Time	Cost
4. *Motions and briefs relating directly to IMC's counterclaim*—Prepare trial brief relating to IMC's counterclaim; prepare any necessary evidentiary briefs.	Attorney time: _____ Paralegal time: _____	$ ____________ $ ____________
5. *SGB personnel and former personnel depositions (liability)*—Prepare for and take depositions of SGB personnel still remaining that we agreed with co-counsel to do for liability case: Haig, Weinberger.	Attorney time: _____ Paralegal time: _____	$ ____________ $ ____________
6. *SGB Damage case*—Work with co-counsel in program of discovery aimed at SGB's damage case. Prepare for and take depositions of SGB's personnel assigned: Meese, Deaver, and perhaps Baker. Work with accounting experts on analysis of SGB damage case and development of testimony necessary to meet it.	Attorney time: _____ Paralegal time: _____	$ ____________ $ ____________
7. *Fruits of SGB discovery assigned to us*—Organize fruits of discovery of SGB personnel whose depositions we were responsible for. Prepare necessary summaries for use in joint briefs. Prepare for trial examination, prepare trial exhibits and deposition excerpts, prepare charts and other demonstrative aids. SGB witnesses involved: Haig, Weinberger, Watt, Regan, Stockman, Meese, Deaver, and Baker.	Attorney time: _____ Paralegal time: _____	$ ____________ $ ____________
8. *Third-party discovery*—Participate in third-party discovery that directly affects IMC's interests, e.g., Darth Vader, Intexco personnel (L. Skywalker, H. Solo).	Attorney time: _____ Paralegal time: _____	$ ____________ $ ____________
9. *Remaining discovery of defendants*—Participate in remaining discovery of defendants that directly affects IMC's interests, e.g., M. Piggy, K. Frog, C. Monster	Attorney time: _____ Paralegal time: _____	$ ____________ $ ____________
10. *PVC discovery*—Participate in PVC discovery that directly affects IMC's interests. Cross-examine to establish affirmative points IMC wants to prove, e.g., P. Lastic Pipe.	Attorney time: _____ Paralegal time: _____	$ ____________ $ ____________

11. *Industry discovery*—Review and analyze documents of other industry members assigned to us, for use in task force projects, for materials in support of economic case, and generally for materials for trial. Other industry members involved: U.S. Industries, Interstellar Conglomerates, Multiphasic Associates, Trans-Pacific Inc., Uniexit Inc. Depose USI as assigned to us, and if Group II companies are deposed, IC, MA, and T-P. Organize all fruits of discovery. Review fruits of industry discovery conducted by others for items of particular use to IMC.

    Attorney time: _____ $ ______________

    Paralegal time: _____ $ ______________

12. *Our economic case*—Work with IMC in-house personnel, co-counsel, Professors Macro, Micro, et al., and Rice Porterhouse & Co. on development of economic case. Prepare witnesses for and participate in expert depositions. Help in preparing for trial testimony, trial exhibits, charts, and other demonstrative aids.

    Attorney time: _____ $ ______________

    Paralegal time: _____ $ ______________

13. *SGB's economic case*—Prepare for and participate in depositions of SGB's economic experts. Work with our experts on analysis of SGB's economic case. Help in preparing for trial examination, trial exhibits, charts, and other demonstrative aids.

    Attorney time: _____ $ ______________

    Paralegal time: _____ $ ______________

14. *Task force projects*—Complete updating of price verification task force project assigned to us. Coordinate with other co-counsel and provide input into other task force projects. Organize fruits of task force projects into trial evidence. Review fruits for matters of direct assistance to IMC's case.

    Attorney time: _____ $ ______________

    Paralegal time: _____ $ ______________

15. *Further document work*—Complete coding of deposition exhibits assigned to us and not yet done. Pursue, as needed, additional documentary materials resulting from discovery program. Anticipate further disputes on productions to date, and possible further requests to be handled (e.g., subpoena on IMC's joint venture with Trans-Pacific).

    Attorney time: _____ $ ______________

    Paralegal time: _____ $ ______________

16. *Requests for admissions*—Prepare such requests and respond to SGB's requests for admissions as part of court's requirements concerning stipulations of fact.	Attorney time: _____ $ ____________ Paralegal time: _____ $ ____________
17. *Tasks required by court's pretrial schedule—Stipulations*—Preparation of proposed stipulations of law and fact and statements of issues; coordination with co-counsel; review of SGB's proposals; negotiations with SGB re stipulations, statements of issues.	Attorney time: _____ $ ____________ Paralegal time: _____ $ ____________
18. *Tasks required by court's pretrial schedule—exhibits/depositions*—Preparation of proposed exhibits, exhibit lists, deposition excerpts, videotapes, interrogatory answers; coordination with co-counsel; review of SGB's proposals; negotiations with SGB re exhibits, exhibit lists, deposition excerpts, etc.; preparation of counter-designations.	Attorney time: _____ $ ____________ Paralegal time: _____ $ ____________
19. *Tasks required by court's pretrial schedule—special pretrial conferences*—Preparation for and participation in pretrial conferences scheduled to narrow issues, settle admissibility of exhibits, establish order of proof, settle jury matters, etc.	Attorney time: _____ $ ____________ Paralegal time: _____ $ ____________
20. *Pretrial briefs*—Work on defendants' joint briefs on defense and counterclaim. (Separate briefs by IMC re its own specific issues are also contemplated.) Review of SGB's briefs, and work on reply briefs.	Attorney time: _____ $ ____________ Paralegal time: _____ $ ____________
21. *Other briefing*—Participation in briefing efforts on motions of particular importance to IMC, e.g., jury trial, bifurcation, severance, motions to limit evidence, or other evidentiary motions.	Attorney time: _____ $ ____________ Paralegal time: _____ $ ____________
22. *Jury instructions*—Coordination with co-counsel in work on defendants' joint jury instructions on defense and counterclaims. Review of SGB's proposals and preparation of counterproposals.	Attorney time: _____ $ ____________ Paralegal time: _____ $ ____________

23. *Other defense committee work*—Participation in joint defense committees other than as indicated above.	Attorney time: _____	$ _____________
	Paralegal time: _____	$ _____________
24. *Counsel meetings*—Participation in joint defense counsel meetings and advance preparation for them.	Attorney time: _____	$ _____________
	Paralegal time: _____	$ _____________
25. *General pretrial conferences and court hearings*—Participation in general pretrial conferences and court hearings, preparation for them, and attendance at counsel meetings related to them.	Attorney time: _____	$ _____________
	Paralegal time: _____	$ _____________
26. *Coordination of activities with co-defendants*—General coordination efforts and communications with respect to various joint defense problems.	Attorney time: _____	$ _____________
	Paralegal time: _____	$ _____________
27. *Monitoring case developments*—Keeping up with correspondence, pleadings, discovery and other pretrial activities, fruits of depositions, etc.	Attorney time: _____	$ _____________
	Paralegal time: _____	$ _____________
Totals	Attorney time: _____	$ _____________
	Paralegal time: _____	$ _____________

FORM 22

Retention and Billing Policy

The Company Office of General Counsel, except as otherwise agreed upon in advance in writing, expects to be charged for services rendered on its behalf solely on the basis of the application of counsel's standard hourly rate for the categories of partners and associates performing the services. Charges for air travel, except on international trips of ten elapsed hours or more, will be at the coach rate.

Procedure

A statement for services rendered may be submitted to the Retaining Company Attorney as often as the Retaining Company Attorney and counsel may desire. As a minimum, the statement shall be submitted at the end of any month in which the total services and disbursements exceed $2500 and at the end of each calendar quarter.

Each statement shall set forth with respect to each matter the statement covers:

- a *brief summary* of the various services performed;
- the number of hours spent by each category of partner and associate;
- the billing rate for each category of partner and associate;
- expenses and disbursements, in detail; and
- the total for each matter for the billing period.

For year-end accounting purposes, a statement as of November 30 will be required no later than December 10. A telephone or TWX estimate of December billings will be required on the last working day of December.

Only statements submitted in accordance with this procedure will be processed for payment.

Any questions concerning this policy and procedure should be addressed to the Retaining Company Attorney.

FORM 23

Model Litigation Budget in a Breach-of-Contract Case

Schedule A: Simple or Traditional Budget

Estimated Attorney's Fees Budget (through Trial)

Phase/Task	Personnel	Time	Hourly Rate	Projections
I. Introductory Phase				
A. Investigative/Research				
1. Research				
a. Research and preparation of memorandum on elements/defenses	Young associate	40 hrs.	$ 60/hr.	$ 2,400
	Young partner	5	$100	500
b. Research and preparation of memorandum on special problems	Young associate	20	$ 60	1,200
	Young partner	4	$100	400
2. Investigation				
a. Preliminary document search, organization, and review	Young associate	50	$ 60	3,000
	Young partner	10	$100	1,000
b. Initial interviews of corporate employees	Young partner	30	$100	3,000
B. Pleadings				
1. Drafting and reviewing original answer	Young associate	2	$ 60	120
	Young partner	3	$100	300
2. Drafting and reviewing amendments	Young partner	3	$100	300

Phase/Task	Personnel	Time	Hourly Rate	Projections
II. Discovery Phase				
A. Paper Discovery				
1. Drafting and reviewing interrogatories	Young associate	25 hrs.	$ 60/hr.	$1,500
	Young partner	10	$100	1,000
2. Responding to interrogatories	Young associate	20	$ 60	1,200
	Young partner	10	$100	1,000
3. Drafting and reviewing requests for admission	Young associate	7	$ 60	420
	Young partner	3	$100	300
4. Responding to requests for admission	Young associate	6	$ 60	360
	Young partner	3	$100	300
5. Drafting and reviewing requests for production	Young associate	20	$ 60	1,200
	Young partner	10	$100	1,000
6. Document search and responding to requests for production	Young associate	60	$ 60	3,600
	Young partner	30	$100	3,000
7. Review of plaintiffs' documents	Young partner	40	$100	4,000
	Young associate	80	$ 60	4,800
8. Preparation, research, and argument of discovery motions	Young partner	5	$100	500
	Young associate	20	$ 60	1,200
B. Oral Discovery				
1. Preparation for and taking of depositions of opposing-party witnesses				
a. Witness A	Young partner	20	$100	2,000
b. Witness B	Young partner	20	$100	2,000
c. Witness C	Young partner	20	$100	2,000
d. Witness D	Young associate	20	$ 60	1,200
e. Witness E	Young partner	30	$100	3,000
f. Witness F	Young partner	20	$100	2,000
g. Witness G	Young associate	25	$ 60	1,500
2. Preparation for and taking of depositions of third-party witnesses				
a. Witness H	Young partner	30	$100	3,000
b. Witness I	Young associate	30	$ 60	1,800
c. Witness J	Young associate	20	$ 60	1,200
d. Witness K	Young partner	20	$100	2,000
	Young associate	15	$ 60	900

Phase/Task	Personnel	Time	Hourly Rate	Projections
3. Preparation of and defending depositions of client's witnesses				
a. Witness A	Young Partner	20 hrs.	$100/hr.	$2,000
	Young associate	15	$ 60	900
b. Witness B	Young Partner	20	$100	2,000
	Young associate	15	$ 60	900
c. Witness C	Young Partner	15	$100	1,500
d. Witness D	Young Partner	25	$100	2,500
e. Witness E	Young Partner	25	$100	2,500
f. Witness F	Young Partner	25	$100	2,500
g. Witness G	Young Partner	35	$100	3,500
	Young associate	15	$ 60	900
h. Witness H	Young Partner	20	$100	2,000
i. Witness I	Young associate	25	$ 60	1,500
j. Witness J	Young associate	25	$ 60	1,500
k. Witness K	Young associate	20	$ 60	1,200
4. Preparation, taking, and defending of depositions of expert witnesses				
a. Witness A	Young partner	40	$100	4,000
b. Witness B	Young partner	25	$100	2,500
c. Witness C	Young partner	20	$100	2,000
d. Witness D	Young associate	20	$ 60	1,200
III. Miscellaneous (general telephone and office conferences and correspondence among counsel, with client, with opposing counsel, and with the court; discovery planning and budgeting, etc.)				4,900
IV. Trial Preparation				
1. Preparation, review, and argument of motion for summary judgment	Young partner	15	$100	1,500
	Young associate	25	$ 60	1,500
2. Preparation, review, and argument of motion in limine	Young associate	3	$ 60	180
	Young partner	2	$100	200
3. Identification and preparation of live witnesses for trial	Young partner	40	$100	4,000
	Young associate	10	$ 60	600
4. Identification of deposition testimony for use at trial, preparation of objections to opposing depositions, and responses to opposing objections	Young partner	10	$100	1,000
	Young associate	20	$ 60	1,200

Phase/Task	Personnel	Time	Hourly Rate	Projections
5. Identification of documents for use at trial, preparation of objections to opposing documents, and responses to opposing objections	Young partner	20 hrs.	$100/hr.	$ 2,000
	Young associate	30	$ 60	1,800
6. Research on evidentiary trial issues and preparation and review of evidentiary trial briefs	Young associate	40	$ 60	2,400
	Young partner	10	$100	1,000
7. Research on substantive trial issues and preparation and review of substantive trial briefs	Young associate	40	$ 60	2,400
	Young partner	10	$100	1,000
8. Research and preparation of proposed charge to the jury	Young partner	10	$100	1,000
	Young associate	30	$ 60	1,800
V. Trial	Young partner	90	$100	9,000
	Young associate	90	$ 60	5,400
			Total	$138,280

Estimated Paralegal Budget (through Trial)

Task	Personnel	Time	Hourly	Projections
Document search and review	Paralegal	200 hrs.	$40/hr.	$ 8,000
Bates numbering documents	Paralegal	40	$40	1,600
General file organization	Paralegal	20	$40	800
Preparation of defendants' document index	Paralegal	60	$40	2,400
Preparation of plaintiffs' document index	Paralegal	60	$40	2,400
Preparation of witness files	Paralegal	90	$40	3,600
Summarizing/indexing depositions (assuming 6 minutes per page for 26 depositions averaging 250 pages)	Paralegal	650	$40	26,000
Organization and preparation of trial exhibits	Paralegal	30	$40	1,200
Trial	Paralegal	70	$40	2,800
			Total	$48,800

Estimated Expense Budget (through Trial)

	Item	Quantity	Unit Cost	Projections
1.	Photocopies	50,000	$ .20	$10,000
2.	Travel (attorneys)			
	a. Air	5 round trips	$ 550 each	2,750
	b. Rental car	2 trips (1 day each)	$ 50/day	100
	c. Taxi	3 trips	$ 80/trip	240
	d. Hotels	5 (1 night each)	$ 90/night	450
3.	Depositions			
	a. Original/copy	13 (average 250 pages)	$ 3.75/page	12,187
	b. Copy only	13 (average 250 pages)	$ .95/page	3,087
4.	Telecopies	30 (10 pages each)	$ 1/page	300
5.	Long-distance telephone calls	90	$ 4 (average)	360
6.	LEXIS/WESTLAW	6 (average 20 min. each)	$ 4/min.	480
7.	Messenger service (overnight package delivery included)	20	$ 20 each	400
8.	Expert witnesses	2 (12 days each)	$1,200/day	28,800
9.	Travel (expert witnesses)			
	a. Air	2 (5 trips each)	$ 550 each	5,500
	b. Rental car	2 (3 trips each)	$ 50/day	300
	c. Taxi	2 (2 trips each)	$ 80/trip	320
	d. Hotels	2 (10 nights each)	$ 90/night	1,800
			Total	$67,075

Schedule B: Issue Budget (Breach of Contract), Alternative A—Lawyer Tasks

Phase/Task	Personnel	Time	Hourly Rate	Projections
A. *Investigative/Research*				
1. Research				
a. Research and preparation of memorandum on elements/defenses	Junior associate	10 hrs.	$ 60/hr.	$ 600
b. Research and preparation of memorandum on special problems	Junior associate	50	$ 60	3,000
2. Investigation				
a. Preliminary document search and review	Senior associate	30 (50%)	$ 80	1,200
b. Client interviews	Young partner	30 (40%)	$100	1,200
c. Third-party witness interviews	Senior associate	20 (30%)	$ 80	480

Phase/Task	Personnel	Time	Hourly Rate	Projections
B. *Pleadings*				
1. Drafting and reviewing original complaint/answer	Senior associate	4 (40%)	$ 80/hr.	$ 128
	Young partner	2 (40%)	$100	80
2. Drafting and reviewing amendments	Young partner	3 (40%)	$100	120
C. *Paper discovery*				
1. Drafting and reviewing interrogatories	Senior associate	15 hrs (40%)	$ 80	480
2. Responding to interrogatories	Senior associate	20 (30%)	$ 80	480
3. Drafting and reviewing requests for admission	Senior associate	4 (30%)	$ 80	96
4. Responding to requests for admission	Senior associate	4 (30%)	$ 80	96
5. Drafting and reviewing requests for production	Senior associate	20 (50%)	$ 80	800
6. Document search and responding to requests for production	Junior associate	60 (50%)	$ 60	1,800
	Senior associate	30 (50%)	$ 80	1,200
7. Preparation, research, and argument of discovery motions	Junior associate	60	$ 60	3,600
	Young partner	20	$100	2,000
D. *Oral Discovery*				
1. Preparation for and taking of depositions of opposing-party witnesses				
a. Witness A	Young partner	30	$100	3,000
b. Witness B	Young partner	30 (60%)	$100	1,800
c. Witness C	Young partner	20 (50%)	$100	1,000
d. Witness D	Senior associate	30 (40%)	$ 80	960
2. Preparation for and taking of depositions of third-party witnesses				
a. Witness A	Young partner	20 hrs.	$100	2,000
b. Witness B	Senior associate	30 (40%)	$ 80	960
c. Witness C	Senior associate	20 (60%)	$ 80	960

Phase/Task	Personnel	Time	Hourly Rate	Projections
3. Preparation of and defending depositions of client witnesses				
a. Witness A	Young partner	60 (80%)	$100/hr.	$ 4,800
b. Witness B	Young partner	40 (40%)	$100	1,600
c. Witness C	Young partner	50 (50%)	$100	2,500
d. Witness D	Senior associate	30	$ 80	2,400
4. Preparation and taking of depositions of expert witnesses				
a. Witness A	Young partner	30	$100	3,000
b. Witness B	Young partner	25	$100	2,500
c. Witness C	Senior associate	20 (50%)	$ 80	800
d. Witness D	Senior associate	20 (50%)	$ 80	800
			Total	$46,440

Schedule C: Issue Budget (Breach of Contract), Alternative B—Lawyer Tasks

Phase/Task	Personnel	Time	Hourly Rate	Projections
A. Investigative/Research				
1. Research				
a. Research and preparation of memorandum on elements/defenses	Junior associate	5 hrs.	$ 60/hr.	$ 300
b. Research and preparation of memorandum on special problems	Junior associate	30	$ 60	1,000
2. Investigation				
a. Preliminary document search and review	Senior associate	20 (50%)	$ 80	800
b. Client interviews	Young partner	20 (40%)	$100	800
c. Third-party witness interviews	Senior associate	15 (30%)	$ 80	360
B. Pleadings				
1. Drafting and reviewing original complaint/answer	Senior associate	3 (30%)	$ 80	72
	Young partner	1.5 (30%)	$100	45
2. Drafting and reviewing amendments	Young partner	1 (30%)	$100	30
C. Paper Discovery				
1. Drafting and reviewing interrogatories	Senior associate	5 (40%)	$ 80	160
2. Responding to interrogatories	Senior associate	15 (30%)	$ 80	360

Phase/Task	Personnel	Time	Hourly Rate	Projections
3. Drafting and reviewing requests for admission	None			
4. Responding to requests for admission	None			
5. Drafting and reviewing requests for production	Senior associate	15 hrs. (50%)	$ 80/hr.	$ 600
6. Document search and responding to requests for production	Junior associate	40 (50%)	$ 60	1,200
7. Preparation, research, and argument of discovery motions	Junior associate	20	$ 60	1,200
	Senior associate	5	$ 80	400
D. Oral Discovery				
1. Preparation for and taking of depositions of opposing-party witnesses				
a. Witness A	Young partner	15 (30%)	$100	450
b. Witness B	Young partner	12 (30%)	$100	360
c. Witness C	Senior associate	8 (30%)	80	192
2. Preparation for and taking of depositions of third-party witnesses				
a. Witness A	Young partner	15 (30%)	$100	450
b. Witness B	Senior associate	15 (40%)	$ 80	480
3. Preparation of and defending depositions of client witnesses				
a. Witness A	Young partner	20 (50%)	$100	1,000
b. Witness B	Young partner	15 (30%)	$100	450
c. Witness C	Young partner	12 (30%)	$100	360
4. Preparation and taking of depositions of expert witnesses				
a. Witness A	Young partner	25	$100	2,500
b. Witness C	Senior associate	25	$ 80	2,000
			Total	$16,369

Schedule D: Lawyer Tasks—Trial and Posttrial

Task	Personnel	Time	Hourly Rate	Projections
A. Trial Preparation				
1. Preparation, review, and argument of motion for summary judgment	Young partner	10 hrs.	$100/hr.	$ 1,000
	Senior associate	20	$ 80	1,600

Task	Personnel	Time	Hourly Rate	Projections
2. Preparation, review, and argument of motion in limine	Junior associate Senior associate	5 hrs. 1	$100/hr. $ 80	$ 500 80
3. Identification and preparation of live witnesses for trial	Young partner	40	$100	4,000
4. Identification of deposition testimony for trial, preparation of objections to opposing depositions, and responses to opposing objections	Senior associate Junior associate	20 20	$ 80 $ 60	1,600 1,200
5. Identification of documents for use at trial, preparation of objections to opposing documents, and responses to opposing objections	Young partner Junior associate	20 20	$100 $ 60	2,000 1,200
6. Research on evidentiary trial issues and preparation and review of evidentiary trial briefs	Junior associate Senior associate	30 10	$ 60 $ 80	1,800 800
7. Research on substantive trial issues and preparation and review of substantive trial briefs	Junior associate Young partner	30 10	$ 60 $100	1,800 1,000
8. Research and preparation of proposed charge to the jury	Young partner Junior associate	10 30	$100 $ 80	1,000 2,400
B. Trial	Young partner Senior associate Junior associate	120 120 40	$100 $ 80 $ 60	12,000 9,600 2,400
C. Posttrial				
1. Research, preparation, and review of posttrial motions and briefs	Junior associate Senior associate Young partner	20 10 10	$ 60 $ 80 $100	1,200 800 1,000
2. Preparation and review of judgment	Young partner	2	$100	200
3. Preparation of findings and conclusions	None			
4. Research, preparation and review of brief for appeal and oral argument	Senior associate Young partner	60 40	$ 80 $100	4,800 4,000
			Total	$57,980

Schedule E: Issue Budget (Breach of Contract), Paralegal Tasks

Task	Personnel	Time	Hourly Rate	Projections
Document search and review	Paralegal A Paralegal B	40 hrs. 20	$25/hr. $35	$1,000 700
Photocopying documents	Paralegal	10	$25	250
Bates numbering documents	Paralegal	10	$25	250
Preparation of document index	Paralegal	8	$25	200
General file organization	Paralegal	10	$25	250
Pleadings organization and indexing	Paralegal	4	$25	100
Discovery documents organization and indexing	Paralegal	4	$25	100
Motion organization and indexing	Paralegal	3	$25	75
Preparation of witness files	Paralegal	20	$25	500
Summarizing and indexing depositions	Paralegal	80	$25	2,000
			Total	$5,425

Schedule F: Expense Budget

Item	Quantity	Unit Cost	Projections
1. Photocopies	30,000	$ .20	$ 6,000
2. Travel (attorneys)			
a. Air	10 round trips	$ 350 each	3,500
b. Rental car	5 trips (1 day each)	$ 50/day	250
c. Taxi	5 trips	$ 30/trip	150
d. Hotels	5 (1 night each)	$ 50/night	250
3. Depositions			
a. Original/copy	20 (average 200 pages)	$ 3.75/page	15,000
b. Copy only	10 (average 200 pages)	$ .95/page	1,900
4. Telecopies	20 (5 pages each)	$ 1/page	100
5. Long-distance telephone calls	100	$ 5 average	500
6. LEXIS/WESTLAW	5 (average 10 min. each)	$ 4/min.	200
7. Messenger service (overnight package delivery included)	25	$ 20 each	500
8. Expert witnesses	3 (5 days each)	$1,000/day	15,000
9. Travel (expert witnesses)			
a. Air	3 (3 trips each)	$ 550 each	4,950
b. Rental car	3 (1 trip each)	$ 50/day	150
c. Taxi	3 (2 trips each)	$ 40/trip	240
d. Hotels	3 (5 nights each)	$ 90/night	1,350
		Total	$50,040

Optional Items

10. Computer support system for document control	
a. Initial setup fee	$ 2,500
b. Input fee (10,000 documents at $1.00 per page)	10,000
c. Inquiry time charges (40 hours at $75 per hour)	3,000
Total	$15,500

11. Social science firm for jury and issue analysis	
a. Jury analysis	$30,000
b. Issue analysis	20,000
Total	$50,000

Schedule G: Proposed Final Budget

A. Pretrial Budget

1. Fraud issue ______________
2. Breach-of-contract issue ______________
3. Tortious interference with contract issue ______________
4. Antitrust issue ______________

Total ______________

B. Trial and Posttrial Budget

1. Trial preparation ______________
2. Trial ______________
3. Posttrial ______________

Total ______________

C. Expense Budget

1. Photocopies ______________
2. Travel (attorneys) ______________
3. Depositions ______________
4. Telecopies ______________
5. Long-distance telephone ______________
6. LEXIS/WESTLAW ______________
7. Messenger service ______________
8. Expert witnesses ______________
9. Travel (expert witnesses) ______________
10. Computer support system ______________
11. Social science firm ______________ ______________

Total ______________

Schedule H: Decision Package—Breach-of-Contract Issue

Purpose/Benefit

This is the strongest theory of recovery for the plaintiff on liability, but it appears to be weak on damages. Most of the plaintiff's damages appear to flow from the tort causes of action (fraud, antitrust, tortious interference). This theory should be pursued because the defendant can be made to look very bad by his breach, and the effect may spill over into the higher-damage theories.

Assumptions

Alternative A represents a fairly high level of activity on this issue. It assumes a staffing of three attorneys (young partner, senior associate, and junior associate) and two paralegals. It also assumes that the depositions of eleven fact witnesses and four expert witnesses will be taken.

Alternative B represents a fairly low level of activities. It assumes the same staffing, but provides for the depositions of only eight fact witnesses and two expert witnesses. This alternative also cuts down significantly on the time spent on other discovery tasks and preparation, including investigation and research.

In both alternatives, it is assumed that the defendant will take the same amount of discovery from the plaintiff as the plaintiff takes from the defendant. If the defendant takes a more aggressive discovery posture on this claim and seeks additional depositions or documents, then the cost of prosecuting this cause of action under either alternative could increase significantly.

Deletion of Tasks—Risks/Cost Savings

Eliminating this issue altogether would eliminate only three depositions in Alternative A from those to be taken in support of the tort claims, and none from Alternative B. If the tortious interference claim is abandoned, two more depositions can be eliminated with this theory. Eliminating this cause of action would, of course, eliminate the research and some paper discovery and investigation.

Alternative A provides for all of the discovery that should reasonably be necessary to prosecute this claim on behalf of the plaintiff. Alternative B provides a low, reasonable approach to the issue, but requires some risk taking. For example, certain fact depositions and some third-party investigation have been deleted because they are likely to be cumulative, but to the extent that such witnesses may have additional, important information, Alternative B risks the loss of that testimony. In addition, the number of expert witnesses has been reduced from two to one on each side, although this is not considered critical. But the amount of time spent on paper discovery, investigation, and research has been significantly reduced from Alternative A to Alternative B, and this could affect the development of the issue. Pursuing Alternative B rather than Alternative A may reduce the chances of the plaintiff's prevailing in this case by as much as 15 percent.

Cost/Benefit Analysis

When the cost of Alternative A is added to the cost of developing the other issues in the case, the litigation expense increases significantly in comparison to the amount at stake. This is particularly true since the greater part of the damages suffered by the plaintiff cannot readily be traced to the breach of contract. Because of its helpfulness in establishing liability on the tort issues, this theory should be asserted and developed. But because of the relatively small amount of damages flowing from the breach, Alternative B should be adopted. The risks of taking the less-thorough approach must be recognized, but the lower cost in comparison to the benefit to be attained makes it the more cost-effective option under the circumstances.

Ranking

The breach-of-contract issue should be ranked second in order of importance among the four theories available to the plaintiff. Alternative B is ranked over Alternative A as the preferable approach.

Schedule I: Estimated Monthly Breakdown of Lawyer and Paralegal Fees and Expenses

____

(Case Name or Project)

____

(Law Firm)

Year: 19__

	Jan.	Feb.	March	April	May	June	July	August	Sept.	Oct.	Nov.	Dec.
Investigative/ research												
Pleadings												
Discovery												
Motions												
Trial preparation												
Trial												
Posttrial												
Expenses												
Other												
Monthly totals												

FORM 24

Letter to Co-Defendants Regarding Selection of Counsel

Version Sent Before Selection of Counsel

TO DISTRIBUTION LIST

Dear ______________:

The ______________ case has been filed in ______________ Court, [city and state] in Judge ______________ Court. In the interest of efficiency, a number of us have agreed to share counsel until a reason not to arises. The nature of this case suggests that cost and trial efficiencies will be beneficial to each of us.

To date no firm has been selected to serve as joint defense counsel; however, I have scheduled a teleconference for [date and time] to discuss this matter.

Based on our discussions, the following procedures are to delineate our proposed sharing of counsel.

1. Once you are served, each of you should contact our joint counsel's firm as soon as possible to advise whether your company is joining in the shared use of counsel in this case. If you are opting out of sharing the firm's services, please let the shared counsel know who your lawyer will be, so that any necessary motions and discovery can be coordinated with your counsel, since joint motions and discovery save costs to all.

   I will volunteer to be a general coordinator of periodic teleconferences or meetings of the full clients' coordinating committee to which each sharing company should designate a single main representative (although multiple attendance and support personnel are welcome). Although a steering committee of those companies willing to contribute their time and personnel to steering and subcommittee (law and technical) activities may be eventually needed, it appears premature to establish that mechanism at this time in this case. For efficiency, some of you may wish to delegate, or serve as delegates on behalf of others in our group, for meetings you cannot participate in due to conflicts in your schedule. Any steering committee we form would be our point of contact only on noncase dispositive, ministerial matters that may arise in communications with the shared outside counsel, with the understanding that anything substantive would be the subject of direct communication between our counsel and each of us.

2. The sharing of counsel will be on an equal-share basis until there is some reason to use another formula. Work of sole benefit or interest to a single company will, of course, be billed to that company's separate account.
3. We will give prior notice to one another of any intentions to offer settlement or withdraw from our sharing of counsel. Any documents put in any repository created by the law firm during the pendency of your involvement in the sharing group will be accessible to you.
4. We will share necessary expert fees and confer with one another for getting unanimity regarding experts, tactics, and other matters.
5. We will avoid bedeviling retained counsel with duplicative inquiries and calls and ask for regular written updates to be issued to each of us for that purpose. We will each keep our own insurance carriers supplied with such information and copies as they wish.
6. Any necessary motion to have claims for contributions among co-defendants be deemed extant by an Agreed Order can be accomplished when appropriate before trial and obviate the unnecessary filing of duplicative claims for contribution among ourselves. No one is waiving any rights to cross-act, etc., by this sharing of counsel.
7. If a conflict between us arises that we cannot resolve among ourselves, anyone uncomfortable with staying with the shared counsel can then bail out and hire a different firm; those still comfortable with the sharing format can continue on with the group's law firm, which will not be recused.
8. A good deal of valuable work product and the benefits of recent cases are and should be made available to our counsel in this case. The method for smoothly and without duplicative efforts providing this data to the selected law firm is one item open for discussion. Additionally, [shared counsel attorney] will present to our full group his plan for an approach

to this case, his fee structure, and identify any partner or associates who would be assisting him with this litigation.

9. The public interest of having publicly owned corporations operating cost-efficiently and the avoidance of cluttering the already overloaded ______________ courts with duplicative efforts in response to such lawsuits all weigh heavily in favor of a joint sharing of counsel in this case.

Feel free to call me at ______________ if you wish to discuss this matter further.

Very truly yours,

Version Sent After Selection of Counsel

TO DISTRIBUTION LIST

Dear ______________ :

The ______________ case has been filed in ______________ Court, [city and state] in Judge ______________ Court. In the interest of efficiency, a number of us have agreed to share counsel until a reason not to arises. The nature of this case suggests that cost and trial efficiencies will be beneficial to each of us.

The counsel receiving the most nominations to serve as joint defense counsel at our teleconference of [date], was [attorney's name] of [law firm name and address].

Based on our discussions, the following procedures will apply to our proposed sharing of counsel.

1. Once you are served, each of you should contact our joint counsel's firm as soon as possible to advise whether your company is joining in the shared use of counsel in this case. If you are opting out of sharing the firm's services, please let the shared counsel know who your lawyer will be, so that any necessary motions and discovery can be coordinated with your counsel, since joint motions and discovery save costs to all.

   I will volunteer to be a general coordinator of periodic teleconferences or meetings of the full clients' coordinating committee to which each sharing company should designate a single main representative (although multiple attendance and support personnel are welcome). Although a steering committee of those companies willing to contribute their time and personnel to steering and subcommittee (law and technical) activities may be eventually needed, it appears premature to establish that mechanism at this time in this case. For efficiency, some of you may wish to delegate, or serve as delegates on behalf of others in our group, for meetings you cannot participate in due to conflicts in your schedule. Any steering committee we form would be our point of contact only on noncase dispositive, ministerial matters that may arise in communications with the shared outside counsel, with the understanding that anything substantive would be the subject of direct communication between our counsel and each of us.

2. The sharing of counsel will be on an equal-share basis until there is some reason to use another formula. Work of sole benefit or interest to a single company will, of course, be billed to that company's separate account.
3. We will give prior notice to one another of any intentions to offer settlement or withdraw from our sharing of counsel. Any documents put in any repository created by the law firm during the pendency of your involvement in the sharing group will be accessible to you.
4. We will share necessary expert fees and confer with one another for getting unanimity regarding experts, tactics, and other matters.
5. We will avoid bedeviling retained counsel with duplicative inquiries and calls and ask for regular written updates to be issued to each of us for that purpose. We will each keep our own insurance carriers supplied with such information and copies as they wish.
6. Any necessary motion to have claims for contributions among co-defendants be deemed extant by an Agreed Order can be accomplished when appropriate before trial and obviate the unnecessary filing of duplicative claims for contribution among ourselves. No one is waiving any rights to cross-act, etc., by this sharing of counsel.
7. If a conflict between us arises that we cannot resolve among ourselves, anyone uncomfortable with staying with the shared counsel can then bail out and hire a different firm; those still comfortable with the sharing format can continue on with the group's law firm, which will not be recused.
8. A good deal of valuable work product and the benefits of recent cases are and should be made available to our counsel in this case. The method for smoothly and without duplicative efforts providing this data to the selected law firm is one

item open for discussion. Additionally, [shared counsel attorney] will present to our full group his plan for an approach to this case, his fee structure, and identify any partner or associates who would be assisting him with this litigation.

9. The public interest of having publicly owned corporations operating cost-efficiently and the avoidance of cluttering the already overloaded _____ courts with duplicative efforts in response to such lawsuits all weigh heavily in favor of a joint sharing of counsel in this case.

Feel free to call me at _______________ if you wish to discuss this matter further.

Very truly yours,

FORM 25

Pretrial Order to Prevent Prejudice to Cooperating Co-Defendants

DISTRICT COURT OF ________
_______ division: _____ COUNTY
CAUSE NO. ___________________

PLAINTIFF

V.

DEFENDANT

CIVIL ACTION—ORDER FOR
DISCOVERY & LITIGATION PROCEDURE

The Court having found that cooperation by defendants will expedite the handling of the within matter and aid judicial economy, the conduct of the defendants working jointly, retrospectively, and prospectively, for purposes of coordinating discovery, trial, sharing counsel, and otherwise minimizing expenses shall not constitute evidence of conspiracy, concertive action, or any other wrongful conduct and shall not be admissible as evidence for any purpose.

____
JUDGE

FORM 26

Letter to Co-Defendants' Counsel Proposing Motion to Have Cross-Actions Deemed Filed and Denied

[Date]

Re: [case name]________________

Dear ______________:

The enclosed Motion and proposed Order for the above-entitled and numbered cause will be filed with the court by [Company] on behalf of [Company] and all Co-defendants on [date] unless some Co-defendant opts out by calling my office at [phone number] before ______________ p.m. on [date].

This Motion and proposed Order to have cross-actions for contribution and indemnification and the Answer thereto deemed filed, served, and answered will obviate the need to physically produce, file, and serve duplicative pleadings. This is done as a cost efficiency and to relieve all of our support people and the District Clerk's office of the unreasonable burden of filing and maintaining duplicative pleadings.

Sincerely,

FORM 27

Motion to Have Cross-Actions Deemed Filed and Denied

IN THE UNITED STATES DISTRICT COURT
FOR THE EASTERN DISTRICT OF TEXAS
BEAUMONT DIVISION

JOHN DOE	§	
	§	CIVIL ACTION NO.
V.	§	B-83-321-CA
	§	
ACME CHEMICAL COMPANY, ET AL.	§	

MOTION TO HAVE CROSS-ACTIONS FOR CONTRIBUTION
AND INDEMNIFICATION BY EACH DEFENDANT
DEEMED FILED AND DEEMED DENIED
BY EACH DEFENDANT

TO THE HONORABLE JUDGE OF SAID COURT:

COMES NOW Exxon Corporation a Defendant in the above-entitled and numbered cause and on behalf of itself and each Defendant files this Motion to have Cross-Actions for Contribution and Indemnification by each Defendant Deemed Filed and Deemed Denied by each Defendant and as grounds would show the Court the following:

I.

It is requested that Cross-Actions for each Defendant for contribution from Co-Defendants pursuant to the applicable provisions of Articles 2212 and 2212(a) of Vernon's Annotated Civil Statutes, together with Cross-Actions for each Defendant for common law indemnification from Co-Defendants shall be deemed filed and deemed denied by each Defendant without the need to physically file and serve said Cross-Actions or the Answers in denial thereof.

II.

This Motion is presented in order to expedite this matter; to aid judicial economy; to enhance the cost-efficient handling of this cause; and to avoid unduly burdening the office of the District Clerk with duplicative multiple filings by the Co-Defendants.

III.

Neither the Plaintiff nor any Defendant opposes this Motion.

WHEREFORE, premises considered, Exxon Corporation on behalf of itself and each Defendant requests this Honorable Court to grant its unopposed Motion to have Cross-Actions for Contribution and Indemnification by each Defendant Deemed Filed and Deemed Denied by each Defendant without the need to physically file and serve said Cross-Actions or the Answers in denial thereof.

Respectfully submitted,

____

Edward Lowenberg
Texas Bar No. 12628000
Donald L. Saunders
Texas Bar No. 17679000
1861 Exxon Building
800 Bell Street
Houston, Texas 77002

ATTORNEYS FOR DEFENDANT
Exxon Corporation

CERTIFICATE OF SERVICE

I hereby certify that a true and correct copy of the foregoing Motion to have Cross-Actions for Contributions and Indemnifications by Each Defendant Deemed Filed and Deemed Denied by Each Defendant was mailed by certified mail, return receipt requested, to all counsel of record on this the 26th day of May, 1983.

____

Edward Lowenberg

FORM 28

Form Agreement among Co-Defendants and Third Parties in a Multidefendant Action and Insurers Regarding Cooperation in Litigation

THIS AGREEMENT made this ________________________ day of ______________ 198X, between defendant *A* corporation and its insurer, defendant *B* corporation and its insurer, and third parties *C* corporation and *D* corporation;

WHEREAS there is now pending in the ______________ Court of ______________, County of ______________, a Complaint brought by [plaintiff] *v. A and B, et al.*, and

WHEREAS Insurer 1 and Insurer 2 are the insurers of *A* and *B* respectively and

WHEREAS it is to the best interests of the parties to this Agreement that *A* and *B* forbear from filing a third-party Complaint against *C* and *D*,

IN CONSIDERATION OF THEIR MUTUAL PROMISES, the parties stipulate and agree as follows:

1. *A* and its insurer and *B* and its insurer agree not to file a third-party Complaint or any other Complaint against *C* and/or *D* as a result of the allegations set forth in the Complaint above.
2. *C* and/or *D* agree to produce the names of experts, including experts' reports, in order to help *A* and *B* defend the above-captioned matter.
3. *C* and/or *D* agree to furnish whatever additional and reasonable assistance is required by *A* and/or *B* or their insurers, to assist in their defense of the above-captioned action.
4. *C* and/or *D* agree to negotiate in good faith with respect to their contribution to any settlement or judgment resulting from the above-captioned action.
5. *A* and *B* agree to keep *C* and/or *D* advised of developments in the above-captioned matter, including settlement discussions.
6. *C* and/or *D* shall have the privilege of designating [attorney] as trial counsel on behalf of *B* and the present attorneys for *B* and/or *A* shall do whatever is necessary to have [attorney], a member of the ______________ Bar, admitted *pro hac vice* to try this case in the State of ______________.

7. *A* and their insurer and *B* and their insurer shall cause their attorneys who are currently attorneys of record to cooperate with *C*, *D*, and [attorney] in the defense of this case.

8. In consideration of the above, *C* and *D* agree to indemnify *A* and their insurer and *B* and their insurer against all judgments that may be rendered against *A* and/or *B* in the above-captioned matter. This indemnity shall only apply if a jury finds that the product causing the death and/or injury to [plaintiff] is [toxic chemical] that is not shown to have originated from some entity other than *C* and *D*. This indemnity shall apply whether the liability of *A* and/or *B* is based on their sole acts or their acts jointly with others. It is the understanding of the parties that this indemnity is to be a full indemnity indemnifying *A* and *B* against all judgments rendered against them involving the product [toxic chemical] that is not shown to have originated from some entity other than *C* and *D*. It is, however, understood between the parties that all legal fees of the law firms heretofore representing *A* and *B* companies will be paid by their respective clients and not by *C* or *D* companies.

9. This Agreement has been executed in counterparts as of the date first hereinafter set forth by authorized representatives of the parties.

A

By: ______________________________
(Attorney)

B

By: ______________________________
(Attorney)

C

By: ______________________________

D

By: ______________________________

FORM 29

Form Agreement among Defendants and Third Parties Concerning Cooperation

AGREEMENT

RE: [Plaintiff v. Defendant *A* et al.] CAUSE NO. ____________, IN THE ____________ COURT FOR THE ____________ DISTRICT OF ____________, ____________ DIVISION

In consideration for [Defendant *A*] agreeing to pay all costs of defense counsel, court costs, and trial expenses in connection with the above-captioned matter, and forbearing from impleading [third party corporation *D*], the parties hereto stipulate and agree as follows:

I.

[*D*] agrees to produce for [*A*] copies of all written materials sent to either co-defendants *B* and *C*, concerning the motor oils, fuels, and lubricants that were manufactured by [*D*] and subsequently delivered to said companies during the pertinent period covered by this lawsuit.

II.

[*D*] agrees to make available, for interviews and depositions (if necessary), those persons employed by [*D*] or who were acting on behalf of [*D*], who discussed with any representative of *B* or with *C* any type of safety or health advice or instructions during the pertinent period covered by this lawsuit.

III.

[*D*] agrees to furnish whatever additional and reasonable assistance is requested by [*A*] to assist in its defense of the captioned action.

IV.

[*D*] agrees to negotiate in good faith with respect to its contribution to any settlement or judgment resulting from the captioned lawsuit. If [*A*] or *B*—should [*D*] take over and defend in *B*'s name—is found liable by either the court or jury, and if [*A*] and [*D*] cannot amicably work out their respective proportionate share of liability, then it is agreed by the parties hereto that the share of liability to be allocated to each party to this agreement will be submitted for Arbitration to the Center for Public Resources, New York, New York. *A* agrees to keep *D* advised of developments in this case, including settlement discussions.

V.

To preserve the status quo concerning statutes of limitations that apply to any potential claims between the parties to this agreement or any separate lawsuits between the parties hereto arising out of the captioned lawsuit, the undersigned, by their respective and duly authorized attorneys, agree that any and all applicable statutes of limitations are hereby tolled as of [date], until such time a final settlement or judgment is rendered in this matter, except as hereinafter provided. This agreement only tolls all applicable statutes of limitations between the parties hereto and does not restrict or in any way limit the rights of the parties hereto to file third-party complaints or separate lawsuits. Any party hereto may terminate this agreement upon ninety days' written notice to all other parties hereto.

By their signature below, those signing indicate (a) that they are authorized to sign the above on behalf of their respective company and (b) that they agree to be bound by the terms and conditions of this agreement, this ____________day of ____________, 198X.

[Defendant *A*]	[Third Party Corporation *D*]
BY: ______________________	BY: ______________________
TITLE ___________________	TITLE ___________________

Forms for Section V:

Alternatives to Litigation

FORM 30

Center for Public Resources Model Procedure for Mediation of Business Disputes

This model represents a useful working tool. Mediation is a most informal and flexible procedure. There is no one right way to conduct a mediation. *Parties are urged to adapt the model to their own circumstances and needs.*

Proposing Mediation

Any party to a business dispute may unilaterally initiate a mediation process by contacting the other party or parties, orally or in writing, and suggesting the use of a neutral mediator to mediate efforts to arrive at a settlement.

Selecting the Mediator

Once the parties have agreed in principle to a mediation process, or at least to seriously consider mediation, they will discuss the desired qualifications of the mediator and who possesses such qualifications. Any party may suggest one or more candidates, or may recommend that the parties choose a mediator from a roster such as the Center for Public Resources (CPR) Judicial Panel. The mediator must be selected by agreement of all parties.

Each party shall promptly disclose to the other party any circumstances known to it that would cause reasonable doubt regarding the impartiality of an individual under consideration or appointed as a mediator. Any such individual shall promptly disclose any such circumstances to the parties. If any such circumstances have been disclosed, before or after the individual's appointment as mediator, the individual shall not serve, unless all parties agree.

The mediator's compensation rate will be determined at or before his* appointment. Such compensation, and all other costs of the process, will be shared equally by the parties, unless they otherwise agree.

*The male pronoun applies to persons of either sex.

Ground Rules of Proceeding

The ground rules of the proceeding will be as follows:

1. The process is voluntary and nonbinding. Each party may withdraw at any time by notifying the mediator and the other party or parties in writing of its intent to withdraw.
2. The mediator shall be neutral and impartial.
3. The mediator controls the procedural aspects of the mediation. The parties will cooperate fully with the mediator.
    - There will be no direct communication between the parties or between their attorneys without the concurrence of the mediator.
    - The mediator is free to meet and communicate separately with each party.
    - The mediator will decide when to hold separate meetings with the parties and when to hold joint meetings. The mediator will fix the time and place of each session and the agenda, in consultation with the parties.
4. Each party may be represented by more than one person, e.g., a business executive and an attorney. At least one representative of each party will be authorized to negotiate a settlement of the dispute.
5. The process will be conducted expeditiously. Each representative will make every effort to be available for meetings.
6. The mediator will not transmit information given him by any party to another party, unless authorized to do so.
7. The entire process is confidential. The parties and the mediator will not disclose information regarding the process, including settlement terms, to third parties, unless the parties otherwise agree. The process shall be treated as a compromise negotiation for purposes of the Federal Rules of Evidence and state rules of evidence. The mediator will be disqualified as a witness, consultant, or expert in any pending or future action relating to the subject matter of the mediation, including those between persons not parties to the mediation.
8. If the dispute goes to arbitration, the mediator shall not serve as an arbitrator, unless the parties otherwise agree.
9. The mediator, if a lawyer, may freely express his views to the parties on the legal issues of the dispute, unless a party objects to his so doing.
10. The mediator may obtain assistance and independent expert

advice with the agreement of and at the expense of the parties.

11. The mediator shall not be liable for any act or omission in connection with his role as mediator.
12. The parties will refrain from court proceedings during the mediation process, insofar as they can do so without prejudicing their legal rights. If litigation is pending between the parties regarding the subject matter of the mediation, the parties may agree to inform the court of the mediation process and the name of the mediator, and they may request a stay of court proceedings. Insofar as possible, discovery will be suspended while the mediation is ongoing.

Once a mediator has been selected, the representatives of the parties will meet jointly with the mediator to discuss these ground rules and any different or additional ground rules the mediator or a party wishes to propose. The parties and the mediator may agree on whether the parties will be the first to make settlement proposals, or whether they wish the mediator to make such a proposal once he has familiarized himself with the dispute.

Submission of Materials to the Mediator

Upon entering into mediation, each party will submit to the mediator such material and information as it deems necessary to familiarize the mediator with the dispute. Submissions may be made in writing and orally.

The mediator may request any party to provide clarification and additional information. The mediator may raise legal questions and arguments and may request any party's attorney to brief legal issues.

The mediator may request each party, separately or at a joint meeting, to present its case informally to the mediator.

Negotiation of Settlement Terms

Once the mediator has familiarized himself with the case, he will hold discussions with the representatives of the parties. The mediator will decide when to meet or confer separately with each party and when to hold joint meetings. The mediator may assist the parties in arriving at a settlement in a variety of ways.

If the parties fail to develop mutually acceptable settlement terms, the mediator before terminating the procedure may submit to the parties a final settlement proposal that he considers equitable to all parties. The parties will carefully consider any such proposal, and at the request of the mediator will discuss the proposal with him.

Efforts to reach a settlement will continue until a settlement is reached, or one of the parties withdraws from the process, or the mediator concludes and informs the parties that further efforts would not be useful.

Settlement

If a settlement is reached, the mediator, or one of the parties at his request, will draft a written settlement document incorporating all settlement terms. This draft will be circulated among the parties, edited as necessary, and, if acceptable, formally executed.

FORM 31

Center for Public Resources Model Procedure for Commercial Agreement Mediation Clause

The Center for Public Resources (CPR) encourages drafting a commercial agreement to incorporate the model procedure by reference. The following language is suggested:

> The parties will attempt in good faith to resolve any controversy or claim arising out of or relating to this agreement by mediation in accordance with the CPR Model Procedure for Mediation of a Business Dispute.

This clause may not create an enforceable right or obligation. However, if a dispute should arise, such a clause, whether enforceable or not, would substantially increase the likelihood that the parties would make a serious effort to arrive at a compromise through mediation, rather than seeking an adjudicative solution. In any event, mediation is more likely to succeed if the parties have a genuine motivation to make it succeed.

The commercial agreement also could provide that, if a dispute arises, negotiations between executives would be the first step; if negotiations become deadlocked, mediation would be the second step.

Transnational Disputes

Litigation or arbitration of disputes between companies in different countries tends to be particularly burdensome, protracted, and damaging to business relationships. The concept of mediation is not alien to many foreign business people, and mediation should be considered as a process for transnational dispute resolution. The CPR model procedure is applicable to transnational disputes. When such a dispute involves two parties of different cultures, it may be helpful to use two mediators—one from each culture.

FORM 32

Center for Public Resources Model Contract Provisions for Minitrials, Negotiation, and Mediation

Minitrial Provisions

1. In the event of any dispute between the parties relating to or arising out of any provision of this Agreement, the representatives of the parties shall meet promptly in a good-faith effort to resolve the dispute extrajudicially. The disputing party shall arrange for this meeting at a time and place mutually acceptable to both parties. Before the meeting, the disputing party shall deliver to the other party a written summary of the evidence and arguments substantiating its dispute.

2. If the dispute is not resolved as a result of the meeting, the parties shall attempt to resolve the dispute by the use of a nonbinding minitrial.

3. The minitrial shall be conducted before a panel composed of senior executive officers of each party who have settling authority to resolve the dispute and a neutral adviser.

4. The parties shall exchange names of potential advisers and select from this pool a mutually acceptable candidate. If the parties cannot agree on the selection of a neutral adviser, the president of the Center for Public Resources or his designee shall select a neutral adviser from the Judicial Panel of the Center for Public Resources.

5. The parties shall promptly agree on the ground rules that will govern the parties' conduct before, during, and after the minitrial. These ground rules shall include a schedule for the exchange of documents, including briefs summarizing each party's respective position on the dispute; the duties and responsibilities of the neutral adviser; the format and location of the minitrial; and mandatory settlement discussions between the senior executives of each party immediately after the minitrial.

6. The parties shall also discuss whether any discovery will be necessary to prepare for the minitrial. If the parties mutually agree that such discovery is necessary, they shall establish an expedited discovery schedule.

7. Either party may resort to judicial proceeding if the good-faith attempt to resolve the dispute by a minitrial is unsuccessful or interim resort

to court is necessary to prevent irreparable injury to a party or to third parties.

Negotiation and Minitrial Provisions

1. In the event of any dispute between the parties relating to or arising out of any provision of this Agreement, the representatives of the parties shall meet in a good-faith effort to resolve the dispute extrajudicially. The disputing party shall give the other party written notice of its dispute. This notice shall include a summary of the evidence and arguments underlying its dispute; arrangements for a meeting to attempt to resolve the dispute to be held within sixty days of receipt of the notice; and the name of the party's representative who will represent the party at the meeting. Within thirty days after the receipt of this notice, the other party shall submit to the disputing party a written summary responding to the evidence and arguments contained in the disputing party's notice and identifying the party's representative who will be its representative at the meeting.

2. The parties' named representatives shall meet at a time and place mutually acceptable to both parties to attempt to settle the dispute in good faith. This meeting shall be held within sixty days after the receipt of the disputing party's written notice of its dispute.

3. If the dispute is not resolved at the meeting, the party shall attempt to resolve the dispute by the use of a nonbinding minitrial.

4. The minitrial shall be conducted before a panel composed of a senior executive officer for each party with authority to settle the dispute and a neutral adviser. The parties may also have present at the minitrial their counsel, technical experts (in-house or retained), and fact witnesses.

5. The parties shall exchange names of potential advisers and select from this pool a mutually acceptable candidate. If the parties cannot agree on the selection of a neutral adviser, the president of the Center for Public Resources or the president's designee shall select a neutral adviser from the Judicial Panel of the Center for Public Resources.

6. The neutral adviser is not to mediate or effect a compromise of the dispute. The neutral adviser is to issue a nonbinding opinion to the parties addressing the merits of each party's claim and assessing which party is likely to prevail at trial on the merits, so that the parties can determine whether and on what basis the dispute may be resolved extrajudicially. The neutral adviser's opinion shall be issued sixty days after the conclusion of the minitrial if the parties are unable to resolve the dispute immediately after the conclusion of the minitrial.

7. The parties shall execute an agreement with the neutral adviser that shall prohibit any ex parte contacts with the neutral adviser without the

explicit consent of the other party and require the neutral adviser to treat any information conveyed to him or her as confidential and prohibit disclosure of any confidential or trade secret information. The agreement shall also provide that the neutral adviser will be disqualified as a trial witness, consultant, or expert for any party, and his or her advisory opinion of the likely outcome of any litigation of the dispute is subject to rule 408 of the Federal Rules of Evidence and inadmissible for any purpose.

8. The parties shall promptly agree on the ground rules that will govern the conduct of the parties before, during, and after the minitrial. These ground rules shall include a schedule for the exchange of documents and short narrative statements summarizing each party's respective position on the dispute; if the parties mutually agree that discovery is necessary to prepare for the minitrial, an expedited discovery schedule; and the format and location of the minitrial.

9. If the parties are unable to agree on the ground rules of the minitrial, the parties shall submit the matter to the neutral adviser for that person's advice and assistance in resolving the disagreement.

10. The senior executive officers of each party shall meet immediately after the conclusion of the minitrial to attempt to resolve the dispute. If they do not resolve the dispute at this meeting, the neutral adviser will submit to the parties his or her nonbinding opinion. Ten days after receiving the neutral adviser's opinion, the parties' senior executive officers shall meet at least one more time to attempt to resolve the dispute.

11. If the parties, in good faith, are unable to resolve the dispute after the meeting(s) of the parties' senior executive officers stated in the last sentence of Paragraph 10, either party may give the other party a written notice of its intention to litigate the dispute in a court of law. The party submitting such notice may not commence litigation until sixty days after the receipt of the notice to litigate.

12. The fees and expenses of the neutral adviser and the minitrial shall be apportioned equally to each party. However, these costs shall be assessed against the losing party if the dispute is not settled and instead proceeds to trial.

13. Interim resort to court is permitted by either party if it is necessary to prevent irreparable injury to that party or to a third party.

Negotiation, Mediation, and Minitrial Provisions

1. In the event of any dispute between the parties relating to or arising out of any provision of this Agreement, the representatives of the parties shall meet promptly in an effort to resolve the dispute extrajudicially.

2. If the dispute is not resolved as a result of such meeting, the dispute shall be referred to the members of the senior management of each party within ten days after the meeting prescribed in Paragraph 1.

3. The members of the senior management of each party shall meet to attempt to resolve the dispute within thirty days after the dispute has been referred to them as prescribed in Paragraph 2.

4. Before the meeting of the members of the senior management of each party, the parties shall exchange a written summary of the issues and the underlying evidence relating to the dispute. The disputing party shall submit its written summary to the other party twenty days before the meeting of senior management. This submission shall set forth the basis of its dispute and identify the member of its senior management authorized to resolve the dispute on its behalf. Ten days thereafter, the other party shall submit its written summary to the disputing party. This submission shall respond to the matters raised in the written summary provided by the disputing party and identify the member of its senior management authorized to resolve the dispute on its behalf.

5. If the dispute is not resolved by the senior management of each party, the parties shall appoint a neutral adviser, who shall within sixty days submit to the parties a nonbinding opinion that addresses the merits of each party's position and assesses which party is likely to prevail at trial on the merits.

6. The parties shall exchange names of potential advisers and select from this pool a mutually acceptable candidate. If the parties cannot agree on the selection of a neutral adviser, the president of the Center for Public Resources or the president's designee shall select a neutral adviser from the Judicial Panel of the Center for Public Resources.

7. The parties shall enter into an agreement with the neutral advisor prohibiting any ex parte contacts with the neutral adviser without the explicit consent of the other party and requiring the neutral adviser to treat any information conveyed to him or her as confidential and prohibit disclosure of any confidential or trade secret information. The agreement shall also provide that the neutral adviser will be disqualified as a trial witness, consultant, or expert for any party, and that his or her advisory opinion of the likely outcome of any litigation of the dispute is subject to rule 408 of the Federal Rules of Evidence and is inadmissible for any purpose.

8. Ten days after the neutral adviser has been designated, each party shall submit to the neutral adviser, as well as to the other party, a written statement summarizing the issues and underlying evidence supporting its position. The written statements are to be no longer than thirty $8^{1}/_{2}'' \times 11''$ double-spaced pages.

9. If the neutral adviser wishes to consult with the parties on any issue relating to the dispute before the minitrial, he or she shall outline general areas of inquiry and, on agreement by both parties, may submit written questions jointly to the parties. The parties shall respond to these ques-

tions in writing and shall provide each other with a copy of any such response.

10. The fees and expenses of the neutral adviser shall be apportioned equally to each side. However, these costs shall be assessed against the losing party if the dispute is not settled and instead proceeds to trial.

11. Ten days after the neutral adviser issues an opinion to the parties, members of the senior management shall meet again in an attempt to resolve the dispute.

12. Either party may resort to judicial proceeding if the good-faith attempts to resolve the dispute stated in Paragraphs 1, 3, and 11 are unsuccessful or interim resort to court is necessary to prevent irreparable injury to a party or to third parties.

FORM 33

Center for Public Resources Model Procedure for Settlement of Transnational Business Disputes

1. Institution of Proceeding

The parties will commence the procedure by signing a written agreement (the "initiating agreement"), substantially in the form attached hereto as Exhibit A. The party proposing the procedure will submit to the other(s) a draft of the initiating agreement. The parties will resolve any differences regarding such draft, whereupon the parties will sign the initiating agreement.

2. Neutral Adviser

The parties will select a mutually acceptable neutral adviser, who shall have the functions stated in this procedure or in the initiating agreement.

Unless the parties otherwise agree, an individual shall not serve as neutral adviser if circumstances exist that would cause reasonable doubt regarding that person's impartiality. Any such circumstances shall be promptly disclosed.

Before the formal meeting, no party, nor anyone acting on its behalf, may unilaterally communicate with the neutral adviser, except as specifically provided for herein or otherwise agreed.

The neutral adviser's fee or time charge rate will be established at the time of his or her appointment.

3. Exchange of Information

Before the formal meeting, and by the date specified in the initiating agreement, the parties shall exchange and submit to the neutral adviser, concise memoranda stating the issues in the dispute and their position, as well as all documents and other exhibits on which the parties intend to rely during such meeting, or that are helpful in understanding their position. Only those documents and exhibits which have an important and direct bearing on the issues in the dispute are to be submitted. Documents and exhibits presented, if not in the language(s) of the procedure, will be accompanied by a translation into the language(s) of the procedure, unless the parties otherwise agree.

4. Formal Meeting

A formal meeting will be held before a panel consisting of the neutral adviser and one management representative of each party who shall have authority to negotiate a settlement on behalf of the party he or she represents. The neutral adviser will supervise the conduct of the formal meeting.

The formal meeting shall be held at the place and time, and in the manner, designated in the initiating agreement.

During the formal meeting, each party will make an oral presentation of its case, and each party shall be entitled to a reply. The presentations and replies may be made in any form and by any individuals other than the management representatives as desired by each party, and may be supported by any of, but only, the memoranda, documents, and other exhibits submitted in accordance with Article 3. The use of witnesses and experts shall be permitted. Presentations may not be interrupted, except that the neutral adviser and the management representatives may ask clarifying questions.

The meeting shall not be recorded. However, persons attending may take notes. Each management representative may have not more than two advisers in attendance.

5. Negotiations between Management Representatives

At the conclusion of the formal meeting, the management representatives shall make all reasonable efforts to agree on a resolution of the dispute. They shall meet one or more times, as necessary. By mutual agreement, other members of their teams and an interpreter may be invited to attend the negotiations. At the request of either management representative, the neutral adviser will attend the negotiations and will give an oral opinion as to the issues raised during the formal meeting. At the request of both management representatives, the neutral adviser also will submit a written opinion as to the aforesaid issues, make a settlement proposal, or mediate the negotiations.

The terms of any settlement are to be set out in a written agreement which is to be signed by the management representatives as soon as possible after the conclusion of the negotiations and will, once signed, be legally binding on the parties.

6. Confidentiality

By entering into this procedure, the parties shall be taken to agree that the entire proceeding is confidential; that the parties, their representatives, and the neutral adviser must keep confidential all statements, whether oral or written, made in this proceeding and all other matters relating to the proceeding, including the settlement agreement, except when and insofar as its disclosure is necessary to implement and enforce such agreement. All such matters will be inadmissible and not subject to discovery in any litigation, arbitration, or other proceeding.

The neutral adviser will be disqualified as a witness, consultant, or expert for any party to this proceeding, and his or her opinions in this proceeding will be inadmissible in any litigation, arbitration, or other proceeding.

7. Legal Proceedings

The parties will not commence or continue arbitration or court proceedings while this proceeding is pending, insofar as they do not thereby materially prejudice their legal position.

If this proceeding should not result in a settlement, the parties may pursue legal remedies following termination of this proceeding.

8. Costs

Unless the parties otherwise agree, the fees and expenses of the neutral adviser, as well as any other expenses of the proceeding, will be borne equally by the parties, and each party shall bear its own costs of the proceeding.

9. Termination of Proceeding

The proceeding shall be deemed terminated if and when the parties have not executed a written settlement agreement within forty-five days following conclusion of the formal meeting (which deadline may be extended by mutual agreement), or either party serves on the other party and on the neutral adviser a written notice of withdrawal from the proceeding.

Exhibit A: Agreement to Initiate CPR Procedure for Settlement of Transnational Business Disputes

Between

______________________________ [Name] ("Party A")
______________________________ [full address].

______________________________ [Name] ("Party B")
______________________________ [full address].

Matter

[Title/subject matter, parties, and date of contract to which dispute relates] ("the Contract").

Dispute

[Brief description of the nature of the dispute, including reference to relevant provision in the Contract] ("the dispute").

Terms of Agreement

1. CPR Procedure

By this agreement we agree to seek to resolve the dispute by adopting and using the CPR Model Procedure for Settlement of Transnational Business Disputes ("the CPR Procedure") as modified by the provisions of this agreement.

2. Management Representatives

[Name of Management Representative of Party A and corporate title.]

[Name of Management Representative of Party B and corporate title.]

Each of the above persons ("the Management Representatives") will represent their respective companies at the formal meeting and will have full authority to settle the dispute.

3. Place and Time of Formal Meeting

A formal meeting ("the formal meeting") will take place in the manner set out in section 4 of the CPR Procedure at:

____ [full address]

at ______________ o'clock on [date].

4. Language of Proceedings

The proceedings are to be conducted in [language(s)].

5. Exchange of Information

The parties shall comply with the provisions of section 3 ("Exchange of Information") of the CPR Procedure by [date].

6. Conduct of Formal Meeting and Negotiations

The formal meeting will be conducted, as provided by section 4 of the CPR Procedure, as follows:

______________ o'clock to ______________ o'clock

Presentation by Party A of its case.

______________ o'clock to ______________ o'clock

Reply by Party B.

______________ o'clock to ______________ o'clock

Presentation by Party B of its case.

______________ o'clock to ______________ o'clock

Reply by Party A.

The Management Representatives will meet for negotiations to settle the dispute at ______________ o'clock on [date—if possible, immediately after formal meeting].

7. Suspension of Legal Proceedings

The following steps will be taken, as provided by section 7 of the CPR Procedure, to suspend the legal proceedings/arbitration (if any) relating to the dispute:

If no legal proceedings/arbitration have been commenced, it is agreed that none will be commenced until the termination of this agreement, in accordance with section 9 of the CPR Procedure.

8. Neutral Adviser

The neutral adviser will be [name—delete if no neutral adviser is to be appointed].

[Or]

The nomination of neutral adviser is to be agreed between the parties by the date specified in paragraph 5 above. The neutral adviser is to be qualified as the following:

[professional qualifications]
[linguistic ability]
[nationality]

SIGNED: ______________________

[name]

For and on behalf of Party A

SIGNED: ______________________

[name]

For and on behalf of Party B

Considerations in Drawing the Agreement

Neutral Expert

If the parties need independent expert advice on critical technical or legal issues, and the neutral adviser does not possess the required expertise, they may agree on the selection of a neutral expert or empower the neutral adviser to select one.

The Locale

Parties of different nationalities often are reluctant to litigate or arbitrate in each other's country. They should be less reluctant to hold this proceeding in each other's country, since the objective is a settlement negotiated by the parties, not adjudication. In any event, the parties may meet in a third country of their choice.

Legal Proceedings

If no litigation is pending between the parties with respect to the subject matter of the dispute, and if a statute of limitations would expire while the procedure is being conducted, the parties should consider the feasibility of suspending such statute of limitations by agreement for the duration of the procedure.

Commercial Agreement Clauses

Persons drafting a commercial agreement are urged to incorporate the model procedure by reference. The following contract clause is suggested:

> The parties will attempt in good faith to resolve any controversy or claim arising out of or relating to this agreement in accordance with the Center for Public Resources (CPR) Model Procedure for Settlement of Transnational Business Disputes.

This clause may well not be legally enforceable. But between reputable companies, an expression of intent, enforceable or not, should carry considerable weight. If a dispute arises, this contract clause would substantially increase the likelihood that the parties would make a serious effort to arrive at a compromise through this process, rather than seeking an adjudicative solution.

The commercial agreement also could provide that if a controversy arises, negotiations between executives would be the first step in attempting resolution; this procedure the second step. A suggested contract clause is attached. The clause represents an expression of intent and states that either party may withdraw at any time and may institute legal proceedings.

Sample Time Schedule

Commencement Date (CD): Date of last signature on the initiating agreement.

CD + 20: Parties agree on neutral adviser.

CD + 30: Parties exchange and send the neutral adviser memoranda and documents and exhibits to be used at the formal meeting.

CD + 45: Formal meeting:

9:00–11:00 Party *A*'s presentation

	11:00–12:00	Party *B*'s reply
	14:00–16:00	Party *B*'s presentation
	16:00–17:00	Party *A*'s reply
CD + 46:	Settlement negotiations begin. Neutral adviser submits oral opinion.	
CD + 49:	Parties agree on settlement terms.	
CD + 50:	A written settlement agreement is prepared and signed.	

Negotiation Clause for Transnational Commercial Agreement

The parties will attempt in good faith to resolve any controversy or claim arising out of or relating to this agreement promptly by negotiations between executives of the parties.

If a controversy or claim should arise, ______________ of *X* Co. and ______________ of *Y* Co., or their respective successors in the positions they now hold (herein called the "project managers"), will meet at least once and will attempt to resolve the matter. Either project manager may request the other to meet within twenty-one days, at a mutually agreed time.

If the matter shall not have been resolved within thirty days of their first meeting, the project managers shall refer the matter to senior executives, who shall have authority to settle the dispute (herein called "the senior executives"). Thereupon, the project managers shall promptly prepare and exchange memoranda stating the issues in dispute and their positions, summarizing the negotiations that have taken place, and attaching relevant documents. The senior executives will meet for negotiations within twenty-one days of the end of the thirty-day period referred to above, at a mutually agreed time.

The first meeting shall be held at the offices of the project manager receiving the request to meet. If more than one meeting is held, the meetings shall be held in rotation at the offices of *X* Co. and *Y* Co.

If the controversy or claim has not been resolved within thirty days of the meeting of the senior executives, either party may initiate the Center for Public Resources (CPR) Model Procedure for Settlement of Transnational Business Disputes.

The parties intend to cooperate in implementing the above procedures; however, either party may withdraw at any time upon written notice to the other from the negotiations or from the aforesaid CPR procedure and may institute [litigation] [arbitration proceedings].

[An arbitration clause may be added here.]

FORM 34

Center for Public Resources Model Agreement for Product Liability Claim Resolution

This model agreement is intended for use by parties to a personal injury product liability controversy who wish to resolve their controversy promptly on the basis of a nonbinding, reasoned, oral determination by an experienced neutral party of the settlement value of their case. The neutral party is chosen by mutual agreement, if need be with the assistance of a "selector." The parties exchange essential information and present their case before the neutral party in highly abbreviated form. The parties are free to modify the model agreement. With minor changes, the model also may be used for non–product liability tort claims.

AGREEMENT made ____[date]____, 19__ between ___[plaintiff]___

of ____

represented by __________[plaintiff's attorney]__________

("Plaintiff"), and __________[defendant]__________

of ____

represented by __________[defendant's attorney]__________

("Defendant").

WHEREAS, Plaintiff has made a claim against Defendant as the result of an incident alleged to have occurred on __[date of incident]__, 19__, in __________[city and state]__________, which is alleged to have involved a product of the Defendant known as __________[product]__________ (the "incident"); and

WHEREAS, the parties wish to attempt to resolve their controversy through a nonbinding process, as described in this agreement.

NOW, THEREFORE, the parties agree as follows:

1. Neutral

1.1. Number.

The proceeding shall be conducted before one neutral.

1.2. Selection

The neutral shall be ____

____

who has agreed to serve and whose compensation has been agreed to between the parties and the neutral.

[**Alternate:**

1.2. Selection.

The parties will attempt to agree on the selection of the neutral. If within ten days from the date of this agreement, the parties shall not have agreed on a neutral and determined his or her willingness to serve, either or both parties may request ______________ (the "selector") to nominate candidates having the qualifications set forth in Paragraph 1.3. Within ten days the selector shall submit to the parties the names of not fewer than three nominees, together with a brief statement of each nominee's qualifications and the per diem or hourly rates charged by such nominee. Each party shall strike from the list the names of any persons who are unacceptable to it and shall number the remaining names to indicate an order of preference. Each party shall mail the list to the selector within seven days of having received it. The selector will designate the neutral from the panel members acceptable to all parties, in accordance with the designated order of mutual preference. If a party does not return the list of nominees within seven days, the selector will assume that all of the nominees are acceptable to that party. If no nominee is acceptable to both parties, the selector will schedule and hold a meeting with the parties to agree on a neutral. If a neutral is not designated within seven days of said meeting, the proceeding shall be deemed terminated.]

1.3. Qualifications of Neutral.

Unless the parties otherwise agree, the selector named in Paragraph 1.2 shall nominate candidates who shall have served as a judge in a court of general jurisdiction, or who are attorneys who have practiced law for at least ten years and who have extensive experience in litigation. Unless the parties otherwise agree, if Plaintiff's claim is in litigation, the neutral shall reside or have an office in the state in which such litigation is pending;

and if no such litigation is pending, in the state in which Plaintiff resides or the state in which the incident occurred.

1.4. Conflict of Interest.

Each party shall promptly disclose to the other party any circumstances known to it that would cause reasonable doubt regarding the impartiality of an individual under consideration or appointed as a neutral. Any such individual shall promptly disclose any such circumstances to the parties. If any such circumstances have been disclosed, before or after the individual's appointment, the individual shall not serve, unless the parties agree in writing.

1.5. Communication with Neutral.

Unless the parties otherwise agree, neither party, nor anyone acting on its behalf, shall unilaterally communicate with the neutral, except as specifically provided for herein.

1.6. Compensation.

The neutral's per diem or hourly charges will be established at the time of appointment.

1.7. Hold Harmless.

The neutral shall not be liable for any act or omission in connection with his or her role as neutral in this proceeding.

2. Disclosure of Information

2.1. Plaintiff's Statement.

Plaintiff's attorney will deliver to Defendant's attorney and to the neutral, within twenty days of the date of this agreement, but not before the selection of a neutral, unless otherwise agreed:

- A description of the time, place and incident out of which the claim arises, including a particularized description of the product allegedly involved
- The amount of the demand, with itemization of special damages and economic losses
- A particularized statement of the nature of the defect, and any test results and written expert's report on which Plaintiff intends to rely at the hearing
- Copies of all medical and hospital records arising out of the incident, and all other documents on which Plaintiff intends to rely at the hearing

Plaintiff's attorney also shall make available to Defendant's attorney at that time for nondestructive study and testing the Defendant's product alleged to be involved in the incident. If Defendant's attorney so requests, Plaintiff's attorney shall make the Plaintiff available for examination at a mutually agreed time and place by a physician selected by Defendant's attorney.

2.2. Defendant's Statement.

Within twenty days (unless otherwise agreed) after receiving Plaintiff's Statement, Defendant's attorney will deliver to Plaintiff's attorney and to the neutral a statement of Defendant's position with respect to the claim, including a particularization of Defendant's defenses and the bases therefor, as well as relevant documents and test results on which Defendant intends to rely at the hearing. Defendant's attorney shall furnish to Plaintiff's attorney as soon as they become available copies of any written expert reports on which Defendant intends to rely at the hearing.

2.3. Discovery.

No discovery shall take place in this proceeding, except as the parties otherwise agree. Any discovery in this proceeding shall be expeditious and aimed at determining essential facts, without prejudice to the parties' right to conduct further discovery if this proceeding should fail to result in a resolution of the case. If litigation between the parties with respect to Plaintiff's claim is pending, any discovery previously taken in such litigation may be used in this proceeding. Discovery taken in this proceeding may be used in litigation between the parties with respect to the incident.

3. Statements and Exhibits

Not less than ten days before the hearing, each party shall deliver to the other, and to the neutral, a concise statement, not exceeding ten 8½″ × 11″ double-spaced pages, setting forth its factual and legal position on the issues of the case, as well as all documents and other exhibits on which the party intends to rely at the hearing.

4. The Hearing

4.1. Purpose.

The hearing is intended to present each party's best case to the other party and the neutral in highly abbreviated form. The hearing is not a trial.

4.2. Place and Time.

Unless the parties otherwise agree, the neutral shall designate by not less than thirty days' written notice to the parties' attorneys the place and time of the hearing; provided that the hearing shall commence not less than thirty days, and not more than sixty days, from the date on which Defendant's Statement is submitted, in accordance with Paragraph 2.2. The neutral may postpone the hearing date for reasons he or she finds compelling.

4.3. Neutral to Preside.

The neutral shall preside at the hearing and shall rule on procedure at the hearing to the extent not set forth in this agreement.

4.4. Presentations.

Plaintiff shall have sixty minutes to present its case-in-chief. Following such presentation, Defendant shall have ninety minutes to present its case-in-chief and to rebut Plaintiff. Thereupon, Plaintiff shall have an additional thirty minutes for rebuttal. Each attorney may use the time allotted in any manner he or she sees fit. Question-and-answer testimony by witnesses will not be taken. The presentation by counsel, however, can be combined, at counsel's discretion, with oral statements by expert and fact witnesses, as well as any form of documentary or visual evidence. Cross-examination is not permitted. The neutral may ask questions for clarification at any time.

4.5. Rules of Evidence.

No rules of evidence, including rules of relevance, will apply, except that the rules pertaining to privileged communications and attorney work product will apply.

4.6. Attendance of Parties.

Plaintiff and an employee or other representative of Defendant authorized to settle the case (other than outside counsel in the case) shall attend the hearing, unless the parties otherwise agree.

4.7. Record.

The hearing shall not be recorded by any means.

5. Determination

5.1. Nature and Announcement of Determination.

The neutral shall make a determination as to the settlement value of the case, in accordance with the law which he or she believes governs. The neutral shall orally communicate such determination, and the reasons underlying the same, to the parties in person, preferably on the day of the hearing, and at the latest on the day following the hearing. Such determination shall not be binding on either party.

5.2. Settlement Negotiations.

If the neutral's determination should not be acceptable to either or both parties, they will engage in settlement negotiations immediately following the announcement of the neutral's determination. The neutral shall be available to mediate such negotiations.

6. Court Proceedings

6.1. Commencement of Litigation and Extension of Limitations Period.

Neither party may commence litigation with respect to the subject matter of the proceeding until the proceeding shall have terminated in accordance with Article 9 hereof. Execution of this agreement shall extend all applicable statutes of limitation by a period equal to the duration of the proceeding, from the date of this agreement until the proceeding is terminated in accordance with Article 9. The parties will take such other action, if any, required to effectuate such extension or waiver of the governing statutory periods.

[ALTERNATE (if litigation is pending):

6.1. Stay of Litigation.

The parties will promptly present a joint motion to the Court in which litigation between the parties is pending to request a stay of all proceedings pending conclusion of this proceeding, provided, however, that the grant of such stay shall not be a condition to the continuation of this proceeding.]

7. Confidentiality

7.1. Compromise Negotiation.

The entire process is a compromise negotiation. The parties will maintain in confidence all offers, promises, conduct, and statements, whether oral or written, made in the course of the proceeding by any of the parties, their agents, employees, experts, and attorneys, and by the neutral for the purpose of these compromise negotiations. Such offers, promises, conduct, and statements shall be treated as if subject to rule 408 of the Federal Rules of Evidence and are inadmissible and not discoverable for any purpose, including impeachment, in litigation between the parties. Evidence that is otherwise admissible or discoverable shall not be rendered inadmissible or nondiscoverable as a result of its presentation or use in this proceeding. Depositions taken in this proceeding may be used in litigation between the parties.

7.2. Neutral as Witness.

The neutral will be disqualified as a trial witness, consultant, or expert for any party, and his or her oral and written determination and opinions will be inadmissible for all purposes in this or any other dispute involving either or both of the parties hereto or in any subsequent proceeding of any kind.

8. Costs

8.1. Division of Costs.

The fees and expenses of the neutral and the selector, and all other expenses of the proceeding, will be borne equally by the parties, unless the parties otherwise agree. Each party shall bear its own costs of the proceeding.

9. Termination

Neither party may terminate the proceeding unilaterally; provided that if the proceeding shall not have been terminated in accordance with the subsequent sentence within 180 days of the date of this agreement, either party may terminate the proceeding at any time thereafter by written notice to the other party and the neutral. The proceeding shall be deemed terminated when [a neutral is not selected by the end of the seven-day period referred to in the last sentence of Alternate Paragraph 1.2 hereof; or] the neutral's determination is made; or the parties enter into a settlement agreement; or the parties agree in writing to discontinue the proceeding; whichever event occurs first.

10. Code of Professional Responsibility

Counsel for the parties expressly acknowledge their obligation under the applicable code of professional responsibility and agree to pursue this process in accordance therewith. Without limiting the foregoing, counsel agree that all written and oral statements made by them will be based upon a good-faith belief in their truth and accuracy.

IN WITNESS WHEREOF, the parties by their attorneys have executed this Agreement as of the date first above written.

____
Plaintiff

By: ______________________________
Plaintiff's Attorney

____
Defendant

By: ______________________________
Defendant's Attorney

Sample Schedule

Commencement Date (CD):	Parties sign agreement.
CD + 10:	If litigation is pending, attorneys move to stay proceedings (¶ 6.1).
CD + 10:	Attorneys agree on neutral (¶ 1.4).
CD + 20:	Plaintiff's Statement is submitted (¶ 2.1).
CD + 30:	Neutral designates place and date for hearing (¶ 4.2).
CD + 40:	Defendant's Statement is submitted (¶ 2.2).
CD + 60:	Parties exchange briefs and exhibits (¶ 3.1).
CD + 70:	Hearing (¶ 4.2):

9:00–10:00	Plaintiff's case-in-chief
10:00–11:30	Defendant's case-in-chief and rebuttal
11:30–12:00	Plaintiff's rebuttal
2:00	Neutral's announcement of determination and reasons therefor to the parties
2:30	Acceptance of determination or negotiations to settle case

FORM 35

Center for Public Resources Model Minitrial Agreement for Business Disputes

1. Institution of Minitrial Proceeding

1.1. Parties to a dispute may commence a minitrial proceeding by entering into a written agreement (the "initiating agreement") to conduct a minitrial. The initiating agreement shall describe the matter in dispute, and shall state either that the parties agree to follow this model agreement, as modified by the initiating agreement, or that the parties agree to other procedures set forth or identified in the initiating agreement. A copy of the initiating agreement will be filed with the Center for Public Resources (CPR), 680 Fifth Avenue, New York, New York 10019.

1.2. Various time periods referred to in this model agreement are measured from the date of the initiating agreement, which hereafter is called the Commencement Date.

2. Minitrial Panel

2.1. The minitrial panel shall consist of a neutral adviser and one member of management from each party. Each such member shall have appropriate authority to negotiate a settlement on behalf of the party he or she represents.

2.2. The parties shall attempt to select a neutral adviser who is mutually acceptable to them, and who may be, but need not be, a member of the CPR Judicial Panel. The functions of the neutral adviser are those stated in this agreement.

2.3. If the parties have not agreed on a neutral adviser within fifteen days from the Commencement Date, any party may request CPR to nominate candidates. Within ten days of receiving such a request, CPR shall submit to the parties the names of not fewer than five nominees, together with a brief statement of each nominee's qualifications and the per diem or hourly rates charged by such nominee. Each party may strike from the list the names of all persons who are unacceptable to it and number the remaining names to indicate an order of preference. Each party shall mail the list to CPR within seven days of having received it. CPR will designate the neutral adviser from the panel members acceptable to all parties, in accordance with the designated order of mutual preference. If a party does not return the list of nominees within seven days, CPR will assume that all of the nominees are acceptable to that party. If no nominee is acceptable to all parties, CPR will schedule a meeting with the parties to agree on a neutral adviser.

2.4. Each party shall promptly disclose to the other party or parties any circumstances known to it that would cause reasonable doubt regarding the impartiality of an individual under consideration or appointed as a neutral adviser. Any such individual shall promptly disclose any such circumstances to the parties. If any such circumstances have been disclosed, the individual shall not serve as neutral adviser, unless all parties agree.

2.5. Before the minitrial information exchange described in Article 6 hereof, and unless all parties otherwise agree, no party, nor anyone acting on its behalf, shall unilaterally communicate with the neutral adviser, except as specifically provided for herein.

2.6. The parties will jointly and promptly send to the neutral adviser such materials as they may agree upon for the purpose of familiarizing him or her with the facts and issues in the dispute.

2.7. The parties may jointly seek the advice and assistance of the neutral adviser or of CPR in interpreting this agreement and on procedural matters. The parties shall comply promptly with all reasonable requests by the neutral adviser for documents or other information relevant to the dispute.

2.8. The neutral adviser's per diem or hourly charge will be established at the time of his or her appointment. Unless the parties otherwise agree, the fees and expenses of the neutral advisor, as well as any other expenses of the minitrial, will be borne equally by the parties, and each party shall bear its own costs of the proceedings.

2.9. On or before thirty days from the Commencement Date, by written notice to each other party and the neutral adviser, each party shall select a member of its management to serve on the panel. If a party later desires to designate a different member of management, it shall promptly notify each other party and the neutral adviser of the substitution.

3. Court Proceedings

3.1. If on the Commencement Date no litigation is pending between the parties with respect to the subject matter of the minitrial, no party shall commence such litigation until the minitrial proceedings have terminated in accordance with Article 9 hereof. Execution of the initiating agreement shall toll all applicable statutes of limitation until the minitrial proceedings have terminated. The parties will take such other action, if any, required to effectuate such tolling.

3.2. If on the Commencement Date litigation is pending between the parties with respect to the subject matter of the minitrial, the parties will promptly (a) present a joint motion to the Court to request a stay of all proceedings pending conclusion of the minitrial proceedings; and (b) request the Court to enter an order protecting the confidentiality of the minitrial and barring any collateral use by the parties of any aspect of the minitrial in any pending or future litigation; provided, however, that the grant of such stay and protective order shall not be a condition to the continuation of the minitrial proceeding.

4. Discovery

4.1. If one or more of the parties have a substantial need for discovery in order to prepare for the minitrial information exchange, the parties shall attempt in good faith to agree on a minimum plan for strictly necessary, expeditious discovery. Should they fail to reach agreement, any party may request a joint meeting with the neutral adviser to explain points of agreement and disagreement. The neutral adviser shall promptly recommend the scope of discovery and time allowed therefor.

4.2. Should the minitrial not result in a settlement of the dispute, discovery taken in preparation for the minitrial information exchange may be used in any pending or future judicial proceeding between the parties relating to the dispute. Such discovery shall not restrict a party's ability to take additional discovery at a later date in any such proceeding, including additional depositions from persons deposed.

5. Briefs and Exhibits

Before the minitrial information exchange, the parties shall exchange, and submit to the neutral adviser, briefs, as well as all documents or other exhibits on which the parties intend to rely during the minitrial information exchange. The parties shall agree upon the length of such briefs, and on the date on which such briefs, documents, and other exhibits are to be exchanged.

6. Conduct of Minitrial Information Exchange

6.1. The minitrial information exchange shall be held before the minitrial panel at a place agreed to by the parties, on a date agreed to by the parties and the neutral adviser.

6.2. During the information exchange, each party shall present its best case, and each party shall be entitled to a rebuttal. The order and permissible length of presentations and rebuttals shall be determined by agreement between the parties.

6.3. The presentations and rebuttals of each party may be made in any form, and by any individuals, as desired by such party. Presentations by fact witnesses and expert witnesses shall be permitted.

6.4. No rules of evidence, including rules of relevance, will apply at the information exchange, except that the rules pertaining to privileged communications and attorney work product will apply.

6.5. The neutral adviser will moderate the information exchange.

6.6. Presentations may not be interrupted, except that during each party's presentation, and following such presentation, any member of the panel may ask clarifying questions of counsel or other persons appearing on that party's behalf. No member of the panel may limit the scope or substance of a party's presentation. Each party may ask questions of opposing counsel and witnesses during scheduled open question-and-answer exchanges, and during that party's rebuttal time if the parties so agree.

6.7. The information exchange shall not be recorded by any means. However, subject to Article 8, persons attending the information exchange may take notes of the proceedings.

6.8. In addition to counsel, each management representative may have advisers in attendance at the information exchange, provided that each other party and the neutral adviser shall have been notified of the identity of such advisers at least ten days before commencement of the information exchange.

7. Negotiations between Management Representatives

7.1. At the conclusion of the information exchange, the management representatives shall meet, by themselves, and shall attempt to agree on a resolution of the dispute. By agreement, other members of their teams may be invited to participate in the meetings.

7.2. At the request of any management representative, the neutral adviser will render an oral opinion as to the likely outcome at trial of each issue raised during the information exchange. Following that opinion, the management representatives will again attempt to resolve the dispute. If all management representatives agree to request a written opinion on such matters, the neutral adviser shall render such a written opinion within fourteen days. Following issuance of any such written opinion, the management representatives will again attempt to resolve the dispute.

8. Confidentiality

8.1. The entire process is a compromise negotiation. All offers, promises, conduct, and statements, whether oral or written, made in the course of the minitrial proceeding by any of the parties, their agents, employees, experts, and attorneys, and by the neutral adviser, who is the parties' joint counsel (or agent if not an attorney) for the purpose of these compromise negotiations, are confidential. Such offers, promises, conduct, and statements are subject to Federal Rule of Evidence 408 and are inadmissible and not discoverable for any purpose, including impeachment, in litigation between the parties to the minitrial or other litigation. However, evidence that is otherwise admissible or discoverable shall not be rendered inadmissible or nondiscoverable as a result of its presentation or use at the minitrial.

8.2. The neutral adviser will be disqualified as a trial witness, consultant, or expert for any party, and his or her oral and written opinions will be inadmissible for all purposes in this or any other dispute involving the parties hereto.

9. Termination of Proceeding

9.1. The minitrial proceedings shall be deemed terminated if and when (a) the parties have not executed a written settlement of their dispute on or before the forty-fifth day following conclusion of the minitrial information exchange (which deadline may be extended by mutual agreement of the parties), or (b) any party serves on each other party and on the neutral adviser a notice of withdrawal from the minitrial proceedings.

Sample Minitrial Schedule

Before the Minitrial Information Exchange

Commencement Date (CD):	Parties sign initiating agreement and file same with CPR (¶ 1.1).
CD + 10:	Parties agree on neutral adviser (NA) (¶ 2.2). If litigation is pending, parties' attorneys move to stay proceedings (¶ 3.2).
CD + 15:	Parties' attorneys agree on discovery plan, including a sixty-day discovery schedule (¶ 4.1).
CD + 20:	Parties' attorneys send material on dispute to NA (¶ 2.6).
CD + 30:	Parties' attorneys agree on place and date for minitrial and on length of presentations, rebuttals, and responses (¶¶ 6.1–6.2). Parties determine form of briefs and date for submission of briefs and exhibits (¶ 5.1).

	Parties give notice of selection of management members of panel (¶ 2.9).
CD + 75:	Discovery is completed.
CD + 90:	Parties exchange briefs and exhibits (¶ 5.1).
CD + 95:	Parties give notice of advisers who will attend information exchange (¶ 6.8).
CD + 105:	Information exchange begins (¶ 6.2).

At the Minitrial Information Exchange

Day 1	9:00–12:00	Plaintiff's case-in-chief.
	1:00– 2:00	Defendant's rebuttal.
	2:00– 3:00	Open question-and-answer exchange.
Day 2	9:00–12:00	Defendant's case-in-chief.
	1:00– 2:00	Plaintiff's rebuttal.
	2:00– 3:00	Open question-and-answer exchange.

After the Minitrial Information Exchange

Day 2:	3:00–5:00 Negotiations.
Days 3–21:	Reserved for negotiations (¶ 7.1).
Day 17:	NA submits written opinion, if requested (¶ 7.2).

Commentary on Model Minitrial Agreement

Counsel drafting a commercial agreement may incorporate the model minitrial agreement by reference. The following language is suggested:

> The parties intend that they will attempt in good faith to resolve any controversy or claim arising out of or relating to this agreement by a minitrial in accordance with the CPR Model Minitrial Agreement.

The Center for Public Resources (CPR) does not consider this clause as creating an enforceable right or obligation. The model agreement is not designed to be self-executing. CPR considers it an essential characteristic of the minitrial that it be entered into voluntarily by parties that wish to resolve a dispute privately, rapidly, and cost-effectively through an informal, collaborative process that will enable them to fashion their own solution. A minitrial is not likely to succeed without the genuine motivation of the parties to make it succeed.

Between reputable companies even an unenforceable statement of intent should carry considerable weight, and if a dispute should arise, such a statement would substantially increase the likelihood that the parties would make a serious effort to arrive at a compromise through the minitrial process, rather than seeking an adjudicative solution.

The commercial agreement also could provide that if a dispute arises, negotiations between executives would be the first step in attempting resolution; a minitrial could be the second step, if such negotiations should not succeed.

The role of CPR in the procedure is very limited. CPR believes that the minitrial should be a truly private process that succeeds through cooperation between the parties and between counsel.

CPR may make reasonable time charges for such services as it is asked to perform.

The paragraph numbers below refer to paragraphs in the model agreement:

1.1 CPR will not charge a fee for filing of the initiating agreement.

2.1 The model agreement provides for the appointment of a neutral adviser. CPR believes that a highly qualified neutral adviser can substantially enhance the prospects for success; however, successful minitrials also have been held without a neutral adviser. The parties have the option of dispensing with a neutral adviser.

2.2 For the neutral adviser's views to carry weight, the neutral adviser must be a person in whose impartiality and judgment all parties have full confidence. It is preferable that the neutral adviser be selected by mutual agreement, rather than through the nomination procedure set forth in paragraph 2.3.

2.9 The negotiations following the information exchange are more likely to succeed if the negotiators are objective and do not feel a need to defend past actions. It is preferable that the management representatives shall not have participated directly or actively in the events underlying the dispute. As a rule, the more senior the management representatives, the greater the range of options for a constructive solution they will perceive.

4.1 Discovery should be limited to that for which each party has a substantial need for purposes of the minitrial information exchange. As a rule, such discovery would be far less extensive than discovery conducted in preparation for a trial. The objective is to enable the parties, through limited discovery on the merits, in a short period to define the issues and to learn the principal strengths and weaknesses of their cases. If litigation between the parties is pending, any prior discovery in that litigation should be taken into account in determining the need for additional discovery.

6.2 The tone of the minitrial should be one of business-like problem solving. Nevertheless, counsel are expected to vigorously advocate their positions during the minitrial information exchange.

7.1 In some circumstances negotiations will be more productive if more than one representative of each party participates.

7.2 The neutral advisor also may assist in bringing about a settlement by mediating the negotiations. The initiating agreement may provide that the neutral adviser will serve as a mediator, or the management representatives may call on him or her to play that role during the negotiations.

Forms for Section VI:

The Use of Computers in Litigation

FORM 36

Computerized Legal Matter Notification Form and Matter Directories

Legal Matter Notification
Section 1: Matter Identification

☐ Open New Matter   Matter Number: ☐☐☐☐☐☐   Date: __/__/__

_ _
Abbreviated Description (30 Characters)

Section 2: Matter Information

_ _

_ _
Complete Matter Description (80 Characters)

Type of Law: ______________________ ☐ ☐ ☐

Group/Division: ______________________ ☐ ☐ ☐

Staff Attorney: ______________________ ☐ ☐ ☐

Staff Legal Assistant: ______________________ ☐ ☐ ☐

Payment Type: ______________________ ☐

Status: ______________________ ☐

Account Number: ___ - ___ - ___

Adverse Party 1: _

Adverse Party 2: _

Adverse Party 3: _

Risk Management No.: __ - ____

Section 3: Litigation Information

Court: _ State: __ Date Served: __/__/__ Trial Date: __/__/__

Answer Date: __/__/__

Court Description:

Clearfield Indicator: _ Major Case Indicator: _ Company Indicator: _

Prayer: $ ______ Prayer Other: ______

Recovery/Exposure: (+)(−) ______

Total Fees: ______ Company Relationship: ______

Status Information

Case Status (50 characters per line):

______

______

______

______

Date Closed: __/__/__ Disposition: __ Disposition Amount: ______

Matter Number: ☐ ☐ ☐ ☐ ☐ ☐

Summary

Case Summary (15 lines):

Section 4: Outside Counsel and Fees Estimate

1st: ______________	☐	☐	☐	☐	☐	$ ________
2d: ______________	☐	☐	☐	☐	☐	$ ________
3d: ______________	☐	☐	☐	☐	☐	$ ________

Plaintiff Firm/Lead Attorney:	Defendant Firm/Lead Attorney:
____________________	____________________
____________________	____________________
____________________	____________________
____________________	____________________
____________________	____________________
Phone: ______________	Phone: ______________

Matter Directories
Database Description

The Legal Department's integrated database organizes data on legal matters and is stored on the Company's mainframe computer. (The Legal Matter Notification sheet is the basic entry document.) The database, however, includes information on:

- New matters—matter numbers, names, types of law, outside counsel, adverse party, court, trial date, status, and summary
- Outside counsel directories
- Budgets and professional fees
- INVALUE and BREAKEVEN models used to determine the economical practicability of lawsuits in which the corporation is involved
- Work-product retrieval (BRANDEIS) system

From data input, the system produces various litigation reports, professional fee analysis reports, management reports, and attorney reports monthly, quarterly, and on demand. In addition, matter directories for quick reference are produced monthly. The database may also be searched instantly for key words as inquiries arise.

The Legal Department is "automated." Attorneys and legal assistants each have either a terminal or a personal computer at their desks, and legal secretaries have either a terminal or a word processor at their desks. All have access to the system and database information. The integrated database is considered, and is treated in all respects, as confidential and protected from the standpoint of both work-product and attorney-client privilege.

In addition, a nonintegrated database is also maintained, which includes information on continuing legal education and on other critical corporate programs under the responsibility of the Legal Department, such as antitrust compliance and environmental compliance.

Types of Law Codes

Code	*Printed Description*	*Expanded Description*
211	Corporate Litigation	Shareholder and corporate derivative litigation, including proxy contests
212	Acquisition Litigation	Contested acquisitions, mergers and takeovers, including tender offers
213	Securities Litigation	Registrations, public offerings, and filings, including allegations of "insider" information or securities fraud
215	Creditor Rights Litigation	Creditor rights litigation, including prejudgment remedies, insolvency and chapter proceedings, personal property foreclosures, and other collection matters
216	Contract Litigation	Commercial contracts, including loan agreements, construction contracts, procurement or sale agreements
217	Products Liability	Products liability litigation, other than siding cases
218	Insulite Siding Lit	Products liability litigation involving Insulite siding
219	Rough Sawn Siding Lit	Products liability litigation involving rough sawn mahogany siding
220	Other Siding Litigation	Products liability litigation involving siding other than Insulite or rough sawn mahogany

Code	*Printed Description*	*Expanded Description*
222	Tax Litigation	Tax litigation, including federal, state, and local income tax; sales, use, and property tax
223	ERISA Litigation	Executive or employee compensation and benefit matters, including interpretation of qualified or nonqualified employee benefit plans
232	Labor Litigation	NLRB representation and unfair labor practices; strikes, boycotts, and injunctions; collective bargaining or wage/hour matters
233	EEO Litigation	Civil rights, discrimination charges, and other EEOC, Title VII, ADEA matters
235	OSHA Litigation	Occupational safety and health matters
236	Employment Litigation	Other employment law matters not specifically covered by one of the defined labor categories
237	Workers' Comp Litigation	Workers' compensation matters
241	Real Property Litigation	Real property litigation, including land-use regulations, title disputes, condemnation, landlord-tenant questions, and real property foreclosures
242	Environmental Litigation	Environmental litigation, including air, water, noise

Code	Printed Description	Expanded Description
		pollution, or toxic substances
243	Energy Litigation	Energy litigation, including cogeneration, hydropower, petroleum, coal, nuclear, biomass, and synthetic fuels
244	Water Rights Litigation	Administrative proceedings to adjudicate water rights disputes
251	Antitrust Litigation	Civil or criminal antitrust, unfair competition, and other trade regulation matters
252	Proprietary Litigation	Trade secrets, infringement of trademarks, copyrights, or patents, whether domestic or foreign
261	Foreign Litigation	Foreign (except Canadian) litigation, including commercial and tax controversies, international law, etc.
262	Transportation Litigation	Transportation and aviation law, including regulation and tariff matters
263	Miscellaneous Litigation	All other litigation matters
264	Personal Injury	Personal injury litigation
265	Property Damage	Property damage litigation
266	Timber Litigation	Timber trespass, lien claims, timber purchase and sale agreements; forest products acts; similar regulatory matters

Directories, Fees Analysis, Calendaring, and Docketing

The following reports illustrate how the database can be manipulated for purposes of litigation management.

1. *Directories*
   - a. DIR-01 Numeric
   - b. DIR-02 Alphabetic
   - c. DIR-03 By outside counsel
   - d. DIR-04 By staff attorney
   - e. DIR-05 By group division
   - f. DIR-06 By type of law
   - g. DIR-07 By status
   - h. DIR-08 Numeric with account number

2. *Litigation*
   - a. LIT-01 Litigation by attorney
   - b. LIT-13 Cross-reference listing

3. *Professional Fees Analysis*
   - a. PFA-06 By type of law
   - b. PFA-10 By group/division
   - c. PFA-11 By matter within staff attorney
   - d. PFA-13 By type of law within division
   - e. PFA-21 By year-to-date descending by matter within group

4. *Litigation Management/Calendaring*
   - a. CAL1 Litigation Section, calendar by date
   - b. CAL2 Litigation Section, calendar by matter
   - c. CAL3 All sections, calendar by attorney

Company Legal Department Matter Directory—Numeric

DIR-01

Matter Number	Counsel	Abbreviated Matter Description	Outside Counsel	Status	Type of Law	Staff Atty	Pay Type	Grp Div
001007	MORGL	XXXXXXX	Morgan, Lewis	9	Commercial law	SKP	2	951
001008	MORGL	XXXXXXX	Morgan, Lewis	9	Commercial law	SKP	2	951
001009	MORGL	XXXXXXX	Morgan, Lewis	9	Commercial law	SKP	2	951
001010	OTHER		Other Counsel	8	Products Liability	SKP	2	813

900

Boise Cascade Corporation Legal Department
Matter Directory—Alphabetic

Matter Number	Counsel	Abbreviated Matter Description	Outside Counsel	Status	Type of Law	Staff Atty	Pay Type	Grp Div
002046	FRASR	XXXXXXX	Fraser & Beatty	3	Environmental litigation	JPB	2	420
	LITIG	XXXXXXX	Litigation Section					
000860	REIDP	XXXXXXX	Reid & Priest	9	Tax litigation	RAW	1	850
000624	GARLI		Garlington, Lohn	9	Products liability	SKP	1	951
001266	WEEKS		Weeks, Thomas	9	Real estate law	JWH	1	510

Matter Directory—By Outside Counsel

DIR-03

Matter Number	Counsel	Abbreviated Matter Description	Outside Counsel	Status	Type of Law	Staff Atty	Pay Type	Grp Div
001347	MCCAL	XXXXXXX	McCalla, Thompson	1	Collective bargaining	SKP	2	430
001397		XXXXXXX		1	Collective bargaining	SKP	2	430
001400	MORGL	XXXXXXX	Morgan, Lewis	8	Labor relations	SKP	1	836

Boise Cascade Corporation Legal Department
Matter Directory—By Staff Attorney

Matter Number	Counsel	Abbreviated Matter Description	Outside Counsel	Status	Type of Law	Staff Atty	Pay Type	Grp Div
000106	DEWEY	XXXXXXX	Dewey, Ballantine	9	Contract litigation	DM	1	850
000112	BRONB	XXXXXXX	Bronson, Bronson	9	Products liability	DM	2	940
000312	BELLB	XXXXXXX	Bell, Boyd	9	Proprietary litigation	DM	1	610

Matter Directory—By Group/Division

DIR-05

Matter Number	Counsel	Abbreviated Matter Description	Outside Counsel	Status	Type of Law	Staff Atty	Pay Type	Grp Div
001740	OTREP	XXXXXXX	Other—Reporters	9	Contract litigation	JWH	1	510
001801	ARMST	XXXXXXX	Armstrong, Teasdale	9	Transportation litigation	RMM	1	510
001831	DYKMA	XXXXXXX	Dykema, Gossett	9	Creditor rights litigation	RMM	1	510
001832	LITIG		Litigation Section	9	Creditor rights litigation	JWH	1	510
001844	MCMAH	XXXXXXX	McMahon, Berger	9	Employment litigation	KBB	1	510
	OTREP	XXXXXXX	Other—Reporters					

Matter Number	Counsel	Abbreviated Matter Description	Outside Counsel	Status	Type of Law	Staff Atty	Pay Type	Grp Div
001971	LITIG	XXXXXXX	Litigation Section	9	Miscellaneous litigation	RBW	1	510
001974	ARMST	XXXXXXX	Armstrong, Teasdale	1	Commercial law	JWH	1	510
	OTCON	XXXXXXX	Other—Consultants					
001978	ARMST	XXXXXXX	Armstrong, Teasdale	9	Contract litigation	SKP	1	510
001983	HEISK	XXXXXXX	Heiskell, Donelson	1	EEO litigation	JTS	1	510
002023	LITIG	XXXXXXX	Litigation Section	9	OSHA litigation	SKP	1	510

Matter Directory—By Type of Law

DIR-06

Matter Number	Counsel	Abbreviated Matter Description	Outside Counsel	Status	Type of Law	Staff Atty	Pay Type	Grp Div
001178	LUKIN	XXXXXXX	Lukins, Annis	1	Timber disputes	JSM	1	110
001180	ADHOC	XXXXXXX	Adhoc ESSB 4663 Comm	1		JSM	1	110
	BCCLD	XXXXXXX	BCC Legal Department					
	FERGU		Ferguson & Burdell					
001192	FERGU		Ferguson & Burdell	9		JSM	1	110

Boise Cascade Corporation Legal Department Matter Directory—Numeric w/Account Numbers

DIR-08

Matter Number	Counsel	Abbreviated Matter Description	Outside Counsel	Account Number	Atty	Pay Type
000758	LITIG	XXXXXXXX	Litigation Section	166-661-010	SKP	1
000759	KNIGH	XXXXXXXX	Knight, Wagner	166-664-010	DGG	1
000760	LITIG	XXXXXXXX	Litigation Section	166-661-010	SKP	1
000761	LITIG		Litigation Section	166-664-010	DGG	1

FORM 37

Computerized Litigation Reports

Litigation Report—LIT-01

Description of Action	Prayer or Action Sought	Estimated Recovery or Exposure	PLF/ DEF.	Out-of-Pocket Costs: This Month	Out-of-Pocket Costs: Year to Date	Out-of-Pocket Costs: Commencement of Suit to Date
SART V REEVES & BCC MATTER: 001492 COURT: F SUBJECT: PRODUCTS LIABILITY LA: PCM DIVISION: HOUSING DIVISION STATE: NY SERVED: 03/27/78 TRIAL: 00/00/00 LAST CHG: 08/22/85 ORIG. MOD: 12,096 REV. MOD: 100 (00/00) STATUS: BCC PREPARED LETTER TO OUTSIDE COUNSEL AND OPPOSING COUNSEL RE RESOLUTION POSSIBILITIES.	75,000	-2,000	D	0	61	551
UPPER TERRACE V RED RIVER MATTER: 000783 COURT: S SUBJECT: OTHER SIDING LITIGATION LA: SMT DIVISION: TIMBER & WOOD PRODUCTS STATE: CT SERVED: 07/18/79 TRIAL: 00/00/00 LAST CHG: 06/25/85 ORIG. MOD: 27,798 REV. MOD: 100(00/00) STATUS: CASE SETTLED AT APPROXIMATE COST TO BCC OF $29,000. BECAUSE OF NOTICE REQUIREMENT TO INDIVIDUAL CONDO OWNERS, CLOSING DOCUMENTS ARE NOT EXPECTED FOR APPROXIMATELY 3 MONTHS.						
MARTIN V SE MUTUAL MATTER: 001956 COURT: S SUBJECT: PERSONAL INJURY LA: JK DIVISION: CLEARFIELD INSURANCE STATE: GA SERVED: 11/25/81 TRIAL: 00/00/00 LAST CHG: 8/22/85 ORIG. MOD: 1,669 REV. MOD: 100 (05/85) STATUS: PLAINTIFF LOST WORKERS' COMP. CASE IN FINAL ROUND. BC WILL TRY TO HAVE CASE DISMISSED VOLUNTARILY; MIGHT CONSIDER NUISANCE VALUE SETTLEMENT.						

Cross-Reference Listing (Adverse Parties)

LIT-13

Cross-Reference/Adverse Party	Matter	Abbreviated Matter Description	S	Opened	Closed	Type	Div	Atty	O/S Atty
XXXXXXX	001261	XXXXXXX	8	00/00/00	00/00/00	115	620	DM	EBERL
	000837		9	02/08/80	10/30/80	264	813	DRA	FERGU
	000718		9	01/19/79	02/01/80	217	951	DRA	DYKMA
	001282		1	00/00/00	00/00/00	135	110	KBB	OTREP

Analysis of Professional Fees by Type of Law (Year to Date)

PFA-06

				Variance from Budget		
January 198X	YTD Fees Paid by Legal Department	YTD Fees Paid by Others	YTD Gross Fees Paid	YTD Fees Paid by Legal Department	YTD Fees Paid by Others	YTD Gross Fees Paid
Antitrust advice	X,XXX	X,XXX	X,XXX	X,XXX	X,XXX	X,XXX
Commercial law						
Environmental/energy law						
Financial law						
Foreign advice						
Labor law						
Litigation						
Other legal matters						
Proprietary law						
Real estate law						
Securities law						
Tax law						
Grand Total	X,XXX	X,XXX	X,XXX	X,XXX	X,XXX	X,XXX

Analysis of Professional Fees by Group/Division (Year to Date)

PFA-10

				Variance from Budget		
January 1984	YTD Fees Paid by Legal Department	YTD Fees Paid by Others	YTD Gross Fees Paid	YTD Fees Paid by Legal Department	YTD Fees Paid by Others	YTD Gross Fees Paid
Timber & Wood Products Group						
Boise Cascade Timberlands	X,XXX	X,XXX	X,XXX	X,XXX	X,XXX	X,XXX
Timber & Wood Products						
Timberland Resources						
Group Total						
Paper Group						
Boise Cascade Canada	X,XXX	X,XXX	X,XXX	X,XXX	X,XXX	X,XXX
Boise Southern Company						
Missisquoi Associates						
Paper Group						
Group Total						

January 1984	YTD Fees Paid by Legal Department	YTD Fees Paid by Others	YTD Gross Fees Paid	Variance from Budget: YTD Fees Paid by Legal Department	Variance from Budget: YTD Fees Paid by Others	Variance from Budget: YTD Gross Fees Paid
Packaging Group						
Boise Cascade France	X,XXX	X,XXX	X,XXX	X,XXX	X,XXX	X,XXX
Composite Can Division						
Corrugated Container Division						
Envelope Division						
Melcarta/Duropack						
Group Total						

Analysis of Professional Fees by Matter Within Staff Attorney (Current Month)

PFA-11

Attorney Name	This Month	Monthly Fees Paid by Legal Department	Monthly Fees Paid by Others	Monthly Gross Fees Paid	Variance from Budget: Monthly Fees Paid by Legal Department	Variance from Budget: Monthly Fees Paid by Others	Variance from Budget: Monthly Gross Fees Paid
—Matter and	Counsel—						
J.T. Sahlberg	Jan. 198X						
XXXXXXXX	BELLB	X,XXX	X,XXX	X,XXX	X,XXX	X,XXX	X,XXX
XXXXXXXX	PHILL						
XXXXXXXX	PINSK						
	DESKY						
	HOLME						
	EBERL						
	LITIG						
	FERGU						
	VINSN						
	LITIG						
	PAULJ						
	KYKMA						
	MINNI						
	GISLA						
	CAMPA						
	WINCM						
	WEEKS						
	CRAIG						
	FELTH						
	STOEL						
	OTREP						

Analysis of Professional Fees by Type of Law Within Division (Year to Date)

PFA-13

Type of Law	YTD Fees Paid by Legal Department	YTD Fees Paid by Others	YTD Gross Fees Paid	Variance from Budget: YTD Fees Paid by Legal Department	Variance from Budget: YTD Fees Paid by Others	Variance from Budget: YTD Gross Fees Paid
January 198X						
Packaging Group						
Composite Can Division						
Antitrust advice	X,XXX	X,XXX	X,XXX	X,XXX	X,XXX	X,XXX
Commercial law						
Labor law						
Litigation						
Proprietary law						
Corrugated Container Division						
Antitrust advice	X,XXX	X,XXX	X,XXX	X,XXX	X,XXX	X,XXX
Commercial law						
Litigation						
Proprietary law						
Envelope Division						
Antitrust advice	X,XXX	X,XXX	X,XXX	X,XXX	X,XXX	X,XXX
Commercial law						
Labor law						
Proprietary law						
Boise Cascade France						
Other Legal Matters	X,XXX	X,XXX	X,XXX	X,XXX	X,XXX	X,XXX

Legal Department Calendar by Date

CAL1

Person	Date	Matter	Matter Name	Description
SKP; PMS;	09/24/8X	812	XXXXXXXX	Trial.
GGH	09/25/8X	1796	XXXXXXXX	Depositions of XXXXXXXXXXXXXX .
JTS; PMS	09/25/8X	2010	XXXXXXXX	Notice of examination prior to trial. Representative of ________ requested to appear on this date.
BJK; JAK	09/27/8X	2070		Motions hearing.
DRA	10/01/8X	30		Appellant's opening brief due.
JTS; PMS	10/01/8X	1718		Check with ________ re reimbursement.
JTS; GGH	10/02/8X	978		Jury trial reset for Tuesday, October 2, 198X, at 1:30 in Pocatello.
JTS	10/04/8X	2149		Answer to complaint due.
KBB; SMT	10/08/8X	2059		Trial date.

CAL1

Person	Date	Matter	Matter Name	Description
SKP	10/09/8X	2127		Hearing.
SKP	10/10/8X	2150		Answer to compaint due.

Legal Department Calendar by Matter

CAL2

Person	Date	Matter	Matter Name	Description
SKP	12/07/8X	1951	XXXXXXXX	Answering brief due.
SKP	12/21/8X	1951	XXXXXXXX	Boise's reply brief due.
SKP	10/15/8X	1995	XXXXXXXX	Trial (October 15–19, 198X).
JTS; PMS	09/25/8X	2010		Notice of examination prior to trial. Representative of ________ requested to appear on this date.
JTS; PMS	11/15/8X	2037		Discovery cutoff.
JTS; PMS	12/10/8X	2037		Trial date.
KBB	10/19/8X	2053		All motions to be filed.
KBB; SMT	10/08/8X	2059		Trial date.
JTS; PMS	10/15/8X	2061		File verified statement or file verified statement 15 days after discovery is terminated, whichever is later.
JTS	10/15/8X	2061		Complainant's statement due.
JTS	11/14/8X	2061		Defendant's statement due.

Legal Department Calendar by Attorney

CAL3

Person	Date	Matter	Matter Name	Description
JTS; PMS	09/25/8X	2010	XXXXXXXX	Notice of examination prior to trial. Representative of ________ requested to appear on this date.
JTS; PMS	10/01/8X	1718	XXXXXXXX	Check with ________ re reimbursement.
JTS; GGH	10/02/8X	978	XXXXXXXX	Jury trial reset for Tuesday, October 2, 198X, at 1:30 in Pocatello.
JTS	10/04/8X	2149		Answer to complaint due.
JTS; PMS	10/15/8X	858		Trial date.
JTS; PMS	10/15/8X	2061		File verified statement or file verified statement 15 days after discovery is terminated, whichever is later.
JTS	10/15/8X	2061		Complainant's statement due.
JTS	11/14/8X	2061		Defendant's statement due.

FORM 38

Computerized Work-Product Retrieval Input Form

Explanation of Work-Product Retrieval—BRANDEIS

BRANDEIS is an acronym for Boise Cascade's Brief Retrieval and Electronic Information Storage System. The system was developed to permit computerized storage and retrieval of attorney work product and published materials.

Information selected for storage and retrieval includes documents prepared by the Legal Department staff, by retained counsel, or by opposing counsel, as well as published materials selected by a member of the Legal Department staff. It is not, however, a forms file and does not include agreements and contracts. Rather, it includes appropriately selected legal research memos, opinion letters, settlement letters, pleadings and briefs, speeches and published summaries, annotations, and articles.

In the future, BRANDEIS will have full-text retrieval capability, but currently the database has been structured as an indexed file supplemented by limited textual abstracts or extracts. Each computer "record" includes identifying information, index subjects, and some sort of textual field. The input form following this explanation is the "record." On the reverse side of the form are spaces for narrative comments about the document, and those who select documents for BRANDEIS are encouraged to note any limitations or exceptional strengths of the particular document. The textual field may contain full text of document, an extract or excerpt of text, or the selector's abstract, summary, or synopsis of the material.

As with most systems, and especially with most computerized legal storage and information retrieval systems, the accuracy and usefulness of the system depends upon the willingness of attorneys and legal assistants to systematically send copies of work product to the relevant files. To guard against failure in that regard, a relatively simple process has been devised to ensure that documents of significant potential use find their way into the database. That process is as follows:

- An input form is attached by legal secretaries to all documents meeting defined criteria.

- Information evident from a quick glance at the document, i.e., author, recipient, and title, is not reentered on the input form.
- Less obvious objective information related to the document, such as legal jurisdiction, adversaries, and matter number, is entered on the input form by the secretary.
- Analytical information about the document, such as indexed subjects, abstracts, and comments, is entered on the input form by the attorney or legal assistant responsible for creating or reviewing that document.
- Attorneys are encouraged to extract rather than abstract published articles. It is quicker to highlight critical portions of text than summarize or synopsize complex articles.
- Those within the Legal Department who agree to provide abstracts or extracts of certain areas of the law are moved to the top of routing lists for articles in those particular areas.
- Input forms and photocopies of all selected documents are sent to the attorney with responsibility for the BRANDEIS system.
- The word-processing system has a compatible interface with the computer on which the database is stored and permits transmittal of either full text, abstracts, or extracts into the BRANDEIS system.

BRANDEIS is similar to LEXIS and WESTLAW, although there are some differences. For example, BRANDEIS has both an electronic and hard-copy component. Thus, there is a computerized database searchable through a number of predefined data fields, as well as a manual file of document folders, arranged in numerical order accompanied by a library-type charge-out procedure to control document flow and ensure timely returns to the manual file.

Attorneys and legal assistants search BRANDEIS before commencing legal research on any issue. They log onto the mainframe computer through one of several CRT terminals in the Legal Department, frame a search request using the same logical connectors found in LEXIS, and then narrow or expand the search request through multiple levels.

In addition, the BRANDEIS database may be searched on the index subject, textual phrases, legal jurisdiction, author, title, or a variety of descriptive fields. The computer will select all documents meeting the search request, and those documents may be displayed on the computer screen or printed out on hard copy as the searcher dictates.

Finally, the BRANDEIS database is a privileged collection of attorney work product, and the system may be used only by attorneys or other members of the Legal Department acting under the direction of an attorney. Although some documents have been published or filed in court, others are not on the public record. The following guidelines govern access to *both* the computer database and the hard-copy file:

- Documents may be retrieved by any member of the Legal Department acting under attorney direction.
- Published articles (ARTI) and filed pleadings (PLEA) may be shown to anyone.

Thus, material retrieved through the BRANDEIS system, whether in electronic or hard-copy form, may have to be summarized or reworked before it can be shared with the client or outside counsel involved in the matter for which it was retrieved. These procedures are necessary in order to preserve both the attorney-client privilege and attorney work-product immunity.

Input Form

________________		____________
BRANDEIS Number	Boise Cascade Corporation Legal Department BRANDEIS System Input Form	File Location

Please enter the enclosed document into the Brief Retrieval AND Electronic Information Storage (BRANDEIS) database. All relevant information (unless obvious) has been highlighted with a yellow marker or indicated on this form:

Author(s): ____

Organization: ____

Title: ____

____

Date: ________________ _____-_____-_____

Recipient(s): ____

Organization: ____

Document Type: [ ] <u>Arti</u>cle [ ] <u>Corr</u>espondence [ ] <u>Memo</u>randum

[ ] <u>Plea</u>ding [ ] <u>Pres</u>entation [ ] <u>Repo</u>rt

Matter Number: ____

Adversaries ____

Jurisdiction: ____

Bibliographic: ____

Indexed Subjects

____

____

____

____

____

____

Textual Retrieval

[ ] Abstract — [ ] Reverse of form [ ] Prepared later

[ ] Extract — Highlighted text (yellow marker)

[ ] Full Text— [ ] Word processing [ ] Rekeyboard (rare use)

Critique

[ ] Valuable [ ] Useful [ ] Limited

Selector: ______________________ Entry: ___-___-___

Please use this side of the form for more lengthy narrative information, and try to keep handwriting legible. The comments section is optional. The abstract section should be used when neither full text nor an extract is attached.

Comments (about 25–50 words)

____

____

____

Document Abstract (about 150–200 words)

____

____

____

____

____

____

____

____

____

____

FORM 39

Microfilm Target Sheet

File Folder Target Sheet

Files of: ____________________________

Department: ____________________________

Executive: ____________________________

File Folder Title: ____

Folder No.

Roll Number	Target Number
Plaintiff Receptacle Number	Box or Receptacle Number

FORM 40

Coding Form

Please *print* all entries!

Document Coding Form
Privileged and Confidential

Identification Number: | | | | | | | | | | |

Production Site: ____________________

Source: Receptacle Number: ________________

Files of: ____

File Title: ______________________________________

Biographical: Author: ____________________________________

Addressee: ________________________________

Copyees: __________________________________

____

Content: Document Title: ______________________________

Document Date: ______________________________

Pages (including attachments): ____________________

FORM 41

Litigation File Inventory

Box No.: ______________________

Office/Department: ____

File Holder: ____

Position: ____

Contents:

Date Range From To

Folder Labels

1.

2.

3.

4.

5.

Classification No.: ____

Reviewer: ______________________

Date of Review: _________________

FORM 42

Computer Screens for File Folder Logs

Coopers & Lybrand
Litigation Services Group
Document Inventory System

Selection Menu

1. Add New Documents
2. Modify Documents
3. Produce Document by Box Number Report
4. Produce Document by Box Number—Expanded
5. Produce Document by Holder Report
6. Produce Document by Holder—Expanded
7. Produce Document by Contents Report

Q. End of Session

Select Desired Function . . .

Coopers & Lybrand
Litigation Services Group
Document Inventory System

Box Number:	Department:
File Holder:	Position:
Date From:	Date To:

Contents

Classification: Reviewer: Review Date:

FORM 43

Output Reports of File Folder Logs

Coopers & Lybrand Litigation Services Group File Inventory Report

Box Number	Department	File Holder	Position	File Contents
*Box Number: L0001				
L0001	LSG	Keane James	Director	Antitrust litigation
L0001	LSG	Keane James	Director	Antitrust, grand jury
L0001	LSG	Keane James	Director	Computerization of law internationally
L0001	LSG	Keane James	Director	Behavior sciences in litigation
L0001	LSG	Keane James	Director	Economics in litigation
L0001	LSG	Keane James	Director	Construction litigation
L0001	LSG	Keane James	Director	Health care litigation
L0001	LSG	Keane James	Director	Environmental litigation
L0001	LSG	Keane James	Director	Expert witnesses
L0001	LSG	Keane James	Director	FOIA litigation
L0001	LSG	Keane James	Director	Cost of litigation
L0001	LSG	Keane James	Director	Damages
L0001	LSG	Keane James	Director	Government litigation
L0001	LSG	Keane James	Director	White-collar crime
L0001	LSG	Keane James	Director	International litigation
L0001	LSG	Keane James	Director	Securities litigation
L0001	LSG	Keane James	Director	Oil and gas litigation
L0001	LSG	Keane James	Director	Patent litigation
L0001	LSG	Keane James	Director	Product liability litigation
L0001	LSG	Keane James	Director	Asbestos litigation
*Box Number: L0002				
L0002	LSG	Keane James	Director	Indexing techniques
L0002	LSG	Keane James	Director	Information science
L0002	LSG	Keane James	Director	Complex litigation rules
L0002	LSG	Keane James	Director	Antitrust grand jury
L0002	LSG	Keane James	Director	Paralegal training
L0002	LSG	Keane James	Director	Discovery procedures
L0002	LSG	Keane James	Director	General counsel office management
L0002	LSG	Keane James	Director	Litigation department management
L0002	LSG	Keane James	Director	Expert witness
L0002	LSG	Keane James	Director	Videotape evidence
L0002	LSG	Keane James	Director	Microfilm
L0002	LSG	Keane James	Director	Video law seminar

Box Number	Department	File Holder	Position	File Contents
*Box Number: L0003				
L0003	LSG	Keane James	Director	Computer law
L0003	LSG	Keane James	Director	Computer services—general
L0003	LSG	Keane James	Director	Litigation support systems
L0003	LSG	Keane James	Director	Flite system USAF
L0003	LSG	Keane James	Director	Quiklaw
L0003	LSG	Keane James	Director	Aspen Systems
L0003	LSG	Keane James	Director	LEXIS
L0003	LSG	Keane James	Director	Informatics
L0003	LSG	Keane James	Director	SBC
L0003	LSG	Keane James	Director	Evidex
L0003	LSG	Keane James	Director	Factmatcher
L0003	LSG	Keane James	Director	CDC
L0003	LSG	Keane James	Director	Vendors, miscellaneous
L0003	LSG	Keane James	Director	Lawtime software
L0003	LSG	Keane James	Director	Law office administration
L0003	LSG	Keane James	Director	Law office management systems
L0003	LSG	Keane James	Director	Legal Automation News
L0003	LSG	Keane James	Director	Computer product directories
L0003	LSG	Keane James	Director	Word processing
L0003	LSG	Keane James	Director	Computer security
L0003	LSG	Keane James	Director	Computer abuse
L0003	LSG	Keane James	Director	Microcomputers
L0003	LSG	Keane James	Director	Litton Mellonics
L0003	LSG	Keane James	Director	Inmagic
L0003	LSG	Keane James	Director	Atlis
L0003	LSG	Keane James	Director	Wang
L0003	LSG	Keane James	Director	Juris
L0003	LSG	Keane James	Director	WESTLAW
L0003	LSG	Keane James	Director	IBM Stairs
*Box Number: L0004				
L0004	LSG	Keane James	Director	Decade of law office automation
L0004	LSG	Keane James	Director	Law firms and acct'g firms—contrast
L0004	LSG	Keane James	Director	Good-bye green eyeshades
L0004	LSG	Keane James	Director	The emerging role of consultants
L0004	LSG	Keane James	Director	Prison riot prosecution planning
L0004	LSG	Keane James	Director	Working with the trial lawyer
L0004	LSG	Keane James	Director	Computers in litigation
L0004	LSG	Keane James	Director	Document management system
L0004	LSG	Keane James	Director	Using the microcomputer in w.p.
L0004	LSG	Keane James	Director	Business end of general counsel office

Coopers & Lybrand Box Inventory Report by File Label

Contents	Box Number	Department	File Holder	Position
Aspen Systems	L0003	LSG	Keane James	Director
Atlis	L0003	LSG	Keane James	Director
Behavior sciences in litigation	L0001	LSG	Keane James	Director
Business end of general counsel office	L0004	LSG	Keane James	Director
CDC	L0003	LSG	Keane James	Director
Complex litigation rules	L0002	LSG	Keane James	Director
Computer abuse	L0003	LSG	Keane James	Director
Computer law	L0003	LSG	Keane James	Director
Computer product directories	L0003	LSG	Keane James	Director
Computer security	L0003	LSG	Keane James	Director

Contents	Box Number	Department	File Holder	Position
Computer services—general	L0003	LSG	Keane James	Director
Computerization of law internationally	L0001	LSG	Keane James	Director
Computers in litigation	L0004	LSG	Keane James	Director
Construction litigation	L0001	LSG	Keane James	Director
Cost of litigation	L0001	LSG	Keane James	Director
Damages	L0001	LSG	Keane James	Director
Decade of law office automation	L0004	LSG	Keane James	Director
Discovery procedures	L0002	LSG	Keane James	Director
Document management system	L0004	LSG	Keane James	Director
Economics in litigation	L0001	LSG	Keane James	Director
Environmental litigation	L0001	LSG	Keane James	Director
Evidex	L0003	LSG	Keane James	Director
Expert witness	L0002	LSG	Keane James	Director
Expert witnesses	L0001	LSG	Keane James	Director
Factmatcher	L0003	LSG	Keane James	Director
Flite system USAF	L0003	LSG	Keane James	Director
FOIA litigation	L0001	LSG	Keane James	Director
General counsel office management	L0002	LSG	Keane James	Director
Good-bye green eyeshades	L0004	LSG	Keane James	Director
Government litigation	L0001	LSG	Keane James	Director
Health care litigation	L0001	LSG	Keane James	Director
IBM stairs	L0003	LSG	Keane James	Director
Indexing techniques	L0002	LSG	Keane James	Director
Informatics	L0003	LSG	Keane James	Director
Information science	L0002	LSG	Keane James	Director
Inmagic	L0003	LSG	Keane James	Director
International litigation	L0001	LSG	Keane James	Director
Juris	L0003	LSG	Keane James	Director
Law firms and acct'g firms—contrast	L0004	LSG	Keane James	Director
Law office administration	L0003	LSG	Keane James	Director
Law office management systems	L0003	LSG	Keane James	Director
Lawtime software	L0003	LSG	Keane James	Director
Legal Automation News	L0003	LSG	Keane James	Director
LEXIS	L0003	LSG	Keane James	Director
Litigation department management	L0002	LSG	Keane James	Director
Litigation support systems	L0003	LSG	Keane James	Director
Litton Mellonics	L0003	LSG	Keane James	Director
Microcomputers	L0003	LSG	Keane James	Director
Microfilm	L0002	LSG	Keane James	Director
Oil and gas litigation	L0001	LSG	Keane James	Director
Paralegal training	L0002	LSG	Keane James	Director
Patent litigation	L0001	LSG	Keane James	Director
Prison riot prosecution planning	L0004	LSG	Keane James	Director
Product liability litigation	L0001	LSG	Keane James	Director
Quiklaw	L0003	LSG	Keane James	Director
SBC	L0003	LSG	Keane James	Director
Securities litigation	L0001	LSG	Keane James	Director
The emerging role of consultants	L0004	LSG	Keane James	Director
Using the microcomputer in w.p.	L0004	LSG	Keane James	Director
Vendors, miscellaneous	L0003	LSG	Keane James	Director
Video law seminar	L0002	LSG	Keane James	Director
Videotape evidence	L0002	LSG	Keane James	Director
Wang	L0003	LSG	Keane James	Director
WESTLAW	L0003	LSG	Keane James	Director
White-collar crime	L0001	LSG	Keane James	Director
Word processing	L0003	LSG	Keane James	Director
Working with the trial lawyer	L0004	LSG	Keane James	Director

FORM 44

Document Information Sheet

Page ______ of ______

NO (Doc. No.): ____________ BATE (Bates Range): ____________ THRU: ____________

Production and File Source

DD (Doc. Date): ______________

FILE (Files of): ______________ Type (Doc. Type): ________ RELV (Relevancy): ________

OFF (Office): ________________ INC (Incomplete)? Y ___ N ___

FTL (Folder Title): ___________ ATT (Attachment)? Y ___ N ___

FNO (Folder No.): ___________ NOAT (No. of Attachments): ___

CNF (Confidential)? Y __ N __ LEG (Legible)? Y __ N __ P __

PRIV (Privileged)? Y ___ N ___ MAR (Marginalia)? Y ___ N ___

Bibliographic Data

AUT (Author): ____ ☐ MULT. AUT. CONT. P. 2

ORG (Aut. Organization): ______________________________

RCP (Recipient/Addressee): ____________________________ ☐ MULT. RCP. CONT. P. 2

TTL (Title/Subject): __________________________________

____

CC (Copy Recipients/Dist.): ____________________________ ☐ MULT. CC. CONT. P. 2

Analysis

TRT (Treatment): Annotation _ Abstract _ Extract _ Full Text _ ☐ SEE DOC.

SUBJ (Subject Codes): _________________________________

SUMM (Annotation/Abstract): ___________________________

____

____

____ ☐ CONT. P. 2

TEXT (Extract/Key Words): ______________________

____

____

______________________ ☐ SEE ATTACHED DOCUMENT

____

XREF (Cross-References): ______________________

______________________ ☐ CONT. P. 2

NOTE (Comments (I.D. by Initials)): ______________________

____

____

____

REVW (Reviewed by): ____________ Date: ____________

ARVW (Atty. Review by): ____________ Date: ____________

☐ Second Page Follows

FORM 45

Microcomputer Data Structure for Litigation Document Analysis

INMAGIC* – DEFINE Data Structure

Enter name of structure: HELMET
Enter description line (optional): HELMET CASE
Enter retrieval key field(s): RECORD
Enter order key field(s): RECORD

Enter	Label	Name	Index	Sort	Emphasis for each field
F/1	REC	RECORD	Y	1	1
F/2	TY	TYPE	Y	1	1
F/3	DT	DATE	Y	4	1
F/4	AU	AUTHOR	Y	5	1
F/5	DEP	DEPONENT	Y	5	1
F/6	RCP	RECIPIENT	Y	5	1
F/7	SPN	SPONSOR	Y	5	1
F/8	WIT	WITNESS	Y	5	1
F/9	MEN	MENTIONED	Y	5	1
F/10	TTL	TITLE	K	1	1
F/11	SUM	SUMMARY	K	1	1
F/12	SUBJ	SUBJECT	Y	5	1
F/13	FRM	FILM FRAME	T	2	1
F/14	INTQ	INTROG	Y	2	1
F/15	EXH	EXHIBIT	Y	2	1
F/16	XREF	CROSSREF	Y	2	1
F/17	NT	NOTE	K	1	1
F/18	PG	PAGE	Y	2	1

*INMAGIC (stands for "INformation MAGIC") is a document retrieval software package broadly used for litigation support. It can be operated on a variety of brands and sizes of computers, including IBM and IBM-compatible microcomputers. INMAGIC is a registered trademark of INMAGIC, Inc., 2067 Massachusetts Ave., Cambridge, Massachusetts 02140-1338, (617)661-8124.

FORM 46

Sample Litigation Support System Records

Exhibit Description with Multiple Cross-References to Depositions

---

RECORD: 3
TYPE: Photograph
DATE: 710903
AUTHOR: Lens, Nick
SUMMARY: Shows Kuiper in process of removing helmet. 3 of 9 Globe photos.
SUBJECT: Helmet removal
RESPONSE TO: School Interrogatory 29
EXHIBIT: Davis DX3
CROSS-REFERENCE: Davis Deposition Transcript 56
Kuiper Dep Tr 72–76
Schimbeno Dep Tr 22–23
Noran Dep Tr 76–77, 86–87
Long Dep Tr 91–94
NOTE: Noran will testify that photos 3 & 4 evidence extension of neck during helmet removal.

RECORD: 100
TYPE: Damage Claim Study
DATE: 30-Nov-1983
AUTHOR: Silverman, Alan
RECIPIENT: Marron, Barry, Esq. (Davis)
Richard, Lawrence, Esq. (MacGregor)
Whitehead, Marc, Esq. (School)

Note: The date format is yy/mm/dd, which is an easier number for computation than 5 April 1979, the date of the Kuiper's deposition. Kuiper's deposition contains cross-references to Exhibits 1–4.

TITLE: Calculation of the Economic Loss Suffered by John Davis
SUMMARY: Economic expert calculates losses before and after trial date of January 1, 198X. Lost earnings: $88,519. Medicals: $151,517. Attendant care: $822,929. Future lost earnings, discounted: $966,419. Future medical costs and attendant care, discounted, are: $3,442,941. Total loss: $5,232,289. Key assumptions are 24 hours of attendant care, 7% inflation, and 8% discount factor.
SUBJECT: Damages

Deposition Digests Showing Multiple Cross-References of Digests to Exhibits

---

RECORD: 5
TYPE: Deposition
DATE: 790106
DEPONENT: Davis, John Jr.
SUMMARY: Coach Kuiper was first one out on field after he was injured. First thing he did was to remove the helmet. The helmet was removed carefully. Dr. Hallin, his father, and the other coaches also came out to him. Kuiper later told Davis he knew something had broken: The crack could be heard all over the field.
SUBJECT: Helmet removal
PAGE: 40–41

RECORD: 6
TYPE: Deposition
DATE: 790405
DEPONENT: Kuiper, Don
SUMMARY: Photo 2 shows Kuiper standing over plaintiff. Doesn't refresh recollection as to what he is doing. Does not recall taking off helmet or anyone else removing it. Believes he was first non–player/referee to arrive on field. Agrees photo 2 appears to show him touching the equipment. Can't recall anyone directing his movements.
SUBJECT: Helmet removal
CROSS-REFERENCE: Davis DX1
Davis DX2
Davis DX3
Davis DX4
PAGE: 72–76

Exhibit Cross-Reference List

Exhibit	Type	Record	Reference
Davis DX1	Photograph	1	1. Davis Dep Tr 56 2. Kuiper Dep Tr 72–77
Davis DX2	Photograph	2	1. Davis Dep Tr 56 2. Kuiper Dep Tr 72–76
Davis DX3	Photograph	3	1. Davis Dep Tr 56 2. Kuiper Dep Tr 72–77 3. Schimbeno Dep Tr 22–23 4. Noran Dep Tr 76–77, 86–87 5. Long Dep Tr 91–94
Davis DX4	Photograph	4	1. Davis Dep Tr 56 2. Kuiper Dep Tr 72–76

Comment: "DX" in the first column stands for deposition exhibit. This is a convention to distinguish between exhibits introduced at trial and those produced or identified in multiple depositions. The first item in the list means that the first photograph was identified as exhibit #1 in the Davis deposition. The last column shows that it was mentioned at page 56 of his deposition. The same exhibit was also mentioned in Kuiper's deposition at pages 72–77, mercifully using the same exhibit number. "Type" describes the dominant characteristic of the item, and "Record" refers to the computer record number from which the information is derived.

Deponent/Subject List

Davis, John Jr. Record #5	SUBJECT: Helmet removal Transcript Pages: 40–41
Kuiper, Don Record #6	SUBJECT: Helmet removal Transcript Pages: 72–76
Hallin, Roger P. M.D. Record #7	SUBJECT: Helmet removal Transcript Pages: 28–29
Noran, Harold H. M.D. Record #8	SUBJECT: Injury aggravation; helmet removal Transcript Pages: 76–77
Noran, Harold H. M.D. Record #9	SUBJECT: Helmet removal Transcript Pages: 86–87
Noran, Harold H. M.D. Record #11	SUBJECT: Injury aggravation; helmet removal Transcript Pages: 98–100

Noran, Harold H. M.D. Record #12	SUBJECT: Injury aggravation; helmet removal Transcript Pages: 116–121
Long, Stephan E. Record #15	SUBJECT: Injury aggravation; helmet removal Transcript Pages: 61–62
Long, Stephan E. Record #17	SUBJECT: Injury aggravation; helmet removal Transcript Pages: 91–94

Listing for the Order of Proof on the Issues of "Helmet Removal" and "Injury Aggravation"

HELMET REMOVAL Record #1 Photograph: Davis DX1	WITNESS: Lens, Nick
HELMET REMOVAL Record #2 Photograph: Davis DX2	WITNESS: Lens, Nick
HELMET REMOVAL Record #3 Photograph: Davis DX3	WITNESS: Lens, Nick
HELMET REMOVAL Record #4 Photograph: Davis DX4	WITNESS: Lens, Nick
HELMET REMOVAL Record #5 Deposition: 40–41	WITNESS: Davis, John
HELMET REMOVAL Record #6 Deposition 72–76	WITNESS: Kuiper, Don
HELMET REMOVAL Record #7 Deposition: 28–29	WITNESS: Hallin, Roger
INJURY AGGRAVATION; HELMET REMOVAL Record #8 Deposition 76–77	WITNESS: Noran, Harold H.
HELMET REMOVAL Record #9 Deposition: 86–87	WITNESS: Noran, Harold H.
INJURY AGGRAVATION Record # 10 Deposition: 77–81	WITNESS: Noran, Harold H.
INJURY AGGRAVATION; HELMET REMOVAL Record #11 Deposition 98–100	WITNESS: Noran, Harold H.
INJURY AGGRAVATION; HELMET REMOVAL Record #12 Deposition: 116–121	WITNESS: Noran, Harold H.
HELMET REMOVAL Record #13 Publication: Long DX1	WITNESS: Long, Stephan E.
INJURY AGGRAVATION Record #14 Publication: Long DX2	WITNESS: Klaff, Edward

INJURY AGGRAVATION;
HELMET REMOVAL — WITNESS: Long, Stephan E.
Record #15 Deposition: 61–62

INJURY AGGRAVATION — WITNESS: Long, Stephan E.
Record #16 Deposition: 75–77

INJURY AGGRAVATION;
HELMET REMOVAL — WITNESS: Long, Stephan E.
Record #17 Deposition: 91–94

Internal Computer Indexes

Key words from the text of the summary, noting the frequency of occurrence

14	HELMET
2	HELMETS
3	HIM
5	HIS
1	HOLD
1	HOURS
1	HOWEVER
5	IF
1	IMMEDIATELY
2	INCHES
2	INCREASED
1	INFLATION
1	INITIAL
3	INJURED
2	INJURIES
4	INJURY

Subject Terms, by Phrase

1	DAMAGES
14	HELMET REMOVAL
1	IMPACT
8	INJURY AGGRAVATION

FORM 47

Production Source Log

Prepared for Plaintiff's Counsel
In re:

Source Log

Company: ______________________________

Production Site and Date: ______________________________

Receptacle Number	Receptacle Description	Department	Files of	Date Rec'd	From Whom	Date Returned	To Whom

FORM 48

Digest Form

Jones v. Consolidated Widgets

DOC. Nos. __________ to __________ SUBJECT: ____________________
Date: ______/______/19___ To: ______________ From: ______________

Doc. Type:	Company:	People:	Mentions:
______Letter	______Con-Widget	______Smith, J.A.	______JTQ Widget
______Memo	______Acme Sales	______Brown, F.D.	______Testing
______Notes	______Car Dealer	______Heywood, C.	______Wear
______Report	______St. Frances Hospital	______Bush, E.P.	______Mileage
______Brochure	______NHTSA	______Johnson, B.B.	______Safety
______Advertising	______	______Clark, T.F.	______Warranty
______Photo	______	______	______Government Investigation
______	______	______	______Recall
______	______	______	______Manufacture
______	______	______	______
______	______	______	

Counts:
______Strict liability
______Negligence (manufacturing)
______Negligence (design)
______Failure to warn
______Express warranty
______Implied warranty
______Punitive damages
______
______

Summary:
____
____
____
____
____
____
____

Digested by: ____________________
Date: ____________________

FORM 49

Document Tracking Form

Receiving Information

Division/Box No.: Division:
Former Division:
Shipping Mode: Shipping No.:
Date Collected: 00/00/00 Date Shipped: 00/00/00
Date Received: 00/00/00
Present Status: to be numbered Date Computer Updated: 00/00/00

Numbering Information

Date Numbered: 00/00/00 Individual Numbering:
Document No.:

Copying Information

Date Prescreened: 00/00/00 Individual Prescreening:
Special Handling? (Y or N)
Describe Special Handling:

Date to Special Handling: 00/00/00 Date Returned from Special Handling: 00/00/00
Date to Copying: 00/00/00 Date Returned from Copying: 00/00/00
Date Shelved: 00/00/00 Shelf Location:

Coding Information

Date to Coding: 00/00/00 Date Returned from Coding: 00/00/00

Documents Returned to Division

Date Returned: 00/00/00

Comments

FORM 50

Document Coding Form

Control Information

Document Nos. ☐☐☐☐☐☐☐☐ to ☐☐☐☐☐☐☐☐ Document Type ☐☐☐

Document Date ☐☐☐☐☐☐ Document Identifier ☐☐☐☐☐☐☐☐☐☐☐☐☐☐☐
YYMMDD

Title (Re)

Attachments

Present ☐ Y/N Ref'd ☐ Y/N Packet Nos. ☐☐☐☐☐☐☐☐ to ☐☐☐☐☐☐☐☐

Administrative Information

Priv. ☐ Y/N Date Coded ☐☐☐☐☐☐ MMDDYY Coder ☐☐☐

Form for Section VII:

Representing Corporate Clients in Various Litigation Settings

FORM 51

Notification to Employees of Criminal Investigation

Dear XYZ Employee:

The United States Department of Justice, in conjunction with the Federal Bureau of Investigation and the Air Force Office of Special Investigations, is currently investigating the Company's allocation of labor costs between various overhead accounts and specific projects for fiscal years 1984–1985.

The Company is cooperating with the government in this investigation by providing information requested by the government.

The Company is represented in this investigation by its Office of General Counsel and by [outside counsel] of the law firm of ____________. In the course of this investigation, you may be contacted by lawyers from the General Counsel's office or the ____________ firm to provide information and documentation to support the Company's efforts. We ask your cooperation in this regard.

Government investigators may also wish to question you in connection with this investigation. Because those inquiries will concern matters that occurred while you were a Company employee, the Company has retained, at its expense, ____________ of the law firm of ____________ to provide legal advice and assistance to those employees who are approached by the government and are not represented by other attorneys. ____________, who is experienced in matters of this kind as a former federal prosecutor and now as a defense attorney, is not representing the Company, but has been retained to provide independent legal counsel to those employees who choose to use his [or her] services. ____________'s representation would include the following activities:

- Advising you of your legal rights and duties in connection with any interview
- Advising whether, and under what conditions, it is in your legal interest to be interviewed
- Appearance on your behalf at any interview, grand jury proceeding, or other investigative proceeding

While the Company recommends that you retain ____________, at the Company's expense, to represent your legal interests in this investigation, it is your right to do so or not. You may also deal directly with government investigators without assistance of counsel, or you may retain your own counsel at your own expense.

If you wish to retain ______________, you may contact him [or her] directly [telephone number] or contact the General Counsel's office [telephone number] to make the necessary arrangements.

____
Vice President and General Counsel

Index

Bold face page numbers indicate forms in Appendix.